Juvenile Delinquency
Theory, Practice, and Law

Seventh Edition

1881

Michigan begins child protection with the Michigan Public Acts of 1881.

1884

The state assumes the authority to take neglected children and place them in an institution. See *Reynolds v. Howe,* 51 Conn. 472, 478 (1884).

1886

First neglect case is heard in Massachusetts.

1889

Board of children's guardians is established in Indiana and given jurisdiction over neglected and dependent children.

1890

Children's Aid Society of Pennsylvania, a foster home for the juvenile delinquent used as an alternative to reform schools, is established.

1891

Supreme Court of Minnesota establishes the doctrine of parental immunity.

1875–1900

Case law begins to deal with parental statutes.

1897

Ex Parte Becknell, a California decision that reverses the sentence of a juvenile who has not been given a jury trial

1899

Illinois Juvenile Court Act

1903–1905

Many other states pass juvenile court acts.

1905

Commonwealth v. Fisher—Pennsylvania Supreme Court upholds the constitutionality of the Juvenile Court Act.

1881   1890   1900

1906

Massachusetts passes an act to provide for the treatment of children not as criminals but as children in need of guidance and aid.

1908

Ex Parte Sharpe defines more clearly the role of the juvenile court to include *parens patriae*.

1910

Compulsory school acts

1918

Chicago area studies are conducted by Shaw and McKay.

1924

Federal Probation Act

1930

Children's Charter

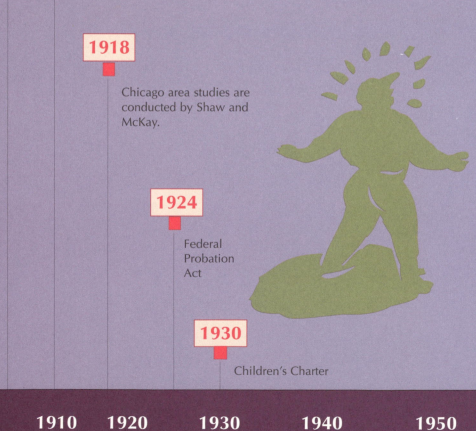

1954

Brown v. Board of Education, a major school desegregation decision

1959

Standard Family Court Act of National Council on Crime and Delinquency establishes that juvenile hearings are to be informal.

| 1910 | 1920 | 1930 | 1940 | 1950 |

Juvenile Delinquency

Theory, Practice, and Law

Seventh Edition

■ **Larry J. Siegel**, Ph.D.

University of Massachusetts—Lowell

■ **Joseph J. Senna**, M.S.W., J.D.

Northeastern University

Wadsworth
Thomson Learning

Australia ▪ Canada ▪ Denmark ▪ Japan ▪
Mexico ▪ New Zealand ▪ Philippines ▪ Puerto Rico ▪ Singapore ▪
South Africa ▪ Spain ▪ United Kingdom ▪ United States

...mon Ryan
...onal Assistant: Ann Tsai
Marketing Manager: Christine Henry
Project Editor: Jennie Redwitz
Print Buyer: Karen Hunt
Permissions Editor: Bob Kauser

Photo credits are on page A-43

Production: Cecile Joyner/The Cooper Company
Designer: Delgado Design, Inc.
Copyeditor: Kay Mikel
Illustrator: Precision Graphics
Cover Design: Delgado Design, Inc.
Cover Image: Jean-Michel Basquiat © 1999 Artists
   Rights Society (ARS), New York/ADAGP, Paris
Image of Basquiat: © William Coupon/Gamma Liaison
Compositor: Thompson Type
Printer: World Color Book Company, Taunton,
   Massachusetts

For permission to use material from this text,
contact us:
   web   www.thomsonrights.com
   fax   1-800-730-2215
   phone   1-800-730-2214

**Library of Congress
Cataloging-in-Publication Data**
Siegel, Larry J.
   Juvenile delinquency : theory, practice, and law /
Larry J. Siegel, Joseph J. Senna. — 7th ed.
      p.   cm.
   Includes bibliographical references and index.
   ISBN 0-534-55728-7
   1. Juvenile delinquency—United States.
2. Juvenile justice, Administration of—United States.
I. Senna, Joseph J.   II. Title.
HV9104.S53   2000
364.36'0973—dc21   99-25735

Instructor's Edition: 0-534-55729-5

Wadsworth/Thomson Learning
10 Davis Drive
Belmont, CA 94002
USA
www.wadsworth.com

International Headquarters
Thomson Learning
290 Harbor Drive, 2nd Floor
Stamford, CT 06902-7477
USA

UK/Europe/Middle East
Thomson Learning
Berkshire House
168-173 High Holborn
London WC1V 7AA
United Kingdom

Asia
Thomson Learning
60 Albert Street #15-01
Albert Complex
Singapore 189969

Canada
Nelson/Thomson Learning
1120 Birchmount Road
Scarborough, Ontario M1K 5G4
Canada

 *This book is printed on acid-free
recycled paper.*

To my wife Therese J. Libby and my children,
Julie, Andrew, Eric, and Rachel

—L.J.S.

To my wife Janet and my children, Christian,
Stephen, Peter, and Joseph

—J.J.S.

About the Cover Artist

In the late 1970s New Yorkers began to notice arcane messages, signed with the name SAMO, on the streets of lower Manhattan: "PLAYING ART WITH DADDY'S MONEY"; "9-5 CLONE"; "PLUSH SAFE . . . HE THINK." Eventually it became known that these writings were the work of a young Brooklyn-born painter of Haitian and Puerto Rican descent named Jean-Michel Basquiat. When his wall paintings garnered favorable notices in the press, Basquiat began to attract the attention of the art world. In 1980 Jean-Michel showed his art for the first time in a Times Square show held in an abandoned warehouse. Important galleries began to show his work, and one owner—Annina Nosei—gave him money for supplies and allowed him to use her gallery's basement as a studio. As he rose to fame in the New York art scene, Basquiat's work began to command impressive prices and glowing reviews. Among his most ardent admirers and collaborators was painter and cultural icon Andy Warhol. Tragically, Basquiat died in 1988 at age 27 at the peak of his artistic powers.

Basquiat's images combine vibrant energy with elements of music and popular culture, African-American heritage, and the turbulence of urban life. He used a variety of mediums, including markers, acrylic, spray paint, color photocopies, and silkscreens. He had a great interest in contemporary culture and was especially interested in jazz and other forms of music—musical symbols are common in his work. It is said that Basquiat frequently painted while listening to jazz, and one of his most famous paintings, "The Horn Players," painted in 1983, is a tribute to saxophonist Charlie Parker and trumpeter Dizzy Gillespie.

Basquiat's work explores the dualities of contemporary society, encompassing both its ills and its rewards. He uses satire, humor, and political commentary to reveal his perspective on the American cultural scene. We have used his painting "Dust Heads" on the cover of this book for two reasons. First, because its vivid imagery captures the essence of the adolescent experience in American culture: exciting, colorful, mercurial, dynamic, in motion, going places. Second, we believe that Jean-Michel Basquiat was a singularly unique and great American painter. We would like to expose as many students as possible to his work so that they may take pleasure, as we do, from his imagery, color sense, and imagination.

About the Authors

Larry J. Siegel was born in the Bronx in 1947. While attending City College of New York in the 1960s he was introduced to the study of crime and justice in courses taught by sociologist Charles Winick. After graduation he attended the newly opened program in criminal justice at the State University of New York at Albany, where he earned both his MA and Ph.D. and studied with famed scholars such as Michael Hindelang, Gilbert Geis, and Donald Newman. After completing his graduate work, Dr. Siegel began his teaching career at Northeastern University, where he worked closely with colleague Joseph Senna on a number of texts and research projects. After leaving Northeastern, he held teaching positions at the University of Nebraska–Omaha and Saint Anselm College in New Hampshire. He is currently a professor at the University of Massachusetts–Lowell.

Dr. Siegel has written extensively in the area of crime and justice, including books on juvenile law, delinquency, criminology, and criminal procedure. He is a court-certified expert on police conduct and has testified in numerous legal cases. He resides in Bedford, New Hampshire, with his wife Therese J. Libby, Esq. and their children.

Joseph J. Senna was born in Brooklyn, New York. He graduated from Brooklyn College, Fordham University Graduate School of Social Service, and Suffolk University Law School. Mr. Senna has spent over fourteen years teaching law and justice courses at Northeastern University. In addition, he has served as an Assistant District Attorney, Director of Harvard Law School Prosecutorial Program, and consultant to numerous criminal justice organizations. His academic specialities include the areas of Criminal Law, Constitutional Due Process, Criminal Justice, and Juvenile Law.

Mr. Senna lives with his wife and sons outside of Boston. He is currently working on a criminal law textbook.

Brief Contents

Detailed Contents

Preface

On August 11, 1998, Circuit Judge Ralph Wilson ordered 14-year-old Mitchell Johnson and 12-year-old Andrew Golden to spend the remainder of their minority in a juvenile correctional facility for a school shooting spree that killed a teacher and four little girls at the Westside Middle School in Jonesboro, Arkansas. Johnson turned to the crowded courtroom and told the victim's friends and relatives that he didn't mean to cause any harm:

"I thought we were going to shoot over their heads," he said after admitting to his role in the shooting. "We didn't think anybody was going to get hurt." Some were not satisfied with his excuse considering that he and Golden used a false fire alarm to lure their schoolmates outside and then fired repeatedly into the terrified mass of students and teachers with high-powered rifles. According to the existing Arkansas law, anyone who commits a serious crime before their fourteenth birthday cannot be tried as an adult. Judge Wilson remanded the boys to the Division of Youth Services, where they will probably be held in a juvenile detention center until their eighteenth birthdays and then released. While the Jonesboro case shocked the nation, it was later overshadowed by an even deadlier school incident, which took place at Columbine High School in Littleton, Colorado. On April 20, 1999, two students, Eric Harris, 18, and Dylan Klebold, 17, members of a mysterious group called the "Trenchcoat Mafia," went on a shooting spree that claimed the lives of at least twelve students and one teacher and wounded twenty-four others, many seriously. Before they could be captured, the boys committed suicide in the school library, leaving authorities to puzzle over the cause of their deadly outburst.

Considering the immediacy and importance of the problem of youth crime, it is not surprising that courses on juvenile delinquency have become popular offerings on the nation's college campuses. This text, *Juvenile Delinquency: Theory, Practice, and Law,* is designed to help students understand the nature of juvenile delinquency, its cause and correlates, as well as the current strategies being used to control or eliminate its occurrence. The text also reviews the legal rules that have been set down to either protect innocent minors or control adolescent misconduct: Can children be required to submit to drug testing in school? Can teachers search suspicious students or use corporal punishment as a method of discipline? Can children testify on closed-circuit TV in child abuse cases? Can a minor be given a death-penalty sentence?

Because the study of juvenile delinquency is a dynamic, ever-changing field of scientific inquiry and because the theories, concepts, and processes of this area of study are constantly evolving, we have updated *Juvenile Delinquency: Theory, Practice, and Law* to reflect the changes that have taken place in the study of delinquent behavior during the past few years. Like its predecessors, the seventh edition includes a review of recent legal cases, research studies, and policy initiatives. It provides a groundwork for the study of juvenile delinquency by analyzing and describing the nature and extent of delinquency, the suspected causes of delinquent behavior, and the environmental influences on youthful misbehavior. It covers what most experts believe are the critical issues in juvenile delinquency and analyzes crucial policy issues including the use of pretrial detention, waiver to adult court, and restorative justice programs.

Goals and Objectives

Our primary goals in writing this seventh edition remain as they have been for previous editions:

1. To be as objective as possible, presenting the many diverse views and perspectives that characterize the study of juvenile delinquency and reflect its interdisciplinary nature.
2. To maintain a balance of theory, law, policy, and practice. It is essential that a text on delinquency not solely be a theory book without presenting the juvenile justice system or contain sections on current policies without examining legal issues and cases.
3. To be as thorough and up-to-date as possible. We have attempted to include the most current data and information available.
4. To make the study of delinquency interesting as well as informative. We want to make readers as interested as possible in the study of delinquency so that they will pursue it on an undergraduate or graduate level.

We have tried to provide a text that is both scholarly and informative, comprehensive yet interesting, well organized and objective yet provocative and thought provoking.

Organization of the Text

The seventh edition of *Juvenile Delinquency* is divided into six main sections:.

Part One examines the concept of delinquency and status offending, the measurement of delinquency, and trends and patterns in the delinquency rate. Chapter 1 contains extensive material on the history of childhood and the legal concept of delinquency and status offending. This material enables the reader to understand how the concept of adolescence evolved over time and how that evolution influenced the development of the juvenile court and the special status of delinquency. Chapter 2 covers the measurement of delinquent behavior, trends and patterns in teen crime and also discusses the correlates of delinquency including race, gender, class, and age and chronic offending.

Part Two describes the various theoretical models that have been used to explain the onset of delinquent behavior. Chapter 3 covers recent individual-level views, which focus on choice, biological, and psychological theories. Chapter 4 looks at social structural theories, which hold that economic, cultural, and environmental influences control delinquent behavior. Chapter 5 reviews those theories which maintain that improper socialization is the key to understanding delinquent behavior. These include learning, control, and developmental theories. Chapter 6, on social reaction theories, includes analysis on labeling and conflict theory.

Part Three covers the environmental and individual correlates of delinquency. Part Three begins with Chapter 7 on gender and delinquency, which explores the sex-based differences that are thought to account for the gender patterns in the delinquency rate. Also in this section are chapters on the influence of families (Chapter 8), gangs (Chapter 9), schools (Chapter 10), and drugs (Chapter 11).

Part Four on juvenile justice advocacy contains material on both the history of juvenile justice and the philosophy and practice of today's juvenile justice system. Chapter 12 gives extensive coverage to the emergence of state control over children in need and the development of the juvenile justice system. It also covers the contemporary juvenile justice system, the major stages in the justice process, the role of the federal government in the juvenile justice system, an analysis of the differences between the adult and juvenile justice system, and extensive coverage of the legal rights of children including a new time line of Constitutional cases.

Part Five on controlling juvenile offenders contains three chapters on the police and court process. Chapter 13 discusses the role of police in delinquency prevention and covers legal issues such as major court decisions on school searches and *Miranda* rights of juveniles. It also contains material on race and gender effects on police discretion. Chapter 14, on early court process, contains information on plea bargaining in juvenile court, the use of detention, and transfer to adult jails. It contains an analysis of the critical factors that influence the waiver decision. Chapter 15, on the juvenile trial and sentencing, contains sections on special problems faced by juvenile court judges, such as substance abuse cases and gangs. It reviews the role of the public defender and federal prosecutor in juvenile court and models of sentencing in juvenile court.

Part Six contains two chapters on the juvenile correctional system. Chapter 16, on community-based treatments, involves material on probation and other community dispositions including restorative justice programs. Chapter 17 reviews juvenile training schools with emphasis on legal issues such as right to treatment and innovative programs such as boot camps.

Once again the book closes with a brief overview of significant findings found within the text.

What's New in This Edition?

There have been a number of important new features added in this edition. Each chapter now includes an Infotrac College Edition exercise that directs students to articles on the World Wide Web that can supplement the material found within the chapter. Infotrac College Edition contains hundreds of thousands of current articles, and many are related to juvenile justice. There are two new boxed features: *Juvenile Law in Review* covers in depth the most important legal cases that shape the juvenile justice system; *Policy and Practice* boxes focus on important programs and policy initiatives that are now being used to help children in need. In addition, each chapter now begins with a "real life" vignette or story that illustrates a real, personal dilemma in the study of juvenile delinquency and helps draw students into the material contained within the chapter.

Each chapter has been thoroughly updated. A few of the more important changes and updates include:

- Chapter 1 now contains material showing that adolescence is a time when juveniles are likely to take risks and get in trouble. It has data from the 1998 report by the National Center for Health Statistics, showing trends in teen-age birth rates. It also covers changes in statutory rape law and the definition of the age of consent.

- Chapter 2 covers juvenile crime trends and reviews recent trends in the juvenile violence rate. It updates information of delinquency trends and has a section on juvenile victimization.

- Chapter 3 now contains a more detailed review of situational crime prevention strategies as well as a new section on evolutionary theory.

- Chapter 4 reports on a 1998 study by the National Center for Children in Poverty, which found that more than 20 percent of American children are living in poverty. New data show that the effects of poverty are most often felt by minority-group members. It reviews Jeffrey Fagan's important research from *Adolescent Violence: A View from the Street,* published in 1998.

- Chapter 5 now looks at the recent developmental theories of crime, including such topics as continuity of crime, multiple pathways to delinquency, problem behavior syndrome, and offense specialization.

- Chapter 6 has a new section on restorative justice, which spells out the under-lining principles of this emerging area of juvenile justice, as well as a detailed analysis of restorative justice in practice, which describes a variety of on-going programs.

- Chapter 7, Gender and Delinquency, has a new section on Deborah Denno's biosocial study of female delinquency.

- Chapter 8, Family and Delinquency, now has a review of the important new book by Judith Rich Harris, *The Nature Assumption,* as well as material on the association between family structure and substance abuse, recent developments in child abuse, and a section on women who have killed their children.

- Chapter 9 has the latest data on the association between gang membership and substance abuse, as well as a detailed analysis of Boston's Youth Violence Strike Force (YVSF), one of the nations' most successful anti-gang units. It also con-tains reviews of school-based anti-gang initiatives.

- Chapter 10 reviews recent research on dropping out and delinquency, school climate and delinquency, the latest trends in academic performance, and new programs designed to reduce school-based delinquency. It contains data from the School Crime Victimization Survey. There is a major section on school-yard bullies and what is being done to control their activities.

- Chapter 11 charts the latest trends in teen drug use, including the ISR and PRIDE surveys. There is a section on what is being done to help families pre-vent substance abuse.

- Chapter 12 describes the historical development of juvenile justice as well as providing an overview of the contemporary juvenile justice system. New mate-rial includes a section on the Juvenile Court in the new millennium, the role of the Supreme Court in framing juvenile law, and the future of juvenile justice strategies.

- Chapter 13 contains new material on policy initiatives in law enforcement, inter-vention strategies, police discretion in juvenile cases, and the effect of race and ethnicity in police decision making.

- Chapter 14 contains new material on trying juveniles in adult court, as well as new approaches to detention.

- Chapter 15 now contains sections on blended sentencing, juvenile delinquency in the Federal Court system, juvenile drug courts, and discussion of whether the juvenile court movement can be considered a "success."

- Chapter 16 reviews new information on probation innovations and community treatment. There is an analysis of the Reclaim program in Ohio, as well as re-cent data on balanced probation and restorative justice programming.

- Chapter 17 reviews the continuing problem of racial disparity in juvenile correc-tions. There is an analysis of what really "works" in juvenile corrections and the call for new legislation on juvenile after-care.

Learning Tools

The text contains the following features designed to help students learn and com-prehend the material:

- Each chapter begins with an outline.
- The book contains more than 200 photos, tables, and charts. The endsheets contain a time line of juvenile justice history that helps students chart the critical incidents in the study of delinquency over the past two hundred years.
- Every chapter contains *Case in Point* boxed inserts on intriguing issues concern-ing juvenile delinquency policy or processes. Within the boxed inserts are criti-

cal thinking sections that help students conceptualize problems of concern to juvenile delinquency.

- As in previous editions, *Focus on Delinquency* boxed inserts focus attention on topics of special importance and concern. For example, in Chapter 8 Juvenile Prostitution is the topic, while in Chapter 4 a Focus on Delinquency looks at the topic of Race and Poverty.
- Juvenile Law in Review boxes include major Supreme Court cases that influence and control the juvenile justice system—for example, *In Re Gault,* which defines the concept of due process for youthful offenders.
- Policy and Practice boxes discuss major initiatives and programs. For example, the one in Chapter 5 describes programs based on the Social Development model of delinquency causation.
- Key terms are defined in the margins throughout the text.
- Each chapter ends with thought-provoking discussion questions.
- A glossary is included, which sets out and defines key terms used in the text.
- A concluding section called American Delinquency summarizes some of the text's major findings and conclusions.

Acknowledgments

The preparation of this text would not have been possible without the aid of our colleagues who helped by reviewing the previous edition and gave us important suggestions for improvement: Earlier reviews were provided by Aric Steven Frazier, David M. Horton, Harold W. Osborne, Barbara Owen, Ray Paternoster, Stanley L. Swart, Pamela Tontodonato; Kim Weaver.

In addition, important information was provided by the following individuals and institutions: Marcus Felson, Marty Schwartz, George Knox, G. David Curry, Joan McDermott, Helene Raskin White, Joe Sanborn, Jim Inciardi, Vic Streib, Malcom Klein, Robert Agnew, Eve Buzawa, Meda Chesney-Lind, Gerald Hotaling, Marv Zalman, John Laub, Rob Sampson, David Farrington, Larry Sherman, Deborah Denno, James A. Fox, Jack McDevitt, Lee Ellis, the staff at the Institute for Social Research at the University of Michigan; the National Center for State Courts; the Police Foundation; the Sentencing Project; Kathleen Maguire and the staff of the Hindelang Research Center at State University of New York—Albany; the National Criminal Justice Reference Service; Deborah Daro and Karen McCurdy of the National Committee for Prevention of Child Abuse; Terence Thornberry and the researchers at the Rochester Youth Study, Albany, New York. We extend a special thanks to Dr. Lynn Sametz for providing the time line data.

And, of course, our colleagues at Wadsworth Publishing did their usual outstanding job of aiding us in the preparation of the text. Sabra Horne, our wonderful editor, is an inspiration and guide; Dan Alpert is more than a developmental editor, he is a friend and mentor; Linda Rill was awesome as usual in doing the photo research (and had the good sense to praise my cooking); Shannon Ryan did a superb job coordinating a challenging supplements program. Cecile Joyner was her usual professional self in handling the production; Christine Henry is great to work with in marketing the text and getting its message out; and Jennie Redwitz is a wonderful addition to the team.

Larry Siegel
Joseph Senna

Reviewers of the current edition

Richard Ball, West Virginia State University
Scott Decker, University of Missouri—St. Louis
Irwin Kantor, Middlesex Community College
Elizabeth McConnell, Valdosta State University
Harold W. Osborne, Baylor University
Sudipto Roy, Indiana State University
Jeff Rush, Jacksonville State University

Reviewers of the previous editions

Fred Andes
Robert Agnew
Sarah Boggs
Thomas Calhoun
Steven Frazier
Fred Hawley
Tonya Hilligoss
Vincent Hoffman
David Horton
Fred Jones
James Larson
Harold Osborne
Barbara Owen
Ray Paternoster
Joseph Rankin
Thomas Segady
Richard Siebert
Paul Steele
Leslie Sue
Stanley Swart
Pam Tontodonato
Paul Tracy
William Waegel
Bill Wagner
Kim Weaver
Mervin White
Michael Wiatrowski

Part One

The Concept of Delinquency

The field of juvenile delinquency has been an important area of study since the turn of the century. Academicians, practitioners, policymakers, and legal scholars have devoted their attention to basic questions about the nature of youth crime: Who commits delinquent acts? How much delinquency occurs each year? Is the rate of delinquent activity increasing or decreasing? How should delinquency be defined? What can we do to prevent delinquency?

Part One reviews these basic questions in detail. In Chapter 1 we discuss the origins of society's concern for children and the development of the concept of delinquency. In Chapter 2 we examine the nature and extent of delinquent behavior, discuss how social scientists gather information on juvenile delinquency, and provide an overview of some of the major trends on juvenile crime.

Why do some kids continually get in trouble with the law, escalate the seriousness of their offenses, and become adult criminals? Why do others desist from delinquent activities? These are the major themes of the newly emerging life course view of delinquency.

Chapter One

Childhood and Delinquency

On March 11, 1998, fifteen-year-old Daphne Abdela pleaded guilty to manslaughter in the first degree. As a juvenile, she would receive a sentence of three and one-third to ten years in prison. At the sentencing hearing the judge told Daphne that she would receive the maximum sentence of ten years. He stated to the courtroom: "A friend of mine described the walls of a courtroom where children are sentenced as walls that weep. Today, they are weeping."

Daphne Abdela was a product of some of New York City's best private schools.[1] Her father was a vice president for an international company, and the family lived in a duplex on New York City's fashionable Central Park West. Friends said her parents were attentive without spoiling her, and outward appearances suggested an idyllic family life.

But Daphne had a hidden, darker side. Often in trouble at school, Daphne's teachers thought she had poor self-control. Despite considerable amounts of counseling and tutoring, Daphne's behavior remained erratic. She could be kind and warm, but on some occasions her friends found her obnoxious, unpredictable, insecure, and craving attention. She was overly self-conscious about her weight and had a drinking problem. Daphne attended AA meetings while her parents searched for a more structured treatment program. She was on the waiting list at Daytop Village, a residential substance abuse treatment program. Her parents seemed intimidated by her, were confused by her complexities, and puzzled over how to control her. Police said that her father even filed a harassment complaint against her once, saying she had slapped him.

Despite repeated promises to get her life together, Daphne chose to hang out most nights in Central Park and drink with neighborhood kids. A visitor can experience more of New York City life in Central Park than in any other part of town. The park attracts

Fifteen-year-old Daphne Abdela was a troubled product of some of New York City's best private schools. Always in trouble, she had poor self-control, was overly self-conscious about her weight, and had a drinking problem. On March 11, 1998, Daphne pleaded guilty to manslaughter in the death of a drinking companion in Central Park. As a juvenile, she received a sentence of 3⅓ to 10 years in prison.

about twenty million people annually to its 843 acres, and Manhattan residents love to spend time there.[2] It is a place where cultural barriers tend to break down.

On more than one occasion Daphne went to the park with Christopher Vasquez, a quiet boy who had his own set of personal problems. His parents had separated, and he suffered severe anxiety attacks and a form of agoraphobia, a fear of public places. He stayed home from school and took two drugs for his emotional problems—Zoloft, an antidepressant, and Lorazepam, a sedative. Chris was fond of roller blading and liked to play roller hockey, but to the other teenagers in the park he was someone who could easily be dominated, especially by the strong-willed Daphne.

Daphne was her usual boisterous self when she arrived in Central Park on the afternoon of May 23, 1997. Flashing her wad of twenties and tens—more than a hundred dollars in all—she shared beer with some of her friends. Then she and Chris Vasquez met up with Michael McMorrow, a forty-four-year-old man with a long history of alcohol problems. McMorrow liked to hang in the park and drink with the kids. After a night of drinking with Daphne and Chris, a fight broke out and McMorrow was stabbed, his throat cut, and his body dumped in the lake. Daphne was arrested soon after the attack when she placed a 911 call to police, telling them that a friend had "jumped in the lake and didn't come out." Police searched the area and found McMorrow's slashed and stabbed body in the water;

he had been disemboweled. One of the investigators said that it was one of the worst things he had ever seen.

In November of 1998 Chris was also found guilty for the homicide.

The Adolescent Dilemma

Is the tragic story of Daphne and Chris unique, or does it reflect the common problems faced by American youth? Daphne grew up in an affluent family, yet she was rebellious and confused. Can destructive personal traits offset the positive social influences of a caring family and an affluent lifestyle? Unlike Daphne, many American children grow up in dysfunctional families headed by substance abusing parents, live in deteriorated neighborhoods, have access to dangerous weapons, are lured by gangs, and are constantly exposed to extremes of poverty and violence (see Table 1.1). Some suffer from deep-seated emotional and personal problems. Can these children succeed despite these environmental deficits?

This latest generation of adolescents has been described as both cynical and political. They seem overly preoccupied with material acquisitions and lack interest in creative expression.[3] By age 18 they have spent more time in front of a TV set than in the classroom; each year they may see up to one thousand rapes, murders, and assaults on TV. What effects do such prolonged exposures to violence have on child development?

And why does the United States, considered the "richest" country on earth and leading the world in many economic and social categories, come up short in many areas of child welfare? As Table 1.2 shows, the United States lags other industrialized nations in important areas of child care and protection, despite having the high-

Table 1.1

MOMENTS IN AMERICA FOR CHILDREN

Every 9 seconds	a child drops out of school.
Every 10 seconds	a child is reported abused or neglected.
✔ Every 15 seconds	a child is arrested.
Every 25 seconds	a child is born to an unmarried mother.
Every 32 seconds	a child sees his or her parents divorce.
✔ Every 36 seconds	a child is born into poverty.
Every 36 seconds	a child is born to a mother who did not graduate from high school.
✔ Every minute	a child is born to a teen mother.
Every 2 minutes	a child is born at low birthweight.
Every 3 minutes	a child is born to a mother who received late or no prenatal care.
✔ Every 3 minutes	a child is arrested for drug abuse.
✔ Every 4 minutes	a child is arrested for an alcohol-related offense.
Every 5 minutes	a child is arrested for a violent crime.
Every 18 minutes	an infant dies.
Every 23 minutes	a child is wounded by gunfire.
Every 100 minutes	a child is killed by gunfire.
Every 4 hours	a child commits suicide.

Source: Children's Defense Fund, *The State of America's Children Yearbook 1998* (Washington, D.C.: Children's Defense Fund, p. 1)

est gross domestic product in the world.[4] Why the United States lags so far behind other countries in these areas is the subject of debate between academics, policy-makers, and juvenile justice officials as well as ordinary citizens concerned about public safety and the health and well-being of children.

The problems of American society and the daily stress of modern life have had a significant effect on our nation's youth. Adolescence is unquestionably a time of transition, a time of trial and uncertainty, a time when youths are extremely vulnerable to emotional turmoil, experiencing anxiety, humiliation, and mood swings. During this period, the self, or basic personality, is still undergoing a metamorphosis and is vulnerable to a host of external factors as well as to internal physiological changes.[5]

Adolescents also undergo a period of biological development that proceeds at a far faster pace than at any other time in their lives except infancy. Over a period of a few years, their height, weight, and sexual characteristics change dramatically. A hundred and fifty years ago girls matured sexually at age 16, but the average age at which girls reach puberty today is 12.5 years. Although they may be capable of having children as early as age 14, many youngsters remain emotionally and intellectually immature long after biological maturity.[6] At age 15 a significant number of teenagers are approaching adulthood unable to adequately meet the requirements and responsibilities of the workplace, the family, and the neighborhood. Many suffer from health problems, are educational underachievers, and are already skeptical about their ability to enter the American mainstream.[7]

In later adolescence (ages 16 to 18) youths may experience a life crisis that psychologist Erik Erikson labeled the struggle between ego identity and role diffusion. **Ego identity** is formed when youths develop a firm sense of who they are

ego identity
According to Erik Erikson, ego identity is formed when persons develop a firm sense of who they are and what they stand for.

Table 1.2

WHERE AMERICA STANDS

Among industrialized countries, the United States ranks:

1st	in gross domestic product
1st	in the number of millionaires and billionaires
1st	in health technology
1st	in military technology
1st	in military exports
1st	in defense spending
10th	in eighth-grade science scores
16th	in living standards among the poorest one-fifth of children
17th	in rates of low-birthweight births
18th	in the income gap between rich and poor children
18th	in infant mortality
21st	in eighth-grade math scores
Last	in protecting our children against gun violence

According to the Centers for Disease Control and Prevention, U.S. children under age 15 are:

12	times more likely to die from gunfire,
16	times more likely to be murdered by a gun,
11	times more likely to commit suicide with a gun, and
9	times more likely to die in a firearm accident

than children in 25 other industrialized countries *combined*.

Source: Children's Defense Fund, *The State of America's Children Yearbook 1998* (Washington, D.C.: Children's Defense Fund, p. 2)

role diffusion

According to Erik Erikson, role diffusion occurs when youths spread themselves too thin, experience personal uncertainty, and place themselves at the mercy of leaders who promise to give them a sense of identity they cannot develop for themselves.

and what they stand for; **role diffusion** occurs when youths experience personal uncertainty, spread themselves too thin, and place themselves at the mercy of leaders who promise to give them a sense of identity they cannot mold for themselves.[8] Could Christopher Vasquez have suffered role diffusion, making him susceptible to the influence of a strong person such as Daphne Abdela? Psychologists also find that late adolescence is a period dominated by the yearning for independence from parental control.[9] Given this explosive mixture of biological change and a desire for autonomy, it isn't surprising that the teenage years are a time of rebelliousness and conflict with authority at home, at school, and in the community.

Youth in Crisis

In 1998 there were about 70 million children in the United States, a number that is projected to increase to 77.6 million by 2020.[10] During the "baby boom" (1946 to 1964), the number of children increased rapidly. This growth rate declined in the 1970s and 1980s but began to increase again in 1990. Children are projected to remain a fairly stable percentage of the total population, making up about 24 percent of the population by the year 2020.

Problems in the home, the school, and the neighborhood, coupled with health and developmental hazards, have placed a significant portion of American youth "at risk." Youths considered at risk are those dabbling in various forms of dangerous conduct such as drug abuse, alcohol use, and precocious sexuality. Due to economic, health, or social problems, many families are unable to provide adequate care and discipline. Although it is impossible to determine precisely the number of at-risk youths in the United States, one estimate is that 25 percent of the population under age 17, or about 17 million youths, are vulnerable to the negative consequences of school failure, substance abuse, and early sexuality. Of these, seven million are extremely vulnerable to delinquency and gang activity.[11] An additional seven million adolescents can be classified as "at moderate risk."[12]

at-risk youths

Young people who are extremely vulnerable to the negative consequences of school failure, substance abuse, and early sexuality.

The most pressing problems facing American youth revolve around four issues.

Poverty. About 20 percent of all children are now living below the poverty line, which is about $16,000 annual income for a family of four. Although the percentage of extremely poor adolescents in the population has remained fairly steady since 1980, the Tufts University Center on Hunger, Poverty, and Nutrition Policy estimates that 20.7 million, or 28 percent, of all minor children will be living in poverty by the year 2012.[13]

Family Problems. Divorce strikes about half of all new marriages, and many families sacrifice time with each other to afford better housing and more affluent lifestyles. Research shows that children in the United States are being polarized into two distinct economic groups: those born into affluent, two-earner, married couple households and those residing in impoverished, single-parent households.[14]

Urban Decay. The destructive environment of deteriorated urban areas prevents too many adolescents from having productive, fulfilling, and happy lives. Many face an early death from random bullets and drive-by shootings. Some are homeless, living desperate lives on the street where they are at risk of drug addiction and sexually transmitted diseases (STDs) including AIDS. One study of 425 homeless "street kids" in New York City found that 37 percent earned money through prostitution and almost one-third had contracted an STD.[15]

Inadequate Education. The U.S. educational system, once the envy of the world, now seems to be failing many young people. We are lagging behind other developed nations in critical areas such as science and mathematics achievement. The rate of *retention* (being forced to repeat a grade) is far higher than it should be in most communities. Retention rates are associated

Although it is impossible to precisely determine the number of at-risk youth in the United States, one estimate is that 25 percent of the population under 17, or more than 7 million youths, are extremely vulnerable to the negative consequences of school failure, substance abuse, and early sexuality. This teen prostitute is at extreme risk of violent crime and victimization.

with another major educational problem: dropping out. It is estimated that about 14 percent of all eligible youths do not finish high school.[16] All young people face stress in the education system, but the risks are greatest for the poor, members of racial and ethnic minorities, and recent immigrants. These children usually attend the most underfunded schools, receive inadequate educational opportunities, and have the fewest opportunities to achieve conventional success.

Considering that youth are at risk during the most tumultuous time of their lives, it comes as no surprise that they are willing, as the Focus on Delinquency box suggests, to engage in risky, destructive behavior.

Are There Reasons for Hope?

Despite the many hazards faced by teens, there are some bright spots on the horizon. According to a 1998 report by the National Center for Health Statistics, teenage birthrates nationwide have declined substantially during the 1990s, with the sharpest declines being experienced by African American girls (see Figure 1.1 on page

RISKY BUSINESS

The Centers for Disease Control (CDC) reports that in the United States 73 percent of all deaths among youths and young adults ten to twenty-four years of age result from only four causes: motor vehicle crashes, other unintentional injuries, homicide, and suicide. The reason may be that many high school students engage in risky behaviors that increase their likelihood of death from violence, accident, or self-destruction. A survey conducted by the CDC found that significant numbers of high school students had engaged in activities that, by most standards, would be considered risky (see Table A).

Why do youths take such chances? Criminologist Nanette Davis suggests there is a potential for "risky" behavior among youths in all facets of American life. Risk is behavior that is emotionally edgy, dangerous, exciting, hazardous, challenging, volatile, and potentially emotionally, socially, and financially costly—sometimes even life-threatening. Youths commonly become involved in risky behavior as they negotiate the hurdles of adolescent life, learning to drive, date, drink, work, relate, and live. Davis finds that social developments in the United States have increased the risks of growing up for all children. Some of the social, economic, and political circumstances that increase adolescent risk taking are:

1. *The uncertainty of contemporary social life.* Planning a future is problematic in a society where job elimination and corporate downsizing are accepted business practices and divorce and family restructuring are epidemic.

2. *Politicians who opt for short-term solutions while ignoring long-term consequences.* For example, politicians may find that fighting minimum wage increases pleases their constituents. Yet a low minimum wage reinforces the belief that economic advancement cannot be achieved through conventional means. This may undermine the working poors' belief in the "American Dream" of economic opportunity and lead to delinquent alternatives such as drug dealing or theft.

Table A   A Profile of High School Students

- 20 percent of the high school students surveyed rarely or never wore seat belts
- 37 percent had ridden with a driver who had been drinking alcohol
- 50.8 percent had drunk alcohol
- 18 percent had carried a weapon
- 26 percent had used marijuana
- 8 percent had attempted suicide during the twelve months preceding the survey
- 50 percent of the high school students had had sexual intercourse
- 43 percent of sexually active students had not used a condom
- 36 percent had smoked cigarettes during the prior month

12).[17] These data indicate that more young girls are using birth control and practicing "safe sex." Fewer children with health risks are being born today than in 1990. This probably means that fewer women are drinking alcohol or smoking cigarettes during pregnancy and that fewer are receiving late or no prenatal care. Since 1990 the number of children immunized against disease has also increased.[18]

Due in large part to improvements in medical technology, infant mortality rates—or the number of children who die before their first birthday—has declined about 30 percent during the past decade (from 10.6 to 7.6 per 1,000 births).[19]

3. *The emphasis on consumerism.* In high school, peer respect is "bought" through the accumulation of material goods. Underprivileged youths are driven to illegal behavior in an effort to engage in conspicuous consumption. Drug deals and theft may be a short-cut to getting coveted name brand clothing and athletic shoes.

4. *Race, class, age, and ethnic inequalities that discourage kids from believing in a better future.* Children are raised to be skeptical that they can receive social benefits from any institution beyond themselves or their immediate family.

5. *Lack of adequate child care.* This has become a national emergency. Lower-class women cannot afford adequate child care. New welfare laws requiring single mothers to work put millions of children in high-risk situations. Children receiving low-quality care can have delayed cognition and language development. They behave more aggressively toward others and react poorly to stress.

6. *Limited access to dominant social institutions.* Gaining access to social institutions is most often a function of social class and occupation. Without such access people are less able to manage risk.

7. *The "cult of individualism."* People become self-involved and self-centered, which hurts collective and group identities. Children are taught to put their own interests above those of others. People occupy their own private worlds without caring for the rights of others.

Some children are extreme risk takers who often take on what appears to adults to be extremely chancy behaviors. Their motives may be survival and acceptance in a hostile environment. For example, joining a gang is very risky. It exposes youths to a variety of dangers including drug use and violence. But not joining a gang may be even riskier because gangs provide protection and comradery. Similarly, although adults consider recreational drug use dangerous and risky, youths may find the risks acceptable because the youth culture has made drug use the norm. Peer acceptance and admiration may outweigh the risk of school failure, family conflict, and personality change associated with drug use.

As children mature into adults, the uncertainty of modern society may prolong their risk-taking behavior. Jobs have become unpredictable, and many undereducated and undertrained youths find themselves competing for the same low-paying job with hundreds of applicants; they are a "surplus product." They may find their only alternative for survival is to return to their childhood home and live off their parents. Under these circumstances, risk taking may be a plausible alternative for fitting into our consumer-oriented society.

Davis calls for a major national effort to "restore" these troubled youths using a holistic, nonpunitive approach that recognizes the special needs of children.

Sources: Laura Kann et al., "Youth Risk Behavior Surveillance—United States, 1997" (Atlanta, Ga.: Centers for Disease Control, 14 August 1998); Nanette Davis, *Youth Crisis: Growing Up in the High-Risk Society* (New York: Praeger, Greenwood Publishing, 1999).

Although education is still a problem area, more parents are reading to their young children, and math achievement is rising in grades 4 through 12. More students are receiving degrees in math and science than in the 1970s and 1980s.[20]

There are also indications that youngsters may be rejecting hard drugs. Teen smoking and drinking rates remain unacceptably high, but fewer kids are getting involved in heroin and crack cocaine use.[21]

Although these signs are encouraging many problem areas remain, and the improvement of adolescent life continues to be a national goal.

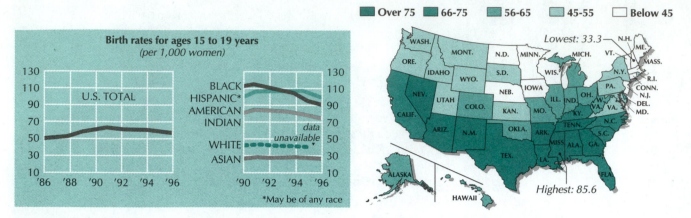

FIGURE 1.1

Teen Birth Trends

Source: Stephanie Ventura, Sally Curten, and T. J. Matthews, *Teenage Birth in the U.S.: National & State Trends, 1990–1996* (Washington, D.C.: National Center for Health Statistics, 1998).

The Study of Juvenile Delinquency

juvenile delinquency
Participation in illegal behavior by a minor who falls under a statutory age limit.

chronic delinquents
Youths who have been arrested five or more times during their minority; this small group of offenders is believed to engage in a significant portion of all delinquent behavior.

aging-out process
The tendency for youths to reduce the frequency of their offending behavior as they age (also called spontaneous remission); aging out is thought to occur among all groups of offenders.

The problems of youth in modern society are both a major national concern and an important subject for academic study. This text focuses on one area of particular concern: **juvenile delinquency,** or criminal behavior committed by minors. The study of juvenile delinquency is important because of both the damage suffered by its victims and the problems faced by its perpetrators.

More than two million youths are arrested each year for crimes ranging in seriousness from loitering to murder.[22] Though most juvenile law violations are minor, some young offenders are extremely dangerous and violent. More than 700,000 youths belong to street gangs and groups that can put fear into an entire city. Youths involved in multiple serious criminal acts—referred to as lifestyle, repeat, or **chronic delinquent** offenders—are now recognized as a serious social problem. State juvenile authorities must deal with these offenders, along with responding to a range of other social problems, including child abuse and neglect, school crime and vandalism, family crises, and drug abuse.

Given the diversity and gravity of these problems, there is an urgent need for strategies to combat such a complex social phenomenon as juvenile delinquency. But formulating effective strategies demands a solid understanding of delinquency's causes. Is delinquency a function of psychological abnormality? a collective reaction by youths against destructive social conditions? the product of a disturbed home life and disrupted socialization? Does serious delinquent behavior occur only in large urban areas among lower-class youths? Or is it spread throughout the entire social structure? What impact does family life, substance abuse, school experiences, and peer relations have on youths and their law-violating behaviors?

We know that most youthful law violators do not go on to become adult criminals; this is known as the **aging-out process.** Yet we do not know why some youths become *chronic career offenders* whose delinquent careers begin early and persist into their adulthood. Why does the onset of delinquency begin so early in some children? Why does the severity of their offenses escalate? What factors pre-

juvenile justice system
The segment of the justice system including law enforcement officers, the courts, and correctional agencies, designed to treat youthful offenders.

dict the *persistence,* or continuation, of delinquency, and conversely, what are the factors associated with its *desistance,* or termination? Unless these questions are studied in an orderly and scientific manner, developing effective prevention and control strategies will be difficult.

The study of delinquency also involves the analysis of law enforcement, court, and correctional agencies designed to treat youthful offenders. This is known collectively as the **juvenile justice system.** How should police deal with minors who violate the law? What are the legal rights of children? For example, should minors who commit murder receive the death penalty? What kind of correctional programs are most effective with delinquent youths? How useful are educational, community, counseling, and vocational development programs? Is it true, as some critics claim, that most efforts to rehabilitate young offenders are doomed to failure?[23] Should we adopt a punishment or a treatment orientation to combat delinquency, or something in between?

In summary, the scientific study of delinquency requires understanding the nature, extent, and cause of youthful law violations and the methods devised for their control. We also need to study important environmental and social issues associated with delinquent behavior, including substance abuse, child abuse and neglect, education, and peer relations. This textbook investigates these aspects of juvenile delinquency along with the efforts being made to treat problem youths and prevent the spread of delinquent behavior. Our study begins with a look back to the development of the concept of "childhood" and how children were first identified as a unique group with their own special needs and behaviors.

The Development of Childhood

The treatment of children as a distinct social group with special needs and behavior is, in historical terms, a relatively new concept. It is only for the past 350 years or so that any formal mechanism existed to care for even the most needy children, including those left orphaned and destitute. How did this concept of concern for children develop?

In Europe during the Middle Ages (A.D. 700 to A.D. 1500), the concept of childhood as we know it today did not exist. In the **paternalistic family** of the time, the father was the final authority on all family matters and exercised complete control over the social, economic, and physical well-being of his wife and children.[24] Children who did not obey were subject to severe physical punishment, even death.

paternalistic family
A family style wherein the father is the final authority on all family matters and exercises complete control over his wife and children.

For medieval children, the passage into adulthood was abrupt. As soon as they were physically capable, children of all classes were expected to engage in adult roles. Among the working classes, males engaged in farming or learning a skilled trade, such as masonry or metal working; females aided in food preparation or household maintenance.[25] Some peasant youths went into domestic or agricultural service on the estates of powerful landowners or in trades or crafts such as a blacksmith or farrier (horseshoer).[26]

Children of the affluent landholding classes also assumed adult roles at an early age. Girls born into aristocratic families were educated at home and married in their early teens. A few were taught to read, write, and do sufficient mathematics to handle household accounts in addition to typical female duties such as supervising servants and ensuring the food supply of the manor.

At age 7 or 8, boys born to landholding families were either sent to a monastery or cathedral school to be trained for lives in the church or selected to be members of the warrior class and sent to serve as squires, or assistants, to experienced knights. At age 21, young men of the knightly classes completed their terms as squires, received their own knighthoods, and returned home to live with their parents. Most remained single because it was widely believed there should only be one married couple residing in a castle. To pass the time and maintain their fighting edge, many entered the tournament circuit, engaging in melees and jousts to win fame and fortune. Upon the death of their fathers, young nobles assumed their inherited titles, married, and began their own families.

Custom and Practice in the Middle Ages

primogeniture
Middle Ages practice of allowing only the family's eldest son to inherit lands and titles.

Custom and practice greatly amplified the hardships suffered by many children during the Middle Ages. Among the landholding classes, **primogeniture** required that the oldest surviving male child inherit family lands and titles. He could then distribute them as he saw fit to younger siblings. There was no absolute requirement, however, that portions of the estate be distributed equally. Many youths received no lands and were forced to enter religious orders, become soldiers, or seek wealthy patrons. Primogeniture often caused intense family rivalry that led to blood feuds and tragedy.

dower system
Middle Ages custom of the bride's family giving the groom monetary compensation before a marriage could take place.

Dower   The **dower system** mandated that a woman's family bestow money, land, or other wealth (called a dowery) on a potential husband or his family in exchange for his marriage to her. In return, the young woman received a promise of financial assistance, called a *jointure,* from the groom's family. Jointure provided a lifetime income if a wife outlived her mate. The dower system had a significant impact on the role of women in medieval society and consequently on the role of children. Within this system, a father or male guardian had the final say in his daughter's choice of marital partner because he could threaten to withhold her dowery. Some women were denied access to marriage simply because of their position in a family. A father with many daughters and few sons might find himself financially unable to obtain suitable marriages. Consequently, the youngest girls in many families were forced to enter convents, were abandoned, or were left at home.

The dower system had far-reaching effects on the position of women in society, forcing them into the role of second class citizens dependent on their fathers, brothers, and guardians. Females who did not conform to what males considered to be acceptable standards of feminine behavior could receive harsh sanctions. The dower system established a sexual double standard that still exists in part today.

Child Rearing and Discipline   The harshness of medieval life influenced child-rearing practices during the fifteenth and sixteenth centuries. For instance, newborns were almost immediately handed over to *wet nurses* who fed and cared for them during the first two years of life. These women often lived away from the family, and parents had little contact with their children. Even the wealthiest families employed wet nurses because it was considered demeaning for a noblewoman to nurse. Wrapping a newborn entirely in bandages, or s*waddling,* was a common practice. The bandages prevented any movement and enabled the wet nurse to manage the child easily. This practice was thought to protect the child, but it most likely contributed to high infant mortality rates because the child could not be kept clean.

Discipline was severe during this period. Young children of all classes, both peasant and wealthy, were subjected to stringent rules and regulations. Children were beaten severely for any sign of disobedience or ill-temper, and many children of this time would be considered abused by today's standards. The relationship between parent and child was remote. Children were expected to enter the world of adults and to undertake responsibilities early in their lives, sharing in the work of

As soon as they were physically capable, children of the Middle Ages were expected to engage in adult roles. Among the working classes, males engaged in peasant farming or learned a skilled trade, such as masonry or metal working; females aided in food preparation or household maintenance. Some peasant youth went into domestic or agricultural service on the estate of a powerful landowner or in trades or crafts, such as blacksmith or farrier (horseshoer).

siblings and parents. Children thought to be suffering from disease or retardation were often abandoned to churches, orphanages, or foundling homes.[27]

The roots of the impersonal relationship between parent and child can be traced to high mortality rates, which made sentimental and affectionate relationships risky. Parents were reluctant to invest emotional effort in relationships that could so easily end due to violence, accidents, or disease. Many believed children must be toughened to ensure their survival in a hostile world, and close family relationships were viewed as detrimental to this process. Also, since the oldest male child was the essential player in a family's well-being, younger male and female siblings were considered economic and social liabilities.

The Development of Concern for Children

Throughout the seventeenth and eighteenth centuries, a number of developments in England heralded the march toward the recognition of children's rights. Some of these events eventually affected the juvenile legal system as it emerged in the United

States. They include (1) changes in family style and child care, (2) the English Poor Laws, (3) the apprenticeship movement, and (4) the role of the chancery court.[28]

Changes in Family Structure   Family structure and the role of children began to change after the Middle Ages. Extended families, which were created over centuries, gave way to the nuclear family structure with which we are familiar today. It became more common for marriage to be based on love and mutual attraction between men and women rather than on parental consent and paternal dominance. This changing concept of marriage—from an economic arrangement to an emotional commitment—also began to influence the way children were treated within the family structure. Although parents still rigidly disciplined their children, they formed closer parental ties and had greater concern for their offsprings' well-being.

Grammar and boarding schools were established and began to flourish in many large cities during this time.[29] Children studied grammar, Latin, law, and logic, often beginning at a young age. Teachers in these institutions often ruled by fear, and flogging was their main method of discipline. Students were beaten for academic mistakes as well as for moral lapses. Such brutal treatment fell on both the rich and the poor throughout all levels of educational life, including boarding schools and universities. This treatment abated in Europe with the rise of the Enlightenment, but it remained in full force in Great Britain until late in the nineteenth century. Although this brutal approach to children may be difficult to understand now, remember that the child in that society was a second-class citizen.

Toward the close of the eighteenth century, the work of such philosophers as Voltaire, Rousseau, and Locke launched a new age for childhood and the family.[30] Their vision produced a period known as the Enlightenment, which stressed a humanistic view of life, freedom, family, reason, and law. The ideal person was sympathetic to others and receptive to new ideas. These new beliefs influenced both the structure and the lifestyle of the family. The father's authority was tempered, discipline in the home became more relaxed, and the expression of love and affection became more commonplace among family members. Upper- and middle-class families began to devote attention to child rearing, and the status of children was advanced.

As a result of these changes, nineteenth-century children began to emerge as a readily distinguishable group with independent needs and interests. Parents often took greater interest in their upbringing. In addition, serious questions arose over the treatment of children in school. Public outcries led to a decrease in excessive physical discipline. Restrictions were placed on the use of the whip, and in some schools the imposition of academic assignments or the loss of privileges replaced corporal punishment. Despite such reforms, many children still led harsh lives. Girls were still undereducated, punishment was still primarily physical, and schools continued to mistreat children.

Poor Laws

English statutes that allowed the courts to appoint overseers over destitute and neglected children, who then placed them in families, workhouses, or apprenticeships.

Poor Laws   Government action to care for needy children can be traced to the Poor Laws of Great Britain. As early as 1535, the English passed statutes known as **Poor Laws.**[31] These laws allowed for the appointment of overseers to place destitute or neglected children as servants in the homes of the affluent. The Poor Laws forced children to serve during their minority in the care of families who trained them in agricultural, trade, or domestic services. The Elizabethan Poor Laws of 1601 were a model for dealing with poor children for more than two hundred years. These laws created a system of church wardens and overseers who, with the consent of justices of the peace, identified vagrant, delinquent, and neglected children and took measures to put them to work. Often this meant placing them in poorhouses or workhouses or apprenticing them to masters.

The Apprenticeship Movement   Apprenticeship in Great Britain existed throughout almost the entire history of the country.[32] Under this practice, children were placed in the care of adults who trained them to discharge various duties and ob-

Work in the newly developing factories taxed young laborers, placing demands on them they were often too young to endure. To alleviate a rapidly developing problem, the Factory Acts of the early nineteenth century limited the hours children were permitted to work and the age at which they could begin work. It also prescribed a minimum amount of schooling to be provided by factory owners.

tain specific skills. Voluntary apprentices were bound out by parents or guardians who wished to secure training for their children. Involuntary apprentices were compelled by the authorities to serve until they were twenty-one or older. The master–apprentice relationship was similar to the parent–child relationship in that the master had complete responsibility for and authority over the apprentice. If an apprentice was unruly, a complaint could be made and the apprentice could be punished. Incarcerated apprentices were often placed in rooms or workshops apart from other prisoners and were generally treated differently from those charged with criminal offenses. Even at this early stage, the conviction was growing that the criminal law and its enforcement should be applied differently to children.

chancery courts
Court proceedings created in fifteenth-century England to oversee the lives of high-born minors who were orphaned or otherwise could not care for themselves.

parens patriae
Power of the state to act in behalf of the child and provide care and protection equivalent to that of a parent.

Chancery Court   Throughout Great Britain in the Middle Ages **chancery courts** were established to protect property rights, although their authority also extended to the welfare of children generally. The major issues in medieval cases that came before the chancery courts concerned guardianship of children who were orphaned. This included safeguarding their property and inheritance rights and appointing a guardian to protect them until they reached the age of majority and could care for themselves.

Chancery courts were founded on the proposition that children and other incompetents were under the protective control of the king; thus, the Latin phrase **parens patriae** was used, which refers to the role of the king as the father of his country. The concept was first used by English kings to establish their right to intervene in the lives of the children of their vassals—children whose position and property were of direct concern to the monarch.[33] In the famous 1827 English case *Wellesley v. Wellesley,* a duke's children were taken away from him in the name and interest of *parens patriae* because of his scandalous behavior.[34] Thus, the concept of *parens patriae* became the theoretical basis for the protective jurisdiction of the chancery courts acting as part of the crown's power. As time passed, the monarchy used *parens patriae* more and more to justify its intervention in the lives of families and children by its interest in their general welfare.[35]

The chancery courts dealt with the property and custody problems of the wealthier classes. They did not have jurisdiction over children charged with criminal conduct. Juveniles who violated the law were handled within the framework of the regular criminal court system. Nonetheless, the concept of *parens patriae,* which was established with the English chancery court system, grew to refer primarily to the responsibility of the courts and the state to act in the best interests of the child.

Childhood in America

While England was using its chancery courts and Poor Laws to care for children in need, the American colonies were developing similar concepts. The colonies were a haven for poor and unfortunate people looking for religious and economic opportunities denied them in England and Europe. Along with early settlers, many children came not as citizens but as indentured servants, apprentices, or agricultural workers. They were recruited from various English workhouses, orphanages, prisons, and asylums that housed vagrant and delinquent youths during the sixteenth and seventeenth centuries.[36]

At the same time, the colonists themselves produced illegitimate, neglected, abandoned, and delinquent children. The initial response to caring for such unfortunate children was to adopt court and Poor Laws systems similar to those in England. Involuntary apprenticeship, indenture, and binding out of children became integral parts of colonization. Poor Law legislation requiring poor and dependent children to serve apprenticeships was passed in Virginia in 1646 and in Massachusetts and Connecticut in 1673.[37]

The master in colonial America acted as a surrogate parent, and in certain instances apprentices would actually become part of the nuclear family structure. If they disobeyed their masters, apprentices were punished by local tribunals. If masters abused apprentices, courts would make them pay damages, return the children to the parents, or find new guardians. Maryland and Virginia developed an orphans' court that supervised the treatment of youths placed with guardians and ensured that they were not mistreated or taken advantage of by their masters. These courts did not supervise children living with their natural parents, leaving intact parents' rights to care for their children.[38]

By the beginning of the nineteenth century, as the agrarian economy began to be replaced by industry, the apprenticeship system gave way to the factory system, and the problems of how to deal effectively with growing numbers of dependent youths increased.

Early American settlers believed hard work, strict discipline, and education were the only reliable methods for salvation. A child's life was marked by work alongside parents, some schooling, prayer, more work, and further study. Work in the factories, however, often taxed young laborers by placing demands on them that they were too young to endure. To alleviate a rapidly developing problem, the Factory Act of the early nineteenth century limited the hours children were permitted to work and the age at which they could begin to work. It also prescribed a minimum amount of schooling to be provided by factory owners.[39] This and related statutes were often violated, and conditions of work and school remained troublesome issues well into the twentieth century. Nevertheless, the statutes were a step in the direction of reform.

Controlling Children

In the United States, as in England, moral discipline was rigidly enforced. Stubborn child laws were passed that required children to obey their parents.[40] It was not uncommon in the colonies for children who were disobedient or disrespectful to their families to be whipped or otherwise physically chastised. Children were often required to attend public whippings and executions because these events were thought to be important forms of moral instruction. Parents referred their children to published writings on behavior and discipline and expected them to follow their precepts carefully. The early colonists, however, viewed family violence as a sin, and child protection laws were passed as early as 1639 (in New Haven, Connecticut). These laws were generally symbolic and rarely enforced. They expressed the community's commitment to God to oppose sin, but offenders usually received lenient sentences.[41]

Although most colonies adopted a protectionist stance, few cases of child abuse were actually brought before the courts. There are several explanations for this neglect. The absence of child abuse cases may reflect the nature of life in what were essentially extremely religious households. Children were productive laborers and respected by their parents. In addition, large families provided many siblings and kinfolk who could care for children and relieve stress-producing burdens on parents.[42]

Another view is that although many children were harshly punished, in early American families the "acceptable" limits of discipline were so high that few parents were charged with assault. Any punishment that fell short of maiming or permanently harming a child was considered within the sphere of parental rights.[43]

The Concept of Delinquency

Considering the rough treatment handed out to children who misbehaved at home or at school, it should come as no surprise that children who actually broke the law and committed serious criminal acts were dealt with harshly. Prior to the twentieth century, little distinction was made between adult and juvenile offenders. Although judges considered the age of an offender when deciding on punishment, both adults and children were eligible for the same forms of punishment—prison, corporal punishment, and even the death penalty. In fact, children were treated with extreme cruelty at home, at school, and by the law.[44]

child savers
Nineteenth-century reformers who developed programs for troubled youth and influenced legislation creating the juvenile justice system; today some critics view them as being more concerned with control of the poor than with their welfare.

Over the years this treatment changed as society became sensitive to the special needs of children. Beginning in the mid-nineteenth century as immigrant youths poured into the United States, there was official recognition that children formed a separate group with their own special needs. Around the nation, in New York, Boston, and Chicago, groups known as **child savers** were being formed to assist children in need. They created community programs to service needy children and lobbied for a separate legal status for children, which ultimately led to development of a formal juvenile justice system. The child-saving movement will be discussed more fully in Chapter 12.

Delinquency and *Parens Patriae*

delinquent
Juvenile who has been adjudicated by a judicial officer of a juvenile court as having committed a delinquent act.

The current treatment of juvenile delinquents is a by-product of this developing national consciousness. The designation **delinquent** became popular at the onset of the twentieth century when the first separate juvenile courts were instituted. The child savers believed treating minors and adults equally violated the humanitarian ideals of American society. Consequently, the newly emerging juvenile justice system operated under the *parens patriae* philosophy. Minors who engaged in extralegal behavior were viewed as victims of improper care, custody, and treatment at home. Illegal behavior was a sign that the state should step in and take control of the youths before they committed more serious crimes. Through its juvenile authorities, the state should act in the **best interests of the child.** This means that children should not be punished for their misdeeds but instead should be given the care and custody necessary to remedy and control wayward behavior. It makes no sense to find children guilty of specific crimes, such as burglary or petty larceny, because that stigmatizes them and labels them as thieves or burglars. Instead, the catch-all term "juvenile delinquency" should be used because it indicates that the child needs the care, custody, and treatment of the state.

best interests of the child
A philosophical viewpoint that encouraged the state to take control of wayward children and provide care, custody, and treatment to remedy delinquent behavior.

The Legal Status of Delinquency

The child savers fought hard for a separate legal status of "juvenile delinquent" early in the twentieth century, but the concept that children could be treated differently before the law can actually be traced to its roots in the British legal tradition. Early British jurisprudence held that children under the age of seven were legally incapable of committing crimes. Children between the ages of seven and fourteen were responsible for their actions, but their age might be used to excuse or lighten their punishment. Our legal system still recognizes that many young people are incapable of making mature judgments and that responsibility for their acts should be limited. Children can intentionally steal cars and know full well that the act is illegal, but they may be incapable of fully understanding the consequences of their behavior and the harm it may cause. Therefore, the law does not punish a youth as it would an adult, and it sees youthful misconduct as evidence of unreasoned or impaired judgment.

Today, the legal status of juvenile delinquent refers to a minor child who has been found to have violated the penal code. Most states define "minor child" as an individual who falls under a statutory age limit, most commonly seventeen or eighteen years of age. Because of their minority status, juveniles are usually kept separate from adults and receive different consideration and treatment under the law. Most large police departments employ officers whose sole responsibility is youth crime and delinquency. Every state has some form of separate juvenile court with its own judges, probation department, and other facilities. Terminology is also different: Adults are *tried* in court; children are *adjudicated*. Adults can be *punished;* children are *treated*. If treatment is mandated, children can be sent to secure detention facilities, but they cannot normally be committed to adult prisons.

Children also have their own unique legal status. A minor apprehended for a criminal act is usually charged with "being a juvenile delinquent" regardless of the crime committed. These charges are confidential, and trial records are kept secret, with the name, behavior, and background of the delinquent offender sealed. Eliminating specific crime categories and maintaining secrecy are efforts to shield children from the stigma of a criminal conviction and to prevent youthful misdeeds from becoming a lifelong burden.

Legal Responsibility of Youths

In our society the actions of adults are controlled by two types of law: criminal law and civil law. Criminal laws prohibit activities that are injurious to the well-being of society and threaten the social order. Drug use, theft, and rape are criminal legal actions brought by state authorities against private citizens. In contrast, civil laws control interpersonal or private activities, and legal actions are usually initiated by individual citizens. The ownership and transfer of property, contractual relationships, and personal conflicts (torts) are subjects of civil law. Also covered under civil law are provisions for the care and custody of those people who cannot care for themselves—the mentally ill, the incompetent, and the infirm.

Today the juvenile delinquency concept occupies a legal status falling somewhere between criminal and civil law. Under *parens patriae,* delinquent acts are not considered criminal violations, nor are delinquents considered "criminals." The legal action against them is considered more similar (though not identical) to a civil action that determines their "need for treatment." This legal theory recognizes that children who violate the law are in need of the same care and treatment as are law-abiding citizens who cannot care for themselves and require state intervention in their lives.

Delinquent behavior is sanctioned less heavily than criminality because the law considers juveniles to be less responsible for their behavior than adults. As a class, adolescents are believed to (1) have a stronger preference for risk and novelty; (2) assess the potentially negative consequences of risky conduct less unfavorably than adults; (3) be more impulsive and more concerned with short-term rather than long-term consequences; (4) have a different appreciation of time and self-control; and (5) be more susceptible to peer pressure.[45] Many adolescents may be more responsible and calculating than adults, but under normal circumstances the law is willing to recognize age as a barrier to having full responsibility over one's actions.

Even though youths have a lesser degree of legal responsibility, they are in fact subject to arrest, trial, and incarceration just as adults are. Their legal predicament has prompted the courts to grant children many of the same legal protections granted to adults accused of criminal offenses. These legal protections include the right to consult an attorney, to be free from self-incrimination, and to be protected from illegal searches and seizures. However, state legislatures are toughening legal codes today and making them more punitive in an effort to "get tough" on dangerous youth.

Appreciation of the criminal nature of the delinquency concept has helped increase the legal rights of minors, but it has also allowed state authorities to declare that some offenders are "beyond control" and cannot be treated as children. This recognition has prompted the policy of **waiver process,** that is, transferring legal jurisdiction over the most serious and experienced juvenile offenders to the adult court for criminal prosecution. So although the *parens patriae* concept is still applied to children whose law violations are considered not to be serious, the more serious juvenile offenders can be declared "legal adults" and placed outside the jurisdiction of the juvenile court.

waiver process
Transferring legal jurisdiction over the most serious and experienced juvenile offenders to the adult court for criminal prosecution.

Status Offenders

In contrast to serious offenses that lead to prosecution of minors as adults, a child can also be sent to the juvenile court for behavior as frivolous as cutting class! In addition, a child can become subject to state authority for committing actions that would not be considered illegal if perpetrated by an adult. Conduct that is illegal only because the child is under age is known as a **status offense.** (Figure 1.2 illustrates some typical status offenses.) The court can also exercise control over dependent children.[46] Eleven states classify these youths using the term "child in need of supervision," whereas the remainder use terms such as "unruly child," "incorrigible child," or "minor in need of supervision."[47]

State control over a child's noncriminal behavior supports the *parens patriae* philosophy because it is assumed to be in the best interests of the child. Usually,

status offense
Conduct that is illegal only because the child is under age.

FIGURE 1.2
Status Offenses

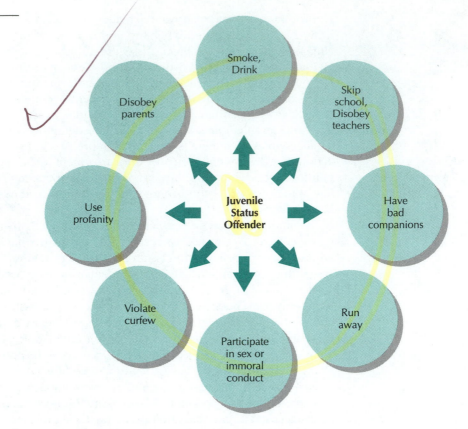

status offenders are directed to the juvenile court when it is determined that their parents are unable or unwilling to care for or control them and that the offenders' behavior is self-destructive or harmful to society.

A historical basis exists for status offense statutes. It was common practice early in the nation's history to place disobedient or runaway youths in orphan asylums, residential homes, or houses of refuge.[48] When the first juvenile courts were established in Illinois, the Chicago Bar Association described part of their purpose as follows:

> The whole trend and spirit of the [1889 Juvenile Court Act] is that the State, acting through the Juvenile Court, exercises that tender solicitude and care over its neglected, dependent wards that a wise and loving parent would exercise with reference to his own children under similar circumstances.[49]

Until relatively recently, however, almost every state treated status offenders and juvenile delinquents alike, referring to them either as **wayward minors** or delinquent children.

A trend begun in the 1960s has resulted in the creation of separate status offense categories that vary from state to state: children, minors, persons, youths, or juveniles in need of supervision (CHINS, MINS, PINS, YINS, or JINS). The purpose of creating separate status offender categories was to shield noncriminal youths from the stigma attached to the label "juvenile delinquent" and to signify that they were troubled youths who had special needs and problems. Table 1.3 shows the differences in these laws in two states. Wisconsin law is more oriented toward protective services than Louisiana law and encompasses more areas of child neglect.

Even where there are separate legal categories for delinquents and status offenders, the distinction between them has become blurred. Some noncriminal conduct may be included in the definition of delinquency, and some less serious criminal offenses occasionally may be labeled as status offenses.[50] In some states the juvenile court judge is granted discretion to substitute a status offense for a delinquency charge.[51] Replacing a juvenile delinquency charge with a status offense

wayward minors
Early legal designation of youths whose violations of the law related to their minority status; now referred to as *status offenders*.

Table 1.3
STATUS OFFENSE LAWS: WISCONSIN AND LOUISIANA

Louisiana

"Child in need of supervision" means a child who needs care or rehabilitation because:

1. Being subject to compulsory school attendance, he is habitually truant from school or willfully violates the rules of the school;

2. He habitually disobeys the reasonable and lawful demands of his parents, and is ungovernable and beyond their control;

3. He absents himself from his home or usual place of abode without the consent of his parent;

4. He purposefully, intentionally and willfully deceives, or misrepresents the true facts to, any person holding a retail dealer's permit, or his agent, associate, employee or representative, for the purposes of buying or receiving alcoholic beverages or beer, or visiting or loitering in or about any place where such beverages are the principal commodities sold or handled;

5. His occupation, conduct, environment or associations are injurious to his welfare; or

6. He has committed an offense applicable only to children.

Wisconsin

The court has exclusive original jurisdiction over a child alleged to be in need of protection or services which can be ordered by the court, and:

1. Who is without a parent or guardian;

2. Who has been abandoned;

3. Who has been the victim of sexual or physical abuse including injury which is self-inflicted or inflicted by another by other than accidental means;

4. Whose parent or guardian signs the petition requesting jurisdiction and states that he or she is unable to care for, control or provide necessary special care or special treatment for the child;

5. Who has been placed for care or adoption in violation of law;

6. Who is habitually truant from school, *after evidence is provided by the school attendance officer that the activities under s. 118.16(5) have been completed;*

7. Who is habitually truant from home and either the child or a parent, *guardian or a relative in whose home the child resides signs* the petition requesting jurisdiction and attests in court that reconciliation efforts have been attempted and have failed;

8. Who is receiving inadequate care during the period of time a parent is missing, incarcerated, hospitalized or institutionalized;

9. Who is at least age 12, signs the petition requesting jurisdiction and attests in court that he or she is in need of special care and treatment which the parent, guardian or legal custodian is unwilling to provide;

10. Whose parent, guardian or legal custodian neglects, refuses or is unable for reasons other than poverty to provide necessary care, food, clothing, medical or dental care or shelter so as to seriously endanger the physical health of the child;

11. Who is suffering emotional damage for which the parent or guardian is unwilling to provide treatment, which is evidenced by one or more of the following characteristics, exhibited to a severe degree: anxiety, depression, withdrawal or outward aggressive behavior;

12. Who, being under 12 years of age, has committed a delinquent act as defined in s. 48.12;

13. Who has not been immunized as required by s. 140.05(16) and not exempted under s. 140.05(16)(c); or

14. Who has been determined, under s. 48.30(5)(c), to be not responsible for a delinquent act by reason of mental disease or defect.

Source: LA. Code Juv.Proc.Ann. art. 13 § 12 (West 1979, amended 1987) and Wis.Stat.Ann. § 48.13 (West 1979, amended 1987).

charge can be used as a bargaining chip to encourage youths to admit to the charges against them in return for a promise of being treated as (less stigmatized) status offenders and receiving less punitive treatment.

The Status Offender in the Juvenile Justice System

Separate status offense categories may avoid some of the stigma associated with the delinquency label, but they have relatively little practical effect on the child's treatment. Youths in either category can be picked up by the police and brought to a police station. They can be petitioned to the same juvenile court, where they have a hearing before the same judge and come under the supervision of the probation department, the court clinic, and the treatment staff. At a hearing, status offenders may see little difference between the treatment they receive and the treatment of the delinquent offenders sitting across the room. Although status offenders are usually not detained or incarcerated with delinquents, they can be transferred to secure facilities if they are repeatedly unruly and considered uncontrollable.

Aiding the Status Offender

Office of Juvenile Justice and Delinquency Prevention (OJJDP)

Branch of the U.S. Justice Department charged with shaping national juvenile justice policy through disbursement of federal aid and research funds.

Efforts have been ongoing to reduce the penalties and stigma borne by status offenders. The **Office of Juvenile Justice and Delinquency Prevention (OJJDP)—** a federal agency created to identify the needs of youths and fund policy initiatives in the juvenile justice system—has made it a top priority to encourage the removal of status offenders from secure lockups, detention centers, and postdisposition treatment facilities that also house delinquent offenders. This has been a highly successful policy initiative, and the number of status offenders kept in secure pretrial detention has dropped significantly.[52]

Those who favor removing status offenders from juvenile court authority charge that their experience with the legal system further stigmatizes these already troubled youths, exposes them to the influence of "true" delinquents, and enmeshes them in a system that cannot really afford to help or treat their needs. Will the youth in this photo suffer from his experience with the police or might his behavior improve?

Despite this mandate, juvenile court judges in many states can still detain status offenders in secure lockups if the youths are found in "contempt of court." The act that created the OJJDP was amended in 1987 to allow status offenders to be detained and incarcerated for violations of "valid court orders."[53] Children have been detained for behavior such as wearing shorts to court, throwing paper on the floor, and, in one Florida case involving a pregnant teenager, for not keeping a doctor's appointment.[54] Activists have attempted to outlaw such practices because it puts noncriminal youth in jeopardy, and the Florida State Supreme Court forbade the practice in *A.A. v. Rolle* (1992).[55] It remains to be seen whether other jurisdictions will follow suit.

Change in the treatment of status offenders reflects the current attitude toward children who violate the law. On one hand, there appears to be a national movement to severely sanction youths who commit serious, violent offenses. On the other hand, a great effort has been made to remove nonserious cases, such as those involving status offenders, from the official agencies of justice and place these youths in informal, community-based treatment programs.

Reforming Status Offense Laws

For the past two decades national commissions have called for reform of status offense laws. More than twenty years ago the National Council on Crime and Delinquency, an influential, privately funded think tank, recommended removing status offenders from the juvenile court.[56] In 1976 the National Advisory Commission on Criminal Justice Standards and Goals, a task force created to develop a national crime policy, opted for the nonjudicial treatment of status offenders: "The only conduct that should warrant family court intervention is conduct that is clearly self-destructive or otherwise harmful to the child." To meet this standard, the commission suggested that the nation's juvenile courts confine themselves to controlling five status offenses: habitual truancy, repeated disregard for parental authority, repeated running away, repeated use of intoxicating beverages, and delinquent acts by youths under the age of ten.[57] The American Bar Association's National Juvenile Justice Standards Project, designed to promote significant improvements in the way children are treated by the police and the courts, called for the end of juvenile court jurisdiction over status offenders: "A juvenile's acts of misbehavior, ungovernability or unruliness which do not violate the criminal law should not constitute a ground for asserting juvenile court jurisdiction over the juvenile committing them."[58]

These calls for reform prompted a number of states, including New York, to experiment with replacing juvenile court jurisdiction over most status offenders with community-based treatment programs.[59] A few states, including Maine, Delaware, Idaho, and Washington, have attempted to eliminate status offense laws and treat these youths as neglected or dependent children, giving child protective services the primary responsibility for their care. However, juvenile court judges strongly resist removal of status jurisdiction. They believe that reducing judicial authority over children will limit juvenile court jurisdiction to only the most hard core juvenile offenders and constrain the court's ability to help youths before they commit serious antisocial acts.[60] Legislative changes may be more cosmetic than practical; when efforts to remedy the child's problems through a social welfare approach fail, the case can be referred to the juvenile court for more formal processing.[61]

Those who favor removing status offenders from juvenile court authority charge that their experience with the legal system further stigmatizes these already troubled youths, exposing them to the influence of "true" delinquents and enmeshing them in a system that cannot really afford to help them.[62] Reformer Ira Schwartz argues that status offenders "should be removed from the jurisdiction of the courts altogether."[63] Schwartz maintains that status offenders would best be served not by juvenile courts but by dispute resolution and mediation programs designed to strengthen family ties because "status offense cases are often rooted in family problems."[64]

Increasing Social Control

Those in favor of retaining the status offense category point to society's responsibility to care for troubled youths. Some have suggested that the failure of the courts to extend social control over wayward youths neglects the rights of concerned parents who are not able to care for and correct their children.[65] Others maintain that the status offense should remain a legal category so that juvenile courts can "force" a youth to receive treatment.[66] Although it is recognized that a court appearance can produce a negative "stigma," the taint may be less important than the need for treatment.[67] Many state jurisdictions, prompted by concern over serious delinquency, have enacted laws that actually expand social control over juveniles.

Curfew Laws   Beginning in 1990 there has been an explosion in the passage of curfew laws aimed at restricting the opportunity kids have for "getting in trouble." A survey of seventy-seven large U.S. cities found that fifty-nine of them have such laws.[68] Currently, more than 125,000 youths are arrested for curfew violations each year; in 1997 there were only about 60,000 arrests for curfew violations. Designed to deter serious delinquency, curfew laws have created large numbers of new status offenders.

Disciplining Parents   Another new approach to controlling status offenders is to actually punish parents for their children's misconduct. Since the early twentieth century, there have been laws aimed at disciplining parents for "contributing to the delinquency of a minor." The first of these statutes was enacted in Colorado in 1903, and today forty-two states and the District of Columbia maintain similar laws. As a group, such "contributing" laws allow parents to be sanctioned in juvenile courts for behaviors associated with or suspected of encouraging their child's misbehavior. Some states, such as Florida, Idaho, and Virginia, take a punitive approach and require parents to reimburse the government for costs associated with the detention or care of their children. Others, such as Maryland, Missouri, and Oklahoma, demand that parents make restitution payments if their children are unable to compensate victims. Sanctions might include having parents pay for damage caused by their children who vandalized a school. All states except New Hampshire have incorporated parental liability laws within their statutes, though most recent legislation places limits on recovery somewhere between $250 (Vermont) and $15,000 (Texas); the average is $2,500. Other states, such as Colorado, Texas, and Louisiana, are more prevention-oriented and require parents as well as children to participate in counseling and community service activities.[69]

An extreme form of discipline for parents also makes them criminally liable for the illegal acts of their children. Since 1990, there have been more than eighteen cases in which parents have been ordered to serve time in jail because their children have been truant from school. Whether such measures are legal and effective remains to be seen. Civil libertarians charge that these laws violate the constitutional right to due process and seem to be used only against lower-class parents. They find little evidence that punishing parents can deter delinquency and conclude that laws sanctioning parents are not only misguided and inadequate but take on an air of vindictiveness.[70] State laws of this kind have been successfully challenged in the lower courts.

Statutory Rape Laws   Juveniles may be considered status offenders if they engage in precocious or underage sexual behavior, especially if it involves an adult partner (referred to as statutory rape). Though the sex is not forced or coerced, the law holds that young girls are incapable of giving informed consent and therefore the act is legally considered nonconsensual. Such laws are consistent with the *parens patriae* concept because they are meant to protect the minor. Typically, state law will define an **age of consent** above which there can be no criminal prosecution for sexual relations. Though each state law is different, most evaluate the age differences between the parties to determine whether an offense has taken place. For example, Indiana law mandates prosecution of men aged 21 or older who have consensual sex with girls younger than age 14. Consensual sex between two minors of the same age would be considered under status offense rather than criminal law. A recent survey conducted by the American Bar Association (ABA) found that prosecution is often difficult in statutory rape cases because the young victims are reluctant to testify, parents often have given their "blessing" to the relationship, and juries are reluctant to convict men involved in consensual sex even with young teenage girls. The ABA report calls for stricter enforcement of these cases and notes that many states are already toughening their laws by raising the age of consent to protect minors from the psychological scars of precocious sexuality with an older predatory partner.[71]

Should the Courts Control Status Offenders?

Research shows that a majority of youths routinely engage in some status offenses and that those who refrain from doing so are an atypical minority.[72] "Illegal" acts such as teen sex and substance abuse have become normative and commonplace. Does it make sense, then, to have the juvenile court intervene with kids who are caught in what has become routine teenage behavior? In contrast, juvenile court jurisdiction over status offenders may be defended if, in fact, their offending patterns are similar to those of delinquents. Is their current offense only the tip of an antisocial "iceberg," or are they actually noncriminal youths who need only the loving hand of a substitute parent figure interested in their welfare?

A number of studies have attempted to answer this question, but their results are at best inconclusive.[73] Some find that status offenders are quite different, whereas others note that many status offenders also have prior arrests for delinquent acts and that many delinquents exhibited behaviors that would define them as status offenders.[74]

These disparate findings may be explained in part by the different "types" of status offenders, some similar to delinquents and others who are quite different.[75] It might be more realistic to divide status offenders into three groups: (1) first offenders, (2) those with prior status offenses, and (3) those with both a delinquent record and a status offense record.[76]. The fact that many young offenders have mixed delinquent–status offender records indicates that these legal categories are not entirely independent. However, it is also recognized that some "pure" first-time status offenders are quite different from delinquents and that a juvenile court experience can be harmful to them and escalate the frequency and seriousness of their law-violating behaviors.[77] The removal of these status offenders from the juvenile court is an issue that continues to be debated. The Case in Point box explores this question.

The predominate view today is that many status offenders and delinquents share similar social and developmental problems and, consequently, that both categories should fall under the jurisdiction of the juvenile court. Not surprisingly, research shows that the legal processing of delinquents and status offenders remains quite similar.[78]

You have just been appointed by the governor as chairperson of a newly formed group charged with overhauling the state's juvenile justice system.

One primary concern is the treatment of status offenders. Kids charged with being runaways, truants, or incorrigible are petitioned to juvenile court under an existing status offense statute. Those adjudicated as minors in need of supervision are usually placed with the county probation department. In serious cases, they may be removed from the home and placed in foster care or a state or private custodial institution. Recently, a great deal of media attention has been given to the plight of runaway children who live on the streets, take drugs, and engage in prostitution.

At an open hearing, advocates of the current system argue that many families cannot provide the care and control needed to keep children out of trouble and that the state must maintain control of at-risk youth. They contend that many status offenders have a history of drug and delinquency problems and are little different from youths arrested on criminal charges. Control by the juvenile court is necessary if the youths are ever to get needed treatment.

Another vocal group argues that it is a mistake for a system that deals with criminal youth to also handle troubled adolescents whose problems are the result of child abuse and neglect. They believe the current statute should be amended to give the state's Department of Social Welfare (DSW) jurisdiction over all noncriminal youths who are in need of assistance. These opponents of the current law point out that, even though status offenders and delinquents are held in separate facilities, those who violate the rules or run away can be transferred to correctional facilities that house criminal youths. Furthermore, the threatening process of lawyers, trials, and court proceedings helps convince these troubled youths that they are "bad kids" and social outcasts and not youths who need a helping hand. If necessary, the DSW could place needy children in community mental health clinics or with foster parents; they would, however, be totally removed from the justice system.

- Should status offenders be treated differently from juvenile delinquents?
- Should distinctions be made between different types of status offenders?
- Are status-type problems best handled by social service agencies?
- What recommendations would you make to the governor?

The "Dilemma" of Delinquency

The media has added to the nation's concerns about delinquency, helping convince the general public that "things are worse than ever." In fact, concern about youthful rebellion is not a recent phenomenon. In the 1950s

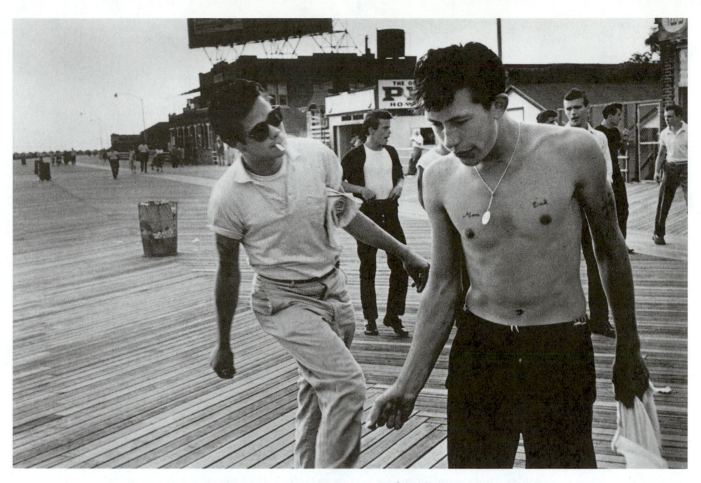

Although the media gives the impression that delinquency is only a contemporary problem, concern about youthful rebellion was common as far back as the 1950s. American teenagers were then viewed as rebellious troublemakers influenced by cult figures, comic books, movies, and advertising. These teens in New York around 1959 were part of what was called the "shook up generation."

social commentators were disturbed about the development of a postwar youth culture.[79] The American teenager was viewed as a rebellious troublemaker influenced by cult figures (especially James Dean and Elvis Presley), comic books, movies, and advertising. Teens spoke a separate language ("blast," "drag," "shook up"), had their own dress code (jeans and "duck tail" haircuts), and listened to the new rock and roll music, which sounded quite alien to their parents who were part of the "swing generation." And though the delinquency rate was still relatively low, an increase in youth crime between 1950 and 1956 prompted angry public outbursts against a "generation gone sour." *New York Times* reporter Harrison Salisbury called teens in the 1950s the "shook up generation."[80]

These concerns prompted a U.S. Senate subcommittee headed by Estes Kefauver to look into the delinquency problem. Psychologist Frederic Wertham published *The Seduction of the Innocent,* which named comic books with a violent theme as a cause of delinquency. The resulting public outrage forced the comic book industry to adopt a code of standards.[81]

Forty years later, many of these problems remain, and some have increased in severity. Many American youths live in neighborhoods where they fear violence walking to school in the morning and where it is common to begin experimenting with drugs and alcohol at an early age. They live in a country whose leaders tell them to practice sexual abstinence yet also tell them that if they have sex, it must be "safe." Early sexual experimentation has also increased the proportion of youth

YOUTH CRIME AROUND THE WORLD

A youngster is robbed on the street by knife-wielding teenagers who covet his designer-labeled backpack; a headmaster is stabbed to death by a pupil outside his school; a thirty-year-old man is trampled to death by teenagers because he tried to talk them out of tipping other people's motorcycles; youngsters set one hundred cars afire in a single year. You may be surprised to learn that these crimes were not reported to the police in the United States; these incidents occurred in Berlin, London, Amsterdam, and Strasbourg, France.

Delinquency rates are on the rise around the world. James Finckenauer reports that Russia has experienced a significant increase in delinquency, with the number of reported acts doubling in the last ten years. Finckenauer found that delinquents account for nearly 20 percent of all serious criminal activity in Russia. Delinquency rates in other western countries, traditionally quite low, have been increasing while at the same time the crime rate among America's teenagers has been falling. Germany has been wracked by well-publicized outbursts of violence against immigrants and minorities by youth gangs of "skinheads." The "skins" are reacting to unemployment and competition for jobs between Germans and immigrants. Some skins are neo-Nazis whose violence is fueled by racial hatred; others are apolitical youths whose violence is motivated by the anger of poverty and ignorance. In addition to these fascist outbursts, juveniles have been involved in about 20 percent of all violent crime in Germany and one-third of all property offenses. Drug abuse is also a common problem. More than 10 percent of German youth have had experience with drugs; Germany has more than one hundred thousand drug addicts today.

Paul Friday reports that crime in Sweden—a country known for its liberal social welfare programs—is also on the increase. Crime patterns in Sweden are similar to those in the United States: the majority of offenders are young males, and a few chronic offenders are responsible for a majority of all known offenses.

There have also been reports of increased criminal activity in Asia. Japan—a nation that prides itself on low crime rates—has experienced an upsurge in juvenile crime. It is estimated that 45 percent of all crimes in Japan are committed by people under age 20, about double what it is in the United States. Because so much of Japanese crime is committed by youths and the juvenile crime rate is escalating, experts predict an overall increase in future crime rates.

What has fueled this increase in teen violence? Although each nation is quite different, all share an explosive mix of racial tension, poverty, envy, drug abuse, broken families, unemployment, and alienation. Some of the areas hardest hit have been undergoing rapid social and economic change—the fall of communism, the end of the Cold War, the effects of the global economy, an influx of multinational immigration—as they move toward increased economic integration, privatization, and diminished social services. Asia is experiencing economic pressures and collapsing economies. In Japan students are under intense pressure to succeed and are often left on their own with relatively little support from parents or peers.

who contract STDs, including AIDS.[82] Although the number of teenage pregnancies has been on the decline, many teens are still getting pregnant. Children born to underage mothers often have low birth weights and are extremely vulnerable to health problems. Teenage mothers are also more likely to drop out of school and face economic disadvantages that hinder their future.

In the 1950s youths were reading comic books, but 1990s teens are listening to heavy metal rock bands such as Marilyn Manson, whose songs dwell on Satanism, drug use, and racial conflict. They watch TV shows and movies that rely on graphic scenes of violence as their main theme. Films such as *Seven* and *Silence of the Lambs* depict brutish acts of decapitation and dismemberment. And the brave new world of cyberspace has exposed our nation's youth to images that their 1950s counter-

As in the United States, middle-class parents can no longer guarantee their children greater prosperity than they enjoyed. Unemployment is high at the same time that slick advertising and peer pressure have convinced youngsters that material goods such as expensive shoes and CD players are a social requirement.

European schools seem ill-equipped to handle teen troublemakers. In Great Britain schools have failed to provide the solid education youngsters need. According to British police, semiliterate school-age truants accounted for 40 percent of street crime in London.

Urban housing projects have become the breeding ground for violent youths. Suburban housing projects in some cities in France have become known as liberated zones of drug dealers, who prey on the unemployed descendants of North African immigrants and the unemployed.

Some European politicians have called for a get-tough policy to combat juvenile crime. In Britain, where property crime rates are now higher than in the United States, the New Labor Party has promised a crackdown on juvenile crime. However, critics argue that the United States has only overcome its crime problems by creating a prison population of more than one million, a far higher incarceration rate than that of Britain, which has a prison population of 60,000.

Does the leveling off in crime rates achieved in the United States mean that American get-tough policies would be appropriate abroad? For some European countries—particularly Germany, with its memories of Nazi and communist dictatorship—the balance between civil liberty and public order may never be allowed to tip very far in favor of police and prosecutors. And many cling to the notion that young criminals need crime prevention programs, personal help, and rehabilitation as much as punishment. In Odense, Denmark, for example, authorities have instituted far-reaching and intrusive cooperation between police, social workers, and government officials, and they make routine visits to the parents of young people to warn parents that their offspring might be on the brink of criminal associations.

Sources: Michael Zielenziger, "Juvenile Crime Jumps to Record High in Japan," *Boston Globe* 19 April 1998; Alan Cowell, "Europe Envies America: Now, Teen-Agers Turn to Crime," *New York Times* 1 February 1998; Reuters, "Singapore Says Delinquency Up," *Boston Globe* 17 February 1996, p. 4; James Finckenauer, *Russian Youth, Law, Deviance and the Pursuit of Freedom* (New Brunswick, NJ: Transaction Books, 1995); Clayton Hartjen, "Legal Change and Juvenile Justice in India," paper presented at the American Society of Criminology Meetings, Boston, MA, November 1995; Alison Hatch and Curt Griffiths, "Youth Crime in Canada: Observations for Cross-Cultural Analysis," *International Journal of Comparative and Applied Criminal Justice* 16: 165–79 (1992); Gunther Kaiser, "Juvenile Delinquency in the Federal Republic of Germany," *International Journal of Comparative and Applied Criminal Justice* 16: 185–97 (1992); Marie Douglas, "Auslander Raus! Nazi Raus! An Observation of German Skins and Jugendgangen," *International Journal of Comparative and Applied Criminal Justice* 16: 129–33 (1992); Paul Friday, "Delinquency in Sweden: Current Trends and Theoretical Implications," *International Journal of Comparative and Applied Criminal Justice* 16: 231–44 (1992); Galan Janeksela, "The Significance of Comparative Analysis of Juvenile Delinquency and Juvenile Justice," *International Journal of Comparative and Applied Criminal Justice* 16: 137–47 (1992), p. 146.

parts could not imagine. How will this exposure affect the current and future generation of American children? Should we, as American citizens, be concerned?

The reaction to juvenile delinquency frequently divides the American public. People are concerned about the problems of youth and want to insulate young people from a life of crime and drug abuse. Research suggests that a majority of the American public still favors policies mandating rehabilitation and treatment of known offenders.[83] Evidence also exists that many at-risk youths can be successfully helped with the proper treatment and care.[84]

However, many Americans are wary of teenage hoodlums and gangs and their violent way of life. How can we control their behavior and protect innocent people? Should we embrace a "get tough" policy in which violent teens are locked up or even face the death penalty? Or should we continue to treat delinquents as troubled teens who need a helping hand from a "wise parent"?

This tension pervades every aspect of the legal treatment of youths. The creation of delinquency statutes and an independent juvenile court at the turn of the century is evidence that society recognizes that children are distinctly different from adults and should be treated separately and with more compassion. At the same time, statutes that allow the transfer of delinquents to adult legal jurisdictions show that the legal system is ready and willing to get tough with juveniles. Despite the lip service paid to society's obligation to help at-risk children, prosecutors appear to be exercising their right to waive youths to the adult justice system more frequently today than in the past.[85] Many juvenile court judges have adopted a punitive attitude and base their sentencing decisions on the need to punish offenders to convince them not to repeat their criminal acts. Also, many judges are more concerned about protecting the rights of victims of crime than rehabilitating or treating juveniles.[86] Similarly, the Supreme Court has legalized the death penalty for children once they reach age 16.[87] The American public is generally in favor of the death penalty, but surveys indicate that a substantial majority oppose capital punishment for minor offenders.[88] Still, more than thirty people are on death row for crimes committed in their minority.

The value conflict in our current response to juvenile delinquency is a potent theme in American jurisprudence.[89] Throughout the country, programs to treat, help, and rehabilitate minor offenders exist side by side with efforts to control, incarcerate, and punish youths who violate the law. Some critics have warned that our treatment of juveniles is becoming more and more intrusive and more likely to enmesh them in the justice process, a condition referred to as **widening the net.**[90] Caring and concerned agents of the juvenile justice system are more likely to refer kids to programs that "help" or "treat" troubled youth rather than those that are more punitive. However, even programs with the best intentions apply labels and stigma and may have a negative effect on their clients. In other words, efforts to "help" at-risk youth may eventually lead to unintended negative and harmful consequences.[91]

The problem of delinquency is not going away soon, and as the Focus on Delinquency box shows, youth crime has become a worldwide problem.

widening the net
Phenomenon that occurs when programs created to divert youths from the justice system actually involve them more deeply in the official process.

SUMMARY

The study of delinquency is concerned with a number of different issues: the nature and extent of the criminal behavior of youths; the causes of youthful law violations; the legal rights of juveniles; and prevention and treatment techniques.

The problems of American youths have become a national concern and an important subject of academic study. The dynamic nature of adolescence, compounded by hardships such as poverty and a deteriorating educational system, have added to teenage stress. Drugs, pregnancy, suicide, and social conflict are all taking their toll on adolescents.

The concept of a separate status of "childhood" has developed slowly over the centuries. In earlier times family life was based on primogeniture and the dower system. Relationships between children and parents were remote. Punishment was severe, and children were expected to take on adult roles early in their lives.

With the start of the seventeenth century came greater recognition of the needs of children. In Great Britain the chancery court movement, the Poor Laws, and apprenticeship programs helped reinforce the idea of children as a distinct social group with unique needs. In colonial America, many of the characteristics of English family living were adopted.

In the nineteenth century, neglected, delinquent, and dependent or runaway children were treated no differently from criminal defendants. Children were often charged and convicted of crimes. During this time, however, philosophical shifts in the perception of crime and delinquency as well as increased support for the concept of *parens patriae* resulted in steps to reduce the responsibility of children under the criminal law in both Great Britain and the United States.

The concept of delinquency was developed in the early twentieth century. Before that time, criminal youths and adults were treated in almost the same fashion. A group of reformers, referred to as child savers, helped create a separate delinquency category to insulate juvenile offenders from the influence of adult criminals.

The separate status of juvenile delinquency is still based on the *parens patriae* philosophy, which holds that children have the right to care and custody and that if parents are not capable of providing that care the state must step in to take control.

Juvenile courts also have jurisdiction over noncriminal status offenders. Status offenses are illegal only because of the minority status of the offender. They include such misbehavior as truancy, running away, and sexual misconduct. Some experts have called for an end to juvenile court control over status offenders, charging that it further stigmatizes already troubled youths. Some research indicates that status offenders are harmed by juvenile court processing. Other research indicates that status offenders and delinquents are actually quite similar.

The treatment of juveniles is an ongoing dilemma in American society. Still uncertain is whether young law violators respond better to harsh punishments or to benevolent treatment.

KEY TERMS

ego identity	primogeniture	waiver process
role diffusion	dower system	status offense
at-risk youths	Poor Laws	wayward minors
juvenile delinquency	chancery courts	Office of Juvenile Justice
chronic delinquents	*parens patriae*	and Delinquency
aging-out process	child savers	Prevention (OJJDP)
juvenile justice system	delinquent	age of consent
paternalistic family	best interests of the child	widening the net

INFOTRAC COLLEGE EDITION EXERCISES

Read the following articles from InfoTrac College Edition:

Cleaning up crime in Boston. (Successful anticrime program helps keep teens out of trouble)(Cover Story) Jon Marcus. *Scholastic Update* Nov 2, 1998

Youth crime, public policy, and practice in the juvenile justice system: Recent trends and needed reforms. Jeffrey M. Jenson, Matthew O. Howard. *Social Work* July 1998

Rough justice in the youth courts. Kirsty Milne. *New Statesman (1996)* Jan 30, 1998

After reading these articles, do you think that current efforts to combat problems with juvenile crime are tending toward punishment or rehabilitation?

Explore other articles on this subject using key words such as: *juvenile rehabilitation, juvenile crime,* and *juvenile delinquency.*

QUESTIONS FOR DISCUSSION

1. Is it fair to have a separate legal category for youths? Considering how dangerous young people can be, does it make more sense to group offenders on the basis of what they have done rather than on their age?
2. At what age are juveniles truly capable of understanding the seriousness of their actions?
3. Is it fair to institutionalize a minor simply for being truant or running away from home? Should the jurisdiction of status offenders be removed from juvenile court and placed with the state Department of Social Services or some other welfare organization?
4. Should delinquency proceedings be secretive? Does the public have a right to know who juvenile criminals are?
5. Can a "get tough" policy help control juvenile misbehavior, or should *parens patriae* remain the standard?
6. Should juveniles who commit felonies such as rape or robbery be treated as adults?

NOTES

1. Adapted from John Sullivan, "Teen Girl Pleads Guilty to Manslaughter in Park Killing," *New York Times* 12 March 1998, p. 1.; N. R. Kleinfield, "Central Park Murder: Lives Tangle in a Hidden World," *New York Times* 1 June 1997, p. 1.
2. Robb Mandelbaum, "A City Runs Through It," *Travel-Holiday,* 181:62–70 (1998).
3. Nanette Davis, *Youth Crisis: Growing Up in the High-Risk Society* (New York: Praeger, Greenwood Publishing, 1998).

4. Children's Defense Fund, *The State of America's Children Yearbook 1998* (Washington, D.C.: Children's Defense Fund, 1998).

5. Susan Crimmins and Michael Foley, "The Threshold of Violence in Urban Adolescents," paper presented at the annual meeting of the American Society of Criminology, Reno, Nev., November 1989.

6. Ibid., p. 21.

7. Task Force on Education of Young Adolescents, *Turning Points, Preparing American Youth for the 21st Century* (New York: Carnegie Council on Adolescent Development, 1989).

8. Erik Erikson, *Childhood and Society* (New York: W. H. Norton, 1963).

9. Roger Gould, "Adult Life Stages: Growth toward Self-Tolerance," *Psychology Today* 8:74–78 (1975).

10. U.S. Bureau of the Census, *Population Estimates and Projections* (Washington, D.C.: U.S. Government Printing Office, 1998).

11. Kevin Thompson, David Brownfield, and Ann Marie Sorenson, "At-Risk Behavior and Gang Involvement: A Latent Structure Analysis," *Journal of Gang Research* 5:1–15 (1998).

12. Task Force on Education of Young Adolescents, *Turning Points*, p. 27.

13. John Cook and Larry Brown, *Two Americas: Alternative Future for Child Poverty in America* (Medford, Mass.: Tufts University Center on Hunger, Poverty and Nutrition, 1993).

14. David Eggebeen and Daniel Lichter, "Race, Family Structure, and Changing Poverty among American Children," *American Sociological Review* 56:801–17 (1991).

15. W. Rees Davis and Michael Clatts, "High Risk Youth and the N.Y.C. Street Economy: Policy Implications," paper presented at the American Society of Criminology Meeting, Boston, Mass., November 1995.

16. Stephanie Venture, Sally Curtin, and T. J. Matthews, *Teen Age Births in the United States: National and State Trends, 1990–1996* (Washington, D.C.: National Center for Health Statistics, 1998).

17. Ibid.

18. National Education Goals Panel, *The National Education Goals Report, Building a Nation of Learners* (Washington, D.C.: U.S. Government Printing Office, 1997), pp. iii–iv.

19. News Release, "Kids Count Survey, 1998" (Annie E. Casey Foundation, Baltimore, Md., May 5, 1998).

20. National Education Goals Panel, *The National Education Goals Report*.

21. Bruce Johnson, George Thomas, and Andrew Golub, "Trends in Heroin Use among Manhattan Arrestees from the Heroin and Crack Era," in James Inciardi and Lana Harrison, eds., *Heroin in the Age of Crack-Cocaine* (Thousand Oaks, Calif.: Sage, 1998), pp. 108–30.

22. Federal Bureau of Investigation, *Crimes in the United States, 1997* (Washington, D.C.: U.S. Government Printing Office, 1998), p. 247.

23. John Whitehead and Steven Lab, "A Meta-Analysis of Juvenile Correctional Treatment," *Journal of Research in Crime and Delinquency* 26:276–95 (1989).

24. See Lawrence Stone, *The Family, Sex, and Marriage in England: 1500–1800* (New York: Harper & Row, 1977).

25. This section relies on Jackson Spielvogel, *Western Civilization* (St. Paul: West, 1991), pp. 279–86.

26. Ibid.

27. See Philipe Aries, *Century of Childhood: A Social History of Family Life* (New York: Vintage, 1962).

28. See Douglas R. Rendleman, "*Parens Patriae:* From Chancery to the Juvenile Court," *South Carolina Law Review* 23:205 (1971).

29. See Stone, *The Family, Sex, and Marriage in England;* and Lawrence Stone, ed., *Schooling and Society: Studies in the History of Education* (Baltimore: John Hopkins University Press, 1970).

30. Ibid.

31. See Wiley B. Sanders, *Some Early Beginnings of the Children's Court Movement in England,* National Probation Association Yearbook (New York: National Council on Crime and Delinquency, 1945).

32. Rendleman, "*Parens Patriae,*" p. 205.

33. Douglas Besharov, *Juvenile Justice Advocacy—Practice in a Unique Court* (New York: Practicing Law Institute, 1974), p. 2.

34. *Wellesley v. Wellesley,* 4 Eng. Rep. 1078 (1827).

35. Rendleman, "*Parens Patriae,*" p. 209.

36. See Anthony Platt, "The Rise of the Child Saving Movement: A Study in Social Policy and Correctional Reform," *Annals of the American Academy of Political and Social Science* 381:21–38 (1969).

37. Robert Bremmer, ed., and John Barnard, Hareven Tamara, and Robert Mennel, asst. eds., *Children and Youth in America* (Cambridge: Harvard University Press, 1970), p. 64.

38. Elizabeth Pleck, "Criminal Approaches to Family Violence, 1640–1980," in Lloyd Ohlin and Michael Tonry, eds., *Family Violence* (Chicago: University of Chicago Press, 1989), pp. 19–58.

39. Ibid.

40. John R. Sutton, *Stubborn Children: Controlling Delinquency in the United States, 1640–1981* (Berkeley: University of California Press, 1988).

41. Pleck, "Criminal Approaches to Family Violence," p. 29.

42. John Demos, *Past, Present and Personal* (New York: Oxford University Press, 1986), pp. 80–88.

43. Elizabeth Pleck, *Domestic Tyranny: The Making of Social Policy against Family Violence from Colonial Times to the Present* (New York: Oxford University Press, 1987), pp. 28–30.

44. Graeme Newman, *The Punishment Response* (Philadelphia: J. B. Lippincott, 1978), pp. 53–79; Philip Aries, *Centuries of Childhood* (New York: Knopf, 1962). The history of childhood juvenile justice is discussed in detail in Chapter 12.

45. Stephen J. Morse, "Immaturity and Irresponsibility," *Journal of Criminal Law and Criminology* 88:15–67 (1997).

46. John L. Hutzler, *Juvenile Court Jurisdiction over Children's Conduct: 1982 Comparative Analysis of Juvenile and Family Codes and National Standards* (Pittsburgh: National Center for Juvenile Justice, 1982), p. 2.

47. Ibid.

48. See, generally, David Rothman, *The Discovery of the Asylum* (Boston: Little, Brown, 1971).

49. Reports of the Chicago Bar Association Committee, 1899, cited in Anthony Platt, *The Child Savers* (Chicago: University of Chicago Press, 1969) p. 119.

50. Susan Datesman and Mikel Aickin, "Offense Specialization and Escalation among Status Offenders," *Journal of Criminal Law and Criminology* 75:1246–75 (1985).

51. Ibid.

52. See, generally, Solomon Kobrin and Malcolm Klein, *National Evaluation of the Deinstitutionalization of Status Offender Programs—Executive Summary* (Los Angeles: Social Science Research Institute, University of Southern California, 1982).

53. 42 U.S.C.A. 5601–5751 (1983 & Supp. 1987).

54. Claudia Wright, "Contempt No Excuse for Locking Up Status Offenders, Says Florida Supreme Court," *Youth Law News* 13:1–3 (1992).

55. *A.A. v. Rolle,* 604 So. 2d 813 (1992).

56. National Council on Crime and Delinquency, "Juvenile Curfews—A Policy Statement," *Crime and Delinquency* 18:132–33 (1972).

57. National Advisory Commission on Criminal Justice Standards and Goals, *Juvenile Justice and Delinquency Prevention* (Washington, D.C.: U.S. Government Printing Office, 1977), p. 311.

58. American Bar Association Joint Commission on Juvenile Justice Standards, *Summary and Analysis* (Cambridge, Mass.: Ballinger, 1977), sect. 1.1.

59. Martin Rouse, "The Diversion of Status Offenders, Criminalization, and the New York Family Court," rev. version, paper

presented at the American Society of Criminology, Reno, Nev., November 1989, p. 12.

60. Barry Feld, "Criminalizing the American Juvenile Court," in Michael Tonry, ed., *Crime and Justice, A Review of Research* (Chicago: University of Chicago Press, 1993), p. 232.

61. Marc Miller, "Changing Legal Paradigms in Juvenile Justice," in Peter Greenwood, ed., *The Juvenile Rehabilitation Reader* (Santa Monica, Calif.: Rand Corporation, 1985) p. V.44.

62. Thomas Kelley, "Status Offenders Can Be Different: A Comparative Study of Delinquent Careers," *Crime and Delinquency* 29:365–80 (1983).

63. Ira Schwartz, *Justice for Juveniles: Rethinking the Best Interests of the Child* (Lexington, Mass: Lexington Books, 1989), p. 171.

64. Ibid.

65. Lawrence Martin and Phyllis Snyder, "Jurisdiction over Status Offenses Should Not Be Removed from the Juvenile Court," *Crime and Delinquency* 22:44–47 (1976).

66. Lindsay Arthur, "Status Offenders Need a Court of Last Resort," *Boston University Law Review* 57:631–44 (1977).

67. Ibid.

68. William Ruefle and Kenneth Mike Reynolds, "Curfews and Delinquency in Major American Cities," *Crime and Delinquency* 41:347–63 (1995).

69. Juvenile Justice Reform Initiatives in the States (Washington, D.C.: Office of Juvenile Justice and Delinquency Prevention, 1997).

70. Gilbert Geis and Arnold Binder, "Sins of Their Children: Parental Responsibility for Juvenile Delinquency," *Notre Dame Journal of Law, Ethics, and Public Policy* 5:303–22 (1991); Christi Harlan and Arthur Hayes, "Jailing Parents," *Wall Street Journal* 18 May 1992, p. B6.

71. Sharon Elstein and Noy Davis, *Sexual Relationships between Adult Males and Young Teen Girls: Exploring the Legal and Social Responses* (Chicago, Ill. American Bar Association, 1997).

72. Carolyn Smith, "Factors Associated with Early Sexual Activity among Urban Adolescents," *Social Work* 42:334–46 (1997).

73. Kelley, "Status Offenders Can Be Different."

74. Charles Thomas, "Are Status Offenders Really So Different?", *Crime and Delinquency* 22:438–55 (1976); Howard Snyder, *Court Careers of Juvenile Offenders* (Washington, D.C.: Office of Juvenile Justice and Delinquency Prevention, 1988), p. 65.

75. Randall Shelden, John Horvath, and Sharon Tracy, "Do Status Offenders Get Worse? Some Clarifications on the Question of Escalation," *Crime and Delinquency* 35:202–16 (1989).

76. Solomon Kobrin, Frank Hellum, and John Peterson, "Offense Patterns of Status Offenders," in D. Schichor and D. Kelly, eds., *Critical Issues in Juvenile Delinquency* (Lexington, Mass.: Lexington Books, 1980), pp. 203–35.

77. Schwartz, *Justice for Juveniles,* pp. 378–79.

78. Chris Marshall, Ineke Marshall, and Charles Thomas, "The Implementation of Formal Procedures in Juvenile Court Processing of Status Offenders," *Journal of Criminal Justice* 11:195–211 (1983).

79. This section leans heavily on James Gilbert, *A Cycle of Outrage, America's Reaction to the Juvenile Delinquent in the 1950's* (New York: Oxford University Press, 1986).

80. Harrison Salisbury, *The Shook-Up Generation* (New York: Harper, 1958).

81. Frederic Wertham, *Seduction of the Innocent* (Port Washington, N.Y.: Kennikat Press, 1953).

82. Ibid.

83. Francis Cullen, Sandra Evans Skovron, Joseph Scott, and Velmer Burton, "Public Support for Correctional Treatment: The Tenacity of Rehabilitative Ideology," *Criminal Justice and Behavior* 17:6–18 (1990).

84. Rhena Izzo and Robert Ross, "Meta-Analysis of Rehabilitation Programs for Juvenile Delinquents," *Criminal Justice and Behavior* 17:134–42 (1990).

85. Dean Champion, "Teenage Felons and Waiver Hearing: Some Recent Trends, 1980–1988," *Crime and Delinquency* 35:577–85 (1989).

86. Gordon Bazemore and Lynette Feder, "Judges in the Punitive Juvenile Court: Organizational, Career and Ideological Influences on Sanctioning Orientation," *Justice Quarterly* 14:87–114 (1997).

87. *Stanford v. Kentucky,* and *Wilkins v. Missouri,* 109 S.Ct. 2969 (1989).

88. Sandra Skovron, Joseph Scott, and Francis Cullen, "The Death Penalty for Juveniles: An Assessment of Public Support," *Crime and Delinquency* 35:546–61 (1989).

89. See, generally, Edmund McGarrell, *Juvenile Correctional Reform: Two Decades of Policy and Procedural Change* (Albany, N.Y.: State University of New York Press, 1988); Barry Krisberg, Ira Schwartz, Paul Litsky, and James Austin, "The Watershed of Juvenile Justice Reform," *Crime and Delinquency* 32:5–38 (1986), at 34.

90. Mark Ezell, "Juvenile Arbitration: Net Widening and Other Unintended Consequences," *Journal of Research in Crime and Delinquency* 26:358–77 (1990).

91. Schwartz, *Justice for Juveniles*, p. 17.

Chapter Two

The Nature and Extent of Delinquency

On Friday June 4, 1998, in a Dallas, Texas, courtroom an eleven-year-old boy was convicted—along with two younger boys ages 7 and 8—of beating and raping a three-year-old girl. The boys took the girl from a van outside her home to a neighborhood creek, where she was beaten with a brick and a shoe, stripped, and sexually assaulted. The younger boys admitted taking part in the attack, but they are too young to face criminal charges under state law. During his trial, the eleven-year-old testified that the seven-year-old sexually assaulted the girl. The two younger boys testified that all three attacked the girl, and a detective testified that all three admitted to the sexual assault. Jurors found the fourth grader guilty of two counts of sexual assault and one count of injuring a child; he faces a possible forty-year prison sentence.[1]

Cases like this horrible assault on a very young girl capture media attention and give the impression that juvenile crime is out of control and that today's youth are much more violent than ever before. Is this impression accurate? How common are serious acts of juvenile delinquency? Who commits delinquent acts, and where are they most likely to occur? Is the juvenile crime rate increasing or decreasing? Are juveniles more likely than adults to become the victims of crime?[2] To understand the causes of delinquent behavior and to devise effective means to reduce or eliminate their occurrence, we must seek answers to these questions.

Delinquency experts have devised a variety of data collection methods that they believe can accurately measure the nature and extent of delinquency. In this chapter we begin with a description of the three most widely used of these data sources: official statistics, self-report data, and victim data (Table 2.1). We also examine the information these resources provide on juvenile crime rates and trends. These data sources will then be used to provide information on the personal characteristics of adolescent law violators, including their age, gender, race, income, and offending patterns.

The Dallas case involving an assault on a very young girl by very young boys gives the public the impression that juvenile violence is out of control and that today's youth are much more violent than ever before. This billboard warning parents about the dangers of violent crime helps fuel public fear. Are such measures warranted?

Table 2.1

SOURCES OF DELINQUENCY DATA

Official Statistics   Official statistics are based on the criminal incidents reported to the nation's police departments. This information is collected and disseminated on an annual basis by the Federal Bureau of Investigation in their Uniform Crime Report (UCR) program. The UCR records both the total number of crimes reported to the police for major offense categories, such as murder and rape, and the total number of arrests made for *any crime* that is cleared, or solved. Because the age of arrestees is recorded, official data can be used to study trends and patterns in the delinquency rate. Youths with arrest records are referred to as "official delinquents." Their actions are considered recorded, or "official, delinquency," and their behavior becomes part of the "official statistics."

Self-Report Data   Self-report data are obtained from anonymous surveys or interviews, often conducted in schools, that query adolescents about their participation in illegal acts such as drug abuse and vandalism. Self-report data are aimed at assessing criminal acts that have gone undetected by the police either because victims fail to report crimes or because the crime is "victimless," for example, drug abuse. Self-report data measure the extent of unrecorded juvenile delinquency, the so-called dark figures of crime. These data can also be used to compare the personal characteristics (for example, race and gender) of official delinquents with youths whose criminal activity remains undetected.

Victim Data   Victim surveys ask those who have experienced crime firsthand to tell about the episode. Victim data include both crimes reported to the police and crimes victims failed to report. They provide important information on where victimization takes place, the likelihood of victimization, and the kinds of personal behaviors and the lifestyle that increase the chances of becoming a crime victim. The most widely used of these is the federally sponsored National Crime Victimization Survey (NCVS), an annual survey of thousands of selected citizens in communities across the nation.

Official Statistics

Federal Bureau of Investigation (FBI)
Arm of the U.S. Department of Justice that investigates violations of federal law, gathers crime statistics, runs a comprehensive crime laboratory, and helps train local law enforcement officers.

Uniform Crime Report (UCR)
Compiled by the FBI, the UCR is the most widely used source of national crime and delinquency statistics.

Part I offenses, index crimes
Offenses include homicide and nonnegligent manslaughter, forcible rape, robbery, aggravated assault, burglary, larceny, arson, and motor vehicle theft; recorded by local law enforcement officers, arrests for these crimes are tallied quarterly and sent to the FBI for inclusion in the UCR.

Part II offenses
All crimes other than Part I offenses; recorded by local law enforcement officers, arrests for these crimes are tallied quarterly and sent to the FBI for inclusion in the UCR.

The standard source of official crime and delinquency statistics is the annual effort of the U.S. Justice Department's **Federal Bureau of Investigation (FBI).** The FBI compiles information gathered by the nation's police departments on the number of criminal acts reported by citizens and the number of persons arrested each year for criminal and delinquent activity. Called the *Uniform Crime Report* **(UCR),** the FBI's effort constitutes our best-known and most widely used source of national crime and delinquency statistics.

The UCR is compiled from statistics sent to the FBI from more than sixteen thousand police departments serving a majority of the population of the United States. It groups offenses into two categories: Part I and Part II offenses. **Part I offenses,** also known as **index crimes,** include homicide and nonnegligent manslaughter, forcible rape, robbery, aggravated assault, burglary, larceny, arson, and motor vehicle theft (Table 2.2). A record is entered by cooperating police agencies every time one of these offenses is reported by a victim or a witness. The FBI receives quarterly tallies of these offenses and publishes the results annually. Data are broken down by city, county, metropolitan area, and geographical divisions of the United States. In addition to these statistics, the UCR provides information on the number and characteristics of individuals who have been arrested for these and all other criminal offenses including vandalism, liquor law violations, and drug trafficking. These are known as **Part II offenses.** The arrest data break down personal information by age, sex, and race.

The UCR expresses crime data in three ways. First, the number of crimes reported to the police and arrests made are given as raw figures (for example, 18,209 murders occurred in 1997). Second, percentage changes in the amount of crime between years are computed (for example, murder decreased 26 percent between 1993 and 1997). Finally, crime rates per one hundred thousand people are computed. That is, when the UCR indicates that the murder rate was 6.8 in 1997, it means that about seven people in every one hundred thousand fell victim to murder between January 1 and December 31 of 1997. The equation used is:

$$\frac{\text{Number of reported crimes}}{\text{Total U.S. population}} \times 100{,}000 = \text{Crime rate}$$

All three methods will be used in the following discussion, which reviews some of the most significant trends reported by the UCR.

Crime Trends in the United States

Crime continues to be one of the leading social problems in the United States. The crime rate skyrocketed between 1960 (3.3 million crimes reported to police agencies) and 1981 (13.4 million crimes recorded). Then, after four years of decline, the rate went up in 1985 and continued to increase for the remainder of the decade. As the 1990s began, the overall crime rate declined, dropping 10 percent between 1993 and 1997 (Figure 2.1).[3] Some large cities, including New York, reported significant declines in the violence rate.

Even though the crime rate has declined, the FBI estimates that about fourteen million serious crimes currently are reported to police annually, more than 5,000 per 100,000 inhabitants.[4]

Table 2.2

PART I INDEX CRIME OFFENSES

Crime	Description
Criminal homicide	a. Murder and nonnegligent manslaughter: the willful (nonnegligent) killing of one human being by another. Deaths caused by negligence, attempts to kill, assaults to kill, suicides, accidental deaths, and justifiable homicides are excluded. Justifiable homicides are limited to (1) the killing of a felon by a law enforcement officer in the line of duty; and (2) the killing of a felon, during the commission of a felony, by a private citizen. b. Manslaughter by negligence: the killing of another person through gross negligence. Traffic fatalities are excluded. While manslaughter by negligence is a Part I crime, it is not included in the Crime Index.
Forcible rape	The carnal knowledge of a female forcibly and against her will. Included are rapes by force and attempts or assaults to rape. Statutory offenses (no force used—victim under age of consent) are excluded.
Robbery	The taking or attempting to take anything of value from the care, custody, or control of a person or persons by force or threat of force or violence and/or by putting the victim in fear.
Aggravated assault	An unlawful attack by one person upon another for the purpose of inflicting severe or aggravated bodily injury. This type of assault usually is accompanied by the use of a weapon or by means likely to produce death or great bodily harm. Simple assaults are excluded.
Burglary/breaking or entering	The unlawful entry of a structure to commit a felony or a theft. Attempted forcible entry is included.
Larceny/theft (except motor vehicle theft)	The unlawful taking, carrying, leading, or riding away of property from the possession or constructive possession of another. Examples are thefts of bicycles or automobile accessories, shoplifting, pocket-picking, or the stealing of any property or article which is not taken by force and violence or by fraud. Attempted larcenies are included. Embezzlement, "con" games, forgery, worthless checks, etc., are excluded.
Motor vehicle theft	The theft or attempted theft of a motor vehicle. A motor vehicle is self-propelled and runs on the surface and not on rails. Specifically excluded from this category are motorboats, construction equipment, airplanes, and farming equipment.
Arson	Any willful or malicious burning or attempt to burn, with or without intent to defraud, a dwelling house, public building, motor vehicle or aircraft, personal property of another, etc.

Source: FBI, *Uniform Crime Report*, 1997, p. 407.

FIGURE 2.1

Crime Rate Trends, 1960–1997

Source: *Uniform Crime Report,* 1997, p. 8.

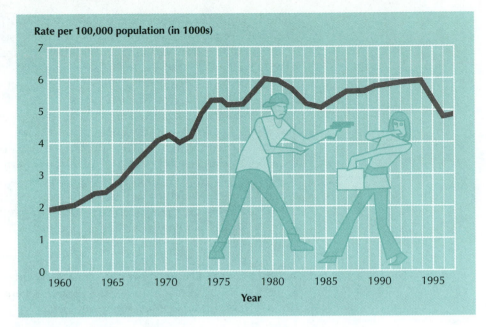

Rate per 100,000 population (in 1000s)

Year

Measuring Official Delinquency

disaggregated
Analyzing the relationship between two or more variables (such as murder convictions and death sentence) while controlling for the influence of a third variable (such as race).

Because the UCR arrest statistics are **disaggregated** (broken down) by suspect's age, they can be used to estimate adolescent participation in official crime. Juvenile arrest data must be interpreted with caution, however. First, the number of teenagers arrested does not represent the actual number of youths who have committed delinquent acts but only those caught and officially processed by the police. Some offenders are never counted because they are never caught. Others are counted more than once because multiple arrests of the same individual for different crimes are counted separately in the UCR. Consequently, the total number of arrests does not equal the number of people who have been arrested. Put another way, if two million arrests of youths under eighteen years of age were made in a given year, we could not be sure if two million individuals had been arrested once or if five hundred thousand chronic offenders had been arrested four times each. In addition, when an arrested offender commits multiple crimes, only the most serious one is recorded. For example, if a juvenile arrested for a rape is found in possession of a gun and drugs, only the rape arrest is recorded. Therefore, if two million juveniles are arrested, the number of crimes committed is at least two million, but it may be much higher.

Despite these limitations, the nature of arrest data remains constant over time. That is, all the factors that influence the validity of UCR arrest statistics are present each year the data are collected. Consequently, arrest data can, at the very least, provide some indication of the nature and trends in juvenile crime.

Keeping these limitations in mind, what does the UCR tell us about delinquency?

Official Delinquency In 1997 (the latest data available) a total of about 15.2 million arrests were made; of these, 2.7 million were for serious Part I crimes and 12.5 million for less serious Part II crimes. By isolating the percentage of juvenile arrests from the total, we see that juvenile offenders make a significant contribution to the nation's crime problem.

The official data reveal that about two million juvenile arrests were made in 1997, or 19 percent of all arrests; about 30 percent of these arrests were for more serious Part I crimes.[5] A disproportionate number of violent crimes are committed each year by young people. The under eighteen population is about one one-twelfth of the U.S. population but is responsible for about 13 percent of the violent crime arrests and one-quarter of the property crime arrests.[6]

In addition to serious crime arrests, about 1.5 million juvenile arrests were made in 1997 for Part II offenses. Included in this total were 136,000 arrests for running away from home, 148,000 for disorderly conduct, 153,000 for drug abuse violations, and 128, 000 for curfew violations.

It comes as no surprise then that crime is a young person's game. As Figure 2.2 shows, most serious property crime activity peaks at age 16, and the peak for violent crime arrests is age 18. Age-level crime rates begin to decline gradually after these peak years, and by age 24 violent crime arrests are about 64 percent what they were at their peak, and property crime arrests 31 percent. The participation by young people in the crime rate is underscored by incidents such as the Dallas rape case described in the opening of this chapter. More than four hundred youths under twelve years of age were arrested for rape in 1997; of these, seventy-five were less than ten years old.

Juvenile Crime Trends   Juvenile crime continues to have a significant influence on the nation's overall crime statistics despite recent optimistic trends. As Figure 2.3 shows, arrests for violent juvenile crime began to increase in 1989, peaked in 1994,

FIGURE 2.2

The Relationship between Age and Serious Crime Arrests

Source: FBI, *Uniform Crime Report,* 1997, pp. 232–33.

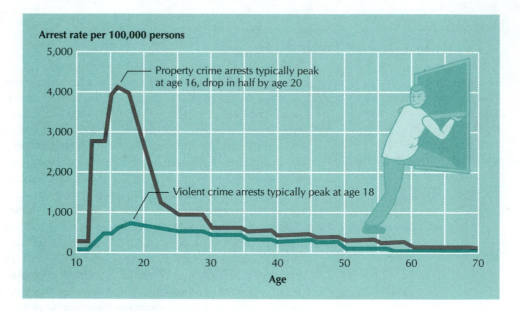

Arrest rate per 100,000 persons

Property crime arrests typically peak at age 16, drop in half by age 20

Violent crime arrests typically peak at age 18

Age

FIGURE 2.3

Juvenile Violent Crime Arrest Rates: United States, 1965–1997

Source: FBI, *Uniform Crime Report,* 1997, p. 280.

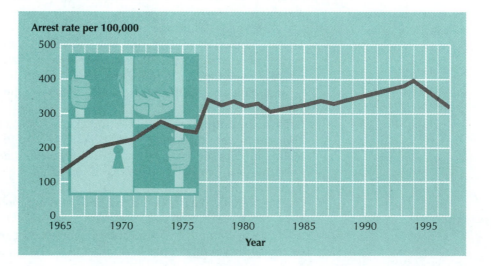

Arrest rate per 100,000

Year

and then began to fall. Property crime arrests have remained more stable but have also declined somewhat during the past few years.

As Figure 2.4 indicates, juvenile murder rates more than doubled between the early 1980s and their peak in 1993; they have since been in decline but remain higher than earlier levels. More than 1,700 youths were arrested for murder and another 3,800 for rape in 1997. Politicians have heralded this recent drop in juvenile delinquency, but the teen crime problem is by no means over.

The official data tell us that juvenile crime rates ebb and flow. What accounts for increases? What factors are related to the recent decreases? This is the topic of the Focus on Delinquency box entitled "The Rise and Fall of Juvenile Crime Rates."

Criticism of Official Data

There has long been criticism over the accuracy of official crime data. Victim surveys show that less than half of all victims report crime to the police. Because official data is derived entirely from police records, we can assume that a significant number of crimes are not accounted for in the UCR. There are also concerns that police departments make systematic errors in recording crime data. In addition, under pressure to prove their effectiveness with ever-decreasing crime statistics, some police commanders may manipulate crime data.[7] In New York, Atlanta, and Boca Raton, Florida, charges of falsely reporting crime statistics have resulted in the resignation or demotion of high-ranking police commanders. Philadelphia had to withdraw its crime figures for 1996, 1997, and the the first half of 1998 due to underreporting and downgrading serious crimes to less serious incidents and to sloppiness.

Using official arrest data to measure delinquency rates is particularly problematic and may be biased because of racial and ethnic discrimination in the arrest process. Arrest records only count adolescents who have been "caught," and these youths may be different from those who evade capture. In addition, victimless crimes such as drug and alcohol use are significantly undercounted using this measure.

Arrest decision criteria vary between police agencies. Some police agencies may practice full enforcement, arresting all teens who violate the law, whereas others may follow a policy of discretion that encourages unofficial handling of juvenile matters through social service agencies. This, too, can influence the arrest data.

Although critics argue that these flaws undermine the validity of official data, some experts believe the accuracy of official statistics may be improving.[8] After more than twenty years of effort to increase the sensitivity of police officers to civil rights, arrests may now be less class- and race-biased and, consequently, are a more valid indicator of the actual participation in delinquent acts.[9]

FIGURE 2.4

Juvenile Murder Rate Trends, 1976–1997

Source: James A. Fox and Martanne Zavitz, *Homicide Trends in the U.S.* (Washington, D.C.: Bureau of Justice Statistics, 1998).

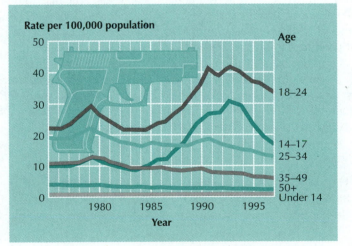

THE RISE AND FALL OF JUVENILE CRIME RATES

Crime rates climb and fall, reflecting a variety of social and economic conditions. Although there is still disagreement over what causes crime rate fluctuations, these factors play a major role in determining patterns and trends.

AGE

Change in the age distribution of the population deeply influences crime and delinquency rates. Juvenile males commit more crime than any other population segment, so as a general rule, the crime rate follows the proportion of young males in the population. The post-war baby-boom generation reached their teenage years in the 1960s, just as the crime rate began a sharp increase. With the "graying" of society in the late 1980s and a decline in the birth rate, it was not surprising that the overall crime rate began to decline. The number of juveniles is expected to increase over the next decade, and some criminologists fear that this will signal a return to escalating crime rates.

ECONOMY

In the short term, a poor economy may actually help lower crime rates. Unemployed parents are at home to supervise children and to guard their homes. Because there is less to spend, a poor economy means that there are actually fewer valuables around worth stealing. In the long term, periods of sustained economic weakness and unemployment eventually lift crime rates. Chronic teenage unemployment may produce a perception of hopelessness that leads to crime and delinquency. The sustained economic growth experienced in the 1990s may have helped reduce crime rates.

Violence may be a function of urban problems and the economic deterioration in the nation's inner cities. Our nation's economy is now fueled by the service and high technology industries. Youths who at one time might have obtained low-skill jobs in factories and shops may find that these legitimate economic opportunities no longer exist. Low-skill manufacturing jobs have been dispersed to overseas plants, and most new jobs that don't require specialized skills are in the low-paying service area. Lack of real economic opportunity may encourage drug dealing, theft, and violence. Although crime rates have been in a recent decline, those left out of the economic recovery are still committing millions of crimes.

DRUGS

Drug use has been linked to fluctuations in the crime and delinquency rates. Drug abusers are particularly crime prone, so as drug use levels increase, so too do crime rates. The increase in teenage violence began in 1985, and it is no coincidence that this period also witnessed increases in drug trafficking and arrests for drug crimes. Teenage substance abusers commit a significant portion of all serious crimes, and inner-city drug abuse problems may account for part of the persistently high violent crime rate. Groups and gangs that are involved in the urban drug trade recruit juveniles because they work cheaply, are immune from heavy criminal penalties, and also because they are "daring and willing to take risks." Arming themselves for protection, these youthful dealers pose a threat to neighborhood adolescents who in turn carry arms for self-protection. The result, an "arms race" that produces an increasing spiral of violence

Drug abuse may also have a more direct influence on teen crime patterns, for example, when alcohol-abusing kids engage in acts of senseless violence. Users may turn to theft and violence for money to purchase drugs and to support their drug habits. Increases in teenage drug use may be a precursor to higher future violence rates.

One reason for the decline in crime rates during the 1990s is linked to a reduction in the use of cocaine and its derivative, crack. As users switch to less expensive drugs, such as heroin, violence rates have declined.

OTHER SOCIAL PROBLEMS

As the level of social problems increases so too do crime rates. Increases in the number of single-parent families, dropout rates, and teen pregnancies may also influence crime rates.

Table A Social Problems Associated with Teen Violence

- child abuse and neglect
- lack of role models
- crisis in leadership
- witnessing violence
- access to guns
- substance abuse
- poverty and lack of resources

- low self-esteem
- the inability to deal with strong negative feelings
- boredom and lack of fun activities
- poor judgment and lack of boundaries
- prejudice and intolerance
- feelings that there is nothing left to lose

Source: Kathleen Heide, "Why Kids Keep Killing: The Correlates, Causes and Challenge of Juvenile Homicide," paper presented at the American Society of Criminology Meeting, Boston, Mass., November 1995.

Cross-national research indicates that child homicide rates are greatest in those nations, including the United States, that have the highest rates of children born out of wedlock and teenage mothers.

In spite of a strong economy, millions of youths now live in poverty, and those numbers are expected to increase dramatically over the next fifteen years. Children living in single-parent homes are twice as likely to be impoverished as those in two-parent homes. Such children are especially at risk to juvenile delinquency, foretelling an increasing crime rate. Some of the social problems associated with teen violence are listed in Table A.

GUNS

Another important influence on violence rates is the number of weapons in the hands of teens. Between 1987 and 1997, the number of children under eighteen arrested on weapons charges rose more than one hundred percent. In 1997, 151 per 100,000 teens were arrested on weapons charges, the highest rate in history. More than 60 percent of the homicides committed by juveniles involve firearms, especially handguns. Guns turn a school yard fight into a homicide. Their presence creates a climate in which kids who would otherwise shun firearms begin to carry them for "self-protection." As the number of guns in the hands of children increases, so do juvenile violence rates.

GANGS

The explosive growth in teenage gangs has also contributed to teen violence rates. Surveys indicate that there are about one-half million gang members in the United States. A large and growing number of juveniles who kill do so in groups of two or more; multiple-offender killings have doubled since the mid-1980s. Gang-related violence is frequently compounded by the use of firearms. A recent study of 4,000 youthful arrestees in eleven major cities found that about one-third who said they were gang members carried a gun all or most of the time.

WHAT THE FUTURE HOLDS

The nation's teenage population will increase by 15 percent, or more than nine million, between now and 2010; those in the high-risk category (ages 15 to 17) will increase by more than three million, or 31 percent. If the increase in at-risk youth is matched by recent increases in drug abuse, economic and social problems, and gang recruitment, we should expect significant increases in the delinquency rate and the overall crime rate during the next fifteen years. If, however, society can find a way to counteract these social problems, to control guns and gangs, and to limit substance abuse, delinquency rates may continue to decline.

Source: Rosemary Gartner, "Family Structure, Welfare Spending, and Child Homicide in Developed Democracies," *Journal of Marriage and the Family* 53:231–40 (1991); Scott Decker and Susan Pennell, *Arrestees and Guns: Monitoring the Illegal Firearms Market* (Washington, D.C.: National Institute of Justice, 1995); G. David Curry, Richard Ball, and Scott Decker, "Estimating the National Scope of Gang Crime from Law Enforcement Data," in C. Ronald Huff, ed., *Gangs in America,* 2d. ed. (Newbury Park, Calif.: Sage, 1996).

Groups that are involved in the urban drug trade recruit juveniles to become part of their gang. Arming themselves for protection, these youthful dealers pose a threat to neighborhood adolescents, who in turn arm themselves for self-protection. The result is an "arms race" that produces an increasing spiral of violence and creates a climate in which kids who would otherwise shun firearms begin to carry them for "self-protection." As the number of guns in the hands of children increases, so do juvenile violence rates.

Self-Reported Delinquency

self-reports
Questionnaire or survey technique that asks subjects to reveal their own participation in delinquent or criminal acts.

Official statistics are useful for examining general trends in the relative frequency of delinquent behavior and geographic patterns of youth crime, but they are an inadequate source of individual-level information. They do not reveal much about the personality, attitudes, and behavior of individual delinquents. To get information at this level, criminologists have developed alternative sources of delinquency statistics, the most commonly used source being **self-reports** of delinquent behavior.

Self-report studies are designed to obtain information from youthful subjects about their violations of the law. This information can be obtained in a variety of ways. For example, youths arrested by police may be interviewed at the station house; an anonymous survey can be distributed simultaneously to every student in a high school; boys in a youth detention center may be asked to respond to a survey; or youths randomly selected from the population of teenagers can be questioned in the privacy of their homes. Self-report information can be collected in one-to-one interviews between the researcher and the subject or through a self-administered questionnaire, but more commonly this information is gathered through a mass distribution of anonymous questionnaires.

Although the format may vary, the benefits and assumptions of self-report surveys remain constant. Self-report surveys can include all segments of the population. This cross-sectional data provides information on offenders who have never been arrested and are therefore not part of the official data. Self-report surveys also measure behavior that is rarely detected by police, such as drug abuse, because the safety of anonymity allows youths to freely describe their illegal activities. Surveys can also include items measuring personality characteristics, behavior, and attitudes, which help us know more about the types of youths who commit delinquent acts.

Table 2.3 shows one format for asking self-report questions. Youths are asked to check the appropriate spaces to indicate how many times they have participated in illegal or deviant behavior. Other formats allow subjects to write in the precise number of times they engaged in each delinquent activity. Note that the sample survey limits the reporting period to the past twelve months, thereby focusing on relatively recent behavior; some surveys question lifetime activity.

Questions not directly related to delinquent activity are often included on self-report surveys. Information on self-image, intelligence, personality, attitudes toward family, friends, and school, leisure activities, and school activities may be collected. Self-report surveys also gather personal information on family background, social status, race, and sex. Reports of delinquent acts can then be correlated with this information to create a much more complete picture of delinquent offenders than official statistics can provide.

dark figures of crime
Incidents of crime and delinquency that go undetected by police.

Criminologists have used self-report studies of delinquency for more than forty years.[10] They are a valuable source of information on the delinquent activities of youths who have had formal contact with the juvenile justice system as well as the **dark figures of crime**—that is, those who have escaped official notice of their delinquent acts.

Self-Report Data

Most self-report studies indicate that the number of children who break the law is far greater than official statistics would lead us to believe.[11] In fact, when truancy,

Table 2.3

SELF-REPORT SURVEY QUESTIONS

Please indicate how often in the past twelve months you did each act. (Check the best answer.)

	Never Did Act	One Time	2–5 Times	6–9 Times	10+ Times
Stole something worth less than $50	___	___	___	___	___
Stole something worth more than $50	___	___	___	___	___
Used cocaine	___	___	___	___	___
Been in a fistfight	___	___	___	___	___
Carried a weapon such as a gun or knife	___	___	___	___	___
Fought someone using a weapon	___	___	___	___	___

alcohol consumption, petty theft, and soft drug use are included in self-report scales, delinquency appears to be almost universal. The most common offenses are truancy, drinking alcohol, using a false ID, shoplifting or larceny under five dollars, fighting, using marijuana, and damaging the property of others.[12] In Chapter 11 self-report data will be used to gauge trends in adolescent drug abuse.

Researchers at the University of Michigan's Institute for Social Research (ISR)[13] conduct one of the most methodologically sound national self-report surveys. This annual survey involves a sample of about three thousand youths and is probably the most complete national survey of juvenlie misbehavior. Table 2.4 contains some of the data from the 1997 ISR survey.

A surprising number of these "typical" teenagers reported involvement in serious criminal behavior during the twelve months before the survey: about 13 percent reported hurting someone badly enough that the victim needed medical care (1 percent said they did this five times or more); about 31 percent reported stealing something worth less than fifty dollars, and another 10 percent stole something worth more than $50; 29 percent reported shoplifting from a store; 14 percent had damaged school property. Of the youths reporting, only 9 percent said they were arrested and taken to a police station.

If the ISR data accurately represent the national distribution of delinquent activities, then the juvenile crime problem is much greater than official statistics would lead us to believe. There are approximately fourteen million youths between the ages of fourteen and seventeen. Extrapolating from the ISR findings, this group accounts for more than 100 percent of all theft offenses reported in the UCR (about eight million). More than 3 percent of the students said they used a knife or a gun in a robbery. At this rate, high school students commit 1.05 million armed robberies per year. In comparison, the UCR tallies about 360,000 armed robberies for all age groups annually.

Although these disturbing statistics show that the delinquency problem is far greater than is indicated by the national arrest statistics, self-reports rarely show the delinquency rate climbing. With the exception of assault, patterns of self-reported delinquency have been rather stable since 1975, and property crime rates—most notably shoplifting—may actually be in decline.[14]

Over the past decade, the ISR surveys indicate a uniform pattern of delinquent behavior: teenager participation in theft, violence, and damage-related crimes seems

Table 2.4

SELF-REPORTED DELINQUENT ACTIVITY

Crime Category	Percent of High School Seniors, Class of 1997, Engaging in Offenses during the Past 12 Months	
	At Least One Offense	Multiple Offenses
Serious fight	8	7
Gang fight	10	8
Hurt someone badly	7	6
Used a weapon to steal	2	2
Stole less than $50	14	17
Stole more than $50	4	6
Shoplift	12	17
Breaking and entering	11	13
Arson	1.5	1
Damaged school property	6	8

Source: *Monitoring the Future, 1997* (Ann Arbor, MI: Institute of Social Research, 1998)

to be stable. Although a self-reported crime wave has not occurred, neither has there been any visible reduction in teenage delinquency. Indeed, these trends may actually have originated more than thirty years ago, as self-report statistics are little changed from similar data obtained in the 1960s.[15] Though self-report data suggest a stable teenage crime rate, these data typically do not include the most serious violent crimes of murder and rape, which official statistics show are increasing.

Validating Self-Reports

Critics of self-report studies suggest that it is not realistic to expect young people to admit illegal acts candidly. These youths have nothing to gain, and those taking the greatest risk are the ones with official records. Conversely, some young people may exaggerate their delinquent acts, forget some of them, or be confused. Methodological problems of self-report surveys include failing to use representative samples or including items that are trivial and without real interest to police ("used a false ID"). Despite these problems, a remarkable degree of uniformity has been found between self-reported answers and official records.[16]

The most common technique for validating self-reports is to compare the answers youths provide with official police records. Some methods of testing the validity of self-reports are illustrated in Table 2.5. In general, these efforts have been supportive of self-report techniques. The most thorough analysis of self-report validity was conducted by Michael Hindelang, Travis Hirschi, and Joseph Weis, who

Table 2.5

METHODS USED TO VALIDATE SELF-REPORTS

Method	Description of Technique
Known group method	Incarcerated youth and "normal" groups are compared to see whether the former report more delinquency
Peer informants	Friends who can verify the honesty of a subject's answers are asked to verify the accuracy of self-reports
Testing across time	Subjects are asked the same questions at different times to see if their answers remain the same
Benchmark questions	Questions are designed to identify those who are lying; a response like "I have never done anything wrong in my life" is suspect
Polygraph test	Subjects are asked questions while hooked up to a polygraph machine
Comparisons with official records	Official police and court records are compared with self-report information

Source: David Farrington, Rolf Loeber, Magda Stouthamer-Loeber, Welmoet Van Kammen, and Laura Schmidt, "Self-Reported Delinquency and a Combined Delinquency Seriousness Scale Based on Boys, Mothers, and Teachers: Concurrent and Predictive Validity for African-Americans and Caucasians," *Criminology* 34:501–25 (1996); Martin Gold, "Undetected Delinquent Behavior," *Journal of Research in Crime and Delinquency* 3:27–46 (1966); David Farrington, "Self-Reports of Deviant Behavior: Predictive and Stable?" *Journal of Criminal Law and Criminology* 64:99–110 (1973); John Clark and Larry Tifft, "Polygraph and Interview Validation of Self-Reported Deviant Behavior," *American Sociological Review* 31:516–23 (1966).

used data gathered in Seattle and at other sites.[17] They concluded that the problems of accuracy in self-reports are "surmountable," that self-reports are more accurate than most criminologists believe, and that self-reports and official statistics are quite compatible. They state:

> the method of self-reports does not appear from these studies to be fundamentally flawed. Reliability measures are impressive and the majority of studies produce validity coefficients in the moderate to strong range.[18]

The Hindelang, Hirschi, and Weis findings are supported by other studies that indicate that the patterns and trends evident in official delinquency are also contained in self-report data.[19]

Research has shown, however, that offenders with the most extensive prior criminality are most likely to "be poor historians of their own crime commission rates."[20] Therefore, self-reports may be measuring only nonserious, occasional delinquents. Hard core chronic offenders may be institutionalized and unavailable for surveys.[21] These institutionalized youths, absent from most self-report surveys, are not only more delinquent than the "average kid" in the general youth population but also are considerably more delinquent than the most delinquent youths identified in the typical self-report survey.[22]

It is also possible that self-reports are weakest in the one area they are most heavily relied on: measuring substance abuse.[23] Drug users may significantly underreport the frequency of their substance abuse. In studies of juvenile detainees, significant numbers of youths who test positive for drug use fail to self-report drug abuse.[24] Although this research involves a sample of incarcerated youths who might be expected to underreport drug use, the findings undercut the validity of self-report surveys. Similar research with adult pretrial detainees also found that self-reports significantly undercounted drug abuse.[25]

In conclusion, self-reports have limited value because they rarely include the most serious offenders, and when they do include them, these reports may be unreliable. Although self-reports continue to be used as a standard method of delinquency research, the results obtained must be interpreted with caution.

Correlates of Delinquency

Official and self-report data tell a great deal about the personal and social factors associated with delinquent behavior. But who are delinquents? What are their personal characteristics? Are they old? young? male? female? rich? poor? What offending patterns are routine?

An important aspect of delinquency research is measurement of the personal traits and social characteristics associated with adolescent misbehavior. If, for example, a strong association exists between delinquent behavior and limited social status, then poverty and economic deprivation must be considered in any explanation of the onset of delinquent behavior. If the crime–poverty association is not found, then forces independent of the socioeconomic structure may be responsible for the onset of youthful law violations. It would be fruitless to concentrate delinquency control efforts in areas such as job creation and vocational training if social status were found to be unrelated to delinquent behavior. Similarly, if only a handful of delinquents are responsible for most serious crimes, then crime control policies might be made more effective by identifying and treating these persistent offenders. The next sections discuss the relationship between delinquency and important personal traits and characteristics such as gender, race, social class, and age.

Although males maintain a significant edge in arrests for most illegal acts, one relationship does reverse this general pattern: girls are more likely than boys to be arrested for being runaways. It is possible that police hold paternalistic attitudes and are more likely to arrest female runaways and process them through the official justice channels. These two runaway girls comfort each other on the streets of New York.

Gender and Delinquency

Official arrest statistics, victim data, and self-reports indicate that males are significantly more criminal and delinquent than females. Today, the UCR results typically show that the teenage gender ratio for serious violent crime arrests is approximately 6 to 1, and for property crime approximately 3 to 1, in favor of males (Table 2.6).

Although males maintain a significant edge in arrests for most illegal acts, one relationship does reverse this general pattern: girls are more likely than boys to be arrested for being runaways. There are two explanations for this. Girls simply could be more likely than boys to run away from home, or, as some scholars have suggested, police may view the female runaway as the more serious problem and therefore be more likely to process females through official justice channels. This may reflect paternalistic attitudes toward girls who are viewed by police as likely candidates for "getting in trouble."[26]

Table 2.6

GENDER DIFFERENCES IN ARRESTS

For Representative UCR Crimes	Male:Female Ratio
Murder	16:1
Robbery	10:1
Assault	4:1
Burglary	9:1
Larceny	2:1
Auto Theft	5:1
Arson	9:1
Runaway	1:1.3

Source: FBI, *Uniform Crime Report*, 1997, pp. 234–36.

Table 2.7

DELINQUENT ACTS

Crime Category	Percentage of High School Seniors Admitting to at Least One Offense during the Past 12 Months, by Gender	
	Males	Females
Serious fight	18	11
Gang fight	23	14
Hurt someone badly	20	5
Used a weapon to steal	5	1
Stole less than $50	40	23
Stole more than $50	14	5
Shoplift	36	24
Breaking and entering	30	17
Arson	4	1
Damaged school property	21	7

Source: *Monitoring the Future, 1997* (Ann Arbor, Mi.: Institute of Social Research, 1998).

These patterns are not unique to the United States. Similar findings have been observed in self-report and official record studies in Great Britain as well. A Home Office study found that the overall male–female offense ratio was about 5 to 1 at ages 10 to 13, and 4 to 1 at ages 14 to 16. The ratio was much higher for serious crimes; for burglary, for example, it was about 17 to 1.[27]

In recent years the number and rate of arrests of female delinquents have been increasing faster than those for males. Between 1988 and 1997, the number of arrests of male delinquents increased about 28 percent, whereas the number of female delinquents arrested increased almost 60 percent. The change in serious violent crime arrests was even more striking: males increased 42 percent and females 100 percent. Self-report data seem to show that the incidence of female delinquency is much higher than previously expected and that, overall, the pattern of delinquency committed by males and females is quite similar. That is, the most common crimes committed by males are also the ones most female offenders commit.[28] Table 2.7 shows the percentage of males and females who admitted engaging in delinquent acts during the past twelve months in the latest ISR survey.

Although the ISR survey shows that many females engage in delinquency, most self-reports indicate that boys are still more likely than girls to be "frequently delinquent" and to engage in serious felony-type acts.[29] So although self-report studies indicate that female delinquency is more prevalent than that reflected in the official statistics and that the content of girls' delinquency is similar to boys', the few adolescents who report frequently engaging in serious violent crime are still predominantly male.[30] (Gender differences in the delinquency rate is the topic of Chapter 7.)

Racial Patterns in Delinquency

It thus seems clear that one cannot paint an accurate picture of crime in the United States without relying to some extent on race and ethnicity.[31]

Table 2.8

JUVENILE ARRESTS FOR SERIOUS CRIMES

Percentage of Total Juvenile Arrests for Serious Crimes, by Race

	Murder	Rape	Robbery	Assault	Burglary	Larceny	Auto Theft	Arson
White	40	56	42	60	73	70	59	79
Black	58	42	55	38	24	26	37	19
Other*	2	2	3	2	3	4	4	2

*Other includes American Indian, Alaskan Native, Asian or Pacific Islander
Source: FBI, *Uniform Crime Report*, 1997, p. 241.

There are approximately 38 million white and 7.5 million African American youths ages 5 to 17, a ratio of about 5 to 1. Yet FBI data show that racial minorities are disproportionately represented in the arrest statistics. African Americans make up about 12.5 percent of the population, but they account for about 31 percent of all arrests and 36 percent of index crime arrests. Table 2.8 presents the relative involvement of African American and white juveniles in the arrest data.

African American youths are arrested for a disproportionate number of serious crimes—murder, rape, robbery, and assault. White youths are arrested for a disproportionate share of arsons. Among Part II crimes, white youths are disproportionately arrested for alcohol-related violations such as driving under the influence, perhaps because they have greater access to automobiles.

The racial gap in the juvenile arrest rate has widened during the past decade. African American youths have experienced a steady increase in their arrest rates, whereas rates for other groups have remained stable. The African American arrest rate for weapon-related crime rose from two hundred to more than five hundred per one hundred thousand during this period.

Self-Report Differences Official statistics show that minority youths are much more likely than white youths to be arrested for serious criminal behavior and that race is an important predictor of delinquent behavior. To many delinquency experts, this pattern merely reflects racism and discrimination in the juvenile justice system. In other words, African American youths show up in the official statistics more often because they are more likely to be formally arrested by the police, who, in contrast, will treat white youths informally.

One way to examine this issue is to compare the racial differences in self-reported data with those found in the official delinquency records. Charges of racial discrimination in the arrest process would be supported by an insignificant difference between minority and white self-reported delinquency statistics.

Early researchers found that the relationship between race and self-reported delinquency was virtually nonexistent.[32] This research suggests that racial differences in the official crime data may be a function of law enforcement practices; arrest rates may reflect the fact that African American youths simply have a much greater chance of being arrested and officially processed.[33]

Self-report studies also suggest that the delinquent behavior rates of African American and white teenagers are generally similar and that differences in arrest statistics may indicate a differential selection policy by police.[34] The ISR survey, for example, generally shows that offending differences between African American and white youths are marginal.[35] However, some experts warn that there are racial differences in the way delinquency is self-reported and that African American youths may underreport more serious crimes, limiting the ability of self-reports to be a valid indicator of racial differences in the crime rate.[36]

Are the Data Valid?   Racial patterns in the delinquency rate have long been the subject of considerable controversy. The view that the disproportionate amount of African American official delinquency is a result of juvenile justice system bias has found some support in research studies. For example, recent research shows that juvenile suspects who belong to ethnic minorities, are male, and are poor are more likely to be formally arrested than suspects who are white, female, and affluent.[37]

In juvenile court minority youths may be punished more severely than white youths; juvenile court judges may believe the offenses committed by African American youths are more serious than those committed by white offenders.[38] Judges seem more willing to give white defendants lenient sentences if, for example, they show strong family ties or live in two-parent households; such considerations are absent from cases involving African American children.[39] Any form of racial bias is crucial because possession of a prior record, even if it is the product of bias, increases the likelihood that upon subsequent contact police will formally arrest a suspect rather than release the individual with a warning or take some other "unofficial" action.[40]

Although some bias does exist in the justice system, there is enough correspondence between official and self-report data to conclude that racial differences in the crime rate are real and are not solely the result of racial bias.[41] In their comprehensive review of race and justice entitled *The Color of Justice,* Samuel Walker, Cassia Spohn, and Miriam DeLone found that African American youths are arrested at a disproportionately high rate and that for crimes such as robbery and assault the evidence is that this is a result of offending rates rather than selection bias or racism on the part of the criminal justice system.[42]

Explaining Racial Patterns   A number of attempts have been made to explain racial differences in the official crime data. If, in fact, the racial differences in the delinquency rate recorded by official data are valid, one view is that they are a function of the ecological differences in U.S. society. African Americans are more likely than whites to be indigent and to reside in areas characterized by (1) deteriorated housing, (2) limited or nonexistent legitimate employment and recreational opportunities, (3) social conflict, (4) high crime rates that predate the current African American ethnic group in residence, (5) an abnormally high incidence of transient or pychopathological individuals, (6) a disproportionate number of opportunities to engage in criminal behavior or form delinquent subcultures, and (7) poverty being the norm rather than the exception.[43]

Related to these factors is the belief that institutionalized racism has produced an African American culture that is separate and in opposition to conventional white middle-class values. The African American inner-city subculture has been solidified by unduly harsh economic conditions; there seems little cause for optimism that this will change in the years to come because most minority youths still see few prospects for economic success.[44] Even when economic data show that they are doing better, news accounts of "protests, riots, and acts of civil disobedience" tell them otherwise.[45] A black teenage underclass has developed whose members lack the basic job skills needed to enter the social mainstream. African Americans are more than three times as likely as whites to be poor, and their median income and net worth is much less than that of whites. African American men are twice as likely to be jobless as white men,[46] and this lack of economic opportunity has directly influenced their crime and delinquency rates.[47]

Racial differentials in the crime rate may also be tied to frustrations over perceived racism, discrimination, and economic disparity. Even during times of economic growth, many poor African Americans believe they are being left out of the mainstream and feel a growing sense of frustration and failure.[48] Such frustration may be magnified by frequent exposure to neighborhood violence. African Americans who live in poor areas with high-crime rates may be disproportionately violent because they are exposed to more violence in their daily lives than other racial and economic groups. Research has shown that such exposure is a significant risk factor for violent behavior.[49]

It should come as no surprise that an element of the population that is shut out of educational and economic opportunities enjoyed by the rest of society may be prone to the lure of illegitimate gain and criminality. Young African American males in the inner city often are resigned to a lifetime of little if any social and economic opportunity. When they are directly exposed to racial prejudice, they are more likely to engage in violent behavior.[50]

The burden of social and economic marginalization may be compounded by the weakening of the African American family structure. Family dissolution in the minority community is tied to low employment rates among minority males, which places a strain on marriages. The relatively large number of female-headed households in minority communities may be one cause of the high mortality rate among African American males. Children in single-parent homes face an increased risk of early death due to disease and violence.[51] When families are weakened or disrupted, their ability to act as social control agents is compromised. It is not surprising then that divorce and separation rates are significantly associated with homicide rates in the African American community.[52]

In summary, official data indicate that African American youths are arrested for more serious crimes than whites. However, a number of self-report studies show that the differences in the rate of delinquency between the races is insignificant and that official differences are an artifact of bias in the justice system: police are more likely to arrest and courts are more likely to convict young African Americans.[53] In contrast, if the official data has validity, the participation of African American youths in serious criminal behavior is generally viewed as a function of their socioeconomic position and the racism they face.

Social Class and Delinquency

One of the most enduring debates among criminologists is over the relationship between economic status and delinquent behavior. Defining this relationship is a key element in the study of delinquency. If youth crime is purely a lower-class phenomenon, then its cause must be rooted in the social forces that are found solely in lower-class areas: poverty, unemployment, social disorganization, culture conflict, and alienation.[54] However, if delinquent behavior is spread throughout the social structure, then its cause must be related to some noneconomic factor: intelligence, personality, socialization, family dysfunction, educational failure, or peer influence. According to this line of reasoning, providing jobs or economic incentives would have little effect on the crime rate.

At first glance the relationship between class and crime seems clear. Youths who lack wealth or social standing, who live in deteriorated inner-city areas, and who rightfully perceive few legitimate opportunities are the most likely to use criminal means to achieve their goals. Despite the inherent logic of this observation, available research data do not consistently support this relationship, and poverty and economic deprivation do not correlate with delinquency. For example, little, if any, consistent evidence exists that unemployment rates are associated with crime rates.[55] Furthermore, many lower-class people live conventional and law-abiding lives, whereas a great number of middle-class people are delinquents and criminals.

Research on Social Class and Delinquency   Research on the class–crime relationship has been confusing and contradictory. Those who use official delinquency data persistently find social class to be a significant predictor of delinquency. Juvenile arrest rates are highest in areas that are economically deprived and socially disorganized.[56] People in lower-class neighborhoods are much more likely to need to call for police services than are residents of affluent suburbs.[57] Theorists who have based their efforts on official police statistics maintain that those who think delinquency is spread throughout the social classes are just "wishful thinkers"; to many experts, "real" delinquency is a lower-class phenomenon.[58]

Pioneering self-report studies—specifically those conducted by James Short and F. Ivan Nye—did not find a direct relationship between social class and the actual commission of delinquent acts.[59] However, they did find that socioeconomic class was related to official processing (chances of arrest and incarceration) by police, court, and correctional agencies.

The pioneering work of Nye and Short sparked numerous self-report studies in the 1960s and 1970s, most of which supported their view of a weak or nonexistent relationship between class and delinquency.[60] Some of the most important work was conducted by sociologist Martin Gold. In his first few studies Gold found that delinquents were predominantly lower-class youth, but his later work with Jay Williams showed no significant self-reported differences among economic classes.[61] The only statistically significant relationship indicated that higher-status white males were more seriously delinquent than other white males.

In the most widely cited research on this issue, Charles Tittle, Wayne Villemez, and Douglas Smith reviewed thirty-five studies containing 363 separate estimates of the relationship between class and crime.[62] Their conclusion was that little, if any, support exists for the position that delinquency is primarily a lower-class phenomenon. Tittle and his associates argue forcefully that official statistics probably reflect class bias in the way police make arrests. A follow-up study conducted by Tittle with Robert Meier once again found no significant association between delinquency and a variety of social class measures.[63] These reviews are usually cited by delinquency experts as the strongest refutation of the assertion that lower-class youths are disproportionately delinquent.[64]

In summary, the widespread use of self-reports uncovered the rather startling fact that poverty was not significantly correlated with delinquency.[65] Most researchers did conclude that lower-class youths were more likely to receive official notice from the justice system and, therefore, were overrepresented as official delinquents. Middle-class delinquency, for the most part, remained hidden.

Reassessing the Class–Delinquency Association   Those who find fault with Tittle's conclusions usually point to the inclusion of trivial offenses, for example, using a false ID, in most self-report instruments. Although middle- and upper-class youths may appear to be as delinquent as those in the lower class, it is because they engage in significant amounts of what are actually status offenses. Lower-class youths are more likely than middle-class youths to engage in serious delinquent acts such as burglary, assault, robbery, sexual assault, and vandalism.[66] Class seems to have less of an effect on property offenses.

How social class is measured also has been found to significantly influence research findings. Some researchers use "status attainment" variables such as parental income and education as measures of social class affiliation whereas others use indicators of sustained underclass status such as years on welfare and unemployment.[67] The basis for measurement will help shape conclusions about the relationship between class and delinquency. Some measures of social status (such as parental occupational status) are not related to serious delinquency, whereas other measures (such as parental unemployment) predict serious offending.[68] The class–delinquency association may also be crime specific. Research in this area is ongoing, but the most recent efforts suggest that middle- and upper-class youths may engage in some forms of minor illegal activity and theft offenses but it is members of the underclass who are responsible for the majority of serious delinquent acts.[69]

Age and Delinquency

Age is generally agreed to be inversely related to criminality.[70] In other words, as youthful offenders age, the likelihood that they will commit offenses declines. Official statistics tell us that young people are arrested at a disproportionate rate to their numbers in the population, and this finding is supported by victim surveys for crimes in which the age of the assailant can be determined. Youths thirteen to seventeen years old collectively make up about 6 percent of the total U.S. population, but they account for about 27 percent of the index crime arrests and 16 percent of the arrests for all crimes. In contrast, adults forty-five years and older, who make up 32 percent of the population, account for only 8 percent of arrests.

Self-report data collected by the Institute of Social Research also indicate that people commit less crime as they mature. The results of a six-year nationwide survey of high school seniors found that the self-reported rates for crimes such as assault, gang fighting, robbery, stealing, and trespass decline substantially between the ages of seventeen and twenty-three.[71] Although there is a generalized decline in criminal activity as youths mature, the incidence of some illegal acts, such as substance abuse, fraud, gambling, and drunkenness, may increase.[72] In addition, in a small segment of the delinquent population criminal behavior remains intact as they reach adulthood. Chronic offending is discussed later in this chapter.

Age Has Nothing to Do with It   The relationship between age and crime is very important to delinquency experts. One of the major criticisms leveled against theories of delinquency causation is that they fail to adequately explain why many youngsters forgo delinquent behavior as they mature, a process referred to as **aging out, desistance,** or **spontaneous remission.** That is, well-known theories that account for the *start,* or onset, of delinquency rarely bother to explain why people *stop* committing crime as they mature.

Criminologists Travis Hirschi and Michael Gottfredson argue that the age–crime relationship is a constant and therefore is irrelevant to the study of crime. They find that regardless of race, sex, social class, intelligence, or any other social variable, people commit less crime as they age.[73] They argue that even the most chronic juvenile offenders will commit less crime as they age.[74] According to this logic, since all people commit less crime as they age, age is irrelevant to the study of crime (see Figure 2.5).

aging out, desistance, spontaneous remission
Frequency of offending or delinquent behavior diminishes as youths mature; occurs among all groups of offenders.

FIGURE 2.5

Gender and Crime over the Life Span

According to Gottfredson and Hirschi, although the crime rate of males and females declines over the life-course, the *difference* in their crime rates remains consistent and stable.

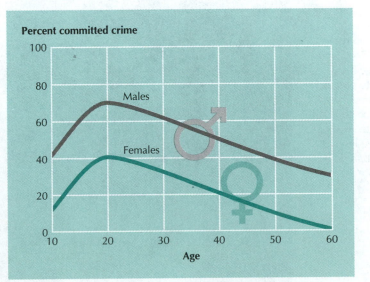

age of onset
Age at which youths begin their delinquent careers; early onset is believed to be linked with chronic offending patterns.

developmental view
The view that factors present at birth and events that unfold over a person's lifetime influence behavior; developmental theory focuses on the onset, escalation, desistance, and amplification of delinquent behaviors.

longitudinal studies
A research design that entails repeated measures over time; for example, a cohort may be measured at several points over their life course to determine risk factors for chronic offending.

Age Matters Those who oppose the Hirschi-Gottfredson view of the age–crime relationship suggest that age is one important determinant of crime but that other factors directly associated with a person's lifestyle also affect offending rates.[75] Crime patterns, then, may evolve over a person's life course. The probability that a person may become a persistent career criminal is influenced by a number of personal and environmental factors.[76] Evidence exists, for example, that the **age of onset** of a delinquent career has an important effect on its length: those who demonstrate antisocial tendencies at a very early age are more likely to commit more crime for a longer duration. According to this **developmental view,** it is important to do **longitudinal studies**—that is, to follow delinquents over their life cycle—to fully understand the factors that influence offending patterns.[77]

In summary, some criminologists believe youths who get involved with delinquency at a very early age and who acquire an official record are most likely to become career criminals. These researchers believe age is a key determinant of delinquency.[78] Those opposed to this view find that the age of onset is irrelevant and that all people commit less crime as they age. These researchers believe the relationship between age and crime is constant and therefore inconsequential to the study of delinquency.[79] The true role of the age variable in the production of criminal careers has been the focus of many lively debates in the literature of crime and delinquency.[80]

Why Do People Age Out of Crime? Delinquency experts have developed a number of reasons for the aging-out process. Here are a few of them:

■ Growing older means having to face the future. Young people, especially the indigent and antisocial, tend to be impatient; they "discount the future."[81] Why should they delay gratification when faced with an uncertain future? With maturity comes a long-term life view and the ability to resist the "quick fix."[82]

■ Maturation coincides with increased levels of responsibility. Some kids view teenage crime as "fun." Petty crimes are a risky and exciting social activity that provides adventure in an otherwise boring and unsympathetic world. As youths grow older, they take on new responsibilities that are inconsistent with criminality.[83] For example, young people who marry, enlist in the armed services, or enroll in vocational training courses are less likely to pursue criminal activities.[84]

Delinquency rates tend to go down as people mature. Increased levels of responsibility result in lower levels of criminality. Young people who marry, enlist in the armed services, and enroll in vocational training courses are less likely to pursue criminal activities. Although having a baby will place great stress upon them, this teen couple will simply have less time to get in trouble than before their child was born.

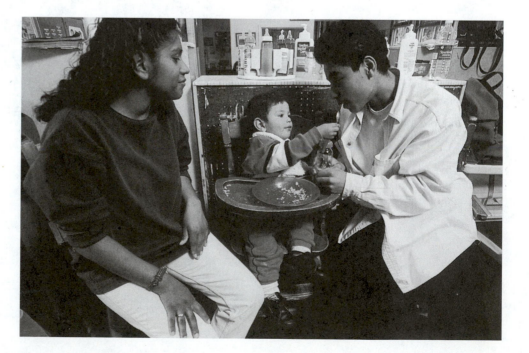

- Personalities can change with age. As youths mature, rebellious youngsters may develop increased self-control and be able to resist antisocial behavior.[85]

- Young adults become more aware of the risks that accompany crime. Once youths reach legal majority, criminal punishment takes a decidedly more serious turn. As adults, they are no longer protected by the kindly arms of the juvenile justice system.[86]

Of course, not all juvenile criminals desist as they age; some go on to become chronic adult offenders. Yet even those who remain active in a criminal career eventually slow down as they age. Crime is too dangerous, physically taxing, and unrewarding, and punishments too harsh and long-lasting to become a way of life for most people.[87]

Chronic Offending: Careers in Delinquency

Official and unofficial data sources indicate that although most adolescents age out of crime, a relatively small number of youths begin to violate the law early in their lives (early onset) and continue at a high rate well into adulthood (persistence).[88] The association between early onset and high rate persistent offending has been demonstrated in samples drawn from a variety of cultures, time periods, and offender types.[89]

These high-rate persisters are resistant to change and seem immune from the effects of punishment. Arrest, prosecution, and conviction do little to slow down their offending careers. These so-called chronic offenders are responsible for a significant amount of all delinquent and criminal activity.

The Glueck Research

Interest in chronic, persistent offending is at an all-time high, but it is not a new concept. In the 1930s Sheldon and Eleanor Glueck of Harvard University popularized research on the life cycle of delinquent careers,[90] following the careers of known delinquents in a series of longitudinal research studies.[91] In their best known study, *Unraveling Juvenile Delinquency*, they carefully matched a sample of five hundred delinquent youths with five hundred nondelinquents to ascertain the personal characteristics that predict persistent offending.

The Gluecks focused on the early onset of delinquency as a harbinger of a criminal career: "[T]he deeper the roots of childhood maladjustment, the smaller the chance of adult adjustment."[92] They also noted the stability of offending careers, concluding that children who are antisocial early in life are most likely to continue their offending careers into adulthood.

Their research findings convinced the Gluecks that the presence of specific personal factors present early in life were the most significant predictors of delinquent careers. They identified a variety of social factors related to persistent offending, the most important of which—family relations—included the quality of discipline and the child's emotional ties with parents. The adolescent raised in a large, single-parent family of limited economic means and educational achievement was most vulnerable to delinquency.

The Gluecks also evaluated biological and psychological traits such as body type, intelligence, and personality and found that physical and mental factors also played a role in determining behavior. Children with low intelligence, a history of mental illness, and a powerful physique were most likely to become persistent offenders. Though more than fifty years old, the Glueck research is now considered a forerunner of current efforts to describe the process of chronic offending and career criminality. The Gluecks' method of giving equal weight to social, biological, and psychological traits corresponds with current thinking on the formation of criminal careers.[93]

The Chronic Juvenile Offender

chronic delinquent offenders
Youths who start their delinquent careers at a young age, have serious and repeated brushes with the law, and build a career in crime; these youths do not age out of crime but continue their criminal behavior into adulthood.

Current interest in the delinquent life cycle was also prompted by the "discovery" in the 1970s of the **chronic delinquent offender.** According to this view, a relatively small number of youthful offenders commit a significant percentage of all serious crimes in the community, and many of these same offenders grow up to become chronic adult criminals who are responsible for a large share of the total adult crime rate.

Chronic offenders can be distinguished from other delinquent youths. Many youthful law violators are apprehended for a single instance of criminal behavior, usually one of minor seriousness such as shoplifting, joyriding, petty larceny, and so on. The chronic offender differs from other offenders in a number of important characteristics. Chronic offenders begin their delinquent careers at a young age (under ten years old; referred to as "early onset"), have serious and persistent brushes with the law, build a career in crime, and may be excessively violent and destructive. Moreover, chronic offenders do not age out of crime but continue their law-violating behavior into adulthood.[94] The important conclusion is that early and repeated delinquent activity is the best predictor of future adult criminality.

A number of important research efforts have set out to chronicle the careers of serious delinquent offenders. The next sections describe these initiatives.

Delinquency in a Birth Cohort The concept of the chronic career offender is most closely associated with the research efforts of Marvin Wolfgang and his associates at the University of Pennsylvania.[95] In 1972 Wolfgang, Robert Figlio, and Thorsten Sellin published a landmark study, *Delinquency in a Birth Cohort,* which has profoundly influenced the very concept of the delinquent offender.

Wolfgang, Figlio, and Sellin used official records to follow the delinquent careers of a cohort of 9,945 boys born in Philadelphia in 1945 from birth until they reached eighteen years of age. Data was obtained from police files and school records. Socioeconomic status was determined by locating the residence of each member of the cohort and assigning him the median family income for that area. About one-third of the boys (3,475) had some police contact. The remaining two-thirds (6,470) had none. Those boys with at least one contact with the police during their minority committed a total of 10,214 offenses. Wolfgang and his colleagues examined the relationship between delinquency and personal traits such as race, class, and education levels. Their most significant findings are contained in Table 2.9.

chronic recidivists
Youths who have been arrested five or more times and perpetuate a striking majority of serious criminal acts; this small group, known as the "chronic 6 percent," is believed to engage in a significant portion of all delinquent behavior.

Chronic Offenders The most significant discovery of Wolfgang and his associates was that of the so-called chronic offender. The cohort data indicated that 54 percent (1,862) of the sample's delinquent youths were repeat offenders; the remaining 46 percent (1,613) were one-time offenders. The repeaters could be further categorized as nonchronic recidivists and **chronic recidivists.** Nonchronic recidivists had been arrested more than once but fewer than five times. The 627 boys labeled chronic recidivists had been arrested five times or more. Although these chronic offenders accounted for only 18 percent of the delinquent population (6 percent of the total sample), they were found to be responsible for 52 percent of all offenses. Known today as the "chronic 6 percent," this group perpetrated a striking majority of the serious criminal acts: 71 percent of the homicides, 82 percent of the robberies, and 64 percent of the aggravated assaults.

Wolfgang and his associates found that arrest and juvenile court experience did little to deter chronic offenders. In fact, disposition was inversely related to chronic delinquency—the greater the punishment, the more likely they were to engage in repeat delinquent behavior. Strict punishment dispositions also increased the probability that further court action would be taken. Two factors stood out as encouraging recidivism: the seriousness of the original offense and the severity of the disposition. The researchers concluded that efforts of the juvenile justice system to control or eliminate delinquent behavior may be futile: not only do a greater proportion of those who receive a severe disposition violate the law, but their violations are serious and frequent.

Birth Cohort II   The juveniles who made up Wolfgang's original birth cohort were born in 1945. Have the behavior patterns of youths changed in subsequent years? To answer this question, Wolfgang and his associates Paul Tracy and Robert Figlio conducted a new, larger birth cohort study (Birth Cohort II) of youths born in Philadelphia in 1958, following them until their maturity.[96] Larger than the original group, the 1958 cohort had 27,160 youths, of which 13,160 were males and 14,000 females.

Table 2.9

FINDINGS OF THE PHILADELPHIA COHORT STUDY

Predictors of Delinquency	Findings
Race	Race was the most significant predictor of eventual police contact. About half of the nonwhite youths had police contact compared to 28 percent of the white youths in the cohort. The association between race and arrest remained significant even when youths from the same socioeconomic levels were compared.
Schooling	The type of school youths attended also influenced whether they would eventually be picked up by police. There was a higher delinquency rate for public school students than for parochial school attendees. Attending a public disciplinary institution increased the chances for a delinquency record even more.
Educational achievement	Levels of education and school achievement were influential factors. Nondelinquents received more education than delinquents (11.24 years completed versus 9.96). The number of delinquents assigned the lowest academic rating was more than double that of nondelinquents. Relatively few delinquents had high academic achievement levels. Nonwhites who suffered academically were especially susceptible to delinquency.
Intelligence	Intelligence (IQ) levels distinguished delinquents from nondelinquents. The average IQ for nondelinquents was 107.87 compared with 100.95 for delinquents.

The second cohort study revealed many of the same trends as its 1945 predecessor. The overall offending patterns in both cohorts were relatively similar. For example, about one-third of the boys in both samples had at least one police contact before their eighteenth birthday. Both studies revealed a greater percentage of delinquent behavior among minority youths, although the racial differences so apparent in the first cohort were less significant in the second. For example, the violent crime ratio, which was 15 to 1 in the first cohort, had declined to about 6 to 1 in the second. In addition, the number of white chronic delinquents increased substantially (by 5 percent), whereas the number of nonwhite chronic offenders declined (by 2 percent). Table 2.10 compares the major findings for each cohort with respect to chronic delinquency.

Despite these similarities, there were some discrepancies between the two cohorts. The second cohort contained female subjects, which allowed for a comparison between male and female delinquency patterns. As might be expected, males were two and a half times more likely than females to become involved in delinquent behavior. In addition, females who did get in trouble with the law were much more likely to be one-time offenders and less likely to be chronic delinquents. However, about 7 percent of the delinquent females were classified as chronic recidivists (147 girls).

Second, of the males in the sample, chronic delinquents (five or more arrests) made up 7.5 percent of the 1958 cohort (compared with 6.3 percent in 1945) and 23 percent of all delinquent offenders (compared with 18 percent in 1945). Chronic male delinquents continued to be responsible for a disproportionate amount of criminal behavior.

Finally, subjects in the 1958 cohort group were involved in significantly more serious crimes (455 per 1,000) than were those in the 1945 group (274 per 1,000).

The 1945 cohort study found that chronic offenders dominate the total juvenile crime rate and continue their law-violating careers as adults. The second cohort study showed that the chronic delinquent syndrome was being maintained in a group of subjects born thirteen years later than the original cohort, and, if anything, they were more violent than their older brothers. Finally, the efforts of the

Table 2.10

COMPARISON OF 1945 AND 1958 PHILADELPHIA COHORTS

	1958 Cohort	**1945 Cohort**
Total sample	27,160	9,945
Total delinquent population	1,159 offenses per 1,000 subjects	1,027 offenses per 1,000 subjects
Proportion of chronic delinquents	7.5 percent of sample 23 percent of delinquent population	6.3 percent of sample 18 percent of delinquent population
Proportion of offenses committed by chronic delinquents	61 percent of all offenses	51.9 percent of all offenses
Proportion of serious crimes committed by chronic delinquents	61 percent of all homicides 73 percent of robberies 65 percent of aggravated assaults	71 percent of all homicides 82 percent of robberies 64 percent of aggravated assaults

justice system seemed to have had little preventive effect on the behavior of chronic offenders.

Wolfgang's two pioneering efforts to identify the chronic career offender have been duplicated in a number of other important research studies.[97] Some have tracked criminal careers using the records of court-processed youths, and others have employed self-report data. These studies show that the chronic offender problem may be larger than previously believed.

Stability in Crime: From Delinquent to Criminal

The original chronic offender research left an important question unanswered: Do chronic juvenile offenders grow up to become chronic adult criminals? A number of research efforts have been aimed at answering this question. In one important study a 10 percent sample of the original Pennsylvania cohort (974 subjects) was followed through their adulthood to age 30.[98] This study supports the premise that juvenile chronic offender patterns are likely to play out into adulthood. Seventy percent of the "persistent" adult offenders had also been chronic juvenile offenders; they had an 80 percent chance of becoming adult offenders and a 50 percent chance of being arrested four or more times as adults. In comparison, subjects with no juvenile arrests had only an 18 percent chance of being arrested as adults. The chronic offenders also continued to engage in the most serious crimes. Though they accounted for only 15 percent of the follow-up sample, the former chronic delinquents were involved in 74 percent of all arrests and 82 percent of all serious crimes, such as homicide, rape, and robbery.

The stability of criminal careers was also detected by Paul Tracy and Kimberly Kempf-Leonard in their important follow-up study of all subjects in the second 1958 cohort. By age 26, Cohort II subjects were displaying the same behavior patterns as their older peers. Few delinquent offenders (about one-third) and even fewer non-delinquent offenders (10 percent) became adult criminals, a finding that supports the aging-out premise. Nonetheless, those delinquents with high rates of juvenile offending, who started their delinquent careers early, committed a violent crime, and continued offending throughout adolescence were most likely to persist in criminal behavior as adults. Tracy and Kempf-Leonard found that delinquents who began their offending careers with serious offenses or who quickly increased the severity of their offending early in life were most likely to persist in their criminal behavior into adulthood. Severity of offending rather than frequency of criminal behavior had the greatest impact on later adult criminality.[99]

Further research on criminal careers provides evidence that chronic juvenile offenders continue their law-violating careers as adults, a concept referred to as the **continuity of crime.** Kids who are disruptive and antisocial as early as age 5 or 6 are most likely to exhibit stable, long-term patterns of disruptive behavior throughout adolescence.[100] They have measurable behavior problems in learning and motor skills, cognitive abilities, family relations, and other areas of social, psychological, and physical functioning.[101] Apprehension and punishment seem to have little effect on their offending behavior. One study followed the offending careers of nearly two thousand serious, chronic youthful offenders for a period of ten years after their release from the California Youth Authority. These youthful offenders were arrested on 24,615 occasions over the period tracked by the study, an average of twelve arrests each. More than 90 percent had been rearrested during the following decade, and they averaged about nine property, four violent, three drug, and six other arrests.[102] This recent research suggests that the best predictor of future behavior is past behavior. Youths who have long juvenile records will most likely continue their offending careers into adulthood.

continuity of crime
The idea that chronic juvenile offenders are likely to continue violating the law as adults.

Policy Implications

The ongoing research efforts to chart the life cycle of crime and delinquency will have a major influence on both theory and policy. Rather than simply asking why youths become delinquent or commit antisocial acts, theorists are charting the onset, escalation, frequency, and cessation of delinquent behavior.

Research on delinquent careers has also influenced delinquency control policy. If a relatively few persistent offenders commit a great number of all delinquent acts and then persist as adult criminals, it follows that steps should be taken to limit their criminal opportunities.[103] One approach is to identify persistent offenders at the beginning stages of their offending careers and provide early intervention and treatment.[104] Identification might be facilitated by research aimed at identifying traits (for example, impulsive personalities) that can be used to classify high-risk offenders.[105] Because many of these youths suffer from a variety of social problems, treatment must be aimed at a broad range of educational, family, vocational, and psychological problems. Focusing on a single problem, such as a lack of employment, may be ineffective.[106]

The concept of the chronic career offender has profoundly influenced the daily operations of the juvenile justice system. Few concepts have shaken the study of crime and delinquency as much as the "discovery" of the chronic or persistent delinquent offender. The belief that a few persistent offenders are responsible for a significant portion of the serious crime in a community has been translated into a number of policy initiatives within the juvenile justice system. First, it has strengthened the position of conservative policymakers who call for a get-tough approach to juvenile delinquency. Although it might seem futile, cruel, and expensive to lock up all juvenile offenders, it makes both economic and practical sense to incarcerate the few chronic offenders who are responsible for most of the crime problem. Increased attention to the problem of career criminals has resulted in development of tough juvenile sentencing codes, as well as the transfer of serious delinquency cases to the adult court.

Of course, even the most sophisticated attempts to predict chronic offending are erroneous more than half the time.[107] Efforts to predict individual cases of chronic offending have proven unreliable.[108] The danger also exists that early identification, arrest, and custody of youths will promote rather than inhibit their delinquent careers.[109] After all, Wolfgang found that intervention had little effect on chronic offenders other than increasing the likelihood of their rearrest. Although an intensive law enforcement policy aimed at multiple offenders may have political appeal, it might actually produce a higher overall delinquency rate.

The discovery of the chronic offender has significantly shifted juvenile justice philosophy away from a liberal treatment orientation and toward a more conservative crime control model. It may also produce a review of the *parens patriae* doctrine and an examination of the jurisdiction of the juvenile court. As Kimberly Kempf-Leonard suggests, it may make sense to reconstruct the criminal court system so that both petty juvenile and adult cases are handled in one court, chronic juvenile and adult felony offenders in another, and status offenders in a third. The problems of juvenile and adult chronic offenders may be similar enough to warrant the attention of the same judicial authority.[110] The Case in Point explores some of these issues.

Juvenile Victimization

Juveniles are also the victims of crime, and data from victim surveys can help us understand the nature of juvenile victimization. Most of what is known about the nature and extent of juvenile victimization comes from an ongoing

You are a newly appointed judge in the county juvenile court.

A twelve-year-old boy, Joseph L., is petitioned to court on a robbery charge. It seems that Joseph, a five-foot-four, 110-pound youngster, used a knife in a school yard robbery. This is already his fifth offense. He was arrested at age 9 on a petty larceny charge, and six months later he was picked up for breaking into a home. At age 10 he was again arrested for a break-in, and at age 11 he assaulted and badly beat a younger boy after school. Despite his youth, the boy seems defiant and unafraid.

At the sentencing hearing the prosecutor presents evidence that Joseph has all the character traits of a chronic offender: early onset of delinquency, multiple arrests, increased seriousness of offenses, a history of school failure, low intelligence, and siblings who are law violators. The prosecution demands a three-year placement in the state correctional facility for dangerous youth. Defense counsel asks for community supervision. She claims that the state's high-security juvenile facility usually houses much older offenders, many of whom are over sixteen. Placement will only exacerbate an already serious situation. Considering the boy's tender age, she argues, the case can better be handled by community treatment agencies.

The prosecution counters that chronic offenders will not be impressed with leniency and that community treatment is therefore a waste of time. Though the prosecutor agrees with defense counsel's claim that placement with older delinquents will certainly diminish any chance of future rehabilitation, he believes this youth has already proven himself beyond control. Society's need for safety outweighs the remote likelihood of rehabilitation, he contends.

A period of incarceration is needed in this case to protect the public from a dangerous chronic offender, but:

■ Is it fair to place this child with older youths in a high-security treatment center?

■ Should the needs of society outweigh a child's right to treatment?

■ Should predictions of future behavior patterns influence the treatment of children?

cooperative effort of the Bureau of Justice Statistics of the U.S. Department of Justice and the U.S. Census Bureau, called the National Crime Victimization Survey (NCVS). The NCVS is a massive annual household survey of the victims of criminal behavior in the United States that measures the nature of the crime and the personal characteristics of victims.

The total annual sample size of the NCVS has been about fifty thousand households containing about one hundred thousand individuals. The sample is broken down into subsamples of ten thousand households (about twenty thousand individuals), and each group is interviewed twice a year; for example, people interviewed in January will be recontacted in July. The NCVS has been conducted annually for more than fifteen years and was revised recently to increase both the validity and the reliability of its estimates.

Victimization in the United States

victimizations

The number of people who are victims of criminal acts; young teens are fifteen times more likely than older adults (age 65 and over) to be victims of crimes.

The National Crime Victimization Survey provides yearly estimates of the total number of personal contact crimes (such as assault, rape, and robbery) and household **victimizations** (such as burglary, larceny, and vehicle theft). According to victims' reports, about thirty-seven million crimes occur annually in the United States.[111] This includes about six million crimes of violence, fourteen million personal thefts, and fourteen million household crimes, such as burglary. These crimes take a terrible toll on victims. If we translate the value of pain, emotional trauma, disability, and risk of death into dollar terms, the cost is $450 billion, or $1,800 for every person in the United States.[112]

At first glance these figures seem overwhelming, but victimization rates are stable or declining for most crime categories. The number of victimizations peaked in the early 1980s, but the NCVS parallels the UCR's finding that crime rates have been in decline for the past few years.

Many of the differences between NCVS data and official statistics can be attributed to the fact that many victims do not report their victimizations to police. About 57 percent of the crimes of violence, 72 percent of the personal crimes of theft, and 66 percent of household crimes go unreported.

Young Victims

The National Crime Victimization Survey data indicate that young people are much more likely to be the victims of crime than adults.[113] Although it is common for the media to portray the elderly as particularly vulnerable to violent personal crime, it is actually teenagers who have the greatest risk of victimization. The chance of victimization declines with age. Young teens are more than fifteen times as likely as people over sixty-five to be victims of personal crimes such as robbery (Figure 2.6). What is both surprising and shocking is that this pattern holds for serious crimes such as rape, aggravated assault, and robbery as well; juvenile victimization is not just a matter of minor school yard assaults (see Figure 2.7).

In addition to these age patterns, NCVS data show that male teenagers have a significantly higher chance than females of becoming victims of violent crime.

FIGURE 2.6

Estimates of Personal Victimization, by Age

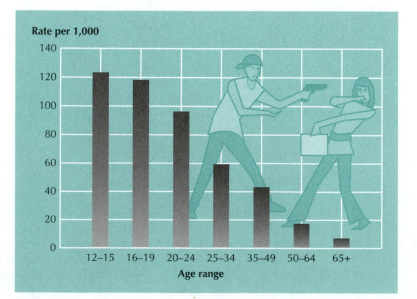

FIGURE 2.7

Murder Victimization Rates, 1976–1997

Source: James A. Fox and Martanne Zavitz, *Homicide Trends in the U.S.* (Washington, D.C.: Bureau of Justice Statistics, 1998).

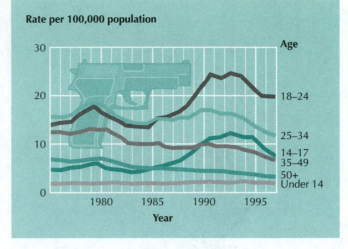

African American teens ages 12 to 15 have a greater chance of becoming victims of violent crimes than white teenagers of the same age, but by age 16 teenagers of both racial groups share an equal victimization risk (118 per 1,000 were violent crime victims).

The vulnerability children have to criminal victimization is affirmed by data acquired from the nation's hospital emergency rooms. Of the more than 1.4 million people who sought treatment for violence-related injuries in a single year (1994), about 400,000 were children and teens under age 19, including more than 15,000 who were treated for injuries sustained during rapes and sexual assaults.[114]

Considering these findings, it is somewhat ironic that, in general, older women are the most likely to have a generalized fear of crime, and teenage males and females are usually found to be the least fearful. Fear of crime is difficult to measure, but there are some indications that those who actually have the lowest risk of crime victimization are the most fearful of crime.[115]

The Victims and Their Criminals

NCVS data can also tell us something about the relationship between victims and offenders. This information is available because victims of violent personal crimes, such as assault and robbery, can identify the age, sex, and race of their attackers.

In general teens tend to be victimized by their peers: a majority of teens were victimized by other teens, whereas victims age 20 and over identified their attackers as being twenty-one or older. However, people in almost all age groups who were victimized by groups of offenders identified their attackers as teenagers. Violent crime victims report that a disproportionate number of their attackers are young, ranging in age from sixteen to twenty-five.

The NCVS data also tell us that victimization in intraracial: African American teens tend to be victimized by other African American teenagers, and whites by whites.

Most teens are victimized by people they know or are acquainted with, and their victimization is more likely to occur during the day. In contrast, adults are more often victimized by strangers and at night. One explanation for this pattern is that youths are at greatest risk from their own family and relatives. (Chapter 8 deals with the disturbing issue of child abuse and neglect.) Another possibility is that many teenage victimizations occur at school. About 13 percent of all crimes of violence take place in school buildings or on school grounds. Teens tend to be victimized in public places such as schools and parks by peers of the same sex, race, and age.

Hospital records show that children are extremely vulnerable to violent crime. About 400,000 children and teens under age 19 are treated for injuries in emergency rooms each year, including more than 15,000 who are treated for injuries sustained during rapes and sexual assaults. There was no help for these two youngsters, Devon, age 6, and Damon, age 5, who were found murdered in their home in Rowlett, Texas, in 1996. They were stabbed to death in their sleep and their mother was the prime suspect.

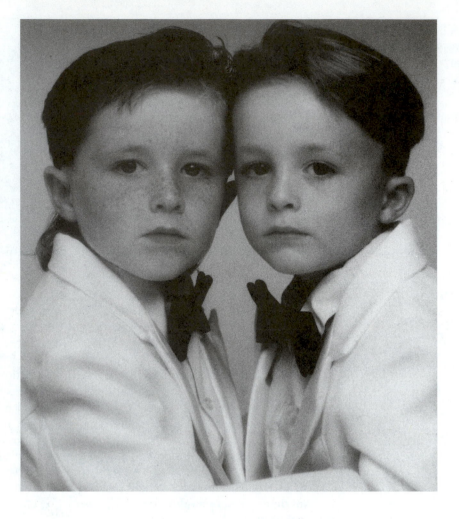

Stranger Attacks   These data contradict the popular belief that children are at great risk of being abducted and harmed by strangers. The number of children seriously harmed (abducted or murdered) by strangers is less than commonly thought.[116] Each year there are about fifty cases in which it can be verified that a child was abducted and feloniously killed by a stranger. In another one hundred cases the surrounding circumstances remain unknown, except that a child was killed by a stranger, for a total of about one hundred and fifty stranger homicides a year. The research indicates that fourteen- to seventeen-year-old youths account for nearly two out of three victims, a risk nearly seven times greater than that faced by children nine years old and younger. Girls are twice as likely as boys to be victims of known stranger homicides, a pattern that contrasts with general homicide rates.

Although stranger victimizations may be less common than once thought, the fact that as many as three children are abducted and killed by strangers every week in the United States is still extremely disturbing. These horrible crimes permanently scar victims' families and friends and probably take a greater toll on the general public than any other crime.

Family and Acquaintance Victimization   Analysis of the National Crime Victimization Survey data indicates that at some time during their lifetime about 80 percent of the twelve-year-old youths in the United States will become victims of completed or attempted violent crimes, 99 percent will experience theft, and 40 percent will be injured during the course of the crime.[117] A recent Bureau of Justice survey found that nearly 20 percent of state prison inmates serving time for violent crimes had victimized someone under age.[118] Figure 2.8 summarizes the findings of this survey. In most instances victim and criminal were either related, living together, or

Characteristics of the offenders

▶ An estimated 18.6 percent of inmates serving time in state prisons in 1991 for violent crimes, or about 61,000 offenders nationwhide, have been convicted of a crime against a victim under age 18.

▶ One in five violent offenders serving time in a state prison reported having victimized a child.

▶ More than half the violent crimes committed against children involved victims age 12 or younger.

▶ Seven in ten offenders with child victims reported that they were imprisoned for a rape or sexual assault.

▶ Two-thirds of all prisoners convicted of rape or sexual assault had committed their crime against a child.

▶ All but 3 percent of offenders who committed violent crimes against children were male.

▶ Violent child victimizers were substantially more likely than those with adult victims to have been physically or sexually abused when they were children, though the majority of violent offenders, regardless of victim age, did not have a history of such abuse.

Characteristics of the victims

▶ Three in ten child victimizers reported that they had committed their crimes against multiple victims; they were more likely than those who victimized adults to have had multiple victims.

▶ Three in four victims of violence were female.

▶ For the vast majority of child victimizers in state prisons, the victim was someone they knew before the crime:
A third had committed their crime against their own child
About half had a relationship with the victim as a friend, acquaintance, or relative other than offspring

▶ About one in seven reported the victim to have been a stranger to them.

▶ Three-quarters of the violent victimizations of children took place in either the victim's home or the offender's home.

▶ Four in ten child victims of violence suffered either forcible rape or another injury.

19 percent of violent state prison inmates committed their crime against a child;

78 percent of those convicted of sexual assault had abused a child.

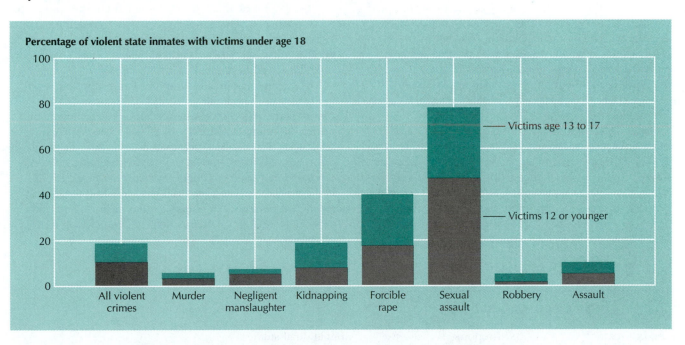

FIGURE 2.8

Child Victimizers: Characteristics of Offenders and Victims

Source: Lawrence Greenfeld, *Child Victimizers: Violent Offenders and Their Victims* (Washington, D.C.: Bureau of Justice Statistics, 1996) p. 1.

acquaintances. In a third of the cases the offender had victimized his or her own child. Only one in seven cases involved a stranger.

Although these rates may seem shocking, compared to other self-report surveys the NCVS seriously *underreports* juvenile victimization. The rate of current and lifetime likelihood of victimization of juveniles may be several times higher than that indicated by the NCVS.[119]

SUMMARY

Official delinquency refers to youths who are arrested by police agencies. What is known about official delinquency comes from the FBI's *Uniform Crime Report* (UCR), an annual tally of crimes reported to police by citizens. In addition, the FBI gathers arrest statistics from local police departments. From these, it is possible to determine the number of youths who are arrested each year, along with their age, race, and gender.

About two million youths are now being arrested annually by police. A disturbing trend has been an increase in the number of juveniles arrested for violent crimes, especially rape and murder. Though it is not certain why this trend has developed, possible explanations include involvement in gang activity, drug abuse, and teen gun ownership.

Dissatsifaction with the validity of the UCR prompted criminologists to develop other means of measuring the true amount of delinquent behavior. Self-reports are surveys of youths in which subjects are asked to describe their misbehavior. Although self-reports indicate that many more crimes are committed than are known to the police, they also show that the delinquency rate is rather stable.

The third method of gathering information on delinquency involves victim surveys. The National Crime Victimization Survey is an annual national survey of the victims of crime conducted by agencies of the federal government. Teenagers are much more likely to become victims of crime than are people in other age groups. All three sources of crime statistics agree on one thing, however; young people commit more crimes than adults.

The data sources tell us that delinquents are disproportionately male, although female delinquency rates are rising at a faster rate. Minority youth are overrepresented in the delinquency rate, especially for violent crime arrests. Experts are split on the cause of racial differences. Some believe they are a function of system bias; others see them as representing actual differences in the delinquency rate. Disagreement also exists over the relationship between class position and delinquency. Some hold that adolescent crime is a lower-class phenomenon, whereas others see it as spread throughout the social structure. Problems in methodology and data collection have obscured the true class–crime relationship. However, official statistics indicate that lower-class youths are responsible for the most serious criminal acts.

Quite a bit of attention has been paid to the age–crime relationship. There is general agreement that delinquency rates decline with age. Some experts believe this phenomenon is universal, whereas others believe a small group of offenders persists in crime at a high rate.

The age–crime relationship has spurred research on the nature of delinquency over the life course. One discovery is the chronic persistent offender, who begins his or her offending career early in life and persists as an adult. The Gluecks first identified the traits of persistent offenders. Wolfgang and his colleagues identified chronic offenders in a series of cohort studies conducted in Philadelphia. Ongoing research has identified the characteristics of persistent offenders as they mature, and both personality and social factors help us predict long-term offending patterns.

KEY TERMS

Federal Bureau of
    Investigation (FBI)
Uniform Crime Report
    (UCR)
Part I offenses
Part II offenses
disaggregated

self-reports
dark figures of crime
aging out
desistance
spontaneous remission
age of onset
developmental view

longitudinal studies
chronic delinquent
    offenders
chronic recidivists
continuity of crime
victimization

A number of criminologists have commented on the likelihood of a juvenile crime wave over the next few years. The basis for this speculation has been the increasing number of young people in this country. Although this phenomenon has yet to materialize, many political campaign platforms have been based on this fear of juvenile crime.

Explore InfoTrac College Edition for articles on juvenile crime statistics. What do the overall trends show? Based on what you find, does it appear that the predictions of a youth crime wave are accurate?

To search for information, use key words such as: *juvenile crime statistics, crime statistics,* and *juvenile delinquency statistics.*

QUESTIONS FOR DISCUSSION

1. What factors contribute to the aging-out process?
2. Why are males more delinquent than females? Is it a matter of lifestyle, culture, or physical properties?
3. Discuss the racial differences found in the crime rate. What factors account for differences in the African American and white crime rates?
4. Discuss the controversy surrounding the role social class plays in delinquency. Do you believe that middle-class youths are as delinquent as lower-class youths?

NOTES

1. "Boy, 11, Faces 40 Years in Sexual Assault Case," *New York Times* 5 June 1998, p. A17.
2. Howard Snyder and Melissa Sickmund, *Juvenile Offenders and Victims: A National Report* (Washington, D.C.: National Center for Juvenile Justice, 1995).
3. FBI News Release, 5 May 1996.
4. Ibid., p. 5.
5. Howard Snyder, *Juvenile Arrests, 1996* (Washington, D.C.: Office of Juvenile Justice and Delinquency Prevention, 1997).
6. All population statistics used in the chapter are from U.S. Bureau of Census, unpublished data, 1994 (Washington, D.C.: U.S. Department of Census, 1995).
7. "Fox Butterfield Possible Manipulation of Crime Data Worries Top Police," *New York Times* 3 August 1998, p.1.
8. For the most complete review, see Michael Hindelang, Travis Hirschi, and Joseph Weis, *Measuring Delinquency* (Beverly Hills, Calif.: Sage, 1981).
9. Walter Gove, Michael Hughes, and Michael Geerken, "Are Uniform Crime Reports a Valid Indicator of the Index Crimes? An Affirmative Answer with Minor Qualifications," *Criminology* 23:451–501 (1985); Michael Hindelang, Travis Hirschi, and Joseph Weis, "Correlates of Delinquency: The Illusion of Discrepancy between Self-Report and Official Data," *American Sociological Review* 44:995–1014 (1979).
10. A pioneering effort of self-report research is A. L. Porterfield's *Youth in Trouble* (Fort Worth, Tex.: Leo Potishman Foundation, 1946); for a review, see Robert Hardt and George Bodine, *Development of Self-Report Instruments in Delinquency Research: A Conference Report* (Syracuse, N.Y.: Syracuse University Youth Development Center, 1965); see also, Fred Murphy, Mary Shirley, and Helen Witmer, "The Incidence of Hidden Delinquency," *American Journal of Orthopsychiatry* 16:686–96 (1946).
11. For example, the following studies have noted the great discrepancy between official statistics and self-report studies: Maynard Erickson and LaMar Empey, "Court Records, Undetected Delinquency, and Decision-Making," *Journal of Criminal Law, Criminology, and Police Science* 54:456–69 (1963);

Martin Gold, "Undetected Delinquent Behavior," *Journal of Research in Crime and Delinquency* 3:27–46 (1966); James Short and F. Ivan Nye, "Extent of Unrecorded Delinquency, Tentative Conclusions," *Journal of Criminal Law, Criminology, and Police Science* 49:296–302 (1958).
12. In addition to the studies listed in note 11, see David Farrington, "Self-Reports of Deviant Behavior: Predictive and Stable?", *Journal of Criminal Law and Criminology* 64:99–110 (1973); Michael Hindelang, "Causes of Delinquency: A Partial Replication and Extension," *Social Problems* 20:471–87 (1973).
13. Jerald Bachman, Lloyd Johnston, and Patrick O'Malley, *Monitoring the Future: Questionnaire Responses from the Nation's High School Seniors, 1995* (Ann Arbor, Mich.: Institute for Social Research, 1996), pp. 102–4.
14. D. Wayne Osgood, Patrick O'Malley, Jerald Bachman, and Lloyd Johnston, "Time Trends and Age Trends in Arrests and Self-Reported Illegal Behavior," *Criminology* 27:389–417 (1989).
15. Rosemary Sarri, "Gender Issues in Juvenile Justice," *Crime and Delinquency* 29:381–97 (1983).
16. Erickson and Empey, "Court Records, Undetected Delinquency, and Decision Making"; H. B. Gibson, Sylvia Morrison, and D. J. West, "The Confession of Known Offenses in Response to a Self-Reported Delinquency Schedule," *British Journal of Criminology* 10:277–80 (1970); John Blackmore, "The Relationship between Self-Reported Delinquency and Official Convictions amongst Adolescent Boys," *British Journal of Criminology* 14:172–76 (1974).
17. Hindelang, Hirschi, and Weis, *Measuring Delinquency.*
18. Ibid., p. 114.
19. Douglas Smith and Laura Davidson, "Interfacing Indicators and Constructs in Criminological Research: A Note on the Comparability of Self-Report and Violence Data for Race and Sex Groups," *Criminology* 24:473–87 (1986); Robert Sampson, "Sex Differences in Self-Reported Delinquency and Official Records: A Multiple Group Structural Modeling Approach," *Journal of Quantitative Criminology* 23:345–68 (1985).
20. Leono Simon, "Validity and Reliability of Violent Juveniles: A Comparison of Juvenile Self-Reports with Adult Self-Reports

Incarcerated in Adult Prisons," paper presented at the American Society of Criminology Meeting, Boston, Mass., November 1995, p. 26.

21. Stephen Cernkovich, Peggy Giordano, and Meredith Pugh, "Chronic Offenders: The Missing Cases in Self-Report Delinquency Research," *Journal of Criminal Law and Criminology* 76:705–32 (1985).

22. Ibid., p. 706.

23. Minu Mathur, Richard Dodder, and Harjit Sandhu, "Inmate Self-Report Data: A Study of Reliability," *Criminal Justice Review* 17:258–67 (1992).

24. Eric Wish, Thomas Gray, and Eliot Levine, *Recent Drug Use in Female Juvenile Detainees: Esitmates from Interviews, Urinalysis and Hair Analysis* (College Park, Md.: Center for Substance Abuse Research, 1996); Thomas Gray and Eric Wish, *Maryland Youth at Risk: A Study of Drug Use in Juvenile Detainees* (College Park, Md.: Center for Substance Abuse Research, 1993).

25. Eric Wish and Christina Polsenberg, "Arrestee Urine Tests and Self-Reports of Drug Use: Which Is More Related to Re-arrest?", paper presented at the American Society of Criminology Meeting, Phoenix, Ariz., November 1993.

26. For a discussion of sex bias, see Meda Chesney-Lind, "Guilty by Reason of Sex: Young Women and the Criminal Justice System," paper presented at the American Society of Criminology Meeting, Toronto, Canada, 1980.

27. Cited in David Farrington, "Juvenile Delinquency," in John Coleman, *The School Years* (London: Routledge, 1992), p. 132.

28. Hindelang, Hirschi, and Weis, *Measuring Delinquency;* Gary Jensen and Raymond Eve, "Sex Differences in Delinquency: An Examination of Popular Sociological Explanation," *Criminology* 13:427–48 (1976); Michael Hindelang, "Age, Sex, and the Versatility of Delinquent Involvements," *Social Problems* 18:522–35 (1979); James Short and F. Ivan Nye, "Extent of Unrecorded Juvenile Delinquency, Tentative Conclusions," *Journal of Criminal Law, Criminology, and Police Science* 49:296–302 (1958).

29. Rosemary Sarri, "Gender Issues in Juvenile Justice," *Crime and Delinquency* 29:381–97 (1983).

30. For a review, see Meda Chesney-Lind and Randall Shelden, *Girls' Delinquency and Juvenile Justice* (Pacific Grove, Calif.: Brooks/Cole, 1992), pp. 7–14.

31. Samuel Walker, Cassia Spohn, and Miriam DeLone, *The Color of Justice* (Belmont, Calif.: Wadsworth, 1996), p. 229.

32. Leroy Gould, "Who Defines Delinquency? A Comparison of Self-Report and Officially Reported Indices of Delinquency for Three Racial Groups," *Social Problems* 16:325–36 (1969); Harwin Voss, "Ethnic Differentials in Delinquency in Honolulu," *Journal of Criminal Law, Criminology, and Police Science* 54:322–27 (1963); Ronald Akers, Marvin Krohn, Marcia Radosevich, and Lonn Lanza-Kaduce, "Social Characteristics and Self-Reported Delinquency," in Gary Jensen, ed., *Sociology of Delinquency* (Beverly Hills, Calif.: Sage, 1981), pp. 48–62.

33. David Huizinga and Delbert Elliott, "Juvenile Offenders: Prevalence, Offender Incidence, and Arrest Rates by Race," *Crime and Delinquency* 33:206–23 (1987); see also, Dale Dannefer and Russell Schutt, "Race and Juvenile Justice Processing in Court and Police Agencies," *American Journal of Sociology* 87:1113–32 (1982).

34. Paul Tracy, "Race and Class Differences in Official and Self-Reported Delinquency," in Marvin Wolfgang, Terrence Thornberry, and Robert Figlio, eds., *From Boy to Man, from Delinquency to Crime* (Chicago: University of Chicago Press, 1987), p. 120.

35. Bachman, Johnston, and O'Malley, *Monitoring the Future,* pp. 102–4.

36. Walker, Spohn, and DeLone, *The Color of Justice,* pp. 46–47.

37. Miriam Sealock and Sally Simpson, "Unraveling Bias in Arrest Decisions: The Role of Juvenile Offender Typescripts," *Justice Quarterly* 15:427–457 (1998).

38. Christina Polsenberg and Kenneth Jackson, "Putting Race into Context: Race, Juvenile Justice Processing and Urbanization," paper presented at the American Society of Criminology Meeting, Boston, Mass., November 1995 (updated version, 1996); for a general review, see Carl Pope and William Feyerherm, "Minority Status and Juvenile Justice Processing (Part I)," *Criminal Justice Abstracts* 22:327–35 (1990); see also Douglas Smith and Jody Klein, "Police Control of Interpersonal Disputes," *Social Problems* 31:468–81 (1984).

39. Christina DeJong and Kenneth Jackson, "Putting Race into Context: Race, Juvenile Justice Processing, and Urbanization," *Justice Quarterly* 15:487–504 (1998).

40. Donna Bishop and Charles Frazier, "The Influence of Race in Juvenile Justice Processing," *Journal of Research in Crime and Delinquency* 25:242–63 (1989).

41. For a general review, see William Wilbanks, *The Myth of a Racist Criminal Justice System* (Pacific Grove, Calif.: Brooks/Cole, 1987).

42. Walker, Spohn, and DeLone, *The Color of Justice,* pp. 47–48.

43. Daniel Georges-Abeyie, cited in James Byrne and Robert Sampson, *The Social Ecology of Crime* (New York: Springer-Verlag, 1986), p. 99.

44. Tom Joe, "Economic Inequality: The Picture in Black and White," *Crime and Delinquency* 33:287–99 (1987).

45. Gary LaFree, Kriss Drass, and Patrick O'Day, "Race and Crime in Postwar America: Determinants of African-American and White Rates, 1957–1988," *Criminology* 30:157–88 (1992).

46. Troy Duster, "Crime, Youth Unemployment, and the Black Urban Underclass," *Crime and Delinquency* 33:300–16 (1987); Joe, "Economic Inequality."

47. Duster, "Crime, Youth Unemployment, and the Black Urban Underclass," pp. 301–3.

48. Melvin Thomas, "Race, Class and Personal Income: An Empirical Test of the Declining Significance of Race Thesis, 1968–1988," *Social Problems* 40:328–39 (1993).

49. Mallie Paschall, Robert Flewelling, and Susan Ennett, "Racial Differences in Violent Behavior among Young Adults: Moderating and Confounding Effects," *Journal of Research in Crime and Delinquency* 35:148–65 (1998).

50. Joan McCord and Margaret Ensminger, "Pathways from Aggressive Childhood to Criminality," paper presented at the American Society of Criminology Meeting, Boston, Mass., November 1995.

51. R. Kelly Raley, "A Shortage of Marriageable Men? A Note on the Role of Cohabitation in Black-White Differences in Marriage Rates," *American Sociological Review* 61:973–83 (1996).

52. Julie Phillips, "Variation in African-American Homicide Rates: An Assessment of Potential Explanations," *Criminology* 35:527–59 (1997).

53. Carl Pope and William Feyerherm, "Minority Status and Juvenile Processing: An Assessment of the Research Literature," paper presented at the American Society of Criminology Meeting, Reno, Nev., November 1989.

54. Jefferey Fagan, Elizabeth Piper, and Melinda Moore, "Violent Delinquents and Urban Youths," *Criminology* 24:439–71 (1986).

55. Robert Nash Parker and Allan Horowitz, "Unemployment, Crime, and Imprisonment: A Panel Approach," *Criminology* 24:751–73 (1986).

56. For a general review of these issues, see James Byrne and Robert Sampson, *The Social Ecology of Crime* (New York: Springer-Verlag, 1986).

57. Barbara Warner and Glenn Pierce, "Reexamining Social Disorganization Theory Using Calls to the Police as a Measure of Crime," *Criminology* 31:493–517 (1993).

58. John Braithwaite, "The Myth of Social Class and Criminality Reconsidered," *American Sociological Review* 46:36–57 (1981).

59. James Short and Ivan Nye, "Reported Behavior as a Criterion of Deviant Behavior," *Social Problems* 5:207–13 (1958).

60. Ivan Nye, James Short, and Virgil Olsen, "Socio-economic Status and Delinquent Behavior," *American Journal of Sociology* 63:381–89 (1958); Robert Dentler and Lawrence Monroe,

"Social Correlates of Early Adolescent Theft," *American Sociological Review* 26:733–43 (1961); John Clark and Eugene Wenninger, "Socio-economic Class and Areas as Correlates of Illegal Behavior among Juveniles," *American Sociological Review* 27:826–34 (1962); William Arnold, "Continuities in Research: Scaling Delinquent Behavior," *Social Problems* 13:59–66 (1965); LaMar Empey and Maynard Erickson, "Hidden Delinquency and Social Status," *Social Forces* 44:1546–54 (1966); Ronald Akers, "Socio-economic Status and Delinquent Behavior: A Retest," *Journal of Research in Crime and Delinquency* 1:38–46 (1964); Voss, "Ethnic Differentials in Delinquency in Honolulu."

61. Martin Gold, "Undetected Delinquent Behavior," *Journal of Research in Crime and Delinquency* 3:35–41 (1966); Jay Williams and Martin Gold, "From Delinquent Behavior to Official Delinquency," *Social Problems* 20:209–29 (1972).

62. Charles Tittle, Wayne Villemez, and Douglas Smith, "The Myth of Social Class and Criminality: An Empirical Assessment of the Empirical Evidence," *American Sociological Review* 43:643–56 (1978).

63. Charles Tittle and Robert Meier, "Specifying the SES/Delinquency Relationship," *Criminology* 28:271–99 (1990); idem, "Specifying the SES/Delinquency Relationship by Social Characteristics of Contexts," *Journal of Research in Crime and Delinquency* 28:430–55 (1991).

64. For supporting research, see Gary Jensen and Kevin Thompson, "What's Class Got to Do with It? A Further Examination of Power-Control Theory," *American Journal of Sociology* 95:1009–23 (1990); Paul Tracy, "Race and Class Differences in Official and Self-Reported Delinquency," in Marvin Wolfgang, Terrence Thornberry, and Robert Figlio, eds., *From Boy to Man, from Delinquency to Crime* (Chicago: University of Chicago Press, 1987), p. 118.

65. See, for example, David Decker, David Shichor, and Robert O"Brien, *Urban Structure and Victimization* (Lexington, Mass.: Lexington Books, 1982).

66. Delbert Eliott and Suzanne Ageton, "Reconciling Race and Class Differences in Self-Reported and Official Estimates of Delinquency," *American Sociological Review* 45:95–110 (1980); for a similar view, see John Braithwaite, "The Myth of Social Class and Criminality Reconsidered," *American Sociological Review* 46:35–58 (1981); Margaret Farnworth, Terence Thornberry, Marvin Krohn, and Alan Lizotte, *Measurement in the Study of Class and Delinquency: Integrating Theory and Research*, working paper no. 4, rev. (Albany, N.Y.: Rochester Youth Development Survey, 1992), p. 19.

67. Simon Singer and Susyan Jou, "Specifying the SES/Delinquency Relationship by Subjective and Objective Indicators of Parental and Youth Social Status," paper presented at the American Society of Criminology Meeting, New Orleans, La., November 1992; David Brownfield, "Social Class and Violent Behavior," *Criminology* 24:421–38 (1986).

68. Margaret Farnworth, Terence Thornberry, Marvin Krohn, and Alan Lizotte, "Measurement in the Study of Class and Delinquency: Integrating Theory and Research," *Journal of Research in Crime and Delinquency* 31:32–61 (1994).

69. G. Roger Jarjoura and Ruth Triplett, "Delinquency and Class: A Test of the Proximity Principle," *Justice Quarterly* 14:765–792 (1997).

70. See, generally, David Farrington, "Age and Crime," in Michael Tonry and Norval Morris, eds., *Crime and Justice, An Annual Review,* vol. 7 (Chicago: University of Chicago Press, 1986), pp. 189–250.

71. Patrick O'Malley, Jerald Bachman, and Lloyd Johnston, "Period, Age and Cohort Effects on Substance Abuse among Young Americans: A Decade of Change, 1976–1986," *American Journal of Public Health* 78:1315–21 (1989); Darrell Steffensmeier, Emilie Allan, Miles Harer, and Cathy Streifel, "Age and the Distribution of Crime," *American Journal of Sociology* 94:803–31 (1989); Alfred Blumstein and Jacqueline Cohen, "Characterizing Criminal Careers," *Science* 237:985–91 (1987).

72. O'Malley, Bachman, and Johnston, "Period, Age, and Cohort Effects on Substance Use among Young Americans."

73. Travis Hirschi and Michael Gottfredson, "Age and the Explanation of Crime," *American Journal of Sociology* 89:552–84 (1983).

74. Michael Gottfredson and Travis Hirschi, "The True Value of Lambda Would Appear to Be Zero: An Essay on Career Criminals, Criminal Careers, Selective Incapacitation, Cohort Studies, and Related Topics," *Criminology* 24:213–34 (1986); further support for their position can be found in Lawrence Cohen and Kenneth Land, "Age Structure and Crime," *American Sociological Review* 52:170–83 (1987).

75. David Greenberg, "Age, Crime and Social Explanation," *American Journal of Sociology* 91:1–21 (1985).

76. Robert Sampson and John Laub, *Crime in the Making: Pathways and Turning Points Through Life* (Cambridge: Harvard University Press, 1993).

77. Farrington, "Age and Crime," pp. 236–37.

78. Marvin Wolfgang, Robert Figlio, and Thorsten Sellin, *Delinquency in a Birth Cohort* (Chicago: University of Chicago Press, 1972); Lyle Shannon, *Assessing the Relationship of Adult Criminal Careers to Juvenile Careers: A Summary* (Washington, D.C.: U.S. Department of Justice, 1982); D. J. West and David P. Farrington, *The Delinquent Way of Life* (London: Heinemann, 1977); Donna Hamparian, Richard Schuster, Simon Dinitz, and John Conrad, *The Violent Few* (Lexington, Mass.: Lexington Books, 1978).

79. Rolf Loeber and Howard Snyder, "Rate of Offending in Juvenile Careers: Findings of Constancy and Change in Lambda," *Criminology* 28:97–109 (1990).

80. Travis Hirschi and Michael Gottfredson, "Age and Crime, Logic and Scholarship: Comment on Greenberg," *American Journal of Sociology* 91:22–7 (1985); idem, "All Wise after the Fact Learning Theory, Again: Reply to Baldwin," *American Journal of Sociology* 90:1330–33 (1985); John Baldwin, "Thrill and Adventure Seeking and the Age Distribution of Crime: Comment on Hirschi and Gottfredson," *American Journal of Sociology* 90:1326–29 (1985).

81. Margo Wilson and Martin Daly, "Life Expectancy, Economic Inequality, Homicide, and Reproductive Timing in Chicago Neighbourhoods," *British Journal of Medicine* 31:1271–74 (1997).

82. Edward Mulvey and John LaRosa, "Delinquency Cessation and Adolescent Development: Preliminary Data," *American Journal of Orthopsychiatry* 56:212–24 (1986).

83. Gordon Trasler, "Cautions for a Biological Approach to Crime," in Sarnoff Mednick, Terrie Moffitt, and Susan Stack, eds., *The Causes of Crime, New Biological Approaches* (Cambridge: Cambridge University Press, 1987), pp. 7–25.

84. Alicia Rand, "Transitional Life Events and Desistance from Delinquency and Crime," in Marvin Wolfgang, Terence Thornberry, and Robert Figlio, eds., *From Boy to Man, from Delinquency to Crime* (Chicago: University of Chicago Press, 1987), pp. 134–63.

85. Marc Le Blanc, "Late Adolescence Deceleration of Criminal Activity and Development of Self- and Social-Control," *Studies on Crime and Crime Prevention* 2:51–68 (1993).

86. Barry Glassner, Margaret Ksander, Bruce Berg, and Bruce Johnson, "A Note on the Deterrent Effect of Juvenile vs. Adult Jurisdiction," *Social Problems* 31:219–21 (1983), at 219.

87. Neal Shover and Carol Thompson, "Age, Differential Expectations, and Crime Desistance," *Criminology* 30:89–104 (1992).

88. D. Wayne Osgood, "The Covariation among Adolescent Problem Behaviors," paper presented at the American Society of Criminology Meeting, Baltimore, Md., November 1990.

89. Stephen Tibbetts, "Low Birth Weight, Disadvantaged Environment and Early Onset: A Test of Moffitt's Interactional Hypothesis," paper presented at the American Society of Criminology Meeting, Boston, Mass., November 1995.

90. For a review of the Gluecks' careers, see John Laub and Robert Sampson, "The Sutherland-Glueck Debate: On the

Sociology of Criminological Knowledge," *American Journal of Sociology* 96:1402–40 (1991).

91. See, for example, Sheldon Glueck and Eleanor Glueck, *500 Criminal Careers* (New York: Knopf, 1930); idem, *One Thousand Juvenile Delinquents* (Cambridge: Harvard University Press, 1934); idem, *Unraveling Juvenile Delinquency* (Cambridge: Harvard University Press, 1950).

92. Sheldon Glueck and Eleanor Glueck, *Predicting Delinquency and Crime* (Cambridge: Harvard University Press, 1967), pp. 82–83.

93. David Rowe and Daniel Flannery, "An Examination of Environmental and Trait Influences on Adolescent Delinquency," *Journal of Research in Crime and Delinquency* 31:374–89 (1994); John Laub and Robert Sampson, "Unraveling Families and Delinquency: A Reanalysis of the Gluecks' Data," *Criminology* 26:355–80 (1988).

94. Arnold Barnett, Alfred Blumstein, and David Farrington, "A Prospective Test of a Criminal Career Model," *Criminology* 27:373–88 (1989).

95. Wolfgang, Figlio, and Sellin, *Delinquency in a Birth Cohort*.

96. Paul Tracy, Marvin Wolfgang, and Robert Figlio, *Delinquency in Two Birth Cohorts, Executive Summary* (Washington, D.C.: U.S. Department of Justice, 1985).

97. Shannon, *Assessing the Relationship of Adult Criminal Careers to Juvenile Careers*; Howard Snyder, *Court Careers of Juvenile Offenders* (Washington, D.C.: Office of Juvenile Justice and Delinquency Prevention, 1988); D. J. West and David P. Farrington, *The Delinquent Way of Life* (London: Heinemann, 1977); Donna Hamparian, Richard Schuster, Simon Dinitz, and John Conrad, *The Violent Few* (Lexington, Mass.: Lexington Books, 1978).

98. See, generally, Marvin Wolfgang, Terence Thornberry, and Robert Figlio, eds. *From Boy to Man, from Delinquency to Crime* (Chicago: University of Chicago Press, 1987).

99. Paul Tracy and Kimberly Kempf-Leonard, *Continuity and Discontinuity in Criminal Careers* (New York: Plenum Press, 1996).

100. R. Tremblay, R. Loeber, C. Gagnon, P. Charlebois, S. Larivee, and M. Le Blanc, "Disruptive Boys with Stable and Unstable High Fighting Behavior Patterns during Junior Elementary School," *Journal of Abnormal Child Psychology* 19:285–300 (1991).

101. Jennifer White, Terrie Moffitt, Felton Earls, Lee Robins, and Phil Silva, "How Early Can We Tell? Predictors of Childhood Conduct Disorder and Adolescent Delinquency," *Criminology* 28:507–35 (1990).

102. Mark Ezell and Amy D'Unger, "Offense Specialization among Serious Youthful Offenders: A Longitudinal Analysis of a California Youth Authority Sample," unpublished report (Durham, N.C.: Duke University, 1998).

103. Kimberly Kempf, "Crime Severity and Criminal Career Progression," *Journal of Criminal Law and Criminology* 79:524–40 (1988).

104. Jeffrey Fagan, "Social and Legal Policy Dimensions of Violent Juvenile Crime," *Criminal Justice and Behavior* 17:93–133 (1990).

105. Peter Greenwood, *Selective Incapacitation* (Santa Monica, Calif.: Rand Corp., 1982).

106. Terence Thornberry, David Huizinga, and Rolf Loeber, "The Prevention of Serious Delinquency and Violence," in James Howell, Barry Krisberg, J. David Hawkins, and John Wilson, eds., *Sourcebook on Serious, Violent, and Chronic Juvenile Offenders* (Thousand Oaks, Calif.: Sage, 1995).

107. Andrew von Hirsch and Donald Gottfredson, "Selective Incapacitation: Some Queries about Research Design and Equity," *New York University Review of Law and Social Change* 12:11–19 (1984).

108. Scott Decker and Barbara Salert, "Predicting the Career Criminal: An Empirical Test of the Greenwood Scale," *Journal of Criminal Law and Criminology* 77:215–36 (1986).

109. Pamela Tontodonato, "Explaining Rate Changes in Delinquent Arrest Transitions Using Event History Analysis," *Criminology* 26:439–59 (1988).

110. Kimberly Kempf, "Career Criminals in the 1958 Philadelphia Birth Cohort," *Criminal Justice Review* 15:212–35 (1990).

111. Ibid.

112. Ted Miller, Mark Cohen, and Brian Wiersema, *The Extent and Costs of Crime Victimization: A New Look* (Washington, D.C.: National Institute of Justice, 1995).

113. Joan Johnson, *Criminal Victimization in the United States* (Washington, D.C.: Bureau of Justice Statistics, 1992).

114. Michael Rand and Kevin Strom, *Violence-Related Injuries Treated in Hospital Emergency Departments* (Washington, D.C: Bureau of Justice Statistics, 1997).

115. Randy LaGrange and Kenneth Ferraro, "Assessing Age and Gender Differences in Perceived Risk and Fear of Crime," *Criminology* 27:697–719 (1989).

116. Gerald Hotaling and David Finkelhor, "Estimating the Number of Stranger Abduction Homicides of Children: A Review of Available Evidence," *Journal of Criminal Justice* 18:385–99 (1990).

117. Herbert Koppel, *Lifetime Likelihood of Victimization* (Washington, D.C.: Bureau of Justice Statistics, Technical Report, 1987).

118. Lawrence Greenfeld, *Child Victimizers: Violent Offenders and Their Victims* (Washington, D.C.: Bureau of Justice Statistics, 1996).

119. L. Edward Wells and Joseph Rankin, "Juvenile Victimization: Convergent Validation of Alternative Measurements," *Journal of Research in Crime and Delinquency* 32:301–4 (1995).

Part Two

Theories of Delinquency

What causes delinquent behavior? Why do some youths enter a life of crime that persists into their adulthood? Are people products of their environment, or is the likelihood of their becoming delinquent determined at birth?

The study of delinquency is essentially interdisciplinary, so it is not surprising that a variety of theoretical models have been formulated to explain juvenile misbehavior. Theories of delinquency reflect many different avenues of inquiry, including biology, psychology, sociology, political science, and economics. Chapter 3 reviews theories that hold that delinquency is essentially an individual factor, caused either by personal choices and decision making or by psychological and biological aspects of human development. Chapters 4, 5, and 6 review sociological theories of delinquency. Chapter 4 reviews those theories that hold that youthful misbehavior is caused by a child's place in the social structure; Chapter 5 covers theories that regard the child's relationships with social institutions and processes as the key to understanding delinquency. Chapter 6 views how delinquents may be victims of either social labeling or social conflict.

The variety of delinquency theories is often confusing. Logic dictates that the competing and contradictory theoretical models presented here cannot all be correct. Yet every branch of the social sciences contains competing theoretical models. Understanding why people behave the way they do and how society functions are issues that are far from being settled.

Chapter Three

Focus on the Individual: Choice and Trait Theories

On October 1, 1997, seventeen-year-old Luke Woodham went on a rampage during which he killed his mother, Mary, and then shot and killed two classmates and wounded seven others. At his trial on June 4, 1998, Luke claimed he was under the spell of demons and had been influenced by an older youth named Grant Boyette. Of the morning Luke plunged a butcher knife into his mother, then drove to school and killed two classmates, he said, "I remember I woke up that morning and I'd seen demons that I always saw when Grant told me to do something. They said I was nothing and I would never be anything if I didn't get to that school and kill those people." Luke belonged to a Satanic cult-like group, and he believed Grant Boyette had placed him under a spell: "I just closed my eyes and fought with myself because I didn't want to do any of it," he said. "When I opened my eyes, my mother was laying in her bed."[1]

Cases such as Luke Woodham's suggest that some delinquents are not merely "products of their environment" but are influenced by their unique abnormal physical and mental makeups. If social and economic factors alone determine behavior, how is it possible that many at-risk youths residing in the most dangerous inner-city neighborhoods live conventional, law-abiding lives? Conversely, why are so many privileged middle-class youths involved in delinquency and substance abuse? Research on persistent offending indicates that relatively few youths in any population become hard core delinquents,[2] and the quality of neighborhood and family life may have little impact on the choices individuals make through the life cycle.[3] To some theorists, the locus of delinquency is rooted in the individual. This sentiment was first expressed by William Healy, writing in 1915 in *The Individual Delinquent*: "The dynamic center of the whole problem of delinquency and crime will ever be the individual offender."

There is more than one explanation of why individuals become crime prone. One position, referred to as **choice theory,** suggests that young offenders choose to engage in antisocial activity because they believe their actions will be beneficial and profitable. Whether they join a gang, steal cars, or sell drugs, their delinquent acts are motivated by the reasoned belief that crime can be a relatively risk-free way to better their personal situation. They have little fear of get-

Luke Woodham is taken into court for jury selection, following his shooting rampage at Pearl High School in Hattiesburg, Mississippi, on October 1, 1997. Cases such as Woodham's suggest that delinquents are not merely "products of their environment" but are influenced by their unique abnormal physical and mental makeups.

choice theory
Holds that youths will engage in delinquent and criminal behavior after weighing the consequences and benefits of their actions; delinquent behavior is a rational choice made by a motivated offender who perceives that the chances of gain outweigh any possible punishment or loss.

trait theory
Holds that youths engage in delinquent or criminal behavior due to aberrant physical or psychological traits that govern behavioral choices; delinquent actions are impulsive or instinctual rather than rational choices.

ting caught or of the consequences of punishment. Some are motivated by fantasies of riches, and others may simply enjoy the excitement and short-term gratification produced by criminal acts such as beating up an opponent or stealing a car.

All youthful misbehavior cannot be traced to rational choice, profit motive, and criminal entrepreneurship, however. Some delinquent acts, especially violent ones, seem irrational, selfish, or hedonistic. Many forms of delinquency, such as substance abuse and vandalism, appear more impulsive than rational, and these antisocial behaviors may be inspired by aberrant physical or psychological traits that govern behavioral choices. Although some youths may choose to commit crime simply because they desire conventional luxuries and power, others may be driven by constitutional abnormalities such as hyperactivity, low intelligence, biochemical imbalance, or genetic defects. This view of delinquency is referred to here generally as **trait theory** because it links delinquency to biological and psychological traits that control human development.

Choice and trait theories share common ground because they focus on the individual's mental and behavioral processes. All people are different, and each person reacts to the same set of environmental and social conditions in a unique fashion. Faced with extreme stress and economic hardship, one person will seek employment, borrow money, save for the future, and live a law-abiding life; another will use antisocial or violent behavior to satisfy his or her needs.

In this chapter we first cover those theoretical models that focus on individual choice. Then, we discuss the view that the biological and psychological development of some youngsters makes them violent, aggressive, and antisocial. Finally, we analyze an attempt to integrate individual choice and trait factors into a singular explanation of the cause of delinquent behavior.

Choice Theory and Classical Criminology

free will
View that youths are in charge of their own destinies and are free to make personal behavior choices unencumbered by environmental factors.

utilitarians
Those who believe that people weigh the benefits and consequences of their future actions before deciding on a course of behavior.

classical criminology
Holds that decisions to violate the law are weighed against possible punishments and to deter crime the pain of punishment must outweigh the benefit of illegal gain; led to graduated punishments based on seriousness of the crime (let the punishment fit the crime).

The first formal explanations of crime and delinquency held that human behavior was a matter of choice. It was assumed that people had **free will** to choose their behavior and that those who violated the law were motivated by personal needs: greed, revenge, survival, or hedonism. Over two hundred years ago, **utilitarian** philosophers Cesare Beccaria and Jeremy Bentham argued that people weigh the benefits and consequences of their future actions before deciding on a course of behavior.[4] Their writings formed the core of what is today referred to as **classical criminology.**

The classical view of crime and delinquency holds that the decision to violate the law comes after a careful weighing of the benefits and costs of criminal behaviors. Most potential law violators would cease their actions if the potential pain associated with a behavior outweighed its anticipated gain; conversely, law-violating behavior seems attractive if the future rewards seem far greater than the potential punishment.[5]

According to the classical view, youths who decide to become drug dealers weigh and compare the possible benefits, such as cash to buy cars, clothes, and other luxury items, with the potential penalties, such as arrest followed by a long stay in a juvenile facility. If they believe drug dealers are rarely caught and even when caught usually avoid severe punishments, youths are more likely to choose to become dealers than if they believe dealers are almost always caught and punished by lengthy prison terms. Put simply, to deter or prevent crime, the pain of punishment must outweigh the benefit of illegal gain.[6]

Classical criminologists argued that punishment should be only severe enough to deter a particular offense and that punishments should be graded according to the seriousness of particular crimes: "Let the punishment fit the crime." For example, Beccaria argued that it would be foolish to punish pickpockets and murderers in a similar fashion because this would encourage thieves to kill the victims or witnesses to their crimes.[7] The popularity of the classical approach was responsible, in part, for development of prisons as an alternative to physical punishment and the eventual creation of criminal sentences geared to the seriousness of crimes.[8] The choice approach dominated the policy of the U.S. justice system for about one hundred and fifty years.

The Rational Delinquent

The view that delinquents are rational decision makers who *choose* to violate the law remains a popular theoretical approach to the study and control of delinquency. Its current popularity is based in part on the disappointing results of rehabilitative strategies. Past efforts to reform known delinquents through treatment, counseling, and other rehabilitation techniques have been regarded by some experts as noble failures.[9] This failure, they argue, is a signal that delinquency is not merely a function of social ills, such as a lack of economic opportunity or family dysfunction. If it were, then educational enrichment, family counseling, job training programs, and the like should be more effective alternatives to crime. In reality, some affluent youths from "good" families choose to break the law, and most indigent adolescents are law abiding. The reasoning goes then that some youths "choose" crime and that their behavior can be controlled only by punishments severe enough to convince them to choose conventional over criminal behaviors.[10] Subscribers to the rational choice model believe the decision to commit a specific type of crime and the subsequent entry into a criminal lifestyle is a matter of personal decision making based on weighing all available information; hence, the term *rational choice*.

The well-publicized resurgence of youthful gang activity has also lent credence to rational choice explanations (see Chapter 9 for more on gangs). The emergence of gangs and their involvement in the drug trade strengthens the case for rational choice: these young, well-armed entrepreneurs are seeking to cash in on a lucrative, albeit illegal, "business enterprise."

Gang leaders are surely "rational decision makers," constantly processing information during their criminal transactions: Who are my enemies? How can I make more money? What are the chances of getting caught? Where can I find a good lawyer?[11] Contemporary gang members involved in drug trafficking have been found to act like "employers," providing their business associates with security and the know-how to conduct "business deals." Gang membership helps kids achieve financial success that would otherwise be impossible. Like legitimate business enterprises, some gangs actively recruit new personnel and cut deals with rivals over products and territory.[12] Similarly, drug dealers have been observed to carefully evaluate the desirability of their "sales area" before getting ready to "deal."[13] Geography is an important issue. Dealers usually choose the middle of a long street to conduct transactions because of the good visibility in both directions; police raids can then be spotted before they occur.[14]

Such illustrations support the belief that law-violating behavior occurs when a reasoning offender decides to take the chance of violating the law after considering his or her personal situation (need for money, learning experiences, opportunities for conventional success), values (conscience, moral values, need for peer approval), and situational factors (how well the target is protected, whether people are at home, how wealthy the neighborhood is, the likelihood of getting caught, the punishment if apprehended).

Conversely, the decision to forgo law-violating behavior may be based on the growing perception that the economic benefits are no longer good or that the probability of successfully completing a crime is less than the chance of being caught and punished. For example, the aging-out process may occur because as delinquents age and mature they begin to realize that the risks of crime are greater than the potential profits. The solution to crime, therefore, may be formulating policies that will cause the potential criminal to choose conventional behaviors over criminal ones.[15]

Choosing Delinquent Acts

The focus of rational choice theory is on the delinquent *act,* not on the delinquent *offender.* The questions these researchers ask include: How are crimes planned? What makes one target inviting and another forbidding? What can be done to prevent each type of burglary? In rational choice theory the concepts of crime and criminality are two separate issues. Criminality is the propensity to engage in criminal or delinquent acts; crimes are events that are in violation of the criminal law.[16] There will always be a population of criminally motivated adolescents, but if they do not have criminal opportunities, they will not be able to act on their inclinations. Similarly, given an open opportunity for illegal gain, even the least criminally inclined youths may be motivated to act. Why a child eventually becomes a delinquent, then, is quite distinct from the reasons a delinquent decides to break into a particu-

FOCUS ON DELINQUENCY

IS DELINQUENCY "SEDUCTIVE"?

Sociologist Jack Katz makes the provocative argument that violating the law can be exciting, and even "seductive," for those willing to take the risk; the seductions of crime result from the thrill associated with successful involvement in delinquent acts.

The key to understanding why young people engage in crime is not as mysterious as some experts make it seem. Delinquency has a here-and-now orientation. Youths become involved in provocative situations that influence their behavior choices: someone challenges their authority, heritage, or reputation, and they vanquish this opponent with a beating; they want to maximize their pleasure by doing something exciting, so they break into and vandalize a school building. Crime is a pleasurable exercise that can relieve tension, increase self-esteem, and in the case of drug use even provide pleasurable physical sensations.

According to Katz, choosing crime satisfies the need to relieve emotional upheavals brought about by moral challenges. Gang members are rejecting society's expectations that they become conventional adults. They violently defend meaningless turf boundaries and get into brawls in an effort to show their indifference to social expectations. Young gang members carry on like the avenging gods of mythology, electing to have life or death control over their victims.

Theft crimes bring what Katz calls "sneaky thrills." For many youngsters shoplifting and theft are attractive because "getting away with it" is a thrilling demonstration of personal competence, especially when the crime is consummated under the eyes of an adult. Getting away with crime is especially thrilling, not so much because it brings material goods but because it shows how competent the young "thief" is and how he or she can flaunt the moral and legal code with impunity.

Katz finds that the central theme in the choice to commit crime is perceived emotional upheaval—humiliation, righteousness, arrogance, ridicule, cynicism, defilement, or vengeance. For example, the assailant interprets the victim's behavior as disrespectful and humiliating, and violence is a way of expressing her resulting rage. When the drunk at a party is told to "shut up and go home" because she is disturbing people, she responds, "So, I'm acting like a fool, am I?" She goes home and returns with a gun because she must "sacrifice" or injure the body of the victim to maintain her "honor."

There is growing evidence that immediate events do in fact play an important role in adolescent misbehavior. People committed to criminal careers seem to take intrinsic pleasure from their behavior; they enjoy taking risks. Youths are most likely to be seduced if they fear neither the risk of apprehension nor its social consequences, such as losing the respect of their peers. Fear of punishment may help neutralize the attractions of crime. Whether it is violent or profit-oriented, crime has an allure that some people cannot resist. Crime may produce a natural "high" and other positive sensations that are instrumental in maintaining and reinforcing criminal behavior.

Sources: Jack Katz, *Seductions of Crime* (New York: Basic Books, 1988); Peter Wood, Walter Gove, James Wilson, and John Cochran, "Nonsocial Reinforcement and Habitual Criminal Conduct: An Extension of Learning," *Criminology* 35:335–66 (1997); Bill McCarthy, "Not Just 'For the Thrill of It': An Instrumentalist Elaboration of Katz's Explanation of Sneaky Thrill Property Crime," *Criminology* 33: 519–39 (1995); Bill McCarthy and John Hagan, "Mean Streets: The Theoretical Significance of Situational Delinquency among Homeless Youths," *American Journal of Sociology* 3:597–627 (1992).

lar house one day or to sell narcotics the next. (See the Focus on Delinquency box for additional reasons some individuals choose delinquent behaviors.)

Routine Activities

routine activities theory
View that crime is a "normal" function of the routine activities of modern living; offenses can be expected if there is a motivated offender and a suitable target that is not protected by capable guardians.

predatory crimes
Violent crimes against persons and crimes in which an offender attempts to steal an object directly from its holder.

To some crime experts, the concept of the motivated offender is insufficient to explain patterns in the delinquency rate. If the number of motivated delinquents is a constant, why do crime rates rise and fall? Why are some areas more crime ridden than others? To answer these questions, attention must be paid to fluctuations in the *opportunity to commit crimes,* controlled in part by both the behavior of potential victims and those charged with their protection (for example, police officers).[17] Crime may occur not only because a criminal decides to break the law but also because victims place themselves at risk when no one is around to protect them.[18]

One prominent statement of this view of crime is **routine activity theory,** developed by Lawrence Cohen and Marcus Felson.[19] At the heart of this theory is the assumption that certain activities or settings lend themselves to conditions conducive to the occurrence of crimes. According to this view, the volume and distribution of **predatory crimes** (violent crimes against persons and crimes in which an offender attempts to steal an object directly from its holder) are influenced by the interaction of three variables that reflect routine activities found in everyday life: the availability of *suitable targets* (such as homes containing easily salable goods), the absence of *capable guardians* (such as home owners and their neighbors, friends, and relatives), and the presence of *motivated offenders* (such as unemployed teenagers). If all of these components are present, there is greater likelihood that a predatory crime will take place (see Figure 3.1).

The routine activities approach gives equal weight to the role of both the victim and the offender in the crime process. Criminal opportunity is significantly influenced by the victim's lifestyle and behavior; the greater the opportunity for criminals and victims to interact, the greater the probability of crime. Reduce the interaction, and the opportunity for crime will decline.[20]

Lack of Capable Guardians According to the routine activities approach, general social change can filter down to influence delinquency rates and patterns. For

Why are some areas more crime ridden than others? It may be because of variations in the opportunity to commit crimes. Places that are unguarded may be more vulnerable to criminal activities. Crime may occur not only because a criminal decides to break the law, but also because victims place themselves at risk and no one is around to protect them from harm.

FIGURE 3.1

Routine Activities Theory Posits the Interaction of Three Factors

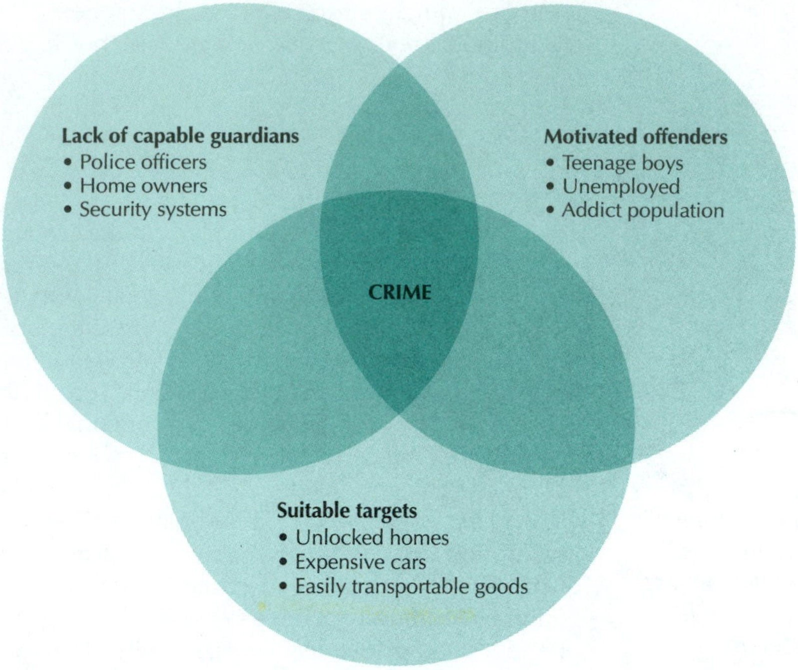

Lack of capable guardians
- Police officers
- Home owners
- Security systems

Motivated offenders
- Teenage boys
- Unemployed
- Addict population

CRIME

Suitable targets
- Unlocked homes
- Expensive cars
- Easily transportable goods

example, one reason the delinquency rate may have trended upward between 1970 and 1990 is because the number of adult caretakers (guardians) at home during the day decreased as more women entered the workforce. With mothers at work and children in day care, homes are left unguarded and become more "suitable targets." Similarly, with the growth of suburbia and the decline of the traditional neighborhood, the number of familiar guardians (family, neighbors, and friends) has diminished.[21]

Suitable Targets   The availability of suitable targets, such as easily transportable commodities, will increase crime rates. Research has generally supported the fact that the more wealth a home contains, the more likely it will be a crime target.[22] As computers, stereo systems and TVs become more commonplace, burglary rates should rise due to the increased availability of high-priced and easily sold goods.[23]

Routine activities theory also recognizes that behavior and lifestyle influence the nature and likelihood of victimization risk. People who routinely go out to public places are most likely to be victimized by strangers; "stay at homes" are most likely to be harmed by family or friends.[24] Maintaining a high-risk lifestyle by frequenting dangerous "hot spots," such as bars and taverns, increases the likelihood of victimization.[25]

Motivated Offenders   Routine activities theory also links the delinquency rates to general social changes that increase the number and motivation of offenders. Structural changes in the population can have an impact on crime rates. Delinquency rates will increase if there is a surplus of youths of the same age category competing for a limited number of jobs and educational opportunities. During any given period, if the number of teenagers exceeds the number of available part-time and after-school jobs, the supply of motivated offenders may be increased simply because many potential offenders are competing for a limited number of legitimate resources.[26]

Lifestyle also affects criminal motivation. Adolescents who spend much time socializing with peers in the absence of authority figures (for example, riding around in cars, going to parties, going out at night for fun), are more likely to engage in deviant behaviors.[27] In the presence of motivated peers, the lack of structure and guardianship leaves more opportunity for antisocial behaviors including substance abuse, crime, and dangerous driving. Participation in unstructured activities helps explain the association between crime rates and gender, age, and status. Teenage boys have the highest crime rates because they are the group most likely to engage in unsupervised socialization. Even for adolescents who engage in what should be "character building" activities—such as having a part-time job after school—the opportunity to socialize with deviant peers combined with a lack of parental supervision increases criminal motivation.[28]

Preventing Delinquency

If delinquency is a rational choice and a routine activity, as some believe, then delinquency prevention is a matter of convincing potential delinquents that they will be severely punished for committing delinquent acts, punishing them so severely that they never again commit crimes, or making it so difficult to commit crimes that the potential gain is not worth the risk. The first of these strategies is called general deterrence, the second is specific deterrence, and the third is called situational crime prevention. Let's look at each of these strategies in more detail.

General Deterrence

general deterrence
Crime control policies that depend on the fear of criminal penalties, such as long prison sentences for violent crimes; aim is to convince law violator that the pain outweighs the benefit of criminal activity.

The **general deterrence** concept holds that the choice to commit delinquent acts can be controlled or structured by the threat of punishment. If people fear the power of the law and believe illegal behavior will result in certain and severe sanctions, they will choose not to commit crimes.[29]

One of the guiding principles of deterrence theory is that the more severe, certain, and swift the punishment, the greater its deterrent effect will be.[30] Even if a particular crime carries a severe punishment, there will be relatively little deterrent effect if most people do not believe they will be caught.[31] Conversely, even a mild sanction may be sufficient to deter crime if people believe punishment is certain. And even the most severe sanctions will have little deterrent effect if they are slow, delayed, or easily put off.

Traditionally, juvenile justice authorities have been reluctant to incorporate deterrence-based punishments on the ground that they interfere with its stated *parens patriae* philosophy. Children are punished less severely than adults, limiting the power of the law to deter juvenile crime. However, the increase in teenage violence, gang activity, and drug abuse in recent years, has prompted a reevaluation of deterrence strategies. Some juvenile courts have shifted from an emphasis on treatment to concerns with public safety.[32] Police are now more willing to use aggressive tactics, such as gang-busting units, to deter membership in drug trafficking gangs, and youthful looking officers have been sent into high schools undercover to identify, contact, and arrest student drug dealers.[33]

Many courts have also attempted to initiate a deterrence strategy. Juvenile court judges have become more willing to waive youths to adult courts; prior record may outweigh an offender's need for services in making this decision.[34] In addition, legislators have passed more restrictive juvenile codes featuring mandatory incarceration, and the number of incarcerated juveniles continues to increase. Adolescents are not even spared capital punishment; the U.S. Supreme Court has upheld the use of the death penalty for youths sixteen years of age.[35] The trend toward a more punitive, deterrence-based juvenile process is discussed further in Chapters 12 through 17.

Do General Deterrence Strategies Work? The effectiveness of deterrence strategies is a topic of considerable debate. A number of studies have contributed data supportive of deterrence concepts. Evidence indicates that the threat of police arrest can deter property crimes,[36] and areas of the country in which punishment is more certain seem to have lower delinquency rates. The more likely people are to anticipate punishment, the less likely they are to commit crimes.[37]

Although these findings are persuasive, there is little conclusive evidence that the threat of apprehension and punishment alone can deter crime.[38] More evidence exists that fear of social disapproval and informal penalties, criticisms, and punishments from parents and friends are greater deterrents to crime than legal punishments.[39]

Because deterrence strategies are based on the idea of a "rational," calculating offender, they may not be effective when applied to immature young people. Minors tend to be less capable of making mature judgments about their behavior choices, and many younger offenders are unaware of the content of juvenile legal codes. Imposition of a deterrence policy (for example, mandatory waiver to the adult court for violent crimes), will have little effect on delinquency rates for these offenders.[40] It seems futile, therefore, to try to deter delinquency through fear of legal punishment. Teens seem more fearful of being punished by their parents or of being the target of disapproval from their friends than they are of the police.[41]

It is also possible that for the highest risk group of young offenders—teens living in economically depressed neighborhoods—the deterrent threat of formal sanctions may be irrelevant. Inner-city youngsters may not have internalized the norms of society that hold that getting arrested is "wrong" (see Chapter 4 for more on inner-city norms and values). Young people in these areas have less to lose if arrested; they have a limited "stake in society" and are not worried about their future. They also may not connect their illegal behavior with punishment because they see many people in their neighborhood committing crimes and not getting caught or being punished.[42]

Research also shows that many juvenile offenders are under the influence of drugs or alcohol when they break the law, a condition that might impair their decision-making ability.[43] Similarly, juveniles often commit crimes in groups, and peer pressure can outweigh the deterrent effect of the law.

In summary, deterring delinquency through the fear of punishment may be of limited value because children may neither fully comprehend the seriousness of their acts nor the consequences they may face.[44] On the surface deterrence appears to have benefit as a delinquency control device, but there is also reason to believe this benefit is limited.

Specific Deterrence

specific deterrence
Sending convicted offenders to secure incarceration facilities so that punishment is severe enough to convince offenders not to repeat their criminal activity.

General deterrence focuses on potential offenders, but specific deterrence targets offenders who have already been convicted. The theory of **specific deterrence** holds that if offenders are punished severely the experience will convince them not to repeat their illegal acts. Juveniles are sent to secure incarceration facilities with the understanding that their ordeal will deter future misbehavior.

Specific deterrence is a popular approach to crime control today, and the admissions rate to confinement facilities has increased sharply during the past decade (see Chapter 17). Unfortunately, relying on punitive measures may expand rather than reduce future delinquency. Institutions quickly become overcrowded, and chronic violent offenders are packed into swollen facilities with nonserious and nonviolent juveniles. The use of mandatory sentences for some crimes (usually violent crimes or drug dealing) means that all youths who are found to have committed those crimes must be institutionalized; first offenders may be treated the same as chronic recidivists.

Rather than reducing delinquency, some believe increased use of punitive measures increases the frequency of delinquent behavior. Research shows that arrest and punishment may even increase the likelihood that inexperienced, or first-time, offenders will commit new crimes.[45] Similarly, chronic offender research indicates that a stay in a juvenile justice facility has little deterrent effect on the likelihood that a persistent delinquent will become an adult criminal.[46] A history of prior arrest, conviction, and punishment has proven to be the best predictor of rearrest among young offenders released from correctional institutions. Rather than deterring future offending, punishment may in fact encourage reoffending.[47]

Why does punishment encourage rather than reduce delinquency? According to some experts, institutionalization cuts youths off from prosocial supports in the community, making them more reliant on deviant peers. Incarceration may also diminish chances for successful future employment, reducing access to legitimate opportunities. Some researchers have found that punishment may reduce the frequency of future offending, but the weight of the evidence suggests that time served has little impact on recidivism.[48] The failure of specific deterrence might help explain why delinquency rates are increasing at the same time that incarceration rates are at an all-time high.

Situational Crime Prevention

Situational crime prevention strategies are designed to make it so difficult to commit specific criminal acts that would-be delinquent offenders will be convinced the risks are greater than the rewards.[49] Rather than deterring or punishing individuals, situational crime reduction strategies aim to reduce the opportunities people have to commit particular crimes. Controlling the situation of crime can be accomplished by increasing the effort or the risks of criminal activity or by reducing the rewards attached to delinquent acts.

Increasing the effort of crime might involve *target-hardening techniques* such as placing steering locks on cars and putting unbreakable glass on storefronts. *Access control* can be maintained by locking gates and fencing yards.[50] The *facilitators of crime* can be controlled by banning the sale of spray paint to adolescents in an effort to cut down on graffiti or having a photo put on credit cards to reduce their value if stolen.

Increasing the risks of crime might involve improving surveillance lighting, creating neighborhood watch programs, controlling building entrances and exits, installing burglar alarms and security systems, or increasing the number of private security officers and police patrols.

Reducing the rewards of crime could include strategies such as making car radios removable so they can be kept in the home at night, marking property so it is more difficult to sell when stolen, and having gender-neutral phone listings to discourage obscene phone calls. Tracking systems, such as those made by the LOJACK Corporation, help police locate and return stolen vehicles.

Community-wide situational crime control strategies have also been proposed. Some possible steps that might help reduce delinquency in a community are listed in Table 3.1. This approach is designed to reduce the overall crime rate by limiting the access of a highly motivated offender group (such as high school youths) to tempting targets. Notice that it is not designed to eliminate a specific crime but to reduce the overall crime rate. In one type of community strategy, prevention efforts target specific locales that are known to be the scene of repeated delinquent activity. By focusing on a particular hot spot—an area which is the site of ongoing teenage crime, for example, a shopping mall, public park, or housing project—law enforcement efforts can be used to "crack down" on ongoing crime problems. Crackdowns seem to be an effective short-term crime reduction strategy, but their

Table 3.1

COMMUNITY-LEVEL SITUATIONAL CRIME PREVENTION EFFORTS

1. Uniform school release schedules so there is no doubt when kids belong in school and when they are truant.

2. Truancy control efforts.

3. After-school activities to keep youths under adult supervision.

4. Organized weekend activities with adult supervision.

5. School lunch programs designed to keep youths in school and away from shopping areas.

6. No-cash policies in schools to reduce youths' opportunities to either be targets or to engage in the consumption of drugs or alcohol.

7. Keep shopping areas and schools separate.

8. Construct housing to maximize guardianship and minimize illegal behavior.

9. Encourage neighborhood stability so residents will be acquainted with one another.

10. Encourage privatization of parks and recreational facilities so people will be responsible for their area's security.

Source: Marcus Felson, "Routine Activities and Crime Prevention," in *Studies on Crime and Crime Prevention, Annual Review,* vol. 1, National Council for Crime Prevention (Stockholm: Scandinavian University Press, 1992), pp. 30–34.

delinquency reduction effect begins to decay once the initial "shock effect" wears off.[51] Crackdowns also may simply displace illegal activity to "safer" areas of the city where there are fewer police and less chance of apprehension.

Do Delinquents Choose Crime?

All the delinquency control methods based on choice theory assume the delinquent to be a motivated offender who breaks the law because he or she perceives an abundance of benefits and an absence of threat. Increase the threat and reduce the benefits, and the delinquency rate should decline.

This logic is hard to refute. After all, by definition, a person who commits an illegal act but who is not "rational" cannot be considered a criminal or delinquent but instead is "not guilty by reason of insanity." To say that delinquents choose their crimes is entirely logical, yet several questions remain unanswered by choice theorists. First, why do some people continually choose to break the law even after suffering its consequences whereas others are content to live law-abiding yet indigent lives? That is, how can "the good boy in the high-crime area" be explained?[52] Conversely, why do affluent youths break the law when they have everything to lose and little more to gain?

Choice theorists also have difficulty explaining seemingly irrational crimes such as vandalism, arson, and even drug abuse. To say a teenager painted swastikas on a synagogue after making a "rational choice" seems inadequate in the face of such a destructive, nonbeneficial act.

The relationships observed by rational choice theorists can be explained in other ways. For example, even though the high victimization rates in lower-class neighborhoods can be explained by an oversupply of motivated offenders, other factors, such as social conflict and disorganization, may also explain this phenomenon.[53]

In summary, choice theories help us understand criminal events and victim patterns (see Table 3.2 for a summary of the different choice theories and strategies). However, the question remains, why are some people motivated to commit crime and delinquency whereas others in similar circumstances remain law abiding?

Table 3.2

CHOICE THEORIES AND STRATEGIES

Choice Theories	Major Premise	Strengths
Rational choice	Law-violating behavior is an event that occurs after offenders weigh information on their personal needs and the situational factors involved in the difficulty and risk of committing a crime.	Explains why high-risk youth do not constantly engage in delinquent acts. Relates theory to delinquency control policy. It is not limited by class or other social variables.
Routine activities	Crime and delinquency are functions of the presence of motivated offenders, the availability of suitable targets, and the absence of capable guardians.	Can explain fluctuations in crime and delinquency rates. Shows how victim behavior influences criminal choice.
Choice Theory Strategies		
General deterrence	People will commit crime and delinquency if they perceive that the benefits outweigh the risks. Crime is a function of the severity, certainty, and speed of punishment.	Shows the relationship between crime and punishment. Suggests a real solution to crime.
Specific deterrence	Punishing people severely will prevent future law violations. People learn from punishment that "crime does not pay."	Provides a simple solution to the crime problem. Punishment can be made proportionate to the seriousness of the crime. Increasing the severity of punishment will reduce crime.
Situational crime prevention	Crime can be controlled by increasing the effort, increasing the risks, and reducing the rewards attached to committing offenses.	Shows the importance of situational factors or the specific circumstances surrounding crimes. Offers concrete crime prevention alternatives.

Why do some people choose crime over legal activities? The remaining sections of this chapter present some possible explanations.

Trait Theories: Biosocial and Psychological Views

Defective intelligence → defective thinking

Choice theorists believe selecting crime is part of an economic strategy, a function of carefully weighing the benefits of criminal over legal behavior. For example, youths decide to commit a robbery if they believe they will make a good profit, have a good chance of getting away, and, even if caught, stand little chance of being severely punished.

But a number of delinquency experts think this model is incomplete. They believe it is wrong to infer that all youths choose crime simply because the advantages outweigh the risks. If that were the case, how could senseless and profitless crimes such as vandalism and random violence be explained? These experts argue that human behavioral choices are a function of an individual's mental and physical makeup. Most law-abiding youths have personal traits that keep them within the mainstream of conventional society. In contrast, youths who choose to engage in repeated aggressive, antisocial, or conflict-oriented behavior manifest abnormal traits that influence their behavior choices.[54] Uncontrollable, impulsive behavior patterns place some youths at odds with society, and they soon find themselves in trouble with the law. Although delinquents may choose their actions, some researchers believe these decisions are a product of all but uncontrollable mental and physical properties and traits. Is it possible that someone like Luke Woodham "chose" to gun down his classmates, or is his behavior a product of a twisted mind?

The idea that delinquents are somehow "abnormal" is not a new one. Some of the earliest theories of criminal and delinquent behavior stressed that crime is a product of personal traits and that measurable physical and mental conditions, such as IQ and body build, determine behavior. This view is generally referred to today as *positivism*. Positivists believe the scientific method can be used to measure the causes of human behavior and that behavior is a function of often uncontrollable factors, such as mental illness.

The source of behavioral control is one significant difference between trait and choice theories. To a choice theorist, reducing the benefits of crime by increasing the likelihood and severity of punishment will eventually lower the crime rate. Trait theory focuses less on the effects of punishment and more on the treatment of abnormal mental and physical conditions as a method of crime reduction.

In the next sections the primary components of trait theory are reviewed.

The Origins of Trait Theory

criminal atavism
The idea that delinquents manifest physical anomalies that make them biologically and physiologically similar to our primitive ancestors, savage throwbacks to an earlier stage of human evolution.

The first attempts to discover why criminal tendencies develop focused on the physical makeup of offenders. Biological traits present at birth were thought to predetermine whether people would live a life of crime.

The origin of this school of thought is generally credited to the Italian physician Cesare Lombroso (1835–1909).[55] Known as the father of criminology, Lombroso put his many years of medical research to use in his theory of **criminal atavism**.[56] Lombroso found that delinquents manifest physical anomalies that make them biologically and physiologically similar to our primitive ancestors. These

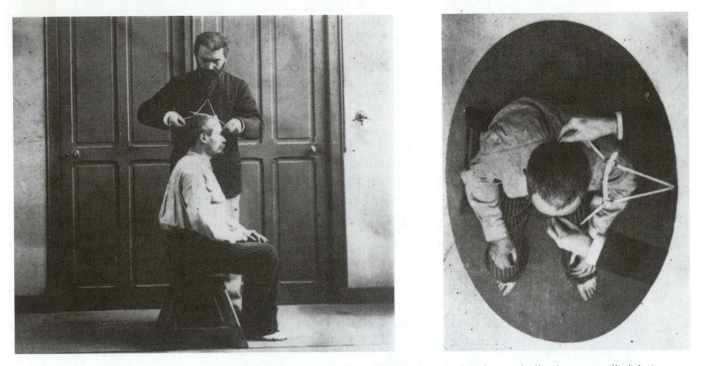

Early bio-criminologists believed that the physical makeup of offenders controlled their behavior. Biological traits present at birth were thought to predetermine whether people would live a life of crime. Here the skull of a criminal is measured in a study to determine if brain size and shape are related to violent behavior.

atavistic individuals are savage throwbacks to an earlier stage of human evolution. Because of this link, the "born criminal" has such physical traits as enormous jaws, strong canines, a flattened nose, and supernumerary teeth (double rows, as in snakes). Lombroso made statements such as: "[I]t was easy to understand why the span of the arms in criminals so often exceeds the height, for this is a characteristic of apes, whose forelimbs are used in walking and climbing."[57]

Contemporaries of Lombroso refined the notion of a physical basis of crime. Raffaele Garofalo (1851–1934) shared Lombroso's belief that certain physical characteristics indicate a criminal or delinquent nature.[58] Enrico Ferri (1856–1929), a student of Lombroso, believed a number of biological, social, and organic factors caused delinquency and crime. Ferri accepted the biological approach to explaining criminal activity, but he attempted to interweave physical, anthropological, and social factors into his explanation of the causes of illegal behavior.[59] The English criminologist Charles Goring (1870–1919) challenged the validity of Lombroso's research and claimed instead that delinquent behaviors bore a significant relationship to a condition he referred to as "defective intelligence."[60] Goring believed delinquent behavior was inherited and could therefore best be controlled by regulating the reproduction of families exhibiting traits such as "feeble-mindedness, epilepsy, insanity, and defective social instinct."[61]

Advocates of the inheritance school studied the family trees of criminal and delinquent offenders and traced the activities of several generations of families believed to have an especially large number of criminal members. The most famous of these studies involved the Jukes and the Kallikaks. Richard Dugdale's *The Jukes: A Study in Crime, Pauperism, Disease, and Heredity* (1875) and Arthur Estabrook's later work, *The Jukes in 1915,* traced the history of the Jukes, a family responsible for a disproportionate amount of crime.[62]

Advocates of the **somatotype school,** or body build school, argued that delinquents and criminals manifest distinct physiques that make them susceptible to particular types of delinquent behavior.[63] William H. Sheldon linked body type to

somatotype school
Argued that delinquents manifest distinct physiques that make them susceptible to particular types of delinquent behavior.

delinquency.[64] *Mesomorphs* have well-developed muscles and an athletic appearance. They are active, aggressive, sometimes violent, and the most likely to become delinquents. *Endomorphs* have heavy builds and are slow-moving and lethargic. *Ectomorphs* are tall and thin and less social and more intellectual than the other types.[65]

These early views that portrayed delinquent behavior as a function of a single factor or trait, such as body build or defective intelligence, had a significant impact on early American criminology, which relied heavily on developing a science of "criminal anthropology."[66] Eventually, these views evoked criticism for their unsound methodology and lack of proper scientific controls. Many trait studies used captive offender populations and failed to compare experimental subjects with control groups of nondelinquents or undetected delinquents.[67] These methodological flaws make it impossible to determine if biological traits produce delinquency. It is equally plausible that police are more likely to arrest—and courts to convict—the mentally and physically abnormal. By the middle of the twentieth century, biological theories had fallen out of favor as an explanation of delinquency.

Contemporary Biosocial Theory

For most of the twentieth century delinquency experts scoffed at the notion that a youth's behavior was controlled by physical conditions present at birth. During this period, the majority of delinquency research focused on social factors, such as poverty and family life, that were believed to be responsible for law-violating behavior. However, a small group of criminologists and penologists kept alive the biological approach.[68] Some embraced sociobiology, a perspective that suggests that behavior will adapt to the environment in which it evolved.[69] Creatures of all species are influenced by their genetic inheritance and their innate need to survive and dominate others. Sociobiology had a tremendous effect on reviving interest in a biological basis for crime and delinquency. If biological (genetic) makeup controls all human behavior, it follows that a person's genes should also be responsible for determining whether he or she chooses law-violating or conventional behavior.[70]

equipotentiality
View that all people are equal at birth and are thereafter influenced by their environment.

Today, those who embrace trait theory reject the traditional assumptions that all humans are born with equal potential to learn and achieve (**equipotentiality**) and that thereafter their behavior is controlled by external or social forces.[71] Traditional criminologists suggest (either explicitly or implicitly) that all people are born equal and that parents, schools, neighborhoods, and friends control subsequent development. But trait theorists argue that no two people (with rare exceptions, such as identical twins) are alike and therefore that each will react to environmental stimuli in a distinct way. They assert that a combination of personal traits and environmental influences produce individual behavior patterns. People with pathological traits, such as brain damage, abnormal personality, or a low IQ, may have a heightened risk for crime. This risk is elevated by environmental stresses such as poor family life, educational failure, substance abuse, and exposure to delinquent peers. The reverse may also apply: a supportive environment may be strong enough to counteract adverse biological and psychological traits.[72]

The interaction between a child's predisposition caused by physical or mental disorders and his or her environment produces delinquency. Children born into disadvantaged environments often do not get the social and familial support they need to overcome their handicaps. Lack of family support can have long-term physical consequences. For example, a child's neural pathways may be damaged by repeated child neglect or abuse. Once experiences are ingrained, the brain "remembers," and a pattern of electrochemical activation is established that remains across the life span.[73] The relatively small number of youths who suffer both physical and social handicaps and who also lack social supports are the ones who become early onset offenders and persist in a life of crime.[74]

biosocial theory
The view that both thought and behavior have biological and social bases.

Contemporary **biosocial theory** explains the onset of antisocial behaviors such as aggression and violence by focusing on the physical qualities of the offenders.[75] The majority of research efforts are concentrated in three distinct areas of study: biochemical reactions, neurological dysfunction, and genetic influences. These three views are discussed in some detail next.

Biochemical Factors

This area of biosocial research concerns the suspected relationship between antisocial behavior and biochemical makeup.[76] One view is that the body chemistry can govern behavior and personality, including levels of both aggression and depression.[77]

You Are What You Eat?   There is evidence that diet may influence behavior through its impact on body chemistry. Of particular concern is an unusually high intake of artificial food coloring, milk, and sweets. Some scientists believe chronic under- or oversupply of vitamins C, B3, and B6 may be related to restlessness and antisocial behavior in youths. Evidence also exists that allergies to foods can influence mood and behavior, resulting in personality swings between hyperactivity and depression.[78]

High intake or excessive exposure to certain common minerals, including magnesium, copper, cadmium, and zinc, has also been linked to aggression.[79] Overexposure to lead, for example, has been traced to learning disabilities, cognitive deficits, lower IQ, and mental dullness, which are considered risk factors for delinquency and violent behavior.[80]

Experimental evidence exists that institutionalized youths have had a long history of poor nutrition, with diets low in protein and high in sugar and other carbohydrates.[81] Some highly sophisticated experiments show that antisocial youths who are given a diet balanced in nutrients have significantly reduced episodes of antisocial behavior and improved scores on psychological inventories.[82] A high-protein, low-carbohydrate, sugarless diet, supplemented by megavitamins, has been found to improve behavior problems including hyperactivity and aggression. Lower intake of refined sugar also seems to have a mediating effect on aggressive behavior.[83] Experiments conducted in schools have linked diets containing lower levels of sugar and preservatives to improved scores on national achievement tests. School achievement has been consistently linked to delinquent behavior, and any improvement in academic performance resulting from dietary changes may help reduce the rate of antisocial activities among the student population.[84]

Dissenting Views   This evidence seems persuasive, but the relationship between biochemical intake and abnormal behavior is far from settled. Some of this research has been criticized as being methodologically unsound, and a number of controlled experiments have failed to substantiate any real link between the two variables.[85] In one important study a group of researchers had twenty-five preschool and twenty-three school-age children described as sensitive to sugar follow a different diet for three consecutive three-week periods. One diet was high in sucrose (a form of sugar), the second substituted aspartame (Nutrasweet) for a sweetener, and the third relied on saccharin (another form of artificial sweetener). Careful measurement of the subjects found little evidence of cognitive or behavioral differences that could be linked to diet. If anything, sugar seemed to have a calming effect on the children.[86]

Additional evidence also questions a diet–delinquency link. The United States, with one of the highest crime and delinquency rates in the world, has a far lower per capita consumption of sugar than other western nations. Furthermore, adolescents, who usually have the highest crime rate, actually have sugar intakes about one-half that of the general population.[87]

Despite these criticisms, the relationship between diet and delinquency remains unresolved. There is little conclusive evidence linking diet and antisocial behavior,[88] but further research of this relationship is certainly warranted.[89]

Hormonal Levels   Hormonal levels are another area of biochemical research. Antisocial behavior allegedly peaks in the teenage years because hormonal activity is at its greatest level during this period. It is argued that increased levels of the male androgen (testosterone) are responsible for excessive levels of violence among teenage boys. Adolescents who experience more intense moods, mood swings, anxiety, and restlessness than people at other points in development also have the highest crime rates.[90] These mood and behavior changes have been associated with family conflict and antisocial behavior.

Hormonal sensitivity may begin at the very early stages of life if the fetus is exposed to abnormally high levels of testosterone while in the uterus. This may trigger a heightened response to the release of testosterone when an adolescent male reaches puberty. Although testosterone levels may appear normal, the young male is at risk for overaggressive behavioral responses.[91]

Hormonal activity as an explanation of gender differences in the delinquency crime rate will be discussed further in Chapter 7.

Neurological Dysfunction

Another focus of biosocial theory is the neurological, or brain and nervous system, structure of offenders. Studies measure indicators of system functioning including brain waves, heart rate, arousal levels, skin conductance and attention span, cognitive ability, and spatial learning and compare them to measures of antisocial behavior.

One view is that the neuroendocrine system, which controls brain chemistry, is the key to understanding violence and aggression. Imbalance in the central nervous system's chemical and hormonal activity has been linked to antisocial behavior and drug abuse.[92]

Another view is that neurological dysfunction, commonly measured with an electroencephalogram (EEG), a CAT scan, or performance indicators (gross motor functions, visual processing, auditory-language functioning), is the key factor causing aggression and violence. Children who manifest behavior disturbances may have identifiable neurological deficits, such as damage to the hemispheres of the brain.[93] This is sometimes referred to as **minimal brain dysfunction (MBD),** an abnormality in the cerebral or brain structure that causes behavior injurious to a person's lifestyle and social adjustment. Impairment is produced by factors such as low birthweight, brain injury, birth complications, and inherited abnormalities.[94] Research indicates that children exhibiting neurological impairment also have an increased risk for a garden variety of developmental problems, such as low IQ scores and cognitive impairment, that have been associated with delinquency.[95]

A number of research efforts have attempted to substantiate a link between neurological impairment and crime. There is evidence that this relationship can be detected quite early and that children who suffer from measurable neurological deficits at birth are more likely to become criminals later in life.[96] Low birthweight is highly correlated with neurological impairment,[97] and low birthweight children are also likely to be early onset delinquents. Clinical analysis of death row inmates found that a significant number had suffered head injuries as children, resulting in

minimal brain dysfunction (MBD)
Damage to the brain itself that causes antisocial behavior injurious to the individual's lifestyle and social adjustment.

damage to their central nervous system and neurological impairment.[98] Measurement of the brain activity of antisocial youths has revealed impairments that might cause them to experience otherwise unexplainable outbursts of anger, hostility, and aggression.[99] Evidence has been found linking brain damage to mental disorders such as schizophrenia and depression.[100] Cross-national studies also support a link between neurological dysfunction and antisocial behavior.[101]

A number of research studies have used an EEG to measure the brain waves and activity of delinquents and then compared them with those of law-abiding adolescents. In what is considered the most significant investigation of EEG abnormality and delinquency, 335 violent delinquents were classified on the basis of their antisocial activities and measured on an EEG.[102] Youths who committed a single violent act had a 12 percent abnormality rate (the same as the general population), but the habitually aggressive youths tested at a 57 percent abnormality rate—a rate almost five times normal. Behaviors believed to be highly correlated with abnormal EEG functions include poor impulse control, inadequate social ability, hostility, temper tantrums, destructiveness, and hyperactivity.[103]

The Learning Disabilities   One specific type of MBD that has generated considerable interest is **learning disability (LD),** a term that has been defined by the National Advisory Committee on Handicapped Children:

> Children with special learning disabilities exhibit a disorder in one or more of the basic psychological processes involved in understanding or using spoken or written languages. They may be manifested in disorders of listening, thinking, talking, reading, writing or arithmetic. They include conditions which have been referred to as perceptual handicaps, brain injury, minimal brain dysfunction, dyslexia, developmental aphasia, etc. They do not include learning problems which are due to visual, hearing or motor handicaps, to mental retardation, emotional disturbance, or to environmental disadvantages.[104]

Learning disabled kids usually exhibit poor motor coordination (for example, problems with poor hand–eye coordination, trouble climbing stairs, or clumsiness), have behavior problems (lack of emotional control, hostility, and cannot stay on task), and produce improper auditory and vocal responses (do not seem to hear or cannot differentiate sounds and noises).

The relationship between learning disabilities and delinquency has been highlighted by studies showing that arrested and incarcerated children have a far higher LD rate than do children in the general population.[105] Although learning disabilities are quite common—approximately 10 percent of all youths have some form of learning disorder—estimates of LD among adjudicated delinquents range from 26 to 73 percent.[106] Do these statistics necessarily mean that learning disabilities somehow cause delinquent behavior?

Typically, there are two possible explanations of the link between learning disabilities and delinquency.[107] One view, known as the *susceptibility rationale,* argues that the link is caused by certain side effects of learning disabilities, such as impulsiveness, poor ability to learn from experience, and an inability to take social cues. In contrast, the *school failure rationale* assumes that the frustration caused by the LD child's poor school performance will lead to a negative self-image and acting-out behavior.

A number of recent research efforts have found that the LD child may not be any more susceptible to delinquent behavior than the non-LD child and that the proposed link between learning disabilities and delinquency may be an artifact of bias in the way the juvenile justice system treats LD youths.[108] Because of social bias, LD youths are more likely to be arrested and, if petitioned to juvenile court, their poor school records can influence the outcome of the case. LD youths bring with them to court a record of school problems and low grades and a history of frustrating efforts by agents of the educational system to help them. When information

learning disability (LD)
Neurological dysfunction that prevents an individual from learning to his or her potential.

is gleaned from the school personnel at juvenile trials, LD children's poor performance may work against them in the court. Consequently, the view that learning disabilities cause delinquency has been questioned, and the view that LD children are more likely to be arrested and officially labeled delinquent demands further inquiry. Self-reports show few differences between the behavior of LD and non-LD youths, a finding that supports the social bias argument.[109]

Despite this evidence, some scholars continue to affirm the presence of an LD–JD link. Psychologist Terrie Moffitt has evaluated the relevant literature on the connection between LD and delinquency and concludes that it is a significant correlate of persistent antisocial behavior (or conduct disorders).[110] She finds that neurological symptoms, such as LD and MBD, correlate highly with factors that create high risk for persistent antisocial behavior: early onset of deviance, hyperactivity, and aggressiveness. Moffitt's review indicates further research is needed on the cause and impact of neurological dysfunction: When do such problems begin? Are they the result of injury during birth? or of child abuse and neglect?[111] Is there a continuum of learning disabilities, and are the most severely disabled also the most

FOCUS ON DELINQUENCY

ATTENTION DEFICIT HYPERACTIVITY DISORDER

Many parents have noticed that their children do not pay attention to them—they run around and do things in their own way. Sometimes this inattention is a function of age; in other instances it is a symptom of a common learning disability referred to as attention deficit hyperactivity disorder (ADHD), a condition in which a child shows a developmentally inappropriate lack of attention, distractibility, impulsivity, and hyperactivity. The various symptoms of ADHD are listed in Table A.

No one is really sure how ADHD develops, but some psychologists believe it is tied to dysfunction in a section of the lower portion of the brain known as the reticular activating system. This area keeps the higher brain centers alert and ready for input. There is some evidence that this area is not working properly in ADHD kids and that their behavior is

Table A Symptoms of ADHD

Lack of Attention

- Frequently fails to finish projects
- Does not seem to pay attention
- Does not sustain interest in play activities
- Cannot sustain concentration on schoolwork or related tasks
- Is easily distracted

Impulsivity

- Frequently acts without thinking
- Often "calls out" in class
- Does not want to wait his or her turn in line or games
- Shifts from activity to activity
- Cannot organize tasks or work
- Requires constant supervision

Hyperactivity

- Constantly runs around and climbs on things
- Shows excessive motor activity while asleep
- Cannot sit still; is constantly fidgeting
- Does not remain in his or her seat in class
- Is constantly on the go like a "motor"
- Difficulty regulating emotions
- Difficulty getting started
- Difficulty staying on track
- Difficulty adjusting to social demands

prone to delinquency?[112] Efforts are being made to introduce new technologies in the measurement of brain function and behavior to investigate early detection, prevention, and control of maladapted behaviors.[113]

In the Focus on Delinquency box, attention deficit hyperactivity disorder, a neurological condition associated with antisocial behavior, is discussed in some detail.

Arousal Theory It has long been suspected that obtaining thrills is a motivator of crime. Adolescents may engage in crimes such as shoplifting and vandalism simply because they offer the attraction of "getting away with it"; delinquency is a thrilling demonstration of personal competence.[114] Is it possible that thrill seekers are people who have some form of abnormal brain functioning that directs their behavior?

Arousal theorists believe that for a variety of genetic and environmental reasons some people's brains function differently in response to environmental stimuli. All of us seek to maintain a preferred or optimal level of arousal: too much stimulation leaves us anxious and stressed out, and too little makes us feel bored

really the brain's attempt to generate new stimulation to maintain alertness. Other suspected origins are neurological damage to the frontal lobes of the brain, prenatal stress, and even food additives and chemical allergies. Some experts suggest that the condition might be traced to the neurological effects of abnormal levels of the chemicals dopamine and norepinephrine.

Children from any background can develop ADHD, but it is five to seven times more common in boys than girls. It does not affect intelligence, and ADHD children often show considerable ability with artistic endeavors. More common in the United States than elsewhere, ADHD tends to run in families, and there is some suggestion of an association with a family history of alcoholism or depression.

Estimates of ADHD in the general population range from 3 to 12 percent, but it is much more prevalent in adolescents, where some estimates reach as high as one-third of the population. ADHD children are most often treated by giving them doses of stimulants, most commonly Ritalin and Dexedrine (or dextroamphetamine), which, ironically, help these children control their emotional and behavioral outbursts. The antimanic, anticonvulsant drug Tegretol has also been used effectively.

ADHD usually results in poor school performance, including a high dropout rate, bullying, stubbornness, mental disorder, and a lack of response to discipline; these conditions are highly correlated with delinquent behavior. A series of research studies now link ADHD to the onset and continuance of a delinquent career and increased risk for antisocial behavior and substance abuse in adulthood. ADHD children are more likely to be arrested, to be charged with a felony, and to have multiple arrests than non-ADHD youths. There is also evidence that ADHD youths who *also* exhibit early signs of MBD and conduct disorder (for example, fighting) are the most at risk for persistent antisocial behaviors continuing into adulthood. Of course many, if not most, children who are diagnosed ADHD do not engage in delinquent behavior, and new treatment techniques featuring behavior modification and drug therapies are constantly being developed to help children who have attention or hyperactivity problems.

Sources: Kimberly Barletto, "Who's at Risk: Delinquent Trajectories of Children with Attention and Conduct Problems," paper presented at the American Society of Criminology Meeting, San Diego, Calif., 1997; Harry Wexler, "Attention Deficit Disorder, Drugs and Crime: The Dangerous Mixture," paper presented at the American Society of Criminology Meeting, Boston, Mass., November 1995; Terrie Moffitt and Phil Silva, "Self-Reported Delinquency, Neuropsychological Deficit, and History of Attention Deficit Disorder," *Journal of Abnormal Child Psychology* 16:553–69 (1988); American Psychiatric Association, *Diagnostic and Statistical Manual of the Mental Disorders*, 4th ed. (Washington, D.C.: American Psychiatric Press, 1994), pp. 60–64.

Arousal theorists believe that, for a variety of genetic and environmental reasons, some people's brains function differently in response to environmental stimuli. All of us seek to maintain a preferred or optimal level of arousal. Too much stimulation may leave us anxious and stressed out; too little may make us bored and weary. Some kids may need the rush that comes from getting into scrapes and conflicts in order to feel relaxed and at ease.

and weary. However, there is variation in the way children's brains process sensory input. Some nearly always feel comfortable with little stimulation, whereas others require a high degree of environmental input to feel comfortable. The latter group become "sensation seekers," who seek out stimulating activities that may include aggressive or violent behavior patterns.[115]

The factors that determine a person's level of arousal are not yet fully understood. Suspected sources include brain chemistry (for example, serotonin levels) and brain structure (the brain has many more nerve cells with receptor sites for neurotransmitters in some people than in others). Another view is that adolescents with low heart rates are more likely to commit crimes because they seek out stimulation to increase their feelings of arousal to normal levels.[116]

Genetic Influences

Individuals who share genes are alike in personality regardless of how they are reared, whereas rearing environment induces little or no personality resemblance.[117]

Biosocial theorists also study the genetic makeup of delinquents.[118] It has been hypothesized that some youths inherit a genetic configuration that predisposes them to violence and aggression.[119] In the same way people inherit genes that control height and eye color, biosocial theorists believe antisocial behavior characteristics and mental disorders also may be passed down.[120] Early theories of heredity suggested that delinquency proneness ran in families. However, most families share a similar lifestyle as well as a similar gene pool, making it difficult to determine whether behavior is a function of heredity or the environment.

Interest in a genetic basis of crime was given new life in 1966 because of the highly publicized killing of eight Chicago nurses by Richard Speck. It was soon reported that Speck possessed an extra male chromosome; instead of the normal 46XY chromosomal structure, his was 47XYY. Though numerous research studies failed to find conclusive proof that males with an extra Y chromosome were disproportionately violent and criminal, interest brought about by the Speck case boosted research on genetic influences on delinquency (it was later revealed that Speck's genetic structure had been misidentified).[121]

Biosocial theorists have once again taken up the study of family transmission of delinquent traits. Some recent research shows a significant association in sibling behavior: brothers and sisters seem to share antisocial lifestyles.[122] Siblings share the same environment, so it is not surprising that their behavior co-varies. To establish the influence of environment and genetics independently, criminologists have studied twins and adopted children.

Twin Studies   One method of studying the genetic basis of delinquency is to compare the behavior of twins to nontwin siblings. If crime is an inherited trait, identical twins should be quite similar in their behavior because they share a common genetic makeup.

Because twins are usually brought up in the same household and share common life experiences, however, any similarity in their delinquent behavior might be a function of comparable environmental influences and not genetics at all. To guard against this, biosocial theorists have compared the behavior of identical monozygotic (MZ) twins with fraternal dizygotic (DZ) twins; the former have an identical genetic makeup, but the latter share only about 50 percent of their genetic combinations. Research has shown that MZ twins are significantly closer in their personal characteristics, such as intelligence, than are DZ twins.[123] Reviews of twin studies found that in almost all cases MZ twins have delinquent and antisocial behavior patterns more similar than that of DZ twins.[124]

Although this seems to support a connection between genetic makeup and delinquency, little conclusive evidence exists of such an actual link. MZ twins are more likely to look alike and to share physical traits than DZ twins, and they are more likely to be treated similarly. Shared behavior patterns may therefore be a function of socialization and not heredity. Critics have also challenged the methodology of these studies and suggest that those that show a conclusive genetic link to behavior use faulty data.[125]

Against this interpretation is research evidence that identical twins reared apart are quite as similar in many traits, including personality, intelligence, and attitudes, as twins who live in the same household.[126] The Minnesota study of twins reared apart found that MZ twins who were separated at birth shared many similarities in personal style and behavior; in contrast, the DZ twins reared apart seldom produced similar behavior patterns.[127] Such findings support a genetic basis of behavior.

Adoption Studies   Another way to determine whether delinquency is an inherited trait is to compare the behavior of adopted children with that of their biological parents. If the criminal behavior of children is more like that of their biological parents (whom they have never met) than that of their adoptive parents (who brought them up), it would indicate that the tendency toward delinquency is inherited rather than shaped by environmental factors.

Studies of this kind have generally supported the hypothesis that there is a link between genetics and behavior.[128] Adoptees share many of the behavioral and intellectual characteristics of their biological parents despite the social and environmental conditions found in their adoptive homes. Genetic makeup is sufficient to counteract or negate even the most extreme environmental conditions, such as malnutrition and abuse.[129]

Some of the most influential research in this area has been conducted by Sarnoff Mednick. In one study Mednick and Bernard Hutchings found that although only 13 percent of the adoptive fathers of a sample of adjudicated delinquent youths had criminal records, 31 percent of their biological fathers had criminal records.[130] Analysis of a control group's background indicated that about 11 percent of all fathers will have criminal records. Hutchings and Mednick were forced to conclude that genetics played at least some role in creating delinquent tendencies, because the biological fathers of delinquents were much more likely than the fathers of noncriminal youths to be criminals.[131]

In addition to a direct link between heredity and delinquency, the literature also shows that behavior traits indirectly linked to delinquency may be at least in part inherited. Biological parents of adopted hyperactive children are more likely to show symptoms of hyperactivity than are the adoptive parents.[132] Several studies have reported a higher incidence of psychological problems in parents of hyperactive children when compared to control groups. All hyperactive children do not become delinquent, but the link between this neurological condition and delinquency has long been suspected.

Similarly, there is evidence (disputed) that intelligence is related to heredity and that low intelligence is a cause of impulsive delinquent acts that are easier to detect and more likely to result in arrest.[133] This connection can create the appearance of a relationship between heredity and delinquency (see later sections for more on IQ and delinquency).

Connecting delinquent behavior to heredity is quite controversial because it implies that the cause of delinquency (a) is present at birth, (b) is "transmitted" from one generation to the next, and (c) is immune to treatment efforts (since genes cannot be altered). Recent evaluations of the gene–crime relationship find that even though a relationship can be detected the better designed research efforts provide less support than earlier and weaker studies.[134] If there is a genetic basis of delinquency, it is likely that genetic factors contribute to certain individual differences that interact with specific social and environmental conditions to bring about antisocial behavior.[135]

Evolutionary Theory

evolutionary theory
Explaining the existence of aggression and violent behavior as positive adaptive behaviors in human evolution; these traits allowed their bearers to reproduce disproportionately, which has had an effect on the human gene pool.

Some theorists have speculated that the human traits that produce violence and aggression have been nurtured and refined through the long process of human evolution.[136] According to **evolutionary theory,** the competition for scarce resources has influenced and shaped human behavior,[137] favoring actions that promote individual well-being and ensuring the survival and reproduction of particular genetic lines. Males who are impulsive risk takers may father more children, which would increase the representation of that trait in the human gene pool. If impulsive behavior is an inherited trait, it is not surprising that human history has been marked by war, violence, and aggression.

Crime rate differences between the genders, then, are less a matter of socialization than of inherent differences in mating patterns between the sexes that have developed over time.[138] Among young men, reckless, life-threatening "risk proneness" is especially likely to evolve in societies where choosing not to compete means an inability to reproduce due to a scarcity of suitable females.[139] Aggressive males have had the greatest impact on the gene pool, and the descendants of these aggressive males now account for the disproportionate amount of male aggression and violence.[140]

This evolutionary model, sometimes called "cheater theory," suggests that a subpopulation of men has evolved with genes that incline them toward extremely low parental involvement. Sexually aggressive, they use their cunning to gain sexual conquests with as many females as possible. Because females would not willingly choose them as mates, they use stealth (that is, cheating) to gain sexual access, including mimicking the behavior of more stable males.[141] Psychologist Byron Roth notes that these flamboyant sexually aggressive males are especially attractive to younger, less intelligent women who begin having children at a very early age.[142] Their fleeting courtship process produces children with low IQs, aggressive personalities, and little chance of proper socialization in father-absent families. Because

Table 3.3

BIOSOCIAL THEORIES

	Major Premise	Strengths
Biochemical	Crime, especially violence, is a function of diet, vitamin intake, hormonal imbalance, or food allergies.	Explains irrational violence. Shows how the environment interacts with personal traits to influence behavior.
Neurological	Criminals and delinquents often suffer brain impairment, as measured by the EEG. Learning disabilities such as attention deficit hyperactive disorder and minimum brain dysfunction are related to antisocial behavior.	Explains irrational violence. Shows how the environment interacts with personal traits to influence behavior.
Genetic	Delinquent traits and predispositions are inherited. Criminality of parents can predict the delinquency of children.	Explains why only a small percentage of youths in a high-crime area become chronic offenders.
Evolutionary	Behavior patterns and reproductive traits, developed over the millennia, control behavior.	Explains male aggressiveness.

the criminal justice system treats them leniently, argues Roth, sexually irresponsible men are free to prey on young girls. Over time, their offspring will provide an ever-expanding supply of people who are both antisocial and sexually aggressive.

Table 3.3 offers a summary of the major biosocial theories of delinquency.

Psychological Theories of Delinquency

Some experts view the cause of delinquency as essentially psychological.[143] After all, most behaviors labeled delinquent—violence, theft, sexual misconduct—seem to be symptomatic of some underlying psychological problem. Psychologists point out that many delinquent youths have poor home lives, destructive relationships with neighbors, friends, and teachers, and conflicts with authority figures in general. These relationships seem to indicate a disturbed personality structure. Furthermore, numerous studies of incarcerated youths indicate that the youths' personalities are marked by negative, antisocial behavior characteristics. And since delinquent behavior occurs among youths in every racial, ethnic, and socioeconomic group, psychologists view it as a function of emotional and

FIGURE 3.2

Psychological Perspectives of
Delinquency

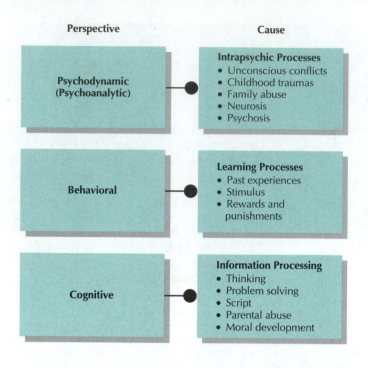

mental disturbance rather than purely a result of social factors, such as racism, poverty, and class conflict. Many delinquents do not manifest significant psychological problems, but enough do to give clinicians a powerful influence on delinquency theory.

Because psychology is a complex and diversified discipline, more than one psychological perspective on crime exists. Three prominent psychological perspectives on delinquency are psychodynamic theory, behavioral theory, and cognitive theory.[144] These three perspectives are outlined in Figure 3.2

Psychodynamic Theory

psychodynamic theory
Branch of psychology that holds that the human personality is controlled by unconscious mental processes developed early in childhood.

Russell Eugene Weston Jr. was a quiet loner who drifted back and forth between a cabin in the Montana mountains and a modest house in rural Illinois.[145] He became an increasingly troubled figure who eventually was hospitalized after writing threatening letters to government officials. On July 25, 1998, he entered the U.S. Capitol, where he went on a shooting rampage during which two capitol police officers were slain and a female tourist was wounded. After his arrest, Weston's family told officials that their son had been diagnosed by a medical professional as a paranoid schizophrenic. His neighbors portrayed the forty-one-year-old Weston as a withdrawn, introverted loner who grew increasingly angry and alienated over the years. "When he was on his medication, he was fine, he would wave and talk," said a longtime resident. "When he was off the medication, he was paranoid, you just didn't know."

According to the **psychodynamic theory,** which originated with the pioneering work of the Austrian physician Sigmund Freud (1856–1939), law violations are a product of an abnormal personality structure formed early in life and which thereafter controls human behavior choices.[146] In extreme cases, such as Ronald Weston's, mental torment drives people into violence and aggression. The basis of psychodynamic theory is the assumption that human behavior is controlled by unconscious mental processes developed early in childhood.

Psychodynamic theory argues that the human personality contains three major components. The *id* is the unrestrained, primitive, pleasure-seeking component

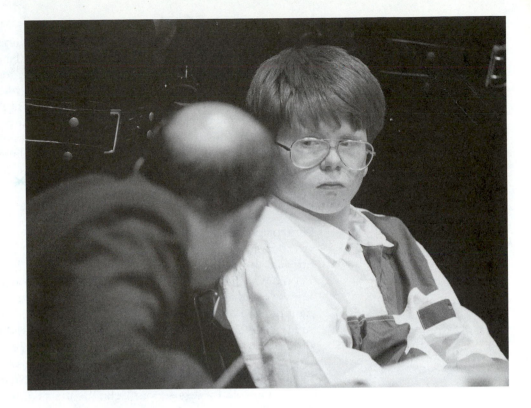

Psychologists point out that many delinquent youths have poor home lives, destructive relationships with neighbors, friends, and teachers, and conflicts with authority figures in general. These relationships seem to indicate a disturbed personality structure that can result in negative, antisocial behavior characteristics. Eric Smith, shown here, was convicted at age 14 of killing a preschooler. Could his behavior possibly have been the product of a normal personality?

with which each child is born. The *ego* develops through the reality of living in the world and helps manage and restrain the id's need for immediate gratification. The *superego* develops through interactions with parents and other significant people and represents the conscience and the moral rules that are shared by most adults.

Psychodynamic theory suggests that unconscious motivations for behavior come from the id's action in response to two primal needs: sex and aggression. Human behavior is often marked by symbolic actions that reflect hidden feelings about these needs. For example, stealing a car may reflect a person's unconscious need for shelter and mobility to escape from hostile enemies (aggression) or perhaps an urge to enter a closed, dark, womb-like structure that reflects the earliest memories (sex).

All three segments of the personality operate simultaneously. The id dictates needs and desires, the superego counteracts the id by fostering feelings of morality and righteousness, and the ego evaluates the reality of a position between these two extremes (see Figure 3.3). If these components are properly balanced, the individual

FIGURE 3.3

The Structure of the Id, Ego, and Superego

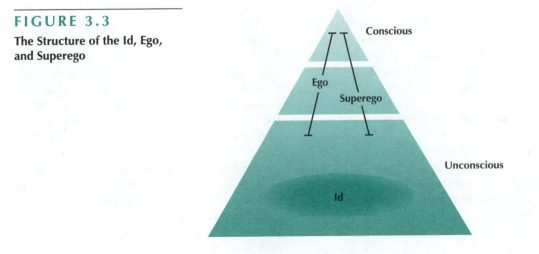

can lead a normal life. If one aspect of the personality becomes dominant at the expense of the others, however, the individual exhibits abnormal personality traits.

Furthermore, the theory suggests that an imbalance in personality traits caused by a traumatic early childhood can result in long-term psychological difficulties. For example, if neglectful parents fail to help the child develop his or her superego adequately, the child's id may become the dominant personality force. The absence of a strong superego results in an inability to distinguish clearly between right and wrong. Later, the youth may demand immediate gratification, lack compassion and sensitivity for the needs of others, disassociate feelings, act aggressively and impulsively, or demonstrate other psychotic symptoms. Antisocial behavior may result from conflict or trauma occurring early in a child's development, and delinquent activity may become an outlet for these violent and antisocial feelings.

Neuroses and Psychosis   According to Freud's version of psychodynamic theory, people who experience feelings of anxiety and are afraid they are losing control are said to be suffering from a form of neurosis and are referred to as *neurotics*. People who have lost total control and who are dominated by their primitive id are known as *psychotics*. Their behavior may be marked by bizarre episodes, hallucinations, and inappropriate responses. Psychosis takes many forms, the most common being labeled *schizophrenia,* a condition marked by illogical thought processes, distorted perceptions, and abnormal emotional expression. According to the classical psychoanalytic view, the most serious types of youthful antisocial behavior (such as murder) might be motivated by psychosis, whereas neurotic feelings would be responsible for less serious delinquent acts and status offenses (such as petty theft and truancy).[147]

Contemporary psychologists generally no longer use the term *neuroses* to describe all forms of unconscious conflict. It is now more common to characterize people with more specific types of disorders, including anxiety disorder, mood disorder, sleep disorder, and so on.

The Psychodynamic Tradition and Delinquency   A number of psychoanalysts have expanded on Freud's original model to explain the onset of antisocial behaviors. Erik Erickson speculated that many adolescents experience a life crisis in which they feel emotional, impulsive, and uncertain of their role and purpose.[148] He coined the phrase **identity crisis** to denote this period of inner turmoil and confusion. Erickson's approach might characterize the behavior of youthful drug abusers as an expression of confusion over their place in society, their inability to direct behavior toward useful outlets, and perhaps their dependence on others to offer them solutions to their problems.

Psychoanalysts view youth crime as a result of unresolved mental anguish and internal conflict. Some children, especially those who have been abused or mistreated, may experience unconscious feelings of resentment, fear, and hatred. If these conflicts cannot be reconciled, regression occurs and the id becomes dominant. This regression accounts for a great number of mental diseases, from neuroses to psychoses, and in many cases it may be related to criminal behavior.[149]

Another psychoanalytic view is that delinquents are id-dominated people who suffer from the inability to control their impulsive drives. Perhaps because they suffered unhappy experiences in childhood or had families who could not provide proper love and care, delinquents have weak or damaged egos and are unable to cope with conventional society.[150] In its most extreme form, delinquency may be viewed as a form of psychosis that prevents delinquent youths from appreciating the feelings of their victims or controlling their own impulsive needs for gratification. For example, in his classic work, psychoanalyst August Aichorn found that social stress alone could not produce such an emotional state. He identifies **latent delinquents** as youths whose troubled family lives lead them to seek immediate gratification without consideration of right and wrong or the feelings of others.[151]

identity crisis
Psychological state, identified by Erikson, in which youth face inner turmoil and uncertainty about life roles.

latent delinquents
Youths whose troubled family life leads them to seek immediate gratification without consideration of right and wrong or the feelings of others.

Others view adolescent antisocial behavior as a consequence for youths who are unable to cope with feelings of oppression. Criminality actually allows youths to strive by producing positive psychic results: helping them to feel free and independent; giving them the possibility of excitement and the chance to use their skills and imagination; providing the promise of positive gain; allowing them to blame others (the police) for their predicament; and giving them a chance to rationalize their own sense of failure ("If I hadn't gotten into trouble, I could have been a success").[152]

The psychodynamic view is supported by research that shows that a number of serious, violent juvenile offenders suffer from some sort of personality disturbance. Violent youths have been clinically diagnosed as "overtly hostile," "explosive or volatile," "anxious," and "depressed."[153] As many as 75 percent of male adolescents accused of murder could be classified as having some mental illness, including schizophrenia.[154] Abused, depressed, and suicidal children may grow up to vent their feelings in a homicidal rage.[155]

Family Life   The psychodynamic approach places heavy emphasis on the family's role in producing a delinquent child. Antisocial youths frequently come from families in which parents are unable to give love, set consistent limits, and provide the controls that allow children to develop the necessary personal tools to cope with the world.[156] The exploitive, destructive behavior of a youth may actually be a symbolic call for help. In fact, some psychoanalysts view delinquent behaviors as being motivated by an unconscious urge to be punished. These children, who feel unloved at home, assume the reason must be their own inadequacy; hence, they deserve punishment.

Behavioral Theory

Not all psychologists agree that behavior is controlled by unconscious mental processes determined by parental relationships developed early in childhood. Behavioral psychologists argue that a person's personality is learned throughout life during interaction with others. Based primarily on the works of the American psychologist John B. Watson (1878–1958) and popularized by Harvard professor B. F. Skinner (1904–1990), **behaviorism** concerns itself solely with measurable events and not the unobservable psychic phenomena described by psychoanalysts.

Behaviorists suggest that individuals learn by observing how people react to their behavior. Behavior is triggered initially by a stimulus or change in the environment. If a particular behavior is reinforced by some positive reaction or event, that behavior will be continued and eventually learned. However, behaviors that are not reinforced or are punished will be extinguished or become extinct. For example, if children are given a reward (ice cream for dessert) for eating their entire dinner, eventually they will learn to eat properly as a matter of habit. Conversely, if children are punished for some misbehavior, they will eventually learn to associate disapproval with that act and avoid it.

behaviorism
Branch of psychology concerned with the study of observable behavior rather than unconscious processes; focuses on particular stimuli and responses to them.

social learning theory
The view that behavior is modeled through observation either directly through intimate contact with others or indirectly through media; interactions that are rewarded are copied, whereas those that are punished are avoided.

Social Learning Theory   Not all behaviorists strictly follow the teachings of Watson and Skinner. Some hold that a person's learning and social experiences, coupled with his or her values and expectations, determine behavior. This is known as **social learning theory.** The most widely read social learning theorists are Albert Bandura, Walter Mischel, and Richard Walters.[157] In general, they hold that children will model their behavior according to the reactions they receive from others, either positive or negative; the behavior of those adults they are in close contact with, especially parents; and the behavior they view on television and in movies. If children observe aggression and see that the aggressive behavior—such as an adult slapping or punching someone during an argument—is approved or rewarded, they will likely react violently during a similar incident. Eventually, the children will master the techniques of aggression and become more confident that their behavior will bring tangible rewards.[158]

By implication, social learning suggests that children who grow up in homes where violence is a way of life may learn to believe that such behavior is acceptable and rewarding. Even if parents tell children not to be violent and punish them if they are, the children will still model their behavior on the observed parental violence. Thus, children are more likely to heed what parents *do* than what they *say*. By middle childhood some children have already acquired an association between their use of aggression against others and the physical punishment they receive at home. Often their aggressive responses are directed at other family members and siblings. The family may serve as a training ground for violence since the child perceives physical punishment as the norm during conflict situations with others.[159]

Adolescent aggression is a result of disrupted dependency relations with parents. This refers to the frustration and anger a child feels when parents provide poor role models and hold back affection and nurturing. Children who lack close dependent ties to their parents may have little opportunity or desire to model themselves after them or to internalize their standards of behavior. In the absence of such internalized controls, the child's aggression is likely to be expressed in an immediate, direct, and socially unacceptable fashion such as violence and aggression.[160]

The Media and Delinquency One aspect of social learning theory that has received a great deal of attention is the belief that children will model their behavior after characters they observe on TV or see in movies. Many parents are concerned about the effects of their children's exposure to violence in the mass media. Often the violence is of a sexual nature, and some experts fear there is a link between sexual violence and viewing pornography.[161]

Children are particularly susceptible to TV imagery. It is believed that many children consider television images to be real, especially if they are authoritatively presented by an adult (as in a commercial). Some children, especially those considered "emotionally disturbed," may be unable to distinguish between fantasy and reality when watching TV shows.[162] Studies have found that frequent TV viewing begins at two and a half years of age and continues at a high level during the preschool and early school years. It has been estimated that children ages 2 to 5 watch TV 27.8 hours each week; children 6 to 11, 24.3 hours per week; and teens, 23 hours per week.[163] But what do they watch? Marketing research indicates that adolescents ages 11 to 14 rent violent horror movies at a higher rate than any other age group; adolescents use older peers and siblings and apathetic parents to gain access to R-rated films. More than 40 percent of U.S. households now have cable TV, which features violent films and shows. Even children's programming is saturated with violence.

What are the alternatives to violent programming? A well-publicized study conducted by researchers at UCLA found that at least 10 network shows made heavy use of violence. Of the 161 television movies monitored (every one that aired that season), 23 raised concerns from viewers about their use of violence, violent theme, violent title, or inappropriate graphicness of a scene. Of the 118 theatrical films monitored, 50 raised concerns about their use of violence. Some television series may contain limited depictions of violence, each of which may be appropriate in its context. However, it was found that commercials for these programs emphasized only the violent scenes with little in the way of context. Even some children's television programs were found to feature "sinister combat" as the theme of the show. The characters were portrayed as happy to fight with little provocation.[164] It is estimated that the average child views 8,000 TV murders before finishing elementary school.

Some critics charge that viewing violent slasher films like *Scream* or *Scream II* cause kids to become violent and aggressive themselves. However, millions of children watch media violence every day yet fail to become violent criminals.

TV and Violence   A number of research methods have been used to measure the effect of TV viewing on violent behavior. One method is to expose groups of people to violent TV shows in a laboratory setting and then compare their behavior to control groups who viewed nonviolent programming; observations have also been made at playgrounds, athletic fields, and residences. Other experiments require individuals to answer attitude surveys after watching violent TV shows. Still another approach is to use aggregate measures of TV viewing; for example, the number of violent TV shows on the air during a given time period is compared to crime rates during the same period.

Most evaluations of experimental data gathered using these techniques indicate that watching violence on TV is correlated with aggressive behaviors.[165] Such august bodies as the American Psychological Association and the National Institute of Mental Health support the TV–violence link.[166] Individuals who view violent TV shows are likely to commence aggressive behavior almost immediately. This phenomenon is demonstrated by numerous reports of copycat behavior after a particularly violent film or TV show is aired. For example, on November 27, 1995, thieves ignited flammable liquid in a New York City subway token booth, seriously injuring the clerk. Their behavior was virtually identical to a robbery scene in the film *Money Train* (with Wesley Snipes and Woody Harrelson) that had been released a few days before.[167]

Rethinking the Media–Violence Link   Though this evidence is persuasive, the relationship between TV viewing and violence is still uncertain. A number of critics say the evidence simply does not support the claim that TV viewing is related to antisocial behavior.[168] Some critics assert that experimental results are inconclusive and short-lived. Children may have an immediate reaction to viewing violence on TV, but aggression is quickly extinguished once the viewing ends.[169] Experiments showing that children act aggressively after watching violent TV shows fail to link aggression to actual criminal behaviors such as rape or assault.

Aggregate data are also inconclusive. Little evidence exists that areas that have the highest levels of violent TV viewing also have rates of violent crime that are above the norm.[170] Millions of children watch violence every night yet fail to become violent criminals. And even if a violent behavior–TV link could be established, it would be difficult to show that antisocial people develop aggressive traits merely from watching TV. Aggressive youths may simply enjoy watching TV shows that conform to and support their behavioral orientation.

Cognitive Theory

cognitive theory
The branch of psychology that studies the perception of reality and the mental processes required to understand the world we live in.

A third area of psychology that has received increasing recognition in recent years is **cognitive theory.** Psychologists with a cognitive perspective focus on mental processes, the way people perceive and mentally represent the world around them, and how they solve problems. The pioneers of this school were Wilhelm Wundt (1832–1920), Edward Titchener (1867–1927), and William James (1842–1920). The cognitive perspective contains several subgroups. Perhaps the most important for criminological theory is the moral and intellectual development branch, which is concerned with how people morally represent and reason about the world.

Jean Piaget (1896–1980), founder of this approach, hypothesized that a child's reasoning processes develop in an orderly fashion, beginning at birth and continuing until age 12 and older.[171] At first, during the *sensorimotor stage,* children respond to the environment in a simple manner, seeking interesting objects and developing their reflexes. By the fourth and final stage, the *formal operations stage,* they have developed into mature adults who can use logic and abstract thought.

Lawrence Kohlberg applied the concept of developmental stages to issues in criminology.[172] He suggested that people travel through stages of moral development during which the basis for moral and ethical decision making changes. It is possible that serious offenders have a moral orientation that differs from that of law-abiding citizens. Kohlberg's stages of development are:

Stage 1: Obedience to power and avoidance of punishment.
Stage 2: Taking responsibility for oneself, meeting one's own needs, and leaving to others the responsibility for themselves.
Stage 3: Being good in the sense of having good motives, having concern for others, and "putting yourself in the other person's shoes."
Stage 4: Maintaining the rules of a society and serving the welfare of the group or society.
Stage 5: Recognizing individuals' rights within a society with agreed-upon rules, a social contract.
Stage 6: An assumed obligation to the principles of justice, equality, and respect for human personality, which apply to all humankind.

Kohlberg classified people according to the stage on this continuum at which their moral development has ceased to grow. In studies conducted by Kohlberg and his associates, criminals were found to be significantly lower in their moral judgment development than noncriminals of the same social background.[173] The majority of noncriminals were classified in stages three and four, whereas a majority of criminals were in stages one and two. Moral development theory suggests that people who obey the law simply to avoid punishment or who have outlooks mainly characterized by self-interest are more likely to commit crimes than those who view the law as something that benefits all of society and who honor the rights of others. Subsequent research has found that a significant number of delinquent youths were in the first two moral development categories, whereas nondelinquents were ranked higher.[174] In addition, higher stages of moral reasoning are associated with honesty, generosity, and nonviolence, which are considered incompatible with delinquency.[175]

Information Processing Cognitive theorists who study information processing try to explain antisocial behavior in terms of perception and analysis of data. When people make decisions, they engage in a sequence of cognitive thought processes. First they encode information so it can be interpreted. Then they search for a proper response and decide on the most appropriate action. Finally, they act on their decision.[176]

Adolescents who use information properly, who are better conditioned to make reasoned judgments, and who can make quick and reasoned decisions when facing emotion-laden events are best able to avoid antisocial behavior choices.[177] In contrast, violence prone adolescents may be using information incorrectly or too slowly when making decisions. They have difficulty making the "right decision" while under stress. One reason is that they may be relying on mental "scripts" learned in early childhood that tell them how to interpret events, what to expect, how they should react, and what the outcome of the interaction should be.[178] Hostile children may have learned improper scripts by observing how others react to events; their own parents' aggressive and inappropriate behavior would have considerable impact. Child abuse victims may have had early and prolonged exposure to violence, which increased their sensitivity to teasing and maltreatment. Oversensitivity to rejection by their peers is a continuation of sensitivity to rejection by parents.[179] Violence becomes a stable behavior because the scripts that emphasize aggressive responses are repeatedly rehearsed as the child matures.

Violence prone kids perceive people as more aggressive than they actually are, and they may feel threatened when there is no reason for alarm. As these children mature, they use fewer cues than most people to process information. Some use violence in a calculating fashion as a means of getting what they want; others react in an overly volatile fashion to the slightest provocation. When they attack victims, they may believe they are defending themselves, even though they are misreading the situation.[180] Adolescents who use violence as a coping technique with others are also more likely to exhibit other social problems such as drugs and alcohol abuse.[181]

There is also evidence that delinquent boys who engage in theft are more likely than nondelinquent youths to exhibit cognitive deficits. For example, delinquent boys have a poor sense of time, leaving them incapable of dealing with or solving social problems in an effective manner.[182]

Cognitive Treatment Treatment based on information processing acknowledges that people are more likely to respond aggressively to a provocation when thoughts intensify the insult or otherwise stir feelings of anger. Cognitive therapists attempt to teach explosive people to control aggressive impulses by experiencing social provocations as problems demanding a solution rather than as insults requiring retaliation. Programs teach problem-solving skills that may include self-disclosure, role playing, listening, following instructions, joining in, and using self-control.[183] Areas for improvement include (1) coping and problem-solving skills; (2) relationships with peers, parents, and other adults; (3) conflict resolution and communication skills and methods for resisting peer pressure related to drug use and violence; (4) consequential thinking and decision-making abilities; (5) prosocial behaviors, including cooperation with others, self-responsibility, respecting others, and public speaking efficacy; and (6) awareness of feelings of others (empathy).[184]

Gerald Patterson and his colleagues at the Oregon Social Learning Center are important figures in the area of cognitive treatment. Their treatment program seems to help parents deal effectively with children who have heretofore been disruptive. It stresses praising desirable behavior and punishing undesirable behavior (such as back talk) with a regimen that includes loss of privileges and short-term isolation in the child's room.[185] Patterson's techniques will be discussed further in Chapter 8. Table 3.4 summarizes the major psychological theories. The next sections discuss two additional targets of psychological research: the proposed links between personality and crime and between intelligence and crime.

Table 3.4

PSYCHOLOGICAL THEORIES

	Major Premise	Strengths
Psychodynamic	The development of the unconscious personality early in childhood influences behavior for the rest of a person's life. Delinquents have weak egos and damaged personalities.	Explains the onset of crime and delinquency. Shows why delinquency and drug abuse cut across class lines.
Behavioral	People commit crime when they model their behavior after others they see being rewarded for the same acts. Behavior is enforced by rewards and extinguished by punishment.	Explains the role of others in the crime process. Shows how family life and media can influence delinquency.
Cognitive	Individual reasoning processes influence behavior. Reasoning is influenced by the way people perceive their environment and by their moral and intellectual development.	Shows why delinquent behavior patterns change over time as people mature and develop their moral reasoning.

Personality and Delinquency

Personality can be defined as the reasonably stable patterns of behavior, including thoughts and emotions, that distinguish one person from another.[186] An individual's personality reflects characteristic ways of adapting to life's demands and problems. The way we behave is a function of how our personality enables us to interpret life events and make appropriate behavioral choices.

Can the cause of delinquency be linked to personality? There has been a great deal of research on this subject and an equal amount of controversy and debate over the findings.[187] In their early work, Sheldon and Eleanor Glueck, who were introduced in the previous chapter, identified a number of personality traits that characterize delinquents:[188]

- self-assertiveness
- defiance
- impulsiveness
- narcissism
- suspicion
- destructiveness
- sadism
- lack of concern for others

- extraversion
- ambivalence
- feeling unappreciated
- distrust of authority
- poor personal skills
- mental instability
- hostility
- resentment

The Gluecks' research is representative of the view that delinquents maintain a distinct personality whose characteristics increase the probability (a) that they will be aggressive and antisocial and (b) that their actions will involve them with agents of social control ranging from teachers to police.

Extraversion and Neuroticism   Since the Gluecks' findings were published, other research efforts have attempted to identify personality traits that would increase the chances for a delinquent career.[189] A common theme is that delinquents are hyperactive, impulsive individuals with short attention spans (attention deficit disorder) who frequently manifest conduct disorders, anxiety disorders, and depression.[190] These traits make them prone to problems ranging from psychopathology to drug abuse, sexual promiscuity, and violence.[191] The well-known psychologist Hans Eysenck identified two important personality traits that he associated with antisocial behavior: extraversion and neuroticism. Eysenck defines **extraverts** as impulsive individuals who lack the ability to examine their own motives and behaviors. **Neuroticism** produces anxiety, tension, and emotional instability.[192] Youths who lack self-insight and are impulsive and emotionally unstable are likely to interpret events differently from youths who are able to give reasoned judgments to life events. The former may act destructively (for example, by using drugs), whereas the latter will be able to reason that such behavior is ultimately self-defeating and life-threatening.

The Antisocial Personality   It has also been suggested that chronic delinquency may result from a personality pattern or syndrome commonly referred to as the **psychopathic personality** or **sociopathic personality** (the terms are used interchangeably). Although no more than 3 percent of the male offending population may be classified as sociopathic, it is possible that a large segment of persistent chronic offenders share this trait.[193]

Psychopathic (sociopathic) youths exhibit a low level of guilt and anxiety and persistently violate the rights of others. Although they may exhibit superficial charm and above-average intelligence, these often mask a disturbed personality that makes them incapable of forming enduring relationships with others. Frequently involved in such deviant behaviors as truancy, running away, lying, substance abuse, and impulsivity, psychopaths lack the ability to empathize with others. From an early age, the psychopath's home life was filled with frustrations, bitterness, and quarreling. Consequently, throughout life the sociopath is unreliable, unstable, demanding, and egocentric. Hervey Cleckley, a leading authority on psychopathy, describes them this way:

> [Psychopaths are] chronically antisocial individuals who are always in trouble, profiting neither from experience nor punishment, and maintaining no real loyalties to any person, group, or code. They are frequently callous and hedonistic, showing marked emotional immaturity, with lack of responsibility, lack of judgment and an ability to rationalize their behavior so that it appears warranted, reasonable and justified.[194]

Youths diagnosed as psychopaths are believed to be thrill-seekers who engage in violent, destructive behavior. Some become gang members and participate in violent and destructive sexual escapades to compensate for a fear of responsibility and an inability to maintain interpersonal relationships.[195] Delinquents have been described as sensation-seekers who desire a hedonistic pursuit of pleasure, an extraverted lifestyle, partying, drinking, and a variety of sexual partners.[196] Psychologists have attempted to treat patients diagnosed as psychopaths by giving them adrenaline, which increases their arousal levels.

The Origins of an Antisocial Personality   A number of factors have been found to contribute to the development of psychopathic personalities. They include having an emotionally disturbed parent, a lack of love, parental rejection during childhood, and inconsistent discipline.[197] Another view, related to the arousal theory discussed earlier in this chapter, is that psychopathy has its basis in a measurable

extravert
A person who behaves impulsively and doesn't have the ability to examine motives and behavior.

neuroticism
A personality trait marked by unfounded anxiety, tension, and emotional instability.

psychopathic personality, sociopathic personality
A person lacking in warmth and affection, exhibiting inappropriate behavioral responses, and unable to learn from experience.

physical condition; psychopaths suffer from lower levels of arousal than those of the general population. Consequently, psychopathic youths may need greater-than-average stimulation to bring them up to comfortable levels.

Psychologist Linda Mealey accepts both these positions when she suggests that there are actually two types of sociopaths, primary and secondary; the first has a genetic basis, whereas the second is environmentally induced. **Primary sociopaths** have inherited traits (that is, a genotype) that predispose them to antisocial behavior. In contrast, **secondary sociopaths** are constitutionally normal but are influenced by negative environmental factors ranging from poor parenting to racial segregation and social conflict.

primary sociopaths
Individuals with an inherited trait that predisposes them to antisocial behavior.

secondary sociopaths
Individuals who are biologically normal but exhibit antisocial behavior due to negative life experiences.

The Delinquency–Personality Link   Numerous attempts have been made to show that psychological tests that measure personality can predict the onset of delinquent behavior. The most common of these is the Minnesota Multiphasic Personality Inventory (MMPI). Developed by R. Starke Hathaway and J. Charnley McKinley, the MMPI has subscales that purport to measure many different personality traits, including psychopathic deviation (Pd scale), schizophrenia (Sc), and hypomania (over activity, Ma).[198]

Early research found that scores on some of the MMPI subscales, especially the Pd scale, predicted delinquency.[199] Over the years a number of researchers claimed that psychological personality tests had the ability to predict future delinquents.[200]

Despite the time and energy put into using MMPI scales to predict delinquency (new versions have been developed over the years), the results are inconclusive. Surveys of the literature of personality testing have not found conclusive evidence that personality traits can predict delinquent involvement.[201] Some delinquents manifested abnormal traits, but others scored no differently than the general population.

The personality tests reviewed in these surveys often had methodological flaws, however, so any negative conclusions must be interpreted with caution. Some recent research efforts have successfully classified offenders and predicted their behavioral traits on the basis of personality inventory scores.[202] Sufficient evidence exists of an association between some kinds of delinquency and personality disturbance to warrant further research on this important yet sensitive issue.

Intelligence and Delinquency

Psychologists have been concerned with the development of intelligence and its subsequent relationship to behavior, noting that children with low IQs are responsible for a disproportionate share of delinquency.

Early criminologists believed low intelligence was a major cause of delinquency. They thought that if one could determine which individuals were less intelligent one might be able to identify potential delinquents before they committed socially harmful acts.[203] Because social scientists had a captive group of subjects in training schools and penal institutions, studies began to appear that measured the correlation between IQ and crime by testing adjudicated juvenile delinquents. Delinquent juveniles were believed to be inherently substandard in intelligence and thus naturally inclined to commit more crimes than more intelligent persons. Thus, juvenile delinquents were used as a test group around which numerous theories about intelligence were built.

Nature Theory   When the newly developed IQ tests were administered to inmates of prisons and juvenile training schools in the first decades of the twentieth century, a large proportion of the inmates scored low on the tests. Henry Goddard found in his studies in 1920 that many institutionalized persons were what he considered "feeble-minded" and thus concluded that at least half of all juvenile delinquents were mental defectives.[204]

Similarly, in 1926 William Healy and Augusta Bronner tested a group of delinquents in Chicago and Boston and found that 37 percent were subnormal in intelligence.[205] They concluded that delinquents were five to ten times more likely to be mentally deficient than nondelinquent boys.

These and other early studies were embraced as proof that low IQ scores indicated potentially delinquent children and that a correlation existed between innate low intelligence and deviant behavior. IQ tests were believed to measure the inborn genetic makeup of individuals, and many criminologists accepted the predisposition of substandard individuals toward delinquency. This view is referred to as the **nature theory** of intelligence.

nature theory
Holds that low intelligence is genetically determined and inherited.

nurture theory
Holds that intelligence is partly biological but mostly sociological; negative environmental factors encourage delinquent behavior and depress intelligence scores for many youths.

Nurture Theory   More culturally sensitive explanations of human behavior in the 1930s led to the **nurture theory** of intelligence. This view holds that intelligence must be viewed as partly biological but primarily sociological. Nurture theorists discredit the notion that people commit crimes because they have low IQs. Instead, they postulate that environmental stimulation from parents, relatives, schools, peer groups, and innumerable others create a child's IQ level and that low IQs result from an environment that also encourages delinquent and criminal behavior.[206] For example, if educational environments could be improved, the result might be both an elevation in IQ scores and a decrease in delinquency.[207]

Studies challenging the assumption that people automatically committed delinquent acts because they had below-average IQs began to appear as early as the 1920s when John Slawson's study of 1,543 delinquent boys in New York institutions found that, although 80 percent of the delinquents achieved lower scores in abstract verbal intelligence than the general population, the delinquents were about normal in mechanical aptitude and nonverbal intelligence. Slawson found no relationship between the number of arrests, the types of offenses, and IQ.[208] In 1931 Edwin Sutherland also evaluated IQ studies of criminals and delinquents and found evidence disputing the association between intelligence and criminality.[209] These findings did much to discredit the notion that a strong relationship exists between IQ and criminality, and for many years the IQ–delinquency link was ignored.

IQ and Delinquency Today   A study published twenty years ago by Travis Hirschi and Michael Hindelang revived interest in the association between IQ and delinquency.[210] After conducting a thorough statistical analysis of IQ and delinquency data, Hirschi and Hindelang concluded both that IQ tests are a valid predictor of intelligence and that "the weight of evidence is that IQ is more important than race and social class" for predicting delinquent involvement. They argued that a low IQ increases the likelihood of delinquent behavior through its effect on school performance. Youths with low IQs do poorly in school, and school failure and academic incompetence are highly related to delinquency.

The Hirschi-Hindelang findings have been supported by a number of research efforts.[211] In their widely read *Crime and Human Nature*, James Q. Wilson and Richard Herrnstein concluded:

> there appears to be a clear and consistent link between criminality and low intelligence. That is, taking all offenders as a group, and ignoring differences among kinds of crime, criminals seem, on the average, to be a bit less bright and to have a different set of intellectual strengths and weaknesses than do noncriminals as a group.[212]

Those social scientists who conclude that IQ influences delinquent behavior are split on the structure of the associations. Some believe IQ has an indirect influence on delinquency. For example, children with low IQs are more likely to engage in delinquent behavior because their poor verbal ability is a handicap in school.

Low IQ leads to school failure, and educational underachievement has consistently been associated with delinquency.[213] Even high-risk youths are less likely to become persistent delinquents if they have relatively high IQs; low IQ increases the probability of a stable delinquent career.[214] The relationship between IQ and delinquency has been found to be consistent after controlling for class, race, and personality traits.[215]

Some experts believe IQ may have a direct influence on the onset of delinquent involvement. The key linkage between IQ and delinquency is the ability to manipulate abstract concepts. Low intelligence limits adolescents' ability to "foresee the consequences of their offending and to appreciate the feelings of victims."[216] Therefore, youths with limited intelligence are more likely to misinterpret events and gestures, act foolishly, take risks, and engage in harmful behavior.

The IQ and Delinquency Controversy The relationship between IQ and delinquency is an extremely controversial issue because it implies a condition is present at birth that accounts for a child's delinquent behavior throughout the life cycle and that this condition is not easily changed or improved. Research shows that measurements of intelligence taken in infancy are a good predictor of later IQ.[217] By implication, if delinquency is not spread evenly through the social structure, neither is intelligence.

There is also research indicating that IQ level has a negligible influence on delinquent behavior.[218] IQ research has also been tainted by charges that tests are culturally biased and invalid, making any existing evidence at best inconclusive.

If, as some believe, the link between IQ and crime is indirect, then delinquency may be a reflection of poor school performance and educational failure.[219] As Wilson and Herrnstein put it, "A child who chronically loses standing in the competition of the classroom may feel justified in settling the score outside, by violence, theft, and other forms of defiant illegality."[220] The relationship runs from low IQ to poor school performance to frustration to delinquency, and school officials need to recognize the problem and plan programs to help underachievers perform better in school. Because the hypothesized relationship between IQ and delinquency, even if proved to be valid, is an indirect one, educational enrichment programs can help counteract any influence intellectual impairment has on the predilection of young people to commit crime.

Critiquing Trait Theory Views

Trait theories have been criticized on a number of grounds. One view is that the research methodologies they employ are weak and invalid. Most research efforts use adjudicated or incarcerated offenders. It is often difficult to determine whether findings represent the delinquent population or merely those most likely to be arrested and adjudicated by officials of the justice system. For example, some critics have described the methods used in heredity studies as "poorly designed, ambiguously reported and exceedingly inadequate in addressing the relevant issues."[221]

Some critics also fear that trait-theory research can be socially and politically damaging. If an above-average number of indigent youths become delinquent offenders, can it be assumed that the less affluent are impulsive, greedy, have low IQs, or are genetically inferior? The implications of this conclusion are unacceptable to many social scientists in light of what is known about race, gender, and class bias.

Critics also suggest that trait theory is limited as a generalized explanation of delinquent behavior because it fails to account for the known patterns of criminal behavior. Delinquent behavior trends seem to conform to certain patterns linked to social and ecological rather than individual factors—that is, to social class, seasonality, population density, and gender roles. Social forces that appear to be influencing the onset and maintenance of delinquent behavior are not accounted for by explanations of delinquency that focus on the individual. If, as is often the case, the delinquency rate is higher in one neighborhood than in another, are we to conclude that youths in the high-crime area are more likely to be watching violent TV shows or eating more sugar-coated cereals than those in low-crime neighborhoods? How can individual traits explain the fact that crime rates vary between cities and between regions?

Defending Trait Theory

> The legitimization of social-psychological, psychiatric, and biosocial approaches to deviant behavior may prove to be an important and productive paradigm shift in the decades ahead.[222]

Theorists who focus on individual behavior contend that critics overlook the fact that their research often gives equal weight to environmental and social as well as to mental and physical factors.[223] For example, some people may have particular developmental problems that place them at a disadvantage in society, limit their chances of conventional success, and heighten their feelings of anger, frustration, and rage. Though the incidence of these personal traits may be spread evenly across the social structure, families in one segment of the population may have the financial resources to treat these problems, whereas families in another segment may lack the economic means and the institutional support needed to help their children. Delinquency rate differences may then result from differential access to opportunities either to commit crime or to receive the care and treatment needed to correct and compensate for developmental problems.

In addition, trait theorists believe that, like it or not, youths are in fact different and may have differing potentials for antisocial acts. For example, gender differences in the violence rate may be explained by the fact that after centuries of aggressive mating behavior, males have become naturally more violent than females.[224] Male aggression may be more a matter of genetic transfer than of socialization or cultural patterns.

Trait Theory and Delinquency Prevention

Many trait theorists are also practitioners and clinicians, so it is not surprising that a great many delinquency prevention efforts are based in psychological and biosocial theory. As a group, trait-theory perspectives on delinquency suggest that prevention efforts should be directed at strengthening a youth's home life and personal relationships. Almost all of these theoretical efforts point to the child's home life as a key factor in delinquent behavior. If parents cannot supply proper nurturing, love, care, discipline, nutrition, and so on, the child cannot develop properly. Whether one believes that delinquency has a biosocial basis, a psychological basis, or a combination of both, it is evident that delinquency prevention efforts should be oriented to reach children early in their development.

County welfare agencies and privately funded treatment centers have offered counseling and other mental health services to families referred by schools, by welfare agents, and by juvenile court authorities. In some instances, intervention is focused on a particular family problem that has the potential for producing delinquent behavior, for example, alcohol and drug problems, child abuse, or sexual abuse. In other situations, intervention is more generalized and oriented toward developing the self-image of parents and children or improving discipline in the family.

Some programs utilize treatment regimens based on specific theories of delinquency causation (such as cognitive or behavioral modification therapies). For example, the Decisions to Actions delinquency prevention program implemented in Kincheloe, Michigan, is organized around cognitive-behavioral restructuring of children's personalities. Its main focus is changing attitudes, beliefs, and views associated with improper feelings and behaviors. Youths are taught to identify poor decision making and to explore the underlying thinking behind these decisions. The youths also are taught relapse prevention techniques that enable them to better manage their emotions, behavior, and environment. The ten-week program includes an assessment process, meetings between the youths and personal mentors, victim empathy sessions where convicted felons speak with the youths, and team-building exercises.[225]

In addition, individual approaches have been used to prevent court-adjudicated youths from engaging in further criminal activities. This is sometimes referred to as **secondary prevention** or **special prevention.** It has become almost universal for incarcerated and court-adjudicated youths to be given some form of mental and physical evaluation before they begin their term of correctional treatment. Such rehabilitation methods as psychological counseling and psychotropic medication (involving drugs such as Valium or Ritalin) are often prescribed. In some instances, rehabilitation programs are provided through "drop-in" centers that service youths who are able to remain in their homes; more intensive programs require residential care and treatment. The creation of such programs illustrates that agents of the juvenile justice system believe many delinquent youths and status offenders have psychological or physical problems and that their successful treatment can help reduce repeat criminal behavior. Faith in this treatment approach suggests widespread agreement among juvenile justice system professionals that the cause of delinquency can be traced to individual pathology. If not, why bother treating them?

The influence of psychological theory on delinquency prevention has been extensive, and programs based on biosocial theory have been dormant for some time. However, institutions are beginning to sponsor demonstration projects designed to study the influence of diet on crime and to determine whether regulating the metabolism can affect behavior. Such efforts are relatively new and untested. Similarly, schools are making an effort to help youths with learning disabilities and other developmental problems. Delinquency prevention efforts based on biocriminological theory are still in their infancy. The Case in Point explores some questions arising out of the biosocial approach.

Some questions remain about the effectiveness of individual treatment as a delinquency prevention technique. Little hard evidence exists that clinical treatment alone can prevent delinquency or rehabilitate known delinquents. Critics still point to the failure of the famous Cambridge-Somerville Youth Study as evidence that clinical treatment has little value. In that effort, 325 high-risk predelinquents were given intensive counseling and treatment, and their progress was compared with a control group that received no special attention. A well-known evaluation of the project by Joan and William McCord found that the treated youths were more likely to become involved in law violation than the untreated controls.[226] By implication, the danger is that the efforts designed to help youths may actually stigmatize and label them, hindering their efforts to live conventional lives.

Critics such as Edwin Schur argue that less is better—that the more we try to help youths, the more likely they will be to see themselves as different, as outcasts, as troublemakers, and so on.[227] Such questions have led to the development of

secondary prevention, special prevention
Psychological counseling, psychotropic medications, and other rehabilitation treatment programs designed to prevent repeat offenses.

You are a state legislator who is a member of the subcommittee on juvenile justice. Your committee has been asked to redesign the state's juvenile code because of public outrage over serious juvenile crime.

At an open hearing, a professor from the local university testifies that she has devised a sure-fire test to predict violence prone delinquents. The procedure involves brain scans, DNA testing, and blood analysis. Used with samples of incarcerated adolescents, her procedure has been able to distinguish with 90 percent accuracy between youths with a history of violence and those who are exclusively property offenders. The professor testifies that if each juvenile offender were tested with her techniques, the violence prone career offender could easily be identified and given special treatment (for example, separated from the general juvenile population or given a longer sentence).

Opponents argue that this type of testing is unconstitutional because it violates the Fifth Amendment right against self-incrimination and can unjustly label nonviolent offenders. Any attempt to base policy on biosocial makeup seems inherently wrong and unfair. Those who favor the professor's approach maintain that it is not uncommon to single out the insane or mentally incompetent for special treatment and that these conditions often have a biological basis. It is better that a few delinquents be unfairly labeled than that seriously violent offenders be ignored before it is too late.

■ Should special laws be created to deal with the "potentially" dangerous offender?

■ Should offenders be typed on the basis of their biological characteristics?

■ Is a 10 percent rate of inaccuracy too high to be considered for a basis of prediction? What would you do if the test were 100 percent reliable?

prevention efforts designed to influence the social as well as the psychological world of delinquent and predelinquent youths (see Chapters 5 and 6).

Both choice and trait theories have been embraced by conservatives because they focus on the individual offender's personal characteristics and traits rather than on the social environment. Both theoretical positions agree that delinquency can be prevented by dealing with the youths who engage in crime, not by transforming the social conditions associated with youth crime. In contrast, more liberal delinquency experts (whose work will be discussed in Chapters 4, 5, and 6), view the environment as the main source of delinquency-producing phenomena.

SUMMARY

Criminological theories that focus on the individual can be classified according to two major groups: choice theories and trait theories.

Choice theory holds that people have free will to control their actions. Delinquency is a product of weighing the risks of crime against its benefits. If the risk is greater than the gain, people will choose not to commit crimes. One way of creating a greater risk is to make sure that the punishments associated with delinquency are severe, certain, and fast.

There are several major subcategories of choice theory. The first, routine activities theory, maintains that a pool of motivated offenders exists and that they will take advantage of suitable unguarded targets.

Deterrence theory holds that if criminals are indeed rational, an inverse relationship should exist between punishment and crime. Deterrence theory has been criticized on the grounds that it wrongfully assumes that criminals make a rational choice before committing crimes and because it does not take into account the social and psychological factors that may influence delinquency. Research designed to test the validity of the deterrence concept has not indicated that deterrent measures actually reduce the delinquency rate.

Specific deterrence theory holds that the crime rate can be reduced if known offenders are punished so severely that they never commit crimes again. However, there is little evidence that harsh punishments actually reduce the crime rate. Incapacitation theory maintains that if deterrence does not work, the best course of action is to incarcerate known offenders for long periods of time so they lack criminal opportunity. Research efforts have not provided clear-cut proof that experiencing punishment actually will reduce crime rates.

Situational crime prevention strategies aim to reduce opportunities for crime to take place. By imposing obstacles that make it difficult to offend, such strategies strive to dissuade would-be offenders.

Choice theorists argue that delinquent behavior can be prevented if youths can be deterred from illegal acts. Consequently, they agree that the punishment for delinquency should be increased. One method is to transfer youths to the criminal courts or to grant the adult justice system original jurisdiction over serious juvenile cases. Similarly, some delinquency experts advocate the use of incapacitation for serious juvenile offenders—for example, using mandatory, long-term sentences for chronic delinquents.

Trait theories hold that personal and environmental factors dictate behavior choices, that delinquents do not choose to commit crimes freely but are influenced by forces beyond their control. Two types of trait theory are biological and psychological.

One of the earliest branches of biological theory was formulated by Cesare Lombroso, who originated the concept of the "born criminal" and linked delinquency to inborn traits. Following his lead were theories based on genetic inheritance and body build. Although biological theory was in disrepute for many years, it has recently reemerged in importance. Biochemical, neurological, and genetic factors have been linked to aggressiveness and violence in youth. However, because biosocial theory has not been subjected to methodologically sound tests, the results remain problematic.

Psychological theories also fall into several categories. Some theorists rely on Freud's psychoanalytic theory and link delinquency to ego development and personality. Others use a behavioral perspective, which emphasizes overt behavior rather than unconscious processes. Social learning theorists hold that children imitate the adult behavior they observe live or on television. Children who are exposed to violence and see it rewarded may become violent as adults. Cognitive psychology is concerned with human development and how people perceive the world. Criminality is viewed as a function of improper information processing or lack of moral development.

Psychological traits, such as personality and intelligence, have been linked to delinquency. One important area of study has been the psychopath, a person who lacks emotion and concern for others. The controversial issue of the relationship of IQ to delinquency has received new interest with the publication of research studies purporting to show that delinquents have lower IQs than nondelinquents.

Many delinquency prevention efforts are based on psychological theory. Judges commonly order delinquent youths to receive counseling and other mental health care. Recently, some adjudicated delinquent offenders have been given biochemical therapy.

KEY TERMS

choice theory	equipotentiality	cognitive theory
trait theory	biosocial theory	extravert
free will	minimal brain dysfunction	neuroticism
utilitarian	(MBD)	psychopathic personality
classical criminology	learning disability (LD)	sociopathic personality
routine activity theory	evolutionary theory	primary sociopaths
predatory crimes	psychodynamic theory	secondary sociopaths
general deterrence	identity crisis	nature theory
specific deterrence	latent delinquents	nurture theory
criminal atavism	behaviorism	secondary prevention
somatotype school	social learning theory	special prevention

Read the following article from InfoTrac College Edition:

Unified Kvetch Theory. (reasons for schoolchildren's criminal behavior) Walter Olson. *Reason* August-Sep 1998

The effectiveness of deterrence theory is quite debatable. Although a number of studies have shown that it works with certain crimes, little evidence exists that deterrence alone can prevent crime. Deterring juveniles may be difficult because they are often subject to more lenient punishment.

Assume that the theory proposed in this article is valid and can reliably explain the majority of youthful criminal offenses. What steps should we take to implement policy associated with this idea? More specifically, how should we go about discouraging such "radical individualism"?

QUESTIONS FOR DISCUSSION

1. Is there such a thing as the "criminal man"?
2. Is crime psychologically abnormal? Can there be "normal" crimes?
3. Apply psychodynamic theory to delinquent acts such as shoplifting and breaking and entering a house.
4. Can delinquent behavior be deterred by the threat of punishment? If not, how can it be controlled?
5. Should we incarcerate violent juvenile offenders for long periods of time, say, ten years or more?
6. Does watching violence on TV and in films encourage youths to be aggressive and antisocial? Do advertisements for beer featuring attractive, scantily dressed young men and women encourage drinking and precocious sex? If not, why bother advertising?
7. Discuss the characteristics of psychopaths. Do you know anyone who fits the description?

NOTES

1. "Teen-Ager Accused of Killing Says He Got Demons' Orders," *New York Times* 5 June 1998.
2. Marvin Wolfgang, Robert Figlio, and Thorsten Sellin, *Delinquency in a Birth Cohort* (Chicago: University of Chicago Press, 1972).
3. Alan Lizotte, Terence Thornberry, Marvin Krohn, Deborah Chard-Wierschem, and David McDowall, "Neighborhood Context and Delinquency: A Longitudinal Analysis," in H. J. Kerner and E. Weitekamp, eds., *Cross-National Longitudinal Research on Human Development and Criminal Behavior* (Dordrecht, The Netherlands: Kluwer Academic Publishers, 1993), pp. 11–15.
4. Jeremy Bentham, in Wilfred Harrison, ed., *A Fragment on Government and an Introduction to the Principles of Morals and Legislation* (Oxford: Basic Blackwell, 1967).
5. See, generally, Ernest Van den Haag, *Punishing Criminals* (New York: Basic Books, 1975).
6. See, generally, James Q. Wilson, *Thinking about Crime* (New York: Basic Books, 1975).
7. Cesare Beccaria, *On Crimes and Punishments,* 6th ed., trans. Henry Paolucci (Indianapolis: Bobbs-Merrill, 1977), p. 43.
8. F. E. Devine, "Cesare Beccaria and the Theoretical Foundations of Modern Penal Jurisprudence," *New England Journal on Prison Law* 7:8–21 (1982).
9. Charles Murray and Louis Cox, *Beyond Probation* (Beverly Hills: Sage, 1979).
10. James Q. Wilson and Richard Herrnstein, *Crime and Human Nature* (New York: Simon and Schuster, 1985), p. 396.
11. Mary Tuck and David Riley, "The Theory of Reasoned Action: A Decision Theory of Crime," in D. Cornish and R. Clarke, eds., *The Reasoning Criminal* (New York: Springer-Verlag, 1986), pp. 156–69.
12. Felix Padilla, *The Gang as an American Enterprise* (New Brunswick, N.J.: Rutgers University Press, 1992); see also,
   Martin Sanchez-Jankowski, *Islands in the Street: Gangs and American Urban Society* (Berkeley: University of California Press, 1991).
13. Bruce Jacobs, "Crack Dealers' Apprehension Avoidance Techniques: A Case of Restrictive Deterrence," *Justice Quarterly* 13:359–81 (1996).
14. Ibid., p. 367.
15. See, generally, Derek Cornish and Ronald Clarke, eds., *The Reasoning Criminal* (New York: Springer-Verlag, 1986); see also Philip Cook, "The Demand and Supply of Criminal Opportunities," in Michael Tonry and Norval Morris, eds., *Crime and Justice,* vol. 7 (Chicago: University of Chicago Press, 1986), pp. 1–28; Ronald Clarke and Derek Cornish, "Modeling Offenders' Decisions: A Framework for Research and Policy," in Michael Tonry and Norval Morris, eds., *Crime and Justice,* vol. 6 (Chicago: University of Chicago Press, 1985), pp. 147–87; Morgan Reynolds, *Crime by Choice: An Economic Analysis* (Dallas: Fisher Institute, 1985).
16. Travis Hirschi, "Rational Choice and Social Control Theories of Crime," in D. Cornish and R. Clarke, eds., *The Reasoning Criminal* (New York: Springer-Verlag, 1986), p. 114.
17. Michael Hindelang, Michael Gottfredson, and James Garofalo, *Victims of Personal Crime: An Empirical Foundation for a Theory of Personal Victimization* (Cambridge, Mass.: Ballinger, 1978).
18. James Massey, Marvin Krohn, and Lisa Bonati, "Property Crime and the Routine Activities of Individuals," *Journal of Research in Crime and Delinquency* 26:378–400 (1989).
19. Lawrence Cohen and Marcus Felson, "Social Change and Crime Rate Trends: A Routine Activities Approach," *American Sociological Review* 44:588–608 (1979).
20. David Maume, "Inequality and Metropolitan Rape Rates: A Routine Activity Approach," *Justice Quarterly* 6:513–27 (1989).

21. Denise Osborn, Alan Trickett, and Rob Elder, "Area Characteristics and Regional Variates as Determinants of Area Property Crime Levels," *Journal of Quantitative Criminology* 8:265–82 (1992).

22. Massey, Krohn, and Bonati, "Property Crime and Routine Activities of Individuals," p. 397.

23. Lawrence Cohen, Marcus Felson, and Kenneth Land, "Property Crime Rates in the United States: A Macrodynamic Analysis, 1947–1977, with Ex-Ante Forecasts for the Mid-1980's," *American Journal of Sociology* 86:90–118 (1980).

24. Steven Messner and Kenneth Tardiff, "The Social Ecology of Urban Homicide: An Application of the 'Routine Activities' Approach," *Criminology* 23:241–67 (1985).

25. Leslie Kennedy and David Forde, "Routine Activities and Crime: An Analysis of Victimization in Canada," *Criminology* 28:137–52 (1990).

26. Robert O'Brien, "Relative Cohort Sex and Age-Specific Crime Rates: An Age-Period-Relative-Cohort-Size Model," *Criminology* 27:57–78 (1989).

27. D. Wayne Osgood, Janet Wilson, Patrick O'Malley, Jerald Bachman, and Lloyd Johnston, "Routine Activities and Individual Deviant Behavior," *American Sociological Review* 61:635–55 (1996).

28. Matthew Ploeger, "Youth Employment and Delinquency: Reconsidering a Problematic Relationship," *Criminology* 35:659–75 (1997).

29. Ernest Van den Haag, "The Criminal Law as a Threat System," *Journal of Criminal Law and Criminology* 73:709–85 (1982).

30. Beccaria, *On Crimes and Punishments*.

31. For the classic analysis on the subject, see Johannes Andenaes, *Punishment and Deterrence* (Ann Arbor: University of Michigan Press, 1974).

32. Gordon Bazemore and Mark Umbreit, "Rethinking the Sanctioning Function in Juvenile Court: Retributive or Restorative Responses to Youth Crime," *Crime and Delinquency* 41: 296–316 (1995).

33. Bruce Jacobs, "Anticipatory Undercover Targeting in High Schools," *Journal of Criminal Justice* 22:445–57 (1994).

34. Leona Lee, "Factors Determining Waiver in a Juvenile Court," *Journal of Criminal Justice* 22:329–39 (1994).

35. *Wilkins v. Missouri; Stanford v. Kentucky*, 109 S.Ct. 2969 (1989).

36. Carol Kohfeld and John Sprague, "Demography, Police Behavior, and Deterrence," *Criminology* 28:111–36 (1990).

37. Steven Klepper and Daniel Nagin, "The Deterrent Effect of Perceived Certainty and Severity of Punishment Revisited," *Criminology* 27:721–46 (1989).

38. See, generally, Raymond Paternoster, "The Deterrent Effect of Perceived Certainty and Severity of Punishment: A Review of the Evidence and Issues," *Justice Quarterly* 42:173–217 (1987); idem, "Absolute and Restrictive Deterrence in a Panel of Youth: Explaining the Onset, Persistence/Desistance, and Frequency of Delinquent Offending," *Social Problems* 36: 289–307 (1989).

39. Wanda Foglia, "Perceptual Deterrence and the Mediating Effect of Internalized Norms among Inner-City Teenagers," *Journal of Research in Crime and Delinquency* 34:414–42 (1997); Donald Green, "Measures of Illegal Behavior in Individual-Level Deterrence Research," *Journal of Research in Crime and Delinquency* 26:253–75 (1989); Charles Tittle, *Sanctions and Social Deviance: The Question of Deterrence* (New York: Praeger, 1980).

40. Eric Jensen and Linda Metsger, "A Test of the Deterrent Effect of Legislative Waiver on Violent Juvenile Crime," *Crime and Delinquency* 40:96–104 (1994).

41. Foglia, "Perceptual Deterrence and the Mediating Effect of Internalized Norms among Inner-City Teenagers."

42. Ibid.

43. Bureau of Justice Statistics, *Prisoners and Drugs* (Washington, D.C.: U.S. Government Printing Office, 1983); idem, *Prisoners and Alcohol* (Washington, D.C.: U.S. Government Printing Office, 1983).

44. Maynard Erickson and Jack Gibbs, "Punishment, Deterrence, and Juvenile Justice," in D. Shichor and D. Kelly, eds., *Critical Issues in Juvenile Justice* (Lexington, Mass.: Lexington Books, 1980), pp. 183–202.

45. Christina Dejong, "Survival Analysis and Specific Deterrence: Integrating Theoretical and Empirical Models of Recidivism," *Criminology* 35:561–76 (1997).

46. Paul Tracy and Kimberly Kempf-Leonard, *Continuity and Discontinuity in Criminal Careers* (New York: Plenum Press, 1996).

47. Pamela Lattimore, Christy Visher, and Richard Linster, "Predicting Rearrest for Violence among Serious Youthful Offenders," *Journal of Research in Crime and Delinquency* 32:54–83 (1995).

48. David Altschuler, "Juveniles and Violence: Is There an Epidemic and What Can Be Done," paper presented at the American Society of Criminology Meeting, Boston, Mass., November 1995; Charles Murray and Louis B. Cox, *Beyond Probation* (Beverly Hills, Calif.: Sage, 1979).

49. Marcus Felson, "Routine Activities and Crime Prevention, in National Council for Crime Prevention, ed., *Studies on Crime and Crime Prevention, Annual Review,* vol. 1 (Stockholm: Scandinavian University Press, 1992), pp. 30–34.

50. Barry Webb, "Steering Column Locks and Motor Vehicle Theft: Evaluations for Three Countries," in Ronald Clarke, ed., *Crime Prevention Studies* (Monsey, N.Y.: Criminal Justice Press, 1994), pp. 71–89.

51. Lawrence Sherman, "Police Crackdowns: Initial and Residual Deterrence," in Michael Tonry and Norval Morris, eds., *Crime and Justice, A Review of Research,* vol. 12 (Chicago: University of Chicago Press, 1990), pp. 1–48.

52. Taken from the famous title of an article by Walter Reckless, Simon Dinitz, and Ellen Murray, "The Good Boy in a High Delinquency Area," *Journal of Criminal Law, Criminology, and Police Science* 48:18–26 (1957).

53. Massey, Krohn, and Bonati, "Property Crime and the Routine Activities of Individuals."

54. David Shantz, "Conflict, Aggression, and Peer Status: An Observational Study," *Child Development* 57:1322–32 (1986).

55. For an excellent review of Lombroso's work, as well as that of other well-known theorists, see Randy Martin, Robert Mutchnick, and W. Timothy Austin, *Criminological Thought, Pioneers Past and Present* (New York: Macmillan, 1990).

56. Marvin Wolfgang, "Cesare Lombroso," in Herman Mannheim, ed., *Pioneers in Criminology* (Montclair, N.J.: Patterson Smith, 1970), pp. 232–71.

57. Gina Lombroso-Ferrero, *Criminal Man According to the Classification of Cesare Lombroso* (1911; reprint, Montclair, N.J.: Patterson Smith, 1972), p. 7.

58. Edwin Driver, "Charles Buckman Goring," in Herman Mannheim, ed., *Pioneers in Criminology* (Montclair, N.J.: Patterson Smith, 1970), pp. 429–42.

59. See, generally, Thorsten Sellin, "Enrico Ferri," in Herman Mannheim, ed., *Pioneers in Criminology* (Montclair, N.J.: Patterson Smith, 1970), pp. 361–84.

60. Driver, "Charles Buckman Goring," pp. 434–35.

61. Ibid., p. 440.

62. See Richard Dugdale, *The Jukes* (New York: Putnam, 1910); Arthur Estabrook, *The Jukes in 1915* (Washington, D.C.: Carnegie Institute of Washington, 1916).

63. Ernst Kretschmer, *Physique and Character,* trans. W. J. H. Spratt (London: Kegan Paul, 1925).

64. William Sheldon, *Varieties of Delinquent Youth* (New York: Harper Bros., 1949).

65. For a review of Sheldon's legacy, see C. Peter Herman, "The Shape of Man," *Contemporary Psychology* 37:525–30 (1992).

66. Nicole Hahn Rafter, "Criminal Anthropology in the United States," *Criminology* 30:525–47 (1992).

67. B. R. McCandless, W. S. Persons, and A. Roberts, "Perceived Opportunity, Delinquency, Race, and Body Build among Delinquent Youth," *Journal of Consulting and Clinical Psychology* 38:281–83 (1972).

68. Edmond O. Wilson, *Sociobiology: The New Synthesis* (Cambridge: Harvard University Press, 1975).

69. For a general review, see John Archer, "Human Sociobiology: Basic Concepts and Limitations," *Journal of Social Issues* 47: 11–26 (1991).

70. Arthur Caplan, *The Sociobiology Debate: Readings on Ethical and Scientific Issues* (New York: Harper and Row, 1978).

71. See C. Ray Jeffrey, "Criminology as an Interdisciplinary Behavioral Science," *Criminology* 16:149–67 (1978).

72. Diana Fishbein, "Selected Studies on the Biology of Crime," in John Conklin, ed., *New Perspectives in Criminology* (Needham Heights, Mass.: Allyn and Bacon, 1996), pp. 26–38.

73. Anthony Walsh and Lee Ellis, "Shoring Up the Big Three: Improving Criminological Theories with Biosocial Concepts," paper presented at the Annual Society of Criminology Meeting, San Diego, Calif., November 1997, p. 15.

74. Terrie Moffitt, "Adolescence-Limited and Life-Course Persistent Antisocial Behavior: A Developmental Taxonomy," *Psychological Review* 100:674–701 (1993).

75. For a thorough review of the biosocial perspective, see Diana Fishbein, "Biological Perspectives in Criminology," *Criminology* 28:27–72 (1990).

76. See, generally, Adrian Raine, *The Psychopathology of Crime* (San Diego, Calif.: Academic Press, 1993); see also Leonard Hippchen, *The Ecologic-Biochemical Approaches to Treatment of Delinquents and Criminals* (New York: Van Nostrand Reinhold, 1978).

77. Paul Marshall, "Allergy and Depression: A Neurochemical Threshold Model of the Relation between the Illnesses," *Psychological Bulletin* 113:23–43 (1993); Elizabeth McNeal and Peter Cimbolic, "Antidepressants and Biochemical Theories of Depression," *Psychological Bulletin* 99:361–74 (1986); for an opposing view, see "Adverse Reactions to Food in Young Children," *Nutrition Reviews* 46:120–21 (1988).

78. Marshall, "Allergy and Depression: A Neurochemical Threshold Model of the Relation between the Illnesses."

79. Raine, *The Psychopathology of Crime*, p. 212.

80. Deborah Denno, "Human Biology and Criminal Responsibility: Free Will or Free Ride?", *University of Pennsylvania Law Review* 137:615–71 (1988).

81. Leonard Hippchen, "Some Possible Biochemical Aspects of Criminal Behavior," *Journal of Behavioral Ecology* 2:1–6 (1981); Sarnoff Mednick and Jan Volavka, "Biology and Crime," in N. Morris and M. Tonry, eds., *Crime and Justice*, vol. 2 (Chicago: University of Chicago Press, 1980), pp. 85–159.

82. Stephen Schoenthaler, "Malnutrition and Maladaptive Behavior: Two Correlational Analyses and a Double-Blind Placebo-Controlled Challenge in Five States," in W. B. Essman, ed., *Nutrients and Brain Function* (New York: Karger, 1987); Alexander Schauss and C. Simonsen, "A Critical Analysis of the Diets of Chronic Juvenile Offenders, Part I," *Journal of Orthomolecular Psychiatry* 8:149–57 (1979).

83. Stephen Schoenthaler and Walter Doraz, "Types of Offenses which Can Be Reduced in an Institutional Setting Using Nutritional Intervention," *International Journal of Biosocial Research* 4:74–84 (1983); and idem, "Diet and Crime," *International Journal of Biosocial Research* 4:29–39 (1983); J. Kershner and W. Hawke, "Megavitamins and Learning Disorders: A Controlled Double-Blind Experiment," *Journal of Nutrition* 109:819–26 (1979).

84. Stephen Schoenthaler, Walter Doraz, and James Wakefield, "The Impact of a Low Food Additive and Sucrose Diet on Academic Performance in 803 New York City Public Schools," *International Journal of Biosocial Research* 8:185–95 (1986).

85. Richard Milich and William Pelham, "Effects of Sugar Ingestion on the Classroom and Playgroup Behavior of Attention Deficit Disordered Boys," *Journal of Counseling and Clinical Psychology* 54:714–18 (1986).

86. Mark Wolraich, Scott Lindgren, Phyllis Stumbo, Lewis Steginck, Mark Appelbaum, and Mary Kiritsy, "Effects of Diets High in Sucrose or Aspartame on the Behavior and Cognitive Performance of Children," *The New England Journal of Medicine* 330: 303–6 (1994).

87. Dian Gans, "Sucrose and Unusual Childhood Behavior," *Nutrition Today* 26:8–14 (1991).

88. Marcel Kinsbourne, "Sugar and the Hyperactive Child," *The New England Journal of Medicine* 330:355–56 (1994).

89. Stephen Schoenthaler, "Institutional Nutritional Policies and Criminal Behavior," *Nutrition Today* 24:16–24 (1985), at 24.

90. Christy Miller Buchanan, Jacquelynne Eccles, and Jill Becker, "Are Adolescents the Victims of Raging Hormones? Evidence for Activational Effects of Hormones on Moods and Behavior at Adolescence," *Psychological Bulletin* 111:62–107 (1992).

91. Fishbein, "Selected Studies on the Biology of Antisocial Behavior."

92. Diana Fishbein, David Lozovsky, and Jerome Jaffe, "Impulsivity, Aggression and Neuroendocrine Responses to Serotonergic Stimulation in Substance Abusers," paper presented at the American Society of Criminology Meeting, Reno, Nev., November 1989.

93. Kytja Voeller, "Right-Hemisphere Deficit Syndrome in Children," *American Journal of Psychiatry* 143:1004–9 (1986).

94. Terrie Moffitt, "Adolescence-Limited and Life-Course Persistent Antisocial Behavior: A Developmental Taxonomy," *Psychological Review* 100:674–701 (1993).

95. Leila Beckwith and Arthur Parmelee, "EEG Patterns of Preterm Infants, Home Environment, and Later IQ," *Child Development* 57:777–89 (1986).

96. Adrian Raine, Patricia Brennan, Brigitte Mednick, and Sarnoff Mednick, "High Rates of Violence, Crime, Academic Problems, and Behavioral Problems in Males with Both Early Neuromotor Deficits and Unstable Family Environments," *Archives of General Psychiatry* 53:544–49 (1966).

97. Stephen Tibbetts, "Low Birth Weight, Disadvantaged Environment and Early Onset: A Test of Moffitt's Interactional Hypothesis," paper presented at the American Society of Criminology Meeting, Boston, Mass., November 1995.

98. Dorothy Otnow Lewis, Jonathan Pincus, Marilyn Feldman, Lori Jackson, and Barbara Bard, "Psychiatric, Neurological, and Psychoeducational Characteristics of 15 Death Row Inmates in the United States," *American Journal of Psychiatry* 143:838–45 (1986).

99. See, generally, R. R. Monroe, *Brain Dysfunction in Aggressive Criminals* (Lexington, Mass.: D. C. Heath, 1978).

100. Adrian Raine et al., "Interhemispheric Transfer in Schizophrenics, Depressives and Normals with Schizoid Tendencies," *Journal of Abnormal Psychology* 98:35–41 (1989).

101. Jean Seguin, Robert Pihl, Philip Harden, Richard Tremblay, and Bernard Boulerice, "Cognitive and Neuropsychological Characteristics of Physically Aggressive Boys," *Journal of Abnormal Psychology* 104:614–24 (1995).

102. D. Williams, "Neural Factors Related to Habitual Aggression—Consideration of Differences between Habitual Aggressives and Others Who Have Committed Crimes of Violence," *Brain* 92:503–20 (1969).

103. Charlotte Johnson and William Pelham, "Teacher Ratings Predict Peer Ratings of Aggression at 3-Year Follow-Up in Boys with Attention Deficit Disorder with Hyperactivity," *Journal of Consulting and Clinical Psychology* 54:571–2 (1987).

104. Cited in Charles Post, "The Link between Learning Disabilities and Juvenile Delinquency: Cause, Effect, and 'Present Solutions'," *Juvenile and Family Court Journal* 31:59 (1981).

105. For a general review, see Concetta Culliver, "Juvenile Delinquency and Learning Disability: Any Link?", paper presented at the Academy of Criminal Justice Sciences, San Francisco, April 1988.

106. Joel Zimmerman, William Rich, Ingo Keilitz, and Paul Broder, "Some Observations on the Link between Learning Disabilities and Juvenile Delinquency," *Journal of Criminal Justice* 9:9–17 (1981); J. W. Podboy and W. A. Mallory, "The Diagnosis of Specific Learning Disabilities in a Juvenile Delinquent

Population," *Juvenile and Family Court Journal* 30:11–13 (1978).

107. Charles Murray, *The Link between Learning Disabilities and Juvenile Delinquency: A Current Theory and Knowledge* (Washington, D.C.: U.S. Government Printing Office, 1976).

108. Robert Pasternak and Reid Lyon, "Clinical and Empirical Identification of Learning Disabled Juvenile Delinquents," *Journal of Correctional Education* 33:7–13 (1982).

109. Zimmerman et al., "Some Observations on the Link between Learning Disabilities and Juvenile Delinquency."

110. Terrie Moffitt, "The Neuropsychology of Conduct Disorder," mimeo (University of Wisconsin-Madison, 1992).

111. Elizabeth Kandel and Sarnoff Mednick, "Perinatal Complications Predict Violent Offending," *Criminology* 29:519–30 (1991).

112. James Creechan, "The Masking of Learning Disabilities and Juvenile Delinquency: The Learning Disabilities–Juvenile Delinquency Amplification Model," paper presented at the Annual Meeting of the American Society of Criminology, New Orleans, November 1992.

113. Diana Fishbein and Robert Thatcher, "New Diagnostic Methods in Criminology: Assessing Organic Sources of Behavioral Disorder," *Journal of Research in Crime and Delinquency* 23:240–67 (1986).

114. Jack Katz, *Seduction of Crime: Moral and Sensual Attractions of Doing Evil* (New York: Basic Books, 1988), pp. 12–15.

115. Lee Ellis, "Arousal Theory and the Religiosity-Criminality Relationship," in Peter Cordella and Larry Siegel, eds., *Contemporary Criminological Theory* (Boston, Mass.: Northeastern University, 1996), pp. 65–84.

116. Adrian Raine, Peter Venables, and Sarnoff Mednick, "Low Resting Heart Rate at Age 3 Years Predisposes to Aggression at Age 11 Years: Evidence from the Mauritius Child Health Project," *Journal of the American Academy of Adolescent Psychiatry* 36:1457–64 (1997).

117. David Rowe, *The Limits of Family Influence: Genes, Experiences and Behavior* (New York: Guilford Press, 1995), p. 64.

118. For a review, see Lisabeth Fisher DiLalla and Irving Gottesman, "Biological and Genetic Contributors to Violence— Widom's Untold Tale," *Psychological Bulletin* 109:125–29 (1991).

119. Ibid.

120. L. Erlenmeyer-Kimling, Robert Golden, and Barbara Cornblatt, "A Taxometric Analysis of Cognitive and Neuromotor Variables in Children in Risk for Schizophrenia," *Journal of Abnormal Psychology* 98:203–8 (1989).

121. A. A. Sandberg, G. F. Koeph, T. Ishiara, and T. S. Hauschka, "An XYY Human Male," *Lancet* 262:448–49 (1961); T. R. Sarbin and L. E. Miller, "Demonism Revisited: The XYY Chromosome Anomaly," *Issues in Criminology* 5:195–207 (1970).

122. David Rowe, Joseph Rogers, and Sylvia Meseck-Bushey, "Sibling Delinquency and the Family Environment: Shared and Unshared Influences," *Child Development* 63:59–67 (1992).

123. David Rowe, "Sibling Interaction and Self-Reported Delinquent Behavior: A Study of 265 Twin Pairs," *Criminology* 23:223–40 (1985); Nancy Segal, "Monozygotic and Dizygotic Twins: A Comparative Analysis of Mental Ability Profiles," *Child Development* 56:1051–58 (1985).

124. Mednick and Volavka, "Biology and Crime"; in Norval Morris and Michael Tonry, eds., *Crime and Justice,* vol. 1 (Chicago; University of Chicago Press, 1980), pp. 85–159; Lee Ellis, "Genetics and Criminal Behavior," *Criminology* 10:43–66 (1982); Karl O. Christiansen, "A Preliminary Study of Criminality among Twins," in S. A. Mednick and Karl O. Christiansen, eds., *The Biosocial Bases of Criminal Behavior* (New York: Gardner Press, 1977).

125. Glenn Walters, "A Meta-Analysis of the Gene–Crime Relationship," *Criminology* 30:595–613 (1992).

126. T. J. Bouchard, D. T. Lykken, D. T. McGue, N. L. Segal, and A. Tellegan, "Sources of Human Psychological Differences: The Minnesota Study of Twins Reared Apart," *Science* 250: 223–28 (1990).

127. D. T. Lykken, M. McGue, A. Tellegen, and T. J. Bouchard Jr., "Emergenesis, Genetic Traits that May Not Run in Families," *American Psychologist* 47:1565–77 (1992).

128. Remi Cadoret, Colleen Cain, and Raymond Crowe, "Evidence for a Gene–Environment Interaction in the Development of Adolescent Antisocial Behavior," *Behavior Genetics* 13:301–10 (1983).

129. Rowe, *The Limits of Family Influence,* p. 110.

130. Bernard Hutchings and Sarnoff Mednick, "Criminality in Adoptees and Their Adoptive and Biological Parents: A Pilot Study," in S. A. Mednick and Karl O. Christiansen, eds., *Biosocial Bases of Criminal Behavior* (New York: Gardner Press, 1977).

131. For similar findings, see William Gabrielli and Sarnoff Mednick, "Urban Environment, Genetics, and Crime," *Criminology* 22:645–53 (1984).

132. Jody Alberts-Corush, Philip Firestone, and John Goodman, "Attention and Impulsivity Characteristics of the Biological and Adoptive Parents of Hyperactive and Normal Control Children," *American Journal of Orthopsychiatry* 56:413–23 (1986).

133. Wilson and Herrnstein, *Crime and Human Nature,* p. 131.

134. Walters, "A Meta-Analysis of the Gene–Crime Relationship."

135. Ibid., p. 108.

136. Lawrence Cohen and Richard Machalek, "A General Theory of Expropriative Crime: An Evolutionary Ecological Approach," *American Journal of Sociology* 94:465–501 (1988).

137. For a general review, see Martin Daly and Margo Wilson, "Crime and Conflict: Homicide in Evolutionary Psychological Theory," in Michael Tonry, ed., *Crime and Justice, An Annual Edition* (Chicago: University of Chicago Press, 1997), pp. 51–100.

138. David Rowe, Alexander Vazsonyi, and Aurelio Jose Figuerdo, "Mating-Effort in Adolescence: A Conditional of Alternative Strategy," *Personal Individual Differences* 23:105–15 (1997).

139. Ibid., p. 71.

140. Lee Ellis, "The Evolution of Violent Criminal Behavior and Its Nonlegal Equivalent," *Crime in Biological Contexts,* pp. 63–65.

141. Ellis and Walsh, "Gene-Based Evolutionary Theories of Criminology."

142. Byron Roth, "Crime and Child Rearing," *Society* 34:39–45 (1996).

143. For a thorough review of this issue, see David Brandt and S. Jack Zlotnick, *The Psychology and Treatment of the Youthful Offender* (Springfield, Ill.: Charles C. Thomas, 1988).

144. Spencer Rathus, *Psychology* (New York: Holt, Rinehart & Winston, 1996), pp. 11–21.

145. Based on James Brooke, Pam Belluck, and John Kifner, and was written by James Brooke, "Man Hospitalized in 1996 for Writing Ominous Letters," *New York Times* 26 July 1998, p.1.

146. See, generally, Sigmund Freud, *An Outline of Psychoanalysis,* trans. James Strachey (New York: Norton, 1963).

147. Seymour Halleck, *Psychiatry and the Dilemmas of Crime* (Berkeley: University of California Press, 1971).

148. See, generally, Erik Erikson, *Identity, Youth, and Crisis* (New York: Norton, 1968).

149. David Abrahamsen, *Crime and Human Mind* (New York: Columbia University Press, 1944), p. 137.

150. See, generally, Fritz Redl and Hans Toch, "The Psychoanalytic Perspective," in Hans Toch, ed., *Psychology of Crime and Criminal Justice* (New York: Holt, Rinehart & Winston, 1979), pp. 193–95.

151. August Aichorn, *Wayward Youth* (New York: Viking Press, 1935).

152. Halleck, *Psychiatry and the Dilemmas of Crime.*

153. James Sorrells, "Kids Who Kill," *Crime and Delinquency* 23:312–20 (1977).

154. Richard Rosner et al., "Adolescents Accused of Murder and Manslaughter: A Five-Year Descriptive Study," *Bulletin of the American Academy of Psychiatry and the Law* 7:342–51 (1979).

155. Milton Rosenbaum and Binni Bennet, "Homicide and Depression," *American Journal of Psychiatry* 143:367–70 (1986).

156. Brandt and Zlotnick, *The Psychology and Treatment of the Youthful Offender,* pp. 72–73.

157. See Albert Bandura and Frances Menlove, "Factors Determining Vicarious Extinction of Avoidance Behavior through Symbolic Modeling," *Journal of Personality and Social Psychology* 8:99–108 (1965); and Albert Bandura and Richard Walters, *Social Learning and Personality Development* (New York: Holt, Rinehart & Winston, 1963).

158. David Perry, Louise Perry, and Paul Rasmussen, "Cognitive Social Learning Mediators of Aggression," *Child Development* 57:700–11 (1986).

159. Bonnie Carlson, "Children's Beliefs about Punishment," *American Journal of Orthopsychiatry* 56:308–12 (1986).

160. Albert Bandura and Richard Walters, *Adolescent Aggression* (New York: Ronald Press, 1959), p. 32.

161. Edward Donnerstein and Daniel Linz, "The Question of Pornography," *Psychology Today* 20:56–59 (1986).

162. Joyce Sprafkin, Kenneth Gadow, and Monique Dussault, "Reality Perceptions of Television: A Preliminary Comparison of Emotionally Disturbed and Nonhandicapped Children," *American Journal of Orthopsychiatry* 56:147–52 (1986).

163. Daniel Anderson, Elizabeth Pugzles Lorch, Diane Field, Patricia Collins, and John Nathan, "Television Viewing at Home: Age Trends in Visual Attention Time with TV," *Child Development* 57:1024–33 (1986).

164. UCLA Center for Communication Policy, *Television Violence Monitoring Project* (Los Angeles, Calif.: University of California Press, 1995); Associated Press, "Hollywood Is Blamed in Token Booth Attack," *Boston Globe,* 28 November 1995, p. 30.

165. Wendy Wood, Frank Wong, and J. Gregory Chachere, "Effects of Media Violence on Viewers' Aggression in Unconstrained Social Interaction," *Psychological Bulletin* 109:371–83 (1991); Lynette Friedrich-Cofer and Aletha Huston, "Television Violence and Aggression: The Debate Continues," *Psychological Bulletin* 100:364–71 (1986).

166. American Psychological Association, *Violence on TV. A Social Issue Release from the Board of Social and Ethical Responsibility for Psychology* (Washington, D.C.: APA, 1985).

167. Associated Press, "Hollywood is Blamed in Token Booth Attack."

168. Jonathon Freedman, "Television Violence and Aggression: What the Evidence Shows," in S. Oskamp, ed., *Applied Social Psychology Annual: Television as a Social Issue* (Newbury Park, Calif.: Sage, 1988), pp. 144–62.

169. Jonathon Freedman, "Effect of Television Violence on Aggressiveness," *Psychological Bulletin* 96:227–46 (1984); idem, "Television Violence and Aggression: A Rejoinder," *Psychological Bulletin* 100:372–78 (1986).

170. Steven Messner, "Television Violence and Violent Crime: An Aggregate Analysis," *Social Problems* 33:218–35 (1986).

171. See, generally, Jean Piaget, *The Moral Judgement of the Child* (London: Kegan Paul, 1932).

172. Lawrence Kohlberg, *Stages in the Development of Moral Thought and Action* (New York: Holt, Rinehart & Winston, 1969).

173. L. Kohlberg, K. Kauffman, P. Scharf, and J. Hickey, *The Just Community Approach in Corrections: A Manual* (Niantic, Conn.: Connecticut Department of Corrections, 1973).

174. Scott Henggeler, *Delinquency in Adolescence* (Newbury Park, Calif.: Sage, 1989), p. 26.

175. Ibid.

176. K. A. Dodge, "A Social Information Processing Model of Social Competence in Children," in M. Perlmutter, ed., *Minnesota Symposium in Child Psychology,* vol. 18 (Hillsdale, N.J.: Erlbaum, 1986), pp. 77–125.

177. Adrian Raine, Peter Venables, and Mark Williams, "Better Autonomic Conditioning and Faster Electrodermal Half-Recovery Time at Age 15 Years as Possible Protective Factors against Crime at Age 29 Years," *Developmental Psychology* 32:624–30 (1996).

178. L. Huesman and L. Eron, "Individual Differences and the Trait of Aggression," *European Journal of Personality* 3:95–106 (1989).

179. Rolf Loeber and Dale Hay, "Key Issues in the Development of Aggression and Violence from Childhood to Early Adulthood," *Annual Review of Psychology* 48:371–410 (1997).

180. J. E. Lochman, "Self and Peer Perceptions and Attributional Biases of Aggressive and Nonaggressive Boys in Dyadic Interactions," *Journal of Consulting and Clinical Psychology* 55:404–10 (1987).

181. Kathleen Cirillo, B. E. Pruitt, Brian Colwell, Paul M. Kingery, Robert S. Hurley, and Danny Ballard, "School Violence: Prevalence and Intervention Strategies for At-Risk Adolescents," *Adolescence* 33:319–31 (1998).

182. Leilani Greening, "Adolescent Stealers' and Nonstealers' Social Problem-Solving Skills," *Adolescence* 32:51–56 (1997).

183. Graeme Newman, *Understanding Violence* (New York: Lippincott, 1979) pp. 145–46.

184. Kathleen Cirillo, B.E. Pruitt, Brian Colwell, Paul M. Kingery, Robert S. Hurley, and Danny Ballard, "School Violence: Prevalence and Intervention Strategies for At-Risk Adolescents," *Adolescence* 33:319–31 (1998).

185. See, generally, G. Patterson, J. Reid, and T. Dishion, *Antisocial Boys* (Eugene, Or.: Castalia, 1992).

186. See, generally, Walter Mischel, *Introduction to Personality,* 4th ed. (New York: Holt, Rinehart & Winston, 1986).

187. D. A. Andrews and J. Stephen Wormith, "Personality and Crime: Knowledge and Construction in Criminology," *Justice Quarterly* 6:289–310 (1989); Donald Gibbons, "Comment—Personality and Crime: Non-Issues, Real Issues, and a Theory and Research Agenda," *Justice Quarterly* 6:311–24 (1989).

188. Sheldon Glueck and Eleanor Glueck, *Unraveling Juvenile Delinquency* (Cambridge: Harvard University Press, 1950).

189. See, generally, Hans Eysenck, *Personality and Crime* (London: Routledge and Kegan Paul, 1977).

190. David Farrington, "Psychobiological Factors in the Explanation and Reduction of Delinquency," *Today's Delinquent* 7:37–51 (1988).

191. Laurie Frost, Terrie Moffitt, and Rob McGee, "Neuropsychological Correlates of Psychopathology in an Unselected Cohort of Young Adolescents," *Journal of Abnormal Psychology* 98:307–13 (1989).

192. Hans Eysenck and M. W. Eysenck, *Personality and Individual Differences* (New York: Plenum, 1985).

193. Linda Mealey, "The Sociobiology of Sociopathy: An Integrated Evolutionary Model," *Behavioral and Brain Sciences* 18:523–40 (1995).

194. Hervey Cleckley, "Psychopathic States," in S. Aneti, ed., *American Handbook of Psychiatry* (New York: Basic Books, 1959), pp. 567–69.

195. Lewis Yablonsky, *The Violent Gang* (Baltimore: Penguin, 1971), pp. 195–205.

196. Helene Raskin White, Erich Labouvie, and Marsha Bates, "The Relationship between Sensation Seeking and Delinquency: A Longitudinal Analysis," *Journal of Research in Crime and Delinquency* 22:197–211 (1985).

197. Rathus, *Psychology,* p. 452.

198. See, for example, R. Starke Hathaway and Elio Monachesi, "The M.M.P.I. in the Study of Juvenile Delinquents," in A. M. Rose, ed., *Mental Health and Mental Disorder* (London: Routledge, 1956).

199. R. Starke Hathaway and Elio Monachesi, *Analyzing and Predicting Juvenile Delinquency with the M.M.P.I.* (Minneapolis: University of Minnesota Press, 1953).

200. Deborah Decker Roman and David Gerbing, "The Mentally Disordered Criminal Offender: A Description Based on Demographic, Clinical and MMPI D," *Journal of Clinical Psychology* 45:983–90 (1989).

201. Karl Schuessler and Donald Cressey, "Personality Characteristics of Criminals," *American Journal of Sociology* 55:476–84 (1950); Gordon Waldo and Simon Dinitz, "Personality Attributes of the Criminal: An Analysis of Research Studies,

1950–1965," *Journal of Research in Crime and Delinquency* 4:185–201 (1967); David Tennenbaum, "Research Studies of Personality and Criminality," *Journal of Criminal Justice* 5:1–19 (1977).

202. Donald Calsyn, Douglass Roszell, and Edmund Chaney, "Validation of MMPI Profile Subtypes among Opioid Addicts Who Are Beginning Methadone Maintenance Treatment," *Journal of Clinical Psychology* 45:991–99 (1989).

203. L. M. Terman, "Research on the Diagnosis of Predelinquent Tendencies," *Journal of Delinquency* 9:124–30 (1925); L. M. Terman, *Measurement of Intelligence* (Boston: Houghton-Mifflin, 1916); for example, see M. G. Caldwell, "The Intelligence of Delinquent Boys Committed to Wisconsin Industrial School," *Journal of Criminal Law and Criminology* 20:421–28 (1929); and C. Murcheson, *Criminal Intelligence* (Worcester, Mass.: Clark University, 1926), pp. 41–44.

204. Henry Goddard, *Efficiency and Levels of Intelligence* (Princeton, N.J.: Princeton University Press, 1920).

205. William Healy and Augusta Bronner, *Delinquency and Criminals: Their Making and Unmaking* (New York: Macmillan, 1926).

206. Kenneth Eels, *Intelligence and Cultural Differences* (Chicago: University of Chicago Press, 1951), p. 181.

207. Sorel Cahahn and Nora Cohen, "Age versus Schooling Effects on Intelligence Development," *Child Development* 60:1239–49 (1989).

208. John Slawson, *The Delinquent Boys* (Boston: Budget Press, 1926).

209. Edwin Sutherland, "Mental Deficiency and Crime," in Kimball Young, ed., *Social Attitudes* (New York: Henry Holt, 1973), chap. 15.

210. Travis Hirschi and Michael Hindelang, "Intelligence and Delinquency: A Revisionist Review," *American Sociological Review* 42:471–586 (1977).

211. Terrie Moffitt and Phil Silva, "IQ and Delinquency: A Direct Test of the Differential Detection Hypothesis," *Journal of Abnormal Psychology* 97:1–4 (1988); E. Kandel, S. Mednick, L. Sorenson-Kirkegaard, B. Hutchings, J. Knop, R. Rosenberg, and F. Schulsinger, "IQ as a Protective Factor for Subjects at a High Risk for Antisocial Behavior," *Journal of Consulting and Clinical Psychology* 56:224–26 (1988); Christine Ward and Richard McFall, "Further Validation of the Problem Inventory for Adolescent Girls: Comparing Caucasian and Black Delinquents and Nondelinquents," *Journal of Consulting and Clinical Psychology* 54:732–33 (1986).

212. Wilson and Herrnstein, *Crime and Human Nature,* p. 148.

213. Terri Moffitt, William Gabrielli, Sarnoff Mednick, and Fini Schulsinger, "Socioeconomic Status, IQ, and Delinquency," *Journal of Abnormal Psychology* 90:152–56 (1981); for a similar finding, see L. Hubble and M. Groff, "Magnitude and Direction of WISC-R Verbal Performance IQ Discrepancies among Adjudicated Male Delinquents," *Journal of Youth and Adolescence* 10:179–83 (1981).

214. Jennifer White, Terrie Moffitt, and Phil Silva, "A Prospective Replication of the Protective Effects of IQ in Subjects at High Risk for Juvenile Delinquency," *Journal of Consulting and Clinical Psychology* 37:719–24 (1989).

215. Donald Lynam, Terrie Moffitt, and Magda Stouthamer-Loeber, "Explaining the Relations between IQ and Delinquency: Class, Race, Test Motivation, School Failure or Self-Control," *Journal of Abnormal Psychology* 102:187–96 (1993).

216. David Farrington, "Juvenile Delinquency," in John C. Coleman, ed., *The School Years* (London: Routledge, 1992), p. 137.

217. Robert McCall and Michael Carriger, "A Meta-Analysis of Infant Habituation and Recognition Memory Performance as Predictors of Later IQ," *Child Development* 64:57–79 (1993).

218. H. D. Day, J. M. Franklin, and D. D. Marshall, "Predictors of Aggression in Hospitalized Adolescents," *Journal of Psychology* 132:427–35 (1998); Scott Menard and Barbara Morse, "A Structuralist Critique of the IQ–Delinquency Hypothesis: Theory and Evidence," *American Journal of Sociology* 89: 1347–78 (1984).

219. Deborah Denno, "Sociological and Human Developmental Explanations of Crime: Conflict or Consensus," *Criminology* 23:711–41 (1985).

220. Ibid., p. 711.

221. Glenn Walters and Thomas White, "Heredity and Crime: Bad Genes or Bad Research," *Justice Quarterly* 27:455–85 (1989), at 478.

222. John Cochran, Peter Wood, and Bruce Arneklev, "Is the Religiosity–Delinquency Relationship Spurious? A Test of Arousal and Social Control Theories," *Journal of Research in Crime and Delinquency* 31:92–113 (1994).

223. Ellis, "Genetics and Criminal Behavior," *Criminology* 10:43–66 (1982), at 58.

224. Lee Ellis, "The Evolution of the Nonlegal Equivalent of Aggressive Criminal Behavior," *Aggressive Behavior* 12:57–71 (1986).

225. Sheryl Ellis, "It Does Take a Village: A Youth Violence Program in Kincheloe, Mich., Galvanizes the Community," *Corrections Today* 60:100–3 (1998).

226. Joan McCord and William McCord, "A Follow-Up Report on the Cambridge-Somerville Youth Study," *Annals* 322:89–98 (1959).

227. Edwin Schur, *Radical Nonintervention: Rethinking the Delinquency Problem* (Englewood Cliffs, N.J.: Prentice-Hall, 1973).

Chapter Four

Social Structure and Delinquency

Lenzie Jones packed his grandchildren's clothes for the movers but did not know what to do with their mother's belongings. She had fled a few days before, after the drug gang she hawked heroin for accused her of stealing and beat her with a baseball bat and a two-by-four.

Angela Smith frantically swatted cockroaches in her kitchen. An inspector was coming to scrutinize her housekeeping. If she failed, she would lose the apartment she had set her heart on.

Juanita Williams, age 74, was so paralyzed over leaving her apartment of twenty-five years that she stayed after the water and gas were shut off, until police officers removed her.

Each of these families currently lives in the Robert Taylor Housing Project, the nation's largest, and are in transition because of a federal program called Hope VI, which is razing deteriorated inner-city projects containing more than one hundred thousand apartments.[1] The Robert Taylor Project, called the "Hole," has been denounced as the "worst slum area in the United States" by the people who run it, the Chicago Housing Authority.

The Hole is located in one of Chicago's toughest areas and has been described as an "urban war zone." Children in the Hole and in other similar project areas lack life's basic needs, witness continual killings and drug dealing, and suffer from absent parents and abject poverty.[2] Police patrols are frustrated by gang lookouts and the ability of dealers to vanish into highrise hideouts. After a shooting, children who attend the elementary school located across a parking lot stay together in groups until patrols are formed to escort them to class. In February 1998 a man was killed crossing from the Hole into another gang's territory. In March postal workers refused to deliver mail for a day because of shooting. On one April weekend, one man was killed and another wounded. In June, a nine-year-old was shot. In August a police officer investigating drug dealing was critically wounded; a sixteen-year-old and two seventeen year-olds were charged.

Negative social conditions have worsened in many blighted urban areas during the past decade, and a ma-

The residents of many urban housing projects face social problems—poverty, despair, violence, deterioration—that are almost unimaginable to most affluent Americans. The move by the government to shut down such blighted projects is an effort to break the cycle of poverty, which presents poor young children with bleak life-chances.

jor effort is needed to revitalize deteriorating neighborhoods.[3] The need is significant because economic and social hardship has been related to psychological adjustment levels: people who live in poverty are more likely to suffer low self-esteem, depression, and loneliness.[4] This federally sponsored plan replaces high-density housing with smaller developments that mix families of different incomes and moves thousands of tenants into privately owned buildings.

Yet such a transition is difficult. Ninety-six percent of Robert Taylor adult residents are unemployed, and little may change if they are simply moved. Some tenants need more basic help: clothes to wear to interviews with prospective landlords, help arranging electric and gas service, classes on housekeeping skills such as cleaning carpets and operating garbage disposals. The goal is to disperse the project's concentrated poverty without introducing or aggravating social problems in the new neighborhoods. But success requires that communities accept as neighbors people they have long been happy to ignore. Already a pattern is emerging of tenants from housing projects being moved mainly into poor neighborhoods, some as rundown and unsafe as the high-rises they left.

Residents of the Hole and other urban housing projects face social problems—poverty, despair, violence, deterioration—that are unimaginable to most affluent Americans. The move by the government to shut down these projects is an effort

culture of poverty
View that lower-class people form a separate culture with their own values and norms, which are sometimes in conflict with conventional society.

underclass
Group of urban poor whose members have little chance of upward mobility or improvement.

to break the cycle of poverty in which poor young girls nurture children with equally bleak life chances.

Recognition of this problem is not new. In 1966 sociologist Oscar Lewis coined the phrase the **culture of poverty** to describe the crushing burden faced daily by the large mass of urban poor.[5] According to Lewis, the culture of poverty is marked by apathy, cynicism, helplessness, and mistrust of institutions such as police, courts, schools, and government. Mistrust of authority prevents the impoverished from taking advantage of the few conventional opportunities available to them. The result is a permanent American **underclass** whose members have little chance of upward mobility or improvement.

Cities are not singular entities but can be further subdivided into blocks, neighborhoods, communities, and metropolitan systems, each with its own special characteristics and problems (Figure 4.1). Nowhere are urban problems more pressing than in the inner-city neighborhoods that experience constant population turnover as their more affluent residents move out to stable community areas or outlying suburbs. As a city becomes "hollowed out," with a deteriorated inner core surrounded by less devastated but declining suburban communities, delinquency rates spiral upward.[6] Those remaining are forced to live in communities with poorly organized social networks, heterogeneous and alienated populations, and high crime.[7]

Members of the urban underclass, typically minority group members, are referred to by sociologist William Julius Wilson as the "truly disadvantaged."[8]

FIGURE 4.1

What Is a Community? Characteristics of a Community Structure

Source: Felton Earls and Albert Reiss, Jr., *Breaking the Cycle: Predicting and Preventing Violence* (Washington, D.C.: National Institute of Justice, 1994), pp. 10–11.

A Community Is a Set of Nested Boxes

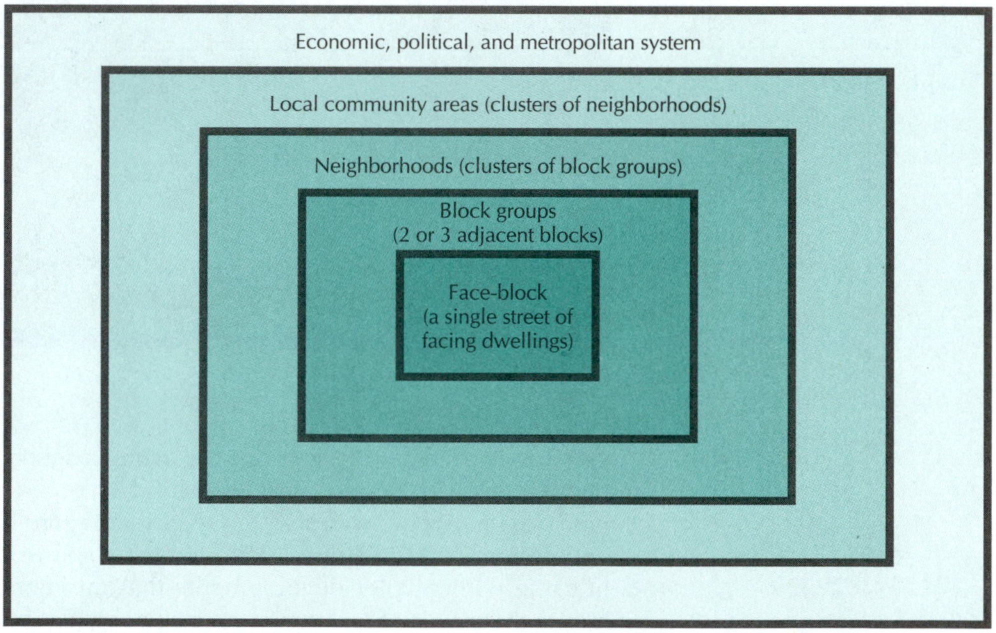

Economic, political, and metropolitan system

Local community areas (clusters of neighborhoods)

Neighborhoods (clusters of block groups)

Block groups (2 or 3 adjacent blocks)

Face-block (a single street of facing dwellings)

The most basic unit is the face-block, those houses or apartments facing each other across a single street.

Block groups of two or three adjacent city blocks represent a normal zone of adult neighborliness. It is also the area from which children draw their first friends.

Neighborhoods, which are clusters of block groups, traditionally refer to small, socially homogeneous areas defined by interaction patterns and geographic landmarks such as parks, main streets, or railroad tracks.

Local community areas encompass several neighborhoods.

Each community is part of a wider economic, political, and metropolitan system. Looking at the political economy of each place brings into the equation factors such as the distance to good jobs, the availability of public transportation, and the quality of basic services as dictated by citywide political decisions.

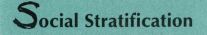

Social Stratification

stratification
Grouping society into classes based on the unequal distribution of scarce resources.

Data gathered from a number of sources support a vision of a racially, socially, and economically stratified American society. **Stratification** refers to the unequal distribution of scarce resources and can involve different dimensions of human behavior. For example, *economic stratification* refers to the unequal distribution of wealth and income; *political stratification* refers to the unequal ability to gain power or hold office; *prestige stratification* involves the ability to be well regarded in the community. Family, education, group or religious affiliation, and race all influence an individual's ability to gain a disproportionate share of wealth, power, and prestige.

The United States is a stratified society. Although most of us have the financial means to enjoy the fruits of U.S. technology and achievement, about fifty million people live below the poverty line. (In 1998 the official poverty line was $16,000 a year for a family of four and $12,500 for a family of three.) Stratification effects are becoming sharper today, with the wealthiest Americans now enjoying a greater share of the economy than ever before. The top 5 percent of the population control more than half of all U.S. wealth; the poorest Americans, the bottom 20 percent, receive less than 5 percent.

Being Poor

The poor in the United States face many of the same hardships encountered by residents of so-called third world countries. They are deprived of a standard of living enjoyed by most other citizens, and the children of the poor suffer from much more than financial hardship. Many, supported by public welfare and private charity throughout their entire lives, have no hope of achieving higher status in conventional society. They attend poor schools, live in substandard housing, and lack good health care. More than half the families are fatherless and husbandless, headed by a female who is the sole breadwinner; many are supported entirely by government welfare aid. Instead of increasing government aid to the needy, however, in the past decade a concerted effort has been made to limit eligibility for public assistance.

According to a 1998 study by the National Center for Children in Poverty, more than 20 percent of U.S. children are living in poverty. The percentage of poor young children with working parents has increased substantially: in 1997, 63 percent of poor children were in families with at least one working parent, compared with 54 percent in 1993.[9]

Children are especially hard hit by poverty. Hundreds of studies have documented the association between family poverty and children's health, achievement, and behavior impairments.[10] Children in poor families suffer many social problems, including inadequate education. Children who grow up in low-income households are less likely to achieve in school and are less likely to complete their schooling than children with more affluent parents.[11] Poor children are also more likely to suffer from health problems and to receive inadequate health care. Unfortunately, the number of children covered by health insurance has decreased and will continue to do so for the foreseeable future.[12] Lack of coverage almost guarantees that these children will suffer health problems that will impede their long-term development. Children who live in extreme poverty or who remain poor for extended periods of time appear to suffer the worst outcomes. Findings suggest that poverty suffered during early childhood may have a greater detrimental impact on children than poverty suffered during the adolescent or teen years.[13] As Figure 4.2 shows, poor children are much more likely than the wealthy to suffer a variety of social ills ranging from

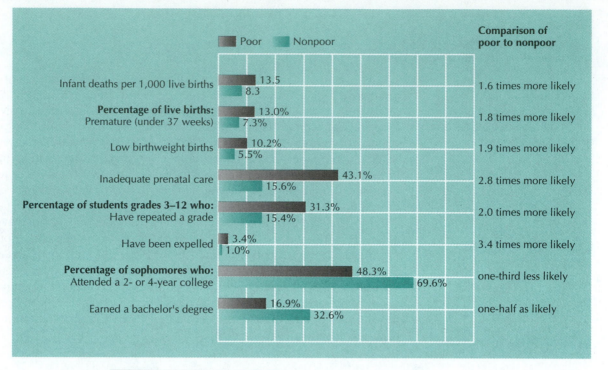

FIGURE 4.2

Problems of Poor and Nonpoor Children: Being Poor Means Much More than Suffering Financial Hardship

Source: Arloc Sherman, *Poverty Matters* (Washington, D.C.: Children's Defense Fund, 1997), p. 3.

low birthweight to never earning a college degree. The cycle of poverty can lead to a variety of adverse outcomes, including life- and health-endangering conditions (Figure 4.3). The Focus on Delinquency box entitled "Race and Poverty" provides further discussion on why minority children often face the greatest burdens of poverty.

Providing adequate care and discipline to children under these circumstances can be an immense undertaking. About five million youths under age 13 are **latchkey children** who are left unattended after school every day. Many children under age 5 are left in the care of strangers and nonfamily members, often in unregulated day-care centers.

latchkey children
Children left unsupervised after school by working parents.

Social Structure and Delinquency

The experience of poverty has taken its toll on all too many adolescents and their families. To some delinquency experts, these unfair and destructive economic and social conditions in the nation's low-income areas are the root cause of delinquency. Although middle- and upper-class children may engage in minor and occasional delinquent acts—vandalism, use of nonaddictive drugs such as marijuana, petty theft, motor vehicle violations—they tend to refrain from the more serious acts of violence, theft, and gang membership. Even those who do engage in delinquent acts are eventually able to age out of criminality and become responsible citizens.[14] In contrast, many inner-city youths with little hope of earning success through legitimate means fall prey to gang membership. Is it any wonder that they turn to crime as a means of survival, self-esteem, and revenge on a society that has turned its back on them?

Lower-class urban areas are also the scene of the highest crime and victimization rates. Official delinquency rates for crimes such as robbery and larceny are

FIGURE 4.3

Examples of Documented Pathways from Poverty to Adverse Child Outcomes

Source: Arloc Sherman, *Poverty Matters* (Washington, D.C.: Children's Defense Fund, 1997), p. 23.

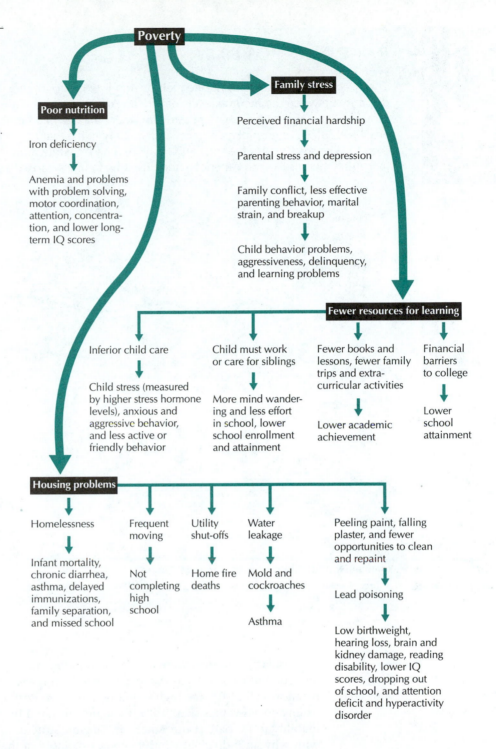

much higher in urban than in suburban and rural areas. Self-report studies also indicate that lower-class youths are the most likely to commit serious delinquent and criminal acts. Nor are these problems unique to the United States; cross-national data show that countries that spend more on child welfare, providing opportunities for the underprivileged, usually have lower crime rates than those that give less attention to welfare programs.[15]

This view of delinquency is essentially *structural* and *cultural*. It holds that delinquency is a consequence of the social and economic inequalities built into the social structure. Even those youths who receive the loving support of parents and family members are at risk of crime, delinquency, and arrest over their life course if they suffer from social disadvantage.[16]

RACE AND POVERTY

The effects of poverty are most often felt by minority group members. There is signficant disparity between the income levels of African Americans and whites and other ethnic groups. About three times as many African American as white families live below the poverty level. Black unemployment rates are typically twice that of white rates. According to the U.S. Census Bureau, the median family income for white families was about $37,000 in 1998, whereas African American and Hispanic families earned about $24,000. Asian

FIGURE A

Median Household Income, by Race and Origin
Source: Census Bureau, Current Population Survey, 1998.

social structure theories
Explain delinquency using socioeconomic conditions and cultural values.

Social structure theories tie delinquency rates to socioeconomic conditions and cultural values. Areas that experience high levels of poverty and social disorganization will also have high delinquency rates. Residents of such areas view prevailing social values skeptically; they are frustrated by their class position and their inability to be part of the American Dream. Structural theories are less concerned with why an individual youth becomes delinquent than with why certain ecological areas experience high delinquency rates.

The Branches of Social Structure Theory

The social structure approach has had a long tradition in juvenile delinquency studies. As Figure 4.4 shows, social structure theories can be classified in three independent, yet interrelated, subgroups: social disorganization, strain, and cultural deviance (also called subcultural theory).

Table A Race and Poverty

	Number (in thousands)	Percentage in Poverty
Hispanic	4,237	40
Black	4,519	39.9
Asian/Pacific Islander	571	19.5
White	9,044	16.3

and Pacific Islanders were the highest earning racial/ethnic group in the United States (see Figure A).

African American income has been on the rise since the early 1990s, but about 26 percent of black households still have no assets, and only 8 percent are worth more than $100,000. In contrast, only 10 percent of white households have no assets, and 32 percent are worth more than $100,000. One reason for this discrepancy is home ownership rates: 42 percent of black and 63 percent of white households live in homes owned by a resident.

There are also significant racial and ethnic differences in the rate of child poverty. As Table A shows, there are distinct differences in the racial and ethnic makeup of adolescent poverty: more than twice as many African American and Hispanic children are likely to be poor than white and Asian children. Economic disparity will continually haunt these young Americans and their future children over the course of their life span. Even if these children value education and other middle-class norms, their difficult life circumstances, including high unemployment rates and single and nontraditional family structures, may prevent them from developing the skills, habits, and styles that lead first to educational success and later to success in the workplace.

Although this picture is bleak, there are some signs of hope. The proportion of African Americans falling into the lowest asset category is in decline, and the percentage with assets over $100,000 has doubled during the past decade.

Sources: James Ainsworth-Darnell and Douglas Downey, "Assessing the Oppositional Culture Explanation for Racial/Ethnic Differences in School Performances," *American Sociological Review* 63:536–53 (1998); Children's Defense Fund, *The State of America's Children, 1998* (Washington, D.C.: Children's Defense Fund, 1998); U.S. Department of Census Data, *Race and Income* (Washington, D.C.: Census Bureau, 1998).

FIGURE 4.4

Branches of Social Structure Theory

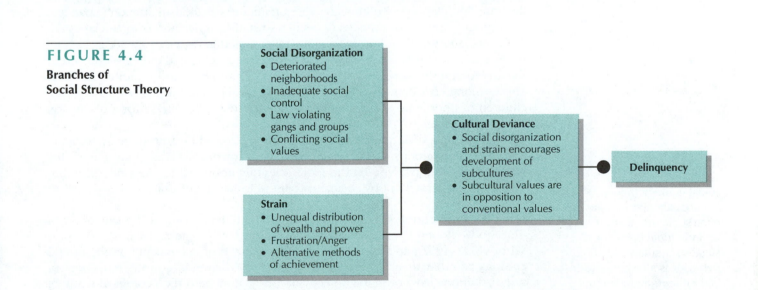

Social Disorganization
- Deteriorated neighborhoods
- Inadequate social control
- Law violating gangs and groups
- Conflicting social values

Strain
- Unequal distribution of wealth and power
- Frustration/Anger
- Alternative methods of achievement

Cultural Deviance
- Social disorganization and strain encourages development of subcultures
- Subcultural values are in opposition to conventional values

Delinquency

social disorganization theory
Posits that delinquency is a product of the social forces existing in inner-city, low-income areas.

Social disorganization theory characterizes delinquency as a product of the social forces existing in inner-city, low-income areas. At risk are neighborhoods that lack or have lost the means to control deviance, protect residents, and regulate social conduct. These areas are plagued by drug-involved juvenile gangs that overwhelm the ability of social institutions, such as the family and the school, to maintain order. The result is stable pockets of crime and deviance. Environmental and ecological factors, such as substandard housing, low income, unemployment, poor schools, broken families, urban density, and overcrowding, are predictive of a high incidence of delinquency.

strain theory
Links delinquency to the strain of being locked out of the cultural and economic mainstream, which creates the anger and frustration that lead to delinquent acts.

The core of **strain theory** is the idea that delinquency is linked to the frustration and anger of the lower class, who are locked out of the economic mainstream of society.[17] Strain results when the desire for middle-class benefits and luxuries cannot be met by legitimate means. Anger and frustration create pressure for corrective action, including attacking the sources of frustration or escaping through use of drugs and alcohol.

cultural deviance theory
Links delinquent acts to the formation of independent subcultures with a unique set of values that clash with the mainstream culture.

subcultures
Groups that are loosely part of the dominant culture but that maintain a unique set of values, beliefs, and traditions.

According to **cultural deviance theory,** adolescent residents of disorganized urban areas perceive tremendous strain and frustration and become alienated from the values of the dominant culture. The result is the formation of independent **subcultures** that maintain their own rules and values in opposition to existing law and custom. Conflict arises when these subcultural values and beliefs clash with those of the general culture. Delinquency is not caused by rebellion against the dominant society, according to this view, but by conformity to the rules of a deviant subculture.

The three branches of structural theory are interrelated; each maintains that a person's place in the social structure controls the direction of his or her behavior and that culture, environment, and the economy interact to influence behavior. Because each theoretical branch provides important concepts for delinquency study, they are set out in detail in the next sections.

Social Disorganization Theory

The roots of the social disorganization tradition can be traced to research conducted in the famed sociology department at the University of Chicago early in the twentieth century. Chicago's evolution as a city was typical of the transition that occurred in many other urban areas as industrialization expanded. Large populations of workers were needed to staff factories and commercial establishments, and waves of European immigrants settled in the city to work in the factories and stockyards. Many of the city's wealthy, established citizens believed in the stereotype that foreign immigrants were crime prone and morally dissolute. These "moral crusaders" created organizations for the very purpose of "saving" the children of poor families from moral decadence. (See Chapter 12 for a discussion of the child savers.)

At that time, delinquency was commonly perceived as a problem of "morally inferior" ethnic groups. This prejudiced view of lower-class immigrant criminality was challenged, however, by the more scientific approach to the study of delinquency being carried out by sociologists at the University of Chicago.

social ecology theory
Focuses attention on the influence social institutions have on individual behavior and suggests that law-violating behavior is a response to social rather than individual forces operating in an urban environment.

The Chicago School The unique research being conducted at the University of Chicago by Robert Ezra Park (1864–1944), Ernest W. Burgess (1886–1966), Louis Wirth (1897–1952), and their colleagues introduced new concepts on the **social ecology** of urban areas. These sociologists focused attention on the influence social institutions have on human behavior. They pioneered the ecological study of crime: that is, law-violating behavior is a function of community-level (not individual-level) social forces operating in an urban environment. They found that a func-

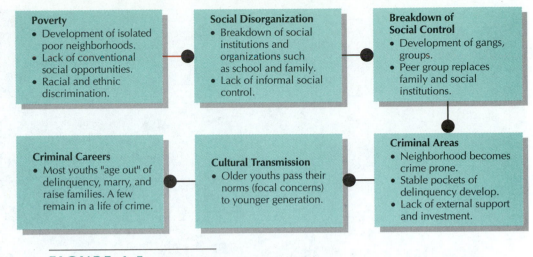

FIGURE 4.5

Social Disorganization Theory

---

social control

Ability of social institutions to influence human behavior; the justice system is the primary agency of formal social control.

natural areas for crime

Inner-city areas of extreme poverty where the critical social control mechanisms have broken down.

tional community has the ability to regulate itself so that common goals (such as living in a crime-free area) can be achieved; this is referred to as **social control.**[18] Those neighborhoods that are incapable of social control because they are wracked by disease, crime, mental disorder, and economic failure are most at risk for criminal interactions.

Natural Areas   The Chicago School researchers found that deteriorated inner-city neighborhoods become **natural areas for crime.** The extraordinarily high level of poverty in these urban neighborhoods causes a breakdown of critical social control institutions including the school and the family. According to Wirth, urban areas undergoing rapid growth in population density and ethnic diversification experience *segmentalization* of life. People look inward for achievement and shun interpersonal relationships. Interactions among residents in large cities are superficial, fleeting, and exploitive.[19] The resulting social disorganization reduces the ability of social institutions to control behavior, thus causing a high-crime rate (see Figure 4.5).

The Area Studies of Shaw and McKay

Today the social disorganization perspective is most closely associated with early research conducted in Chicago by sociologists Clifford Shaw and Henry McKay.[20] Shaw and McKay collected extensive crime data, including the records of almost twenty-five thousand alleged delinquents brought before the Juvenile Court of Cook County from 1900 to 1933. Their ongoing analysis convinced them that the then-popular individual-level explanations of delinquency, which rested on factors such as IQ or body build, were fallacious. Instead, delinquency stemmed from the ecological conditions of the city itself. They saw that Chicago had developed into distinct neighborhoods, some marked by wealth and luxury, others by overcrowding, poor health and sanitary conditions, and extreme poverty. These rundown areas were believed to be the spawning grounds of delinquency.

transitional neighborhood

Area undergoing a shift in population and structure, usually from middle-class residential to lower-class mixed use.

Shaw and McKay viewed delinquency as a product of the **transitional neighborhood**—ecologically distinct areas that changed from affluent to decayed. Here, factories and commercial establishments were interspersed with private residences. In such environments teenage gangs developed as a means of survival, economic gain, defense, and friendship. Gang youths developed a unique set of cultural values that conflicted with generally accepted social norms and traditions. Gang leaders

Delinquency is a product of the social forces existing in inner-city slum areas. Within these areas, the unsupervised behavior of juvenile gangs and groups overwhelms the ability of social institutions, such as the family and the school, to maintain order. The result is stable pockets of crime and deviance. Environmental and ecological factors such as substandard housing, low income, high unemployment levels, deteriorated housing, substandard schools, broken families, urban density, and overcrowding are predictive of a high incidence of gang delinquency. These young men are suspected members of a New York City Chinese gang.

cultural transmission
Cultural norms and values that are passed down from one generation to the next.

recruited younger members, passing on delinquent traditions and ensuring survival of the gang from one generation to the next—a process referred to as **cultural transmission.**

Concentric Zones   While mapping crime and delinquency rates in Chicago, Shaw and McKay noted that distinct ecological areas had developed in the city. These comprised a series of concentric zones, each with a stable delinquency rate (see Figure 4.6).[21] The areas of heaviest delinquency concentration appeared to be the transitional, inner-city zones where large portions of foreign-born citizens lived. The zones farthest from the city's center were the least prone to delinquency. Analysis of these data indicated a surprisingly stable pattern of delinquent activity in the ecological zones over a sixty-five-year period. Shaw and McKay noted that delinquency rates in these areas were unaffected by population makeup and transition. It seemed that high-risk areas—not high-risk people—were associated with delinquency rates.

Social Values and Crime Rates   Shaw and McKay did not restrict their analysis to ecological factors alone. They found a significant correlation between social values and crime rates as well. Areas with low delinquency rates were marked by "uniformity, consistency, and universality of conventional values and attitudes."[22] In these low-crime areas, middle-class child-rearing practices prevailed, and residents con-

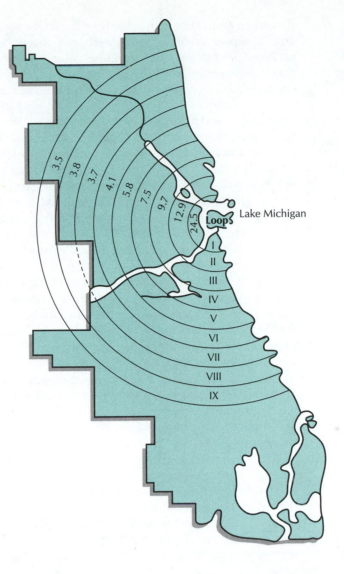

formed to the legal code. In contrast, conflicting moral values and powerful attractions to deviant modes of behavior existed in high-crime areas. In disorganized neighborhoods, delinquency provided a means for financially deprived youths to gain prestige, economic achievement, and other satisfactions. Deviant values emerge and become pervasive when the community is neither capable of helping residents realize their legitimate goals nor able to control the behavior of those who embrace illegal activities for personal gain.

Parent–child relationships were seen by Shaw and McKay as having an important influence on the development of social values. In zones with low delinquency rates, parents stressed values such as attending school and church and involvement in community organizations. In high-rate, transitional areas a diversity of values existed. Some youths were taught to strive for basic middle-class goals; others were exposed to the rackets and illegal activities such as theft.

Shaw and McKay concluded that in transitional neighborhoods deviant and conventional values compete with one another. Adolescents exposed to both value systems are often forced to choose between them and, consequently, may seek out groups that share particular ideas and behavior. Those who choose illegitimate values may find membership in law-violating groups and gangs an essential element of life in these areas (see Chapter 9 on gang behavior).

Value Conflict Because of their deviant values, youths from transitional neighborhoods often come into conflict with existing middle-class norms, including those demanding strict obedience to the legal code. Such value conflicts set delinquents and their peer group even further from conventional society. The result is a fuller acceptance of deviant goals and behavior. Shunned by the mainstream, neighborhood street gangs become fixed institutions, recruiting new members and passing on delinquent traditions from one generation to the next.

The quality of social organizations and institutions also varies considerably between high- and low-crime areas. In high-crime areas, conflicting social values neutralize the influence of social control organizations. A close-knit family, which should serve as a buffer against delinquency, exercises little social control in disorganized areas. Families in transitional areas often contain adult members who are themselves profiting from theft, violence, and drug dealing. In these circumstances, family ties can actually encourage delinquency. Even those social control agents with an expressed agenda of crime control and prevention, such as schools and community centers, have only limited influence because they are staffed and funded by outsiders who are not trusted by neighborhood residents.

Legacy of Shaw and McKay Most important among the many achievements of Shaw and McKay was locating the cause of delinquency within the domain of social ecology. The Shaw-McKay model replaced the view that delinquents were either biological throwbacks, intellectually impaired, or psychologically damaged. Their research refuted the assumption that delinquency is a property of any one minority or ethnic group.

Because the basis of their theory was that neighborhood disintegration and urban decay are the primary causes of delinquent behavior, Shaw and McKay paved the way for the many community action and treatment programs developed in the last half-century. Shaw himself founded one very influential community-based treatment program, the Chicago Area Project, which will be discussed later in this chapter.[23]

Another important feature of Shaw and McKay's work was its depiction of delinquent gang membership as a "normal" response to the adverse social conditions in impoverished urban areas. Gangs provide social and economic advantages that would otherwise be denied youths in these areas. Shaw, McKay, and other Chicago-based theorists, such as Frederick Thrasher, viewed gang members as neither troubled nor depressed.[24] Their illegal behavior was merely a way of achieving excitement, social success, and financial gain when all other avenues seemed to be closed.

Shaw and McKay's work has been subject to criticism. Dependence on official statistics is always suspect because high-crime rates in the inner-city may be a function of police arrest practices. The stable patterns of inner-city delinquency depicted by Shaw and McKay may not actually exist. Social mobility and change in neighborhood composition may, in fact, influence crime rates.[25] Self-report studies indicate that many middle-class suburban youths commit crimes, a finding that suggests that the cause of delinquency may have little to do with economic deprivation and social disorganization.

These criticisms aside, by introducing a new variable—the ecology of the city—into the study of delinquency, Shaw and McKay paved the way for a whole generation of criminologists to focus on the social influences of delinquent behavior.

Contemporary Social Ecology

During the mid-twentieth century, Shaw and McKay's legacy was continued in area studies conducted by Bernard Lander in Baltimore, David Bordua in Detroit, and Roland Chilton in Indianapolis. As a group, they showed that ecological conditions such as substandard housing, low income, and unrelated people living together predicted a high incidence of delinquency.[26]

Today the social disorganization view is still the subject of a great deal of scholarship. Researchers are now using complex statistical models to determine the effects ecological and social conditions have on delinquent crime patterns.[27] A growing body of important studies indicate that the social context of urban areas has significant influence on delinquency rates.[28] This new research on the social ecology of delinquency suggests that social forces operating within depressed urban areas help generate the conditions favorable to drug abuse and delinquency. The next sections describe some of the most significant areas of research.

Relative Deprivation   According to Judith and Peter Blau, a sense of social injustice occurs in communities in which the poor and the wealthy live close to one another. Income inequality causes feelings of **relative deprivation.** The relatively deprived are prone to have feelings of anger and hostility, which precede criminal behavior.

The Blaus believe adolescents residing in poor inner-city areas will experience delinquency-producing status frustration because their neighborhoods are contiguous to some of the most affluent areas in the United States. Deprived teenagers can observe wealth and luxury close up, but they have no hope of actually achieving riches themselves. This condition is felt most acutely by racial and ethnic minorities who live in low-status areas and in substandard housing.[29] Psychologists warn that under these circumstances young males will begin to fear and envy "winners" who are doing very well at their expense. If they fail to take risky, aggressive tactics, they are surely going to lose out in social competition and have little chance of future success.[30]

Research supportive of the Blaus' relative deprivation model has been conducted by a number of criminologists who have linked income inequality to high delinquency rates.[31] Richard Block found that the variable best able to predict crime rates was the proximity in which poor and wealthy people lived to one another.[32] Inequality seems significantly related to crime rates, especially in areas where residents have high achievement aspirations but few economic opportunities.[33]

These studies support the premise that youths living in deteriorated urban areas of the city that are close to more affluent neighborhoods will be the most likely to resort to crimes such as homicide, robbery, and aggravated assault to express their frustration or achieve monetary gain.

Community Change   Some social ecologists contend that, like people, urban areas and neighborhoods have a life cycle during which they undergo significant change: from affluent to impoverished, from impoverished to rehabilitated or **gentrified,** from residential to commercial, from stable to transient. It has been observed that as communities go through these structural changes, levels of social disorder and delinquency also change.[34] Neighborhood deterioration precedes increasing rates of crime and delinquency.[35]

Communities on the down-swing are most likely to experience rapid increases in the number of single-parent families, a change in housing from owner- to renter-occupied units, a loss of semiskilled and unskilled jobs, and a growth in discouraged unemployed workers who are no longer seeking jobs.[36] These communities also tend to develop "mixed-use" areas in which commercial and residential properties stand side by side. Areas in which retail establishments go bankrupt, are abandoned, and deteriorate physically have the highest crime rates and the most calls for police services.[37]

The changing racial makeup of communities may also influence crime and delinquency rates. Areas undergoing change in their racial composition will experience corresponding increases in delinquency rates.[38] This phenomenon may reflect community fear of racial conflict. Adults may encourage teens to terrorize the newcomers and commit hate crimes; the result is conflict, violence, and disorder.

Wealth and Opportunity   Although Shaw and McKay did not assume a direct relationship between economic status and criminality, they did imply that areas wracked

relative deprivation
Condition that exists when people of wealth and poverty live in close proximity to one another; the relatively deprived are apt to have feelings of anger and hostility, which may produce criminal behavior.

gentrified
The process of transforming a lower-class area into a middle-class enclave through property rehabilitation.

by poverty would also experience social disorganization. Research has confirmed that neighborhoods that provide few employment opportunities for youths and adults are the most vulnerable to predatory crime. Unemployment helps destabilize households, and unstable families are more likely to contain children who choose violence and aggression as a means of dealing with limited opportunity.[39]

A lack of employment opportunity also limits the respect and authority of parents and neighborhood adults, reducing their ability to guide and influence children. Because adult authority figures cannot serve as role models, the local culture is left to the domination of youth gangs whose members are both feared and respected. Predatory crime increases to levels that cannot easily be controlled by police. Although even the most deteriorated neighborhoods have a surprising degree of familial and kinship strength, the consistent pattern of crime and neighborhood disorganization that follows periods of high unemployment can neutralize an area's inherent social control capability.

Does Delinquency Cause Poverty?

It is commonly assumed that poverty causes delinquency. But it is just as likely that the reverse is true and that delinquency causes poverty.

High-crime-rate areas can become impoverished because the fear of crime reduces investment and commerce. Middle-class people flee the area in search of safer surroundings, and people won't enter the area to shop or do business.[40] The decline in consumer confidence and business activity further reduces employment opportunities, effectively eliminating many area residents from the job market. Periods of sustained criminality and fear put ever greater strain on the economic life of the area, encouraging area youth to join gangs for economic survival. A cycle of crime and poverty is introduced that becomes difficult to break or reduce.

Social Embeddedness   John Hagan, a noted criminologist, has found that some youths become *embedded* in a delinquent way of life. They have criminal parents, deviant friends, and an ongoing involvement in antisocial behavior. Their lifestyle reduces any chance they may have of gaining steady adult employment, further sustaining their criminal embeddedness.

In contrast, some children in high-crime neighborhoods are fortunate enough to have parents whose connections help them become embedded in conventional society. They maintain connections with community leaders, develop political ties, and can tap into the local job "network." Their parents social embeddedness later helps these children enter the workforce and lead successful lives. If they "get in trouble," they can use family contacts with agents of the criminal justice system to get off lightly. Even in the most deprived neighborhoods, parents who are socially rather than criminally embedded can help their children avoid delinquent careers.[41]

Fear   Disorganized neighborhoods suffer social and physical incivilities—rowdy youth, trash and litter, graffiti, abandoned storefronts, burned-out buildings, littered lots, strangers, drunks, vagabonds, loiterers, prostitutes, noise, congestion, angry words, dirt, and stench. The presence of such incivilities helps convince residents of disorganized areas that their neighborhood is dangerous and that they face a considerable chance of becoming crime victims; not surprisingly, when crime rates are actually high in these disorganized areas, fear levels undergo a dramatic increase.[42] Perceptions of crime and victimization produce *neighborhood fear*.[43]

Fear of crime and delinquency is much higher in disorganized neighborhoods than in affluent suburbs.[44] Members of the underclass fear crime and have little confidence that the government can do anything to counter the drug dealers and juvenile gangs that terrorize the neighborhood.[45] People tell others of their personal experiences of being victimized, spreading the word that the neighborhood is getting dangerous and that the chances of future victimization are high.

Residents of areas with high death rates and short life expectancies may alter their behavior out of fear. Why plan for the future when there is a significant likelihood that they may never see it? In such areas young boys and girls may adjust psychologically by taking risks and discounting the future. Teenage birth rates soar, and so do violence rates.[46]

When fear grips a neighborhood, people do not want to leave their homes at night, so they withdraw from community life. Fear has been related to distress, inactivity, and decline in personal health.[47] High levels of fear are also related to deteriorating business conditions, increased population mobility, and the domination of street life by violent gangs and groups.

Social Controls   Most neighborhood residents share the common goal of living in a crime-free area. Some communities rely on institutions such as families and schools to regulate the behavior of residents. When community social control efforts are blunted, delinquency rates increase and neighborhood cohesiveness is weakened, setting the stage for an endless cycle of community deterioration.

Neighborhoods maintain a variety of agencies and institutions of social control. Some operate on the primary or personal level and involve peers, families, and relatives. These sources exert informal control over behavior by either awarding or withholding approval, respect, and admiration. Informal control mechanisms include direct criticism, ridicule, ostracism, desertion, and physical punishment.[48] Communities also use internal networks and local institutions to control delinquency; these include business associations, schools, churches, and voluntary organizations.[49]

Stable neighborhoods are able to marshal external sources of social control; for example, they can use their political clout to get state and city funding for job programs and economic development. Access to these external control sources has been found to mediate delinquency rates.[50] One source of external control may be the ability to increase levels of police services. The presence of police sends a message that the area will not tolerate deviant behavior. Current and potential delinquents may avoid such areas and concentrate on easier and more appealing "targets."[51]

Disorganized neighborhoods cannot mount an effective social control effort. Because the population is transient, interpersonal relationships tend to be superficial and cannot help reduce deviant behavior. Social institutions, such as schools and churches, cannot work effectively in a climate of alienation and mistrust. In such neighborhoods, the absence of political power brokers limits access to external funding and police protection.

Disorganized neighborhoods cannot mount an effective social control effort. Since the population is transient, interpersonal relationships tend to be superficial and cannot help reduce deviant behavior. Social institutions, such as schools and churches, cannot work effectively in a climate of alienation and mistrust. In such neighborhoods, the absence of political power brokers limits access to external funding and police protection. When social institutions are strong, neighborhood crime rates can be stabilized. Here, teenagers perform a comedy skit at a benefit for the Foundation for the Junior Blind in Los Angeles.

Social control is also weakened because unsupervised peer groups and gangs, which flourish in disorganized areas, disrupt the influence of neighborhood control agents.[52] Children surveyed in disorganized areas report that they are unable to become involved with conventional social institutions and are therefore vulnerable to interpersonal aggression and delinquency.[53]

Rage, Distrust, and Hopelessness   Kids in socially disorganized areas experience rage, distrust, and hopelessness. They are socialized in a world where adults maintain a siege mentality, believing there are government plots to undermine the neighborhood (for example, "the AIDS virus was created to kill us off"; "the government brings drugs into the neighborhood to keep people under control").[54] Young people growing up in these areas become very angry, believing no one in power cares about their plight. There is "free-floating anger," which causes adolescents to strike out at the merest hint of provocation.[55]

Social scientist Felton Earls is now conducting a government-funded longitudinal study of pathways to violence among eight thousand Chicago area youths in eighty randomly selected neighborhoods.[56] Interviews with youths (ages 9 to 15) have so far revealed that large numbers of these children have been victims of or witnesses to violence and that many carry weapons themselves. The researchers found a strong correlation between exposure to violence and self-reports of violent behavior: between 30 and 40 percent of the children who reported exposure to violence also displayed significant violent behavior themselves. The research also shows that girls are involved in violence as much as boys, although the nature of the violence is quite different. Girls are more likely than boys to be victims of sexual violence, and boys are more likely to see or to participate in fights, stabbings, or shootings.

Children living in these conditions become "crusted over." They do not let people get close to them, nor do they give expression to their childhood. Their peer relations are exploitive, and they develop a sense of hopelessness at a very young age. Parents and teachers seem to focus on their failures and problems rather than on their achievements, leaving them vulnerable to the lure of delinquent gangs and groups.[57]

Social Support/Altruism   A multitude of stressors in modern society—family conflict, divorce and separation, school failure—have been linked to social problems ranging from depression, anxiety, and suicide attempts to drug use and criminality.[58] Social supports from a community can help young people cope with life's stress, and adults can provide the external support systems that will enable youths to desist from criminality by helping them become more resilient and self-confident. Residents can teach one another that they have moral and social obligations to their fellow citizens, and children can learn to be sensitive to the rights of others and to respect differences. Areas and neighborhoods that place more stress on caring for fellow citizens seem, not surprisingly, less crime prone than those emphasizing self-reliance.[59] The government can also be a force for social altruism by providing economic and social supports. Though welfare programs are often attacked by conservative politicians, there is evidence that as the amount of welfare increases in a neighborhood crime rates decline.[60] Government assistance may help people improve their social status while at the same time reducing stress, frustration, and anger.

The writings of the social ecology school show that social disorganization produces criminality and that the quality of community life, including levels of change, fear, incivility, poverty, and deterioration, has a direct influence on the crime rate. It is not some individual property or trait that causes some people to commit crime but the quality and ambience of the community in which they reside.

Recent attempts to define the influence of social ecology on area delinquency rates support the core social disorganization model: deteriorated and disorganized areas are unable to assemble social forces sufficient to control the behavior of their residents. Rather than dissuade neighborhood youths from joining gangs and com-

You have just been appointed as a presidential adviser on urban problems.

The president informs you that he wants to initiate a demonstration project in a major city aimed at showing that government can do something to reduce poverty, crime, and drug abuse. The area he has chosen for development is a large inner-city neighborhood with more than one hundred thousand residents. It suffers from disorganized community structure, poverty, and hopelessness. Predatory delinquent gangs run free and terrorize local merchants and citizens. The school system has failed to provide opportunities and educational experiences sufficient to dampen enthusiasm for gang recruitment. Stores, homes, and public buildings are deteriorated and decayed. Commercial enterprise has fled the area, and civil servants are reluctant to enter the neighborhood.

There is an uneasy truce between the varied ethnic and racial groups that populate the area. Residents feel that little can be done to bring the neighborhood back to life.

You are faced with suggesting an urban redevelopment program that can revitalize the area and eventually bring down the crime rate. You can bring any element of the public and private sector to bear on this rather overwhelming problem—including the military! You can also ask private industry to help in the struggle, promising them tax breaks for their participation.

- What programs do you feel could break the cycle of urban poverty?
- Would reducing the poverty rate produce a lowered delinquency rate?
- Is there a place for private industry in social reorganization?

mitting crime, social forces in these areas encourage and sustain antisocial behavior. The Case in Point box explores the question of how to reverse this negative outcome of social disorganization.

Strain Theory

Strain-based explanations form the second major category of social structure theories. The core concept of strain theory is that most people share similar values and aspirations. After all, advertisers spend billions of dollars each year on media advertising to convince people to drive the right car, wear the right clothes, and live in the right neighborhood. Most children attend schools and religious institutions that teach the same conventional values: honesty, forgiveness, concern, and abstinence. However, relatively few people have the ability or means

Strain occurs because legitimate avenues for success may be all but closed to some young people, such as these teen runaways living under a highway in California. Because legal and socially acceptable means for obtaining success do not exist, individuals may either use deviant methods to achieve their goals or reject socially accepted goals and substitute deviant ones.

to achieve substantial economic and social success, and this unequal opportunity breeds anger, resentment, and aggression.

According to strain theorists, the means for success are stratified by socioeconomic class. Strain is not typical in middle- and upper-class communities where education and prestigious occupations are readily obtainable. In lower-class areas, however, strain occurs because legitimate avenues for success are all but closed to young people (Figure 4.7). Without legal and socially acceptable means for obtaining success, individuals may either use deviant methods to achieve their goals or reject socially accepted goals and substitute deviant ones (for example, becoming drug users or alcoholics).

Strain theory is compatible with social disorganization views because they both link structural variables—poverty, economic opportunity, the availability of goods and services—to crime and delinquency rates. Also, the likelihood of strain is greatest in deteriorated inner-city areas.

The two models differ in their orientation. Social disorganization theories emphasize group processes and how they affect neighborhood delinquency rates, whereas strain theories focus on how a sense of alienation, rage, and frustration influences individual offending patterns.

We now turn to the best known formulation of strain theory, Robert Merton's theory of anomie.

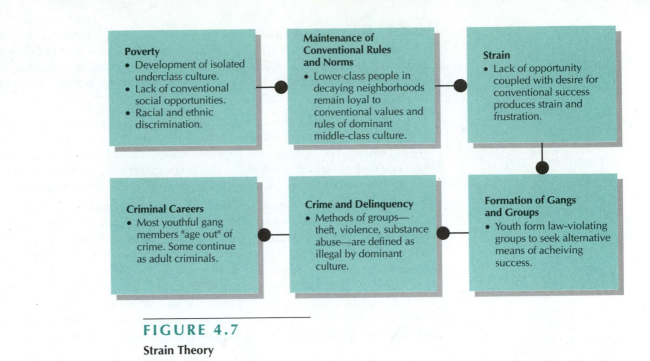

FIGURE 4.7
Strain Theory

Merton's Theory of Anomie

anomie
Normlessness produced by rapidly shifting moral values; according to Merton, anomie occurs when personal goals cannot be achieved using available means.

Strain theories probably owe their popularity to the distinguished U.S. sociologist Robert Merton.[61] In 1938 Merton proposed a revised version of the concept of **anomie** that has proven to be one of the most durable theoretical concepts in twentieth-century social thought.[62]

French sociologist Émile Durkheim first employed the concept of anomie to describe the social malaise that accompanies the breakdown of existing social rules and values brought about by rapid social change.[63] When established norms, customs, and practices are made obsolete, the result is a collective sense of social insecurity and normlessness. Anomic conditions arise when the rule of law is weakened and becomes powerless to maintain social control. Under these conditions, crime can be considered a "normal" response to existing social conditions. A good example of anomie can be seen in the former Soviet Union, where the fall of communism has been followed by the rise of numerous criminal gangs, economic chaos, and political unrest. The Russian people are suffering from a sense of normlessness, striving to cope with the crisis by storing various goods and withdrawing their life savings from banks.[64]

Merton adapted the concept of anomie to the highly competitive postindustrial U.S. society, which he believed also produces a sense of alienation and hopelessness. He argued that two elements of modern culture interact to produce potentially anomic conditions: culturally defined *goals* of acquiring wealth, success, and power; and socially permissible *means,* such as hard work, education, and thrift. According to Merton, U.S. society is goal-oriented, and wealth and material goods are coveted most of all. Unfortunately, legitimate means of acquiring wealth are stratified across class and status lines. Those with little formal education and few economic resources soon find that they are denied the ability to acquire money and other success symbols legally.[65] Denied access to the legitimate opportunity structure, these individuals experience a sense of anger, frustration, normlessness, and anomie. Anomie can lead to criminal or delinquent solutions to the problem of attaining goals, to the rejection of goals, or to substitution of deviant goals for conventional ones.[66]

Social Adaptations   How do we negotiate the tension between our drive to succeed and the actual opportunities available to us? Merton identified five possible modes of adaptation or adjustment: conformity, innovation, ritualism, retreatism, and rebellion. Each represents a way of coping with a balance or imbalance of goals and means.

1. *Conformity:* Conformity occurs when an individual desires conventional social goals and can attain them legitimately through conventional means; goals and means are in balance. For example, middle-class, college-bound students will obey the law because they recognize that their access to education will provide them with a lucrative career. Conformity is the most common form of adaptation in a stable society.

2. *Innovation:* Innovation occurs when an individual accepts the goals of society but rejects or is incapable of gaining them through legitimate means. The sense of anomie that develops because of the imbalance between goals and means can be relieved by adopting innovative behaviors, such as stealing cars, selling drugs, or committing armed robberies. Of the five adaptations, innovation is most closely associated with delinquent behavior. The struggle to achieve the American Dream places such an enormous burden on those lacking economic opportunity that delinquent modes of adaptation are not a surprising result. This condition accounts for the high rate of delinquency in poor areas, where access to legitimate means is

FOCUS ON DELINQUENCY

CRIME AND THE AMERICAN DREAM

Crime and the American Dream, by Steven Messner and Richard Rosenfeld, is an important addition to the conceptualization of strain theory. Their vision of why U.S. crime and delinquency rates are so high focuses on the function of *cultural* and *institutional* influences in American society.

Messner and Rosenfeld agree with Merton's view that the success goal is pervasive in U.S. culture. They refer to this as the American Dream, a term they employ as both a goal and a process. As a goal, the American Dream involves the accumulation of material goods and wealth under conditions of open individual competition. As a process, it involves the socialization of youth to pursue material success above all else and to believe that prosperity is a universally achievable goal. Anomic conditions occur because the desire to succeed at any cost drives people apart, weakens the collective sense of community, fosters ambition, and restricts the desirability of other kinds of achievement, such as a "good name" and a respected reputation.

That Americans are conditioned to succeed "at all costs" should come as no surprise because our capitalist system encourages innovation in the pursuit of monetary rewards. Billionaire businessmen such as Steve Forbes, Ross Perot, Bill Gates, and Donald Trump are considered national heroes whose wealth and lifestyle are universally admired. They become cultural icons and leaders who many believe deserve to be elected president because of their business success.

What is distinct about U.S. society, according to Messner and Rosenfeld, and what most likely determines our exceedingly high national crime rate, is that anomic conditions have been allowed to "develop to such an extraordinary degree." Why has this happened? Messner and Rosenfeld believe there are three reasons why institutions that might otherwise control the exaggerated emphasis on financial success have been rendered powerless or obsolete:

1. *Noneconomic functions and roles have been* devalued. Performance in other institutional settings—the family, school, or community—is assigned a lower priority than the goal of financial success. Human service jobs such as social work and teaching are considered significantly less important than jobs as entertainers or athletes. In U.S. society it seems normal and rational for citizens to demand that the board of education ask public

severely limited. The infusion of the success goal in U.S. culture and its effect on crime is discussed in the Focus on Delinquency box entitled "Crime and the American Dream."

3. *Ritualism:* Ritualism refers to the diminution of the success goals in favor of a strict set of manners and customs that provide pleasure even when the rituals serve no practical purpose. Such practices are common in cults, feudal societies, clubs, college fraternities, and social organizations. Sometimes ritualism can lead to tragedy when members become obsessed with their cults' bizarre demands. For example, in 1997 thirty-nine members of the California-based Heaven's Gate group killed themselves in a mass suicide so that they could enter a spaceship that their leader, Marshall Applewhite, told them was approaching earth.[67]

4. *Retreatism:* Retreatism entails a rejection of both the goals and the means of society. Merton suggested that people who adjust in this fashion are "in society but not of it."[68] Included in this category are "psychotics, psychoneurotics, chronic autists, pariahs, outcasts, vagrants, tramps, chronic drunkards, and drug addicts."[69] People who perceive anomie because they have embraced socially acceptable goals but are denied the means to attain them may become retreatists. Because they are morally or otherwise incapable of violence or theft, they attempt to escape their lack of success by withdrawing, either mentally or physically.

school teachers to take pay cuts or go for years without a raise. But these same people complain loudly when the owner of a local baseball team allows a slugger to sign with another team rather than pay him $10 million per year.

2. *When conflicts emerge, noneconomic roles become subordinate to and must* accommodate *economic roles.* The schedules, routines, and demands of the workplace take priority over those of the home, the school, the community, and other aspects of social life. For example, many parents are willing to leave very young children in day care for ten hours per day or more to pursue the careers that can bring them increased levels of luxury.

3. *Economic standards and norms* penetrate *into noneconomic realms.* Economic terms become part of the common language: people want you to get to the "bottom line"; spouses view themselves as "partners" who "manage" the household. Business leaders run for public office promising to "run the country like a corporation."

According to Messner and Rosenfeld, the relatively high U.S. delinquency rates can be explained by the interrelationship of culture and institutions. At the cultural level, the dominance of the American Dream mythology ensures that a great many more children than can be satisfied by legitimate means will hunger for material goods. Anomie becomes the norm because no matter how much the typical American has, it's never enough. Youths always want the most stylish fashions, the newest music, and the hottest car. As soon as cultural values change, so does their need for material possessions.

At the institutional level the dominance of economic concerns weakens the informal social control exerted by the family and the school. Parents lose their authority when they cannot provide children with economic luxuries. Teachers lose their influence when adolescents no longer believe education will get them what they want.

Cultural and institutional conditions reinforce each other in a never-ending loop: culture determines institutions and institutional change influences culture.

The Messner-Rosenfeld version of anomie builds on Merton's views by trying to explain why the success goal has reached such a place of prominence in U.S. culture. The message "to succeed by any means necessary" has become a national icon.

Source: Steven Messner and Richard Rosenfeld, *Crime and the American Dream,* 2nd ed. (Belmont, Calif.: Wadsworth, 1996).

5. *Rebellion:* A rebellious adaptation involves reacting to anomie by substituting an alternative sets of goals and means for the accepted ones of society. This adaptation is typical of revolutionaries, who promote radical change in the existing social structure and advocate alternative lifestyles, goals, and beliefs. Revolutionary groups and cults have abounded in the United States, some espousing the violent overthrow of the existing social order and others advocating the use of nonviolent, passive resistance to change society. Rebels may perceive anomie because they feel that the government is corrupt or because they want to create alternate opportunities and lifestyles within the existing system.

Analyzing Anomie   Anomie theory helps explain the dynamic relationship between social and individual sources of criminal behavior. People who lack socially acceptable means of success become frustrated and respond with innovations such as theft or extortion, retreat into drugs or alcohol, or rebel and join hate, revolutionary, or cult groups. Considering the economic stratification in U.S. society, anomie predicts that crime and delinquency will prevail in lower-class culture, which it does.

Although highly influential, a number of questions are left unanswered by anomie theory:

■ Merton did not explain why people choose different adaptations to anomie: Why does one adolescent choose innovation and become a thief and another become a "retreatist" and take drugs?

■ The theory also does not adequately explain the "aging-out phenomenon": Does the fact that crime rates decline with age imply that perceptions of anomie also diminish as people mature? Merton never addresses the dynamics of anomie.

■ Anomie theory focuses on behavior of the lower class and is less useful as an explanation of middle-class or white-collar crime. It also does not address gender differences in the crime rate. If female crime rates are lower, women must be more likely to embrace conformity. Yet women are less likely to have opportunities for success due to gender discrimination.

■ Critics have also suggested that people actually pursue a number of different life goals and that the economic success goal is merely one among many. Other goals include educational, athletic, and social success and prominence. Achieving these goals is not a matter of social class alone; other factors, including physical ability, intelligence, personality, and family life, can either hinder or assist in their attainment.[70]

Research on how perceptions of anomie influence delinquent behavior has yielded mixed results. Some researchers have found that correlations between scales measuring anomie and criminality are lower than expected, whereas others have found an association between perceptions of anomie and deviant behavior.[71] Despite these ambiguous findings, Merton's original formation of anomie has remained one of the most enduring concepts in the social sciences. It has recently been broadened and updated in the writings of sociologist Robert Agnew, whose general strain theory is discussed next.

General Strain Theory (GST)

Agnew has broadened Merton's vision of anomie and strain so that it might better explain all forms of delinquent behavior.[72] According to Agnew, there are actually three sources of strain (Figure 4.8).

1. *Strain caused by the failure to achieve positively valued goals.* This category of strain includes the disjunction between aspirations and expectations (goals and

Sources of Strain	Negative Affect States	Antisocial Behavior
• Failure to achieve goals • Removal of positive stimuli • Presentation of negative stimuli	• Anger • Frustration • Disappointment • Depression • Fear	• Drug abuse • Delinquency • Violence • Dropping out

FIGURE 4.8

General Strain Theory (GST)

means); this is what Merton spoke of in his theory of anomie. Such strain will occur when youths aspire for wealth and fame but, because they are poor and undereducated, assume that such goals are impossible to achieve. Also falling within this general category is the strain induced by the disjunction between expectations and actual achievements; for example, when a person compares him- or herself to peers who seem to be doing a lot better financially or socially. A similar form of strain occurs when youths perceive that they are not being treated fairly or that the "playing field" is being tilted against them. Perceptions of inequity may result in adverse reactions ranging from running away from its source to lowering the benefits of others through physical attacks or vandalism of their property. For example, the student who believes he is being "picked on" unfairly by a teacher slashes the tires on the teacher's car for revenge.

2. *Strain as the removal of positively valued stimuli from the individual.* Strain may occur because of the actual or anticipated removal or loss of a positively valued stimulus.[73] For example, the loss of a girl- or boyfriend can produce strain, as can the death of a loved one, moving to a new neighborhood or school, or the divorce or separation of parents. The loss of positive stimuli may lead to delinquency as the adolescent tries to prevent the loss, retrieve what has been lost, obtain substitutes, or seek revenge against those responsible for the loss.

3. *Strain as the presentation of negative stimuli.* Strain may also be caused by negative or noxious stimuli. Included within this category are such pain-inducing social interactions as child abuse and neglect, criminal victimization, physical punishment, family and peer conflict, school failure, and interaction with stressful life events ranging from verbal threats to air pollution. For example, children who are abused at home may take their rage out on younger children at school or become involved in violent delinquency.[74]

Although these three main sources of strain are independent from one another, they may overlap and be cumulative. For example, insults from a teacher may be viewed as an unfair application of negative stimuli that interferes with academic aspirations. The greater the intensity and frequency of strain experiences, the greater their impact and the more likely they are to cause delinquency.

negative affective states
Anger, depression, disappointment, fear, and other adverse emotions that derive from strain.

Negative Affective States   According to Agnew, adolescents engage in delinquency as a result of **negative affective states**—the anger, frustration, disappointment, depression, fear, and other adverse emotions that derive from strain. Of these, anger is the key linkage between strain and delinquency.

Each type of strain will increase the likelihood that people will experience anger. Anger increases perceptions of injury and of being wronged. It produces a desire for revenge, energizes individuals to take action, and lowers inhibitions; violence and aggression seem justified if you have been wronged and are righteously angry.

Strain can be considered a predisposing factor for delinquency when it is chronic and repetitive and creates a hostile, suspicious, and aggressive attitude. An individual strain episode may be the situational event, or "trigger," that produces violent or otherwise antisocial behavior.

According to Agnew, adolescents who experience strain develop a sense of anger, frustration, normlessness, and anomie. They may take their frustrations out in violent behavior or vandalism.

Coping with Strain Even though it may be socially disapproved, delinquency provides relief and satisfaction for an adolescent living an otherwise stress-filled life. Children who can "take care of themselves" in the school yard may find that their use of violence for self-protection increases their feelings of self-worth. Violent responses may be used as self-protective measures from strain caused by negative stimuli. For example, children who report that they hit or strike their parents also report that they have been the targets of parental violence, such as hitting or slapping. Fighting back is associated with a reduction of assaultive behavior by parents. What may be viewed as a violent response to strain in this scenario actually helps remedy a problem.[75]

Agnew recognizes that not all youths who experience strain become delinquents. Some are able to marshal their emotional, mental, and behavioral resources to cope with the anger and frustration produced by strain. Some defenses are *cognitive*. Individuals may be able to rationalize their frustrating situation: Economic success is "just not that important"; I may be poor, but the "next guy is worse off"; and when things don't work out, "I got what I deserved."

Others seek *behavioral solutions*. They run away from adverse conditions or seek revenge against those who caused the strain. Behavioral techniques range from physical exercise to drug abuse. In some cases people can cope with strain through legitimate behavior, but others fall back on deviant or antisocial coping mechanisms such as using drugs to cope with emotional pain.

GST acknowledges that the ability to cope with strain is mediated by social and economic capital. The economically deprived are less likely than the affluent to develop effective coping mechanisms. Youths who form associations with delinquent peers are less likely to cope than those who avoid forming relationships with others who reinforce their frustration and anger.

Coping with strain may also be influenced by the source of strain. Individuals who can identify a target to blame for their problems are more likely to respond with retaliatory action (for example, "Joe stole my girl away by lying about me, so I beat him up!"). When individuals internalize blame, delinquent behavior is less likely to occur (for example, "I lost my girlfriend because I was unfaithful, it's all my fault"). When the source of strain is difficult to pinpoint (for example, "I feel depressed because my parents got divorced"), aggressive responses are less frequent.[76]

Evaluating GST Agnew's work is quite important because it both expands on Merton's characterization of strain and directs future research agendas. It also adds to the body of literature describing how social and life history events influence offending patterns. Sources of strain vary over the life course, and so too should delinquency rates—and they do.

There is also empirical support for GST. Adolescents who report feeling "hassled" because they can't get along with their peers and who experience "negative life events" such as being a victim of crime or of a serious illness are also the ones most likely to engage in delinquency.[77]

Independent research efforts have supported Agnew's vision of delinquency. Some research shows that indicators of strain—family breakup, unemployment, moving, feelings of dissatisfaction with friends and school—are positively related to delinquency.[78] Adolescents who report feelings of stress and anger are more likely to interact with delinquent peers and engage in delinquent behaviors.[79] In some cases delinquent behaviors may actually help to mediate strain: delinquency is an effective coping mechanism that helps relieve feelings of anger and resentment.[80] Strain then may be reduced by attacking others, stealing, or vandalizing property.

A number of questions are left unanswered by GST. As Agnew himself has acknowledged, GST fails to adequately explain gender differences in the delinquency rate. Females experience as much or more strain, frustration, and anger as males, yet their delinquency rate is much lower. Is it possible that there are gender differences in either the perception of strain or the ability to cope with its adverse effects? Research testing the GST indicates that the same sources of strain have similar overall effects on both males and females.[81] How, then, can gender differences in the crime rate be explained? Even when presented with similar types of strain, males and females respond with a different constellation of negative emotions.[82] Females may be socialized to internalize stress, blaming themselves for their problems, whereas males can relieve strain by striking out at others. It is also possible that the influences of strain are crime specific. Males may be more susceptible or deeply influenced by the types of strain associated with some crimes (such as violence), whereas females may be affected by others (such as drug abuse). Why particular types of strain should affect the sexes differently remains to be determined by future research.[83]

Cultural Deviance Theories

Cultural deviance theories (sometimes called *subcultural theory*) hold that delinquency is a result of youths' desire to conform to the cultural

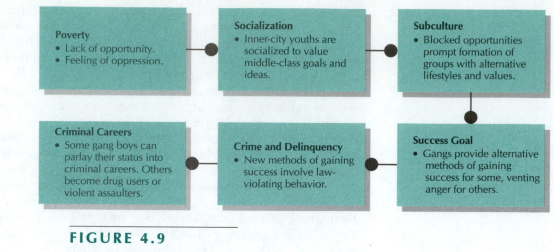

FIGURE 4.9
Cultural Deviance Theory

values of their immediate environment that are in conflict with those of the greater society. Conformity to the rules, values, and norms of unconventional groups with whom youths are in close contact results in violation of the rules of conventional society. According to this view, delinquent behavior is caused by proper socialization within a "deviant" social group or culture. Juvenile delinquency is merely "marching to a different drummer."[84]

Cultural deviance theories suggest that youths from disorganized areas violate the law because they adhere to the unique, independent value system existing within lower-class areas. Lower-class values include being tough, never showing fear, living for today, and disrespecting authority. In a socially disorganized neighborhood, conventional values such as honesty, obedience, and hard work make little sense to youths whose successful adult role models may include the neighborhood gun runner, drug dealer, or pimp (see Figure 4.9).

Cultural deviance theory provides a link between the concepts of social disorganization and strain theory. Subcultural theorists argue that youths who live in impoverished areas lack the means to acquire conventional success goals. Because they develop feelings of anomie and strain, impoverished youths create a unique set of cultural values and standards of their own. Instead of aspiring to be "preppies" or "yuppies," lower-class kids want to be considered tough, street-smart, and to have a bad "rep." In other words, feelings of strain and anomie encourage lower-class youths to form independent subcultures that provide them with support and nurturance. They may be failures in conventional society, but they are the kings and queens of the neighborhood.

Development of Subcultures

culture conflict
When the values of a subculture clash with those of the dominant culture.

In 1938 sociologist Thorsten Sellin identified the social factors that promote and sustain independent subcultures.[85] He found that newly arrived immigrant groups brought with them views and beliefs that clashed with the dominant values of U.S. society. For example, some European and Latin cultures demand that males seek violent revenge for perceived slights or insults to female family members. They could not understand it when police arrested them for killing someone who had insulted their daughter or sister. The result was **culture conflict** between agents of the middle class and residents of poverty areas.

subculture of violence
An identified urban-based subculture in which young males are expected to respond with violence to the slightest provocation.

focal concerns
The value orientation of lower-class culture that is characterized by a need for excitement, trouble, smartness, fate, and personal autonomy.

In 1967 Marvin Wolfgang and Franco Ferracuti identified a **subculture of violence,** whose norms stressed a potent theme of violence and revenge. Young males living in this urban-based subculture were expected to respond with violence to the slightest provocation.[86]

According to a classic paper by sociologist Walter Miller, lower-class areas manifest a distinct cultural climate that remains stable over long periods of time.[87] In these areas a unique group of value-like **focal concerns** dominate life. These concerns have evolved specifically to fit conditions in lower-class environments. The major focal concerns Miller identifies are trouble, toughness, smartness, excitement, fate, and autonomy (see Table 4.1).

According to Miller, clinging to lower-class focal concerns promotes behavior that often runs afoul of the law. Toughness may mean displaying fighting prowess; street smarts leads to drug deals; excitement may result in drinking, gambling, or drug abuse. It is this obedience to the prevailing cultural demands of lower-class society, and not alienation from conventional society, that causes urban crime. Research does in fact show that members of the lower-class value toughness and want to show they are courageous in the face of provocation. Adherence to these lower-class values or focal concerns are linked to violent behavior patterns.[88]

Table 4.1

MILLER'S LOWER-CLASS FOCAL CONCERNS

Trouble   Getting into trouble includes behavior such as fighting, drinking, and sexual misconduct. In lower-class communities people are evaluated by their actual or potential involvement in trouble-making activity. Dealing with trouble can confer prestige (for example, when a man gets a reputation for being able to handle himself well in a fight). Not being able to handle trouble, and having to pay the consequences, can make a person look foolish and incompetent.

Toughness   Lower-class males want local recognition of their physical and spiritual toughness. They refuse to be sentimental or soft and instead value physical strength, fighting ability, and athletic skill. Those who cannot meet these standards risk getting a reputation for being weak, inept, and effeminate.

Smartness   Members of lower-class culture want to maintain an image of being "street-wise" and savvy, using their "street smarts," and having the ability to outfox and "out-con" the opponent. Though formal education is not admired, knowing essential survival techniques—gambling, conning, and outsmarting the law—is a requirement.

Excitement   Members of the lower-class search for fun and excitement to enliven an otherwise drab existence. The search for excitement may lead to gambling, fighting, getting drunk, and sexual adventures. In-between, lower-class citizens may simply "hang out" and "be cool."

Fate   Lower-class citizens believe their lives are in the hands of strong spiritual forces that guide their destinies. Getting lucky, finding good fortune, and hitting the jackpot are all daily dreams.

Autonomy   Being independent of authority figures, such as the police, teachers, and parents, is required; losing control is an unacceptable weakness, incompatible with toughness.

Source: Walter Miller, "Lower-Class Culture as a Generating Milieu of Gang Delinquency," *Journal of Social Issues* 14:5–19 (1958).

Subcultural Values Today

How relevant is Miller's research to today's juveniles? Many of the focal concerns he found in the 1950s still hold sway in lower-class subcultures. Significant numbers of lower-class adolescents are carrying guns today, ready to display their toughness if provoked. Substance abuse is on the rise in lower-class areas as youths look for excitement. Smartness leads inner-city kids to devalue formal education and become dropouts. Trouble means drinking, getting high, and engaging in precocious sex. Gangs and groups in these areas maintain their own language, signs, codes, and moral rules.

Youths living in today's disorganized areas consider themselves part of an urban underclass whose members must use their wits to survive (smartness) or they will succumb to poverty, alcoholism, and drug addiction. [89] Exploitation of women abounds in a culture wracked by unemployment and limited economic opportunity. Sexual conquest (trouble) is one of the few areas open to lower-class males for achieving self-respect (status). The absence of male authority figures contributes to the fear that marriage will limit freedom (autonomy). Peers heap scorn on anyone who allows himself to get "trapped" by a female, fueling the number of single-parent households.[90] Youths who are committed to the norms and values of this deviant subculture are also more likely to disdain or disparage agents of conventional society such as police and teachers.[91]

A number of studies of urban youths confirm Miller's view that street smarts is an important focal concern not only to make money but also to achieve self-respect. In his respected study of street gangs, Mercer Sullivan found that success in crime is called "getting paid" or "getting over," which means not only financial reward but achieving a sense of triumph over the grim urban environment.[92]

Toughness is still admired by urban street youths. In a recent interview study of violent young men in New York, sociologist Jeffery Fagan found that the most compelling function violence served was to develop a status as a "tough" person. A reputation for toughness helped youths gain social power and insulated them from becoming victims themselves. Violence was also seen as a means to acquire the symbols of wealth (nice clothes, flashy cars, access to clubs), to control or humiliate another person, to defy authority, to settle drug-related "business" disputes, to attain retribution, to satisfy the need for thrills or risk-taking, or to respond to challenges to one's manhood.[93]

Cohen's Theory of Delinquent Subculture

Albert K. Cohen first articulated the theory of delinquent subculture in his 1955 book, *Delinquent Boys*.[94] Cohen's main purpose was to explain the disproportionate amount of official delinquent behavior found in poor neighborhoods. In contrast to Walter Miller, who viewed delinquency as conforming to the norms of a lower-class subculture, Cohen's central position is that delinquent behavior of lower-class youths is actually a protest against the norms and values of the middle-class U.S. culture. Because social conditions make them incapable of achieving success in a legitimate fashion, lower-class youths experience a form of culture conflict that Cohen labels *status frustration*. As a result, many youths join together in teenage gangs and engage in behavior that is nonutilitarian, malicious, and negativistic.[95]

Cohen views delinquents as forming a separate subculture and possessing a value system directly in opposition to that of the larger society. He describes the subculture as one that takes "its norms from the larger culture but turns them upside down. The delinquent's conduct is right, by the standards of his subculture, precisely because it is wrong by the norms of the larger cultures."[96]

Causes of Delinquency According to Cohen, the development of the delinquent subculture is a function of the social and familial conditions children experience as they mature in deteriorating inner-city environments. Delinquency is not a product of inherent class inferiority but rather is a function of the social and economic limitations suffered by members of the less fortunate groups in U.S. society. The numbing burden of poverty is the real villain in the creation of delinquent careers.[97]

By implication, Cohen suggests that lower-class families are incapable of teaching their offspring proper socialization techniques for entry into the dominant middle-class culture. Lower-class families, permanently cut off from middle-class norms and values, produce children who lack the basic skills necessary to achieve social and economic success in our demanding society. Developmental disabilities produced by such an upbringing include a lack of educational training, poor speech and communication skills, and an inability to delay gratification.[98]

Middle-Class Measuring Rods Lower-class children find it especially difficult to positively impress authority figures such as teachers, employers, or supervisors. Cohen calls the standards these authority figures set **middle-class measuring rods** and maintains that the conflict lower-class youths feel when they fail to meet these standards is a primary cause of delinquency.

Middle-class measuring rods develop because the most important institutions in society—schools, religious institutions, businesses, the military, the justice system, and so on—are dominated by middle-class values. Clients of these institutions (for example, students, workers, soldiers) are expected to display middle-class values, manners, and behaviors, including verbal skills, ambition, and the ability to delay gratification. When lower-class youths cannot meet these criteria, their failures become part of an enduring public record that is consulted whenever they apply for a job, seek educational advancement, or wish to join a social organization. This failure to meet middle-class measuring rods becomes an enduring part of the permanent record of lower-class youths, following them throughout life and thwarting personal ambitions.

Corner Boys, College Boys, and Delinquent Boys Cohen's position is that lower-class boys who suffer the rejection of middle-class decision makers are deeply affected by their lack of social recognition.[99] Typically, they may elect to adopt one of three alternative behavior models: the corner boy role, the college boy role, or the delinquent boy role.

The **corner boy** is not delinquent but may engage in some marginal behavior. For example, he is a truant and petty drug user but would never get involved in drug trafficking, armed robbery, or other felony crimes. The corner boy spends his time hanging out with his peers, upon whom he depends for support, motivation, and interest. His values, therefore, are those of this group. Eventually, the corner boy will marry a local girl and obtain a menial job with few prospects for advancement or success.

The **college boy** embraces the cultural and social values of the middle class. He actively strives to conform to "middle-class measuring rods" to move up the social ladder. Ill-equipped academically, socially, and linguistically to achieve the rewards of middle-class life, the college boy is fated for frustration and disappointment. Some make it in the middle-class world, but most remain on its margin.

As if sensing that they are headed for eventual disappointment, the **delinquent boy** adopts a set of norms and principles in direct opposition to middle-class society.[100] Living for today only, delinquent boys hold a "devil may care" attitude that Cohen calls short-run hedonism. Members of the delinquent subculture are also careful to maintain **group autonomy.** They join gangs and groups that resist control efforts by authority figures. The gang is autonomous, independent, and the focus of "attraction, loyalty, and solidarity."[101]

Although the delinquent boy may be negativistic and malicious, he may still harbor admiration for the norms and values of the mainstream culture. He may really

---

middle-class measuring rods
Standards by which teachers and other representatives of state authority evaluate students' behavior; when lower-class youths cannot meet these standards they are subject to failure, which brings on frustration and anger at conventional society.

corner boy
Not a delinquent but may engage in marginal behavior; eventually will marry a local girl and obtain a menial job with few prospects for advancement or success.

college boy
Strives to conform to middle-class values and to move up the social ladder but is ill-equipped to succeed and fated to become frustrated and disappointed.

delinquent boy
Adopts a set of norms and values in direct opposition to middle-class society and resists control efforts by authority figures.

group autonomy
Maintaining subcultural values and attitudes that reinforce the independence of the group and separate it from other cultural groups.

want to be a success, but the deck is stacked against him. To deal with this conflict, delinquent boys resort to a process Cohen calls **reaction formation**—rejecting outright the conventional goals and values they may desire but know they can never achieve.[102] For the delinquent boy, this takes the form of irrational, malicious, unaccountable hostility to the norms of respectable middle-class society.[103]

Opportunity Theory

In their influential 1960 work, *Delinquency and Opportunity,* Richard Cloward and Lloyd Ohlin added significantly to the knowledge of delinquent subcultures.[104] Cloward and Ohlin agree with strain theory that access to the legitimate means of achieving social goals is stratified by class.[105] However, they maintain that access to *illegitimate* means are stratified as well. Opportunities for "successful" criminal careers in organized crime or professional theft and drug dealing gangs are not open to everyone. Both legitimate and illegitimate opportunities are closed to youths in the most disorganized inner-city areas.

Gang Subcultures   A key element in opportunity theory is the assumption that a strong relationship exists between environment and crime. In wealthy or middle-class areas educational and vocational opportunities abound, and youths can avail themselves of conventional means of getting ahead, such as going to college. However, in low-income areas, legitimate means are more difficult to come by; therefore, youths must seek illegitimate avenues of success.

Cloward and Ohlin propose that illegitimate avenues of success are also "blocked" for many youths. In fact, they are available only to children growing up in relatively stable areas where adult criminals have developed ongoing criminal enterprises. Accommodations have already been reached—through bribery and corruption—with crooked police and court officials, local businessmen who are willing to buy stolen merchandise with no questions asked, and bondsmen who are willing to post bail in the case of an unforseen arrest. Criminal activity—organized crime, drug trafficking, loan sharking, car theft rings, gambling—can provide a stable income and an alternative avenue to legitimate success. Children growing up in stable but crime-ridden areas admire these successful criminals and attach themselves to the gang. Learning the ropes and helping out, they fit right into this *criminal subculture.* At first they may join youth gangs specializing in theft, extortion, and other profitable criminal activities. Later, if they prove their worth, they can become part of the even more profitable adult crime organizations.

Not all youths in such areas join criminal gangs. Some remain loyal to the values and rules of conventional society. Others are temperamentally incapable of following either criminal or conventional rules. They take drugs and alcohol and stress playing it cool and being high and strung out. Cloward and Ohlin call their world the *retreatist subculture.*

Some poverty areas are so unstable and disorganized that even illegitimate means to success are blocked. Youths in these areas become members of the *conflict subculture.*[106] They form fighting gangs to defend their turf and engage in extortion and violent crimes. The conflict subculture provides little in the way of economic incentives, but it allows boys the opportunity for success and for ego gratification by enabling them to show their bravery, strength, and fighting prowess.[107]

Analyzing Opportunity Theory   More than thirty years ago Cloward and Ohlin's view of urban delinquency was considered a milestone for guiding delinquency prevention efforts: if youths could be provided with economic opportunities, they would forgo criminal activity and live conventional lives. Social programs of the time were geared to providing these alternatives, but they proved less than successful. Providing economic opportunity alone may not be sufficient to reduce delinquency rates.

Research testing the main premises of opportunity theory has also been inconclusive.[108] Recent surveys of gang delinquency have shown that gangs are more pervasive than Cloward and Ohlin imagined, that more than one type of gang (conflict, violent, drug dealing, social) exists in a particular area, and that the commitment of gang boys to one another is less intense than opportunity theory would suggest.[109]

Several contrasting studies appear to support opportunity theory.[110] Research efforts have found that lower-class delinquents report less perception of opportunity than middle-class youths who engage in conventional behavior patterns.[111] Some recent evidence from gang research projects is also supportive of opportunity theory. Studies of gang boys in Detroit by Carl Taylor and in Chicago by Felix Padilla suggest that gangs form as quasi "business enterprises" to provide economic opportunity via drug dealing to youths who otherwise would be left out of the economic mainstream.[112] They found evidence that gang boys do in fact share the economic values of the American middle class but lack the opportunity to achieve success through conventional means. Although the gang boys Padilla studied certainly know that what they are doing is in violation of social norms and laws, they believe it is really the only course of action readily open to them (gang delinquency is discussed further in Chapter 9).[113]

Social Structure Theory and Delinquency Prevention

Social structure theories suggest that the best method of primary delinquency prevention is local community organization. Such efforts should be two-pronged. First, deteriorated neighborhoods must be refurbished to provide an environment that meets the basic needs of the residents. Second, educational and job opportunities must be created to provide legitimate alternatives to delinquent gangs. To achieve these goals, financial support must be made available to needy families to sustain their ability to survive.

Delinquency prevention through community organizations was pioneered in Chicago by Clifford Shaw in the 1930s. In 1933 Shaw initiated the Chicago Area Project, which was designed to produce social change in communities that suffered from high delinquency rates and gang activity. As part of the project, qualified local leaders coordinated social service centers that promoted community solidarity and counteracted social disorganization. More than twenty different programs were developed, featuring discussion groups, counseling services, hobby groups, school-related activities, and recreation. There is still some question of whether these programs had a positive influence on the delinquency rate. Some evaluations indicated positive results, but others showed that the Chicago Area Project efforts did little to reduce juvenile criminality.[114]

In the 1950s delinquency prevention programs sought to reach out to youths who were unlikely to use community centers. Instead of having troubled youths come to them, **detached street workers** were sent out into inner-city neighborhoods, creating close relationships with juvenile gangs and groups in their own milieu.[115] The best known detached street worker program was Boston's Mid-City Project, which dispatched trained social workers to seek out and meet with youth gangs three to four times a week on the gangs' own turf. Their goal was to modify the organization of the gang and allow gang members a chance to engage in more

detached street workers
Social workers who go out into the community and establish close relationships with juvenile gangs with the goal of modifying gang behavior to conform to conventional behaviors and to help gang members get jobs and educational opportunities.

conventional behaviors. The detached street workers tried to help gang members get jobs and educational opportunities. They acted as go-betweens for gang members with agents of the power structure—lawyers, judges, parole officers, and the like. Despite these efforts, an evaluation of the program by Walter Miller failed to show that it resulted in a significant reduction in criminal activity.[116]

The heyday of delinquency prevention programs based on social structure theory was in the 1960s. The approach seemed quite compatible with the rehabilitative policies of the Kennedy (New Frontier) and Johnson (Great Society/War on Poverty) administrations. Delinquency prevention programs received a great deal of federal funding. The most ambitious of these was the New York City-based Mobilization for Youth (MOBY). Funded by more than $50 million, MOBY attempted an integrated approach to community development. Based securely on Cloward and Ohlin's concept of providing opportunities for legitimate success, MOBY organizers created new employment opportunities in the community, coordinated social services, and sponsored social action groups such as tenants' committees, legal action services, voter registration, and political action committees. But MOBY died for lack of funding amid serious questions about its utility and use of funds.

The concept of community organization and change to combat delinquency fell into disfavor in the 1970s and 1980s. However, attempts to improve the lives of families and to prevent and control delinquency have not ended. One approach has been directed at helping families in need by giving them the resources to sustain and improve their lives. If opportunities are available, families will be better able to control their children and remain a primary source of social control.

Another approach has been to help children develop strategies to resolve conflict peacefully and to deal effectively with neighborhood violence. The mass media has been enlisted to discourage violence. Nonetheless, in recent years the focus of delinquency prevention efforts has shifted from the neighborhood reclamation projects of the 1960s to more individualized, family-centered treatments (see Chapters 5 and 8).

SUMMARY

Social structure theories hold that delinquent behavior is an adaptation to conditions that predominate in lower-class environments. Social structure theory has three main branches (see Table 4.2). The first, social disorganization, suggests that economically deprived areas lose their ability to control and direct the behavior of their residents. Gangs and groups flourish in these disorganized areas. Deviant values are transmitted from one generation to the next. Shaw and McKay found this cultural transmission process to be typical of youthful street gangs. They found in their study that delinquency rates varied widely throughout Chicago. Adolescents who live in high-crime-rate areas have a greater probability of becoming delinquent and being arrested and later incarcerated. Delinquency is a product of the socialization mechanisms within a neighborhood. Unstable neighborhoods have the greatest chance of producing delinquents. More recent ecological theories have expanded on this early research and shown how community fear, unemployment, change, and attitudes influence behavior patterns.

The second branch of social structure theory is made up of strain theories. These hold that lower-class youths may actually desire legitimate goals but that their unavailability causes rage, frustration, and substitution of deviant behavior. Robert Merton linked strain to anomie, a condition caused when there is a conflict or disjunction between goals and means. In his general strain theory, Robert Agnew identifies two more sources of strain, the removal of positive reinforcements and the addition of negative ones. He shows how strain causes delinquent behavior by creating negative affective states, and he outlines the means adolescents employ to cope with strain.

The third branch of structural theory is cultural deviance or subcultural theory. This maintains that the result of social disorganization and strain is the development of independent subcultures that hold values in opposition to mainstream society. Walter Miller argues that almost all lower-class citizens maintain separate value systems, which he calls focal concerns. Albert Cohen identifies a delinquent subculture that is negativistic and destructive. Sociologists Richard Cloward and Lloyd Ohlin take this idea one step further by suggesting that some neighborhoods deny their residents the opportunity for even illegal gain, thereby creating the rise in violence and drug-related subcultures.

The social structure view is still influential today. Modern theorists consider the high level of crime in certain areas to be a function of social disorganization, relative deprivation, and neighborhood transition.

Over the years, a number of delinquency prevention efforts have been based on a social structure approach.

Table 4.2

SOCIAL STRUCTURE THEORIES

Theory	Major Premise	Strengths
Social Disorganization Theories		
Social disorganization	The breakdown of informal and formal social control in deteriorated inner-city areas results in the formation of gangs and increasing rates of delinquency.	Accounts for urban crime rates and trends.
Relative deprivation	Crime occurs when the wealthy and poor live in close proximity to one another.	Explains high-crime rates in deteriorated inner-city areas located near more affluent neighborhoods.
Strain Theories		
Anomie	People who adopt the goals of society but lack the means to attain them seek alternatives, such as crime.	Points out how competition for success creates conflict and crime. Suggests that social conditions can account for crime.
General strain theory	Strain has a variety of sources. Strain causes crime in the absence of adequate coping mechanisms.	Identifies the complexities of strain in modern society. Expands on anomie theory. Shows the influences of social events on behavior over the life course. Can explain middle- and upper-class crime.
Cultural Deviance Theories		
Subcultural theory	Citizens who obey the street rules of lower-class life (focal concerns) find themselves in conflict with the dominant culture.	Identifies more coherently the elements of lower-class culture that push people into committing street crimes.
Cohen's theory of delinquent subculture	Status frustration of lower-class boys, created by their failure to achieve middle-class success, causes them to join gangs.	Shows how the conditions of lower-class life produce crime. Explains violence and destructive acts. Identifies conflict of lower class with middle class.
Cloward and Ohlin's theory of opportunity	Blockage of conventional opportunities causes lower-class youths to join criminal, conflict, or retreatist gangs. Criminal opportunities are limited.	Shows that even illegal opportunities are structured in society. Indicates why people become involved in a particular type of criminal activity.

K E Y   T E R M S

culture of poverty	social ecology	subculture of violence
underclass	social control	focal concerns
stratification	natural areas for crime	middle-class measuring
latchkey children	transitional neighborhood	rods
social structure theories	cultural transmission	corner boy
social disorganization	relative deprivation	college boy
theory	gentrified	delinquent boy
strain theory	anomie	group autonomy
cultural deviance theory	negative affective states	reaction formation
subcultures	culture conflict	detached street workers

Read the following article from InfoTrac College Edition:

Understanding disproportionate minority confinement. (Juvenile Justice News) Karen B. Shepard. *Corrections Today* June 1995

A number of theories have associated poverty and minority status with higher rates of crime and, consequently, incarceration. Although all have associated weaknesses, they are still used as popular explanations of the plight of the lower classes and minorities. These theories are just as applicable for describing adult crime as they are for understanding juvenile delinquency.

After reading the article above, use one of the social structure theories outlined in Chapter 4 to help define the causes for increased minority incarceration.

QUESTIONS FOR DISCUSSION

1. Is there a transitional area in your town or city?
2. Is it possible that a distinct lower-class culture exists? Do you know anyone who has the focal concerns Miller talks about?
3. Have you ever perceived anomie? What causes anomie? Is there more than one cause of strain?
4. How does poverty cause delinquency?
5. Do middle-class youths become delinquent for the same reasons as lower-class youths?
6. Does relative deprivation produce delinquency?

NOTES

1. Adapted from Pam Belluck, "Razing the Slums to Rescue the Residents," *New York Times* 6 September 1998.
2. Katherine A. Gilbert, "Learning in a War Zone," *The Christian Century* 23 October 1996, pp. 998–1001.
3. Julian Chow and Claudia Coulton, "Was There a Social Transformation of Urban Neighbourhoods in the 1980s?" *Urban Studies* 35:1358–75 (1998).
4. Laura G. De Haan and Shelley MacDermid, "The Relationship of Individual and Family Factors to the Psychological Well-Being of Junior High School Students Living in Urban Poverty," *Adolescence* 33:73–90 (1998).
5. Oscar Lewis, "The Culture of Poverty," *Scientific American* 215:19–25 (1966).
6. Rodrick Wallace, "Expanding Coupled Shock Fronts of Urban Decay and Criminal Behavior: How U.S. Cities Are Becoming 'Hollowed Out'," *Journal of Quantitative Criminology* 7:333–55 (1991).
7. Ken Auletta, *The Under Class* (New York: Random House, 1982).
8. William Julius Wilson, *The Truly Disadvantaged* (Chicago: University of Chicago Press, 1987).
9. Tamar Lewin, "Number of Children in Poverty Declines," *New York Times* 15 March 1998, p. 4.
10. Jeanne Brooks-Gunn and Greg J. Duncan, "The Effects of Poverty on Children," *The Future of Children* 7:34–39 (1997).
11. Greg Duncan, W. Jean Yeung, Jeanne Brooks-Gunn, and Judith Smith, "How Much Does Childhood Poverty Affect the Life Chances of Children?", *American Sociological Review* 63:406–23 (1998).
12. Ibid., p. 29.
13. Brooks-Gunn and Duncan, "The Effects of Poverty on Children."
14. Herman Schwendinger and Julia Siegel Schwendinger, *Adolescent Subcultures and Delinquency* (New York: Prager, 1985).
15. Joanne Savage and Bryan Vila, "Lagged Effects of Nurturance on Crime: A Cross-National Comparison," paper presented at the American Society of Criminology Meeting, Boston, Mass., November 1995.
16. G. R. Patterson, L. Crosby, and S. Vuchnich, "Predicting Risk for Early Police Arrest," *Journal of Quantitative Criminology* 8:335–53 (1992).
17. Robert Agnew, "Foundation for a General Strain Theory of Crime and Delinquency," *Criminology* 30:47–87 (1992), at 48.
18. Robert Bursik and Harold Grasmick, "The Multiple Layers of Social Disorganization," paper presented at the Annual Meeting of the American Society of Criminology, New Orleans, November 1992; Robert Bursik and Harold Grasmick, "Longitudinal Neighborhood Profiles in Delinquency: The Decomposition of Change," *Journal of Quantitative Criminology* 8:247–56 (1992).
19. Louis Wirth, "Urbanism as a Way of Life," *American Journal of Sociology* 44:1–24 (1938).
20. Clifford R. Shaw and Henry D. McKay, *Juvenile Delinquency and Urban Areas,* rev. ed. (Chicago: University of Chicago Press, 1972).
21. Ibid., p. 52.
22. Ibid., p. 170.
23. Solomon Kobrin, "Chicago Area Project—A Twenty-Five Year Assessment," *Annals of the American Academy of Political and Social Science* 322:20–29 (1950).
24. Frederick Thrasher, *The Gang* (Chicago: University of Chicago Press, 1927).
25. Robert Bursik and James Webb, "Community Change and Patterns of Delinquency," *American Journal of Sociology* 88:24–42 (1982).
26. Bernard Lander, *Toward an Understanding of Juvenile Delinquency* (New York: Columbia University Press, 1954); David Bordua, "Juvenile Delinquency and 'Anomie': An Attempt at Replication," *Social Problems* 6:230–38 (1958); Roland Chilton, "Continuities in Delinquency Area Research: A Comparison of Studies in Baltimore, Detroit, and Indianapolis," *American Sociological Review* 29:71–73 (1964).
27. For a general review, see James Byrne and Robert Sampson, eds., *The Social Ecology of Crime* (New York: Springer-Verlag, 1985).
28. Leo Carroll and Pamela Irving Jackson, "Inequality, Opportunity, and Crime Rates in Central Cities," *Criminology* 21:178–94 (1983).
29. Judith Blau and Peter Blau, "The Cost of Inequality: Metropolitan Structure and Violent Crime," *American Sociological Review* 147:114–29 (1982).

30. Margo Wilson and Martin Daly, "Life Expectancy, Economic Inequality, Homicide, and Reproductive Timing in Chicago Neighbourhoods," *British Journal of Medicine* 314:1271–74 (1997).

31. Robert Sampson, "Structural Sources of Variation in Race-Age-Specific Rates of Offending across Major U.S. Cities," *Criminology* 23:647–73 (1985).

32. Richard Block, "Community Environment and Violent Crime," *Criminology* 17:46–57 (1979).

33. Richard Rosenfeld, "Urban Crime Rates: Effects of Inequality, Welfare Dependency, Region and Race," in James Byrne and Robert Sampson, eds., *The Social Ecology of Crime* (New York: Springer-Verlag, 1985), pp. 116–30.

34. Ora Simcha-Fagan and Joseph Schwartz, "Neighborhood and Delinquency: An Assessment of Contextual Effects," *Criminology* 24:667–703 (1986).

35. Leo Scheurman and Solomon Kobrin, "Community Careers in Crime," in Albert Reiss and Michael Tonry, eds., *Communities and Crime* (Chicago: University of Chicago Press, 1986), pp. 67–100.

36. Ibid., p. 96.

37. Ellen Kurtz, Barbara Koons, and Ralph Taylor, "Land Use, Physical Deterioration, Resident-based Control, and Calls for Service on Urban Streetblocks," *Justice Quarterly* 15:121–49 (1998).

38. Janet Heitgerd and Robert Bursik Jr., "Extracommunity Dynamics and the Ecology of Delinquency," *American Journal of Sociology* 92:775–87 (1987).

39. Richard McGahey, "Economic Conditions, Organization, and Urban Crime," in Albert Reiss and Michael Tonry, eds., *Communities and Crime* (Chicago: University of Chicago Press, 1986), pp. 231–70.

40. Allen Liska and Paul Bellair, "Violent-Crime Rates and Racial Composition: Convergence Over Time," *American Journal of Sociology* 101:578–610 (1995).

41. John Hagan, "The Social Embeddedness of Crime and Unemployment," *Criminology* 31:465–92 (1993).

42. Pamela Wilcox Rountree and Kenneth Land, "Burglary Victimization, Perceptions of Crime Risk, and Routine Activities: A Multilevel Analysis across Seattle Neighborhoods and Census Tracts," *Journal of Research in Crime and Delinquency* 33:147–80 (1996).

43. Randy LaGrange, Kenneth Ferraro, and Michael Supancic, "Perceived Risk and Fear of Crime: Role of Social and Physical Incivilities," *Journal of Research in Crime and Delinquency* 29:311–34 (1992).

44. See, generally, Wesley Skogan, "Fear of Crime and Neighborhood Change," in Albert Reiss and Michael Tonry, eds., *Communities and Crime* (Chicago: University of Chicago Press, 1986), pp. 191–232; Stephanie Greenberg, "Fear and Its Relationship to Crime, Neighborhood Deterioration and Informal Social Control," in James Byrne and Robert Sampson, eds., *The Social Ecology of Crime* (New York: Springer-Verlag, 1985), pp. 47–62.

45. Jeffery Will and John McGrath, "Crime, Neighborhood Perceptions, and the Underclass: The Relationship between Fear of Crime and Class Position," *Journal of Criminal Justice* 23:163–76 (1995).

46. Wilson and Daly, "Life Expectancy, Economic Inequality, Homicide, and Reproductive Timing In Chicago Neighborhoods."

47. Catherine Ross, "Fear of Victimization and Health," *Journal of Quantitative Criminology* 9:159–65 (1993).

48. Donald Black, "Social Control as a Dependent Variable," in D. Black, ed., *Toward a General Theory of Social Control* (Orlando: Academic Press, 1990).

49. Bursik and Grasmick, "The Multiple Layers of Social Disorganization," pp. 8–10.

50. Robert Bursik Jr. and Harold Grasmick, "Economic Deprivation and Neighborhood Crime Rates, 1960–1980," *Law and Society* 27:263–84 (1993).

51. Rodney Stark, "Deviant Places: A Theory of the Ecology of Crime," *Criminology* 25:893–911 (1987).

52. Robert Sampson and W. Byron Groves, "Community Structure and Crime: Testing Social Disorganization Theory," *American Journal of Sociology* 94:774–802 (1989).

53. Denise Gottfredson, Richard McNeill, and Gary Gottfredson, "Social Area Influences on Delinquency: A Multilevel Analysis," *Journal of Research in Crime and Delinquency* 28:197–206 (1991).

54. Elijah Anderson, *Streetwise: Race, Class and Change in an Urban Community* (Chicago: University of Chicago Press, 1990), pp. 243–44.

55. Michael Greene, "Chronic Exposure to Violence and Poverty: Interventions that Work for Youth," *Crime and Delinquency* 39:106–24 (1993).

56. Felton Earls, *Linking Community Factors and Individual Development* (Washington, D.C.: National Institute of Justice, 1998).

57. Greene, "Chronic Exposure to Violence and Poverty: Interventions that Work for Youth," pp. 110–11.

58. Carolyn Smith and Bonnie Carlson, "Stress, Coping, and Resilience in Young Children," *Social Service Review* 71:231–56 (1997).

59. Mitchell Chamlin and John Cochran, "Social Altruism and Crime," *Criminology* 35:203–27 (1997).

60. James DeFronzo, "Welfare and Homicide," *Journal of Research in Crime and Delinquency* 34:395–406 (1997).

61. See, for example, Robert Merton, *Social Theory and Social Structure* (Glencoe, Ill.: Free Press, 1957).

62. Robert Merton, "Social Structure and Anomie," *American Sociological Review* 3:672–82 (1938).

63. For samples of his work, see Émile Durkheim, *The Rules of Sociological Method*, 8th ed. (Glencoe, Ill.: Free Press, 1950); idem, *Suicide* (Glencoe, Ill.: Free Press, 1951).

64. Mikhail Ivanov, "The Rip-Off of a Nation," *Russian Life* 41:8–12 (1998).

65. Ibid., p. 680.

66. Ibid.

67. Stephen J. Hedge, "www.masssuicide.com," *U.S. News & World Report* 7 April 1997, pp. 26–31.

68. Robert Merton, "Social Structure and Anomie," in Marvin Wolfgang, Leonard Savitz, and Norman Johnston, eds., *The Sociology of Crime and Delinquency* (New York: Wiley, 1970), p. 242.

69. Ibid.

70. Robert Agnew, "Goal Achievement and Delinquency," *Sociology and Social Research* 68:435–51 (1984); see also, Margaret Farnworth and Michael Leiber, "Strain Theory Revisited: Economic Goals, Educational Means and Delinquency," *American Sociological Review* 54:263–74 (1989).

71. Scott Menard, "A Developmental Test of Mertonian Anomie Theory," *Journal of Research in Crime and Delinquency* 32:136–74 (1995).

72. Agnew, "Foundation for a General Strain Theory of Crime and Delinquency."

73. Ibid., p. 57.

74. Timothy Brezina, "Adolescent Maltreatment and Delinquency: The Question of Intervening Processes," *Journal of Research in Crime and Delinquency* 35:71–99 (1998).

75. Timothy Brezina, "The Functions of Aggression: Violent Adaptations to Interpersonal Violence," paper presented at the American Society of Criminology Meeting, San Diego, Calif., 1997.

76. Paul Mazerolle and Alex Piquero, "Linking General Strain with Anger: Investigating the Instrumental, Escapist, and Violent Adaptations to Strain," paper presented at the American Society of Criminology Meeting, Boston, Mass., November 1995.

77. Robert Agnew and Helene Raskin White, "An Empirical Test of General Strain Theory," *Criminology* 30:475–99 (1992).

78. Raymond Paternoster and Paul Mazerolle, "General Strain Theory and Delinquency: A Replication and Extension," *Journal of Research in Crime and Delinquency* 31:235–63 (1994).

79. Teresa Lagrange and Robert Silverman, "Perceived Strain and Delinquency Motivation: An Empirical Evaluation of General

Strain Theory," paper presented at the American Society of Criminology Meeting, Boston, Mass., November 1995.

80. Timothy Brezina, "Adapting to Strain: An Examination of Delinquent Coping Responses," *Criminology* 34:39–61 (1996).

81. John Hoffman and S. Susan Su, "The Conditional Effects of Stress on Delinquency and Drug Use: A Strain Theory in Assessment of Sex Differences," *Journal of Research in Crime and Delinquency* 34:46–78 (1997); Paul Mazerolle, "Gender, General Strain and Delinquency: An Empirical Examination," *Justice Quarterly* 15:65–93 (1998).

82. Lisa Broidy, "The Role of Gender in General Strain Theory," paper presented at the American Society of Criminology Meeting, Boston, Mass., November 1995.

83. Robert Agnew, "Gender and Crime: A General Strain Theory Perspective," paper presented at the American Society of Criminology Meeting, Boston, Mass., November 1995.

84. Joseph Weis and John Sederstrom, *The Prevention of Serious Delinquency: What to Do?* (Washington, D.C.: Government Printing Office, 1981), p. 30.

85. Thorsten Sellin, *Culture Conflict and Crime*, Bulletin No. 41 (New York: Social Science Research Council, 1938).

86. Marvin Wolfgang and Franco Ferracuti, *The Subculture of Violence* (London: Tavistock, 1967).

87. Walter Miller, "Lower Class Culture as a Generating Milieu of Gang Delinquency," *Journal of Social Issues* 14:5–19 (1958).

88. Fred Markowitz and Richard Felson, "Social-Demographic Attitudes and Violence," *Criminology* 36:117–38 (1998).

89. James Short, "Gangs, Neighborhoods and Youth Crime," *Criminal Justice Research Bulletin* 5:1–11 (1990); Sam Houston University, Criminal Justice Research Center, Huntsville, Texas.

90. Ibid.

91. Michael Leiber, Mahesh Nalla, and Margaret Farnworth, "Explaining Juveniles' Attitudes Toward the Police," *Justice Quarterly* 15:151–73 (1998).

92. Mercer Sullivan, *"Getting Paid": Youth Crime and Work in the Inner City* (Ithaca, N.Y.: Cornell University Press, 1990).

93. Jeffrey Fagan, *Adolescent Violence: A View from the Street*, NIJ Research Preview (Washington, D.C.: National Institute of Justice, 1998).

94. Albert Cohen, *Delinquent Boys* (New York: Free Press, 1955).

95. Ibid., p. 25.

96. Ibid., p. 28.

97. Ibid., pp. 73–74.

98. Ibid., p. 86.

99. Ibid., p. 128.

100. Ibid., p. 30.

101. Ibid., p. 31.

102. Ibid., p. 133.

103. Albert Cohen and James Short, "Research on Delinquent Subcultures," *Journal of Social Issues* 14:20 (1958).

104. Richard Cloward and Lloyd Ohlin, *Delinquency and Opportunity* (New York: Free Press, 1960).

105. See Edwin Sutherland, *Principles of Criminology*, 4th ed. (Philadelphia: J.B. Lippincott, 1947).

106. Clarence Schrag, *Crime and Justice, American Style* (Washington, D.C.: U.S. Government Printing Office, 1971), p. 67.

107. See, for example, Irving Spergel, *Racketville, Slumtown, and Haulburg* (Chicago: University of Chicago Press, 1964).

108. Leon Fannin and Marshall Clinard, "Differences in the Conception of Self as a Male among Lower- and Middle-Class Delinquents," *Social Problems* 13:205–15 (1965).

109. Jeffery Fagan, "The Social Organization of Drug Use and Drug Dealing among Urban Gangs," *Criminology* 27:633–69 (1989).

110. Judson Landis and Frank Scarpitti, "Perceptions Regarding Value Orientation and Legitimate Opportunity: Delinquents and Non-Delinquents," *Social Forces* 84:57–61 (1965).

111. James Short, Ramon Rivera, and Ray Tennyson, "Perceived Opportunities, Gang Membership, and Delinquency," *American Sociological Review* 30:56–57 (1965).

112. Carl Taylor, *Dangerous Society* (East Lansing: Michigan State University Press, 1990); Felix Padilla, *The Gang as an American Enterprise* (New Brunswick, N.J.: Rutgers University Press, 1992).

113. Padilla, *The Gang as an American Enterprise*, p. 4.

114. For an intensive look at the Chicago Area Project, see Steven Schlossman and Michael Sedlak, "The Chicago Area Project Revisited," *Crime and Delinquency* 29:398–462 (1983).

115. See New York City Youth Board, *Reaching the Fighting Gang* (New York: New York City Youth Board, 1960).

116. Walter Miller, "The Impact of a 'Total Community' Delinquency Control Project," *Social Problems* 10:168–91 (1962).

Chapter Five

Social Process Theories: Learning, Control, and Developmental

Little League umpire Clayton J. Haen required four stitches to close his wounds after he was attacked by a coach who questioned his judgment during a Sturgeon Bay, Wisconsin, Little League game on June 29, 1998. It all started when the Lions' Club team lost again to the best team in the league. The Lions' Club first base coach (whose son was pitching!) believed the opposing pitcher was not keeping his back foot on the pitching rubber (balking) as required by Little League rules. After the Lions' Club had lost, 9–6, the players shook hands, but the coach cursed umpire Haen in front of the children, shoved him, and followed him into the equipment room. The coach's wife tried to get between them but failed to prevent the fight. "He must be left-handed," Haen said afterward, "because he came around her shoulder and got me in the eye."

Attacks on umpires during children's sporting events have become commonplace.[1] In Wagoner, Oklahoma, a thirty-six-year-old tee-ball coach was convicted in 1997 of choking a fifteen-year-old umpire during a game. In Riverdale, Georgia, a coach shot a father in the arm after the father had complained that his son was not pitching enough. In Houston, Texas, criminal background checks are used by the leagues to weed out volunteers with a record of violence, alcohol abuse, sexual abuse, or theft. A league in suburban Chicago has a zero-tolerance policy against yelling, and a few leagues have quit keeping score, hoping to tamp down on the competitive fervor.

What kind of messages do children receive when their parents are overly aggressive or use violence to settle their problems? If a parent is willing to punch out a Little League umpire for making a bad call, should we be surprised when children use the same tactics in school yard disagreements? For some theorists delinquency is less a matter of where a child lives than a function of how that child is raised: the child's life experiences, the quality of the child's relationships, and what the child learns from his or her parents and friends. According to this view, the onset of delinquency may be traced to learning delinquent attitudes from peers, becoming detached from school, or experiencing conflict in the home. Although social

Little League umpire Clayton J. Haen required four stitches to close his wounds after he was attacked by a coach who questioned his judgment during a Sturgeon Bay, Wisconsin, Little League game. What kind of messages do children receive when their parents are overly aggressive or use violence to settle their problems? If a parent is willing to "punch out" a Little League umpire over a call, should we be surprised when their children use the same tactics in school yard disagreements?

socialization

Process of human development and enculturation that is influenced by key social processes and institutions.

position is certainly important—whether a child's family is rich or poor—**socialization** is considered to be the key determinant of behavior. If the socialization process is incomplete or negatively focused, it can produce an adolescent with a poor self-image who is alienated from conventional social institutions and who feels little attachment to a law-abiding lifestyle.

Socialization is the process of guiding people into socially acceptable behavior patterns through the distribution of information, approval, rewards, and punishments. It involves learning the techniques needed to survive, function, and thrive in society through interaction with significant individuals and institutions. Socialization is a developmental process, evolving over time, that is directed and influenced by an array of family and peer group members, neighbors, teachers, and other authority figures.

Early socialization experiences run deep, and they have a lifelong influence on self-image, beliefs, values, and behavior. Even children living in the most deteriorated inner-city urban environments will not get involved in delinquency if their socialization experiences are positive and supportive.[2] After all, most inner-city youths do not commit serious crimes, and relatively few of those who do go on to become career criminals.[3] More than fourteen million youths live in poverty today, but the great majority do not become chronic offenders. Only those who suffer improper socialization are at risk to crime.

Social Processes and Delinquency

social process theories
Posit that the interactions a person has with key elements of the socialization process determine his or her future behavior.

Social process theories are grounded in the extensive literature examining the relationship between socialization and delinquent behavior. Numerous research studies have found that as children mature elements of society with which they have close and intimate contact influence their behavior patterns. The primary influence is the family. When parenting is inadequate, absent, or destructive, a child's normal maturation processes will be interrupted and damaged. Although much debate still occurs over which elements of the parent–child relationship are most critical, there is little question that family relationships have a significant influence on antisocial behavior.[4] Family breakup, conflict, and abuse are common occurrences, and the association between family dysfunction and delinquency is critical. Child protective services receive about three million complaints per year, and about seven hundred thousand children are in foster care or some other form of substitute shelter.[5] (See Chapter 8 for a review of the family's role in delinquency causation.)

The literature linking delinquency to poor school performance, educational disabilities, and inadequate educational facilities is also quite extensive. Youths who feel that teachers do not care, who consider themselves hopeless academic failures, and who eventually drop out of school are more likely to become involved in a delinquent way of life than adolescents who are educationally gifted and successful.[6] (Chapter 10 reviews the relationship between schools and delinquency.)

Still another suspected element of deviant socialization are peer group relations that stress substance abuse, theft, and violence. Youths who become involved with peers who engage in antisocial behavior may learn the techniques and attitudes that support delinquency and soon may find themselves cut off from more conventional associates and institutions.[7] (Chapter 9 reviews peer relations and delinquency.)

Social process theory portrays the delinquent youth as someone whose personality and behavior—formed in the crucible of social relationships and societal processes—is at odds with conventional society. The social process perspective has three main branches (see Figure 5.1). The first, **learning theory,** holds that delinquency is learned through close relationships with others. Both the techniques of crime and the attitudes necessary to support delinquency are learned. Learning theories assume that children are born "good" and then learn from others to be "bad." They reflect the concerned mother's lament that her formerly well-behaved daughter is "being ruined by her friends" and that her son is "picking up bad habits from his friends."

learning theory
Posits that delinquency is learned through close relationships with others; asserts that children are born "good" and learn to be "bad" from others.

control theory
Posits that delinquency results from a weakened commitment to the major social institutions (family, peers, and school); lack of such commitment allows youths to exercise antisocial behavioral choices.

The second branch, **control theory,** views delinquency as a result of a weakened commitment to the major institutions of society—family, peers, and school. Because their bonds to these institutions of informal social control are severed, some adolescents feel free to exercise antisocial behavior choices. Unlike learning theories, control theories assume that people are born "bad"—impulsive and egocentric—and that they then learn to control themselves through the efforts of wise parents and understanding teachers.

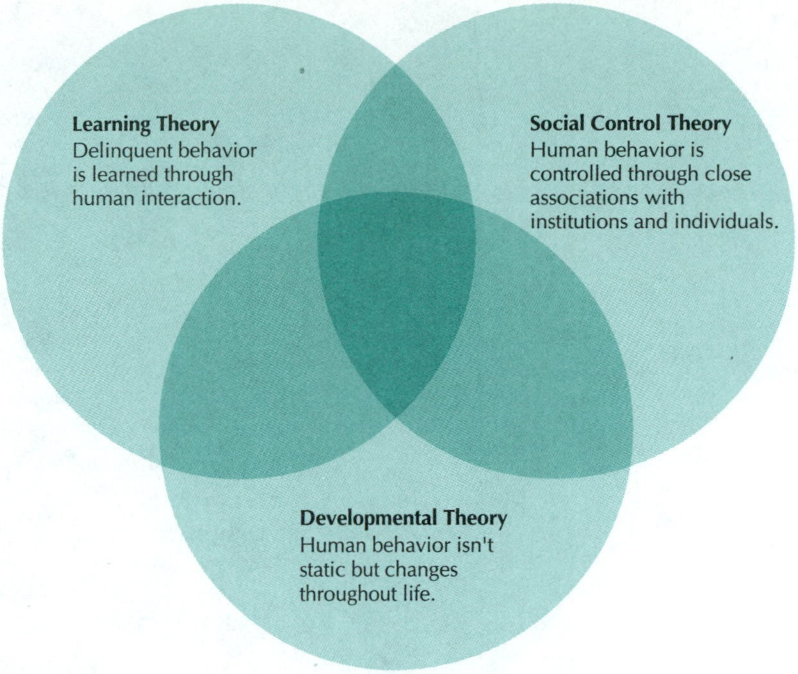

Learning Theory
Delinquent behavior
is learned through
human interaction.

Social Control Theory
Human behavior is
controlled through close
associations with
institutions and individuals.

Developmental Theory
Human behavior isn't
static but changes
throughout life.

developmental theories
Asserts that personal characteristics guide human development and influence behavioral choices but that these choices may change over the life course.

The third branch, **developmental theories,** challenges the view that children can be classified as either delinquents or nondelinquents and that this status is stable over the life course. Developmental theorists are concerned not only with the processes that initiate the onset of delinquency but with the processes that terminate it: Why do people age out or desist from crime? The natural history of criminal careers is also an important part of developmental theory. Why do some delinquents escalate their criminal activities as others are decreasing or limiting their law violations? Why do some youths specialize in a particular crime, whereas others become generalists? Why do some delinquents limit their criminal activity but then resume it once again? Research now shows that some offenders begin their criminal careers at a very early age, whereas others begin at a later point in their lives. How can early and late onset of delinquency be explained?[8]

These questions are central to social process theorists. Let's take a closer look at each of these branches of social process theory.

Learning Theories

Learning theory holds that children living in even the most deteriorated urban areas can successfully resist inducements to crime if they have learned proper moral values, attitudes, and behaviors from their parents, peers, teachers, and neighbors. Delinquency, in contrast, develops by learning the norms, values, and behaviors associated with criminal activity (see Figure 5.2). Social learning can involve the actual techniques of crime (how to hot-wire a car or smoke crack) as well as the psychological aspects of criminality (how to deal with the guilt or shame associated with illegal activities). The former are needed to commit crimes, whereas the latter are required to cope with the emotional turmoil that is the inevitable consequence of law-violating behavior. The next sections describe

FIGURE 5.2
Learning Theory of
Delinquency

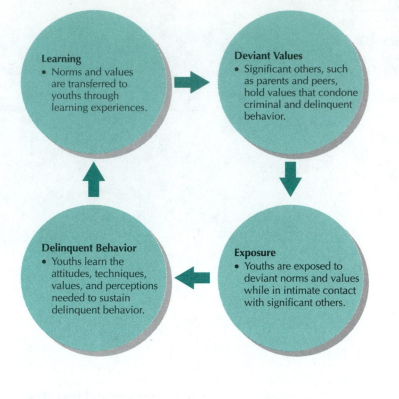

the three most important branches of learning theory: differential association theory, differential reinforcement theory, and neutralization theory.

Differential Association Theory

differential association theory
Asserts that criminal behavior is learned primarily within interpersonal groups and that youths will become delinquent if definitions they have learned favorable to violating the law exceed definitions favorable to obeying the law within that group.

Edwin Sutherland, long considered the preeminent U.S. criminologist, first formulated **differential association theory** in 1939 in his book *Principles of Criminology*.[9] The theory appeared in its final form in 1947. Differential association theory was applied to all criminal and delinquent behavior patterns and has remained broad-based ever since. After Sutherland's death in 1950, his work was continued by his longtime associate Donald Cressey. Cressey was so successful in explaining and popularizing his mentor's ideas that differential association theory remains one of the most enduring explanations of delinquent behavior.

Principles of Differential Association Theory   The basic principles of differential association theory can be summarized in nine statements.[10]

1. *Criminal behavior is learned.* This statement differentiates Sutherland's theory from prior attempts to classify delinquent behavior either as an individual trait or as a product of the social environment. By suggesting that delinquent and criminal behavior is actually learned, Sutherland implied that it can be classified like any other learned behavior—such as writing, painting, or reading. This statement also reveals that Sutherland was aware of and influenced by aspects of (psychological) social learning theory (see Chapter 3).

2. *Criminal behavior is learned in interaction with other persons in a process of communication.* Sutherland believed delinquent behavior is actively learned. An individual does not become a delinquent simply by living passively in a high-crime environment. Youths participate in the process with other individuals who

serve as teachers and guides to delinquent behavior. Delinquency is a group process and cannot appear spontaneously.

3. *Criminal behavior learning occurs principally within intimate personal groups.* Children's contacts with their closest social companions—family, friends, and peers—have the greatest influence on learning deviant behavior and attitudes. Relationships with these individuals can color and control the interpretation of everyday events, helping youths to overcome social controls and embrace delinquent values and behavior. The intimacy of these associations far outweighs the importance of any other form of communication, for example, movies or television. Even on those rare occasions when violent films seem to provoke mass delinquent episodes, the outbreaks can be explained more readily as a reaction to peer group pressure than as a reaction to the films themselves.

4. *Criminal behavior learning includes techniques of committing the crime, which are sometimes very complicated and sometimes very simple, and the specific direction of motives, drives, rationalizations, and attitudes.* Like any learned behavior, the actual techniques of criminality must be acquired and learned. For example, young delinquents learn from their associates the proper way to pick a lock, shoplift, buy and use guns, and deal drugs. The proper way to get high, to smoke a joint, or to use a crack pipe are behavior patterns usually acquired from older or more experienced companions.[11] In addition, delinquents must acquire the proper personal attitudes to sustain a delinquent career. They must learn how to react properly to their criminal acts—when to defend or rationalize their behavior and when to be proud and boastful of their criminal gain; when to show remorse and when to be defiant.

5. *The specific direction of motives and drives is learned from various favorable and unfavorable definitions of the legal codes.* The reaction to social rules and laws is not uniform across society, and youths constantly come in contact with people who maintain different views on the utility of obeying the legal code. Parents and teachers may say one thing, peers another. Children experience what Sutherland calls *culture conflict* when definitions of right and wrong are extremely varied, contradictory, and confusing.

6. *A person becomes delinquent if definitions favorable to violating the law exceed definitions favorable to obeying the law.* According to Sutherland's theory, individuals will become delinquent when they are in contact with persons, groups, or events that produce an excess of "definitions toward delinquency" and, concomitantly, when they are isolated from counteracting forces that promote conventional behaviors. A definition *toward* delinquency occurs when a youth is exposed to deviant behaviors (for example, parents who use alcohol or drugs) or attitudes (for example, friends who discuss the rewards of a shoplifting spree). A definition *against* delinquency occurs when friends or parents demonstrate their disapproval of crime (see Figure 5.3). Of course, neutral behavior (such as reading a book) also exists, and Cressey argues that it is important "especially as an occupier of the time of a child so that he is not in contact with criminal behaviors during the time he is so engaged in the neutral behavior."[12]

7. *Differential associations may vary in frequency, duration, priority, or intensity.* Whether a child learns to obey the law or to disregard it is influenced by the quality of his or her social interactions. Those of lasting duration will have greater influence than those that are shorter. Frequent contacts have greater effect than rare and haphazard ones. Sutherland did not specify what he meant by "priority," but Cressey and others have interpreted this term to mean the age of children when they first encounter definitions toward criminality.[13] Contacts made early in life will probably have a greater and more far-reaching influence than those developed later in life. "Intensity" is generally interpreted to mean the importance and prestige attributed to the individual or groups from whom the definitions are learned.

FIGURE 5.3

Differential Association Theory

Differential association theory assumes that delinquent behavior will occur when the definitions favoring delinquency outweigh the definitions against delinquency.

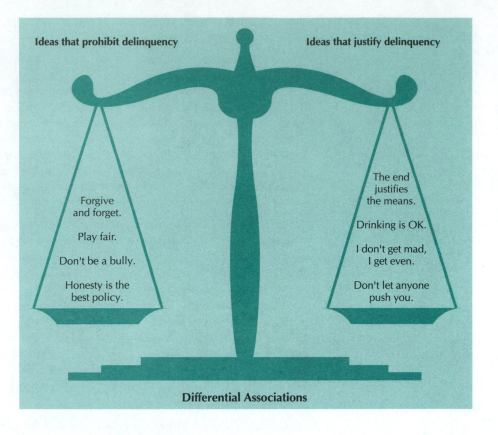

Ideas that prohibit delinquency | Ideas that justify delinquency

Forgive and forget.
Play fair.
Don't be a bully.
Honesty is the best policy.

The end justifies the means.
Drinking is OK.
I don't get mad, I get even.
Don't let anyone push you.

Differential Associations

For example, the influence of a father, mother, or trusted friend will far outweigh that of more socially distant figures.

8. *The process of learning criminal behavior by association with criminal and anticriminal patterns involves all the mechanisms involved in any other learning.* This statement suggests that learning criminal behavior patterns is similar to all other learning experiences and is not a matter of mere imitation.

9. *Criminal behavior is an explanation of general needs and values, but it is not explained by those needs and values because noncriminal behavior is an explanation of the same needs and values.* By this principle Sutherland suggested that the motives for delinquent behavior cannot logically be the same as those for conventional behavior. He ruled out such motives as a desire to accumulate money or social status, a sense of personal frustration, a low self-concept, or any other similar motive as causes of delinquency. They are just as likely to produce such noncriminal behavior as getting a better education or working harder on a job. It is only learning deviant norms through contact with an excess of definitions toward criminality that produces delinquent behavior.

Testing Differential Association Theory   A number of important research efforts have been devoted to testing the validity of differential association theory. These findings support Sutherland's basic tenets:

■ Adolescents who maintain close relations with deviant peers will learn delinquent values.[14]

■ The duration, priority, and intensity of interaction with delinquent peers and the consequent exposure to their deviant attitudes has been positively correlated with delinquent behavior.[15]

■ The association between exposure to deviant definitions and delinquency holds true across racial, age, and class lines.[16]

Learning theories such as differential association stress that human behavior is learned through group process and social interaction. They suggest that in order to begin a delinquent career, youthful law violators must first learn the attitudes, morals, skills, behaviors, and techniques necessary to both commit crimes and then to cope with the emotional turmoil that is the inevitable consequence of their behavior.

■ A number of research efforts have found that adolescent substance abusers maintain strong ties to drug-abusing peers and that shared interests in illegal activities brings drug users closer together.[17]

■ Youths are deterred from criminality by the threat of peer and family disapproval.[18]

■ Youths who believe their friends and family hold attitudes in support of deviance will feel free to violate the law; in contrast, those who believe their friends and family hold conventional attitudes and will condemn their behavior are deterred from criminal violations.[19]

Is Differential Association Theory Valid?   Despite these affirmations, some criminologists have been critical of the principles and meaning of differential association theory, and efforts to verify these principles have not all been successful.[20] Some of these criticisms may be unwarranted, however, because they stem from misconceptions about the core principles of differential association theory.[21] For example, some criminologists claim that the theory is concerned solely with the number of personal contacts and associations a delinquent has with other criminal or delinquent offenders.[22] If this assumption were true, those most likely to become criminals would be police, judges, and correctional authorities because they are constantly associating with criminals. Sutherland stressed "excess definitions toward criminality," not mere association with criminals. Personnel of the juvenile justice system do have extensive associations with criminals, but these are more than counterbalanced by their associations with law-abiding citizens.

Another misconception is that definitions toward delinquency are acquired by learning the values of a deviant subculture.[23] Although differential association theory stresses an excess of definitions toward delinquency, it does not specify that they must come solely from lower-class criminal sources. This distinguishes Sutherland's work from social structure theories. Outwardly law-abiding middle-class parents can encourage delinquent behavior by their own drinking, drug use, or family violence. And both middle- and lower-class youths are exposed to media images that express open admiration for violent heroes, such as those played by Jackie Chan or Jean-Claude Van Damme, who take the law into their own hands. Deviant learning then can affect middle-class as well as lower-class youth.[24]

A number of valid criticisms of Sutherland's work and its legacy have been noted, however. Differential association theory fails to explain why one youth who is exposed to delinquent definitions eventually succumbs to them whereas another, living under similar conditions, avoids antisocial behavior.[25] It also fails to account for the origin of delinquent definitions. How did the first "teacher" learn delinquent attitudes and definitions so they could be passed on?

There are other unanswered questions about differential association theory. We cannot be sure that Sutherland's assumptions about cause and effect are valid. Even if delinquent youths have many like-minded friends and report exposure to an excess of prodelinquent definitions, it is difficult to determine whether these associations and definitions caused law-violating behavior or were the result of it. It is possible that youngsters who continually break the law develop a group of like-minded peers who support their behavior (that is, birds of a feather flock together) rather than being a process whereby "innocent" youths are "seduced" into crime by exposure to the deviant attitudes of more delinquent peers.[26]

Another apparently valid criticism of differential association theory is that it assumes criminal and delinquent acts to be rational and systematic. This ignores spontaneous and wanton acts of violence and damage that appear to have little utility or purpose such as the isolated psychopathic killing, which is virtually unsolvable because of the killer's anonymity and lack of delinquent associations.

The most serious criticism of differential association theory concerns the vagueness of its terms, which makes it very difficult to test its assumptions. For example, what constitutes an "excess of definitions toward criminality"? How can we determine whether an individual actually has a prodelinquent imbalance of these definitions? It is simplistic to assume that, by definition, all delinquents have experienced a majority of definitions toward delinquency and all nondelinquents a minority of them. Unless the terms employed in the theory can be defined more precisely, its validity remains a matter of guesswork.

To overcome these criticisms, future research may be directed at creating more accurate means with which to test these basic principles.[27] One approach is to follow a cohort over time to assess the impact of delinquent friends and associations: Does repeated exposure to excess definitions toward deviance escalate deviance through the life course? Some recent research by Mark Warr illustrates the utility of this approach. Warr found that adolescents who acquire delinquent friends are also the ones most likely to eventually engage in delinquent behavior—a finding that supports differential association theory. Warr notes that delinquent friends are "sticky"; once gotten, they are hard to shake. They help lock youths into antisocial behavior patterns throughout the life course. In fact, youths who maintain deviant friendships and close relationships with deviant peers are likely to continue their offending careers as they mature.[28] Deviant friends help counteract the crime-reducing effects of the aging-out process.[29] As youths mature, however, the impact of even the "stickiest" friends eventually lessens. Those who get married and raise a family find that their exposure to deviant peers is reduced and so too is their involvement in delinquency.[30] The Warr research is important because it shows the effect of delinquent associations over time.

Despite its critics, differential association theory maintains an important place in the study of delinquent behavior, in part because it provides a consistent explanation of all types of delinquent and criminal behavior. Unlike the social structure theories discussed previously, differential association theory is not limited to the explanation of a single facet of antisocial activity, for example, lower-class gang activity. The theory can also account for the extensive delinquent behavior found even in middle- and upper-class areas where youths may be exposed to a variety of prodelinquent definitions from sources such as overly opportunistic parents and friends.

Differential Reinforcement Theory

differential reinforcement theory
A refinement of differential association theory that asserts that behavior is shaped by the reactions of others to that behavior; youths who receive more rewards than punishments for conforming behavior will be the most likely to remain nondelinquent.

A number of attempts have been made to reformulate the concept of differential association. The most important being Robert Burgess and Ronald Akers's effort to frame Sutherland's model in a behavioral theory format labeled **differential reinforcement theory.** They suggest that delinquent behavior, like all behavior, is shaped by the stimuli or reactions of others to that behavior.[31] Like Sutherland, these theorists believe social behavior is learned through direct conditioning or modeling others' behavior. They have amplified this model with the assumption that behavior is strengthened through reward or positive reinforcement and weakened by loss of reward (negative punishment) or actual punishment (positive punishment). Youths who receive more rewards than punishments for conforming behavior will be the most likely to remain nondelinquent—a process called differential reinforcement. Reinforcements, both positive and negative, are usually received in group settings. The most powerful influences are peers and family, but a youth may also be affected by school, social groups, church groups, and other institutions.

In an empirical analysis of differential reinforcement, Ronald Akers and his associates found that survey items measuring differential reinforcement predicted significant amounts of marijuana use and alcohol abuse.[32] Other social scientists have confirmed that peer influence and differential reinforcements help shape adolescent behavior.[33] For example, the onset of cigarette smoking and substance abuse has been linked to the behavior and attitudes of parents and friends.[34]

Akers's work has emerged as an important view of the cause of criminal activity. It is one of the few prominent theoretical models that successfully blends sociological and psychological learning concepts. It also complements rational choice theory because both suggest (a) that people learn the techniques and attitudes necessary to commit crime and (b) that criminal knowledge is gained through experience. After considering the outcome of their past experiences, potential offenders decide which criminal acts will be profitable and which are dangerous and should be avoided.[35] Why do people make rational choices about crime?—because they have learned to balance risks against the potential for criminal gain.

Neutralization Theory

neutralization theory
Holds that youths adhere to conventional values while "drifting" into periods of illegal behavior; for drift to occur, youths must first neutralize conventional legal and moral values.

drift
Idea that youths move in and out of delinquency and that their lifestyles can embrace both conventional and deviant values.

Neutralization theory is identified with the writings of David Matza and his associate Gresham Sykes.[36] In furthering Sutherland's views, Sykes and Matza suggest that delinquents hold attitudes and values similar to those of law-abiding citizens but that they learn techniques that enable them to neutralize those values and attitudes temporarily and drift back and forth between legitimate and delinquent behavior. The techniques used by delinquents to weaken the hold of social values are learned through interaction with others.

Elements of Neutralization Theory In his major work, *Delinquency and Drift*, Matza suggests that most individuals spend their lives behaving on a continuum somewhere between total freedom and total restraint. **Drift** is the process by which an individual moves from one extreme of behavior to another, behaving sometimes in an unconventional, free, or deviant manner and at other times with constraint and sobriety.

The subculture of delinquency, in which criminal behavior is regularly supported, encourages drift in young people. Matza views the subculture as amorphous and without formal rules or values (except those bestowed on it by sociologists). He characterizes it as an informal, relatively inarticulate oral tradition. Members of the subculture infer the behavior they are to follow from behavior cues of their comrades, including slogans and actions.[37]

Writing with Gresham Sykes, Matza subsequently rejected the central ideas held by cultural deviance theorists that the subculture of delinquency maintains an independent set of values and attitudes that place the delinquent in direct opposition to the values of the dominant culture. Rather, Matza and Sykes point to the complex pluralistic culture in our society that is both deviant and ethical. Although most youths actually appreciate goal-oriented middle-class values, they may feel that expressing conventional virtues and engaging in accepted behavior would be frowned on by their peers. They search for adventure, excitement, or thrills. They admire **subterranean values** that are not inherently deviant but, in extreme cases, may encourage deviant behavior, such as partying and drinking. Subterranean values are familiar to and tolerated by a broad segment of the adult population. However, when pursued in a socially disapproved or sanctioned fashion, they can lead to social problems: It is OK to drink but not to become a substance abuser; playing "hooky" to go to the beach is acceptable, dropping out of school is not.

In a later paper, Matza further defines his concept of the teenage subculture as a conventional version of the delinquent's traditional behavior. That subculture emphasizes fun and adventure, and its members are persistently involved in status offenses, such as smoking, drinking, gambling, and making out. They disdain schoolwork and scholars and are overly concerned with proving their masculinity or femininity.[38]

Techniques of Neutralization Sykes and Matza suggest that juveniles develop a distinct set of justifications for their behavior when it violates accepted social norms. These neutralization techniques allow youths to temporarily drift away from the rules of the normative society and participate in subterranean behaviors. Sykes and Matza base their theoretical model on these observations:[39]

1. Delinquents sometimes voice a sense of guilt over their illegal acts. If a stable delinquent value system existed in opposition to generally held values and rules, delinquents likely would not exhibit any remorse for their acts other than regret at being apprehended.
2. Juvenile offenders frequently respect and admire honest, law-abiding persons. "Really honest" persons are often revered, and if for some reason they are accused of misbehavior, the delinquent is quick to defend their integrity. Those admired may include sports figures, clergy, parents, teachers, and neighbors.
3. Delinquents draw a line between those whom they can victimize and those whom they cannot. Members of youths' ethnic groups, churches, or neighborhoods are off limits as far as crime goes. This practice implies that delinquents are aware of the wrongfulness of their acts. Why else would they limit them?
4. Delinquents are not immune to the demands of conformity. Most delinquents frequently participate in many of the same social functions as law-abiding youths, for example, school, church, and family activities.

Sykes and Matza argue that these observations substantiate their assertion that delinquents operate as part of the normative culture and adhere to its values and standards. How, then, do they account for delinquency? They suggest that delinquency is a result of the neutralization of accepted social values through employment of a standard set of rationalizations for illegal behavior. Thus, most youths generally adhere to the rules of society but learn certain techniques to temporarily release themselves from their moral constraints—denial of responsibility, denial of injury, denial of a victim, condemnation of the condemners, and appeals to higher authorities.[40] These are described in Table 5.1.

subterranean values
The ability of youthful law violators to repress social norms.

Table 5.1

SYKES AND MATZA'S TECHNIQUES OF NEUTRALIZATION

Denial of responsibility   Delinquents sometimes claim that their unlawful acts were simply not their fault, that they were due to forces beyond their control or were an accident.

Denial of injury   By denying the wrongfulness of an act, delinquents are able to rationalize their illegal behavior. For example, stealing is viewed as "borrowing," vandalism is considered mischief that got out of hand. Society often agrees with delinquents, labeling their illegal behavior "pranks" and thereby reaffirming that delinquency can be socially acceptable.

Denial of victim   Delinquents sometimes rationalize their behavior by maintaining that the victim of crime "had it coming." For example, a school is vandalized because a student believes he was treated unfairly.

Condemnation of the condemners   Delinquents view the world as a corrupt place with a dog-eat-dog moral code. Police and judges are on the take, teachers show favoritism, and parents take out their frustrations on their children, so it is ironic and unfair for these authorities to turn around and condemn youthful misconduct. By shifting the blame to others, delinquents are able to repress the feeling that their own acts are wrong.

Appeal to higher loyalties   Delinquents argue that they are caught in the dilemma of being loyal to their own peer group while at the same time attempting to abide by the rules of the larger society. The needs of the group take precedence over the rules of society because the demands of the former are immediate and localized.

Sources: Gresham Sykes and David Matza, "Techniques of Neutralization: A Theory of Delinquency," *American Sociological Review* 22:664–70 (1957); and David Matza, *Delinquency and Drift* (New York: Wiley, 1964).

In summary, the theory of neutralization presupposes a condition in which such statements as "I didn't mean to do it," "I didn't really hurt anybody," "They had it coming to them," "Everybody's picking on me," and "I didn't do it for myself" are used by youths to rationalize violating accepted social norms and values so that they can enter, or drift, into delinquent modes of behavior (see Figure 5.4).

Testing Neutralization   Empirical tests of the assumptions of neutralization theory have so far proven to be inconclusive.[41] One area of research has been directed at determining whether there really is a need for adolescent law violators to neutralize moral constraints. If delinquents belong to subcultures that maintain values "in opposition" to accepted social norms, then there is really no need to neutralize. So far the evidence is mixed. Some studies support the opposing values argument, showing that delinquent youths approve of criminal behavior such as theft and violence. Other studies find evidence that youths oppose and disapprove of illegal behavior even though they may be active participants in crime.[42] Some studies indicate that delinquents generally approve of social values such as honesty and fairness; others come to the opposite conclusion.[43] Although the research findings may be ambiguous, the weight of the evidence is (a) that most adolescents generally disapprove of deviant behaviors such as violence and (b) that neutralizations do in fact enable youths to engage in socially disapproved of behavior.[44]

FIGURE 5.4
Techniques of Neutralization

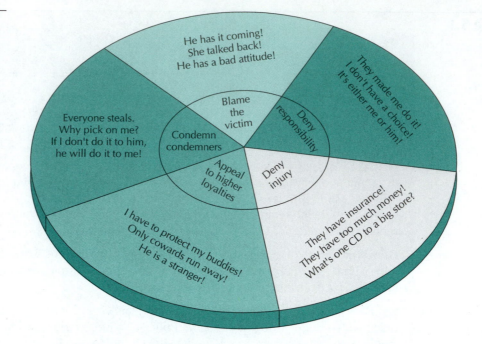

New evidence shows that delinquents drift in and out of antisocial behavior. Jeffery Fagan recently interviewed 150 young men living in some of New York City's toughest areas and found that many alternated between "decent" and "street" codes of behavior, language, and dress. The street code's rules for getting and maintaining respect through aggressive behavior forced many "decent" youths to situationally adopt a tough demeanor and perhaps behave violently to survive an otherwise hostile and possibly dangerous environment.[45]

The theory of neutralization is a major contribution to the literature of crime and delinquency. It can explain various aspects of criminal behavior including the aging-out process. Neutralization theory implies that youths can forgo criminal behavior when they reach their majority because they never really rejected the morality of normative society. It helps to explain the behavior of the occasional, or nonchronic, delinquent who is able to successfully age out of crime. While they are young, they can devise justifications and excuses to neutralize guilt, which enables them to continue to feel good about themselves.[46] But if teens are not committed to criminality, as they mature they simply drift back into conventional behavior patterns.

Control Theories

control theories
Suggest that many forms of delinquent behavior are attractive to all teenagers, but only those who have few social supports (through family, friends, and teachers) feel free to violate the law.

Control theories suggest that many forms of delinquent behavior—using drugs, engaging in sexual acts, skipping school, fighting, getting drunk, and so on—are attractive to almost every teenager. These acts represent the exciting, illicit, adventurous behavior that is glorified by popular culture in movies, TV, and rock music. Why, then, do most youths obey conventional rules and grow up to be law-abiding adults?

For a social control theorist the answer lies in the strength and direction of youths' ties with conventional groups, individuals, and institutions. Those who have close relationships with their parents, friends, and teachers and who maintain a positive self-image will be able to resist the lure of deviant behaviors. To protect

FIGURE 5.5

Elements of the Social Bond

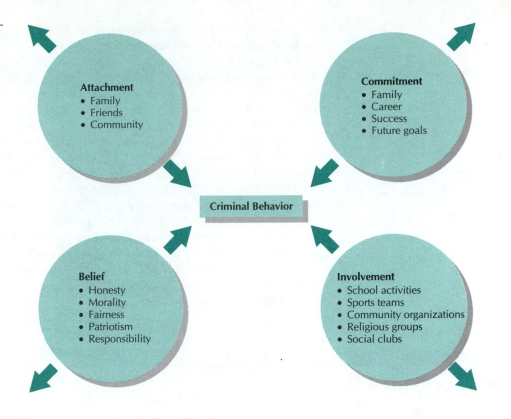

their good standing in the community, they refuse to risk detection and punishment for delinquent offenses. However, youths without these social supports feel free to violate the law; if caught, they have nothing to lose (see Figure 5.5).

Self-Concept and Delinquency

commitment to conformity
The strength of the ties of youths to conventional social institutions predicts their likely behavior; those with poor or negative ties are more likely to indulge in delinquent acts.

containment theory
Asserts that a strong self-image insulates youths from the pressure to engage in illegal acts; youths with poor self-concepts and low self-esteem are more likely to engage in crime.

Control theorists began by speculating that delinquency was a product of a weak self-concept and poor self-esteem. Youths who felt good about themselves were able to resist the temptations of the streets; those with poor self-images were more likely to succumb. As early as 1951, Albert Reiss described how delinquents had weak "ego ideals" and lacked the "personal controls" to produce conforming behavior.[47] In a similar vein, Scott Briar and Irving Piliavin described how delinquents have a weak **commitment to conformity.**[48] Youths who fear that apprehension for criminal activity will damage their self-image will be most likely to conform to social roles. In his **containment theory,** Walter Reckless argued that a strong self-image insulates youths from the pressures and pulls of criminogenic influences in the environment.[49] In a series of studies conducted in the school setting, Reckless and his colleagues found that nondelinquents were able to maintain a positive self-image in the face of environmental pressures toward delinquency.[50]

Self-Enhancement Theory   Howard Kaplan found that youths with poor self-concepts are most likely to engage in delinquent behavior and that successful participation in criminality actually helps raise their self-esteem.[51] Kaplan argues that adolescents structure their behavior to enhance their self-image and to minimize negative self-attitudes. Youths will conform to social rules of society, seek membership in normative groups, and perform conventional tasks as long as their efforts pay off in positive, esteem-enhancing feedback. If they feel threatened, rebuked, or belittled, they may experience "self-rejection" (such as "I feel I don't have much to be proud of" or "I certainly feel useless at times"). Youths then may turn to deviant groups to meet their need for self-esteem. Although conventional society may reject them, their new criminal friends give them positive feedback and support. To further enhance their new identity, youths may engage in deviant behaviors.[52] Youths who have both the lowest self-image and the greatest need for approval are the ones most likely to seek self-enhancement from delinquency.[53]

Does low self-esteem lead to criminality? Some scholars still question whether committing crime can actually raise self-image, but there seems to be a significant association between self-image and delinquency.[54] There is also evidence that, as predicted by Kaplan, associating with antisocial peers can actually raise self-esteem and contribute to self-enhancement. Outcast youths may find emotional comfort not necessarily by committing crimes but by maintaining favorable relations with others who are similarly shunned by society.[55]

A strong self-concept may be one factor that controls human behavior, but it may not be the only factor. In the most important statement of control theory, Travis Hirschi identified other social factors that help restrain youths from engaging in antisocial behaviors. A more complete discussion of Hirschi's important work is the topic of the next section.

Hirschi's Control Theory

Travis Hirschi's version of control theory, first articulated in his classic book *Causes of Delinquency,* links delinquent behavior to the bond an individual maintains with society. When that bond weakens or breaks, the constraints society places on its members are lifted, and an individual may violate the law. Unlike some of the other theoretical models discussed here, Hirschi's control theory assumes that all individuals are potential delinquents and criminals ("born bad") and that social controls, not moral values, maintain law and order. Without controls and in the absence of sensitivity to and interest in others, a youth is free to commit criminal acts.[56]

Hirschi speculates that a consistent value system exists and that all people in society are exposed to it. Delinquents defy this moral code because their attachment to society is weak. Hirschi views the youthful law violator as someone who lacks commitment to social norms and beliefs. The major elements of his argument are (1) that there is a "variation in belief in the moral validity of social rules,"[57] (2) that this variation is brought about by a weakening of the attachment of the individual to elements of society, and (3) that this condition produces delinquent behavior.

social bond

Ties a person to the institutions and processes of society; elements of the bond include attachment, commitment, involvement, and belief.

Hirschi argues that the **social bond** a person maintains with society is divided into four main elements: attachment, commitment, involvement, and belief (see Figure 5.5).

1. *Attachment:* Attachment refers to a person's sensitivity to and interest in others. Psychologists believe that without a sense of attachment a person becomes a psychopath and loses the ability to relate coherently to the world. The acceptance of social norms and the development of a social conscience depend on attachment to and caring for other human beings. Hirschi views parents, peers, and schools as the most important social institutions with which a person should maintain ties. Attachment to parents is the most important. Even if a family is shattered by divorce and separation, a child must retain a strong attachment to one or both parents. Without attachment to the family, a child is unlikely to develop feelings of respect for others in authority.

2. *Commitment:* Commitment encompasses the time, energy, and effort expended in pursuit of conventional lines of action. It embraces activities such as getting an education and saving money for the future. Control theory holds that if people

Hirschi argues that youths who maintain close involvements with social institutions such as school and religion are less likely to commit delinquent acts. Delinquent youths, on the other hand, are often uninvolved in conventional activities. Do you agree with Hirschi, or do you believe that getting involved has little influence on behavior? Are the children shown here, members of the Boys & Girls Club of New Haven, Connecticut, insulated from delinquency because of their strong attachments to adults?

build up a strong involvement in life, property, and reputation they will be less likely to engage in acts that will jeopardize their position. Conversely, a lack of commitment to conventional values may foreshadow a condition in which risk-taking behavior, such as delinquency, becomes a reasonable alternative.

3. *Involvement:* An individual's heavy involvement in conventional activities does not leave time for illegal behavior. Hirschi believes involvement—in school, recreation, and family—insulates youths from the potential lure of delinquent behavior that idleness encourages.

4. *Belief:* People who live in common social settings often share a similar moral doctrine and revere human values such as sharing, sensitivity to the rights of others, and admiration for the legal code. If these beliefs are absent or weakened, individuals are more likely to share in antisocial acts.

Hirschi further suggests that the interrelationship of elements of the social bond influences whether an individual pursues delinquent or conventional activities. For example, boys or girls who feel kinship with and sensitivity toward their parents and friends should be more likely to desire and work toward legitimate goals. Youths who reject social relationships will probably lack commitment to conventional goals and are more likely to be involved in unconventional activities.

Empirical Research on Control Theory One of Hirschi's most significant contributions to delinquency research is his impartial verification of the principal hypothesis of control theory. He administered a complex self-report survey to a sample of more than four thousand junior and senior high school students in Contra Costa County, California.[58] In a detailed analysis of the data, Hirschi found considerable evidence to support the control theory model. Let's look at some of his more important findings in detail.

Hirschi compared youths' attachment to their family ("Would you like to be the kind of person your father is?" and "When you come across things you don't understand, does your mother [father] help you with them?") with their deviant behavior. He found that youths who were strongly attached to their parents—even criminal parents—were less likely to participate in delinquent behavior.

Hirschi also found that lack of attachment to the school and to education ("Do you care what teachers think of you?" and "It is none of the school's business if a student wants to smoke outside the classroom") is a strong predictor of delinquent behavior.

Youths with poor basic academic skills are likely to become detached from school and involved in delinquency. Hirschi traces this important relationship as follows: "The causal chain runs from academic incompetence to poor school performance to disliking of school to rejection of the school's authority to the commission of delinquent acts."[59]

Hirschi also examined the attachment of youths to their friends and other peers, using questions such as "Would you like to be the kind of person your best friends are?" He found that youths who maintain close associations with friends are less likely to commit delinquent acts. Delinquent youths, in contrast, often maintain weak and distant relationships with their peers. Among Hirschi's most important discoveries are these:

- Contrary to subcultural theories, the gang rarely recruits "good" boys or influences them to turn "bad."

- Boys who maintain middle-class values are relatively unaffected by the delinquent behavior of their friends, although having delinquent friends was generally related to criminality.

- The idea that delinquents have warm, intimate relationships with one another is a myth.

- "The child with little stake in conformity is susceptible to pro-delinquent influences in his environment; the child with a large stake in conformity is relatively immune to these influences."[60]

- Involvement in school inhibits delinquency. Youths who smoke, drink, date, ride around in cars, and find adolescence "boring" are more prone to delinquency.

- There was little difference in the beliefs of delinquents and nondelinquents; delinquents often respected middle-class attitudes.

Hirschi's data lend important support to the validity of control theory. Although the statistical significance of his findings was sometimes less than he expected, his research data are extremely consistent. Only in very rare instances do his findings contradict the theory's most critical assumptions.

Corroborating Research   Hirschi's version of social control theory has been corroborated by research showing that delinquent youths often feel detached from society.[61] Their relationships within the family, peer group, and school often appear strained, indicative of a weakened social bond.[62]

Associations between indicators of attachment, belief, commitment, and involvement with measures of delinquency have tended to be positive and significant.[63] Teens who are attached to their parents are also able to develop the social skills that equip them both to maintain harmonious social ties and to escape life stresses such as school failure.[64] In contrast, family detachment, including intrafamily conflict, abuse of children, and lack of affection, supervision, and family pride, are predictive of delinquent conduct.[65] Youths who are detached from the educational experience are at risk to criminality; those who are committed to school are less likely to engage in delinquent acts.[66] Corroborating evidence has also been found outside the United States. Lack of attachment to family, peers, and school has been found to predict delinquency in cross-cultural samples of youths.[67]

Other research efforts have shown that holding positive beliefs are inversely related to criminality. Children who are involved in religious activities and hold conventional religious beliefs are less likely to become involved in substance abuse.[68] Similarly, youths who are involved in conventional leisure activities, such as supervised social activities and noncompetitive sports, are less likely to engage in delinquency than those who are involved in unconventional leisure activities and unsupervised, peer-oriented social pursuits.[69]

Dissenting Opinions   More than seventy attempts have been made to corroborate social control theory by replicating Hirschi's original survey techniques.[70] There has been significant empirical support for Hirschi's work, and it remains one of the pillars of delinquency theory. However, there are also those who question some or all of its elements:

1. *Loners?* Hirschi maintains that delinquents are detached loners whose bond to their family and friends has been broken. Some critics have questioned (1) whether delinquents do in fact have strained relations with family and peers and (2) whether they may be influenced by close relationships with deviant peers and family members. A number of research efforts do show that delinquents maintain relationships and are influenced by membership in a deviant peer group.[71] Delinquents may not be "lone wolves" whose only personal relationships are exploitive; their friendship patterns seem quite close to those of conventional youths.[72] For example, research shows that young male drug abusers maintain even more intimate relations with their peers than do nonabusers; illicit drug use can be used to predict strong social ties and high levels of intimacy.[73] Attachment to deviant peers seems to motivate the decision to commit crime; deviant friends facilitate delinquent acts.[74]

2. *Deviant attachments.* Hirschi suggests that all attachments, even deviant ones, are beneficial. Critics disagree, suggesting that attachment to deviant others increases delinquent involvements. Youths who are attached to drug-abusing parents are more likely to use drugs themselves.[75]

3. *All bond elements are not equal.* Some research efforts also question whether elements of the social bond such as "belief" or "involvement" actually influence delinquent behaviors. Hirschi himself found little evidence that delinquents reject conventional values and beliefs. People who commit crimes do not necessarily believe criminal activity is "good" or proper.[76] Although there is little clear-cut evidence that involvement in conventional activities precludes deviant behaviors, there is the possibility that it may be positively related to delinquency. When children are involved in behaviors outside the home, parental supervision is reduced and the opportunity to commit crimes increases.[77]

4. *Changing bonds?* Hirschi's theory ignores changes in social bonds. Do social bonds change over the life course? Once they are "broken," can they be "repaired"? Hirschi assumes that bonds are constant, but empirical evidence describes bonds that ebb and flow over the life course. As children mature, so too does the nature of their social bonds. In mid-adolescence, for example, children are more likely to be influenced by their parents and teachers, whereas in late adolescence they become more deeply influenced by their peers.[78]

5. *Cannot explain serious crimes.* Some critics charge that control theory is restricted to only minor acts and cannot explain serious felonies. It may also be age and gender relative, having more explanatory power for some groups than for others. Control variables have been better able to explain female delinquency than male delinquency and minor delinquency (such as alcohol and marijuana abuse) than more serious delinquent acts.[79] Hirschi's model may have more utility as an explanation of the onset of delinquency, a period when youthful offenders are both engaging in petty offenses and questioning their commitment and attachment to social institutions. It has less explanatory value for hard core antisocial acts such as murder or rape committed by chronic offenders.

6. *Does delinquency weaken bonds?* The fact that delinquents have weakened social bonds is in itself insufficient proof of the validity of control theory. The weakening of social bonds may be a *result* of delinquent behavior and not its *cause*. It would not be surprising that youths who engage in repeated criminal activity have poor relationships at home and at school. To confirm control theory, it must be shown that a weakened social bond preceded the delinquent behavior. Robert Agnew questions the control theory assumption that a weak bond to society

causes delinquency.[80] He suggests an opposing chain of events: chronic delinquents may find that their bonds to parents, schools, and society are becoming weak and attenuated; in other words, delinquency causes the weakening of social bonds and not vice versa.[81]

In summary, some research efforts have given support to the core concepts of social control theory, but other efforts have questioned its explanatory power. However, even its detractors recognize that control theory has been the most influential model of delinquency for the past twenty-five years.

The General Theory of Crime

In an important work called *A General Theory of Crime,* Travis Hirschi and his colleague Michael Gottfredson refined and extended Hirschi's original concept of social control and social bonds.[82] In this work Hirschi recognizes that an important element of control is the self-discipline people develop early in life, which guides their behavior thereafter.

In their general theory of crime (GTC), Gottfredson and Hirschi argue that to properly understand the nature of crime and delinquency we must differentiate offenders from their acts. *Crimes,* such as robberies or burglaries, are illegal events or deeds committed by people who perceive them to be advantageous. For example, burglaries are typically committed by male adolescents seeking cash, liquor, and entertainment. The delinquency provides "easy short-term gratification."[83] In contrast, *criminals* are those people who maintain a status that maximizes the possibility that they will engage in crimes. Adolescents with delinquent inclinations do not constantly commit crimes; their days are filled with nondelinquent behaviors such as going to school, parties, concerts, and church. But given the same set of life circumstances, they have a much higher probability of committing illegal acts than do nondelinquents.

Self-Control   What causes youths to become excessively delinquency prone? According to the GTC, the explanation for individual differences in the tendency to commit delinquent acts can be found in an adolescent's level of **self-control.** People with limited self-control have impulsive personalities. They tend to be insensitive, physical (rather than intellectual), risk taking, short-sighted, and nonverbal.[84] They have a "here-and-now" orientation and refuse to work for distant goals; they lack diligence, tenacity, and persistence in a course of action. Children lacking self-control also tend to be adventureous, active, physical, and self-centered. In their adulthood, they have unstable marriages, jobs, and friendships.[85] Criminal acts are attractive to them because they provide easy and immediate gratification or, as Gottfredson and Hirschi put it, "money without work, sex without courtship, revenge without court delays."[86]

Considering their desire for the "quick fix," it should come as no surprise that people lacking self-control will also engage in risky, exciting, thrilling "imprudent" behaviors that provide them with immediate short-term gratification, for example, reckless driving, smoking, drinking, gambling, illicit sexuality, or having out-of-wedlock children. Even if these acts are not criminal per se, they direct the impulsive youth down a path that leads to future criminality[87] (see Figure 5.6). Desiring immediate satisfaction, these youths are more likely to engage in criminal acts requiring stealth, danger, agility, speed, and power than in conventional acts that demand long-term study and require cognitive and verbal skills.

Self-Control and Social Bonds   The general theory argues that poor self-control is a function of inadequate child-rearing practices. Parents who refuse or are unable

self-control
Ability to control impulsive and often imprudent behaviors that offer immediate short-term gratification.

FIGURE 5.6

The General Theory of Crime

Impulsive Personality
- Physical
- Insensitive
- Risk-taking
- Short-sighted
- Nonverbal

Low Self-Control
- Poor parenting
- Deviant parents
- Lack of supervision
- Active
- Self-centered

Weakening of Social Bonds
- Attachment
- Involvement
- Commitment
- Belief

Criminal Opportunity
- Gangs
- Free time
- Drugs
- Suitable targets

Crime and Deviance
- Delinquency
- Smoking
- Drinking
- Sex
- Crime

to monitor a child's behavior, fail to recognize deviant behavior when it occurs, and neglect to punish that behavior will produce children who lack self-control. Kids who lack self-control are unlikely to be attached to parents, committed to orthodox value and beliefs, and involved in conventional activities. There may be a reciprocal relationship between social control and social bonds. An attenuated bond to society further weakens self-control; people with low self-control have difficulty maintaining adequate bonds to society.[88] The causal chain then may flow from (1) an impulsive personality, to (2) poor parenting practices, to (3) lack of self-control, to (4) the withering of social bonds, to (5) increased criminal opportunity, to (6) amplification of deviance and maintenance of a deviant career throughout the life span.[89]

Gottfredson and Hirschi conclude that the cause of persistent delinquency—the lack of self-control—is established during the early formative years and controls behavior throughout the life course.

An Analysis of Self-Control Theory   Gottfredson and Hirschi's general theory of crime answers many of the questions left open by the original control model. By separating the concepts of "delinquency" and "delinquents," Gottfredson and Hirschi help explain why some kids who lack self-control can escape criminality—they

Capricious acts of vandalism bolster Gottfredson and Hirschi's claim that criminals are impulsive individuals who lack self-control. Is it at all possible that the people who vandalized this vehicle could be well reasoned and thoughtful?

lack criminal opportunity. Similarly, even those people with strong bonds to social institutions and good self-control may on occasion engage in law-violating behavior: If the opportunity is strong enough, the incentives may overcome self-control. This explains why the so-called good kid, who has a favorable school record and positive parental relationships, can get involved in drugs or vandalism, or why the corporate executive with a spotless record gets caught up in business fraud. Even successful executives may find their self-control inadequate if the potential for illegal gain runs into the tens of millions of dollars.

Gottfredson and Hirschi argue vehemently that life events *do not* influence the *propensity* to commit crime; the tendency to commit crime is stable. It is criminal opportunities—the occasion to commit crime—that vary significantly over the life course. Individual crime rates fluctuate with criminal opportunities.

Testing GTC   The GTC is considered an extremely important contribution to the literature of crime and delinquency. Research has confirmed that adolescents who are egocentric and impulsive, with weak or strained ties to society, have a greater likelihood of anti-social behavior.[90] Moreover, there is evidence that variables measuring lack of self-control are correlated with criminal behavior.[91] For example, kids who take drugs and commit crimes are impulsive and enjoy engaging in risky behaviors.[92] Male and female drunk drivers have likewise been found to be impulsive individuals who manifest low self-control.[93] Research on known offenders indicates that they display an impulsive personality structure, enjoy risk-taking behavior, and hold values and attitudes that suggest impulsivity.[94]

There is also evidence verifying the positive association Gottfredson and Hirschi assume exists between poor parental supervision and management, lack of self-control, and subsequent deviant behavior.[95] And, as the general theory maintains, kids whose problems develop very early in life seem to be the ones most resistant to change in treatment and rehabilitation programs.[96]

Dissenting Opinion   Although much research is generally supportive of GTC, some areas need further testing and evaluation. One issue is whether the core principles of GTC are universal. There is evidence that criminals in other countries do not lack self-control, indicating that GTC may be culturally limited.[97] Behavior that may be considered imprudent and risky in one culture may be socially acceptable in another and therefore cannot be explained by a "lack of self-control."[98]

Some critics contend that changing life circumstances affect the propensity to commit crime and that the propensity to commit crime is not stable and unchanging. One area of controversy is the influence of delinquent peers. Research shows that as children mature peer influence over delinquent behavior choices continues to grow. In contrast, the GTC suggests that the influence of friends should be stable and unchanging.[99] Those already delinquent may choose delinquent friends, and their new "friends" may encourage and escalate their involvement with crime.[100] Changing life circumstances such as starting and leaving school, abusing substances and "getting straight," and starting or ending personal relationships all have been found to influence the propensity to offend and the frequency of offending.[101] But do such changes affect the *propensity* to commit crime, or do they merely influence the *opportunity* as Gottfredson and Hirschi suggest?

Finally, some research results acknowledge that even though poor self-control and criminal opportunity are important factors in delinquency they alone cannot predict the onset of a criminal career.[102] Other forces must be brought into play in the creation of delinquency, and these forces still need to be identified. Continued efforts are needed to test the GTC and to establish the validity of its core concepts.

Developmental Perspectives

Both learning and control theories divide the adolescent population into two separate groups: offenders and nonoffenders. They then offer an explanation of why youths fall into one group or the other. Delinquents lack control or have learned criminal values; nondelinquents have absorbed noncriminal values. Some criminologists believe these "either-or" models are too static and that they fail to explain all the nuances of a delinquent career. For example, what causes onset of delinquency, and what sustains criminality over the person's life course? What is the natural history of a delinquent career? What causes some youths to begin a delinquent career and then to stop or desist from crime? Why do some youthful law violators sustain and even escalate their antisocial behavior patterns in adulthood?

Criminologists who pose such questions and attempt to find answers for them are known as developmental theorists. According to their perspective, as adolescence begins, children are expected to engage in social processes that will determine their future well-being. They begin thinking about careers, leaving their parental homes, finding permanent relationships, and eventually marrying and beginning their own families.[103] These transitions are expected to take place in an orderly fashion beginning with high school graduation, entering the workforce, getting married, and having children. Some individuals are incapable of normal maturation because of family, environmental, and personal problems. In some cases transitions can be too early, for example, when adolescents engage in precocious sex. In other cases they may come to late, for example, when a student fails to graduate on time. Sometimes disruption in one life area can do harm in another area. For example, having a baby while a teenager will most likely disrupt educational and career development.

Disruptions in life transitions are destructive and promote criminality. Those who are already at risk because of socioeconomic problems or family dysfunction are the most susceptible to these awkward transitions. The cumulative impact of these disruptions sustains criminality from childhood into adulthood.

Because a transition from one stage of life to another can be a bumpy ride, the propensity to commit crimes can be considered a **developmental process.** Some people commit offenses at a steady pace, whereas others escalate the rate of their criminal involvement. Offenders may specialize in one type of crime or become generalists who commit a variety of illegal acts. Delinquents may be influenced by family matters, financial needs, and changes in lifestyle and interests.

Developmental theorists recognize that a variety of factors influence behavior.[104] Early in the life course family relations may be most influential; in later adolescence school and peer relations predominate; in adulthood vocational achievement and marital relations may be the most critical influence. For example, some antisocial youths who are "in trouble" throughout their adolescence may manage to find stable work and maintain intact marriages as adults; these life events help them desist from crime. In contrast, the less fortunate who develop arrest records and get involved with the "wrong crowd" later can only find menial jobs and are at risk for criminal careers. Social forces that are critical at one stage of life may have little meaning or influence at another.

This vision of delinquent career development can be traced back to the research efforts of Sheldon and Eleanor Glueck. As you may recall, the Gluecks conducted a series of longitudinal research studies, following the offending careers of known delinquents. They focused on early onset of delinquency as a harbinger of a criminal career: "The deeper the roots of childhood maladjustment, the smaller the chance of adult adjustment."[105] They also noted the stability of offending careers: children who are antisocial early in life are the ones most likely to continue their offending careers in adulthood.

After years of neglect there has been renewed interest in understanding the development of delinquent careers. The "discovery" of the chronic offender (see Chapter 2) has focused attention on the onset, nurturance, and termination of delinquent careers. Because they acknowledge that multiple social, personal, physical, and economic processes influence behavior, the Glueck's work is being carefully reconsidered by contemporary developmental theorists.[106]

The main issues that concern developmental theorists today are continuity of crime, multiple pathways, problem behavior syndrome, and offense specialization.

developmental process
At different stages of the life course a variety of factors can influence behavior; factors influential at one stage of life may not be significant at a later stage.

Continuity of Crime

Research on chronic offenders finds that a majority of the most serious juvenile offenders continue their law-violating careers as adults, a concept referred to as the continuity of crime (Chapter 2). Children who are found to be disruptive and antisocial as early as age 5 or 6 are the ones most likely to exhibit stable, long-term patterns of disruptive behavior throughout adolescence.[107] According to psycholo-

Table 5.2

PROBLEM AREAS OF LONG-TERM CHRONIC OFFENDERS

Poor learning and motor skills

Inadequate cognitive abilities

Disrupted family relations

Improper social, psychological, and physical functioning

Alcohol abuse

Economically dependent

Low aspirations

High probability of divorce or separation

Weak employment record

Engage in a garden variety of criminal acts including theft, drug, and violent offenses

Apprehension and punishment seems to have little effect on offending behavior

Sources: Jennifer White, Terrie Moffitt, Felton Earls, Lee Robins, and Phil Silva, "How Early Can We Tell? Predictors of Childhood Conduct Disorder and Adolescent Delinquency," *Criminology* 28:507–35 (1990); Joan McCord, "Family Relationships, Juvenile Delinquency, and Adult Criminality," *Criminology* 29:397–417 (1991).

gist Terrie Moffitt, most adolescents stop offending in their teens, but a small group of "life-course persistent" delinquents offend well into their adulthood[108] (see Table 5.2). Life-course persisters combine family dysfunction with severe neurological problems that predispose them to antisocial behavior patterns. These afflictions can be the result of damaging social and physical problems such as maternal drug abuse, poor perinatal nutrition, or exposure to toxic agents such as lead; they may have lower verbal ability, which inhibits reasoning skills, learning ability, and school achievement.[109]

A number of research efforts have substantiated the continuity of crime concept. The Cambridge Study in Delinquent Development, directed by David Farrington, has followed the offending careers of 411 London boys born in 1953.[110] Beginning at age 8 and continuing to age 32, the boys were interviewed eight times over a period of twenty-four years. The results of the Cambridge study validate both the existence of chronic offenders and the continuity of offending. In a small group of adolescents, early onset leads to persistent delinquency; persistent delinquency leads to adult misbehavior. The traits of the persisters in the Cambridge study are shown in Figure 5.7.

Different Classes of Delinquents   Developmental theorists also recognize that not all juvenile offenders are early onset. Although some are "precocious," beginning their criminal careers at a very early age, others are "late bloomers" who stay out of trouble until their teenage years. Some offenders may "peak" at an early age, whereas others persist into adulthood. Research shows a number of different classes of criminal careers that correspond to changes in the life course (see Table 5.3). As the table indicates, offending patterns can vary according to age of onset. Some youths maximize their offending rates at a relatively early age (15–18) and then reduce their criminal activity; others persist into their twenties. Whether they are chronic offenders or "adolescent peaked,"[111] those who begin their criminal activity later in adolescence tned to offend at a lower rate.

Early onset delinquents seem to be more strongly influenced by individual level traits: low verbal ability, hyperactive personality, and negative or impulsive personality. In contrast, late adolescent delinquents are more strongly influenced by their delinquent peers. Early onset delinquents also appear to be more violent than the late starters who are more likely to get involved in nonviolent crimes such as theft.[112]

Age 8

The persister receives poor parental supervision, including harsh or erratic punishments; his parents are likely to be in conflict and to separate. He tends to associate with friends who are also delinquents. By age 8 he is already exhibiting antisocial behavior, including dishonesty and aggressiveness. At school he tends to have low educational achievement and attainment and is restless, troublesome, hyperactive, impulsive, and often truant.

Age 18

After leaving school the persistent delinquent tends to maintain a relatively low-status job and suffer periods of unemployment. Deviant behavior tends to be versatile, rather than specialized, for example, property offenses, violence, vandalism, drug use, excessive drinking, and sexual promiscuity. He lives away from home and has conflict with his parents. He tends to get tattoos and enjoys "hanging out" with peers. He gets involved in fights, carries weapons, and uses them in violent encounters. The frequency of his offending reaches a peak in his teenage years (about age 17 or 18), then declines in his twenties, when he marries or lives with a woman.

Age 32

By the time he reaches his thirties, the former delinquent is likely to be separated or divorced from his wife, is an absent parent, and is a poor role model for his children. His employment record remains spotty, and he moves often to rental units rather than owning his own home. HIs life is still characterized by evenings out, heavy drinking, substance abuse, and more violent behavior than that of his contemporaries.

FIGURE 5.7

Traits of the Persistent Delinquent

Source: David Farrington, "The Development of Offending and Antisocial Behavior from Childhood to Adulthood," paper presented at the Congress on Rethinking Delinquency, University of Minho, Braga, Portugal, July 1992.

Table 5. 3

DIFFERENT CLASSES OF DELINQUENCY

Delinquent Classes	Onset	Offending Rate
Adolescent Peaked	Early	High
(delinquency maximizes ages 15–18)	Late	Low
Chronic Offender	Early	High
(delinquency maximizes ages 17–21)	Late	Low

Source: Amy D'Unger, Kenneth Land, Patricia McCall, and Daniel Nagin, "How Many Latent Classes of Delinquent/Criminal Careers? Results from Mixed Poisson Regression Analyses," *American Journal of Sociology* 103:1593–1630 (1998).

Multiple Pathways to Delinquency

Some developmental theorists are concerned with charting the paths taken by youths as they enter into a delinquent way of life. Rather than being unidirectional, there may be multiple routes to a delinquent career. Using data from a longitudinal cohort study conducted in Pittsburgh (The Pittsburgh Youth Study), Rolf Loeber and his associates identified three paths that lead to a delinquent career:[113]

■ *Authority conflict pathway:* begins at an early age with stubborn behavior, leading to defiance (doing things your own way, refusing to do things, disobedience) and then to authority avoidance (staying out late, truancy, and running away). Defiance of parents and authority avoidance leads to more serious offenses including drug use.

■ *Covert pathway:* begins with minor underhanded behavior (lying, shoplifting) that leads to property damage (setting fires, damaging property) and eventually escalates to more serious forms of delinquency ranging from joyriding, pickpocketing, larceny, and fencing to bad checks, bad credit cards, car theft, drug dealing, and breaking and entering.

■ *Overt pathway:* consists of an escalation of delinquent acts beginning with aggression (annoying others, bullying) and leads to physical fighting (fighting and gang fighting) and violence (attacking someone, strong-arming, forced theft).

Each of these paths may lead a youth into a sustained deviant career (see Figure 5.8), but the Loeber research indicates that some troubled adolescents take two and even three paths simultaneously. They are stubborn, lie to teachers and parents, are bullies, and commit petty thefts—these are the adolescents most likely to become persistent offenders.

The pathways research is important because it shows that delinquency does escalate as children travel the life course and that antisocial behaviors are varied, rather than unidimensional, allowing offenders more than one path as they shift from delinquent to criminal.

Problem Behavior Syndrome

problem behavior syndrome (PBS)
Convergence of a variety of psychological problems and family dysfunctions including substance abuse and criminality.

Some developmental theorists claim that adolescent criminality may be one segment of a general **problem behavior syndrome (PBS).** Unconventional adolescent behavior patterns that are thought to cluster together include being the target of physical and sexual abuse, smoking and substance abuse, precocious sexual experimentation, pregnancy, school failure, suicide attempts, risk taking and thrill seeking, theft, violence, suicide, and mental illness.[114] Other elements associated with PBS include family-related problems such as parental conflict, large family size, low income, and broken home as well as individual-level factors including poor concentration, hyperactivity, and impulsivity.[115] Table 5.4 lists some of the problem behaviors that have been found to cluster together in samples of delinquent youths.

There is significant empirical evidence supporting PBS. A number of research efforts have found that youths who are involved in crime also are likely to engage in a variety of other antisocial behaviors.[116] In fact, more than half of all youths with mental or substance abuse problems have been found to suffer from at least one other co-occurring disorder.[117] For example, teenage boys who engage in antisocial behavior such as fathering children out of wedlock are also more likely to have had a court appearance, to have dropped out of school, to have been involved in drinking, and to have trafficked in drugs. They are three times more likely to have been involved in car theft and forced entry than nonsexually precocious youths.[118]

Delinquency may be one of a cluster of antisocial behaviors that either have a common cause or can be part of a collective lifestyle.[119] Adolescents entering into a delinquent career at a very young age may be the ones most at risk to PBS be-

FIGURE 5.8

Three Pathways to Boys' Disruptive Behavior and Delinquency

Source: Barbara Tatem Kelley, Rolf Loeber, Kate Keenan, and Mary DeLamatre, "Developmental Pathways in Boys' Disruptive and Delinquent Behavior," *Juvenile Justice Bulletin* (November 1997), p. 3.

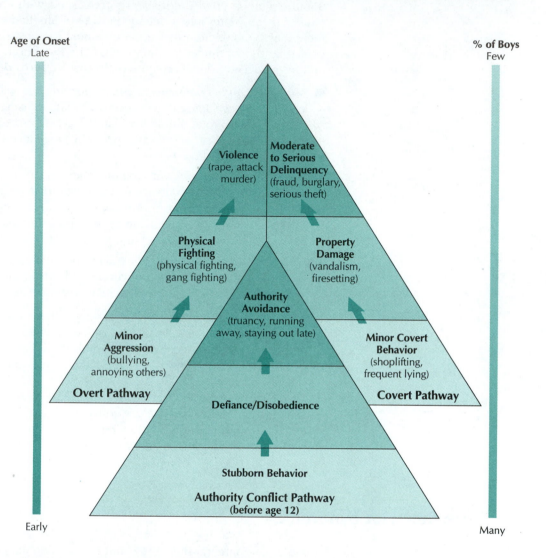

Table 5.4

PROBLEM BEHAVIOR SYNDROME: RISK FACTORS

History of Misconduct	Psychological Disorders	Family Problems
Delinquency	Psychological distress	Parental conflict
Drug dealing	Suicide attempts	Large families
Substance abuse	Poor concentration	Low income
Violence	Hyperactivity	Broken home
School misconduct	Impulsivity	
	Poor communication skills	
	Lack of empathy	

cause they accumulate delinquent friends who support their deviant activities as they mature.[120] Classification of delinquents based on the nature and extent of their problem behaviors may make it easier for correctional personnel to plan effective treatments.[121]

Offense Specialization

As their delinquent careers develop, most persistent offenders do not seem to specialize in any one type of behavior but, as they mature, engage in a variety of delinquent acts and antisocial behaviors. For example, they begin by cheating on tests and bullying others in the school yard. Over time, they use drugs, commit burglaries, and steal cars.

There may be some exceptions to this rule, however. Recent evidence indicates that over time some chronic offenders may begin to specialize in particular forms of delinquency.[122] Some may be involved in serious crimes such as drug trafficking and violence, whereas others are "nuisance offenders" who repeatedly engage in status and neglect-type offenses such as running away and truancy.[123]

Constructing Developmental Theories

A number of theories have been constructed based on developmental views. They are inherently multidimensional, suggesting that criminality has multiple roots including maladaptive personality traits, educational failure, and poor family relations. Criminality, according to this view, cannot be attributed to a single cause, nor does it represent a single underlying tendency.[124] People are influenced by different social processes as they mature; a factor that may have an important influence at one stage of life (for example, delinquent peers) may have little effect later on.[125]

Developmental theorists conclude that multiple social, personal, and economic factors can influence criminality and that as these factors change over time so, too, does criminal involvement.[126] As people make important transitions in life—from child to adolescent, from adolescent to adult, from unwed to married—the nature of social interactions change and behavior is altered. Let's examine three prominent developmental theories in more detail.

The Social Development Model

social development model (SDM)
An array of personal, psychological, and community-level risk factors that make some children susceptible to development of antisocial behaviors.

According to the **social development model (SDM),** developed by Joseph Weis, J. David Hawkins, Richard Catalano, and their associates, a number of personal, psychological, and community-level risk factors make some children susceptible to the development of antisocial behaviors over the course of their lives.[127] The antisocial behavior of children with preexisting risk factors are either reinforced or neutralized through their community- and individual-level interactions.

According to the Social Development Model (SDM), there are a number of personal, psychological, and community level "risk factors" that make some children susceptible to the development of antisocial behaviors over the course of their lives. Children with pre-existing risk factors find that their antisocial behavior is either reinforced or neutralized through community and individual level interactions. Actor/Latino activist Edward Olmos, shown here, is an example of someone who was able to overcome these risk factors and succeed in society. He now helps at-risk youths succeed and reach their potential.

Stating that the key to delinquency prevention is found in the socialization experience, SDM stresses formation of prosocial bonds with society—an element it shares with Hirschi's control theory. For these bonds to be formed, the family must provide prosocial opportunities and reinforce them by consistent positive feedback. The process begins when a child forms an attachment to his or her parents. This attachment will have a profound influence on a child's behavior throughout the life course, determining both the nature of the school experience as well as personal beliefs and values. For those with strong family relationships, school will be a meaningful experience marked by academic success and commitment to education. These children will be more likely to develop conventional beliefs and values, become committed to conventional activities, and form attachments to conventional others.

Children's antisocial behavior also depends on the quality of their attachments to others. If they remain unattached or develop attachments to deviant others, their own behavior may become antisocial. SDM suggests that interaction with antisocial peers and adults promotes participation in delinquency and substance abuse over the life course.[128]

As Figure 5.9 shows, involvement in pro- or antisocial behavior determines the quality of attachments. Those adolescents who perceive opportunities and rewards for antisocial behavior will form deep attachments to deviant peers and become committed to a delinquent way of life. In contrast, those who perceive opportunities for prosocial behavior will take a different path, getting involved in conventional activities and forming attachments to prosocial activities and others.

Many of the core assumptions of SDM have been tested empirically, and their validity has been verified.[129] The path predicted by SDM seems an accurate picture of the onset and continuation of delinquency and drug abuse. The social development model has also guided treatment interventions that promote development of strong bonds to family and school, showing youths how to use these bonds to resist any opportunity or motivation to take drugs or to engage in delinquent behaviors. Preliminary evaluation of one program, the Seattle Social Development Project, indicates that SDM-based interventions can help reduce delinquency and drug abuse.[130] In the Policy and Practice box entitled "The Social Development Model," Richard Catalano describes some of the most successful delinquency prevention strategies based on the social development model.

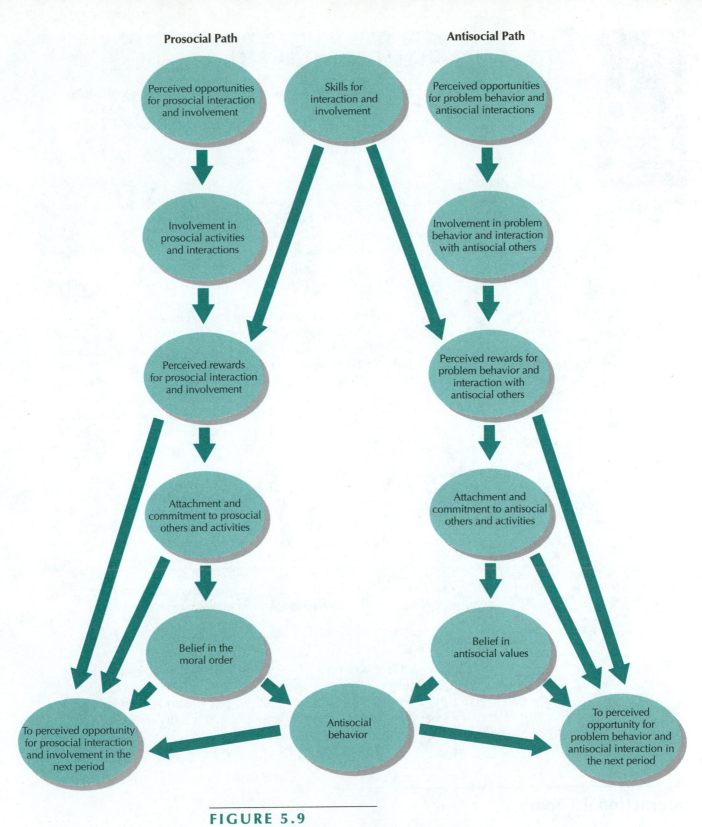

Prosocial Path   **Antisocial Path**

FIGURE 5.9

The Social Development Model of Antisocial Behavior

Source: Seattle Social Development Project.

THE SOCIAL DEVELOPMENT MODEL

The social development model has been used as a basis for a number of ongoing delinquency programs. Here, Richard Catalano, one of the creators of the model, describes some of the delinquency prevention interventions that might be successful with children who are at especially high risk for criminal activity.

PRENATAL AND INFANCY PROGRAMS

There are a variety of programs in this area. In one program visiting nurses are sent into homes of pregnant adolescents who are often single, unmarried, low-income teenage moms. This occurs during the prenatal period, when they are still carrying the baby. The nurses talk about the effects of alcohol, drugs, and cigarettes on the child and encourage the mothers to stop doing those kinds of things. After the baby is born, follow-up continues on a monthly basis for two years, which can help parents with infant bonding and family management.

At the end of five years of this program there were reduced rates of child abuse and neglect, longer periods between pregnancies, and fewer future pregnancies for the teenage mom. This program has positive effects on the mom as well as reducing family management problems like severe punishment. Fifteen years later the youths have about 40 percent less involvement in delinquent behaviors than the experimental group. Children who were taught social cognitive skills at age 3 and 4 and whose parents were taught family management skills are 50 percent less likely to be arrested and are about 40 percent less likely to be involved in violent activities. They also have higher rates of graduation from high school.

PARENT TRAINING

Long-term prevention requires parent training. There are several kinds of programs where the evidence is fairly clear. Basic family management programs, including teaching parents how to set rules, have reduced conduct disorders and increased social competence among children and provided better family management skills among parents.

The next level is making sure parents know how to help their children and how to support their children's academic success. These kinds of programs show better outcomes in academic achievement as well as increases in family management skills.

CHANGE IN SCHOOLS

Something has to happen to the school organization. One successful program does three things. It gets teachers, administrators, and parents talking to each other. It gets parents involved in the daily management of the school. Finally, it gets everyone involved in a set of activities and processes that include parents, counselors, and teachers working with those higher-risk-behavior problem children.

Interactional Theory

interactional theory
Asserts that youths' interactions with institutions and events over the life course determine criminal behavior patterns and that these patterns of behavior evolve over time.

Another important attempt at developmental theory is Terence Thornberry's **interactional theory**[131] (see Figure 5.10). Thornberry suggests that the onset of crime can be traced to a deterioration of the social bond during adolescence, which is marked by a weakened attachment to parents, commitment to school, and belief in conventional values. Like the social development model, interactional theory recognizes the influence risk factors such as lower-class status can have on delinquency: youths growing up in socially disorganized areas are at the greatest risk of

CLASSROOM ORGANIZATION, MANAGEMENT, AND INSTRUCTIONAL STRATEGIES

We know a lot from the educational literature about how to teach, but we don't always use this knowledge in our schools. There is a lot of good educational literature about effective teaching practices, effective classroom management practices, and effective involvement practices for children. You can teach teachers to teach better and to manage their classrooms better, and as a result students will have higher grades. Students develop more commitment to school and are pregnant or father children less often. They commit fewer violent activities, and there are smaller numbers of heavy drinkers. You can get these results by making basic changes in how teachers teach, how they manage their classrooms, and how they organize their classrooms.

CLASSROOM CURRICULA FOR PROMOTING SOCIAL COMPETENCE

There are a series of social competencies that children need to have in schools: how to share, how to talk to others, how to cooperate, and later on, how to develop relationships. A variety of classroom curricula promote social competence beginning with preschool. One program has developed skills to teach children social and emotional competencies as early as first, second, and third grade. In middle school a program teaches youths social resistance skills as well as skills to develop relationships and set norms regarding substance use and violence. Life skills training teaches problem-solving social skills as well as social resistance skills and norm setting to high school students. These skills have had long-term effects in reducing drug use and other adolescent problem behavior.

SCHOOL BEHAVIOR MANAGEMENT STRATEGIES

A whole school approach identifies children who are bad actors—those who have truancy, academic, and behavior problems in school. With these youths we work with some simple reinforcers in the school setting, getting parents and teachers involved in giving out very small monetary rewards as well as extra school trips and extra field trips at the end of the year if the youths improve their attendance, academic performance, and school behavior. This type of approach has been very successful in reducing delinquent behaviors.

COMMUNITY-BASED YOUTH PROGRAMS

In this area we work with youths in seventh, eighth, ninth, tenth, eleventh, and sometimes twelfth grades. Recreational programs are fairly popular interventions, but they only work under certain conditions. After-school recreation programs can be effective only if they teach youths skills and how to do things. Second, this kind of program has to put youths in contact with existing sports leagues or hobby groups in the community. The program has two goals: to teach the skills and then to network them to existing organizations. These kinds of programs have an incredible impact on youth violence, reducing it to a great extent.

Source: Adapted from "Communities that Care," Dr. Richard Catalano, Professor, School of Social Work, University of Washington, Seattle, and Associate Director of the Social Development Research Group, School of Social Work (Seattle, Wash., 1998).

having a weakened social bond and subsequently becoming delinquent. The onset of a criminal career is supported by residence in a social setting in which deviant values and attitudes can be learned and reinforced by delinquent peers.

Interactional theory also holds that serious delinquent youths form belief systems that are consistent with their deviant lifestyle. They seek out the company of others who share their interests and who are likely to reinforce their beliefs about the world and support their delinquent behavior.[132] According to interactional theory, delinquents seek out a criminal peer group in the same fashion that chess buffs look for others who share their passion for the game. Deviant peers do not turn

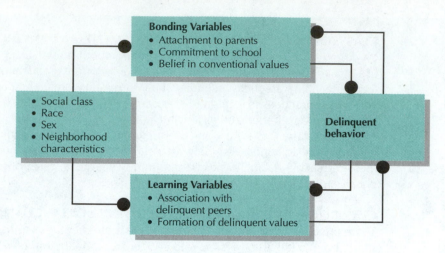

FIGURE 5.10

Overview of the Interactional Theory of Delinquency

Source: Terence Thornberry, Margaret Farnsworth, Alan Lizotte, and Susan Stern, "A Longitudinal Examination of the Causes and Correlates of Delinquency," working paper no. 1, Rochester Youth Development Study (Albany, N.Y.: Hindelang Criminal Justice Research Center, 1987), p. 11.

"innocent" boys into delinquents; they support and amplify the behavior of youths who have already accepted a delinquent way of life.

Life Course View   A key assumption of this theory—and what makes it unique— is that causal influences on delinquency are reciprocal. (This is the reason for the bidirectional arrows in Figure 5.10.) Weakened bonds to society lead youths to develop relationships with deviant peers and get involved in high-rate delinquency. More frequent occurrences of delinquent behavior further weaken these bonds, making it difficult to reestablish links to conventional peers. Delinquency promoting factors tend to reinforce one another in a never ending loop, which helps sustain a chronic criminal career.

Interactional theory has a developmental emphasis because it holds that adolescents pass through different stages of reasoning and sophistication as they mature. Thornberry applies this concept by suggesting that criminality is a developmental process that takes on different meanings and forms over the life course. During early adolescence, attachment to the family is the single most important determinant of whether a youth will adjust to conventional society and be shielded from delinquency. By mid-adolescence the influence of the family is replaced by the world of friends, school, and youth culture. In adulthood people's behavioral choices are shaped by their place in conventional society and their own nuclear family. The process is reciprocal: people are shaped by the quality of their social world, and the quality of their social world is influenced by their behavior.

Testing Interactional Theory   Thornberry's model is being evaluated and tested with a group of youths in Rochester, New York, who are being followed through the cycle of their offending careers; most results seem to support interactional theory. In one analysis Thornberry and his colleagues examined the influence of peer associations on delinquency and found that they conformed to interactional principles: associating with delinquent peers leads to increases in delinquency; increased delinquency leads to associations with delinquent peers. As this process unfolds over the life course, antisocial youths become part of a deviant peer network that reinforces their behavior, whereas conventional youths are reinforced by their conventional friends.[133] Thornberry and his colleagues have found similar patterns for family and school relations. Delinquency is related to weakened attachments to family and to the educational process, and delinquent behavior further weakens the bonds to family and school.[134] Other researchers have supported an interactional relationship between delinquent behavior and moral values (delinquency weakens moral beliefs and weakened beliefs encourage delinquency).[135]

In summary, interactional theory rests on life course assumptions: events and relationships that develop during a person's life cycle influence his or her behavior.

Age-Graded Theory

age-graded theory
Identifies turning points (such as marriage and career) that can cause delinquents to reverse course and desist from further criminal behavior.

If there are various pathways to crime and delinquency, are there trails back to conformity? In an important work, *Crime in the Making,* Robert Sampson and John Laub identify the turning points in a criminal career.[136] Although they agree that background factors such as family status and personality traits can affect entry into a delinquent career, Sampson and Laub also find that the stability of delinquent behavior can be affected by events that occur later in life, even after a chronic delinquent career has been undertaken (see Figure 5.11). Two critical turning points identified by their **age-graded theory** are marriage and career. Youths who had problems with the law are able to desist from crime as adults if they become attached to a spouse who supports and sustains them, even when the partner knows they had been in trouble when they were younger. Getting married not only introduces youths to a more stable lifestyle but limits their interactions with friends and peer group members whose carefree lifestyle might otherwise support deviant behaviors.[137] They may encounter employers who are willing to give them a chance despite their record. People who cannot sustain secure marital relations or are failures in the labor market are less likely to desist from crime.

According to Sampson and Laub, these life events help people build relations with individuals and institutions that are life-sustaining, a concept they refer to as

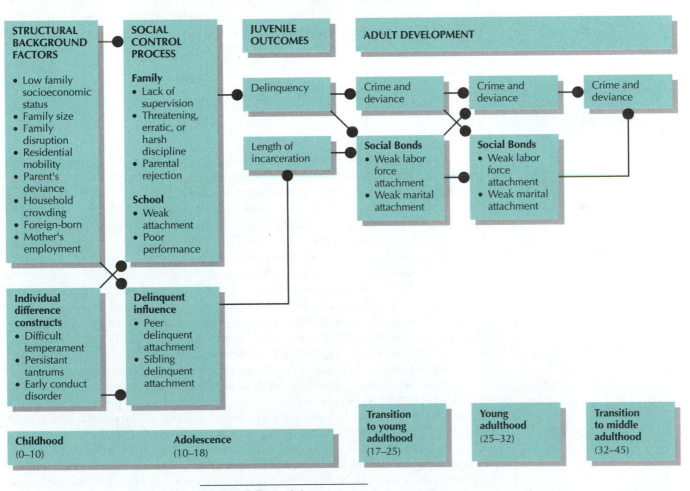

FIGURE 5.11

Sampson and Laub's Age-Graded Theory

Source: Robert Sampson and John Laub, *Crime in the Making* (Cambridge, Mass.: Harvard University Press, 1993), pp. 244–45.

"social capital." Building this social capital supports conventional behavior and inhibits deviant behavior. For example, a successful marriage creates social capital when it improves a person's stature and feelings of self-worth and encourages others to "take a chance" on the individual. There is growing evidence that youths who accumulate social capital in childhood (for example, by doing well in school or having a supportive family) are likely to maintain steady work as adults; employment may help insulate them from crime.[138] In the same way, having a good career can inhibit crime by creating a stake in conformity. Why commit crime when you are doing well at your job? These relationships are reciprocal. If a person is chosen as an employee, he or she returns the "favor" by doing the best job possible. If the person is chosen as a spouse, he or she blossoms into a devoted partner. Building social capital reduces the likelihood of deviance.

Sampson and Laub's research indicates that events that occur in later adolescence and adulthood do influence the direction of delinquent and criminal careers. Life events can help to either terminate or sustain deviant careers. The factors that produce crime and delinquency at one point in the life cycle may not be relevant at another; as people mature, the social, physical, and environmental influences on their behavior are transformed. Although latent traits may be important, they alone are not enough to control human behavior over the lifespan. Adolescents may show a propensity to offend early in their lives, but the nature and frequency of their activities are affected by outside forces beyond their control, such as getting arrested and being punished for crime.[139] Having established that change is possible, some important questions still need answering: Why do some youths change and others resist? Why do some people enter strong marriages and others fail? Why are some troubled youths able to conform to the requirements of a job or career when others cannot?

Policy Implications

The three types of social process theories suggest that delinquency can be prevented by strengthening the relationship between youths and the institutions primarily responsible for their socialization. This objective can be reached either by strengthening the institutions themselves or by helping youths better handle preexisting conditions. For example, the neighborhood school might be improved by getting teachers to realize that all students can and should be educated, by expanding preschool education programs, by developing curricula and educational materials relevant to students' lives, by developing teaching methods appropriate to the students, by developing individualized curricula, by stressing teacher development, and so on. At the same time, school-based delinquency prevention efforts must be available to help the youth who is manifesting problems in school, experiencing school failure, and finding that his or her bond to the educational system has eroded. Individual counseling and remedial services are needed for troubled youths. The Case in Point raises some prevention issues.

Prevention programs must also work to strengthen the internal structure of families in crisis. Because attachment to parents who can provide proper socialization is a cornerstone of all social process theories, developing good family relations is an essential element of delinquency prevention. This should not mean, however, that all families are expected to conform to a particular lifestyle or pattern. What is most important is that the family become a living unit that provides care and support for its members. What should be developed is a family structure that can encourage the positive self-image the child needs to resist the forces promoting delinquency in his or her environment.

Agents of the juvenile justice system must also recognize that their actions have a bearing on the future behavior of youths. For example, if a youth feels that he or

CASE IN POINT

You have just been appointed the head of curriculum for the local school system. The school board is interested in creating courses that will reduce the incidence of student delinquency and drug abuse. They fear that TV shows, popular music, and films that glorify the use of drugs teach children that substance abuse and crime are exciting and socially desirable activities. They feel the school must present courses that can counteract the weight of these destructive influences.

You are faced with designing a program that can teach students to "say no" to drugs and crime. One of your advisers suggests that the best approach is to teach children about the effects of drugs through media and live presentations in which former users discuss their experiences and problems. She believes learning about the evils of drugs can counteract the drug culture influences of commercial TV and rock and roll. In contrast, another adviser argues that the best approach is a series of workshops that help students develop a bond with their parents and their community and learn the value of commitment to conventional behavior and actions. These workshops would stress techniques of interfamily communications and life skills. Although both of these approaches have merit, only one can be chosen to serve as the basis of the new course.

■ What type of information would you present to the students?

■ Can students learn not to commit crimes and take drugs?

■ Who could best help students learn not to use drugs or engage in delinquency? other students? parents? teachers? ex-offenders?

she is not being treated fairly by police or court officials, that youth may seek out peers who share similar views. Consequently, the youth will be likely to experience an excess of definitions toward delinquency as well as a weakening of belief in conventional social rules and values.

Because many high-risk children suffer from PBS, treatment must be aimed at a variety of educational, family, vocational, and psychological problems. Focusing on a single problem, such as a lack of employment, may be ineffective.[140] Some efforts have been directed at primary prevention (before the onset of delinquency); others have focused on secondary prevention (treating troubled youths) and tertiary prevention (helping ex-offenders "go straight").

Prevention programs have also focused on providing services for youngsters who have been identified as delinquents or predelinquents. Such services usually include counseling, job placement, legal assistance, and so on. There aim is to reach out to troubled youths and provide them with the life skills necessary to function in their often troubling environment before they get in trouble with the law. For example, New York City's Beacon Community Center Program has, since 1991, provided city youths with a variety of interrelated services. The more than thirty Beacon programs give youths the tools to help them avoid crime and violence and to solve problems. Among the array of services and programs provided are mentoring,

HEAD START

Head Start is probably the best known effort to help lower-class youths achieve proper socialization and, in so doing, reduce their potential for future criminality.

Head Start programs were instituted in the 1960s as part of the Johnson administration's War on Poverty. In the beginning Head Start was a two-month summer program for children about to enter school that was aimed at embracing the "whole child." Comprehensive programming helped improve physical health, enhance mental processes, and improve social and emotional development, self-image, and interpersonal relationships. Preschoolers were provided with an enriched educational environment to develop their learning and cognitive skills. They were given the opportunity to use pegs and pegboards, puzzles, toy animals, dolls, letters and numbers, and other materials that middle-class children take for granted and that give them a leg up in the educational process.

Today, there are more than eighteen hundred centers around the nation, with 36,000 classrooms serving about eight hundred thousand children and their families on a budget of more than $4 billion annually. In addition to school-based programs, Head Start offers 571 home-based programs providing services to about forty thousand children by 4,562 home visitors.

Services have been expanded beyond the two-month summer program; more than thirteen million children have been served by Head Start since it began. Head Start programs receive 80 percent of their funding from the federal government; the other 20 percent comes from the local community.

Head Start teachers hope to provide a variety of learning experiences appropriate to the child's age and development. These experiences help the child to read books, to understand cultural diversity, to express feelings, and to play with and relate to peers in an appropriate fashion. Students are guided in developing gross and fine motor skills and self-confidence. Health care is also an issue, and most children enrolled in the program receive comprehensive health screening, physical and dental examinations, and appropriate followup. Many programs provide meals to ensure that the children receive proper nourishment.

Head Start programs now serve parents in addition to their preschoolers. Some programs allow parents to enroll in classes that cover parenting, literacy, nutrition/weight loss, domestic violence prevention, and other social issues; social services, health, nutrition, and educational services are also available. The programs offered by Head Start are summarized in Table A.

Considerable controversy has surrounded the success of the Head Start program. In 1970 the Westinghouse Learning Corporation issued a definitive evaluation of the Head Start effort and concluded that there was no evidence of lasting cognitive gains on the part of the participating children. Initial gains seemed to evaporate during the elementary school years, and by the third grade the performance of the Head Start children was no different from their peers.

Although disappointing, this evaluation focused on IQ levels and gave short shrift to improvement in social competence and other survival skills. More recent research has produced dramatically different results. One report found that by age 5, children who experienced the enriched day care offered by Head Start averaged more than ten points higher on their IQ scores than their peers who did not participate in the program. Other

tutoring, employment training and counseling, and cultural and recreational activities. Many of these services are aimed at strengthening protective factors (such as bonding with role models and developing healthy peer groups). Targeted efforts include antiviolence programs and campaigns, conflict resolution training, public education about drugs, substance abuse treatment, community beautification projects, and athletic activities involving youths and local police officers.[141]

Table A   Head Start Services

Education: Head Start's educational program is designed to meet the needs of each child, the community served, and its ethnic and cultural characteristics. Every child receives a variety of learning experiences to foster intellectual, social, and emotional growth.

Health: Head Start emphasizes the importance of the early identification of health problems. Every child is involved in a comprehensive health program, which includes immunizations and medical, dental, mental health, and nutritional services.

Parent Involvement: An essential part of Head Start is involvement of parents in parent education, program planning, and operating activities. Many parents serve as members of policy councils and committees and have a voice in administrative and managerial decisions. Participation in classes and workshops on child development and staff visits to the home allow parents to learn about the needs of their children and about educational activities that can take place at home.

Social Services: Specific services are geared to each family after its needs are determined. They include community outreach, referrals, family need assessments, recruitment and enrollment of children, and emergency assistance and crisis intervention.

research that carefully compared Head Start children to similar youths who did not attend the program found that the former made significant intellectual gains. Head Start children were less likely to be retained in a grade or placed in classes for slow learners, they outperformed peers on achievement tests, and they were more likely to graduate from high school. Head Start children also make strides in nonacademic areas: they have better health, immunization rates, and nutrition, and they have enhanced emotional characteristics after leaving the program. Research also shows that the Head Start program can have important psychological benefits for the mothers of participants, such as decreasing depression and anxiety and increasing feelings of life satisfaction. Although findings in some areas may be tentative, they are all in the same direction—Head Start enhances school readiness and has enduring effects on social competence.

If, as many experts believe, there is a close link between school performance, family life, and crime, programs such as Head Start can help some potentially criminal youths avoid problems with the law. Their success indicates that programs that help socialize youngsters can be used to combat urban criminality. Although some problems have been identified in individual centers, the government has shown its faith in Head Start as a socialization agent by planning to expand services in the coming years; total funding could reach $8 billion.

Sources: Fact Sheet, Administration for Children and Families, Administration on Children, Youth and Families (Washington, D.C.: Department of Health and Human Services, 1998); Robert E. Slavin, "Can Education Reduce Social Inequity?", *Educational Leadership* 55:6–10 (1997); Edward Zigler and Sally Styfco, "Head Start, Criticisms in a Constructive Context," *American Psychologist* 49:127–32 (1994); Nancy Kassebaum, "Head Start, Only the Best for America's Children," *American Psychologist* 49:123–26 (1994); Faith Lamb Parker, Chaya Piorkowski, and Lenore Peay, "Head Start as Social Support for Mothers: The Psychological Benefits of Involvement," *American Journal of Orthopsychiatry* 57:220–33 (1987).

In addition to these local efforts, the federal government has sponsored several national delinquency prevention efforts using the principles of social process theory. These include vocational training programs, such as the Comprehensive Employment Training Act, as well as educational enrichment programs, such as Head Start for preschoolers (see the Policy and Practice box entitled "Head Start" for more on this program).

SUMMARY

Social process theories explain delinquency as a function of the human interactions that occur daily in society. These theories reject the view that delinquents are born criminals or that delinquent behavior is purely a function of the socioeconomic structure of society.

Some social process theories stress the learning of delinquent or nondelinquent behavior. For example, Sutherland's theory of differential association suggests that delinquency is almost purely a learning process. Similarly, David Matza's neutralization approach describes how youngsters are able to learn techniques that can effectively neutralize the constraints of conventional values.

A second branch of social process theory is concerned with the forces of social control. Theorists such as Travis Hirschi view delinquency as a result of the inability of conventional institutions and relationships to restrain the behavior of youths. Although Hirschi's social control theory does not stress learning per se, it is evident that the weakening of the social bond is a long-term development that involves delinquent youths in an escalating process of antisocial behavior accompanied by a continuous diminution of their attachment to society. In Gottfredson and Hirschi's general theory of crime, impulsivity is identified as the key factor that produces a lack of control. Youths who lack self-control may find that their bond to society is weak and attenuated.

Developmental theories try to identify the social processes that affect change in delinquent and criminal behaving over the life course. Social development theory finds that youths' place in the social structure, coupled with their interpersonal problems, help weaken their prosocial bonds to society. This increases the probability that they will engage in delinquency. Interactional theory argues that these relationships change over the life course and that the processes and institutions that influence behavior at one point in time might have little influence at another time. Sampson and Laub expand this view in their age-graded theory by identifying factors that help youths desist from crime as they mature. These factors include marriage, employment, and military service.

Prevention programs based on social process theories usually prescribe treatment designed to strengthen family ties, improve school performance, or develop a youth's bond to society. Newer programs recognize that delinquency is a multifaceted problem and that programs must be multidimensional. They provide education, counseling, and job training both to youths and to their families.

KEY TERMS

socialization
social process theories
learning theory
control theory
developmental theories
differential association
    theory
differential reinforcement
    theory

neutralization theory
drift
subterranean values
control theories
commitment to
    conformity
containment theory
social bond

self-control
developmental process
problem behavior
    syndrome (PBS)
social development
    model (SDM)
interactional theory
age-graded theory

INFOTRAC COLLEGE EDITION EXERCISES

Read the following article from InfoTrac College Edition:

Delinquency and shame: data from Hong Kong. (shame as a way to control delinquency) Jon Vagg. *British Journal of Criminology* Spring, 1998

Social control theory, in relation to the prevention of juvenile delinquency, has provided a number of interesting theoretical propositions. One of these, shaming theory, can be defined as follows: those individuals who have a greater stake in conformity, due to factors such as community and family ties, will be less likely to commit delin-quent acts. If youths engage in criminal behavior, creating guilt through shaming may lower future occurrences of delinquent behavior. While this concept is highly debated, this approach has been in limited use recently for controlling youth crime.

What implications does Vagg's study have for juvenile delinquency prevention in this country? Emphasize the cultural differences between the United States and Asian countries.

QUESTIONS FOR DISCUSSION

1. Identify the processes that produce delinquent behaviors.
2. Have you ever rationalized your deviant acts? What neutralization techniques did you use?
3. Does self-esteem really influence behavior? Can antisocial acts actually improve self-image?
4. Comment on the statement "Delinquents are made, not born."
5. Of all attachments, which are the most important?
6. According to the general theory of crime, stable, unchanging personality traits produce delinquent behaviors. Comment then on this observation: "People don't change, opportunities do."

NOTES

1. Bill Dedman, "Where Children Play, Grown-Ups Often Brawl," *New York Times* 29 July 1998, p. A10.
2. A. Leigh Ingram, "Type of Place, Urbanism, and Delinquency: Further Testing of the Determinist Theory," *Journal of Research in Crime and Delinquency* 30:192–212 (1993).
3. Alan Lizotte, Terence Thornberry, Marvin Krohn, Deborah Chard-Wierschem, and David McDowall, "Neighborhood Context and Delinquency: A Longitudinal Analysis," in H. J. Kerner and E. Weitekamp, eds., *Cross-National Longitudinal Research on Human Development and Criminal Behavior* (Dordrecht, The Netherlands: Kluwer Academic Publishers, 1993), pp. 1–11.
4. Lawrence Rosen, "Family and Delinquency: Structure or Function," *Criminology* 23:553–73 (1985).
5. Howard Snyder and Melissa Sickmund, *Juvenile Offenders and Victims: A National Report* (Washington, D.C.: Office of Juvenile Justice and Delinquency Prevention, 1995), pp. 37–40.
6. Kenneth Polk and Walter Schafer, eds., *Schools and Delinquency* (Englewood Cliffs, N.J.: Prentice Hall, 1972).
7. Thomas Berndt, "The Features and Effects of Friendship in Early Adolescence," *Child Development* 53:1447–60 (1982).
8. Gerald Patterson and Karen Yoerger, "Developmental Models for Delinquent Behavior," in Sheilagh Hodgins, ed., *Mental Disorder and Crime* (Newbury Park, Calif.: Sage, 1993), pp. 150–59.
9. Edwin Sutherland, *Principles of Criminology* (Philadelphia: J.B. Lippincott, 1939).
10. Edwin Sutherland and Donald Cressey, *Criminology,* 8th ed. (Philadelphia: J.B. Lippincott, 1970), pp. 75–77.
11. Howard Becker, *Outsiders* (New York: Free Press, 1963).
12. Sutherland and Cressey, *Criminology,* pp. 77–79.
13. Ibid.
14. Albert Reiss and A. Lewis Rhodes, "The Distribution of Delinquency in the Social Class Structure," *American Sociological Review* 26:732 (1961).
15. Matthew Ploeger, "Youth Employment and Delinquency: Reconsidering a Problematic Relationship," *Criminology* 35:659–75 (1997); Elton Jackson, Charles Tittle, and Mary Jean Burke, "Offense-Specific Models of the Differential Association Process," *Social Problems* 33:335–56 (1986); James Short, "Differential Association as a Hypothesis: Problems of Empirical Testing," *Social Problems* 8:14–25 (1960).
16. Ross Matsueda and Karen Heimer, "Race, Family Structure and Delinquency: A Test of Differential Association and Control Theories," *American Sociological Review* 52:826–40 (1987).
17. James Orcutt, "Differential Association and Substance Abuse: A Closer Look at Sutherland (with a Little Help from Becker)," *Criminology* 25:341–58 (1987); Denise Kandel, "Friendship Networks, Intimacy, and Illicit Drug Use in Young Adulthood: A Comparison of Two Competing Theories," *Criminology* 29:441–69 (1991); Marvin Krohn and Terence Thornberry, "Rochester Youth Development Study, Network Theory:
A Model for Understanding Drug Abuse among African-American and Hispanic Youth," working paper no. 10 (Albany, N.Y.: Hindelang Research Center, 1991).
18. Donald Green, "Measures of Illegal Behavior in Individual-Level Deterrence Research," *Journal of Research in Crime and Delinquency* 26:253–75 (1989).
19. Gerben J. N. Bruinsma, "Differential Association Theory Reconsidered: An Extension and Its Empirical Test," *Journal of Quantitative Criminology* 8:29–46 (1992); Charles Tittle, *Sanctions and Social Deviance: The Question of Deterrence* (New York: Praeger, 1980).
20. Reed Adams, "The Adequacy of Differential Association Theory," *Journal of Research in Crime and Delinquency* 11:1–8 (1974).
21. The most influential critique of differential association is contained in Ruth Kornhauser, *Social Sources of Delinquency* (Chicago: University of Chicago Press, 1978).
22. These misconceptions are derived from Donald Cressey, "Epidemiologies and Individual Conduct: A Case from Criminology," *Pacific Sociological Review* 3:47–58 (1960).
23. Kornhauser, *Social Sources of Delinquency*; in contrast, see Ross Matsueda, "The Current State of Differential Association Theory," *Crime and Delinquency* 34:277–306 (1988).
24. Craig Reinerman and Jeffrey Fagan, "Social Organization and Differential Association: A Research Note from a Longitudinal Study of Violent Juvenile Offenders," *Crime and Delinquency* 34:307–27 (1988).
25. Sue Titus Reed, *Crime and Criminology,* 2nd ed. (New York: Holt, Rinehart & Winston, 1979), p. 234.
26. Robert Burgess and Ronald Akers, "A Differential Association-Reinforcement Theory of Criminal Behavior," *Social Problems* 14:128–47 (1966).
27. Matsueda, "The Current State of Differential Association Theory."
28. Graham Ousey and David Aday Jr., "The Interaction Hypothesis: A Test Using Social Control Theory and Social Learning Theory," paper presented at the American Society of Criminology Meeting, Boston, Mass., November 1995.
29. Mark Warr, "Age, Peers and Delinquency," *Criminology* 31: 17–40 (1993).
30. Mark Warr, "Life-Course Transitions and Desistance from Crime," *Criminology* 36:183–216 (1998).
31. Robert Burgess and Ronald Akers, "Differential Association—Reinforcement Theory of Criminal Behavior," *Social Problems* 14:128–47 (1968).
32. Ronald Akers, Marvin Krohn, Lonn Lonza-Kaduce, and Marcia Radosevich, "Social Learning and Deviant Behavior: A Specific Test of a General Theory," *American Sociological Review* 44: 636–55 (1979).
33. Richard Lawrence, "School Performance, Peers and Delinquency: Implications for Juvenile Justice," *Juvenile and Family Court Journal* 42:59–69 (1991).
34. Marvin Krohn, William Skinner, James Massey, and Ronald Akers, "Social Learning Theory and Adolescent Cigarette

Smoking: A Longitudinal Study," *Social Problems* 32:455–71 (1985); L. Thomas Winfree Jr., Christine Sellers, and Dennis Clason, "Social Learning and Adolescent Deviance Abstention: Toward Understanding the Reasons for Initiating, Quitting, and Avoiding Drugs," *Journal of Quantitative Criminology* 9:101–123 (1993).

35. John Hamlin, "Misplaced Role of Rational Choice in Neutralization Theory," *Criminology* 26:425–38 (1988).

36. Gresham Sykes and David Matza, "Techniques of Neutralization: A Theory of Delinquency," *American Sociological Review* 22:664–70 (1957); David Matza, *Delinquency and Drift* (New York: Wiley, 1964).

37. Matza, *Delinquency and Drift*, p. 51.

38. David Matza, "Subterranean Traditions of Youth," *Annals* 378:116 (1961).

39. Sykes and Matza, "Techniques of Neutralization."

40. Ibid.

41. Ian Shields and George Whitehall, "Neutralization and Delinquency among Teenagers," *Criminal Justice and Behavior* 21:223–35 (1994); Robert A. Ball, "An Empirical Exploration of Neutralization Theory," *Criminologica* 4:22–32 (1966); see also, M. William Minor, "The Neutralization of Criminal Offense," *Criminology* 18:103–20 (1980); Robert Gordon, James Short, Desmond Cartwright, and Fred Strodtbeck, "Values and Gang Delinquency: A Study of Street Corner Groups," *American Journal of Sociology* 69:109–28 (1963).

42. Michael Hindelang, "The Commitment of Delinquents to Their Misdeeds: Do Delinquents Drift?", *Social Problems* 17:500–9 (1970); Robert Regoli and Eric Poole, "The Commitment of Delinquents to Their Misdeeds: A Reexamination," *Journal of Criminal Justice* 6:261–69 (1978).

43. Larry Siegel, Spencer Rathus, and Carol Ruppert, "Values and Delinquent Youth: An Empirical Reexamination of Theories of Delinquency," *British Journal of Criminology* 13:237–44 (1973).

44. Robert Agnew, "The Techniques of Neutralization and Violence," *Criminology* 32:555–80 (1994).

45. Jeffrey Fagan, *Adolescent Violence: A View from the Street*, NIJ Research Preview (Washington, D.C: National Institute of Justice, 1998).

46. John Hamlin, "Misplaced Role of Rational Choice in Neutralization Theory," *Criminology* 6:425–38 (1988).

47. Albert Reiss, "Delinquency as the Failure of Personal and Social Controls," *American Sociological Review* 16:196–207 (1951).

48. Scott Briar and Irving Piliavin, "Delinquency: Situational Inducements and Commitment to Conformity," *Social Problems* 13:35–45 (1965–66).

49. Walter Reckless, *The Crime Problem* (New York: Appleton-Century Crofts, 1967), pp. 469–83.

50. Among the many research reports by Reckless and his colleagues are Frank Scarpitti, Ellen Murray, Simon Dinitz, and Walter Reckless, "The Good Boy in a High Delinquency Area: Four Years Later," *American Sociological Review* 23:555–58 (1960); Walter Reckless, Simon Dinitz, and Ellen Murray, "The Good Boy in a High Delinquency Area," *Journal of Criminal Law, Criminology, and Police Science* 48:12–26 (1957); idem, "Self-Concept as an Insulator against Delinquency," *American Sociological Review* 21:744–46 (1956); Walter Reckless and Simon Dinitz, "Pioneering with Self-Concept as a Vulnerability Factor in Delinquency," *Journal of Criminal Law, Criminology, and Police Science* 58:515–23 (1967); Walter Reckless, Simon Dinitz, and Barbara Kay, "The Self-Component in Potential Delinquency and Potential Non-Delinquency," *American Sociological Review* 22:566–70 (1957).

51. Howard Kaplan, *Deviant Behavior in Defense of Self* (New York: Academic Press, 1980); idem, "Self-Attitudes and Deviant Response," *Social Forces* 54:788–801 (1978).

52. Ibid.

53. L. Edward Wells, "Self-Enhancement through Delinquency: A Conditional Test of Self-Derogation Theory," *Journal of Research in Crime and Delinquency* 26:226–52 (1989).

54. John McCarthy and Dean Hoge, "The Dynamics of Self-Esteem and Delinquency," *American Journal of Sociology* 90:396–410 (1984); L. Edward Wells and Joseph Rankin, "Self-Concept as a Mediating Concept in Delinquency," *Social Psychology Quarterly* 46:11–22 (1983).

55. Sung Joon Jang and Terence Thornberry, "Self-Esteem, Delinquent Peers, and Delinquency: A Test of the Self-Enhancement Thesis," *American Sociological Review* 63:586–98 (1998).

56. Ibid.

57. Ibid., p. 8.

58. Travis Hirschi's data are examined in his *Causes of Delinquency* (Berkeley, Calif.: Univerity of California Press, 1969).

59. Ibid., p. 132.

60. Ibid., pp. 160–61.

61. Michael Wiatroski, David Griswold, and Mary K. Roberts, "Social Control Theory and Delinquency," *American Sociological Review* 46:525–41 (1981).

62. Patricia Van Voorhis, Francis Cullen, Richard Mathers, and Connie Chenoweth Garner, "The Impact of Family Structure and Quality on Delinquency: A Comparative Assessment of Structural and Functional Factors," *Criminology* 26:235–61 (1988).

63. Marc Le Blanc, "Family Dynamics, Adolescent Delinquency, and Adult Criminality," paper presented at the Society for Life History Research Conference, Keystone, Colorado, October 1990, p. 6.

64. Teresa Lagrange and Robert Silverman, "Perceived Strain and Delinquency Motivation: An Empirical Evaluation of General Strain Theory," paper presented at the American Society of Criminology Meeting, Boston, Mass., November 1995.

65. Patricia Van Voorhis, Francis Cullen, Richard Mathers, and Connie Chenoweth Garner, "The Impact of Family Structure and Quality on Delinquency: A Comparative Assessment of Structural and Functional Factors," *Criminology* 26:235–61 (1988).

66. Patricia Jenkins, "School Delinquency and the School Social Bond," *Journal of Research in Crime and Delinquency* 34:337–67 (1997).

67. Marianne Junger and Ineke Haen Marshall, "The Interethnic Generalizability of Social Control Theory: An Empirical Test," *Journal of Research in Crime and Delinquency* 34:79–112 (1997); Marianne Junger and Wim Polder, "Some Explanations of Crime among Four Ethnic Groups in the Netherlands," *Journal of Quantitative Criminology* 8:51–78 (1992); Josine Junger-Tas, "An Empirical Test of Social Control Theory," *Journal of Quantitative Criminology* 8:18–29 (1992).

68. John Cochran and Ronald Akers, "An Exploration of the Variable Effects of Religiosity on Adolescent Marijuana and Alcohol Use," *Journal of Research in Crime and Delinquency* 26:198–225 (1989).

69. Robert Agnew and David Peterson, "Leisure and Delinquency," *Social Problems* 36:332–48 (1989).

70. For a review of existing research, see Kimberly Kempf, "The Empirical Status of Hirschi's Control Theory," in Bill Laufer and Freda Adler, eds., *Advances in Criminological Theory* (New Brunswick, N.J.: Transaction Publishers, 1992).

71. Richard Lawrence, "Parents, Peers, School and Delinquency," paper presented at the American Society of Criminology Meeting, Boston, Mass., November 1995.

72. Peggy Giordano, Stephen Cernkovich, and M. D. Pugh, "Friendships and Delinquency," *American Journal of Sociology* 91:1170–1202 (1986).

73. Denise Kandel and Mark Davies, "Friendship Networks, Intimacy, and Illicit Drug Use in Young Adulthood: A Comparison of Two Competing Theories," *Criminology* 29:441–67 (1991).

74. Leslie Samuelson, Timothy Hartnagel, and Harvey Krahn, "Crime and Social Control among High School Dropouts," *Journal of Crime and Justice,* 18:129–61 (1990).

75. Gary Jensen and David Brownfield, "Parents and Drugs," *Criminology* 21:543–54 (1983); see also, M. Wiatrowski,

D. Griswold, and M. Roberts, "Social Control Theory and Delinquency," *American Sociological Review* 46:525–41 (1981).

76. Kimberly Kempf Leonard and Scott Decker, "The Theory of Social Control: Does It Apply to the Very Young?", *Journal of Criminal Justice* 22:89–105 (1994).

77. Velmer Burton, Francis Cullen, T. David Evans, R. Gregory Dunaway, Sesha Kethineni, and Gary Payne, "The Impact of Parental Controls on Delinquency," *Journal of Criminal Justice* 23:111–26 (1995).

78. Randy LaGrange and Helene Raskin White, "Age Differences in Delinquency: A Test of Theory," *Criminology* 23:19–45 (1985).

79. Marvin Krohn and James Massey, "Social Control and Delinquent Behavior: An Examination of the Elements of the Social Bond," *Sociological Quarterly* 21:529–43 (1980).

80. Robert Agnew, "Social Control Theory and Delinquency: A Longitudinal Test," *Criminology* 23:47–61 (1985).

81. For a similar result, see A. E. Liska and M. D. Reed, "Ties to Conventional Institutions and Delinquency: Estimating Reciprocal Effects," *American Sociological Review* 50:547–60 (1985).

82. Michael Gottfredson and Travis Hirschi, *A General Theory of Crime* (Stanford, Calif.: Stanford University Press, 1990).

83. Ibid., p. 27.

84. Ibid., p. 90.

85. Ibid., p. 89.

86. Ibid.

87. David Forde and Leslie Kennedy, "Risky Lifestyles, Routine Activities, and the General Theory of Crime," *Justice Quarterly* 14:265–94 (1997).

88. Michael Polakowski, "Linking Self- and Social Control with Deviance: Illuminating the Structure Underlying a General Theory of Crime and Its Relation to Deviant Activity," *Journal of Quantitative Criminology* 10:41–76 (1994).

89. Bruce Link, Elmer Streuning, Francis Cullen, Patrick Shrout, and Bruce Dohrenwend, "A Modified Labeling Theory Approach to Mental Disorders: An Empirical Assessment," *American Sociological Review* 54:400–23 (1989).

90. Marc Le Blanc, Marc Ouimet, and Richard Tremblay, "An Integrative Control Theory of Delinquent Behavior: A Validation 1976–1985," *Psychiatry* 51:164–76 (1988).

91. Polakowski, "Linking Self- and Social Control with Deviance: Illuminating the Structure Underlying a General Theory of Crime and Its Relation to Deviant Activity."

92. John Gibbs and Dennis Giever, "Self-Control and Its Manifestations among University Students: An Empirical Test of Gottfredson and Hirschi's General Theory," *Justice Quarterly* 12: 231–55 (1995); David Brownfield and Ann Marie Sorenson, "Self-Control and Juvenile Delinquency: Theoretical Issues and an Empirical Assessment of Selected Elements of a General Theory of Crime," *Deviant Behavior* 14:243–64 (1993); Harold Grasmick, Charles Tittle, Robert Bursik, and Bruce Arneklev, "Testing the Core Empirical Implications of Gottfredson and Hirschi's General Theory of Crime," *Journal of Research in Crime and Delinquency* 30:5–29 (1993); John Cochran, Peter Wood, and Bruce Arneklev, "Is the Religiosity-Delinquency Relationship Spurious? A Test of Arousal and Social Control Theories," *Journal of Research in Crime and Delinquency* 31: 92–123 (1994).

93. Carl Keane, Paul Maxim, and James Teevan, "Drinking and Driving, Self-Control, and Gender: Testing a General Theory of Crime," *Journal of Research in Crime and Delinquency* 30:30–46 (1993).

94. Judith DeJong, Matti Virkkunen, and Marku Linnoila, "Factors Associated with Recidivism in a Criminal Population," *The Journal of Nervous and Mental Disease* 180:543–50 (1992); David Cantor, "Drug Involvement and Offending among Incarcerated Juveniles," paper presented at the American Society of Criminology Meeting, Boston, Mass., November 1995.

95. Dennis Giever, "An Empirical Assessment of the Core Elements of Gottfredson and Hirschi's General Theory of Crime," paper presented at the American Society of Criminology Meeting, Boston, Mass., November 1995.

96. Linda Pagani, Richard Tremblay, Frank Vitaro, and Sophie Parent, "Does Preschool Help Prevent Delinquency in Boys with a History of Perinatal Complications?," *Criminology* 36:245–68 (1998).

97. Otwin Marenin and Michael Resig, "A General Theory of Crime and Patterns of Crime in Nigeria: An Exploration of Methodological Assumptions," *Journal of Criminal Justice* 23:501–18 (1995).

98. Bruce Arneklev, Harold Grasmick, Charles Tittle, and Robert Bursik, "Low Self-Control and Imprudent Behavior," *Journal of Quantitative Criminology* 9:225–46 (1993).

99. Ousey and Aday, "The Interaction Hypothesis: A Test Using Social Control Theory and Social Learning Theory."

100. Ross Matsueda and Kathleen Anderson, "The Dynamics of Delinquent Peers and Delinquent Behavior," *Criminology* 36:269–308 (1998).

101. Julie Horney, D. Wayne Osgood, and Ineke Haen Marshall, "Criminal Careers in the Short Term: Intra-Individual Variability in Crime and Its Relations to Local Life Circumstances," *American Sociological Review* 60:655–73 (1995).

102. Douglas Longshore, "Self-Control and Criminal Opportunity: A Prospective Test of the General Theory of Crime," *Social Problems* 45:102–14 (1998).

103. Marvin Krohn, Alan Lizotte, and Cynthia Perez, "The Interrelationship between Substance Use and Precocious Transitions to Adult Sexuality," *Journal of Health and Social Behavior* 38:87–103 (1997) at 88.

104. G. R. Patterson, Barbara DeBaryshe, and Elizabeth Ramsey, "A Developmental Perspective on Antisocial Behavior," *American Psychologist* 44:329–35 (1989).

105. Sheldon Glueck and Eleanor Glueck, *Unraveling Juvenile Delinquency* (Cambridge: Harvard University Press, 1950), p. 59.

106. Robert Sampson and John Laub, "Crime and Deviance in the Life Course," *American Review of Sociology* 18:63–84 (1992).

107. R. Tremblay, R. Loeber, C. Gagnon, P. Charlebois, S. Larivee, and M. Le Blanc, "Disruptive Boys with Stable and Unstable High Fighting Behavior Patterns during Junior Elementary School," *Journal of Abnormal Child Psychology* 19:285–300 (1991).

108. Terrie Moffitt, "Natural Histories of Delinquency" in Elmar Weitekamp and Hans-Jurgen Kerner, eds., *Cross-National Longitudinal Research on Human Development and Criminal Behavior* (Dordrecht, Netherlands: Kluwer, 1994), pp. 3–65.

109. Rolf Loeber and Magda Stouthamer-Loeber, "Development of Juvenile Aggression and Violence," *American Psychologist* 53:242–59 (1998).

110. See, generally, D. J. West and David P. Farrington, *The Delinquent Way of Life* (London: Hienemann, 1977); the findings here are reported in David Farrington, "The Development of Offending and Antisocial Behavior from Childhood to Adulthood," paper presented at the Congress on Rethinking Delinquency, University of Minho, Braga, Portugal, July 1992.

111. Amy D'Unger, Kenneth Land, Patricia McCall, and Daniel Nagin, "How Many Latent Classes of Delinquent/Criminal Careers? Results from Mixed Poisson Regression Analyses," *American Journal of Sociology* 103:1593–1630 (1998).

112. Dawn Jeglum Bartusch, Donald Lynam, Terrie Moffitt, and Phil Silva, "Is Age Important? Testing a General versus a Developmental Theory of Antisocial Behavior," *Criminology* 35:13–48 (1997).

113. Rolf Loeber, Phen Wung, Kate Keenan, Bruce Giroux, Magda Stouthamer-Loeber, Wemoet Van Kammen, and Barbara Maughan, "Developmental Pathways in Disruptive Behavior," *Development and Psychopathology* 5:351–71 (1993).

114. Michael Maxfield and Cathy Spatz Widom, "Childhood Victimization and Patterns of Offending through the Life Cycle: Early Onset and Continuation," paper presented at the American Society of Criminology Meeting, Boston, Mass., November 1995; Richard Jessor, John Donovan, and Francis Costa,

Beyond Adolescence: Problem Behavior and Young Adult Development (New York: Cambridge University Press, 1991).

115. David Farrington and Rolf Loeber, "Transatlantic Replicability of Risk Factors in the Development of Delinquency," paper presented at the American Society of Criminology Meeting, Boston, Mass., November 1995.

116. D. Wayne Osgood, "The Covariation among Adolescent Problem Behaviors," paper presented at the annual meeting of the American Society of Criminology, Baltimore, November 1990.

117. Paul Greenbaum, Lynn Foster-Johnson, and Amelia Petrila, "Co-Occurring Addictive and Mental Disorders among Adolescents: Prevalence Research and Future Directions," *American Journal of Orthopsychiatry* 66:52–60 (1996).

118. Magda Stouthamer-Loeber and Evelyn Wei, "The Precursors of Young Fatherhood and Its Effect on Delinquency of Teenage Males," *Journal of Adolescent Health* 22:56–65 (1998); Richard Jessor, John Donovan, and Francis Costa, *Beyond Adolescence: Problem Behavior and Young Adults* (New York: Cambridge University Press, 1991); David Rowe, Alexander Vazsonyi, and Aurelio Jose Figueredo, "Mating Effort in Adolescence: Conditional or Alternative Strategy," paper presented at the American Society of Criminology Meeting, Boston, Mass., November 1995.

119. For a review, see Tina Mawhorr, "Social Skill Deficits and Juvenile Delinquency: Are Delinquents Really Social Misfits?," paper presented at the American Society of Criminology Meeting, Boston, Mass., November 1995.

120. Lening Zhang, William Wieczorek, and John Welte, "The Impact of Age of Onset on Substance Use on Delinquency," *Journal of Research in Crime and Delinquency* 34:253–68 (1997).

121. Richard Dembo, Glenn Turner, James Schmeidler, Camille Chin Sue, Polly Borden, and Darrell Manning, "Development and Evaluation of a Classification of High Risk Youths Entering a Juvenile Assessment Center," *Substance Abuse and Misuse* 31:303–22 (1996).

122. Robert Bursik, "The Dynamics of Specialization in Juvenile Offenses," *Social Forces* 58:851–64 (1980).

123. Randall Shelden, "The Chronic Delinquent: Some Clarifications of a Vague Concept," *Juvenile and Family Court Journal* 40:37–44 (1989).

124. Joan McCord, "Family Relationships, Juvenile Delinquency, and Adult Criminality," *Criminology* 29:397–417 (1991).

125. Paul Mazerolle, "Delinquent Definitions and Participation Age: Assessing the Invariance Hypothesis," *Studies on Crime and Crime Prevention* 6:151–68 (1997).

126. Robert Sampson and John Laub, "Crime and Deviance in the Life Course," *American Review of Sociology* 18:63–84 (1992).

127. Joseph Weis and J. David Hawkins, *Reports of the National Juvenile Justice Assessment Centers, Preventing Delinquency* (Washington, D.C.: U.S. Department of Justice, 1981); Joseph Weis and John Sederstrom, *Reports of the National Juvenile Justice Assessment Centers, The Prevention of Serious Delinquency: What to Do* (Washington, D.C.: U.S. Department of Justice, 1981).

128. Julie O'Donnell, J. David Hawkins, and Robert Abbott, "Predicting Serious Delinquency and Substance Use among Aggressive Boys," *Journal of Consulting and Clinical Psychology* 63:529–37 (1995).

129. Ibid., pp. 534–36.

130. J. David Hawkins, Richard Catalano, Diane Morrison, Julie O'Donnell, Robert Abbott, and L. Edward Day, "The Seattle Social Development Project," in Joan McCord and Richard Tremblay, eds., *The Prevention of Antisocial Behavior in Children* (New York: Guilford, 1992), pp. 139–60.

131. Terence Thornberry, "Toward an Interactional Theory of Delinquency," *Criminology* 25:863–81 (1997).

132. Matsueda and Anderson, "The Dynamics of Delinquent Peers and Delinquent Behavior."

133. Terence Thornberry, Alan Lizotte, Marvin Krohn, Margaret Farnworth, and Sung Joon Jang, *Delinquent Peers, Beliefs, and Delinquent Behavior: A Longitudinal Test of Interactional Theory*, working paper no. 6, rev., Rochester Youth Development Study (Albany, N.Y.: Hindelang Criminal Justice Research Center, 1992).

134. Terence Thornberry, Alan Lizotte, Marvin Krohn, Margaret Farnworth, and Sung Joon Jang, "Testing Interactional Theory: An Examination of Reciprocal Causal Relationships among Family, School and Delinquency," *Journal of Criminal Law and Criminology* 82:3–35 (1991).

135. Scott Menard and Delbert Elliott, "Delinquent Bonding, Moral Beliefs and Illegal Behavior: A Three Wave-Panel Model," *Justice Quarterly* 11:173–88 (1994) at 185–87.

136. Robert Sampson and John Laub, *Crime in the Making: Pathways and Turning Points through Life* (Cambridge, Mass.: Harvard University Press, 1993).

137. Warr, "Life-Course Transitions and Desistance from Crime."

138. Avshalom Caspi, Terrie Moffitt, Bradley Entner Wright, and Phil Silva, "Early Failure in the Labor Market: Childhood and Adolescent Predictors of Unemployment in the Transition to Adulthood," *American Sociological Review* 63:424–51 (1998).

139. Raymond Paternoster, Charles Dean, Alex Piquero, Paul Mazerolle, and Robert Brame, "Generality, Continuity, and Change in Offending," *Journal of Quantitative Criminology* 13:231–66 (1997).

140. Terence Thornberry, David Huizinga, and Rolf Loeber, "The Prevention of Serious Delinquency and Violence," in James Howell, Barry Krisberg, J. David Hawkins, and John Wilson, eds., *Sourcebook on Serious, Violent, and Chronic Juvenile Offenders* (Thousand Oaks, Calif.: Sage, 1995).

141. Adapted from Daniel McGillis, *Beacons of Hope: New York City's School-Based Community Centers* (Washington, D.C.: National Institute of Justice, 1996).

Chapter Six

Social Reaction Theories: Labeling and Conflict

Russell Eugene Weston Jr. was described as a quiet loner who drifted back and forth between a cabin in the Montana mountains and a modest house in rural Illinois.[1] On July 25, 1998, he entered the U.S. Capitol building and went on a shooting rampage during which two Capitol police officers were slain and a female tourist was wounded.[2] Weston's murderous spree may have been the result of mental disturbance, but it is also possible that his outburst was triggered by his life as an outsider.[3]

Weston's neighbors portrayed the forty-one-year-old as a withdrawn, introverted man who grew increasingly angry and alienated over the years. When invitation letters went out for a twenty-year reunion of his high school class, Weston sent his back scrawled with obscenities and a warning never to contact him again. A classmate from the seventh grade remembered Weston mostly as "one of the forgotten middle kids, kind of on the fat side, not a sports guy, never went out with any girls. Only had a couple of friends." Then around the eleventh grade "he started getting into the drug scene, smoking marijuana. He and a group of other kids, they all went out to this place in Montana. They wanted to get away, to be free. It was to be some kind of self-sufficient commune. I heard he had a gold claim out there."[4]

Although Weston's behavior may reflect mental problems, could it be that he and others like him, after years of taunting and torment, are reacting to being on the margin of society? Is their behavior a product of social conflict and alienation?

The two theoretical models discussed in this chapter, although quite different from each other, share one important characteristic that differentiates them from all other theories of delinquency. Most other theories portray youthful law violators as individuals who cannot conform to the rules of society. In contrast, social reaction theories focus on the role

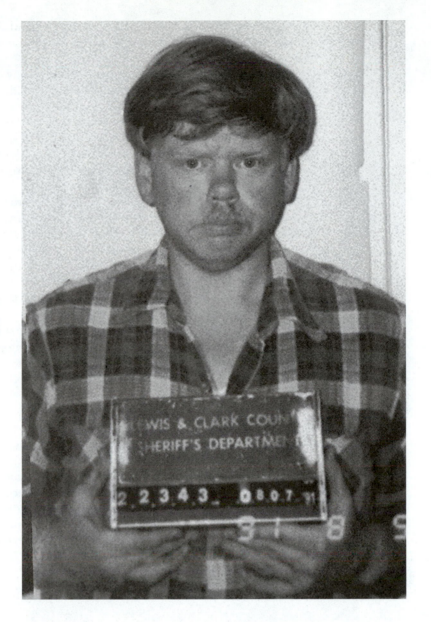

Russell Eugene Weston Jr. went on a shooting spree in the Capitol building, slaying two Capitol Hill police officers. Could his personality disorder have been triggered by a lifetime of negative social labels and stigma?

social and economic institutions play in *producing* delinquent behaviors and how the application of the rule of law in U.S. society influences delinquent behavior. At the core of these theories is the idea that the way *society* reacts to individuals and the way *individuals* react to society determines behavior. Social reactions determine which behaviors are considered criminal or conventional; they also determine individual behavior and can contribute to the formation of delinquent careers.

Both of these perspectives on delinquency theory and policy were developed in the late 1960s and early 1970s. In this period of social ferment, many traditional social institutions were questioned and criticized. The role of government became suspect because of the generally unpopular war in Vietnam and the corruption uncovered in the Nixon administration. Likewise, legal and academic scholars voiced growing concerns with the juvenile justice system because of its alleged inefficiency and discriminatory practices. Even the educational system was criticized for its failure to provide equal educational opportunities for all.[5]

Considering the climate of those times, it is not surprising that social scientists questioned the role powerful social institutions play in shaping society and influencing the behavior of people living within it. Scholars critical of big government, educational, corporate, and criminal justice organizations claimed that the efforts of these institutions actually helped produce crime and delinquency. Those holding power were accused of striving for control over the lower class and protecting the interests of the wealthy and powerful.

According to these critical scholars, those in power used their influence to control the criminal law for their own benefit.[6] The illegal behaviors of the have-not members of society were heavily punished, yet the violations of the upper classes—tax evasion, stock market manipulation, price fixing, political corruption, and so on—were often immune from prosecution or considered civil violations and punished financially. Critics argued that those in power used their control over social institutions to stigmatize the powerless and brand them as outcasts from society. Even when sincere efforts were made to help the less fortunate, the outcome was to enmesh them further in a deviant or outcast status. For example, educational enrichment efforts, such as the Head Start program (discussed in Chapter 5), were suspected of helping identify children as intellectually deficient and in need of special attention; efforts to provide mental health services branded individuals as "sick" or "crazy." Out of this critical inquiry two potent themes emerged: (1) concepts of law and justice are differently applied in U.S. society, and (2) those who become involved with the justice system are soon branded deviants or outcasts and launched into a deviant "career."

This type of analysis was soon applied to the study of delinquent behavior. It was alleged that delinquency results from the reactions of politically powerful individuals and groups, especially government social control agencies, to society's less fortunate members. Delinquents are not inherently wrong or "evil" but are youths who have had a deviant status conferred on them for socially unacceptable behavior by those holding economic, political, and social power. These reactions are stratified by class: lower-class youngsters are stigmatized, arrested, tried, and punished; middle-class youths are sent on their way by a benign, understanding police officer or juvenile court judge.[7] Thus, it is not the quality of the delinquent act itself that is important but the way society and its institutions react to the act.

In this chapter we will first review labeling theory, which maintains that official reactions to delinquent acts help label youths as criminals, troublemakers, and outcasts, locking them into a cycle of escalating delinquent acts and social sanctions. Then we will turn to conflict theory, which holds that the decision to confer a delinquent label is a product of the capitalist system of economic production and its destructive influence on human behavior.

Labeling Theory

labeling theory
Posits that society creates deviance through a system of social control agencies that designate (or label) certain individuals as delinquent, thereby stigmatizing youths and encouraging them to accept this negative personal identity.

Labeling theory is concerned with the consequences of stigmatization by agents of social control, including official institutions such as the police and the courts and unofficial institutions such as parents and neighbors. Labeling theory differs from the theories we've discussed previously in that it emphasizes the sustenance of criminal behavior rather than its origins. Thus, it is more a theory of delinquent career formation than one that predicts the onset of individual delinquent behaviors.[8]

According to labeling theory, youths may violate the law for a variety of reasons, including but not limited to poor family relationships, neighborhood conflict, peer pressure, psychological or biological abnormality, and prodelinquent learning experiences. Regardless of the cause, if a youth's delinquent behavior is detected, the offender will be given a negative social label that can follow him or her throughout life. These labels include "troublemaker," "juvenile delinquent," "mentally ill," "retarded," "criminal," "junkie," and "thief."

Applying Labels

The way labels are applied and the nature of the labels themselves are likely to have important future consequences for the delinquent. The degree to which youngsters are perceived as deviants may affect their treatment at home, at work, and at school. Young offenders may find that their parents consider them a detrimental influence on younger brothers and sisters. Neighbors may tell their children to avoid this "troublemaker." Teachers may place them in classes or tracks reserved especially for students with behavior problems, minimizing their chances of obtaining higher education. The delinquency label may also restrict eligibility for employment and negatively affect the attitudes of society in general, and, depending on the severity of the label, youthful offenders will be subjected to official sanctions ranging from mild reprimands to incarceration.

Beyond these immediate results, and depending on the visibility of the label and the manner and severity with which it is applied, youths will have an increasing commitment to delinquent careers. As the negative feedback of law enforcement agencies, parents, friends, teachers, and other figures strengthens this commitment, delinquents may begin to reevaluate their identity and come to see themselves as criminals, troublemakers, or "screw-ups." Thus, through a process of identification and sanctioning, reidentification, and increased sanctioning, young offenders become transformed. They are no longer children in trouble; they are "delinquents," and they accept that label as a personal identity—a process called self-labeling[9] (see Figure 6.1).

Who Defines Deviance?

Another important principle of the labeling approach is that the concepts of crime and delinquency are not absolute or permanent but vary according to social norms, customs, and the power structure of society. Those in power control what is considered "right" and "wrong," what is legal and illegal. Acts become outlawed because people in power view them as harmful behaviors.

A number of pioneering labeling theorists helped define this perspective by declaring that deviance is not an absolute concept but rather is relative in both place and time. "Deviance is not a property inherent in certain forms of behavior," argues sociologist Kai Erikson in a classic statement. "It is a property conferred

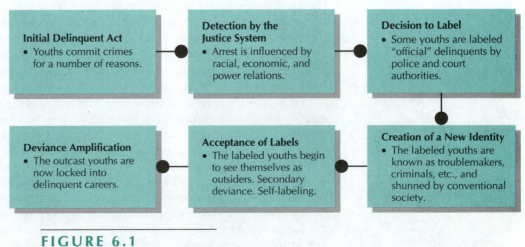

FIGURE 6.1

Labeling Theory

upon those forms by the audiences which directly or indirectly witness them."[10] Behavior is considered wrong or deviant only when it departs from expected social behavior patterns and elicits a reaction that serves to isolate or punish the individuals engaged in the behavior.[11] For example, body piercing may be considered a deviant act if only a few youths try it; it becomes normative when popular entertainers begin piercing and millions of their loyal fans follow suit.

In what is probably the best known statement by a labeling theorist, Howard Becker described how deviance is created by labels:

> Deviance is *not* a quality of the act the person commits, but rather a consequence of the application by others of rules and sanctions to an "offender." The deviant is one to whom that label has successfully been applied; deviant behavior is behavior that people so label.[12]

moral entrepreneurs
Interest groups that attempt to control social life by promoting their own personal set of moral values and establishing them as law.

Becker argues that legal and social rules are created by **moral entrepreneurs,** people who are concerned about social morality and who work to control its definition and application. Moral entrepreneurs attempt to influence the views of the power elite—those who control the government, industry, education, and the media—as well as shape the attitudes of the general public. Their goal is to determine the direction and content of the criminal law and, in so doing, identify what society considers "right" and "wrong." For example, during our own lifetimes, some of us have witnessed the legalization of abortion, the banning of school prayer, the control of handguns, changes in the age limit for the use of alcohol, and the fight to ban gay marriages. Becker and other labeling theorists help us recognize that concepts of deviance are not written in stone but evolve over time.

The Effect of Labeling

The labeling approach focuses primarily on society's reaction to deviant behavior and the effect that reaction has on people who are labeled. What effect does social stigma have on the people who are labeled?

We often form enduring opinions of others based on brief first impressions.[13] If interactions involve perceptions of deviance, individuals may be assigned negative informal labels, such as "troublemaker," "nerd," or "crazy." Individuals who are suspected of harboring such behavior "problems" are carefully scrutinized by those they interact with; people are cautious with them, search for signs of deviance, or shun them outright.[14]

Official labels may be applied when people run afoul of socially accepted rules, laws, or conventions. Official or formal labels may include "criminal," "mentally ill," or "dropout." Official labels are often bestowed during "ceremonies" designed to redefine deviants' identity and remove them from the normative social structure, for example, during trials or civil commitment hearings or school disciplinary board hearings.[15] The net effect of this legal and social process is a *durable negative label and an accompanying loss of status*. The labeled deviant becomes a social outcast who is prevented from enjoying higher education, well-paying jobs, and other societal benefits. Because this label is "official," few will question the accuracy of the negative assessment. People who may have been "suspicious" in the past now feel justified in their early assessments: "I always knew he was a bad kid."

A good example of the official labeling ceremony occurs in juvenile courts. Here young offenders find (perhaps for the first time) that authority figures, in the person of the juvenile court judge, consider them incorrigible outcasts who must be separated from the right-thinking members of society. To reach that decision, the judge relies on the testimony of a parade of witnesses—parents, teachers, police officers, social workers, and psychologists—all of whom may testify that the offenders are unfit to be part of conventional society.[16] As the label "juvenile delin-

Labeling theorists believe that negative labels create a self-fulfilling prophecy. If children continually receive negative feedback from parents, teachers, judges, and others whose opinions they take to heart, they will eventually interpret this rejection as accurate and self-defining. In contrast, children who constantly receive positive feedback, such as these champion athletes, will define themselves as successful and behave accordingly.

quent" is conferred on offenders, their identities may forever be transformed from "kids who have done something bad" to "bad kids."[17]

self-fulfilling prophecy
Deviant behavior patterns that are a response to an earlier labeling experience; youths act out these social roles even if they were falsely bestowed.

Self-Fulfilling Prophecy   Labeling theorists believe negative labels create a **self-fulfilling prophecy.**[18] If children continually receive negative feedback from parents, teachers, judges, and others whose opinion they take to heart, they will eventually interpret this rejection as accurate and self-defining. Ultimately, their behavior will begin to conform to these negative expectations; they become the person others perceive them to be: "Teachers already think I'm stupid, so why should I bother to study." The self-fulfilling prophecy leads to a damaged self-image and an increase in antisocial behaviors.[19]

Self-Rejection   Labeling and stigmatization help create a new, deviant identity. Those exposed to negative social sanctions experience both self-rejection and a lower self-image. Self-rejecting attitudes ("At times I think I am no good at all") result in both a weakened commitment to conventional values and behaviors and the acquisition of motives to deviate from social norms ("Everyone is against me, so why should I obey the rules?").[20]

This attitude and value transformation is amplified by the bond social outcasts form with similarly labeled peers.[21] Labeled delinquents will seek out other outcasts from conventional society who are similarly stigmatized.[22] Associating with deviant peers helps reinforce conventional society's preexisting negative evaluations: "We were right all along about him, look who his friends are!"

Delinquent peers may help the labeled youths "reject their rejectors": Teachers are "stupid," they are told; cops are "dishonest"; parents "just don't understand."[23] Group identity enables outcast youths to be defiant, to show contempt for the source of the negative labels, and to distance themselves from the source of condemnation. These actions help solidify both the grip of deviant peers and the impact of the negative labels.[24]

Primary and Secondary Deviance

primary deviance
Deviant acts that do not redefine the self- and public image of the offender.

The shape of the labeling process was refined by Edwin Lemert in his formulation of primary and secondary deviance, a significant concept in the development of delinquency theory.[25] Lemert argues that deviant acts actually form two distinct classes, primary and secondary. **Primary deviance** describes youths who engage in "bad acts" but are not considered "bad people." They are not labeled deviant by others, nor do they apply self-labels. For example, a student who successfully shoplifts a CD from the college store and avoids detection is not recognized by others as deviant, nor does the student recognize him- or herself as a "thief" or a "criminal." Later the student may say, "I can't believe I was so stupid and took such a risk." But the act of theft has little impact on the student's current or future status; that student can go on to graduate without consequence. Later, when attending law school, this deviant behavior is rationalized by the offender as a youthful prank, a mistake, or a slip in an otherwise unblemished life: "Everyone shoplifts once. What's the big deal? I was immature. I'd never do it now." Although primary acts may be considered serious, they do not materially affect self-concept.

Lemert attaches little importance to primary deviance, but he argues that deviations become significant when the deviant behavior is repetitive, highly visible, and subject to severe social reaction. This stage is referred to as **secondary deviance.** The secondary deviant is not someone who has done a bad act; he is now considered a "bad person." The college boy who is caught while shoplifting a book may find himself expelled from school and facing criminal charges. Thereafter he will be watched and suspected, stigmatized and labeled. He may then incorporate this new deviant identity into his own psyche: "Maybe I am a thief and untrustworthy; after all, that's what everyone says about me!" Had he not been caught and labeled, his deviant act would soon have been forgotten; he would have remained a primary deviant.

secondary deviance
Deviant acts that redefine the offender's self- and public image, forming the basis for the youth's self-concept.

A Spoiled Identity All life roles of secondary deviants revolve around the new, albeit damaged, identity they have accepted.[26] Their resocialization is controlled by the disgrace, punishment, segregation, and stigma that typically accompany deviant labels. Self-labeling, combined with social stigma, transforms the person into one who

> employs his behavior (deviant) or a role based upon it as a means of defense, attack, or adjustment to the overt and covert problems created by the consequent societal reaction to him.[27]

The delinquent may use this damaged identity as a coping mechanism, for example, by joining with others so labeled in a deviant subculture such as a gang or a drug clique. So although the intent of deviant labels may be to reduce unwanted behavior, their actual effect is to encourage its continuity.

Lemert's model helps to explain how the labeling process encourages further episodes of deviant behavior. The model portrays immersion in a deviant identity as a cycle of events (Figure 6.2) in which a deviant act (A) leads to a social reaction (B), which leads to self-conception as a "deviant" (C), which leads to increased, more serious deviant acts (D) and to greater and more severe social reactions, including legal reprisals (E), until identification with a deviant identity becomes complete (F), a state of events that increases the probability of future deviant acts.[28] Lemert's conceptualization of the labeling process and his description of primary and secondary deviance are major theoretical underpinnings of the labeling approach.

Differential Social Control Why do some youths become secondary deviants? According to Karen Heimer and Ross Matsueda's concept of *differential social control,* deviant self-evaluations reflect appraisals made by others. Youths who view themselves as delinquents are giving an inner voice to their perceptions of how

FIGURE 6.2

Lemert's Cycle of Secondary Deviance

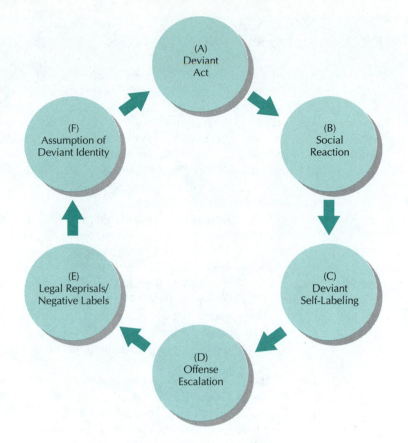

parents, teachers, peers, and neighbors feel about them. Youths who believe others view them as antisocial or as troublemakers take on roles that reflect this assumption; they expect to be suspected and then rejected. This process is referred to as **reflective role-taking.** Labeled youths may then join up with similarly outcast delinquent peers who facilitate their behavior. Eventually, antisocial behavior becomes habitual and automatic.[29]

reflective role-taking
A process whereby youths take on antisocial roles assigned to them by others.

A unique aspect of Heimer and Matsueda's model is that it acknowledges the effect of social control mechanisms on deviance formation. Tempering or enhancing the effect of reflective role-taking are informal and institutional social control processes. Families, schools, peers, and the social system can either help control youths and dissuade them from crime or encourage and sustain deviance. When these groups are dysfunctional (for example, parents use drugs), they encourage rather than control antisocial behavior.

Youths who believe their parents and friends consider them deviants and troublemakers are the ones most likely to engage in delinquency. A damaged self-image, influenced and directed by social interaction, controls the content of behavior and produces secondary deviants.[30]

The Juvenile Justice Process and Labeling

Is it possible that the juvenile justice process actually increases the probability that at-risk youths will continue their offending careers? In fact, the justice system has long been accused of bestowing destructive deviant labels on children who are suspected of being delinquents. In a classic work, Frank Tannenbaum first suggested that social typing, which he called "dramatization of evil," transforms the offender's identity from a doer of evil to an "evil person."[31] Tannenbaum emphasized

PROSECUTOR'S PRECHARGING DIVERSION PROGRAM

A number of juvenile justice systems have experimented with alternatives to official processing to avoid the problems of stigma and labeling. One such program, in operation since 1993, is located in the prosecutor's office of Arkansas's Sixth Judicial District. The prosecutor was prompted to create the program because the juvenile court system had become overwhelmed. The congestion was causing a tremendous delay in getting juveniles into the court system and was affecting the quality of treatment of juveniles once they were brought to trial. It was clear that an alternative system was needed to cut down on the number of cases filed in juvenile court and to provide more appropriate treatment for juveniles charged with less serious offenses.

The Prosecutor's Precharging Diversion Program is designed to provide youthful offenders with sentencing diversion as an option to formal adjudication in juvenile court. The program's primary purpose is to discourage juvenile crime and recidivism and to teach meaningful lessons about accepting responsibility and developing self-esteem. It is aimed at youths ages 12 through 17 who have been charged with a nonviolent misdemeanor or certain felony offenses in Pulaski County, Arkansas (Little Rock area). The nature of the offense is reviewed by deputy prosecutors to determine whether basic eligibility criteria have been met. If the youth is eligible for the Precharging Diversion Program, the parents are contacted and a meeting is arranged to enroll the juvenile in the forty-five-day program.

Once enrolled, the youth is required to report to a " peer group judgment panel" for the purpose of alternative sentencing. Made up of youths who have successfully completed the Precharging Diversion Program and have received appropriate training, the peer group judgment panel assigns youths to a constructive treatment regimen designed to cover the following areas: paying back the victim, making new friends, improving education achievement, and learning respect for the law.

The juvenile is also required to perform a certain number of hours of community service to be supervised by the community or a nonprofit organization. These activities could include removing graffiti, cleaning up city parks, or washing police cars. Three to sixteen hours of community service must be performed, and tasks are designed to be performed on the weekend. Currently, youths are assigned to work in facilities such as the Arkansas Food Bank, the Rice Depot Food Bank, the school district building, and the Union Rescue Mission.

The program requires juveniles to participate in area programs and presentations designed to acquaint youths with constructive community relationships. They also must uti-

the role of the juvenile justice system in this scheme: "The entire process of dealing with young delinquents is mischievous insofar as it identifies *him* to *himself* and to the environment as a delinquent person."[32]

Theorists have built on the work of Tannenbaum, continuing to describe the impact of juvenile justice processing on delinquent labeling and consequent illegal behavior. Delinquents, the argument goes, are in reality the finished products of the juvenile justice "assembly line."[33] Although youths enter as children in trouble, they emerge as individuals transformed by decision makers into bearers of criminal histories, which are likely to reinvolve them in criminal activity. Once labeled, the police and other authority figures begin to anticipate that these troublemakers will continue their life of crime.[34] Labeled delinquents are assumed to engage in a full range of violence, theft, and drug abuse. Although they have not necessarily demonstrated these characteristics by their behavior, they become "perennial suspects."[35] The system designed to reduce delinquency may help produce hardened, stigma-bearing young criminals.

lize the library or other literary programs available to complete an autobiography or a book report. Youths learn firsthand about the consequences of criminal activity through presentations by Arkansas Department of Corrections inmates.

Having successfully completed these different phases of the Prosecutor's Precharging Diversion Program, the juvenile learns the importance of accountability and responsibility by sitting in judgment over incoming youths who will be participating in the program. The juvenile sits as a member of a peer group judgment panel on three occasions and imposes alternative sentences as outlined here. This final portion of the program is especially important because it gives the juvenile a sense of coming full circle, and it helps the youth perform the critical analysis process, which is designed to result in the acceptance of responsibility for wrongful conduct. Failure to complete the program results in prosecution in juvenile court.

Outside of Little Rock, the diversion program has been expanded to include a Teen Court. Youths in trouble with the law can be brought before the Teen Court if they admit to the acts they are accused of and agree to go before the court to be sentenced. Local youths are recruited to serve as teen attorneys to represent their peers who are in trouble with the law. Teens act as bailiffs and clerks of court; the only adult is a juvenile prosecutor who acts as the judge. After the teen court process, sentences range from six hours of community service for a disorderly conduct charge to thirty-six hours for multiple possession of drugs and alcohol. Juveniles are also required to participate in self-help programs and peer group review panels.

Part of the success of the Prosecutor's Precharging Diversion Program has been that the peer group review panel typically comprises at-risk youths who have made strides toward turning their lives around. Youths who have been in trouble with the law are true peers of the juvenile referred by the prosecutor's office and relate more easily to the referred juvenile. The program seems to reduce juvenile crime without the need for bestowing permanent labels.

Programs such as the Prosecutor's Precharging Diversion Program help reduce stigma and labeling, but do they truly have a deterrent effect? This program is used with nonviolent first offenders, but could it also be offered to more serious offenders such as violent youths? What would victims think? What do you think?

Sources: Innovative Courts Programs, Bureau of Justice Assistance, Office of Justice Programs, Washington, D.C., 1995; personal communication with Matt Jordan, Precharging Diversion Supervisor, Sixth Judicial District, Little Rock, Arkansas, October 30, 1998.

degradation ceremony
Going to court, being scolded by a judge, or being found delinquent after a trial are examples of public ceremonies that can transform youthful offenders by degrading their self-image.

Degradation Ceremonies   According to the labeling perspective, the actions of the juvenile justice system, outwardly aimed at delinquency prevention, actually gains the opposite effect by turning the self-perception of a youthful suspect into that of a delinquent.[36] In another classic paper, sociologist Harold Garfinkel addressed why this occurs when he described what he called a successful **degradation ceremony,** during which the public identity of an offender is transformed into "something looked on as lower in the social scheme of social types."[37] Garfinkel concludes that this process may be similar in form and function to what is currently practiced in juvenile court. Going to a juvenile court, being scolded by a judge, having charges read, and being found delinquent after a trial process are all conditions that should produce "successful degradation." Recognizing the role stigma plays in maintaining and developing a delinquent career has prompted some juvenile justice agencies to break this destructive cycle by creating programs designed to limit delinquent labels. One such effort is described in the Policy and Practice box entitled "Prosecutor's Precharging Diversion Program."

Labeling theory predicts two relationships with regard to juvenile justice processing: the delinquency label will be bestowed on the powerless members of society in a discriminatory fashion, and the more frequent, prolonged, or decisive the contacts with the juvenile justice system, the more likely it is that an offender will ultimately accept the delinquency label as a personal identity and enter into a life of crime. These two anticipated relationships are discussed next.

Discrimination in the Labeling Process   One of the cornerstones of the labeling perspective is that the likelihood of becoming labeled is skewed along racial and class lines; the burden falls most heavily on the disadvantaged, the poor, and the powerless. Because they are often stereotyped, young, male, inner-city, minority group members are more likely than others to be labeled delinquent.[38]

There is much evidence in support of the labeling hypothesis. Research shows that police are more likely to arrest and officially process males, minority group members and those in the lower economic classes than youths who do not share these traits.[39]

Evidence also exists that offenders whose families have economic or political power are likely to be given a mere warning by police officers rather than being processed to the juvenile court.[40] And the juvenile court is believed to respond more favorably to youths from middle-class homes than to those from the lower class. Living in a single-parent home, especially if a child is a minority group member, has been related to discrimination in the juvenile justice system. Under these circumstances, minority youths were found to be more at risk than white youths.[41]

Although this evidence is persuasive, some critics dispute the charge that the justice system operates in a distinctly discriminatory fashion.[42] Some evidence suggests that decisions related to official juvenile justice processing are influenced more by crime-related issues, such as offense seriousness and prior record, than by personal factors, such as racial or economic bias.[43] The factors most closely related to the decision of police to take formal action reflect legal and crime-related variables: prior offense record, association with known delinquents, involvement in gang violence, and drug involvement. Such findings have led some to believe that youths who commit multiple crimes with their friends, use drugs, and get into fights will also get arrested, regardless of their race or class. If this is the case, labels are merely a by-product of a delinquent career and not its cause.

Are They Really Transformed?   A cornerstone of labeling theory is that the end product of an official label is a "transformed" identity. However, studies attempting to measure the identity transformation of adolescents at the onset and conclusion of official contact have been inconclusive.[44] Some research shows that youths actually feel relief after the conclusion of their juvenile justice experience rather than shame, stigma, or a diminution of their self-image as labeling theorists would predict.[45]

Despite such skeptical conclusions, a body of empirical evidence shows that negative labels can lead to self-labeling and deviance amplification.[46] Youths labeled troublemakers in school are the ones most likely to drop out, and dropping out has been linked to delinquent behavior.[47] Similarly, male drug users labeled as addicts by social control agencies eventually become self-labeled and increased their drug use.[48]

The labeling process may start early with informal social labels. Parents may negatively label their children who suffer a variety of problems, including antisocial behavior and school failure.[49] This process is important because once they are labeled as troublemakers, adolescents begin to reassess their self-image. Parental labeling may facilitate intrafamily alienation; children experience damaged self-images and become more prone to delinquency.[50]

Even if official labels do not cause youths to restructure their self-image, there is little question that they seem to amplify rather than extinguish offending careers. Research now shows that children who are labeled by the juvenile justice system are more likely than nonlabeled youths to seek out deviant peers and to engage in subsequent antisocial behavior.[51] Official labeling may produce a cumulative disadvantage that provokes some youths into repeating their antisocial behaviors.[52] Labeling may reduce their standing in the community, reduce their social capital, and thereby help sustain delinquency over time.[53] This effect may explain, in part, why the specific deterrent effect of severe and repeated punishment often fails to materialize: deterrent effects are negated or overcome by the force of stigmatization. In other words, the fear of punishment is outweighed by the deviance amplification effects of stigma.

Evaluation of Labeling Theory

Although quite influential in the 1970s, labeling theory has declined in importance as a primary theory of delinquency since then. Four major criticisms of the labeling approach have led to this decline.

1. Labeling theorists failed to explain the onset of the first or primary deviation. Why is it that some people engage in the initial deviant act that leads to their label, whereas others in the same circumstances stick to conventional behaviors?[54] As criminologist Ronald Akers puts it: "One sometimes gets the impression from reading the literature that people go about minding their own business and then—'wham'—bad society comes along and slaps them with a stigmatized label."[55]

2. According to labeling theory, the overrepresentation of males, minorities, and the poor in the crime rate is a function of discriminatory labeling by social control agents. However, as we've seen, empirical research has failed to consistently show that labels are bestowed in a discriminatory fashion.[56] About 40 percent of the research studies indicate a racial effect on juvenile justice decision making, and 60 percent do not; about one-third of research studies show a socioeconomic influence on labeling, but the remaining two-thirds refute this conclusion.[57] Therefore, a majority of empirical research efforts suggest that supposed label-producing actions such as arrest, prosecution, and sentencing are more closely related to the seriousness of the criminal act and the youth's prior record than to personal characteristics.

Discrimination in the labeling process is a cornerstone of the theory because it indicates that the manner in which labels are bestowed is the key issue in determining criminality. If people were labeled only because they deserved negative social reactions (that is, they committed serious crimes), the theory would be invalid because the labeling process would be an effect of crime rather than its cause.[58]

3. Not all studies that evaluate the effects of official labeling support a deviance amplification effect. Some youngsters undergoing the labeling process may not be as deeply affected by their experiences as labeling theory predicts.[59]

4. Criminologists found that the labeling concept that "no act is inherently evil or criminal" is naive. This point is driven home by sociologist Charles Wellford, who argues rather conclusively that some crimes, such as rape and homicide, are almost universally sanctioned.[60] He says, "Serious violations of the law are universally understood and *are*, therefore, *in that sense*, intrinsically criminal."[61]

These criticisms led to a decline in labeling theory as an explanation of delinquent behavior. Enthusiasm for the labeling approach also diminished because the general public and academic community seem more concerned with crime control and the best method of curbing delinquent youths rather than worrying about the stigma such treatment might produce. In one influential work, *Beyond Delinquency*, sociologists Charles Murray and Louis Cox found that youths assigned to a treatment program designed to reduce labels were more likely to later commit delinquent acts than a comparison group who were placed in a traditional and more punitive state training school. The implication was that the deterrent threat of punishment had a greater impact on youths and that the crime-producing influence of negative labels was actually minimal.[62]

Labeling Theory Reconsidered   Just when it seemed that labeling theory was about to be dropped as an explanation of delinquency, it has become the object of renewed interest by the academic community. Criminologists Raymond Paternoster and Leeann Iovanni suggest that the labeling perspective can offer important insights:

1. It identifies the role played by social control agents in the process of delinquency causation; delinquent behavior cannot be fully understood if the agencies and individuals empowered to control and treat it are ignored.
2. It recognizes that delinquency is not a disease or pathological behavior; it focuses attention on the social interactions and reactions that shape individuals and their behavior.
3. It distinguishes between delinquent acts (primary deviance) and delinquent careers (secondary deviance) and shows that these are separate problems that must be treated differently.[63]

Paternoster and Iovanni's support for labeling theory reinforces the current attention being paid to the development and maintenance of delinquent careers as opposed to the onset of delinquent acts. Labeling theory provides a model for understanding why some misbehaving youths continue down the path of ever-escalating antisocial behaviors whereas most are able to successfully desist from crime. The Case in Point box touches on the controversy surrounding labeling theory.

Social Conflict Theory

social conflict theory
Asserts that society is in a state of constant internal conflict, and focuses on the role of social and governmental institutions as mechanisms for social control.

Unlike traditional theoretical perspectives that try to explain why an individual violates the law, **social conflict theory** focuses on the role social and governmental institutions play in creating and enforcing laws that control behavior and morality. According to this view, society is in a constant state of internal conflict, and different groups strive to impose their will on others. Those with money and power succeed in shaping the law to meet their needs and to maintain their interests. Those whose behavior cannot conform to the needs of the power elite are defined as delinquents and criminals. Conflict criminologists do not view delinquents as rebels who cannot conform to proper social norms, nor do they try to devise innovative ways of controlling youthful misbehavior. Their interests lie in evaluating how the criminal law is used as a mechanism of social control and in describing how social, political, and economic power is used to control and shape society.

The Emergence of Critical Criminology

Like labeling theory, conflict theory had its roots in the widespread social and political upheavals of the 1960s.[64] These forces included the Vietnam war, the counterculture movement, and various forms of political protest. Conflict theory flourished within this framework because it provided a theoretical basis to challenge the legit-

You are planning director for the state department of juvenile justice correctional services. One of your main concerns is the effect of stigma on the criminal offending patterns of delinquent youths. Some of your advisers suggest that processing youths through the juvenile correctional justice system produces deviant identities that lock them into a criminal way of life. Rather than rehabilitate, the system produces hard core delinquents who are likely to recidivate. They point to studies that show that an experience with the juvenile justice system has relatively little impact on chronic offenders and, if anything, is associated with escalating the seriousness of their criminal behavior.

Some of the more conservative members of your staff are opposed to making the reduction of stigma and labeling a top correctional concern. They remind you that an experience with the juvenile justice system may actually help deter crime. They point to studies that suggest that youths who have been processed through the correctional system are less likely to recidivate than youths who receive lesser punishments, such as community corrections or probation. In addition, they believe hard core, violent offenders deserve to be punished; excessive concern for the offender and not their acts ignores the rights of victims and society in general.

These opposing views have left you in a quandary. On one hand, the system must be sensitive to the adverse effects of stigma and labeling. On the other hand, the need for control and deterrence must not be ignored. Despite your dilemma, you must come up with a plan that satisfies both positions.

- What types of correctional programs might avoid excessive stigma yet control juvenile offenders?

- Should more concern be given to control or to labeling?

imacy of the government's creation and application of law. Students protesting the war, and who later were appalled at the political maneuvering of the Nixon administration, adopted a left-wing ideology. Many went on to graduate school in the social sciences, where they embraced political and social theories critical of the power elite, those who have the political and economic power to shape society to reflect their personal standards and beliefs. Some went on to teaching careers where they could continue their left-wing scholarship.

These critical thinkers hurled challenges at the academic world, the center of most theoretical thought in criminology. They claimed that it was archaic, conservative, and out of tune with recent changes in society.[65] **Critical criminologists** questioned the fundamental role criminologists play in uncovering the causes of crime and delinquency. At a time of general turmoil in society, they called for sweeping innovation in academic settings—including changes in the way courses were taught, grading, and tenure. Criminologists were asked to evaluate their own lives and activities to understand their personal role in the crime problem. Was it possible that they were acting as agents of the state, taking money from government agencies to achieve more effective repression of the poor and laboring classes?[66] These

critical criminologists
Analysts who review historical and current developments in law and order to expose the interests of the power elite and ruling classes.

social conflict theorists called for rethinking the entire field of law and criminology.[67] From this intellectual ferment emerged a number of branches of social conflict theory.

The Branches of Conflict Theory

Several views exist about what produces social conflict. Those who follow the writings of German social philosopher Karl Marx focus their attention on the economic conditions of the capitialist system. Marx believed capitalism turned workers into a dehumanized mass who were at the mercy of their employers. Theorists who use Marxian analysis reject the notion that law is designed to maintain a tranquil and fair society and that criminals are malevolent people who wish to trample the rights of others. Marxian criminologists suggest that law and justice are not neutral devices that serve the interest of society but are *instruments of power* used to protect the power elite's interests.[68] Racism, sexism, imperialism, unsafe working conditions, inadequate child care, substandard housing, industrial pollution, and war making as a tool of foreign policy are "true crimes"; the crimes of the helpless—burglary, robbery, and assault—are more expressions of rage over unjust conditions than actual crimes.[69] According to the Marxists, crime and delinquency are the natural consequence of the unequal distribution of wealth and power in postindustrial capitalist society.

In contrast, Weberian conflict theorists believe conflict between the haves and have-nots of society can occur in any social system and is not solely a product of capitalism. This view relies heavily on the writings of Max Weber (1864–1920), a German economist and social historian who believed all social and legal systems are controlled by intergroup competition and conflict. Weber argued that there were multiple sources of competition; groups compete not solely for economic dominance but over ethical and religious ideas as well.

According to conflict theory, society is in a constant state of turmoil. Different groups strive to impose their will on others. Those in power shape the law to meet their needs and maintain their interests. This relationship has existed in every time and in every place. This scene shows the process of rendering justice in 1389.

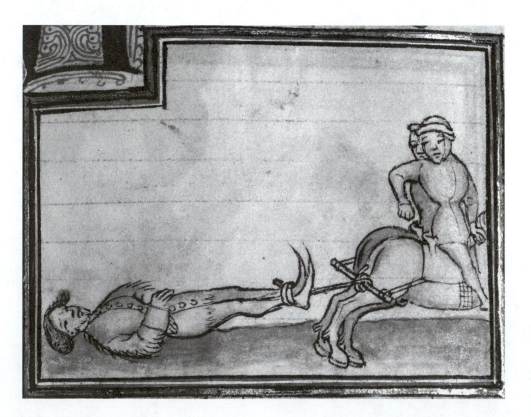

Despite the significant dogmatic differences between them, all social conflict theorists agree that those in power define the behavior of the poor as criminal and delinquent while shaping the law to define their own actions as acceptable and appropriate.

The social conflict approach is different from the labeling perspective despite their common emphasis on reactions of society and its institutions. Social conflict theorists charge that labeling advocates do not go far enough in exposing the crime-producing elements of U.S. culture, that they seem content merely to analyze the behavior of strange and different people. In contrast, social conflict thinkers use historical research and political analysis to understand the social relationships, power relations, and institutional arrangements that produce delinquent and criminal behavior.

Elements of Social Conflict Theory

Social conflict theory examines the relationship between the ruling class and the process by which deviance is defined and controlled in capitalist society (Figure 6.3). By broadening the search for an explanation of deviance to include its defining process, social conflict theorists depart from the narrower focus of earlier positivist models of deviant behavior, which viewed deviance as a function of the problems people have relating to society. If crime occurs, it may be because society has let its own citizens down and not vice versa.

Social Control   Conflict theorists are interested in the nature and purpose of social control. They believe those in power use the justice system to maintain their relative status while keeping others in a subservient position: men use their economic power to control and subjugate women; members of the majority group want to stave off economic advancement of minorities; capitalists want to reduce the power of workers to ensure they are willing to accept low wages.

Conflict theory centers around a view of society in which an elite class uses the criminal law as a means of meeting and controlling threats to its status. The ruling class is a self-interested collective whose primary interest is self-gain.[70]

FIGURE 6.3
Social Conflict Theory

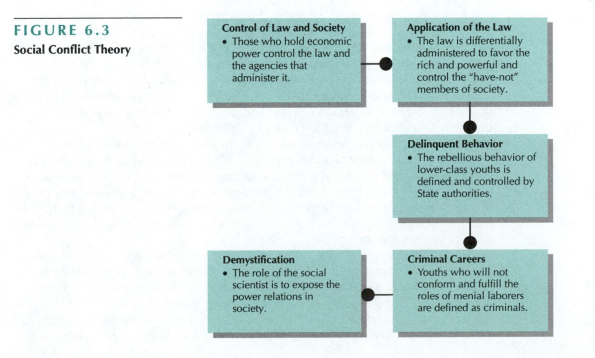

Control of Law and Society
• Those who hold economic power control the law and the agencies that administer it.

Application of the Law
• The law is differentially administered to favor the rich and powerful and control the "have-not" members of society.

Delinquent Behavior
• The rebellious behavior of lower-class youths is defined and controlled by State authorities.

Demystification
• The role of the social scientist is to expose the power relations in society.

Criminal Careers
• Youths who will not conform and fulfill the roles of menial laborers are defined as criminals.

Law and Justice   Social conflict theorists view the criminal law and the criminal justice system as vehicles for controlling the poor, have-not members of society. They help the powerful and the rich to impose their particular morality and standards of good behavior on the entire society; protect their property and physical safety from attack by the have-nots, even though the cost may be high in terms of the legal rights of those it perceives as a threat; and extend the definition of illegal or criminal behavior to encompass those who might threaten the status quo.[71] The ruling elite draws the lower-middle class into this pattern of control, leading it to believe it also has a stake in maintaining the status quo.[72] According to social conflict theory, the poor may or may not commit more crimes than the rich, but they certainly are arrested and punished more often. The poor are driven to crime because:

- Middle- and upper-class rules and laws have little relationship to the lifestyle of the poor.
- A natural frustration exists in a society where affluence is well publicized but unattainable to the majority of citizens.
- A deep-rooted hostility is generated among members of the lower class toward a social order they are not allowed to shape or participate in.[73]

Conflict theorists seriously contradict the long-held presumption that the U.S. system of law and justice is humane and fair to all citizens. Conflict theory asks us to reevaluate many basic beliefs. For example, that laws protecting private property may actually be designed to preserve the dominance of a ruling elite seems to strike at the very heart of our moral beliefs. For this reason alone, conflict theory has had a profound effect on mid-twentieth-century criminological thought.

Demystification   Social conflict theorists strive to demystify law and science. This complex concept entails a number of different actions. For one thing, conflict criminologists charge that an inordinate amount of scientific effort is devoted to unmasking the social conditions of lower-class citizens with the ostensible purpose of improving their lives. Such studies include examinations of lower-class family life, measurements of intelligence, school performance, and so on. Conflict criminologists argue, however, that these efforts actually serve to stifle the lower classes by "proving" that they are more delinquent and less intelligent and that they have poorer school performance than the middle class. They point out that the tests and instruments used to conduct these studies are biased and inaccurate.[74] Thus, in one sense, demystification entails uncovering the real reasons behind scientific research.

Another aspect of demystification involves identifying the historical development of criminal law. By drawing attention to the "real" reasons such laws as tax codes and statutes prohibiting theft and drug use were created, we will gain a broader understanding of the purpose and intent of these laws. If it is found that theft laws, for example, were originally created to maintain the wealth and capital of the rich, then those who violate the law should not perceive themselves as evil, immoral, or wrong but rather as victims of an unjust system.

Demystification also involves identifying hidden power relations in society. For example, radical feminist scholars have focused their attention on how male power (patriarchy) is used to control both the economic means of production and the sexuality of women, ensuring continued male dominance. Radical feminists have helped identify the extent of sexual violence and battering (offenses that are frequently unreported), showing that men physically and sexually victimize women in their attempt to maintain control.[75]

Finally, the demystification of capitalist society reveals the controlling nature of the "professional mystique."[76] It is alleged that our society grants inordinate power to professionals to judge and control the population. When teachers, doctors, lawyers, and psychologists judge persons to be crazy, stupid, sick, unfit, delinquent, or criminal, that label becomes their social identity. Conflict criminologists charge that professionals often suppress and distort the truth, "unmasking" powerless people so that their positions of social inferiority are maintained. The system quickly condemns those who speak against it as "subversive," traitorous," or "mentally ill."

The Conflict Concept of Delinquency

Conflict theorists view delinquency as a normal response by youths to the social conditions created by capitalist society.[77] In fact, the very creation of a unique legal category, "delinquency," is a function of the class consciousness that occurred around the turn of the century.[78] In his book, *The Child Savers,* Anthony Platt documented the creation of the delinquency concept and the role played by wealthy child savers in forming the philosophy of the juvenile court. Platt believed the child-saving movement's real goal was to maintain order, stability, and control while preserving the existing class system and distribution of wealth.[79] He and others have concluded that the child savers were anything but—they were, in reality, powerful and wealthy citizens who aimed to control the behavior of weak and disenfranchised youths.[80]

Today, conflict criminologists still view delinquent behavior as a function of the capitalist system's inherent social and economic inequity. They argue that capitalism accelerates the trend toward replacing human labor with machines so that youths are removed from a useful place in the labor force.[81] From early childhood, the values of capitalism are reinforced. Social control agencies such as schools prepare youths for placement in the existing capitalist system by presenting them with behavior models that will help them conform to later job expectations. For example, rewards for good schoolwork correspond to the rewards a manager uses with subordinate employees. In fact, most schools are set up to reward and nurture youths who show early promise in self-discipline, achievement, and motivation and who are therefore judged likely to perform well in the capitalist system. Youths who are judged inferior as potential job prospects (Herman and Julia Schwendinger refer to them as "prototypical marginals") become known to the school community as "losers," "burnouts," and "punks" and eventually wind up in delinquent roles.[82]

Class and Delinquency   The capitalist system affects youths at each level of the class structure differently. In the lowest classes, youths form delinquent gangs, which can be found in the most desolated ghetto areas of the nation. These violent gangs serve outcast youths as a means of survival in a system that offers no other reasonable alternative. Other lower-class youths, who live in more stable areas, are usually on the fringe of criminal activity because the economic system excludes them from meaningful opportunity.

Conflict theory also acknowledges middle-class delinquency. The alienation of individuals from one another, the never-ending competitive struggle, and the absence of human interest and feeling—all inherent qualities of capitalism—contribute to middle-class delinquency. Because capitalism is such a dehumanizing system, it is not surprising that even middle-class youths turn to drugs, gambling, and illicit sex to find escape and excitement.

Controlling Delinquents   Conflict theorists suggest that rather than inhibiting delinquent behavior the juvenile justice system actually may help to create and sustain such behavior. They claim that the capitalist state fails to control delinquents because it is actually in the state's own best interest to maintain a large number of outcast deviant youths. These youths can then be employed as low-paid marginal workers, willing to work for minimum wage in jobs no one else wants. Thus, labeling by the juvenile justice system fits within the capitalist managers' need to maintain an underclass of cheap labor to be employed in its factories and fast-food restaurants.

Emerging Concepts of Conflict Theory

Conflict theory does indeed question the many instances of misguided "official wisdom" that pervade our society, but despite its lofty goals and ideals critics question its lack of empirical verification.[83] Most research has been by necessity historical and theoretical. Most conflict scholarship and theories lack the specific propositions sociologists require to test theories properly.[84]

Criticism of conflict theory has also been directed at its utopianism. To blame the state for all evil seems to ignore the great variety of human differences. Conflict theory also overlooks the fact that a great deal of delinquent behavior is committed by lower-class youths who target their indigent peers. Members of the lower class fear violent local gangs more than they do capitalist profiteers.

As it evolved, conflict theory has been subdivided, branching off in new directions. One important area is **feminist theory,** which examines the relationship between sex roles, the economic system, and delinquency. These views will be discussed in more detail in Chapter 7. Two other important views, left realism and peacemaking, are discussed in some detail next.

feminist theory
Asserts that the patriarchal social system oppresses women, creating gender bias and encouraging violence against women.

Left Realism   Some radical scholars are now addressing the need for the left to respond to the increasing power of right-wing conservatives. They are troubled by the emergence of a strict "law and order" philosophy, which encompasses a policy of waiving juveniles to adult court where they may be punished severely. At the same time, they find the focus of most left-wing scholarship—the abuse of power by the ruling elite—too narrow. It is wrong, they argue, to ignore the problem of inner-city gang crime and violence, which all too often targets indigent people.[85] Those who share these concerns are referred to as "left realists."[86]

Left realism is most often connected to the writings of British scholars John Lea and Jock Young. In their well-respected 1984 work, *What Is to Be Done about Law and Order?,* they reject the utopian views of "idealistic" Marxists who portray street criminals as revolutionaries.[87] They take the "realistic" approach that street criminals prey on the poor and the disenfranchised, thus making them doubly abused, first by the capitalist system and then by members of their own class.

left realism
Asserts that crime is a function of relative deprivation and that criminals prey on the poor.

Lea and Young's view of crime causation borrows from conventional sociological theory and closely resembles the relative deprivation approach discussed in Chapter 4. As they put it, "The equation is simple: relative deprivation equals discontent; discontent plus lack of political solution equals crime."[88]

Left realists argue that crime victims in all classes need and deserve protection; crime control should reflect community needs. They do not view police and the courts as inherently evil tools of capitalism whose tough tactics alienate the lower classes. These institutions would in fact offer life-saving public services if their use of force could be reduced and their sensitivity to the public increased.[89] Another approach is preemptive deterrence, in which community organization efforts eliminate or reduce crime before it becomes necessary to employ police force. If the number of marginalized youths (that is, youths who feel they are not part of society and have nothing to lose by committing crime) could be reduced, delinquency rates would decline.[90]

To left realists, street crime is real; the fear of violence among the lower classes has allowed the right wing to seize "law and order" as a political issue.[91] Gangs are not made up of Robin Hoods—revolutionaries who steal from the rich—most gang members prey on others of their own race and class and are happy to keep the proceeds for themselves. Gang members may be the ultimate capitalists, hustling their way to obtain the coveted symbols of success.[92]

Although implementation of a socialist economy would help eliminate the crime problem, left realists recognize that something must be done in the meantime to control crime under the existing capitalist system. To create crime control policy, left realists welcome not only radical ideas but build on the work of strain theorists, social ecologists, and other mainstream views. Community-based efforts seem to hold the most promise as crime control techniques.

Left realism has been critiqued by radical thinkers as legitimizing the existing power structure: by supporting conventional definitions of law and justice, it suggests that the deviant, and not the capitalist system, is the root cause of society's problems. Is it not advocating the very institutions that "currently imprison us and our patterns of thought and action"?[93] In rebuttal, a left realist would charge that it is unrealistic to speak of a socialist state lacking a police force or system of laws and justice; the criminal code does in fact represent public opinion.

peacemakers
Assert that peace and humanism can reduce crime and offers a new approach to crime control through mediation.

Peacemaking   **Peacemakers** hope to promote a peaceful and just society. They draw their inspiration from a variety of religious and philosophical teachings ranging from Quakerism to Zen. According to peacemakers, human suffering has risen out of the disunity and separation that characterizes postmodern society and can be ended only with the "return of all sentient beings to a condition of wholeness."[94]

Like labeling theorists, peacemakers view the efforts of the state to punish and control delinquent youths as crime-encouraging rather than crime-discouraging. If our social, economic, and political system could be transformed into an engine that eliminates suffering and promotes peace and justice, crime rates would ultimately decline.

When these views were first articulated more than fifteen years ago in a series of books written by Larry Tifft and Dennis Sullivan, they received little attention.[95]

Peacemakers hope to promote a peaceful and just society. They draw their inspiration from a variety of religious and philosophical teachings. They believe that social, economic, and political systems can be transformed in order to eliminate suffering and promote peace and justice. One technique for addressing problems is mediating conflict between people before it escalates out of control. This group of seventh and eighth graders are trying to "unknot" themselves without letting go of one another's hands in an activity to promote working together to solve problems.

In his book, *The Mask of Love,* Sullivan recognized the futility of correcting and punishing criminals in the context of our conflict-ridden society:

> The reality we must grasp is that we live in a culture of severed relationships, where every available institution provides a form of banishment but no place or means for people to become connected, to be responsible to and for each other.[96]

This theme of mutual aid rather than coercive punishment as the key to a harmonious society has been adopted by advocates of the peacemaking movement, who are now trying to find humanist solutions to delinquency drug abuse and other social problems.[97] Rather than punishment and prison, they advocate policies such as mediation and conflict resolution. Peacemakers embrace having young offenders meet with their victims to understand their problems and perhaps to repay them for their loss and suffering. Rather than harsh treatment and punishment, peacemakers advocate reconciliation and restitution.[98]

Social Reaction Theories and Delinquency Prevention

Labeling and social conflict theories have had an important influence on delinquency prevention policy during the past two decades. These theoretical models have drawn attention to the biases in the juvenile justice system and how interacting with the system can actually produce rather than eliminate delinquent behavior.

The system of juvenile justice began to acknowledge the problems of labeling and stigmatization in 1967, when the President's Commission on Law Enforcement and the Administration of Justice first identified the consequences of negative labeling. In its report on juvenile delinquency, the commission stated:

> The affixing of that label (delinquency) can be a momentous occurrence in a youngster's life. Thereafter he may be watched; he may be suspect; his every misstep may be evidence of his delinquent nature. He may be excluded more and more from legitimate activities and opportunities. Soon he may be designed and dealt with as a delinquent and will find it very difficult to move into a law-abiding path even if he can overcome his own belligerent reaction and self-image and seeks to do so.[99]

These sentiments helped set the course for juvenile justice policy. National programs were created to insulate youths from the labeling processes of the juvenile justice system. Edwin Schur, in his widely read book *Radical Nonintervention,* captured the essence of the social reaction and social conflict approach to delinquency by suggesting that even efforts to treat and rehabilitate delinquents are essentially harmful because they stigmatized youth:

> A great deal of the labeling of delinquents is socially unnecessary and counterproductive. Policies should be adopted, therefore, that accept a greater diversity in youth behavior; special delinquency laws should be exceedingly narrow in scope or else abolished completely, along with preventive efforts that single out specific individuals and programs that employ "compulsory treatment."[100]

Schur argued that the treatment orientation of the juvenile court, directed at dealing with the problems of the "whole" person, merely identified these adolescents as troubled youths who needed state aid.

As the dangers of stigma and labeling became known, a massive effort was made on the local, state, and federal levels to limit the interface of youths with the juvenile justice system. One approach was to divert youths from official processing channels at the time of their initial contact with police authorities. The usual practice is to have police refer children to community treatment facilities and clinics rather than to the juvenile court.

In a similar vein, children who were petitioned to juvenile court might be eligible for an additional round of court-based diversion programs. For example, restitution allows children to pay back the victims of their crimes for the damage (or inconvenience) they have caused instead of receiving an official delinquency label.

If a youth was found delinquent, efforts were made to reduce stigma by using alternative sanction programs such as boot camp or intensive probation monitoring. Alternative community-based sanctions substituted for the more heavily intrusive state training schools, a policy known as **deinstitutionalization.** Whenever possible, anything producing stigma was to be avoided, a philosophy of justice referred to as nonintervention.

deinstitutionalization
Removing juveniles from adult jails and placing them in community-based programs to avoid the stigma attached to these facilities.

The federal government was a prime mover in the effort to divert children from the justice system. The Office of Juvenile Justice and Delinquency Prevention sponsored numerous diversion and restitution programs around the nation. In addition, it made one of its most important priorities the removal of juveniles from adult jails and the discontinuance of housing status offenders and juvenile delinquents together. These programs were designed to limit, whenever possible, the juvenile's interaction with the formal justice system, to reduce stigma, and to make use of informal, nonpunitive treatment modalities.[101] Diversion and deinstitutionalization are covered in more detail in Chapter 14.

Although diversion and restitution continue to be used widely, the impetus for the movement seems to have waned. The philosophy of nonintervention has been criticized on several levels. First, it institutionalized a practice that had been carried out informally for years. Police officers and probation officers commonly released children they felt were deserving of a second chance, and only a small percentage of all offenders were continued through the juvenile justice process.[102] Second, many diversion program clients were young, first offenders who had been routinely released informally by the police; hard core delinquents were not eligible for diversion programs. Consequently, the nonintervention movement actually created a whole new class of juvenile offenders who heretofore might have avoided prolonged contact with juvenile justice agencies; critics referred to this as *widening the net*.[103] Finally, evaluation of existing programs did not indicate that they could reduce the recidivism rate of clients.[104] As a result of these "failures," policy initiatives have now shifted toward greater intervention and more restrictive juvenile justice sanctions. However, many of the nonintervention programs begun in the 1970s still operate today.

In the 1990s the peacemaking movement has had a significant impact on justice policy. The writings of peacemakers emphasize mutual aid rather than coercive punishment as the key to a harmonious society. They try to find humanistic solutions to crime and other social problems.[105] Their influence has been realized in the restorative justice movement, which is discussed in the next section.

Restorative Justice

A young man sits, in a circle of chairs surrounded by community members, elders, the young man's sister, a judge and a probation officer. The Keeper, a respected community member skilled in peacemaking and consensus-building, opens the session with a prayer and a reminder that the circle has been convened to address the behavior of this young man, who killed his sister's cat in a drunken outburst. An eagle feather is passed around the circle. As the feather is passed, each member of the circle expresses his or her feelings about the crime and raises questions or concerns. The young man expresses regret about his actions and a desire to change his harmful behavior. His sister talks about her anger and sadness, while acknowledging her love for her brother. An elder mentions that the youngster owes something to the animal kingdom and suggests building a bird feeder and feeding the birds. Another community member comments on the inability of the boy to cry and suggests grief and anger counseling. Attendance at Alcoholics Anonymous and community service also are suggested. One community member volunteers to help the young man with the bird feeder and several others offer to accompany him on his first visit to the counselor when he acknowledges that it may be difficult for him to go alone.[106]

restorative justice
Nonpunitive strategies for dealing with juvenile offenders that make the justice system a healing process rather than a punishment process.

If conflict is the source of delinquency, conflict resolution or reduction may be the key to its demise. This is the aim of **restorative justice,** an approach that relies on nonpunitive strategies for delinquency prevention and control.[107] Restoration involves turning the justice system into a "healing" process rather than a distributor of retribution and revenge. Most people involved in offender–victim relationships actually know one another or are related in some way. Restorative justice attempts to address the issues that produced conflict between these people rather than to treat one as a victim deserving sympathy and the other as a delinquent deserving punishment. Rather than take sides and choose whom to isolate and punish, society should try to reconcile the parties involved in conflict.[108]

Restorative justice is based on a social rather than a legal view of delinquency. The restoration of social relationships damaged by delinquent acts can only be healed in smaller, less formal and more cohesive social groups, such as families, congregations, and residential communities.[109] Restorative justice stands in opposition to views of juvenile justice that purposely limit consideration of the unique personal and social qualities of particular offenders. As a result of its preoccupation with the protection of society, the juvenile justice system has become more conservative and relies increasingly on punishment strategies (for example, incarceration) to control law violating. The present system of justice encourages youths to deny, justify, or excuse their actions, thereby precluding the acceptance of responsibility.

Restorative programs for juveniles typically involve diversion from the formal court process and the use of programs that encourage meeting and reconciliation between offenders and victims. Programs include victim advocacy, mediation programs, and sentencing circles, in which crime victims and their families are brought together with offenders to formulate a peaceful and equitable solution to their problems. Many of these programs originate in the practices of Native American and Native Canadian people who have traditionally used restoration techniques in their justice systems. Here, Simon Roberts is shown leaving Pine Lodge Pre-Release Facility in Medical Lake, Washington, after serving time for a 1993 assault on a pizza deliveryman when he was 16 years old. He was banished to an Alaskan island, then sent to prison.

In addition, the central role of trained professionals (prosecution and defense attorneys) in the juvenile justice process severely limits the possibility of direct exchanges between the victim and the offender. Because the adversaries are narrowly defined as the "accused" and the "State," little or no consideration can be given to community concerns and participation. These limitations impede the effectiveness of traditional programs designed to reduce delinquent activities.

Restorative justice depends on returning law-violating youths to the community where they can resume a productive role. The effectiveness of this approach ultimately depends on the stake a person has in the community or in a particular social group. If an adolescent does not value his or her membership in the group, the youth will be unlikely to accept responsibility, show remorse, or repair the injuries caused by his or her actions. Even the most effective restorative justice programs will be unable to reach those persons who are disengaged from all community institutions. Therefore, community involvement is an essential ingredient of the restorative justice approach. The principles that define restorative justice are outlined in Table 6.1.

Table 6.1
PRINCIPLES OF RESTORATIVE JUSTICE

Crime and delinquency are fundamentally a violation of people and interpersonal relationships.	Victims and the community have been harmed and are in need of restoration. Victims include the target of the offense but also include family members, witnesses, and the community at large.
	Victims, offenders, and the affected communities are the key stakeholders in justice. The state must investigate crime and ensure safety, but it is not the center of the justice process. Victims are the key, and they must help in the search for restoration, healing, responsibility, and prevention.
Violations create obligations and liabilities.	Offenders have the obligation to make things right as much as possible. They must understand the harm they have caused. Their participation should be as voluntary as possible; coercion is to be minimized.
	The community's obligations are to both victims and offenders as well as the general welfare of its members. This includes the obligation to reintegrate the offender in the community and to ensure the offender the opportunity to make amends.
Restorative justice seeks to heal and put right the wrongs.	Victims needs are the focal concern of the justice process. Safety is a top priority, and victims should be empowered to participate in determining their needs and case outcomes.
	The exchange of information between victim and offender should be encouraged; when possible, face-to-face meetings might be undertaken. There should be mutual agreement over imposed outcomes.
	Offenders' needs and competencies need to be addressed. Healing and reintegration are emphasized; isolation and removal from the community are restricted.
	The justice process belongs to the community; members are encouraged to "do justice." The justice process should be sensitive to community needs and geared at preventing similar harm in the future. Early interventions are encouraged.
	Justice is mindful of the outcomes, intended and unintended, of its responses to crime and victimization. It should monitor case outcome and provide necessary support and opportunity to all involved. The least restrictive intervention should be used, and overt social control should be avoided.

Source: Howard Zehr and Harry Mika, "Fundamental Concepts of Restorative Justice," *Contemporary Justice Review* 1:47–55 (1998).

RESTORATIVE JUSTICE IN PRACTICE

Juvenile justice systems are now beginning to embrace restorative justice models. Maryland has revised its juvenile justice act to integrate principles of restorative justice in the administration of justice. Delinquents are now subject to sanctions geared toward community protection and public safety, accountability on the part of the offender, and efforts to promote character development and competency. Programs now in operation include these:

Operation Spotlight: Asks juvenile justice professionals to join communities and local law enforcement agencies to target serious and violent juvenile offenders who are at risk for delinquent behavior. Information and monitoring, support services, and family intervention are shared among the participants. This program targets youths with intensive supervision, family intervention, and recidivism prevention programming.

Earn It: Creates partnerships with area institutions such as businesses and churches to provide youths with job training and employment. The program ensures that youths are held accountable to their victims by garnishing their wages to make restitution payments. This program also provides juvenile justice youths with mentors in the business community.

Justice in Cluster Education (JUICE): Deters youths on juvenile probation from further disruptive behavior and prevents at-risk youths from entering the juvenile justice system by placing probation specialists directly in local schools where they can provide enhanced probation supervision and monitor attendance, office referrals, and suspensions.

Youth mentorship programs: Recruits college students and community members as paid interns to assist with supervising juveniles on probation. The students act as role models, tutors, and mentors. This program also helps attract students to juvenile justice careers and provides community members with the opportunity to take an active role in local delinquency prevention efforts.

Day treatment programs: Community-based alternatives to residential placements. They provide education, counseling, life skills training, drug screening, and education. They offer extensive and comprehensive supervision and aftercare.

Impact programs: High-intensity, short-term residential placements that provide services in victim awareness and anger management for youths with an immediate need for control. With average lengths of stay ranging from thirty to ninety days, youths released from these programs are given specialized, extended aftercare placements.

The restorative justice movement has a number of different sources. Negotiation, mediation, consensus-building, and peacemaking have been part of the dispute resolution process in European and Asian communities for centuries.[110] Native American and Native Canadian people have long used participation of community members in the adjudication process (for example, sentencing circles, sentencing panels, and elders' panels).[111] Members of the U.S. peacemaking movement have also championed the use of nonpunitive alternatives to justice. Gordon Bazemore and other policy experts helped formulate a version of restorative justice known as "the balanced approach" to juvenile justice, which emphasizes that victims, offenders, and the community itself should all benefit from interactions with the juvenile justice system.[112] The balanced approach attempts to link community protection, competency building, and victims' rights. Offenders must take responsibility for their actions, a process that can both increase self-esteem and decrease recidivism.[113] In contrast, an overreliance on punishment can be counterproductive. Bazemore warns:

Youth leadership challenge programs: Combines military-style training with a leadership curriculum and more traditional juvenile rehabilitation programs. They challenge youths to become responsible members of society. Strict regimentation promotes self-discipline, self-esteem, and self-worth.

Perseverance, Responsibility, Integrity, Discipline, and Esteem (PRIDE): These sixteen-week programs also rely on extended aftercare to reinforce discipline and core values.

Electronic monitoring: Used as an alternative to detention for youths awaiting juvenile court hearings, Maryland is also using this technology to enhance supervision of youths in programs such as probation, aftercare, and day treatment.

Project Attend: Creates partnerships with local school systems and law enforcement agencies in school clusters where chronic truancy is a serious problem. This program improves the attendance and academic achievement of identified chronic truants by including families and matching them with appropriate service providers.

After School Education Training (ASET): Provides at-risk youths and their families with educational support and family counseling through local schools and health departments. Transportation and meals are provided for trips arranged for the youths and their families.

Reflections: A week-long outdoor learning experience in western Maryland's mountains where youths on probation or at risk of delinquency participate in confidence-building physical activities, nature and wildlife presentations, counseling, and substance abuse education.

Success Through Accelerated-Education and Responsibility (STAR): Diverts youths from the juvenile justice system and exposes them to more productive activities. Operated in partnership with a Baltimore nonprofit group called Professional Black Men, this program includes group sessions for youths and parents, mentoring services, field trips, exposure to the business community, individual counseling, and graduation incentives.

How can restorative justice programs be "sold" to a public that seems to be becoming more conservative and punitive toward crime? How could taxpayers be convinced to embrace programs geared to violent offenders that stress restoration over punishment? What do you think about these issues?

Source: Adapted from Stuart O. Simms, "Restorative Juvenile Justice: Maryland's Legislature Reaffirms Commitment to Juvenile Justice Reform," *Corrections Today* 59:94–98 (1997).

Punishment, by stigmatizing, humiliating, and isolating the offender, may have a counter-deterrent effect by minimizing prospects that the offender may gain or regain both self-respect and the respect of the community.[114]

To counteract the negative effects of punishment, restorative justice programs for juveniles typically involve diversion from the formal court process, programs that encourage meeting and reconciliation between offenders and victims, victim advocacy, mediation programs, and sentencing circles, in which crime victims and their families are brought together with offenders and their families in an effort to formulate a sanction that addresses the needs of each party. Some of the restorative justice programs used in Maryland are discussed in the Policy and Practice box entitled "Restorative Justice in Practice." Further discussion of restorative justice programs can be found in Chapters 12 through 17.

SUMMARY

Social reaction theories view delinquent behavior as a function of the influence powerful members of society have over less fortunate youths (see Table 6.2). Two main branches of the theory are currently popular. Labeling theory views deviant behavior as a product of the deviant labels society imposes on its least powerful citizens. Deviant labels mark people as social outcasts and create barriers between them and the general social order. Eventually, deviant labels transform the offenders' personalities, and they come to accept their new "criminal" or "delinquent" identities as self-definitions.

Labeling theorists suggest that delinquent labels lock individuals out of the mainstream of society, thereby assuring that they will turn to additional illegal behavior for survival. Who is to be labeled and the type of labeling depends on a youth's position in the social structure. The poor and powerless are much more likely to be labeled than the wealthy and powerful.

Edwin Lemert has distinguished between primary and secondary deviants. Primary deviants are people who cling to a conventional self-image; secondary deviants are people who have accepted the traits implied by deviant labels bestowed on them. Howard Becker has analyzed the dif-

ferent forms labeling takes with respect to the individual audience's reactions to labeling.

Relatively few studies have empirically validated the labeling perspective. Research efforts aimed at the influence of juvenile justice processing on delinquent youths fail to find that labels produce their expected damaging results. Despite the lack of empirical verification, there has been a renewal of interest in labeling theory because it helps explain the behavior of chronic offenders.

Social conflict theory holds that the class conflicts present in modern society produce crime and delinquency. The law and legal systems are controlled by those in power, whose aim is to maintain their hold over society. Consequently, their activities are immune, whereas the deviant behaviors of the lower classes are severely punished. Delinquency occurs when lower-class youngsters rebel against the constraints placed on them by those in power. The role and economic position youths have in our modern, postindustrial capitalist society influences their delinquent behavior choices.

Labeling and social control theories have had an important effect on delinquency prevention policy. Efforts have been made to eliminate, whenever possible, the

Table 6.2

SOCIAL REACTION THEORIES

Theory	Major Premise	Strengths
Labeling	Youths are locked into a delinquent career when their behavior is labeled by agents of the justice system and they reorganize their identities around a deviant role.	Explains delinquent careers and the role of social control agents in sustaining deviance.
Conflict	Crime is a function of class conflict. The definition of the law is controlled by people who hold social and political power.	Accounts for class differences in the delinquency rate. Shows how class conflict influences behavior.
Radical Feminism	The capitalist system creates patriarchy, which oppresses women.	Explains gender bias, violence against women, and repression.
Left Realism	Crime is a function of relative deprivation; criminals prey on the poor.	Represents a compromise between conflict and traditional criminology.
Peacemaking/ Restorative Justice	Peace and humanism can reduce crime; conflict resolution strategies can work.	Offers a new approach to crime control through mediation.

stigma of the juvenile justice system. This has meant diverting offenders before trial, limiting detention, and de-institutionalization. Peacemakers advocate mediation and restitution rather than punishment for delinquent acts. This has given rise to the restorative justice movement, which emphasizes nonpunitive alternatives to traditional juvenile justice sanctions.

KEY TERMS

labeling theory
moral entrepreneurs
self-fulfilling prophecy
primary deviance
secondary deviance

reflective role-taking
degradation ceremony
social conflict theory
critical criminologists
feminist theory

left realism
peacemakers
deinstitutionalization
restorative justice

INFOTRAC COLLEGE EDITION EXERCISES

Peacemaking criminologists' views of punishment tend toward reconciliation and "mutual aid." Treatment approaches advocated by this point of view range from mediation to conflict resolution. However, with much of the violent juvenile crime seen on nightly broadcasts, the public view of dealing with juveniles might be characterized as punitive.

Explore the concept of restorative justice by reviewing articles from InfoTrac College Edition. What implications, if any, does this form of justice have on juvenile offenders? How can we reconcile the belief in "making peace" with the facts of schoolyard shootings and predatory juvenile offenders?

QUESTIONS FOR DISCUSSION

1. What are some common labels used in the school setting? How can these hurt youths?
2. Can labels be beneficial to a person? What are some positive effects of labeling?
3. Is it possible to overcome labels? What methods could a person employ to counteract labels?
4. Are there laws that seem to be designed to protect the rich? Is it possible that laws are actually applied fairly?
5. Are there factors in our economy that make Marx's predictions about capitalism obsolete?
6. What steps should the justice system take to restore outcast youths to society? Should the victims' wishes and feelings be taken into consideration?

NOTES

1. Based on James Brooke, Pam Belluck, and John Kifner, and written by James Brooke, "Man Hospitalized in 1996 for Writing Ominous Letters," *New York Times* 26 July 1998, p. 1.
2. Associated Press, "Judge Approves Family Visit for Suspect," *USA Today* 7 August 1998, p.1.
3. Ibid., p. 2.
4. Brooke, Belluck, and Kifner, "Man Hospitalized in 1996 for Writing Ominous Letters," p. 1.
5. Charles Silberman, *Crises in the Classroom: The Remaking of American Education* (New York: Random House, 1971); idem, "Murder in the Classroom: How the Public Schools Kill Dreams and Mutilate Minds," *Atlantic* 255:82–94 (1970).
6. Richard Quinney, *The Social Reality of Crime* (Boston: Little, Brown, 1970); William Chambliss and Robert Seidman, *Law, Order, and Power* (Reading, Mass.: Addison-Wesley, 1971).
7. These sentiments are contained in some pioneering studies of police discretion, such as Nathan Goldman, *The Differential Selection of Juvenile Offenders for Court Appearance* (New York: National Council on Crime and Delinquency, 1963).
8. For a review of this position, see Anne R. Mahoney, "The Effect of Labeling upon Youths in the Juvenile Justice System: A Review of the Evidence," *Law and Society Review* 8:583–614 (1974); see also, David Matza, *Becoming Deviant* (Englewood Cliffs, N.J.: Prentice-Hall, 1974).
9. The self-labeling concept originated in Edwin Lemert, *Social Pathology* (New York: McGraw-Hill, 1951); see also, Frank Tannenbaum, *Crime and the Community* (Boston: Ginn, 1936).
10. Kai Erikson, "Notes on the Sociology of Deviance," *Social Problems* 10:307–14 (1962).
11. Edwin Schur, *Labeling Deviant Behavior* (New York: Harper & Row, 1972), p. 21.
12. Howard Becker, *Outsiders: Studies in the Sociology of Deviance* (New York: Macmillan, 1963), p. 9.

13. Nalini Ambady and Robert Rosenthal, "Half a Minute: Predicting Teacher Evaluations from Thin Slices of Nonverbal Behavior and Physical Attractiveness," *Journal of Personality and Social Psychology* 64:431–41 (1993).

14. Monica Harris, Richard Milich, Elizabeth Corbitt, Daniel Hoover, and Marianne Brady, "Self-Fulfilling Effects of Stigmatizing Information on Children's Social Interactions," *Journal of Personality and Social Psychology* 33:41–50 (1992).

15. Harold Garfinkle, "Conditions of Successful Degradation Ceremonies," *American Journal of Sociology* 61:420–24 (1956).

16. M. A. Bortner, *Inside a Juvenile Court: The Tarnished Ideal of Individualized Justice* (New York: University Press, 1982).

17. Edwin Lemert, *Human Deviance, Social Problems, and Social Control* (Englewood Cliffs, N.J.: Prentice-Hall, 1967), p. 15.

18. Charles H. Cooley, *Human Nature and the Social Order* (New York: Scribner, 1902).

19. Ross Matsueda, "Reflected Appraisals, Parental Labeling, and Delinquency: Specifying a Symbolic Interactionist Theory," *American Journal of Sociology* 97:1577–1611 (1992).

20. Howard Kaplan and Hiroshi Fukurai, "Negative Social Sanctions, Self-Rejection, and Drug Use," *Youth and Society* 23:275–98 (1992).

21. Howard Kaplan, *Toward a General Theory of Deviance: Contributions from Perspectives on Deviance and Criminality* (College Station, Tex.: Texas A & M University, n.d.).

22. Harris et al., "Self-Fulfilling Effects of Stigmatizing Information on Children's Social Interactions," pp. 48–50.

23. Kaplan, *Toward a General Theory of Deviance*.

24. Howard Kaplan, Robert Johnson, and Carol Bailey, "Deviant Peers and Deviant Behavior: Further Elaboration of a Model," *Social Psychology Quarterly* 30:277–84 (1987).

25. Lemert, *Social Pathology*.

26. Ibid., p. 73

27. Ibid., p. 75.

28. Ibid.

29. Karen Heimer and Ross Matsueda, "Role-Taking, Role-Commitment and Delinquency: A Theory of Differential Social Control," *American Sociological Review* 59:400–37 (1994).

30. Karen Heimer, "Gender, Race, and the Pathways to Delinquency: An Interactionist Explanation," in John Hagan and Ruth Peterson, eds., *Crime and Inequality* (Stanford, Calif.: Stanford University Press, 1995).

31. Tannenbaum, *Crime and the Community*.

32. Ibid., p. 27.

33. Aaron Cicourel, *The Social Organization of Juvenile Justice* (New York: Wiley, 1968).

34. Matza, *Becoming Deviant*.

35. Ibid., p. 78.

36. Stanton Wheeler and Leonard Cottrell, "Juvenile Delinquency: Its Prevention and Control," in Donald Cressey and David Ward, eds., *Delinquency, Crime, and Social Processes* (New York: Harper & Row, 1969), p. 609.

37. Garfinkel, "Conditions of Successful Degradation Ceremonies," p. 424.

38. Ross Matsueda, "Reflected Appraisals, Parental Labeling, and Delinquency: Specifying a Symbolic Interactionist Theory," *American Journal of Sociology* 97:1577–1611 (1992).

39. See, generally, Carl Pope and William Feyerherm, "Minority Status and Juvenile Justice Processing," *Criminal Justice Abstracts* 22:327–36 (1990); Carl Pope, "Race and Crime Revisited," *Crime and Delinquency* 25:347–57 (1979).

40. Nathan Goldman, *The Differential Selection of Juvenile Offenders for Court Appearance* (New York: National Council on Crime and Delinquency, 1963).

41. Carl Pope, "Juvenile Crime and Justice," in Brian Forst, ed., *The Socioeconomics of Crime and Justice* (New York: M. E. Sharpe, in press).

42. See, for example, William Wilbanks, *The Myth of a Racist Criminal Justice System* (Pacific Grove, Calif.; Brooks/Cole, 1987).

43. Merry Morash, "Establishment of a Juvenile Police Record," *Criminology* 22:97–111 (1984).

44. Paul Lipsett, "The Juvenile Offender's Perception," *Crime and Delinquency* 14:49 (1968).

45. Richard Anson and Carol Eason, "The Effects of Confinement on Delinquent Self-Image," *Juvenile and Family Court Journal* 37:39–47 (1986); Gerald O'Connor, "The Effect of Detention upon Male Delinquency," *Social Problems* 18:194–97 (1970); David Street, Robert Vintner, and Charles Perrow, *Organization for Treatment* (New York: Free Press, 1966); Jack Foster, Simon Dinitz, and Walter Reckless, "Perception of Stigma Following Public Intervention for Delinquent Behavior," *Social Problems* 20:202 (1972); Gary Jensen, "Labeling and Identity," *Criminology* 18:121–29 (1980); Eloise Snyder, "The Impact of the Juvenile Court Hearing on the Child," *Crime and Delinquency* 17:180–82 (1971).

46. Howard Kaplan and Robert Johnson, "Negative Social Sanctions and Juvenile Delinquency: Effects of Labeling in a Model of Deviant Behavior," *Social Science Quarterly* 72:98–122 (1991); Suzanne Ageton and Delbert Elliott, *The Effect of Legal Processing on Self-Concept* (Boulder, Colo.: Institute of Behavioral Science, 1973).

47. Christine Bowditch, "Getting Rid of Troublemakers: High School Disciplinary Procedures and the Production of Dropouts," *Social Problems* 40:493–507 (1993).

48. Melvin Ray and William Downs, "An Empirical Test of Labeling Theory Using Longitudinal Data," 23:169–94 (1986).

49. Ruth Triplett, "The Conflict Perspective, Symbolic Interactionism, and the Status Characteristics Hypothesis," *Justice Quarterly* 10:540–58 (1993).

50. Ross Matsueda, "Reflected Appraisals, Parental Labeling, and Delinquency: Specifying a Symbolic Interactionist Theory," *American Journal of Sociology* 97:1577–1611 (1992).

51. De Li, "Legal Sanctions and Youth Status Achievement: A Longitudinal Study," Center for Justice Research and Development, Lamar University, Beaumont, Tex., April 1998; Charles Tittle, "Two Empirical Regularities (Maybe) in Search of an Explanation: Commentary on the Age/Crime Debate," *Criminology* 26:75–85 (1988).

52. Robert Sampson and John Laub, "A Life-Course Theory of Cumulative Disadvantage and the Stability of Delinquency," in Terence Thornberry, ed., *Developmental Theories of Crime and Delinquency* (New Brunswick, N.J., 1997), pp. 133–61.

53. Douglas Smith and Robert Brame, "On the Initiation and Continuation of Delinquency," *Criminology* 4:607–30 (1994).

54. Schur, *Labeling Delinquent Behavior*, p. 14.

55. Ronald Akers, "Problems in the Sociology of Deviance," *Social Forces* 46:463 (1968).

56. Peter Manning, "On Deviance," *Contemporary Sociology* 2:697–99 (1973).

57. Charles Tittle and Debra Curran, "Contingencies for Dispositional Disparities in Juvenile Justice," *Social Forces* 67:23–58 (1988).

58. Charles Wellford, "Labeling Theory and Criminology: An Assessment," *Social Problems* 22:335–47 (1975), at 337.

59. David Bordua, "On Deviance," *Annals* 312:121–23 (1969).

60. Wellford, "Labeling Theory and Criminology."

61. Ibid.

62. Charles Murray and Lewis Cox, *Beyond Probation* (Beverly Hills, Calif.: Sage, 1979).

63. Raymond Paternoster and Leeann Iovanni, "The Labeling Perspective and Delinquency: An Elaboration of the Theory and an Assessment of the Evidence," *Justice Quarterly* 6:358–94 (1989).

64. Gresham Sykes, "The Rise of Critical Criminology," *Journal of Criminal Law and Criminology* 65:211–17 (1974).

65. See, for example, Dennis Sullivan, Larry Tifft, and Larry Siegel, "Criminology, Science and Politics," in Emilio Viano, ed., *Criminal Justice Research* (Lexington, Mass.: Lexington Books, 1978).

66. Ibid., p. 10.

67. Robert Meier, "The New Criminology: Continuity in Criminology Theory," *Journal of Criminal Law and Criminology* 67:461–69 (1997), at 463.

68. Walter DeKeseredy and Martin Schwartz, *Contemporary Criminology* (Belmont, Calif.: Wadsworth, 1996), p. 77.
69. Michael Lynch and W. Byron Groves, *A Primer in Radical Criminology*, 2nd ed. (Albany, N.Y.: Harrow and Heston, 1989), pp. 32–33.
70. Meier, "The New Criminology," p. 463.
71. Sykes, "The Rise of Critical Criminology," pp. 211–13.
72. Ibid.
73. Ibid.
74. Sullivan, Tifft, and Siegel, "Criminology, Science, and Politics," p. 11.
75. See, for example, Kathleen Daly and Meda Chesney-Lind, "Feminism and Criminology," *Justice Quarterly* 5:497–538 (1988); see also, K. Daly, *Gender, Crime and Punishment* (New Haven, Ct.: Yale University Press, 1994).
76. Ibid.
77. Robert Gordon, "Capitalism, Class, and Crime in America," *Crime and Delinquency* 19:174 (1973).
78. Richard Quinney, *Class, State, and Crime* (New York: Longman, 1977), p. 52.
79. Anthony Platt, "The Triumph of Benevolence: The Origins of the Juvenile Justice System in the United States," in Richard Quinney, ed., *Criminal Justice in America: A Critical Understanding* (Boston: Little, Brown, 1974), p. 367; see also, Anthony Platt, *The Child Savers* (Chicago: University of Chicago Press, 1969).
80. Barry Krisberg and James Austin, *Children of Ishmael* (Palo Alto, Calif.: Mayfield, 1978), p. 2.
81. Herman Schwendinger and Julia Schwendinger, "Delinquency and Social Reform: A Radical Perspective," in Lamar Empey, ed., *Juvenile Justice,* (Charlottesville: University of Virginia Press, 1979) p. 250.
82. Ibid., p. 252.
83. Carl Klockars, "The Contemporary Crises of Marxist Criminology," in James Inciardi, ed., *Radical Criminology: The Coming Crisis* (Beverly Hills, Calif.: Sage, 1980), pp. 92–123.
84. Allan Horowitz, "Marxist Theory of Deviance and Teleology: A Critique of Spitzer," *Social Problems* 24:362 (1977).
85. Anthony Platt, "Criminology in the 1980s: Progressive Alternatives to 'Law and Order,'" *Crime and Social Justice* 21–22: 191–99 (1985).
86. See, generally, Roger Matthews and Jock Young, eds., *Confronting Crime* (London: Sage, 1986); for a thorough review of left realism, see Martin Schwartz and Walter DeKeseredy, "Left Realist Criminology: Strengths, Weaknesses and the Feminist Critique," *Crime, Law and Social Change* 15:51–72 (1991).
87. John Lea and Jock Young, *What Is to Be Done about Law and Order?* (Harmondsworth, England: Penguin, 1984).
88. Ibid., p. 88.
89. Richard Kinsey, John Lea, and Jock Young, *Losing the Fight against Crime* (London: Blackwell, 1986).
90. DeKeseredy and Schwartz, *Contemporary Criminology*, p. 249.
91. Martin Schwartz and Walter DeKeseredy, "Left Realist Criminology: Strengths, Weaknesses and the Feminist Critique," *Crime, Law and Social Change* 15:51–72 (1991).
92. Ibid., p. 54.
93. Schwartz and DeKeseredy, "Left Realist Criminology," p. 58.
94. Richard Quinney, "The Way of Peace: On Crime, Suffering and Service," in Harold Pepinsky and Richard Quinney, eds., *Criminology as Peacemaking* (Bloomington: Indiana University Press, 1991), pp. 8–9.
95. See, for example, Larry Tifft and Dennis Sullivan, *The Struggle to Be Human: Crime, Criminology, and Anarchism* (Orkney Islands, Over-the-Water-Sanday: Clienfuegos Press, 1979); and Dennis Sullivan, *The Mask of Love* (Port Washington, N.Y.: Kennikat Press, 1980).
96. Sullivan, *The Mask of Love,* p. 141.
97. Harold Pepinsky and Richard Quinney, eds., *Criminology as Peacemaking* (Bloomington, Indiana University Press, 1991).
98. Martin Schwartz and David Friedrichs, "Postmodern Thought and Criminological Discontent: New Metaphors for Understanding Violence," *Criminology* 32:221–46 (1994).
99. President's Commission on Law Enforcement and the Administration of Justice, *Task Force Report: Juvenile Delinquency and Youth Crime* (Washington, D.C.: U.S. Government Printing Office, 1967), p. 43.
100. Edwin Schur, *Radical Nonintervention* (Englewood Cliffs, N.J.: Prentice-Hall, 1973), p. 88.
101. Malcolm Klein, "Deinstitutionalization and Diversion of Juvenile Offenders: A Litany of Impediments," in Norval Morris and Michael Tonry, eds., *Crime and Justice,* vol. 1 (Chicago: University of Chicago Press, 1979).
102. LaMar Empey, "Revolution and Counter Revolution: Current Trends in Juvenile Justice," in David Shichor and Delos Kelly, eds., *Critical Issues in Juvenile Delinquency* (Lexington, Mass.: Lexington Books, 1980), pp. 157–82.
103. James Austin and Barry Krisberg, "The Unmet Promise of Alternatives to Incarceration," *Crime and Delinquency* 28: 3–19 (1982).
104. William Selke, "Diversion and Crime Prevention," *Criminology* 20:395–406 (1982).
105. Pepinsky and Quinney, *Criminology as Peacemaking.*
106. Adapted from Kay Pranis, "Peacemaking Circles: Restorative Justice in Practice Allows Victims and Offenders to Begin Repairing the Harm," *Corrections Today* 59:72–76 (1997).
107. Kathleen Daly and Russ Immarigeon, "The Past, Present and Future of Restorative Justice: Some Critical Reflections," *Contemporary Justice Review* 1:21–45 (1998).
108. Gene Stephens, "The Future of Policing: From a War Model to a Peace Model," in Brendan Maguire and Polly Radosh, eds., *The Past, Present and Future of American Criminal Justice* (Dix Hills, NY: General Hall, 1996), pp. 77–93.
109. Peter Cordella, "Justice," unpublished paper, Manchester, N.H.: St. Anselm College, 1997; see also, Herbert Bianchi, *Justice as Sanctuary* (Bloomington: Indiana University Press, 1994); Nils Christie, "Conflicts as Property," *The British Journal of Criminology* 17:1–15 (1977); L. Hulsman, "Critical Criminology and the Concept of Crime," *Contemporary Crises* 10:63–80 (1986).
110. Pranis, "Peacemaking Circles," p. 74.
111. Carol LaPrairie, "The 'New' Justice: Some Implications for Aboriginal Communities," *Canadian Journal of Criminology* 40:61–79 (1998).
112. Gordon Bazemore, "What's New About the Balanced Approach?", *Juvenile and Family Court Journal* 48:1–23 (1997); Gordon Bazemore and Mara Schiff, "Community Justice/Restorative Justice: Prospects for a New Social Ecology for Community Corrections," *International Journal of Comparative and Applied Criminal Justice* 20:311–35 (1996).
113. Jay Zaslaw and George Ballance, "The Socio-Legal Response: A New Approach to Juvenile Justice in the '90s," *Corrections Today* 58:72–75 (1996).
114. Gordon Bazemore, "Restorative Justice and Earned Redemption: Communities, Victims, and Offender Reintegration," *American Behavioral Scientist* 41:768–814 (1998).

Part Three

Environmental Influences on Delinquency

Gender relations, as well as interactions with parents, peers, schools, and substance abuse, exert a powerful influence on children. Youths who fail at home, at school, and in the neighborhood are at risk for sustained delinquent careers. However, these social relationships are complex and are subject to various interpretations. For example, there may be little question that educational underachievement is related to delinquency, but significant disagreement exists over the cause and direction of the relationship. A conflict theorist might view children's school failure as a consequence of class conflict and discrimination. A biosocial theorist may view it as a function of learning disabilities or some other neurological dysfunction. Although both experts conclude that children who do poorly in school are among the most likely to violate the law, their explanations of school failure and its relationship to delinquency are markedly different. Similarly, the influences of family life, substance abuse, and peer relations can also be viewed in a number of different ways, depending on the observer's orientation.

Beyond their theoretical importance, the family, the school, and the peer group occupy significant positions in daily social life and can help insulate children from delinquency or encourage illegal activities. Many delinquency prevention efforts focus on improving family relations, supporting educational achievement, and reducing substance abuse. Part Three has five chapters devoted to the influences critical social forces have on delinquency. Chapter 7 explores gender relations and their relationship to delinquency. Chapter 8 is devoted to the family; Chapter 9 focuses on the peer group and gangs. Chapter 10 examines the relationship between education and delinquency, and Chapter 11 discusses substance abuse. Among the special topics considered are child abuse and neglect, school-based crime, gang control efforts, and the relationship between delinquency and drug abuse.

Chapter 7

Gender and Delinquency

*I*f you could travel back in time to Athens in the fifth century B.C., you would discover a society in which women had virtually no social or political rights. Women were controlled by men at nearly every stage of their lives. The most important duty for a woman in ancient Greece was to bear children—preferably male. An unwanted newborn daughter might be disposed of by placing her in a clay pot and simply abandoning her in a public area. These "exposed" female infants either died from their ordeal, were rescued by childless women, or, most often, were brought up as slaves.

*I*n ancient Athens men spent most of their time away from their homes, enjoying sporting activities and the baths at the local gymnasium after their daytime activities were completed. Women were left to raise the children, spin, weave, and sew the family's clothes, and supervise the daily running of the household. In all but the poorest homes wives were aided by female slaves who were available to cook, clean, and carry water from the fountain.[1]

Gender disparity could also be found in the way children were raised. Athenians did not favor large families, being unwilling to divide their assets among many sons and loath to pay the doweries of daughters.

Young girls received few of the advantages of boys. At first education was limited to aristocratic males, but by the fourth century B.C. all but the poorest boys went to school. At age 18 males spent two years in a gymnasium, a state school devoted to physical and intellectual development. More advanced education in philosophy, mathematics, logic, and rhetoric was available to the sons of the affluent in highly select gymnasia such as the Academy of Plato and the Lycaeum of Aristotle. When their education was complete, males were able to enjoy the richness of Athenian culture, socializing in the gymnasiums and baths, doing their civic duty, working, and even shopping.

In contrast, girls in ancient Greece received no formal education, although some of the wealthiest might be taught to read and write by female tutors. Women were forbidden from performing physical exercises in public, and once married, young women were mostly confined to their homes and even restricted to specific quarters referred to as the "gynaikeion." Although forbidden to go out in public, women might visit female friends in their homes if accompanied by at least one female slave.

Gender-based differences in socialization, education, and upbringing were not unique to ancient Greece but were a fixture of social life in most early societies. Traditionally, girls were restricted and were prevented from enjoying the privileges of boys. Even though such distinctions do not exist in modern society, the idea of male domination has not disappeared. It should come as no surprise, then, that beyond their obvious biological differences, inequalities still exist in the way boys and girls are socialized by their parents and treated by social institutions. Do these gender differences also manifest themselves in the delinquency rate? What significance do gender roles have on illegal behavior choices?

As we saw in Chapter 2, significant gender differences in the delinquency rate exist: Males are much more likely than females to engage in repeat and serious offending. Official statistics show that girls are arrested far less often than boys and then for relatively minor offenses; correctional data show that about 95 percent of incarcerated inmates are males.

Nor is this relationship a recent occurrence. To early criminologists, the female offender was an aberration who engaged in crimes that usually had a sexual connotation—prostitution, running away (which presumably leads to sexual misadventure), premarital sex, incorrigibility, and later, crimes of sexual passion (killing a boyfriend or a husband).[2] Delinquency experts often ignored female offenders, assuming either that they rarely violated the law or, if they did, that their illegal acts were status-type offenses. Female delinquency was viewed as moral, emotional, or family-related, and such problems were not an important concern of traditional criminologists. In fact, the few "true" female delinquents were considered anomalies whose criminal or delinquent activity was a function of their abandoning accepted feminine roles and taking on masculine characteristics, a concept referred to as the "masculinity hypothesis."[3]

Because female delinquency was considered unimportant, most early theories of delinquency focused on male misconduct and were tested with samples of male delinquents. Quite often these models did not adequately explain gender differences in the delinquency rate. For example, strain theory (Chapter 4) holds that delinquency results from the failure to achieve socially desirable material goals. Using this logic, females should be more criminal than males because they face *gender discrimination,* a barrier to success unknown to males. Some criminologists interpret such exceptions to the rules as an indication that theoretical explanations of male criminality do not apply to females and that separate explanations for male and female delinquency are required.[4]

Unlike earlier generations of criminologists, interest in the association between gender and delinquency is emerging. In part, this interest has been fueled by observations of contemporary crime trends and patterns. Official crime data indicate that although the female delinquency rate is still much lower than the male rate it is growing at a faster pace. Female crime patterns in the UCR are remarkably similar to those of males—larceny and aggravated assault, the crimes for which most males are arrested (as measured by the UCR), are also the most common offenses for which females are arrested. Although young girls still commit less crime than young males, members of both sexes are quite similar in the onset, development, and dynamic of their offending careers.[5] In societies and groups with high rates of male crime and delinquency, so too are there high rates of female crime and delinquency. Over time, male and female arrest rates rise and fall in a parallel fashion.[6]

Another reason for the interest in gender studies is that conceptions of gender differences have changed. A feminist approach to understanding crime is now firmly established. The stereotype of the female delinquent as a purely sexual deviant is no longer taken seriously.[7] The result has been an increased effort to conduct gender-related research to adequately understand and explain differences and similarities in male and female offending patterns.

This chapter provides an overview of gender factors in delinquency. We first discuss some of the gender differences in development and offending patterns. Then we turn to a more detailed discussion of the explanations for these differences as we examine the (1) trait view, (2) the socialization view, (3) the liberal feminist view, and (4) the radical feminist view.

Gender Differences in Development

Research on the developmental differences between adolescent males and females is a relatively new area of study, but from the information now available we know that gender differences may exist as early as infancy when boys are able to express positive and negative emotions at higher rates. Infant girls show greater self-control over their emotions, whereas boys are more easily angered and depend more on inputs from their mothers.[8] There are indications that gender differences in socialization and development do exist and that these differences may have an effect on juvenile offending patterns.[9]

Socialization Differences

Psychologists believe that the significant differences in the way females and males are socialized affect their development. Males learn to value separation and independence, whereas females are taught that their self-worth depends on their ability to sustain relationships. Girls, therefore, run the risk of losing themselves in their relationships with others, and boys may experience a chronic sense of alienation. Because so many personal and romantic relationships go sour, females also run the risk of feeling alienated and strained because of the failure to achieve relational success.[10]

Although there are few gender-based differences in aggression during the first few years of life, girls are socialized to be less aggressive than boys, and girls are supervised more closely by parents.[11] Differences in aggression become noticeable between ages 3 and 6 when children are first socialized into organized peer groups such as the day-care center or school. Males are more likely to display physical aggression, whereas females display relational aggression—excluding disliked peers from play groups, gossiping, and interfering with social relationships.[12]

As they mature, girls learn to respond to provocation by feeling anxious and depressed, unlike boys who are encouraged to retaliate.[13] Overall, women are much more likely to feel distressed than men, experiencing sadness, anxiety, and uneasiness.[14] Although females get angry as often as males, many have been taught to blame themselves for harboring such negative feelings. Females are, therefore, much more likely than males to respond to anger with feelings of depression, anxiety, fear, and shame. Females are socialized to fear that their anger will harm valued relationships; males are encouraged to react with "moral outrage," blaming others for their discomfort.[15]

Females are also more likely than males to be targets of sexual and physical abuse. Female victims have been shown to suffer more seriously from these attacks, sustaining long-term damage to their self-image; victims of sexual abuse find it difficult to build autonomy and life skills.

Cognitive Differences

There are also measurable cognitive differences between adolescent males and females. Girls have been found to be superior to boys in verbal ability; boys test higher in visual-spatial performance. Girls acquire language faster, learning to speak earlier and faster, with better pronunciation. Girls are far less likely than boys to have reading problems, but boys do much better on standardized math tests, which is attributed by some experts to their strategies for approaching math problems. In most cases cognitive differences are small, narrowing, and usually attributed to cultural expectations. When given training, girls can increase their visual-spatial skills, making their abilities indistinguishable from those of boys.

Personality Differences

Girls are often stereotyped as talkative, but research shows that in many situations boys spend more time talking than girls do. Females are more willing to reveal their feelings and more likely than males to express concern for the well-being of others. Females are more concerned about finding the "meaning of life" and less interested in competing for material success.[16] Males are more likely to introduce new topics and to interrupt conversations.

Adolescent females use different knowledge than males and have different ways of interpreting their lives and their interactions with others. These gender differences in achieving self-understanding may later have an impact on self-esteem and self-concept. Research shows that as adolescents develop through the life course male self-esteem and self-concept rise, whereas female self-confidence is lowered.[17] However, females display more self-control than males, a factor that has been related to criminality.[18] These differences are summarized in Table 7.1.

What Causes Gender Differences?

Why do these gender differences occur? Some experts suggest that the reason may be neurological. Males and females have somewhat different brain organizations; females are more "left brain"-oriented and males more "right brain"-oriented. (The left brain is believed to control language and the right spatial relations.) Others point to the hormonal and biochemical differences between the sexes as the key to understanding their behavior.

A third nonbiological view is that gender differences are a result of the interaction of socialization, learning, and enculturation. Boys and girls may behave differently because they have been exposed to different styles of socialization, learned different values, and have been given different cultural experiences. It follows, then, that if members of both sexes were treated evenly and equally exposed to the factors that produce delinquency their delinquency rates would be equivalent.[19]

Table 7.1

DIFFERENCES BETWEEN MALE AND FEMALE SOCIALIZATION

Females	Males
Self-worth depends on ability to sustain relationships	Taught to value separation and independence
Less aggressive; more likely to show relational aggression	More aggressive; aggression takes a physical form
Blame self when angry	React with moral outrage; others are responsible
More likely to be depressed or anxious	Less prone to sadness or fear
More likely to be abuse victims	Less likely to be targets of abuse

gender-schema theory
Asserts that our culture polarizes males and females, forcing them into exclusive gender roles of "feminine" or "masculine"; these gender scripts provide the basis for deviant behaviors.

Gender-schema theory recognizes the different socialization processes of males and females. According to psychologist Sandra Bem, our culture polarizes males and females by forcing them to obey mutually exclusive gender roles or "scripts." Girls are expected to be "feminine," exhibiting traits such as being tender, sympathetic, understanding, and gentle. In contrast, boys are expected to be "masculine," exhibiting assertiveness, forceful competitiveness, and dominance. Children internalize these scripts and accept gender polarization as normal behavior. Children's self-esteem becomes wrapped up in how close their behavior conforms to the proper sex role stereotype. When children begin to perceive themselves as either *boys* or *girls* (which occurs at about age 3), they actively search for information to help them define their role; they begin to learn what behavior is appropriate for their sex and what is gender-inconsistent behavior.[20] Girls are expected to

Males seem more aggressive and assertive and less likely to form attachments to others, factors that might increase their crime rates. One reason may be that sons try to emulate their fathers' macho behavior, and the fathers are then pleased when their sons act "manly." Gender-based differences in behavior may be intergenerational, passed down from father to son in an unending cycle.

behave according to the appropriate script and to seek approval of their behavior: Are they acting as girls should at that age? Masculine behavior is to be avoided. In contrast, males look for cues from their peers to define their masculinity; aggressive behavior may be rewarded with peer approval, whereas sensitivity is viewed as nonmasculine.[21]

Gender Differences and Delinquency

There appear to be measurable differences in personality, cognitive ability, and socialization between males and females. These distinctions may explain in part the significant gender differences in the delinquency rate.

Males seem more aggressive and assertive and less likely to form attachments to others, factors that might increase their crime rates. Males view aggression as an appropriate means to gain status and power. Boys are also more likely than girls to socialize with deviant peers, and when they do, they display personality traits that make them more susceptible to delinquency. Boys have a more cavalier attitude and are more interested in their own self-interest.

Girls are shielded by their moral sense, which directs them to care about people and to avoid harming others. Their moral sensitivity may help counterbalance the effects of poverty and family problems.[22] Females are more verbally proficient, a skill that may help them deal with conflict without resorting to violence. They are taught to be less aggressive and view belligerence as a lack of self-control.[23] When girls are aggressive, they are more likely than boys to hide their behavior from adults; girls who "bully" others are less likely than boys to admit their behavior.[24]

Cognitive and personality differences are magnified when, at an early age, children begin to internalize gender-specific behaviors. Boys who aren't tough and aggressive are labeled "sissies" and "crybabies." Girls are given different messages; they are expected to form closer bonds with their friends and to share feelings. Recent research by Stacey Nofziger finds that grasp of one's **gender identity** is the most important predictor of intersex differences in the delinquency rate. Members of both sexes who identify with "masculine traits," such as dominance and forcefulness, are more likely to engage in delinquent acts than those who admire "feminine traits," such as affection and compassion. Because boys are more likely to identify with masculine traits, their crime rates are higher. Sex may only have an impact on delinquency, she concludes, to the extent that females learn to be "feminine" and males "masculine."[25]

gender identity
The gender characteristics individuals identify in their own behaviors; members of both sexes who identify with "masculine" traits are more likely to engage in delinquent acts.

Gender Patterns in Delinquency

Over the past decade females have increased their participation in delinquent behaviors at a faster rate than males. Arrest data indicate that juvenile females make up a greater percentage of the arrest statistics today than they did thirty years ago. In 1967 females constituted 13 percent of all juvenile index crime arrests; today they make up 25 percent of the total. The most recent arrest data (Figure 7.1) show that between 1993 and 1997 the teenage male arrest rate increased about 9 percent and the female rate increased 26 percent.[26]

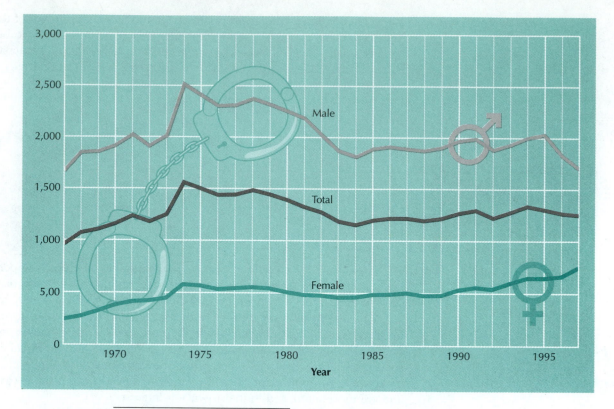

FIGURE 7.1

Juvenile Index Crime Arrest Rates by Sex (per 100,000)
Source: *Uniform Crime Report,* 1997.

Females are also becoming involved more often in the most serious offenses including murder, armed robbery, and aggravated assault.[27] As Figure 7.2 shows, in 1967 about 5 percent of female arrests were for violent crime; by 1997 that percentage had doubled to almost 10 percent (male violent crime arrest rates also doubled during this period from 9 percent to 17 percent).

The patterns of male and female criminality also appear to be converging. Self-report data indicate that the rank ordering of male and female deviant behaviors are quite similar. The illegal acts most common for boys—petty larceny, using a false ID, and smoking marijuana—are also the ones most frequently committed by girls.

Violent Behavior

If men were to relinquish the ideal that aggression is a legitimate means of social coercion and a source of status, a range of social problems from schoolyard bullying and domestic violence to terrorism and international conflicts might be brought under control.[28]

Gender differences in the delinquency rate may be narrowing, but there is little question that males continue to be overrepresented in arrests for the most violent crimes. For example, almost all homicide offenders are males. In 1997, of the 1,669 juveniles arrested for murder, only 106 were female.[29] Homicide rates increase with age throughout the adolescent years. As might be expected, the increase for males is significantly higher than that of females.

Males and females who engage in extreme violence show gender-based differences in terms of the victims they target and the weapons they use. The typical

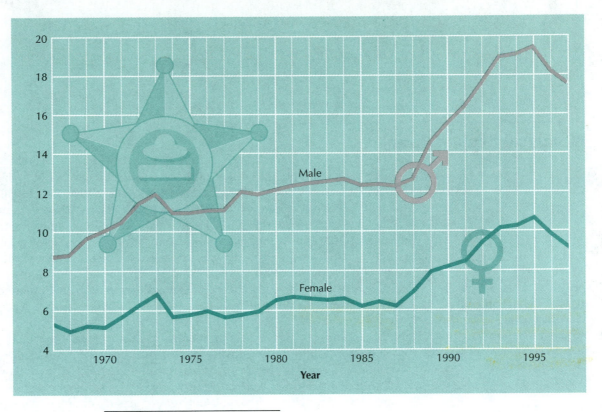

FIGURE 7.2

Violent Crime Arrests by Sex as a Percentage of all Index Crime Arrests for Juveniles
Source: *Uniform Crime Report*, 1997.

male juvenile kills a friend or an acquaintance with a handgun during an argument. In contrast, the typical female is as likely to kill a family member as a friend or an acquaintance and is more likely to use a knife. Both males and females tend to kill males, generally their brothers, fathers, or friends.

Why do these differences occur, and why are girls increasing their involvement in most delinquent activities at a faster pace than boys? The wide range of opinions on these important questions will be presented in the remaining sections of this chapter.

Trait Views of Female Delinquency

There has been a long tradition of tracing the onset of gender differences in the delinquency rate to physical and mental traits that are either uniquely male or female. The argument that biological and psychological differences between males and females can explain differences in crime rates is not a new one. The earliest criminologists, such as Cesare Lombroso whose theories were introduced in Chapter 3, focused their attention on physical characteristics believed to be precursors of crime. Lombroso's concept of the "born criminal" rested on male-oriented physical and mental traits such as extraordinary strength and agility, lack of emotion, and insensibility to pain. In contrast, female delinquents were treated as a bizarre aberration. Because the female crime rate was so low and because most girls were not delinquents, those whose behavior deviated from what was considered appropriate for females were believed to be inherently evil or physically maladapted.

Biological Explanations

masculinity hypothesis
View that women who commit crimes have biological and psychological traits similar to those of men.

With the publication in 1895 of his book *The Female Offender,* Lombroso (with William Ferrero) extended his pioneering work on criminality to females.[30] Lombroso maintained that women were lower on the evolutionary scale than men, more childlike, less sensitive, and less intelligent.[31] Women who committed crimes (most often prostitution and other sex-related offenses) could be distinguished from "normal" women by physical characteristics—excessive body hair, wrinkles, crow's feet, and an abnormal cranium, for example.[32] In physical appearance, delinquent females appeared closer both to criminal and noncriminal men than to other women. The **masculinity hypothesis** suggested that delinquent girls had excessive male characteristics.[33]

Lombroso's suggestion that women were lower on the evolutionary scale than men is puzzling because he viewed atavism or primitivism as the key element in producing criminal behavior, yet the crime rate of females is lower than that of males. Lombroso explained this apparent inconsistency by arguing that most girls are restrained from committing delinquent acts by counterbalancing traits such as "piety, maternity, want of passion, sexual coldness, weakness, and undeveloped intelligence."[34] The delinquent female lacks these traits and is therefore "unrestrained in her childlike, unreasoned passions." Lombroso also believed much female delinquency is masked and hidden.

Lombroso did recognize, however, that there were far fewer female than male delinquents. He suggested that this was a function of the relative homogeneity and uniformity among females; the female "born criminal" was indeed a rare creature. But he also believed that if a girl did become a delinquent her behavior might become even more vicious than that of males.[35]

Lombroso's early work on the physical abnormalities of deviant girls portrayed female offenders as suffering from weak egos, abnormal or impulsive personalities, and other psychological problems. Another theme begun by Lombroso was that female delinquency was almost always linked to anatomy and sexuality.

Lombrosian thought had a significant influence on how the female delinquent was viewed for much of the twentieth century. Delinquency rate differentials were explained in terms of gender-based physical differences. For example, in 1925 Cyril Burt linked female delinquency to menstruation.[36] Similarly, William Healy and Augusta Bronner's research suggested that males' physical superiority enhanced their criminality. Their research showed that about 70 percent of the delinquent girls they studied had abnormal, masculine weight and size characteristics, a finding that supported the "masculinity hypothesis."[37] In a later work, *The Criminality of Women* (1950), Otto Pollak linked the onset of female criminality to the impact of biological conditions such as menstruation, pregnancy, and menopause:[38]

> Thefts, particularly shoplifting, arson, homicide, and resistance against public officials seem to show a significant correlation between the menstruation of the offender and the time of the offense. The turmoil of the onset of menstruation and the puberty of girls appears to express itself in the relatively high frequency of false accusations and—where cultural opportunities permit—of incendiarism. Pregnancy in its turn is a crime-promoting influence with regard to attacks against the life of the fetus and the newborn. The menopause finally seems to bring about a distinct increase in crime, especially in offenses resulting from irritability such as arson, breaches of the peace, perjury, and insults.[39]

Pollak argued that most female delinquency goes unrecorded because the female is the instigator rather than the perpetrator of illegal behavior.[40] Females first use their sexual charms to instigate crime and then beguile males in the justice system to obtain deferential treatment. This observation is referred to as the **chivalry hypothesis,** which holds that gender differences in the delinquency rate can be explained by the fact that female criminality is overlooked or forgiven by male agents of the criminal justice system. Those who believe in the chivalry hypothesis point to data that show that even though women make up about 20 percent of all arrestees they account for less than 5 percent of all inmates. Police and other justice system personnel may still be less willing to arrest and penalize female offenders than male offenders.[41]

chivalry hypothesis
View that low female crime and delinquency rates are a reflection of the leniency with which police treat female offenders.

Psychological Explanations

Psychologists also viewed the physical differences between male and female as a basis for their behavior differentials. Sigmund Freud maintained that girls interpret their lack of a penis as a sign that they have been punished. Boys fear that they also can be punished by having their penis cut off, and thus they learn to fear women. From this conflict comes *penis envy,* and the girl's wish to become a boy. Penis envy often produces an inferiority complex in girls, forcing them to make an effort to compensate for their "defect." One way to compensate is to identify with their mothers and accept a maternal role as wife and child bearer. Also, girls may become narcissistic and attempt to compensate for their lack of a penis by dressing well and beautifying themselves.[42]

Freud also claimed that if a young girl does not overcome her penis envy neurotic episodes may follow: "If a little girl persists in her first wish—to grow into a boy—in extreme cases she will end as a manifest homosexual, and otherwise she will exhibit markedly masculine traits in the conduct of her later life, will choose a masculine vocation, and so on."[43]

Freud's concept of penis envy has been strongly questioned by contemporary psychoanalysts and psychologists who scoff at the notion that little girls feel inferior to little boys and charge that Freud's thinking was influenced by the sexist culture of his age.[44]

At mid-century, psychodynamic theorists suggested that girls are socialized to be passive and in need of affection, which helps to explain their low crime rate. However, this personality condition also makes some females susceptible to being manipulated by men; hence, their participation in sex-related crimes such as prostitution. A girl's wayward behavior, psychoanalysts suggested, was restricted to neurotic theft (kleptomania) and to overt sexual acts, which were symptoms of some unresolved personality maladaption.[45]

According to these early versions of the psychoanalytic approach, gender differences in the delinquency rate can be traced to differences in psychological orientation. Male delinquency reflects aggressive personality traits, whereas female delinquency is a product of a young girl's psychosexual development, a function of repressed sexuality, gender conflict, and abnormal socialization.

Contemporary Trait Views

Contemporary biosocial and psychological theorists have continued the tradition of attributing gender differences in delinquency to physical and emotional traits (for

THE BIOSOCIAL STUDY OF FEMALE DELINQUENCY

The biosocial study followed nearly one thousand Philadelphia residents from birth through early adulthood. Participants came from families involved in the Philadelphia Collaborative Perinatal Project at Pennsylvania Hospital between 1959 and 1966. This was part of a nationwide study of biological and environmental influences on the pregnancies of sixty thousand women, as well as the physical, neurological, and psychological development of their children. Upon registration for the Perinatal Project, each mother underwent a battery of interviews and physical examinations that provided data for each pregnancy, including the mother's reproductive history, recent and past medical history, and labor and delivery events. Data recorded for each child included information on neurological examinations conducted at birth, throughout the hospital stay, at four months, and at ages 1 and 7. Additionally, the children had their speech, language, and hearing examined at ages 3 and 8. Philadelphia public school records were used to collect data on academic achievement and evidence of learning or disciplinary problems. In addition, official police records were collected for all subjects from ages 7 to 22.

The biosocial study found that nine factors, some social and some biological, had an important impact on the likelihood that a female would engage in delinquent behavior: (1) disciplinary problems in school, (2) lack of foster parents, (3) abnormal movement, (4) neurological abnormalities, (5) left foot preference, (6) father absence, (7) low language achievement, (8) normal intellectual status, and (9) right eye preference.

The data yielded a number of surprises, including the discovery that foster care had a more positive effect on behavior than keeping a child with her own family! Many of the children who were placed in foster care in the biosocial study came from disruptive and abusive homes where at least one parent was absent. Their early family experiences appear to have had a significant effect on their later delinquency. This conclusion is confirmed by the significant association found between father absence and delinquency.

The biosocial study also assessed neurological impairment and its relationship to delinquency. A number of different tests were used to measure abnormality. Researchers would ask a test child to hold out both arms horizontally for thirty seconds to ease the detection of abnormal posture, chorea (rapid involuntary jerks), and athetosis (slow, spasmodic repetitions). They recorded many different types of abnormal movements, including tremors, tics, and mirror movements. They also noted neurological abnormalities, condi-

an example of this research see Figure 7.3). These more contemporary views recognize that it is the interaction of biological and psychological traits with the social environment that produces delinquency. The Focus on Delinquency box entitled "The Biosocial Study of Female Delinquency" describes a major study of the biological and social factors that influence the formation of delinquency.[46]

precocious sexuality
Sexual experimentation in early adolescence.

Precocious Sexuality   Early theorists linked female sexuality and delinquency to the effects of early or **precocious sexuality.** According to this view, girls who experience an early onset of physical maturity are most likely to engage in antisocial behavior.[47] Female delinquents were believed to be promiscuous and somewhat more sophisticated and mature than male delinquents.[48] Linking female delinquency to sexuality was responsible, in part, for the view that female delinquency is symptomatic of maladjustment and social isolation.[49]

Equating female delinquency purely with sexual activity is no longer taken seriously, but early sexuality has been linked to other social problems such as a higher risk of teen pregnancy and sexually transmitted diseases.[50] Empirical evidence suggests that girls who reach puberty at an early age are at the highest risk for delinquency.[51] One reason is that "early bloomers" may be more attractive to older adolescent boys, and increased contact with this high-risk group places the

tions that are often related to central nervous system disorders, such as abnormalities of skull size and shape, spinal anomalies, and primary muscle disease. Neurological abnormalities and factors associated with attention deficit disorder were found to be important predictors of female delinquency and violence. Those physical factors—number of neurological abnormalities, mixed cerebral dominance as indicated by left-footedness and right-eyedness, and abnormal movements—can interfere with language achievement. Poor language skills were found to have a positive correlation with female delinquency.

The study found that delinquency and violence are associated with learning difficulties and low achievement for females but are not associated with the more serious types of mental impairments such as mental retardation or abnormal intellectual status. This finding is consistent with other analyses, indicating generally that the more violent and chronic delinquents had lower achievement test scores but that they were not significantly represented in programs for the mentally retarded.

Which female juvenile delinquents later became adult offenders? Four factors showed direct effects on the number of adult offenses among females: seriousness of juvenile offenses, number of disciplinary problems in school, low number of juvenile offenses, and father's low educational level. As with males, the seriousness of delinquent offenses was significant; however, unlike males, those most apt to continue to commit crime during adulthood were not always those who committed the most crime during their youth. This result is not surprising, however, because females commit a relatively larger number of petty or status offenses such as shoplifting. Therefore, unlike males, chronic female offenders were not always the most serious offenders. In addition, disciplinary problems in school had a long-term effect on adult offending. This is evidence that early problem behavior is predictive of problems in adulthood.

The biosocial study is important because it involves careful and precise measurements of physical traits and conditions. It shows that both social factors and physical traits have important effects on both female delinquency and, later, on adult criminality. Can such physical traits be neutralized by social support? Do you believe it is impossible to overcome biological limitations? What do you think about this important issue?

Sources: Deborah W. Denno, *Biology and Violence: From Birth to Adulthood* (London: Cambridge University Press, 1990); Deborah W. Denno, "Gender, Crime, and the Criminal Law Defenses," *Journal of Criminal Law and Criminology* 85: 80–180 (1994).

girls in jeopardy for antisocial behavior. The delinquency gap between early and late bloomers narrows when the latter group reaches sexual maturity and increases their exposure to boys.[52] Biological and social factors seem to interact to postpone or accelerate female delinquent activity. The Case in Point explores this issue.

Hormonal Differences   As you may recall from Chapter 3, some biosocial theorists link antisocial behavior to hormonal influences.[53] The argument is that male sex hormones (androgens) account for more aggressive male behavior and that gender-related hormonal differences can also explain the gender gap in delinquency.[54] Females may be biologically "protected" from deviant behavior in the same way they are immune from some diseases that strike males. Sensation seeking, impulsivity, aggression, dominance, and lesser verbal skills are androgen-related male traits that are related to antisocial behaviors.

Gender differences in the crime rate may be a function of androgen levels; these hormones cause areas of the brain to become less sensitive to environmental stimuli, making males more likely to seek high levels of stimulation, such as the "rush" that accompanies crime, and to tolerate more pain in the process.[55] Androgens are also linked to brain seizures, which result in greater emotional volatility, especially when stresses are present. Some experts believe androgens affect the brain structure

A longitudinal study that followed children born on the Hawaiian island of Kauai in 1955 for thirty-two years found that the most reliable traits for predicting delinquency in boys included the following:

- Disordered care-taking
- Lack of educational stimulation in the home
- Reading problems
- A need for remedial education by age 10
- Late maturation
- An unemployed, criminal, or absent father

In addition, boys appeared to be particularly vulnerable to early childhood learning problems, leading to school failure. A combination of reaching puberty late and lack of a significant male role model also encouraged the persistence of antisocial behavior throughout adolescence.

In the same longitudinal study, researchers found that delinquent girls tend to have the following traits:

- A history of minor congenital defects
- Low development scores by age 2
- A need for mental health services by age 10
- Earlier-than-average onset of puberty

Researchers hypothesize that birth defects and slow early development could lead to poor self-esteem, whereas early sexual development may encourage sexual relationships with older males and conflict with parents.

FIGURE 7.3

Trait Differences in Male and Female Delinquents

Source: Felton Earls and Albert Reiss, *Breaking the Cycle: Predicting and Preventing Crime* (Washington, D.C.: National Institute of Justice, 1994), pp. 24–25.

itself (the left hemisphere of the neocortex), effectively reducing sympathetic feelings toward others that help to inhibit the urge to victimize.[56]

A great deal of research has been done on the relationship between hormone levels and aggression. In general, females who test higher on testosterone (an androgen) are more likely to engage in stereotypical male behaviors.[57] Females who have naturally low androgen levels are less aggressive than males, whereas those who have elevated levels will take on characteristically male traits, including aggression.[58]

Some females are overexposed to male hormones in utero. Females affected this way may become "constitutionally masculinized" and at risk to delinquency. They may develop abnormal hair growth, large musculature, low voice, irregular menstrual cycle, fertility disorders, and hyperaggressiveness; this condition can also develop as a result of steroid use or certain medical disorders.[59] Diana Fishbein has reviewed the literature in this area and finds that after holding constant a variety of factors (including IQ, age, and environment) females exposed to male hormones in utero are more likely to engage in physically aggressive behavior later in life.[60]

Premenstrual Syndrome Early biotheorists suspected that premenstrual syndrome (PMS) was a direct cause of the relatively rare instances of female violence and aggression:

> For several days prior to and during menstruation, the stereotype has been that "raging hormones" doom women to irritability and poor judgment—two facets of premenstrual syndrome.[61]

The link between PMS and delinquency was popularized by Katharina Dalton, whose studies of English women led her to conclude that females are more likely to commit suicide and be aggressive and otherwise antisocial before or during menstruation.[62]

As the principal of a northeast junior high school, you get a call from a parent who is disturbed because he has heard a rumor that the students plan to publish a story with a sexual theme in the literary digest. The work is written by a junior high school girl who became pregnant during the year and underwent an abortion. You ask for and receive a copy of the narrative.

The girl's theme is a cautionary tale of young love that results in an unwanted pregnancy. The author details her abusive home life, which led her to engage in an intimate relationship with another student, her pregnancy, her conflict with her parents, her decision to abort, and the emotional turmoil that the incident created. She tells students to use contraception if they are sexually active and recommends appropriate types of birth control. There is nothing provocative or sexually explicit in the work.

Some teachers argue that girls should not be allowed to read this material because it has a sexual content that they must be protected from and that in a sense it advocates defiance of parents. Also, some parents may object to a story about precocious sexuality because they fear it may encourage their children to "experiment," and such behavior is linked to delinquency and drug abuse. Those who advocate publication believe girls have a right to read about such important issues and decide on their own course of action. Censorship would also be a violation of the author's First Amendment rights?

■ Should you force the story's deletion because its theme is essentially sexual and controversial?

■ Should you allow publication because it deals with the subject matter in a mature fashion?

■ Do you think reading and learning about sexual matters encourages or discourages experimentation in sexuality?

Today there is conflicting evidence on the relationship between PMS and female delinquency. Diana Fishbein, a noted expert on biosocial theory, concludes that there is an association between elevated levels of female aggression and menstruation. Research efforts show that a significant number of incarcerated females committed their crimes during the premenstrual phase and that at least a small percentage of women appear vulnerable to cyclical hormonal changes that make them more prone to anxiety and hostility.[63] Fishbein notes that the great majority of females who suffer anxiety and hostility prior to and during menstruation do not actually engage in criminal behavior.[64]

Existing research has been criticized on the basis of methodological inadequacy.[65] A valid test of the association must consider its time-ordering: it is possible that the psychological and physical stress of antisocial behavior produces early menstruation and not vice versa.[66]

Aggression   According to some biosocial theorists, gender differences in the delinquency rate can be explained by inborn differences in aggression between males and females.[67]

The adolescent girl who is growing up in a troubled home or one marked by abuse, conflict, or neglect may be prone to delinquency. If a girl grows up in an atmosphere of sexual tension, where hostility exists between her parents or where the parents are absent, she likely will turn to outside sources, such as older males, for affection and support.

> Males and females differ with respect to biological vulnerabilities, reflected in consistent findings that males are inherently more likely to be aggressive.[68]

Some psychologists have suggested that these gender-based differences in aggression are present very early in life, appearing before socialization can influence behavior. Males seem to be more aggressive in all human societies for which data is available; gender differences in aggression can even be found in nonhuman primates.[69]

Some biosocial theorists argue that gender-based differences in aggression reflect the essential physical dissimilarities in the male and female reproductive systems. Males are naturally more aggressive because they wish to possess and control as many sex partners as possible to increase their chances of producing offspring. Females have learned to control their aggressive impulses because multiple mates do not increase their chances of conception. Instead they concentrate their efforts on acquiring things that will help them to successfully rear their offspring, such as a reliable mate who will supply material resources.[70]

The weight of the evidence is that males are more aggressive than females. However, evidence also exists that females are more likely to act aggressively under some circumstances than others. For instance:

- Males are more likely than females to report physical aggression in their behavior, intentions, and dreams.

- Females are more likely to feel anxious or guilty about behaving aggressively, and these feelings tend to inhibit aggression.

- Females behave as aggressively as males when they have the means to do so and believe their behavior is justified.

- Females are more likely to empathize with the victim—to put themselves in the victim's place.

- Sex differences in aggression decrease when the victim is anonymous; anonymity may prevent females from empathizing with the victim.[71]

- Females may feel more freedom than males to express anger and aggression in the family setting.[72]

In summary, biosocial theorists find that qualities of male biological traits make males "naturally" more aggressive than females; under some circumstances, however, females may actually be more aggressive than males.

Socialization Views

Socialization views are based on the idea that a child's social development, which is influenced and controlled by family, peers, teachers, and society, may be the key to understanding delinquent behavior. If a child experiences impairment, trauma, family disruption, and so on, the child will be more susceptible to delinquent associations and criminality.

Linking crime rate variations to gender differences in socialization is not a recent discovery. In a 1928 work, *The Unadjusted Girl,* W. I. Thomas forged a link between socialization, sexuality, and delinquency. He suggested that some impoverished girls who have not been socialized under middle-class family controls can become impulsive thrill seekers. According to Thomas, female delinquency is linked to the "wish" for luxury and excitement.[73] Inequities in the social class system condemn poor girls from demoralized families to use sex as a means to gain amusement, adventure, pretty clothes, and other luxuries. Precocious sexuality makes these disadvantaged girls vulnerable to older men who, taking advantage of their naiveté, lead them down the path to crime and decadence.[74]

Socialization and Delinquency

Scholars concerned with gender differences in the crime rate are interested in the distinction between the lifestyles of males and females. Girls may be supervised more closely than boys and are expected to stay at home more often. If girls behave in a socially disapproved fashion, their parents may be more likely to notice and take action. Adults may be more tolerant of deviant behavior in boys than in girls and expect boys to act tough and to take risks.[75] Closer supervision restricts the opportunity for crime and the time available to mingle with delinquent peers. It follows, then, that the adolescent girl who is growing up in a troubled home—one marked by abuse, conflict, or neglect—and who lacks concern and supervision may be more prone to delinquency.[76]

Focus on Socialization   In the 1950s a number of researchers began to focus on gender-specific socialization patterns as a key determinant of antisocial behavior. They made three assumptions about gender differences in socialization: families exert a more powerful influence on girls than on boys; girls do not form close same-sex friendships and generally compete with their peers; and female criminals are primarily sexual offenders. Let's examine these three assumptions made by the researchers.

First, parents are stricter with girls because they perceived them as vulnerable and in need of control. In some families adolescent girls rebel against strict controls. In other families parents are absent or unavailable, and girls turn to the streets for support and companionship. Second, girls rarely form close relationships with female peers because they view them as rivals for the few males who would make eligible marriage partners.[77] Instead, girls enter into sexual affairs with older men who exploit them, involve them in sexual deviance, and father their illegitimate children.[78] The result is prostitution, petty theft, drug abuse, and marginal lives. Their daughters then would repeat this pattern in a never-ending cycle of despair and exploitation.

Perhaps the best known work focusing on gender differences as a cause of delinquency is Gisela Konopka's *The Adolescent Girl in Conflict* (1966). More than thirty years ago Konopka integrated psychoanalytic views with sociological concepts in an effort to explain the onset of deviant behavior in girls.[79]

Konopka suggested that female delinquency has its roots in a girl's feeling of uncertainty and loneliness. During her adolescence, a girl's major emotional need is to be accepted by members of the opposite sex. If normal channels (such as family and friends) for receiving such approval are impaired, she may fight isolation by joining a "crowd" or engaging in gratuitous sexual relationships. This behavior eventually leads to "rejection by the community, general experience of having no recognized success . . . and more behavior which increases the feeling of worthlessness."[80]

Konopka identified a number of factors that produce the onset of female delinquent behavior.[81] The onset of puberty in girls is traumatic because of the often cruel way in which it is received by parents and the fear it creates in girls. The social identification process can be dramatic and difficult because of a girl's competitiveness with her mother. In fatherless homes, girls have an especially hard time because "the road to a healthy development toward womanhood through affection for the male and identification with the female simply does not exist."[82] The absence of socioeconomic mobility can also create problems. Delinquent girls are believed to suffer from a lack of training and education. This locks them into low-paying jobs with little hope for advancement. These conditions lead girls to relieve their thwarted ambition through aggressive or destructive behavior. The world then presents a hostile environment to some girls; adult authority figures tell them what to do, but no one is there to listen to their needs.

Broken Homes/Fallen Women   A number of experts shared Konopka's emphasis on the family and society as a primary influence on delinquent behavior. Male delinquents were typically portrayed as rebels who, testing their masculinity, esteemed "toughness," "excitement," and other lower-class values. Males succumbed to the lure of gang delinquency when they perceived few legitimate opportunities. In contrast, female delinquents were portrayed as troubled adolescents who suffered inadequate home lives and, more often than not, were victims of sexual and physical abuse. Ruth Morris described delinquent girls as unattractive, poorly groomed youths who reside in homes marked by family tensions or absent parents.[83] In an oft-cited work, *The Delinquent Girl* (1970), Clyde Vedder and Dora Somerville suggest that female delinquency is usually a problem of adjustment to family and social pressure; an estimated 75 percent of institutionalized girls have family problems.[84] They also suggest that girls have serious problems in a male-dominated culture with rigid and sometimes unfair social practices.

Eleanor and Sheldon Glueck also distinguished between the causes of male and female delinquency. They linked male delinquency to muscular body type, impulsive personality, a hostile, defiant attitude, destructive traits, and a poor home life.[85] Delinquent males had been reared in homes of "little understanding or affection, stability or moral fibre," by parents who were unfit to be role models.[86] In contrast, when they examined the life histories of institutionalized female offenders in their classic work *Five Hundred Delinquent Women,* they found that a significant majority of these women had been involved in sexual deviance that began early in their teens.[87] The Gluecks concluded that sexual delinquency and general behavior maladjustment developed in girls simultaneously with unstable home lives.[88]

Other early efforts linked "rebellious" or sexually precocious behavior to sexual conflicts in the home and to incestuous relationships.[89] Broken or disrupted homes were found to predict female delinquency.[90] Females petitioned to juvenile court were more likely than males to be charged with ungovernable behavior, running away, and sex offenses. They also were more likely to reside in single-parent homes.[91] Studies of incarcerated juveniles found that most of the male delinquents were incarcerated for burglary, robbery, and other theft-related offenses, but female delinquents tended to be involved in incorrigibility, sex offenses, and truancy. The conclusion: boys became delinquent to gain status and demonstrate their masculinity by adventurous behavior; girls were delinquent because of hostility toward parents and a consequent need to obtain gratification and attention from others.[92]

Contemporary Socialization Views

The view that females are more deeply affected by family disruption and conflict than males has not been abandoned. Investigators continue to support the view that female delinquents have more dysfunctional home lives than male offenders.[93] Institutionalized girls tell of lives filled with severe physical and sexual abuse. Females who are "official" delinquents openly discuss being survivors of rape and incest. In addition to tragic home lives, delinquent girls report social and community experiences that were frustrating or even degrading.[94]

Girls seem to be more deeply affected than boys by child abuse, and the link between abuse and female delinquency seems stronger than it is for male delinquency.[95] A significant amount of female delinquency can be traced to physical and sexual abuse in the home.[96] Meda Chesney-Lind, a prominent feminist scholar, has described this association: "Young women on the run from homes characterized by sexual abuse and parental neglect are forced, by the very statutes designed to protect them, into the life of an escaped convict."[97]

Joan Moore's analysis of gang girls in East Los Angeles found that many came from troubled homes. Sixty-eight percent of the girls she interviewed were afraid of their fathers, and 55 percent reported fear of their mothers. One girl told Moore about the abuse she received from her mother:

> She would hit me, pinch me, and pull my hair, and then she'd have my brother— the oldest one—get a whip, and whip me, and then I'd have stripes all over my body like a zebra, and I went to school like that.[98]

Many of the girls Moore spoke with reported that their parents were overly strict and controlling despite the fact that they engaged in drug abuse and criminality themselves. Moore also details accounts of incest and sexual abuse; about 30 percent of the gang girls reported that family members had made sexual advances. Considering the restrictions placed on these girls and the high incidence of incest, it comes as no surprise that three-quarters reported having run away at least once. Moore concludes:

> clearly more women than men came from troubled families. They were more likely to have been living with a chronically sick relative, one who died, one who

was a heroin addict, or one who was arrested. . . . This seems on the face of it to imply that the gang represents [for girls] . . . a refuge from family problems.[99]

In summary, the socialization approach holds that family interaction and child-parent relations are the key to understanding female delinquency. If a girl grows up in an atmosphere of sexual tension, where hostility exists between her parents or where the parents are absent, she is likely to turn to outside sources for affection and support. Girls are expected to follow very narrowly defined behavioral patterns. In contrast, it is not unusual or unexpected for boys to stay out late at night, drive around with friends, or get involved in other unstructured behaviors linked to delinquency. If, in their reaction to loneliness, frustration, and parental hostility, girls begin to engage in the same "routine activities" as boys (staying out late at night, drinking, partying, and riding around with their friends), they run the risk of engaging in similar types of delinquent or wayward behavior.[100]

The socialization approach holds that the psychological pressure of a poor home life is likely to have an even more damaging effect on females than on males. Because girls are less likely than boys to have the support of close-knit peer associations, they are more likely to need close parental relationships to retain emotional stability. In fact, girls may become sexually involved with boys to receive support from them, a practice that only tends to magnify their problems.

Liberal Feminist Views

All of us, despite our differences, are constantly growing and trying to understand each other's oppression, be it as working class women, black or brown women, gay women or middle class women. We are, by struggling, finding new ways of caring about each other, and it is this that gives us hope of having a movement, finally, which will provide for all of our needs.[101]

This statement represented the sentiments of women who were active participants in the feminist movement in its formative years. Feminist leaders have fought to help women break away from their traditional roles of homemaker and mother and secure for themselves economic, professional, educational, and social advancement. There is little question that the women's movement has revised the way women perceive their roles in society, and it has significantly altered the relationships of women to many important social institutions.

Liberal feminism also has influenced thinking about the nature and extent of delinquency. A number of scholars, including Rita Simon and Freda Adler, have drawn national attention to the changing pattern of female criminality and offered new explanations for the differences between male and female delinquency rates.[102] Their position is that economic conditions and sex role differences are a greater influence on delinquency rates than socialization. After all, improper socialization affects both males and females and therefore cannot be the sole explanation for gender differences in the crime rate.

According to liberal feminists, females are less delinquent than males because their social roles provide them with fewer opportunities to commit crime. As the roles of girls and women become more similar to those of boys and men, so too will their crime patterns. Female criminality is actually motivated by the same crime-producing influences as male criminality. This view was spelled out most clearly more than twenty years ago in Freda Adler's book *Sisters in Crime* (1975), which explained how sex role differences influence crime and delinquency.

liberal feminism

Asserts that females are less delinquent than males because their social roles provide them with fewer opportunities to commit crimes; as the roles of girls and women become more similar to those of boys and men, so too will their crime patterns.

Sisters in Crime

Adler's major thesis was that by striving for social and economic independence women have begun to alter the social institutions that had protected males in their traditional positions of power. "The phenomenon of female criminality," she claims, "is but one wave in this rising tide of female assertiveness."[103]

Adler argued that female delinquency patterns and rates would be affected by the changing role of women in society. As females entered new occupations and participated in sports, education, politics, and other "traditionally" male endeavors, they would also become involved in crimes that had heretofore been male-oriented; delinquency rates would then converge. She noted that girls were already becoming increasingly involved in traditionally masculine crimes such as stealing, gang activity, and fighting.

Adler predicted that the women's liberation movement would produce even steeper increases in the rate of female delinquency because it created an environment in which the social roles of girls and boys converge. Boys, she argued, have traditionally entered puberty ill-prepared for the world of aggression and competition they encounter in the activities of their peer groups. The consequent emotional strain leads them to engage in delinquent activities. In contrast, girls have always maintained traditional, relatively static behavior patterns. These patterns protected them from the pressures of transition into the adult world. However, Adler argued, "the modern girl . . . is passing from childhood to adulthood via a new and uncharted course. . . . She is partly pushed and partly impelled into fields previously closed to women. . . . Clearly, the developmental difficulties which encouraged male delinquency in the past are exerting a similar influence on girls."[104]

Adler proclaimed that the changing female role will eventually produce female delinquents and criminals who are quite similar to their male counterparts:

> Women are no longer behaving like subhuman primates with only one option. Medical, educational, political and technological advances have freed women from unwanted pregnancies, provided them with male occupational skills, and equalized their strengths with weapons. Is it any wonder that once women were

According to liberal feminists, females are less delinquent than males because their social roles provide them with fewer opportunities to commit crime. As the roles of girls and women become more similar to those of males, so too will their crime patterns. Female criminality is actually motivated by the same crime-producing influences as male criminality. The fact that female delinquency is rising at a faster rate than male delinquency reflects the convergence of their social roles.

armed with male opportunities, they should strive for status, criminal as well as civil, through established male hierarchial channels.

In the cities . . . young girls are now taking to the streets just as boys have traditionally done. It has now become quite common for adolescent girls to participate in muggings, burglaries, and extortion rings which prey on schoolmates.[105]

Support for Liberal Feminism

A number of well-known studies support the feminist view of gender differences in the delinquency rate.[106] More than twenty years ago Rita Simon explained how the consistent increase in female criminality is a function of the changing role of women. She claimed that as women were empowered economically and socially they would be less likely to feel victimized, dependent, and oppressed. Consequently, women would be less likely to attack their traditional targets: their husbands, lovers, pimps (that is, men with whom they are emotionally involved and dependent upon), and their babies (those recently born and those not yet delivered).[107] Instead, their new role as family breadwinner might encourage women to engage in traditional male economic crimes such as larceny and car theft.

Simon's view has been supported in part by Roy Austin's analysis of the effect the women's liberation and economic emancipation movement has had on the female crime rate.[108] Using 1966 as a jumping-off point (because the National Organization for Women was founded in that year), Austin's research shows that patterns of serious female crime (robbery and auto theft) correlate with indicators of female emancipation (namely, the divorce rate and participation in the labor force). Although Austin admits this research does not conclusively prove that female crime is related to economic and social change, it certainly identifies behavior patterns that support that hypothesis.

In addition to these efforts, a number of self-report studies support the liberal feminist view by showing that gender differences in delinquency patterns are fading; that is, the delinquent acts committed most (petty larceny) and least often (heroin addiction, armed robbery) by girls are nearly identical to those reported most and least often by boys.[109] The pattern of female delinquency, if not the extent, is now similar to that of male delinquency,[110] and with few exceptions the factors that seem to motivate both male and female criminality (family dysfunction, educational failure, impulsive personality) seem quite similar.[111]

As the sex roles of males and females have become less distinct, their offending patterns have become more similar. Girls may be joining gangs and committing crimes to gain economic advancement and not because they perceive a lack of parental support and affection. Both of these patterns are predicted by liberal feminists.

Critiques of Liberal Feminism

Not all delinquency experts believe changing sex roles actually influence female crime rates. Some argue that the delinquent behavior patterns of girls have remained static and have not been influenced by the women's movement. Females involved in violent crime more often than not have some connection to a male business or intimate partner who influences their behavior. One recent study of women who kill in the course of their involvement in the drug trade found that rather than act in their own self-interest they kill on behalf of a man or out of fear of a man.[112]

Others dispute whether overall changes in the female delinquency rate correspond to the feminist movement. They argue that self-report studies show that female participation in most crime patterns has remained stable for the past ten years, with increases in the area of drug use and alcohol abuse.[113] It is possible that the women's movement has not influenced female crime rates as much as previously thought.[114] Perhaps the greater participation by females in the UCR arrest data is more a function of how police are treating females—that is, the end of chivalry—rather than an actual change in female behavior patterns.

In summary, gender differences in the crime rate have not changed as much as liberal feminist writers had predicted.[115] Consequently, the argument that female crime and delinquency will be elevated by the women's movement has not received unqualified support.

Is Convergence Possible?

Will the gender differences in the delinquency crime rate eventually disappear as liberal feminists have predicted? Are gender differences permanent and unchanging? Not all experts have abandoned the convergence argument, suggesting that in the long run male and female delinquency rates will become quite similar.[116] For example, female gang membership has increased, and gang activity is associated with increased levels of crime and drug abuse.[117]

Perhaps crime convergence has been delayed by a slower-than-expected change in gender roles; the women's movement has not yet achieved its full impact on social life.[118] Although expanding their economic role, women have not abandoned their conventional role as family caretakers and home providers. Women today are being forced to cope with added financial and social burdens. If gender roles were truly equivalent, crime rates might eventually converge. As our society shifts toward more balanced gender roles, there may be significant changes in female delinquency rates.

Radical Feminist Views

radical feminists, Marxist feminists
Hold that gender inequality stems from the unequal power of men and women and the subsequent exploitation of women by men; the cause of female delinquency originates with the onset of male supremacy and the efforts of males to control females' sexuality.

A number of feminist writers take a more revolutionary view of gender differences in crime. These scholars can be categorized as **radical** or **Marxist feminists.** They believe gender inequality stems from the unequal power of men and women in a capitalist society and the exploitation of females by fathers and husbands: women are considered a "commodity" worth possessing, like land or money.[119] The cause of female delinquency originates with the onset of male supremacy (*patriarchy*), the subsequent subordination of women, male aggression, and the efforts of men to control females sexually.[120]

Radical feminists focus on the social forces that shape girls' lives and experiences to explain female criminality.[121] They attempt to show how the sexual victimization of girls is often a function of male socialization and that young males learn to be aggressive and exploitive of women. James Messerschmidt, an influential feminist scholar, has formulated a complex theoretical model to show how misguided concepts of what "masculinity" is flows from the inequities built into "patriarchal capitalism." Men dominate business and power in capitalist societies, and males who cannot function well within its parameters are at risk to crime. Women are inherently powerless in such a male-dominated society, and their crimes reflect their limitations for both legitimate and illegitimate opportunity.[122]

This view is supported by a national survey conducted by the Center for Research on Women at Wellesley College, which found that 90 percent of adolescent girls are sexually harassed in school, with almost 30 percent reporting having been psychologically pressured to "do something sexual" and 10 percent physically forced into sexual behaviors.[123]

According to the radical view, male exploitation acts as a trigger for female delinquent behavior and status offending. Female delinquents recount being so severely sexually harassed at school that they were forced to carry knives for their own safety. Some have reported that their much older boyfriends, sometimes in their thirties, who "knew how to treat a girl" would often draw them into criminal activity such as drug trafficking, which eventually entangled them in the juvenile justice system.[124]

When female adolescents run away and use drugs, they may be reacting to abuse at home or at school. Their attempts at survival are then labeled deviant or delinquent; victim blaming is not uncommon.[125] Research shows that a significant number of girls who require emergency room treatment for sexual abuse later engage in violence as a teen or as an adult; many of these abused girls actually form a romantic attachment with the abusive partner.[126] The Wellesley survey of sexual harassment found that teachers and school officials ignore about 45 percent of the complaints made by female students. Because agents of social control often choose to ignore reports of abuse and harassment, young girls may feel trapped and desperate.

Crime and Patriarchy

A number of theoretical models have attempted to use a radical or Marxist feminist perspective to explain gender differences in the delinquency rate. For example, in *Capitalism, Patriarchy, and Crime,* Marxist James Messerschmidt argues that capitalist society is marked by both patriarchy and class conflict. Capitalists control the labor of workers, and men control women both economically and biologically.[127] This "double marginality" explains why females in a capitalist society commit fewer crimes than males: they are isolated in the family and have fewer opportunities to engage in elite deviance (white-collar and economic crimes); they are also denied access to male-dominated street crimes. Because capitalism renders women powerless, they are forced to commit less serious, nonviolent, and self-destructive crimes such as abusing drugs.

Power-Control Theory

power-control theory
Holds that gender differences in the delinquency rate are a function of class differences and economic conditions that influence the structure of family life.

In one prominent radical feminist work, John Hagan and his associates have speculated that gender differences in the delinquency rate are a function of class differences and economic conditions that in turn influence the structure of family life. Hagan calls his view **power-control theory.**[128]

According to this view, class position influences delinquency by controlling the quality of family life. In **paternalistic families,** fathers assume the traditional role of breadwinners, and mothers have menial jobs or remain at home. In these homes mothers are expected to control the behavior of their daughters while granting greater freedom to sons. The parent–daughter relationship can be viewed as a prepa-

paternalistic families
Fathers are breadwinners and mothers have menial jobs and stay at home; mothers are expected to control the behavior of their daughters while granting greater freedom to their sons.

egalitarian families
Husband and wife share power at home; daughters gain a kind of freedom similar to that of sons and their law-violating behaviors mirror those of their brothers.

ration for the "cult of domesticity," which makes daughters' involvement in delinquency unlikely. Hence, males exhibit a higher degree of delinquent behavior than their sisters.

In contrast, in **egalitarian families**—those in which the husband and the wife share similar positions of power at home and in the workplace—daughters gain a kind of freedom that reflects reduced parental control. These families produce daughters whose law-violating behaviors mirror those of their brothers. Ironically, these kinds of relationships also occur in female-headed households with absent fathers. Similarly, Hagan and his associates found that when both fathers and mothers hold equally valued managerial positions the similarity between the rates of their daughters' and sons' delinquency is greatest. Therefore, middle-class girls are the most likely to violate the law because they are less closely controlled than their lower-class sisters.

Some of the basic premises of power-control theory, such as the relationship between social class and delinquency, have been challenged. For example, the theory holds that upper-class youths may engage in more petty delinquency than lower-class youths because they are brought up to be "risk takers" who do not fear the consequences of their misdeeds; such relationships may not exist.[129] However, ongoing research by Hagan and his colleagues has tended to support the core relationship between family structure and gender differences in the delinquency rate.[130]

Power-control theory is important because it encourages a new approach to the study of delinquency, one that addresses gender differences, class position, and family structure. It also helps to explain the relative increase in female delinquency by stressing the significance of changing feminine roles in modern society. With the increase in single-parent homes brought about by the significant numbers of unwed teenage mothers and the high divorce rate, the patterns Hagan has identified may also undergo change. The decline of the patriarchal family may produce looser family ties on girls, changing sex roles, and increased delinquency.

Gender and the Juvenile Justice System

Not only do gender differences have an effect on juvenile crime rates and patterns but they also may have a significant impact on the way children are treated by the juvenile justice system when they are apprehended. Several feminist scholars argue that girls are not only the victims of injustice at home but also risk being victimized by agents of the juvenile justice system. In many respects the treatment girls receive today is not too dissimilar from the "sexualization" of female delinquency found by Odem and Schlossman in 1920. (See the Focus on Delinquency box entitled "Guardians of Virtue" for more on this topic.) Paternalistic attitudes and the sexual double standard increase the likelihood that girls will be referred to juvenile court for status-type offenses and, after adjudication, receive a disposition involving incarceration.

Are girls "victims" of the juvenile justice system? In her classic 1973 study, Meda Chesney-Lind found that police in Honolulu, Hawaii, were likely to arrest female adolescents for sexual activity and to ignore the same behavior among male delinquents.[131] Some 74 percent of the females in her sample were charged with sexual activity or incorrigibility; in comparison, only 27 percent of the males were so charged. Similar to the Los Angeles juvenile justice practices of the 1920s, the Honolulu court ordered 70 percent of the females to undergo physical examinations but required only 15 percent of the males to undergo this embarrassing procedure. Girls were also more likely to be sent to a detention facility before trial, and the length of their detention averaged three times that of the boys.

FOCUS ON DELINQUENCY

GUARDIANS OF VIRTUE

The view that female delinquency is sexual in nature and that the great majority of female delinquents' troubles can be linked to their sexual precociousness influenced the treatment of young female offenders in the first juvenile courts. Mary Odem and Steven Schlossman explored this "sexualization" of female delinquency in their study of more than two hundred girls petitioned to the Los Angeles Juvenile Court in 1920.

Odem and Schlossman argue that in the first decades of the twentieth century delinquency "experts" identified young female "sex delinquents" as a major social problem that required a forceful public response. These experts spoke of a rise in illicit sexual activity among young working-class females. This phenomenon was perceived, in part, to be a product of the newfound freedoms enjoyed by girls after the turn of the century. Young females were getting jobs in stores and offices where they were more likely to meet eligible young men. Recreation now included dance halls, movie theaters, beaches, and amusement parks—areas fraught with the danger of "sexual experimentation." Civic leaders, concerned about immorality, mounted a social hygiene campaign that identified the "sex delinquent" as a moral and sexual threat to American society and advocated a policy of "eugenics"—sterilization to prevent these inferior individuals from having children.

The Los Angeles juvenile justice system responded to this "epidemic" of sexuality by targeting the lower-class female population. At first, female civic leaders and social workers campaigned for special attention to be given to female delinquency in an effort to combat "moral ruin." Los Angeles responded by hiring the first female police officers in the nation to deal with girls under arrest as well as female judges to hear girls' cases in juvenile court. The city also developed a nationally recognized female detention center and a girl's reformatory.

The first female officer in the country was Alice Stebbins Wells, appointed on September 13, 1910. A social worker, Wells argued that she could better serve her clients if she had full police powers. She and her fellow female officers inspected dance halls, cafes, theaters, and other public amusement places to ferret out girls who were in danger of moral ruin, sending some home and bringing the incorrigible to the detention center.

Female "referees" were appointed to hear cases involving girls, and female probation officers were assigned to supervise them. The influx of new cases prompted the county to open custodial institutions for girls, including the El Retiro School, which was considered the latest in modern rehabilitative treatment.

When Odem and Schlossman evaluated the juvenile court records of delinquent girls who entered the Los Angeles Juvenile Court in 1920, they found that the majority were petitioned either for suspected sexual activity or for behavior that placed them at risk of sexual relations. Despite the limited seriousness of these charges, the majority of girls were detained prior to their trials, and while in Juvenile Hall, all were given a compulsory pelvic exam. Girls adjudged sexually delinquent on the basis of the exam were segregated from the merely incorrigible girls to prevent moral corruption. Those testing positive for venereal disease were confined in Juvenile Hall Hospital, usually for one to three months.

After trial, 29 percent of these female adolescents were committed to custodial institutions, a high price to pay for moral transgressions. While society was undergoing a sexual revolution, the juvenile court seemed wedded to a philosophy of controlling "immoral" young women, a policy that was to last more than thirty years.

Source: Mary Odem and Steven Schlossman, "Guardians of Virtue: The Juvenile Court and Female Delinquency in Early 20th-Century Los Angeles," *Crime and Delinquency* 37:186–203 (1991).

Chesney-Lind concluded that female adolescents are granted a much narrower range of acceptable behavior than male adolescents. Any sign of misbehavior in girls is seen as a substantial challenge to authority and to the viability of the sexual double standard.

Are Standards Changing?

More than twenty years after the Chesney-Lind research brought attention to the gender "double standard" in juvenile court, distinctions are still being made between male and female offenders. Girls are still more likely than boys to be petitioned to court and punished for the status offense of incorrigibility.[132] Girls are still disadvantaged if their behavior is viewed as morally incorrect by government officials. Girls who are held in contempt of court for failing to obey a judge's orders are much more likely than boys to be sentenced to incarceration in a secure detention facility, a state of affairs that "reflect the continuation of protectionist policies toward female status offenders."[133] This finding has been substantiated by

Several feminist scholars believe that girls are at risk when they enter the juvenile court. They argue that girls are not only the victims of injustice at home but also risk being victimized by agents of the juvenile justice system. Paternalistic attitudes and the sexual "double standard" increase the likelihood that girls will be referred to juvenile court for status-type offenses and, after adjudication, receive a disposition involving incarceration.

multiple studies showing that girls are much more likely than boys to be sanctioned for status offenses.[134]

Girls may still be subject to harsh punishments if they are considered dangerously immoral. Girls arrested on status offense charges are more likely than boys to have descriptions of their physical attractiveness placed in case files. There still appears to be an association between male standards of "beauty" and sexual behavior: judges, social workers, and other criminal justice professionals may look on attractive girls who engage in sexual behavior more harshly, punishing them while overlooking some of the same behaviors in less attractive girls. In some jurisdictions girls are still being incarcerated for noncriminal status offenses because their behavior does not measure up to (male) decision makers' concepts of proper female behavior.[135] Even though girls are still less likely to be arrested than boys, those who fail to measure up to male stereotypes of "proper" female behavior, such as girls with prior records, are more likely to be sanctioned than male offenders.[136]

Once in the system, females receive fewer benefits and services than their male counterparts. Institutionalized girls report receiving fewer privileges, less space, less equipment, fewer programs, and less treatment than institutionalized boys.[137] They resent the fact that boys have more educational, recreational, and occupational opportunities. Why do these differences persist?—because juvenile correctional authorities continue to subscribe to stereotyped beliefs about the needs of young girls that have little to do with reality.

Although these arguments are persuasive, some recent national data gathered for the federal government by the Pittsburgh-based National Center for Juvenile Justice show that there is little gender-based difference today in state processing of status offenders. Both girls and boys seem to have an equal chance of proceeding to formal adjudication and being sent to out-of-the-home placements for status offenses.[138] This suggests that the gender bias in some areas of the juvenile justice process may be in decline.

SUMMARY

The relationship between gender and delinquency has become a topic of considerable interest to criminologists and other experts interested in youth crimes. At one time, attention was directed solely at male offenders, and the rare female delinquent was considered an oddity. The nature and extent of female delinquent activities have changed, and girls are now engaging in more frequent and serious illegal activity. Consequently, interest in gender issues in delinquency has increased.

Sociologists and psychologists now recognize that there are distinct differences in attitudes, values, and behavior between boys and girls. Females process information differently from males and have different cognitive and physical strengths. These differences may, in part, explain gender differences in the delinquency rate.

Theories that seek to explain the cause of these gender differences fit into several major categories. Trait views are concerned with biological and psychological differences between the sexes. Early efforts by Cesare Lombroso and his followers place the blame for delinquency on physical differences between males and females. Girls who were delinquent had inherent masculine characteristics. Later, biosocial theorists viewed girls' psychological makeup, hormonal, and physical characteristics as key to their delinquent behavior.

Socialization has also been identified as a cause of delinquency. Males are socialized to be tough and aggressive, whereas females are instructed to be more passive and obedient. The adolescent female offender was portrayed as a troubled girl who lacked love at home and supportive peer relations. These theories treated female delinquents as sexual offenders whose criminal activities were linked to destructive relationships with men.

More recent views of gender and delinquency incorporate the changes brought about by the women's movement. It is argued that as the social and economic roles of women change so will their crime patterns. Although a number of research studies support this view, some theorists question its validity. The female crime rate has increased and female delinquency patterns now resemble those of male delinquency, but the gender gap has not narrowed after more than two decades. Hagan's power-control theory helps us understand why these differences exist and whether change may be coming.

The treatment girls receive by the juvenile justice system has also been the subject of debate. Originally, it was thought that police treated girls with chivalry and protected them from the stigma of a delinquency label. Contemporary criminologists charge, however, that girls are actually discriminated against by agents of the justice system.

KEY TERMS

gender-schema theory
gender identity
masculinity hypothesis
chivalry hypothesis

precocious sexuality
liberal feminism
radical feminists
Marxist feminists

power-control theory
paternalistic families
egalitarian families

INFOTRAC COLLEGE EDITION EXERCISES

The view of female criminality, once considered simply an aberration, has been subject recently to a great deal of study. The understanding of gender differences related to crimes committed has aided in our general understanding but has apparently done little to change our conception of the female offender. Although this gender bias may be in decline, female offenders still present a different problem for our criminal justice system.

Review articles from InfoTrac College Edition that pertain to delinquent female offenders. Summarize some of the problems facing the criminal justice system with regard to female offenders.

To search for information, use key words such as: *delinquent female offenders, female criminals,* and *female delinquents.*

QUESTIONS FOR DISCUSSION

1. Are girls delinquent for different reasons than boys? Do girls have a unique set of problems?
2. As sex roles become more homogenous, do you believe female delinquency will become identical to male delinquency in rate and type?
3. Does the sexual double standard still exist?

4. Are lower-class girls more strictly supervised than upper- and middle-class girls? Is control stratified across class lines?
5. Are girls the victims of unfairness at the hands of the justice system, or do they benefit from "chivalry"?

NOTES

1. Peter Connolly and Hazel Dodge, *The Ancient City* (London: Oxford University Press, 1998), pp. 32–44.
2. Cesare Lombroso, *The Female Offender* (New York: Appleton, 1920); W. I. Thomas, *The Unadjusted Girl* (New York: Harper & Row, 1923).
3. Cesare Lombroso and William Ferrero, *The Female Offender* (New York: Philosophical Library, 1895).
4. James Messerschmidt, *Masculinities and Crime: Critique and Reconceptualization of Theory* (Lanham, Md.: Rowman and Littlefield, 1993).
5. Paul Mazerolle, Robert Brame, Ray Paternoster, Alex Piquero, and Charles Dean, "Onset Age, Persistence, and Offending Versatility: Comparisons across Sex," paper presented at the annual Society of Criminology Meeting, San Diego, Calif., November 1997.
6. Kathleen Daly, "From Gender Ratios to Gendered Lives: Women's Gender in Crime and Criminological Theory," in Michael Tonry, ed., *The Handbook of Crime and Punishment* (New York: Oxford University Press, 1998).
7. Rita James Simon, *The Contemporary Woman and Crime* (Washington, D.C.: U.S. Government Printing Office, 1975).
8. Rolf Loeber and Dale Hay, "Key Issues in the Development of Aggression and Violence from Childhood to Early Adulthood," *Annual Review of Psychology* 48:371–410 (1997).
9. This section relies on Spencer Rathus, *Psychology in the New Millennium* (Fort Worth, Tex.: Harcourt, Brace College Pub-

lishers, 1996); see also, Darcy Miller, Catherine Trapani, Kathy Fejes-Mendoza, Carolyn Eggleston, and Donna Dwiggins, "Adolescent Female Offenders: Unique Considerations," *Adolescence* 30:429–35 (1995).
10. Allison Morris, *Women, Crime and Criminal Justice* (Oxford, England: Basil Blackwell, 1987).
11. Dennis Giever, "An Empirical Assessment of the Core Elements of Gottfredson and Hirschi's General Theory of Crime," paper presented at the American Society of Criminology Meeting, Boston, Mass., November 1995.
12. Loeber and Hay, "Key Issues in the Development of Aggression and Violence from Childhood to Early Adulthood," p. 378.
13. John Mirowsky and Catherine Ross, "Sex Differences in Distress: Real or Artifact?", *American Sociological Review* 60: 449–68 (1995).
14. Ibid., pp. 460–65.
15. For a review of this issue, see Anne Campbell, *Men, Women and Aggression* (New York: Basic Books, 1993).
16. Ann Beutel and Margaret Mooney Marini, "Gender and Values," *American Sociological Review* 60:436–48 (1995).
17. American Association of University Women, *Shortchanging Girls, Shortchanging America* (Washington, D.C.: American Association of University Women, 1991).
18. John Gibbs, Dennis Giever, and Jamie Martin, "Parental Management and Self-Control: An Empirical Test of Gottfredson

and Hirschi's General Theory," *Journal of Research in Crime and Delinquency* 35:40–70 (1998); Velmer Burton, Francis Cullen, T. David Evans, Leanne Fiftal Alarid, and R. Gregory Dunaway, "Gender, Self-Control, and Crime," *Journal of Research in Crime and Delinquency* 35:123–47 (1998).

19. David Rowe, Alexander Vazsonyi, and Daniel Flannery, "Sex Differences in Crime: Do Means and Within-Sex Variation Have Similar Causes?," *Journal of Research in Crime and Delinquency* 32:84–100 (1995).

20. Sandra Bem, *The Lenses of Gender* (New Haven: Yale University Press, 1993).

21. Walter DeKeseredy and Martin Schwartz, "Male Peer Support and Woman Abuse," *Sociological Spectrum* 13:393–413 (1993).

22. Daniel Mears, Matthew Ploeger, and Mark Warr, "Explaining the Gender Gap in Delinquency: Peer Influence and Moral Evaluations of Behavior," *Journal of Research in Crime and Delinquency* 35:251–66 (1998).

23. Messerschmidt, *Masculinities and Crime: Critique and Reconceptualization of Theory.*

24. D. J. Pepler and W. M. Craig, "A Peek Behind the Fence: Naturalistic Observations of Aggressive Children with Remote Audiovisual Recording," *Developmental Psychology* 31:548–53 (1995).

25. Stacey Nofziger, "Sex and Gender Identity: A Gendered Look at Delinquency," paper presented at the American Society of Criminology Meeting, Boston, Mass., November 1995 (rev. version, January 1996).

26. Federal Bureau of Investigation, *Crime in the United States, 1997* (Washington, D.C.: U.S. Government Printing Office, 1998), pp. 288–95.

27. George Calhoun, Janelle Jurgens, and Fengling Chen, "The Neophyte Female Delinquent: A Review of the Literature," *Adolescence* 28:461–71 (1993).

28. Anne Campbell and Steven Muncer, "Men and the Meaning of Violence," in John Archer, ed., *Male Violence* (London: Routledge, 1995), at p. 346.

29. FBI: *Crime in the United States, 1997,* p. 22.

30. Lombroso and Ferrero, *The Female Offender.*

31. Ibid., p. 122.

32. Ibid., pp. 51–52.

33. For a review, see Anne Campbell, *Girl Delinquents* (Oxford: Basic Blackwell, 1981), pp. 41–48.

34. Ibid., p. 151.

35. Ibid., pp. 150–52.

36. Cyril Burt, *The Young Delinquent* (New York: Appleton, 1925); see also, Warren Middleton, "Is There a Relation between Kleptomania and Female Periodicity in Neurotic Individuals?", *Psychology Clinic* (December 1933) pp. 232–47.

37. William Healy and Augusta Bronner, *Delinquents and Criminals, Their Making and Unmaking* (New York: Macmillan, 1926).

38. Otto Pollak, *The Criminality of Women* (Philadelphia: University of Pennsylvania Press, 1950).

39. Ibid., p. 158.

40. Ibid., p. 10.

41. Miriam Sealock and Sally Simpson, "Unraveling Bias in Arrest Decisions: The Role of Juvenile Offender Typescripts," *Justice Quarterly* 15:427–57 (1998); Christina Polsenberg and Kenneth Jackson, "Putting Race into Context: Race, Juvenile Justice Processing and Urbanization," paper presented at the American Society of Criminology Meeting, Boston, Mass., November 1995 (rev. version, January 1996); for a general review, see Carl Pope and William Feyerherm, "Minority Status and Juvenile Justice Processing (Part I)," *Criminal Justice Abstracts* 22:327–35 (1990); see also, Douglas Smith and Jody Klein, "Police Control of Interpersonal Disputes," *Social Problems* 31:468–81 (1984).

42. Sigmund Freud, *An Outline of Psychoanalysis,* trans. James Strachey (New York: Norton, 1949), p. 278.

43. Dorie Klein, "The Etiology of Female Crime: A Review of the Literature," in Freda Adler and Rita Simon, eds., *The Criminology of Deviant Women* (Boston: Houghton Mifflin, 1979), pp. 69–71.

44. Phyliss Chesler, *Women and Madness* (Garden City, N.Y.: Doubleday, 1972); Karen Horney, *Feminine Psychology* (New York: Norton, 1967).

45. Peter Blos, "Preoedipal Factors in the Etiology of Female Delinquency," *Psychoanalytic Studies of the Child* 12:229–42 (1957).

46. See, generally, Ralph Weisheit and Sue Mahan, *Women, Crime and Criminal Justice* (Cincinnati: Anderson Publishing, 1988).

47. Sheldon Glueck and Eleanor Glueck, *Five Hundred Delinquent Women* (New York: Knopf, 1934).

48. J. Cowie, V. Cowie, and E. Slater, *Delinquency in Girls* (London: Heinemann, 1968).

49. Anne Campbell, "On the Invisibility of the Female Delinquent Peer Group," *Women and Criminal Justice* 2:41–62 (1990).

50. Carolyn Smith, "Factors Associated with Early Sexual Activity among Urban Adolescents," *Social Work* 42:334–46 (1997).

51. For a review, see Christy Miller Buchanan, Jacquelynne Eccles, and Jill Becker, "Are Adolescents the Victims of Raging Hormones? Evidence for Activational Effects of Hormones on Moods and Behavior at Adolescence," *Psychological Bulletin* 111:63–107 (1992).

52. Avshalom Caspi, Donald Lyman, Terrie Moffitt, and Phil Silva, "Unraveling Girls' Delinquency: Biological, Dispositional, and Contextual Contributions to Adolescent Misbehavior," *Developmental Psychology* 29:283–89 (1993).

53. Eleanor Maccoby and Carol Jacklin, *The Psychology of Sex Differences* (Stanford, Calif.: Stanford University Press, 1974).

54. Alan Booth and D. Wayne Osgood, "The Influence of Testosterone on Deviance in Adulthood: Assessing and Explaining the Relationship," *Criminology* 31:93–118 (1993).

55. Walter Gove, "The Effect of Age and Gender on Deviant Behavior: A Biopsychosocial Perspective," in A. S. Rossi, ed., *Gender and the Life Course* (New York: Aldine, 1985), pp. 115–44.

56. Lee Ellis, "Evolutionary and Neurochemical Causes of Sex Differences in Victimizing Behavior: Toward a Unified Theory of Criminal Behavior and Social Stratification," *Social Science Information* 28:625–26 (1989).

57. D. H. Baucom, P. K. Besch, and S. Callahan, "Relationship between Testosterone Concentration, Sex Role Identity, and Personality among Females," *Journal of Personality and Social Psychology* 48:1218–26 (1985).

58. Lee Ellis, "Evidence of Neuroandrogenic Etiology of Sex Roles from a Combined Analysis of Human, Nonhuman Primate and Nonprimate Mammalian Studies," *Personality and Individual Differences* 7:519–52 (1986).

59. Diana Fishbein, "Selected Studies on the Biology of Antisocial Behavior," in John Conklin, ed., *New Perspectives in Criminology* (Needham Heights, Mass.: Allyn and Bacon, 1996), pp. 26–38.

60. Diana Fishbein, "The Psychobiology of Female Aggression," *Criminal Justice and Behavior* 19:99–126 (1992).

61. Spencer Rathus, *Psychology,* 3rd ed. (New York: Holt, Rinehart & Winston, 1987), p. 88.

62. See, generally, Katharina Dalton, *The Premenstrual Syndrome* (Springfield, Ill.: Charles C. Thomas, 1971).

63. Fishbein, "Selected Studies on the Biology of Antisocial Behavior."

64. Fishbein, "Selected Studies on the Biology of Antisocial Behavior"; Karen Paige, "Effects of Oral Contraceptives on Affective Fluctuations Associated with the Menstrual Cycle," *Psychosomatic Medicine* 33:515–37 (1971).

65. B. Harry and C. Balcer, "Menstruation and Crime: A Critical Review of the Literature from the Clinical Criminology Perspective," *Behavioral Sciences and the Law* 5:307–22 (1987).

66. Julie Horney, "Menstrual Cycles and Criminal Responsibility," *Law and Human Nature* 2:25–36 (1978).

67. Lee Ellis, "The Victimful-Victimless Crime Distinction and Seven Universal Demographic Correlates of Victimful Criminal Behavior," *Personality and Individual Differences* 9:525–48 (1988).

68. Horney, "Menstrual Cycles and Criminal Responsibility," p. 116.

69. Eleanor Maccoby and Carol Jacklin, *The Psychology of Sex Differences* (Stanford, Calif.: Stanford University Press, 1974).

70. Ellis, "Evolutionary and Neurochemical Causes of Sex Differences in Victimizing Behavior," pp. 605–36.

71. Ann Frodi, J. Maccauley, and P. R. Thome, "Are Women Always Less Aggressive than Men? A Review of the Experimental Literature," *Psychological Bulletin* 84:634–60 (1977).

72. Buchanan, Eccles, and Becker, "Are Adolescents the Victims of Raging Hormones?", p. 94.

73. Thomas, *The Unadjusted Girl*.

74. Ibid., p. 109.

75. David Farrington, "Juvenile Delinquency," in John Coleman, ed., *The School Years* (London: Routledge, 1992), p. 133.

76. Ibid.

77. Ruth Morris, "Female Delinquents and Relational Problems," *Social Forces* 43:82–89 (1964).

78. Cowie, Cowie, and Slater, *Delinquency in Girls,* p. 27.

79. Gisela Konopka, *The Adolescent Girl in Conflict* (Englewood Cliffs, N.J.: Prentice-Hall, 1966).

80. Ibid., p. 40.

81. Peter Kratcoski and Lucille Kratcoski, *Juvenile Delinquency* (Englewood Cliffs, N.J.: Prentice-Hall, 1979), pp. 146–47.

82. Konopka, *The Adolescent Girl in Conflict,* p. 50.

83. Morris, "Female Delinquency and Relational Problems."

84. Clyde Vedder and Dora Somerville, *The Delinquent Girl* (Springfield, Ill.: Charles C. Thomas, 1970).

85. Sheldon Glueck and Eleanor Glueck, *Unraveling Juvenile Delinquency* (Cambridge, Mass.: Harvard University Press, 1950).

86. Ibid., pp. 281–82.

87. Glueck and Glueck, *Five Hundred Delinquent Women.*

88. Ibid., p. 90.

89. Ames Robey, Richard Rosenwal, John Small, and Ruth Lee, "The Runaway Girl: A Reaction to Family Stress," *American Journal of Orthopsychiatry* 34:763–67 (1964).

90. William Wattenberg and Frank Saunders, "Sex Differences among Juvenile Court Offenders," *Sociology and Social Research* 39:24–31 (1954).

91. Don Gibbons and Manzer Griswold, "Sex Differences among Juvenile Court Referrals," *Sociology and Social Research* 42: 106–10 (1957).

92. Gordon Barker and William Adams, "Comparison of the Delinquencies of Boys and Girls," *Journal of Criminal Law, Criminology, and Police Science* 53:470–75 (1962).

93. George Calhoun, Janelle Jurgens, and Fengling Chen, " The Neophyte Female Delinquent: A Review of the Literature," *Adolescence* 28:461–71 (1993).

94. Joanne Belknap, Kristi Holsinger, and Melissa Dunn, "Understanding Incarcerated Girls: The Results of a Focus Group Study," *Prison Journal* 77:381–405 (1997).

95. Kimberly Barletto, "Who's at Risk: Delinquent Trajectories of Children with Attention and Conduct Problems," paper presented at the American Society of Criminology Meeting, San Diego, Calif., 1997; Veronica Herrera, "Equals in Risk? The Differential Impact of Family Violence on Male and Female Delinquency," paper presented at the annual Society of Criminology Meeting, San Diego, Calif., November 1997.

96. Meda Chesney-Lind, "Girls' Crime and Women's Place: Toward a Feminist Model of Female Delinquency," paper presented at the American Society of Criminology Meeting, Montreal, November 1987.

97. Ibid., p. 20.

98. Joan Moore, *Going Down to the Barrio: Homeboys and Homegirls in Change* (Philadelphia: Temple University Press, 1991), p. 93.

99. Ibid., p. 101.

100. D. Wayne Osgood, Janet Wilson, Patrick O'Malley, Jerald Bachman, and Lloyd Johnston, "Routine Activities and Individual Deviant Behaviors," *American Sociological Review* 61:635–55 (1996).

101. Deborah Babcox and Madeline Belken, *Liberation: NOW* (New York: Dell, 1971).

102. Simon, *The Contemporary Woman and Crime;* Freda Adler, *Sisters in Crime* (New York: McGraw-Hill, 1975).

103. Adler, *Sisters in Crime.*

104. Ibid., p. 104.

105. Ibid., pp. 10–11.

106. Rita James Simon, "Women and Crime Revisited," *Social Science Quarterly* 56:658–63 (1976).

107. Ibid., pp. 660–61.

108. Roy Austin, "Women's Liberation and Increase in Minor, Major, and Occupational Offenses," *Criminology* 20:407–30 (1982).

109. Michael Hindelang, "Age, Sex, and the Versatility of Delinquency Involvements," *Social Forces* 14:525–34 (1971).

110. Martin Gold, *Delinquent Behavior in an American City* (Pacific Grove, Calif.: Brooks/Cole, 1970), p. 118; John Clark and Edward Haurek, "Age and Sex Roles of Adolescents and Their Involvement in Misconduct: A Reappraisal," *Sociology and Social Research* 50:495–508 (1966); Nancy Wise, "Juvenile Delinquency in Middle-Class Girls," in E. Vaz, ed., *Middle Class Delinquency* (New York: Harper & Row, 1967), pp. 179–88; Gary Jensen and Raymond Eve, "Sex Differences in Delinquency: An Examination of Popular Sociological Explanations," *Criminology* 13:427–48 (1976).

111. Beth Bjerregaard and Carolyn Smith, "Gender Differences in Gang Participation and Delinquency," *Journal of Quantitative Criminology* 9:329–50 (1993).

112. Henry Brownstein, Barry Spunt, Susan Crimmins, and Sandra Langley, "Women Who Kill in Drug Market Situations," *Justice Quarterly* 12:472–98 (1995).

113. Darrell Steffensmeier and Renee Hoffman Steffensmeier, "Trends in Female Delinquency," *Criminology* 18:62–85 (1980); see also, idem, "Crime and the Contemporary Woman: An Analysis of Changing Levels of Female Property Crime, 1960–1975," *Social Forces* 57:566–84 (1978); Darrell Steffensmeier and Michael Cobb, "Sex Differences in Urban Arrest Patterns, 1934–1979," *Social Problems* 29:37–49 (1981).

114. Darrell Steffensmeier, "National Trends in Female Arrests, 1960–1990: Assessment and Recommendations for Research," *Journal of Quantitative Criminology* 9:411–37 (1993).

115. Carol Smart, "The New Female Offender: Reality or Myth?", *British Journal of Criminology* 19:50–59 (1979).

116. Roy Austin, "Recent Trends in Official Male and Female Crime Rates: The Convergence Controversy," *Journal of Criminal Justice* 21:447–66 (1993).

117. Beth Bjerregaard and Carolyn Smith, "Gender Differences in Gang Participation, Delinquency, and Substance Abuse," *Journal of Quantitative Criminology* 9:329–55 (1993).

118. Austin, "Recent Trends in Official Male and Female Crime Rates," p. 464.

119. Julia Schwendinger and Herman Schwendinger, *Rape and Inequality* (Beverly Hills, Calif.: Sage, 1983).

120. For a review of feminist theory, see Sally Simpson, "Feminist Theory, Crime and Justice," *Criminology* 27:605–32 (1989).

121. Ibid., p. 611.

122. Messerschmidt, *Masculinities and Crime: Critique and Reconceptualization of Theory.*

123. Center for Research on Women, *Secrets in Public: Sexual Harassment in Our Schools* (Wellesley, Mass.: Wellesley College, 1993).

124. Belknap, Holsinger, and Dunn, "Understanding Incarcerated Girls: The Results of a Focus Group Study."

125. Kathleen Daly and Meda Chesney-Lind, "Feminism and Criminology," *Justice Quarterly* 5:497–538 (1988).

126. Jane Siegel and Linda Meyer Williams, "Aggressive Behavior among Women Sexually Abused as Children," paper presented

at the American Society of Criminology Meeting, Phoenix, Az., 1993 (rev. version).

127. James Messerschmidt, *Capitalism, Patriarchy and Crime* (Totowa, N.J.: Rowman and Littlefield, 1986); for a critique of this work, see Herman Schwendinger and Julia Schwendinger, "The World According to James Messerschmidt," *Social Justice* 15:123–45 (1988).

128. John Hagan, A. R. Gillis, and John Simpson, "The Class Structure and Delinquency: Toward a Power-Control Theory of Common Delinquent Behavior," *American Journal of Sociology* 90:1151–78 (1985); John Hagan, John Simpson, and A. R. Gillis, "Class in the Household: A Power-Control Theory of Gender and Delinquency," *American Journal of Sociology* 92:788–816 (1987).

129. Gary Jensen and Kevin Thompson, "What's Class Got to Do with It? A Further Examination of Power-Control Theory," *American Journal of Sociology* 95:1009–23 (1990); Kevin Thompson, "Gender and Adolescent Drinking Problems: The Effects of Occupational Structure," *Social Problems* 36:30–44 (1989); for some critical research, see Simon Singer and Murray Levine, "Power-Control Theory, Gender and Delinquency: A Partial Replication with Additional Evidence on the Effects of Peers," *Criminology* 26:627–48 (1988).

130. John Hagan, A. R. Gillis, and John Simpson, "Clarifying and Extending Power-Control Theory," *American Journal of Sociology* 95:1024–37 (1990).

131. Meda Chesney-Lind, "Judicial Enforcement of the Female Sex Role: The Family Court and the Female Delinquent," *Issues in Criminology* 8:51–59 (1973).

132. Donna Bishop and Charles Frazier, "Gender Bias in Juvenile Justice Processing: Implications of the JJDP Act," *Journal of Criminal Law and Criminology* 82:1162–86 (1992).

133. Ibid., p. 1186.

134. Jean Rhodes and Karla Fischer, "Spanning the Gender Gap: Gender Differences in Delinquency among Inner City Adolescents," *Adolescence* 28:880–89 (1993).

135. Jill Leslie Rosenbaum and Meda Chesney-Lind, "Appearance and Delinquency: A Research Note," *Crime and Delinquency* 40:250–61 (1994).

136. Sealock and Simpson, "Unraveling Bias in Arrest Decisions: The Role of Juvenile Offender Typescripts."

137. Belknap, Holsinger, and Dunn, "Understanding Incarcerated Girls: The Results of a Focus Group Study."

138. General Accounting Office, *Juvenile Justice: Minimal Gender Bias Occurred in Processing Noncriminal Juveniles* (Gaithersburg, Md.: General Accounting Office, 1995).

Chapter Eight

The Family and Delinquency: Makeup, Influence, and Abuse

arie Noe was considered by her Philadelphia neighbors to be a martyr who had stoically endured the cruel fate of losing a staggering ten sons and daughters to early death. *Life* magazine featured the woman as a tragic figure in 1963 after six of her children had died. The first baby was stillborn, and the second child died a few hours after birth. The other eight infants went home healthy, but died soon after. It was a fate almost too cruel to be believed.[1] But prosecutors were suspicious because they know that the unexplained deaths of babies, especially when their mothers are poorly educated, may sometimes be the result of abuse.[2] Still, it was surprising when on August 7, 1998, Mrs. Noe was indicted for murder and called by prosecutors "as much a mass murderer as Ted Bundy."

When Marie Noe was arraigned in Philadelphia's Common Pleas by Judge Carolyn Engel Temin, prosecutors asked that the court show her "no mercy" after reanalysis of the children's autopsies revealed that their deaths were caused by suffocation and not sudden infant death syndrome (SIDS), as first thought.[3] Mrs. Noe's crimes were undetected, the authorities surmised, because medical authorities in the 1950s and 1960s were reluctant to make accusations against parents in cases of crib death. The medical community is now willing to acknowledge that some SIDS cases may be infanticide, the murder of infants.

The Noe case is certainly an extreme example of child abuse. Although such cases are rare, mistreatment of a child can have a profound effect later in life. Children growing up in households characterized by abuse, conflict, and tension, whose parents are absent or separated, and who lack familial love and support will be the ones most likely to engage in violence and delinquency.[4] Conversely, a supportive family life can be very beneficial to children in any social environment or group.

The family is the key social institution that provides the nurturant socialization of young children.[5] Interactions between parents, children, and their siblings provide opportunities for children to acquire or inhibit antisocial behavior patterns.[6] Even children living in so-called high-crime areas are better able to re-

Marie Noe after her arrest on August 7, 1998. Noe is believed to have murdered six of her own children.

nuclear family
A family unit composed of parents and their children; this smaller family structure is subject to great stress due to the intense, close contact between parents and children.

sist the temptation of the streets if they receive fair discipline, care, and support from parents who provide them with strong, positive role models.[7] The relationship between family life and delinquency is not unique to U.S. culture; cross-national data support a significant association between family variables and delinquency.[8]

The assumed relationship between delinquency and family life is critical today because the traditional American family is rapidly changing. Extended families, once common because of the economic necessity of sharing housing with many family members, are now for the most part anachronisms. In their place is the isolated **nuclear family,** described as a "dangerous hot-house of emotions" because of the intensely close contact between parents and children; in these families problems are unrelieved by contact with other kin living nearby.[9]

The nuclear family is showing signs of breakdown. Much of the parental responsibility for child rearing is delegated to baby-sitters, television, and day-care providers. Despite these changes, some families are able to adapt and continue functioning as healthy and caring units, producing well-adjusted children. Others have crumbled under the stress, severely damaging the present and the future of their children.[10] This is particularly true when child abuse and neglect become part of family life.

Because these domestic issues are so critical for understanding juvenile delinquency, this entire chapter is devoted to an analysis of the family's role as a delinquency producing or inhibiting social institution. In this chapter we first cover the changing face of the American family. We then review how family structure and function influence delinquent behavior. The relationship between child abuse, neglect, and delinquency is covered in some depth. Finally, programs designed to improve family functioning are briefly reviewed.

The Changing American Family

The concept of the American family is changing. The so-called traditional family, with a male breadwinner and a female who cares for the home and the children, is a thing of the past. No longer can this paternalistic family structure, as depicted in 1960s television sitcoms like *Father Knows Best* and *Leave It to Beaver*, be considered the norm. Changing sex roles have created a family where women play a much greater role in the economic process than ever before; this social evolution has created a more egalitarian family structure in which both spouses contribute to the family's economic and social well-being. More than 70 percent of all mothers of schoolage children are now employed, up from 50 percent in 1970 and 40 percent in 1960.[11] The changing economic structure may be reflected in shifting sex roles. Fathers are now spending more time with their children on workdays than they did twenty years ago (2.3 hours versus 1.8), and women are spending somewhat less time (3.3 hours versus 3.0).[12] On their days off, both working men and women spend about an hour more with their children than they did twenty years ago, with women devoting about eight hours, and men six. So, although the time spent with children may be less than is desirable, it has actually increased over the past twenty years.

Family Makeup

The very makeup and definition of the family are undergoing change. Approximately 50 percent of all new marriages end in divorce. The divorce rate is now about one for every two new marriages. Children of divorce often feel "caught" between their parents, especially in families marked by high levels of hostility and low levels of cooperation. Feeling caught or trapped is related to adjustment problems and, later, to deviant behavior.[13] Children of divorce are more likely to undergo marital breakup as adults, creating a cycle of family dissolution.[14]

People are waiting longer to marry and are having fewer children. Single-parent households have become common.[15] In 1970, 12 percent of children lived with one parent. Today that number is about 30 percent, and at least half of all children will live part of their childhood with one parent only. More single women than ever are deciding to keep and raise their children; about 30 percent of all births are to unmarried women. Although the teen birth rate has been declining, more than five hundred thousand babies are born to teenaged mothers every year, about two hundred thousand to girls under age 18.

Child Care

Charged with caring for children is a day-care system whose workers are often paid minimum wage. Of special concern are the hundreds of thousands of "family day-care homes" in which a single provider takes care of three to nine children. Several states do not license or monitor these small private providers. Even in those states that do mandate registration and inspection of day-care providers, it is estimated that 90 percent or more of the facilities operate "underground." It is not uncommon for one adult to care for eight infants, an impossible task regardless of training or concern; the development of many children is being compromised in day care.[16] The average cost for child care is about $4,000 per child each year—and it is much higher for families in metropolitan areas. With such a high price tag, children from working poor families are most likely to suffer from inadequate child care programs; these children often spend time in makeshift, temporary arrangements that let their parents work but that lack the stimulating environment children need to thrive.[17] About three and a half million children under age 13 spend some time at home alone each week while their parents are at work.

Economic Stress

The American family is also undergoing economic stress. The vast majority of indigent families live in substandard housing without adequate health care, nutrition, or child care. Those whose incomes place them above the poverty line are deprived of government assistance that might help their children develop into productive adults. Recent political trends suggest that the social "safety net" is under attack, and poor families can expect less government aid in the coming years.

Will this economic pressure be reduced in the future? The baby boom generation is aging, and the number of senior citizens is on the rise. As people retire, there will be fewer workers to cover the costs of Social Security, medical care, and nursing home care. These costs will put greater economic stress on already burdened American families. Voter sentiment has an impact on the allocation of public funds, and there is concern that an older generation, worried about health care costs, may be reluctant to spend tax dollars on at-risk kids.

The Effects of Child Neglect and Abuse

The Marie Noe case may be extreme, but neglect and abuse of children are widespread and serious problems in the United States. Each year one million children or more are maltreated in a variety of ways, ranging from gross neglect and starvation to overt physical and mental cruelty.[18] Juvenile courts throughout the nation annually hear approximately half a million child neglect and abuse cases. As child abuse experts Richard Gelles and Murray Straus put it:

> Parent-to-child violence is so common and so widely approved that one needs few case studies to make the point. In general, the large majority of Americans believes that good parenting requires some physical punishment. . . . Among the thousands of people we have interviewed, it was the absence of physical punishment that was thought to be deviant, not the hitting of children.[19]

Children who are victims of abuse suffer physical and psychological damage, both when the abuse takes place and later in life. Evidence supports a link between the abuse of young children and their subsequent violent and aggressive behavior as juvenile delinquents and status offenders.

The Family's Influence on Delinquency

Most experts, though not all, believe a destructive and disturbed home environment can have such a significant impact on delinquency because

DO PARENTS CONTROL BEHAVIOR?

Who plays a greater role in shaping the long-term behavior of children: peers or parents? Although most experts might question her opinions, psychologist Judith Rich Harris's highly controversial book, *The Nature Assumption,* made headlines around the nation (including the cover of *Newsweek*) when it appeared in 1998 because it challenged the long-cherished belief that parents play an important, if not the most important, role in a child's upbringing. Instead of family influence, Harris claims that genetics and total social environment determine, to a large extent, how a child turns out. The child's innate temperament is influenced primarily by peer relations rather than by parents. Children's interpersonal relations ultimately determine the kind of people they will be when they mature.

Harris reasons that parenting skills may be irrelevant to future success because researchers have been unable to find any child-raising method or style that predicts children's accomplishments or failures once they mature and leave home. Besides, most parents don't have a single child-rearing style, and they may impose an individual style on the family. For example, some parents are more permissive with their mild-mannered children and more strict and punitive with those who are temperamental or defiant. Even siblings raised in the same family under relatively similar conditions can turn out quite differently. Moreover, there is evidence that the way children are raised has little or no influence on personality. According to Harris, children sent to day care are quite similar to those who remain at home; having a working mother seems to have little long-term effect. Family structure also does not seem to matter: adults growing up in single-parent homes are as likely to be successful as those who were raised in two-parent households.

Harris also questions the abuse–delinquency link. Despite the finding by some experts that abused children are more likely to engage in antisocial behaviors, the majority of children growing up in troubled or abusive households are noncriminal and do not suffer lasting psychological damage. The literature also recognizes that many children who are raised in nurturing homes by caring parents take drugs, join gangs, and are continually involved in antisocial behavior.

Harris finds little or no association between the personality traits of adopted children and their adoptive parents. Nor is there much of a confluence between the personality of adopted children and other siblings in the home, as might be expected if "home environment" had a strong influence on personality and development. One reason is that parents' behavior affects children mainly when they are with their parents. When they are alone or playing with other children, parental influence wanes.

If parenting has little direct influence on children's long-term development, what does? To Harris, genetics plays the most important role in behavior, but genes alone do not determine behavior. The child's total social environment is the other great shaper of behav-

the family is the primary unit in which children learn the values, attitudes, and processes that guide their actions throughout their lives. (See the Focus on Delinquency entitled "Do Parents Control Behavior?" for more on this topic.)

Four broad categories of family dysfunction seem to promote delinquent behavior: families disrupted by spousal conflict or breakup, families involved in interpersonal conflict, negligent parents who are not attuned to their children's behavior and emotional problems (in this context are included quality factors such as attentiveness, nurturing, open communication, and effective supervision), and families that contain deviant parents who may transmit their behavior to their children[20] (see Figure 8.1). Each of these factors may also interact to intensify individual effects; for example, drug abusing deviant parents may be more likely to engage in family conflict, child neglect, and marital breakup. We now turn to the specific types of family problems that have been linked to delinquent behavior.

ior. Children may act one way at home but may be totally different at school or with their peers. Some who are mild mannered around the house are "hell-raisers" in the school yard; others may bully their siblings but remain docile with friends. Children may conform to parental expectations at home, but they leave these behaviors behind in their own social environment.

Outside the home the need to conform to peer group values replaces parental influence as the key determinant of behavior. Children know peers are quick to scapegoat anyone who is different—anyone who has different interests, clothes, or mannerisms. Watch what happens when a boy tells a group of thirteen-year-old peers that he loves opera and ballet and not baseball or football. Children can be cruel and abusive to peers who are different, and survival becomes a matter of conforming. Children develop their own culture with unique traditions, words, rules, and activities that often defy parental and adult values. What parent encourages their children to pierce their body or get a tattoo? Parents encourage their children to do the things that will make them successful adults, but youngsters are more concerned with becoming successful children!—and that often means rejecting the role models their parents so admire. Some social values (for example, honesty and loyalty) are shared by parents and their children, but when values clash, the peer group wins out.

There are exceptions to this pattern. Harris concedes that some children are square pegs who follow the beat of their own drum. Others have special skills or an especially close bond to their parents that enables them to resist peer pressure. But as a general rule, children are more oriented to their peers than to their parents.

Those who question Harris's conclusions point out that her reasoning implies that many favorite social programs are doomed to failure. School antidrug programs are geared to mainstream parental values. If peer groups disparage these values, children are unlikely to be receptive to the programs that promote them. *The Nature Assumption* also contradicts the extensive literature that concludes that parenting matters and that improving the quality of parent–child relationships can have a significant impact on delinquency. By implication, Harris's theory absolves from blame those parents who abuse or neglect their children. If parents are close to their children, Harris claims, it should be because they want to be companions and friends and not because it will help their life chances. Harris's book is proof that the age-old debate on nature versus nurture is far from resolved. Despite the attention Harris's ideas have received, most research on parenting continues to assert the significance of the parent–child bond.

Source: Judith Rich Harris, *The Nurture Assumption, Why Children Turn Out the Way They Do* (New York: The Free Press, 1998).

Family Breakup: Broken Homes

broken home
Home in which one or both parents is absent due to divorce or separation; children in such an environment may be prone to antisocial behavior.

One of the most enduring controversies in the study of juvenile delinquency is the relationship between a parent being absent from the home and the onset of delinquent behavior. Research indicates that parents whose marriage is secure, who maintain communications and avoid conflict, also produce children who are secure and independent.[21] In contrast, children growing up in homes with one or both parents absent due to divorce or separation may be prone to antisocial behavior.

A number of prominent delinquency experts have contended that a **broken home** is a strong determinant of a child's law-violating behavior. The connection seems self-evident because a child is first socialized at home and from the beginning

FIGURE 8.1

Family Influences on Behavior

Each of these four factors
has been linked to antisocial
behavior and delinquency.
Interaction between these factors may escalate delinquent
activity.

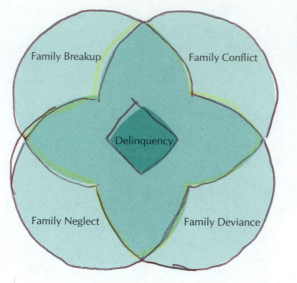

blended families
Nuclear families that are the
product of divorce and remarriage; blending one parent
from each of two families and
their combined children into
one family unit.

learns behaviors, values, and beliefs from parents. Any disjunction in an orderly family structure should have a negative impact on the child's life.

The question of the suspected broken home–delinquency relationship is now especially important because, if current trends continue, less than half of all children born today will live continuously with their own mother and father throughout childhood. And because stepfamilies or so-called **blended families** are less stable than families consisting of two biological parents, an increasing number of children will experience family breakup two or even three times during childhood.[22]

A number of clinical studies indicate that children who have experienced family breakup are more likely to demonstrate behavior problems, inappropriate conduct, and hyperactivity when compared to children in intact families.[23] Family breakup is often associated with discord, conflict, hostility, and aggression; children of divorce are suspected of having greater autonomy, lax supervision, weakened attachment, and greater susceptibility to peer pressure.[24] However, despite the strong hypothetical case linking broken homes to delinquency, the bulk of empirical research on the matter has been inconclusive.

Broken Home Research The relationship between broken homes and delinquency was established in early research, which suggested that a significant association existed between parental absence and youthful misconduct.[25] Other efforts showed that parental absence seemed to affect girls, white youths, and the affluent more than it did males, minorities, and the indigent.[26] But the link was clear: children growing up in broken homes were much more likely to fall prey to delinquency than those who lived in two-parent households.

The early studies that established the link between broken homes and delinquency used the records of police, courts, and correctional institutions.[27] This research may be tainted by sampling bias. Youths from broken homes may get arrested, petitioned to juvenile court, and institutionalized more often than youths from intact families, but this does not necessarily mean they actually engage in more frequent and serious delinquent behavior. Official statistics may reflect the fact that agents of the justice system treat children from disrupted households more severely because they cannot call on parents for support. The *parens patriae* philosophy of the juvenile courts calls for official intervention when parental supervision is considered inadequate.[28]

Numerous subsequent studies, using both official and self-report data, failed to establish any clear-cut relationship between broken homes and delinquent behavior.[29] Boys and girls from intact families seem as likely to self-report delinquency as those whose parents are divorced or separated. Children from broken homes are still more likely to show up in the official statistics. Researchers concluded that the absence of parents has a greater effect on agents of the justice system than it does on the behavior of children.[30]

Broken Homes Reconsidered   Although there is still debate over the true nature of the relationship between a broken home and delinquency, a number of recent studies have found that family breakup does have a direct influence on adolescent misbehavior. For example, family structure has been linked to rebellious acts or status offenses such as running away and truancy.[31] This association is illustrated with data obtained from a national study of more than twenty-two thousand adolescents who were questioned about their use of illegal substances.[32] Table 8.1 gives the ratios for substance abuse for children living in two-parent families and those living in other types of family structure. As the table shows, children living with their mothers only are almost twice as likely to use marijuana as those living with both parents. Those in the "other parental" category—father and stepmother, mother and nonrelative, and father only—are almost three times as likely to abuse substances.

Similarly, an ongoing research project being conducted by sociologist Sara McLanahan has examined the effect of parental absence on child development using several large national data sets. McLanahan finds that children who grow up apart from their biological fathers typically do less well than children who grow up with both biological parents. They are less likely to finish high school and attend college, less likely to find and keep a steady job, and more likely to become teen mothers. Although most children who grow up with a single parent do quite well, differences between children in one- and two-parent families are significant, and there is fairly good evidence that father absence per se is responsible for at least some significant social problems.[33]

Attachment to One Parent   Even if a broken home–delinquency link could be identified, it is possible that children who are strongly attached to a single parent might be insulated from delinquency. Some experts have argued that caregivers in

Table 8.1

LIKELIHOOD OF USING ALCOHOL OR OTHER DRUGS BASED ON FAMILY STRUCTURE

Family Structure	Ratio of Likelihood of Substance Use (Comparison Is to Adolescents Living with Two Parents)			
	Alcohol Use	Cigarette Use	Marijuana Use	Any Illicit Drug Use
Mother + stepfather	1.5:1	1.8:1	1.5:1	1.6:1
Mother only	1.7	1.7	1.9	1.6
Mother + other relative	1.5	1.6	2.0	1.7
Other parental	2.1	2.5	2.9	2.4
Other	1.8	2.0	2.4	2.4

Source: Robert Johnson, John Hoffman, and Dean Gerstein, *The Relationship between Family Structure and Adolescent Substance Abuse* (Washington, D.C.: Office of Applied Studies, Substance Abuse and Mental Health Services Administration, 1996). Prepared by the Center for Substance Abuse Research, 1997.

Note: "Other parental" includes Father + stepmother, Mother + nonrelative, and Father only arrangements. "Other" includes Other relative only and Spouse present arrangements. All data are from 1991–1993 NHSDA data, are adjusted for age, race/ethnicity, and family income, and are statistically significant at the .05 level. N=22,237.

single-parent households who maintain high levels of supervision help reduce the likelihood that their children will have police contacts.[34]

However, there are also those who suggest that a single parent, no matter how competent, cannot make up for the absence of a second parent. Even if single mothers (or fathers) could possibly make up for the loss of a second parent, it is simply too difficult to do so, and the chances of failure are great.[35] Single parents may find it difficult to provide adequate supervision. It is therefore not surprising, they claim, that children who are strongly attached to two parents have a lower probability of self-reporting delinquency than those attached to a single parent. Similarly, children who live in single parent homes and who are strongly attached to the custodial parent have a greater chance of committing delinquent acts than children living in intact homes who are strongly attached to both parents.[36] Such studies provide further support for a link between family structure and the potential for delinquent behaviors.

Educational Encouragement   The McLanahan research found that children living in single-parent homes face a significantly higher risk of becoming school dropouts; dropping out is a factor linked to delinquency (see Chapter 10). Living without a father increases the risk of dropping out of school by 150 percent among white children. Father absence has less impact on minority youths, but it still increases the school failure risk among African Americans and Hispanics by 75 percent and 96 percent, respectively. White students are generally less likely to drop out than minorities, but white children from one-parent households are significantly more likely to drop out than blacks from two-parent homes, and they are nearly as likely to experience school failure as blacks from similarly disrupted families.[37] A number of other indicators also support the detrimental effects of father absence. Students from two-parent families have higher grade point averages than students from one-parent families. They also have higher test scores, higher college expectations, and better school attendance records.

One reason is that children who live with single parents receive less encouragement and less help with schoolwork.[38] Children in two-parent households are more likely to want to go on to college than children in single-parent homes.[39] Poor school achievement and limited educational aspirations have been associated with delinquent behavior. Single parents who become involved in their children's education may counteract this effect and help improve their children's school achievement.

Economic Factors   The relationship between broken homes and delinquency may also be mediated by economic factors. The social and economic conditions present in disorganized areas—poverty, unemployment, and alienation—may be the cause of both delinquent behaviors and marital breakup.[40] Divorce and separation often result in the acceleration of economic hardship. White single mothers find that their incomes decline about 30 percent, to an average of $13,500, after divorce; nonwhite single mothers average $9,000 annually. Many divorced mothers are forced to move to cheaper residences located in deteriorated, disorganized neighborhoods, which places children at risk of delinquency.

Family Conflict

intrafamily conflict
An environment of discord and conflict within the family; children who grow up in dysfunctional homes often exhibit delinquent behaviors, having learned at a young age that aggression pays off.

Not all unhappy marriages end in divorce; some continue in an atmosphere of discord and conflict. **Intrafamily conflict** is an all too common experience in many American families.[41] The link between parental conflict and delinquency was established almost forty years ago when pioneering research by F. Ivan Nye found that a child's perception of his or her parents' marital happiness was a significant predictor of self-reported delinquency.[42]

Contemporary studies have also found that children who grow up in maladapted homes and who witness discord or violence later exhibit patterns of emotional disturbance, behavior problems, and social conflict.[43] There seems to be little difference between the behavior patterns of children who merely *witness* intrafamily violence and those who are its *victims*.[44] In fact, some research efforts show that observing the abuse of a parent (mother) is actually a more significant determinant of future delinquency than being the target of child abuse.[45]

Research efforts have consistently supported the relationship between family conflict, hostility, low warmth and affection, and delinquency.[46] Adolescents who are incarcerated report growing up in dysfunctional homes, some in what can be described as an "animal-like environment."[47] Parents of beyond control youngsters have been found to be inconsistent rule-setters, to be less likely to praise, encourage, and show interest in their children, and to display high levels of hostile detachment.[48] To avoid escalation of a child's aggression, these parents may give in to their children's demands rather than risk a confrontation or to reduce their own discomfort. These children learn that aggression pays off.[49]

Although damaged parent–child relationships are generally associated with delinquency, it is difficult to assess the causal relationship. It is often assumed that preexisting family problems cause delinquency, but it may also be true that children who act out put enormous stress on a family. When parents are besieged by highly challenging adolescents, they may feel overwhelmed and shut their child out of their lives. Adolescent misbehavior may be a precursor of family conflict; dissension and strife lead to more adolescent misconduct, producing an endless cycle of family stress and delinquency.[50]

Family Conflict versus Broken Homes   Which is worse, growing up in a home marked by extreme conflict or growing up in a broken home? Should parents stay together "for the sake of the children"? Research shows that children in both broken homes and high-conflict intact homes were considerably worse off than children in low-conflict, intact families.[51] However, children in high-conflict intact families appear to exhibit lower levels of adjustment and well-being than children in families where the parents had divorced; family conflict may have a more damaging effect on children than divorce. Some other important findings on family structure and delinquency are set out in Table 8.2. Divorce is harmful, but family conflict may have a more negative impact on children than family separation.

Table 8.2

THE FAMILY STRUCTURE–DELINQUENCY LINK

- Children growing up in families disrupted by parental death are better adjusted than children of divorce. Parental absence is not a per se cause of antisocial behavior.

- Remarriage did not mitigate the effects of divorce on youth: children living with a stepparent exhibit (a) as many problems as youths in divorce situations and (b) considerably more problems than do children living with both biological parents.

- Continued contact with the noncustodial parent has little effect on a child's well-being.

- Evidence that the behavior of children of divorce improves over time is inconclusive.

- Postdivorce conflict between parents is related to child maladjustment.

Source: Paul Amato and Bruce Keith, "Parental Divorce and the Well-Being of Children: A Meta-Analysis," *Psychological Bulletin* 110:26–46 (1991).

The Quality of Parent–Child Relations

Many child development experts believe children need a warm, close, supportive relationship with their parents.[52] Close relations with family are important throughout childhood and until late adolescence when the influence of peer group relations is heightened.

A number of independent research studies support the link between the quality of family life and delinquency. Children who feel inhibited with their parents and therefore refuse to discuss important issues with them are more likely to engage in deviant activities and status offenses. Poor child–parent communications have been related to dysfunctional activities such as running away, and in all too many instances these children enter the ranks of homeless street youths who get involved in theft and prostitution to survive.[53] In contrast, even those children who appear to be at risk are better able to resist involvement in delinquent activity when they report a strong attachment to their parents.[54] The importance of close relations with the family may diminish over time as children reach their late adolescence and develop stronger peer group relations, but most experts believe family influence on behavior remains considerable throughout the life span.[55]

Discipline   Studies using both self-report and official samples show that the parents of delinquent youths tend to be inconsistent disciplinarians, either overly harsh

The effects of a supportive family life can be very beneficial to children in any social environment or group. Even those children living in so-called high-crime areas are better able to resist the temptation of the streets if they receive fair discipline, care, and support from parents who provide them with strong, positive role models.

or extremely lenient in their disciplinary practices.[56] But what conclusions can we draw from this observation?

The link between discipline and deviant behavior is still uncertain. Attitudes toward physical discipline have changed little during the past twenty-five years, and most Americans still support the use of corporal punishment to discipline children. The use of physical punishment cuts across racial, ethnic, and religious groups.[57]

Good intentions notwithstanding, there is growing evidence of a "violence begetting violence" cycle. Children who are subject to even minimum amounts of physical punishment may be more likely to use violence themselves in personal interactions. Murray Straus reviewed the concept of discipline in a series of cross-sectional surveys and found a powerful relationship between exposure to physical punishment and later aggression throughout the life course.[58] Nonviolent societies are also ones in which parents rarely punish their children physically; there is a link between corporal punishment, delinquency, anger, spousal abuse, depression, and adult crime.[59] Research conducted in ten European countries shows that the degree to which parents and teachers approve of corporal punishment is related to the overall homicide rate and also to the homicide rate for infants.[60]

Physical punishment weakens the bond between parent and child, lowers the child's self-esteem, labels him or her "bad," and undermines his or her faith in justice. It is not surprising, then, that Straus finds a high correlation between exposure to physical discipline and street crime. It is possible that physical punishment and overly strict parenting encourage children to become more furtive and secretive and eventually dishonest in their activities.[61] Overly strict discipline may have an even more insidious link to antisocial behaviors: abused children have a significantly higher risk of brain damage and neurological dysfunction than the nonabused, and brain abnormalities have been linked to violent crime.[62]

Supervision   Evidence also exists that inconsistent supervision can promote delinquency. In his early research, F. Ivan Nye found that mothers who threatened discipline but failed to carry it out were more likely to have delinquent children than those who were consistent in their discipline.[63] Contemporary research supports this finding with evidence that assaultive boys tend to grow up in homes in which there are poor problem-solving skills and inconsistent discipline.[64]

There is ample evidence that close, effective parental supervision can reduce children's involvement in delinquency and drug abuse. Youths who believe their parents care little about their activities and companions are more likely to engage in criminal acts than those who believe their actions will be closely monitored.[65] But simply having parents present in the household is not always enough. Effective supervision is not merely a function of the number of parents in the home but reflects the style, quality, and intent of parenting.[66] Parents who closely supervise their children also have closer and more affective ties with them, helping to reduce their delinquent behavior.[67]

Family Size   Parents may find it hard to control and discipline their children because they have such large families that economic and time resources are spread too thin (resource dilution). Larger families are more likely to produce delinquents than smaller ones, and middle children are more likely to engage in delinquent acts than first- or last-born children.

Some sociologists assume that family size has a direct effect on delinquency, attributing this phenomenon to the stretched resources of the large family and the relatively limited supervision parents can provide for each child.[68] It is also possible that the relationship is indirect, caused by the connection of family size to some external factor associated with criminality; for example, resource dilution has been linked to educational underachievement, long considered a correlate of delinquency.[69] Middle children may suffer because they are the most likely to be home when large numbers of siblings are also at home and economic resources are the most stressed.[70]

The current trend is that relatively affluent, two-wage-earner families are having fewer children, whereas indigent, single-parent households are growing larger. Children are at a greater risk today of being both poor and delinquent because indigent families are the ones most likely to have more children.[71]

Parental Deviance

A number of studies have found that parental criminality and deviance have a powerful influence on delinquent behavior.[72] Parental deviance disrupts the family's role as an agent of informal social control, increasing the likelihood of chronic offending.[73] Some of the most important data on parental deviance was gathered by Donald J. West and David P. Farrington as part of the long-term Cambridge Youth Survey. Their cohort data (see Chapter 2) indicate that a significant number of delinquent youths have criminal fathers.[74] About 8 percent of the sons of noncriminal fathers eventually became chronic offenders, compared to 37 percent of youths with criminal fathers.[75] In another important analysis, Farrington found that one type of parental deviance, school yard aggression or bullying, may be both inter- and intra-generational. Bullies have children who bully others, and these "second-generation bullies" grow up to become the fathers of children who are also bullies, in what seems like a never-ending cycle (see Chapter 10 for more on bullying).[76]

The cause of intergenerational deviance is still uncertain. Genetic, environmental, psychological, and child-rearing factors may all play a role in the linkage between generations. One finding that supports a genetic basis is that fathers of youths who suffer attention deficit hyperactivity disorder (ADHD), a condition closely linked to delinquency, are five times more likely to suffer antisocial personality disorder (APD) than fathers of non-ADHD youths.[77] This linkage may be viewed as evidence that aggressive behavioral tendencies are inherited. Similarly, research on the sons of alcoholics show that these youths suffer from many neurological impairments related to chronic delinquency.[78] It is possible that prolonged parental alcoholism causes genetic problems related to developmental impairment or that the children of substance-abusing parents are more prone to neurological impairment before, during, or after birth.

The quality of family life may also be key. Criminal parents may be least likely to have close, intimate relationships with their offspring, and research confirms that substance-abusing or criminal parents are more likely to use harsh and inconsistent discipline, a factor closely linked to delinquent behavior.[79] This association may be reinforced by stigmatization of children of known deviants. Social control agents may be quick to fix a "delinquent" label on the children of known law violators; "the acorn," the reasoning goes, "does not fall far from the tree."[80]

Although there is some agreement that criminal parents produce delinquent offspring, the specific nature and cause of the relationship is still unknown.[81]

Sibling Influences Most research on the family's influence on delinquency is directed at parental effects, but some evidence exists that siblings may also have an important influence on behavior. Siblings who report warm, mutual relationships and share friends are the most likely to behave in a similar fashion; those who maintain a close relationship also report similar rates of drug abuse and delinquency.[82]

Like intergenerational deviance, a number of interpretations of this data are possible. Siblings who live in the same environment are influenced by similar social and economic factors. Another possibility is that deviant siblings grow closer because of shared interests. It is possible that the relationship is due to interpersonal interactions: older siblings and their peers are admired and imitated by younger siblings. What seems to be a genetic effect may actually be the result of warm and close sibling interaction.

In summary, the research on delinquency and family relationships offers ample evidence that family life can be a potent force on a growing child's development. The delinquent child is likely to grow up in a large family with parents who may drink, participate in criminal acts, are harsh and inconsistent disciplinarians, are cold and unaffectionate, have marital conflicts, and are poor role models. Over all, the quality of a child's family life seems to be more important than its structure.

Child Abuse and Neglect

Family violence—particularly violence against children—is a critical priority for criminal justice officials, political leaders and the public we serve.[83]

Concern about the quality of family life has recently increased because of disturbing reports that many children are physically abused or neglected by their parents and that this harsh treatment has serious consequences for their future behavior. Because of this topic's great importance, the remainder of this chapter is devoted to the issue of child abuse and neglect and its relationship to delinquent behavior.

Historical Foundation

Parental abuse and neglect is not a modern phenomenon. From infanticide to severe physical beatings for disciplinary purposes, maltreatment of children has occurred throughout history. Some concern for the negative effects of such maltreatment was voiced in the eighteenth century in the United States, but concerted efforts to deal with the problem of endangered children did not begin until 1874.

In that year residents of a New York City apartment building reported to a public health nurse, Etta Wheeler, that a child in one of the apartments was being abused by her stepmother. The nurse found a young child named Mary Ellen Wilson who had been repeatedly beaten and chained to her bed and was malnourished from a continuous diet of bread and water. Even though the child was seriously ill, the police agreed with her parents that the law entitled the parents to raise Mary Ellen as they saw fit. The New York City Department of Charities claimed it had no custody right over Mary Ellen.

According to legend, Mary Ellen's removal from her parents had to be arranged through the Society for Prevention of Cruelty to Animals (SPCA) on the ground that she was a member of the animal kingdom, which the SPCA was founded to protect. The truth, however, is less sensational: Mary Ellen's case was heard by a judge. Because the child needed protection, she eventually was placed in an orphanage.[84] The case and subsequent jail sentence for Mary Ellen's stepmother received a great deal of press coverage. Not coincidentally, the Society for Prevention of Cruelty to Children was founded the following year, marking the extension of humane organizations from animals to humans.[85]

Little legal or medical research into the problems of maltreated children occurred in the twentieth century before the work of Dr. C. Henry Kempe of the University of Colorado. In 1962 Kempe reported the results of a survey of medical and law enforcement agencies that indicated that the child abuse rate was much higher than had been thought. He coined a new term, **battered child syndrome,** which he applied to cases of nonaccidental physical injury of children by their parents or guardians.[86] Kempe's work sparked a flurry of research into the problems of the

battered child syndrome
Nonaccidental physical injury of children by their parents or guardians.

In 1874 Henry Bugh and Etta Angell Wheeler persuaded a New York court to take a child, Mary Ellen, away from her mother on the grounds of child abuse. This is the first recorded case in which a court was used to protect a child. Mary Ellen is shown at age 9 when she appeared in court showing bruises from a whipping and several gashes from a pair of scissors. The other photograph shows her a year later.

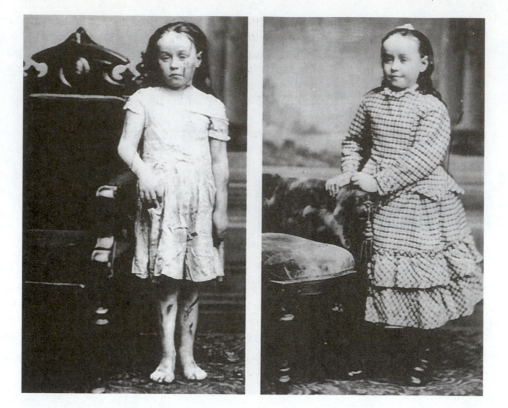

battered child, and a network of law enforcement, medical, and social service agencies was formed to deal with battered children.[87]

Professionals dealing with such children soon discovered the limitations of Kempe's definition as they came face to face with a wide range of physical and emotional abuse inflicted on children by their parents. As Kempe himself recognized in 1976:

> The term "battered child" has been dropped. . . . When coined 15 years ago, its purpose was to gain the attention of both physicians and the public. We feel, now, that enough progress has been made to move on to a more inclusive phrase—child abuse and neglect. The problem is clearly not just one of *physical* battering. Save for the children who are killed or endure permanent brain damage . . . the most devastating aspect of abuse and neglect is the permanent adverse effects on the developmental process and the child's emotional well-being.[88]

Kempe's pioneering efforts paved the way for a national consciousness on child abuse.

Defining Abuse and Neglect

child abuse
Any physical, emotional, or sexual trauma to a child, including neglecting to give proper care and attention, for which no reasonable explanation can be found.

The definition of battered children has expanded, and the term **child abuse** is now a generic expression that includes neglect as well as overt physical beating. Specifically, it now describes any physical or emotional trauma to a child for which no reasonable explanation, such as an accident or ordinary disciplinary practices, can be found. Child abuse is generally seen as a pattern of behavior rather than a single beating or act of neglect. The effects of a pattern of behavior are cumulative. That is, the longer the abuse continues, the more severe the effect on the child.[89]

Although the terms *child abuse* and **neglect** are sometimes used interchangeably, they represent different forms of maltreatment. Neglect is the more passive term, referring to deprivations children suffer at the hands of their parents—lack of

neglect
Passive neglect by a parent or guardian, depriving children of food, shelter, health care, and love.

food, shelter, health care, and love. *Abuse* is a more overt form of physical aggression against the child, one that often requires medical attention. The distinction between the two terms is often unclear, however, because in many cases both occur simultaneously.

Physical abuse includes throwing, shooting, stabbing, burning, drowning, suffocating, biting, or deliberately disfiguring a child. The greatest number of injuries result from beatings with various kinds of implements and instruments. Some children have been strangled or suffocated with pillows held over their mouths or plastic bags thrown over their heads; a number have been drowned in bathtubs.[90]

Physical neglect results from parents' failure to provide adequate food, shelter, or medical care for their children, as well as failure to protect them from physical danger.

Emotional abuse or neglect frequently accompanies physical abuse; it is manifested by constant criticism and rejection of the child.[91] Those who suffer emotional abuse have significantly lower levels of self-esteem as adults.[92]

Emotional neglect includes inadequate nurturing or affection, inattention to a child's emotional development, and lack of concern about maladaptive behavior.

Sexual abuse refers to the exploitation of children through rape, incest, and molestation by parents, family members, friends, or legal guardians.

Finally, **abandonment** refers to the situation in which parents physically leave their children with the intention of completely severing the parent–child relationship.[93]

There are a variety of legal definitions of abuse, but almost all contain concepts such as nonaccidental physical injury, physical neglect, emotional abuse or neglect, sexual abuse, and abandonment.[94] For example, the federal government's definition is included in Table 8.3.

abandonment
Parents physically leave their children with the intention of completely severing the parent–child relationship.

Table 8.3

THE FEDERAL DEFINITION OF CHILD ABUSE AND NEGLECT

Child abuse and neglect is

- Any recent act or failure to act resulting in imminent risk of serious harm, death, serious physical or emotional harm, sexual abuse, or exploitation

- of a child (a person under age 18, unless the child protection law of the state in which the child resides specifies a younger age for cases not involving sexual abuse)

- by a parent or caretaker (including any employee of a residential facility or any staff person providing out-of-home care) who is responsible for the child's welfare

Sexual abuse is

- Employment, use, persuasion, inducement, enticement, or coercion of any child to engage in, or assist any other person to engage in, any sexually explicit conduct or any simulation of such conduct for the purpose of producing any visual depiction of such conduct

- Rape, and in cases of caretaker or interfamilial relationships, statutory rape, molestation, prostitution, or other forms of sexual exploitation of children, or incest with children

Source: The Child Abuse Prevention and Treatment Act (CAPTA), as amended and reauthorized in October 1996 (Public Law 104-235, Section 111; 42 U.S.C. 5106g).

Sexual Abuse

Sexual abuse has become an issue of growing national concern. This form of abuse can vary in content and style. It may range from rewarding a child for sexual behavior that is inappropriate for his or her level of development to using force or the threat of force for the purposes of sex. Sexual abuse can involve children who are well aware of the sexual content of their actions and others too young to have any real idea of what their actions mean. It can involve a variety of acts from inappropriate touching and fondling to forcible sexual penetration.

The effects of sexual abuse can be devastating. Abused children suffer disrupted ego development and personality development.[95] Guilt and shame are commonly experienced by survivors, and psychological trauma sometimes continues into adulthood. The ego of the victim may be overwhelmed by rage and horror over the incident, and the experience can have long-lasting repercussions (see Table 8.4).

Research indicates a correlation between the severity of abuse and its long-term effects: the less serious the form of abuse, the more quickly the child can recover.[96]

Table 8.4
LONG-TERM EFFECTS OF SEXUAL ABUSE

Traumatic Sexualization

The process in which a child's sexual identity is shaped in an inappropriate and dysfunctional way by the result of the abuse episode.

- Abused children suffer disrupted ego and personality development and psychological trauma that can continue into adulthood.
- Traumatic sexualization can lead children to victimize peers and act promiscuously, for example, trading sex for affection.
- Signs of postabuse trauma are hallucinations, nightmares, and periods of profound rage.

Betrayal

The discovery by abused children that someone whom they trusted and on whom they are dependent caused them harm.

- The end result of feelings of betrayal can be depression, disillusionment, hostility, and anger. Others react with imparied judgment and insecurity, making them vulnerable to further abuse.

Powerlessness

The process in which the child's will, desires, and sense of competence are negated.

- Associated with anxiety, phobias, clinging behavior, hypersensitivity, and lack of coping skills.
- Sexually assaulted males report emotional distress and social isolation; they are more likely to have deviant peers and engage in delinquent activities.
- Girls who were sexually abused as children are more suicidal as adults than the nonabused.

Stigmatization

The negative connotations, such as shame and guilt, that are communicated to children around their experiences and that then become incorporated into their self-image.

Sources: Michael Wiederman, Randy Sansone, and Lori Sansone, "History of Trauma and Attempted Suicide among Women in a Primary Care Setting," *Violence and Victims* 13:3–11 (1998); Susan Leslie Bryant and Lillian Range, "Suicidality in College Women Who Were Sexually and Physically Abused and Physically Punished by Parents," *Violence and Victims* 10:195–215 (1995); Jill Kuhn, Charleanea Arellano, and Ernest Chavez, "Correlates of Sexual Assault in Mexican American and White Non-Hispanic Adolescent Males," *Violence and Victims* 13:11–21 (1998); Angela Browne and David Finkelhor, "Impact of Child Sexual Abuse: A Review of the Research," *Psychological Bulletin* 99:66–77 (1986); Kathleen Kendall-Tackett, Linda Meyer Williams, and David Finkelhor, "Impact of Sexual Abuse on Children: A Review and Synthesis of Recent Empirical Studies," *Psychological Bulletin* 113:164–80 (1993).

Children who are frequently abused over long periods of time and who suffered actual penetration of sexual organs are most likely to experience long-term trauma, including posttraumatic stress syndrome, precocious sexuality, and poor self-esteem.[97] Some victims find themselves sexualizing their own children in ways that lead them to sexual or physical abuse. Several studies have found a close association between sexual abuse and adolescent prostitution.[98] See the following Focus on Delinquency entitled "Juvenile Prostitution" for more on this topic. And finally, girls who were sexually and physically abused as children are more often suicidal as adults than the nonabused.[99]

The Extent of Child Abuse

How extensive is the incidence of child abuse? It is almost impossible to give an accurate estimate of the extent of child abuse. Many victims are so young that they have not learned to speak or communicate. Some are too embarrassed or afraid. Many incidents occur behind closed doors, and even when another adult witnesses inappropriate or criminal behavior the adult may not want to get involved in what is considered a "family matter."

Some of the first and most explosive indications of the severity of the problem of child abuse came from a widely publicized 1980 national survey conducted by sociologists Richard Gelles and Murray Straus.[100] Gelles and Straus estimated that between 1.4 million and 1.9 million children in the United States were subject to physical abuse from their parents. This physical abuse was rarely a one-time act. The average number of assaults per year was 10.5, and the median was 4.5. Gelles and Straus also found that 16 percent of the couples in their sample reported spousal abuse; 50 percent of the multichild families reported attacks between siblings; 20 percent of the families reported incidents in which children attacked parents.[101]

FOCUS ON DELINQUENCY

JUVENILE PROSTITUTION

[P]rostitutes place themselves at risk the moment they enter the business. They are exploited and victimized by pimps, johns, cops, robbers, muggers, drug addicts, drug dealers, and more. There is a high rate of rape among girl prostitutes as most ply their trade in high-risk crime areas.*

One of the most devastating forms of child sexual exploitation is juvenile prostitution. The National Center on Child Abuse and Neglect defines juvenile prostitution as "the use of, or participation by, children under the age of majority in sexual acts with adults or other minors where no force is present." The lack of force may make the relationship between a juvenile prostitute and the customer appear to be an equal economic exchange; however, victims' advocates acknowledge that in reality the juvenile is a victim, often of an abusive family life, low self-esteem, and a lack of economic alternatives.

HOW PREVALENT IS JUVENILE PROSTITUTION?

It is difficult to measure the number of children who are actually involved in prostitution. Estimates from law enforcement officials, social service providers, and researchers have ranged from tens of thousands to 2.4 million children annually. A reasonable estimate is that there are between one hundred thousand and three hundred thousand juvenile prostitutes per year. Although experts debate the extent of the problem, according to the UCR

(continued on the following page)

(continued from the previous page)

about fifteen hundred girls eighteen and under are arrested each year for prostitution in the United States, a few as young as ten and eleven years old.

Even this estimate indicates a consistent nationwide problem of child sexual exploitation through prostitution. Where do these children come from, and how do they get recruited into prostitution? Youth service professionals suggest several traits or characteristics shared by juvenile prostitutes. Often, these children come from dysfunctional families. Having suffered physical, sexual, or emotional abuse, a majority of child prostitutes are runaways trying to escape their home environment. About 75 percent of juvenile prostitutes are believed to be runaways or "throwaways," having been encouraged or forced to leave home by their families.

Research suggests that most of the children who become prostitutes suffer from a negative self-image. Whether by parents, school officials, or peers, these youngsters have been convinced that they have little self-worth. Many of the children "want to be wanted," and the attention of customers and pimps can foster the illusion that these people really care.

This negative self-image coupled with a lack of marketable skills may force children into prostitution as a means of economic survival. Pimps and other prostitutes may offer food and shelter in exchange for money raised through prostitution. Once the juveniles have entered this lifestyle, they may find it difficult to get out.

Some may suffer more severe forms of mental disorders, including schizophrenia, depression, and emotional instability. Of course, these problems may result from the dysfunctional family life of youths who get involved in prostitution.

WHO ARE THE PIMPS?

Recognizing that runaway children are emotionally and financially desperate, pimps exploit these needs for their own personal gain. Almost always men, they will often wait in bus terminals and train stations, offering juveniles traveling alone some companionship and a place to stay. Initially, attention and affection are provided "with no strings attached." Once the juveniles become indebted to him, the pimp "turns them out" in prostitution as a form of repayment.

To increase his profits, a pimp may be a member of an organized ring, sending the juvenile on a circuit that could encompass numerous locations over several states. A booking agent often works as the middleman, organizing the circuit schedule and providing a facade of legitimacy between the pimp and the police. Interestingly, most research disputes the myth that pimps kidnap totally innocent children, raping them and turning them out into prostitution. Most youths become prostitutes by choice, but once in the life, they may find themselves subject to the pimp's "control, rules, orders, drugs, violence, and manipulation."

WHAT ARE THE RISKS?

Aside from the emotional traumas associated with life as a juvenile prostitute, numerous physical risks endanger the child as well. Sexually transmitted diseases, including AIDS and early pregnancy, are constant dangers as is long-term physical damage. Juveniles rarely seek medical help for fear they may be brought to the attention of authorities.

Along with the risks of disease come the risks of violence, both from pimps and from customers. Although pimps claim they protect the juveniles, the pimps may allow customers to "rough up" the youths "to teach them a lesson." Some pimps may use cruel and bizarre punishments, such as forcing juveniles to sit on a hot stove to punish them for not meeting their quotas or for causing problems. More commonly, a pimp controls the juveniles through battering or the threat of violence. Prostitutes are also easy targets for muggers and other criminals. These juveniles are often out late at night with large amounts of cash and are unlikely to report a victimization to the police. Prostitutes are also common targets of serial murderers.

IS JUVENILE PROSTITUTION COMMON AROUND THE WORLD?

Child prostitution is now a worldwide problem. Girls from Latin America are being sold for sex in Europe and the Middle East. South Asian girls wind up in Northern Europe and the Middle East, and Russian and Ukranian girls are sold in Hungary, Poland, and the Baltic states. In Asia an estimated one million children are part of the sex trade. Thailand is the leader, but prostitution is a growing problem in India, Bangladesh, and the Philippines as well. Sex tours are a common practice in these nations and the United Nations has called for sanctions to punish operators.

Child prostitution is not unique to undeveloped countries. Prostitution is also common in Japan. Lured from the suburbs by quick and easy cash, fifteen-year-olds walk the streets in their school uniforms. Each year Japanese police arrest thousands of girls under age 18 for prostitution, but those arrested represent only a small percentage of the total. Most school-girl prostitutes in Tokyo belong to "dating clubs" whose members cannot be detained on any charges because prostitution is legal unless arranged by a pimp. Girls in junior high school have joined telephone clubs where men can wait for calls from teenage girls; there are also dating clubs featuring young girls. Some clubs have hundreds of girls on the payroll. Other girls bypass the clubs, either posting beeper or phone numbers on bulletin boards or walking the streets in their school uniforms.

WHAT CAN BE DONE LEGALLY?

In 1997, the Japanese began an attempt to control child prostitution in Tokyo, arresting men if they engaged the services of young girls. Then in 1999 growing concern led the government to prohibit sexual relations with a minor under 17 years of age. It remains to be seen whether such attempts will be successful at controlling juvenile prostitution.

In the United States each state and the federal government have criminalized some aspects of child prostitution. The federal government's primary law criminalizing child prostitution is the Mann Act, which prohibits interstate or foreign transportation of individuals under the age of 18 to engage in prostitution or any sexual activity for which any person can be charged with a criminal offense. The federal statutes controlling child prostitution include:

18 USC § 2422 Coercion and enticement. Prohibits enticing, persuading, inducing, etcetera any person to travel across a state boundary for prostitution or for any sexual activity for which any person may be charged with a crime.

18 USC § 2423 Transportation of minors. Prohibits transporting a minor across state lines for prostitution or any sexual purpose for which any person may be charged with a crime.

18 USC § 2243 Sexual abuse of a minor or ward. This criminalizes assaults on children and youths on federal property or on airliners etcetera.

State laws focus on persons who advance, promote, or induce prostitution and sometimes allow for the prosecution of patrons of child prostitutes under child sexual abuse or statutory rape laws. But these laws rarely punish parents who offer their children for money. Stricter enforcement of these laws and additional ones punishing parents may help eradicate this extreme form of abuse.

Sources: Steven Butler, "Prostitution Has Its Limits," *U.S. News & World Report* 14 April 1997; "UN Cites Sharp Rise in Child Labor: Prostitution," *Boston Globe* 12 November 1996, p. A6; Education Development Center, Inc., *Child Sexual Exploitation: Improving Investigations and Protecting Victims* (Boston, Mass., Author, 1995); Valerie Reitman, "Japan's New Growth Industry: Schoolgirl Prostitution, Prevention Efforts Are Blocked by Lax Laws and Mothers' Groups," *Wall Street Journal* 2 October 1996, p. A14; * R. Barri Flowers, *Female Crime, Criminals and Cellmates* (Jefferson, N.C.: McFarland & Co., 1995), p. 156; Jennifer Williard, *Juvenile Prostitution* (Washington, D.C.: National Victim Resource Center, 1991).

Newspaper headlines featuring child abuse have become commonplace because the number of children killed by their parents has increased by more than 50 percent since 1985.

The Gelles and Straus survey was an important milestone in identifying child abuse as a national phenomenon. Subsequent national surveys conducted in 1985 and 1992 indicated that the incidence of very severe violence toward children had declined.[102] One reason was that parental approval of corporal punishment, which had stood at 94 percent in 1968, had decreased to 68 percent by 1994.[103] Recognition of the problem may have helped moderate existing cultural values and awakened parents to the dangers of physically disciplining children. Nonetheless, more than one million children were still being subjected to severe violence annually.[104] If the definition of "severe abuse" used in the survey had included hitting with objects such as a stick or a belt, the actual number of child victims would have been closer to seven million per year.

Attempts to determine the extent of sexual abuse indicate that perhaps one in ten boys and one in three girls have been the victims of some form of sexual exploitation. An oft-cited survey by Diana Russell found that 16 percent of women reported sexual abuse by a relative, and an additional 4.5 percent reported abuse by a father or stepfather.[105] It has been estimated that 30 to 75 percent of women in treatment for substance-abuse disorders had experienced childhood sexual abuse and rape.[106]

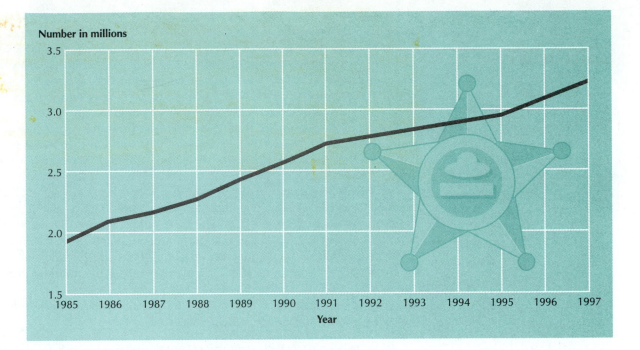

Number in millions

FIGURE 8.2

Number of Child Abuse Cases Reported

Source: David Wiese and Ching-Tung Lung, *Current Trends in Child Abuse and Fatalities: The Results of the 1997 Annual Fifty-State Survey* (Chicago: National Committee to Prevent Child Abuse, 1998).

Not all child abuse and neglect cases are reported to authorities, but those that are take on added importance because they become the focus of state action. A number of national organizations have been collecting data on reported child abuse. One important source of such information is the National Committee to Prevent Child Abuse (NCPCA). The committee conducts an annual survey of child protection service (CPS) agencies to determine the number and trends of reported child abuse victims. In 1997 (the last data available) an estimated 3,195,000 children were reported to CPS agencies as alleged victims of child maltreatment (see Figure 8.2). Nationwide, the rate of children reported for child abuse or neglect increased 4 percent between 1992 and 1997, from 45 per 1,000 children in 1992 to 47 per 1,000 in 1997. Overall, the total number of reports nationwide has increased 41 percent since 1988.[107] A little more than one million cases, or about one-third of those reported, are later substantiated by authorities, a number that corresponds with the results of the surveys conducted by Gelles, Straus, and their associates.

The Causes of Child Abuse and Neglect

Parental maltreatment of children is a complex problem with neither a single cause nor a single solution. It cuts across racial, ethnic, religious, and socioeconomic lines, affecting the entire spectrum of society. Abusive parents cannot be categorized by sex, age, or educational level. They are persons from all walks of life, with varying cultural and economic backgrounds.

Of all factors associated with child abuse, three are discussed most often: (1) parents who themselves suffered abuse as children tend to abuse their own children;

(2) the presence of an unrelated adult increases the risk of abuse; and (3) isolated and alienated families tend to become abusive. A cyclical pattern of family violence seems to be perpetuated from one generation to another within families. Evidence indicates that a large number of abused and neglected children grow into adolescence and adulthood with a tendency to engage in violent behavior. The behavior of abusive parents can often be traced to negative experiences in their own childhood—physical abuse, lack of love, emotional neglect, and incest. These parents become unable to separate their own childhood traumas from their relationships with their children. An extreme example of the intrafamily transmission of abuse is the subject of the Focus on Delinquency box entitled "Women Who Have Killed Their Children."

Abusive parents often have unrealistic perceptions of normal childhood development. When their children are unable to act appropriately—when they cry, throw food, or strike their parents—the parents may react in an abusive manner.[108] For parents such as these, "the axiom about not being able to love when you have not known love yourself is painfully borne out in their case histories. . . . They spend their days going around the house, ticking away like unexploded bombs. A fussy baby can be the lighted match."[109]

Parents may also become abusive if they are isolated from friends, neighbors, or relatives who can provide a lifeline in times of crisis:

> Potentially or actually abusing parents are those who live in states of alienation from society, couples who have carried the concept of the shrinking nuclear family to its most extreme form, cut off as they are from ties of kinship and contact with other people in the neighborhood.[110]

Many abusive and neglectful parents describe themselves as highly alienated from their extended families, and they lack close relationships with persons who could provide help and support in stressful situations.[111] The relationship between alienation and abuse may be particularly acute in homes where there has been divorce or separation or in which parents have never actually married; abusive punishment in single-parent homes has been found to be twice that of two-parent families.[112] Parents who are unable to cope with stressful lives or events—divorce, alcoholism, financial stress, poor housing conditions, recurring mental illness, and drug addiction—are the most at risk.[113]

In summary, Richard Gelles and Murray Straus describe the abusive parent as:

> . . . a single parent who was young (under thirty) had been married for less than ten years, had his or her first child before the age of eighteen, and was unemployed or employed part-time. If he or she worked, it would be at a manual labor job . . . women are slightly more likely to abuse their children than men. The reason is rather obvious: Women typically spend more time with children.[114]

Substance Abuse and Child Abuse   Abusive and neglectful families suffer from severe stress, and it is therefore not surprising that they frequently harbor members who turn to drugs and alcohol. Substance abuse is the cause of child maltreatment most often cited by CPS professionals (63 percent).[115]

Research studies have found a strong association between child abuse and parental alcoholism.[116] In addition, evidence exists of a significant relationship between cocaine and heroin abuse and the neglect and physical abuse of children. In Massachusetts almost 90 percent of the confirmed cases of abuse and neglect involving a victim under one year in age occurred in families in which one or more members were drug users; about 68 percent of the abused infants were diagnosed as suffering congenital drug addiction.[117]

States are just beginning to respond to women with substance abuse problems who also abuse their children. For example, Illinois employs Project SAFE (Substance Abuse Free Environment) to provide drug- and alcohol-involved women with intensive treatment and training in parenting skills.[118]

WOMEN WHO HAVE KILLED THEIR CHILDREN

The most serious form of child abuse and neglect is the killing of a child by a parent. It seems inconceivable that a mother would kill her child; the nurturance and protection of young children seems both instinctual and universal. What, then, would prompt a woman to kill her child who is both helpless and dependent on her for care and survival?

To answer this question, Susan Crimmins, Sandra Langley, Henry Brownstein, and Barry Spunt interviewed forty-two women in New York state prisons who had been convicted of manslaughter or murder in the deaths of their children. The women told of a consistent history of social and psychological trauma leading up to their fatal act. More than two-thirds were characterized as "motherless mothers" who had absent or abusive mothers themselves. More than one-third reported that their mothers were alcoholics.

About three-quarters of these women had been physically or sexually abused as children. For many, the pattern was carried over into abusive spousal relations: the great majority of these women (79 percent) had been abused by a partner. It should come as no surprise that 41 percent had attempted suicide. All forty-three women interviewed experienced more than one incident that damaged their self-image prior to their child killing. Given their rough start in life, it is not difficult to imagine how the stress of caring for a child under extreme life conditions might prove overwhelming.

About three-quarters of the women were biological parents; the others killed foster or adopted children or the children of neighbors or relatives. When asked why they killed, most reported extreme psychological stress (due to depression or schizophrenia); about one-third linked their behavior to alcohol or drug abuse. Isolation in childhood carried over to motherhood, and they felt isolated and alone. These women had learned to "suffer in silence."

The link these women shared was a traumatic childhood filled with abuse, brutality, and loss that extended to an adulthood of social isolation and unmet emotional needs. This isolation, coupled with their learned ability to suffer without complaint, served to further erode their already poor self-esteem. Their own behavior was the product of years of frustration and having learned to use violence to settle disputes in their own families. Isolated, rejected, and feeling low self-worth, these women could not form empathy for others. This generated additional feelings of rage and despair, which later erupted into violent, aggressive behavior.

Can such appalling behavior be prevented? Early identification and aggressive prevention services might help break this cycle of violence. Self-esteem builders and self-care programs for new mothers are probable solutions, as is nursery care for newborns whose mothers are believed to be high risk.

Source: Susan Crimmins, Sandra Langley, Henry Brownstein, and Barry Spunt, "Convicted Women Who Have Killed Children: A Self-Psychology Perspective," *Journal of Interpersonal Violence* 12:49–69 (1997).

Stepparents and Abuse Research indicates that stepchildren share a greater risk for abuse than do biological offspring.[119] Stepparents may have less emotional attachment to the children of another and be restrained in their affection. All too often the biological parent has to choose between the new mate and the child, sometimes even becoming an accomplice in the exploitation and abuse.[120]

Stepchildren are overrepresented in cases of **familicide,** mass murders in which a spouse and one or more children are slain. It is also more common for fathers who kill their biological children to commit suicide than those who kill stepchildren, an indication that their act was motivated by hostility and not personal despair.[121].

familicide
Mass murders in which a spouse and one or more children are slain.

Social Class and Abuse Surveys indicate a high rate of reported abuse and neglect cases among people in lower economic classes. Children from families earning less

Research on sexual abuse indicates that perhaps one in ten boys and one in three girls have been victims of some form of sexual exploitation. Children who are frequently abused over long periods of time experience long-term trauma, including posttraumatic stress syndrome, precocious sexuality, and poor self-esteem.

than $15,000 per year experience more abuse and suffer greater injury than children living in more affluent homes.[122] More than 40 percent of CPS workers indicate that most of their clients either live in poverty or face increased financial stress due to unemployment and economic recession.[123] These findings suggest that parental mal-treatment of children is predominantly a lower-class problem. Is this conclusion valid?

One view is that the survey statistics are generally accurate and that lower-class parents are in fact more abusive of their children. Low-income families, especially those headed by a single parent, are often subject to greater levels of environmental stress and have fewer resources available to deal with such stress than families with higher incomes.[124] A relationship seems to exist between the burdens of raising a child without adequate economic and social resources and the use of excessive force and discipline. Self-report surveys do show that indigent parents are significantly more likely than affluent parents to hold attitudes that condone physical chastisement of children.[125]

Another view is that child abuse rates are so high among the lower class because poor families are more often dealt with by public agencies that automatically report suspected cases to CPS agencies. For example, higher-income families can afford private medical treatment, which shields their problems from public view.[126] CPS agents and judges may look differently on abuse cases that involve well-educated suburban dwellers than they do on those involving members of the lower class. Attending physicians may label a child of middle-class parents "accident-prone" under circumstances in which they would judge a lower-class child "abused."[127] Although these prejudices may mask child abuse among the middle class, many cases of lower-class abuse may also go unreported. Police may be less likely to report child abuse by lower-class or minority families because they perceive that violence is more "normal" in these families and that minority children "need" harsher discipline than children in more affluent families.[128]

There is a third, biosocial explanation for the apparent class differences in child abuse.[129] It is possible that the treatment of children is related to the actual "cost" to parents of perpetuating their genes through raising offspring. Higher rates of maltreatment in low-income families reflect the stress caused by the burdensome "investment" of resources lower-class parents make in raising their children. In contrast, middle-class parents devote a smaller percentage of their total resources to raising a family and therefore are less likely to perceive economic and social stress. According to this view, child abuse rates should be highest among lower-class families with a large number of children: few resources must be spread among a large number of children, limiting the resources available for each one's well-being. Higher abuse rates of emotionally and physically handicapped children may occur because these youngsters are poor prospects for "investment" by parents because their chances of becoming "successful" adults are limited.[130]

The Child Protection System: Philosophy and Practice

For most of the nation's history, courts have operated on the assumption that parents have the right to bring up their children as they see fit. Though child protection agencies have been dealing with the problems of abuse and neglect since the late nineteenth century, recent awareness of child abuse and neglect has prompted judicial authorities to take increasingly bold steps to ensure the safety of children.[131] The age-old assumption that the parent–child relationship is inviolate has been challenged. In 1974 Congress passed the Child Abuse Prevention and Treatment Act (CAPTA), which provides funds to states to bolster their services for maltreated children and their parents.[132] CAPTA provides federal funding to states in support of prevention, assessment, investigation, prosecution, and treatment activities. It also provides grants to public agencies and nonprofit organizations for demonstration programs and projects

CAPTA has been the impetus for all fifty states to improve the legal framework of their child protection systems. Abusive parents are subject to prosecution in criminal courts under the traditional statutes against assault, battery, and homicide. Many states have specific child abuse statutes that make it a felony to injure and abuse children.

State laws specifically prescribe procedures for investigation and prosecution of cases. The legal rights of both parents and children are constitutionally protected. In the cases of *Lassiter v. Department of Social Services* and *Santosky v. Kramer,* the U.S. Supreme Court recognized the child's right to be free from parental abuse and set down guidelines for a termination-of-custody hearing, including the right to legal representation.[133] States provide a guardian *ad litem* for the child (a lawyer appointed by the court to look after the interests of those who do not have the capacity to assert their own rights). States also ensure confidentiality of reporting and mandate professional training and public education programs.[134]

Investigating and Reporting Abuse   One major problem in enforcing abuse and neglect statutes is that maltreatment of children can easily be hidden from public view. Although state laws require doctors, teachers, and others who work with children to report suspected cases to child protection agencies, many maltreated children are out of the law's reach because they are too young for school or because their parents do not take them to a doctor or a hospital. Parents abuse their children in private and, even when confronted, often accuse their children of lying or blame the children's medical problems on accidents of legitimate discipline. Legal and social service agencies must find more effective ways to locate abused and neglected children and to handle such cases once they are found.

All fifty states have statutes requiring that persons suspected of abuse and neglect be reported. Many have made failure to report child abuse a criminal offense. Though such statutes are rarely enforced, teachers have been arrested for failing to report abuse or neglect cases.[135]

Once reported to a child protection service agency via a "hotline" or some other procedure, the case is screened by an intake worker and then turned over to an investigative caseworker. Protective service workers often work with law enforcement officers and other agency personnel. If the caseworker determines that the child is in imminent danger of severe harm, the caseworker may immediately remove the child from the home. A court hearing must then be held shortly after to approve the custody. Stories of children abruptly and erroneously taken from their homes abound, but it is much more likely that these "gatekeepers" will consider cases unfounded and take no further action. More than 50 percent of all reported cases are so classified.[136] Among the most common reasons for screening out cases is that the reporting party is involved in a child custody case and the screener believes the accusation is a consequence of marital turmoil.[137]

Even when there is compelling evidence of abuse, most social service agencies will try to involve the family in voluntary treatment and counseling without court intervention. Case managers will do periodic follow-ups to determine if treatment plans are being followed. If parents are uncooperative or if the danger to the children is so great that they must be removed from the home, a complaint will be filed in the criminal, family, or juvenile court system.

The Process of State Intervention   Although procedures vary from state to state, most follow a similar legal process once a social service agency files a court petition alleging abuse or neglect.[138] This process is diagrammed in Figure 8.3.

If the allegation of abuse is confirmed by investigating child welfare authorities, the child may be removed and placed in some form of protective custody or left temporarily with the parents. Most state statutes require that the court be notified "promptly" or "immediately" if the child is removed; some states, including Arkansas, North Carolina, and Pennsylvania, have gone as far as requiring that no more than twelve hours elapse before official action is taken. If the child has not been removed from the home, state authorities are given more time to notify the court of suspected abuse. For example, Louisiana and Maryland set a limit of thirty days to take action, whereas Wisconsin mandates that state action take no more than twenty days once the case has been investigated.

When an abuse or neglect petition is prosecuted, an **advisement hearing** (also called a preliminary protective hearing or temporary custody hearing, in the event that the child has been removed from the home) is held. At this hearing the court will review the facts of the case, determine whether removal is justified, and notify the parents of the nature of the charges against them. Parents have the right to counsel in all cases of abuse and neglect, and many states require the court to appoint an attorney for the child as well. The child's attorney, a guardian *ad litem,* often acts as an advocate for the child's welfare as well as providing legal assistance. If the parents admit the allegations, the court enters a consent decree, and the case is continued for disposition. Approximately half of all cases are settled by admission at the advisement hearing. If the parents deny the petition, an attorney is appointed for the child, and the case is continued for a pretrial conference.

At the **pretrial conference,** the attorney for the social service agency presents an overview of the case and summarizes the evidence. Such matters as admissibil-

advisement hearing
A preliminary protective or temporary custody hearing in which the court will review the facts and determine whether removal of the child is justified and notify parents of the charges against them.

pretrial conference
The attorney for the social services agency presents an overview of the case and a plea bargain or negotiated settlement can be agreed to in a consent decree.

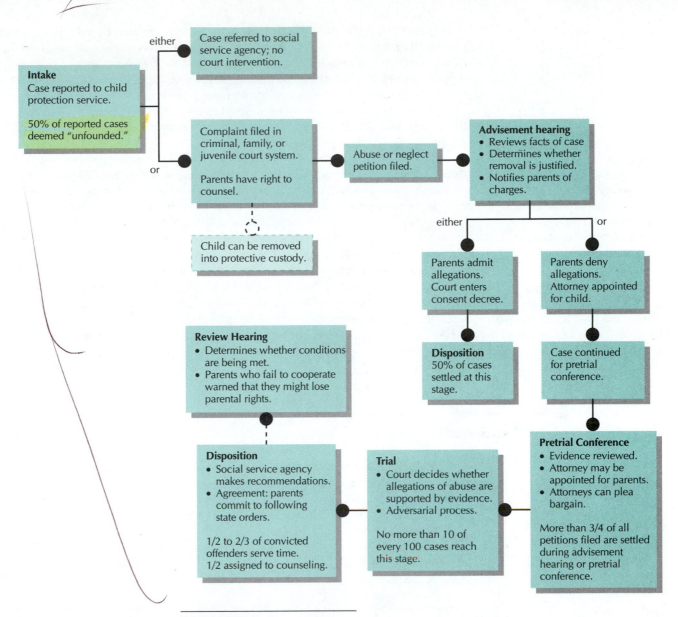

Intake
Case reported to child protection service.

50% of reported cases deemed "unfounded."

either → Case referred to social service agency; no court intervention.

or → Complaint filed in criminal, family, or juvenile court system.

Parents have right to counsel.

Child can be removed into protective custody.

Abuse or neglect petition filed.

Advisement hearing
- Reviews facts of case
- Determines whether removal is justified.
- Notifies parents of charges.

either → Parents admit allegations. Court enters consent decree.

or → Parents deny allegations. Attorney appointed for child.

Disposition
50% of cases settled at this stage.

Case continued for pretrial conference.

Review Hearing
- Determines whether conditions are being met.
- Parents who fail to cooperate warned that they might lose parental rights.

Disposition
- Social service agency makes recommendations.
- Agreement: parents commit to following state orders.

1/2 to 2/3 of convicted offenders serve time. 1/2 assigned to counseling.

Trial
- Court decides whether allegations of abuse are supported by evidence.
- Adversarial process.

No more than 10 of every 100 cases reach this stage.

Pretrial Conference
- Evidence reviewed.
- Attorney may be appointed for parents.
- Attorneys can plea bargain.

More than 3/4 of all petitions filed are settled during advisement hearing or pretrial conference.

FIGURE 8.3

The Process of State Intervention in Cases of Abuse and Neglect

ity of photos and written reports are settled. At this point in the process the attorneys can plea bargain or negotiate a settlement of the case. About three-fourths of the cases that go to pretrial conference are settled by a consent decree. About eighty-five out of every one hundred petitions filed will be settled at either the advisement hearing or the pretrial conference.

Of the fifteen remaining cases, five will generally be settled before trial. Usually no more than ten cases out of every one hundred actually reach the trial stage of the process. These few cases are tried within the regular adversary process in which the court determines whether the allegations of abuse or neglect are supported by evidence.

Disposition From the perspective of both the child and the parents, the most crucial part of an abuse or neglect proceeding is the independent **disposition hearing.** At this hearing the social service agency presents its case plan, which includes recommendations such as conditions for returning the child to the parents or a visitation plan if the child is to be taken from the parents, and so on. The plan

disposition hearing
The social service agency presents its case plan and recommendations for care of the child and treatment of the parents, including incarceration and counseling or other treatments.

is discussed with the parents, and an agreement is reached by which the parents commit themselves to following the state orders. Between one-half and two-thirds of all convicted parents will be required to serve time in incarceration; almost half will be assigned to a form of counseling and treatment. As far as the children are concerned, some may be placed in temporary state or foster care; in other cases parental rights are permanently terminated and the child is placed in the custody of the state child protective service agency. Legal custody can then be assigned to a relative or some other person.

In making their decisions juvenile or family courts are generally guided by three interests: the role of the parents, protection for the child, and the responsibility of the state. Frequently, these interests conflict. In fact, at times even the interests of the two parents are not in harmony. Ideally, the state attempts to balance the parents' natural right to control their child's upbringing with the child's right to grow into adulthood free from severe physical or emotional harm. This is generally referred to as the **balancing-of-the-interest approach.**

Periodically, **review hearings** are held to determine if the conditions of the case plan are being met. Parents who fail to cooperate are warned that they may lose their parental rights. Most abuse and neglect cases are concluded within a year. Either the parents lose their rights and the child is given a permanent placement, or the child is returned to the parents and the court's jurisdiction ends. The Case in Point box explores some questions about state intervention.

balancing-of-the-interest approach
Efforts of the courts to balance the parents' natural right to raise a child with the child's right to grow into adulthood free from physical abuse or emotional harm.

review hearing
Periodic meetings to determine whether the conditions of the case plan for an abused child are being met by the parents or guardians of the child.

The Abused Child in Court

One of the most significant problems associated with the prosecution of child abuse and sexual abuse cases is the trauma a child must go through in a court hearing. Children get confused and frightened and may change their testimony, resulting in dropped charges or mistrial. Much controversy has arisen over the accuracy of children's reports of family violence and sexual abuse, resulting in hung juries in some well-known cases, including the McMartin Day Care case in California.[139] As one expert, Judge Lindsay Arthur of the National Council of Juvenile and Family Court Judges, put it:

> The system may interview the child time and again, each time making her relive the experience, keeping the wound open. It may force her down to court waiting rooms where she sits uncomfortably without even the accoutrements of a dentist's office for hours and then often to be told that the case was continued and to come back next week. She may be put on a witness stand, in a big formal room, with what seems like a thousand eyes staring at her, and a bailiff in full uniform ready to lock her up, and a judge in a black robe towering above her. She may find that the newspapers and television are full of her name and pictures and stories about what happened to her which they obtained from the official records. And this may make her the focus of her classmates with all the brutal teasing that can involve.
>
> The system may also suddenly arrest her father and just as suddenly release him. It may plea bargain away her future hope of rehabilitation without even talking to her, in the name of speedy justice.[140]

State jurisdictions have instituted a number of innovative procedures to minimize the trauma to the child. Most have enacted legislation allowing videotaped statements or interviews with child witnesses taken at a preliminary hearing or at a formal deposition to be admissible in court. Videotaped testimony spares child witnesses the trauma of testifying in open court. States that allow videotaped testimony usually put some restrictions on its use: some prohibit the government from calling the child to testify at trial if the videotape is used; some states require a finding that

You are an investigator with the county Bureau of Social Services, and a case has been referred to you by the middle school's head guidance counselor.

A young girl, Emily M., has been showing up at school in a dazed and listless condition. She has had a hard time concentrating in class and seems withdrawn and uncommunicative. The thirteen-year-old has missed more than a normal share of school days and has often been late to class. Last week she seemed so lethargic that her homeroom teacher sent her to the school nurse. A physical examination revealed that she was malnourished and in poor physical health. She also had evidence of bruising that could only come from a beating. Emily told the nurse that she had been punished by her parents for doing poorly at school and for failing to do her chores at home.

When her parents were called to the school to meet with the principal and head guidance counselor, they claimed to be members of a religious order that believes strongly that children should be punished severely for their misdeeds. Emily had been placed on a restricted diet as well as beaten with a belt to correct her misbehavior. When the guidance counselor asked them if they would be willing to go into family therapy, they were furious and told her to "mind her own business." It's a sad day, they said, when "God-fearing American citizens cannot bring up their children according to their religious beliefs." The girl is in no immediate danger insofar as her punishment has not been life-threatening.

The case is referred to your office. When you go to see the parents at home, they refuse to make any change in their behavior and claim they are in the right and you represent all that is wrong with society. The lax discipline you want imposed leads to drugs, sex, and other teenage problems.

- Should you get a court order removing Emily from her home and requiring the parents to go to counseling?

- Should you report the case to the district attorney's office so it could proceed criminally against her parents under the state's Child Protection Act?

- Should you take no further action, reasoning that Emily's parents have the right to discipline their child as they see fit?

- Should you talk with Emily and see what she wants to happen?

the child is "medically unavailable" because of the trauma of the case before videotaping can be used; some require that the defendant be present during the videotaping; a few specify that the child not be able to see or hear the defendant.[141]

More than two-thirds of the states now allow a child's testimony to be given on closed-circuit television (CCTV). The child is able to view the judge and attorneys, and the courtroom participants are able to observe the child. The standards for CCTV testimony vary widely. Some states, such as New Hampshire, assume that any child

A counselor shows a doll to a victim of child abuse. Children in sexual abuse cases may use anatomically correct dolls to demonstrate happenings that they cannot describe verbally. The Victims of Child Abuse Act of 1990 allows children to use dolls when testifying in federal courts; at least eight states have passed similar legislation.

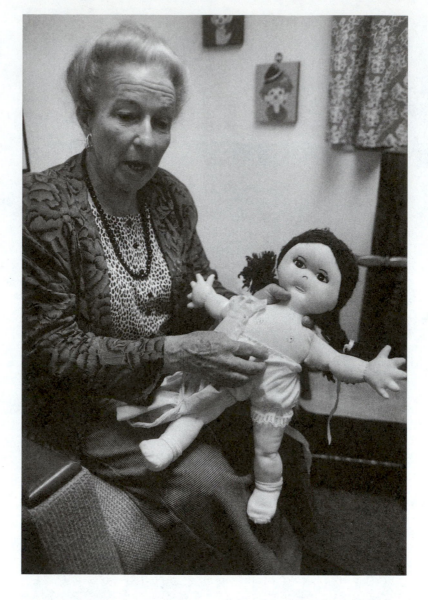

witness under age 12 would benefit from not having to appear in court. Others require an independent examination by a mental health professional to determine whether there is a "compelling need" for CCTV testimony.

In addition to innovative methods of testimony, children in sexual abuse cases have been allowed to use anatomically correct dolls to demonstrate happenings that they cannot describe verbally. The Victims of Child Abuse Act of 1990 allows children to use these dolls when testifying in federal courts; at least eight states have passed similar legislation.[142] Similarly, states have relaxed their laws of evidence to allow out-of-court statements by the child to a social worker, teacher, or police officer to be used as evidence (such statements would otherwise be considered **hearsay**). Typically, corroboration is required to support these statements if the child does not also testify.

The prevalence of sexual abuse cases has created new problems for the justice system. All too often accusations are made in conjunction with marital disputes and separation. The fear is growing that children may become unwitting pawns in custody battles; the mere suggestion of sexual abuse is enough to galvanize social service workers and to affect the outcome of a bitter divorce action. The juvenile justice system must develop techniques that can get at the truth of the matter without creating a lifelong scar on the child's psyche.

hearsay
Out-of-court statements made by one person and recounted in court by another; such statements are generally not allowed as evidence except in child abuse cases wherein a child's statements to social workers, teachers, or police may be admissible.

Legal Issues A number of cases have been brought before the Supreme Court testing the right of children to present evidence at trial using nontraditional methods and settings. Two issues stand out. One is the ability of physicians and mental health professionals to testify about statements made to them by victims of child abuse, especially when the children are incapable of testifying. The second concerns the way children testify in court and the leeway given prosecutors to make them feel at ease.

In a 1992 case, *White v. Illinois*, the Court significantly eased the prosecution of child abuse cases by ruling that the state's attorney is required neither to produce young victims at trial nor to demonstrate the reason they were unavailable to serve as witnesses.[143] *White* involved the use as testimony of statements given by the child to the child's baby-sitter and mother, a doctor, a nurse, and a police officer concerning the facts and identity of the alleged assailant in a sexual assault case. The prosecutor twice tried to call the child to testify, but both times the four-year-old experienced emotional difficulty and could not appear in court. The case outcome then hinged solely on the testimony of the five witnesses who repeated in court the statements made to them by the child.

By allowing others to testify as to what the child said, a practice typically prohibited by rules against hearsay evidence, *White* removed the requirement that prosecutors produce child victims in court. This facilitates the prosecution of child abusers in cases where a court appearance by a victim would prove too disturbing or where the victim is too young to understand the court process.[144] In its decision the Court noted that statements made to doctors during medical exams or those made when a victim is upset or excited carry more weight than ones made after careful reflection. The Court ruled that such statements can be repeated during trial because the circumstances in which they were made (for example, during an examination in an emergency room) could not be duplicated simply by having the child testify to them in court.

In-Court Statements Children who are victims of sexual or physical abuse often make poor witnesses because they are traumatized and overwhelmed by court processes. Yet their testimony may be crucial to convict child abusers. In an important 1988 case, *Coy v. Iowa*, the Court placed limitations on efforts to protect child witnesses in court. During testimony in a sexual assault case, a "one-way" glass screen was set up so that the child victims would not be able to view the defendant (the defendant, however, could view the witnesses as they testified).[145] The Iowa statute that allowed the protective screen assumed that children would be traumatized by their courtroom experience. The Court ruled that unless there was a finding that the child witness needs special protection, the Sixth Amendment of the Constitution grants defendants "face-to-face" confrontation with their accusers. *Coy* was viewed as a setback in the prosecution of child abuse cases. In her dissenting opinion, Justice Sandra Day O'Connor suggested that if courts found it necessary, it would be appropriate to allow children to testify via CCTV or videotape.

Justice O'Connor's views became law in the landmark case of *Craig v. Maryland*.[146] In this case a day-care operator was convicted of sexually abusing a six-year-old child; one-way CCTV testimony was used during the trial. The decision was overturned in the Maryland Court of Appeals on the grounds that the procedures used were insufficient to show that the child could only testify in this manner (via one-way CCTV) because a trial appearance would be too traumatic. On appeal, the Court ruled that the Maryland statute that allows CCTV testimony is sufficient because it requires a determination be made that the child will suffer emotional distress if forced to testify and would not therefore be able to communicate with a jury. In its decision the Court noted that CCTV could serve as the equivalent of in-court testimony and, properly applied, would not interfere with the defendant's right to confront witnesses.

Since *Coy v. Iowa*, the Supreme Court has significantly increased the legal tools prosecutors can employ in child abuse cases. This opens the door for prosecutions in cases that would have been impossible to pursue before.

Disposition of Abuse and Neglect Cases

Just as disagreement is widespread about when state intervention into family life is appropriate, there is also considerable controversy over what forms of intervention are helpful in abuse and neglect cases. Today, social service agents avoid removing children from the home whenever possible and instead try to employ counseling and support techniques to control abusive relationships. In serious cases the state may remove children from their parents and place them in shelter care or foster homes. Placement of these children in foster care is intended to be temporary, but it is not uncommon for children to remain in foster care for three years or more. Furthermore, children are likely to be shifted from one temporary home to another during this period, which severely deprives them of a stable home. Although out-of-home placements may not be as traumatic as previously believed, those children who are moved around more than three times were twice as likely to get arrested as children who had more stable foster home placements.[147]

Ultimately, the court has the power to permanently terminate the rights of parents over their children, but because the effects of destroying the family unit are serious and far-reaching, the court does so only in the most severe cases. Judicial hesitancy is illustrated in a Virginia appellate case in which grandparents contested a father being awarded custody of his children. Even though he had a history of alcohol abuse, had already been found to be an unfit parent, and was awaiting appeal of his conviction for killing the children's mother, the trial court claimed that he had turned his life around.[148]

Despite such occurrences, efforts have been ongoing to improve the child protection system and to reduce the chance of repeat abuse. Jurisdictions have expedited case processing, instituted court procedures designed not to frighten child witnesses, coordinated investigations between various social service and law enforcement agencies, and assigned an advocate or guardian *ad litem* to support the child in need of protection.

Abuse, Neglect, and Delinquency

The immediate effects of abuse and neglect are evident—physical injury, malnutrition, depression, even death. Less obvious are the suspected long-term effects. Psychologists suggest that maltreatment encourages children to use aggression as a means of solving problems and prevents them from feeling empathy for others. It diminishes their ability to cope with stress and makes them vulnerable to the aggression and violence in the culture. Abused children have fewer positive interactions with peers, are less well liked, and are more likely to have disturbed social interactions.[149]

The link between maltreatment and delinquency is also supported by a number of criminological theories. For example:

Social Control Theory. By disrupting normal relationships and impeding socialization, maltreatment reduces the social bond and frees individuals to become involved in deviance.

Social Learning Theory. Maltreatment leads to delinquency because it teaches children that aggression and violence are justifiable forms of behavior.

General Strain Theory. Maltreatment creates the "negative affective states" that are related to strain, anger, and aggression.

Because an association between abuse and each of these models has been found, it seems possible that the strong link between maltreatment and delinquency can occur for different reasons.[150]

A significant amount of literature suggests that abuse and neglect may have a profound effect on behavior in later years. Exposure to excessive physical aggression and emotional chaos in early life provides a foundation for several varieties of violent and antisocial behavior. Sociologists Richard Gelles and Murray Straus state that "with the exception of the police and the military, the family is perhaps the most violent social group, and the home the most violent social setting, in our society."[151] Similarly, Ray Helfer and C. Henry Kempe contend:

> The effects of child abuse and neglect are cumulative. Once the developmental process of a child is insulted or arrested by bizarre child rearing patterns, the scars remain. One should not be surprised, then, to find that the large majority of delinquent adolescents indicate that they were abused as children.[152]

Aggressive, delinquent behavior is the means by which many abused or neglected children act out their hostility toward their parents. Some join gangs, which furnish a sense of belonging and allow pent-up anger to be expressed in group-approved delinquent acts.

Clinical Histories   A considerable body of research examines the clinical histories of known delinquents, typically employing samples of court-adjudicated or incarcerated youths. Studies of juvenile offenders have confirmed that between 70 and 80 percent may have had abusive backgrounds. Many of these juveniles reported serious injury including bruises, lacerations, fractures, and being knocked unconscious by a parent or guardian.[153] Likewise, studies of persons convicted of murder reveal "a demonstrable association between homicide and maltreatment in early childhood."[154] Among children who kill or who attempt murder, the most common factor is said to be "the child's tendency to identify himself with aggressive parents, and pattern after their behavior."[155] One study of several cases of murder and murderous assault by juveniles indicated that in all cases "one or both parents had fostered and condoned murderous assault."[156] Adolescent boys who had committed homicide also reported being beaten more often by their brothers and sisters.[157]

Cohort Studies   Although these findings are persuasive, they do not necessarily prove that maltreatment causes delinquency. It is possible that child abuse is a reaction to misbehavior and is caused by delinquency and not vice versa. In other words, it is possible that angry parents attack their delinquent and drug-abusing children and that child abuse is a *result* of delinquency, not its cause.

One way of solving this methodological dilemma is to follow a cohort of youths who had been reported as victims of child abuse and neglect early in their lives and compare them with a similar cohort of unabused youths. One study conducted by Jose Alfaro in New York found that about half of all children reported to area hospitals as abused children later acquired arrest records. A significant number of boys (21 percent) and girls (29 percent) petitioned to juvenile court had prior histories as abuse cases. Children treated for abuse or neglect were disproportionately involved in violent offenses, including homicide, rape, and assault.[158]

In an important cohort study, Cathy Spatz Widom followed the offending careers of 908 youths reported as abused from 1967 to 1971 and compared them with a control group of 667 unabused youths. Widom found that the abuse and neglect involved a variety of perpetrators, including parents, relatives, strangers, and even grandparents. Twenty-six percent of the abused and neglected sample had juvenile arrests, compared to 17 percent of the comparison group; 29 percent of those who were abused and neglected had adult criminal records, compared to 21 percent of the control group. Widom further found that race, gender, and age also affected the probability that abuse would lead to delinquency. The highest risk group was older, black males who had suffered abuse; about 67 percent of this group went on to become adult criminals. In contrast, only 4 percent of young, white, unabused females became adult offenders.[159] Her conclusion: Being abused or neglected significantly increased the likelihood of arrest both as a juvenile and as an adult.[160]

Widom also tested the hypothesis that victims of childhood violence resort to violence themselves as they mature. The children in her sample who suffered from physical abuse were the most likely to get arrested for violent crimes; their violent crime arrest rate was double that of the control group. Although this relationship was not unexpected, more surprising was the discovery that neglected children maintained significantly higher rates of violence than children in the comparison group. Clearly, family trauma of all kinds may influence violence.

Child Victims and Persistent Offending   Widom also interviewed a sample of five hundred subjects twenty years after their childhood victimization. Preliminary analysis of this sample indicates that the long-term consequences of childhood victimization continues throughout the life cycle. Potential problems associated with abuse and neglect include mental health concerns, such as depression and suicide attempts; educational problems, including low IQ and poor reading ability; health and safety problems, including substance abuse; and occupational difficulties, including under- and unaggressive employment.

In a more recent analysis of these data, Widom and Michael Maxfield found that by the time they reached age 32 abused children had a higher frequency of adult offending than the unabused. People who began their offending careers as adults were also more likely to have been abused as children. Widom and Maxfield conclude that early intervention with at-risk children may be necessary to stop this cycle of violence.[161]

Sexual Abuse   Cohort research shows that sexually abused youths are much more likely to suffer an arrest than unabused children. The risk is greatest if the abuse took place when the child was less than seven years of age and the offense was committed by a male. Children who suffered multiple incidents of abuse had an increased risk of criminal involvement.[162] Sexually abused girls share a significant risk of becoming violent over the life course. There is also evidence that sexual abuse victims are more likely to later abuse others, especially if they were exposed to or observed firsthand other forms of family violence (for example, spouse abuse or sibling abuse) aside from their own sexual abuse.[163]

Self-report studies also confirm that child maltreatment increases the likelihood of delinquency. The most severely abused youths—those whose treatment was serious enough to warrant an official intervention by child protection services—are at the greatest risk for long-term serious delinquency.[164]

The Abuse–Delinquency Link

These research findings do not necessarily mean that most abused or neglected children eventually become delinquent. Many do not, and many seriously delinquent youths come from what appear to be model homes. Though Widom found that more abused children in her cohort became involved in crime and delinquency than did the unabused, the majority of *both* groups were neither delinquent nor adult offenders. She concludes: "The strength of the cycle of violence may be of less magnitude than some might have expected."[165]

Although these studies suggest an abuse–delinquency link, others find that the association is either nonsignificant or inconsistent, for example, having a greater influence on girls than boys.[166] Abused adolescents seem to get involved in more status-type offenses, such as running away, than in delinquency, perhaps indicating that abused children are more likely to "flee than fight."[167]

The abuse–delinquency link may be less than anticipated because of definitional ambiguity: some youths may not consider themselves abused under the definitions provided by researchers and therefore cannot relate their experiences to current behavior. For example, underage males who have been involved in sexual relations with older females may not consider themselves abused even though their experience falls under the legal and moral definition of "abuse."[168] This type of relationship made headlines in 1997–98 when Mary Kay LeTourneau, a thirty-five-year-old Seattle teacher pleaded guilty to the sexual abuse of a thirteen-year-old male student. The boy's response was to defend the relationship and insist that he had initiated it. "All that matters," he told one reporter, "was that we loved each other."[169] LeTourneau's community release was revoked in 1998 when it was discovered she had resumed the relationship and was pregnant with the boy's child.

The Family and Delinquency Prevention

Since the family is believed to play such an important role in the production of youth crime, it follows that improving family functioning can help prevent delinquency. Counselors commonly work with the families of antisocial youths as part of a court-ordered treatment strategy. Family counseling and therapy are almost mandatory when the child's acting-out behavior is suspected to be the result of family-related problems such as child abuse or neglect.[170] Some jurisdictions have integrated family counseling services into the juvenile court.[171]

Early Childhood Intervention

Another approach to involving the family in delinquency prevention is to attack the problem before it occurs. Early childhood prevention programs that target at-risk youths can relieve some of the symptoms associated with chronic delinquency.[172] Frequent home visits by trained nurses and other helpers to infants aged zero to 2 years reduce child abuse and other injuries to the infants. Preschool and weekly home visits by preschool teachers to children under age 5 substantially reduce arrests at least through age 15. Family therapy and parent training about delinquent and at-risk preadolescents reduce risk factors for delinquency such as aggression and hyperactivity.[173]

Among the best known of these early prevention programs is the Syracuse University Family Development Research Program. This program identifies high-risk, indigent women during the later stages of their pregnancies. After the women give birth, paraprofessionals are assigned to work with the mothers, encouraging sound parent–child relationships, providing nutrition information, and helping them to establish relationships with social service agencies. In addition to services for the mother, the program provides four-and-one-half years of quality child care at Syracuse University Children's Center. A ten-year follow-up compared children involved in the Syracuse program with a matched control group and found that those receiving intervention were less likely to be involved in criminal activity, were more likely to express positive feelings about themselves, and were able to take a more active role in dealing with personal problems. Girls seemed to especially benefit from the program, doing better in school and getting higher teacher evaluations; parents were more likely to express prosocial attitudes.[174]

The Perry Preschool in Michigan has provided disadvantaged students with a two-year program of educational enrichment supplemented with weekly home visits designed to improve child care; children in the program accumulated half the arrests of a matched comparison group and appeared to be better motivated.[175] The highly successful Hawaii Healthy Start program has helped thousands of families considered at risk to abuse and neglect.[176]

Improving Parenting Skills

The most widely cited parenting skills program is the one created at the Oregon Social Learning Center (OSLC) by Gerald R. Patterson and his associates.[177] Patterson's long-term research into the lifestyles of antisocial children convinced him that poor parenting skills were associated with antisocial behavior occurring in the home and at school. Family disruption and coercive exchanges between parents and children led to increased family tension, poor academic performance, and negative peer relations. The primary cause of the problem seemed to be that parents did not know how to deal effectively with their children. Parents sometimes ignored their children's behavior, but at other times the same childish actions would trigger an explosive rage. Some parents would discipline their children for reasons that had little to do with the children's behavior but rather reflected their own frustrations and conflicts.

The children reacted to indifferent parenting in a regular progression, from learning to be noncompliant at home to learning to be physically assaultive. Their "coercive behavior," which included whining, yelling, and temper tantrums, would sometimes be acquired by other family members, exacerbating the already explosive situation. Eventually, family conflict would escalate and flow out of the home and into the school and social environment.

The OSLC program uses behavior modification techniques to help parents of antisocial children acquire proper care and disciplinary methods. Parents are asked to select several particular behaviors for change. Staff counselors first analyze family dynamics and then work with parents to construct a change program. Parents are asked to closely monitor the particular behaviors and to count the weekly frequency of their occurrence. OSLC personnel teach both social skills to reinforce positive behaviors and constructive disciplinary methods to discourage negative ones. Incentive programs are initiated in which a child can earn points or praise for such desirable behaviors as being cooperative and doing chores. Points can be exchanged for allowance, prizes, or privileges. Parents are also taught effective disciplinary techniques that stress firmness and consistency rather than "nattering" (low intensity, nonverbal, or negative verbal behaviors, such as scowling or scolding) or explosive discipline, such as hitting, making humiliating remarks, or screaming. One important technique is the "time out" in which the child is removed for brief isolation in a quiet room. Parents are taught the importance of setting rules and sticking to them. The OSLC has also developed programs especially designed to help high-risk families, such as the Adolescent Transitions Program (ATP), which teaches parents skills to deal with especially troubled adolescents.

The Oregon program is not unique; there are similar methods of parent training being used with high-risk youths elsewhere. For example, Functional Family Therapy (FFT) is designed either to teach family members parenting skills they lack or to help them to better manage the skills they already possess. The program helps teach parents communications skills, provides technical aids that assist in reinforcing functional behavior, and helps institute interpersonal family tasks. Functional Family Therapy can effectively reduce recidivism of young offenders.[178]

Evidence suggests that early intervention in delinquency cases may be the most effective method and that the later the intervention, the more difficult the change process. Psychologist Edward Zigler and his associates found that early and intensive interventions in family functioning can result in significant improvement in parent–child relations and a concomitant reduction in antisocial activities.[179]

The parent training method used by the OSLC may be the most cost-effective method of early intervention.[180] A recent Rand survey found that parent training costs about one-twentieth what a home visit program costs and is more effective in preventing serious crimes. The Rand study estimates that 501 serious crimes could be prevented for every million dollars spent on parent training, a far cheaper solution to the crime problem than the use of long-term incarceration, which would cost about $16,000 to prevent a single crime![181]

SUMMARY

Poor family relationships have long been linked to the problem of juvenile delinquency. Early theories viewed the broken home as a cause of youthful misconduct, but subsequent research indicates that divorce, separation, or parental death plays a smaller role in influencing delinquent acts than was previously thought. More recently, experts have suggested that broken homes may have a greater effect than once believed. They argue that despite good intentions it is simply more difficult for one parent to provide the same degree of control, discipline, and support as two. The quality of family life also has a great influence on a child's behavior. Studies have explored the effect of discipline, parental misconduct, and family harmony on youth crime.

Concern over the relationship between family life and delinquency has been heightened by reports of widespread child abuse and neglect. Cases of abuse and neglect have been found in every level of the economic strata, and it has been estimated that there are three million reported cases of child abuse each year, of which one million are confirmed by child welfare investigators.

Two factors are seen as causing child abuse. First, parents who themselves suffered abuse as children tend to abuse their own children. Second, isolated and alienated families tend to become abusive.

Local, state, and federal governments have attempted to alleviate the problem of child abuse. The major issue has been state interference in the family structure. All fifty states have statutes requiring that suspected cases of abuse and neglect be reported.

A number of studies have linked abuse and neglect to juvenile delinquency. They show that a disproportionate number of court-adjudicated youths had been abused or neglected. Although the evidence so far is not conclusive, it suggests that a strong relationship exists between child abuse and neglect and subsequent delinquent behavior.

To make it easier to prosecute abusers, the Supreme Court has legalized the use of closed-circuit TV in some abuse cases. Most states allow children to use anatomically correct dolls when testifying in court.

The important role of the family in delinquency formation has been addressed in various prevention efforts. Family counseling and therapy are often used in cases involving antisocial youths. Parenting skills programs such as the Oregon Social Learning Center aim to prevent delinquency before it occurs.

KEY TERMS

nuclear family
broken home
blended families
intrafamily conflict
battered child syndrome
child abuse

neglect
abandonment
familicide
advisement hearing
pretrial conference
disposition hearing

balancing-of-the-interest
    approach
review hearings
hearsay

INFOTRAC COLLEGE EDITION EXERCISES

Due to the overwhelming influence that parents have on their childrens' values, attitudes, and thought processes, researchers believe that destructive home environments can influence criminal behavior. A majority of the work in this area has linked juvenile delinquency with abuse and neglect. However, the evidence is still inconclusive.

Explore the relationship between family structure and delinquent behavior. Review relevant articles from Info-Trac College Edition.

To search for information, use key words such as: *juvenile delinquency and family* and *delinquent behavior and family*.

QUESTIONS FOR DISCUSSION

1. What is the meaning of the terms *child abuse* and *child neglect*?
2. Social agencies, police departments, and health groups all indicate that child abuse and neglect are increasing. What is the incidence of such action by parents against children? Are the definitions of child abuse and child neglect the key elements in determining the volume of child abuse cases in various jurisdictions?
3. What causes parents to abuse their children?

4. What is meant by the child protection system? Do courts act in the best interest of the child when they allow an abused child to remain with the family?
5. Should children be allowed to testify in court via closed-circuit TV? Does this approach prevent defendants in child abuse cases from confronting their accusers?
6. Is corporal punishment ever permissible as a disciplinary method?

NOTES

1. Dirk Johnson, "Mother Goes from Martyr to Defendant in Infanticide," *New York Times* 7 August 1998, p. 1.
2. Associated Press, "Young Moms' Kids at Murder Risk," *USA Today* 22 October 1998, p. 1.
3. Clea Benson, "Marie Noe Released Until Her Trial," *Philadelphia Inquirer* 27 August 1998.
4. For a general review of the relationship between families and delinquency, see Alan Jay Lincoln and Murray Straus, *Crime and the Family* (Springfield, Ill.: Charles C. Thomas, 1985); Rolf Loeber and Magda Stouthamer-Loeber, "Family Factors as Correlates and Predictors of Juvenile Conduct Problems and Delinquency," in Michael Tonry and Norval Morris, eds., *Crime and Justice,* vol. 7 (Chicago: University of Chicago Press, 1986), pp. 29–151.
5. Paul Amato and Bruce Keith, "Parental Divorce and the Well-Being of Children: A Meta-Analysis," *Psychological Bulletin* 110:26–46 (1991).
6. Rolf Loeber and Magda Stouthamer-Loeber, "Development of Juvenile Aggression and Violence," *American Psychologist* 53:242–59 (1998), at 250.
7. Joan McCord, "Family Relationships, Juvenile Delinquency and Adult Criminality," *Criminology* 29:397–417 (1991); Scott Henggeler, ed., *Delinquency and Adolescent Psychopathology: A Family Ecological Systems Approach* (Littleton, Mass.: Wright-PSG, 1982).
8. David Farrington, "Juvenile Delinquency," in John Coleman, ed., *The School Years* (London: Routledge, 1992), pp. 139–40.
9. Ruth Inglis, *Sins of the Fathers: A Study of the Physical and Emotional Abuse of Children* (New York: St. Martin's Press, 1978), p. 131.
10. See Joseph J. Costa and Gordon K. Nelson, *Child Abuse and Neglect: Legislation, Reporting, and Prevention* (Lexington, Mass.: D.C. Heath, 1978), p. xiii.
11. S. E. Shank, "Women and the Labor Market: The Link Grows Stronger," *Monthly Labor Review* 111:3–8 (1988).
12. Tamar Lewin, "Men Assuming Bigger Role at Home, New Survey Shows," *New York Times* 15 April 1998, p. A18.
13. Christy Buchanan, Eleanor Maccoby, and Sanford Dornbusch, "Caught between Parents: Adolescents' Experience in Divorced Homes," *Child Development* 62:1008–29 (1991).
14. Pamela Webster, Terri Orbuch, and James House, "Effects of Childhood Family Background on Adult Marital Quality and Perceived Stability," *American Journal of Sociology* 101:404–32 (1995).
15. Children's Defense Fund, *The State of America's Children 1995* (Washington, D.C.: Children's Defense Fund, 1995), p. 5.
16. Edward Zigler, "Addressing the Nation's Child Care Crisis, the School of the Twenty-First Century," *American Journal of Orthopsychiatry* 59:484–91 (1989), at 486.
17. News Release, "Kids Count Survey 1998," Annie E. Casey Foundation, Baltimore, Md., May 5, 1998.

18. David Wiese and Deborah Daro, *Current Trends in Child Abuse Reporting and Fatalities: The Results of the 1994 Annual Fifty-State Survey* (Chicago: National Committee to Prevent Child Abuse, 1995).
19. Richard Gelles and Murray Straus, *Intimate Violence* (New York: Simon and Schuster, 1988), p. 27.
20. Loeber and Stouthamer-Loeber, "Family Factors," pp. 39–41.
21. Paul Howes and Howard Markman, "Marital Quality and Child Functioning: A Longitudinal Investigation," *Child Development* 60:1044–51 (1989).
22. Barbara Dafoe Whitehead, "Dan Quayle Was Right," *Atlantic Monthly* 271:47–84 (1993).
23. C. Patrick Brady, James Bray, and Linda Zeeb, "Behavior Problems of Clinic Children: Relation to Parental Marital Status, Age, and Sex of Child," *American Journal of Orthopsychiatry* 56:399–412 (1986).
24. Scott Henggeler, *Delinquency in Adolescence* (Newbury Park, Calif.: Sage, 1989), p. 48.
25. Sheldon Glueck and Eleanor Glueck, *Unraveling Juvenile Delinquency* (Cambridge: Harvard University Press, 1950); Ashley Weeks, "Predicting Juvenile Delinquency," *American Sociological Review* 8:40–46 (1943).
26. Jackson Toby, "The Differential Impact of Family Disorganization," *American Sociological Review* 22:505–12 (1957); Ruth Morris, "Female Delinquency and Relation Problems," *Social Forces* 43:82–89 (1964); Roland Chilton and Gerald Markle, "Family Disruption, Delinquent Conduct, and the Effects of Sub-classification," *American Sociological Review* 37:93–99 (1972).
27. For a review of these early studies, see Thomas Monahan, "Family Status and the Delinquent Child: A Reappraisal and Some New Findings," *Social Forces* 35:250–58 (1957).
28. Clifford Shaw and Henry McKay, *Report on the Causes of Crime, Social Factors in Juvenile Delinquency,* vol. 2 (Washington, D.C.: U.S. Government Printing Office, 1931), p. 392.
29. John Laub and Robert Sampson, "Unraveling Families and Delinquency: A Reanalysis of the Gluecks' Data," *Criminology* 26:355–80 (1988); Lawrence Rosen, "The Broken Home and Male Delinquency," in M. Wolfgang, L. Savitz, and N. Johnston, eds., *The Sociology of Crime and Delinquency* (New York: Wiley, 1970), pp. 489–95.
30. Christina DeJong and Kenneth Jackson, "Putting Race into Context: Race, Juvenile Justice Processing, and Urbanization," *Justice Quarterly* 15:487–504 (1998).
31. L. Edward Wells and Joseph Rankin, "Families and Delinquency: A Meta-Analysis of the Impact of Broken Homes," *Social Problems* 38:71–90 (1991).
32. Robert Johnson, John Hoffman, and Dean Gerstein, "The Relationship between Family Structure and Adolescent Substance Abuse" (Washington, D.C.: Office of Applied Studies, Substance Abuse and Mental Health Services Administration, 1996).

33. Sara McLanahan, "Father Absence and the Welfare of Children," working paper prepared for the John D. and Catherine MacArthur Research Foundation, Chicago, Ill., 1998.
34. Loeber and Stouthamer-Loeber, "Family Factors," p. 78.
35. James Q. Wilson and Richard Herrnstein, *Crime and Human Nature* (New York: Simon and Schuster, 1985), p. 249.
36. Joseph Rankin and Roger Kern, "Parental Attachments and Delinquency," *Criminology* 32:495–515 (1994).
37. McLanahan, "Father Absence and the Welfare of Children."
38. Marvin Krohn, Terence Thornberry, Lori Collins-Hall, and Alan Lizotte, "School Dropout, Delinquent Behavior, and Drug Use," in Howard Kaplan, ed., *Drugs, Crime and Other Deviant Adaptations: Longitudinal Studies* (New York: Plenum Press, 1995), pp. 163–83.
39. Nan Marie Astone and Sara McLanahan, "Family Structure, Parental Practices and High School Completion," *American Sociological Review* 56:309–20 (1991).
40. Mary Pat Traxler, "The Influence of the Father and Alternative Male Role Models on African-American Boys' Involvement in Antisocial Behavior," paper presented at the Annual Meeting of the American Society of Criminology, New Orleans, November 1992.
41. Judith Smetena, "Adolescents' and Parents' Reasoning about Actual Family Conflict," *Child Development* 60:1052–67 (1989).
42. F. Ivan Nye, "Child Adjustment in Broken and Unhappy Unbroken Homes," *Marriage and Family* 19:356–61 (1957); idem, *Family Relationships and Delinquent Behavior* (New York: Wiley, 1958).
43. Michael Hershorn and Alan Rosenbaum, "Children of Marital Violence: A Closer Look at the Unintended Victims," *American Journal of Orthopsychiatry* 55:260–66 (1985).
44. Peter Jaffe, David Wolfe, Susan Wilson, and Lydia Zak, "Similarities in Behavior and Social Maladjustment among Child Victims and Witnesses to Family Violence," *American Journal of Orthopsychiatry* 56:142–46 (1986).
45. Veronica Herrera, "Equals in Risk? The Differential Impact of Family Violence on Male and Female Delinquency," paper presented at the Annual Society of Criminology Meeting, San Diego, Calif., November 1997.
46. Henggeler, *Delinquency in Adolescence,* p. 39.
47. Jill Leslie Rosenbaum, "Family Dysfunction and Female Delinquency," *Crime and Delinquency* 35:31–44 (1989), at 41.
48. Paul Robinson, "Parents of 'Beyond Control' Adolescents," *Adolescence* 13:116–19 (1978).
49. Loeber and Stouthamer-Loeber, "Development of Juvenile Aggression and Violence," p. 251.
50. Carolyn Smith, Sung Joon Jang, and Susan Stern, "The Effect of Delinquency on Families," *Family and Corrections Network Report* 13:1–11 (1997).
51. Amato and Keith, "Parental Divorce and the Well-Being of Children."
52. Adrian Raine, Patricia Brennan, and Sarnoff Mednick, "Interaction between Birth Complications and Early Maternal Rejection in Predisposing Individuals to Adult Violence: Specificity to Serious, Early-Onset Violence," *American Journal of Psychiatry* 154:1265–71 (1997).
53. Bill McCarthy and John Hagan, "Mean Streets: The Theoretical Significance of Situational Delinquency among Homeless Youth," *American Journal of Sociology* 98:597–627 (1992).
54. Carolyn Smith, Alan Lizotte, Terence Thornberry, and Marvin Krohn, "Resilience to Delinquency," *The Prevention Researcher* 4:4–7 (1997).
55. Sung Joon Jang and Carolyn Smith, "A Test of Reciprocal Causal Relationships among Parental Supervision, Affective Ties, and Delinquency," *Journal of Research in Crime and Delinquency* 34:307–36 (1997).
56. Gerald Patterson and Magda Stouthamer-Loeber, "The Correlation of Family Management Practices and Delinquency," *Child Development* 55:1299–1307 (1984); Gerald R. Patterson, *A Social Learning Approach: Coercive Family Process,* vol. 3 (Eugene, Ore.: Castalia, 1982).
57. Christopher Ellison and Darren Sherkat, "Conservative Protestantism and Support for Corporal Punishment," *American Sociological Review* 58:131–44 (1993).
58. Murray Straus, "Discipline and Deviance: Physical Punishment of Children and Violence and Other Crime in Adulthood," *Social Problems* 38:101–23 (1991).
59. Murray A. Straus, "Spanking and the Making of a Violent Society; The Short- and Long-Term Consequences of Corporal Punishment," *Pediatrics* 98:837–43 (1996).
60. Ibid.
61. Loeber and Stouthamer-Loeber, "Development of Juvenile Aggression and Violence," p. 251.
62. Nathaniel Pallone and James Hennessy, "Brain Dysfunction and Criminal Violence," *Society* 35:21–27 (1998).
63. Nye, *Family Relationships and Delinquent Behavior.*
64. Rolf Loeber and Thomas Dishion, "Boys Who Fight at Home and School: Family Conditions Influencing Cross-Setting Consistency," *Journal of Consulting and Clinical Psychology* 52:759–68 (1984).
65. Lisa Broidy, "Direct Supervision and Delinquency: Assessing the Adequacy of Structural Proxies," *Journal of Criminal Justice* 23:541–54 (1995).
66. Stephen Cernkovich and Peggy Giordano, "Family Relationships and Delinquency," *Criminology* 25:295–321 (1987).
67. Jang and Smith, "A Test of Reciprocal Causal Relationships among Parental Supervision, Affective Ties, and Delinquency."
68. Linda Waite and Lee Lillard, "Children and Marital Disruption," *American Journal of Sociology* 96:930–53 (1991).
69. Douglas Downey, "When Bigger Is Not Better: Family Size, Parental Reources, and Children's Educational Performance," *American Sociological Review* 60:746–61 (1995).
70. G. Rahav, "Birth Order and Delinquency," *British Journal of Criminology* 20:385–95 (1980); D. Viles and D. Challinger, "Family Size and Birth Order of Young Offenders," *International Journal of Offender Therapy and Comparative Criminology* 25:60–66 (1981).
71. David Eggebeen and Daniel Lichter, "Race, Family Structure, and Changing Poverty among American Children," *American Sociological Review* 56:801–17 (1991).
72. For an early review, see Barbara Wooton, *Social Science and Social Pathology* (London: Allen and Unwin, 1959).
73. Laub and Sampson, "Unraveling Families and Delinquency," p. 375.
74. D. J. West and D. P. Farrington, eds., "Who Becomes Delinquent?", in *The Delinquent Way of Life* (London: Heinemann, 1977); D. J. West, *Delinquency, Its Roots, Careers, and Prospects* (Cambridge: Harvard University Press, 1982).
75. West, *Delinquency,* p. 114.
76. David Farrington, "Understanding and Preventing Bullying," in Michael Tonry, ed., *Crime and Justice,* vol. 17 (Chicago: University of Chicago Press, 1993), pp. 381–457.
77. Leonore Simon, "Does Criminal Offender Treatment Work?", *Applied and Preventive Psychology* Summer:1–22 (1998).
78. Philip Harden and Robert Pihl, "Cognitive Function, Cardiovascular Reactivity, and Behavior in Boys at High Risk for Alcoholism," *Journal of Abnormal Psychology* 104:94–103 (1995).
79. Laub and Sampson, "Unraveling Families and Delinquency," p. 370.
80. D. P. Farrington, Gwen Gundry, and D. J. West, "The Familial Transmission of Criminality," in Alan Lincoln and Murray Straus, eds., *Crime and the Family* (Springfield, Ill.: Charles C. Thomas, 1985), pp. 193–206.
81. See, generally, Wooton, *Social Science and Social Pathology;* H. Wilson, "Juvenile Delinquency, Parental Criminality, and Social Handicaps," *British Journal of Criminology* 15:241–50 (1975).
82. David Rowe and Bill Gulley, "Sibling Effects on Substance Use and Delinquency," *Criminology* 30:217–32 (1992); see also, David Rowe, Joseph Rogers, and Sylvia Meseck-Bushey, "Sibling Delinquency and the Family Environment: Shared and Unshared Influences," *Child Development* 63:59–67 (1992).

83. Charles De Witt, director of the National Institute of Justice, quoted in National Institute of Justice, Research in Brief, *The Cycle of Violence* (Washington, D.C.: National Institute of Justice, 1992), p. 1.

84. Richard Gelles and Claire Pedrick Cornell, *Intimate Violence in Families,* 2nd ed. (Newbury Park, Calif.: Sage, 1990), p. 33.

85. Lois Hochhauser, "Child Abuse and the Law: A Mandate for Change," *Harvard Law Journal* 18:200 (1973); see also, Douglas J. Besharov, "The Legal Aspects of Reporting Known and Suspected Child Abuse and Neglect," *Villanova Law Review* 23:458 (1978).

86. C. Henry Kempe, F. N. Silverman, B. F. Steele, W. Droegemueller, and H. K. Silver, "The Battered-Child Syndrome," *Journal of the American Medical Association* 181:17–24 (1962).

87. Vincent J. Fontana, "The Maltreated Children of Our Times," *Villanova Law Review* 23:448 (1978).

88. Ray E. Helfer and C. Henry Kempe, eds., *Child Abuse and Neglect: The Family and the Community* (Cambridge, Mass.: Ballinger, 1976), p. xix.

89. Brian G. Fraser, "A Glance at the Past, a Gaze at the Present, a Glimpse at the Future: A Critical Analysis of the Development of Child Abuse Reporting Statutes," *Chicago-Kent Law Review* 54:643 (1977–78).

90. Vincent J. Fontana, "To Prevent the Abuse of the Future," *Trial* 10:14 (1974).

91. See, especially, Inglis, *Sins of the Fathers,* chap. 8.

92. William Downs and Brenda Miller, "Relationships between Experiences of Parental Violence during Childhood and Women's Self-Esteem," *Violence and Victims* 13:63–78 (1998).

93. Ruth S. Kempe and C. Henry Kempe, *Child Abuse* (Cambridge: Harvard University Press, 1978), pp. 6–7.

94. Ibid.

95. Herman Daldin, "The Fate of the Sexually Abused Child," *Clinical Social Work Journal* 16:20–26 (1988).

96. Judith Herman, Diana Russell, and Karen Trocki, "Long-Term Effects of Incestuous Abuse in Childhood," *American Journal of Psychiatry* 143:1293–96 (1986).

97. Kathleen Kendall-Tackett, Linda Meyer Williams, and David Finkelhor, "Impact of Sexual Abuse on Children: A Review and Synthesis of Recent Empirical Studies," *Psychological Bulletin* 113:164–80 (1993).

98. Magnus Seng, "Child Sexual Abuse and Adolescent Prostitution: A Comparative Analysis," *Adolescence* 24:665–75 (1989); Dorothy Bracey, *Baby Pros: Preliminary Profiles of Juvenile Prostitutes* (New York: John Jay Press, 1979).

99. Kendall-Tackett, Williams, and Finkelhor, "Impact of Sexual Abuse on Children," p. 171.

100. Murray Straus, Richard Gelles, and Suzanne Steinmentz, *Behind Closed Doors: Violence in the American Family* (Garden City, N.Y.: Anchor Books, 1980); Richard Gelles and Murray Straus, "Violence in the American Family," *Journal of Social Issues* 35:15–39 (1979).

101. Gelles and Straus, "Violence in the American Family," p. 24.

102. Gelles and Straus, *Intimate Violence,* pp. 108–9; Murray A. Straus and Glenda Kaufman Kantor, "Trends in Physical Abuse by Parents from 1975 to 1992: A Comparison of Three National Surveys," paper presented at the Annual Meeting of the American Society of Criminology, Boston, 1995.

103. Murray A. Straus and Anita K. Mathur, "Social Change and Trends in Approval of Corporal Punishment by Parents from 1968 to 1994," in D. Frehsee, W. Horn, and K. Bussman, eds., *Violence Against Children* (New York: Walter de Gruyter, 1996) pp. 91–105.

104. Murray Straus, *Beating the Devil Out of Them: Corporal Punishment in American Families* (San Francisco, Calif.: Lexington/Jossey-Bass, 1994); Richard Gelles and Murray Straus, *Is Violence Toward Children Increasing? A Comparison of 1975 and 1985 National Survey Rates* (Durham, N.H.: Family Violence Research Program, 1985).

105. Diana Russell, *Sexual Exploitation: Rape, Child Sexual Abuse, and Workplace Harassment* (Beverly Hills, Calif.: Sage, 1984).

106. Maria Root, "Treatment Failures: The Role of Sexual Victimization in Women's Addictive Behavior," *American Journal of Orthopsychiatry* 59:543–49 (1989).

107. Ching-Tung Wang and Deborah Daro, *Current Trends in Child Abuse Reporting and Fatalities: The Results of the 1997 Annual Fifty State Survey* (Chicago, Ill.: The Center on Child Abuse Prevention Research, National Committee to Prevent Child Abuse, 1998).

108. Carolyn Webster-Stratton, "Comparison of Abusive and Nonabusive Families with Conduct-Disordered Children," *American Journal of Orthopsychiatry* 55:59–69 (1985); Fontana, "To Prevent the Abuse of the Future," p. 16; Fontana, "The Maltreated Children of Our Times," p. 451; Brandt F. Steele and Carl B. Pollock, "A Psychiatric Study of Parents Who Abuse Infants and Small Children," in Ray Helfer and C. Henry Kempe, eds., *The Battered Child* (Chicago: University of Chicago Press, 1968), pp. 103–45.

109. Inglis, *Sins of the Fathers,* p. 68.

110. Ibid., p. 53.

111. Brandt F. Steele, "Violence within the Family," in Ray E. Helfer and C. Henry Kempe, eds., *Child Abuse and Neglect: The Family and the Community* (Cambridge, Mass.: Ballinger, 1976), p. 13.

112. William Sack, Robert Mason, and James Higgins, "The Single-Parent Family and Abusive Punishment," *American Journal of Orthopsychiatry* 55:252–59 (1985).

113. Fontana, "The Maltreated Children of Our Times," pp. 450–51; see also, Blair Justice and Rita Justice, *The Abusing Family* (New York: Human Sciences Press, 1976); Steele, "Violence within the Family," p. 12; Nanette Dembitz, "Preventing Youth Crime by Preventing Child Neglect," *American Bar Association Journal* 65:920–23 (1979).

114. Gelles and Straus, *Intimate Violence,* p. 85.

115. Wang and Daro, *Current Trends in Child Abuse,* p. 11.

116. Nancy Smyth, Brenda Miller, Paula Janicki, and Pamela Mudar, "Mothers' Protectiveness and Child Abuse: The Impact of Her History of Childhood Sexual Abuse and an Alcohol Diagnosis," paper presented at the American Society of Criminology Meeting, Boston, Mass., November 1995; Richard Famularo, Karen Stone, Richard Barnum, and Robert Wharton, "Alcoholism and Severe Child Maltreatment," *American Journal of Orthopsychiatry* 56:481–85 (1987).

117. Jordana Hart, "Child Abuse Found Tied to Drug Use," *Boston Globe* 2 June 1989, p. 23.

118. Wang and Daro, *Current Trends in Child Abuse,* p. 18.

119. Martin Daly and Margo Wilson, "Violence against Stepchildren," *Current Directions in Psychological Science* 5:77–81 (1996).

120. Ibid.

121. Margo Wilson, Martin Daly, and Atonietta Daniele, "Familicide: The Killing of Spouse and Children," *Aggressive Behavior* 21:275–91 (1995).

122. Wang and Daro, *Current Trends in Child Abuse,* p. 10.

123. Ibid., p. 12.

124. Richard Gelles, "Child Abuse and Violence in Single-Parent Families: Parent Absence and Economic Deprivation," *American Journal of Orthopsychiatry* 59:492–501 (1989).

125. Susan Napier and Mitchell Silverman, "Family Violence as a Function of Occupation Status, Socioeconomic Class, and Other Variables," paper presented at the American Society of Criminology Meeting, Boston, Mass., November 1995.

126. Karla McPherson and Laura Garcia, "Effects of Social Class and Familiarity on Pediatricians' Responses to Child Abuse," *Child Welfare* 62:387–93 (1983).

127. S. Bittner and E. H. Newberger, "Pediatric Understanding of Child Abuse," *Pediatrics in Review* 7:197–207 (1981); see also, E. H. Newberger and P. Bourne, "The Medicalization

and Legalization of Child Abuse," *American Journal of Orthopsychiatry* 48:593–607 (1978).

128. Cecil Willis and Richard Wells, "The Police and Child Abuse: An Analysis of Police Decisions to Report Illegal Behavior," *Criminology* 26:695–716 (1988).

129. Robert Burgess and Patricia Draper, "The Explanation of Family Violence," in Ohlin and Tonry, eds., *Family Violence* (Chicago: University of Chicago Press, 1989), pp. 59–117.

130. Ibid., pp. 103–4.

131. Linda Gordon, "Incest and Resistance: Patterns of Father–Daughter Incest, 1880–1930," *Social Problems* 33:253–67 (1986).

132. P.L. 93–247 (1974); P.L. 104–235 (1996).

133. 452 U.S. 18, 101 S.Ct. 2153 (1981); 455 U.S. 745, 102 S.Ct. 1388 (1982).

134. For a survey of each state's reporting requirements, abuse and neglect legislation, and available programs and agencies, see Costa and Nelson, *Child Abuse and Neglect.*

135. Martha Brannigan, "Arrests Spark Furor over the Reporting of Suspected Abuse," *Wall Street Journal* 7 June 1989, p. B8.

136. Debra Whitcomb, *When the Victim Is a Child* (Washington, D.C.: National Institute of Justice, 1992), p. 5.

137. "False Accusations of Abuse Devastating to Families," *Crime Victims Digest* 6 (2):4–5 (1989).

138. This section relies heavily on Shirley Dobbin, Sophia Gatowski, and Margaret Springate, "Child Abuse and Neglect," *Juvenile and Family Court Journal* 48:43–54 (1997).

139. For an analysis of the accuracy of children's recollections of abuse, see Candace Kruttschnitt and Maude Dornfeld, "Will They Tell? Assessing Preadolescents' Reports of Family Violence," *Journal of Research in Crime and Delinquency* 29:136–47 (1992).

140. Lindsay Arthur, "Child Sexual Abuse: Improving the System's Response," *Juvenile and Family Court Journal* 37:27–36 (1986).

141. Ibid.

142. Whitcomb, *When the Victim Is a Child,* p. 33.

143. *White v. Illinois,* 502 U.S. 346; 112 S.Ct. 736 (1992).

144. Myrna Raeder, "*White's* Effect on the Right to Confront One's Accuser," *Criminal Justice* (Winter) 1993, pp. 2–7.

145. *Coy v. Iowa,* 487 U.S. 1012 (1988).

146. *Maryland v. Craig,* 110 S.Ct. 3157 (1990).

147. Cathy Spatz Widom, *The Cycle of Violence* (Washington, D.C.: National Institute of Justice, 1992), p. 1.

148. *Walker v. Fagg,* 400 S.E. 2d 708 (Va. App. 1991).

149. Mary Haskett and Janet Kistner, "Social Interactions and Peer Perceptions of Young Physically Abused Children," *Child Development* 62:679–90 (1991).

150. Timothy Brezina, "Adolescent Maltreatment and Delinquency: The Question of Intervening Processes," *Journal of Research in Crime and Delinquency* 35:71–99 (1998).

151. Gelles and Straus, "Violence in the American Family."

152. Helfer and Kempe, *Child Abuse and Neglect,* pp. xvii–xviii.

153. National Center on Child Abuse and Neglect, Department of Health, Education, and Welfare, *1977 Analysis of Child Abuse and Neglect Research* (Washington, D.C.: U.S. Government Printing Office, 1978), p. 29.

154. Steele, "Violence within the Family," p. 22.

155. L. Bender and F. J. Curran, "Children and Adolescents Who Kill," *Journal of Criminal Psychopathology* 1:297 (1940), cited in Steele, "Violence within the Family," p. 21.

156. W. M. Easson and R. M. Steinhilber, "Murderous Aggression by Children and Adolescents," *Archives of General Psychiatry* 4:1–11 (1961), cited in Steele, "Violence within the Family," p. 22; see also, J. Duncan and G. Duncan, "Murder in the Family: A Study of Some Homicidal Adolescents," *American Journal of Psychiatry* 127:1498–1502 (1971); C. King, "The Ego and Integration of Violence in Homicidal Youth," *American Journal of Orthopsychiatry* 45:134–45 (1975); James Sorrells, "Kids Who Kill," *Crime and Delinquency* 23:312–26 (1977).

157. C. H. King, "The Ego and the Integration of Violence in Homicidal Youth," *American Journal of Orthopsychiatry* 45:134–45 (1975).

158. Jose Alfaro, "Report of the Relationship between Child Abuse and Neglect and Later Socially Deviant Behavior," unpublished paper (Albany, N.Y.: n.d.) pp. 175–219.

159. Cathy Spatz Widom, "Child Abuse, Neglect, and Violent Criminal Behavior," *Criminology* 27:251–71 (1989).

160. Widom, *The Cycle of Violence,* p. 1.

161. Michael Maxfield and Cathy Spatz Widom, "Childhood Victimization and Patterns of Offending through the Life Cycle: Early Onset and Continuation," paper presented at the American Society of Criminology Meeting, Boston, Mass., November 1995.

162. Jane Siegel and Linda Meyer Williams, "Violent Behavior among Men Abused as Children," paper presented at the American Society of Criminology Meeting, Boston, Mass., November 1995; Jane Siegel and Linda Meyer Williams, "Aggressive Behavior among Women Sexually Abused as Children," paper presented at the American Society of Criminology Meeting, Phoenix, Arizona, 1993 (rev. version).

163. David Skuse, Arnon Bentovim, Jill Hodges, Jim Stevenson, Chriso Andreou, Monica Lanyado, Michelle New, Bryn Williams, and Dean McMillan, "Risk Factors for Development of Sexually Abusive Behaviour in Sexually Victimised Adolescent Boys: Cross Sectional Study," *British Medical Journal* 317:175–80 (1998).

164. Carolyn Smith and Terence Thornberry, "The Relationship between Childhood Maltreatment and Adolescent Involvement in Delinquency," *Criminology* 33:451–77 (1995).

165. Widom, "Child Abuse, Neglect, and Violent Criminal Behavior," p. 267.

166. Bruce Rind, Philip Tromovitch, and Robert Bauserman, "A Meta-Analytic Examination of Assumed Properties of Child Sexual Abuse Using College Samples," *Psychological Bulletin* 124:22–53 (1998); Kimberly Barletto, "Who's at Risk: Delinquent Trajectories of Children with Attention and Conduct Problems," paper presented at the American Society of Criminology Meeting, San Diego, Calif., 1997; Veronica Herrera, "Equals in Risk? The Differential Impact of Family Violence on Male and Female Delinquency," paper presented at the Annual Society of Criminology Meeting, San Diego, Calif., November, 1997.

167. Matthew Zingraff, "Child Maltreatment and Youthful Problem Behavior," *Criminology* 31:173–202 (1993).

168. Rind, Tromovitch, and Bauserman, "A Meta-Analytic Examination of Assumed Properties of Child Sexual Abuse Using College Samples," p. 46.

169. Frank Bruni, "In an Age of Consent, Defining Abuse by Adults," *New York Times* 9 November 1997, p. A18.

170. Leonard Edwards and Inger Sagatun, "Dealing with Parent and Child in Serious Abuse Cases," *Juvenile and Family Court Journal* 34:9–14 (1983).

171. Susan McPherson, Lance McDonald, and Charles Ryer, "Intensive Counseling with Families of Juvenile Offenders," *Juvenile and Family Court Journal* 34:27–34 (1983).

172. The programs in this section are described in Edward Zigler, Cara Taussig, and Kathryn Black, "Early Childhood Intervention, a Promising Preventative for Juvenile Delinquency," *American Psychologist* 47:997–1006 (1992).

173. Lawrence W. Sherman, Denise C. Gottfredson, Doris L. MacKenzie, John Eck, Peter Reuter, and Shawn D. Bushway, *Preventing Crime: What Works, What Doesn't, What's Promising* (Washington, D.C: National Institute of Justice, 1998).

174. Peter Greenwood, Karyn Model, and C. Peter Rydell, *The Cost-Effectiveness of Early Intervention as a Strategy for Reducing Violent Crime* (Santa Monica, Calif.: Rand, 1995).

175. Ibid., p. 7.

176. Ralph Earle, *Helping to Prevent Child Abuse and Future Criminal Consequences: Hawaii Healthy Start* (Washington, D.C.: National Institute of Justice, 1995).

177. See, generally, Gerald Patterson, "Performance Models for Antisocial Boys," *American Psychologist* 41:432–44 (1986); idem, *Coercive Family Process* (Eugene, Ore.: Castalia, 1982).

178. Donald Gordon, "Functional Family Therapy for Delinquents," in Robert Ross, Daniel Antonowicz, and Gurmeet Dhaliwal, eds., *Going Straight: Effective Delinquency Prevention and Offender Rehabilitation* (Ontario, Canada: Air Training and Publications, 1995), pp. 163–77.

179. Zigler, Taussig, and Black, "Early Childhood Intervention, a Promising Preventative for Juvenile Delinquency," pp. 1000–4.

180. N. A. Wiltz and G. R. Patterson, "An Evaluation of Parent Training Procedures Designed to Alter Inappropriate Aggressive Behavior in Boys," *Behavior Therapy* 5:215–21 (1974).

181. Peter Greenwood, Karyn Model, and C. Peter Rydell, *The Cost-Effectiveness of Early Intervention as a Strategy for Reducing Violent Crime* (Santa Monica, Calif.: Rand, 1995).

Chapter Nine

Peers and Delinquency: Juvenile Gangs and Groups

Gang activity is a way of life for residents living in two Staten Island, New York, public housing projects.[1] The "Bloods" sell crack in Markham Gardens, and the "Wolfpack" controls the drug market in "the Projects," as neighboring West Brighton Houses is known. The rivalry between the two gangs exploded on July 16, 1998, with the slaying of Eric Trotman, a member of the Bloods. When word spread through Markham Gardens that Shatiek Johnson, a Wolfpack member, was the shooter, the Bloods "put out a contract" on him. Ten days later police officer Gerard Carter and his partner, Eric Storch, were patrolling the courtyard in West Brighton Houses when they saw a youth who fit the description of Shatiek. The two officers kept driving, again checking the picture before returning to the courtyard. Then, according to police reports, Shatiek suddenly opened fire through the windshield, striking Officer Carter in the head. Charged with second-degree murder for the slaying of Officer Carter and gang member Trotman, Shatiek, who is not yet eighteen, faces a sentence of twenty-five years to life on each count.

The nation has been bombarded with stories like that of Shatiek Johnson, giving people the impression that the United States is being threatened by a horde of gun-wielding gang boys. There has been an outcry from politicians to increase punishment for the "little monsters" and to save the "fallen angels" or the victimized youths who are innocent.[2] Although the media may exaggerate the juvenile gang problem, or at least use it to increase ratings, Shatiek's story is not dissimilar from that of many other children raised in tough housing projects where distrust of outsiders is normative and residents fear gang retribution if they complain or speak out. With an absent father and a single mother who could not control her five sons, Shatiek lived in a world of drugs, gangs, and shootouts long before he was old enough to vote. His father was a convicted drug dealer, and two of his brothers were in prison for violent crimes. By age 15, Shatiek had been convicted of manslaughter for the beating death of a homeless man in a dispute over $10. Shatiek pleaded guilty to manslaughter and was given a one- to three-year sentence at a youth detention center. He was denied parole in February 1997 but was released on April 10, 1998, because of state guidelines that mandate freeing any prisoner who has served two-thirds of his sentence without any major infractions in prison. Now charged with second-degree murder in the slaying of Officer Carter and gang member Trotman, Shatiek faces a sentence of twenty-five years to life on each count.

Although killing a police officer is a capital crime under New York law, Shatiek is not yet eighteen and cannot, therefore, receive the death penalty. However, his crimes have encouraged New York political leaders to demand the abolition of parole or early release of violent criminals. New York City Mayor Rudolph W. Giuliani issued a statement on the case which said in part:

> How many more police officers and innocent civilians will we allow to be killed or critically injured by criminals who have been released prematurely from prison before we repair the system that lets them loose? We have made unprecedented progress in reducing crime. . . . But we have to realize that these gains can't be sustained—much less continued—unless we fix the state criminal justice system that recycles criminals rather than giving them the punishment they deserve. . . . We must also correct the deep flaws in our juvenile justice system, so that 15-, 16-, and 17-year-old juveniles who kill people and commit other violent crimes are penalized as adults, and their records made public. . . . Pretending that a crime never happened, as we do now, reflects a destructive philosophy and perpetuates the criminal mindset in the juvenile offender.[3]

Cases like that of Shatiek Johnson illustrate why few issues in the study of delinquency are more important today than the problems presented by law-violating gangs and groups.[4] Although some gangs are made up of only a few loosely organized neighborhood youths, others have thousands of members who cooperate in highly complex illegal enterprises. A significant portion of all drug distribution in the nation's inner cities is believed to be gang controlled; gang violence accounts for more than one thousand homicides each year. Correctional surveys indicate that about 19 percent of all male and 3 percent of all female inmates are gang members.[5]

Social service and law enforcement groups have made a concerted effort to contain gangs and to reduce their criminal activity using approaches ranging from treatment-oriented settlement houses to deploying tactical gang control units. The problem of gang control is a difficult one: gangs flourish in inner-city areas that offer lower-class youths few conventional opportunities. Gang members are resistant to offers of help that cannot deliver legitimate economic hope. Although gang members may be subject to arrest, prosecution, and incarceration, a new crop of young recruits is always ready to take the place of their fallen comrades. Those sent to prison find that upon release their former gangs are only too willing to have them return to action.

In this chapter we review the nature and extent of gang and group delinquency. The chapter begins with a discussion of peer relations and shows how group relations influence delinquent behavior. Then we explore the definition, nature, and structure of delinquent gangs. In addition, theories of gang formation, the extent of gang activity, and gang-control efforts are presented.

Adolescent Peer Relations

Psychologists have long recognized that as children mature the nature of their friendship patterns also evolves. Although parents are the primary source of influence and attention in children's early years, between ages 8 and 14 children seek out a stable peer group, and both the number and the variety of friendships increase as children go through adolescence. Friends soon begin to have a greater influence over decision making than parents.[6] By their early teens, children report that their friends give them emotional support when they are feeling bad and that they can confide intimate feelings to peers without worrying about their confidences being betrayed.[7]

cliques
Small groups of friends who share intimate knowledge and confidences.

crowds
Loosely organized groups who share interests and activities.

As they go through adolescence, children form **cliques,** small groups of friends who share activities and confidences.[8] They also belong to **crowds,** loosely organized groups of children who share interests and activities such as sports, religion, or hobbies. Popular youths can be members of a variety of same-sex cliques and crowds while also joining with groups containing members of the opposite sex. Intimate friends play an important role in social development, but adolescents are also deeply influenced by this wider circle of friends. Adolescent self-image is in part formed by perceptions of one's place in the social world—whether the individual is considered an accepted insider or an unpopular outcast.[9]

In later adolescence, acceptance by their peers has a major impact on socialization. Popular youths do well in school and are socially astute. In contrast, children who are rejected by their peers are more likely to display aggressive behavior and to disrupt group activities by bickering or behaving antisocially.[10] Lower-class youths, lacking in educational and vocational opportunities, may place even greater emphasis on friendship than middle-class youths who can easily replace friends as they change locale and involvements (for example, as they go off to college).[11]

Peer relations, then, are a significant aspect of maturation. Some experts, such as Judith Rich Harris (see Chapter 8), believe peers exert a powerful influence on youths and pressure them to conform to group values and suggest that peer influence may be more important than parental nurturance in the development of long-term behavior.[12] Peers guide each other and help each other learn to share and cooperate, to cope with aggressive impulses, and to discuss feelings they would not dare bring up at home. Youths can compare their own experiences with peers and learn that others have similar concerns and problems; they realize that they are not alone.[13]

Peer Relations and Delinquency

Experts have long debated the exact relationship between peer group interaction and delinquency, but research shows that peer group relationships are closely tied to delinquent behaviors: youths who report inadequate or strained peer relations, who say they are not popular with the "opposite sex," are the ones most likely to become delinquent.[14] Adolescents who maintain delinquent friends are more likely to engage in antisocial behavior and drug abuse.[15] Reviews of the research show that delinquent acts tend to be committed in small groups rather than alone, a process called **co-offending.**[16] Group process may involve family members as well as peers; brothers are likely to commit offenses with brothers of a similar age.[17]

co-offending
Committing criminal acts in groups.

Delinquent groups tend to be small and transitory.[18] Youths often belong to more than a single deviant group or clique and develop an extensive network of delinquent associates. Multiple memberships are desirable because delinquent groups tend to "specialize" in different types of delinquent activity: one group may concentrate on shoplifting whereas another performs home invasions. Group roles can vary, and an adolescent who assumes a leadership role in one group may be a follower in another.[19]

The Impact of Peer Relations   Does having antisocial peers cause delinquency, or are delinquents antisocial youths who seek out like-minded companions? Three opposing viewpoints exist on this question.

Control theorists, such as Travis Hirschi, argue that delinquents are as detached from their peers as they are from other elements of society. Although delinquent youths may acknowledge that they have "friends," their actual personal relationships are cold and exploitative. In an oft-cited work, James Short and Fred Strodtbeck describe the importance delinquent youths attach to their peer groups while at the same time observing that delinquents lack the social skills to make their peer relations rewarding or fulfilling.[20] According to this view, antisocial adolescents seek out like-minded peers for criminal associations. If delinquency is committed in groups, it is because "birds of a feather flock together" and not because deviant peers cause otherwise law-abiding youths to commit crimes.

Structural and learning theorists, in contrast, view the delinquency experience as one marked by close peer group support. They link delinquency to the rewards gained by associating with like-minded youths, learning deviant values and behaviors from peers, and being influenced by "peer pressure." Youths who maintain friendships with antisocial peers are more likely to become delinquent regardless of their own personality makeup or the type of supervision they receive at home.[21] Even previously law-abiding youths are more likely to get involved in delinquency and substance abuse if they become associated with antisocial friends who initiate them into delinquent careers.[22]

A third view is that peers and delinquency are mutually supporting. Antisocial youths join up with like-minded friends; deviant peers sustain and amplify delinquent careers.[23] The more antisocial the peer group, the more likely that its members will engage in delinquency. Nondelinquent friends help to moderate delinquency.[24] As children move through the life course, friends influence their behavior, and their behavior influences their friends.[25] These antisocial friends help youths maintain delinquent careers and stop the aging-out process.[26] If adulthood brings close and sustaining ties to marriage and family and the time spent with peers declines, so too will the level of deviant behavior.[27] But the aging-out process may be neutralized by maintaining delinquent friends who reinforce patterns of delinquent behavior.

Delinquent Peers   The weight of the empirical evidence indicates that youths who are loyal to delinquent friends, belong to gangs, have "bad companions," and are otherwise involved with deviant peers are the ones most likely to commit crimes.[28] Nonetheless, having deviant peers does not necessarily mean the relationships are close, intimate, and influential. Are delinquents actually close to their peers?

Research shows that both delinquents and nondelinquents have similar types of friendship patterns.[29] Delinquent youths reported that their peer relations contained elements of caring and trust and that they could be open and intimate with their friends. Delinquent youths also reported getting more intrinsic rewards from their peers than did nondelinquents. However, there were some differences between the peer relations of delinquents and nondelinquents. Delinquents reported more conflict with their friends, more feelings of jealousy and competition, and, not unexpectedly, more pronounced feelings of loyalty in the face of trouble. These findings support the view that delinquent peer group relations play an important part in their lifestyle and stand in contrast to the viewpoint that youthful law violators are loners without peer group support.

Comparable relationships have been found in studies of peer relations among young drug-involved males.[30] Alcohol and marijuana users have friendships that are more intimate and varied than those of nonusers.[31]

These findings seem to contradict the control theory model, which holds that delinquents are loners who are detached from their peers, and support the cultural deviance view that delinquents form close-knit peer groups and cliques that sustain their behavior. Adolescents are influenced by social relationships as they go through their life cycle, and these relationships can influence their behavior patterns.

Youth Gangs

As youths move through adolescence, they gravitate toward cliques that provide them with support, assurance, protection, and direction. Peer group membership allows youths to devalue enemies, achieve status, and develop

gangs
Groups of youths who collectively engage in delinquent behaviors.

self-assurance. In some instances the peer group provides the social and emotional basis for antisocial activity including crime and substance abuse. When this happens, the clique is transformed into a **gang.**

The youth gang is sometimes viewed as a uniquely American phenomenon, but youth gangs have also been reported in England, Germany, Italy, New Zealand, Australia, and other nations.[32] Nor are gangs a recent phenomenon. In the 1600s London was terrorized by organized gangs who called themselves "Hectors," "Bugles," "Dead Boys," and other colorful names. In the seventeenth and eighteenth centuries English gangs wore distinctive belts and pins marked with serpents, animals, stars, and the like.[33]

Today, the delinquent gang is a topic of considerable interest to many Americans. Such a powerful mystique has grown up around gangs that mere mention of the word "gang" evokes images of black-jacketed youths roaming the streets at night in groups bearing such colorful names as the Latin Kings, Mafia Crips, Bounty Hunters, and Savage Skulls. Films, television shows, novels, and even Broadway musicals such as *Menace II Society, Boyz N the Hood, New Jack City, Trespass, Fresh, Clockers, Outsiders, West Side Story,* and *Colors* have popularized the youth gang.[34]

Considering the suspected role gangs play in violent crime and drug activity, it is not surprising that gangs have recently become the target of a great deal of research interest.[35] The secretive, constantly changing nature of juvenile gangs makes them a difficult focus of study. Nonetheless, important attempts have been made to gauge their size, location, makeup, and activities.

What Are Gangs?

What exactly are delinquent gangs? Gangs are groups of youths who collectively engage in delinquent behaviors. Yet there is a distinction between group delinquency and gang delinquency. Group delinquency consists of a short-lived alliance created to commit a particular crime or to engage in a random violent act. In contrast, gang delinquency involves long-lived, complex institutions that have a distinct structure and organization, including identifiable leadership, division of labor (some members are fighters, others burglars, and some are known as deal makers), rules, rituals, and possessions (such as a headquarters and weapons).

Despite the familiarity of gangs to the American public, delinquency experts are often at odds over the precise definition of a gang. The term is sometimes used broadly to describe any congregation of youths who have joined together to engage in delinquent acts. However, police departments often use a narrower definition, designating as gangs only cohesive groups that hold and defend territory, or turf.[36]

interstitial group
Delinquent group that fills a crack in the social fabric and maintains standard group practices.

Academic experts have also created a variety of definitions to distinguish delinquent gangs from delinquent groups. The core elements generally included in the concept of the gang are that it is an **interstitial group** and that it maintains standard group processes such as recruiting new members, setting goals (controlling the neighborhood drug trade), assigning roles (appointing someone to negotiate with rivals), and developing status (grooming young members for leadership roles).[37] Table 9.1 provides several definitions of teen gangs by leading experts on delinquency.

Although a great deal of divergence over the definition of "gang" exists, Malcolm Klein argues that two factors stand out:

- Members have self-recognition of their gang status and use special vocabulary, clothing, signs, colors, graffiti, and names. Members set themselves apart from the community and are viewed as a separate entity by others. Once they get the label of gang, members eventually accept and take pride in their status.
- There is a commitment to criminal activity, though even the most criminal gang members spend the bulk of their time in noncriminal activities.[38]

Table 9.1

DEFINITIONS OF TEEN GANGS

Frederick Thrasher
An interstitial group originally formed spontaneously and then integrated through conflict. It is characterized by the following types of behavior: meeting face to face, milling, movement through space as a unit, conflict, and planning. The result of this collective behavior is the development of tradition, unreflective internal structure, esprit de corps, solidarity, morale, group awareness, and attachment to local territory.

Malcolm Klein
Any denotable adolescent group of youngsters who (a) are generally perceived as a distinct aggregation by others in their neighborhood; (b) recognize themselves as a denotable group (almost invariable with a group name); and (c) have been involved in a sufficient number of delinquent incidents to call forth a consistent negative response from neighborhood residents and/or law enforcement agencies.

Desmond Cartwright
An interstitial and integrated group of persons who meet face to face more or less regularly and whose existence and activities are considered an actual or potential threat to the prevailing social order.

Walter Miller
A self-formed association of peers, bound together by mutual interests, with identifiable leadership, well-developed lines of authority, and other organizational features, who act in concert to achieve a specific purpose or purposes, which generally include the conduct of illegal activity and control over a particular territory, facility, or type of enterprise.

G. David Curry and Irving Spergel
Groups containing law-violating juveniles and adults that are complexly organized, although sometimes diffuse, and sometimes cohesive, with established leadership and membership rules. The gang also engages in a range of crime (but with significantly more violence) within a framework of norms and values in respect to mutual support, conflict relations with other gangs, and a tradition of turf, colors, signs, and symbols. Subgroups of the gang may be deferentially committed to various delinquent or criminal patterns, such as drug trafficking, gang fighting, or burglary.

James Short
Gangs are groups of young people whose members meet together with some regularity, over time, on the basis of group-defined criteria of membership and group-defined organizational characteristics. In the simplest terms, gangs are unsupervised (by adults), self-determining groups that demonstrate continuity over time.

Sources: Frederick Thrasher, *The Gang* (Chicago: University of Chicago Press, 1927), p. 57; Malcolm Klein, *Street Gangs and Street Workers* (Englewood Cliffs, N.J.: Prentice Hall, 1971), p. 13; Desmond Cartwright, Barbara Tomson, and Hersey Schwarts, eds., *Gang Delinquency* (Pacific Grove, Calif.: Brooks/Cole, 1975), pp. 149–50; Walter Miller, "Gangs, Groups, and Serious Youth Crime," in David Schicor and Delos Kelly, eds., *Critical Issues in Juvenile Delinquency* (Lexington, Mass.: Lexington Books, 1980); G. David Curry and Irving Spergel, "Gang Homicide, Delinquency, and Community," *Criminology* 26:382 (1988); James Short, "The Level of Explanation Problem Revisited—The American Society of Criminology 1997 Presidential Address," *Criminology* 36:3–36 (1998), p. 16.

Near Groups and Youth Groups

near groups
Relatively unstructured short-term groups with fluid membership.

barrio
A Latino term meaning neighborhood

The standard definition of a gang implies that it is a cohesive group that maintains rules and customs and develops ongoing traditions. The media often portray the gang as a "substitute family" for inner-city youths, replacing a torn or dysfunctional nuclear family, and youths become members for life.

Not all gang experts share this view. Sociologist Lewis Yablonsky believes gangs can best be described as **near groups.** According to Yablonsky, human collectives tend to range from highly cohesive, tight-knit organizations to mobs with anonymous members who are motivated by emotions and disturbed leadership. Because youth gangs fall between the two extremes, they can be characterized as near groups. They usually have diffuse role definition, limited cohesion, impermanence, minimal consensus of norms, shifting membership, disturbed leadership, and limited definitions of membership expectations.[39]

In Yablonsky's view, the gang maintains only a small core of totally committed members who need the gang for satisfaction and other personal reasons. These core members work constantly to keep the momentum of the gang going. On a second level are affiliated youths, who participate in gang activity only when the mood suits them. At a third level are peripheral members, who participate in a particular situation or fight but who usually do not identify with the gang.

The near group model has been supported by the research of James Diego Vigil.[40] Vigil found that boys in Latino **barrio** (Hispanic neighborhood) gangs could be separated into "regular" (inner core), "peripheral" (strong identity but less frequent activity), "temporary" (short-term membership), and "situational" (those who party with the gang but avoid violent confrontations) members. Surveys of Denver gang youths have also found that most adolescents hold membership for about one year and thereafter express the desire not to be in a gang.[41]

Current research indicates that although some gangs remain near groups, without regular meetings, cohesive membership, written rules or stable leadership, others have become quite organized and stable. These gangs resemble traditional organized crime families more than temporary youth groups. Some, such as Chicago's Latin Kings and Gangster Disciples, have members who pay regular dues, are expected to attend gang meetings regularly, and carry out political activities to further gang ambitions.[42]

The Study of Juvenile Gangs and Groups

The study of juvenile gangs and groups was prompted by the Chicago School sociologists in the 1920s. Researchers such as Clifford Shaw and Henry McKay were concerned about the nature of the urban environment and how it influenced young people. Delinquency was believed to be a product of unsupervised groups made up of children of the urban poor and immigrants.

Frederick Thrasher initiated the study of the modern gang in his analysis of more than thirteen hundred youth groups in Chicago. His report on this effort, *The Gang,* was published in 1927.[43] Thrasher found that the social, economic, and ecological processes that affect the structure of great metropolitan cities create interstitial areas, or cracks, in the normal fabric of society, characterized by weak family controls, poverty, and social disorganization. According to Thrasher, groups of youths develop spontaneously to meet such childhood needs as play, fun, and adventure—activities that sometimes lead to delinquent acts.

Impoverished areas present many opportunities for conflict between groups of youths and between youth groups and adult authority. If this conflict continues, the groups become more solidified and their activities become primarily illegal.

The groups thus develop into gangs, with a name and a structure oriented toward delinquent behavior.

To Thrasher, the gang provides the young, lower-class boy with an opportunity for success. Adult society does not meet the needs of lower-class youths, and the gang solves the problem by offering what society fails to provide—excitement, fun, and opportunity. The gang is not a haven for disturbed youths but rather an alternative lifestyle for normal boys.

Thrasher's work has had an important influence on the accepted view of the gang. Recent studies of delinquent gang behavior are similar to Thrasher's in their emphasis on the gang as a means for lower-class boys to achieve advancement and opportunity as well as to defend themselves and to attack rivals.

Gangs in the 1950s and 1960s   In the 1950s and early 1960s the threat of gangs and gang violence swept the public consciousness. Rarely did a week go by without a major city newspaper featuring a story on the violent behavior of fighting gangs and their colorful leaders and names—the Egyptian Kings, the Vice Lords, the Blackstone Rangers. Social service and law enforcement agencies directed major efforts to either rehabilitate or destroy the gangs. Movies such as *The Wild Ones* and *Blackboard Jungle* were made about gangs, and the Broadway musical *West Side Story* romanticized violent gangs.

In his classic 1967 work, *Juvenile Gangs in Context,* Malcolm Klein summarized existing knowledge about gangs.[44] He concluded that gang membership was a way for individual boys to satisfy certain personal needs that were related to the development of youths caught up in the emotional turmoil typical of the period between adolescence and adulthood. A natural inclination to form gangs is reinforced by the perception that the gang represents a substitute for unattainable middle-class rewards. The experience of being a member of a gang will dominate a youngster's perceptions, values, expectations, and behavior. Finally, the gang is self-reinforcing:

> It is within the gang more than anywhere else that a youngster may find forms of acceptance for delinquent behavior—rewards instead of negative sanctions. And as the gang strives for internal cohesion, the negative sanctions of the "outside world" become interpreted as threats to cohesion, thus providing secondary reinforcement for the values central to the legitimization of gang behavior.[45]

By the mid-1960s the gang menace seemed to have disappeared. Some experts attribute the decline of gang activity to successful gang-control programs.[46] Others believe gangs were eliminated because police gang-control units infiltrated gangs, arrested leaders, and constantly harassed members.[47] Gang boys were more likely to be sanctioned by the juvenile justice system, and they received more severe sentences than nongang youths.[48] Another explanation for the decline in gang activity is the increase in political awareness that developed during the 1960s. Many gang leaders became involved in the social or political activities of ethnic pride, civil rights, and antiwar groups. In addition, many gang members were drafted. Still another explanation is that gang activity diminished during the 1960s because many gang members became active users of heroin and other drugs, which curtailed their group-related criminal activity.[49]

Gangs Reemerge   Interest in gang activity began anew in the early 1970s. Walter Miller comments on the New York scene:

> All was quiet on the gang front for almost 10 years. Then, suddenly and without advance warning, the gangs reappeared. Bearing such names as Savage Skulls and Black Assassins, they began to form in the South Bronx in the spring of 1971, quickly spread to other parts of the city, and by 1975 comprised 275 police-verified gangs with 11,000 members. These new and mysteriously merging gangs were far more lethal than their predecessors—heavily armed, incited and directed by violence-hardened older men, and directing their lethal activities far more to the victimization of ordinary citizens than to one another.[50]

Gang activity, by such groups as the Savage Skulls (pictured), reemerged in the 1970s in major cities, including New York, Detroit, El Paso, Los Angeles, and Chicago. In addition, such cities as Cleveland and Columbus, Ohio, and Milwaukee, Wisconsin, which had not experienced serious gang problems before, saw the development of local gangs.

Gang activity also reemerged in other major cities, including Detroit, El Paso, Los Angeles, and Chicago. Today, the number of gang youths appears to be, at least in these major cities, at an all-time high.[51] In addition, Cleveland and Columbus, Ohio, and Milwaukee, Wisconsin, which had not experienced serious gang problems before, saw the development of local gangs.[52] Large urban gangs sent representatives to organize chapters in distant areas or to take over existing gangs. For example, Chicago gangs moved into Dade County, Florida, and demanded cooperation and obedience from local gangs. Two major Chicago gangs, the Gangster Disciples and their rivals the Vice Lords, established branches in Milwaukee.[53] Members of the two largest gangs in Los Angeles, the Crips and the Bloods, began operations in midwestern cities with the result that local police departments with little experience in gang control were confronted with well-organized, established gang activities. Even medium-sized cities, such as Columbus, Ohio, saw gangs emerge from local dance and "rap" groups and neighborhood street-corner groups.[54]

The explosion of gang activities in the 1980s was reflected in the renewed media interest in gang activity. The *Los Angeles Times* printed 36 gang-related stories in 1977, and 15 in 1978. By 1988, 69 articles appeared, and in 1989 the number of stories concerning police sweeps, revenge shootings, and murder trials had risen to 267.[55] In some communities the fear of gangs, fanned by media attention, created a "moral panic" that prompted increased funding for police and prosecutors.[56] Clearly, gangs had captured the national attention.

Why Did Gang Activity Increase?

One compelling reason for the increase in gang activity may be the involvement of youth gangs in the distribution and sale of illegal drugs.[57] Early gangs relied on group loyalty and protection of turf to encourage membership, but modern gang members are lured by the quest for drug profits. In some areas gangs have replaced traditional organized crime families as the dominant suppliers of cocaine and crack. The traditional weapons of gangs—chains, knives, and homemade guns—have been replaced by the "heavy artillery" drug money can buy, Uzi and AK–47 automatic weapons. Felix Padilla studied a Latino gang in Chicago and found that the gang represents a "viable and persistent business enterprise within the U.S. economy, with its own culture, logic, and systematic means of transmitting and reinforcing its fundamental business virtues."[58]

Ironically, efforts by the FBI and other federal agencies to crack down on traditional organized crime families in the 1980s have opened the door to more violent youth gangs that control the drug trade on a local level and will not hesitate to use violence to maintain and expand their authority. The division between organized crime and gang crime is becoming increasingly narrow.

Economic Conditions   Drug trafficking may be an important reason for gang activity, but it is by no means the only reason. Not all gang members sell or use drugs, and many dealers are not gang members. Gang activity may also be on the rise because of economic and social dislocation. In her analysis of gangs in postindustrial America, Pamela Irving Jackson found that gang formation is the natural consequence of the evolution from a manufacturing economy with a surplus of relatively high-paying jobs to a low-wage service economy.[59] U.S. cities, which traditionally required a large population base for their manufacturing plants, now face incredible economic stress as these plants shut down. In this uneasy economic climate, gangs form and flourish while the moderating influence of successful adult role models and stable families declines. From this perspective youth gangs are a response to the glooming of the U.S. economy and its industrial base.

Family Crisis   The ongoing crisis in the American family was discussed in Chapter 8, and many commentators link gang membership to the disorganization of the family. Gang members come from families that are torn by parental absence, substance abuse, poverty, and criminality.[60] The gang serves as a substitute family that contributes the same kind of support, security, and caring that the traditional, intact nuclear family is supposed to provide.

Although this argument is compelling, a sizable portion of gang members come from stable and adequate families, and a significant number of youths from dysfunctional families avoid gang involvement. In some families one brother or sister is "ganged up" whereas another evades gang membership. The gang may be a substitute family for some, but it clearly does not have that appeal for all.

Contemporary Gangs

Thousands of gangs, with hundreds of thousands of members, are operating around the country today. The gang, however, cannot be viewed as a uniform or homogenous social concept. Gangs vary by activity, makeup, location, leadership style, and age. The next sections describe some of the most salient features of this heterogeneous social phenomenon.

Extent

Estimating the extent of the gang problem today is exceedingly difficult. With the variety of definitions of gang membership in use, youths who would be considered gang members in one jurisdiction may be ignored in another. For example, some cities have no "gang" problems but do have drug "crews" and "posses"—groups with more than a passing resemblance to gangs. Youths who say they are gang members might belong to an informal group that falls outside the generally accepted definition of gangs. In addition, gang membership is constantly changing; a continual influx and outflow of members makes creating accurate population estimates extremely problematic.

Despite these difficulties, a number of attempts have been made to inventory gang populations, and all indications are that there has been a major increase in gang membership. Walter Miller conducted two national surveys of gang membership, the first in 1975 and a second in 1982. The 1972 survey indicated gang membership at 55,000, a number that had increased to about 98,000 youths seven years later.[61] The National Assessment of Gang Activity, a comprehensive investigation of the nation's gang problem, found that more than 90 percent of the nation's largest cities reported the presence of youth gangs or groups by 1992.[62] It estimated that nationwide there were 4,881 gangs with 249,324 members. An extension and replication of the national assessment in 1994 indicated as many as 555,181 gang members.[63] Malcolm Klein conducted a national survey and found that 94 percent of the 189 U.S. cities with populations of 100,000 have gang problems; Los Angeles alone has more than a thousand gangs![64] Klein's estimate of 500,000 gang members coincides with the national assessments.[65] The most recent national gang survey estimates that as of 1996 there were 846,000 gang members in more than 31,000 identifiable gangs.[66] Clearly, there has been a pattern of steadily increasing gang memberships (Table 9.2).

Even the 846,000 number may be understated considering the results of a national survey of students ages 12 to 19 who were asked about gang activity in their schools.[67] About 28 percent of students report the presence of street gangs, and almost half the Hispanic students surveyed reported a street gang presence. Students from affluent families were much less likely to experience gang activity than those from lower-income families.

Types

Gangs have been categorized by their activity: some are devoted to violence and to protecting neighborhood boundaries, or turf; others are devoted to theft; some specialize in drug trafficking; others are primarily social groups concerned with recreation rather than crime.[68]

Table 9.2

ESTIMATES OF U.S. GANG MEMBERSHIP, RESULTS OF NATIONAL SURVEYS

Researcher	Year Conducted	Number of Gang Members
Walter Miller	1975	55,000
Walter Miller	1982	98,000
National Gang Assessment	1992	249,324
National Gang Assessment	1994	555,181
Malcolm Klein	1995	500,000
National Gang Assessment	1996	846,000

retreatists
Gangs whose members
actively engage in substance
abuse.

In their early work Richard Cloward and Lloyd Ohlin recognized that some gangs specialized in violent behavior, others were **retreatists** whose members actively engaged in substance abuse, and a third type were criminal gangs that devoted their energy to crime for profit.[69] It has become increasingly difficult to make the criminal, retreatist, and conflict distinctions because so many gang members are now involved in all three behaviors, but experts continue to find that on an aggregate level gangs can be characterized according to their dominant behavioral activities. For example, Jeffrey Fagan analyzed gang behavior in Chicago, San Diego, and Los Angeles and found that most gangs fall into one of these four categories:

Social gang: Involved in few delinquent activities and little drug use other than alcohol and marijuana. Membership is more interested in the social aspects of group behavior.

Party gang: Concentrates on drug use and sales but forgoes most delinquent behavior except vandalism. Drug sales are designed to finance members' personal drug use.

Serious delinquent gang: Engages in serious delinquent behavior while eschewing most drug use. Drugs are used only on social occasions.

Organized gang: Heavily involved in criminality and drug use and sales. Drug use and sales reflect a systemic relationship with other criminal acts. For example, violent acts are used to establish control over drug sale territories. Highly cohesive and organized, this gang is on the verge of becoming a formal criminal organization.[70]

Fagan's findings have been duplicated by other gang observations around the United States. After observing gangs in Columbus, Ohio, C. Ronald Huff found that they could be organized into "hedonistic gangs" (similar to "party gangs"), "instrumental gangs" (similar to "serious delinquent gangs") and "predatory gangs," whose heavy crime and crack use make them similar to the "organized gang" found by Fagan in Chicago and on the west coast.[71] Carl Taylor adds to this list the *scavenger gang,* a group of impulsive youths who have no common bond beyond surviving in a tough urban environment. These youths are typically low achievers who prey on any target they encounter. Taylor contrasts the scavenger gang with the *organized/corporate gang,* whose structure and goal orientation make it similar to a *Fortune* 500 company in its relentless pursuit of profit and market share.[72]

Cheryl Maxson, a noted gang researcher, finds that gangs can be organized into groups based on their size, age range, duration of existence, territory, and criminal acts (Table 9.3).[73] By far the most common is the compressed gang; the collective gang is the least common, followed by specialty gangs. Contrary to public opinion, less than half of the specialty gangs are involved in drug distribution.[74] These more recent observations seem to validate Cloward and Ohlin's research findings from thirty years ago, which suggested that many gangs "specialize" in their activities. However, this does not mean that most gangs are "generalists," whose members engage in a variety of criminal activities ranging from violent turf battles to drug dealing as well as social activities including helping members' families and organizing parties.[75]

Location

transitional neighborhood
Area undergoing a shift in
population and structure, usually from middle-class residential to lower-class mixed use.

The gang problem was traditionally considered an urban, lower-class phenomenon. Two types of urban areas are gang prone. The first is the **transitional neighborhood,** which is marked by rapid population change in which diverse ethnic and racial groups find themselves living side by side and in competition with one another.[76] Intergang conflict and homicide rates are high in these areas, which house the urban "underclass."[77]

Table 9.3

GANG STRUCTURES

Traditional gangs	In existence for twenty years or more and containing clear subgroups based on age. Sometimes subgroups are separated by neighborhoods rather than age. Have large age range (members are from ages 10 to 30) and are very large, with hundreds of members. Territorial, with well-defined home turf.
Neotraditional gangs	Newer territorial gangs that are smaller and that may evolve into traditional gangs over time.
Compressed gangs	Smaller gangs with less than fifty members, a short history, no subgroups, a narrow age range, and a less-defined territory.
Collective gangs	Larger groups that resemble a "shapeless mass" of adolescent and young adult members but that have not developed the distinguishing characteristics of other gangs.
Specialty gangs	Crime-focused gangs that are more criminal than social; smaller in size and age range than other gangs, and have a well-defined territory, which can be based either on geography or on the particular form of crime the gang specializes in (for example, drug territories).

Source: Cheryl Maxson, "Investigating Gang Structures," *Journal of Gang Research* 3:33–40 (1995).

disorganized neighborhood
Inner-city areas of extreme poverty where the critical social control mechanisms have broken down.

The second gang prone urban area is the **disorganized neighborhood,** where population shifts have slowed down, permitting patterns of behavior and traditions to develop over a number of years. Most typical are the poverty-stricken areas of New York and Chicago and the Mexican American barrios of the southwestern states and California.[78] These areas contain large, structured gang clusters that are resistant to most attempts by law enforcement and social service agencies to modify or disband them.

Shifting Gang Locales Transitional and disorganized neighborhoods are not the only environments that produce gangs. In recent years there has been a massive movement of people out of the central city to outlying communities and suburbs. Many of these people have been from the upper or middle class, but lower-income residents have also been affected. In some cities once-fashionable outlying neighborhoods have declined, and downtown, central city areas have undergone extensive urban renewal. Central, inner-city districts of major cities such as New York and Chicago have become devoted to finance, retail stores, restaurants, and entertainment.[79] Two aspects of this development inhibit gang formation: first, there are few residential areas and thus few adolescent recruits, and second, there is intensive police patrol. In some areas, such as Miami and Boston, the poor inner-city populations have shifted from the downtown to outer-city, ring-city, or suburban areas—that is, to formerly middle-class areas now in decay. Some mid-sized cities now contain the types of gangs that only a few years ago were restricted to large metropolitan areas.

Suburban housing projects are also gang prone. Thus, although gangs are still located in areas of urban blight today, these neighborhoods are often at some distance from their traditional inner-city locations.[80]

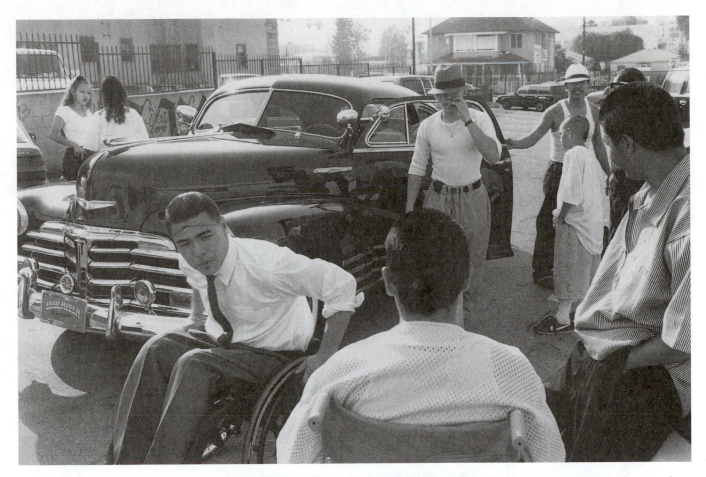

Barrio gangs are made up of Hispanic boys and girls whose ethnic ancestry can be traced to one of several Spanish-speaking cultures, from regions such as Puerto Rico and Mexico. They are known for their fierce loyalty to their original or "home" gang; this affiliation is maintained even if they move to a new neighborhood that contains a rival gang.

Migration   Some of the gangs in smaller cities and towns appear to be home grown, but because these groups copy clothing, insignia, and hand signs of big city gangs, authorities sometimes leap to the conclusion that they are recent arrivals rather than formed and populated by local youths.[81]

Although small town gangs may be local in origin, gang migration may also help to account for the national growth in gang activity (see Figure 9.1). About seven hundred U.S. cities have experienced some form of gang migration during the past decade, either short term, for example, to sell drugs, or long term to form permanent gangs. Most of the new arrivals are from Los Angeles gangs, although Chicago, New York, and Detroit are also sources of migrators. The most common reason for migrating is social—that is, their family relocated or they came to stay with relatives. Others have a specific criminal purpose, such as expanding drug sales and markets. Most of the migrators are African American or Hispanic males who maintain close ties with members of their original gangs "back home."[82] Although retention of gang identity is important, some migrants join local gangs, shedding old ties and gaining new affiliations. Gang migration remains a serious problem, but most cities had local gangs prior to the onset of migration and most likely would have had a gang problem regardless of migration. The number of migrants is relatively small in proportion to the overall gang population, supporting the contention that most gangs are actually "home grown."

Neighborhood Reactions   The presence of gangs in areas unaccustomed to delinquent group activity can have a devastating effect on community life. In his famous

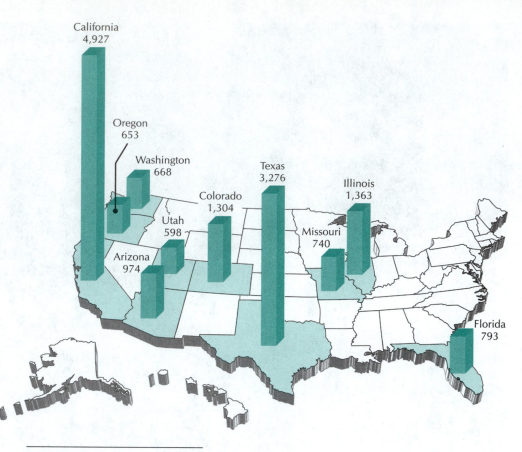

FIGURE 9.1

Top Ten States by Number of Gangs Reported

Source: Institute for Intergovernmental Research, *National Youth Gang Survey, 1995* (Washington, D.C.: OJJDP, 1997), p. 10.

study of Milwaukee gangs, John Hagedorn found that a great deal of neighborhood hostility was evoked when gangs formed in this midwestern city.[83] Community resistance to gangs arose for a number of reasons. First, Milwaukee's gangs had little neighborhood turf affiliation and were formed solely to profit from illegal gain and criminal activity. Second, the gangs were formed at the same time minority students were being bused to implement desegregation. Gang recruitment took place on the buses and in schools and not on neighborhood streets. Gang membership, therefore, cut across neighborhoods, rendering local social control ineffective. Finally, the neighborhoods most likely to be plagued by gang violence were strained economically. Residential segregation and a lack of affordable housing prevented many working-class residents from leaving. The result was mixed neighborhoods of struggling working-class and poor families coexisting with drug houses, gangs, and routine violence. Frightened residents had little recourse but to call police when they heard gunshots; neighborhoods became uneasy and unstable.

Age

The ages of gang members range widely, perhaps from as young as eight to as old as fifty-five.[84] However, members of offending groups are usually no more than a few years apart in age, with a leader or "instigator" who may be more experienced and a few years older.[85]

A recent survey of 3,348 youths that included almost 2,000 gang members, conducted by the National Gang Crime Research Center, found that youths first hear about gangs at around nine years of age, get involved in violence at ten or eleven, and join their first gang at twelve years of age. Half of the gang members interviewed had, by age 13, (a) fired a pistol, (b) seen someone killed or seriously injured by gang violence, (c) gotten a permanent gang tattoo, and (d) been arrested.[86]

Increasing Ages   Gang experts believe the average age of gang members has been increasing yearly, a phenomenon explained in part by the changing structure of the U.S. economy.[87] Desirable unskilled factory jobs that would entice older gang members to leave the gang have been lost. Replacing these legitimate jobs are low-level drug dealing opportunities that require a gang affiliation. William Julius Wilson found that the inability of inner-city males to obtain adequate employment prevents them from attaining adult roles: for example, they cannot afford to marry and raise families. Criminal records acquired at an early age quickly lock these youths out of the job market; remaining in a gang into their adulthood has become an economic necessity.[88]

In his Milwaukee research, John Hagedorn also found that economic deterioration has had an important impact on the age structure of gang membership. Whereas in the past older members could easily slip into the economic mainstream, less than one in five founding members of the youth gangs Hagedorn studied were able to find full-time employment by their mid-twenties; 86 percent had spent considerable time in prison. "Old heads"—older members with powerful street reputations—were held in high esteem by young gang members. In the past, ex-members served as a moderating influence, helping steer gang members into conventional roles and jobs. Today, young adults continue their relationships with their old gangs and promote the values of hustling, drug use, and sexual promiscuity. As a result, gang affiliations can last indefinitely, and it is not unusual to see intergenerational membership, with the children and even grandchildren of gang members affiliating with the same gang.[89] When Hagedorn and his associates interviewed 101 older gang members from fourteen Milwaukee area gangs, he found that there are actually four types of adult gang members:

- *Legits* have left the gang and "hood" behind.
- *Dope fiends* are addicted to cocaine and need drug treatment.
- *New Jacks* have given up on the legitimate economy and see nothing wrong in selling cocaine to anyone.
- *Homeboys,* the majority of all adult gang members, work regular jobs, but when they cannot make enough money they sell cocaine. They want out of the drug trade and wish to have a "normal" life but believe ganging is the only way to make ends meet.[90]

Gender

Of the more than one thousand groups included in Thrasher's original survey, only half a dozen were female gangs. Females were traditionally involved in gang activities in one of three ways: as auxiliaries (or branches) of male gangs, as part of sexually mixed gangs, or as autonomous gangs. Auxiliaries are a feminized version of the male gang name, such as the Lady Disciples of the Devil's Disciples. Some gangs are integrated, containing both male and female members. Mary Glazier's study of a small-town Pennsylvania gang, the Hit and Run, found that girls were invited to become gang members because it was considered unacceptable for male members to fight with females who gave them trouble; girl members were given that responsibility.[91]

The number and extent of girl gangs is increasing. In the Grape Street area of Los Angeles, a female gang member is about to kick another young woman. This is not a random or spontaneous attack but part of the "court in" ceremony in which new members are initiated into the gang.

Independent or autonomous female gangs are now becoming more common.[92] Although initial female gang participation may be forged by links to male gang members, once in gangs, girls form close ties with other female members. Peer interactions form the basis for independent female gangs and group criminal activity.[93]

What benefits does gang membership offer to females? According to the "liberation" view, ganging can provide girls with a sense of "sisterhood," independence, and solidarity as well as a chance to earn profit through illegal activities such as drug dealing. In contrast, the "social injury" view suggests that the deficits of gang membership are greater than its benefits. Female members are still sexually exploited by males and are sometimes forced to exploit other females. Girls who are members of male gang auxiliaries may be particularly prone to exploitation. They report that males in the gang control the girls in the auxiliary gangs by determining the arenas within which they can operate, for example, the extent to which they are allowed to become involved in intergang violence. Males also play a divisive role in the girls' relationships with each other; this manipulation is absent for girls in independent gangs.[94]

Females join gangs in an effort to cope with a bleak and harsh life and the prospects of an equally dismal future.[95] Girls in gangs seem less violent than boys and are more likely to engage in theft offenses than violent crimes.[96] This may be indicative of the desire of female gang members to use their status for economic gain to improve their lifestyle and enhance their future.

It is still difficult to determine the precise number of female gangs or the size of their membership. National surveys of gang activity, which rely on surveys by law enforcement agencies, indicate that females committed 5 percent or less of all reported gang crimes and that more than 90 percent of gang members are male.[97] However, some local gang surveys that rely on interview and self-report data indicate that the number of female gang members may be on the rise in some areas of the country.[98]

Carl Taylor's analysis of Detroit gangs found that girls were very much involved in gang activity.[99] An important analysis of Denver youths found that the number of female gang members is higher than previously thought: approximately 25 percent of the gang members they surveyed were female.[100] A recent survey of almost six thousand youths in forty-two schools located in eleven cities found that almost 40 percent of the gang members were female.[101] It is possible that law enforcement agencies undercount female gang membership and that in actuality more young girls are gang affiliated than previously believed.[102]

Formation

It has long been suggested that gangs form to defend their turf from outsiders; thus, gang formation involves a sense of territoriality. Most gang members live in close proximity to one another, and their sense of belonging and loyalty extend only to their small area of the city. At first a gang may form when members of an ethnic minority newly settled in the neighborhood join together for self-preservation. As the group gains numerical domination over an area, it may view the neighborhood as its territory, or turf, which needs to be defended. Defending turf involves fighting rivals who want to make the territory their own.

Once formed, gangs grow when youths who admire the older gang members and wish to imitate their lifestyle "apply" and are accepted for membership. Sometimes the new members will be given a special, diminished identity within the gang that reflects their inexperience and apprenticeship status. Joan Moore and her associates found that once formed **klikas,** or youth cliques, in Hispanic gangs remain together as unique groups with separate names (for example, the Termites), separate identities, and distinct experiences; they also have more intimate relationships among themselves than among the general gang membership.[103] She likens *klikas* to a particular class in a university, such as the class of '94, not a separate organization but one that has its own unique experiences.

Moore also found that gangs can expand by including members' kin, even if they do not live in the immediate neighborhood, and rival gang members who wish to join because they admire the gang's way of doing things. Adding outsiders gives the gang the ability to take over new territory. However, it also brings with it new problems because outsider membership and the grasp for new territory usually results in greater conflicts with rival gangs.

klikas
Subgroups of same-aged youths in Hispanic gangs that remain together and have separate names and a unique identity within the gang.

Leadership

Most experts describe gang leaders as cool characters who have earned their position by demonstrating a variety of abilities—fighting prowess, verbal quickness, athletic distinction, and so on.[104]

Experts emphasize that gang leadership is held by one person and varies with particular activities, such as fighting, sex, and negotiations. In fact, in some gangs each age level of the gang has its own leaders. Older members may be looked up to, but they are not necessarily considered leaders by younger members. In his analysis of Los Angeles gangs, Malcolm Klein observed that many gang leaders shrink from taking a leadership role and actively deny leadership. Klein overheard one gang boy claim, "We got no leaders, man. Everybody's a leader, and nobody can talk for nobody else."[105] The most plausible explanation of this ambivalence is the boy's fear that during times of crisis his decisions will conflict with those of other leaders and he will lose status and face.

There appear, then, to be diverse concepts of leadership, depending on the organizational structure of the gang. Less organized gangs are marked by diffuse and shifting leadership. Larger and more organized gangs have a clear chain of command and leaders who are supposed to "give orders," plan activities, and control members' behavior.[106]

Communications

Gangs today seek recognition both from their rivals and from the community as a whole. Image and reputation depend on a gang's ability to communicate to the rest of the world.

FIGURE 9.2

Gang Symbols Used in Graffiti
Source: Austin, Texas, Police Department Gang Control Unit, 1996.

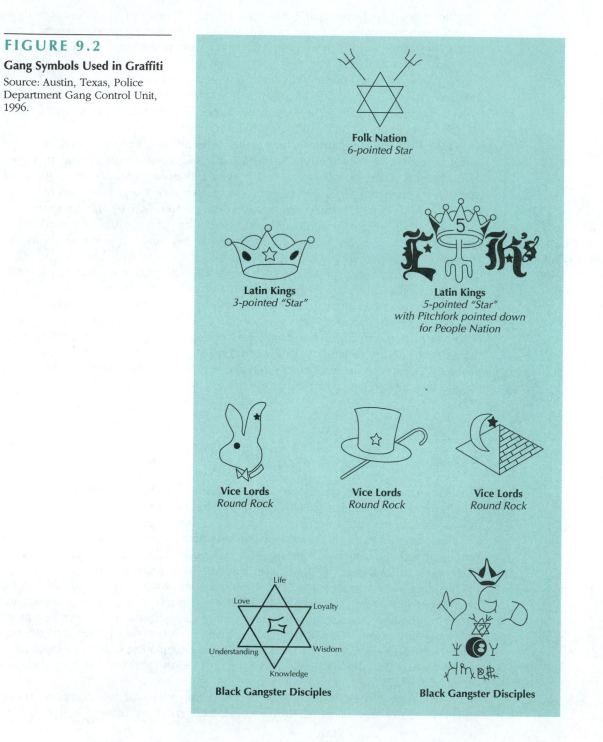

graffiti
Inscriptions or drawings made on a wall or structure and used by delinquents for gang messages and turf definition.

One major source of gang communication is **graffiti** (see Figure 9.2). These wall writings are especially elaborate among Latino gangs, who call their inscriptions *placasos* or *placa,* meaning sign or plaque.[107] Latino gang graffiti usually contains the writer's street name and the name of the gang. Strength or power is frequently asserted through the use of the term *rifa,* which means to rule, and *controllo,* indicating that the gang controls the area. Another common inscription is "p/v," meaning *por vida;* this refers to the fact that the gang expects to control the area "for life." If the numeral 13 is used, it signifies that the gang is *loco,* or "wild." Crossed-out graffiti indicates that a territory is being contested by a rival gang, whereas undisturbed writing indicates that the gang's power has gone unchallenged.

Gangs also communicate by ritualistic argot (a secret vocabulary). "Gangbangers" may refer to their "crew," "posse," "troop," or "tribe." Within larger gangs are "sets," who hang in particular neighborhoods, and "tips," which are small groups formed for particular purposes. Table 9.4 illustrates a variety of gang slang.

representing
Tossing or flashing gang signs in the presence of rivals, often escalating into a verbal or physical confrontation.

Flashing or tossing gang signs (Figure 9.3) in the presence of rivals is often viewed as a direct challenge that can escalate into a verbal or physical confrontation. In Chicago gangs call this **representing.** Gang members will proclaim their

Table 9.4

GANG SLANG

Busted/popped a cap: Shot at someone

Buster: Youngster trying to be a gang member/Fake gang member

Camarada: Friend

Cap: A retort or to shoot at

Carnal: Brother

Carnala: Sister

Chale: No

Chavala: Little girl

Check it out: Listen to what I have to say

Chill out: Stop it/ Don't do that/ Calm down

Chingasos: Fighting

Chiva: Heroin

Chivero: Heroin addict

Chota: Police

C.K.: Crip killer

Click up: To get along well with a homeboy

Cluck: Cocaine smoker

Colors: Gang colors (on shoes, rag, shoelaces, etc.)

O.G.: Original gangster, which you are considered to be when you have killed someone; true; original; someone who is true to the game, who never sold out

Peace out: Bye

Peace-N: Not looking for trouble

Pedo: Fight

Phat, that's: Incredible; great

Piedra: Rock cocaine, crack

Popo: Police

Por vida (P/V): Forever

Put in some work: Do a shooting

Quette: Gun

Rock star: Cocaine prostitute or user

Rooster: Piru blood street gang

Ruka: Gang chick

Salty, you: Think you know everything

Source: Austin, Texas, Police Department Gang Control Unit, 1998.

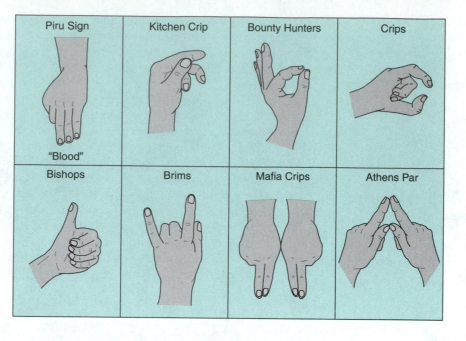

affiliation ("Latin King Love!" "Stone Killers!") and ask victims "Who do you ride?" or "What do you be about?" An incorrect response will provoke an attack.[108] False representing can be used to intentionally misinform witnesses and victims, exposing imposters or neutrals trying to make safe passage through gang-controlled territory.

Still another method of communication is clothing. In some areas gang members communicate their membership by wearing jackets with the name of their gang embroidered on the back. In Boston neighborhoods certain articles of clothing (for example, sneakers or sports jackets with a particular team logo) are worn to identify gang membership.[109] In Los Angeles the two major black gangs are the Crips and the Bloods, each containing many thousands of members. Crips are identified with the color blue and will wear some article of blue clothing—hat, belt, or jacket—to communicate their allegiance; their rivals, the Bloods, identify with the color red.[110]

Criminality

In the 1600s English gangs broke windows, demolished taverns, assaulted local watchmen, and fought intergang battles.[111] Today, gang criminality has numerous patterns.[112]

Some gangs specialize. For example, drug-oriented gangs concentrate on the sale of marijuana, PCP, cocaine (crack), and amphetamines ("crystal"); organized gangs use violence to control a drug territory. But although it has become common to associate gangs with drug activity, not all gangs are major players in drug trafficking and those that are tend to distribute small amounts of drugs at the street level rather then being involved in importation or trafficking large quantities of illegal substances. The world of major dealing belongs to adults, not to street gang youths.[113]

Other gangs are eclectic, engaging in a wide variety of criminal activity ranging from felony assaults to drug dealing.[114] Regardless of their type, gang members typically commit more crimes than any other youths in the social environment; gang membership enhances any preexisting propensity to commit crime.[115]

Data from the Rochester Youth Development Study (RYDS), a longitudinal cohort study of one thousand youths in upstate New York, support the gang–crime association theory. As Figure 9.4 shows, although only 30 percent of the youths in the sample report being gang members, they account for 65 percent of all reported

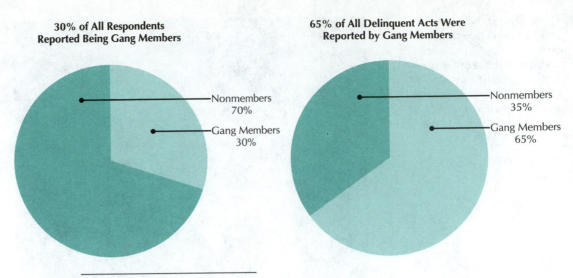

**30% of All Respondents
Reported Being Gang Members**

Nonmembers
70%

Gang Members
30%

**65% of All Delinquent Acts Were
Reported by Gang Members**

Nonmembers
35%

Gang Members
65%

FIGURE 9.4

Percentage of Crimes Reported by Gang Members in the Rochester Youth Development Study

Sources: Terence Thornberry and James Burch, "Gang Members and Delinquent Behavior," Juvenile Justice Bulletin (Office of Juvenile Justice and Delinquency Prevention, June 1997); created by Center for Substance Abuse Research, University of Maryland, 1997.

Note: All data are based on self-reported behaviors. The question asked to determine gang membership was, "Are you a member of a street gang or a posse?"

delinquent acts. The RYDS data show that gang members account for 86 percent of all serious crimes, 63 percent of the alcohol use, and 61 percent of the drug abuse.[116]

Gang Violence   Research indicates that gang violence is impulsive and emotional and therefore comes in spurts. It typically involves defense of the gang and gang members' reputations.[117] Once a spurt ends, the level of violence may recede, but it remains at a level higher than it was previously, constantly escalating with each battle. Spurts usually are not citywide but occur in specific neighborhoods during periods of intense competition over the expansion and defense of gang territory. Peaks in gang homicides tend to correspond to a series of escalating confrontations, usually over control of territory—either traditional street gang turf or an entrepreneurial drug market.[118] Violence often takes the form of boundary disputes. The most dangerous areas are along disputed boundaries where a drug hot spot intersects with a turf hot spot. There are also "marauder" patterns in which members of rival gangs travel to the hub of their enemy's territory in search of potential victims.[119]

Because of the violent nature of their vocation, gang members are heavily armed, dangerous, and more violent than nonmembers. It should come as no surprise that a nationwide survey of arrestees found that half of those who owned or carried guns claimed to be gang members.[120]

Violence is a core fact of gang formation and life; it is what allows gangs to spread from one neighborhood to another.[121] Gang members always feel threatened by other gangs and are wary of encroachments on their turf. It is not surprising that gangs try to recruit youths who are already gun owners; new members are likely to increase gun ownership and possession once they join a gang.[122] Gang members face a far greater chance of death at an early age than do nonmembers.[123]

Honor, Courage, and Prestige   Scott Decker studied gangs in St. Louis, Missouri, and has found that violence is a central feature of gang life, essential to the transformation of a peer group into a "gang." When asked why he calls the group he belongs to a gang, one member replied: "Violence, I guess. There is more violence than a family. With a gang it's like fighting all the time, killing, shooting."[124]

Decker found that gang violence can take on a number of different forms. When joining the gang, members may be forced to partake in violent rituals to

Gang violence is impulsive and emotional and therefore comes in "spurts." It typically involves defense of the gang and the gang membership's reputation. Gang violence is self-perpetuating, constantly escalating with each battle, and often resulting in tragic deaths.

prove their courage and reliability. Gang members are ready to fight when others attack them or when they believe their territory or turf is being encroached upon. Defaced gang signs or graffiti demand a violent response. Retaliatory violence may be directed against rival gang members accused of insults or against those involved in personal disputes. Gang members also expect to fight when they go to certain locations that are "off limits" or attend events such as house parties where violence is routine.

Gang members are sensitive to any rivals who question their honor or courage. Once an insult is perceived or a challenge is offered, the gang's honor cannot be restored until the "debt" is repaid. Police efforts to cool down gang disputes only delay the inevitable revenge, a beating or a drive-by shooting. Random acts of revenge have become so common that physicians now consider the consequences of drive-by shootings as a significant health problem, is a major contributor to early morbidity and mortality among adolescents and children in Los Angeles and other major gang cities.[125]

Retaliation is often directed against gang members who step out of line. If subordinates disobey orders, perhaps by using rather than selling drugs, they may be subject to harsh disciplinary action by other gang members. Violence is used to maintain the gang's internal discipline and security.

Another common gang crime is extortion, called "turf tax," which involves forcing people to pay the gang to be protected from dangerous neighborhood youths

prestige crimes
Stealing or assaulting someone to gain prestige in the neighborhood; often part of gang initiation rites.

(presumably themselves). **Prestige crimes** occur when a gang member steals or assaults someone, even a police officer, to gain prestige in the gang and the neighborhood. These crimes may be part of an initiation rite or an effort to establish a special reputation, a position of responsibility, or a leadership role; to prevail in an internal power struggle; or to respond to a challenge from a rival (proving the youth is not chicken).

Ethnic and Racial Composition

Most gangs seem to be racially exclusive. Although Lewis Yablonsky found racially mixed violent gangs, the majority of gang observers all view gangs as racially homogeneous groups: all white (English, Italian, Irish, or Slavic origin), all black (African origin), all Hispanic/Latino (Mexican, Puerto Rican, Panamanian, Colombian, and other Spanish-speaking people), or all Asian (Chinese, Japanese, Korean, Taiwanese, Samoan, and Vietnamese).[126] Most intergang conflict appears to be among groups of the same ethnic and racial background.[127]

The ethnic distribution of gangs corresponds to their geographic location. For example, in Philadelphia and Detroit the overwhelming number of gang members are African American. In New York and Los Angeles, Latino gangs predominate, and San Francisco's small gang population is mostly Asian.[128] Newly emerging immigrant groups are making their presence felt in gangs. Authorities in Buffalo, New York, estimate that 10 percent of their gang population is Jamaican. Cambodian and Haitian youths are joining gangs in Boston. A significant portion of Honolulu's gangs are Samoans (19 percent) and Filipinos (46 percent).[129]

The national assessment was able to acquire data on the ethnic distribution of gangs from twenty-six large cities. As Figure 9.5 shows, a significant majority of gang members are Hispanic and African American, followed by Anglo and Asian. Although Anglos make up only a small percentage of all gang youths, those jurisdictions (eleven) that record year-to-year change in the ethnicity of gang populations indicate that their numbers are now growing at a faster rate than other groups. The Focus on Delinquency box examines barrio gangs.

African American Gangs   The first black youth gangs were organized in the early 1920s and specialized in common street crime activities.[130] Since they had few rival

FIGURE 9.5

Racial Composition of Gangs

Source: John Moore and Craig Terrett, *Highlights of the 1996 National Youth Gang Survey* (Washington, D.C.: OJJDP, 1998).

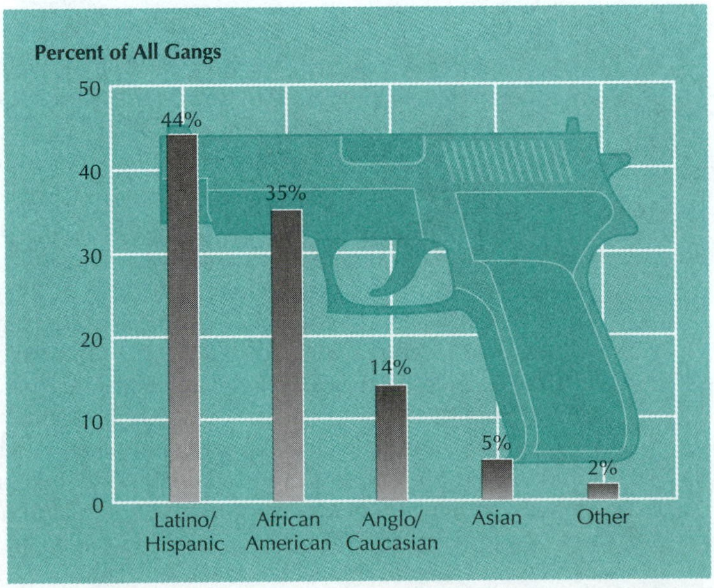

Percent of All Gangs

Latino/Hispanic	African American	Anglo/Caucasian	Asian	Other
44%	35%	14%	5%	2%

BARRIO GANGS

Latino barrio gangs have evolved over time, sustained by continuous waves of poorly educated Mexican immigrants. Each new wave of immigrants settles in existing barrios or creates new ones. There, youngsters subscribe to the *cholo* (marginalized) subculture, which has its own set of slang, clothing, style, and values. The *cholo* subculture places a high value on friendship, often imputing family and kinship relationships to peers by calling them "brother" or "cousin." Scholastic achievement is devalued and replaced with "partying." Employment is valued only if it requires little effort and brings in enough cash to party. An important aspect of the *cholo* culture is demonstrating *machismo,* or manliness. Barrio youths try to impress their peers and rivals with their ability to drink more than others, their fighting and sexual prowess, and their heart. The *cholo* culture helps these immigrants bridge the gap between the Mexican culture, which they left, and the U.S. culture, into which they have trouble assimilating.

Barrio gangs are not a recent development. Aggressive male youth groups have been a feature of the Mexican community as far back as the nineteenth century. The early barrio gangs were made up of young laborers whose behavior was oriented more around sports and socializing than criminality.

Then, in the 1940s, the *pachuco* fad swept through the community; its advocates wore outlandish outfits (zoot suits) and spoke a unique Spanish-English slang. A well-publicized murder case and some urban disturbances helped brand the *pachucos* as vicious "rat packs." Though most zoot-suiters (who can be compared to members of the heavy metal music culture today) were not gang members or necessarily involved in crime, the press focused attention on them as a major social problem and a popular stereotype was created. Mexican American youths became suspect regardless of their actual interest in gangs.

In the 1950s increasing stigmatization and isolation encouraged the development of deviance. Drug use, which had been quietly tolerated in an earlier generation, was now the target of police crackdowns, and many barrio residents went to prison. Mexican Americans gained the stereotype of "evil dope dealers," and the early naiveté of the *cholo* lifestyle was ended.

In the 1960s the Chicano political movement had an important influence on gangs. First, gangs were romanticized as social bandits in the tradition of earlier Mexican opposition to Anglo authority. Second, gangs (and their adult ex-offender members, the *pintos*) began to be viewed as the fighting branch of the movement that protected the community

organizations in their inner-city locales, they were able to concentrate on criminal activity rather than defending their turf. By the 1930s the expanding number of rival gangs spawned competition, and inner-city gang warfare became commonplace.

In Los Angeles, which is today a hot spot of gang activity, the first black youth gang formed in the 1920s was the Boozies, named after a family that provided a significant portion of its membership. This gang virtually ran the inner city until the 1930s, when rivals began to challenge its criminal monopoly. In the next twenty years, a number of black gangs, including the Businessmen, Home Street, Slauson, and Neighborhood, emerged and met with varying degrees of criminal success.

In the 1970s the dominant Crips gang was formed and began to spread over much of Los Angeles. Other neighborhood gangs merged into the Crips or affiliated with it by adding "Crips" to their name, so that the Main Street gang became the Main Street Crips. The dominance of the Crips has since been challenged by its archrivals, the Bloods. Both of these groups, whose total membership exceeds twenty-five thousand youths, resemble organized crime families and are heavily involved in drug trafficking.

In Chicago the Blackstone Rangers dominated illicit activities for almost twenty-five years, beginning in the 1960s and lasting into the early 1990s when its leader,

from the police. Protecting the community (*la raza*) was an extension of protecting their turf or neighborhood. Youth gangs and their extensions became enmeshed in community affairs, and their problems with the law came to be identified with the problems of the community as a whole.

In the last ten years the nature of the Chicano gang has changed significantly. The image of the gang changed within the community, and its purpose was similarly reoriented. A number of reasons exist for this transformation. Publicity about violent Mexican American prison gangs, such as La Familia, helped create the image that all Chicano gangs were criminally oriented. The *cholo* culture was viewed as a liability of the Chicano movement. When political activism cooled and street demonstrations ended, gang members were not needed as community protectors. The gangs became more closely identified with criminals than with social activists. Hanging around and partying were and remain the major activity of these gangs, with drugs as a continuous part of the scene. East Los Angeles gang members continued to heavily use PCP and heroin (cocaine was more sparingly used). A new wave of Mexican immigrants rejected the gang culture, and leaders of the existing community requested police protection from the gangs. As gang isolation increased, so too did gang violence and criminality. Once leaders in a sociopolitical movement, gang members have now become members of an ostracized underclass.

Los Angeles barrio gangs are now being influenced by economic restructuring. The kin-based job-finding networks that helped ease gang members into conventional society has broken down as employers hired the waves of immigrants who have flooded California. Without employment opportunities, young adults hang out with the gang cliques. Their presence empowers the gang and makes it seem more like a family with "older brothers" readily available to guide younger members. Because these gang veterans remain involved with the affairs of recruits, "street socialization" in the gang has become more competitive with conventional socialization in the family and the school.

Sources: Joan Moore, "Isolation and Stigmatization in the Development of an Underclass: The Case of Chicano Gangs in East Los Angeles," *Social Problems* 33:1–12 (1985); idem, *Homeboys: Gangs, Drugs and Prison in the Barrios of Los Angeles* (Philadelphia: Temple University Press, 1979); idem, *Going Down to the Barrio: Homeboys and Homegirls in Change* (Philadelphia: Temple University Press, 1991); James Diego Vigil, *Barrio Gangs: Street Life and Identity in Southern California* (Austin: University of Texas Press, 1988); James Diego Vigil and John Long, "Emic and Etic Perspectives on Gang Culture: The Chicano Case," in C. Ronald Huff, ed., *Gangs in America* (Newbury Park, Calif.: Sage, 1990), pp. 55–70; James Diego Vigil, "*Cholos* and Gangs: Culture Change and Street Youth in Los Angeles," in C. Ronald Huff, ed., *Gangs in America* (Newbury Park, Calif.: Sage, 1990), pp. 116–28.

Jeff Fort, and many of his associates were indicted and imprisoned.[131] The Rangers, who later evolved into the El Rukn gang, worked with "legitimate" businessmen to import and sell heroin. Earning millions in profits, they established businesses that helped them launder drug money. Among their enterprises was a security company that allowed members to bear arms legally. Though many of the convictions were later overturned, the power of El Rukn was ended (Fort remains in a high-security prison).

The Rangers' chief rivals, the Black Gangster Disciples, are now the dominant gang in Chicago. Most street gangs are too "disorganized" to become stable crime groups, but the Gangster Disciples have a structure, activities, and relationships similar to traditional organized gangs like the Mafia. Gangster Disciple members are actively involved in politics in an effort to gain power and support. Members meet regularly, commit crimes as a group, and maintain ongoing relationships with other street gangs and with prison-based gangs. The Gangster Disciples have extensive ownership of "legitimate" private businesses and deal with other businessmen. They offer "protection" against rival gangs and supply stolen merchandise to customers and employees.[132]

African American gang members, especially those in Los Angeles, have some unique behavioral characteristics. They frequently use nicknames, often based on a behavioral trait, to identify themselves. "Little 45" might be used by someone whose favorite weapon is a large handgun. Although TV shows portray gangs as wearing distinctive attire and jackets, in reality members usually favor nondescript attire to reduce police scrutiny; after all, a routine police search can turn up narcotics or weapons. However, gang members frequently have distinctive hairstyles, featuring shaving, corn rows, shaping, or braids, that are designed to look like their leaders'. Tattooing is popular, and members often wear colored scarves or "rags" to identify their gang affiliation. In Los Angeles, Crips use blue or black rags, and Bloods normally carry red.

It is also common for black gang members to mark their territory with distinctive graffiti. The messages are crude rather than sophisticated: drawings of guns, dollar signs, proclamations of individual power, and profanity.

Hispanic Gangs   Hispanic gangs are made up of youths whose ethnic ancestry can be traced to one of several Spanish-speaking cultures, such as Puerto Rico or Mexico. They are known for their fierce loyalty to their original or "home" gang; this affiliation is maintained even if they move to a new neighborhood that contains a rival gang. Admission to the gang usually involves an initiation ritual in which boys are required to show their fearlessness and prove their *machismo,* or manliness. The most common test requires novices to fight several established members or to commit some crime, such as a purse snatching or robbery. The code of conduct associated with membership means never ratting on a brother or even a rival, facing death or prison without betraying their sense of honor.

In some areas, such as Miami, Hispanic gangs are rigidly organized and have a fixed leadership hierarchy. However, in southern California, which has the largest concentration of Hispanic youth gangs, leadership is fluid. No youth is "elected" to a post such as president or warlord. During times of crisis, those with particular skills will assume command on a situational basis.[133] For example, one boy will lead in combat while another negotiates drug deals.

Hispanic gang members are known for their distinctive dress codes. Some wear knit, dark-colored watch caps pulled down over the ears with a small roll at the bottom. Others wear a folded bandana over the forehead and tied in back. Another popular headpiece is the "stingy brim" fedora or a baseball cap with the wearer's nickname and gang affiliation written on the cap's turned up bill. Members favor tank-style T-shirts or open Pendleton shirts that give them quick access to weapons.

Members also proclaim their affiliations by marking off territory with colorful and intricate graffiti. Hispanic gang graffiti has very stylized lettering, frequently uses three-dimensional designs, and proclaims members' organizational pride and power.

Hispanic gangs have a strong sense of territory or turf, and a great deal of gang violence is directed at warding off any threat to their control. Slights by rivals, including putdowns, stare downs ("mad-dogging"), defacing gang insignia, and territorial intrusions, can set off a violent and bloody gang confrontation. Newer gangs carry out this violence with high-powered automatic weapons, a far cry from the zip guns and gravity knives of the past.

Asian Gangs   Asian gangs are prominent in New York, Los Angeles, San Francisco, Seattle, and Houston. The earliest gangs, Wah Ching, were formed in the nineteenth century by Chinese youths affiliated with adult crime groups (*tongs*). In the 1960s two other gangs formed in San Francisco, the Joe Boys and Yu Li, and they now operate, along with the Wah Ching, in many major U.S. cities. National attention focused on the activities of these Chinese gangs in 1977 when a shootout in the Golden Dragon restaurant in San Francisco left five dead and eleven wounded. On the East Coast prominent Asian gangs include Flying Dragon, Green Dragon, Ghost Shadows, Fu Ching, So On Leong, Tong So On, and Born to Kill (a Vietnamese gang).[134]

In an important work Ko-Lin Chin has described the inner workings of Chinese youth gangs today.[135] Chin finds that these gangs have unique properties, such as their reliance on raising capital from the Chinese community through extortion and then investing this money in legitimate business enterprises. Chinese gangs recruit new members from the pool of disaffected youths who have problems at school and consider themselves among the few educational failures in a culture that prizes academic achievement.

In addition to Chinese gangs, Samoan gangs, primarily the Sons of Samoa, have operated on the west coast, as have Vietnamese gangs whose influence has been felt in Los Angeles, New York, and Boston. James Diego Vigil and Steve Chong Yun studied Vietnamese gangs and found that their formation can be tied to external factors including racism, economic problems, and school failure and to internal problems including family stress and failure to achieve the level of success enjoyed by other Asians. Vietnamese gangs are formed when youths feel they need their *ahns,* or brothers, for protection and have unsatisfied needs for belonging.[136]

Asian gangs tend to victimize members of their own ethnic group. Because of group solidarity and distrust of outside authorities, little is known about their activities.

Anglo Gangs   The first American youth gangs were made up of white ethnic youths of European ancestry, especially Irish and Italian immigrants. During the 1950s, such ethnic youth gangs commonly competed with African American and Hispanic gangs in the nation's largest cities.

Today, Anglo gang activity is not uncommon, especially in smaller towns.[137] Many are organized as derivatives of the English punk and **skinhead** movement of the 1970s. In England these youths, generally the daughters and sons of lower-class parents, sported wildly dyed hair often shaved into "mohawks," military clothes, iron cross earrings, and high-topped military boots. Music was a big part of their lives, and the band that characterized their lifestyle was the punk band the Sex Pistols, led by Johnny Rotten and Sid Vicious. Their creed was antiestablishment, and their anger was directed toward foreigners, who they believed were taking their jobs.

The punker-skinhead style was brought to the United States by bands that replicated the Sex Pistols' antisocial music, stage presence, and dress; these included the Clash, the Dead Kennedys, and Human Sexual Response. The music, philosophy, and lifestyle of these rock bands inspired the formation of a variety of white youth gangs. However, unlike their British brothers, American white gang members are often alienated middle-class youths rather than poor lower-class youths out of society's mainstream. These gang members include "punkers" or "stoners" who dress in the latest heavy metal rock fashions and engage in drug- and violence-related activities. Some of these gangs espouse religious beliefs involving the occult and Satanic worship.[138] Some skinhead groups are devoted to racist, white supremacist activities; these youths are being actively recruited by adult hate groups (see Chapter 2).

Another variety of white youth gang engages in satanic rituals and becomes obsessed with occult themes, suicide, ritual killings, and animal mutilations. Members of these gangs get seriously involved in devil worship, tattoo themselves with occult symbols, and gouge their bodies to draw blood for satanic rituals.

Although national surveys do not show an upsurge in Anglo gang activity, a recent survey of almost six thousand youths in forty-two schools located in eleven cities found that about 25 percent of youths who claimed to be gang members were white, a far higher number than that found in the national surveys.[139]

skinhead
Member of white supremacist gang, identified by a shaved skull and Nazi or Ku Klux Klan markings.

Why Do Youths Join Gangs?

What causes youths to join gangs? Though gangs flourish in lower-class, inner-city areas, gang membership cannot be assumed to be solely a function of lower-class subcultural identity. Many lower-class youths do not join gangs, and middle-class youths are found in suburban skinhead and stoner groups. Let's look at some of the suspected causes of gang delinquency.

Anthropological View

Writing about gangs in the 1950s, Herbert Block and Arthur Niederhoffer suggested that gangs appeal to adolescents' deep-seated longing for the tribal group process that sustained and nurtured their ancestors.[140] Block and Niederhoffer found that gang processes and functions do seem similar to the puberty rites of some tribal cultures; like their ancient counterparts, gang rituals help the child bridge the gap between childhood and adulthood. For example, uniforms, tattoos, and other identifying marks are an integral part of gang culture. Gang initiation ceremonies are similar to activities of young men in Pacific Island cultures. Many gangs put new members through a hazing as an initiation to the gang to make sure they have "heart," a feature similar to tribal rites. In tribal societies, initiation into a cult is viewed as the death of childhood. By analogy, younger boys in lower-class urban areas yearn for the time when they can join the gang and really start to live. Membership in the adolescent gang "means the youth gives up his life as a child and assumes a new way of life."[141] Gang names are suggestive of "totemic ancestors" because they usually are symbolic (Cobras, Jaguars, and Kings, for example).

The Gang Prevention and Intervention survey found that over two-thirds of gang members have family members who are or were in gangs; fully two-thirds of gang members reported having members in their gang whose parents are also active members. These data indicate that ganging has become a family tradition passed on as a "rite of passage" from one generation to the next.[142] James Diego Vigil has described the rituals of gang initiation, which include physical pummeling to show that the gang boy is brave and ready to leave his matricentric (mother-dominated) household; this process seems reminiscent of tribal initiation rights.[143] For gang members these rituals become an important part of gang activities. Hand signs and graffiti have a tribal flavor. Gang members adopt nicknames and street identities that reflect personality or physical traits: the more volatile are called "Crazy," "Loco," or "Psycho," and those who wear glasses or read books are dubbed "Professor."[144]

Social Disorganization/Sociocultural View

Sociologists have commonly viewed the shattering, destructive sociocultural forces in disorganized, poor inner-city areas as the major cause of gang formation. Thrasher introduced this concept in his pioneering work on gangs, and it is a theme found in the classic studies of Richard Cloward and Lloyd Ohlin and of Albert K. Cohen.[145] Irving Spergel's consummate study, *Racketville, Slumtown, and Haulburg*, found that Slumtown—the area with the lowest income and the largest population— had the highest number of violent gangs.[146] According to Spergel, the gang gives lower-class youths a means of attaining personal reputations and peer group status. Malcolm Klein's oft-cited research of the late 1960s and 1970s also found that typical gang members came from dysfunctional and destitute families, had family members with criminal histories, and lacked adequate educational and vocational role models.[147]

The social disorganization/sociocultural view retains its prominent position today. Vigil paints a vivid picture of the forces that drive youths into gangs in his well-respected work *Barrio Gangs*.[148] Vigil's gang members are pushed into membership because of poverty and minority status. Those who join gangs are the most marginal youths in their neighborhoods and are outcasts in their own families. Vigil finds that all barrio dwellers experience some forms of psychological, economic, cultural, or social "stressors" that hinder their lives. Gang members are usually afflicted with more than one of these problems, causing them to suffer from "multiple marginality." Barrio youths join gangs seeking a sense of belonging; gangs offer a set of peers with whom friendship and family-like relationships are expected.[149]

Overall, the sociocultural view assumes that gangs are a natural and normal response to the privations of lower-class life and that gangs are a status-generating medium for boys whose aspirations cannot be realized by legitimate means. Youths who join gangs may hold conventional values (for example, want to become financially successful) but they are either unwilling or unable to accomplish this goal through conventional means (such as schooling).[150] Gangs are not solely made up of youths from dysfunctional families who seek deviant peers to compensate for parental brutality or incompetence. Gangs form in poor neighborhoods and recruit youths from many different kinds of families. Rather than an alternate family, the gang is a coalition of troubled youths who are socialized mainly by the streets rather than by conventional institutions.[151]

Anomie In his recent book on gangs, Irving Spergel suggests that youths are encouraged to join gangs during periods of social, economic, and cultural turmoil, conditions thought to produce anomie.[152] For example, gangs were present during the Russian Revolution of 1917 and then again during the chaos that followed the crumbling of the Soviet Union in the early 1990s. The rise of right-wing youth gangs in Germany is associated with social and political change brought about by the unification of East and West Germany. Skinhead groups have formed in Germany in response to the immigration from Turkey and North Africa. In the United States, Spergel notes, gangs have formed in areas where rapid population change has unsettled community norms:

> Immigration or emigration, rapidly expanding or contracting populations, and/or the incursion of different racial/ethnic groups or even different segments or generations of the same racial/ethnic population, can create fragmented communities and gang problems.[153]

Psychological View

A minority position on the formation of gangs is that gangs serve as an outlet for psychologically disturbed youths. One proponent of this view is Lewis Yablonsky, whose theory of violent gang formation holds that violent gangs recruit their members from among the more sociopathic youths living in disorganized, poverty-stricken communities.[154] Yablonsky views the sociopathic youth as one who lacks "social feelings"; he "has not been trained to have human feelings or compassion or responsibility for another."[155] Yablonsky supports this contention by pointing to the eccentric, destructive, and hostile sexual attitudes and behavior of gang youths, who are often violent and sadistic. He sums up the sociopathic character traits of gang boys as (1) a defective social conscience marked by limited feelings of guilt for destructive acts against others, (2) limited compassion or empathy for others, (3) behavior dominated by egocentrism and self-seeking goals, and (4) the manipulation of others for immediate self-gratification (for example, sexually exploitive modes of behavior) without any moral concern or responsibility.

Yablonsky's view is substantiated by cross-cultural studies that have found that gang members suffer from psychological deficits including impulsivity and poor personality control.[156]

Malcolm Klein's more recent analysis of Los Angeles gangs finds that many street gang members suffer from psychological and neuropsychological deficits, including low self-concept, social disabilities or deficits, poor impulse control, and limited life skills. Adolescents who display conduct disorders, early onset of antisocial behavior, and violent temperaments are at the greatest risk for later gang membership.[157] Yet Klein does not consider most gang youths abnormal or pathological. To help them, he believes psychological therapy is less important than providing gang members with vocational training, educational skills, and improving their chances for legitimate opportunities.[158]

Rational Choice View

Some youths may join gangs after making the rational choice that gang membership may benefit their law-violating careers and be a source of income. Members of the underclass, who perceive few opportunities in the legitimate economic structure, will turn to gangs as a method of obtaining desired goods and services, either directly through theft and extortion or indirectly through the profits generated by drug dealing and weapon sales. In this case, joining a gang can be viewed as an "employment decision," with the gang providing its "partners" with the security of knowing they can call on the services of talented "associates" to successfully carry out business ventures. Mercer Sullivan's study of Brooklyn gangs found that members call success at crime "getting paid," a term that imparts an economic edge to gang activity. Gang boys also refer to the rewards of crime as "getting over," which refers to their triumph and pride at "beating the system" and succeeding even though they are far from the economic mainstream.[159] According to this view, the gang boy has long been involved in criminal activity *prior* to his gang membership, and he joins the gang as a means of improving his illegal "productivity."[160]

Gang membership is *not* a necessary precondition for delinquency; already delinquent youths may join gangs because membership facilitates or enhances their criminal careers. Felix Padilla found this when he studied the Diamonds, a Latino gang in Chicago.[161] Joining the gang was a decision made after a careful assessment of legitimate economic opportunities. The gang represented a means of achieving aspirations that were otherwise closed off. The Diamonds made collective business decisions, and individuals who made their own deals were severely penalized. The gang maintained a distinct organizational structure and carried out other functions similar to those of legitimate enterprises, including personnel recruitment and financing business ventures with internal and external capital.

The rational choice view is also endorsed by Martin Sanchez-Jankowski in his important book *Islands in the Street*.[162] Sanchez-Jankowski found gangs to be organizations made up of adolescents who maintain a "defiant individualist character." These individuals maintain distinct personality traits: wariness or mistrust of the outside world, self-reliance, isolation from society, good survival instincts, defiance against authority, and a firm belief that only the strong survive. Youths holding these views and possessing these character traits make rational decisions to join a gang because the gang presents an opportunity to improve the quality of their lives. The gang offers otherwise unobtainable economic and social opportunities, including both support for crime and access to parties, social events, and sexual outlets. Gangs that last the longest and are the most successful offer incentives to these ambitious but destitute youths and can control their behavior. Sanchez-Jankowski's views, important for understanding the economic and social incentives of gang membership, have been supported by independent research data.[163]

The rational choice view holds that gangs provide support for criminal opportunities that might not otherwise be available. Some recent research by Terence Thornberry and his colleagues at the Rochester Youth Development Study support this model. They found that before youths become gang members their substance abuse and delinquency rates are no higher than nongang members. When they are in the gang, their crime and drug abuse rates increase significantly, only to decrease when they leave the gang. Thornberry concludes that gangs facilitate criminality rather than provide a haven for youths who are disturbed or already highly delinquent.

This research is important because it lends support to the life course model: events that take place during the life cycle, such as joining a gang, have a significant impact on criminal behavior and drug abuse.[164] Criminal behavior is not determined solely by factors that are present at birth or soon after.

Personal Safety   According to Spergel, some adolescents choose to join gangs from a "rational calculation" to achieve personal safety rather than profit.[165] Youths who are new to a community may believe they will become the targets of harassment or attack if they remain "unaffiliated." Motivation may have its roots in interrace or interethnic rivalry; youths who are white, African American, Asian, or Hispanic and who reside in an area dominated by a different racial or ethnic group may be persuaded that gang membership is an efficient means of collective protection. Ironically, gang members are more likely to be attacked than nonmembers.

Fun and Support   Some youths join gangs simply to "party" and have fun.[166] They enjoy hanging out with others like themselves and want to get involved in exciting experiences. Youths can learn the meaning of friendship and loyalty through gang membership. There is evidence that youths learn progang attitudes from their peers and that these attitudes direct them to join gangs.[167]

Some experts suggest that youths join gangs in an effort to obtain the family-like atmosphere all too often absent from their own homes. Many gang members reported that they have limited contact with their fathers and mothers, many of whom are unskilled laborers or are unemployed and battling substance abuse problems.[168]

Controlling Gang Activity

Two basic methods are used to control gang activity. The first involves priority targeting by local criminal justice agencies, and the second involves a variety of social service efforts. These methods will be discussed in the next sections.

Law Enforcement Efforts

In recent years gang control has often been left to local police departments. Gang control takes three basic forms:

Youth services programs, in which traditional police personnel, usually from the youth unit, are given responsibility for gang control. No personnel are assigned exclusively or mainly to gang-control work.

Gang details, in which one or more police officers, usually from youth or detective units, are assigned exclusively to gang-control work.

Gang units, established solely to deal with gang problems, to which one or more officers are assigned exclusively to gang-control work.[169]

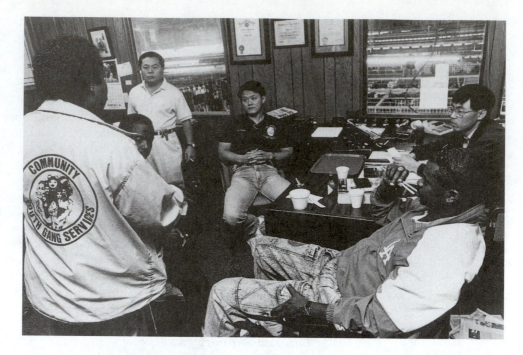

Police departments around the nation now maintain specialized units, such as this one in Los Angeles, that focus on gang problems. They maintain intelligence on gang members and train officers to deal with gang problems. Some identify street gang members and enter their names in a computer bank that is programmed to alert the unit if the youths are picked up or arrested. Some departments also sponsor general prevention programs that can help control gang activities.

The national assessment found that fifty-three of the seventy-two police departments surveyed maintained separate gang-control units. They are involved in activities such as processing information on youth gangs and gang leaders; prevention efforts, such as mediation programs; enforcement efforts to suppress criminal activity and apprehend those believed to have committed crimes; and follow-up investigations directed at apprehending gang members alleged to have committed crimes. About 85 percent of these units have special training in gang control for their personnel, 73 percent have specific policies directed at dealing with gang boys, and 62 percent enforce special laws designed to control gang activity.[170]

A good example of one of these units is the more than four hundred-officer Chicago Police Department gang crime section, which maintains intelligence on gang problems and trains officers to deal with gang problems. Through its gang target program, officers identify street gang members and enter their names in a computer bank that is programmed to alert the unit if the youths are picked up or arrested. Some departments also sponsor general prevention programs that can help control gang activities, including school-based lectures, police–school liaisons, information dissemination, recreation programs, and street worker programs that offer counseling, assistance to parents, and community organization, among other services.

Some police departments engage in "gang-breaking" activities, in which police focus on the gang leaders and make special efforts to arrest, prosecute, convict, and incarcerate them whenever possible. For example, Los Angeles police conduct intensive antigang "sweeps" in which more than a thousand officers are put on the street to round up and intimidate gang members. Police say the sweeps let the gangs know "who the streets belong to" and show neighborhood residents that someone cares.[171] Despite such efforts, the police response to the gang and youth group problem seems fragmented at best; even in Los Angeles, gang membership and violence remain at all-time highs. Few departments have written policies or procedures on how to deal with youths, and many do not provide gang-control training.

Gang sweeps and other traditional police tactics may not work on today's drug gangs. These organized criminal enterprises may best be dealt with as traditional organized crime families. In these cases, it might be useful to (1) develop informants through criminal prosecutions, payments, and witness protection programs; (2) rely heavily on electronic surveillance and long-term undercover investigations; and (3) use special statutes that create criminal liabilities for conspiracy, extortion, or en-

BOSTON'S YOUTH VIOLENCE STRIKE FORCE

The Youth Violence Strike Force (YVSF) is one of the primary enforcement strategies Boston is pursuing to combat youth gang violence. The YVSF is a multiagency coordinated task force made up of forty-five full time Boston police officers and fifteen officers from outside agencies. The membership of the YVSF includes the Massachusetts State Police, the Department of Treasury's Bureau of Alcohol, Tobacco, and Firearms (ATF), police departments from neighboring jurisdictions, Massachusetts Corrections, Probation, Parole, and Division of Youth Service (juvenile corrections) officers, and other agencies as appropriate. It works closely with the Suffolk County district attorney and state attorney general offices and participates in the Department of Justice's Anti-Violent Crime Initiative (AVCI) led locally by the United States Attorney. The YVSF, which has focused on areas of the city where youth-related violence is prevalent, made 1,358 arrests in 1995 and 689 arrests in 1996 through July 31. The YVSF investigates youth crimes, arrests those responsible, and breaks up the environment for crime. One important accomplishment of the YVSF was creation of a comprehensive computer database, which has allowed tough enforcement efforts against the leaders of gangs and positive intervention in the lives of those who are at risk of becoming hard core gang members.

In addition, the Youth Violence Strike Force, in cooperation with the City of Boston and the Department of Justice, has used criminal and civil forfeiture laws to help secure the safety of the community by taking over drug dens and renovating them as new homes. More than 150 drug dens have been closed through joint federal, state, and local cooperation, and nearly 50 are being renovated, including one in the Dorchester neighborhood of Boston that will provide low-income elderly housing.

The Youth Violence Strike Force takes tough action every day against gangs and gang members across Boston. Yet the strike force officers view their work in prevention as equally important, and many of these officers help sponsor prevention activities in the community. For example, members of the YVSF have been working in partnership with several law enforcement, social service, and private institutions to raise funds for a series of "Kids at Risk" programs provided to youths during the summer. These include professionally run camping programs, membership at the Boys and Girls Clubs and YMCA, and attendance at basketball camp or the Boston Police's Teen Summer Academy.

Source: Janet Reno, *Youth Violence: A Community-Based Response, One City's Success Story* (Washington, D.C.: Office of the Attorney General, 1996); updated, personal communication Boston Police Department, September 2, 1998.

gaging in criminal enterprises.[172] Of course, these policies are expensive and difficult to implement and may be needed only against the most sophisticated gangs. In addition, as new community policing strategies are implemented in which police officers are assigned to keep the peace in local neighborhoods (see Chapter 13 for more on community policing), it may be possible to garner sufficient local support and information to counteract gang influences. The Policy and Practice box describes one of the more successful police-sponsored gang-control efforts.

Community Control Efforts

In addition to law enforcement activities, there have been a number of community-based gang-control efforts. In some efforts social welfare professionals offer direct assistance to at-risk youths. This is not a new initiative. During the late nineteenth

detached street worker
Social workers who go out into the community and establish close relationships with juvenile gangs with the goal of modifying gang behavior to conform to conventional behaviors and to help gang members get jobs and educational opportunities.

century, social workers of the YMCA worked with youths in Chicago gangs.[173] During the 1950s, at the height of perceived gang activity, the **detached street worker** program was developed in major centers of gang activity.[174] This unique approach sent social workers into the community to work with gangs on their own turf. The worker attached him- or herself to a gang, participated in its activities, and tried to get to know its members. The purpose was to act as an advocate of the youths, to provide them with a positive role model, to help orient their activities in a positive direction, and to treat individual problems.

Detached street worker programs are sometimes credited with curbing gang activities in the 1950s and 1960s, although their effectiveness has been challenged on the ground that they helped legitimize delinquent groups by turning them into neighborhood organizations.[175] Some critics believed the detached street workers helped maintain group solidarity and as a result new members were drawn to gangs.

Today there are numerous community-level programs designed to limit gang activity. Some, such as the "Neutral Zone" in Mountlake Terrace, Washington (a Seattle suburb), employ recreation areas open in the evening hours that provide supervised activities as an alternative to street life.[176] In some areas citywide coordinating groups help orient gang-control efforts. For example, the Chicago Intervention Network operates field offices around the city in low-income, high-crime areas that provide a variety of services including neighborhood watches, parent patrols, alternative youth programming, and family support efforts.

Some community efforts are partnerships with juvenile justice agencies. In Los Angeles County the Gang Alternative Prevention Program (GAPP) provides intensive supervision of at-risk juveniles who are on probation for relatively minor crimes. GAPP provides prevention services to juveniles before they become entrenched in gangs, including (1) individual and group counseling, (2) bicultural and bilingual services to adolescents and their parents, and (3) special programs such as tutoring, parent training, job development, and recreational, educational, and cultural experiences.[177]

Still another approach has been to involve schools in gang-control programs. Some invite law enforcement agents to lecture students on the dangers of gang involvement and to teach them gang resistance techniques. Others create mechanisms to support parents and provide resources that can help parents prevent their children from joining gangs or, if they already are members, get them out. In the Policy and Practice box entitled "School-Based Gang Resistance Programs," the well-known GRIP program is described in some detail.

Why Gang Control Is Difficult

Experts have charged that the lack of legitimate economic opportunity for unskilled adolescents creates a powerful incentive for them to become involved in the illegal economy. To reduce the gang problem, hundreds of thousands of high-paying jobs are needed. Economic opportunities might prove to be particularly effective as surveys reveal that many gang members might leave gangs if education and vocational opportunities existed.[178]

This solution does not, however, seem practical or probable. As you may recall (Chapter 4), the more embedded youths become in criminal enterprise, the less likely they are to find meaningful adult work. It is unlikely that gang members can suddenly be transformed into highly paid professionals. A more reasonable and effective alternative would be to devote a greater degree of available resources to the most deteriorated urban areas, even if it requires pulling funds from groups that have traditionally been recipients of government aid, such as the elderly.[179]

Although social solutions to the gang problem seem elusive, the evidence shows that gang involvement is a socioecological phenomenon and must be treated as

SCHOOL-BASED GANG RESISTANCE PROGRAMS

In an attempt to curb gang membership and to discourage future gang involvement, the city of Paramount, California, initiated the Gang Resistance Is Paramount (GRIP) program, (formerly known as Alternatives to Gang Membership), which combines the resources of families, schools, and local government. The program attempts to discourage future gang membership by teaching children the harmful consequences of this lifestyle and by persuading them to choose positive alternatives.

The program includes three major components. The first involves neighborhood meetings that provide parents with support, assistance, and resources as they try to prevent their children from joining gangs. These meetings, conducted in both English and Spanish, often use audiovisual materials and focus on educating parents about gang activity, increasing family involvement, supporting sports and recreation programs, and increasing neighborhood unity to combat gang proliferation.

The second component comprises a fifteen-week course for fifth grade students and a ten-week course for second grade students. The lessons deal with graffiti, peer pressure, tattoos, the impact of gang activity on family members, drug abuse, and alternative activities and opportunities.

Finally, a school-based follow-up program is implemented at the ninth grade level to reinforce what children have learned in the elementary grades. The program builds self-esteem and also focuses on the consequences of a criminal lifestyle, the benefits of higher education, and future career opportunities.

Evaluations of GRIP indicate that it can be effective in keeping children out of gangs and that its positive effects do not erode over time.

Source: June Arnette and Marjorie Walsleben, *Combating Fear and Restoring Safety in Schools* (Washington, D.C.: Office of Juvenile Justice and Delinquency Prevention, 1998), pp. 6, 13.

such. Youths who live in deteriorated areas where their need for economic growth and self-fulfillment cannot be met by existing social institutions join gangs when gang members are there to recruit them at home or at school.[180] Social causes demand social solutions. Programs that enhance the lives of adolescents at school or in the family are the key to reducing gang delinquency.

SUMMARY

Gangs are a serious problem in many cities, yet little is known about them. Most gang members are males, ages 14 to 21, who live in urban ghetto areas. Ethnic minorities make up the majority of gang members. Gangs can be classified by their structure, behavior, or status. Some are believed to be social groups, others are criminally oriented, and still others are violent.

Gangs developed early in the nation's history and reached their heyday in the 1950s and early 1960s. After a lull of ten years, gang operations began to increase again in the late 1970s. Today, an estimated five hundred thousand youths belong to gangs. Hundreds of thousands of crimes, including drive-by shootings, are believed to be committed annually by gangs. Although most gang members are male, the number of females in gangs is growing at a

faster pace. African American and Hispanic gangs predominate, but Anglo and Asian gangs are also quite common.

We are still not sure what causes gangs. One view is that they serve as a bridge between adolescence and adulthood in communities where adult control is lacking. Another view suggests that gangs are a product of lower-class social disorganization and serve as an alternative means of advancement for disadvantaged youths. Still another view is that some gangs are havens for psychotic and disturbed youths.

Police departments have tried a number of gang-control techniques, but their efforts have not been well organized. A recent national survey found relatively few training efforts designed to help police officers deal with the gang problem.

KEY TERMS

cliques	barrio	graffiti
crowds	retreatists	representing
co-offending	transitional neighborhood	prestige crimes
gangs	disorganized	skinhead
interstitial group	neighborhood	detached street worker
near groups	*klikas*	

INFOTRAC COLLEGE EDITION EXERCISES

Read the following article from InfoTrac College Edition:

Representations of gangs and delinquency: wild in the streets? (Losing a Generation: Probing the Myths and Reality of Youth and Violence) Paul A. Perrone, Meda Chesney-Lind. *Social Justice* Winter 1997

Much of the information the general public receives regarding gangs and their activity comes from the media. Not surprisingly, the reality of what's actually happening is often quite different. As the public is quite sensitive (and

rightly so) to gang issues, groups of kids who are creating mischief are often viewed as "gang activity." The book describes the difference between a bunch of kids getting together and creating trouble and structured criminal activity such as group delinquency and gang delinquency.

The article above explores the media's influence on the perception of youth gangs and violence. What are the main points of the article? Assuming that our perceptions of events are shaped primarily by the media, how should we address the phenomena of gang violence?

QUESTIONS FOR DISCUSSION

1. Do gangs serve a purpose? Differentiate between a gang and a fraternity.
2. Discuss the differences between violent, criminal, and drug-oriented gangs.
3. How do gangs in suburban areas differ from inner-city gangs?
4. Do delinquents have cold and distant relationships with their peers?

5. Can gangs be controlled without changing the economic opportunity structure of society? Are there any truly meaningful alternatives to gangs today for lower-class youths?
6. Can you think of other rituals in society that reflect an affinity or longing for more tribal times? (*Hint:* Have you ever pledged a fraternity or sorority, gone to a wedding, or attended a football game?)

NOTES

1. Jim Yardley, "A Violent Life: Gangs and Guns Shaped a Suspect in the Death of an Officer," *New York Times* 10 August 1998, p. A16.
2. Paul Perrone and Meda Chesney-Lind, "Representations of Gangs and Delinquency: Wild in the Streets?" *Social Justice* 24:96–117 (1997).
3. Mayor Rudolph W. Giuliani, "Early Release from Prison Causes Another Preventable Tragedy," Mayor's Radio Station WINS Address, 2 August 1998.
4. For a general review, see Scott Cummings and Daniel Monti, *Gangs: The Origin and Impact of Contemporary Youth Gangs in the United States* (Albany, N.Y.: State University of New York Press, 1993); this chapter also makes extensive use of George Knox et al., *Gang Prevention and Intervention: Preliminary Results from the 1995 Gang Research Task Force* (National Gang Crime Research Center, 9501 S. King Drive, Chicago, Ill., 1995).
5. George Knox et al., *Preliminary Results of the 1995 Adult Corrections Survey* (Chicago, Ill.: National Gang Research Center, 1995); G. David Curry, Robert J. Fox, Richard Ball, and Daryl

Stone, *National Assessment of Law Enforcement Anti-Gang Information Resources, Final Report* (Morgantown, W.V.: National Assessment Survey, 1992), Table 6, pp. 36–37.
6. Thomas Berndt, "The Features and Effects of Friendships in Early Adolescence," *Child Development* 53:1447–69 (1982).
7. Thomas Berndt and T. B. Perry, "Children's Perceptions of Friendships as Supportive Relationships," *Developmental Psychology* 22:640–48 (1986).
8. Spencer Rathus, *Understanding Child Development* (New York: Holt, Rinehart & Winston, 1988), p. 462.
9. Peggy Giordano, "The Wider Circle of Friends in Adolescence," *American Journal of Sociology* 101:661–97 (1995).
10. Ibid., p. 463.
11. See, generally, Penelope Eckert, *Jocks and Burnouts: Social Categories and Identity in the High School* (New York: Teachers College Press, 1989).
12. Judith Rich Harris, *The Nurture Assumption: Why Children Turn Out the Way They Do* (New York: The Free Press, 1998).
13. Ibid., p. 463.

14. Robert Agnew and Timothy Brezina, "Relational Problems with Peers, Gender and Delinquency," *Youth and Society* 29:84–111 (1997).

15. David Cantor, "Drug Involvement and Offending among Incarcerated Juveniles," paper presented at the American Society of Criminology Meeting, Boston, Mass., November 1995.

16. Albert Reiss, "Co-Offending and Criminal Careers," in Michael Tonry and Norval Morris, eds., *Crime and Justice,* vol. 10 (Chicago: University of Chicago Press, 1988).

17. David Farrington and Donald West, "The Cambridge Study in Delinquent Development: A Long-Term Follow-Up of 411 London Males," in H. J. Kerner and G. Kaiser, eds., *Criminality: Personality, Behavior, and Life History* (Berlin: Springer-Verlag, 1990).

18. Mark Warr, "Organization and Instigation in Delinquent Groups," *Criminology* 34:11–37 (1996).

19. Ibid., pp. 31–33.

20. James Short and Fred Strodtbeck, *Group Process and Gang Delinquency* (Chicago: Aldine, 1965).

21. Kate Keenan, Rolf Loeber, Quanwu Zhang, Magda Stouthamer-Loeber, and Welmoet Van Kammen, "The Influence of Deviant Peers on the Development of Boys' Disruptive and Delinquent Behavior: A Temporal Analysis," *Development and Pyschopathology* 7:715–26 (1995).

22. John Cole, Robert Terry, Shari-Miller Johnson, and John Lochman, "Longitudinal Effects of Deviant Peer Groups on Criminal Offending in Late Adolescence," paper presented at the American Society of Criminology Meeting, Boston, Mass., November 1995.

23. Terence Thornberry, and Marvin Krohn, "Peers, Drug Use and Delinquency," in David Stoff, James Breiling, and Jack Maser, eds., *Handbook of Antisocial Behavior* (New York: Wiley, 1997), pp. 218–33; Thomas Dishion, Deborah Capaldi, Kathleen Spracklen, and Fuzhong Li, "Peer Ecology of Male Adolescent Drug Use," *Development and Psychopathology* 7:803–24 (1995).

24. Sara Battin, Karl Hill, Robert Abbott, Richard Catalano, and J. David Hawkins, "The Contribution of Gang Membership to Delinquency Beyond Delinquent Friends," *Criminology* 36: 93–116 (1998).

25. Terence Thornberry, Alan Lizotte, Marvin Krohn, Margaret Farnworth, and Sung Joon Jang, "Delinquent Peers, Beliefs, and Delinquent Behavior: A Longitudinal Test of Interactional Theory," working paper no. 6, rev. (Albany, N.Y.: Rochester Youth Development Study, Hindelang Criminal Justice Research Center, 1992), pp. 8–30.

26. Mark Warr, "Age, Peers and Delinquency," *Criminology* 31:17–40 (1993).

27. Mark Warr, "Life-Course Transitions and Desistance from Crime," *Criminology* 36:502–36 (1998).

28. Cindy Hanson, Scott Henggeler, William Haefele, and J. Douglas Rodick, "Demographic, Individual, and Family Relationship Correlates of Serious Repeated Crime among Adolescents and Their Siblings," *Journal of Consulting and Clinical Psychology* 52:528–38 (1984).

29. Peggy Giordano, Stephen Cernkovich, and M. D. Pugh, "Friendships and Delinquency," *American Journal of Sociology* 91:1170–1202 (1986).

30. Denise Kandel, "Friendship Networks, Intimacy and Illicit Drug Use in Young Adulthood: A Comparison of Two Competing Theories," *Criminology* 29:441–69 (1991).

31. Marvin Krohn and Terence Thornberry, "Network Theory: A Model for Understanding Drug Abuse among African-American and Hispanic Youth," working paper no. 10 (Albany, N.Y.: Rochester Youth Development Study, Hindelang Criminal Justice Research Center, 1991).

32. Irving Spergel, *The Youth Gang Problem: A Community Approach* (New York: Oxford University Press, 1995).

33. Ibid., p. 3.

34. Other well-known movie representations of gangs include *The Wild Ones* and *Hell's Angels on Wheels,* which depict motorcycle gangs, and *Saturday Night Fever,* which focused on neighborhood street toughs; see also, David Dawley, *A Nation of Lords* (Garden City, N.Y.: Anchor, 1973).

35. For a recent review of gang research, see James Howell, "Recent Gang Research: Program and Policy Implications," *Crime and Delinquency* 40:495–515 (1994).

36. Walter Miller, *Violence by Youth Gangs and Youth Groups as a Crime Problem in Major American Cities* (Washington, D.C.: U.S. Government Printing Office, 1975).

37. Ibid., p. 20.

38. Malcolm Klein, *The American Street Gang, Its Nature, Prevalence and Control* (New York: Oxford University Press, 1995), p. 30.

39. Lewis Yablonsky, *The Violent Gang* (Baltimore: Penguin, 1966), p. 109.

40. James Diego Vigil, *Barrio Gangs* (Austin: Texas University Press, 1988), pp. 11–19.

41. Finn-Aage Esbensen and David Huizinga, "Gangs, Drugs and Delinquency in a Survey of Urban Youth," *Criminology* 31:565–87 (1993).

42. Scott Decker, Tim Bynum, and Deborah Weisel, "A Tale of Two Cities: Gangs and Organized Crime Groups," *Justice Quarterly* 15:395–425 (1998).

43. Frederick Thrasher, *The Gang* (Chicago: University of Chicago Press, 1927).

44. Malcolm Klein, ed., *Juvenile Gangs in Context* (Englewood Cliffs, N.J.: Prentice-Hall, 1967), pp. 1–12.

45. Ibid., p. 6.

46. Irving Spergel, *Street Gang Work: Theory and Practice* (Reading, Mass.: Addison-Wesley, 1966).

47. Miller, *Violence by Youth Gangs,* p. 2.

48. Marjorie Zatz, "*Los Cholos:* Legal Processing of Chicago Gang Members," *Social Problems* 33:13–30 (1985).

49. Miller, *Violence by Youth Gangs,* pp. 1–2.

50. Ibid.

51. "LA Gang Warfare Called Bloodiest in 5 Years," *Boston Globe,* 18 December 1986, p. A4.

52. John Hagedorn, *People and Folks: Gangs, Crime and the Underclass in a Rustbelt City* (Chicago: Lake View Press, 1988).

53. National School Safety Center, *Gangs in Schools, Breaking Up Is Hard to Do* (Malibu, Calif.: Pepperdine University, 1988), p. 8.

54. C. Ronald Huff, "Youth Gangs and Public Policy," *Crime and Delinquency* 35:524–37 (1989).

55. Joan Moore, *Going Down to the Barrio: Homeboys and Homegirls in Change* (Philadelphia: Temple University Press, 1991), p. 3.

56. Richard McCorkle and Terance Miethe, "The Political and Organizational Response to Gangs: An Examination of 'Moral Panic' in Nevada," *Justice Quarterly* 15:41–64 (1998).

57. Irving Spergel, *Youth Gangs: Problem and Response* (Chicago: University of Chicago, School of Social Service Administration, 1989).

58. Felix Padilla, *The Gang as an American Enterprise* (New Brunswick, N.J.: Rutgers University Press, 1992), p. 3.

59. Pamela Irving Jackson, "Crime, Youth Gangs, and Urban Transition: The Social Dislocations of Postindustrial Economic Development," *Justice Quarterly* 8:379–97 (1991).

60. Moore, *Going Down to the Barrio,* pp. 89–101.

61. Miller, *Violence by Youth Gangs;* idem., *Crime by Youth Gangs and Groups in the United States* (Washington, D.C.: Office of Juvenile Justice Delinquency Prevention, 1982).

62. Curry, Fox, Ball, and Stone, *National Assessment.*

63. G. David Curry, *Gang Crime and Law Enforcement Record Keeping* (Washington, D.C.: National Institute of Justice, 1994).

64. G. David Curry, Richard Ball, and Scott Decker, "Estimating the National Scope of Gang Crime from Law Enforcement Data," in C. Ronald Huff, ed., *Gangs in America,* 2nd ed. (Newbury Park, Calif.: Sage, 1996).

65. Klein, *The American Street Gang,* pp. 31–35.

66. John Moore and Craig Terrett, *Highlights of the 1996 National Youth Gang Survey* (Washington, D.C.: OJJDP, 1998).

67. Kathryn A. Chandler, Chris Chapman, Michael R. Rand, and Bruce M. Taylor, "Students' Reports of School Crime: 1989 and 1995" (Washington, D.C: Bureau of Justice Statistics, 1998).
68. Jeffery Fagan, "The Social Organization of Drug Use and Drug Dealing among Urban Gangs," *Criminology* 27:633–69 (1989).
69. Richard Cloward and Lloyd Ohlin, *Delinquency and Opportunity* (New York: Free Press, 1960), pp. 1–12.
70. Fagan, "The Social Organization of Drug Use and Drug Dealing among Urban Gangs."
71. Huff, "Youth Gangs and Public Policy," pp. 528–29.
72. Carl Taylor, *Dangerous Society* (East Lansing: Michigan State University Press, 1990).
73. Cheryl Maxson, "Investigating Gang Structures," *Journal of Gang Research* 3:33–40 (1995).
74. Personal communication, Malcolm Klein, 12 December 1995.
75. Scott Decker, Tim Bynum, and Deborah Weisel, "A Tale of Two Cities: Gangs and Organized Crime Groups," *Justice Quarterly* 15:395–425 (1998), at 410.
76. Saul Bernstein, *Youth in the Streets: Work with Alienated Youth Gangs* (New York: Associated Press, 1964).
77. William Julius Wilson, *The Truly Disadvantaged* (Chicago: University of Chicago Press, 1987).
78. Vigil, *Barrio Gangs*.
79. Miller, *Violence by Youth Gangs,* pp. 17–20.
80. Jerome Needle and W. Vaughan Stapleton, *Reports of the National Juvenile Justice Assessment Centers, Police Handling of Youth Gangs* (Washington, D.C.: Office of Juvenile Justice and Delinquency Prevention, 1983), p. 12.
81. Richard Zevitz and Susan Takata, "Metropolitan Gang Influence and the Emergence of Group Delinquency in a Regional Community," *Journal of Criminal Justice* 20:93–106 (1992).
82. Cheryl Maxson, Kristi Woods, and Malcolm Klein, "Street Migration in the United States: Executive Summary" (Los Angeles: Center for the Study of Crime and Social Control, University of Southern California, 1995).
83. John Hagedorn, "Gangs, Neighborhoods and Public Policy," *Social Problems* 20:529–41 (1991).
84. National School Safety Center, *Gangs in Schools,* p. 7.
85. Mark Warr, "Organization and Instigation in Delinquent Groups," *Criminology* 34:11–37 (1996).
86. Knox et al., *Gang Prevention and Intervention,* p. vii.
87. Spergel, *Youth Gangs,* p. 7; Hagedorn, *People and Folks.*
88. Wilson, *The Truly Disadvantaged.*
89. National School Safety Center, *Gangs in Schools,* p. 7.
90. John Hagedorn, Jerome Wonders, Angelo Vega, and Joan Moore, "The Milwaukee Drug Posse Study," unpublished leaflet, n.d.
91. Mary Glazier, "Small Town Delinquent Gangs: Origins, Characteristics and Activities," paper presented at the American Society of Criminology Meeting, Boston, Mass., November 1995.
92. G. David Curry, "Female Gang Involvement," *Journal of Research in Crime and Delinquency* 35:100–119 (1998).
93. Moore, *Going Down to the Barrio;* Anne Campbell, *The Girls in the Gang* (Cambridge, Mass.: Basil Blackwood, 1984).
94. Karen Joe Laidler and Geoffrey Hunt, "Violence and Social Organization in Female Gangs," *Social Justice* 24:148–87 (1997).
95. Karen Joe and Meda Chesney-Lind, "'Just Every Mother's Angel': An Analysis of Gender and Ethnic Variations in Youth Gang Membership," *Gender and Society* 9:408–30 (1995).
96. Curry, "Female Gang Involvement."
97. Moore and Terrett, *Highlights of the 1996 National Youth Gang Survey;* Irving Spergel, "Youth Gangs: Continuity and Change," in Michael Tonry and Norval Morris, eds., *Crime and Justice,* vol. 12 (Chicago: University of Chicago Press, 1990), pp. 171–275.
98. Gary Jensen, "Defiance and Gang Identity: Quantitative Tests of Qualitative Hypothesis," paper presented at the American Society of Criminology Meeting, Boston, Mass., November 1995; Finn Esbensen, Terence Thornberry, and David Huizinga, "Gangs," in David Huizinga, Rolf Loeber, and Terence Thornberry, eds., *Urban Delinquency and Substance Abuse: Technical Report* (Washington, D.C.: Office of Juvenile Justice and Delinquency Prevention, 1991).
99. Taylor, *Dangerous Society,* p. 109.
100. Finn-Aage Esbensen and David Huizinga, "Gangs, Drugs and Delinquency in a Survey of Urban Youth," *Criminology* 31: 565–87 (1993).
101. Finn-Aage Esbensen, "Race and Gender Differences between Gang and Nongang Youths: Results from a Multisite Survey," *Justice Quarterly* 15:504–25 (1998).
102. Curry, "Female Gang Involvement."
103. Joan Moore, James Diego Vigil, and Robert Garcia, "Residence and Territoriality in Chicano Gangs," *Social Problems* 31:182–94 (1983).
104. William F. Whyte, *Street Corner Society* (Chicago: University of Chicago Press, 1955).
105. Malcolm Klein, "Impressions of Juvenile Gang Members," *Adolescence* 3:59 (1968).
106. Decker, Bynum, and Weisel, "A Tale of Two Cities."
107. Los Angeles County Sheriff's Department, *Street Gangs of Los Angeles County, White Paper* (Los Angeles: LACSD, n.d.), p. 14.
108. LeRoy Martin, *Collecting, Organizing and Reporting Street Gang Crime* (Chicago: Chicago Police Department, 1988).
109. Patricia Wen, "Boston Gangs: A Hard World," *Boston Globe* 10 May 1988, p. 1.
110. Rick Graves and Ed Allen, *Black Gangs and Narcotics and Black Gangs* (Los Angeles: Los Angeles County Sheriff's Department, n.d.).
111. Spergel, *Youth Gang Problem,* p. 3.
112. Joseph Sheley, Joshua Zhang, Charles Brody, and James Wright, "Gang Organization, Gang Criminal Activity, and Individual Gang Members' Criminal Behavior," *Social Science Quarterly* 76:53–68 (1995).
113. Malcolm Klein, Cheryl Maxson, and Lea Cunningham, "Crack, Street Gangs and Violence," *Criminology* 4:623–50 (1991); Mel Wallace, "The Gang-Drug Debate Revisited," paper presented at the Annual Meeting of the American Society of Criminology, New Orleans, November 1992.
114. Kevin Thompson, David Brownfield, and Ann Marie Sorenson, "Specialization Patterns of Gang and Nongang Offending: A Latent Structure Analysis," *Journal of Gang Research* 3:25–35 (1996).
115. Sara Battin, Karl Hill, Robert Abbott, Richard Catalano, and J. David Hawkins, "The Contribution of Gang Membership to Delinquency Beyond Delinquent Friends," *Criminology* 36:93–116 (1998).
116. Terence Thornberry and James Burch, *Gang Members and Delinquent Behavior* (Washington, D.C.: Office of Juvenile Justice and Delinquency Prevention, 1997).
117. James C. Howell, "Youth Gang Drug Trafficking and Homicide: Policy and Program Implications," *Juvenile Justice Journal* 4:3–5 (1997).
118. Ibid.
119. Ibid.
120. Scott Decker, Susan Pennell, and Ami Caldwell, *Arrestees and Guns: Monitoring the Illegal Firearms Market* (Washington, D.C: National Institute of Justice, 1996).
121. Scott Decker, "Collective and Normative Features of Gang Violence," *Justice Quarterly* 13:243–64 (1996).
122. Beth Bjerregaard and Alan Lizotte, "Gun Ownership and Gang Membership," *Journal of Criminal Law and Criminology* 86:37–53 (1995).
123. Pamela Lattimore, Richard Linster, and John MacDonald, "Risk of Death among Serious Young Offenders," *Journal of Research in Crime and Delinquency* 34:187–209 (1997).
124. Decker, "Collective and Normative Features of Gang Violence," p. 253.
125. H. Range Hutson, Deirdre Anglin, and Michael Pratts Jr., "Adolescents and Children Injured or Killed in Drive-By Shootings in Los Angeles," *The New England Journal of Medicine* 330:324–27 (1994).

126. Miller, *Violence by Youth Gangs,* pp. 2–26.
127. Malcolm Klein, "Violence in American Juvenile Gangs," in Donald Muvihill, Melvin Tumin, and Lynn Curtis, eds., *Crimes of Violence National Commission on the Causes and Prevention of Violence,* vol. 13 (Washington, D.C.: U.S. Government Printing Office, 1969), p. 1429.
128. Kevin Cullen, "Gangs Are Seen as Carefully Organized," *Boston Globe,* 7 January 1987, p. 17.
129. Curry, Fox, Ball, and Stone, *National Assessment,* pp. 60–61.
130. The following description of ethnic gangs leans heavily on the material developed in National School Safety Center, *Gangs in Schools,* pp. 11–23.
131. Spergel, *The Youth Gang Problem,* pp. 136–37.
132. Decker, Bynum, and Weisel, "A Tale of Two Cities."
133. Los Angeles County Sheriff's Department, *Street Gangs of Los Angeles County.*
134. Zheng Wang, Indiana University of Pennsylvania, personnel communication, 3 February 1993.
135. Ko-Lin Chin, *Chinese Subculture and Criminality: Non-traditional Crime Groups in America* (Westport, Conn.: Greenwood Press, 1990).
136. James Diego Vigil and Steve Chong Yun, "Vietnamese Youth Gangs in Southern California," in C. Ronald Huff, ed., *Gangs in America* (Newbury Park, Calif.: Sage, 1990), pp. 146–63.
137. See Glazier, "Small Town Delinquent Gangs."
138. For a review, see Lawrence Trostle, *The Stoners, Drugs, Demons and Delinquency* (New York: Garland, 1992).
139. Esbensen, "Race and Gender Differences between Gang and Nongang Youths."
140. Herbert Block and Arthur Niederhoffer, *The Gang: A Study in Adolescent Behavior* (New York: Philosophical Library, 1958).
141. Ibid., p. 113.
142. Knox et al., *Gang Prevention and Intervention,* p. 44.
143. James Diego Vigil, "Group Processes and Street Identity: Adolescent Chicano Gang Members," *Ethos* 16:421–45 (1988).
144. James Diego Vigil and John Long, "Emic and Etic Perspectives on Gang Culture: The Chicano Case," in C. Ronald Huff, ed., *Gangs in America* (Newbury Park, Calif.: Sage, 1990), p. 66.
145. Albert Cohen, *Delinquent Boys* (New York: Free Press, 1955), pp. 1–19.
146. Irving Spergel, *Racketville, Slumtown, and Haulburg: An Exploratory Study of Delinquent Subcultures* (Chicago: University of Chicago Press, 1964).
147. Malcolm Klein, *Street Gangs and Street Workers* (Englewood Cliffs, N.J.: Prentice-Hall, 1971), pp. 12–15.
148. Vigil, *Barrio Gangs.*
149. Vigil and Long, "Emic and Etic Perspectives on Gang Culture," p. 61.
150. David Brownfield, Kevin Thompson, and Ann Marie Sorenson, "Correlates of Gang Membership: A Test of Strain, Social Learning, and Social Control," *Journal of Gang Research* 4:11–22 (1997).
151. John Hagedorn, Jose Torres, and Greg Giglio, "Cocaine, Kicks, and Strain: Patterns of Substance Use in Milwaukee Gangs," *Contemporary Drug Problems* 25:113–45 (1998).
152. Spergel, *The Youth Gang Problem,* pp. 4–5.
153. Ibid.
154. Yablonsky, *The Violent Gang,* p. 237.
155. Ibid., pp. 239–41.
156. Marc Le Blanc and Nadine Lanctot, "Social and Psychological Characteristics of Gang Members according to the Gang Structure and Its Subcultural and Ethnic Making," paper presented at the American Society of Criminology Meeting, Maimi, Fl. 1994.
157. Klein, *The American Street Gang.*
158. Ibid., p. 163.
159. Mercer Sullivan, *Getting Paid: Youth Crime and Work in the Inner City* (Ithaca, NY: Cornell University Press, 1989), pp. 244–45.
160. Esbensen and Huizinga, "Gangs, Drugs and Delinquency in a Survey of Urban Youth," p. 583; G. David Curry and Irving Spergel, "Gang Involvement and Delinquency among Hispanic and African-American Adolescent Males," *Journal of Research in Crime and Delinquency* 29:273–91 (1992).
161. Padilla, *The Gang as an American Enterprise,* p. 103.
162. Martin Sanchez-Jankowski, *Islands in the Street: Gangs and American Urban Society* (Berkeley: University of California Press, 1991).
163. Gary Jensen, "Defiance and Gang Identity: Quantitative Tests of Qualitative Hypothesis," paper presented at the American Society of Criminology Meeting, Boston, Mass., November 1995.
164. Terence Thornberry, Marvin Krohn, Alan Lizotte, and Deborah Chard-Wierschem, "The Role of Juvenile Gangs in Facilitating Delinquent Behavior," *Journal of Research in Crime and Delinquency* 30:55–87 (1993).
165. Spergel, *The Youth Gang Problem,* pp. 93–94.
166. Ibid., p. 93.
167. L. Thomas Winfree Jr., Teresa Vigil Backstrom, and G. Larry Mays, "Social Learning Theory, Self-Reported Delinquency and Youth Gangs, A New Twist on a General Theory of Crime and Delinquency," *Youth and Society* 26:147–77 (1994).
168. Karen Joe Laidler and Geoffrey Hunt, "Violence and Social Organization in Female Gangs," *Social Justice* 24:148–87 (1997).
169. Needle and Stapleton, *Police Handling of Youth Gangs,* p. 19.
170. Curry, Fox, Ball, and Stone, *National Assessment,* p. 65.
171. Scott Armstrong, "Los Angeles Seeks New Ways to Handle Gangs," *Christian Science Monitor* 23 April 1988, p. 3.
172. Mark Moore and Mark A. R. Kleiman, *The Police and Drugs* (Washington, D.C.: National Institute of Justice, 1989), p. 8.
173. Barry Krisberg, "Preventing and Controlling Violent Youth Crime: The State of the Art," in Ira Schwartz, ed., *Violent Juvenile Crime* (Minneapolis: University of Minnesota, Hubert Humphrey Institute of Public Affairs, n.d.).
174. See, generally, Spergel, *Street Gang Work.*
175. For a revisionist view of gang delinquency, see Hedy Bookin-Weiner and Ruth Horowitz, "The End of the Youth Gang," *Criminology* 21:585–602 (1983).
176. Quint Thurman, Andrew Giacomazzi, Michael Reisig, and David Mueller, "Community-Based Gang Prevention and Intervention: An Evaluation of The Neutral Zone," *Crime and Delinquency* 42:279–96 (1996).
177. Michael Agopian, "Evaluation of the Gang Alternative Prevention Program," paper presented at the American Society of Criminology Meeting, Boston, Mass., November 1995.
178. James Houston, "What Works: The Search for Excellence in Gang Intervention Programs," paper presented at the American Society of Criminology Meeting, Boston, Mass., November 1995.
179. Hagedorn, "Gangs, Neighborhoods and Public Policy."
180. Curry and Spergel, "Gang Involvement and Delinquency among Hispanic and African-American Adolescent Males."

Chapter Ten

Schools and Delinquency

Sean O'Brien, a seventeen-year-old student at Westlake High School (near Cleveland) had a beef with the school band instructor, whom he thought tended to blame him unfairly for problems around school. In response, Sean set up a home-based Internet website that insulted the teacher, describing him as "an overweight middle-aged man who doesn't like to get haircuts."[1] Sean posted a photo of the teacher and said that he "likes to involve himself in everything you do." Sean included the teacher's home address and phone number. When word of the website got out around school, the administration suspended Sean for ten days, told him to remove the website, and threatened to expel him. Sean and his parents sued the district for $550,000, accusing them of violating Sean's right to free speech. In an out-of-court settlement reached in April 1998, the district reinstated Sean, issued an apology, and paid him $30,000 in damages. Sean could have reestablished his website but did not do so. Sean split the money with his lawyers and donated a portion to the ACLU. Afterward, he told reporters that the incident was troubling. "I guess it would've been nice if the whole thing didn't happen and I just went to school like normal."

Fran Cook, a Spanish teacher in Alexandria, Kentucky, won $25,000 in punitive damages and $8,500 in emotional damages in 1995 after she filed a lawsuit against a student in her class. The jury stated on the record that the student in question "exceeded the bounds of common decency" not only for his classroom behavior but also when he left a note after he graduated urging other students to talk about different methods of murdering Ms. Cook in her classroom.[2]

These cases illustrate the varied and complex issues schools must face in modern society. Should a student be allowed to have an off-campus Internet website mocking teachers? If so, should a teacher be allowed to have a website that discusses or mocks his or her students and gives examples of their poor writing styles and behavioral misadventures? School officials whose interest and training may be focused on education and learning must make daily decisions on discipline and crime prevention. Most degree programs in education do not cover these topics.

Because the schools are responsible for educating virtually everyone during most of their formative years, and because so much of an adolescent's time is spent in school, it would seem logical that some relationship exists between delinquent behavior and what is happening—or not happening—in classrooms throughout the United States. This relationship was pointed out as early as 1939 when a study by the New Jersey Delinquency Commission found that of 2,021 inmates of prisons and correctional institutions in that state 2 out of every 5 had first been committed for **truancy.**[3]

Numerous studies have confirmed that delinquency is related to **academic achievement,** and experts have concluded that many of the underlying problems of delinquency are intimately connected with the nature and quality of the school experience.[4]

truancy
Staying out of school without permission.

academic achievement
Being successful in a school environment.

Some find that school-related variables are more important contributing factors to delinquent behavior than the effects of either family or friends.[5] Although there are differences of opinion, most theorists agree that the education system bears some responsibility for the high rate of juvenile crime (see Table 10.1).

In this chapter we examine the relationship between the school and delinquency. We first explore how educational achievement and delinquency are related and what factors in the school experience appear to contribute to delinquent behavior. Next, we turn to delinquency within the school setting itself—vandalism, theft, violence, and so on. Finally, we look at the attempts made by the schools to prevent and control delinquency.

The School in Modern American Society

The school plays a significant role in shaping the values and norms of American children.[6] In contrast to earlier periods, when formal education was a privilege of the upper classes, the U.S. system of compulsory public education has made schooling a legal obligation. Today, more than 90 percent of school-aged children attend school, compared with only 7 percent in 1890.[7] In contrast to the earlier, agrarian days of U.S. history when most adolescents shared in the work of the family and became socialized into adulthood as part of the workforce, today's young people, beginning as early as age 3 or 4, spend most of their time in school. The school has become the primary instrument of **socialization**, the "basic conduit through which the community and adult influences enter into the lives of adolescents."[8]

socialization
The process of learning the values and norms of the society or the subculture to which the individual belongs.

Because young people spend a longer time in school, the period of their adolescence is prolonged. As long as students are still economically dependent on their families and have not entered the work world, they are not considered adults—in their own minds or in the estimation of the rest of society. The responsibilities of adulthood come later to modern-day youths than to those in earlier generations,

Poor academic performance has been directly linked to delinquent behavior: there is general consensus that students who are chronic underachievers in school are also among the most likely to be delinquent. Researchers commonly find that school failure is a stronger predictor of delinquency than such personal variables as economic class membership, racial or ethnic background, or peer group relations.

Table 10.1

View	Educational Impact
Choice	People commit crime because of poor social control. The school can educate youths about the pains of punishment and through disciplinary procedures teach youths that behavior transgressions lead to sanctions. Education can stress moral development.
Biosocial and Psychological	The school can compensate for psychological and biological problems. For example, youths with low IQs or learning disabilities can be put in special classes to ease their frustration and reduce their delinquency-proneness.
Social Structure	The school is a primary cause of delinquency. Middle-class school officials penalize lower-class youths, intensifying their rage, frustration, and anomie.
Social Process	A lack of bond to the school and nonparticipation in educational activities can intensify delinquency-proneness. The school fails to provide sufficient definitions toward conventional behavior to thwart delinquency.
Labeling	Labeling by school officials solidifies negative self-images. The stigma associated with school failure locks youth into a delinquent career pattern.
Conflict	Schools are designated to train lower-class youngsters for menial careers and upper-class youths to be part of the privileged society. Rebellion against these roles promotes delinquency.
Developmental	The school experience plays an important role in the developmental process. School failure can encourage delinquent careers by reducing social capital and by increasing attachments to failure-prone or deviant peers.

and some experts see this prolonged childhood as one factor that contributes to the irresponsible, childish, and often irrational behavior of many juveniles who commit delinquent acts.

Socialization and Status

Another significant aspect of the educational experience of American youths is that it is overwhelmingly a peer encounter. Children spend their school hours with their peers, and most of their activities after school take place with school friends. Young people rely increasingly on school friends and consequently become less and less interested in adult role models. The norms and values of the peer culture are often at odds with those of adult society, and a pseudoculture with a distinct social system develops, offering a united front to the adult world. Law-abiding behavior or conventional norms may not be among the values promoted in such an atmosphere. Youth culture may instead admire bravery, defiance, and having fun much more.

In addition to its role as an instrument of socialization, the school has become a primary determinant of economic and social status. In this highly technological age, education is the key to a job that will mark its holder as "successful." No longer can parents ensure the status of their children through social class origin alone. Educational achievement has become of equal, if not greater, importance as a determinant of economic success.

Schools, then, are geared toward success defined in terms of academic achievement, which provides the key to profit and position in society. Adolescents derive much of their identity from what happens to them in school. Virtually all adolescents must participate in the educational system. Not only is it required by law but also our notion of success is defined in terms of the possession of a technical or professional skill that can be acquired only through formal education.

This emphasis on the value of education is fostered by parents, the media, and the schools themselves. Regardless of their social or economic background, most children grow up believing education is the key to success. Despite their apparent acceptance of the value of education, many youths do not meet acceptable standards of school achievement. Whether failure is measured by test scores, not being promoted, or dropping out, the incidence of school failure continues to be a major social problem for U.S. society. A single school failure often leads to a pattern of chronic academic failure. The links between school failure, academic and social aspirations, and delinquency will be explored more fully in the next sections.

Education in Crisis

The critical role schools play in adolescent development is underscored by the problems faced by the U.S. education system. Budget cutting has severely reduced educational resources in many communities and curtailed state support for local school systems. Spending on elementary and secondary education (as a percentage of the U.S. gross national product) trails that of other nations.

There has been some improvement in measured performance in reading, math, and science achievement during the past decade, but the United States still lags many nations in key educational achievement measures. For example, eighth graders in the United States lag behind students in some less affluent nations (Hungary, Slovak Republic, and Bulgaria) in science achievement, and as Figure 10.1 shows, the math achievement of U.S. eighth graders is actually less than the international average. One reason for the lack of achievement may be that many secondary school math and science teachers did not major, or even minor, in the subjects they teach; less than half the math teachers in California, Delaware, Washington and Alaska have at least a minor in mathematics.[9] This low national level of academic performance, and the resulting educational problems, seems critical when considering delinquent behavior in our schools.

Academic Performance and Delinquency

The general path towards occupational prestige is education, and when youth are deprived of this avenue of success through poor school performance there is a greater likelihood of delinquent behavior.[10]

FIGURE 10.1

Average Scores of Eighth Graders on Standardized Mathematics Achievement Tests

Source: *National Education Goals Report 1997* (Washington, D.C.: U.S. Government Printing Office, 1997), p. 8.

Singapore	643	
Korea	607	
Japan	605	
Hong Kong	588	
Belgium-Flemish	565	
Czech Republic	564	
Slovak Republic	547	
Switzerland	545	
(Netherlands), (Slovenia)	541	
(Bulgaria)	540	
(Austria)	539	
France	538	
Hungary	537	
Russian Federation	535	
(Australia)	530	
Ireland, Canada	527	
(Belgium-French)	526	
	522	(Thailand), (Israel)
Sweden	519	
	513	◄ **International Average**
	509	(Germany)
	508	New Zealand
	506	England
	503	Norway
	502	(Denmark)
	500	**United States**
	498	(Scotland)
	493	Latvia [LSS]
	487	Spain, Iceland
	484	(Greece)
	482	(Romania)
Lithuania	477	
Cyprus	474	
Portugal	454	
Iran, Islamic Republic	428	
(Kuwait)	392	
(Colombia)	385	
(South Africa)	354	

☐ Countries higher than the United States

☐ Countries similar to the United States

☐ Countries lower than the United States

Poor academic performance has been directly linked to delinquent behavior: there is general consensus that students who are chronic underachievers in school are also among the most likely to be delinquent.[11] In fact, researchers commonly find that school failure is a stronger predictor of delinquency than personal variables such as economic class membership, racial or ethnic background, or peer group relations. Studies that compare the academic records of delinquents and nondelinquents—including their scores on standardized tests of basic skills, failure rate, teacher ratings, and other academic measures—have found that delinquents are often academically deficient, a condition that may lead to their leaving school and becoming involved in antisocial activities.[12] Children who report that they do not like school, do not do well in school, and do not concentrate on their homework are most likely to self-report delinquent acts.[13] In contrast, at-risk youths who do well in school, even those with histories of abuse and neglect, are often able to avoid delinquent involvement.[14]

An association between academic failure and delinquency is commonly found among chronic offenders. Those leaving school without a diploma were significantly more likely to become involved in chronic delinquency than high school graduates.[15] Only 9 percent of the chronic offenders in Wolfgang's Philadelphia cohort graduated from high school, compared with 74 percent of nonoffenders.[16] Chronic offenders also had significantly more disciplinary actions and remedial/disciplinary placements than nonoffenders.[17]

The relationship between school achievement and persistent offending is supported by surveys of prison inmates that indicate that only 40 percent of incarcerated felons had twelve or more years of education, compared with about 80 percent of the general population.[18]

School Failure and Delinquency

school failure
Failing to achieve success in school can result in frustration, anger, and reduced self-esteem, which may contribute to delinquent behavior.

Although there is general agreement that **school failure** and delinquency are related, some question remains concerning the nature and direction of this relationship. One view is that the school experience is a direct cause of delinquent behavior. Children who fail at school soon feel frustrated, angry, and rejected. Believing they will never achieve success through conventional means, these children seek out like-minded companions and together engage in antisocial behaviors. Educational failure, beginning early in the life course, evokes negative responses from important people in the child's life, including teachers, parents, and prospective employers. These reactions help solidify feelings of social inadequacy and, in some cases, lead the underachieving student into a pattern of chronic delinquency.

A second view is that school failure leads to psychological and behavioral dysfunction, which are the actual causes of antisocial behavior. For example, academic failure reduces self-esteem; studies using a variety of measures of academic competence and self-esteem clearly demonstrate that good students have a better attitude about themselves than do poor students.[19] Reduced self-esteem has also been found to contribute to delinquent behavior.[20] The association then runs from school failure to low self-concept to delinquency. Schools may mediate these effects by taking steps to stabilize or improve the self-image of academically challenged children.

A third view is that school failure and delinquency share a common cause; they are all part of the problem behavior syndrome (PBS). Therefore, it would be erroneous to conclude that school failure *precedes* antisocial behavior. In this view, the correlates of school failure and delinquency are these:

- Delinquents may have lower IQs than nondelinquents, a factor that might also explain their poor academic achievement.

- Delinquent behavior has been associated with a turbulent family life, a condition that most likely leads to academic underachievement.

- Delinquency has been associated with low self-control and impulsivity, traits that also may produce school failure.

- The adolescent who both fails at school and engages in delinquency may be experiencing drug use, depression, malnutrition, abuse, and disease, all symptoms of a generally troubled lifestyle.[21]

The Causes of School Failure

Despite disagreement over the direction the relationship takes, there is little argument that delinquent behavior is influenced by a child's educational experiences. A number of factors have been linked to the onset of school failure; the most prominent are discussed in some detail in the next sections.

Social Class and School Failure   During the 1950s, research by Albert Cohen indicated that delinquency was fundamentally a phenomenon of working-class students who were poorly equipped to function in middle-class schools. Cohen referred to this phenomenon as a failure to live up to "middle-class measuring rods."[22] Jackson Toby reinforced this concept of class-based delinquency, contending that the disadvantages lower-class children have in school (for example, lack of verbal skills, parental education, and motivation) are a direct result of their position in the social structure and that they implicitly foster delinquency.[23] These views have been supported by the greater than average dropout rates among lower-class children.

One reason lower-class children may do poorly in school is that economic problems require them to take part-time jobs to help support the family. Working while in school seems to lower commitment to educational achievement and is associated with higher levels of delinquent behavior.[24]

Some theorists contend that the high incidence of failure among lower-class youths is actually fostered by the schools themselves.[25] Youths from impoverished backgrounds often find the school experience frightening—constant testing and the threat of failure are clear and ever-present dangers.[26] Research data confirm not only that such children begin school at lower levels of achievement but also that without help their performance progressively deteriorates the longer they stay in school. If this is true, the school itself becomes an active force in the generation of delinquency insofar as it is linked to failure.[27]

Does Class Really Matter? Not all experts agree with the social class, school failure, delinquency hypothesis. A number of early research studies found that boys who do poorly in school, regardless of their socioeconomic background, are more likely to be delinquent than those who perform well.[28] There is evidence that affluent students are equally or even more deeply affected by school failure than lower-class youths and that middle-class youths who do poorly in school are actually more likely to become delinquent than their lower-class peers.[29]

Arthur Stinchcombe's classic research on rebellion in a high school indicated that upper-class youths who were school failures were, in fact, more prone to be delinquent than lower-class **underachievers.** Stinchcombe concluded that a lack of consistency between school achievement and occupational goals was a more important contributor to delinquent behavior than social class. Youths who wanted to get ahead but lacked the necessary grades were the most prone to rebel. According to Stinchcombe, "[t]he key fact is the future of students, not their origins. Since we know that origins partly determine futures, social class will be an important variable, but in an unusual way."[30]

underachievers
Those who do not achieve success in school at the level of their expectations.

Academic Pressure Why might some affluent youths who fail at school be more vulnerable to delinquency than lower-class underachievers? Although the pressure to succeed cuts across class lines, there is a significant difference in the degree to which youths think it's important to do well. This difference is based on parental occupation, with lower-class youths significantly less likely to indicate that getting good grades or going to college is important.[31] Affluent children, the majority of whom live in intact homes, are generally given more encouragement at home to do well in school and are more likely to be high achievers.[32] School failure may cause more damage to their overinflated expectations while having a lesser effect on lower-class youths who maintain limited educational goals (a finding that supports Agnew's general strain theory discussed in Chapter 4).[33]

tracking
Dividing students into groups according to their ability and achievement levels.

Tracking Most researchers have looked at academic **tracking**—dividing students into groups according to ability and achievement level—as a contributor to student delinquency.[34]

> Placement in non-college tracks of the contemporary high school means consignment to an educational oblivion without apparent purpose or meaning.[35]

Studies overwhelmingly indicate that noncollege track preparatory students experience greater academic failure and progressive deterioration of achievement, participate less frequently in extracurricular activities, have an increased tendency to drop out, engage in more frequent misbehavior in school, and commit more delinquent acts. These differences are at least partially caused by assignment to a low academic track, whereby the student is effectively locked out of a chance to achieve educational success. Some effects of tracking as it relates to delinquency are included in Table 10.2.[36]

Some school officials begin stereotyping and tracking students in the lowest grade levels.[37] Educators separate youths into special groups that have innocuous names (such as "special enrichment program") but that may carry with them the

Table 10.2

EFFECTS OF SCHOOL TRACKING

Self-fulfilling prophecy	Lower track students, from whom little achievement and more misbehavior are expected, tend to live up to these often unspoken assumptions about their behavior.
Stigma	The labeling effect of placement in a low track leads to loss of self-esteem, which increases the potential for academic failure and troublemaking both in and out of school.
Student subculture	Students segregated in lower tracks develop a value system that often rewards misbehavior rather than the academic success they feel they can never achieve.
Future rewards	Lower track students are less inclined to conform because they see no future rewards for their schooling; their futures are not threatened by a record of deviance or low academic achievement.
Grading policies	Lower track students tend to receive lower grades than other students, even for work of equal quality, based on the rationale that students who are not college-bound are "obviously" less bright and do not need good grades to get into college.
Teacher effectiveness	Teachers of high-ability students make more of an effort to teach in an interesting and challenging manner than those who instruct lower-level students.

Source: Walter E. Schafer, Carol Olexa, and Kenneth Polk, "Programmed for Social Class: Tracking in High School," in Kenneth Polk and Walter E. Shafer, eds., *Schools and Delinquency* (Englewood Cliffs, N.J.: Prentice-Hall, 1972), pp. 34–54.

taint of failure and academic incompetence. Junior and senior high school students may be tracked within individual subjects based on their perceived ability. Classes may be labeled in descending order: advanced placement, academically enriched, average, basic, and remedial. It is common for students to have all their courses in only one or two tracks.[38]

The effects of negative school labels ("failure," "slow," "special needs") accumulate over time. If a student fails academically, this often means that he or she is destined to fail again. These repeated instances of failure can help to produce the career of the "misfit," "delinquent," or "dropout."[39] Using a tracking system keeps certain students from having any hope of achieving academic success, thereby causing a lack of motivation, failure, and rebellion, all of which may foster delinquent behavior.[40]

Another disturbing outcome of tracking is that students are often stigmatized as academically backward if they voluntarily attend a program or institution designed to help underachievers.[41] Teachers consider remedial reading programs to be dumping grounds for youths with "bad attitudes." Consequently, teachers expect youths who attended special education programs to be disruptive in the classroom.[42] Those who oppose tracking also believe it retards the academic progress of many students, especially those in average and low groups.[43] Tracking may instill feelings of lower self-esteem, promote school misbehavior, and lead to dropping out. Tracking also appears to lower the aspirations of students who are not in the top groups. Perhaps most important, tracking separates students along socio-economic lines—dividing the rich from the poor, whites from minorities. The end result is that poor and minority children are found far more often than others in the bottom tracks. As a result, they are likely to suffer far more negative consequences of schooling than are their more fortunate peers.[44]

School officials who believe tracking is necessary should be cautioned to create tracks that are flexible, that encourage achievement, and that allow student mobility in and between tracks.[45]

Alienation   Alienation of students from the educational experience has also been identified as a link between school failure and delinquency. Students who report they neither like school nor care about their teachers' opinions are more likely to exhibit delinquent behaviors.[46] In contrast, youths who like school and report greater involvement in school activities are less likely to engage in delinquent behaviors.[47] Commitment to school, coupled with the belief their school is being fairly run and that school rules are being consistently applied, helps youths resist criminality.[48] Attachment to teachers also helps insulate high-risk adolescents from delinquency.[49]

Alienation has been linked to the isolation and impersonality that result from the large size of many modern public schools. Schools are getting larger because smaller school districts have been consolidated into multijurisdictional district schools for most of the twentieth century. In 1900 there were one hundred and fifty thousand school districts; today there are approximately sixteen thousand.[50] Although larger schools are more economical to construct, their climate is often impersonal, and relatively few students can find avenues for meaningful participation. The resulting resentment can create an environment in which violence and vandalism are likely to occur. Smaller schools offer a more personal environment, in which students can experience more meaningful interactions with the rest of the educational community. Furthermore, in a smaller school teachers and other school personnel have the opportunity to deal with early indications of academic or behavior problems, thus acting to prevent delinquency.

Student Role   Students can also be alienated by the role that is traditional in our schools: students are expected to be passive, docile receivers of knowledge and are seldom encouraged to take responsibility for their own learning. In many schools students have little voice in decision making. When students feel excluded from the educational process, they may withdraw from or become overly hostile toward the school and all it represents. Those students who believe school rules are unfair and are unevenly applied are most likely to engage in school misconduct and to commit delinquent acts.[51]

Irrelevant Curriculum   Alienation may be a function of students' inability to see the relevance or significance of what they are taught in school. The gap between their education and the real world leads some students to feel that the school experience is little more than a waste of time.[52]

Many students, particularly those from low-income families, believe schooling has no payoff in their future. Because this legitimate channel appears to be meaningless, "the illegitimate alternative becomes increasingly more attractive and delinquency sometimes results."[53] In his pioneering research, Stinchcombe found that rebelliousness in school was closely linked to the perception that school was irrelevant to future job prospects. He found that students who did not plan to attend college or to use their high school education directly in their careers were particularly rebellious.[54]

This middle- and upper-class bias is clearly evident in the preeminent role of the college preparatory curriculum and the second-class position of vocational and technical programs in many school systems. Furthermore, methods of instruction as well as curriculum materials reflect middle-class mores, language, and customs that have little meaning for the disadvantaged child. Middle-class bias in schools relates not only to class and ethnic background but to intellectual style as well.[55]

For some students, then, school is alien territory—a place where they feel unwelcome either because they lack academic skills or because they are different from the role models the school holds out to them. Disruption of classes, vandalism, and violence in schools may be attempts to obtain enjoyment in otherwise lifeless institutions.[56] For the alienated student, delinquency often appears to be an attractive alternative to the hostile—or, at best, boring—atmosphere of the school.

Student Subculture   Alienated students attending isolated, impersonal schools that have curriculums irrelevant to their needs will develop support groups that encourage unconventional values. In fact, evidence exists that in many schools alienated youths form a subculture and work in concert to subvert the educational system. Members of this subculture participate in higher-than-normal amounts of delinquent activity. The problem is not that individual students feel isolated from the educational process but that a loosely structured subculture of youths supporting each other's deviance exists. Individualized treatment efforts will have little effect if they do not take these subcultural influences into account.

Dropping Out

These educational problems all too often translate into dropping out before completion of high school. More than three million Americans ages 16 to 24 have left school permanently without a diploma; of these more than one million withdrew before completing tenth grade.[57]

The burden of dropping out, and its consequent social costs of lower pay and higher unemployment, falls most heavily on the minority community. Although the African American dropout rate has declined substantially over the past two decades (falling faster than the white dropout rate), minority students still drop out at an unacceptably high rate. About 17 percent of African Americans aged 16 to 24 are dropouts; the Hispanic dropout rate for this age group is 38 percent.[58]

dropouts
Youths who leave school before completing their required program of education.

Dropping Out and Delinquency   It is not unusual to later find **dropouts** in police files. Less than half of adult arrestees have a twelfth grade education or more.[59] A twelve-city study that tested juvenile arrestees for drug use found that those who no longer attended school were much more likely to abuse drugs than those who did attend.[60] At eleven of twelve sites, youths who no longer attended school tested higher on cocaine abuse. Cocaine use was up to 3.7 times higher for those not attending school compared to school attendees; marijuana use among those who did not attend school was up to 2.2 times higher than the rate for arrestees who reported attending school.[61]

It is generally recognized that dropping out of school is fraught with negative social consequences, and the impact of dropping out on delinquent behavior has generated much debate. There are two views on this association. *Strain theory* holds that once the pressure and conflict of the school experience end the probability of continued delinquency among disaffected students should be reduced. In contrast, *control theory* suggests that any action that weakens or severs ties with conventional society helps establish a youth in a delinquent way of life; dropping out should, therefore, increase delinquent behaviors.

Some early research efforts supported the strain theory view by finding that delinquent behavior actually decreases once a child leaves the school environment.

In an oft-cited study of twenty-six hundred male and female students, Delbert Elliott and Harwin Voss found:

> The rate of delinquency for dropouts increases during the period immediately preceding their leaving school, but once they drop out, both police-recorded and self-admitted delinquency decline rapidly.[62]

Sociologist Daniel Glaser also noted that this phenomenon seems to cut across socioeconomic lines: "In *every* neighborhood and *every* socioeconomic class, most of those who are first arrested *while still in school* are less frequently arrested after they drop out."[63]

Some recent research contradicts strain theory with findings that dropouts are more likely both to engage in antisocial behavior immediately after leaving school and to persist in their criminal behavior throughout their adulthood.[64] This behavior may be linked to problem behavior syndrome: teens who drop out are also more likely to commit crimes, take drugs, and suffer from an abundance of other social problems.[65] Persistent drug abusers are more likely to drop out than nonabusers and to maintain the same level of substance abuse after leaving school.

Why Do Kids Drop Out?   The confusion about the link between dropouts and delinquency may be explained in part by the fact that youths drop out of school for a variety of reasons. When surveyed, most say they left either because they simply did not like school or because they wanted to get a job. Others had behavioral problems: they could not get along with teachers, had been expelled, or were under suspension. Almost half of all female dropouts left school because they were pregnant or had already given birth to a child.[66]

Poverty and family dysfunction increase the chances of dropping out among all racial and ethnic groups. Dropouts are more likely than graduates to have lived in single-parent families headed by parents who were educational underachievers themselves.[67]

Being Forced to Drop Out   Some youths have no choice but to drop out. They are pushed out of school because they lack attention or have poor attendance records. Teachers label them "troublemakers," and school administrators then use suspensions, transfers, and other means to "convince" these unwanted students that leaving school is their only real option. Because minority students often come from circumstances that interfere with their attendance, they are more likely to be labeled "insubordinate" or "disobedient." Class- and race-based disciplinary practices may help sustain high dropout rates in the minority community.[68]

Not all Dropouts Are Equal   Their personal characteristics and the reasons students choose to drop out of school may have a significant impact on their future law violations. For example, dropping out seems to have a greater impact on middle-class students than on those who are members of the lower class.[69] Youths who left school because of problems at home, for financial reasons, or because of poor grades were unlikely to increase their delinquent activity after leaving school. In contrast, those who dropped out to get married or because of pregnancy were more likely to increase their violent activities; this offending pattern may be linked to family or spousal abuse. Those who left school early because they were expelled did not increase their violent activity but were more likely to engage in theft and drug abuse. Leaving school, per se, was not a cause of future misconduct, but youths with a long history of misconduct while in school often continued their antisocial behavior after dropping out. Dropouts engaged in more antisocial activity than graduates, but the reason youths dropped out influenced their offending patterns.[70]

Dropping Out and School Policy   This debate has serious implications for educational policy in the United States. Evidence that delinquency rates decline after students leave school has caused some educators and juvenile justice personnel to question the wisdom of compulsory education statutes. Some experts, such as Jackson Toby, argue that the effort to force unwilling teenagers to stay in school is counterproductive and that truancy and delinquency might be lessened by allowing them instead to assume a productive position in the workforce.[71] For many youths, leaving school can actually have the beneficial effect of escape from a stressful, humiliating situation that has little promise of offering them any future benefits. Toby proposes a radical solution to the dropout problem—make high schools voluntary and require students to justify the public expenses allocated for their education.[72] Rather than keeping reluctant students in school, youths should have to work hard to retain their educational funding!

However, if the recent findings prove to be accurate, dropping out may offer few short- or long-term benefits and therefore must be avoided at all costs. Programs to keep children in school, to provide them with tutoring, and to create school programs conducive to continued educational achievement may help lower delinquency rates.

Delinquency within the School

The nation was shocked on March 25, 1998, when a thirteen-year-old boy (who had vowed to kill all the girls who had broken up with him) and his eleven-year-old cousin opened fire on students outside a middle school in Jonesboro, Arkansas, killing four girls and a teacher and wounding ten other people.[73] The Jonesboro killings were premeditated murder: the two boys, dressed in camouflage clothing, apparently lay in wait in a wooded area near the school after setting off a fire alarm, which forced students and faculty members outside. Similar multiple school shootings have occurred in the past few years, including well-publicized ones in West Paducah, Kentucky, and Pearl, Mississippi (see Figure 10.2). Then on April 20, 1999, the nation's most deadly school incident to date took place at Columbine High School in Littleton, Colorado. Two students, Eric Harris, 18, and Dylan Klebold, 17, members of a mysterious group called the "Trenchcoat Mafia," went on a shooting spree that claimed the lives of at least 12 students and one teacher and wounded 24 others, many seriously. The boys committed suicide in the school library, leaving authorities to puzzle over the reasons for their deadly act.

These terrible incidents may be occurring because it is now commonplace for students to carry weapons in school. The students most likely to own guns and to bring them to school are those who have engaged in other forms of deviant behavior, including selling drugs, assault, and battery.[74]

The federal government published its pioneering study of school crime, *Violent Schools—Safe Schools* (1977), more than twenty years ago.[75] This survey found that although teenagers spend only 25 percent of their time in school 40 percent of the robberies and 36 percent of the physical attacks involving this age group occur there. This early study focused attention on crime in schools, and three recent surveys highlight the problem of school-based crime in the 1990s. Let's take a closer look at each of them.

School Crime Victimization Survey Released in 1998, the School Crime Victimization Survey is a joint effort by the Justice Department and the Education Department that compares crime in schools between 1989 and 1996.[76]

In 1996 students ages 12 through 18 were victims of about 255,000 incidents of nonfatal serious violent crime at school, including rape, sexual assault, robbery, and aggravated assault (Figure 10.3). The percentages of twelfth graders who have been injured (with or without a weapon) at school has not changed notably over the past twenty years, although slightly more are now threatened with injury (see Figure 10.4). Five percent of all twelfth graders reported that they had been injured with

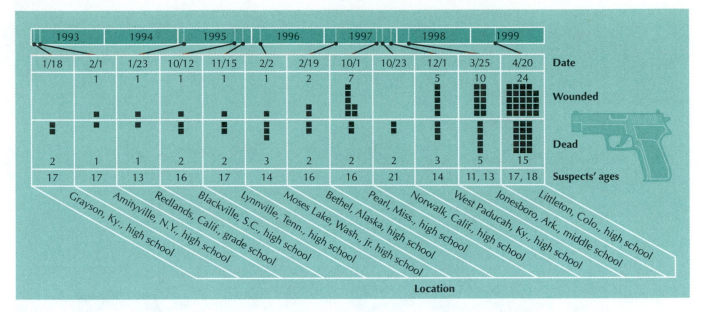

	1993	1994		1995		1996		1997		1998		1999	
Date	1/18	2/1	1/23	10/12	11/15	2/2	2/19	10/1	10/23	12/1	3/25	4/20	
Wounded		1	1	1	1	1	2	7		5	10	24	
Dead	2	1	1	2	2	3	2	2	2	3	5	15	
Suspects' ages	17	17	13	16	17	14	16	16	21	14	11, 13	17, 18	

Location:
Grayson, Ky., high school;
Amityville, N.Y., high school;
Redlands, Calif., high school;
Blackville, S.C., grade school;
Lynnville, Tenn., high school;
Moses Lake, Wash., jr. high school;
Bethel, Alaska, high school;
Pearl, Miss., high school;
Norwalk, Calif., high school;
West Paducah, Ky., high school;
Jonesboro, Ark., middle school;
Littleton, Colo., high school

FIGURE 10.2
School Shootings

Shootings by students or former students on school property in the past five years in which at least two people were killed or wounded. All the assailants were male.
Source: *New York Times* 27 March 1998, p. A14.

Students flee from Columbine High School in Littleton, Colorado, after two students, Eric Harris, 18, and Dylan Klebold, 17, members of a mysterious group called the "Trenchcoat Mafia," went on a shooting spree on April 20, 1999. Twelve students and one teacher were killed; twenty-four others were wounded. This was one of a spate of school yard killings that shocked the nation in the 1990s.

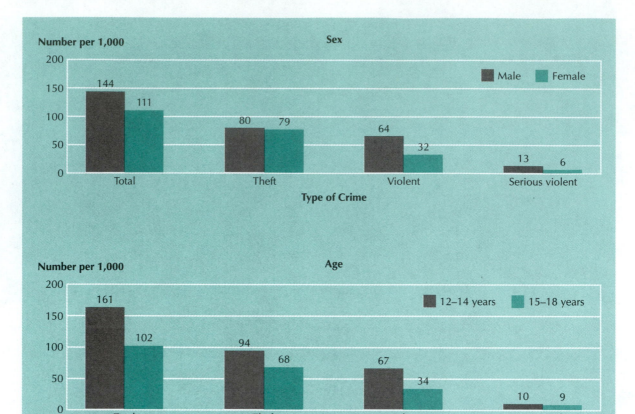

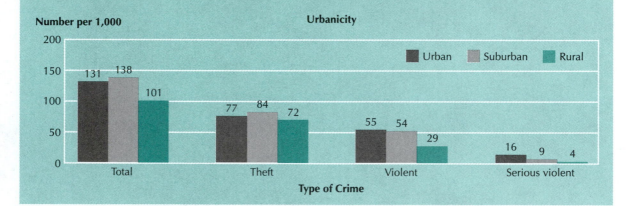

FIGURE 10.3

Number of Nonfatal Crimes against Students Ages 12 through 18 Occurring at School or Going to or from School per 1,000 Students, by Type of Crime and Selected Student Characteristics, 1996

Source: Kaufman et al., *Indicators of School Crime and Safety, 1998* (Washington, D.C.: Department of Justice and Bureau of Justice Statistics, 1998), p. 4.

Note: Serious violent crimes include rape, sexual assault, robbery, and aggravated assault. Violent crimes include serious violent crimes and simple assault.

a weapon such as a knife, gun, or club during the past twelve months while they were at school—that is, inside or outside the school building or on a school bus—and 12 percent reported that they had been injured on purpose without a weapon while at school. Between 1992 and 1994 (the latest data available) sixty-three students were murdered at school and thirteen committed suicide.[77]

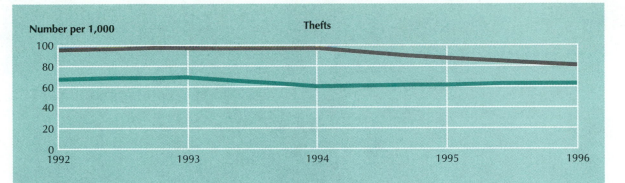

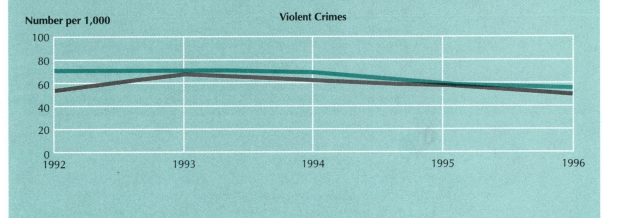

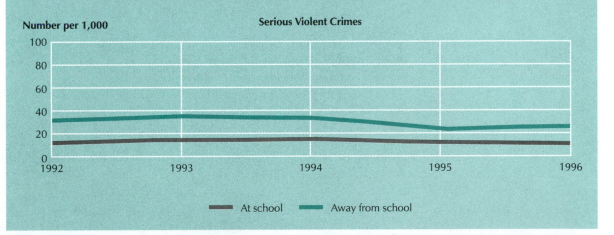

FIGURE 10.4

Number of Nonfatal Crimes against Students Ages 12 through 18 per 1,000 Students, by Type of Crime and Location, 1992–96

Source: Kaufman et al., *Indicators of School Crime and Safety, 1998* (Washington, D.C.: Department of Justice and Bureau of Justice Statistics, 1998), p. 3.

Note: Violent crimes include serious violent crimes and simple assault. Serious violent crimes include rape, sexual assault, robbery, and aggravated assault. "At school" includes on school property or on the way to or from school.

In 1996–97, 10 percent of all public schools reported at least one serious violent crime to the police or a law enforcement representative (Figure 10.5). Principals' reports of serious violent crimes included murder, rape or other types of sexual battery,

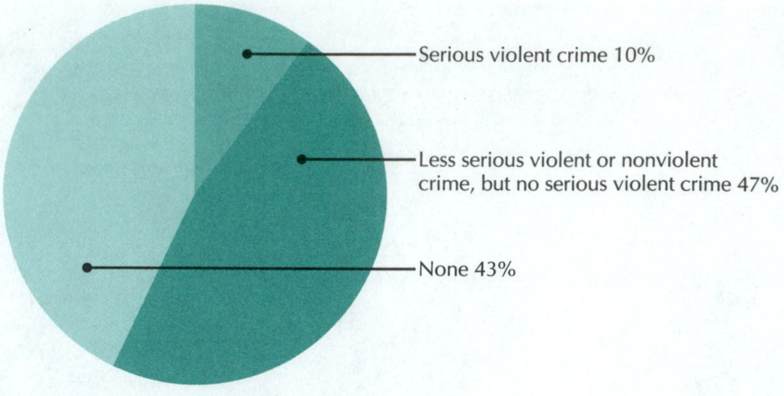

FIGURE 10.5

Percentage Distribution of Public Schools According to Types of Crimes Reported to Police, 1996–97

Source: Kaufman et al., *Indicators of School Crime and Safety, 1998* (Washington, D.C.: Department of Justice and Bureau of Justice Statistics, 1998), p. 14.

Note: Serious violent crimes include murder, rape or other type of sexual battery, suicide, physical attack or fight with a weapon, or robbery. Less serious violent or nonviolent crimes include physical attack or fight without a weapon, theft/larceny, and vandalism. Schools were asked to report crimes that took place in school buildings, on school buses, on school grounds, and at places holding school-sponsored events.

suicide, physical attacks, or fights with a weapon, or robbery. Another 47 percent of public schools reported a less serious violent or nonviolent crime (but not a serious violent one). Crimes in this category include physical attacks or fights without a weapon, theft/larceny, and vandalism.[78]

Students were not the only crime victims on school grounds. Over the five-year period from 1992 to 1996, teachers were victims of 1,581,000 nonfatal crimes at school, including 962,000 thefts and 619,000 violent crimes (rape or sexual assault, robbery, or aggravated and simple assault). This translates to about 316,000 nonfatal crimes per year over this time period.[79]

Considering these findings, it is not surprising that the number of students who felt unsafe at school rose from 6 percent in 1989 to 9 percent in 1995. The percentage of students fearing they would be attacked while traveling to and from school rose from 4 to 7 percent.[80] Another reason for the increase in fear may be that more students are now reporting the presence of street gangs in school, from 15 percent of students in 1989 to 28 percent by 1995.[81]

National Center for Education Statistics Survey   Another overview of school crime in the United States was prepared by the Department of Education's National Center for Education Statistics. This study surveyed principals at 1,234 of the nation's 87,000 public schools.[82] Though only crimes reported to police were included in the survey, the study found that 190,000 fights without a weapon occurred in the 1996–97 school year, along with 116,000 incidents of theft and 98,000 incidents of vandalism. Among the more serious crimes, about 4,000 rapes were reported as well as 7,000 robberies and 11,000 fights or attacks with a weapon. As Figure 10.6 shows, many schools face additional behavior problems such as tardiness, absenteeism, physical conflicts, and smoking.

As might be expected, older youths are more likely to engage in serious criminal acts. Whereas 4 percent of elementary school principals report having incidents of serious crime during the year, 19 percent of the middle schools and 21 percent of the high schools experience significant crimes. In a similar fashion, larger schools, especially those in urban areas, are most likely to experience crime problems. A third of the schools with one thousand students or more had at least one serious

FIGURE 10.6

Percent of Public Schools Reporting that Specific Discipline Issues Were a Serious or Moderate Problem at the School, by Instructional Level, 1996–97

Source: Sheila Heaviside and Shelly Burns, "Violence and Discipline Problems in U.S. Public Schools, 1996–1997," (Washington, D.C.: Department of Education, 1998), p. 17.

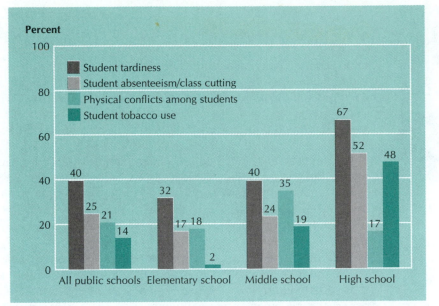

violent crime; in contrast, among the schools with fewer than three hundred students, only 4 percent reported serious crimes. Although more than three-quarters of the schools had some form of antiviolence program, only 2 percent of schools had become so concerned that they had hired guards and started metal checks. Considering the extent of school crime, it is not surprising that about 35 percent of students and 15 percent of teachers report being victims of crime on school property each year.[83]

Sometimes violence is manifested in the form of bullying, the subject of the Focus on Delinquency box entitled "Bullying in School."

School Substance Abuse Survey Violence and delinquency are not the only forms of antisocial behavior occurring on school grounds. The National Center for Addiction and Substance Abuse (CASA) at Columbia University in New York asked more than one thousand teenagers, about one thousand parents, and twelve hundred

A national survey conducted by the national Center for Addiction and Substance Abuse (CASA) at Columbia University in New York found that school-based substance abuse levels were shockingly high. Teens say they are more likely to encounter drugs on school grounds or in their schools than on their neighborhood streets.

BULLYING IN SCHOOL

Experts define bullying among children as repeated, negative acts committed by one or more children against another. These negative acts may be physical or verbal in nature (for example, hitting or kicking, teasing or taunting) or they may involve indirect actions such as manipulating friendships or purposely excluding other children from activities. Implicit in this definition is an imbalance in real or perceived power between the bully and the victim.

Recent research in the United States and abroad has documented that bullying is a common and potentially damaging form of violence among children. Not only does bullying harm both its intended victims and the perpetrators, it also may affect the climate of schools and, indirectly, the ability of all students to learn to the best of their abilities. There is also evidence of a link between bullying and later delinquent and criminal behavior.

Although there have been few studies of the prevalence of bullying among U.S. schoolchildren, available data suggest that bullying is quite common in U.S. schools. In a study of 207 junior high and high school students from small midwestern towns, 88 percent reported having observed bullying, and 77 percent indicated that they had been victims of bullying during their school careers. A study of 6,500 students in fourth to sixth grades in the rural south indicated that one in four students had been bullied with some regularity within the past three months and that one in ten had been bullied at least once a week. Approximately one in five children admitted that they had bullied another child with some regularity in the previous three months.

Bullying contributes to a climate of fear and intimidation in schools. Furthermore, contrary to popular belief, bullying occurs more frequently on school grounds than on the way to and from school.

Studies of bullying suggest that there are short- and long-term consequences for both the perpetrators and the victims of bullying. Students who are chronic victims of bullying experience more physical and psychological problems than their peers who are not harassed by other children. These chronic victims tend not to grow out of the role of victim; longitudinal studies have found that victims of bullying in early grades also reported being bullied several years later. Studies also suggest that chronically victimized students may be at increased risk for depression, poor self-esteem, and other mental health problems, including schizophrenia, as adults.

It is not only victims who are at risk for short- and long-term problems; bullies also are at increased risk for negative outcomes. One researcher found that those elementary students who were bullies attended school less frequently and were more likely to drop out than other students.

Several studies suggest that bullying in early childhood may be a critical risk factor for the development of future problems with violence and delinquency. For example, research conducted in Scandinavia found that bullies were several times more likely than their non-bullying peers to commit antisocial acts, including vandalism, fighting, theft, drunkenness, and truancy, and to have an arrest by young adulthood. Another study of more than five

teachers and principals about their attitude toward cigarettes, alcohol, and illegal drugs (marijuana, heroin, cocaine, and acid).

The CASA survey found that school-based substance abuse levels were shockingly high; 76 percent of high school students and 46 percent of middle school students say their schools are not drug-free. Teens are more likely to encounter drugs on school grounds or in their schools than on their neighborhood streets: more high school students have witnessed drug sales at school (41 percent) than in their neighborhoods (25 percent). Twenty-five percent of teachers say some students who appear to be drunk or high show up in their classes monthly or more fre-

hundred children found that aggressive behavior at age 8 was a powerful predictor of criminality and violent behavior at age 30.

CAN BULLYING BE PREVENTED?

The first and best known intervention to reduce bullying among school children was launched by Dan Olweus in Norway and Sweden in the early 1980s. Inspired by the suicides of several severely victimized children, Norway supported development and implementation of a comprehensive program to address bullying among children in school. The program involved interventions at multiple levels:

Schoolwide interventions. A survey of bullying problems at each school, increased supervision, schoolwide assemblies, and teacher in-service training to raise the awareness of children and school staff regarding bullying.

Classroom-level interventions. Establishment of classroom rules against bullying, regular class meetings to discuss bullying at school, and meetings with all parents.

Individual-level interventions. Discussions with students identified as bullies and victims.

This program was highly effective in reducing bullying and other antisocial behavior among students in primary and junior high schools. Within two years of implementation, both boys' and girls' self-reports indicated that bullying had decreased by half. These changes in behavior were more pronounced the longer the program was in effect. Moreover, students reported significant decreases in rates of truancy, vandalism, and theft and indicated that their school's climate was significantly more positive as a result of the program. Not surprisingly, those schools that had implemented more of the program's components experienced the most marked changes in behavior.

The core components of the Olweus antibullying program have been adapted for use in several other countries, including Canada, England, and the United States. Results of the antibullying efforts in these countries have been similar to the results experienced in the Scandinavian countries, with the efforts in Toronto schools showing somewhat more modest results. Again, as in the Scandinavian study, schools that were more active in implementing the program observed the most marked changes in reported behaviors.

Only one U.S. program has been based explicitly on the comprehensive model developed by Olweus. Gary B. Melton, Susan P. Limber, and colleagues at the Institute for Families in Society of the University of South Carolina in Columbia have adapted Olweus's model for use in rural middle schools in South Carolina. Interventions are focused at the level of the individual, the classroom, the school, and the community at large. A comprehensive evaluation involving 6,500 children is currently under way to measure the effects of the program.

Source: Adapted from Susan P. Limber and Maury M. Nation, "Bullying among Children and Youth," in June Arnette and Marjorie Walsleben, ed., *Combating Fear and Restoring Safety in Schools* (Washington, D.C.: Office of Juvenile Justice and Delinquency Prevention, 1998); see Dan Olweus, "Victimization by Peers: Antecedents and Long-Term Outcomes," in K. H. Rubin and J. B. Asendorf, eds., *Social Withdrawal, Inhibitions, and Shyness* (Hillsdale, N.J.: Erlbaum, 1993), pp. 315–41.

quently. High school students estimate that on average 50 percent of their classmates are using drugs at least once a month. About one-fourth of middle school teachers and one-third of high school teachers have reported a student for using illegal drugs during the school year.

CASA found that the school experience is as powerful an influence on substance abuse as the family and lists seven signs of trouble in school: smoking, drinking, drugs, weapons, expulsion for drugs, student death in drug- or alcohol-related incidents, and students showing up in class drunk or stoned.[84] Considering these problems, it is not surprising that teens, parents, teachers, and principals support firm steps to keep drugs out of schools, including random locker searches, zero tolerance policies, and drug testing of student athletes. More than half of the students (52 percent) and principals (53 percent) support drug testing of all students, compared with 42 percent of parents and 38 percent of teachers.

Who Commits School Crime?

social disorganization
Neighborhood or area marked by culture conflict, lack of cohesiveness, a transient population, and insufficient social organizations; these problems are reflected in the problems at schools in these areas.

Who commits school crime, and what are the factors associated with high crime rates in schools? Schools experiencing crime and drug abuse may be suffering from a condition referred to as **social disorganization.** Schools with a high proportion of students behind grade level in reading; many students from families on welfare; and schools located in a community with high unemployment, crime, poverty and divorce rates are also at risk to delinquency.[85] In contrast, schools with high achieving and interested students, drug- and alcohol-free environments, positive social climates, strong discipline, and involved parents have fewer behavioral problems within the student body.[86]

A number of researchers have observed that school crime and disruption are functions of the community in which the school is located. In other words, crime in schools does not occur in isolation from crime in the community.[87] In one important analysis, Joan McDermott found that the perpetrators and the victims of school crime cannot be divided into two separate groups.[88] Many young offenders have been victims of delinquency themselves and fear being victimized again. McDermott concludes that school-based violent and theft-related crimes have "survival value"—striking back against another, weaker victim is emotionally satisfying or simply a method of regaining lost possessions or self-respect.

McDermott also found that crime and fear in schools reflect the patterns of antisocial behavior that exist in the surrounding neighborhood. Schools in high-crime areas experience more crime than schools in safer areas; there is less fear in schools in safer neighborhoods than in high-crime ones. Students who report being afraid in school are actually *more afraid* of being in city parks, streets, or subways.

Other research efforts confirm the community influences on school crime. Communities with a high percentage of two-parent families experience fewer school problems; neighborhoods with poor housing quality, high population density, and transient populations also have problem prone schools.[89] One study of violent crimes in the schools of Stockholm, Sweden, found that although only one-fifth of schools were located in areas of social instability and disorganization almost a third of school crime happened in these schools.[90]

McDermott's analysis suggests that it may be futile to attempt to eliminate school crime without considering the impact prevention efforts will have on the community.

Reducing School Crime

Schools around the country have mounted a campaign to reduce the incidence of delinquency and drug abuse taking place on campus. Nearly all states have developed some sort of crime-free, weapon-free, or safe school zone statute.[91] Most have defined these zones to include school transportation and locations of school-sponsored functions. Schools are also cooperating with court officials, probation officers, and other youth professionals to share information and to monitor students who have criminal records or who are in treatment for crime-related activities. School districts are formulating crisis prevention and intervention policies and are directing individual schools to develop similar policies and individual safe school plans.

Some schools have instituted strict controls over student activity, for example, making locker searches, preventing students from having lunch off campus, requiring that all visitors report to the school office, and using patrols to monitor drug use (Table 10.3). According to the 1998 National Center survey on school violence, a majority of schools have adopted a **zero tolerance policy** that mandates predetermined consequences or punishments for specific offenses, most typically possession of drugs (88 percent), weapons (91 percent), or tobacco (79 percent), or engaging in violent behaviors (79 percent).[92] Some of the punishments used to control these behaviors are illustrated in Figure 10.7.

zero tolerance policy
Mandating specific consequences or punishments for delinquent acts and not allowing anyone to avoid these consequences.

School Security Efforts Schools have tried a variety of ideas to increase school safety. Almost every school attempts to restrict entry of dangerous persons by having visitors sign in before entering, and most close the campus for lunch to keep students out of off-campus trouble.[93] Schools have attempted to ensure the physical safety of students and school staff by using mechanical security devices such as surveillance cameras, electronic barriers to keep out intruders, and roving security guards. Law and order approaches have relied on metal detectors to identify gun-wielding students. About 4 percent of schools now use random metal detector checks, and 1 percent employ daily checks; metal detectors are much more common in large schools, especially where serious crime has taken place (15 percent).[94]

Table 10.3

PERCENTAGE OF PUBLIC SCHOOLS REPORTING THAT THEY USE VARIOUS TYPES OF SECURITY MEASURES AT THEIR SCHOOLS, BY SELECTED SCHOOL CHARACTERISTICS: 1996–97

School characteristics	Visitors must sign in	Closed campus for most students during lunch	Controlled access to school buildings	Controlled access to school grounds	One or more drug sweeps	Random metal detector checks on students	Students must pass through metal detectors each day
All public schools	96	80	53	24	19	4	1
Instructional level							
Elementary school	96	76	57	25	5	1	(*)
Middle school	96	93	51	22	36	7	1
High school	97	78	40	25	45	9	2
School enrollment							
Less than 300	91	67	40	16	22	(*)	1
300–999	98	84	57	24	15	4	1
1,000 or more	99	82	55	49	34	15	3
Locale							
City	100	81	62	35	12	8	2
Urban fringe	98	85	68	31	13	3	(*)
Town	96	77	49	20	23	2	1
Rural	92	75	33	13	27	2	(*)

Source: Phillip Kaufman et al., *Indicators of School Crime and Safety, 1998* (Washington, D.C.: U.S. Department of Education and Bureau of Justice Statistics, 1998), p. 125.

FIGURE 10.7

Percent of Specified Disciplinary Actions Taken by Public Schools for Specific Offenses, by Type of Action Taken, 1996–97

Source: Sheila Heaviside and Shelly Burns, "Violence and Discipline Problems in U.S. Public Schools, 1996–1997," (Washington, D.C.: Department of Education, 1998), p. 17.

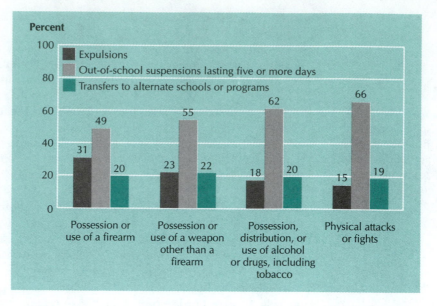

One program in New York City uses random searches with inexpensive hand-held detectors at the start of the school day. Students report a greater sense of security, and attendance has increased.[95] Some districts have gone so far as to infiltrate youthful undercover detectives on school grounds. These detectives pose as pupils, attend classes, mingle with students, contact drug dealers, make buys, and arrest campus dealers.[96]

Schools have employed a variety of security setups, some have independent security divisions, others hire private guards, and still others cooperate with local law enforcement agencies. For example, in Houston, Texas, it is routine to employ armed guards in full uniform during the day. Nor does security end in the evening. In San Diego an elaborate security system makes use of infrared beams and silent alarms to protect school grounds from vandals and unwelcome visitors.[97] Rather than suspending violators, some school districts now send them to a separate center for evaluation and counseling so they are kept separate from the law-abiding students.[98] In New York City the school board maintains a force of 3,200 officers in its Division of School Safety; they patrol the more than one thousand public schools armed only with handcuffs. The New York City Police Department is scheduled to take significant control over recruitment, screening, and training of school security officers, although assignment of regular police officers would be limited to the 130 schools they already help patrol at the invitation of principals.[99]

Table 10.4 summarizes some of the school-based efforts now in use to combat delinquency within the schools.

Critics claim that even though these methods are effective, they reduce staff and student morale. Tighter security, stricter rule enforcement, and fortress-like alterations in a school's physical plant may reduce acts of crime and violence in school only to displace them to the community. Similarly, expelling or suspending troublemakers puts them on the street with nothing to do. Lowering the level of crime in schools may have no real impact on reducing the total amount of crime committed by young people. In fact, schools that employ strict controls are also the ones most likely to suffer increases in school-based victimization (most likely because security is aimed at a preexisting and expanding school crime problem).[100]

Social Programs   Another approach to reducing school crime consists of improving the school climate and increasing educational standards. Programs have been designed to improve the standards of the teaching staff and administrators and the educational climate in the school, increase the relevance of the curriculum, and provide law-related education classes.[101]

Table 10.4

SCHOOL-BASED DELINQUENCY CONTROL EFFORTS

- School bus drivers are tested for drug and alcohol use.

- Criminal background checks are completed on teachers and school staff members before a work assignment is made.

- Neighborhood Watch programs are established in areas near schools.

- Parents are recruited to provide safe houses along school routes and to monitor "safe corridors" or walkways to and from school.

- Parent volunteers monitor hallways, cafeterias, playgrounds, and school walkways to increase visibility of responsible adults.

- Block safety watch programs are carried out by area residents at school bus stops as a crime deterrent for schoolchildren and area residents.

- School grounds are fenced to secure campus perimeters.

- Bathroom doors are replaced with zigzag entrances to make it easier to monitor sounds, and roll-down doors are installed to secure bathrooms after hours.

- One main door is designated for entry to school; exits are equipped with push bars, and all other doors are locked to outside entry.

- Bulletproof windows are installed.

- Schools are equipped with closed-circuit video surveillance systems to reduce property crimes such as break-ins, theft, vandalism, and assaults.

- Landscaping is designed to create an inviting appearance without offering a hiding place for trespassers or criminals.

- Motion-sensitive lights illuminate dark corners in hallways or on campus.

- Convex mirrors monitor blind spots in school hallways.

- Classrooms are equipped with intercom systems connected to the central school office.

- Two-way radios are issued to security patrols or campus staff members.

- Cellular phones are available for use in crises or emergency situations.

- Photo identification badges are required for students, teachers, and staff, and identification cards are provided for visitors on campus.

Source: June L. Arnette and Marjorie C. Walsleben, *Combating Fear and Restoring Safety in Schools* (Washington, D.C.: Office of Juvenile Justice and Delinquency Prevention, 1998).

Controlling school crime is ultimately linked to the community and to family conditions. When communities undergo changes such as increases in unemployment and in the number of single-parent households, both school disruption and community crime rates may rise.[102] The school environment can be made safer only if community issues are addressed: for example, by taking steps to keep intruders out of school buildings, putting pressure on local police to develop community safety programs, increasing correctional services, strengthening laws on school safety, and making parents bear greater responsibility for their children's behavior.[103]

Schools must also use the resources of the community when controlling school crime. Most school districts refer problem students to social services outside the school. About 70 percent of public schools provide outside referrals for students with substance abuse problems, and 90 percent offer drug education within the school.[104]

The Role of the School in Delinquency Prevention

For the past two decades numerous national organizations and political groups have called for reforming the educational system to make it more responsive to the needs of students. Educational leaders now recognize that children undergo enormous pressures while in school that can lead to physical, emotional, and social problems. At one extreme are the pressures to succeed academically and earn admission to a top college; at the other are the crime and substance abuse students face on school grounds. It is difficult to talk of achieving academic excellence in a deteriorated school dominated by violence prone gang members. (See the Case in Point for more on this topic.)

A report by the Carnegie Corporation, a leading educational foundation, found that the United States is indeed facing an educational crisis. Student dissatisfaction with school, which begins to increase after elementary school, is accompanied by a growing aversion for teachers and many academic subjects. The rate of student alienation and the social problems that accompany it—absenteeism, dropping out, and substance abuse—all increase as students enter junior high.

Educators have attempted to play a role in delinquency prevention by creating programs that will benefit youths and provide them with opportunities for conventional success in the outside world, but change has been slow in coming. Not until the mid-1980s did concern about the educational system—prompted by the findings of the National Commission on Excellence in Education in *A Nation at Risk*—focus efforts on change.[105]

Skepticism exists over whether the U.S. school system, viewed by critics as overly conservative and archaic, can play a significant role in delinquency prevention. Some experts contend that no significant change in the lives of youths is possible by merely changing the schools; the entire social and economic structure of society must be altered if schools are to help students realize their full potential.[106] Others suggest that smaller alternative schools, which create a positive learning environment with low student–teacher ratios, an informal classroom structure, and individualized, self-paced learning, may be the answer. Although in theory such programs may help promote academic performance and reduce delinquency, evaluations suggest that attending alternative programs has little effect on delinquency rates.[107]

A danger also exists that the pressure being placed on schools to improve the educational experience of students can produce unforeseen problems for staff members. For example, there have been recent reports of teachers being prosecuted for encouraging students to cheat on tests and providing them with answer sheets. The pressure to improve student performance on standardized tests was the motive for the faculty cheating.[108]

School-Based Prevention Programs   Education officials have instituted numerous programs to make schools more effective instruments of delinquency prevention.[109] The most prevalent strategies include:

Cognitive: Increase students' awareness about the dangers of drug abuse and delinquency.

As principal of a suburban regional high school, you are faced with a growing drug use problem among the student body. There is evidence of dealing on campus, and parents have complained that their children are bringing home drugs they bought at school. Last week, a fifteen-year-old overdosed and almost lost her life. At a school board meeting, frustrated parents charge that this kind of behavior may be OK in the city but not here in a suburban community where people come to get away from drugs and delinquency. There is some angry talk that if you can't handle the situation a new school chief should be found who can.

The local police offer a solution for the drug problem: institute a tough security policy that makes use of hidden cameras in public areas such as the parking lot and cafeteria; allow random searches of student lockers and desks; hire a security director who will search students suspected of selling or possessing drugs; turn over to the police all evidence for prosecution; and suspend students possessing drugs on campus for the school year.

Some teachers feel these draconian policies are misplaced in a suburban school. They believe the relatively few offenders should be placed in counseling programs. Instead of security guards, the school should hire a drug awareness education teacher who can teach youths about the dangers of taking drugs.

■ Should a school drug prevention program stress law enforcement or education?

■ Is it fair to search student lockers at random?

■ Are hidden cameras an intrusion of student privacy or a needed security measure?

Affective: Improve students' psychological assets and self-image, giving them the resources to resist antisocial behavior.

Behavioral: Train students in techniques to resist peer pressure.

Environmental: Establish school management and disciplinary programs that deter crime, such as locker searches.

Therapeutic: Treat youths who have already manifested problems.[110]

More specific suggestions include creating special classes or schools with individualized educational programs that foster success rather than failure for nonadjusting students.[111] Efforts can be made to help students learn to deal constructively with academic failure when it does occur.

More personalized student–teacher relationships have been recommended. This effort to provide young persons with a caring, accepting adult role model will, it is hoped, strengthen the controls against delinquency.

School counselors acting as liaisons between the family and the school might be effective in preventing delinquency. These counselors try to ensure cooperation between the parents and the school and to secure needed services—academic, social, and psychological—for troubled students before serious delinquency becomes a problem.

Experiments have been proposed that integrate job training and experience with the usual classroom instruction, allowing students to see education as a meaningful and relevant prelude to their future careers. Job training programs could emphasize public service, encouraging students to gain a sense of attachment to their communities while acquiring useful vocational training.

Demonstration Projects A number of experimental programs have attempted to prevent or reduce delinquency by manipulating factors in the learning environment. One such project, known as Project PATHE (Positive Action through Holistic Education), was operated experimentally in four middle schools and three high schools in South Carolina."[112] Based on control theory, Project PATHE sought to reduce delinquency by raising students' stake in conformity. This project focused on four related elements: strengthening students' commitment to school, providing successful school experiences, encouraging attachment to conforming members of the educational community, and increasing students' participation in school activities. By increasing students' sense of social competence, belonging, and usefulness, the project sought to promote a positive school experience for students. The PATHE program has undergone extensive evaluation by sociologist Denise Gottfredson, who found that the schools in which it was used experienced a moderate reduction in delinquency and school misconduct.[113]

A similar program, the Seattle Social Development Project, is based on the social development model discussed in Chapter 5. Teachers trained especially for the project learned classroom management techniques that reward appropriate student behavior and minimize disruption. Students were taught cooperatively in small groups, and the groups were given the goal of helping each other master the curriculum. Students were also singled out for cognitive and social skills training to help them master problem-solving, communication, negotiation, and conflict-resolution skills. Family training classes were offered, teaching parents how to properly reward and encourage desirable behavior and how to provide negative consequences for undesirable behavior in a consistent fashion. Other parent training focused on improving their children's academic performance while reducing at-risk behaviors such as drug abuse. Evaluations of the Seattle program show that children in the intervention group enhanced their school commitment and class participation. Substance abuse rates were lowered for the girls, and the boys increased their social and school work skills.[114]

Schools may not be able to reduce delinquency single-handedly, but a number of viable alternatives to their present operations could aid a communitywide effort to lessen the problem of juvenile crime.

A recent review of successful, unsuccessful, and promising school-based programs was conducted by Lawrence Sherman and his associates. He found that a number of policies work to reduce school crime but others do not. Some of his findings are contained in Table 10.5.

One program that holds promise is the Communities in Schools effort to reduce dropping out. This program is described in the Policy and Practice box entitled "Keeping Children in School."

Legal Rights within the School

As education officials have attempted to restore order within the school, their actions often have run into opposition from the courts, which are concerned with maintaining the legal rights of minors. The U.S. Supreme Court has

Table 10.5

PROGRAMS THAT WORK IN SCHOOLS AND OTHERS THAT DO NOT

What Works

■ Building school capacity to initiate and sustain innovation through the use of school teams or other organizational development strategies reduces crime and delinquency.

■ Clarifying and communicating norms about behavior through rules, reinforcement of positive behavior, and schoolwide initiatives (such as antibullying campaigns) reduces crime and delinquency.

■ Teaching social competency skills in programs like Life Skills Training (LST), which teaches stress management, problem solving, self-control, and emotional intelligence, reduce delinquency and substance abuse.

■ Training or coaching in thinking skills for high-risk youths using behavior modification techniques or rewards and punishments reduce substance abuse.

What Doesn't Work

■ Individual and peer counseling does not reduce substance abuse or delinquency and can increase delinquency.

■ Drug Abuse Resistance Education (DARE), a curriculum taught by uniformed police officers primarily to fifth and sixth graders over seventeen lessons, fails to reduce drug abuse when the original DARE curriculum (pre-1993) is used.

■ Instructional programs focusing on information dissemination, fear arousal, moral appeal, self-esteem, and affective education fail to reduce substance abuse.

■ School-based leisure time enrichment programs, including supervised homework and self-esteem exercises, fail to reduce delinquency risk factors or drug abuse.

Source: Lawrence W. Sherman, Denise C. Gottfredson, Doris L. MacKenzie, John Eck, Peter Reuter, and Shawn D. Bushway, *Preventing Crime: What Works, What Doesn't, What's Promising* (Washington, D.C: National Institute of Justice, 1998).

sought to balance the civil liberties of students with the school's mandate to provide a reasonable and safe educational environment. In some instances the Court has sided with students; in others, the balance has shifted toward the educational establishment. The main issues concerning the rights of children and the schools include compulsory attendance, free speech in school, and school discipline.

Compulsory School Attendance

Compulsory school attendance statutes have been in effect in the United States for more than half a century.[115] Children are required by law to attend school until a given age, normally sixteen or seventeen.[116] Violations of compulsory attendance laws generally result in complaints that can lead to court action. However, some

KEEPING CHILDREN IN SCHOOL

Millions of Americans have not completed high school; they are dropouts. Research indicates that they will earn less over their lifetimes and be at risk for criminality. Four in ten dropouts said they left high school because they were failing or they did not like school, and just as many males as females reported they were leaving school because of personality conflicts with teachers. More males than females dropped out because of school suspension or expulsion.

A popular program designed to reduce dropping out is the Communities in Schools (CIS) network (formerly known as Cities in Schools), a web of local, state, and national partnerships working together to meet four basic needs of at-risk youths and help them stay in school. This program focuses on these four areas:

- A personal one-on-one relationship with a caring adult
- A safe place to learn and grow
- A marketable skill to use upon graduation
- A chance to give back to peers and community

A student's "decision" to drop out of school may have its origin in a garden variety of social and emotional problems: family problems, drug and alcohol abuse, illiteracy, or teenage pregnancy. Therefore, the entire community—not just the schools—must take responsibility for preventing youths from dropping out of school. CIS brings together businesses and public and private agencies (such as welfare and health professionals, employment counselors, social workers and recreation leaders), the clergy, and members of community groups, and puts them where they're needed—in the schools. CIS treats the student and his or her family in a holistic manner, bringing together in one place a support system of caring adults who ensure that the student has access to the resources that can help him or her build self-worth and the skills needed to embark on a more productive and constructive life.

Most CIS programs take place inside traditional schools, but another method of service delivery has resulted in the CIS academy, an easily identifiable freestanding facility or wing of an existing school that is sponsored largely by an individual corporation or organization.

THE CIS DELIVERY SYSTEM

In general, CIS projects are grouped into three broad categories:

- Projects at traditional school sites that pattern themselves as closely as possible on the normal classroom routine.
- Projects in which repositioned health and human services staff assume the primary role.
- Projects that function as alternative schools.

The first two categories apply to the classroom model, and the third to the academy model, discussed below.

The Classroom Model

The CIS classroom model allows students to sign up for the program as an elective class. Instruction focuses on life skills education, such as employment topics, remedial education, and tutoring. CIS classrooms often involve community volunteers who mentor and tutor students. The classroom model also can provide in-school activities such as conflict resolution, violence abatement, and community service.

Patterned closely on the normal classroom routine, these activities are led by teachers assigned specifically to the CIS program by the school district. In certain situations repositioned health and human services staff assume the primary leadership role.

The Academy Model

The CIS academy model has all the basic elements of the CIS classroom model but is organized as an alternative school where all students are part of the CIS program. These academies can be "schools within schools," located in a separate wing or section of the school where the CIS students attend classes together, or can occupy a completely separate building. A student who meets CIS program eligibility criteria and has parental permission is assigned a case manager who assesses the student's needs. The case manager then contacts the proper agencies to provide the specific services needed. Through the CIS program, the young person can receive counseling either individually or as part of a group. If the CIS program cannot provide a needed service directly, the student—and sometimes parents and family members—is referred to an appropriate service agency.

DOES CIS WORK?

CIS programs serve a target population of at-risk youths and youths who have already crossed the line into risky behaviors and consequences. Most of these students would be expected to leave school before graduation. Evaluations of the program show that

- High proportions of CIS students remain in school or graduate.
- Eighty percent of the students who participated in CIS services were still in school or had graduated.
- The cumulative dropout rate for CIS students is about 7 percent annually.
- CIS students with serious and moderately severe problems in attendance and academic performance improved their performance in these areas.
- About 70 percent of students with high absenteeism prior to participation in CIS improved their attendance, and 60 percent with low initial grades improved.
- Seventy-nine percent of those students with the lowest grades (GPA below 1.0) raised their GPA, with an average increase of a full grade point.
- The majority of students believed they had benefited from CIS and expressed high levels of satisfaction with the program.

The CIS program is a good example of how strengthening an adolescent's bond to a critical element of the social process can improve his or her life chances. But adolescents continue to drop out of school, and those who drop out have a greater chance of committing crime than high school graduates. What factors do you think influence the graduation–crime association? Do youths drop out because they are already troubled and antisocial, or does dropping out produce delinquent behaviors?

Sources: Clyde A. Winters, "Learning Disabilities, Crime, Delinquency, and Special Education Placement," *Adolescence* (Summer) 32:451–58 (1997); Sharon Cantelon and Donni LeBoeuf, *Keeping Young People in School: Community Programs that Work* (Washington, D.C.: National Institute of Justice, 1997).

Students in Rochester, New York, are shown protesting a school ruling over the presence of metal detectors. The Supreme Court allows school officials to control student speech while on school premises if it interferes with the school's mission to implant "the shared values of a civilized social order." Student protests off-campus are still an open question. In the future, the courts may be asked to rule whether schools can control such forms of speech or whether they are shielded by the First Amendment.

children are truant because of emotional problems or learning disabilities, and when these children are then brought into the court system, it is for problems beyond their control. Emotionally disturbed and nonconforming children may be pushed out of school, which deprives them of an education. It is clear that school systems often ignore the difficult student, who may be classified as "bad" or "delinquent."

In 1925 the Supreme Court determined that compulsory education did not necessarily have to be provided by a public school system and that parochial schools could be a reasonable substitute.[117] From that time through the 1970s, the courts upheld the right of the state to make education compulsory. Then, in 1972, in *Wisconsin v. Yoder,* the Supreme Court made an exception to the general compulsory education law by holding that traditional Amish culture was able to give its children the skills that would prepare them for adulthood within Amish society. Thus, the removal of Amish children from school after the completion of the eighth grade was justified.[118] It is not clear, however, whether this decision speaks directly to the issue of compulsory education or whether it is simply another instance of freedom of religion. Therefore, the state's role in requiring school attendance is still unsettled.

Free Speech

Freedom of speech is granted and guaranteed in the First Amendment to the U.S. Constitution. This right has been divided into two major categories as it affects chil-

passive speech
A form of expression protected by the First Amendment but not associated with actually speaking words; examples include wearing symbols or protest messages on buttons or signs.

dren in schools. The first category involves what is known as **passive speech,** a form of expression not associated with actually speaking words: examples include wearing armbands or political protest buttons. The most important U.S. Supreme Court decision concerning a student's right to passive speech was in 1969 in the case of *Tinker v. Des Moines Independent Community School District*.[119] This case involved the right to wear black armbands to protest the war in Vietnam. Two high school students, ages 16 and 17, were told they would be suspended if they demonstrated their objections to the Vietnam war by wearing black armbands. They attended school wearing the armbands and were suspended. According to the Court, for the state (in the person of a school official) to justify prohibiting an expression of opinion, it must be able to show that its action was caused by something more than a mere desire to avoid the discomfort and unpleasantness that accompany the expression of an unpopular view. Unless it can be shown that the forbidden conduct will interfere with the discipline required to operate the school, the prohibition cannot be sustained. In *Tinker,* the Court said there was no evidence that school authorities had reason to believe wearing armbands would substantially interfere with the work of the school or infringe on the rights of the students.[120]

This decision is significant because it recognizes the child's right to free speech in a public school system. Justice Abe Fortas stated in his majority opinion, "Young people do not shed their constitutional rights at the schoolhouse door."[121] *Tinker* established two things: (1) a child is entitled to free speech in school under the First Amendment of the U.S. Constitution, and (2) the test used to determine whether the child has gone beyond proper speech is whether he or she materially and substantially interferes with the requirements of appropriate discipline in the operation of the school.

The concept of free speech articulated in *Tinker* was used again in 1986 in *Bethel School District No. 403 v. Fraser*.[122] This case upheld a school system's right to suspend or otherwise discipline a student who uses obscene or profane language and gestures. Matthew Fraser, a Bethel high school student, used sexual metaphors in making a speech nominating a friend for student office. His statement included these remarks:

> I know a man who is firm—he's firm in his pants, he's firm in his shirt, his character is firm—but most . . . of all, his belief in you, the students of Bethel, is firm.
>
> Jeff Kuhlman is a man who takes his point and pounds it in. If necessary, he'll take an issue and nail it to the wall. He doesn't attack things in spurts—he drives hard, pushing and pushing until finally—he succeeds.
>
> Jeff is a man who will go to the very end—even the climax, for each and every one of you.
>
> So vote for Jeff for A.S.B. vice-president—he'll never come between you and the best our high school can be.

The Court found that a school has the right to control lewd and offensive speech that undermines the educational mission. The Court drew a distinction between the sexual content of Fraser's remarks and the political nature of Tinker's armband. It ruled that the pervasive sexual innuendo of the speech interfered with the school's mission to implant "the shared values of a civilized social order" in the student body.

active speech
Expressing an opinion by speaking or writing; freedom of speech is a protected right under the First Amendment to the U.S. Constitution.

In a 1988 case, *Hazelwood School District v. Kuhlmeier,* the Court extended the right of school officials to censor **active speech** when it ruled that the principal could censor articles in a student publication.[123] In this case students had written about their personal experiences with pregnancy and parental divorce. The majority ruled that censorship was justified because school-sponsored publications, activities, and productions were part of the curriculum and therefore designed to impart knowledge. Control over such school-supported activities could be differentiated from the action the Tinkers initiated on their own accord. In a dissent, Justice William J. Brennan accused school officials of favoring "thought control."

The Court has dealt with speech on campus, but it may now be asked to address off-campus speech issues as well. As you may recall, students have been suspended for posting messages school officials consider defamatory on Internet websites.[124] In the future the Court may be asked to rule on whether schools can control such forms of speech or whether this speech is shielded by the First Amendment.

School Discipline

in loco parentis
In the place of the parent; rights given to schools that allow them to assume parental duties in disciplining students.

Most states have statutes permitting teachers to use corporal punishment to discipline students in public school systems. Under the concept of **in loco parentis,** discipline is one of the assumed parental duties given to the school system. In two decisions, the Supreme Court upheld the school's right to use corporal punishment. In the case of *Baker v. Owen* the Court stated:

> We hold that the Fourteenth Amendment embraces the right of parents generally to control the means and discipline of their children, but that the state has a countervailing interest in the maintenance of order in the schools . . . sufficient to sustain the right of teachers, and school officials must accord to students minimal due process in the course of inflicting such punishment.[125]

In 1977 the Supreme Court again spoke on the issue of corporal punishment in school systems in the case of *Ingraham v. Wright,* which upheld the right of teachers to use corporal punishment.[126] In this case students James Ingraham and Roosevelt Andrews sustained injuries as a result of a paddling at the Charles Drew Junior High School in Dade County, Florida. The legal problems raised in the case were (1) whether corporal punishment by teachers was a violation of the Eighth Amendment against cruel and unusual punishment, and (2) whether the due process clause of the Fourteenth Amendment required that the students receive proper notice and a hearing prior to receiving corporal punishment. The Court held that neither the Eighth nor the Fourteenth Amendment was violated in this case. Even though Ingraham suffered hematomas on his buttocks as a result of twenty blows with a wooden paddle and Andrews was hurt in the arm, the Supreme Court ruled that such punishment was not a constitutional violation. The Court established the standard that only reasonable discipline is allowed in school systems, but it excepted the degree of punishment administered in this case. The key principle in *Ingraham* is that the reasonableness standard the Court articulated represents the judicial attitude that the scope of the school's right to discipline a child is by no means more restrictive than the right of the child's own parents to impose corporal punishment. Today twenty-four states still use physical punishment.

Other issues involving the legal rights of students include their due process rights when interrogated, when corporal punishment is to be imposed, and when suspension and expulsion are threatened. When students are questioned by school personnel, no warning as to their legal rights to remain silent or right to counsel need be given. However, when school security guards, on-campus police officials, and public police officers question students, such constitutional warnings are required. In the area of corporal punishment, procedural due process established with the case of *Baker v. Owen* requires that students at least be forewarned about the possibility of corporal punishment as a discipline. In addition, the *Baker* case requires that there be a witness to the administration of corporal punishment and allows the student and the parent to elicit reasons for the punishment.

With regard to suspension and expulsion, the Supreme Court ruled in 1976 in the case of *Goss v. Lopez* that any time a student is to be suspended for up to a period of ten days he or she is entitled to a hearing.[127] The hearing would not include a right to counsel or a right to confront or cross-examine witnesses. The Court went on to state in *Goss* that the extent of the procedural due process requirements would be established on a case-by-case basis. That is, each case would represent its own facts and have its own procedural due process elements.

In summary, schools have the right to discipline students, but students are protected from unreasonable, excessive, and arbitrary discipline.

Privacy

Students have the right to expect that their records will be kept private and not distributed publicly by school officials. Although state laws generally govern the disclosure of information from juvenile court records, a 1974 federal law—the Family Educational Rights and Privacy Act (FERPA)—restricts disclosure of personally identifiable information from a student's education records without parental consent.[128] FERPA defines an education record to include all records, files, documents, and other materials, such as films, tapes, or photographs, containing information directly related to a student that an education agency maintains. In 1994 Congress recognized that schools can have a crucial role in aiding the juvenile justice system. It passed the Improving America's Schools Act, which allowed educational systems to disclose education records under these circumstances: (1) state law specifically authorizes the disclosure, (2) the disclosure is to a state or local juvenile justice system agency, (3) the disclosure relates to the juvenile justice system's ability to provide preadjudication services to a student, and (4) state or local officials certify in writing that the institution or individual receiving the information has agreed not to disclose it to a third party other than another juvenile justice system agency.[129]

SUMMARY

For several decades criminologists have attempted to explain the relationship between schools and delinquency. Although no clear causal relationship has been established, research points to many definite links between the delinquent behavior of juveniles and their experiences within the educational system.

Contemporary youths spend much of their time in school because education has become increasingly important as a determinant of social and economic success. Educational institutions are one of the primary instruments of socialization, and it is believed this role is bound to affect the amount of delinquent behavior by school-aged children.

Those who claim a causal link between schools and delinquency cite two major factors in the relationship. The first is academic failure, which arises from a lack of aptitude, labeling, or class conflict and which results in tracking. The second factor is alienation from the educational experience, which is the result of the impersonal nature of schools, the traditionally passive role assigned to students,

and students' perception of their education as irrelevant to their future lives.

Student misbehaviors, which may have their roots in the school experience itself, range from minor infractions of school rules (for example, smoking and loitering in halls) to serious crimes such as assault, burglary, arson, drug abuse, and vandalism of school property.

Dissatisfaction with the educational experience frequently sets the stage for more serious forms of delinquency both in and out of school. Some dissatisfied students choose to drop out of school as soon as they reach the legal age, and research has shown a rapid decline in delinquency among those who do drop out.

School administrators have attempted to eliminate school crime and prevent delinquency. Among the measures taken are security squads, electronic surveillance, and teacher training. Curriculums are being significantly revised to make the school experience more meaningful.

KEY TERMS

truancy
academic achievement
socialization
school failure

underachievers
tracking
dropouts
social disorganization

zero tolerance policy
passive speech
active speech
in loco parentis

Read the following article from InfoTrac College Edition:

Patterns of school crime: a replication and empirical extension. Peter Lindstrom. *British Journal of Criminology* Winter 1997

A number of horrific incidents in America's school over the past few years have created the need for alternative methods of protecting our students. Often, schools have approached this problem from a "target hardening" perspective. Many high schools have installed metal detectors and hired security guards to patrol campuses. Based on the findings of Lindstrom in the article above, what other approaches, aside from target hardening, should we explore in this country to lower the number of incidents of school violence?

Q U E S T I O N S   F O R   D I S C U S S I O N

1. Was there a delinquency problem in your high school? If so, how was it dealt with?
2. Should disobedient youths be suspended from school? Does this solution hurt or help?

3. What can be done to improve the delinquency prevention capabilities of schools?
4. Is school failure responsible for delinquency, or are delinquents simply school failures?

N O T E S

1. Terry Mcmanus, "Home Web Sites Thrust Students Into Censorship Disputes," *New York Times* 13 August 1998, p. E9.
2. Stephen Goode, "Teachers Strike Back at Disruptive Students," *Insight on the News* 4 December 1995, pp. 14–16.
3. *Justice and the Child in New Jersey,* report of the New Jersey Juvenile Delinquency Commission (1939), cited in Paul H. Hahn, *The Juvenile Offender and the Law* (Cincinnati: Anderson, 1978), p. 110.
4. U.S. Senate Subcommittee on Delinquency, *Challenge for the Third Century: Education in a Safe Environment* (Washington, D.C.: U.S. Government Printing Office, 1977), p. 1.
5. Delbert S. Eliott and Harwin L. Voss, *Delinquency and the Dropout* (Lexington, Mass.: Lexington Books, 1974), p. 204.
6. See, generally, Richard Lawrence, *School Crime and Juveniles* (New York: Oxford University Press, 1998).
7. U.S. Office of Education, *Digest of Educational Statistics* (Washington, D.C.: U.S. Government Printing Office, 1969), p. 25.
8. Kenneth Polk and Walter E. Schafer, eds., *Schools and Delinquency* (Englewood Cliffs, N.J.: Prentice-Hall, 1972), p. 13.
9. National Education Goals Report, *Goals Report, 1997* (Washington, D.C.: U.S. Government Printing Office, 1997).
10. Simon Singer and Susyan Jou, "Specifying the SES/Delinquency Relationship by Subjective and Objective Indicators of Parental and Youth Social Status," paper presented at the annual meeting of the American Society of Criminology, New Orleans, November 1992.
11. For reviews see, Bruce Wolford and LaDonna Koebel, " Kentucky Model for Youths at Risk" *Criminal Justice* 9:5–55 (1995); J. David Hawkins, Richard Catalano, Diane Morrison, Julie O'Donnell, Robert Abbott, and L. Edward Day, "The Seattle Social Development Project," in Joan McCord and Richard Tremblay, eds., *The Prevention of Antisocial Behavior in Children* (New York: Guilford, 1992), pp. 139–60.
12. Frank W. Jerse and M. Ebrahim Fakouri, "Juvenile Delinquency and Academic Deficiency," *Contemporary Education* 49:108–9 (1978).
13. Terence Thornberry, Alan Lizotte, Marvin Krohn, Margaret Farnworth, and Sung Joon Jang, "Testing Interactional Theory: An Examination of Reciprocal Causal Relationships among Family, School and Delinquency," *Journal of Criminal Law and Criminology* 82:3–35 (1991).

14. Carolyn Smith, Alan Lizotte, Terence Thornberry, and Marvin Krohn, "Resilience to Delinquency," *The Prevention Researcher* 4:4–7 (1997); Matthew Zingraff, Jeffrey Leiter, Matthew Johnsen, and Kristen Myers, "The Mediating Effect of Good School Performance on the Maltreatment–Delinquency Relationship," *Journal of Research in Crime and Delinquency* 31:62–91 (1994).
15. Lyle Shannon, *Assessing the Relationship of Adult Criminal Careers to Juvenile Careers: A Summary* (Washington, D.C.: U.S. Government Printing Office, 1982).
16. Marvin Wolfgang, Robert Figlio, and Thorsten Sellin, *Delinquency in a Birth Cohort* (Chicago: University of Chicago Press, 1972).
17. Ibid., p. 94.
18. Bureau of Justice Statistics, *Prisons and Prisoners* (Washington, D.C.: U.S. Government Printing Office, 1982), p. 2.
19. Martin Gold, "School Experiences, Self-Esteem, and Delinquent Behavior: A Theory for Alternative Schools," *Crime and Delinquency* 24:294–95 (1978).
20. Ibid.
21. Michael Gottfredson and Travis Hirschi, *A General Theory of Crime* (Stanford, Calif.: Stanford University Press, 1990); J. D. McKinney, "Longitudinal Research on the Behavioral Characteristics of Children with Learning Disabilities," *Journal of Learning Disabilities* 22:141–50 (1990).
22. Albert K. Cohen, *Delinquent Boys* (New York: Free Press, 1955); see also, Kenneth Polk, Dean Frease, and F. Lynn Richmond, "Social Class, School Experience, and Delinquency," *Criminology* 12:84–95 (1974).
23. Jackson Toby, "Orientation to Education as a Factor in the School Maladjustment of Lower-Class Children," *Social Forces* 35:259–66 (1957).
24. John Paul Wright, Francis Cullen, and Nicolas Williams, "Working while in School and Delinquent Involvement: Implications for Social Policy," *Crime and Delinquency* 43:203–21 (1997).
25. William Glaser, *Schools without Failure* (New York: Harper & Row, 1969).
26. Gold, "School Experiences, Self-Esteem, and Delinquent Behavior," p. 292.
27. Ibid., pp. 283–85.
28. Polk, Frease, and Richmond, "Social Class, School Experience, and Delinquency," p. 92.

29. Delos Kelly and Robert Balch, "Social Origins and School Failure," *Pacific Sociological Review* 14:413–30 (1971).

30. Arthur L. Stinchcombe, *Rebellion in a High School* (Chicago: Quadrangle Press, 1964), p. 70.

31. Singer and Jou, "Specifying the SES/Delinquency Relationship by Subjective and Objective Indicators of Parental and Youth Social Status," p. 11.

32. Nan Marie Astone and Sara McLanahan, "Family Structure, Parental Practices and High School Completion," *American Sociological Review* 56:309–20 (1991).

33. Robert Agnew, "Foundation for a General Strain Theory of Crime and Delinquency," *Criminology* 30:47–87 (1992), at 48.

34. For an opposing view, see Michael Waitrowski, Stephen Hansell, Charles Massey, and David Wilson, "Curriculum Tracking and Delinquency," *American Sociological Review* 47:151–60 (1982).

35. Kenneth Polk, "Class, Strain, and Rebellion among Adolescents," in Kenneth Polk and Walter E. Schafer, eds., *Schools and Delinquency* (Englewood Cliffs, N.J.: Prentice-Hall, 1972), p. 34.

36. Based on Walter E. Schafer, Carol Olexa, and Kenneth Polk, "Programmed for Social Class: Tracking in High School," in Kenneth Polk and Walter E. Schafer, eds., *Schools and Delinquency* (Englewood Cliffs, N.J.: Prentice-Hall, 1972), pp. 34–54.

37. Delos Kelly and William Pink, "School Crime and Individual Responsibility: The Perpetuation of a Myth," *Urban Review* 14:47–63 (1982).

38. Jeannie Oakes, *Keeping Track, How Schools Structure Inequality* (New Haven, Conn.: Yale University Press, 1985), p. 48.

39. Ibid., p. 57.

40. Delos Kelly, *Creating School Failure, Youth Crime, and Deviance* (Los Angeles: Trident Shop, 1982), p. 11.

41. Delos Kelly and W. Grove, "Teachers' Nominations and the Production of Academic Misfits," *Education* 101:246–63 (1981).

42. Delos Kelly, "The Role of Teachers' Nominations in the Perpetuation of Deviant Adolescent Careers," *Education* 96:209–17 (1976).

43. Oakes, *Keeping Track*, p. 48.

44. Ibid.

45. Adam Gamoran, "The Variable Effects of High School Tracking," *American Sociological Review* 57:812–28 (1992).

46. Travis Hirschi, *Causes of Delinquency* (Berkeley, Calif.: University of California Press, 1969), pp. 113–24, 132.

47. Richard Lawrence, "Parents, Peers, School and Delinquency," paper presented at the American Society of Criminology Meeting, Boston, Mass., November 1995.

48. Patricia Jenkins, "School Delinquency and the School Social Bond," *Journal of Research in Crime and Delinquency* 34:337–67 (1997).

49. Smith, Lizotte, Thornberry, and Krohn, "Resilience to Delinquency"; Zingraff, Leiter, Johnsen, and Myers, "The Mediating Effect of Good School Performance on the Maltreatment–Delinquency Relationship."

50. Emil Haller, "High School Size and Student Indiscipline: Another Aspect of the School Consolidation Issue," *Educational Evaluation and Policy Analysis* 14:145–56 (1992).

51. Patricia Harris Jenkins, "School Delinquency and Belief in School Rules," paper presented at the annual meeting of the American Society of Criminology, New Orleans, November 1992.

52. *Learning into the 21st Century, Report of Forum 5* (Washington, D.C.: White House Conference on Children, 1970).

53. Polk and Schafer, *Schools and Delinquency*, p. 72.

54. Stinchcombe, *Rebellion in a High School*, p. 70; Daniel Glaser, *Crime in Our Changing Society* (New York: Holt, Rinehart & Winston, 1978), pp. 162–63.

55. Polk and Schafer, *Schools and Delinquency*, p. 23.

56. Mihaly Czikszentmihalyi and Reed Larson, "Intrinsic Rewards in School Crime," *Crime and Delinquency* 24:322 (1978).

57. National Center for Educational Statistics, *Dropout Rates in the United States, 1992* (Washington, D.C.: U.S. Department of Education, 1993).

58. National Education Goals Panel, *Data for the National Education Goals Report, Volume One: National Data* (Washington, D.C.: National Education Goals Panel, 1995).

59. *Drug Use Forecasting: 1994 Annual Report on Adult and Juvenile Arrestees* (Washington, D.C.: National Institute of Justice, 1995).

60. Ibid.

61. Ibid.

62. Eliott and Voss, *Delinquency and the Dropout*.

63. Glaser, *Crime in Our Changing Society*, p. 164.

64. Terence Thornberry, Melanie Moore, and R. L. Christenson, "The Effect of Dropping Out of High School on Subsequent Criminal Behavior," *Criminology* 23:3–18 (1985).

65. Marvin Krohn, Terence Thornberry, Lori Collins-Hall, and Alan Lizotte, "School Dropout, Delinquent Behavior, and Drug Use," in Howard Kaplan, ed., *Drugs, Crime and other Deviant Adaptations: Longitudinal Studies* (New York: Plenum Press, 1995), pp. 163–83.

66. Howard Snyder and Melissa Sickmund, *Juvenile Offenders and Victims: A National Report* (Washington, D.C.: Office of Juvenile Justice and Delinquency Prevention, 1995), p. 15.

67. Jay Teachman, Kathleen Paasch, and Karen Carver, "Social Capital and the Generation of Human Capital," *Social Forces* 75:1343–60 (1997); Michel Janosz, Marc Le Blanc, Bernard Boulerice, and Richard Tremblay, *What Information Is Really Needed to Predict School Dropout? A Replication on Two Longitudinal Samples* (University of Montreal, School of Psychoeducation, 1995).

68. Christine Bowditch, "Getting Rid of Troublemakers: High School Disciplinary Procedures and the Production of Dropouts," *Social Problems* 40:493–508 (1993).

69. G. Roger Jarjoura, "The Conditional Effect of Social Class on the Dropout–Delinquency Relationship," *Journal of Research in Crime and Delinquency* 33:232–55 (1996).

70. G. Roger Jarjoura, "Does Dropping Out of School Enhance Delinquent Involvement? Results from a Large-Scale National Probability Sample," *Criminology* 31:149–72 (1993).

71. Jackson Toby, *Violence in Schools* (Washington, D.C.: National Institute of Justice, 1983), p. 2.

72. Jackson Toby, "Getting Serious about School Discipline," *The Public Interest* 133:68–74 (1998).

73. Rick Bragg, "4 Girls and a Teacher Are Shot to Death in an Ambush at a Middle School in Arkansas," *New York Times* 25 March 1998, p.1.

74. Charles Callahan and Frederick Rivara, "Urban High School Youth and Handguns," *Journal of the American Medical Association* 267:3038–42 (1992).

75. National Institute of Education, U.S. Department of Health, Education and Welfare, *Violent Schools—Safe Schools: The Safe Schools Study Report to the Congress,* vol. 1 (Washington, D.C.: U.S. Government Printing Office, 1977).

76. Phillip Kaufman, Xianglei Chen, Susan P. Choy, Kathryn A. Chandler, Christopher D. Chapman, Michael R. Rand, and Cheryl Ringel, *Indicators of School Crime and Safety, 1998* (Washington, D.C.: U.S. Department of Education and Bureau of Justice Statistics, 1998).

77. Ibid., p. 20.

78. Ibid., p. 32.

79. Ibid., p. 25.

80. Ibid., p. 30.

81. Ibid., p. 34.

82. Sheila Heaviside and Shelley Burns, *Violence and Discipline Problems in U.S. Public Schools: 1996–1997* (Washington, D.C.: Department of Education 1998).

83. National Education Goals Report, *Goals Report, 1997*, p. 63.

84. Luntz Research Companies and QEV Analytics, *Back to School 1997—The CASA National Survey of American Attitudes on Substance Abuse III: Teens and Their Parents, Teachers and Principals* (New York: National Center for Addiction and Substance Abuse, Columbia University, 1998).

85. Gary Gottfredson and Denise Gottfredson, *Victimization in Schools* (New York: Plenum Press, 1985), p. 18.

86. Nancy Weishew and Samuel Peng, "Variables Predicting Students' Problem Behaviors," *Journal of Educational Research* 87:5–17 (1993).

87. James Q. Wilson, "Crime in Society and Schools," in J. M. McPartland and E. L. McDill, eds., *Violence in Schools: Perspective, Programs and Positions* (Lexington, Mass.: D.C. Heath, 1977), p. 48.

88. Joan McDermott, "Crime in the School and in the Community: Offenders, Victims, and Fearful Youth," *Crime and Delinquency* 29:270–83 (1983).

89. Daryl Hellman and Susan Beaton, "The Pattern of Violence in Urban Public Schools: The Influence of School and Community," *Journal of Research in Crime and Delinquency* 23:102–27 (1986).

90. Peter Lindstrom, "Patterns of School Crime: A Replication and Empirical Extension," *British Journal of Criminology* 37:121–31 (1997).

91. June L. Arnette and Marjorie C. Walsleben, *Combating Fear and Restoring Safety in Schools* (Washington, D.C.: Office of Juvenile Justice and Delinquency Prevention, 1998).

92. Heaviside and Burns, *Violence and Discipline Problems in U.S. Public Schools.*

93. Ibid., p. 20.

94. Ibid.

95. American Academy of Pediatrics Committee on School Health, "Violence in Schools: Current Status and Prevention," *School Health: Policy and Practice* (Elk Grove Village, Ill.: American Academy of Pediatrics Committee on School Health), pp. 363–80, at 369.

96. Bruce Jacobs, "Anticipatory Undercover Targeting in High Schools," *Journal of Criminal Justice* 22:445–57 (1994).

97. Kevin Bushweller, "Guards with Guns," *The American School Board Journal* 180:34–36 (1993).

98. Bella English, "Hub Program to Counsel Violent Pupils," *Boston Globe* 24 February 1987, p. 1.

99. Randal C. Archibold, "City Schools Tentatively Agree to Let the Police Run Security," *New York Times* 29 August 1998.

100. Steven Lab and John Whitehead, *The School Environment and School Crime: Causes and Consequences* (Washington, D.C.: National Institute of Justice, 1992), p. 5.

101. Jackie Kimbrough, "School-Based Strategies for Delinquency Prevention," in Peter Greenwood, ed., *The Juvenile Rehabilitation Reader* (Santa Monica, Calif: Rand Corp., 1985), pp. ix, 1–22.

102. Hellman and Beaton, "The Pattern of Violence in Urban Public Schools," pp. 122–23.

103. Julius Menacker, Ward Weldon, and Emanuel Hurwitz, "Community Influences on School Crime and Violence," *Urban Education* 25:68–80 (1990).

104. Wendy Mansfield and Elizabeth Farris, *Public School Principal Survey on Safe, Disciplined and Drug-Free Schools* (Washington, D.C.: U.S. Government Printing Office, 1992), p. iii.

105. National Commission on Excellence in Education, *A Nation at Risk* (Washington, D.C.: U.S. Government Printing Office, 1983).

106. Alexander Liazos, "Schools, Alienation, and Delinquency," *Crime and Delinquency* 24:355–61 (1978).

107. Stephen Cox, William Davidson, and Timothy Bynum, "A Meta-Analytic Assessment of Delinquency-Related Outcomes of Alternative Education Programs," *Crime and Delinquency* 41:219–34 (1995).

108. Gary Putka, "Cheaters in Schools May Not Be Students But Their Teachers," *Wall Street Journal* 2 November 1989, p. 1.

109. U.S. Senate Subcommittee on Delinquency, *Challenge for the Third Century,* p. 95.

110. William Bukoski, "School-Based Substance Abuse Prevention: A Review of Program Research," *Journal of Children in Contemporary Society* 18:95–116 (1985).

111. See, generally, J. David Hawkins and Denise Lishner, "Schooling and Delinquency," in E. H. Johnson, ed., *Handbook on Crime and Delinquency* (Westport, Conn.: Greenwood Press, 1987).

112. Denise Gottfredson, "An Empirical Test of School-Based Environmental and Individual Interventions to Reduce the Risk of Delinquent Behavior," *Criminology* 24:705–31 (1986).

113. Denise Gottfredson, "Changing School Structures to Benefit High Risk Youth," in Peter Leone, ed., *Understanding Troubled and Troubling Youth* (Newbury Park, Calif.: Sage, 1990), pp. 246–71.

114. Julie O'Donnell, J. David Hawkins, Richard Catalano, Robert Abbott, and L. Edward Day, "Preventing School Failure, Drug Use, and Delinquency among Low-Income Children: Long-Term Intervention in Elementary Schools," *Journal of Orthopsychiatry* 65:87–100 (1995).

115. S. Arons, "Compulsory Education: The Plain People Resist," *Saturday Review* 15:63–69 (1972).

116. Ibid.

117. See *Pierce v. Society of Sisters,* 268 U.S. 610, 45 S.Ct. 571, 69 L.Ed. 1070 (1925).

118. 406 U.S. 205, 92 S.Ct. 1526, 32 L.Ed.2d 15 (1972).

119. 393 U.S. 503, 89 S.Ct. 733 (1969).

120. Ibid.

121. Ibid., p. 741.

122. *Bethel School District No. 403 v. Fraser,* 478 U.S. 675, 106 S.Ct. 3159, 92 L.Ed.2d 549 (1986).

123. *Hazelwood School District v. Kuhlmeier,* 484 U.S. 260, 108 S.Ct. 562, 98 L.Ed.2d 592 (1988).

124. Terry Mcmanus, "Home Web Sites Thrust Students into Censorship Disputes," *New York Times* 13 August 1998, p. E9.

125. *Baker v. Owen,* 423 U.S. 907, 96 S.Ct. 210, 46 L.Ed.2d 137 (1975).

126. *Ingraham v. Wright,* 430 U.S. 651, 97 S.Ct. 1401 (1977).

127. *Goss v. Lopez,* 419 U.S. 565, 95 S.Ct. 729 (1976).

128. Michael Medaris, *A Guide to the Family Educational Rights and Privacy Act* (Washington, D.C.: Office of Juvenile Justice and Delinquency Prevention, 1998).

129. Ibid.

Chapter Eleven

Drug Use and Delinquency

Victor Brancaccio, a Port St. Lucie, Florida, teenager with a long history of substance abuse and emotional disturbance, took offense when Mollie Mae Frazier, an eighty-one-year-old widow, scolded him for rapping the lyrics of the tune *Stranded on Death Row* as he walked down the street.[1] Victor dragged Mollie Mae into a field, punched and kicked her repeatedly, jumped on her rib cage, and finally bashed in her skull with a toy gun. The brutality of Victor's act prompted Florida Representative Bill McCollum to say, "In America today, no population poses a greater threat to public safety than juvenile criminals."[2]

Sentenced to life in prison for killing Mollie Mae, Victor was granted a new trial in 1998 when a Florida appeals court ruled that the trial judge erred in not giving the jury a specific instruction to consider whether Victor was "involuntarily intoxicated" by either alcohol or the antidepressant Zoloft at the time of the murder. Victor's defense team claimed that his excessive drinking, combined with prescription mood-altering drugs, left him unable to understand the wrongfulness of his acts. Technically, they argued, Victor was mentally ill at the time of his violent attack.

Ironically, Victor is suing the psychiatric hospital that had been treating him at the time, claiming he would not have assaulted the woman had the hospital not discharged him when his insurance expired.

Victor claims that excessive drinking and drug taking set him off and turned him into what his doctors described as a "walking time bomb." How did a seventeen-year-old, especially one under psychiatric care and with an arrest record, get alcohol in the first place? Was there no treatment available? This case highlights the significant problems posed by teenage **substance abuse.**

There is little question that adolescent substance abuse and its association with youth crime and delinquency continue to be vexing problems. Along with major metropolitan areas such as Los Angeles, New York, and Washington, D.C., almost every town, village, and city in the United States has confronted some type of teenage substance abuse problem. Nor is the United States alone in experiencing a problem with substance abuse. In Australia 19 percent of youths in detention centers report having used heroin at least once, and in the Canadian province of British Columbia where marijuana and powder crack use are considered serious urban problems, almost half of all youths report using drugs. South Africa reports an increase in teen cocaine and heroin abuse, and Thailand has a serious heroin and methamphetamine problem.[3]

Far too many adolescents are involved with drugs and alcohol. Self-report surveys indicate that more than half of high school seniors have tried drugs and more than 90 percent use alcohol.[4] All too often, ado-

Victor Brancaccio was convicted of murdering Mollie Mae Frazier, an 81-year-old widow who scolded him for rapping as he walked down the street. Victor dragged Mollie Mae into a field, punched and kicked her repeatedly, jumped on her rib cage, and finally bashed in her skull with a toy gun. Brancaccio claimed that he was "involuntarily intoxicated" by alcohol and the antidepressant Zoloft and unable to understand the wrongfulness of his acts.

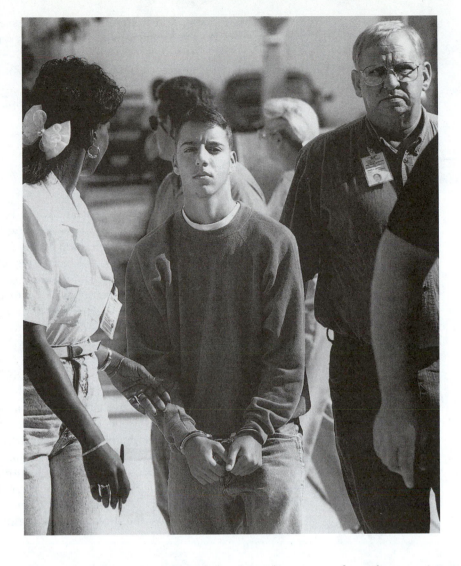

substance abuse
Using drugs or alcohol in such a way as to cause physical harm to yourself.

lescents who remain at high risk for drug abuse come from the most impoverished communities and experience a multitude of problems, including school failure and family conflict.[5] Equally troubling is the association between drug use and crime: drug users commit a significant amount of all crimes, and a significant portion of known criminals are drug abusers.[6] Research indicates that more than half of all juvenile arrestees in some cities test positive for cocaine.[7] Self-report surveys show that drug abusers are more likely to become delinquents than are nonabusers.[8] The pattern of drug use and crime makes teenage substance abuse a key national concern.

In this chapter we address some of the most important issues involving teenage substance abuse. First we review the kinds of drugs children and adolescents are using and how often they are using them. Then we discuss who uses drugs and what causes substance abuse. After describing the association between drug abuse and criminal and delinquent behavior, we conclude the chapter with a review of the efforts being made to control the use of drugs in the United States.

Substances of Abuse

A wide variety of substances generically referred to as "drugs" are sold and used by teenagers. Some drugs are addicting, others are not.

Some create hallucinations, others cause a depressed relaxing stupor, and a few give an immediate exhilarating uplift. In this section we will identify the most widely used substances and discuss their effects. All of these drugs can be abused, and because of the danger they present, many of these substances have been banned from private use. Others are available legally only with physician supervision, and a few are available to adults but prohibited for minor children.

Marijuana and Hashish

hashish
A concentrated form of cannabis made from unadulterated resin from the female cannabis plant.

marijuana
The dried leaves of the cannabis plant.

Commonly called "pot" or "grass," marijuana is produced from the leaves of *cannabis sativa,* a plant grown throughout the world. **Hashish** (hash) is a concentrated form of cannabis made from unadulterated resin from the female plant. The main active ingredient in both marijuana and hashish is tetrahydrocannabinol (THC), a mild hallucinogen that alters sensory impressions.

Marijuana is the drug most commonly used by teenagers. Smoking large amounts of pot or hash can cause drastic distortions in auditory and visual perception, even producing hallucinatory effects. Small doses produce an early excitement ("high") that gives way to a sedated effect and drowsiness. Pot use is also related to decreased physical activity, overestimation of time and space, and increased food consumption. When the user is alone, marijuana produces a quiet, dreamy state. In a group users commonly become giddy and lose perspective.

Marijuana is not physically addicting, but its long-term effects have been the subject of much debate. During the 1970s, it was reported that smoking pot caused a variety of serious physical and mental problems, including brain damage and mental illness. Although the dangers of pot and hash may have been significantly overstated, use of these drugs does present some health risks, including an increased risk of lung cancer, chronic bronchitis, and other diseases. Marijuana smoking should be avoided by prospective parents as it lowers sperm counts in male users and females experience disrupted ovulation and a greater chance of miscarriage.[9]

Cocaine

cocaine
A powerful natural stimulant derived from the coca plant.

Cocaine is an alkaloid derivative of the coca plant first isolated in 1860. When discovered, it was considered a medicinal breakthrough that could relieve fatigue, depression, and various other symptoms, and it quickly became a staple of popular patent medicines. When its addictive qualities and dangerous side effects became apparent, its use was controlled by the Pure Food and Drug Act of 1906.

Cocaine is the most powerful natural stimulant. Its use produces euphoria, laughter, restlessness, and excitement. Overdoses can cause delirium, increased reflexes, violent manic behavior, and possible respiratory failure.

Cocaine can be sniffed, or "snorted," into the nostrils or injected. The immediate feeling of euphoria or rush is short-lived, and heavy users may snort coke as often as every ten minutes. Another highly dangerous practice is "speedballing"—injecting a mixture of cocaine and heroin.

freebase
Purified cocaine crystals that are crushed and smoked to provide a more powerful high than cocaine.

A number of deadly derivatives of cocaine have become popular on the street in recent years. For example, **freebase** is a chemical produced by treating street cocaine with a liquid to remove the hydrochloric acid with which pure cocaine is bonded during manufacture. The freebase is then dissolved in a solvent, usually ether, that crystallizes the purified cocaine. The resulting crystals are crushed and smoked in a special glass pipe, which provides a high more immediate and more powerful than snorting street-strength coke.

crack
A highly addictive crystalline form of cocaine containing remnants of hydrochloride and sodium bicarbonate, which emits a crackling sound when smoked.

Crack, like freebase, is processed street cocaine. Its manufacture involves using ammonia or baking soda to remove the hydrochlorides and create a crystalline form of cocaine that can then be smoked. However, unlike freebase, crack is not a pure form of cocaine and contains both remnants of hydrochloride and residue from the baking soda (sodium bicarbonate). In fact, crack gets its name from the fact that the sodium bicarbonate often emits a crackling sound when the substance is smoked. Also referred to as "rock," "gravel," and "roxanne," crack was introduced and gained popularity on both coasts simultaneously in the mid-1980s. It is relatively inexpensive, can provide a powerful high, and is considered to be highly psychologically addictive.

Heroin

Narcotic drugs have the ability to produce insensibility to pain and to free the mind of anxiety and emotion. Users experience a rush of euphoria, relief from fear and apprehension, release of tension, and elevation of spirits. This short period of euphoria is followed by a period of apathy during which users become drowsy and may nod off. Heroin, the most commonly used narcotic in the United States, is produced from opium, a drug derived from the opium poppy flower. Dealers further cut the drug with neutral substances (sugar or lactose), and street heroin is often only 1 to 4 percent pure.

heroin
A narcotic made from opium and then cut with sugar or some other neutral substance until it is only 1 to 4 percent pure.

Heroin is probably the most dangerous commonly used drug. Users rapidly build up a tolerance for it, fueling the need for increased doses to obtain the desired effect. Some users change their method of ingestion in an effort to recapture the desired "kick." At first heroin is usually sniffed or snorted; as tolerance builds, it is "skin popped" (shot into skin, but not into a vein); and finally it is injected into a vein, or "mainlined."[10]

addict
A person with an overpowering physical or psychological need to continue taking a particular substance or drug.

Through the progressive use of heroin, the user becomes an **addict**—a person with an overpowering physical and psychological need to continue taking a particular substance or drug by any means possible. If addicts cannot get enough heroin to satisfy their habit, they will suffer withdrawal symptoms, which include irritability, emotional depression, extreme nervousness, pain in the abdomen, and nausea.

Alcohol

alcohol
Fermented or distilled liquids containing ethanol, an intoxicating substance.

Alcohol remains the drug of choice for most teenagers. More than 70 percent of high school seniors reported using alcohol in the past year, and more than 80 percent say they have tried it sometime during their lifetime; by the twelfth grade about two-thirds of American youth report that they have "been drunk."[11] More than twenty million Americans are estimated to be problem drinkers, and at least half of these are alcoholics.

The cost of alcohol abuse in the United States is extremely high. Alcohol may be a factor in nearly half of all murders, suicides, and accidental deaths.[12] Alcohol-related deaths number one hundred thousand a year, far more than that of all other illegal drugs combined. About 1.4 million drivers are arrested each year for driving under the influence, and close to a million more are arrested for other alcohol-related violations.[13] The economic cost of America's drinking problem is equally staggering. An estimated $117 billion is lost each year, including $18 billion from premature deaths, $66 billion in reduced work effort, and $13 billion for treatment.[14]

Considering these problems, why do so many youths drink alcohol to excess? Youths who use alcohol report that it reduces tension, diverts worries, enhances

Alcohol abuse remains a serious problem among teens. Police in Florida are shown here stopping an automobile containing the potentially deadly combination of teens and alcoholic beverages.

pleasure, improves social skills, and transforms experiences for the better.[15] Although these reactions may follow the limited use of alcohol, alcohol in higher doses acts as a sedative and a depressant. Long-term use has been linked with depression and numerous physical ailments ranging from heart disease to cirrhosis of the liver (though some research links moderate drinking to a reduction in the probability of heart attack).[16] Many teens also think drinking stirs their romantic urges, but the weight of scientific evidence indicates that alcohol decreases sexual response.[17]

Anesthetics

anesthetic drugs
Nervous system depressants.

Anesthetic drugs are used as nervous system depressants. Local anesthetics block nervous system transmissions; general anesthetics act on the brain to produce a generalized loss of sensation, stupor, or unconsciousness. The most widely abused anesthetic drug is *phencyclidine* (PCP), known on the street as "angel dust." PCP can be sprayed on marijuana or other plant leaves and smoked, drunk, or injected. Originally developed as an animal tranquilizer, PCP creates hallucinations and a spaced-out feeling that causes heavy users to engage in extremely violent acts. The effects of PCP can last up to two days, and the danger of overdose is extremely high.

Inhalants

inhalants
Volatile liquids that give off a vapor, which is inhaled, producing short-term excitement and euphoria followed by a period of disorientation.

Some youths inhale vapors from lighter fluid, paint thinner, cleaning fluid, or model airplane glue to reach a drowsy, dizzy state that is sometimes accompanied by hallucinations. **Inhalants** produce a short-term sense of excitement and euphoria followed by a period of disorientation, slurred speech, and drowsiness. Amyl nitrite ("poppers") is a commonly used volatile liquid packaged in capsule form, which is inhaled when the capsule is broken open.

Sedatives and Barbiturates

sedatives
Drugs of the barbiturate family that depress the central nervous system into a sleep-like condition.

Sedatives, the most commonly used drugs of the barbiturate family, depress the central nervous system into a sleep-like condition. On the illegal market, sedatives are called "goofballs" or "downers," and they are often known by the color of the capsules: "reds" (Seconal), "blue devils" (Amytal), and "rainbows" (Tuinal).

Sedatives can be prescribed by doctors as sleeping pills. Illegal users employ them to create relaxed, sociable, and good-humored feelings; overdoses can cause irritability, repellent behavior, and eventual unconsciousness. Barbiturates are probably the major cause of drug-overdose deaths.

Tranquilizers

tranquilizers
Drugs that reduce anxiety and promote relaxation.

Tranquilizers relieve uncomfortable emotional feelings by reducing anxiety and promoting relaxation. Legally prescribed tranquilizers, such as Ampazine, Thorazine, Pacatal, and Sparine, were originally designed to control the behavior of people suffering from psychoses, aggressiveness, and agitation. Less powerful tranquilizers, such as Valium, Librium, Miltown, and Equanil, are used to combat anxiety, tension, fast heart rate, and headaches. The use of increased dosages of illegally obtained tranquilizers can lead to addiction, and withdrawal can be painful and hazardous.

Hallucinogens

hallucinogens
Natural or synthetic substances that produce vivid distortions of the senses without greatly disturbing consciousness.

Hallucinogens, either natural or synthetic, produce vivid distortions of the senses without greatly disturbing the viewer's consciousness. Some produce hallucinations, and others cause psychotic behavior in otherwise normal people.

One common hallucinogen is mescaline, named after the Mescalero Apaches, who first discovered its potent effect. Mescaline occurs naturally in the peyote, a small cactus that grows in Mexico and the southwestern United States. After initial discomfort, mescaline produces vivid hallucinations in all ranges of colors and geometric patterns, a feeling of depersonalization, and out-of-body sensations.

A second group of hallucinogens are synthetic alkaloid compounds, such as psilocybin. These compounds can be transformed into lysergic acid diethylamide, commonly called LSD. This powerful substance (eight hundred times more potent than mescaline) stimulates cerebral sensory centers to produce visual hallucinations in all ranges of colors, to intensify hearing, and to increase sensitivity. Users often report a scrambling of sensations; they may "hear colors" and "smell music." Users also report feeling euphoric and mentally superior, although to an observer they appear disoriented and confused. Unfortunately, anxiety and panic may occur during the LSD experience, and overdoses can produce psychotic episodes, flashbacks, and even death.

Stimulants

stimulants
Synthetic substances that produce an intense physical reaction by stimulating the central nervous system.

Stimulants ("uppers," "speed," "pep pills," "crystal") are synthetic drugs that stimulate action in the central nervous system. They produce an intense physical reaction: increased blood pressure, breathing rate, and bodily activity, and mood elevation. One widely used amphetamine produces psychological effects such as increased confidence, euphoria, fearlessness, talkativeness, impulsive behavior, and loss of appetite. Commonly used stimulants include Benzedrine ("bennies"), Dexedrine ("dex"), Dexamyl, Bephetamine ("whites"), and Methedrine ("meth," "speed," "crystal meth").

Methedrine is probably the most widely used and most dangerous amphetamine. Some people swallow it; heavy users inject it for a quick rush. Long-term heavy use can result in exhaustion, anxiety, prolonged depression, and hallucinations. A new form of methamphetamine is a crystallized substance with the street name of "ice" or "crystal." Originally popular on the west coast and in Hawaii, it was created in Asian labs; it is called "batu" by Filipinos, "shaba" by the Japanese, and "hirropon" by Koreans. Smoking this crystal causes weight loss, kidney damage, heart and respiratory problems, and paranoia—all symptoms of its better known competitor, crack.[18]

Steroids

anabolic steroids
Drugs used by athletes and body builders to gain muscle bulk and strength.

Teenagers use highly dangerous **anabolic steroids** to gain muscle bulk and strength for athletics and body building.[19] Black market sales of these drugs approach $1 billion annually. Although not physically addicting, steroids can become an "obsession" among teens who desire athletic success. Long-term users may spend up to $400 a week on steroids and may support their habit by dealing the drug.

Steroids are dangerous because of the significant health problems associated with their long-term use: liver ailments, tumors, hepatitis, kidney problems, sexual dysfunction, hypertension, and mental problems such as depression. Steroid use runs in cycles, and other drugs such as Clomid, Teslac, and Halotestin, which carry their own dangerous side effects, are often used to curb the need for high dosages of steroids. Finally, steroid users often share needles, which puts them at high risk for contracting HIV, the virus that causes AIDS.

Cigarettes

Worldwide, approximately twenty-five countries have established laws to prohibit the sale of cigarettes to minors. The reality, however, is that in many countries children and adolescents have easy access to tobacco products.[20] In the United States the Synar Amendment was enacted in July 1992. This federal law requires states to enact and enforce laws restricting the sale and distribution of tobacco products to youths under the age of eighteen. States are required to reduce the illegal sales rates to minors to no more than 20 percent within several years. FDA rules require age verification by photo ID for anyone under the age of twenty-seven who is purchasing tobacco products. It also has banned vending machines and self-service displays except in "adults only" facilities where children are not allowed entry.

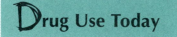

Drug Use Today

Surveys show that marijuana continues to be the most widely used drug and that synthetic (laboratory-made) drugs have become more popular.

Some western states report that methamphetamine ("speed," "crank") use is increasing and that its low cost and high potency has encouraged manufacturers ("cookers") to increase production and distribution efforts. Other synthetics include PCP and LSD, the use of which is not widespread nationally but focused in particular areas of the country. For example, California leads the nation in the manufacture of PCP; about two-thirds of all drug labs seized are in California.[21]

Synthetics are popular because labs can easily be hidden in rural areas, and traffickers do not have to worry about border searches or payoffs to foreign growers and middlemen. Users like synthetics because they are cheap and produce a powerful, long-lasting high that can be greater than that provided by more expensive natural products such as cocaine.

Crack cocaine use, which reached epidemic proportions in the 1980s has been in decline in recent years. Heavy criminal penalties, tight enforcement, and social disapproval have helped to lower crack use in the 1990s.[22] Although it was feared that abusers would turn to heroin as a replacement, there has been little indication of a new "heroin epidemic." Heroin use has stabilized in most of the country, although there are still hundreds of thousands of regular users concentrated in larger cities such as New York.[23] Arrest data show that most frequent users are older offenders who started their heroin abuse decades ago. There is reason to believe heroin use is in decline among adolescents, possibly because it has acquired an extremely negative street image among inner-city youths. Most youths know that heroin is addictive, a hard to break habit, destructive to health, and that needle sharing leads to HIV. Research conducted in New York City shows that most youths avoid heroin, shun users and dealers, and wish to avoid becoming addicts.[24]

Despite concern over these "hard drugs," the most persistent teenage substance abuse problem today is alcohol. Teenage alcoholism is sometimes considered less of a social problem than other types of substance abuse, but it actually produces far more deaths and problems. Teenage alcohol abusers suffer depression, anxiety, and other symptoms of mental distress. Also, it is well-established that alcoholism runs in families; today's teenage abusers may become the parents of the next generation of teenage alcoholics.[25]

Drug Use Surveys

A number of attempts have been made to survey teenage drug abuse. There are two primary sources of data on trends. The federal government sponsors an annual survey conducted by social scientists at the University of Michigan's Institute for Social Research (ISR). Since 1975, the Michigan research team has conducted a series of annual surveys that now include some fifty thousand students at four hundred public and private secondary schools.[26] Participants—and the research team reports that students are enthusiastic participants—are queried about their lifetime, monthly, and annual use of sixteen commonly abused drugs and substances (including cigarettes and alcohol). Early surveys were limited to seniors, but the surveys now include eighth and tenth graders. In addition to the annual survey, about twenty-four hundred members of each class surveyed are followed up for ten years after high school to determine the lifetime incidence of their drug usage.

The second data source is the Parents Resource Institute for Drug Abuse (PRIDE). This is an Atlanta-based nonprofit group that has conducted annual surveys of more than two hundred thousand junior and senior high school students in thirty-four states for the last four years. Let's take a closer look at these two surveys.

ISR Survey

The ISR survey is most often used to follow the course of teenage substance abuse in the United States. The most recent ISR survey available (1997) indicates that fewer adolescents are taking drugs today than twenty years ago, that there was a disturbing up-tick in drug use between 1991 and 1996, and that drug use now seems to have stabilized.

As Figure 11.1 shows, drug use peaked in the late 1970s and early 1980s and then began a decade-long decline. However, by the early 1990s the number of youths in the eighth, tenth and twelfth grades who used any form of drug began to increase. Especially disturbing is the trend for the youngest students (ages 13 and 14) to report an increase in their lifetime, monthly, and annual use of illicit drugs. By eighth grade more than half the students had tried alcohol: about 1 percent drank on a daily basis, and about 15 percent said they had had five or more drinks in the past two weeks.

Cigarette smoking has also increased in the 1990s. About 9 percent of eighth graders and 25 percent of twelfth graders now report smoking during the past thirty days. Among high school seniors, the number who have tried cigarettes during their lifetime has stabilized at about two-thirds. However, the seniors who have tried cigarettes in the past month and who smoke every day has been on the increase; about 14 percent of high school seniors say they now smoke every day. The fact that drug use was essentially unchanged between 1996 and 1997 comes as a welcome relief (Figure 11.2), but drug abuse remains a significant problem for our youth.

PRIDE Survey

The most recent PRIDE survey also indicates increases in drug activity in the last few years, specifically for marijuana, hallucinogens, cocaine, and inhalants. Students also reported increasing their use of cigarettes. The most recent survey (1998) found that about 39 percent of high school seniors reported having smoked marijuana in the past year and about one-quarter smoked monthly.[27] However, like the ISR sur-

FIGURE 11.1

Trends in Annual Prevalence of an Illicit Drug Use Index for Twelfth Graders

Source: Institute for Social Research, *1997 Survey of High School Students* (Ann Arbor, Mich.: University of Michigan News and Information Services, 1998).

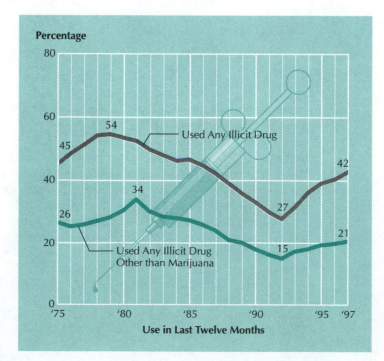

FIGURE 11.2

Trends in Annual Use of Selected Drugs by Grade, 1975–1997

Source: Institute for Social Research, *1997 Survey of High School Students* (Ann Arbor, Mich.: University of Michigan News and Information Services, 1998).

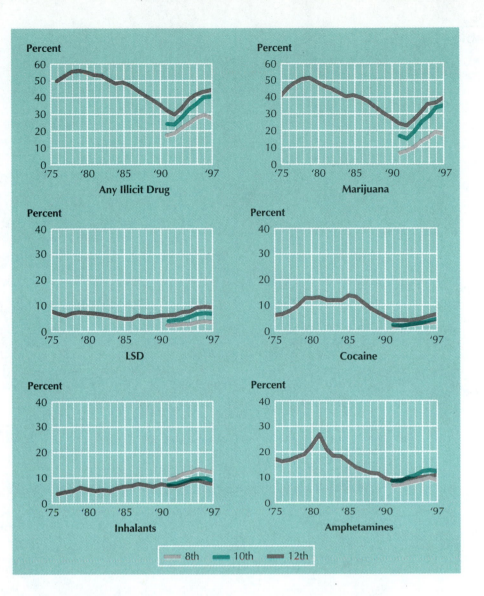

vey, the PRIDE survey of 154,350 students in grades 6 through 12 found that drug use by teens is now stabilizing after six years of gain. In the latest survey, in seven grades studied there were no statistically significant increases in drug use except in the twelfth grade. Decreases were found for the categories "any illicit drug," "any alcohol," and "cigarettes" for junior high (grades 6–8) and senior high (grades 9–12). This is the first across-the-board decline in alcohol, tobacco, and other drug use (annual and monthly) since the 1990–91 school year. Twelfth graders reported slight increases in cigarette, cocaine, uppers, and downers usage both monthly and annually.

Table 11.1 compares the annual use rates for any drug for the eighth, tenth, and twelfth grades in the ISR and PRIDE surveys. Note the rapid increase followed by stabilization in 1996–97. Note also that the surveys are quite close in their estimations of drug abuse. The fact that two national surveys, conducted independently, generate the same pattern and trends in drug abuse helps bolster their validity.

Why Has Teenage Drug Use Fluctuated?

If the national survey results are valid, teenage drug use has undergone a period of significant change. When drug use declined in the 1980s, one reason may have

Table 11.1

COMPARING ANNUAL DRUG USE: PRIDE VERSUS ISR

Year	1996–97			1995–96		
Grade	8	10	12	8	10	12
PRIDE	27.9	39.1	41.6	25.9	38.0	40.8
ISR	22.1	38.5	42.4	23.6	37.5	40.2
Difference	–5.8	–0.6	+0.8	–2.3	–0.5	–0.6

Year	1994–95			1993–94		
Grade	8	10	12	8	10	12
PRIDE	21.3	32.3	35.8	19.3	28.6	31.9
ISR	21.4	33.3	39.0	18.5	30.0	35.8
Difference	+0.1	+1.0	+3.2	–0.8	+1.4	+3.9

Year	1992–93			1991–92		
Grade	8	10	12	8	10	12
PRIDE	15.0	22.6	28.2	13.5	21.1	25.1
ISR	15.1	24.7	31.0	12.9	20.2	27.1
Difference	+0.1	+2.1	+2.8	–0.6	–0.9	+2.0

Year	1990–91		
Grade	8	10	12
PRIDE	13.0	20.5	24.8
ISR	11.3	21.4	29.4
Difference	–1.7	+0.9	+4.6

Source: PRIDE, *1997 Survey of High School Drug Abuse* (Atlanta, Ga.: PRIDE, Inc., 1998).

been changing perceptions about the harmfulness of cocaine and marijuana. As students came to view these drugs as harmful, they tended to use them less. With the widespread publicity linking drug use, needle sharing, and the AIDS virus in the 1980s, it comes as no surprise that youths began to see drug taking as more dangerous and risky than they had in the 1970s. In the 1990s, however, the perceived risks of drug use have been declining. For example, in 1991 the ISR reported that 79 percent of seniors thought they ran a "great risk" if they were regular marijuana users; by 1997 only about 60 percent felt that way.

In addition, as drug use declined, youths reported greater disapproval of drug use among their friends, and peer pressure may help account for lower use rates. National ad campaigns to "just say no to drugs" and to stop friends from drinking and driving also may have helped reduce peer approval of substance abuse. In the 1990s the number of youths disapproving of drugs has declined (though a majority still disapprove); with lower disapproval has come increased usage.

It also appears that it is becoming easier to obtain drugs, especially for younger adolescents. For example, the 1992 ISR survey found that 42 percent of eighth graders said it was easy to obtain pot; three years later more than half (52 percent) claimed obtaining marijuana was easy. A recent survey of high school students also suggests that drugs are actually more readily available today than they were in the 1980s.[28] By grade 12 more than 80 percent of high school youths today say drugs are available at school, up from about 7 percent in 1989.

It should come as no surprise that a cohort of young people who perceive little peer rejection for drug use and who consider drugs risk-free and easily available will increase the frequency of their substance abuse. Today's teens may know less about the dangers of drug abuse, and as a result, they may not be deterred from experimentation. The media's antidrug messages have declined in the 1990s; at the same time, rock and rap bands have frequently placed prodrug messages in their lyrics. In addition, parents may now be unwilling or reluctant to educate their children about the dangers of substance abuse because as "baby boomers" they were drug abusers in the 1960s and 1970s.[29] The PRIDE survey found that only one-third of parents talk to kids about drugs. One-third of parents do not set clear rules, and half of those that do set rules refuse to discipline their children when they break them. The PRIDE survey also found that those children who discuss drug use with parents are much less likely to be abusers than those who receive little direction.

Are the Survey Results Accurate?

Student drug surveys must be interpreted with caution. First, it may be overly optimistic to expect that heavy crack, "crystal," and PCP users are going to cooperate with a drug use survey, especially one being conducted by a government agency. Even if willing, these students are more than likely to be absent from school during testing periods. Also, drug abusers are more likely to be forgetful and to give inaccurate accounts of their substance abuse.

Another problem is that the absentee and dropout rate among drug users is so high that it is likely that the most deviant and drug-dependent portion of the adolescent population is omitted from the sample. Research indicates that more than half of all youths arrested dropped out of school before the twelfth grade, and more than two-thirds of these arrestees are drug users.[30] Eric Wish has found that the number of juvenile detainees (those arrested and held in a lockup) who test positively for cocaine is many times higher than those reporting recent use in the ISR survey. For example, about 22 percent of young detainees in Washington, D.C., and 18 percent in Phoenix, tested positively for cocaine—a use rate many times higher than that of the general high school population.[31] The inclusion of eighth graders in the ISR sample is one way of getting around the dropout problem. Nonetheless, these surveys by their design exclude some of the most drug prone young people.

Any school- or home-based survey will be tainted by measurement problems such as underreporting, overreporting, and the omission of some high-risk cases, but these methodological and measurement problems are consistent over time and therefore do not hinder the *measurement of change* in the national substance abuse rate. That is, prior surveys also omitted dropouts and other high-risk youths and were otherwise tainted by over- and underreporting subjects. However, because the populations being measured are equivalent, any change in the substance abuse rate over time is probably genuine. So while the validity of these surveys may be in doubt, they are probably reliable indicators of trends in substance abuse.

Why Do Youths Take Drugs?

To most people, the "why" of teenage drug abuse remains a puzzle: Why do youths engage in an activity that is sure to bring them overwhelming personal problems? It is hard to imagine that even the youngest drug users are unaware of the social, physical, and legal problems associated with substance abuse. Although it is easy to understand dealers' desires for quick profits, how can we explain users' casual disregard for long- and short-term consequences?

Social Disorganization

One explanation ties drug abuse to poverty, social disorganization, and a feeling of hopelessness. The involvement in drug use by young minority group members has been tied to factors such as racial prejudice, "devalued identities," low self-esteem, poor socioeconomic status, and the stress of living in a harsh urban environment.[32] The association between drug use, race, and poverty has been linked to the high level of mistrust, negativism, and defiance found in lower socioeconomic areas.[33]

Despite a long association between social disorganization and drug use, the empirical data on the relationship between class and crime has so far been inconclusive. For example, the *National Youth Survey* (NYS), a well-respected longitudinal study of delinquent behavior conducted by Delbert Elliott and his associates, found little if any association between drug use and social class. The NYS found that drug use is higher among urban youths, but little evidence existed that minority youths or members of the lower class were more likely to abuse drugs than white youths and the more affluent.[34] Research by the Rand Corporation indicates that many drug-dealing youths (about two-thirds) had legitimate jobs at the time they were arrested for drug trafficking.[35] Therefore, it would be difficult to describe drug abusers simply as unemployed dropouts who are trying to escape the reality of a misspent youth.

Peer Pressure

Drug use is typically a peer experience. Research shows that adolescent drug abuse is highly correlated with the behavior of best friends, especially when parental supervision is weak or nonexistent.[36] Youths in deteriorated inner-city areas where

The two young girls shown here are cooperating in a drug experience. Shared feelings and a sense of intimacy lead youths to become fully enmeshed in the "drug-use subculture." Drug users do in fact have intimate and warm relationships with substance-abusing peers, which help support their habits and behaviors.

feelings of alienation and hopelessness run high often come in contact with established drug users who teach them that drugs provide an answer to their feelings of personal inadequacy and stress.[37] Perhaps they join with peers to learn the techniques of drug use; their friendships with other drug-dependent youths give them social support for their habit. Empirical research efforts show that a youth's association with friends who are substance abusers increases the probability of drug use.[38] The relationship is reciprocal: adolescent substance abusers seek out friends who engage in these behaviors, and associating with drug abusers leads to increased levels of drug abuse.

Peer networks that support drug use may be the most significant influence on long-term substance abuse. Shared feelings and a sense of intimacy lead youths to become fully enmeshed in what has been described as the "drug-use subculture."[39] Research now indicates that drug users do in fact have intimate and warm relationships with substance-abusing peers who help support their habits and behaviors.[40] This street identity and lifestyle provide users with a clear role they can fulfill, activities and behaviors they enjoy, and an opportunity for attaining social status among their peers.[41] One reason it is so difficult to treat hard core users is that quitting drugs means leaving the "fast life" of the streets.

Family Factors

Another explanation is that drug users have a poor family life and a troubled adolescence. Studies have found that the majority of drug users have had an unhappy childhood, which included harsh physical punishment and parental neglect and rejection.[42] The drug abuse and family quality association may involve both racial and gender differences: females and whites who were abused as children are more likely to have alcohol and drug arrests as adults; abuse was less likely to affect drug use in males and African Americans.[43] It is also common to find substance abusers within large families and with parents who are divorced, separated, or absent.[44]

Social psychologists suggest that drug abuse patterns may also result from the observation of parental drug use.[45] Youths who learn that drugs provide pleasurable sensations may be the most likely to experiment with illegal substances; a habit may develop if the user experiences lower anxiety, fear, and tension levels.[46] Research shows, for example, that gang members raised in families with a history of drug use were more likely than other gang members to use cocaine and to use it seriously. In contrast, severe family distress was not related to onset, duration, or seriousness of cocaine use in either males or females.[47] Observing drug abuse may be a more important cause of personal drug abuse than other family-related social problems.

Other family factors associated with teen drug abuse include ineffective discipline skills including parental conflict over child-rearing practices, failure to set rules, and unrealistic demands followed by harsh physical punishments. Low parental attachment, rejection, and excessive family conflict have all been linked to subsequent adolescent substance abuse.[48]

Genetic Factors

The association between parental drug abuse and adolescent behavior may have a genetic basis. Research has shown that the biological children of alcoholics reared by nonalcoholic adoptive parents more often develop alcohol problems than the natural children of the adoptive parents.[49] A number of studies comparing alcoholism among identical and fraternal twins have found that the degree of concordance (both siblings behaving identically) is twice as high among the identical twin groups.[50]

A genetic basis for drug abuse is also supported by recent evidence showing that future substance abuse problems can be predicted by behavior exhibited as early as six years of age. The individual traits predicting future abuse occur before and are independent from peer relations and environmental influences.[51]

Emotional Problems

Not all drug-abusing youths reside in lower-class urban areas; the problem of middle-class substance abuse is very real. To explain drug abuse across social classes, some experts have linked drug use to personality disturbance and emotional problems that can strike youths in any economic class. Psychodynamic explanations of substance abuse suggest that drugs help youths control or express unconscious needs and impulses. Some psychoanalysts believe adolescents who internalize their problems may use drugs and alcohol to reduce their feelings of inadequacy and insecurity. Introverted people may use drugs as an escape from real or imagined feelings of inferiority or insecurity.[52] Another view is that adolescents who externalize their problems and blame others for their perceived failures are likely to engage in antisocial behaviors, including substance abuse. Research exists supportive of each of these positions.[53]

addiction prone personality
The view that the cause of substance abuse can be traced to a personality that has a compulsion for mood-altering drugs.

Drug abusers are also believed to exhibit psychopathic or sociopathic behavior characteristics, forming what is called an **addiction prone personality.**[54] Drinking alcohol may reflect a teen's need to remain dependent on an overprotective mother or an effort to reduce the emotional turmoil of adolescence.[55]

Research on the psychological characteristics of narcotics abusers does, in fact, reveal the presence of a significant degree of personal pathology. Personality testing of known users suggests that a significant percentage suffer from psychotic disorders, including various levels of schizophrenia. Studies have found that addicts suffer personality disorders characterized by a weak ego, a low frustration tolerance, anxiety, and fantasies of omnipotence. Up to half of all drug abusers may also be diagnosed with antisocial personality disorder (ASPD), which is defined as a pervasive pattern of disregard for and violation of the rights of others.[56]

Problem Behavior Syndrome

For many adolescents substance abuse is just one of many problem behaviors that begin early in life and remain throughout the life course.[57] Longitudinal studies show that youths who abuse drugs are maladjusted, alienated, emotionally distressed, and have many social problems.[58] Having a deviant lifestyle means associating with delinquent peers, living in a family in which parents and siblings abuse drugs, having a low commitment to education, being alienated from the dominant values of society, and engaging in delinquent behaviors at an early age.[59] Youths who abuse drugs lack commitment to religious values, disdain education, and spend most of their time in peer activities.[60] Youths who take drugs do poorly in school, have high dropout rates, and maintain their drug use after they leave school.[61]

Gateway Drugs

gateway drug
A substance that leads to use of more serious drugs; alcohol use has long been thought to lead to more serious drug abuse.

Alcohol has long been considered a **gateway drug.** That is, drug involvement begins with drinking alcohol (or smoking) at an early age, which progresses to experimentation with marijuana and hashish and finally to cocaine and even heroin. Although the gateway concept is still being debated, there is little disagreement that serious drug users are also heavily involved with alcohol.[62] Most recreational users

Losers and burnouts are failures at both drug dealing and crime. They do not have the savvy to join gangs or groups and instead begin committing unplanned, opportunistic crimes that increase their chances of arrest. Their heavy drug use both increases their risk of apprehension and decreases their value for organized drug-distribution networks. Being stoned all the time, they risk serious injuries and death.

do not progress to "hard stuff," but few addicts begin their drug involvement with narcotics. Most first experiment with recreational drugs. By implication, if teen smoking and drinking could be reduced, the gateway to hard drugs would be narrowed.

Research on serious adolescent drug users in Miami found that youths who began their substance abuse careers early—by experimenting with alcohol at age 7, getting drunk at age 8, having alcohol with an adult present by age 9, and becoming regular drinkers by the time they were eleven years old—later became crack users.[63] Drinking with an adult present, presumably a parent, was a significant precursor of future substance abuse and delinquency.[64] Survey data substantiate the gateway model. For example, as Figure 11.3 shows, drug users in New York City were more likely to progress from alcohol to marijuana to hard drugs than to begin their substance abuse careers in any other way.

Rational Choice

Youths may choose to use drugs and alcohol because they want to enjoy their anticipated effects. They want to get high, relax, improve their creativity, escape reality, and increase their sexual responsiveness. Research indicates that adolescent alcohol abusers believe getting high will make them powerful, increase their sexual

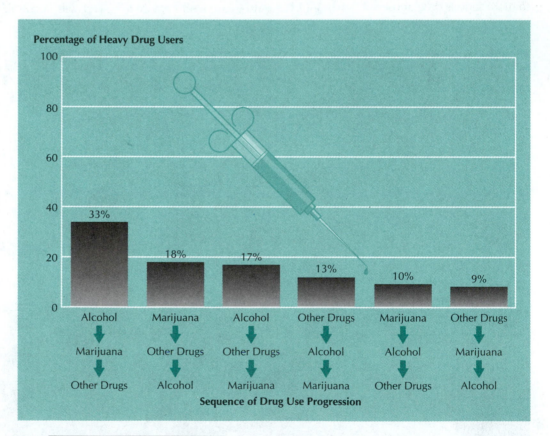

FIGURE 11.3

Sequence of Drug Use Progression by Heavy Drug Users, New York City, 1984–1987 (N=285)

Source: Mary Ellen Mackesy-Amiti, Michael Fendrich, and Paul Goldstein, "Sequence of Drug Use among Serious Drug Users: Typical vs. Atypical Progression," *Drug and Alcohol Dependence* 45: 185–96 (1997). Figure created by the Center for Substance Abuse Research, College Park, Maryland.

performance, and facilitate their social behavior; they care little about negative future consequences.[65] Substance abuse, then, may be a function of the rational, albeit mistaken, belief that substance abuse benefits the user.

Adolescents Who Use Drugs

What are the patterns of teenage drug use? Are all abusers similar, or are there different types of drug involvement? Research indicates that drug-involved youths do take on different roles, lifestyles, and behavior patterns, some of which are described in the next sections.[66]

Adolescents Who Distribute Small Amounts of Drugs

Many adolescents who use and distribute small amounts of drugs do not commit any other serious delinquent acts. Most of these petty dealers occasionally sell marijuana, "crystal," and PCP to support their own drug use. Their customers are almost always known to them and include friends, relatives, and acquaintances. Deals are arranged over the phone, in school, or at public hangouts and meeting places; however, the actual distribution takes place in more private arenas such as at home or in cars.

Petty dealers do not consider themselves "seriously" involved in drugs. One girl commented:

> I don't consider it dealing, I'll sell hits of speed to my friends and joints and nickel bags [of marijuana] to my friends, but that's not dealing.

Included in Inciardi, Horowitz, and Pottieger's sample of crack-using adolescents in Miami was Erica, a sixteen-year-old who modeled, played field hockey, and was a cheerleader. "I'm not really *in* the crack business," she told the investigators. "I just know someone who is and help him out once in a while." When Erica is paid for her services with crack, she may sell it to her friends.[67]

Petty dealers are insulated from the juvenile justice system because their activities rarely result in apprehension and sanction. In fact, few adults notice their activities because these adolescents are able to maintain a relatively conventional lifestyle. In several jurisdictions, however, agents of the justice system are cooperating in the development of educational programs to provide nonusers with the skills to resist the "sales pitch" of petty dealers they meet at school or in the neighborhood.

Adolescents Who Frequently Sell Drugs

A small number of adolescents, most often multiple-drug users or heroin or cocaine users, are high-rate dealers who bridge the gap between adult drug distributors and the adolescent user. Though many are daily users, they are not strung-out junkies, and they take part in many normal adolescent activities, including going to school and socializing with friends.

Frequent dealers often have adults who "front" for them—that is, sell them drugs for cash. The teenagers then distribute the drugs to friends and acquaintances. They return most of the proceeds to the supplier, keeping a commission for themselves.

They may also keep drugs for their personal use, and, in fact, some consider their drug dealing as a way of "getting high for free." Winston, age 17, told Inciardi and his associates:

> I sell the cracks for money and for cracks. The man, he give me this *much*. I sell most of it and I get the rest for me. I like this much. Every day I do this.[68]

Inciardi and his associates found that frequent dealers were also likely to be regular users of crack. About 80 percent of the youths who dealt crack regularly were daily users.[69]

Frequent dealers are more likely to sell drugs in public and can be seen in known drug hangouts in parks, schools, or other public places. Deals occur irregularly, so the chance of apprehension is not significant, nor is the payoff substantial. A recent survey by Robert MacCoun and Peter Reuter found that drug dealers make about $30 per hour when they are working and clear on average about $2,000 per month. These amounts are certainly greater than most dealers could hope to have earned in legitimate jobs, but they are not enough to afford a steady stream of luxuries. Most small-time dealers also hold conventional jobs.[70]

Teenage Drug Dealers Who Commit Other Delinquent Acts

A more serious type of drug-involved youth is the one who uses and distributes multiple substances and commits both property and violent crimes. These youngsters make up about 2 percent of the teenage population, but they may commit up to 40 percent of the robberies and assaults and about 60 percent of all teenage felony thefts and drug sales. Few gender or racial differences exist among these youths: girls are as likely as boys to become high-rate, persistent drug-involved offenders, white youths as likely as black youths, middle-class adolescents raised outside cities as likely as lower-class city children.[71]

In cities these youths frequently are hired by older dealers to act as street-level drug runners. Each member of a crew of three to twelve youths will handle small quantities of drugs, perhaps three bags of heroin, which are received on consignment and sold on the street; the supplier receives 50 to 70 percent of the drug's street value. The crew members also act as lookouts, recruiters, and guards. Although they may be recreational drug users themselves, crew members refrain from using addictive drugs such as heroin; some major suppliers will only hire "drug-free" youths to make street deals. Between drug sales, the young dealers commit robberies, burglaries, and other thefts.

Most youngsters in the street drug trade have few success skills and either terminate their dealing or become drug-dependent. A few, however, develop excellent entrepreneurial skills. Those that are rarely apprehended by police earn the trust of their older contacts and advance in the drug business. They develop their own crews and handle more than half a million dollars a year in the drug business. Some are able to afford the BMW or Mercedes, the fine jewelry, and the expensive clothes that signify success in the drug trade.

Drug-Involved Gangs

Youths involved in teenage gangs commonly become serious suppliers of narcotics. At one time, primacy in the U.S. drug trade was maintained by traditional organized crime families, which used their control of the Asian heroin market as a principal source of mob income. The monopoly of these families, however, has been broken. Efforts to jail crime bosses, coupled with the popularity and growth of cocaine and synthetic drugs (which are less easily controlled by a single source), have shattered this distribution monopoly. Stepping into the void have been local gangs who use their drug income to expand their base and power. Prominent among these are biker gangs such as the Hell's Angels, Outlaws, and Bandidos, who have become active in the manufacture and distribution of synthetics. The Jamaican Posse and Latino gangs control a large part of the east coast cocaine business, and Chinese groups now import much of the nation's heroin supply.

Teenage gangs have also emerged as major players in the drug trade. Most prominent are the two largest Los Angeles youth gangs, the Bloods and the Crips, whose total membership is estimated to be more than twenty thousand (actual membership is impossible to determine).

In Los Angeles itself, these drug-dealing gangs maintain "rock houses" or "stash houses." The houses receive drug shipments arranged by gang members who have the overseas connections and financial backing needed to wholesale drugs. The wholesalers pay the gang for permission to deal in their territory and hire members as a security force. Lower-echelon gang members help transport the drugs and work the houses, retailing cocaine and other drugs to neighborhood youths. Each member makes a profit for every ounce of "rock" sold. Police estimate that youths who work in "rock houses" will earn $700 and up for a twelve-hour shift.[72]

There is still some question of the role of gangs in drug dealing. As you may recall, some gang experts now question whether gangs are responsible for as much drug dealing as the media would have us believe. Others show that tightly organized "super" gangs that control citywide drug dealing are being phased out and replaced with loosely organized neighborhood groups. The turbulent environment of drug dealing is better handled by flexible, informal organizations than by rigid, vertically organized gangs with a leader who is far removed from the action.[73]

Losers and Burnouts

Some drug-involved youths are losers and burnouts, failures at both dealing and crime. They do not have the savvy to join gangs or groups and instead begin committing unplanned, opportunistic crimes that increase their chances of arrest. Their heavy drug use increases their risk of apprehension and decreases their value for organized drug distribution networks.

Drug-involved "losers" can earn a living by steering customers to a seller in a "copping" area, touting drug availability for a dealer, or acting as a lookout. However, they are not considered trustworthy or deft enough to handle drugs or money. They may bungle other criminal acts, which solidifies their reputation as undesirable:

> Buster is almost always stoned on ludes and beer. He is continually getting caught robbing and is in and out of treatment centers. Once he and another boy robbed a jewelry store. They smashed the window with a brick and the window fell on them, knocking them both out. The store owner called the cops and an ambulance.[74]

Though these persistent offenders get involved in drugs at a very early age, they receive little attention from the justice system until they have developed an extensive arrest record. By then they are approaching the end of their minority and will either spontaneously desist or become so deeply entrapped in the drug–crime subculture that little can be done to treat or deter their illegal activities.

About two-thirds of substance-abusing youths continue to use drugs after they reach adulthood, but about half of them desist from other criminal activities. Those who persist in both substance abuse and crime as adults maintain these characteristics:

- They come from poor families.
- Other criminals are members of their families.
- They do poorly in school.
- They started using drugs and committing other delinquent acts at a relatively early age.
- They use multiple types of drugs and commit crimes frequently.
- They have few opportunities in late adolescence to participate in legitimate and rewarding adult activities.[75]

Some evidence exists that these drug-using persisters have low nonverbal IQs and poor physical coordination. Nonetheless, there is little scientific evidence to explain why some drug-abusing youths drop out of crime while others remain active into their adulthood.

Drug Use and Delinquency

An association between drug use and delinquency has been established, and this connection can take a number of different forms. Crime may be an instrument of the drug trade: Violence erupts when rival drug gangs use their automatic weapons to settle differences and establish territorial monopolies. In New York City authorities report that crack gangs will burn down their rival's headquarters, even if people living on the premises are not connected to the drug trade. It is estimated that between 35 and 40 percent of New York's homicides are drug-related.[76]

The association may be economically motivated. Drug users may commit crimes to pay for their habits.[77] One study conducted in Miami found that 573 narcotics user *annually* committed more than 200,000 crimes to obtain cash to purchase drugs, including 6,000 robberies, 6,700 burglaries, and 70,000 larceny offenses. Similar research with a sample of 356 addicts accounted for 118,000 crimes annually.[78] If such proportions hold true, the nation's estimated 700,000 heroin addicts alone may be committing more than one hundred million crimes each year, and this estimate ignores the criminal activity of cocaine and crack abusers.

Drug users may be more willing to take risks because their inhibitions are lowered by substance abuse. Cities with high rates of cocaine abuse are also more likely to experience higher levels of armed robbery; burglary rates are unaffected by cocaine use. It is possible that crack and cocaine users are more willing to engage in a risky armed robbery to get immediate cash than a burglary, which requires more planning and effort.[79]

The relationship between alcohol and drug abuse and delinquency has been substantiated by a number of research studies. Some have found that youths who abuse alcohol are also the ones most likely to engage in violence; later, as adults, those with long histories of drinking are also more likely to report violent offending patterns.[80] The federal government's Drug Use Forecasting (DUF) program tests arrestees in major cities to determine their drug involvement. The results have been startling. In some cities, such as San Diego, New York, and Philadelphia, more than 70 percent of all arrestees, both male and female, test positively for some drug, and this association crosses both gender and racial boundaries.[81]

There is also evidence that incarcerated youths are much more likely to be involved in substance abuse than adolescents in the general population. For example, research by David Cantor on the drug use of incarcerated youths in Washington, D.C. found their drug involvement more than double that of nonincarcerated area youths.[82]

Drugs and Chronic Offending

It is possible that most delinquents are not actually drug users but that police are just more likely to apprehend muddled-headed substance abusers than clear-thinking "abstainers." A second, and probably more plausible, interpretation of the existing data is that the drug abuse–crime connection is so powerful because many delinquents and criminals are in fact substance abusers. Some recent research by Bruce Johnson and his associates confirms this suspicion. Using data from a nationally drawn self-report survey, these researchers found that less than 2 percent of the youths who responded to the survey (a) report using cocaine or heroin and (b) commit two or more index crimes each year. However, these drug-abusing adolescents accounted for 40 to 60 percent of all the index crimes (robbery, theft, drug sales) reported in the sample. Less than one-quarter of these hard core delinquents committed crimes solely to support a drug habit. These data suggest that a small core of substance-abusing adolescents commits a significant proportion of all serious crimes. It is also evident that a behavior, drug abuse, that develops later in adolescence influences the frequency and extent of delinquent activity through the life course.[83]

The relationship between drug abuse and chronic offending is aptly illustrated by Inciardi, Horowitz, and Pottienger's interviews with crack-involved youths in Miami. The 254 kids in their sample reported committing an astounding 223,439 criminal offenses during the twelve months prior to their interviews. It is not surprising, considering that they averaged 879 offenses each, that 87 percent of the sample had been arrested. The greater the involvement in the crack business, the greater the likelihood of committing violent crime. About 74 percent of the hard core dealers committed robbery, and 17 percent engaged in assault. Only 12 percent of the nondealers committed robbery, and 4 percent engaged in assault.

Explaining Drug Use and Delinquency

The general association between delinquency and drug use has been well established in a variety of cultures.[84] It is still far from certain, however, whether (a) drug use *causes* delinquency, (b) delinquent behavior patterns *lead* youths to engage in substance abuse, or (c) both drug abuse and delinquency are *functions* of some other factor that is responsible for both behaviors.[85]

Some of the most sophisticated research on this topic has been conducted by Delbert Elliott and his associates at the Institute of Behavioral Science at the University of Colorado.[86] Using data from the National Youth Survey, a longitudinal study of self-reported delinquency and drug use, Elliott and his colleagues David Huizinga and Scott Menard found a strong association between delinquency and drug use.[87] However, they also found that the direction of the relationship is unclear. As a general rule, drug abuse appears to be a *type* of delinquent behavior and not a *cause* of delinquency. Most youths become involved in delinquent acts before they are initiated into drugs later in their adolescence; it is difficult, therefore, to conclude that drug use causes crime.

According to the Elliott research, both drug use and delinquency seem to reflect a developmental problem. Rather than causing one another, drug use and delinquency are part of a disturbed socialization and lifestyle. This research reveals some important associations between substance abuse and delinquency:

1. Alcohol abuse seems to be a cause of marijuana and other drug abuse because (a) most drug users started with alcohol and (b) youths who abstain from alcohol almost never take drugs.
2. Marijuana use is a cause of multiple-drug use: about 95 percent of youths who use more serious drugs, such as crack, started on pot; only 5 percent of serious drug users never smoked pot.
3. Youths who commit felonies started off with minor delinquent acts. Few (1 percent) delinquents report committing felonies only.

The Elliott research has been supported by a number of other studies that also indicate that delinquency and substance abuse are actually part of a general pattern of deviance or problem behavior syndrome. Helene Raskin White, Robert Padina, and Randy LaGrange found that both forms of deviance are related to symptoms of social disturbance, such as association with an antisocial peer group and educational failure.[88] Similar research by Eric Wish also shows a pattern of deviance escalation in which troubled youths start by committing petty crimes and drinking alcohol and then proceed to both harder drugs and more serious crimes. Both their drug abuse and the delinquency are part of an urban underclass lifestyle involving limited education, few job skills, unstable families, few social skills, and patterns of law violations.[89]

It is also possible that drug abuse and delinquency have independent causes. White has also found that the onset of both delinquency and drug abuse can be traced to the "preferred" deviant behavior of peers: youths whose friends are substance abusers are more likely to abuse substances themselves; adolescents whose peers engage in delinquent behavior are more likely to become delinquents.[90]

By implication, these studies indicate that restricting or reducing substance abuse may have little effect on delinquency rates because drugs are a *symptom* and not a *cause* of youthful misbehavior.

Drug Control Strategies

The United States is in the midst of a well-publicized "war on drugs." Billions are being spent each year to reduce the importation of drugs, deter would-be drug dealers, and treat users. Yet, as most of us know, drug control efforts have been less than successful. Although the overall incidence of drug use has declined, drug use has concentrated in the nation's poorest neighborhoods, with a consequent association between substance abuse and crime.

A number of different drug control strategies have been tried with varying degrees of success. Some are designed to deter drug use by stopping the flow of drugs into the country, apprehending and punishing dealers, and cracking down on street-level drug deals. Another approach is to prevent drug use by educating would-be users and convincing them to "say no to drugs." A third approach is to treat users so they can terminate their addictions. Some of the more important of these efforts are discussed in the following sections.

Law Enforcement Efforts

A variety of law enforcement strategies are aimed at both reducing the supply of drugs and, at the same time, deterring would-be users from drug abuse.

Source Control   One approach to drug control is to deter the sale and importation of drugs through the systematic apprehension of large-volume drug dealers, coupled with enforcement of strict drug laws that carry heavy penalties. This approach is designed to punish known drug dealers and users and to deter those who are considering entering the drug trade.

A major effort has been made to cut off supplies of drugs by destroying overseas crops and arresting members of drug cartels; this approach is known as *source control*. The federal government has been encouraging exporting nations to step up efforts to destroy drug crops and to prosecute dealers. Three South American nations—Peru, Bolivia, and Colombia—have agreed to coordinate control efforts with the United States. However, translating words into deeds is a formidable task. Drug lords are willing and able to fight back through intimidation, violence, and corruption. The United States was forced to invade Panama with twenty thousand troops in 1989 to stop its leader, General Manuel Noriega, from trafficking in cocaine.

Adding to control problems is the fact that the drug trade is an important source of revenue for drug-producing countries and destroying it undermines their economy. For example, about 60 percent of the raw coca leaves used to make cocaine for the United States are grown in Peru. The drug trade supports two hundred thousand Peruvians and brings in over $3 billion annually. In Bolivia, which supplies 30 percent of the raw cocaine for the U.S. market, three hundred thousand people are supported with profits from the drug trade; coca is the country's single leading export. About 20 percent of Colombia's overseas exports are made by drug cartels, which refine the coca leaves into cocaine before shipping it to the United States.[91] And even if the government of one nation is willing to cooperate in vigorous drug suppression efforts, suppliers in other nations, eager to cash in on the seller's market, would be encouraged to turn more acreage over to coca, poppy, or marijuana production.

Border Control   Law enforcement efforts have also been directed at interdicting drug supplies as they enter the country. Border patrols and military personnel using sophisticated hardware have been involved in massive interdiction efforts; many impressive billion-dollar seizures have been made. It is estimated that between one-quarter and one-third of the annual cocaine supply shipped to the United States is seized by drug enforcement agencies. Yet U.S. borders are so vast and unprotected that meaningful interdiction is impossible; between 240 and 340 tons of cocaine and 33 tons of heroin are imported each year with a street value of $38 billion.[92]

If all importation were ended, homegrown marijuana and lab-made drugs, such as "crystal," LSD, and PCP, could become the drugs of choice. Even now, their easy availability and relatively low cost are increasing their popularity among teenagers; they are a $10 billion business in the United States today.

Targeting Dealers   Law enforcement agencies have also made a concerted effort to focus on drug trafficking at the national, state, and local levels. Efforts have been made to bust large-scale drug rings. The long-term consequence has been to decentralize drug dealing and to encourage teenage gangs to become major suppliers. Ironically, it has proven easier for federal agents to infiltrate and prosecute traditional organized crime groups than to take on drug-dealing youth gangs.

Police can also target, intimidate, and arrest street-level dealers and users in an effort to make drug use so much of a hassle that consumption is cut back and the crime rate reduced. Some street-level enforcement efforts have had success, but others are considered failures. "Drug sweeps" have clogged courts and correctional facilities with petty offenders while proving a costly drain on police resources. These sweeps are also suspected of creating a displacement effect: stepped-up efforts to curb drug dealing in one area or city may simply encourage dealers to seek out friendlier "business" territory.[93] People arrested, tried, and punished on drug-related charges are the fastest growing segment of both the juvenile and adult justice systems. National surveys have found that juvenile court judges are prone to use a get-tough approach on drug-involved offenders. They are more likely to be adjudicated, waived to adult court, and receive out-of-home placements than other categories of delinquent offenders, including those who commit violent crimes.[94] Despite these efforts, juvenile drug use continues to grow, indicating that a get-tough policy is not sufficient to deter or eliminate drug use.

Education Strategies

Another approach to reducing teenage substance abuse relies on school-based educational programs. School districts have included drug education programs as a standard part of their curriculum. Drug education now begins in kindergarten and extends through the twelfth grade. More than 80 percent of public school districts include these components in all of their schools: teaching students about the causes and effects of alcohol, drug, and tobacco use; teaching students to resist peer pressure; and referring students for counseling and treatment outside the educational system.[95] Education programs such as Project ALERT, based in middle schools in California and Oregon, appear to be successful in training youths to avoid recreational drugs and to resist peer pressure to use cigarettes and alcohol.[96] The most widely used drug prevention program, DARE, is discussed in the Policy and Practice box entitled "Drug Abuse Resistance Education."

Community Strategies

Another type of drug control effort relies on the involvement of local community groups. Representatives of various local government agencies, churches, civic organizations, and similar institutions are being brought together to create drug prevention awareness programs. Their activities often include creation of drug-free school zones, which encourage police to keep drug dealers away from the areas near schools; Neighborhood Watch programs, which are geared to spotting and reporting drug dealers; citizen patrols, which frighten dealers away from children in public housing projects; and community centers, which provide an alternative to the street culture.

Community-based programs reach out to high-risk youths, getting them involved in after-school programs; offering family and individual counseling sessions; delivering clothing, food, and medical care when needed; and encouraging school achievement through tutoring and other services. Community programs also sponsor drug-free activities involving the arts, clubs, and athletics. Evaluations of community programs have shown that they may encourage antidrug attitudes and help insulate participating youths from an environment that encourages drugs.[97] The Policy and Practice box entitled "Helping Families Prevent Teenage Drug Use" describes two successful community drug programs.

DRUG ABUSE RESISTANCE EDUCATION

The most widely known drug education program, Drug Abuse Resistance Education (DARE), is an elementary school course designed to give students the skills to resist peer pressure to experiment with tobacco, drugs, and alcohol. It is unique because uniformed police officers carry the antidrug message to students before they enter junior high school. The program focuses on five major areas:

- Providing accurate information about tobacco, alcohol, and drugs
- Teaching students techniques to resist peer pressure
- Teaching students respect for the law and for law enforcers
- Giving students ideas for alternatives to drug use
- Building the self-esteem of students

DARE is based on the concept that young people need specific analytical and social skills to resist peer pressure and to say no to drugs. Instructors work with children to raise their self-esteem, provide them with decision-making tools, and help them identify positive alternatives to substance abuse. Millions of students have already taken the DARE program. More than 40 percent of all school districts incorporate assistance from local law enforcement agencies in their drug-prevention programming. New community policing strategies commonly incorporate the DARE program in their efforts to provide services to local neighborhoods at the grassroots level.

DARE is quite popular with both schools and police agencies, but a highly sophisticated evaluation of the program by Dennis Rosenbaum and his associates found that it had only a marginal impact on student drug use and attitudes. DARE may work better in some settings and with some groups than others, but Rosenbaum found it had little overall effect on substance abuse rates. Although national evaluations have questioned the validity of DARE, it continues to be employed in a great many school districts around the United States.

Sources: Dennis Rosenbaum, Robert Flwewlling, Susan Bailey, Chris Ringwalt, and Deanna Wilkinson, "Cops in the Classroom: A Longitudinal Evaluation of Drug Abuse Resistance Education (DARE), *Journal of Research in Crime and Delinquency* 31:3–31 (1994); David Carter, *Community Policing and D.A.R.E.: A Practitioner's Perspective* (Washington, D.C.: Bureau of Justice Assistance, 1995), p. 2; Judi Carpenter, *Public School District Survey on Safe, Disciplined and Drug-Free Schools* (Washington, D.C.: U.S. Government Printing Office, 1992), p. 111.

Treatment Strategies

multisystemic treatment (MST)
Addresses a variety of family, peer, and psychological problems by focusing on problem solving and communication skills training.

Several approaches are used to treat known users. Some efforts stem from the perspective that users have low self-esteem; these use various techniques to build up the user's sense of himself or herself. Some make use of traditional psychological counseling, and others, such as the **multisystemic treatment (MST)** technique developed by psychologist Scott Henggeler, direct attention to a variety of family, peer, and psychological problems by focusing on problem solving and communication skills.[98] Henggeler has found that adolescent abusers who have gone through MST programs are significantly less likely to recidivate than youths in traditional counseling services.[99]

Another approach has been to involve users in outdoor activities, wilderness training, and after-school community programs.[100]

Drug Abuse Resistance Education (DARE) is an elementary school course designed to give students the skills for resisting peer pressure to experiment with tobacco, drugs, and alcohol. It is unique because it employs uniformed police officers to carry the anti-drug message to the students before they enter junior high school. Critics question whether the program is actually as effective as advertised.

More intensive efforts use group therapy in which leaders, many of whom have been substance abusers, try to give users the skills and support that can help them reject the social pressure to use drugs. These programs are based on the Alcoholics Anonymous philosophy that users must find within themselves the strength to stay clean and that peer support from those who understand their experiences can be a successful way to achieve a drug-free life.

Residential programs are used with more heavily involved drug abusers, and a large network of drug treatment units geared to juveniles has developed. Some are detoxification units that use medical procedures to wean patients from the more addicting drugs. Others are therapeutic communities that attempt to deal with the psychological causes of drug use. Hypnosis, aversion therapy (getting users to associate drugs with unpleasant sensations, such as nausea), counseling, biofeedback, and other techniques are often used.

Little evidence exists that these residential programs, despite their good intentions, can efficiently terminate teenage substance abuse. Many are restricted to families whose health insurance will pay for short-term residential care; when the

HELPING FAMILIES PREVENT TEENAGE DRUG USE

One approach to teen drug prevention is to focus on strengthening families and helping them to aid their children to resist drugs. Two successful programs are described here:

STRENGTHENING FAMILIES

The Strengthening Families program contains three elements: a parent training program, a children's skills training program, and a family skills training program. In each of the fourteen weekly sessions, parents and children are trained separately in the first hour. During the second hour, parents and children come together in the family skills training portion. Afterward, the families share dinner and a film or other entertainment.

Parent training improves parenting skills and reduces substance abuse by parents. Children's skills training decreases children's negative behaviors and increases their socially acceptable behaviors through work with a program therapist. Family skills training improves the family environment by involving both generations in learning and practicing their new behaviors.

This intervention approach has been evaluated in a variety of settings and with several racial and ethnic groups. The primary outcomes of the program include reductions in family conflict, improvement in family communication and organization, and reductions in youth conduct disorders, aggressiveness, and substance abuse.

FOCUS ON FAMILIES

Focus on Families is a selective program for parents receiving methadone treatment and for their children. The primary goal is to reduce parents' use of illegal drugs by teaching them skills for relapse prevention and coping. Parents are also taught how to manage their families better. The parent training consists of a five-hour family retreat and thirty-two parent training sessions of one and a half hours each. Children attend twelve of the sessions to practice developmentally appropriate skills with their parents.

Session topics include family goal-setting, relapse prevention, family communication, family management, creating family expectations about alcohol and other drugs, teaching children skills (such as problem solving and resisting drug offers), and helping children succeed in school. Booster sessions and case management services also are provided.

Early results indicate that parents' drug use is dramatically lowered and parenting skills significantly better than are seen in control groups; the program's effects on children have not yet been assessed, however.

Source: National Institute of Drug Abuse, *Preventing Drug Use among Children and Adolescents* (Washington, D.C.: National Institute of Drug Abuse, 1997).

insurance coverage ends, the children are released, even though their treatment program is not completed. Adolescents do not often enter these programs voluntarily, and most have little motivation to change.[101] A stay can help stigmatize residents as "druggies" and "addicts" even though they never used hard drugs; while in treatment, they may be introduced to hard core users with whom they will associate upon release. Evaluations of residential programs show that abuse is sometimes curtailed during the residential phase of treatment but once residence terminates and the offender is returned to the community the drug abuse continues. Even programs that feature intensive aftercare treatment show little evidence that substance abuse can be reversed through correctional treatment.[102]

The president has appointed you as the new "Drug Czar" to lead the fight against drugs. You have $10 billion under your control with which to wage a campaign against drugs. You know that drug use is unacceptably high, especially among poor, inner-city youths, that a great deal of all criminal behavior is drug-related, and that drug dealing gangs are expanding around the United States.

At an open hearing, drug control experts express their policy strategies. One group favors putting the money into hiring new law enforcement agents who will patrol borders, target large dealers, and make drug raids here and abroad. They also call for such get-tough measures as the creation of strict drug laws, the mandatory waiver of young drug dealers to the adult court system, and the death penalty for drug-related gang killings.

A second group believes the best way to deal with drugs is to spend the money on community treatment programs, expanding the number of beds in drug detoxification units and funding research on how to clinically reduce drug dependency.

A third group argues that neither punishment nor treatment can restrict teenage drug use and that the best course is to educate at-risk youths about the dangers of substance abuse and then legalize all drugs but control their distribution. This course of action will help both to reduce crime and violence among drug users and to balance the national debt, as drugs could be heavily taxed.

- Should drugs be legalized?
- Can law enforcement strategies reduce drug consumption?
- Is treatment an effective drug control technique?

What Does the Future Hold?

The United States appears willing to go to great lengths to fight the drug war. Law enforcement efforts, along with the institution of prevention programs and drug treatment projects, have been stepped up (see the Case in Point). Yet all drug control strategies are doomed to fail as long as youths want to take drugs and dealers find that their sales efforts are a lucrative source of income. Prevention, deterrence, and treatment strategies ignore the core reasons for the drug problem: poverty, hopelessness, boredom, alienation, and family disruption. As the gap between rich and poor widens and the opportunities for legitimate advancement decrease, it should come as no surprise that adolescent drug use continues. It is a sad fact that a smaller percentage of the poor and minority group members are attending college today than were ten years ago. The social failures of American society are being translated into teenage substance abuse.

Some commentators have called for the **legalization of drugs.** This approach can have the short-term effect of reducing the association between drug use and crime (since, presumably, the cost of drugs would decrease), but it may have grave

legalization of drugs
Decriminalizing drug use to reduce the association between drug use and crime.

social consequences. Drug use would most certainly increase, creating an overflow of unproductive, drug-dependent people who must be cared for by the rest of society. The problems of teenage alcoholism should serve as a warning of what can happen when controlled substances are made readily available. However, the implications of drug decriminalization should be further studied: what effect would a policy of partial decriminalization (for example, legalizing small amounts of marijuana) have on drug use rates? Does a get-tough policy on drugs help to "widen the net"? Are there alternatives to the criminalization of drugs that could help reduce their use?[103] The Rand Corporation study of drug dealing in Washington, D.C. suggests that law enforcement efforts can have little influence on drug abuse rates as long as dealers can earn more than the minimal salaries they might earn in the legitimate world. Only by improving job prospects and giving youths legitimate future alternatives can hard core users be made to desist and willingly forgo drug use.[104]

SUMMARY

Drug abuse has been closely linked to juvenile delinquency. Among the most popular drugs are marijuana; cocaine and its derivative, crack; "crystal"; LSD; and PCP. However, the most commonly used drug is alcohol, which contributes to almost one hundred thousand deaths per year.

Self-report surveys indicate that after years of decline more teenagers are using drugs today than earlier in the decade. In addition, surveys of arrestees indicate that a significant proportion of teenagers are current drug users and that many are high school dropouts. The number of drug users may be even higher because surveys of teen abusers may be missing the most delinquent and drug-abusing youths.

A variety of youths use drugs. Some are occasional users who might sell to friends. Others are seriously involved in both drug abuse and delinquency; many of these are gang members. There are also "losers" who filter in and out of the juvenile justice system. A small percent-

age of teenage users remain involved with drugs into their adulthood.

Despite years of research, it is not certain whether drug abuse causes delinquency. Many adolescents who break the law later abuse drugs. Some experts believe there is a "common cause" for both delinquency and drug abuse, such as alienation, anger, and rage.

Many attempts have been made to control the drug trade. Some have attempted to inhibit the importation of drugs from overseas, others are aimed at closing down major drug rings, and a few have tried to stop street-level dealing. There have also been attempts to treat known users through rehabilitation programs and to reduce juvenile use by educational efforts. Communities beset by drug problems have mounted grassroots drives to reduce the incidence of drug abuse. So far, these efforts have not been totally successful, although the overall use of drugs may have, in fact, declined somewhat.

KEY TERMS

substance abuse
hashish
marijuana
cocaine
freebase
crack
heroin
addict

alcohol
anesthetic drugs
inhalants
sedatives
tranquilizers
hallucinogens
stimulants
anabolic steroids

addiction prone
  personality
gateway drug
multisystemic treatment
  (MST)
legalization of drugs

INFOTRAC COLLEGE EDITION EXERCISES

Read the following article from InfoTrac College Edition:

Field: juvenile crime bill doesn't do justice to drug issues. (addiction field's attitude on juvenile drug prevention and treatment laws) *Alcoholism & Drug Abuse Week* August 18, 1997

The text points out that no one has made a clear link between juvenile crime and drug abuse. However, many community groups and grass-roots political commissions have pushed for increased treatment programs in response to the growing problem of narcotic use among youths. Read the above article and comment on the recently passed Juvenile Justice and Delinquency Prevention Act.

What are some of the strengths of the argument, made in the same article, about the promise of the community-level drug treatment programs?

QUESTIONS FOR DISCUSSION

1. Discuss the differences between the various categories and types of substances of abuse. Is the term *drugs* too broad to have real meaning?

2. Why do you think youths take drugs? Do you know anyone with an addiction prone personality?

3. What policy might be the best strategy to reduce teenage drug use: source control? reliance on treatment? national education efforts? community-level enforcement?

4. Under what circumstances, if any, might the legalization or decriminalization of drugs be beneficial to society?

5. Do you consider alcohol a drug? Should greater control be placed on the sale of alcohol?

6. Do TV shows and films glorify drug usage and encourage youths to enter the drug trade? Should all images of drinking and smoking be banned from TV? What about advertisements that try to convince youths how much fun it is to drink beer or smoke cigarettes?

7. Why do you think teenage drug use is on the rise? Does the fluctuation of substance abuse rates indicate that social and genetic or personality factors control drug use rates?

NOTES

1. Associated Press, "Florida Murder Revisited: Did Medication Play a Part?", *Boston Globe* 5 October 1998, p. 6.
2. Richard Lacayo, "Teen Crime, Congress Wants to Crack Down on Juvenile Offenders But Is Throwing Teens into Adult Courts—and Adult Prisons—the Best Way?", *Time* 21 July 1997, p. 67.
3. National Institute on Drug Abuse, Community Epidemiology Work Group, *Epidemiological Trends in Drug Abuse* (Washington, D.C.: National Institute on Drug Abuse, 1997), advance report.
4. University of Michigan, Institute for Social Research, News Release, 11 December 1995.
5. Peter Greenwood, "Substance Abuse Problems among High-Risk Youth and Potential Interventions," *Crime and Delinquency* 38:444–58 (1992).
6. U.S. Department of Justice, *Drugs and Crime Facts, 1988* (Washington, D.C.: Bureau of Justice Statistics, 1989), pp. 3–4.
7. Thomas Feucht, Richard Stephens, and Michael Walker, "Drug Use among Juvenile Arrestees: A Comparison of Self-Report, Urinalysis and Hair Assay," *Journal of Drug Issues* 24:99–116 (1994).
8. Mary Ellen Macksey-Amiti and Michael Fendrich, "Delinquent Behavior and Inhalant Use among High School Students," paper presented at the American Society of Criminology Meeting, Boston, Mass., November 1995.
9. Dennis Coon, *Introduction to Psychology* (St. Paul: West, 1992), p. 178.
10. Alan Neaigus, Aylin Atillasoy, Samuel Friedman, Xavier Andrade, Maureen Miller, Gilbert Ildefonso, and Don Des Jarlais, "Trends in the Noninjected Use of Heroin and Factors Associated with the Transition to Injecting," in James Inciardi and Lana Harrison, eds., *Heroin in the Age of Crack-Cocaine* (Thousand Oaks, Calif.: Sage, 1998), pp. 108–30.
11. University of Michigan, News Release, pp. 1–3.
12. Special Issue, "Drugs—The American Family in Crisis," *Juvenile and Family Court* 39:45–46 (1988).
13. Federal Bureau of Investigation, *Crime in the United States, 1994* (Washington, D.C.: U.S. Government Printing Office, 1995), p. 221.
14. Robyn Cohen, *Drunk Driving* (Washington, D.C.: Bureau of Justice Statistics, 1992), p. 2.

15. D. J. Rohsenow, "Drinking Habits and Expectancies about Alcohol's Effects for Self versus Others," *Journal of Consulting and Clinical Psychology* 51:752–56 (1983).
16. William Castelli, cited in G. Kolata, "Study Backs Heart Benefits in Light Drinking," *New York Times* 3 August 1988, p. A24.
17. Spencer Rathus, *Psychology*, 4th ed. (New York: Holt, Rinehart & Winston, 1990), p. 161.
18. Mary Tabor, "'Ice' in an Island Paradise," *Boston Globe* 8 December 1989, p. 3.
19. Paul Goldstein, "Anabolic Steroids: An Ethnographic Approach," unpublished paper (Narcotics and Drug Research, Inc., March 1989).
20. Centers for Disease Control, *Center Facts about Access to Tobacco by Minors* (Atlanta, Ga.: Centers for Disease Control, 23 May 1997).
21. Matt Lait, "California's New Role: Leading PCP Supplier," *Washington Post* 17 April 1989, p. 1.
22. Andrew Lang Golub and Bruce Johnson, "Crack's Decline: Some Surprises across U.S. Cities," *National Institute of Justice Research in Brief* (Washington, D.C.: National Institute of Justice, 1997); Bruce Johnson, Andrew Lang Golub, and Jeffrey Fagan, "Careers in Crack, Drug Use, Drug Distribution, and Nondrug Criminality," *Crime and Delinquency* 41:275–95 (1995).
23. Ibid., p. 10.
24. Bruce Johnson, George Thomas, and Andrew Golub, "Trends in Heroin Use among Manhattan Arrestees from the Heroin and Crack Era," in James Inciardi and Lana Harrison, eds., *Heroin in the Age of Crack-Cocaine* (Thousand Oaks, Calif.: Sage, 1998), pp. 108–30.
25. Robert Brooner, Donald Templer, Dace Svikis, Chester Schmidt, and Spyros Monopolis, "Dimensions of Alcoholism: A Multivariate Analysis," *Journal of Studies on Alcohol* 51: 77–81 (1990).
26. ISR data here is from the *1997 Survey of High School Students* (Ann Arbor, Mich.: University of Michigan News and Information Services, 1998).
27. PRIDE, *1997 Survey of High School Drug Abuse* (Atlanta, Ga.: PRIDE, Inc., 1998).
28. Kathryn A. Chandler, Chris Chapman, Michael R. Rand, and Bruce M. Taylor, *Students' Reports of School Crime: 1989 and 1995* (Washington, D.C: Bureau of Justice Statistics, 1998).

29. Ibid., pp. 6–7.

30. Joyce Ann O'Neil and Eric Wish, *Drug Use Forecasting, Cocaine Use* (Washington, D.C.: U.S. Government Printing Office, 1989), p. 7.

31. Eric Wish, "U.S. Drug Policy in the 1990's: Insights from New Data from Arrestees," *International Journal of the Addictions* 25:1–15 (1990).

32. G. E. Vallant, "Parent-Child Disparity and Drug Addiction," *Journal of Nervous and Mental Disease* 142:534–39 (1966).

33. Charles Winick, "Epidemiology of Narcotics Use," in D. Wilner and G. Kassenbaum, eds., *Narcotics* (New York: McGraw-Hill, 1965), pp. 3–18.

34. Delbert Elliott, David Huizinga, and Scott Menard, *Multiple Problem Youth: Delinquency, Substance Abuse and Mental Health Problems* (New York: Springer-Verlag, 1989).

35. Peter Reuter, Robert MacCoun, and Patrick Murphy, *Money from Crime: A Study of the Economics of Drug Dealing in Washington, D.C.* (Santa Monica, Calif.: Rand, 1990).

36. Thomas Dishion, Deborah Capaldi, Kathleen Spracklen, and Fuzhong Li, "Peer Ecology of Male Adolescent Drug Use," *Development and Psychopathology* 7:803–24 (1995).

37. C. Bowden, "Determinants of Initial Use of Opioids," *Comprehensive Psychiatry* 12:136–40 (1971).

38. Terence Thornberry and Marvin Krohn, "Peers, Drug Use and Delinquency," in David Stoff, James Breiling, and Jack Maser, eds., *Handbook of Antisocial Behavior* (New York: Wiley, 1997), pp. 218–33.

39. R. Cloward and L. Ohlin, *Delinquency and Opportunity: A Theory of Delinquent Gangs* (Glencoe, Ill.: Free Press, 1960).

40. Denise Kandel and Mark Davies, "Friendship Networks, Intimacy and Illicit Drug Use in Young Adulthood: A Comparison of Two Competing Theories," *Criminology* 29:441–71 (1991).

41. James Inciardi, Ruth Horowitz, and Anne Pottieger, *Street Kids, Street Drugs, Street Crime: An Examination of Drug Use and Serious Delinquency in Miami* (Belmont, Calif.: Wadsworth, 1993), p. 43.

42. D. Baer and J. Corrado, "Heroin Addict Relationships with Parents during Childhood and Early Adolescent Years," *Journal of Genetic Psychology* 124:99–103 (1974).

43. Timothy Ireland and Cathy Spatz Widom, *Childhood Victimization and Risk for Alcohol and Drug Arrests* (Washington, D.C.: National Institute of Justice, 1995).

44. See S. F. Bucky, "The Relationship between Background and Extent of Heroin Use," *American Journal of Psychiatry* 130:709–10 (1973); I. Chien, D. L. Gerard, R. Lee, and E. Rosenfield, *The Road to H: Narcotics Delinquency and Social Policy* (New York: Basic Books, 1964).

45. J. S. Mio, G. Nanjundappa, D. E. Verlur, and M. D. DeRios, "Drug Abuse and the Adolescent Sex Offender: A Preliminary Analysis," *Journal of Psychoactive Drugs* 18:65–72 (1986).

46. G. T. Wilson, "Cognitive Studies in Alcoholism," *Journal of Consulting and Clinical Psychology* 55:325–31 (1987).

47. John Hagedorn, Jose Torres, and Greg Giglio, "Cocaine, Kicks, and Strain: Patterns of Substance Use in Milwaukee Gangs," *Contemporary Drug Problems* 25:113–45 (1998).

48. For a thorough review, see Karol Kumpfer, "Impact of Maternal Characteristics and Parenting Processes on Children of Drug Abusers," paper presented at the American Society of Criminology Meeting, Boston, Mass., November 1995.

49. D. W. Goodwin, "Alcoholism and Genetics," *Archives of General Psychiatry* 42:171–74 (1985).

50. Ibid.

51. Patricia Dobkin, Richard Tremblay, Louise Masse, and Frank Vitaro, "Individual and Peer Characteristics in Predicting Boys' Early Onset of Substance Abuse: A Seven-Year Longitudinal Study," *Child Development* 66:1198–1214 (1995).

52. Ric Steele, Rex Forehand, Lisa Armistead, and Gene Brody, "Predicting Alcohol and Drug Use in Early Adulthood: The Role of Internalizing and Externalizing Behavior Problems in Early Adolescence," *American Journal of Orthopsychiatry* 65:380–87 (1995).

53. Ibid., pp. 380–81.

54. Jerome Platt and Christina Platt, *Heroin Addiction* (New York: Wiley, 1976), p. 127.

55. Rathus, *Psychology*, p. 158.

56. Eric Strain, "Antisocial Personality Disorder, Misbehavior and Drug Abuse," *Journal of Nervous and Mental Disease* 163: 162–65 (1995).

57. Patricia Dobkin, Richard Tremblay, Louise Masse, and Frank Vitaro, "Individual and Peer Characteristics in Predicting Boys' Early Onset of Substance Abuse: A Seven-Year Longitudinal Study," *Child Development* 66:1198–1214 (1995).

58. J. Shedler and J. Block, "Adolescent Drug Use and Psychological Health: A Longitudinal Inquiry," *American Psychologist* 45:612–30 (1990).

59. Greenwood, "Substance Abuse Problems among High-Risk Youth and Potential Interventions," p. 448.

60. John Wallace and Jerald Bachman, "Explaining Racial/Ethnic Differences in Adolescent Drug Use: The Impact of Background and Lifestyle," *Social Problems* 38:333–57 (1991).

61. Marvin Krohn, Terence Thornberry, Lori Collins-Hall, and Alan Lizotte, "School Dropout, Delinquent Behavior, and Drug Use," in Howard Kaplan, ed., *Drugs, Crime and Other Deviant Adaptations: Longitudinal Studies* (New York: Plenum Press, 1995), pp. 163–83.

62. Mary Ellen Mackesy-Amiti, Michael Fendrich, and Paul Goldstein, "Sequence of Drug Use among Serious Drug Users: Typical vs. Atypical Progression," *Drug and Alcohol Dependence* 45:185–96 (1997).

63. Inciardi, Horowitz, and Pottieger, *Street Kids, Street Drugs, Street Crime,* p. 135.

64. Ibid., p. 136.

65. B. A. Christiansen, G. T. Smith, P. V. Roehling, and M. S. Goldman, "Using Alcohol Expectancies to Predict Adolescent Drinking Behavior after One Year," *Journal of Counseling and Clinical Psychology* 57:93–99 (1989).

66. The following sections lean heavily on Marcia Chaiken and Bruce Johnson, *Characteristics of Different Types of Drug-Involved Youth* (Washington, D.C.: National Institute of Justice, 1988).

67. Inciardi, Horowitz, and Pottieger, *Street Kids, Street Drugs, and Street Crime,* p. 100.

68. Ibid., p. 100.

69. Ibid., p. 101.

70. Robert MacCoun and Peter Reuter, "Are the Wages of Sin $30 an Hour? Economic Aspects of Street-Level Drug Dealing," *Crime and Delinquency* 38:477–91 (1992).

71. Chaiken & Johnson, *Characteristics of Different Types of Drug-Involved Youth,* p. 12.

72. Rick Graves and Ed Allen, *Narcotics and Black Gangs* (Los Angeles: Los Angeles County Sheriff's Department, n.d.).

73. John Hagedorn, "Neighborhoods, Markets, and Gang Drug Organization," *Journal of Research in Crime and Delinquency* 31:264–94 (1994).

74. Ibid., p. 13.

75. Chaiken and Johnson, *Characteristics of Different Types of Drug-Involved Youth,* p. 14.

76. Eric Baumer, Janet Lauritsen, Richard Rosenfeld, and Richard Wright, "The Influence of Crack Cocaine on Robbery, Burglary, and Homicide Rates: A Cross-City, Longitudinal Analysis," *Journal of Research in Crime and Delinquency* 35:316–40 (1998).

77. Ibid.

78. James Inciardi, "Heroin Use and Street Crime," *Crime and Delinquency* 25:335–46 (1979); idem, *The War on Drugs* (Palo Alto, Calif.: Mayfield, 1986); see also, W. McGlothlin, M. Anglin, and B. Wilson, "Narcotic Addiction and Crime," *Criminology* 16:293–311 (1978); George Speckart and M. Douglas Anglin, "Narcotics Use and Crime: An Overview of Recent Research Advances," *Contemporary Drug Problems* 13:741–69 (1986); Charles Faupel and Carl Klockars, "Drugs-Crime Connections: Elaborations from the Life Histories of Hard-Core Heroin Addicts," *Social Problems* 34:54–68 (1987).

79. Eric Baumer, "Poverty, Crack and Crime: A Cross-City Analysis," *Journal of Research in Crime and Delinquency* 31:311–27 (1994).

80. Marvin Dawkins, "Drug Use and Violent Crime among Adolescents," *Adolescence* 32:395–406 (1997); Robert Peralta, "The Relationship between Alcohol and Violence in an Adolescent Population: An Analysis of the Monitoring the Future Survey," paper presented at the annual Society of Criminology Meeting, San Diego, Calif., November 1997; Helene Raskin White and Stephen Hansell, "The Moderating Effects of Gender and Hostility on the Alcohol-Aggression Relationship," *Journal of Research in Crime and Delinquency* 33:450–70 (1996); D. Wayne Osgood, "Drugs, Alcohol, and Adolescent Violence," paper presented at the annual meeting of the American Society of Criminology, Miami, Fl., 1994).

81. National Institute of Justice, *Drug Use Forecasting, 1997 Annual Report* (Washington, D.C.: National Institute of Justice, 1998).

82. David Cantor, "Drug Involvement and Offending of Incarcerated Youth," paper presented at the American Society of Criminology Meeting, Boston, Mass., November 1995.

83. B. D. Hohnson, E. Wish, J. Schmeidler, and D. Huizinga, "Concentration of Delinquent Offending: Serious Drug Involvement and High Delinquency Rates," *Journal of Drug Issues* 21:205–29 (1991).

84. W. David Watts and Lloyd Wright, "The Relationship of Alcohol, Tobacco, Marijuana, and Other Illegal Drug Use to Delinquency among Mexican-American, Black, and White Adolescent Males," *Adolescence* 25:38–54 (1990).

85. For a general review of this issue, see Helene Raskin White, "The Drug Use–Delinquency Connection in Adolescence," in Ralph Weisheit, ed., *Drugs, Crime and Criminal Justice* (Cincinnati: Anderson, 1990), pp. 215–56; Speckart and Anglin, "Narcotics Use and Crime"; Faupel and Klockars, "Drugs–Crime Connections."

86. Delbert Elliott, David Huizinga, and Susan Ageton, *Explaining Delinquency and Drug Abuse* (Beverly Hills, Calif.: Sage, 1985).

87. David Huizinga, Scott Menard, and Delbert Elliott, "Delinquency and Drug Use: Temporal and Developmental Patterns," *Justice Quarterly* 6:419–55 (1989).

88. Helene Raskin White, Robert Padina, and Randy LaGrange, "Longitudinal Predictors of Serious Substance Use and Delinquency," *Criminology* 25:715–40 (1987).

89. Wish, "U.S. Drug Policy in the 1990's."

90. Helene Raskin White, "Marijuana Use and Delinquency: A Test of the 'Independent Cause' Hypothesis," *Journal of Drug Issues* 21:231–56 (1991).

91. Drug Enforcement Administration, *National Drug Control Strategy* (Washington, D.C.: U.S. Government Printing Office, 1989).

92. William Rhodes et. al. *What America's Users Spend on Illegal Drugs, 1988–1993* (Cambridge, Mass.: Abt Associates, 1995).

93. Mark Moore, *Drug Trafficking* (Washington, D.C: National Institute of Justice, 1988).

94. Jeffrey Butts and Melissa Sickmund, *Offenders in Juvenile Court, 1989* (Washington, D.C.: Office of Juvenile Justice and Delinquency Prevention, 1992), p. 1.

95. Ibid.

96. Phyllis Ellickson and Robert Bell, *Prospects for Preventing Drug Use among Young Adolescents* (Santa Monica, Calif.: Rand Corp., 1990).

97. Wayne Lucan and Steven Gilham, "Impact of a Drug Use Prevention Program: An Empirical Assessment," paper presented at the annual meeting of the American Society of Criminology, New Orleans, November, 1992.

98. Scott Henggeler, *Delinquency and Adolescent Psychopathology: A Family–Ecological Systems Approach* (Littleton, Mass.: Wright-PSG, 1982).

99. Scott Henggeler, "Effects of Multisystemic Therapy on Drug Use and Abuse in Serious Juvenile Offenders: A Progress Report from Two Outcome Studies," *Family Dynamics of Addiction Quarterly* 1:40–51 (1991).

100. Eli Ginzberg, Howard Berliner, and Miriam Ostrow, *Young People at Risk: Is Prevention Possible?* (Boulder, Colo.: Westview Press, 1988), p. 99.

101. Ibid.

102. Miriam Sealock, Denise Gottfredson, and Catherine Gallagher, "Addressing Drug Use and Recidivism in Delinquent Youth: An Examination of Residential and Aftercare Treatment Programs," paper presented at the American Society of Criminology Meeting, Boston, Mass., November 1995.

103. Kathryn Ann Farr, "Revitalizing the Drug Decriminalization Debate," *Crime and Delinquency* 36:223–37 (1990).

104. Reuter, MacCoun, and Murphy, *Money from Crime,* pp. 165–68.

Part Four

Juvenile Justice Advocacy

Part Four provides a general overview of the juvenile justice system, including its process, history, and legal rules.

Since 1900, juveniles who violate the law have been treated differently from adults. A separate juvenile justice system has been developed that features its own judiciary, rules, and processes.

The separation of juvenile and adult offenders reflects society's concern for the plight of children. Since many experts believe children can be reformed or rehabilitated, it makes sense to treat their law violations more leniently than those of adults. Care, protection, and treatment are the bywords of the juvenile justice system. Of course, to some influential critics, the serious juvenile offender is not deserving of this approach. Consequently, efforts have been made recently to "toughen up" the juvenile system and treat some delinquents much more like adult offenders.

Chapter 12 reviews the history and development of juvenile justice. Emphasis is placed on developments throughout the nineteenth century that led to the establishment of the modern juvenile court system. Chapter 12 also provides an overview of the juvenile justice system and describes its major components, processes, goals, and institutions. It describes the organization of juvenile court, the legal rights of minors and the role of the U.S. Supreme Court in juvenile justice.

12 The History and Development of Juvenile Justice

Chapter Twelve

The History and Development of Juvenile Justice

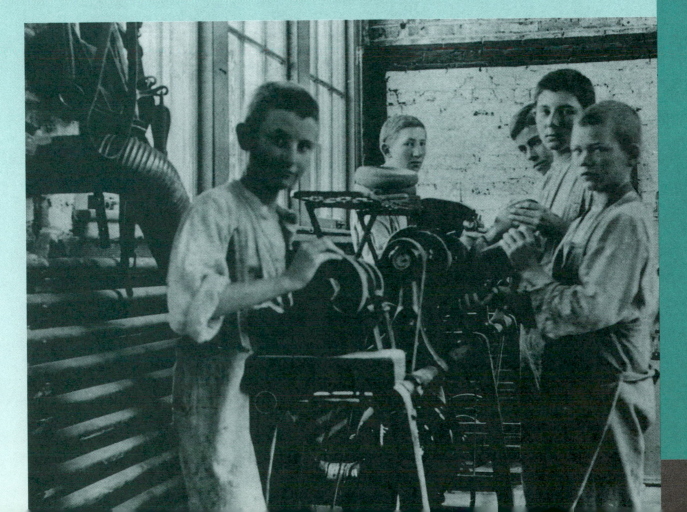

A sixteen-year-old male was brought handcuffed and sullen into the New York Family Court, Juvenile Division, in 1997, charged with being a juvenile delinquent by virtue of driving a stolen vehicle. It was a crime in which nobody was hurt and nothing was stolen, yet another number in the statistics of juvenile crime in the United States.

This youth's road from school to court can tell us more about the realities of the juvenile justice system than any diagram in this chapter. The quality of juvenile justice in New York is not much better nor much worse than in any other major American city. Most of the staff are typically overworked, understaffed, and pushing large numbers of young people into the adult criminal justice system. In this case the juvenile protested his innocence to the police even after he pleaded guilty. No one believed his story, and his case was processed through the juvenile justice system.

Who was this youth? Donald grew up in a New York City ghetto. His mother struggled to raise him. Her husband had deserted her and their four children when Donald was a young boy. She kept the family together, bore two more children by another man, and worked some of the time to supplement the family's income. This family lived in a gang-infested section of New York, and Donald grew up in a public housing project.

No one knew exactly when Donald started skipping school. By the tenth grade he was a high school dropout, swallowed up by the streets of the city. He had a few early run-ins with the juvenile court for truancy and disorderly conduct, routine occurrences for kids from the ghetto. Then he was arrested for shoplifting, wound up pleading guilty, and was given two years' probation. Probation, in theory, is a means of community supervision and rehabilitation. But probation officers in New York City and in other areas around the country are spread thin across many cases. Donald reported to his probation officer occasionally, usually for ten-minute meetings. Once he was referred to a job counselor, but he never went.

At age 16 he was in trouble again. It was past midnight when the police spotted the car parked in a deserted street in lower Manhattan. When the patrol car approached, the car sped off, with two other youths in the front seat. Donald was apprehended driving the car a few blocks from where the police initially saw the vehicle.

At the station house, Donald was placed in the youth detention home when the police couldn't reach his mother. Taken to court, and after speaking with a public defender, Donald was released to the custody of his mother to await his trial for vehicle theft.

Charged with driving the stolen car, Donald met with a new public defender for a few minutes before his trial began. Fortunately, he had not languished in a detention center like some young defendants. Because of extremely limited resources, the public defender system for juveniles often encourages children to plead guilty rather than go to trial. In Donald's case the public defender didn't outline any defense strategy or suggest checking the police report or even ask if any witnesses might be called. Because Donald didn't think driving a stolen car was a major offense, he reluctantly agreed to plead guilty, saving the court time and money. Donald certainly had a right to legal representation. In 1967, in an important case known as *In re Gault,* the U.S. Supreme Court ruled that children had a right to counsel; although Donald had a lawyer, he never went to trial because he elected to plead guilty.

After talking with his public defender and the probation department, the juvenile court judge ordered that Donald be committed to the New York Department of Youth Services until eighteen years of age. Donald was evaluated and placed in a nonsecure group setting where he was given counseling and participated in educational and job training programs. He was subsequently released, six months before his eighteenth birthday. Donald did not participate in any aftercare program.

Only a small percentage of arrested juveniles are removed from the community. In Donald's case, his prior record resulted in the judge's decision to place him in a group home.

The treatment of Donald is typical of nonsecure juvenile offenders with previous records in large urban areas. According to the Office of Juvenile Justice and Delinquency Prevention, serious nonviolent offenders are involved in crimes such as burglary, motor vehicle theft, larceny, and drug trafficking, or status offenses such as truancy. The juvenile process is applied in different ways, depending on the type of case. Over two-thirds of all juvenile crimes are for property and person-oriented offenses; 9 percent involve drugs. Violent juvenile crimes, which represent about 7 percent of all juvenile arrests, are not only complicated cases but also require access to counsel and trial.

Juvenile sentences can range from community programs to incarceration or even transfer to the adult court. The type of sentence varies according to the severity of the offense.

The story of Donald illustrates the complex process of the American juvenile justice system. Will someone like Donald actually be rehabilitated or will he become an adult offender? This chapter describes the organizations, laws, and sequential stages of the juvenile process, some of which are illustrated by Donald's case.

Youth crime is considered a major social problem in the United States, yet many communities have seen significant declines in serious violent crime among teenagers in recent years, including declines in juvenile killings. But even as rates of urban juvenile delinquency are declining, hundreds of thousands of cases like Donald's have rekindled public debate over the juvenile justice system. According to experts, the country has a long way to go before claiming victory over juvenile delinquency.[1] What kinds of punishment can society use to fit these crimes? How can such senseless crimes be prevented? What reforms must be made in the juvenile justice system of the new millennium to rehabilitate Donald? Formulating effective policies to meet such challenges requires a clear understanding of the history and development of juvenile justice.

This chapter begins with a discussion of the major social changes that took place during the nineteenth century leading to creation of the first modern juvenile court in Chicago in 1899. We then cover the reform efforts of the twentieth century, including the movement to grant children the procedural rights that are typically given to adult offenders. This discussion includes descriptions of some of the landmark Supreme Court decisions that have influenced present day juvenile justice procedures.

The second part of this chapter presents an overview of the contemporary juvenile justice system and the various philosophies, processes, organizations, and legal constraints that dominate its operations. The process that takes a youthful offender through a series of steps beginning with arrest and concluding with reentry into society is described. What happens to young people who violate the law? Do they have legal rights? How are they helped? How are they punished? Should juvenile killers be released from custody prior to their eighteenth birthday? Should the goal of the system be rehabilitation or punishment of youthful offenders?

To help address such questions we have included a discussion of the similarities and differences between the adult and juvenile justice systems. This discussion draws attention to the important principle that children are treated separately in our society. By establishing legislation to segregate delinquent children from adult offenders, society has placed greater importance on the delinquent being a "child" rather than being a "criminal." Consequently, rehabilitation rather than punishment has traditionally been the goal. Today, with children committing more serious and violent crimes, the juvenile justice system is having great difficulty finding solutions to handling these offenders.

In the final section, on the future of juvenile justice, we discuss the need for a comprehensive juvenile justice strategy and the role of the federal government in juvenile justice reform—the key element in funding state juvenile justice and delinquency prevention efforts.

The Development of Juvenile Justice in the Nineteenth Century

At the beginning of the nineteenth century, delinquent, neglected, dependent, and runaway children in the United States were treated the same as adult criminal offenders.[2] Like children in England, they were often charged and convicted of crimes, including capital offenses, and received harsh sentences similar to those imposed on adults. The adult criminal code applied to children, and no juvenile court existed.

Throughout the early nineteenth century, various pieces of legislation were introduced to humanize criminal procedures for children. The concept of probation, introduced in Massachusetts in 1841, was geared toward helping young people avoid the trauma of imprisonment. The many books and reports written during this time heightened public interest in juvenile child care.

Despite this interest, no special facilities existed for the care of youths in trouble with the law, nor were there separate laws or courts to control their behavior. Youths who committed petty crimes, such as stealing, gambling, or vandalism, were viewed as wayward children or victims of neglect and were placed in community asylums or homes. Youths who were involved in more serious crimes were subject to the same punishments as adults—imprisonment, whipping, or death.

Several events led to reforms in the field of child care and nourished the eventual development of the U.S. juvenile justice system: (1) urbanization, (2) the child-saving movement and growing interest in the concept of **parens patriae,** and (3) development of institutions and organizations for the care of delinquent and neglected children.

parens patriae
Power of the state to act in behalf of the child and provide care and protection equivalent to that of a parent.

Urbanization

Especially during the first half of the nineteenth century, the United States experienced rapid population growth, primarily because of an increase in the birthrate and expanding European immigration. Members of the rural poor and immigrant groups settled in developing urban commercial centers that promised jobs in manufacturing. In 1790, 5 percent of the population lived in cities, and 95 percent lived in rural areas. By 1850, the share of the urban population had increased to 15 percent; it jumped to 40 percent in 1900, and 51 percent in 1920.[3] New York had more than quadrupled its population in the thirty-year stretch between 1825 and 1855, from 166,000 in 1825 to 630,000 in 1855.[4]

This growing urbanization gave rise to increased numbers of young people at risk who flooded cities and overwhelmed the existing system of work and training. To accommodate groups of dependent and destitute youths, local jurisdictions developed poorhouses (or almshouses) and workhouses. The poor, the insane, the diseased, and vagrant and destitute children were housed here in crowded and unhealthy conditions.

By the late eighteenth century many began to question the family's ability to exert social control over their children. Villages developed into urban commercial centers and work began to center around factories, not the home. The children of destitute families left home or were cast loose to make out as best they could; wealthy families could no longer absorb vagrant youth as apprentices or servants.[5] Chronic poverty became an American dilemma, spurring the federal census department to create a new category of underclass citizens labeled "paupers." The affluent began to voice concern over the increase in the number of people in what they considered to be the *dangerous classes*—the poor, single, criminal, mentally ill, and unemployed.

Increased urbanization and industrialization also generated the belief that certain segments of the population—namely, youths in urban areas and immigrants—were susceptible to the influences of their decayed environment. Many believed that environment, not innate immorality or physical degeneracy, influenced criminal deviance and immorality. The children of these classes were considered a group that might be "saved" by a combination of state and community intervention.[6] Intervention in the lives of these potentially "dangerous classes" to help alleviate their burdens became acceptable for wealthy, civic-minded citizens. Such efforts included shelter care for youths, educational and social activities, and settlement houses, a term used around the turn of the twentieth century to describe shelters or nonsecure residential facilities for vagrant children.

The Child-Saving Movement

The problems generated by large scale urban growth sparked tremendous interest in the welfare of the "new" Americans whose arrival fueled this expansion. In 1817 prominent New Yorkers formed the Society for the Prevention of Pauperism, perhaps the first organized group to focus on the needs of the underclass. Although they concerned themselves with attacking taverns, brothels, and gambling parlors, they also were concerned that the moral training of children of the dangerous classes was inadequate. Soon other groups concerned with the plight of poor children began to form in major urban areas. Their main focus was on extending government control over a whole range of youthful activities that had previously been left to private or family control, including idleness, drinking, vagrancy, and delinquency.

These activists became known as child savers. Prominent among them were penologist Enoch Wines; Judge Richard Tuthill; Lucy Flowers, of the Chicago Women's Association; Sara Cooper, of the National Conference of Charities and Corrections; and Sophia Minton, of the New York Committee on Children.[7] Poor children could become a financial and social burden, and the child savers believed these children presented a threat to the moral fabric of American society and should be controlled because their behavior could lead to the destruction of the nation's economic system.

Child-saving organizations influenced state legislatures to enact laws giving courts the power to commit children who were runaways, criminal offenders, or out of the control of parents to specialized institutions. The most prominent of the care facilities developed by child savers was the **House of Refuge** in New York, which opened in 1825.[8] It was founded on the concept of protecting potential criminal youths by taking them off the streets and reforming them in a family-like environment.

When the House of Refuge opened, the majority of children admitted were status offenders placed there because of vagrancy or neglect. However, the institution was run more like a prison, with work and study schedules, strict discipline, and absolute separation of the sexes. Such a harsh program drove many children to run away, and the House of Refuge was forced to take a more lenient approach. Children were placed in the institution by court order, sometimes over parents' objections. Their length of stay depended on need, age, and skill. Once there, youths were required to do piecework provided by local manufacturers or to work part of the day in the community.

Despite criticism of the program, the concept enjoyed expanding popularity. In 1826 the Boston City Council founded the House of Reformation for juvenile offenders. Similar institutions were opened in Massachusetts and New York in 1847.[9] The courts committed children found guilty of criminal violations or found to be

House of Refuge
A care facility developed by the child savers to protect potential criminal youths by taking them off the street and providing a family-like environment.

The House of Refuge was one of the earliest juvenile institutions in the United States to offer residents vocational training.

beyond the control of their parents to these schools, which were both privately and publicly supported. Because the child savers considered parents of delinquent children to be as guilty as convicted offenders, they sought to have the reform schools establish control over the children. As scholar Robert Mennel states, "By training destitute and delinquent children, and by separating them from their natural parents and adult criminals, refuge managers believed they were preventing poverty and crime."[10]

The philosophy of *parens patriae* was extended to refuge programs, which were given parental control over a committed child. Robert Mennel summarizes this attitude:

> The doctrine of *parens patriae* gave refuge managers the best of two worlds, familial and legal: it separated delinquent children from their natural parents and it circumvented the rigor of criminal law by allowing courts to commit children, under loosely worded statutes, to specially created schools instead of jails.[11]

Were They Really Child Savers?

Great debate continues over the true aims and objectives of the early child savers. Some historians conclude that they were what they seemed: concerned citizens motivated by humanitarian ideals.[12] Modern scholars, however, have reappraised the child-saving movement. In his groundbreaking book *The Child Savers,* critical thinker Anthony Platt paints a picture of the child savers as representative of the ruling class who were galvanized by the threat of newly arriving immigrants and the urban poor to take action to preserve their way of life.[13] He claims

> The child savers should not be considered humanists: (1) their reforms did not herald a new system of justice but rather expedited traditional policies which had been informally developed during the nineteenth century; (2) they implicitly assumed that natural dependence of adolescents and created a special court to impose sanctions on premature independents and behavior unbecoming to youth; (3) their attitudes toward delinquent youth were largely paternalistic and romantic but their commands were backed up by force; (4) they promoted correctional programs requiring longer terms of imprisonment, longer hours of labor, and militaristic discipline, and the inculcation of middle class values and lower class skills.[14]

Other critical thinkers followed Platt in finding that child saving was motivated more by self-interest than by benevolence. For example, Randall Shelden and Lynn Osborne traced the early child-saving movement in Memphis, Tennessee, and found that its leaders were a small group of upper-class citizens who desired to control the behavior and lifestyles of another class of citizens: lower-class youth. The outcome was ominous. Most cases petitioned to the juvenile court (which opened in 1910) were for petty crimes, truancy, and other status-type offenses, yet 25 percent of the youths were committed to some form of incarceration; more than 96 percent of the actions with which females were charged were status offenses.[15]

In summary, these scholars believe that the reformers applied the concept of *parens patriae* for their own purposes, including the continuance of middle- and upper-class values, the control of political systems, and the furtherance of a child labor system consisting of marginal and lower-class skilled workers.

In the course of "saving" children by turning them over to houses of refuge, procedures of criminal law did not apply, meaning that children were not granted the same constitutional protections as adults. But this process of institutional control over children in the name of the state and family did not proceed without some significant legal challenges (see Table 12.1). Two of the more critical cases are

Table 12.1

NOTABLE EARLY LEGAL DECISIONS IN JUVENILE JUSTICE

Case	Holding
Wellesley v. Wellesley (1827)	In this English case, the children of a duke were removed from his custody by the chancery court in the name of *parens patriae* because of his poor behavior.
Ex Parte Crouse (1839)	In a case involving the commitment of a girl to an institution without a trial, the Pennsylvania Supreme Court held that a child did not require the protection of due process of law and that the House of Refuge could supersede the authority of the parent.
O'Connell v. Turner (1870)	The Illinois Supreme Court declared that a child's vagrancy sentence to a reform school was unconstitutional—the opposite result achieved in *Ex Parte Crouse*—the state did not have the authority under *parens patriae* to remove poor children from their parents.
Commonwealth v. Fisher (1905)	The Pennsylvania Supreme Court upheld the constitutionality of the newly enacted Juvenile Court Act to commit a child to the House of Refuge until his or her twenty-first birthday.
Ex Parte Sharpe (1908)	The Idaho Supreme Court upheld the right of the state juvenile court to act in a protective way by applying the *parens patriae* doctrine concerning the role of juveniles. This decision gave further impetus to the development of the juvenile court movement in the United States.

described in the Juvenile Law in Review box entitled "Legal Challenges to the Child Savers."

The Development of Juvenile Institutions

As is evident from Table 12.1, state intervention in the lives of children continued throughout the latter portion of the nineteenth century and well into the twentieth century. The child savers influenced state and local governments to create institutions, called reform schools, exclusively devoted to the care of vagrant and delinquent youths. State institutions opened in Westboro, Massachusetts, in 1848 and in Rochester, New York, in 1849.[16] Institutional programs began in Ohio in 1850 and in Maine, Rhode Island, and Michigan in 1906. Children lived in congregate conditions and spent their days working in the institution, learning a trade where possible, and receiving some basic education. They were racially and sexually segregated; discipline, often involving whipping and isolation, was harsh; and their physical care was poor. Beverly Smith found that girls admitted to the Western House of Refuge in Rochester, New York, during the 1880s were often labeled as deviant or criminal but were in reality abused, orphaned, and neglected. They too were subject to harsh working conditions, strict discipline, and intensive labor.[17] Most of these institutions received state support, unlike the privately funded houses of refuge, homes, and settlement houses.

Although some viewed houses of refuge and reform schools as humanitarian answers to poorhouses and prisons for vagrant, neglected, and delinquent youths, many were opposed to such programs. As an alternative, New York philanthropist Charles Brace helped develop the **Children's Aid Society** in 1853.[18] Brace's formula for dealing with neglected and delinquent youths was to rescue them from the harsh environment of the city and provide them with temporary shelter care. He then sought to place them in private homes throughout the nation. This program was very similar to today's foster home programs. As legal scholar Sanford Fox points out, "The great value to be placed on family life for deviant and crime-prone children was later explicitly set forth in the juvenile court act."[19]

Although the child reformers provided services for children, they could not eliminate juvenile delinquency. Most reform schools lacked the social and financial resources needed to hold and reform youthful law violators. Large numbers of children needing placement burdened the public coffers supporting such programs. So, although state control over vagrant, delinquent, and neglected children was more widespread after the Civil War, it was also more controversial. As the nation

Children's Aid Society
Child-saving organization that took children from the streets of large cities and placed them with farm families on the prairie.

This engraving depicts the work of the Children's Aid Society, founded in 1853.

LEGAL CHALLENGES TO THE CHILD SAVERS

In *Ex Parte Crouse* (1839) a man attempted to free his daughter from the Philadelphia House of Refuge, which claimed the right of parental control over her because of unmanageable behavior. The father argued that her commitment without a trial by jury was unconstitutional. In its decision in the case the Pennsylvania Supreme Court held that the House of Refuge was specifically planned to reform, restrain, and protect children from depraved parents or their environment.*

Crouse, the twelve-year-old girl, was classified as a pauper for the purpose of court jurisdiction. The petition (the juvenile equivalent of an indictment), brought by her mother, alleged that she was a poor person and therefore subject to the court. She was then committed to the Philadelphia House of Refuge, even though delinquency laws did not exist and she had committed no violation of the criminal law. Crouse's father objected to the court action and filed a writ of habeas corpus (a kind of appeal that forces the government to show why they are keeping someone in custody) seeking an explanation for her commitment.

The problem in this case was whether the state of Pennsylvania had the right to take custody of Crouse under the guise of helping her, even though she had committed no crime. The Superior Court decided that placing the child in the House of Refuge did not violate her constitutional rights.

The Court concluded that Crouse was being cared for and not punished and therefore could be placed in an institution even without due process of law. The *Crouse* decision established the key legal concept of *parens patriae,* which became the basis of the juvenile court movement. *Crouse* was the first legal challenge to the practice of institutionalizing children who had committed no crime. It gave the state almost complete authority to intervene in the parent–child relationship because of the state's role as *parens patriae.* The court stated:

> The right of parental control is a natural, but not an inalienable one. It is not accepted by the Declaration of Rights out of the subjects of ordinary legislation; and it consequently remains subject to the ordinary legisla-

Society for the Prevention of Cruelty to Children (SPCC)
First established in 1874, these organizations protected children subjected to cruelty and neglect at home or at school.

grew, it became evident that private charities and public organizations were unable to care adequately for the growing number of troubled youths.

In 1874 the first **Society for the Prevention of Cruelty to Children (SPCC)** was established in New York; by 1900 there were 300 such societies in the United States.[20] Leaders of the SPCCs were concerned that neglected and abused boys would grow up to join the ranks of the dangerous classes, becoming lower-class criminals, and that mistreated young girls might become sexually promiscuous women. A growing post-Civil War crime rate and concern about a rapidly shifting and changing population served to swell SPCC membership. In addition, these organizations protected children subjected to cruelty and neglect at home and at school.

SPCC groups influenced state legislatures to pass statutes protecting children from exploitive or neglectful parents, including those who did not provide them with adequate food and clothing or made them beg or work in places where liquor was sold.[21] Criminal penalties were created for negligent parents, and provisions were established for removing children from the home. In some states, such as New York, agents of the SPCC could actually arrest abusive parents; in others, they would inform the police about suspected abuse cases and accompany officers when they made an arrest.[22]

tive power which, if wantonly or inconveniently used, would soon be constitutionally restricted, but the competency of which, as the government is constituted, cannot be doubted.[†]

The Crouse decision demonstrated that children could be deprived of the constitutional liberties guaranteed to adults.

O'Connell v. Turner, another significant case, went against the *Crouse* decision by deciding in favor of the parent and child against the state.[‡] In 1870 Daniel O'Connell was committed to the Chicago Reform School on the ground that he was a vagrant or destitute youth without proper parental care. The parents fought the child's commitment because he had not been convicted of a crime and had been apprehended and confined under a general grant of power to arrest for simple misfortune. The basic legal problem was whether children could be committed to reform schools in the absence of criminal conduct or because of gross misconduct on the part of their parents.

The law was held to be unconstitutional, and on subsequent appeal, the court ordered Daniel O'Connell discharged. As Justice Thornton noted in the case, "The warrant of commitment does not indicate that the arrest was made for a criminal offense. Hence, we conclude that it was made under the general grant of power to arrest and confine for misfortune."[**] The fact that the court in this case distinguished between criminal acts and acts arising from misfortune was significant: All legislation dealing with misfortune cases was subsequently appealed as a direct result of the O'Connell decision. Also, as scholar Sanford Fox indicates, the O'Connell case changed the course of events in Illinois. The Chicago Reform School closed in 1872, and the case encouraged procedural due process reform for committed youths.[††]

Sources: [*]4 Whart. 9 (1839); see also Randall G. Sheldon, "Confronting the Ghost of Mary Ann Crouse: Gender Bias in the Juvenile Justice System," *Juvenile and Family Court Journal* 49: 11–27 (1998); [†]Ibid., p. 11; [‡]*O'Connell v. Turner*, 55 Ill. 280 (1870); [**]Ibid., p. 283; [††]Sanford J. Fox, "Juvenile Justice Reform: A Historical Perspective," *Stanford Law Review* 22:1187 (1970).

**JUVENILE LAW
IN REVIEW**

The organization and control of SPCCs varied widely. For example, the New York City SPCC was a city agency supported by municipal funds. It conducted investigations of delinquent and neglected children for the court and had little to do with the city's other social welfare agencies. In contrast, the Boston SPCC emphasized delinquency prevention and worked closely with social welfare groups; the Philadelphia SPCC emphasized family unity and was involved with other charities.[23]

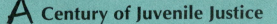

A Century of Juvenile Justice

Although reform groups continued to lobby for government control over children, committing of children under the doctrine of *parens patriae* without due process of law began to be questioned. What care was in the best interest of the child? Could the state incarcerate children who had not violated the criminal law? Should children be held in the same facilities that housed adults? These and other questions began to plague reformers and those interested in the plight of children. Serious problems challenged the effectiveness of the existing system: institutional deficiencies; the absence of due process for poor, ignorant, and noncriminal delinquents; and the treatment of these children by inadequate private child welfare organizations all spurred the argument that a juvenile court should be established.

Increasing delinquency rates also hastened the development of a juvenile court. Theodore Ferdinand's analysis of the Boston juvenile court found that in the 1820s and 1830s very few juveniles were charged with serious offenses. By 1850 juvenile delinquency was the fastest growing component of the local crime problem.[24] Ferdinand concluded that the sizable flow of juvenile cases strengthened the argument that juveniles needed their own special court attuned to their needs.

Table 12.2
EXCERPTS FROM THE ILLINOIS JUVENILE COURT ACT OF 1899

Section 1. Definitions. This act shall apply only to children under the age of sixteen (16) years not now or here-after inmates of a State institution, or any training school for boys or industrial school for girls or some institution incorporated under the laws of this State, except as provided in sections twelve (12) and eighteen (18). For the purposes of this act the words dependent child and neglected child shall mean any child who for any reason is destitute or homeless or abandoned; or dependent upon the public for support; or has not proper parental care or guardianship; or who habitually begs or receives alms; or who is found living in any house of ill fame or with any vicious or disreputable person; or whose home, by reason of neglect, cruelty or depravity on the part of its parents, guardian or other person in whose care it may be, is an unfit place for such a child; and any child under the age of eight (8) years who is found peddling or selling any article or singing or playing any musical instrument upon the streets or giving any public entertainment. The words delinquent child shall include any child under the age of sixteen (16) years who violates any law of this State or any city or village ordinance. The word child or children may mean one or more children, and the word parent or parents may be held to mean one or both parents, when consistent with the intent of this act. The word association shall include any corporation which includes in its purposes the care or disposition of children coming within the meaning of this act. . . .

Section 3. Juvenile Court. In counties having over 500,000 population the judges of the circuit court shall, at such times as they shall determine, designate one or more of their number whose duty it shall be to hear all cases coming under this act. A special courtroom, to be designated as the juvenile courtroom, shall be provided for the hearing of such cases, and the findings of the court shall be entered in a book or books to be kept for that purpose and known as the "Juvenile Record," and the court may, for convenience, be called the "Juvenile Court."

Section 4. Petition to the Court. Any reputable person, being resident in the county, having knowledge of a child in his county who appears to be either neglected, dependent or delinquent, may file with the clerk of court having jurisdiction in the matter a petition in writing, setting forth the facts, verified by affidavit. It shall be sufficient that the affidavit is upon information and belief. . . .

Section 6. Probation Officers. The court shall have authority to appoint or designate one or more discreet persons of good character to serve as probation officers during the pleasure of the court; said probation officers to receive no compensation from the public treasury. In case a probation officer shall be appointed by any court, it shall be the duty of the clerk of the court, if practicable, to notify the said probation officer in advance when any child is to be brought before the said court; it shall be the duty of the said probation officer to make such investigation as may be required by the court; to be present in court in order to represent the interests of the child when the case is heard; to furnish the court such information and assistance as the judge may require; and to take such charge of any child before and after trial as may be directed by the court.

The Illinois Juvenile Court Act and Its Legacy

Illinois Juvenile Court Act of 1899

A major event in the history of juvenile justice, this act served as a model for other states, establishing the special status of juveniles and the emphasis on helping to treat rather than punish young offenders.

The child-saving movement culminated in the passage of the **Illinois Juvenile Court Act of 1899** (see Table 12.2). This was a major event in the history of the juvenile justice movement in the United States. Its significance was such that, by 1917, juvenile courts had been established in all but three states.

The principles motivating the Illinois reformers at that time were these:

1. Children, because of their minority status, should not be held as accountable as adult transgressors;
2. The objective of the juvenile justice system is to help the youngster, to treat and rehabilitate rather than punish;

Section 7. Dependent and Neglected Children. When any child under the age of sixteen (16) years shall be found to be dependent or neglected within the meaning of this act, the court may make an order committing the child to the care of some suitable State institution, or to the care of some reputable citizen of good moral character, or to the care of some training school or an industrial school, as provided by law, or to the care of some association willing to receive it embracing in its objects the purpose of caring or obtaining homes for dependent or neglected children, which association shall have been accredited as hereinafter provided. . . .

Section 9. Disposition of Delinquent Children. In the case of a delinquent child the court may continue the hearing from time to time and may commit the child to the care and guardianship of a probation officer duly appointed by the court and may allow said child to remain in its own home, subject to the visitation of the probation officer; such child to report to the probation officer as often as may be required and subject to be returned to the court for further proceedings, whenever such action may appear to be necessary, or the court may commit the child to the care and guardianship of the probation officer, to be placed in a suitable family home, subject to the friendly supervision of such probation officer, or it may authorize the said probation officer to board out the said child in some suitable family home, in case provision is made by voluntary contribution or otherwise for the payment of the board of such child, until a suitable provision may be made for the child in a home without such payment; or the court may commit the child, if a boy, to a training school for boys, or if a girl, to an industrial school for girls. Or, if the child is found guilty of any criminal offense, and the judge is of the opinion that the best interest requires it, the court may commit the child to any institution within said county incorporated under the laws of this State for the care of delinquent children, or provided by a city for the care of such offenders, or may commit the child, if a boy over the age of ten (10) years, to the State reformatory, or if a girl over the age of ten (10) years, to the State Home for Juvenile Female Offenders. In no case shall a child be committed beyond his or her minority. A child committed to such institution shall be subject to the control of the board of managers thereof, and the said board shall have power to parole such child on such conditions as it may prescribe, and the court shall, on the recommendation of the board, have power to discharge such child from custody whenever in the judgment of the court his or her reformation shall be complete; or the court may commit the child to the care and custody of some association that will receive it, embracing in its objects the care of neglected and dependent children and that has been duly accredited as hereinafter provided. . . .

Section 11. Children under Twelve Years Not to Be Committed to Jail. No court or magistrate shall commit a child under twelve (12) years of age to a jail or police station, but if such child is unable to give bail it may be committed to the care of the sheriff, police officer or probation officer.

Source: Illinois Statute 1899, Section 131.

3. Disposition should be predicated on analysis of the youth's special circumstances and needs; and
4. The system should avoid the punitive, adversary, and formalized trappings of the adult criminal process with all its confusing rules of evidence and tightly controlled procedures.

Just what were the ramifications of passage of the Illinois Juvenile Court Act? The traditional interpretation is that the reformers were genuinely motivated to pass legislation that would serve the best interests of the child. U.S. Supreme Court Justice Abe Fortas took this position in the landmark 1967 *In re Gault* case:

> The early reformers were appalled by adult procedures and penalties and by the fact that children could be given long prison sentences and mixed in jails with hardened criminals. They were profoundly convinced that society's duty to the child could not be confined by the concept of justice alone. . . . The child—essentially good, as they saw it—was to be made to feel that he was the object of the state's care and solicitude, not that he was under arrest or on trial. . . . The idea of crime and punishment was to be abandoned. The child was to be treated and rehabilitated and the procedures from apprehension through institutionalization were to be clinical rather than punitive.[25]

The child savers believed that children were influenced by their environments and emphasized individual values and judgments about children and their care. Society was to be concerned with where children came from, what their problems were, and how these problems could be handled in the interests of the children and the state.

Interpretations of its intentions and effects differ, but unquestionably, the Illinois Juvenile Court Act established juvenile delinquency as a legal concept and the juvenile court as a judicial forum. For the first time the distinction was made between children who were dependent and neglected and those who were delinquent. Delinquent children were those under the age of sixteen who violated the law. Most important, the act also established a court specifically for children and an extensive probation program whereby children were to be the responsibility of probation officers. In addition, the legislation allowed children to be committed to institutions and reform programs under the laws and control of the state.

The key provisions of the act were these:

- A separate and independent court was established for delinquent, dependent, and neglected children.

- Special legal and social procedures were developed to govern the adjudication and disposition of juvenile matters.

- Children were to be separated from adults in courts and in institutional programs.

- Probation programs were to be developed to assist the court in making decisions in the best interests of the state and the child.

Following passage of the Illinois Juvenile Court Act, similar legislation was enacted throughout the nation. The special courts these laws created maintained jurisdiction over predelinquent (neglected and dependent) and delinquent children. Juvenile court jurisdiction was based primarily on a child's noncriminal actions and status, not strictly on a violation of criminal law. The *parens patriae* philosophy predominated, ushering in a form of personalized justice characterized by a procedural laxity and informality that did not provide juvenile offenders with the full array of constitutional protections available to adult criminal offenders. The court's process was paternalistic rather than adversarial. Attorneys were not required, and hearsay evidence, inadmissible in criminal trials, was admissible in the adjudication of juvenile offenders. Verdicts were based on a "preponderance of the evidence" instead of the stricter standard used by criminal courts, "beyond a reasonable doubt," and children were often not granted any right to appeal their convictions.

These characteristics allowed the juvenile court to function in a nonlegal manner and to provide various social services to children in need.

The major functions of the juvenile justice system were to prevent juvenile crime and to rehabilitate juvenile offenders. The roles of the two most important actors—the juvenile court judge and the probation staff—were to diagnose the child's condition and prescribe programs to alleviate it. Until 1967, judgments about children's actions and consideration for their constitutional rights had been secondary.

By the 1920s noncriminal behavior in the form of incorrigibility and truancy from school was added to the jurisdiction of many juvenile court systems. Of particular interest was the sexual behavior of young girls, which fell under the jurisdiction of the new courts. Mary Odem and Steven Schlossman have shown how the juvenile court articulated and enforced a strict moral code on working-class girls, not hesitating to incarcerate those who were sexually active.[26] Programs of all kinds, including individualized counseling and institutional care, were used to "cure" juvenile criminality. An entire group of new "experts"—criminologists, sociologists, social workers, probation officers, and psychologists—emerged to deal with delinquency and noncriminal behavior. Much of their effort involved seeking to rehabilitate children brought before the court.

By 1925 juvenile courts existed in virtually every jurisdiction in every state. Although the juvenile court concept expanded rapidly, it cannot be said that each state implemented the philosophy of the court thoroughly. Some jurisdictions established elaborate juvenile court systems, whereas others passed legislation but provided no services. Some courts had trained juvenile court judges; others had nonlawyers sitting in juvenile cases. Some courts had extensive probation departments; others had untrained probation personnel.

Great diversity also marked juvenile institutions. Some maintained a lenient treatment orientation, but others relied on harsh physical punishments, including beatings, straightjacket restraints, immersion in cold water, and solitary confinement in a dark cell with a diet of bread and water.

These conditions were exacerbated by the rapid growth in the juvenile institutional population. Between 1890 and 1920, the number of institutionalized youths jumped 112 percent, a rise that far exceeded the increase in the total number of adolescents in the United States.[27] Despite the juvenile court movement, private institutions were not squeezed out by public institutions; in fact, they grew much faster and larger. Although social workers, community activists, and court personnel deplored the increased institutionalization of youth, the growth was due in part to the successful efforts by reformers to close poorhouses, thereby creating a need for more juvenile institutions to house their displaced populations. In addition, the lack of a coherent national policy on needy children allowed private entrepreneurs to open institutions and fill the void.[28] Although the increase in institutionalization seemed contrary to the goal of rehabilitation, such an approach was preferable to the unhealthy environment of poorhouses and the streets.

Reforming the System

Reform of this system was slow in coming: After all, why criticize a reform movement designed to treat and not punish? In 1912 the U.S. Children's Bureau was formed as the first federal child welfare agency. By the 1930s the bureau began to investigate the state of juvenile institutions and tried to expose some of their more repressive aspects through a series of books and research reports.[29] After World War II, critics such as Paul Tappan and Francis Allen began to identify problems in the juvenile justice system, among which were the neglect of procedural rights and the warehousing of youth in dangerous and ineffective institutions. Status offenders commonly were housed with delinquents and given sentences that were more punitive than those given to delinquents.[30]

From its origin, the juvenile court system denied children procedural rights normally available to adult offenders. Due process rights such as representation by counsel, a jury trial, freedom from self-incrimination, and freedom from unreasonable search and seizure were not considered essential for the juvenile court system because the primary purpose of the system was not punishment but rehabilitation. However, the dream of trying to rehabilitate children was not achieved. Individual treatment approaches failed, and delinquency rates soared. In many instances, the courts deprived children of their liberty and treated them unfairly.

Reform efforts, begun in earnest in the 1960s, changed the face of the juvenile justice system. In 1962 New York passed legislation creating a family court system.[31] The new family court was to assume responsibility for all matters involving family life, with particular emphasis on delinquent, dependent, and neglected children and paternity, adoption, and support proceedings involving parents. In addition, the legislation established the PINS classification (person in need of supervision). This category, covering noncriminal behavior, included individuals involved in such actions as truancy, running away, and incorrigibility. By using labels like PINS and CHINS (children in need of supervision) to establish jurisdiction over children and their families, juvenile courts expanded their role as social agencies. Because noncriminal children were now involved in the juvenile court system to a greater degree, many juvenile courts had to improve their social services. Efforts were made to play down the authority of the court as a court of law and to personalize the system of justice for children. These reforms were soon followed by a "due process revolution," which ushered in an era of procedural rights for court-adjudicated youth. The next section discusses some key cases that transformed the practice of juvenile justice.

The Role of the Supreme Court in Juvenile Law

Perhaps the single most significant factor in overhauling the juvenile justice system in the twentieth century has been the review of juvenile court procedures by the appellate courts. In the hundred or so years that the juvenile court system has been in operation, the U.S. Supreme Court has heard very few cases dealing with juvenile delinquency proceedings (see Figure 12.1). Despite the relatively small number of cases, the Supreme Court has made its mark on the juvenile justice system. Within one decade (1966 to 1975) the Supreme Court, under the leadership of Earl Warren and Warren Burger, handed down five major decisions affecting the equal rights of children within the jurisdiction of the juvenile court. Here is a brief description of each of these cases:

> ***Kent v. United States* (1966)** established that procedures concerning waiver (whether the juvenile court would hear a case or waive it to an adult court for trial) must include a hearing, a right to counsel, and access to social records. This case was an important forerunner to the most significant juvenile decision by the Supreme Court, *In re Gault.*[32]
>
> ***In re Gault* (1967)** held that juveniles at trial faced with incarceration were entitled to many of the rights granted adult offenders. These included counsel, notice of the charges, cross-examination of witnesses, and protection against self-incrimination. *Gault* was the most far-reaching of the Supreme Court decisions and mandated a more formalized juvenile court system.[33]
>
> ***In re Winship* (1970)** ruled that the standard of proof in a delinquency proceeding that could result in a child's commitment must be "proof beyond a reasonable doubt" and not a "preponderance of the evidence," the more lenient standard used for civil court cases. According to the Court, civil labels and good intentions do not obviate the need for criminal due process safeguards in juvenile courts.[34]

DUE PROCESS CASES (guarantees of procedural fairness under Fifth and Fourteenth Amendments)

1966	1967	1970	1971	1975
Kent	In re Gault	In re Winship	McKeiver	Breed
v.			v.	v.
United States			Pennsylvania*	Jones
(Waiver)	(Trial)	(Standard of Proof)	(Jury Trial)	(Double Jeopardy)

CRIME CONTROL CASES

1977	1979	1979	1982	1984
Oklahoma Publishing Co.	Smith	Fare	Eddings	Schall
v.	v.	v.	v.	v.
District Court	Daily Mail Pub. Co.	Michael	Oklahoma	Martin
(Free Press)	(Free Press)	(Interrogation)	(Capital Punishment)	(Preventive Detention)

1984	1988	1989	1995	1995
New Jersey	Thompson**	Stanford	Vernonia School District	United States
v.	v.	v.	v.	v.
T.L.O.	Oklahoma	Kentucky	Action	Lopez
(School Search)	(Capital Punishment)	(Capital Punishment)	(Drug Testing)	(Commerce Clause)

FIGURE 12.1

Time Line of Major Constitutional Decisions in Juvenile Justice

Notes: *no right to jury trial and went against due process model; **exception to crime control model when Supreme Court concluded death penalty in the case violated Eighth Amendment.

***McKeiver v. Pennsylvania* (1971)** held that juveniles were not to be afforded the constitutional right to a jury in a delinquency proceeding. The Court felt that this aspect of the adversarial process was not appropriate for the juvenile justice system going against the trend of increased due process.[35]

***Breed v. Jones* (1975)** established that the double jeopardy clause of the Fifth Amendment of the U.S. Constitution extends to juvenile offenders. It provides that no person shall be subject to the same offense to be twice put in jeopardy of life or limb and prevents a second prosecution for the same offense. Juveniles, henceforth, could not be tried in a juvenile court and then transferred to an adult court for a similar action.[36]

Since 1975, the Supreme Court has decided a number of other important cases dealing with juvenile offenders. Many of the decisions made in this later period are indicative of a shift away from due process.

Oklahoma Publishing Co. v. District Court (1977) ruled that a state court could not prohibit the publication of information obtained in an open juvenile proceeding. When photographs were taken and published of an eleven-year-old boy suspected of homicide and the local court prohibited further disclosure, the publishing company claimed that the court order was a restraint in violation of the First Amendment. The Supreme Court agreed.[37]

Smith v. Daily Mail Publishing Co. (1979) involved the discovery and subsequent publication of the identity of a juvenile suspect in violation of a state statute prohibiting publication. The Supreme Court declared the statute unconstitutional because it believed the state's interest in protecting the child was not of such magnitude as to justify the use of a criminal statute.[38] Criminal trials are open to the public, but juvenile proceedings are meant to be private and confidential, which ordinarily does not violate the First Amendment right to free press discussed in the above two cases.

Fare v. Michael C. (1979) held that a child's request to see his probation officer at the time of interrogation did not operate to invoke his Fifth Amendment right to remain silent. According to the Court, the probation officer cannot be expected to offer the type of advice that an accused would expect from an attorney.[39] The landmark *Miranda v. Arizona* case ruled that a request for a lawyer is an immediate revocation of a person's right to silence, but this rule is not applicable for a request to see the probation officer.

Eddings v. Oklahoma (1982) ruled that a defendant's age should be a mitigating factor in deciding whether to apply the death penalty.[40]

Schall v. Martin (1984) upheld a statute allowing for the placement of children in preventive detention before their adjudication. The Court concluded that it was not unreasonable to detain juveniles for their own protection.[41]

New Jersey v. T.L.O. (1984) determined that the Fourth Amendment applies to school searches. The Court adopted a "reasonable suspicion" standard, as opposed to the stricter standard of "probable cause," to evaluate the legality of searches and seizures in a school setting.[42]

Thompson v. Oklahoma (1988) ruled that imposing capital punishment on a juvenile murderer who was fifteen years old at the time of the offense violated the Eighth Amendment's constitutional prohibition against cruel and unusual punishment.[43]

Stanford v. Kentucky and *Wilkins v. Missouri* (1989) concluded that the imposition of the death penalty on a juvenile who committed a crime between the ages of sixteen and eighteen was not unconstitutional and that the Eighth Amendment's cruel and unusual punishment clause did not prohibit capital punishment.[44]

Vernonia School District v. Acton (1995) held that the Fourth Amendment's guarantee against unreasonable searches is not violated by the suspicionless drug testing of all students choosing to participate in interscholastic athletics. The Supreme Court expanded the power of public educators to ensure safe learning environments in schools.[45]

United States v. Lopez (1995) ruled that Congress exceeded its authority under the Commerce Clause when it passed the Gun-Free School Zone Act, which made it a federal crime to possess a firearm within one thousand feet of a school.[46]

The future course of constitutional decisions affecting the rights of juveniles is difficult to ascertain while William Rehnquist is chief justice and other conservatives,

In the 1982 case *Eddings v. Oklahoma,* the U.S. Supreme Court ruled that a defendant's age should be a mitigating factor in deciding whether to apply the death penalty. Should very young juvenile killers be eligible for capital punishment, or are they too immature to appreciate the seriousness of their misdeeds?

APRIL 6, 1998 $2.95

TIME

Mitchell Johnson, 13, and Andrew Golden, 11. Right, Golden as a toddler

Armed & Dangerous

An up-close look at the lives of two gun-happy kids and the murderous ambush of their Arkansas classmates

such as Antonin Scalia, Anthony Kennedy, and Clarence Thomas, are on the bench. Another unknown is what role Justices Ruth Bader Ginsburg and Stephen Breyer, the newest members of the Supreme Court, appointed by President Clinton in 1993 and 1995, respectively, will play in children's rights issues. Since the 1960s the Court has reinforced the idea that due process and fair treatment must be accorded juveniles throughout the entire juvenile justice process. However, the Court also seems to be saying that the special status of minors gives the state the right to exercise legal controls from which an adult would be exempted.

The *McKeiver, Schall, T.L.O.,* and *Vernonia School District* decisions appear to reflect a shift back to the informality and paternal protection of the juvenile court in preference to further formalizing court proceedings. Whether this trend will continue remains to be seen. However, as Justice Harry A. Blackmun stated in the *McKeiver* case, "If the formalities of the criminal adjudicative process are to be superimposed upon the juvenile court system, there is little need for its separate existence. Perhaps that ultimate disillusionment will come one day, but for the moment we are disinclined to give impetus to it."[47] Considering the makeup and direction of today's Court, we might expect to see Justice Blackmun's prediction one day come true.[48] For the time being, however these cases affirm the Supreme Court's interest in applying constitutional principles of due process to juvenile justice while maintaining the *parens patriae* philosophy.

Given the more conservative mood of the nation and its legal system today, it is unlikely that any liberalization of the legal rights of juveniles will take place in the near future. If anything, the Supreme Court will give states more opportunities to control minors.[49]

In summary, the early cases from *Kent* to *Breed* provided due process protections for children; the latter cases, such as *Schall, T. L. O.,* and *Stanford,* rejected the rehabilitation ideal in favor of an accountability and punishment philosophy.[50]

In the following section on the contemporary juvenile system, we will explore the specific impact some of these decisions have had on the juvenile court process.

The Contemporary Juvenile Justice System

Today's juvenile justice system is very much a legal system. The Supreme Court has played a significant, if not monumental, role in the formulation of juvenile law and procedure over the past thirty years. Nevertheless, the courts have neither repudiated the goal of rehabilitating children nor subjected children totally to the procedures and philosophy of the adult criminal justice system.

The juvenile justice system exists in all states by statute. Each jurisdiction has a juvenile code and a special court structure to accommodate children in trouble. Nationwide, the juvenile justice system consists of thousands of public and private agencies, with a total budget amounting to hundreds of millions of dollars. Most of the nation's twenty thousand police agencies have juvenile components, and more than three thousand juvenile courts and about an equal number of juvenile correctional facilities exist throughout the nation. There are thousands of juvenile police officers, more than three thousand juvenile court judges, more than sixty-five hundred juvenile probation officers, and thousands of juvenile correctional employees.[51]

About 2.2 million juveniles are arrested annually; Figure 12.2 depicts the approximate number of juvenile offenders removed at various stages of the juvenile justice process.[52]

These figures do not take into account the large number of children who are referred to community diversion and mental health programs. There are thousands of these programs throughout the nation, and thousands of youth are being held in the community-based institutions that administer them. This multitude of agencies and people dealing with juvenile delinquency and status offenses has led to development of what professionals in the field view as an incredibly expansive and complex juvenile justice system. The "Focus on Delinquency" on pages 454–455 takes a closer look at the nature of this system.

The Juvenile Justice Process

How are children processed by the agencies and organizations of the juvenile justice system?[53] Most children initially come in contact with the juvenile justice system as a result of contact with a police officer. When a juvenile commits a serious crime, the police are empowered to make an arrest. Less serious offenses may also require police action, but in these instances, instead of being arrested, the child may be warned, the parents may be called, or a referral may be made to a juvenile social service program. Only about half of all children arrested by the police are

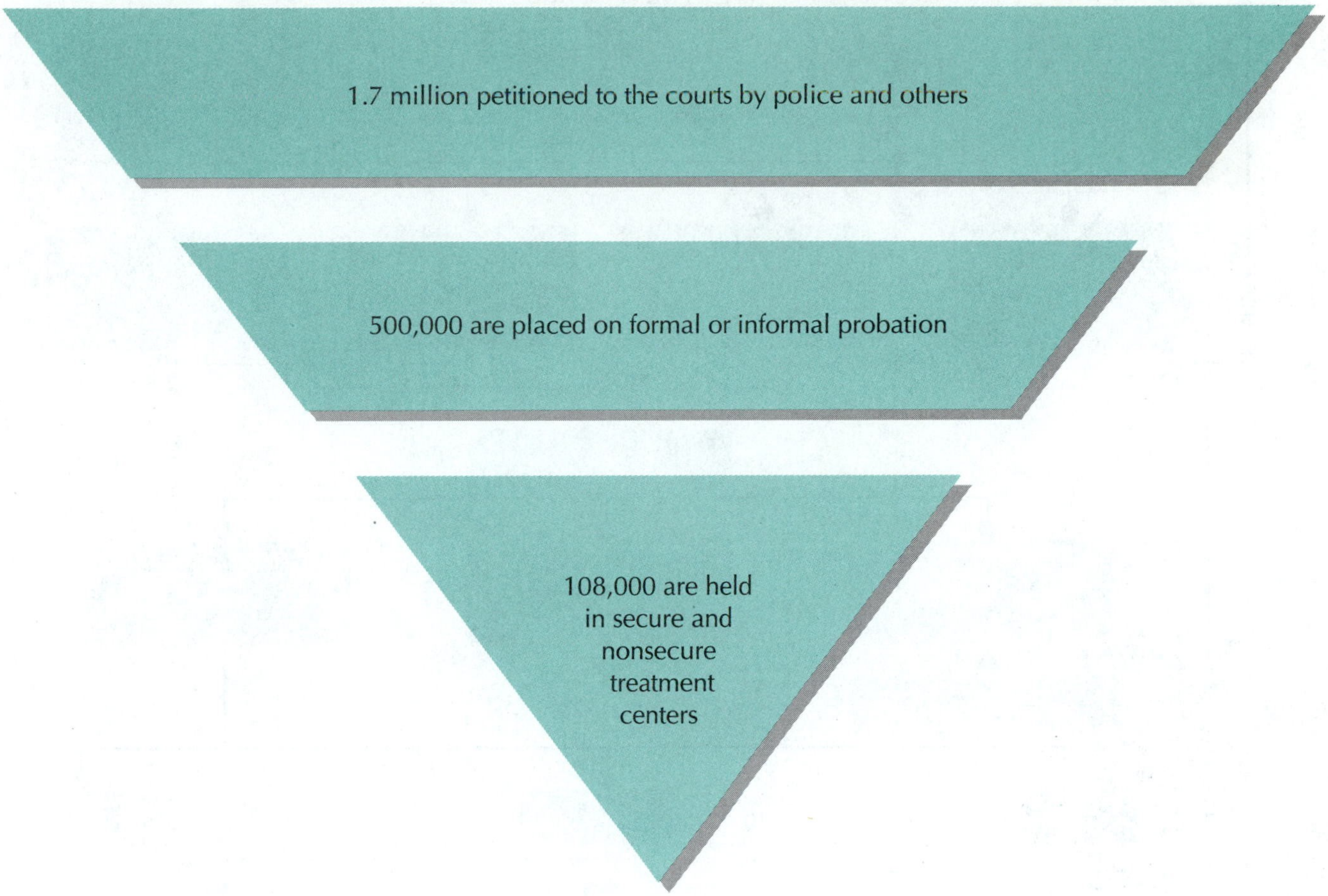

1.7 million petitioned to the courts by police and others

500,000 are placed on formal or informal probation

108,000 are held in secure and nonsecure treatment centers

FIGURE 12.2

Disposition of the 2.2 Million Juveniles Arrested Annually

juvenile justice process
Under the paternal *(parens patriae)* philosophy, juvenile justice procedures are informal and nonadversarial, invoked *for* the juvenile offender rather than *against* him or her; a petition instead of a complaint is filed; courts make findings of involvement or adjudication of delinquency instead of convictions; and juvenile offenders receive dispositions instead of sentences.

detention hearing
A hearing by a judicial officer of a juvenile court to determine whether a juvenile is to be detained or released while juvenile proceedings are pending in the case.

actually referred to the juvenile court. Figure 12.3 outlines the **juvenile justice process,** and a detailed analysis of the stages in this process is presented in the next sections.

Police Investigation   When a juvenile commits a crime, police agencies have the authority to investigate the incident and then to decide whether to release the child or to detain and refer him or her to the juvenile court. This is often a discretionary decision based not only on the nature of the offense committed but also on the conditions existing at the time of the arrest. Such factors as the type and seriousness of the offense, the child's past contacts with the police, and whether or not the child denies committing the crime determine whether a petition is filed. Juveniles who are in the custody of the police have basic constitutional rights similar to those of adult offenders. Children are protected against unreasonable search and seizure under the Fourth and Fourteenth Amendments of the constitution. The Fifth Amendment places limitations on police interrogation procedures.

If the police decide to file a petition, the child is referred to juvenile court. The primary decision at this point is whether the child should remain in the community or be placed in a detention facility or shelter home. In the past, too many children were routinely taken to court and held in detention facilities to await court appearances. Normally, a **detention hearing** is held to determine whether to remand the child to a shelter or to release the child. At this point the child has a right to counsel and other procedural safeguards. A child who is not detained is usually released to his or her parent or guardian. Most state juvenile court acts provide for a child to

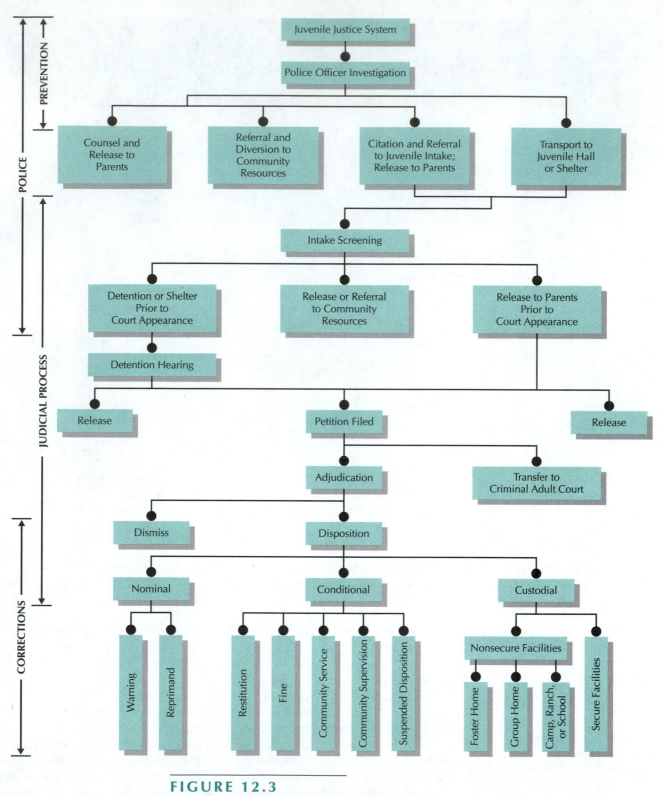

FIGURE 12.3

The Juvenile Justice System

return home to await further court action, except when it is necessary to protect the child, when the child presents a serious danger to the public, or when it is not certain that the child will return to court for further adjudication. In many cases the police will refer the child to a community service program at intake instead of filing a formal charge.

Pretrial Procedures   In most juvenile court jurisdictions the adjudication process begins with some sort of initial hearing. At this hearing juvenile court rules of procedure normally require that the juveniles be informed of their right to a trial, that the plea or admission be voluntary, and that they understand the charges and consequences of the plea. The case will often not be further adjudicated if a child admits to the crime at the initial hearing.

In some cases youths may be detained at this stage pending a trial. Juveniles who are detained are eligible for bail in a handful of jurisdictions. Plea bargaining may also occur in the juvenile process at any stage of the proceedings. A plea bargain is an agreement between the prosecution and the defense by which the juvenile agrees to plead guilty for certain considerations, such as a lenient sentence. This issue is explored in more depth in Chapter 14, which discusses pretrial procedures.

If the child denies the allegation of delinquency, an **adjudicatory hearing** or trial is scheduled. Under extraordinary circumstances, a juvenile who commits a serious crime may be transferred or waived to an adult court instead of being adjudicated. Today, most jurisdictions have laws providing for such transfers. Whether such a transfer occurs depends on the type of offense, the youth's prior record, the nature of past treatment efforts, the availability of treatment services, and the likelihood that the youth will be rehabilitated in the juvenile court system.

Adjudication   The adjudication is the trial stage of the juvenile court process. If the child does not admit guilt at the initial hearing and is not transferred to an adult court, an adjudication hearing is held to determine the facts of the case. The court hears evidence on the allegations in the delinquency petition. This is a trial on the merits (dealing with issues of law and facts), and rules of evidence similar to those of criminal proceedings generally apply. At this stage of the proceeding, the juvenile offender is entitled to many of the procedural guarantees given adult offenders. These rights include the right to representation by counsel, freedom from self-incrimination, the right to confront and cross-examine witnesses, and, in certain instances, the right to a jury trial. In addition, many states have their own procedures concerning rules of evidence, competence of witnesses, pleadings, and pretrial motions. At the end of the adjudicatory hearing, the court enters a judgment against the juvenile.

Disposition   If the adjudication process finds the child delinquent, the court must then decide what should be done to treat the child. Most juvenile court acts require a dispositional hearing separate from the adjudication. This two-stage decision is often referred to as a **bifurcated process.** The dispositional hearing is less formal than adjudication. Here, the judge imposes a **disposition** on the juvenile offender in light of the offense, the youth's prior record, and his or her family background. The judge has broad discretion and can prescribe a wide range of dispositions ranging from a simple warning or reprimand to community service or probation to more intense social control measures, such as institutional commitment, including group home, foster care, or secure facility care. In theory the judge's decision serves the best interests of the child, the family, and the community. Many juvenile statutes require that the judge consider the least restrictive dispositional alternative before imposing any sentence. The disposition is one of the most important stages in the juvenile process, and it may be the court's last opportunity to influence the offender's behavior. Disposition is concerned primarily with treating the juvenile and controlling antisocial behavior.

Some jurisdictions allow for a program of juvenile aftercare or parole. A youth can be paroled from an institution and placed under the supervision of a parole officer. This means that he or she will complete the period of confinement in the community and receive assistance from the parole officer in the form of counseling, school referral, and vocational training.

In most states, juveniles have been granted the right to appeal. Although most state statutes provide for appellate review of juvenile cases, this hasn't yet been

---

adjudicatory hearing
The fact-finding process wherein the juvenile court determines whether there is sufficient evidence to sustain the allegations in a petition.

bifurcated process
The procedure of separating adjudicatory and dispositionary hearings so different levels of evidence can be heard at each.

disposition
The equivalent of sentencing for adult offenders, the juvenile disposition is aimed at rehabilitation rather than retribution.

THE JUVENILE JUSTICE SYSTEM: KEY PLAYERS, PROGRAMS, AND COSTS

PREVENTING DELINQUENCY

Under the Juvenile Justice and Delinquency Prevention Act of 1974 (PL. 93–45), the appropriation amendment for 1996–97 grants approximately $200 million for state juvenile justice programs. A portion of these funds are used for exemplary juvenile delinquency prevention programs. In addition, the Violent Crime Control and Law Enforcement Act of 1994 (PL. 103–322) provides federal funding for juvenile prevention programs.

Hundreds of thousands of children and families are serviced in primary prevention programs targeted at families, schools, and the community. More than 400,000 children live in foster care, and programs such as Permanent Families for Abused and Neglected Children help to prevent delinquency in these children. Court Appointed Special Advocates (CASA) ensure that the courts are familiar with the needs of these children. Schools provide Cities in Schools, law-related education, and peer leadership programs to reduce school violence and prevent students from dropping out. Youth gangs are often served by youth service bureaus, Jobs for Youth, and detached worker programs. Drug prevention programs, such as Drug Abuse Resistance Education (DARE), help kids say no to drugs. Drug-free school zones and citizens' patrols help link youth prevention agencies and organizations.

JUVENILE LAW ENFORCEMENT

Of the thirteen thousand municipal police agencies, approximately 75 percent provide special programs and services for juvenile offenders. Police officers concerned with juveniles often have a multiplicity of roles and duties. Cost of police services for children is undetermined, but more time is being spent dealing with troubled and violent youths committing serious crimes. Police officers make more than 2.9 million juvenile arrests, of which 600,000 are for serious crimes. The community policing concept is being utilized to decentralize policing and make its services more amenable to juvenile delinquency prevention.

DETENTION AND PRETRIAL SERVICES

In the United States, there are more than 3,300 jails and about 830 juvenile detention facilities. Many juveniles, upwards of 1,500, are housed in jails on any given day. From 200,000 to 300,000 are being jailed with adults each year. Upwards of 500,000 youths are held in detention facilities each year. Thousands of juveniles receive diversion as an alternative to official procedures. More than 16,000 are tried as adults. The amount of plea bargaining is uncertain because a significant number of juveniles enter guilty pleas admissions in the juvenile court. All states and the District of Columbia have waiver proceedings to the criminal court.

PROSECUTORS AND PUBLIC DEFENDERS

Of the thirty thousand lawyers in the justice system, including prosecutors and public defenders, only a small percentage work in the juvenile courts. They handle from 500,000 to

recognized as a federal constitutional right. The juvenile appeal process will be covered in detail in Chapter 15.

Juveniles who are committed to programs of treatment and control have a legal right to treatment. The right to treatment for juveniles requires that states provide suitable rehabilitation programs that include counseling, education, and vocational services. Appellate courts have ruled that if such minimum treatment is not provided, individuals must be released from confinement.

600,000 delinquency and status offense cases annually in addition to thousands of informally handled cases. The public defense system provides the bulk of legal representation to children in the juvenile courts. In some areas, only 50 percent of the children in court receive the assistance of counsel. Costs range from $35 to $75 per hour for legal services.

JUVENILE COURTS

Jurisdiction ordinarily is defined by state statute. There are independent juvenile court systems, family court structures, and juvenile sessions of adult courts. Two factors, age and status, bring children under juvenile court jurisdiction. Judges, juvenile probation officers, court clerks, and juvenile prosecutors control and influence court cases.

In a noted 1967 case, *In re Gault,* the Supreme Court declared that youths have a right to a lawyer and other legal protections. The juvenile courts handle about 1.7 million delinquency cases each year in addition to about 160,000 status offense cases.

COMMUNITY TREATMENT

The most common community disposition employed by the juvenile court is probation. More than 500,000 youths are supervised on juvenile probation. Caseloads range from 60 to 80 youths per officer. Intensive probation services utilize very small caseloads and intense scrutiny. Statutory restitution programs exist in all fifty states. Residential programs include group homes, boarding schools, foster programs, and rural residences such as farms and camps.

Community programs often cost half as much per child as a secure training school. Recidivism rates tend to be lower generally in the community treatment programs than in large-scale institutional settings.

JUVENILE CORRECTIONS (INSTITUTIONAL CARE)

There are about 1,100 public and 2,000 private juvenile facilities; more than 100,000 children are held in all types of facilities during a year. Public facilities have a one-day count of 69,000, and 34,000 children are confined in private juvenile facilities. The one-day count for African American youth is twice as high as the rate for Hispanic youth and almost four times as high as the rate for white youth. Average length of stay is about eight months. The budget for juvenile corrections in the states is approximately $2.7 billion annually.

Staff include custody, administrative, and treatment personnel. Institutional placement costs currently are about $25,000 to $40,000 annually per child. States are spending more than $380 million on contracts with private facilities for such specialized services as marine programs and wilderness camps.

Many states indicate a problem with overcrowding. Juveniles in state custody range in age from eleven to eighteen years of age. Delinquent offenders constitute nearly 75 percent of all juvenile commitments.

Sources: Melissa Sickmund, Howard Snyder, and Eileen Poe-Yamagata, *Juvenile Offenders and Victims: 1997 Update on Violence* (Washington, D.C.: OJJDP, 1997); Jeffrey Butts, "Juvenile Court Processing of Delinquency Cases, 1985–1994," Fact Sheet 57 (Washington, D.C.: OJJDP, 1997); Joseph Moore, "Juveniles in Public Facilities—1995," Fact Sheet 69 (Washington, D.C.: OJJDP, 1997).

This overview of the juvenile justice process hints at the often conflicting values at the heart of our contemporary juvenile justice system. Efforts to ensure that juveniles are given appropriate treatment are consistent with the doctrine of *parens patriae* that predominated in the first half of the twentieth century. The current system is also a product of the "due process revolution" of the sixties and seventies, which resulted in granting to juveniles many of the same constitutional protections available to adult offenders. (See Table 12.3 for a time line of the underlying

Table 12.3

Time Frame	Activity
Prior to 1900s	Juveniles treated similarly to adult offenders. No distinction by age or capacity to commit criminal acts.
From 1899 to 1950s	Children treated differently, beginning with the Illinois Juvenile Court Act of 1899. By 1925 juvenile court acts are established in virtually every state.
1950s to 1970s	Recognition by experts that the rehabilitation model and the protective nature of *parens patriae* have failed to prevent delinquency.
1960s to 1970s	Constitutional due process is introduced into the juvenile justice system. The concept of punishing children or protecting them under *parens patriae* is under attack by the courts.
1970s to 1980s	Failure of rehabilitation and due process protections to control delinquency leads to a shift to a crime control and punishment philosophy similar to that of the adult criminal justice system.
Early 1990s	Mixed constitutional protections with some treatment. Uncertain goals and programs; the juvenile justice system relies on punishment and deterrence.
Mid-1990s to 2000	Attention given to strategy that focuses on reducing the threat of juvenile crime and expanding options for handling juvenile offenders. Emphasis is placed on "what works" and implementing the best intervention and control programs. Effort is made to utilize the restorative justice model, which involves balancing the needs of the victim, the community, and the juvenile.

ideologies of juvenile justice during the twentieth century.) Today, no single ideology or program dominates the juvenile justice system, which increasingly has taken on many of the characteristics of the adult court system. However, a number of goals and prevention strategies have been proposed in recent years. Table 12.4 shows the interrelationships of the component stages of the juvenile justice system and some theoretical models or perspectives that experts believe will reduce juvenile crime. Two essential foundations, the crime control perspective which emphasizes protection of society through sanctions, and the due process perspective, which is concerned with fairness and individual rights are inherent in all the models in varying degrees. The next section examines the similarities and differences between the present day juvenile and adult (criminal systems).

Criminal Justice versus Juvenile Justice

The components of the adult and juvenile criminal processes are similar. Both include some form of police investigation, arrest, pretrial procedures, adjudication,

Table 12.4
THEORETICAL MODELS OF JUVENILE JUSTICE

Model	Description	Stage
Rehabilitation	Emphasis on treatment and individual needs of the juvenile; *Parens patriae* philosophy; best interest of child is paramount.	
	Referral to social services, discretion, and referral; limited use of detention, waiver, and plea bargaining.	Police
	Use of intake procedures, discretion, and referral; limited use of detention, waiver, and plea bargaining.	Pretrial
	Procedural due process and fairness in a "helping court"; concern about diversion and community treatment.	Adjudication
	Use of indeterminate sentencing (sentence tailored to individual offender needs); institutional care only as last resort; bifurcated hearing with focus on community alternatives.	Disposition
Justice	Goal is public protection, accountability, and "just deserts"; due process considerations also important; actions similar to adult criminal justice system; decisions based on nature of offense; primary concern is with delinquency and serious crimes (as opposed to status offenses).	
	Officers have limited discretion; strict application of *Miranda* and search and seizure rules.	Police
	Increased role of prosecutor, full procedural safeguards; fact-finding is important. Plea bargaining acceptable; use of detention and waiver procedure.	Pretrial
	Juvenile guaranteed full procedural due process; admission of guilt allowed with proper rules of procedure; fairness and efficiency are goals of court; use of rules of evidence; procedure similar to that in adult court.	Adjudication
	Decisions based primarily on offense, as opposed to individual's need; punishment is goal of the juvenile justice code; determinate sentencing (less flexibility, one size fits all) to ensure accountability for behavior.	Disposition
Restorative Justice	Youth, victim, and community receive balanced attention.	
	Public safety through increased involvement with the community; police collaborate with the community on prevention strategies.	Police
	Reintegration of offenders; restoration of victims and offender; awareness of harm done.	Pretrial
	Due process of law; focus on separating violent offenders from the community; recognition of citizen and victim reports.	Adjudication
	Limited use of incarceration for public protection, not punishment; active role for offenders, victims, and community in prevention activities and sanctions.	Disposition
Hybrid	Combines treatment and punishment; goals often in conflict with each other; no consensus on purpose and nature of juvenile justice.	
	Juvenile codes recognize discretion and need for public protection; arrest, search, seizure, and *Miranda* rules apply in all cases.	Police
	High priority given to crime control policy; detention used with required hearing and due process; effort to retain the traditional goal of rehabilitation through diversion and discretion.	Pretrial
	Formal trial; focus on fact-finding and due process; concern for rules of law and procedure at expense of individual interests.	Adjudication
	Stress on sanctions proportionate to seriousness of youth's crime; effort to balance community treatment and public protection, use of wide range of dispositional alternatives.	Disposition

disposition, and post disposition. However, the juvenile system has a separate, complementary (almost parallel) organizational structure. In many communities juvenile justice is administered by people who bring special skills to the task. Also, more kinds of facilities and services are available to juveniles than to adults.

One major concern of the juvenile court reform movement was to make certain that the stigma attached to a person who became a convicted criminal offender would not be affixed to young people in juvenile proceedings. Thus, even the language used in the juvenile court differs from that used in the adult criminal court (see Table 12.5). Juveniles are not formally indicted for a crime; they have a **petition** filed against them. Secure pretrial holding facilities are called detention centers rather than jails. Similarly, the criminal court trial is called a hearing in the juvenile justice system. The Focus on Delinquency box on pages 460–461 compares the similarities and differences between these two systems.

Legal expert Barry Feld, one of the leading scholars of the juvenile court, believes that over the years the juvenile justice system has taken on more of the char-

petition
Document filed in juvenile court alleging that a juvenile is a delinquent, a status offender, or a dependent and asking that the court assume jurisdiction over the juvenile.

Table 12.5

COMPARISON OF TERMS USED IN ADULT AND JUVENILE JUSTICE SYSTEMS

	Juvenile Terms	Adult Terms
The Person and the Act	Delinquent child	Criminal
	Delinquent act	Crime
Preadjudicatory Stage	Take into custody	Arrest
	Petition	Indictment
	Agree to a finding	Plead guilty
	Deny the petition	Plead not guilty
	Adjustment	Plea bargain
	Detention facility; child care shelter	Jail
Adjudicatory Stage	Substitution	Reduction of charges
	Adjudication or fact-finding hearing	Trial
	Adjudication	Conviction
Postadjudicatory Stage	Dispositional hearing	Sentencing hearing
	Disposition	Sentence
	Commitment	Incarceration
	Youth development center; treatment; training school	Prison
	Residential child care facility	Halfway house
	Aftercare	Parole

acteristics of the adult courts. He refers to this as the "criminalizing" of the juvenile court.[54] Robert Dawson suggests that because the legal differences between the juvenile and criminal systems are narrower than they ever have been, it may be time to abolish the juvenile court and merge it into the larger criminal justice system.[55] During the last twenty years especially, the juvenile court system has come to resemble more closely the adult court system.

The Future of Juvenile Justice

The outlook for juvenile crime rates over the next decade is uncertain. The violent juvenile crime rate fell in the late 1990s, but many experts predict a future surge in juvenile delinquency. Serious crimes such as robbery, rape, and weapons-related offenses are increasingly part of the juvenile crime scene.

A Comprehensive Juvenile Justice Strategy

At a time when much attention is focused on the small group of serious juvenile offenders, a comprehensive juvenile justice strategy has been called for to deal with all aspects of juvenile crime. This strategy focuses on crime prevention and expanding options for handling juvenile offenders. It addresses the links between crime and poverty, child abuse, community violence, drugs, weapons, and school behavior. Programs are based on a continuum of care that begins in early childhood and progresses through late adolescence. The components of this strategy include: (1) prevention in early childhood; (2) intervention methods for at-risk teenage youths;

Elements of a comprehensive juvenile justice strategy are (1) prevention in early childhood; (2) intervention methods for at-risk teenage youths; (3) graduated sanctions to hold juvenile offenders accountable for juvenile crimes; (4) proper utilization of juvenile detention and confinement; and (5) the placement of serious juvenile offenders into adult courts. Here a youth worker lends a helping hand to a youngster, allowing him to build stronger ties to society.

SIMILARITIES AND DIFFERENCES BETWEEN JUVENILE AND ADULT JUSTICE SYSTEMS

Since its creation, the juvenile justice system has sought to maintain its independence from the adult justice system. Yet there are a number of similarities that characterize the institutions, processes, and law of the two systems.

SIMILARITIES BETWEEN THE JUVENILE AND ADULT JUSTICE SYSTEMS

Police officers, judges, and correctional personnel use discretion in decision making in both the adult and the juvenile systems.

The right to receive Miranda warnings applies to juveniles as well as to adults.

Juveniles and adults are protected from prejudicial lineups or other identification procedures.

Similar procedural safeguards protect juveniles and adults when they make an admission of guilt.

Prosecutors and defense attorneys play equally critical roles in juvenile and adult advocacy.

Juveniles and adults have the right to counsel at most key stages of the court process.

Pretrial motions are available in juvenile and criminal court proceedings.

Negotiations and plea bargaining exist for juvenile and adult offenders.

Juveniles and adults have a right to a hearing and an appeal.

The standard of evidence in juvenile delinquency adjudications, as in adult criminal trials, is proof beyond a reasonable doubt.

Juveniles and adults can be placed on probation by the court.

Both juveniles and adults can be placed in pretrial detention facilities.

Juveniles and adults can be kept in detention without bail if they are considered dangerous.

After trial, both can be placed in community treatment programs.

---

(3) graduated sanctions to hold juvenile offenders accountable for juvenile crimes; (4) proper utilization of juvenile detention and confinement; and (5) the placement of serious juvenile offenders in adult courts.[56] Professionals in law enforcement, the courts, and corrections favor this approach, as well as heads of organizations such as the American Bar Association, OJJDP, and the National Council of Juvenile Court Judges.

Prevention   Research has identified certain risk factors that may suggest future delinquency. For young children, these factors include abuse and neglect, domestic violence, family conflict, unpreparedness for school, and health problems. Early childhood services may prevent delinquency from occurring and make a child less vulnerable to future criminality. State legislatures are increasingly investing in state funded early education programs like Head Start to reduce juvenile crime, and Smart Start is designed to make certain children are healthy before starting school. Home visiting programs for new parents target families at risk because of child abuse and neglect.

Intervention   Many jurisdictions are developing new intervention programs for teenage youths. An example of a national program that has been effective is the Big Brother/Big Sister Program, a structured relationship that matches a volunteer adult with a youngster. More and more cities are finding that night curfews can also reduce gang violence and vandalism. Curfews may also contribute to a feeling of safety among residents in high-crime neighborhoods. The actual impact of cur-

DIFFERENCES BETWEEN THE JUVENILE AND ADULT JUSTICE SYSTEMS

The primary purpose of juvenile procedures is protection and treatment. With adults, the aim is to punish the guilty.

Age determines the jurisdiction of the juvenile court. The nature of the offense determines jurisdiction in the adult system. Juveniles can be ordered to the criminal court for trial as adults.

Juveniles can be apprehended for acts that would not be criminal if they were committed by an adult (status offenses).

Juvenile proceedings are not considered criminal; adult proceedings are.

Juvenile court procedures are generally informal and private. Those of adult courts are more formal and are open to the public.

Courts cannot release identifying information about a juvenile to the press, but they must release information about an adult.

Parents are highly involved in the juvenile process but not in the adult process.

The standard of arrest is more stringent for adults than for juveniles.

Juveniles are released into parental custody. Adults are generally given the opportunity for bail.

Juveniles have no constitutional right to a jury trial. Adults have this right. Some state statutes provide juveniles with a jury trial.

Juveniles can be searched in school without probable cause or a warrant.

A juvenile's record is generally sealed when the age of majority is reached. The record of an adult is permanent.

A juvenile court cannot sentence juveniles to county jails or state prisons; these are reserved for adults.

The U.S. Supreme Court has declared that the Eighth Amendment does not prohibit the death penalty for crimes committed by juveniles ages 16 and 17, but it is not a sentence given to children under age 16.

few laws on juvenile crime control is hard to document, however, and more research is needed to determine their effectiveness. Efforts also are being made to deter young people from becoming involved with gangs because gang members ordinarily have higher rates of serious violent behavior.

Graduated Sanctions   Graduated sanction programs for juveniles are another solution being explored by states across the country. Types of graduated sanctions include: (1) immediate sanctions for nonviolent offenders; (2) intermediate sanctions such as probation and electronic monitoring, which target repeat minor offenders and first-time serious offenders; and (3) secure institutional care, which is reserved for repeat serious offenders and violent offenders. A survey conducted on more than 3,000 intervention programs found that about 425 of these programs showed success in juvenile treatment and control.[57] As a result, considerable information is available to states to develop comprehensive graduated sanctions. Graduated sanctions provide a range of opportunity-based options appropriate for different types of juvenile offenders; these are explored in detail in Chapters 16 and 17.

Institutional Programs   Another key to a comprehensive strategy is improving institutional programs. Many experts believe juvenile incarceration is overused, particularly for nonviolent offenders. That is exactly why the concept of deinstitutionalization was established by the Juvenile Justice and Delinquency Act of 1974. Considerable research supports the fact that warehousing juveniles without proper treatment does little to deter future delinquent and criminal behavior. The most effective secure detention and corrections programs are those that provide individual services for a small number of participants. Large training schools have not reduced recidivism.

Treating Juveniles Like Adults   Treating juveniles like adults is the last component to an overall strategy for juvenile justice. This policy affects the numbers and types of juvenile cases going to adult courts. As we previously indicated, the number of delinquency cases waived to criminal court grew from 7,200 to 12,200 cases between 1985 and 1995. Little is known about what happens to juveniles sent to criminal courts. In the meantime, new laws have expanded the pool of cases eligible for judicial waiver. As a result, more juvenile offenders are being sentenced as adults and incarcerated in adult prisons.[58]

Getting tough on juvenile crime is the primary motivation for moving cases to the adult criminal justice system. Some commentators argue that transferring juveniles is a statement that juvenile crime is taken seriously by society; others believe the fear of being transferred serves as a deterrent. In addition to the increase in adult court waivers, some of the major new trends affecting juvenile justice today include: (1) parental responsibility statutes that aim to hold parents responsible for children's offenses; (2) juvenile gun control programs;[59] and (3) analysis of the future of the juvenile court movement.[60] These ideas are discussed in detail in several of the following chapters.

Federal Funding for Juvenile Justice

President's Commission on Law Enforcement and the Administration of Justice
This 1967 commission suggested that we must provide juveniles with opportunities for success, including jobs and education, and that we must develop effective law enforcement procedures to control hard core youthful offenders.

Law Enforcement Assistance Administration (LEAA)
Unit in the U.S. Department of Justice established by the Omnibus Crime Control and Safe Streets Act of 1968 to administer grants and provide guidance for crime prevention policy and programs.

National Advisory Commission on Criminal Justice Standards and Goals
Established in 1973, the commission's report identified major strategies for juvenile justice and delinquency prevention.

Proponents of juvenile justice reform have been aided considerably by federal and state financial support. Since the 1960s, four major efforts have been funded by the government to support the goals of juvenile justice and delinquency reform. First, in 1967 the **President's Commission on Law Enforcement and the Administration of Justice,** a product of the Johnson administration's concern for social welfare, issued its well-thought-out and documented report on juvenile delinquency and its control.[61] Influenced by Cloward and Ohlin's then-popular opportunity theory, the commission suggested that the juvenile justice system must provide underprivileged youths with opportunities for success, including jobs and education. The commission also recognized the need to develop effective law enforcement procedures to control hard core youthful offenders and at the same time grant them due process of law when they came before the courts.

During the 1960s, the concern was primarily for individual treatment and the rights of juvenile offenders. Child advocates and federal lawmakers were interested in merging the goal of rehabilitation with due process of law. The presidential commission report of 1967 acted as a catalyst for passage of the federal Juvenile Delinquency Prevention and Control (JDP) Act of 1968. This law created a Youth Development and Delinquency Prevention Administration, which concentrated on helping states develop new juvenile justice programs, particularly involving diversion of youth, decriminalization, and "decarceration." In 1968 Congress also passed the Omnibus Safe Streets and Crime Control Act.[62] Title I of this law established the **Law Enforcement Assistance Administration (LEAA)** to provide federal funds to improve the adult and juvenile justice systems. In 1972 Congress amended the JDP Act of 1968 to allow the LEAA to focus its funding on juvenile justice and delinquency prevention programs. State and local governments were required to develop and adopt comprehensive plans to obtain federal assistance.

Because crime continued to receive much publicity, a second effort called the **National Advisory Commission on Criminal Justice Standards and Goals** was established in 1973 by the Nixon administration.[63] Its report on juvenile justice and delinquency prevention identified such major strategies as (1) preventing delinquent behavior before it occurs, (2) developing diversion activities, (3) establishing dispositional alternatives, (4) providing due process for all juveniles, and (5) controlling the violent and the chronic delinquent.

This commission's recommendations formed the basis for additional legislation, the landmark **Juvenile Justice and Delinquency Prevention Act of 1974.**[64] (See the following Policy and Practice box for more on this act.) This important act eliminated the old Youth Development and Delinquency Prevention Administration and replaced it with the Office of Juvenile Justice and Delinquency Prevention (OJJDP) within the LEAA. In 1980 the LEAA was phased out, and the OJJDP became an independent agency in the Department of Justice, Attorney General's Office. The role of the OJJDP was to develop and implement worthwhile programs to prevent and reduce juvenile crimes.

Juvenile Justice and Delinquency Prevention Act of 1974
This act established the OJJDP as an independent agency charged with developing and implementing programs to prevent and reduce juvenile crime.

Throughout the 1970s, its two most important goals were (1) removing juveniles from detention in adult jails and (2) eliminating the incarceration together of delinquents and status offenders. During this period, the OJJDP stressed the creation of formal diversion and restitution programs around the United States.

A third effort took place in the 1980s, when the OJJDP shifted its priorities to the identification and control of chronic, violent juvenile offenders. This goal was in line with the Reagan and Bush administrations' more conservative views of justice. The federal government poured millions of dollars into research projects designed to study chronic offenders, predict their behavior, and evaluate programs created to control their activities.

Since 1974, the Juvenile Justice and Delinquency Prevention Act has had a significant impact on juvenile justice policy. It has been an important instrument for removing status offenders from jails and detention centers and has provided funds for innovative and effective programs. Congress has approved the OJJDP reauthorization through the year 2000.

Violent Crime Control and Law Enforcement Act of 1994
This act made available increased funding for juvenile justice and delinquency prevention.

The latest effort, in 1995, made available further funding for juvenile justice and delinquency prevention through the **Violent Crime Control and Law Enforcement Act of 1994.**[65] Known as the largest piece of crime legislation in the history of the United States, it was touted by the Clinton administration for providing 100,000 new police officers and billions of dollars for prisons and prevention programs for both adult and juvenile offenders. A revitalized juvenile justice system needs both a comprehensive strategy to prevent and control delinquency and a consistent program of federal funding.[66]

S U M M A R Y

The study of juvenile justice is concerned with juvenile delinquency and antisocial behavior and the agencies involved in their prevention, control, and treatment. The juvenile justice system is also a process consisting of the steps from the initial investigation of a juvenile crime through the appeal of a case. These steps are the police investigation, the intake procedure in the juvenile court, the pretrial procedures used for juvenile offenders, adjudication, disposition, and the postdispositional procedures.

The processing and terminology of the juvenile system can be compared and contrasted with that of the adult criminal justice system. The juvenile court is the heart of the juvenile process. Each jurisdiction organizes its court differently and has varying criteria. The most important factors determining jurisdiction are the age of the offender and the nature of his or her offense.

Over the past four decades, the courts have moved to eliminate the traditional view that a youth brought into the juvenile justice system has no rights. Both the U.S. Supreme Court and the lower courts have granted juveniles procedural safeguards and the protection of due process in juvenile courts. Major Supreme Court and lower court decisions pertaining to the entire juvenile process have laid down the constitutional requirements for juvenile proceedings. It is important to recognize that in years past the protections currently afforded to both adults and children were not available to children.

How the juvenile justice system deals with the adolescent is also determined by the ever-changing theoretical perspectives and models of the system and its individual agencies. Elements of a comprehensive strategy for juvenile justice into the twenty-first century include: (1) delinquency prevention, (2) intervention programs, (3) the use of graduated sanctions, (4) improvement of institutional programs, and (5) treating juveniles like adults.

Juvenile justice is a very complex system and process

THE JUVENILE JUSTICE AND DELINQUENCY PREVENTION ACT OF 1974— TWENTY-FIVE YEARS LATER

HISTORY OF FEDERAL JUVENILE JUSTICE LEGISLATION

More than twenty-five years have passed since enactment of the JJDP Act. It was the first major federal law to address juvenile delinquency in a comprehensive manner by providing funds to promote improvements in state and local juvenile justice systems. However, it was not the first federal juvenile delinquency law. In 1912 Congress created the Children's Bureau to improve the operations of America's emerging juvenile court system. Little else happened until the mid-twentieth century when the Truman administration convened the National Conference on Children and Youth in 1948 to examine ways to prevent juvenile crime. Although the conference recommended the federal government play a greater role in juvenile justice, Congress did nothing.

When juvenile gang activity became a serious state and local problem in the 1960s, the Kennedy administration worked with Congress to enact the Juvenile Delinquency and Youth Offenses Control Act of 1961. This act provided funds to states for projects to improve methods of preventing and controlling juvenile crime. The Neighborhood Youth Corps, the Legal Services Corporation, and Head Start (an early childhood and education program) evolved from this federal delinquency initiative. In 1966 President Johnson established the Commission on Law Enforcement and Administration of Justice. The Commission's Task Force on Juvenile Delinquency proposed four major strategies to reduce juvenile crime: (1) decriminalization of status offenses; (2) diversion of youth from the court system into alternative programs; (3) deinstitutionalization by using community homes rather than large training schools; and (4) extending due process rights to juveniles. The Juvenile Delinquency Prevention and Control Act of 1968 was passed to achieve these goals. In the same year Congress passed the Omnibus Crime Control and Safe Streets Act, which involved the U.S. Department of Justice in the juvenile justice system. By this time numerous federal agencies had become involved with delinquency prevention. A consensus emerged that federal juvenile justice programs were unfocused and ineffective. Thus, congressional work began on new landmark legislation for the juvenile justice system.

LEGISLATIVE REFORM

By 1974 juvenile delinquency had become a serious nationwide problem. Two themes set the stage for the JJDP Act. First, financial assistance alone was inadequate to combat juvenile crime—comprehensive planning was needed. Second, some practices, such as confining status offenders with delinquents and adult offenders, had to be halted. With these considerations included, the JJDP Act was passed in 1974. The act provided federal funds to divert juveniles from correctional settings into community programs and restitution projects. In particular, Section 223(a)12 and 13 of the act required states to remove status offenders from secure confinement and to separate adults and juvenile offenders as a condition of receiving federal funds. The act also required that states allocate 75 percent of the federal funds they received to such community-based programs and promoted the need for small public and private community facilities.

With congressional support, funding was increased from $25 million in 1974 to $75 million in 1977 and to $100 million by 1980. During this time, status offense cases referred to the juvenile courts decreased, the rate of detention of status offenders decreased, as did the total number of cases referred to the juvenile courts. Unfortunately, from 1980

whose many strategies are translated into day-to-day operations and programs. If professionals responsible for the administration of juvenile justice are to make progress in combating delinquency, they must establish clearly defined goals for the system. In addition, certain key agencies, such as the juvenile court and correctional institutions, must explore how they can deal with youths more comprehensively and effectively.

to 1987 the budget of the Office of Juvenile Justice and Delinquency Prevention (the administrative arm of the act) decreased to $66 million because the focus had shifted from delinquency prevention to criminal justice.

The 1988 and 1992 amendments to the JJDP Act reestablished the importance of juvenile delinquency prevention. Congress was concerned about addressing the problems of juvenile gangs, youth development, due process, and the overrepresentation of minorities in the juvenile justice system. The new amendments also required the OJJDP to submit to Congress an annual report detailing the number of juveniles in custody, the types of offenses for which they were charged, and their race and gender. Funding opportunities became available for states willing to embark on innovative activities, such as improving health services in corrections, removing gender bias from the justice system, and creating community correctional alternatives for violent juveniles. Since the Clinton administration made crime one of its priorities, the OJJDP budget increased to $140 million in 1995. After twenty-five years, the act continues to provide funding for juvenile justice reform.

ACCOMPLISHMENTS AND RECOMMENDATIONS

Today, virtually all the states are in compliance with the federal mandates for removing status offenders from secure incarceration, as well as separating juveniles from convicted adults and removing youths from adult jails. From the early 1980s to 1992 the average one-day count of juveniles in adult jails fell from 12,000 to 2,000. In addition, although the percentage of violent juvenile crime has increased, the overall rate for juvenile crime has remained stable over the last five years. Many states are also working to address the problem of disproportionate minority confinement (DMC). In a 1992 amendment to the JJDP Act, Congress required that DMC be elevated to a case requirement, with future funding eligibility tied to state compliance. More than two-thirds of the states are implementing plans to deal with the disparate treatment of minorities in the juvenile justice system.

The key question is what does the future hold for the JJDPA? Juvenile crime is a high priority in every state. Deinstitutionalization of status offenders remains a central theme. Expanding community-based programs and services for juveniles as alternatives to institutional care is equally important. It would also be helpful if the federal government extended the mandate of the JJDP Act to cover funding under the Violent Crime Control and Law Enforcement Act of 1994, where funds are also available for juvenile delinquency prevention programs.

In conclusion, a White House Conference on Juvenile Justice is needed to review the nation's juvenile justice system. Such a conference would assess the programs sponsored by JJDP Act and determine which have worked and which have not. Other important issues that need to be examined include (1) trends of binding juveniles over to adult courts at younger ages; (2) placing continued emphasis on prevention as the most cost-effective way to reduce juvenile crime; (3) reforming secure juvenile correctional facilities and finding institutions where corrections truly works; and (4) developing further strategies to address disproportionate minority confinement.

The JJDP Act has proven itself and offers tremendous support to states in reforming the juvenile justice system. Today, all the states pursue the act's goals and objectives. For over twenty-five years, the act has provided a unique federal–state partnership by assisting states in carrying out their responsibilities in combating juvenile delinquency.

Sources: Juvenile Justice and Delinquency Prevention Act of 1974, PL. 93–415; Gordon Raley, "The JJDP Act: A Second Look," *Juvenile Justice Journal* 2:11–18 (1995).

It is doubtful any real progress in improving the juvenile justice system could be made without significant support from the federal government. By reauthorizing the Juvenile Justice and Delinquency Prevention Act of 1974 and by passing the Violent Crime Control and Law Enforcement Act of 1994, Congress has made a historic financial effort to address juvenile justice reform.

KEY TERMS

parens patriae
House of Refuge
Children's Aid Society
Society for the Prevention
of Cruelty to Children
Illinois Juvenile Court Act
of 1899
juvenile justice process
detention hearing
adjudicatory hearing

bifurcated process
disposition
petition
President's Commission
on Law Enforcement
and the Administration
of Justice
Law Enforcement
Assistance
Administration (LEAA)

National Advisory
Commission on
Criminal Justice
Standards and Goals
Juvenile Justice and
Delinquency Prevention
Act of 1974
Violent Crime Control
and Law Enforcement
Act of 1994

INFOTRAC COLLEGE EDITION EXERCISES

Read the following article from InfoTrac College Edition:

Young people's understanding and assertion of their rights to silence and legal counsel. (Canada) Rona Abramovitch, Michele Peterson-Badali, Meg Rohan. *Canadian Journal of Criminology* Jan 1995

The text mentions that the court has worked to get rid of the traditional view that youths in the juvenile system have no rights. As of late, juveniles have been granted procedural safeguards and increased protection of due process. The U.S. Supreme Court has also laid down the constitutional requirements for juvenile proceedings.

Although it was not conducted in this country, what implications might Abramovitch et al.'s study have when commenting on the success of the movement to assert juvenile rights?

QUESTIONS FOR DISCUSSION

1. What factors precipitated the development of the Illinois Juvenile Court Act of 1899?
2. The formal components of the criminal justice system are often considered to be the police, the court, and the correctional agency. How do these components compare with the major areas of the juvenile justice system? Is the operation of justice similar in the juvenile and adult systems?
3. What are the basic elements of each model of juvenile justice?
4. Should there be a juvenile justice system, or should juveniles who commit serious crimes be treated as adults and the others be handled by social welfare agencies?
5. The Supreme Court has made a number of major decisions in the area of juvenile justice. What are these

decisions? What is their impact on the juvenile justice system?
6. What is the meaning of the term "procedural due process of law"? Explain why and how procedural due process has had an impact on juvenile justice.
7. One of the most significant reforms in dealing with the juvenile offender was the opening of the New York House of Refuge in 1825. What were the social and judicial consequences of this reform on the juvenile justice system?
8. How would each model of juvenile justice consider the use of capital punishment as a criminal sanction for first degree murder by a juvenile offender?
9. What role has the federal government played in the juvenile justice system over the last twenty-five years?

NOTES

1. Timothy Egan, "From Adolescent Angst to Shooting up Schools," *New York Times,* 14 June 1998, p. 1; James Alan Fox, "Again School Attacks Show Need for New Strategies," *Boston Sunday Globe,* 24 May 1998, p. D1–2; Patricia King and Andrew Murr, "A Son Out of Control," *Newsweek,* 1 June 1998, pp. 32–33; Jerome Shestack, "What about Juvenile Justice," *American Bar Association Journal* 84:8 (1998).

2. Robert M. Mennel, "Origins of the Juvenile Court: Changing Perspectives on the Legal Rights of Juvenile Delinquents," *Crime and Delinquency* 18:68–78 (1972).

3. Anthony Salerno, "The Child Saving Movement: Altruism or Conspiracy," *Juvenile and Family Court Journal* 42:37 (1991).

4. Ronald Bayer, "The Darker Side of Urban Life: Slums in the City," in Frank Copp and P. C. Dolce, eds., *Cities in Transi-*

tion: From the Ancient World to Urban America (Chicago: Nelson Hall, 1974), p. 220.

5. Robert Mennel, "Attitudes and Policies towards Juvenile Delinquency," in Michael Tonry and Norval Morris, eds., *Crime and Justice*, vol. 5 (Chicago: University of Chicago Press, 1983), p. 198.

6. Anthony M. Platt, *The Child Savers: The Invention of Delinquency* (Chicago: University of Chicago Press, 1969).

7. Ibid.

8. Sanford J. Fox, "Juvenile Justice Reform: A Historical Perspective," *Stanford Law Review* 22:1187 (1970).

9. Robert S. Pickett, *House of Refuge—Origins of Juvenile Reform in New York State, 1815–1857* (Syracuse, N.Y.: Syracuse University Press, 1969).

10. Mennel, "Origins of the Juvenile Court," pp. 69–70.

11. Ibid., pp. 70–71.

12. Salerno, "The Child Saving Movement," p. 37.

13. Platt, *The Child Savers: The Invention of Delinquency.*

14. Ibid., p. 116.

15. Randall Shelden and Lynn Osborne, "'For Their Own Good': Class Interests and the Child Saving Movement in Memphis, Tennessee, 1900–1917," *Criminology* 27:747–67 (1989).

16. U.S. Department of Justice, Juvenile Justice and Delinquency Prevention, *Two Hundred Years of American Criminal Justice: An LEAA Bicentennial Study* (Washington, D.C.: LEAA, 1976).

17. Beverly Smith, "Female Admissions and Paroles of the Western House of Refuge in the 1880s, An Historical Example of Community Corrections," *Journal of Research in Crime and Delinquency* 26:36–66 (1989).

18. Fox, "Juvenile Justice Reform," p. 1229.

19. Ibid., p. 1211.

20. Elizabeth Pleck, "Criminal Approaches to Family Violence, 1640–1980," in Lloyd Ohlin and Michael Tonry, eds., *Family Violence* (Chicago: University of Chicago Press, 1989), pp. 19–58.

21. Elizabeth Pleck, *Domestic Tyranny: The Making of Social Policy against Family Violence from Colonial Times to the Present* (New York: Oxford University Press, 1987), pp. 28–30.

22. Linda Gordon, *Family Violence and Social Control* (New York: Viking Press, 1988).

23. Kathleen Block and Donna Hale, "Turf Wars in the Progressive Era of Juvenile Justice: The Relationship of Private and Public Child Care Agencies," *Crime and Delinquency* 37:225–41 (1991).

24. Theodore Ferdinand, "Juvenile Delinquency or Juvenile Justice: Which Came First?" *Criminology* 27:79–106 (1989).

25. *In re Gault,* 387 U.S. 1, 87 S.Ct. 1428, 18 L.Ed. 2d 527 (1967).

26. Mary Odem and Steven Schlossman, "Guardians of Virtue: The Juvenile Court and Female Delinquency in Early 20th-Century Los Angeles," *Crime and Delinquency* 37:186–203 (1991).

27. John Sutton, "Bureaucrats and Entrepreneurs: Institutional Responses to Deviant Children in the United States, 1890–1920," *American Journal of Sociology* 95:1367–1400 (1990).

28. Ibid., p. 1383.

29. Margueritte Rosenthal, "Reforming the Juvenile Correctional Institution: Efforts of the U.S. Children's Bureau in the 1930's," *Journal of Sociology and Social Welfare* 14:47–74 (1987); see also David Steinhart, "Status Offenses," The Center for the Future of Children, The Juvenile Court (Los Altos, Calif.: David and Lucille Packard Foundation, 1996).

30. For an overview of these developments, see Theodore Ferdinand, "History Overtakes the Juvenile Justice System," *Crime and Delinquency* 37:204–24 (1991).

31. N.Y. Fam. Ct. Act, Art. 7, Sec. 712 (Consol. 1962).

32. *Kent v. U.S.*

33. *In re Gault,* 387 U.S. 1, 19, 87 S.Ct. 1428 (1967).

34. *In re Winship,* 397 U.S. 358, 90 S.Ct. 1068 (1970).

35. *McKeiver v. Pennsylvania,* 403 U.S. 528, 91 S.Ct. 1976 (1971).

36. *Breed v. Jones,* 421 U.S. 519, 95 S.Ct. 1779 (1975).

37. *Oklahoma Publishing Co. v. District Court,* 430 U.S. 308, 97 S.Ct. 1045, 51 L.Ed. 2d (1977).

38. *Smith v. Daily Mail Publishing Co.,* 443 U.S. 97, 99 S.Ct. 2667, 61 L.Ed. 2d 399 (1979).

39. *Fare v. Michael C.,* 442 U.S. 707, 99 S.Ct. 2560 (1979).

40. *Eddings v. Oklahoma,* 455 U.S. 104, 102 S.Ct. 869, 71 L.Ed. 2d 1 (1982).

41. *Schall v. Martin,* 467 U.S. 253, 104 S.Ct 2403 (1984).

42. *New Jersey v. T.L.O.,* 469 U.S. 325, 105 S.Ct. 733 (1985).

43. *Thompson v. Oklahoma,* 487 U.S. 815, 108 S.Ct. 2687, 101 L.Ed. 2d 702 (1988).

44. *Stanford v. Kentucky,* 492 U.S., 109 S.Ct. 2969 (1989).

45. *Vernonia School District v. Acton,* 515 U.S. 646 115 S.Ct. 2386, 132 L.Ed.2d 564 (1995).

46. *United States v. Lopez,* 115 S.Ct. 1624 (1995).

47. *McKeiver v. Pennsylvania,* at 538.

48. For differing views of juvenile justice legal policy, see H. Ted Rubin, *Behind the Black Robe—Juvenile Court Judges and the Court* (Beverly Hills, Calif.: Sage, 1985).

49. Samuel Davis, *The Rights of Juveniles,* 2nd. ed. (update 1994; New York: Clark Boardman, Co. 1984), pp. 7–12.

50. Jay S. Albanese, *Dealing with Delinquency—The Future of Juvenile Justice* (Chicago: Nelson-Hall, 1992), p. 122; Barry Feld, "The Juvenile Court Meets the Principle of the Offense: Legislative Changes in Juvenile Waiver Statutes," *Journal of Criminal Law and Criminology* 78:471 (1987); Joseph Sanborn Jr., "Constitutional Problems of Juvenile Delinquency Trials," *Judicature* 78:78 (1994).

51. Kathleen Maguire and Ann Pastore, eds., *Sourcebook of Criminal Justice Statistics, 1994* (Washington, D.C.: U.S. Government Printing Office, 1995).

52. Information in this section comes from a variety of sources, including Maguire and Pastore, *Sourcebook of Criminal Justice Statistics, 1996* (Washington, D.C.: U.S. Government Printing Office, 1997); Howard Snyder, Melissa Sickmund, and Eileen Poe-Yamagata, *Juvenile Offenders and Victims: 1997 Update* (Washington, D.C.: Office of Juvenile Justice and Delinquency Prevention, 1997); *Crime in the United States: Uniform Crime Reports, 1996* (Washington, D.C.: U.S. Government Printing Office, 1997).

53. For an excellent review of the juvenile process, see Adrienne Volenik, *Checklists for Use in Juvenile Delinquency Proceedings* (Washington, D.C.: American Bar Association, 1985); see also, Jeffrey Butts and Gregory Halemba, *Waiting for Justice—Moving Young Offenders through the Juvenile Court Process* (Pittsburgh, Pa.: National Center for Juvenile Justice, 1996).

54. Barry Feld, "Criminology and the Juvenile Court: A Research Agenda for the 1990s," in Ira M. Schwartz, *Juvenile Justice and Public Policy—Toward a National Agenda* (New York: Lexington Books, 1992), p. 59.

55. Robert O. Dawson, "The Future of Juvenile Justice: Is It Time to Abolish the System?" *Journal of Criminal Law and Criminology* 81:136–55 (1990); see also, Leonard P. Edwards, "The Future of the Juvenile Court: Promising New Directions in the Center for the Future of Children," *The Juvenile Court* (Los Altos, Calif.: David and Lucille Packard Foundation, 1996).

56. National Conference of State Legislatures, *A Legislator's Guide to Comprehensive Juvenile Justice, Juvenile Detention and Corrections* (Denver: Col.: National Conference of State Legislators, 1996).

57. James Howell, ed., *Guide for Implementing the Comprehensive Strategy for Serious, Violent, and Chronic Juvenile Offenders* (Washington D.C.: OJJDP, 1995).

58. Carol J. DeFrances and Kevin Strom, *Juveniles Prosecuted in the State Criminal Courts* (Washington, D.C.: Bureau of Justice Statistics, 1997).

59. Office of Justice Programs, *Reducing Youth Gun Violence* (Washington D.C.: U.S. Department of Justice, OJJDP, 1996).

60. *Program Summary, 1995 National Youth Gang Survey* (Washington D.C.: OJJDP, August 1997).

61. President's Commission on Law Enforcement and the Administration of Justice, *The Challenge of Crime in a Free Society* (Washington, D.C.: U.S. Government Printing Office, 1967).

62. Public Law 90–351, Title I—Omnibus Safe Streets and Crime Control Act of 1968, 90th Congress, June 1968.

63. National Advisory Commission on Criminal Justice Standards and Goals, *A National Strategy to Reduce Crime* (Washington, D.C.: U.S. Government Printing Office, 1973).

64. Juvenile Justice and Delinquency Prevention Act of 1974, Public Law 93–415 (1974). For a critique of this legislation, see Ira Schwartz, *Justice for Juveniles—Rethinking the Best Interests of the Child* (Lexington, Mass.: D. C. Heath, 1989), p. 175.

65. For an extensive summary of the Violent Crime Control and Law Enforcement Act of 1994, see *Criminal Law Reporter* 55:2305–2430 (1994).

66. Shay Bilchik, "A Juvenile Justice System for the 21st Century," *Crime and Delinquency* 44:89 (1998).

Part Five

Controlling Juvenile Offenders

Controlling juvenile delinquency is a complex task. Adults who violate the law are subject to clearly defined sanctions, but the *parens patriae* philosophy demands that the state always consider the best interests of the child when controlling juvenile behavior. The line between treatment and punishment, however, is often a narrow one. When do the sincere efforts to help troubled youngsters actually become a crushing burden on them? Is it possible that the doctrine of *parens patriae* goes too far? These questions are central in juvenile justice policymaking.

Part Five contains three chapters devoted to the process and policies used to control juvenile offenders. Chapter 13 covers police treatment of delinquent and status offenders. It includes information on the police role; the organization of police services, police, and the rule of law; and prevention efforts. Chapter 14 addresses the important topic of early court processing, describing current issues such as diversion programs, removal of minor offenders from secure detention facilities, and transferring youths to adult courts. Chapter 15 discusses the equally important topic of juvenile trial and disposition, considering the role of the prosecutor, the juvenile court judge, and the defense attorney at adjudication and disposition.

Chapter 13

Police Work
with Juveniles

On July 28, 1998, a day after she was reported missing, eleven-year-old Ryan Harris was found dead in an abandoned lot. She had been hit in the head with a blunt object and suffocated, and her body showed signs of sexual abuse. Seven days later, two boys, ages 7 and 8, who live close to where Ryan's body was found, were questioned by police for five hours, without their parents or legal counsel present. The two boys were charged with juvenile delinquency (committing a criminal homicide under age) after allegedly making statements during police questioning giving information that the police said "only the perpetrators would know." The local prosecutors believed that evidence was sufficient to show the boys were responsible for the murder of Ryan Harris.

Because of their age and the nature of the crime, the juvenile court judge ruled that the boys should be held for psychiatric examinations. The boys were released into their parents' custody but ordered to stay home and to wear electronic monitors on their ankles for supervision during the pretrial period. Arrest of the two preteen boys in Chicago made headlines around the nation. How could children so young commit such a brutal crime? Defense lawyers appointed by the juvenile court forced prosecutors to turn over all available evidence against the boys before proceeding to trial, claiming the children were innocent. A legal battle ensued over the boys' confessions (which many believed were coerced), lack of physical evidence, and information that the victim had been seen in the presence of one or possibly two other men before she was murdered.

There were questions about the boys' culpability from the beginning. It was hard to imagine the pair dragging Ryan's body from the place where she was said to have been knocked off her bike to the opposite side of the street where she was eventually found. Dissension existed among the police investigators, with some of the uniform police admitting that they may have wrongly accused the boys. It was also known that a police detective in the Harris case had coaxed a confession from an eleven-year-old under strikingly similar circumstances in 1994. Yet the po-

Kip Owen, the prosecutor in the Ryan Harris case, is shown here with state attorneys Michael Oppenheimer and Michele Simmons, as they speak to the media on the second day of hearings of two young boys charged in the death of the eleven-year-old Chicago girl. The Harris case is a good example of why children require greater protection than adults when they are placed in police custody. Panicked and bewildered, they may make incriminating statements, which later prove to be false and misleading.

lice insisted the boys knew too many forensic details to have never been at the crime scene.

Two months after the arrest the juvenile prosecutors dropped the charges against the two boys, citing a crime lab report that confirmed that semen was found on Ryan's undergarments. (Rarely do boys the age of these suspects produce semen.) Although prosecutors refused to rule out the possibility that the boys could be recharged if new evidence surfaced, the children were free to return to school.

This case raised serious questions over the lack of constitutional procedures in charging juveniles with felony crimes. Were the seven- and eight-year-old suspects competent to stand trial? A competent person must have a reasonable understanding of the proceedings against him or her. Did the children give statements to the police without a parent or attorney present? In other words, did they waive their so-called *Miranda* warnings pertaining to their privilege against self-incrimination (the right to remain silent and the right to the presence and advice of an attorney before any custodial interrogation takes place)? If no parent or lawyer was present, how could such young children voluntarily, knowingly, and intelligently waive their rights? Was it possible that the confession was coerced or unreliable because the juveniles were frightened or confused by the police interrogation? (The police argued that the interrogation was not as coercive as defense lawyers later alleged.) What types of constraints were needed for the boys as conditions of their release during the pretrial period? Is electronic monitoring an appropriate short-term intervention for young children?

How the juvenile offender reacts to police authority often determines the police officer's response to his or her behavior. In the Harris case, the police were adamant that the boys knew too much about the murder not to be involved.

At first the police thought the two young boys were responsible. Then adult suspects entered the picture. To solve the mystery of Ryan Harris, the police and the community will need to acknowledge, learn from, and move beyond the mistakes that were made.

This chapter focuses on police work in juvenile justice and delinquency prevention. It covers the role and responsibilities of the police; the history of policing juveniles; the organization and management of police–juvenile operations; the legal aspects of police work, including custodial interrogation and search and seizure; the concept of police discretion; and the relationship between police and community efforts to prevent crime.

The Police and Juvenile Offenders

The modern juvenile justice system is the core from which all efforts to control juvenile crime emerge. Although other segments of society—the family, the political system, the schools, and religious institutions—play a role, it is with the juvenile justice system that most social control rests. As its law enforcement and social control arm, the police, therefore, become the frontline agency for prevention and control of juvenile delinquency.

In the minds of most citizens, the primary responsibility of the police is to protect the public. From the vast array of films, books, and TV shows that depict the derring-do of police officers in the field, the public has obtained an image of "crime fighters" who "always get their man." Since the tumultuous 1960s, however, the public has become increasingly aware that the reality of police work is quite a bit different from its fictional glorification. When police departments failed to bring the crime rate down despite massive government subsidies, when citizens complained of civil rights violations, and when tales of police corruption became widespread, it was evident that a crisis was imminent in American policing.

During the 1980s and 1990s, a new view of policing emerged around the nation. Rather than foster the view of the police officer as a hell-bent-for-leather crime fighter who only tracks down serious criminals or stops armed robberies in progress, many police departments adopted the concept that the police role should be to maintain order in the community, interact with citizens, and be a visible and accessible component of the community. The argument is that police efforts can be successful only when conducted in partnership with concerned and active citizens. This movement is referred to as **community policing.**[1]

community policing
Police strategy that emphasizes fear reduction, community organization, and order maintenance rather than crime fighting.

Interest in the community policing concept does not mean that the crime control model of law enforcement is history. An ongoing effort is being made to improve the crime-fighting capability of police agencies, and there are some indications that the effort is paying off. Research indicates that aggressive, formal action by the police can help reduce the incidence of repeat offending, and technological innovations such as computerized fingerprinting systems may bring about greater police efficiency.[2] Nonetheless, after thirty years of attempting to improve police effectiveness through a combination of policy and technical advancement, little evidence exists that adding police or improving their skills has had a major impact on their crime-fighting success.

During this era in which experts are rethinking the basic police role, the relationship between police and juvenile offenders has become quite complex. Working with juvenile offenders may be especially challenging for police officers because the desire to help young people and to steer them away from criminal careers may seem to conflict with the traditional police duties of crime prevention and order maintenance. Because police officers represent the authority of the community, even the most casual meeting between a police officer and a young person can have a profound effect on the youth's future. In addition, the police are faced with a nationwide adolescent drug problem, increases in the violent crime arrest rate for teens, and renewed gang activity. Efforts are being made to improve adult crime control efforts of the police, but it also may be necessary to increase specialized services for juveniles.

Police Roles

juvenile officers
Police officers who specialize in dealing with juvenile offenders; they may operate alone or as part of a juvenile police unit within the department.

How do juvenile officers spend their time, and what roles do they perform in the police and criminal justice system? **Juvenile officers** either operate alone as specialists within a police department or as part of the juvenile unit of a police department. Their role is similar to that of officers working with adult offenders—to intervene if the actions of a citizen produce public danger or disorder. Most officers regard the violations of juveniles as nonserious unless they are committed by chronic troublemakers or involve significant damage to persons or property. Juveniles who misbehave are often ignored or treated informally. Police encounters with juveniles are generally the result of reports made by citizens, and the bulk of such encounters pertain to matters of minor legal consequence.[3]

Of course, police must also deal with serious juvenile offenders whose criminal acts are similar to those of adults, but these are only a small minority of the offender population. Thus, police who deal with delinquency must concentrate on being peacekeepers and crime preventers.[4]

role conflicts
Conflicts police officers face that revolve around the requirement to perform their primary duty of law enforcement and a desire to aid in rehabilitating youthful offenders.

law enforcement
The primary duty of all police officers to fight crime and keep the peace.

Handling juvenile offenders can produce major **role conflicts** for the police. They may experience tension between wanting to perform what they consider their primary duty, **law enforcement,** and the need to aid in the rehabilitation of youthful offenders. A police officer's actions in cases involving adults are usually controlled by the rule of criminal law and his or her own personal judgment, or discretion. (The concept of discretion is discussed later in this chapter.) In contrast, a case involving a juvenile often demands that the officer consider the "best interests of the child" and how the officer's actions will influence the child's future life and well-being. Consequently, police are much less likely to refer juvenile offenders to courts. It is estimated that between 30 and 40 percent of all juvenile arrests by police are handled informally without judicial action within the police department or are referred to a community service agency (see Figure 13.1). These informal dispositions are the result of the police officer's discretionary authority.[5]

Police intervention in situations involving juveniles can be difficult, frustrating—and emotional. The officer often encounters hostile or belligerent behavior from the juvenile offender as well as agitated witnesses to the encounter. Overreaction by the officer can result in a major, violent incident. Even if the officer succeeds in quieting or dispersing the crowd of witnesses, the juveniles will probably reappear the next day, often in the same place.[6]

Role conflicts are often exacerbated because most police–juvenile encounters involve confrontations brought about by loitering, disturbing the peace, and rowdiness rather than by serious law violations. Dealing with youth problems brings police officers little job satisfaction. For example, over the last decade, public concern has risen about today's out-of-control youth. Yet, because of legal constraints and family interference, the police are often limited in how they can respond to such status offenders.[7]

What role should the police play in mediating problems with youths—hardline law enforcer or social service-oriented delinquency prevention worker? The President's Crime Prevention Council sees the solution as lying somewhere in-between. Most police departments operate juvenile programs that combine law enforcement and delinquency prevention roles, and the police work with the juvenile court to determine a role that is most suitable for the community.[8] In fact, police officers also may act as juvenile prosecutors in some rural courts when attorneys are not available. Thus, the police–juvenile role extends from the on-the-street encounter to the station house to the juvenile court. For juvenile matters involving minor criminal

FIGURE 13.1

The Police Response to Juvenile Crime

To understand how police deal with juvenile crime, picture a funnel, with the result shown here. For every five hundred juveniles taken into custody, a little more than 60 percent are sent to the juvenile court, and almost 33 percent are released.

Source: Melissa Sickmund, Howard Snyder, and Eileen Poe-Yamagata, *Juvenile Offenders and Victims: 1997* (Washington, D.C.: OJJDP, 1997).

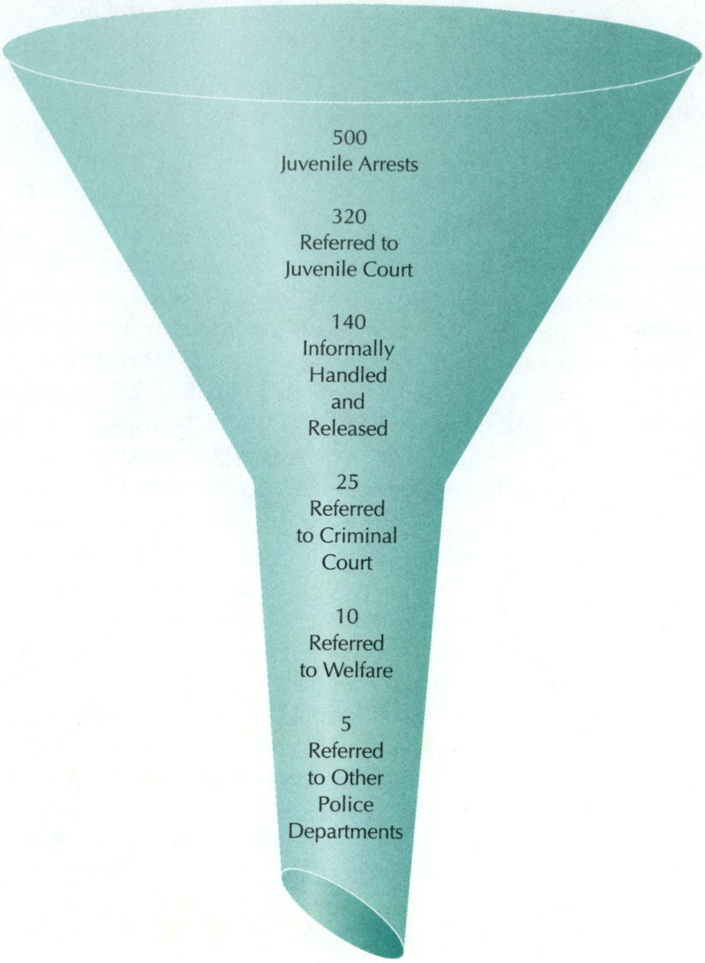

500
Juvenile Arrests

320
Referred to
Juvenile Court

140
Informally
Handled
and
Released

25
Referred
to Criminal
Court

10
Referred
to Welfare

5
Referred
to Other
Police
Departments

conduct or incorrigible behavior, the police ordinarily select the "least restrictive alternative" course of action. Such courses include nonintervention, temporary assistance, or referral to community agencies. In contrast, violent juvenile crime requires that the police investigate, arrest, and even detain youths while providing constitutional safeguards similar to those available to adult offenders.

The Police and Violent Juvenile Crime

Violent juvenile offenders are defined as those juvenile's adjudicated delinquent for crimes of homicide, rape, robbery, aggravated assault, and kidnapping. Law enforcement agencies made more than 2.8 million arrests of persons under age 18 in 1997; nearly 3 percent were for violent crimes.[9] Also, juveniles accounted for nearly 19 percent of all violent crime arrests in 1996. The substantial growth in juvenile violent crime arrests that began in the late 1980s peaked in 1994 and then began to fall in 1995 (see Figure 13.2). For the first time in ten years, arrests of juveniles for violent crimes have begun to decline during the middle of the past decade.[10]

In spite of these findings, the outlook is ominous. A continued surge of violence is predicted as the children of baby boomers enter their prime crime years. Some experts predict that if trends continue as they have over the past ten years juvenile arrests for violent crime will double by the year 2010 (see Chapter 2).[11]

As a result of these dire predictions, police and other justice agencies are experimenting with different methods of controlling violent youth. Some of these

FIGURE 13.2

Juvenile Violent Crime Rates

After more than a decade of consistency, the juvenile violent crime arrest rate began to increase in 1989, peaked in 1994, then fell in 1995 and again in 1996, returning to the 1991 level. Between 1994 and 1996, the juvenile arrest rate for Violent Crime Index offenses dropped 12 percent, to a level of 465 arrests for every 100,000 persons ages 10–17. The 1996 level is, however, about 50 percent above rates of the early 1980s. Rates fell once again in 1997.

Source: Howard Snyder, "Juvenile Arrests 1996," *Juvenile Justice Bulletin* (Washington, D.C.: OJJDP, 1997), p. 4.

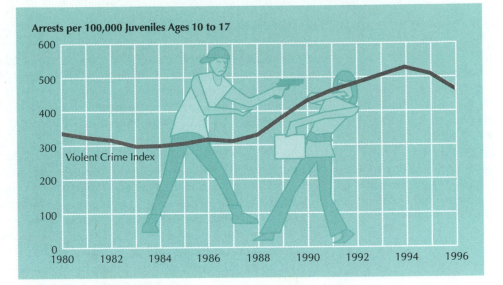

Arrests per 100,000 Juveniles Ages 10 to 17

Violent Crime Index

methods, such as placing more officers on the beat, have existed for decades; others rely on state-of-the-art computer technology to pinpoint the exact locations of violent crimes and to develop immediate countermeasures. Research shows that these police practices have been used with some degree of success to reduce violent juvenile crime: (1) intensified motorized patrol; (2) field interrogation (the police practice of ordering persons to briefly stay and answer questions in regard to suspicious behavior); (3) foot patrol and neighborhood storefront police stations; (4) citizen contact patrols (citizen volunteer groups patrolling high crime neighborhoods); and (5) community mobilization, including neighborhood block watch programs and citizen patrols. These strategies address problems of community disorganization and, when combined with other laws and policies, such as restricting the possession of firearms, can be effective deterrents against juvenile violence. Although many of these policing strategies are not new, implementing them as one element of an overall police plan may have an impact on preventing juvenile violence.

In general, one of the most promising police programs dealing with violent juvenile crime involves intensified motorized patrols in marked cars at night in high-crime locations coupled with field interrogations.[12] These tactics indicate that an increased police presence judiciously directed at high-risk times, areas, and persons can deter juvenile violence. Much more research is needed, however, to ensure the long-term effectiveness of this or any other police strategy.

Finally, one key component of any innovative police program dealing with violent juvenile crime is improved communications between the police and the community. Community policing is discussed in more detail at the conclusion of this chapter.

The History and Organization of Juvenile Policing

Specialized police services for juveniles is a relatively recent phenomenon. At one time citizens were responsible for protecting themselves and maintaining order.

The History of Policing Juveniles

pledge system
Early English system in which neighbors protected each other from thieves and warring groups.

watch system
Replaced the pledge system in England; watchmen patrolled urban areas at night to provide protection from harm.

The origin of U.S. police agencies can be traced to early English society.[13] Before the Norman conquest of England, the **pledge system** assumed that neighbors would protect each other from thieves and warring groups. Individuals were entrusted with policing themselves and resolving minor problems. By the thirteenth century, however, the **watch system** was created to help police England's larger communities, and watchmen patrolled areas at night to provide protection from harm. Men were organized in church parishes to guard at night against disturbances and breaches of the peace under the direction of a local constable. This was followed by establishment of the constable, who was responsible for dealing with more serious crimes. By the seventeenth century, the constable, the justice of the peace, and the night watcher formed the nucleus of the local police system.

When the industrial revolution brought thousands of people from the countryside to work in English urban factories, the need for police protection increased. As a result, the first organized police force was established in London in 1829. The early "bobbies," as they were called, were often corrupt, unsuccessful at stopping crime, and influenced by the wealthy for personal and political gain.[14]

Law enforcement in colonial America followed the British model. In the colonies the local sheriff became the most important police official. By the mid-1800s formal city police departments had formed in Boston, New York, and Philadelphia. Police work was primitive, officers patrolled on foot, and conflicts often arose between untrained officers and the public.

By this time children began to be treated as a distinguishable group. The Poor Laws, the apprenticeship movement, and the restricted family structure (described in Chapter 1) all had an impact on the juvenile legal system. When children violated the law, they were often treated in the same way as adult offenders. But even at this stage a belief existed that the enforcement of criminal law should be applied differently to children.

During the latter portion of the nineteenth century, the problems of how to deal effectively with growing numbers of unemployed, undisciplined, and homeless youths increased; these problems spilled over into the twentieth century. Twentieth-century groups, such as the Wickersham Commission of 1931 and the International Association of Chiefs of Police, became the leading voices for police reform.[15] Their efforts resulted in creation of specialized police units, known as delinquency control squads.

The most famous police reformer of the 1930s was August Vollmer. As the police chief of Berkeley, California, Vollmer instituted numerous professional reforms, including university training, modern management techniques, prevention programs, and juvenile aid bureaus.[16] These bureaus were generally the first organized special police services for juvenile offenders, although specialized police work with youths dates back to the first juvenile court in 1899 in Illinois.

Beginning in the 1960s, policing entered a turbulent period. The U.S. Supreme Court handed down decisions designed to restrict police operations and discretion. Civil unrest produced growing tensions between police and the public. Urban police departments were unable to handle the growing crime rate. Federal funding from the Law Enforcement Assistance Administration (LEAA) was a catalyst for developing hundreds of new police programs, innovations in police operations, and enhancement of police services for children. Even the police role seemed to change from one where the police were simply crime fighters to one in which the police were to have a greater awareness of community issues and crime prevention. This resulted in the emergence of the community policing concept.

By the 1980s most urban police departments recognized that the problem of juvenile delinquency required special attention, although the degree of commitment to this objective varied from one department to another.

The role of the juvenile police officer (one assigned to juvenile work) has taken on added importance, particularly with the increase in violent juvenile and gang-related crime. Today the majority of the nation's urban law enforcement agencies have specialized juvenile police programs. Typically, such programs involve (1) prevention (for example, programs involving a police athletic league, Project DARE, and community outreach) and (2) law enforcement work (for example, juvenile court, school policing, or gang control). Other recent serious problem targets include child abuse, domestic violence, and locating missing children.

Public interest in juvenile delinquency has focused less on police practices than on the juvenile court process, and law enforcement agents continue to make up the front end of the juvenile justice system. They are the primary referral source for juvenile law violators and exercise discretion as to whether to arrest a youth. They also often determine whether an arrested youth should be diverted to a community agency or referred to court.

Organization of Police Services for Juveniles

The problem of juvenile delinquency and youth crime received little attention from most municipal police departments. Even when juvenile crime was increasing during the 1960s, 1970s, and 1980s, police resources were generally directed to adult offenders. However, the alarming increase in serious juvenile crime in the past few years has made it obvious that the police can no longer neglect youthful antisocial behavior. Departments need to assign resources to the problem and have the proper organization for coping with it. The theory and practice of police organization have recently undergone many changes, and as a result, police departments are giving greater emphasis to the juvenile function.

The organization of juvenile work depends on the size of the police department, the kind of community in which the department is located, and the amount and quality of resources available in the community. Today most police agencies recognize that juvenile crime requires special attention. The police who work with juvenile offenders usually have special skills and talents that go beyond those generally associated with regular police work. In large urban police departments, juvenile services are often established through a special unit. Ordinarily this unit is the responsibility of a command-level police officer. The unit commander assigns officers to deal with juvenile problems throughout the police department's jurisdiction. Police departments with very few officers have little need for an internal division with special functions. Most small departments make one officer responsible for handling juvenile matters for the entire community.

The number of police officers assigned to juvenile work has increased in recent years. The International Association of Chiefs of Police found that approximately 500 departments of the 1,400 surveyed in 1960 had juvenile units. By 1970 the number of police departments with a juvenile specialist had doubled.[18] A large proportion of justice agencies have written policy directives for handling juvenile offenders. Figure 13.3 illustrates the major elements of a police department organization dealing with juvenile offenders.

In neither large nor small departments can it be assumed that only police officers assigned to work with juveniles will be involved in handling juvenile offenses. When officers on patrol encounter a youngster committing a crime, they are responsible for dealing with the problem initially. However, they generally refer the case to the juvenile unit or to the juvenile police officer to follow up. The juvenile officer must choose a course of action in cases that cannot be handled with on-the-scene referrals to families or social agencies.

Most juvenile officers are appointed after they have had some general patrol experience. A desire to work with juveniles and a basic understanding of human behavior, along with an aptitude for working with young people, are generally

FIGURE 13.3

Typical Urban Police Department Organization with Juvenile Justice Component

considered essential for the job. Officers must also have a thorough knowledge of the rule of law, especially the constitutional protections available to juveniles.

Police and the Rule of Law

While serving as a primary source of referral and diversion of youth from juvenile court, the police are simultaneously required to investigate criminal activity and take juveniles into custody in appropriate cases. Their actions are controlled by statute, constitutional case law, and judicial review. Police methods of investigation and control in dealing with juvenile offenders include (1) the arrest procedure, (2) search and seizure, and (3) custodial interrogation.

The Arrest Procedure

When a juvenile is apprehended, the police must decide whether to release him or her or make a referral to the juvenile court. Cases involving serious crimes against property or persons are often referred to court. Less serious cases, such as minor disputes between juveniles, school and neighborhood complaints, petty shoplifting, runaways, and assaults and batteries of minors, are often diverted from court action.

arrest

Taking a person into the custody of the law to restrain the accused until he or she can be held accountable for the offense in court proceedings.

probable cause

Reasonable ground to believe the existence of facts that an offense was committed and that the accused committed that offense.

Most states require that the law of **arrest** be the same for both adults and juveniles. To make a legal arrest, an officer must have **probable cause** to believe that an offense took place and that the suspect is the guilty party. Probable cause is usually defined as falling somewhere between a mere suspicion and absolute certainty. In misdemeanor cases the police officer must personally observe the crime to place a suspect in custody. For a felony the police officer may make the arrest without having observed the crime if he or she has probable cause to believe the crime has occurred and the person being arrested has committed it.

The main difference between arrests of adult and juvenile offenders is the broader latitude police have to control youthful behavior. Police can arrest youths for status offenses such as truancy, running away, and possession of alcohol; adults would be immune to arrest for such acts. Most existing juvenile codes, for instance, provide broad authority for the police to take juveniles into custody.[19] Such statutes are designed to give the police the authority to act *in loco parentis* (Latin term referring to "in place of the parent"). According to Samuel Davis, the broad power

Table 13.1

UNIFORM JUVENILE COURT ACT, SECTION 13. (TAKING INTO CUSTODY)

a. A child may be taken into custody:
1. pursuant to an order of the court under this Act;
2. pursuant to the laws of arrest;
3. by a law enforcement officer (or duly authorized officer of the court) if there are reasonable grounds to believe that the child is suffering from illness or injury or is in immediate danger from his surroundings, and that his removal is necessary; or
4. by a law enforcement officer (or duly authorized officer of the court) if there are reasonable grounds to believe that the child has run away from his parents, guardian, or other custodian.

b. The taking of a child into custody is not an arrest, except for the purpose of determining its validity under the constitution of this State or of the United States.

Source: National Conference of Commissioners on Uniform State Laws, *Uniform Court Act* (Chicago: National Conference on Uniform State Laws, 1968), Sect. 13.

granted to police is consistent with the notion that a juvenile is not arrested but "taken into custody," which implies a protective rather than a punitive form of detention.[20] Once a juvenile is formally arrested, however, the constitutional safeguards of the Fourth and Fifth Amendments available to adults are applicable to the juvenile as well.

Section 13 of the Uniform Juvenile Court Act, created by the National Conference of Commissioners on Uniform State Laws, is an excellent example of the statutory provisions typically used in state codes regarding juvenile arrest procedures (see Table 13.1).

There is currently a trend toward treating juvenile offenders more like adults. Related to this overall get-tough attitude about juvenile crime are efforts by the police today to provide a more legalistic and less informal approach to the arrest process, and a more balanced approach to case disposition.[21]

By the end of the 1997 legislative session, over half the states had begun using the balanced restorative justice model in the purpose clause to the their juvenile court acts. The balanced approach has three components: accountability, competency development, and community protection (see Chapter 12 as well as the Policy and Practice box here).

Search and Seizure

search and seizure
The U.S. Constitution protects citizens from any search and seizure by police without a lawfully obtained search warrant; such warrants are issued when there is probable cause to believe that an offense has been committed.

Do juveniles have the same constitutional right to be free from unreasonable **search and seizure** as adults? In general, a citizen's privacy is protected by the Fourth Amendment of the Constitution, which states:

The right of the people to be secure in their persons, houses, papers, and effects, against unreasonable searches and seizures, shall not be violated, and no warrants shall issue, but upon probable cause, supported by oaths or affirmation, and particularly describing the place to be searched, and the persons or things to be seized.[22]

BALANCED AND RESTORATIVE JUSTICE FOR JUVENILES

Public safety is best achieved by collaborative efforts of justice systems and community groups to develop preventive capacity. Incarceration is a limited, expensive, and "last resort" solution for most juvenile offenders; structuring time and providing a clear continuum of sanctions and incentives provide the best approach. The public has a right to a safe and secure community. The community has a responsibility to actively promote healing and restoration.

POLICY GOALS

Reduced recidivism, especially while juveniles are under supervision in the community; increase in citizen feelings of safety and confidence in the juvenile justice system; creation of community "guardians" and improved preventive capacity of schools, families, and community agencies; increase in offender bonding and reintegration; direct involvement of community members.

PRACTICE PRIORITIES

Intensive structuring of juveniles' time and opportunities for bonding through participation in productive activities involving conventional adults (for example, work experiences, alternative service); clear policy options for consequences for noncompliance with supervision requirements and incentives for compliance; engage community "guardians" in the process; collaborate with community policing units; school prevention programs such as conflict resolution and anger management; parent training courses; incarceration for offenders who represent risk to community safety with intensive aftercare; use of volunteer community members.

Source: Gordon Bazemore and Mark Umbrert, *Balanced and Restorative Justice for Juveniles—A Framework for Juvenile Justice in the 21st Century* (Washington, D.C.: OJJDP, 1997); *Guide for Implementing the Balanced and Restorative Justice Model* (Washington, D.C.: U.S. Department of Justice, 1998).

Most courts in state jurisdictions have held that the Fourth Amendment ban against unreasonable search and seizure applies to juveniles in delinquency proceedings and that illegally seized evidence is inadmissible in a juvenile trial. To exclude incriminating evidence, a juvenile's attorney makes a pretrial motion to suppress the evidence—the same procedure that is used in the adult criminal process. Virtually all lower court decisions that have considered this issue have conveyed the view that the same standard must apply to juveniles as well as adults. In *State v. Lowry,* the court stated,

> Is it not more outrageous for the police to treat children more harshly than adult offenders, especially when such is violative of due process and fair treatment? Can a court countenance a system, where, as here, an adult may suppress evidence with the usual effect of having the charges dropped for lack of proof, and on the other hand a juvenile can be institutionalized—lose the most sacred possession a human being has, his freedom—for "rehabilitative" purposes because the Fourth Amendment right is unavailable to him?[23]

A full discussion of search and seizure is beyond the scope of this text, but it is important to note that the Supreme Court has ruled that police may stop a suspect and search for and seize evidence without a search warrant under certain circumstances. A person may be searched after a legal arrest but then only in the immediate area of the suspect's control. For example, after an arrest for possession of drugs,

Officers search students at a high school. The Supreme Court allows police officers and security agents greater latitude in searching students than they would have with other citizens, on the grounds that the campus must be a safe and crime-free environment.

the pockets of a suspect's jacket may be searched;[24] an automobile may be searched if there is probable cause to believe a crime has taken place;[25] a suspect's outer garments may be frisked if police are suspicious of his or her activities;[26] and a search may be conducted if a person volunteers for the search.[27] These rules are usually applied to juveniles as well as to adults.

One major issue of search and seizure in juvenile law is the right of school officials to search students and their possessions on school grounds and to turn over evidence to the police. Searches of students' persons or lockers become necessary when it is believed that students are in the process of violating the law. Drug abuse, theft, assault and battery, and racial conflicts in schools have increased the need to take action against troublemakers. School administrators have questioned students about their illegal activities, conducted searches of students' persons and possessions, and reported suspicious behavior to the police.

In the 1984 landmark decision in *New Jersey v. T.L.O.,* the Supreme Court helped clarify one of the most vexing problems of school searches: whether the Fourth Amendment's prohibition against unreasonable searches and seizures applies to school officials as well as to police officers.[28] In this important case, set out in the Juvenile Law in Review box, the Court found that students are in fact constitutionally protected from illegal searches but that school officials are not bound by the same restrictions as law enforcement agents. Police need "probable cause" before they can conduct a search, but educators can legally search students when there

NEW JERSEY V. T.L.O. (1984)

FACTS

On March 7, 1980, a teacher at Piscataway High in Middlesex County, New Jersey, discovered two girls smoking in a lavatory. Because this was in violation of school rules, he reported the incident to the principal's office, and the girls were summoned to meet with assistant vice principal Theodore Choplick, who questioned them about their behavior. When one of the girls (T.L.O.) claimed she had done nothing wrong, the assistant vice principal demanded to see her purse. When he examined it, he found a pack of cigarettes and also noticed a package of cigarette rolling papers, which are generally associated with the use of marijuana. He then searched the purse thoroughly and found some marijuana, a pipe, a substantial amount of money, a list of students who owed T.L.O. money, and letters implicating her in marijuana dealing. Choplick then informed both T.L.O.'s mother and the police of the evidence he uncovered. Later, at the police station, T.L.O. confessed to dealing drugs on campus.

Based on her confession and the evidence recovered from her purse, the state proceeded against T.L.O. in the juvenile court. Her motion to suppress the evidence taken during the school search was rejected by the trial court on the grounds that school officials could search students if they had reasonable cause to believe that the search was necessary to maintain school discipline or enforce school policies; consequently, T.L.O. was found delinquent and sentenced to a year's probation. T.L.O.'s subsequent appeal of the decision was eventually upheld by the New Jersey Supreme Court on the grounds that Choplick's search of T.L.O.'s purse was not justified under the circumstances of the case. The state appealed to the U.S. Supreme Court.

DECISION

The Supreme Court held that the prohibitions against illegal search and seizure apply to school as well as law enforcement officials. Teachers are not merely substitute parents but agents of the state who are required to carry out state policy and law. Students do not give up their constitutional rights when they walk on school property. However, school officials also have to maintain an atmosphere that is conducive to learning. A balance

are reasonable grounds to believe the students have violated the law or broken school rules. In creating this distinction the Court recognized the needs of school officials to preserve an environment conducive to education and to secure the safety of their students.

One of the most significant questions left unanswered by *New Jersey v. T.L.O.* is whether teachers and other school officials can search school lockers and desks. Here, the law has been controlled by state decisions, and each jurisdiction may create its own standards. Some allow teachers a free hand in opening lockers and desks.[29] However, not all school districts allow warrantless searches, holding as New Jersey did in *State v. Engerud:*

[W]e are satisfied that in the context of this case the student had an expectation of privacy in the contents of his locker. . . . For the four years of high school, the school locker is a home away from home. In it the student stores the kind of personal "effects" protected by the Fourth Amendment. [30]

must be achieved between a student's right to privacy and the school's need to provide a safe, secure environment. Therefore, the Court ruled that teachers do not need to obtain a warrant before searching a student who is under their authority. In addition, the search need not be based on probable cause to believe that a crime has taken place; rather the legality of the search of a student should depend simply on its reasonableness, considering the scope of the search, the age and sex of the student, and the behavior that prompted it to be made. Of considerable importance is the fact that school searches were found to be justified if a student was suspected of violating the law or of violating school rules. Considering this standard, the search of T.L.O. was found to be justified because the report of her smoking created a reasonable suspicion that she had cigarettes in her purse, and the discovery of the rolling papers then gave rise to a reasonable suspicion that she was in possession of marijuana.

SIGNIFICANCE OF THE CASE

By giving teachers and other school officials the right to search students if they are suspected of being in violation of school rules, the Court established a significant difference between the due process rights of adults and juveniles. An adult could not be legally searched by an agent of the government under the same circumstances under which T.L.O. was searched. Thus, the *T.L.O.* decision is in keeping with the judicial philosophy espoused in cases such as *Schall v. Martin* and *McKeiver v. Pennsylvania,* which find that juveniles, for their own protection, may be denied certain constitutional safeguards available to adults.

As a practical matter, *New Jersey v. T.L.O.* opens the door for greater security measures being taken on school grounds. It represents the Court's recognition that the nation's educational system is under siege and that educators need greater freedom to maintain school security. Underlying the decision is a recognition of the inherent rights of the mass of law-abiding students to receive an education unimpeded by the disruptive activities of a few troublemakers.

JUVENILE LAW IN REVIEW

Source: *New Jersey v. T.L.O.,* 469 U.S. 253, 104 S.Ct. 2403 (1984).

These and other lower court decisions have helped establish, limit, and define the scope of the school's authority to search lockers and desks.[31]

However, faced with increased crime by students in public schools, particularly illicit drug use, school administrators today are inclined to enforce drug control statutes and administrative rules.[32] Some urban schools are using breathalyzers, drug-sniffing dogs, hidden video cameras, and routine searches of students' pockets, purses, lockers, and cars.[33] In general, courts consider such searches permissible when they are not overly offensive and where there are reasonable grounds to suspect that the student may have violated the law.[34] School administrators are walking a tightrope between the students' constitutional rights to privacy and school safety.[35]

Of the many reported cases decided by state appellate courts since 1985 that applied the *T.L.O.* standard, intervention by school officials was upheld in virtually all of them. The apparent basis for the opinions was the court's interest in preserving safety in the school system. As Judge White in *T.L.O.* stated,

VERNONIA SCHOOL DISTRICT 47J V. WAYNE AND JUDY ACTON, GUARDIANS AD LITEM FOR JAMES ACTON (1995)

FACTS

In 1989 the Vernonia School District, an Oregon public school system, implemented a suspicionless drug urinalysis program for all students participating in interscholastic athletics. The program was a response to a rise in disciplinary problems the district believed to be related to an increase in drug use among students. When speakers, classes, and even drug-sniffing canines failed to deter student drug use, the school board approved a policy requiring student athletes to submit to random urinalysis as a condition of being allowed to play school sports.

The district's program required testing all interscholastic athletes at the beginning of the season for each athlete's sport. In addition, each week during the sport season 10 percent of the participants were selected randomly for testing. Those selected for testing provided a urine sample, and adult monitors were present while each randomly selected student produced his or her sample. Males were observed; females were not. Strict procedures were followed to ensure tamper-free samples.

Each urine sample was tested for amphetamines, cocaine, and marijuana. A positive test result triggered a second test. Any student who tested positive could continue participating in sports if the student agreed to take part in a six-week counseling program. Refusal to participate resulted in a student's suspension for the current and following season. A second violation resulted in automatic suspension for two seasons, and a third violation resulted in automatic suspension for three seasons.

This case began when James Acton, a seventh grader, was not permitted to play football when both he and his parents refused to consent to the test. No evidence suggested that James had ever used drugs or that school officials had any reason to suspect him of drug use. The Actons filed suit in federal district court, claiming that the district's program violated the search and seizure protections of the Fourth Amendment and the Oregon Constitution. The district court upheld the schools' testing program, but the Ninth Circuit Court of Appeals reversed the case.

DECISION

In a 6–3 decision, the U.S. Supreme Court overturned the Court of Appeals and found that the district's policy did not violate the Fourth and Fourteenth

---

Maintaining order in the classroom has never been easy, but in recent years, school disorder has often taken particularly ugly forms: drug use and violent crime in the schools have become major social problems.[36]

Faced with this crisis, state courts have not hesitated to lessen the applicability of the Fourth Amendment in a school setting.

In summary, the courts have examined the extent of the student's Fourth Amendment protection against unreasonable search and seizure as compared with the extent of the school's authority to conduct searches in the interest of safety. Have children lost some of their constitutional rights at the schoolhouse gate as a result of the *T.L.O.* decision? Perhaps. In 1995 the Supreme Court extended the schools' authority to search by legalizing a random drug-testing policy for student

Amendments of the U.S. Constitution. The Court applied a balancing test and weighed the student's privacy interests against the legitimate interests of the district. Applying this test, the Court stated that the privacy rights implicated by the testing program were minimal. In this regard the Court pointed out that public school students, as minors under compulsory attendance laws, have less Fourth Amendment protection than adults, particularly because they have been committed by their parents to the custody and control of school authorities. In addition, the Court minimized the privacy intrusion by observing that "school sports are not for the bashful and that student athletes routinely showered and changed clothes in front of each other."

With regard to deterrence, the Court stated that the district was responding to an immediate crisis. The Court concluded that deterring drug use by our nation's schoolchildren was "at least as important" as the interests deemed valid by the Court in the nonschool drug testing cases, such as the suspicionless alcohol and drug testing of railroad employees and of Customs Service employees. According to Justice Scalia, "It was self-evident that a drug problem fueled by the role model effect of athletes' drug use is effectively addressed by making sure that athletes do not use drugs." The Court's decision meant that James Acton was required to agree to be tested or forgo playing football.

SIGNIFICANCE OF THE CASE

As a result of *Vernonia*, schools may employ safe school programs such as drug testing procedures so long as the policies satisfy the reasonableness test. The landmark decision of *New Jersey v. T.L.O.*, which announced the reasonable suspicion standard, remains in force, and the list of permissible drug programs will likely expand. In other words, this decision should bring forth a spate of suspicionless searches in public schools across the country. Metal detection procedures, the use of drug-sniffing dogs, and random locker searches will be easier to justify. The *Vernonia* case underscores the importance of eradicating drug use in the nation's school systems. In upholding random, suspicionless drug testing for student athletes, the Supreme Court extended the schools' authority to search one step further, despite court-imposed constitutional safeguards for children. Underlying this decision, like that of *New Jersey v. T.L.O.*, is a recognition that the use of drugs is a serious threat to public safety and to the rights of children to receive a decent and safe education.

Source: *Vernonia School District v. Acton,* 515 U.S. 646, 115 S.Ct. 2386, 132 L.Ed. 2d 564 (1995).

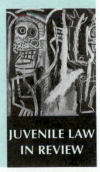

JUVENILE LAW IN REVIEW

athletes. The Supreme Court's recent decision in *Vernonia School District 47J v. Acton* expanded the power of educators to ensure safe learning environments in schools (see the Juvenile Law in Review box).[37]

Restoring safety in schools is a major goal of law enforcement personnel and educators. Strategies that have been identified by the OJJDP as ways to reduce violence in schools include (1) establishing rules against bullying for perpetrators and victims of such behavior (antibullying programs); (2) reducing the existence of youth gangs at schools (gang resistance education and training); (3) maintaining security and preventing weapons from being brought to school (passage of state and gun-free school zones legislation); and (4) stopping the use and trafficking of drugs and alcohol in schools (drug-free school zones). For more on these strategies, see Chapter 10.[38]

Custodial Interrogation

Parents are usually contacted immediately after a child is taken into custody. In years past, the police often questioned juveniles without their parents or even an attorney present. Any incriminatory statements or confessions the juveniles made could be used in evidence at trial. However, in 1966 the landmark Supreme Court case *Miranda v. Arizona* placed constitutional limitations on police interrogation procedures used with adult offenders. *Miranda* held that persons in police custody must be told the following:

- They have the right to remain silent.
- Any statements they make can be used against them.
- They have the right to counsel.
- If they cannot afford counsel, it will be furnished at public expense.[39]

Miranda warning
Supreme Court decisions require police officers to inform individuals under arrest of their constitutional rights; warning must also be given when suspicion begins to focus on an individual in the accusatory stage.

custodial interrogation
Questions posed by the police to a suspect held in custody in the prejudicial stage of the juvenile justice process; juveniles have the same rights against self-incrimination as adults do when being questioned.

totality of the circumstances doctrine
Legal doctrine that mandates that a decision maker consider all the issues and circumstances of a case before judging the outcome; the suspect's age, intelligence, and competency may be issues that influence his or her understanding and judgment.

These ***Miranda* warnings,** which secure the adult defendant's Fifth Amendment privilege against self-incrimination, have been made applicable to children taken into custody. The Supreme Court case of *In re Gault* stated that constitutional privileges against self-incrimination are applicable in juvenile cases as well as in adult cases. Because *In re Gault* implies that *Miranda v. Arizona* applies to **custodial interrogation** in criminal procedure, state court jurisdictions apply the requirements of *Miranda* to juvenile proceedings as well. Since the *Gault* decision in 1967, virtually all of the courts that have ruled on the question of the *Miranda* warning have concluded that the warning does apply to the juvenile process.

One difficult problem associated with the custodial interrogation of juveniles has to do with their waiver of *Miranda* rights: Under what circumstances can juveniles knowingly and willingly waive the rights given them by *Miranda v. Arizona* and discuss their actions with the police without benefit of a lawyer? Is it possible for a youngster, acting alone, to be mature enough to appreciate the right to remain silent? This is precisely the issue discussed in the Ryan Harris murder case at the beginning of the chapter.

Most courts have concluded that parents or attorneys need not be present for children to effectively waive their rights.[40] In a frequently cited California case, *People v. Lara,* the court said that the question of a child's waiver is to be determined by the **totality of the circumstances doctrine.**[41] This means that the validity of a waiver rests not only on the age of the child but also on a combination of other factors, including the education of the accused, the accused's knowledge of the charge and of the right to remain silent and have an attorney present, whether the youth was allowed to consult with family or friends, whether the interrogation took place before or after charges were filed, the method of interrogation, and whether the accused refused to give statements on prior occasions.[42]

The general rule is that juveniles can waive their rights to protection from self-incrimination but that the validity of this waiver is determined by the circumstances of each case.

The waiver of *Miranda* rights by a juvenile is probably one of the most controversial legal issues addressed in the state courts. It has also been the subject of federal constitutional review. In two cases, *Fare v. Michael C.* and *California v. Prysock,* the Supreme Court has attempted to clarify children's rights when they are interrogated by the police. In *Fare v. Michael C.* the Court ruled that a child's asking to speak to his probation officer was not the equivalent of asking for an attorney; consequently, admissions he made to the police absent legal counsel were held to be admissible in court.[43] In *California v. Prysock* the Court was asked to rule on the adequacy of a *Miranda* warning given Randall Prysock, a youthful murder suspect.[44] After reviewing the taped exchange between the police interrogator and the boy, the Court upheld Prysock's conviction when it ruled that even though the *Miranda* warning was given in slightly different language and out of exact context, its meaning was plain and easily understandable, even to a juvenile.

Taken together, *Fare* and *Prysock* make it seem indisputable that juveniles are at least entitled to receive the same *Miranda* rights as adults and ought to be entitled to even greater consideration to ensure that they understand their legal rights.

Miranda v. Arizona is a historic and often symbolic decision that continues to serve to protect the rights of all suspects, both adults and children, placed in custody.[45]

Discretionary Justice

discretion
Use of personal decision making and choice in carrying out operations in the criminal justice system, such as deciding whether to make an arrest or when to accept a plea bargain.

Today juvenile offenders receive nearly as much procedural protection as adult offenders. However, the police have broader authority in dealing with juvenile misconduct under most juvenile codes than they have when dealing with adults. Granting such **discretion** to juvenile officers raises some important questions: When should a police officer act to assist a juvenile in need against his or her will? Under what circumstances should an officer arrest status offenders? Should a summons be used in lieu of arrest? Under what conditions should a juvenile be taken into protective custody?

When police officers confront a case involving a juvenile offender, they rely on their discretion to choose an appropriate course of action. Police discretion is selective enforcement of the law by duly authorized police agents. Legal experts and scholars have elaborated on this definition in various ways. Roscoe Pound defined discretion as the authority conferred by law to act in certain conditions or situations in accordance with an official's or agency's own considered conscience or judgment.[46] Pound's use of the word "conscience" implies that discretion operates in the twilight zone between law and morals. According to Kenneth Davis, discretion

A teen in Los Angeles in police custody hopes that the officers will release him with a warning. His friends are also concerned about their futures. Police have discretion to take formal action against youthful offenders or to release them with a warning or take some other informal action.

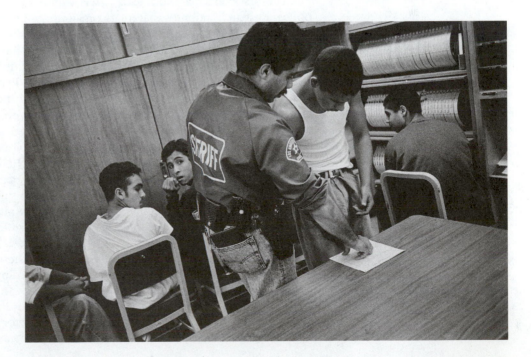

gives officers a choice from among possible courses of action within the limits on their power.[47] Joseph Goldstein has termed the exercise of police discretion a prime example of **low-visibility decision making** in the criminal justice system.[48] Low-visibility decision making refers to decisions made by public officials in the criminal or juvenile justice systems that the public is not in a position to understand, regulate, or criticize.

Police discretion is probably one of the most controversial and important of all police practices. Discretion exists not only in the police function but also in prosecutorial decision making, judicial judgments, and corrections. Discretion results in the law being applied differently in similar situations. For example, two teenagers are caught in a stolen automobile; one is arrested, the other is released. Two youths are drunk and disorderly; one is sent home, the other is booked and sent to juvenile court. A group of youngsters is involved in a gang fight; only a few are arrested, the others are released.

Police officers in both the adult and juvenile systems use a high degree of discretion in carrying out their daily tasks. In particular, much discretion is exercised in juvenile work because of the informality that has been built into the system in an attempt to individualize justice. According to Victor Streib, arbitrary discretion is a characteristic of the informal juvenile system.[49] Furthermore, Streib says, police intake officials, prosecutors, judges, and correctional administrators make final, largely unreviewed decisions about children that often are almost totally unsupervised in any meaningful way.

The daily procedures of juvenile personnel are not subject to administrative scrutiny or judicial review, except when they clearly violate a youth's constitutional rights. As a result, discretion sometimes deteriorates into discrimination, violence, and other abusive practices on the part of the police. As Herbert Packer has stated, the real danger in discretion is that it allows the law to discriminate against precisely those elements in the population—the poor, the ignorant, the unpopular—who are least able to draw attention to their plight and to whose sufferings the vast majority of the population is not responsive.[50]

The problem of discretion in juvenile justice is one of extremes. Too little discretion ties the hands of decision makers and provides little flexibility to treat juvenile offenders as individuals. Too much discretion can lead to juvenile injustice. Guidelines and controls are needed to structure the use of discretion.

The first contact a youth usually has with the juvenile justice system is with the police. Research indicates that a large majority of police decisions at this initial contact involve discretion.[51] Some of these studies show that many juvenile offenders are never referred to the juvenile court system for formal action.

In a classic study, Nathan Goldman examined the arrest records for more than one thousand juveniles from four communities in Pennsylvania to determine what factors operated in police referrals of juveniles to the court.[52] He concluded that more than 64 percent of police contacts with juveniles were handled informally without court referral. Subsequent research offered additional evidence of discretionary decision making and informal disposition of juvenile cases.[53] Paul Strasburg found that only about 50 percent of all children who come in contact with the police ever get past the initial stage of the juvenile justice process.[54] More current data show an increase in the number of cases referred to the juvenile court system for formal action. The FBI generally estimates about two-thirds of all juvenile arrests are referred to juvenile court jurisdiction.[55] The disposition of juvenile offenders taken into custody is illustrated in Figure 13.4.

Despite the variations between the estimates, these studies indicate that the police use significant discretion in their decisions regarding juvenile offenders. Research generally shows that differential decision making goes on without clear guidance and uniformity. Figure 13.5 illustrates the alternatives in the police–juvenile decision-making process. The next sections describe the factors that influence police discretion and review the policies and programs for its control.

FIGURE 13.4

Police Dispositions of Juvenile Offenders Taken into Custody

Sources: Jeffrey Butts, "Juvenile Court Processing of Delinquency Cases, 1985–1994," Fact Sheet 57 (Washington, D.C.: OJJDP, 1998); Melissa Sickmund et al., *Juvenile Court Statistics 1995* (Washington, D.C.: Bureau of Justice Statistics, 1998).

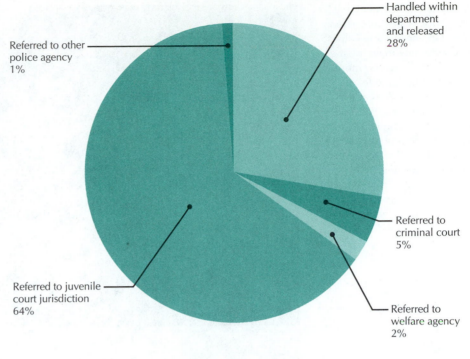

Referred to other police agency
1%

Handled within department and released
28%

Referred to criminal court
5%

Referred to welfare agency
2%

Referred to juvenile court jurisdiction
64%

FIGURE 13.5

Ladder of Police–Juvenile Decision Making

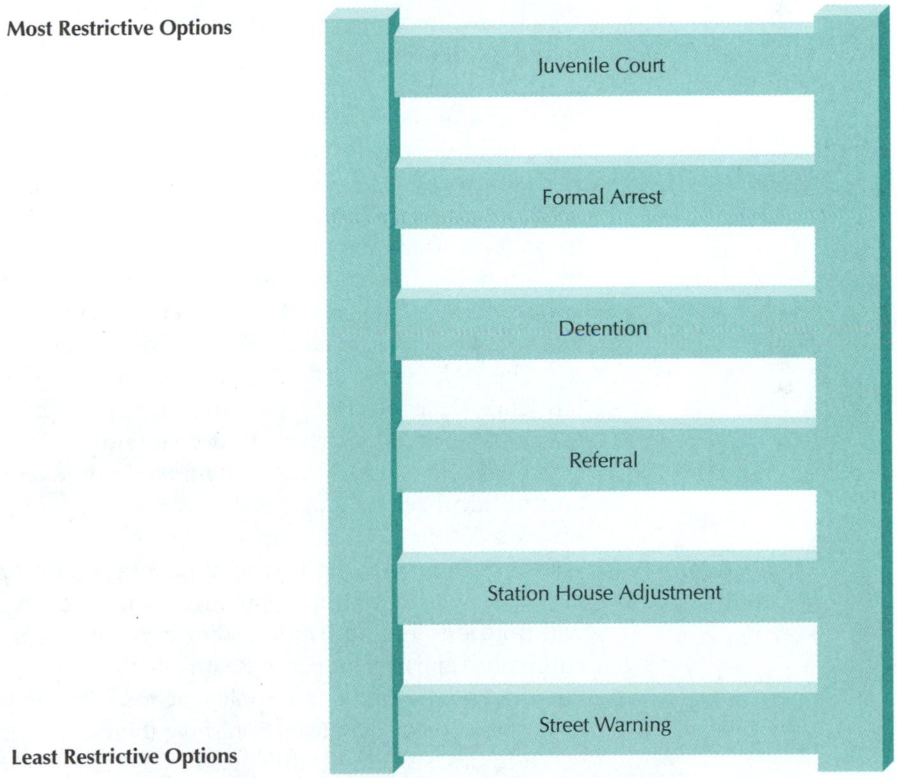

Most Restrictive Options

Juvenile Court

Formal Arrest

Detention

Referral

Station House Adjustment

Street Warning

Least Restrictive Options

Environmental Factors

How does a juvenile police officer decide what to do with a juvenile offender? As might be expected, the seriousness of the crime, the situation in which it occurred, and the legal record of the juvenile significantly affect decision making. Police are much more likely to take formal action if the crime is serious and has been reported

A number of environmental factors influence police discretion, including the norms and values of the community in which the officer works. Some communities tolerate a fair amount of personal freedom. And in these liberal environments, the police may be inclined to release juveniles into the community rather than arrest them. Other officers may work in extremely conservative communities that expect a no-nonsense approach to police enforcement. Here, police may be more inclined to arrest a juvenile.

by a victim who is a respected member of the community and if the offender is well known to them.[56] However, these factors are not the only ones that have been found to influence discretion.

The norms and values of the community in which the officer works also affects the decision. For instance, some officers work in communities that tolerate a fair amount of personal freedom. In liberal environments, the police may be inclined to release juveniles into the community rather than arrest them. Other officers may work in extremely conservative communities that expect a no-nonsense approach to police enforcement. Here, police may be more inclined to arrest a juvenile. Although police use formal arrest procedures more often in lower-class than in middle- and upper-class neighborhoods, there is little clear-cut evidence that an area's general racial or ethnic makeup affects arrest decision making.

The policies, practices, and customs of the local police department also may influence decisions. Juvenile officers may be pressured to make more arrests or to refrain from making arrests under certain circumstances. Directives and orders instruct officers to be alert to certain types of juvenile violations. The chief of police and political officials of a community might initiate policies governing the arrest practices of the juvenile department. For example, if local merchants complain that youths congregating in a shopping center parking lot are inhibiting business, police may be called on to make arrests in order to get the point across that loitering will not be tolerated. Under other circumstances, a more informal warning might be given. Similarly, a rash of deaths caused by teenage drunk driving may galvanize the local media to demand police action. The mayor and the police chief, sensitive to possible voter dissatisfaction, may therefore demand that formal police action be taken in cases of drunk driving.

Another source of influence is pressure from individual superiors, such as police supervisors. The sergeant, for example, may initiate formal or informal directives regarding handling youths in a given community. Some supervising officers may believe it is important to curtail disorderly conduct, drinking, or drug use. In addition, officers may be influenced by the discretionary decisions made by their peers.

A final environmental factor affecting the performance of officers is their perception of community alternatives to police intervention. Police officers may use arrest because they believe nothing else can be done and that arrest is the best possible example of good police work.[57] Other juvenile officers may favor referring juveniles to social service agencies, particularly if they believe a community has a variety of good resources. These referrals save the police officer both time and effort: records do not have to be filled out, and court appearances can be avoided. The availability of such options allows for greater latitude in police decision making.[58] Goldman discovered that community attitudes, political pressures, and the bias of the individual police officer may also influence whether a juvenile offender is arrested, taken into custody, or released.

Situational Factors

In addition to the environment, a variety of situational factors affect a police officer's decisions. Situational factors are those attached to a particular crime, such as specific traits of offenders. Studies show that police officers rely heavily on the demeanor and appearance of the juvenile in making decisions. For example, Aaron Cicourel found that the decision to arrest is often based on situational factors such as dress, attitude, speech, and level of hostility toward the police.[59] Piliavin and Briar found that police perceptions of the attitudes of offenders toward the police, the law, and their own behavior were the most important factors in the decision to process or release an offender.[60]

Most studies conclude that whether the decisions involve juvenile or adult offenders, these variables are important in the police discretionary process:[61]

- The attitude of the complainant
- The type and seriousness of the offense
- The race, sex, and age of the offender
- The attitude of the offender
- The history of the offender's prior contacts with the police
- The perceived willingness of the parents to assist in discipline and in solving the problem (in the case of a child)
- The setting or location in which the incident occurs
- Whether the offender denies the actions or insists on a court hearing (in the case of a child)
- The likelihood that a child can be served by a referral agency in the community

Bias and Police Discretion

Do police allow racial, gender, or organizational bias to affect their decisions on whether to arrest youths? A great deal of debate has been generated over this very critical issue. Some experts believe that police decision making is deeply influenced by the offender's personal characteristics, whereas others maintain that crime-related variables are actually more significant.

Racial Bias It has long been charged that police discriminate against minorities and are more likely to act formally with African American suspects and use their discretion to benefit whites.[62] Research on this controversial issue has yielded mixed conclusions. Some studies indicate that the police are more likely to take offense and demeanor into account than race. T. Edwin Black and Charles Smith found that polite, respectful youths were more likely to get the benefit of police discretion, whether they were African American or white, than youths who displayed a "bad attitude." Black and Smith's national assessment of juvenile justice processing found that there was no difference in the proportion of African Americans and whites arrested and referred to court, regardless of the nature of the offense.[63] However, the same study found that Hispanics and other ethnic minority groups faced a greater likelihood of court referral than either African American or white youths.

Some research efforts do show evidence of police discrimination against African American youths.[64] However, even research supportive of police discrimination does not always indicate that it is overt and unidimensional. For example, Fagan and his associates found that police are more likely to formally process minorities except for crimes of violence, where the pattern is reversed and white offenders are referred to juvenile court at a higher rate.[65] David Griswold states, "The preponderance, as well as the strength, of the evidence leans toward a view that the police do not discriminate against minorities and that factors other than race weigh most heavily in the police decision-making process."[66]

In contrast to Black and Smith's study, Donna Bishop and Charles Frazier found that race can have a direct effect on decisions made at several junctures of the juvenile justice process.[67] Their research examines the impact of a juvenile's race on decisions from intake to disposition, based on a cohort group of more than fifty thousand youths in a large southern city. According to Bishop and Frazier, African Americans are more likely than whites to be recommended for formal processing, referred to court, adjudicated delinquent, and given harsher dispositions for comparable offenses. In the arrest category, specifically, being African American increases the probability of formal police action.[68]

One of the most significant research efforts on differential processing of minorities is a report from the National Coalition of State Juvenile Justice Advisory Groups.[69] The report points out that minority youth, particularly African Americans and Hispanics, are overrepresented at various stages of the juvenile justice system. The coalition suggests two possible explanations for this disparity: (1) differential rates in arrest, incarceration, and even release are the result of a racist system or (2) the differential rates are the result of greater involvement by minorities in juvenile crime.[70] According to the report, to rectify this imbalance, the social structure of society must be altered by improving the educational system, creating more job opportunities, and providing more services for minority families. The report also recommends that the Office of Juvenile Justice and Delinquency Prevention examine police surveillance and apprehension procedures to determine the causes of differential treatment and to reduce or eliminate any subtle discrimination that may exist in the early stages of the juvenile process.[71]

Another important study by the National Council on Crime and Delinquency revealed an equally significant overrepresentation by black youths at every point in the California juvenile justice system. Although less than 9 percent of the state youth population, black youths accounted for 19 percent of juvenile arrests. According to the study, the causes for the racial disparity included (1) institutional racism, (2) environmental factors, (3) family dysfunction, (4) cultural barriers, and (5) school failure.[72] A 1997 OJJDP report shows a similarly prominent disproportionality: black youths were 15 percent of the juvenile population of the United States but were involved in 28 percent of all juvenile arrests. They were most disproportionately involved in arrests for murder (58 percent), forcible rape (45 percent), robbery (60 percent), aggravated assault (42 percent), motor vehicle theft (38 percent), fraud (42 percent), and gambling (71 percent).[73]

In summary, studies of racial bias in police decision making have revealed the following:

1. Some researchers have concluded that the police discriminate against black and other minority youths.
2. Other researchers do not find evidence of discrimination.
3. Racial disparity is most often seen at the arrest stage but probably exists at other processing points.

RACE, GENDER, AND ETHNICITY IN JUVENILE POLICE DECISION MAKING

Does police discretion work against the young, males, the poor, and minority group members, or does it favor special interest groups? Current research has uncovered information supporting both sides.

Although the police are involved in at least some discrimination against racial minorities who are juveniles, the frequency and scope of such discrimination may be less than anticipated. Some of today's literature shows that the police are likely to interfere with or arrest poor African American youths. The police frequently stop and question youths of color walking down the streets of their neighborhoods or hanging around street corners. If this is the case, then race plays a role in police discretion.

In contrast to these findings, data from other studies indicate that racial bias does not influence the decision to arrest and move a youngster through the juvenile justice system. The attitude of the youth, prior record, seriousness of crime, setting or location of the crime, and other variables control police discretion, not race, ethnicity, or gender. Another problem in determining the impact of race or gender on police discretion is that the victim's race, not the juvenile offender's, may be the key to racial bias. Police officers may take differential action when the victim is white rather than when the victim is a minority group member.

Police bias may also be a result of organizational and administrative directions as opposed to bias by an individual officer "on the beat" or in a cruiser. For example, the police departments have been found to use "racial" profiles for stopping and questioning suspects.

Obviously, not all officers operate unfairly or with a racial bias. Quite possibly the impact of race on juvenile police discretion varies from jurisdiction to jurisdiction and from one group of juveniles to another. Many African American youngsters, for example, view their gang affiliation as a means of survival. Teenage gang members and their families often feel frustrated about the lack of opportunities and their experiences as being targets of discrimination.

Despite all the research findings, uncertainty about the extent and degree of racial bias continues to plague the juvenile justice system. Unfortunately, minority youth are involved in a disproportionate percentage of all juvenile arrests. This often gives the impression that racial, gender, and ethnic bias exists in urban police departments.

What do you think? Do the police take race into account when making decisions to arrest juveniles suspected of violating the law?

Sources: For an extensive review of research on police discretion (adult and juvenile) since 1980, see Eric Riksheim and Steven Chermak, "Causes of Police Behavior Revisited," *Journal of Criminal Justice* 21:353–82 (1993); also William Brown, "The Fight for Survival: African American Gang Members and their Families in a Segregated Society," *Juvenile and Family Court Journal* 49:1–15 (1998); Bohsui Wu, "The Effect of Race on Juvenile Justice Processing," *Juvenile and Family Court Journal* 48:43–53 (1997); Richard Sutphen, David Kurtz, and Martha Giddings, "The Influence of Juveniles' Race on Police Decision-Making: An Exploratory Study," *Juvenile and Family Court Journal* 44:69–78 (1997).

---

4. The higher arrest rates of minorities are related to interpersonal, family, community, and organizational differences. Other influences may include police discretion with juveniles, street crime visibility, and high crime rates within a particular group. Such factors, however, may also be linked to a general societal discrimination.

For further information on racial bias in police decisions, see the Focus on Delinquency box entitled "Race, Gender, and Ethnicity in Juvenile Police Decision Making." Further research is needed to better understand and document what appears to be findings of disproportional arrests of minority juvenile offenders.[74]

chivalry hypothesis, paternalism hypothesis
View that the low crime rates and delinquency of females are a reflection of the leniency with which police treat female offenders.

Gender Bias   Is there a difference between police treatment of male and female offenders? Some experts favor the **chivalry** or **paternalism hypothesis,** which holds that police are more likely to act paternally toward young girls and not arrest them. Others believe that police may be more likely to arrest female offenders because their actions violate police officers' cherished stereotypes of the female.

There is some research support for various forms of gender bias. The nature of this bias may vary according to the seriousness of the offense and the age of the offender. Some of the conclusions reached in these studies are:

1. Police tend to be more lenient toward females than males with regard to acts of delinquency.

   Researcher Merry Morash found that young boys who engage in "typical male" delinquent activities are much more likely to develop police records than females.[75]

2. In contrast, females who have committed minor or status offenses seem to be referred to juvenile court more often than males.

   Meda Chesney-Lind has found that adolescent female status offenders are arrested for less serious offenses than boys.[76]

3. Younger female offenders are treated by police in a harsher manner than their older female counterparts—an apparent confirmation of the paternalism theory.

   Research by Christy Visher showed that police officers took a more paternalistic (stricter) position toward young females to "deter any further violation of appropriate sex role behavior." Visher found that age and race were more important factors in arrest decisions for females as compared to males.[77]

4. Recent evidence has confirmed earlier studies showing that the police and most likely the juvenile courts apply a double standard in dealing with male and female juvenile offenders.

   Bishop and Frazier, in a 1992 study, found that both female status offenders and male delinquents are differently disadvantaged in the juvenile justice system.[78]

5. In contrast to these findings, some research indicates that males and females receive similar treatment from police.

   Black and Smith's national assessment study found that the "sex of the offender alone appears to have no influence on whether an offender, after being arrested, is referred to the court."[79]

To a large degree, then, current research findings on police gender bias are inconclusive. However, there appears to be general agreement that police are less likely to process females for delinquent acts and that they discriminate against them by arresting them for status offenses.

Organizational Bias   The policies used in some police departments may result in biased law enforcement practices. Research conducted by a number of police experts, including Douglas Smith, has found that police departments can be characterized by their professionalism (having the skills and knowledge needed for the positions) and degree of bureaucratization.[80] Departments that are highly bureaucratized (excessive use of rules and regulations) and at the same time unprofessional are the ones most likely to be insulated from the communities they serve. (Smith labels these departments "militaristic.") According to Smith, isolation can result in the introduction of racial and class bias into the social control process.

The direction of organizational policy may be fueled by the perceptions of police decision makers. A number of experts have found that law enforcement administrators have a stereotyped view of the urban poor as troublemakers who must be kept under control.[81] Consequently, lower-class neighborhoods experience much greater police scrutiny than middle-class areas, and their residents face a proportionately greater chance of arrest and official processing. Youths who fit the "common image"—for example, males who hang with a tough crowd—significantly increase their chances of being arrested and being officially labeled.

This relationship has been explored in some important research conducted by Robert Sampson. Using both self-reports and official data, Sampson found that teenage residents of neighborhoods with low socioeconomic status had a significantly greater chance of acquiring police records than youths living in higher socioeconomic areas, regardless of the actual crime rates in these areas. Furthermore, Sampson found that this relationship held up even when sex, individual income, race, gang membership, and delinquent peers were controlled.[82] Sampson found that a juvenile's socioeconomic status had an impact on the decision to officially process an arrested youth to the juvenile court. This research indicates that although police officers may not discriminate on an individual level, departmental policy that focuses attention on lower-class areas may result in class and racial bias in the police processing of delinquent youth.

In summary, the policies, practices, and customs of the local police department influence discretion. Conditions vary from department to department and depend strongly on the judgment of the chief and others in the organizational hierarchy.

Considerations of race, economic status, or gender should not determine how the police exercise their authority. Because the police retain a large degree of discretionary power, the ideal goal of nondiscrimination is often difficult to achieve in actual practice. However, policies to limit police discretion can help to eliminate bias.

CASE IN POINT

You are a newly appointed police officer assigned to a juvenile unit of a medium-sized urban police department.

Wayne W. is a fourteen-year-old white boy who was caught shoplifting with two friends of the same age and sex. Wayne attempted to leave a large department store with a $40 shirt and was apprehended by a police officer in front of the store. Wayne seemed quite remorseful about the offense. He said several times that he did not know why he did it and that he had not planned to do it. He seemed upset and scared and, although admitting the offense, did not want to go to court.

Wayne had three previous contacts with the police: one for malicious mischief when he destroyed some property, another involving a minor assault of a boy, and a third involving another shoplifting charge. In all three cases Wayne promised to refrain from ever committing such acts again, and as a result, he was not required to go to court. The other shoplifting offense involved a baseball worth only $10.

Wayne appeared at the police department with his mother because his parents are divorced. She did not seem overly concerned about the case and felt that her son was not really to blame. She argued that he was always getting in trouble and that she was not sure how to control him. She blamed most of his troubles with the law on his being in the wrong crowd.

Store management had left matters in the hands of the police and agreed to support their decision. The other two boys did not steal anything and claimed that they had no idea that Wayne was planning anything when they entered the store. Neither had any criminal record.

■ Should Wayne be sent to court for trial?

■ What other remedy might be appropriate?

Limiting Police Discretion

A number of leading organizations have suggested the use of guidelines to limit police discretion. The American Bar Association (ABA) states, "Since individual police officers may make important decisions affecting police operations without direction, with limited accountability and without any uniformity within a department, police discretion should be structured and controlled."[83] There is almost a unanimous opinion that steps must be taken to provide better control and guidance over police discretion in street and station house adjustments of juvenile cases.

One of the leading exponents of police discretion is Kenneth Culp Davis, who has done much to raise the consciousness of criminal justice practitioners about discretionary decision making. Davis recommends controlling administrative discretion through (1) the use of more narrowly defined laws, (2) the development of written policies, and (3) the recording of decisions by criminal justice personnel.[84] Narrowing the scope of juvenile codes, for example, would limit and redefine the broad authority police officers currently have to take youths into custody for criminal and noncriminal behavior. Such practices would provide fair criteria for arrests, adjustment, and police referral of juvenile offenders and would help eliminate largely personal judgments based on the race, attitude, or demeanor of the juvenile.[85] Discretionary decision making in juvenile police work can be better understood by analyzing the Case in Point and by examining Figure 13.6.

One discretionary option available to juvenile officers is diversion to community agency. The interaction between police and the community is the topic of the next section.

Police Work and Delinquency Prevention

delinquency prevention programs
Programs developed by the police in cooperation with social service agencies to provide needed services to juveniles.

community services
Local delinquency prevention services such as recreational programs and drug and alcohol information programs in schools that help meet the community's needs for youths.

Police need to develop programs and relationships with social service agencies to effectively provide services to juveniles while enforcing the law. Because police officers are responsible for the care of juveniles taken into custody, it is essential that they work closely with social service groups on a day-to-day basis. In addition, the police must assume a leadership role in identifying the needs of children in the community and helping the community meet those needs. In helping to develop **delinquency prevention programs,** the police must work closely with youth service bureaus, schools, recreational facilities, welfare agencies, and employment programs.[86]

Using **community services** for delinquent and nondelinquent juveniles has many advantages. Such services allow young people to avoid the stigma of being processed by a police agency. They also improve the community's awareness of the complex needs of young people. Service providers help cultivate a sense of public responsibility and support for community programs. Another advantage of using community services is that they make it possible to restrict court referral by the police to cases involving serious crime.

One of the most important institutions playing a role in delinquency prevention is the school. Liaison prevention programs between the police and the schools have been implemented in many communities throughout the United States. Liaison officers from schools and police departments have played a leadership role in developing recreational programs for juveniles. In some instances they have actu-

FIGURE 13.6

Discretionary Justice with Juveniles

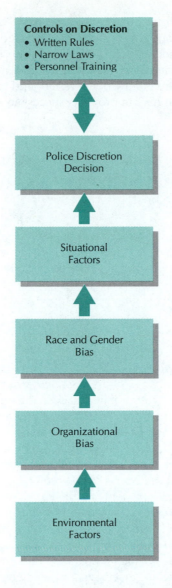

Controls on Discretion
• Written Rules
• Narrow Laws
• Personnel Training

Police Discretion Decision

Situational Factors

Race and Gender Bias

Organizational Bias

Environmental Factors

TOP program

Police and community prevention effort in which teens are hired to patrol the city's parks and recreation areas.

Project DARE

An elementary school drug abuse resistance education program designed to prevent teenage drug abuse by giving youths the skills they need to resist peer pressure to experiment with drugs.

ally operated such programs. In others they have encouraged community support for recreational activities, including Little League baseball, athletic clubs, camping outings, and police athletic and scouting programs.

One prominent example of a successful ongoing police–community prevention effort is the privately funded **TOP program** in Rochester, New York. TOP stands for Teens on Patrol.[87] Each summer, about one hundred youths are hired to patrol the city's parks and recreational areas. The young people help keep the parks "cool" and also learn a lot about police officers; in fact, a number of TOP graduates have gone on to become police officers.

Project DARE (drug abuse resistance education) is a well-respected and effective effort by local police departments to prevent teenage drug abuse. This is an elementary school course designed to give students the skills to resist peer pressure to experiment with tobacco, drugs, and alcohol. It is unique because it employs uniformed police officers who carry the antidrug message to students before they enter junior high school. The program provides information about tobacco, alcohol, and drugs; teaches students techniques to resist peer pressure and to respect law and order; gives students alternatives to drug use; and helps students build self-esteem. DARE programs have been adopted by hundreds of police departments throughout the country. A recent study of the DARE program by the National

Institute for Justice found that more than half (52 percent) of the school districts nationwide have adopted this program. This study also found that the program is best at increasing students' knowledge about substance abuse and at enhancing social skills. However, its effect on reducing student drug use seems insignificant. A revised DARE program is now being tested, and supporters are hopeful that a new interactive orientation may improve its success in reducing student drug use.[88]

POLICY AND PRACTICE

PROMISING DELINQUENCY PREVENTION PROGRAMS IN LAW ENFORCEMENT

A growing body of research supports the idea that delinquency prevention programs involving the police have several advantages: (1) they are often a cost-effective means of reducing youth misbehavior; (2) the programs can focus on children of any age; (3) many programs concentrate on the parents of children in trouble or on the communities in which they live; and (4) although the success rate of many programs has lacked empirical support, others have been proven to have an impact on juvenile misconduct. Let's take a closer look at some major categories of delinquency prevention efforts.

NEIGHBORHOOD VIOLENCE PROGRAMS

Many children live in unsafe neighborhoods. A large percentage of children witness muggings, shootings, and murders. As a result of living with violence, youths experience what psychologists call posttraumatic stress disorder (PTSD). Research supports the belief that children exposed to chronic violence often lose hope and develop an aggressive style of life that includes substance abuse, delinquency, and depression. Children can be so traumatized by neighborhood violence that violence itself becomes a survival mechanism.

In response to concerns about the effects of community violence on juveniles, the New Haven, Connecticut, police department and the Yale University Child Center developed a police program that involves twenty-four-hour crisis intervention for children and families who witness violence. During its five years of operation, the Community Policing Project trained police personnel and provided consultation services to more than six hundred children. This project is being replicated in other major cities throughout the country. Preliminary research indicates that such counseling can play a major role in crime prevention.

MENTORING PROGRAMS

The Juvenile Mentoring Program (JUMP) is a federal program administered by the Office of Juvenile Justice and Delinquency Prevention. As supported by JUMP, mentoring is a one-on-one relationship between a pair of unrelated individuals, one adult and one juvenile, that takes place on a regular basis over an extended period of time. It is almost always characterized by a special bond of mutual commitment and an emotional bond based on respect, loyalty, and identification.

Children need caring adults in their lives, and providing mentors or role models is one way to fill this need for at-risk children. The special bond of commitment fostered by the mutual respect inherent in effective mentoring can be the tie that binds a young person to a better future. OJJDP's Juvenile Mentoring Program, involving police officers as mentors, is designed to reduce delinquency and to improve school attendance for at-risk youth.

With nearly a century of experience, Big Brothers/Big Sisters of America is probably the best known mentoring program in the United States. The extensive evaluation of this pioneer program provides new insights that merit our attention for the role of the police officer as a mentor.

OJJDP's two-year evaluation of JUMP suggests that strengthening the role of mentoring as a component of youth programming may pay handsome dividends in improved school

Today, many experts consider delinquency prevention efforts to be crucial to the development of a comprehensive approach to the problem of youth crime. Although such efforts are broad-based and cut across the entire juvenile justice system, police programs have become increasingly popular in recent years. See the Policy and Practice box entitled "Promising Delinquency Prevention Programs in Law Enforcement" for more on this topic.

performance and reduced antisocial behavior, including alcohol and other drug abuse. In the 1992 reauthorization of the Juvenile Justice and Delinquency Prevention Act of 1974, Congress added "mentoring" to its funded programs. To date, Congress has made $19 million available to fund JUMP.

CURFEW

Curfews have reemerged recently as a popular option for legislators in their efforts to deter juvenile delinquency. Imposed on and off since the turn of the century, curfews tend to receive attention when there is a need for police involvement and more stringent efforts at social control. In a 1995 survey of 1,000 cities with populations of more than 30,000, it was reported that more than 70 percent of the cities have a curfew ordinance in place.

Curfew laws vary with respect to the locale affected, the time frame, and the sanctions. Most restrict minors to their homes or property between the hours of 11 P.M. to 6 A.M. Sanctions for curfew violations by youths range from fines to being charged with a misdemeanor violation and include participation in diversion programs and, in some jurisdictions, jail time for parents.

Community leaders support the role of the police in curfew crime prevention programs. Curfew enforcement activities are implemented through regular law enforcement and special policing units. Two keys to the success of any curfew statute are (1) sustained local police enforcement and (2) community involvement. Other factors that contribute to implementation of successful curfew policies by the police include (1) using a curfew center to hold violators visiting their parents, (2) staffing centers with social service staff, and (3) creating programs for repeat offenders.

Empirical studies addressing the impact of juvenile curfew ordinances are limited, although some communities that have recently adopting curfews have had success. The Dallas, Texas, police department found that juvenile victimization during curfew hours declined by 17.7 percent, and juvenile arrests during curfew hours dropped by 14 percent. A New Orleans curfew with intense police supervision was influential in decreasing the incidence of youth crime arrests by 27 percent one year after its adoption. In 1994 the Chicago police department supported an experimental project called Operation Time-Out in one of the city's high-crime districts. Data showed a decrease of over 20 percent in the number of serious juvenile crimes reported. As a result of this success, Operation Time-Out has been added to four additional police districts. In addition, initial evidence from communities profiled by the U.S. Department of Justice indicates that a community-based curfew enforced by the police provides a great benefit in preventing juvenile delinquency.

Curfew ordinances are in effect in many of the largest U.S. cities. Although some curfews have been challenged on constitutional grounds (violations of the First, Fourth, and Fourteenth Amendments to the U.S. Constitution), narrowly created laws can withstand such challenges.

Sources: Jean Grossman and Eileen Garry, "Mentoring—A Proven Delinquency Prevention Strategy" (Washington, D.C.: OJJDP Juvenile Justice Bulletin, 1997); Donni LeBoeuf, "Curfew: An Answer to Juvenile Delinquency" (Washington, D.C.: OJJDP Juvenile Justice Bulletin, 1996); U.S. Department of Justice, *Juvenile Justice Reform Initiatives in the States, 1994–1996* (Washington, D.C.: OJJDP, 1997); National Conference of State Legislatures, "A Legislative Guide to Comprehensive Juvenile Justice" (Denver, CO: National Conference of State Legislatures, 1996).

Police officers in a DARE program work with fifth graders. While DARE is the most popular anti-drug program, there is still some question whether it effectively limits teen drug use.

Community Policing in the Millennium

One of the most important changes in U.S. law enforcement is the emergence of the community policing model of crime prevention. This concept is based on the premise that police departments do not make efficient crime-fighting organizations when they operate in isolation. However, if they gain the trust and assistance of concerned citizens, the police can carry out their duties more effectively. Under this model, the main police role should be to increase feelings of community safety and encourage area residents to cooperate with their local police agencies.[89] Advocates of community policing regard the approach as useful in juvenile justice for a number of reasons:

1. Moving officers from a position of anonymity in the patrol car to direct engagement with a community gives police more immediate information about problems unique to a neighborhood and insights into their solutions.
2. Freeing officers from the emergency response system permits them to engage more directly in proactive crime prevention.
3. Making police operations more visible to the public increases police accountability to the public.
4. Decentralizing operations allows officers to develop a greater familiarity with the specific workings and needs of various neighborhoods and constituencies in the community and to adapt procedures to accommodate those needs.
5. Encouraging officers to view citizens as partners improves relations between police and the public.
6. Moving decision making and discretion downward to patrol officers places more authority in the hands of the people who best know the community's problems and expectations.[90]

The community policing model has been translated into a number of different policy initiatives. It has encouraged police departments around the country to get patrol officers out of patrol cars—where they were viewed as faceless strangers insulated from the community—and into the streets via **foot patrol.** Hundreds of experimental foot patrol programs have been implemented around the country, and evaluation by the National Neighborhood Foot Patrol Center at Michigan State University indicates that they are highly successful.[91]

foot patrol
Police patrolling an area by walking around the community rather than driving about in patrol cars.

In addition, the police have encouraged and worked with citizen groups to create neighborhood watches and crime prevention groups. The Police Foundation, a nonprofit organization that conducts research on police issues, has reviewed such efforts and found them to be effective methods of increasing citizen cooperation. One of the best known programs is the Philadelphia Block Watch, which cooperates with the police in a number of different delinquency control and victim-aid projects. Another is the Innovative Neighborhood-Oriented Policing (INOP) program.[92] The main objectives of the INOP program are to foster community policing initiatives and to implement drug reduction efforts aimed at juveniles and adults.[93]

In summary, important efforts have been made by local police departments to involve citizens in the process of delinquency control. Community policing is a philosophy that promotes community, government, and police partnerships that address both adult and juvenile crime. It cuts across a vulnerable population of gang-involved youth, dropouts, and first-time offenders.[94]

Although little clear-cut evidence exists that these efforts can lower crime rates, they seem to be effective methods of improving perceptions of community safety and the quality of community life while involving citizens in the wider juvenile justice network. Under the community policing philosophy, juvenile prevention programs may become more effective crime control measures. According to Susan Guarino-Ghezzi, innovative police programs that combine reintegration of youth into the community after institutionalization with police surveillance and increased communication are vital components for improving police effectiveness with juveniles.[95]

SUMMARY

As society has become more complex and rates of delinquency and status offenses have soared, the police have become more important than ever to the juvenile justice system. It is almost always the police officer who has the initial contact with the large number of young people committing antisocial acts. This contact can have a significant impact on an offender's future.

Numerous factors influence the decisions that the police make about juvenile offenders. They include the seriousness of the offense, the harm inflicted on the victim, and the likelihood that the juvenile will break the law again.

The recruitment, selection, and training of juvenile police officers is essential to good police organizations. Police officers must be familiar with procedural law, because their contact with young people includes the legal aspects of arrest, custodial interrogation, and lineups. Through the *Miranda v. Arizona* decision, the U.S. Supreme Court established a clearly defined procedure for custodial interrogation and police investigations. Such practices are applicable to juvenile suspects. Search and

seizure actions, lineups, and other police procedures are also subject to court review.

Another important issue is police discretion in dealing with juvenile offenders. Discretion is a low-visibility decision made in the administration of adult and juvenile justice. Discretionary decisions are made without guidelines or policy statements from the police administrator. Discretion is essential in providing individualized justice, but problems such as discrimination, unfairness, and bias toward particular groups of juveniles must be controlled.

Finally, experts are concerned about the significant amount of crime committed by juveniles. New initiatives in law enforcement to reduce the incidence of youth crime include (1) crime prevention and education programs, (2) mentoring programs, (3) curfew laws, and (4) gang control and drug and firearm interventions. The community policing philosophy, which emphasizes partnerships between police and citizens, has been applied to both adult and juvenile crime.

KEY TERMS

community policing
juvenile officers
role conflicts
law enforcement
pledge system
watch system
arrest
probable cause

search and seizure
Miranda warning
custodial interrogation
totality of the
    circumstances doctrine
discretion
low-visibility decision
    making

chivalry hypothesis,
    paternalism hypothesis
delinquency prevention
    programs
community services
TOP program
Project DARE
foot patrol

Delinquency prevention programs straddle the line between treatment and punishment. Often, sensational and isolated cases of extreme youth violence are cited as cause for getting tough on juvenile crime. While these crimes are no doubt horrific, the reality of dealing with juvenile crime is quite different.

Pretend that you are a member of the President's Crime Control Commission. You have been assigned the task of coming up with solutions to the recent juvenile crime wave. You have decided to review a number of juvenile delinquency prevention programs and present findings on those that are successful in their attempts to lower rates of youth crime.

Search for articles in InfoTrac College Edition regarding crime and juvenile delinquency prevention programs. Choose any number of articles with programs that you feel are working. Summarize their main points, focusing on the specific approach each program takes to reduce juvenile crime. Be sure to state why you feel they are successful.

To search for information, use key words such as: *juvenile crime prevention* and *juvenile delinquency prevention*.

QUESTIONS FOR DISCUSSION

1. The term *discretion* is often defined as selective decision making by police and others in the juvenile justice system who are faced with alternative modes of action. Discuss some of the factors affecting the discretion of the police when dealing with juvenile offenders.

2. What role should police organizations play in delinquency prevention and control? Is it feasible to expect police departments to provide social services to children and families? How should police departments be better organized to provide for the control of juvenile delinquency?

3. What qualities should a police juvenile officer have? Should a college education be a requirement?

4. For the first time in a decade arrests of juveniles for violent crime has declined. What do you believe caused this decline?

5. In light of the traditional and protective roles assumed by law enforcement personnel in juvenile justice, is there any reason to have a *Miranda* warning for youths taken into custody?

6. Can the police and community be truly effective in forming a partnership to reduce juvenile delinquency? Discuss the role of the juvenile police officer in preventing and investigating juvenile crime.

NOTES

1. Herman Goldstein, "Toward Community-Oriented Policing: Potential Basic Requirements and Threshold Questions," *Crime and Delinquency* 33:630 (1987); see also, Janet Reno, "Taking America Back for Our Children," *Crime and Delinquency* 44:75 (1998).

2. Lawrence Sherman and Richard Berk, "The Specific Deterrent Effects of Arrest for Domestic Assault," *American Sociological Review* 49:261–72 (1984).

3. Donald Black and Albert J. Reiss Jr., "Police Control of Juveniles," *American Sociological Review* 35:63 (1970); Richard Lundman, Richard Sykes, and John Clark, "Police Control of Juveniles: A Replication," *Journal of Research on Crime and Delinquency* 15:74 (1978).

4. American Bar Association, *Standards Relating to Police Handling of Juvenile Problems* (Cambridge, Mass.: Ballinger, 1977), p. 1.

5. FBI, *Uniform Crime Reports 1991* (Washington, D.C.: U.S. Government Printing Office, 1990). More than 40 percent of police–juvenile contacts are referred to juvenile court; see also David Huizinga and Finn Esbensen, "An Arresting View of Juvenile Justice," *National School Safety Center Journal,* Spring 1992, pp. 13–17.

6. Samuel Walker, *The Police of America* (New York: McGraw-Hill, 1983), p. 133.

7. Karen A. Joe, "The Dynamics of Running Away, Deinstitutionalization Policies and the Police," *Juvenile Family Court Journal* 46:43–55 (1995).

8. R. Kobetz and B. Borsage, *Juvenile Justice Administration* (Gaithersburg, Md.: IACP, 1973), p. 112; see also, The President's Crime Prevention Council, "Preventing Crime and Promoting Responsibility—50 Programs that Help Communities Help Their Youth" (Washington D.C.: President's Crime Prevention Council, 1995).

9. Howard N. Snyder and Melissa Sickmund, *Juvenile Offenders and Victims: A National Report* (Washington, D.C.: Office of Juvenile Justice and Delinquency Prevention, 1995), p. 100; see also, "Serious and Violent Juvenile Offenders," *Juvenile Justice Bulletin* (Washington, D.C., OJJDP, May 1998); "State Legislative Responses to Violent Juvenile Crime, 1996–97 Update," *Juvenile Justice Bulletin* (Washington, D.C.: OJJDP, November 1998).

10. "What's Behind the Recent Drop in Juvenile Violent Crime," *Juvenile Justice Journal* 3:21–22 (1997).

11. National Conference of State Legislatures, *A Legislators Guide to Comprehensive Juvenile Justice, Interventions for Youth at Risk* (Denver, CO, NCSL, 1996).

12. John Wilson and James Howell, "Serious and Violent Juvenile Crime: A Comprehensive Strategy," *Juvenile and Family Court Journal* 45:3–35 (1995); James Howell, ed., *Guide for Implementing a Comprehensive Strategy for Serious Violent and Chronic Juvenile Offenders* (Washington, D.C.: OJJDP, 1995).

13. This section relies on sources such as Malcolm Sparrow, Mark Moore, and David Kennedy, *Beyond 911, A New Era for Policing* (New York: Basic Books, 1990); Daniel Devlin, *Police*

Procedure, Administration, and Organization (London: Butterworth, 1966); Robert Fogelson, *Big City Police* (Cambridge, Mass., Harvard University Press, 1977); Roger Lane, *Policing the City, Boston 1822–1885* (Cambridge, Mass., Harvard University Press, 1967); Roger Lane, "Urban Police and Crime in Nineteenth-Century America," in Norval Morris and Michael Tonry, eds., *Crime and Justice,* vol. 2 (Chicago: University of Chicago Press, 1980), pp. 1–45; J. J. Tobias, *Crime and Industrial Society in the Nineteenth Century* (New York: Schocken Books, 1967); Samuel Walker, *A Critical History of Police Reform: The Emergence of Professionalism* (Lexington, Mass.: Lexington Books, 1977); idem, *Popular Justice* (New York: Oxford University Press, 1980); President's Commission on Law Enforcement and the Administration of Justice, *Task Force Report: The Police* (Washington, D.C.: U.S. Government Printing Office, 1967), pp. 1–9.

14. See, generally, Walker, *Popular Justice,* p. 61.

15. Law Enforcement Assistance Administration, *Two Hundred Years of American Criminal Justice* (Washington, D.C.: U.S. Government Printing Office, 1976).

16. See August Vollmer, *The Police and Modern Society* (Berkeley: University of California Press, 1936).

17. See O. W. Wilson, *Police Administration,* 2nd ed. (New York: McGraw-Hill, 1963).

18. National Advisory Commission on Criminal Justice Standards and Goals, *Task Force Report on Juvenile Justice and Delinquency Prevention* (Washington D.C.: Law Enforcement Assistance Administration, 1976), p. 258.

19. Linda Szymanski, *Summary of Juvenile Code Purpose Clauses* (Pittsburgh, Pa.: National Center for Juvenile Justice, 1988); see also, for example, GA Code Ann. 15; Iowa Code Ann. 232.2; Mass. Gen. Laws, ch. 119, 56.

20. Samuel M. Davis, *Rights of Juveniles—The Juvenile Justice System* (New York: Clark-Boardmen, revised June 1989), Sec. 3.3.

21. National Council of Juvenile and Family Court Judges, *Juvenile and Family Law Digest* 29:1–2 (1997).

22. See Fourth Amendment, U.S. Constitution.

23. *State v. Lowry,* 230 A.2d 907 (1967).

24. *Chimel v. Cal.,* 395 U.S. 752, 89 S.Ct. 2034 (1969).

25. *United States v. Ross,* 456 U.S. 798, 102 S.Ct. 2157 (1982).

26. *Terry v. Ohio,* 392 U.S.1, 88 S.Ct. 1868 (1968).

27. *Bumper v. North Carolina,* 391 U.S. 543, 88 S.Ct. 1788 (1968).

28. *New Jersey v. T.L.O.,* 469 U.S. 325, 105 S.Ct. 733 (1985).

29. *People v. Overton,* 24 N.Y.2d 522, 301 N.Y.S.2d 479, 249 N.E.2d 366 (1969); Brenda Walts, "*New Jersey v. T.L.O.*: Questions the Court Did Not Answer about School Searches," *Law and Education Journal* 14:421 (1985).

30. *State v. Engerud,* 94 N.J. 331 (1983).

31. *In re Donaldson,* 75 Cal.Rptr. 220 (1969); *People v. Bowers,* 77 Misc.2d 697, 356 N.Y.S.2d 432 (1974); *In re W.,* 29 Cal.App.3d 777, 105 Cal.Rptr. 775 (1973); *Comm. of Pa. v. Dingfelt,* 227 Pa.Supr.380, 323 A.2d 145 (1974).

32. See D. A. Walls, "*New Jersey v. T.L.O.*: The Fourth Amendment Applied to School Searches," *Oklahoma University Law Review* 11:225–41 (1986); Robert Shepard Jr., "Juvenile Justice—Search and Seizures Involving Juveniles," *American Bar Association Journal on Criminal Justice* 5:27–29 (1990); note, "The Standard of Individualized Suspicion with Fourth Amendment Searches," *Journal of Criminal Law and Criminology* 86: 1265–93 (1996).

33. K. A. Bucker, "School Drug Tests: A Fourth Amendment Perspective," *University of Illinois Law Review* 5:275 (1987).

34. J. Hogan and M. Schwartz, "Search and Seizure in the Public Schools," *Case and Comment* 90: 28–32 (1985); M. Meyers, "*T.L.O. v. New Jersey*—Officially Conducted School Searches and a New Balancing Test," *Juvenile Family Journal* 37:27–37 (1986); Samantha Shulter, "Random, Suspicionless Drug Testing of High School Athletes," *Journal of Criminal Law and Criminology* 86:1241–61 (1996).

35. For an interesting article suggesting that school officials should not be permitted to search students without suspicion that each student searched has violated the drug or weapons law, see J. Braverman, "Public School Drug Searches," *Fordham Urban Law Journal* 14:629–84 (1986).

36. 469 U.S., at 339; see also, National School Safety Center, *School Safety Update* (Malibu, Calif.: Pepperdine University, 1991); U.S. Department of Justice, *School Crime—A National Victimization Survey* (Washington, D.C.: Bureau of Justice Statistics, 1991).

37. *Vernonia School District 47J v. Acton,* 115 S.Ct. 2394 (1995); Bernard James and Jonathan Pyatt, "Supreme Court Extends School's Authority to Search," *National School Safety Center News Journal* 26:29 (1995).

38. June Arnett and Marjorie Walsleben, *Combating Fear and Restoring Safety in Schools* (Washington D.C.: OJJDP, 1998).

39. *Miranda v. Arizona,* 384 U.S. 436, 86 S.Ct. 1602 (1966).

40. *Commonwealth v. Gaskins,* 471 Pa. 238, 369 A.2d 1285 (1977); *In re E.T.C.,* 141 Vt. 375, 449 A.2d 937 (1982).

41. *People v. Lara,* 67 Cal.2d 365, 62 Cal.Rptr. 586, 432 P.2d 202 (1967).

42. *West v. United States,* 399 F.2d 467 (5th Cir. 1968).

43. *Fare v. Michael C.,* 442 U.S. 707, 99 S.Ct. 2560 (1979).

44. *California v. Prysock,* 453 U.S. 355, 101 S.Ct. 2806 (1981).

45. See, for example, Larry Holtz, "*Miranda* in a Juvenile Setting—A Child's Right to Silence," *Journal of Criminal Law and Criminology* 79:534–56 (1987).

46. Roscoe Pound, "Discretion, Dispensation, and Mitigation: The Problem of the Individual Special Case," *New York University Law Review* 35:936 (1960).

47. Kenneth C. Davis, *Discretionary Justice: A Preliminary Inquiry* (Baton Rouge: Louisiana State University Press, 1969); H. Ted Rubin, *Juvenile Justice: Police, Practice and Law* (Santa Monica, Calif.: Goodyear, 1979).

48. Joseph Goldstein, "Police Discretion Not to Invoke the Criminal Process: Low-Visibility Decisions in the Administration of Justice," *Yale Law Journal* 69:544 (1960).

49. Victor Streib, *Juvenile Justice in America* (Port Washington, N.Y.: Kennikat, 1978).

50. Herbert Packer, *The Limits of the Criminal Sanction* (Palo Alto, Calif.: Stanford University Press, 1968).

51. Black and Reiss, "Police Control of Juveniles"; Richard J. Lundman, "Routine Police Arrest Practices," *Social Problems* 22: 127–41 (1974).

52. Nathan Goldman, *The Differential Selection of Juvenile Offenders for Court Appearance* (Washington, D.C.: National Council on Crime and Delinquency, 1963).

53. Irving Piliavin and Scott Briar, "Police Encounters with Juveniles," *American Journal of Sociology* 70:206–14 (1964); Theodore Ferdinand and Elmer Luchterhand, "Inner-City Youth, the Police, Juvenile Court, and Justice," *Social Problems* 8:510–26 (1970).

54. Paul Strasburg, *Violent Delinquents: Report to Ford Foundation from Vera Institute of Justice* (New York: Monarch, 1978), p. 11; Robert Terry, "The Screening of Juvenile Offenders," *Journal of Criminal Law, Criminology, and Police Science* 58:173–81 (1967).

55. FBI, *Crime in the U.S.: Uniform Crime Reports, 1996* (Washington, D.C.: U.S. Government Printing Office, 1997).

56. Douglas Smith and Christy Visher, "Street-Level Justice: Situational Determinants of Police Arrest Decisions," *Social Problems* 29:167–78 (1981).

57. Douglas Smith and Jody Klein, "Police Control of Interpersonal Disputes," *Social Problems* 31:468–81 (1984).

58. Goldman, The Differential Selection of Juvenile Offenders for Court Appearance, p. 25; Norman Werner and Charles Willie, "Decisions of Juvenile Officers," *American Journal of Sociology* 77:199–214 (1971).

59. Aaron Cicourel, *The Social Organization of Juvenile Justice* (New York: Wiley, 1968).

60. Piliavin and Briar, "Police Encounters with Juveniles," p. 214.

61. James Fyfe, David Klinger, and Jeanne Flaving, "Differential Police Treatment of Male-on-Female Spousal Violence," *Criminology* 35:455–73 (1997).

62. Dale Dannefer and Russel Schutt, "Race and Juvenile Justice Processing in Police and Court Agencies," *American Journal of Sociology* 87:1113–32 (1982); Smith and Visher, "Street-Level Justice: Situational Determinants of Police Arrest Decisions"; also, Ronald Weitzer, "Racial Discrimination in the Criminal Justice System: Findings and Problems in the Literature," *Journal of Criminal Justice* 24:309–22 (1996).

63. T. Edwin Black and Charles Smith, *A Preliminary National Assessment of the Numbers and Characteristics of Juveniles Processed in the Juvenile Justice System* (Washington, D.C.: U.S. Government Printing Office, 1980), p. 39.

64. Terence Thornberry, "Race, Socioeconomic Status, and Sentencing in the Juvenile Justice System," *Journal of Criminal Law and Criminology* 70:164–71 (1979); Dannefer and Schutt, "Race and Juvenile Justice Processing in Police and Court Agencies"; Jeffrey Fagan, Ellen Slaughter, and Eliot Hartstone, "Blind Justice? The Impact of Race on the Juvenile Justice Process," *Crime and Delinquency* 33:224–58 (1987).

65. Fagan, Slaughter, and Hartstone, "Blind Justice? The Impact of Race on the Juvenile Justice Process," pp. 237–38.

66. David Griswold, "Police Discrimination: An Elusive Question," *Journal of Police Science and Administration* 6:65–66 (1978).

67. Donna M. Bishop and Charles E. Frazier, "The Influence of Race in Juvenile Justice Processing," *Journal of Research in Crime and Delinquency* 25:242–61 (1988).

68. Ibid., p. 258; see also Melissa Sickmund, *Juvenile Court Statistics 1995* (Washington D.C.: OJJDP, 1998), p. 28.

69. National Coalition of State Juvenile Justice Advisory Groups, *A Delicate Balance* (Bethesda, Md.: National Coalition of State Juvenile Justice Advisory Groups, 1989).

70. Ibid., p. 4.

71. Ibid., p. 2. Although not specifically dealing with juveniles, the issue of differential processing for young African American males is addressed in the following study, which found that nearly one of every four African American men in their twenties is caught up in the criminal justice system: Marc Mauer, *Young Black Men and the Criminal Justice System* (Washington, D.C.: The Sentencing Project, 1990).

72. National Council on Crime and Delinquency, *The Over-Representation of Minority Youth in the California Juvenile Justice System* (San Francisco: NCCD, 1992).

73. Melissa Sickmund, Howard Snyder, and Eileen Poe-Yamagata, *Juvenile Offenders and Victims—1997 Update on Violence* (Washington D.C.: OJJDP 1997) p. 17.

74. See Samuel Walker, Cassie Spohn, and Miriam DeLone, *The Color of Justice, Race Ethnicity and Crime in America* (Belmont, Calif.: Wadsworth, 1996).

75. Merry Morash, "Establishment of a Juvenile Record: The Influence of Individual and Peer Group Characteristics," *Criminology* 22:97–112 (1984).

76. Meda Chesney-Lind, "Judicial Enforcement of the Female Sex Role: The Family Court and Female Delinquency Issues," *Criminology* 8:51–71 (1973); idem, "Young Women in the Arms of Law," in L. Bowker, ed., *Women, Crime and the Criminal Justice System,* 2nd ed. (Lexington, Mass.: Lexington Books, 1978).

77. Christy Visher, "Arrest Decisions and Notions of Chivalry," *Criminology* 21:5–28 (1983); see also, Darlene Conley, "Adding Color to a Black and White Picture: Using Qualitative Data to Explain Racial Disproportionality in the Juvenile Justice System," *Journal of Research in Crime and Delinquency* 31:135–48 (1994).

78. Donna Bishop and Charles Frazier, "Gender Bias in Juvenile Justice Processing: Implications of the JJDP Act," *Journal of Criminal Law and Criminology* 82:1162–86 (1992).

79. Black and Smith, *A Preliminary National Assessment of the Numbers and Characteristics of Juveniles Processed in the Juvenile Justice System,* p. 37.

80. Douglas Smith, "The Organizational Context of Legal Control," *Criminology* 22:19–38 (1984); see also, Stephen Mastrofski and Richard Ritti, "Police Training and the Effects of Organization on Drunk Driving Enforcement," *Justice Quarterly* 13:291–320 (1996).

81. John Irwin, *The Jail: Managing the Underclass in American Society* (Berkeley: University of California Press, 1985).

82. Robert Sampson, "Effects of Socioeconomic Context of Official Reaction to Juvenile Delinquency," *American Sociological Review* 51:876–85 (1986).

83. American Bar Association, *Standards of Criminal Justice: Standards Relating to Urban Police Function* (New York: Institute of Judicial Administration, 1972), Standard 4.2, p. 121.

84. Kenneth C. Davis, *Police Discretion* (St. Paul, Minn.: West, 1975).

85. Robert Shepard Jr., ed., *Juvenile Justice Standards Annotated—A Balanced Approach* (Chicago, IL: ABA, 1996).

86. Sherwood Norman, *The Youth Service Bureau—A Key to Delinquency Prevention* (Hackensack, N.J.: National Council on Crime and Delinquency, 1972), p. 8.

87. Karin Lipson, "Cops and TOPS: A Program for Police and Teens that Works," *Police Chief* 49:45–46 (1982).

88. National Institute for Justice, *The Dare Program: A Review of Prevalence, User Satisfaction and Effectiveness* (Washington, D.C.: U.S. Department of Justice, 1994); also Dennis Rosenbaum et al., "Cops in the Classroom: A Longitudinal Evaluation," *Journal of Research in Crime and Delinquency* 31:3–31 (1994).

89. For an analysis of this position, see George Kelling and James Q. Wilson, "Broken Windows: The Police and Neighborhood Safety," *Atlantic Monthly* 249:29–38 (1982).

90. U.S. Department of Justice, "Community Policing," *National Institute of Justice Journal,* 225:1–32 (1992).

91. Robert Trojanowicz and Hazel Harden, *The Status of Contemporary Community Policing Programs* (East Lansing: Michigan State University Neighborhood Foot Patrol Center, 1985).

92. Peter Finn, "Block Watches Help Crime Victims in Philadelphia," *National Institute of Justice Reports,* December: 2–10 (1986).

93. James Q. Wilson, "Drugs and Crime," in Michael Tonry and James Q. Wilson, eds., *Crime and Justice—A Review of Research,* vol. 13 (Chicago: University of Chicago Press, 1990).

94. Susan Guarino-Ghezzi, "Reintegrative Police Surveillance of Juvenile Offenders: Forging an Urban Model," *Crime and Delinquency* 40:131–53 (1994).

95. The President's Crime Prevention Council, *Preventing Crime and Promoting Responsibility: 50 Programs that Help Communities Help Their Youth* (Washington, D.C.: U.S. Government Printing Office, 1995).

Chapter Fourteen

Pretrial Procedures

*I*n July of 1995 Edward O'Brien, a fifteen-and-a-half-year-old boy, was arraigned and subsequently indicted for murder in Middlesex County, Massachusetts. Edward was accused of stabbing and killing a forty-two-year-old mother of four children in her home. In pretrial court proceedings, the juvenile court ruled to deny transfer of this case to the adult court. The prosecutor subsequently appealed this decision, and Edward was tried as an adult, convicted of murder, and sent to state prison for life.

*C*ases like Edward O'Brien's raise a number of complex legal and philosophical problems that defy easy solution. A frequently debated question is whether a youth who is accused of such heinous actions as Edward's should be tried as an adult. If so, how are such decisions to be determined?

According to Massachusetts law, a juvenile can be tried as an adult only after a court finds the child dangerous and incapable of rehabilitation. In such cases the burden of proof is on the defendant to prove that he or she is not dangerous and is amenable to treatment. Such a determination is made at a **transfer hearing,** a court procedure to decide whether a juvenile case will be transferred to an adult court. At O'Brien's transfer hearing both prosecution and defense called numerous witnesses and presented documentary evidence, including forty-nine different exhibits, for court review.

The court took into account factors such as the nature and seriousness of the crime, O'Brien's delinquency record (there was none), his age at the time of arrest (fifteen and a half, although he was a young man of great physical stature), and his family history (deemed "uneventful" by the court). After examining these variables, the court denied transfer to the adult court and ordered that the defendant be tried within the juvenile justice system.

Edward O'Brien, a fifteen-and-a-half-year-old boy, was convicted of the murder of a mother of four children in her home. Should youthful murderers such as O'Brien be routinely charged and tried as adults?

transfer hearing
Preadjudicatory hearing in juvenile court for the purpose of determining whether juvenile court should be retained over a juvenile or waived and the juvenile transferred to adult court for prosecution.

But this was not to be the case. Immediately after the juvenile court ruling, the district attorney filed an appeal, which overturned the initial judgment. O'Brien was tried as an adult, convicted of murder, and sent to state prison for life.

How effective are such transfers to the adult system? Do they help to keep violent offenders off our nation's streets? Or do they subvert a young offender's chances of rehabilitation and reintegration into society? These important questions will be addressed in this chapter, along with other aspects of the juvenile preadjudicatory process.

The period between arrest and adjudication is one of the most critical points in the juvenile justice process. We begin with a discussion of preadjudicatory detention—the involuntary holding of a child by the state in physically restrictive facilities. This will be followed by a description of the events that take place prior to trial, including intake and diversion programs, pretrial release, and plea bargaining. The chapter concludes with a discussion of trying juveniles in adult courts—the phenomenon that led to the incarceration of Edward O'Brien.

The Concept of Detention

detention
Temporary care of a child alleged to be delinquent who requires secure custody in physically restricting facilities pending court disposition or execution of a court order.

Detention is the temporary care of children by the state in physically restricted facilities pending court disposition or transfer to another agency.[1] Traditional detention facilities for children are designed as secure environments. Many of the secure detention facilities in the United States have locked doors, fences or walls, screens or bars, and other barriers designed to prevent detainees from leaving the facility at will. Detention facilities of this kind normally handle juveniles at different stages of the juvenile justice process. Some juveniles are kept in detention to await their court hearings. Others have had a trial but have not been sentenced or are awaiting the imposition of their sentence. A third group of children have had sentences imposed and are awaiting admittance to a correctional training school. Thus, as the American Bar Association states, "the term 'pre-trial detainee' is inaccurate to describe the many juveniles in detention whose cases have already been adjudicated but whose disposition remains unimplemented."[2]

Detention should not be viewed as punishment. A juvenile is normally not a sentenced offender when placed in detention. Thus, a detention facility is not to be used as a permanent correctional facility but as a source of temporary care for children who require secure custody.

Most experts in juvenile justice advocate that detention be limited to alleged delinquent offenders who require secure custody for the protection of themselves and others. In the past, however, children who were neglected and dependent, as well as status offenders, were placed in secure detention facilities. To remedy this situation, an ongoing national effort is being made to remove status offenders and neglected or abused children from detention facilities that also house juvenile delinquents. In addition, alternatives to detention centers—temporary foster homes, detention boarding homes, and programs of neighborhood supervision—have been developed in numerous jurisdictions. These alternatives enable youths to live in a more homelike setting while the courts dispose of their cases. New types of public and private residential facilities also are being created; some young persons who cannot return home are being held in dormitories and multiple-resident dwellings.[3] Other types of residential care programs should be distinguished from detention. We use the term **shelter care** to describe the temporary care of children in physically unrestricting facilities.

shelter care
A place for temporary care of children in physically unrestricting facilities.

National Detention Trends

Despite these efforts to remove nondelinquent youths, the most recent available data show the number of juveniles held in short-term detention facilities increased by 31 percent between 1986 and 1995, rising from 244,000 to 320,800 youths. About 500,000 admissions occur each year, of which 320,000 involve delinquency and 10,000 status offenses.[4] Other admissions involve children who have been neglected or abused by parents or guardians. In addition, increases occurred in all offense categories, with drug offenses showing the greatest increase (see Tables 14.1 and 14.2).

During this period, the number of juveniles detained for drug-related offenses more than doubled. There was a 75-percent increase in the detention rate for person-oriented cases, and a 22-percent rise for public order offenders. In contrast, the rate of detention for property-related offenses has dropped in recent years, most likely as a result of using alternative detention resources.

Tables 14.3 and 14.4 show population trends for detained status offenders for the same period. Although the detention rate for status offenders dropped substantially between 1986 and 1991 (from 12,700 to 7,200), the number had risen to 9,900

Table 14.1

PERCENTAGE CHANGE IN DETAINED DELINQUENCY CASES, 1986–1995

Most Serious Offense	Number of Cases			Percentage Change	
	1986	1991	1995	1986–95	1991–95
Total Delinquency	244,000	293,000	320,000	31	9
Person	48,400	69,800	84,900	75	22
Property	123,800	145,400	132,300	7	–9
Drugs	18,400	23,900	38,600	110	61
Public Order	53,300	54,800	64,900	22	18

Source: Melissa Sickmund, *Juvenile Court Statistics 1995* (Pittsburgh, Pa.: National Center for Juvenile Justice, 1998).

Note: Detail may not add to totals due to rounding. Percentage calculations are based on unrounded numbers.

Table 14.2

PERCENTAGE OF DELINQUENCY CASES DETAINED, BY RACE, 1986–1995

Most Serious Offense	1986	1991	1995
White	18	18	15
Person	21	22	19
Property	15	15	12
Drugs	20	25	15
Public Order	24	23	17
Black	28	27	27
Person	31	30	28
Property	24	22	23
Drugs	43	49	42
Public Order	32	27	29
Other Races	25	24	20
Person	34	29	26
Property	21	21	17
Drugs	20	34	17
Public Order	32	27	21

Source: Melissa Sickmund, *Juvenile Court Statistics 1995* (Pittsburgh, Pa.: National Center for Juvenile Justice, 1998).

by 1995.[5] Throughout this period, runaways accounted for the largest group of status offender detainees. In 1995 liquor law violators also formed a significant segment (25 percent).[6] The typical delinquent detainee was male, over fifteen years of age, and charged with a property crime, whereas the typical status offender was female, under sixteen years of age, and a runaway.[7]

This rise in the juvenile detention rate is occurring at a time when the overall population of juvenile offenders is decreasing. Experts believe the steady increase in detention use may result from (1) a steady rise in the rate of serious juvenile offenses

Table 14.3

PERCENTAGE CHANGE IN DETAINED PETITIONED STATUS OFFENSE CASES, 1986–1995

Most Serious Offenses	Number of Cases			Percentage Change	
	1986	1991	1995	1986–95	1991–95
Total Status Offenses	12,700	7,200	9,900	−22	37
Runaway	5,600	2,400	2,900	−48	21
Truancy	1,400	700	700	−51	0
Ungovernable	3,200	900	1,300	−60	45
Liquor	1,700	1,500	2,400	47	63
Miscellaneous	900	1,800	2,600	196	49

Source: Melissa Sickmund, *Juvenile Court Statistics 1995* (Pittsburgh, Pa.: National Center for Juvenile Justice, 1998).

Note: Detail may not add to totals because of rounding. Percentage change calculations are based on unrounded numbers.

Table 14.4

OFFENSE PROFILE OF DETAINED PETITIONED STATUS OFFENSE CASES, 1986–1995

Most Serious Offense	1986 (percent)	1991 (percent)	1995 (percent)
Runaway	44	33	29
Truancy	11	10	7
Ungovernable	25	12	13
Liquor	13	21	25
Miscellaneous	7	24	26
Number of Cases Involving Detention	12,700	7,200	9,900

Source: Melissa Sickmund, *Juvenile Court Statistics 1995* (Pittsburgh, Pa.: National Center for Juvenile Justice, 1998).

Note: Detail may not total 100 percent due to rounding.

from 1985 to 1995, (2) an increasing number of drug-related crimes, and (3) the involvement of younger children in the juvenile justice system.[8] However, some things about juvenile detention have not changed: nearly half of all youths in juvenile detention are in four states (California, Michigan, Ohio, and Florida); there is great variation among states in the age cutoff for juvenile versus adult court jurisdiction, which influences detention center custody rates; and there appears to be a serious problem of overrepresentation of minorities in secure detention.[9]

Detention of youths continues to be a major issue in the juvenile justice system, and reducing its use has not been an easy task.

The Decision to Detain

The majority of children taken into custody by the police are released to their parents or guardians. Some are held overnight in a detention facility until their parents can be notified of the arrest. Police officers normally take a child to a place of detention only after other alternatives have been exhausted. Many juvenile courts in large urban areas have staff members, such as intake probation officers, on duty twenty-four hours a day to screen detention admissions.

Ordinarily, delinquent children are detained if the police believe they are inclined to run away while awaiting trial, if they are likely to commit an offense dangerous to themselves or the community, or if they are violators from other jurisdictions. In an analysis of detention decisions in a single county in Alabama, Belinda McCarthy found that juveniles were indeed being detained because they were a threat to the community, because their own safety was endangered, and because they tended to commit more serious crimes. Variables such as offender race, class, and gender did not seem to play a role in detention decision making.[10]

In contrast to McCarthy's findings, critics charge that the discretion used when selecting youths for detention often works against the poor and minorities. A study by the Humphrey Institute of Public Affairs found that minority youths are placed in secure detention facilities at a rate three to four times higher than white youths.[11] Other researchers also report that differential detention rates are produced by economic, family, and community forces. For example, of almost twenty-five hundred cases taken from the juvenile court records of six New Jersey counties, researchers Russell Schutt and Dale Dannefer found that detention decisions favor protecting some classes of juveniles rather than ensuring them due process.[12] African American and Hispanic juveniles were quite likely to be detained even if they lived with two parents, but white juveniles were subject to detention only if they lived with one parent.

The criteria used in deciding whether a child should be placed in detention are far from clear, in part because there are no uniform standards to guide detention decisions. Charles Frazier and Donna Bishop analyzed data on all juveniles processed in a single state over a two-year period and failed to uncover any pattern

Delinquent children may be detained if the police believe that they might run away while awaiting trial, that they are likely to commit an offense dangerous to themselves or the community, or if they are violators from other jurisdictions. Here police officers may be likely to detain this juvenile because he had a gun in his possession.

that could help explain how detention decisions were made.[13] Frazier and Bishop concluded that detention decisions were based solely on judicial discretion. Similarly, a study of New York State's juvenile offender law in Westchester County, New York, concluded that detention decisions lack clearly defined statutory criteria that could result in a reduction in the number of youths admitted to secure detention facilities.[14]

Today many courts are striving to implement the recommendations of the National Council on Crime and Delinquency (NCCD) and other standard-setting groups, which suggest that youths should be detained only if they (1) are likely to commit a new offense, (2) present a danger to themselves or the community, or (3) are likely to run away or fail to appear at subsequent court hearings. David Steinhart's analysis of the use of NCCD detention criteria in San Francisco describes the decline in admissions in that facility.[15]

A child should not be held in a detention facility or shelter care unit for more than twenty-four hours. Most jurisdictions require that a formal petition be filed (a written request to the court equivalent to a complaint) against the child invoking the jurisdiction of the juvenile court within twenty-four hours to extend the detention period. To detain a juvenile, there must be clear evidence of probable cause that the child has committed the offense and that he or she will flee the area if not detained. Furthermore, once a child has been held, the period of detention should not be continued without a **detention hearing.**[16] Although the requirements for detention hearings vary considerably among the states, most jurisdictions require that they occur almost immediately after the child's admission to a detention facility and provide the youth with notice and counsel.

detention hearing
A hearing by a judicial officer of a juvenile court to determine whether a juvenile is to be detained or released while juvenile proceedings are pending in the case.

The probation department of the juvenile court may help the judge decide whether or not to keep a child in detention. A probation officer in the intake department usually assists the court in making a decision about the child's release.

Detention also has been criticized for placing children who have not yet been found to be delinquent in a harsh environment that is more often than not lacking in any rehabilitative services. As one national survey of detention conditions put it, "The custody was a matter of lock and key, and the instructive experience was more the exception than the rule. . . . Repeatedly, detention emerged as a form of punishment without conviction—and often without crime."[17] The cost of detention, overcrowding, poor policy decisions, and overrepresentation by minorities in secure facilities are reasons the system needs reform.

New Approaches to Detention

Efforts have been ongoing to improve the process and conditions of detention. The Juvenile Detention Committee of the American Correctional Association has developed standards for detention that establish fair and uniform positive expectations for its use. These standards state:

> Juvenile detention is the temporary and secure custody of children accused or adjudicated of conduct subject to the jurisdiction of the family/juvenile court who require a physically restricting environment for their own or the community's protection while pending legal action. Further, juvenile detention should provide and maintain a wide range of helpful services that include, but are not limited to, the following: education, visitation, private communications, counseling, continuous supervision, medical and health care, nutrition, recreation, and reading. To advise the court on the proper course of action required to restore the child to a productive role in the community, detention should also include or provide a system for clinical observation and diagnosis that complements the wide range of helpful services.[18]

Some evidence indicates that preadjudicatory facilities are meeting this goal. The consensus of professional opinion today is that juvenile detention centers should be reserved for those youths who present a clear and substantial threat to the community. As a result, attention is being focused on development of new, more lenient approaches to detention care, such as day resource centers, detention alternative programs, and family shelters.[19] These centers are nonsecure, unlocked places of care and custody for children that provide some short-term social services and other treatment programs. In some states, nonsecure holdover facilities are being used to service juveniles for a limited period. Special intake programs are also used to screen children to locate more secure housing whenever possible.

In addition, some pretrial detention centers are providing extensive education programs. The Spofford Juvenile Center in the Bronx, New York, is the only pretrial detention center in New York with an educational program approved by the state.[20] The center's instructional program includes a five-and-a-half-hour day, with a curriculum of reading and language arts, math, social studies, science, health and safety education, library skills, physical education, art, and music. Because students remain in detention for varying lengths of time, the curriculum is organized in short modules so that students whose stays are brief can still complete a body of work. The Los Patrinos Juvenile Hall School in Downey, California, also operates with a highly transient population. Yet it has been successful in offering comprehensive instruction in basic academic subjects and technological and functional living skills. It emphasizes helping students develop positive self-concepts and improved relationships with others.[21] In New Hampshire young people spend an average of twenty-one days in the Awaiting Disposition of the Court (ADC) unit. The unit's on-site educational program employs a nontraditional, holistic learning approach designed to generate student opinions, cultivate discussions, and stimulate responses. Several educational themes or modules have been designed both to provide factual information and to promote student discussions on a variety of topics, including U.S. history, basic psychology, and family problems.[22] Other preadjudicatory alternatives to secure detention include (1) in-home monitoring, (2) home detention, (3) day center electronic monitoring, (4) high intensity community supervision, and (5) comprehensive case management programs.

Ira Schwartz describes juvenile detention as the underbelly of the juvenile justice system.[23] Because these institutions are often hidden from public scrutiny, many juveniles are confined in antiquated and poorly managed facilities. Schwartz indicates that there is an overreliance on detention and that improvements can result from adequate policy decision making by juvenile justice officials (see the Policy and Practice box entitled "Reforming the Juvenile Detention System").

Undoubtedly, juveniles pose special detention problems. But some efforts are being made to improve programs and to reduce pretrial detention use, especially in secure settings. Of all the problems associated with detention, however, none is as critical as the issue of placing youths in adult jails.

Detention in Adult Jails

A significant problem in juvenile justice is placing youths under eighteen years of age in adult jails. This is usually done in rural areas where no other facility exists. Almost all experts in the field of juvenile justice agree that placing children under the age of eighteen in any type of jail facility should be prohibited. Juveniles in adult jails can easily be victimized by other inmates and staff.

Juveniles detained in adult jails often live in squalid conditions and are subjected to physical and sexual abuse. Also, children confined to adult institutions are

REFORMING THE JUVENILE DETENTION SYSTEM

Juvenile detention facilities hold more children than do any other type of juvenile institution. What are the determinants of juvenile detention rates? Are any jurisdictions reducing the use of secure detention? How can we implement changes in detention policy? In *Reforming Juvenile Detention—No More Hidden Closets,* Ira Schwartz brings together a series of essays that assess today's juvenile detention system and suggest strategies and solutions to deal with the detention crisis.

Schwartz confirmed that on any given day almost twenty thousand children are in the detention system and more than five hundred thousand are admitted every year; there are more than 422 detention facilities, twice the number of training schools for juveniles. Although national rates declined in the early 1980s, the rate of admission to detention facilities began to rise sharply in the late 1980s. This increase has led to serious overcrowding in detention facilities throughout the country.

There has also been a change in the racial composition of detained juvenile offenders. Although there has been a decline in the proportion of white children detained, this has been offset by an increase for African American males. Overrepresentation of minorities in the juvenile justice system is a major issue, and its causes are being explored by the Office of Juvenile Justice and Delinquency Prevention.

Schwartz and his colleagues point out several important reasons officials should be concerned about the rising detention rates of children in the juvenile justice system. First, the cost for detention is considerable; expenditures for juvenile detention have more than doubled in the last decade to more than $500 million. Second, detention can often have harmful effects on children because of poor institutional conditions and abusive treatment. Third, many children stay in detention longer than anticipated, putting great stress on the available bed space and causing severe overcrowding.

The number of admissions to detention is determined largely by policy decisions in the juvenile justice system. A chapter in Schwartz's book by Terry Martin describing the detention process in Cleveland, Ohio, points out that fluctuations in admissions to juvenile detention facilities are driven by judicial attitudes regarding who should be confined

more likely to commit suicide than those placed in detention centers exclusively for juveniles. Over the years, jails have been the least progressive of all correctional institutions in the United States. Most jails were constructed in the nineteenth century, and few have been substantially improved in the twentieth century. Many are in poor physical condition. Jails throughout the nation are overcrowded, have no rehabilitation programs, provide little or no medical attention, and make no effort to provide adequate plumbing, ventilation, or heating. Many are fire hazards. Courts throughout the nation have ruled that conditions in certain jails make incarceration a cruel and unusual punishment, a violation of the Eighth and Fourteenth Amendments of the U.S. Constitution. Regardless of the conditions, the argument can be made that jailing juveniles with adults must be viewed as cruel and unusual punishment, considering their special status.

Until a few years ago, placing juveniles in adult facilities was common, but efforts have been made recently to change this situation. The impetus for removing juveniles from adult jails comes from the Office of Juvenile Justice and Delinquency Prevention. In 1989 the Juvenile Justice and Delinquency Prevention Act (JJDPA) of 1974 was amended to require that the states remove all juveniles from adult jails and lockups. The act states,

> Juveniles alleged to be or found to be delinquent [and status offenders and non-offenders] shall not be detained or confined in any institution in which they have contact with adult persons incarcerated because they have been convicted of

rather than by the rates of serious juvenile violent offenses and property crimes. In a critical article by William Barton, Ira Schwartz, and Franklin Orlando describing detention conditions in Broward County (Ft. Lauderdale), Florida, the authors indicate that dangerous overcrowding was addressed by developing objective intake criteria, increasing the use of release on recognizance, and establishing community-based alternatives. David Steinhart also describes the developments leading to the decline in admissions to detention facilities in San Francisco. Admissions were brought under control through the development, implementation, and monitoring of detention intake screening criteria.

Schwartz and his coauthors not only bring to light the problems and inefficiencies in juvenile detention but suggest an agenda for detention reform. The nine-step program calls for (1) conducting a comprehensive study of the detention system, (2) adopting objective detention intake criteria, (3) developing twenty-four-hour face-to-face detention intake screening and crisis intervention services, (4) eliminating the practice of committing youths to serve time in detention, (5) creating a detention population management position, (6) developing partnerships between public and private agencies in the delivery of alternative services, (7) enacting legislation that limits the use of detention, (8) creating alternatives to detention and criteria for their use, and (9) developing a mechanism for overseeing and monitoring the detention system.

Although not all experts would agree with Schwartz's entire agenda for reform, there is convincing evidence that detention can be an inappropriate and even degrading experience for many children and requires improvement. At the least, detention should perform the role for which it was intended—to detain juveniles who are a real risk to the community and who are unlikely to appear in court. Implementation of effective policy changes in the juvenile courts would certainly assist in reducing the size of the detention population and in providing secure detention for youths who need it.

Sources: William Barton, Ira Schwartz, and Franklin Orlando, "Objective Juvenile Detention: The California Experience," in Ira Schwartz and William H. Barton, eds., *Reforming Juvenile Detention—No More Hidden Closets* (Columbus: Ohio State University Press, 1994); David Roush and Trudy Wyss, *A Resource Manual for Juvenile Detention and Corrections: Effective and Innovative Programs* (Washington D.C.: OJJDP, 1995).

a crime or are awaiting trial on criminal charges or with the part-time or full-time security staff (including management) or direct-care staff of a jail or lockup for adults.[24]

According to federal guidelines, all juveniles in state custody must be separated from adult offenders or the state could lose federal juvenile justice funds. The OJJDP defines separation as the condition in which juvenile detainees have either totally independent facilities or shared facilities that are designed so that juveniles and adults neither have accidental contact nor share programs or treatment staff.[25]

Much debate has arisen over whether the initiative to remove juveniles from adult jails has succeeded, as the number of youths being held in adult facilities is not known. Some indications are that the numbers have declined significantly from the almost five hundred thousand a year recorded in 1979.[26] Today, some experts estimate that about one hundred thousand juveniles are detained annually in adult jails during the year.

These figures may be misleading, however, because they do not include youths held in urban jails for under six hours or in rural ones for under twenty-four hours, youths transferred to adult courts, youths in four states that do not cooperate with the federal jail removal initiative, or youths in states that consider anyone over sixteen or seventeen to be an adult. The Community Research Center in Champaign, Illinois, which monitors the jailing of delinquent youths, believes that about two hundred thousand youths are still being jailed with adults each year.[27] Other researchers believe that close to half a million youths are detained in adult pre-adjudicatory facilities (jails or lockups) each year.[28] National trends in juvenile detention rates suggest that the actual number of detainees may have occasionally decreased over the last decade but that the length of time juveniles are held in jails and other secure facilities has increased.

Eliminating the confinement of juveniles in adult institutions continues to be a difficult ongoing task. In a recent comprehensive study of the jailing of juveniles in Minnesota, Ira Schwartz found that even in a state recognized nationally for juvenile justice reform the rate of admission of juveniles to adult jails remains unacceptably high.[29] His research also revealed that the rate of admission was not related to the seriousness of the offense and that minority youths spent greater amounts of time in jail for the same offenses than white offenders.[30]

Schwartz suggests (1) that government enact legislation prohibiting the confinement of juveniles in jail, (2) that appropriate juvenile detention facilities be established, (3) that funds be allocated for such programs, (4) that racial disparity in detention be examined, and (5) that responsibility for monitoring conditions of confinement be fixed by statutes and court decisions.[31]

There are some promising trends in detention reform. Some states including California, for example, passed legislation ensuring that no minor under juvenile court jurisdiction can be incarcerated in any adult jail.[32] In the landmark federal court case *Hendrickson v. Griggs,* the court found that Iowa had not complied with the juvenile jail removal mandate of the Juvenile Justice and Delinquency Prevention Act and ordered local officials to develop a plan for bringing the state into conformity with the law.[33] As a result, states will face increasing legal pressure to meet jail removal requirements.

Because the actual number of juvenile detainees in adult jails is uncertain, it remains a difficult job to monitor improvement in this area. For example, in 1996 a one-day count of youths under the age of eighteen in local adult jails was 8,100.[34] With federal help, some progress appears to have been made in removing juveniles from adult facilities, but thousands each year continue to be held in close contact with adults, and thousands more are held in facilities that, although physically separate, put them in close proximity to adults. To the youths held within their walls, there may appear to be little difference between the juvenile detention facilities and the adult jail.

Deinstitutionalization of Status Offenders

One of the most important juvenile justice policy initiatives of the past two decades has been the removal of status offenders from secure detention facilities that also house delinquents. Along with removing all juveniles from adult jails, the OJJDP has made deinstitutionalization of status offenders a cornerstone of its policy. The Juvenile Justice and Delinquency Prevention Act of 1974 prohibits the secure placement of status offenders in detention facilities.

deinstitutionalization
Closing institutions and moving inmates to community-based programs.

Removing status offenders from secure detention facilities serves two purposes: (1) it reduces interaction with serious delinquent offenders, and (2) it insulates status offenders from the stigma and negative labels associated with being a detainee in a locked facility. **Deinstitutionalization** has its roots in labeling theory and the conflict perspective, both of which were described in Chapter 6. To counteract the effects of labeling, stigma, and delinquent learning opportunities, alternatives to secure detention facilities—counseling, after school programs, shelter care, and foster care—have been developed for nondelinquent youths.

The national effort seems to be paying important dividends. About twenty years ago 3,800 status offenders were in some sort of public secure confinement; in the early 1980s this number dropped to about 1,000. Since then, the number of status offenders being held in some sort of secure confinement has remained stable or decreased slightly.[35] Courts generally try to place status offenders in private rather than public facilities.

Deinstitutionalization: A National Project

Almost twenty years ago the OJJDP funded a national Deinstitutionalization of Status Offenders (DSO) Project to demonstrate the feasibility of removing status offenders from secure lockups and to evaluate the effects of deinstitutionalization.[36] Since their inception, DSO programs have netted mixed results. One problem was the variant definitions of status offenders held by different agencies. Some agencies limited their programs to "pure" status offenders, those who had no record of prior delinquency involvement, whereas others included "mixed offenders," those with a record of prior delinquency. The evaluation found that the pure status offender was relatively rare; most current status offenders had prior delinquent experiences. Another problem was the "net widening" that resulted with announcement of the new program. Police became more willing to send youths to the juvenile court rather than handle the cases themselves once they learned of the services available through the new program. Thus, the number of youths processed to court increased in a number of cities, impeding the antilabeling, antistigma aspects of the program.

Another problem was uncovered by Bortner, Sutherland, and Winn, who examined a midwestern community before and after it attempted to deinstitutionalize status offenders. Their study concluded that there was very little overall change in the processing of status offenders. Of greater concern was the fact that African American status offenders were detained more often than whites and that their detention rates actually increased after the DSO effort had been implemented. On a more positive note, the researchers found that after the deinstitutionalization effort was undertaken, the use of formal hearings and severe dispositions for both African American and white youths dropped substantially.[37]

Anne Schneider has conducted the most comprehensive evaluation of DSO programs on a national level. She found that the DSO programs were successful overall in significantly reducing—but not eliminating—the number of status offenders held in secure detention and the number of status offenders institutionalized after trial. However, the recidivism rate was unaffected by the DSO project, and at some sites it actually increased. That is, status offenders placed in nonsecure facilities separate from delinquents were sometimes more likely to commit repeat offenses than those held in secure detention centers.[38]

This finding suggests that removing status offenders from detention is not a panacea for preventing juvenile crime. However, it was as effective as secure detention. Because shelter care and foster care are much less expensive to maintain than a secure detention facility, deinstitutionalization is at least a more cost-effective juvenile justice policy.

For girls deinstitutionalization may be much less successful. According to Federle and Chesney-Lind, the deinstitutionalization movement of the JJDPA has resulted in girls being removed to mental health and child welfare programs. They conclude that the system appears to be perpetuating the paternalism that has historically characterized juvenile justice for girls. The issue of increasing gender-specific programs for females in the juvenile justice system cannot be ignored because female involvement in the system continues on a steady upward course.[39]

The debate over the most effective way to handle juvenile status offenders continues, especially when it comes to the concept of deinstitutionalization. Some critics have argued that the juvenile court is essentially unable to take effective action in status offender cases and that it should be stripped of jurisdiction over these non-criminal youths. Most judges would prefer to retain jurisdiction so they can help children and families resolve problems that cause runaways, truancy, and other status offense behaviors.[40]

The Intake Process

intake
Process during which a juvenile referral is received and a decision is made to file a petition in juvenile court to release the juvenile, to place the juvenile under supervision, or to refer the juvenile elsewhere.

Police officers may use their discretion to refer a child to the intake division of the juvenile court. The term **intake** refers to the screening of cases by the juvenile court system. The child and his or her family are screened by intake officers, who are often probation staff members, to determine whether the services of the juvenile court are needed. Intake officers may (1) send the youth home with no further action, (2) divert the youth to a social agency, (3) petition the child to the juvenile court, or (4) file a petition and hold the youth in detention. The intake process reduces demands on limited court resources, screens out cases that are not within the court's jurisdiction, and enables assistance to be obtained from community agencies without court intervention.

Juvenile court intake is now provided for by statute in almost all of the states. Also, most of the model acts and standards in juvenile justice suggest developing extensive juvenile court intake proceedings to channel children into programs that do not involve judicial action.[41] Intake procedures are desirable because:

■ Filing complaints against children in court may do more harm than good as rehabilitation often fails in the juvenile court system.

■ Processing children in the juvenile court labels them as delinquent, stigmatizes them, and thus reinforces their antisocial behavior.

■ Nonjudicial handling of children gives them and their families an opportunity to work voluntarily with a social service agency.

■ Intake screening of children helps conserve already overburdened resources in the juvenile court system.

These teens are waiting during the intake process in the juvenile court in Orlando, Florida. The intake process refers to the screening of cases by the juvenile court system. Intake officers, who are often probation staff members, determine whether the services of the juvenile court are needed.

Intake screening allows juvenile courts to enter into consent decrees with juveniles without filing petitions and without formal adjudication. (The consent decree is a court order authorizing disposition of the case without a formal label of delinquency. It is based on an agreement between the intake department of the court and the juvenile who is the subject of the complaint.)

Notwithstanding all of its advantages, intake also has some problems. Because half of all juveniles who are arrested and brought to court are handled nonjudicially, intake sections are constantly pressured to provide services for a large group of children. Intake programs also need to be provided twenty-four hours a day in many urban courts so dispositions can be resolved quickly on the day the child is referred to court. Poorly qualified employees in intake sections are another serious flaw in many court systems.

Although almost all state juvenile court systems provide intake and diversion programs, there are few formal criteria and procedures for selecting children for such nonjudicial alternatives. Normally, the intake probation officer undertakes a preliminary investigation to obtain information about the child and the family prior to making a decision. Written guidelines are needed to assist intake personnel in their duties and to alert juveniles and their families to their procedural rights. Some jurisdictions have attempted to provide guidelines for intake decision making. Guidelines used to determine whether a juvenile case is suitable for adjustment or whether court jurisdiction should be invoked include (1) age of the child, (2) conduct, (3) prior or pending juvenile complaints, (4) the substantial likelihood that the child will cooperate with the adjustment process, and (5) the substantial likelihood that the child is in need of and can receive appropriate services without court intervention.

A number of legal problems are also associated with the intake process. Among them are whether the child has a right to counsel at this stage, whether the child is protected against self-incrimination at intake, and to what degree the child needs to consent to nonjudicial disposition as recommended by the intake probation officer.

Finally, intake dispositions are often determined by the prior juvenile court record rather than by the seriousness of the current offense or the social background of the child. This practice, according to some experts, departs from the court's traditional philosophy of *parens patriae*. It is important that the juvenile court intake examine its function and make certain its decisions are consistent with its philosophy.[42]

The shift from *parens patriae* and rehabilitation has led to changes in the intake process in various jurisdictions. One important trend has been the increased influence of prosecutors on decision making. Traditionally, the intake process has been controlled by probation personnel whose decisions heavily influenced the presiding juvenile court judge's view of which cases to handle formally and which should be settled without court action. This approach to intake, in which probation personnel seek to dispense the least disruptive amount of rehabilitative justice, is being replaced in some jurisdictions by a model in which a prosecutor, who may be more concerned with protecting the public and controlling offenders, is the central figure. Some states now require that intake officers get approval from the prosecutor before either accepting or rejecting a delinquency petition. Other states allow the complaining party to appeal petitions rejected by intake officers to the prosecutor.[43]

The county's chief legal officer, the district attorney, is now playing a greater role in the juvenile court process. There is evidence of a shift from the rehabilitation model to the balanced approach in juvenile justice. As Ted Rubin puts it,

> The prosecutor's authority in the juvenile intake process is likely to develop into a controlling one, stimulated by the prosecutor's public protection image, the increased interest in handling juveniles according to offense and prior record, and diminished confidence in the ideal of rehabilitation.[44]

(A more detailed analysis of the role of the prosecutor is found in Chapter 15.)

Diversion

diversion

Officially halting or suspending a formal criminal or juvenile justice proceeding at any legally prescribed processing point after a recorded justice system entry, and referral of that person to a treatment or care program or a recommendation that the person be released.

One of the most important alternatives chosen at intake is nonjudicial disposition or, as it is variously called, nonjudicial adjustment, handling or processing, informal disposition, adjustment, or diversion. **Diversion** is the most common term used to refer to screening out children from the juvenile court without judicial determination.

Numerous national groups, commentators, lawyers, and criminal justice experts have sought to define the concept of diversion since its inception in the mid-1960s. We suggest that juvenile diversion is the process of placing youths suspected of law-violating behavior into treatment-oriented programs prior to formal trial and disposition to minimize their penetration into the justice system and thereby avoid any potential stigma and labeling.

Diversion implies more than simply screening out cases that are trivial or unimportant and for which no additional treatment is needed. Screening involves abandoning efforts to apply any coercive measures to a defendant. In contrast, diversion, encourages an individual to participate in some specific program or activity by expressed or implied threat of further prosecution. Juvenile justice experts define diversion as "the channeling of cases to noncourt institutions in instances where these cases would ordinarily have received an adjudicatory hearing by a court."[45] Whatever definition is used, diversion generally refers to formally acknowledged and organized efforts to process juvenile and adult offenders outside the justice system.[46]

Diversion has become one of the most popular reforms in juvenile justice since it was recommended by the President's Crime Commission in 1967. Arguments for the use of diversion programs contend that:

- It keeps the juvenile justice system operating; without it, the system would collapse from voluminous caseloads.

- It is considered more effective than the juvenile justice treatment system.

- It gives legislators and other government leaders the opportunity to reallocate resources to programs that may be more successful in the treatment of juvenile offenders.

- Its costs are significantly less than the per capita cost of institutionalization.

- It helps youths avoid the stigma of being labeled delinquent, which is believed to be an important factor in developing a delinquent career.[47]

Police-based diversion models include family crisis intervention projects, referral programs, and youth service bureaus. A youth service bureau is a neighborhood agency that coordinates all community services for young people and provides programs lacking in the community, especially those designated for predelinquent youths. Court-based diversion models have been used extensively for status offenders, minor first offenders, children involved in family disturbances, and children involved in offenses such as shoplifting or minor assault and battery. Specific diversion programs include intervention projects involving employment, referral for educational programs, and placement of juveniles who are involved with drugs in drug-related programs.

Most court-based diversion programs employ a particular formula for choosing youths for diversion. Criteria such as being a first offender, a nonviolent offender, or a status offender, and being drug- or alcohol-dependent are used to select clients. In some programs youths will be asked to partake of services voluntarily in lieu of a court appearance. In other programs prosecutors will agree to defer, and then dismiss, a case once a youth has successfully completed a treatment program. Finally, some programs can be initiated by the juvenile court judge after the case has been brought to his or her attention at an initial hearing.[48]

In summary, diversion programs have been created to remove nonserious offenders from the formal justice system, to provide them with nonpunitive treatment services, and to help them avoid the stigma of a delinquent label.

Issues in Diversion: Widening the Net

widening the net
Phenomenon that occurs when programs created to divert youths from the justice system actually involve them more deeply in the official process.

Diversion has been viewed as a promising alternative to official procedures, but over the years its basic premises have been questioned by a number of experts.[49] The most damaging criticism has been that diversion programs, rather than reducing stigma and system penetration, are increasing it by involving children in the juvenile justice system who previously would have been released without official notice. This phenomenon is referred to as **widening the net.** Various studies indicate that police and court personnel are likely to use diversion program services for youths who ordinarily would have been turned loose at the intake or arrest stage.[50] For example, in an analysis of diversion programs in Florida, and after controlling for such social and legal variables as race, sex, age, offense severity, and prior record, Frazier and Cochran found that diverted youths experienced at least as much involvement with the juvenile justice system as did youths who were not selected for diversion.[51] Similarly, after reviewing existing research on the effectiveness of employing diversion with status offenders, Anderson and Schoen found little evidence that diversion programs have met their stated goals. They conclude that although diversion should not be dismissed as an "unrealistic or harmful fad" neither should it be judged as a "satisfactory approach to juvenile delinquency."[52]

Why does net widening occur? One explanation is that police and prosecutors find diversion a more attractive alternative to both official processing and outright release—diversion helps them resolve the conflict between doing too much or too little. Also, many local diversion programs receive outside (federal, state, or private) funds. Local officials worry that they will lose these funds if client quotas for "warm bodies" are not maintained by police and court systems. Police and judges who are reluctant to give up control of offenders they believe need more formal treatment refer youths whom they might have released with a warning in the past. As Rausch and Logan put it,

> In essence, the diverted population was drawn from a pool of offenders who, prior to the implementation of diversion programs, would probably have been released or left alone. The effect of such a policy has been to expand control over a larger, less seriously involved sector of the juvenile population.[53]

Similarly, Frazier and Cochran found that net widening may result from the fact that diversion staff members often have social service backgrounds: "Most staff believed that the more attention given a youth and the longer the period of time over which the attention was given, the better the prospects for a successful outcome.[54]

Diversion has also been criticized as ineffective and unproductive; that is, youths being diverted make no better adjustment in the community than those who go through official channels. However, not all delinquency experts are critical of diversion. Arnold Binder and Gilbert Geis claim that the many benefits of diversion more than balance its negative qualities.[55] They challenge the net-widening concept as being naive: How do we know that diverted youths would have had less interface with the justice system if diversion didn't exist? They suggest that, even if juveniles escape official labels for their current offense, it may be inevitable that they would eventually fall into the hands of the police and juvenile court. They also point out that the rehabilitative potential of diversion should not be overlooked (see the Case in Point box).

You are the intake worker assigned to the local juvenile court. Charles is a thirteen-year-old who was arrested for shoplifting in a department store. He was appearing before the juvenile court for trial and disposition of this, his first delinquency offense. Charles lives with his mother and three younger siblings in a public housing project. His parents are separated, and Charles hasn't seen his father in more than a year. Charles is in the eighth grade, seems bright, but frequently fights in school. The school report indicates that Charles is a sad, lonely child with a hot temper.

The intake worker and the defense attorney indicate that Charles wants to remain at home, and both recommend closing the delinquency case. The prosecutor and arresting police officer believe that Charles is an aggressive, acting-out youth whose behavior is unpredictable and who is in need of juvenile court supervision.

■ Do you believe that Charles would benefit from a diversion program?

■ How would you assess the juvenile court's role in this type of case?

Although diversion programs are not the panacea their originators believed them to be, at least they offer an alternative to official processing. They can help the justice system devote its energies to more serious offenders while providing counseling and other rehabilitative services to needy youths.

In summary, an examination of the history of diversion indicates that most programs widen the net of the justice system and that their ability to reduce recidivism remains uncertain. According to Mark Ezell, the central theme in the juvenile court movement is the endless search for effective alternatives.[56] Juvenile diversion programs represent one alternative to the traditional process.

Of course, every year thousands of juvenile offenders fail to qualify for such alternatives. The remaining sections of this chapter focus on what happens to these children.

The Petition and Pretrial Release

complaint
Report made by the police or some other agency to the court that initiates the intake process.

A **complaint** is the report that the police or some other agency makes to the court to initiate the intake process. Once the agency makes a decision in intake that judicial disposition is required, a **petition** is filed. The petition is the formal legal complaint that initiates judicial action against a juvenile charged with actions alleging juvenile delinquency or noncriminal behavior such as status offenses. The petition includes basic information such as the name, age, and residence

petition
Document filed in juvenile court alleging that a juvenile is a delinquent, a status offender, or a dependent and asking the court to assume jurisdiction over the juvenile or to transfer the juvenile to adult court.

of the child; the parents' names; and the facts alleging the child's delinquency. The police officer, a family member, or a social service agency can file a petition.

If, after being given the right to counsel, the child admits the allegation in the petition, an initial hearing is immediately scheduled for the child to make the admission before the court, and information is gathered to develop a treatment plan.

If the child does not admit to any of the facts in the petition, a date for a scheduled adjudicatory hearing on the petition is set. This hearing, whose purpose is to determine the merits of the petition, is similar to the adult trial. Once a hearing date has been set, the probation department, which is the agency providing social services to the court, is normally asked to prepare a social study report. This predisposition report contains relevant information about the child along with recommendations for treatment and service. This report, often known as the probation or social investigation report, is discussed in detail in Chapter 16.

When a date has been set for the hearing on the petition, parents or guardians and other persons associated with the petition (witnesses, the arresting police officer, and victims) are notified of the hearing. On occasion, the court may issue a summons—a court order requiring the juvenile or others involved in the case to appear for the hearing. The statutes of the juvenile code in a given jurisdiction govern the contents of the petition. Some jurisdictions, for instance, allow for a petition to be filed based on the information and belief of the complainant alone. Others require that the petition be filed under oath or that an affidavit accompany the petition. Some jurisdictions authorize only one official, such as a probation officer or prosecutor, to file the petition. Others allow numerous officials, including family and social service agencies, to set forth facts in the petition. Pretrial release (bail) is also reviewed at this time.

Bail for Children

bail
Amount of money that must be paid as a condition of pretrial release to ensure that the accused will return for subsequent proceedings; bail is normally set by the judge at the initial appearance, and if unable to make bail, the accused is detained in jail.

Bail is money or some other security provided to the court to ensure the appearance of a defendant at every subsequent stage of the justice process. Its purpose is to obtain the release from custody of the person charged with the crime. Once the amount of bail is set by the court, the defendant is required to pay a percentage of the entire amount in cash or securities or to pay a professional bail bonding agency to submit a bond as a guarantee for returning to court. If a person is released on bail but fails to appear in court at the stipulated time, the bail deposit is forfeited. The person, if apprehended, is then confined in a detention facility until the court appearance.

With a few exceptions, persons other than those accused of murder are entitled to reasonable bail, as stated in the Eighth Amendment of the U.S. Constitution. There is some controversy today about whether a constitutional right to bail exists or whether the court can impose excessive bail resulting in a person's confinement. In most cases a defendant has the right to be released on reasonable bail. Many jurisdictions require a bail review hearing by a higher court when a person is detained because he or she is unable to pay an excessive bail. Whether a defendant will appear at the next stage of the juvenile or criminal proceeding is a key issue in determining bail. Bail cannot be used to punish an accused person, nor can it be denied or revoked simply at the discretion of the court.

Many experts believe bail is one of the worst aspects of the criminal justice system. It discriminates against the poor, and it is costly to the government, which must pay for detention facilities for offenders who are unable to make bail and who could otherwise be in the community. It is dehumanizing to those who must stay in jail because they cannot raise bail. It is even believed that people who await trial in jail have a higher proportion of subsequent convictions than people who are released on bail.

Once bail is set by the court, the defendant is required to pay a percentage of the entire amount in cash or securities or to pay a professional bail bonding agency to submit a bond as a guarantee for returning to court. If a person is released on bail but fails to appear in court at the stipulated time, the bail deposit is forfeited. The person, if apprehended, is then confined in a detention facility until the court appearance. The issue of bail for children is quite controversial, and, while most youngsters are released to the custody of their parents, thousands are detained in secure facilities prior to their hearing in juvenile court.

As we discussed earlier in this chapter, juvenile detention prior to adjudication is one of the most serious problems facing the juvenile justice system. Large numbers of juveniles are incarcerated in inadequate facilities, which can lead to many harmful effects. Despite these facts, many states refuse juveniles the right to bail. They argue that juvenile proceedings are civil (private wrong as opposed to public offense), not criminal, and that detention is rehabilitative, not punitive. In addition, they argue that juveniles do not need a constitutional right to bail because statutory provisions allow children to be released in parental custody. Furthermore, they believe it would be more productive to reduce the number of detention facilities and the children in them than to develop a bail program.

In view of the recognized deficiency of the adult bail system, some experts believe alternative release programs should be developed within the juvenile justice system. These programs include release on recognizance, release to a third party, and the use of station house summonses or citation programs in lieu of arrest. Release on recognizance (R.O.R.) is the pretrial release of a defendant from court without posting a bail bond or any security but only on the promise of the defendant to return to court for trial. A summons or citation is also an order requiring the appearance of the defendant at court, but it is usually initiated at the police station.

Some states do provide bail programs for children. Bail is used only to ensure the presence of the accused at trial; the presumption exists that the accused should be released solely on the basis of being able to make bail. Mark Solar and his colleagues point out that state juvenile bail statutes are divided into three categories: (1) those guaranteeing the right to bail, (2) those that grant the court discretion to give bail, and (3) those that deny a juvenile the right to bail.[57] The consensus generally is that allowing bail for juveniles is in conflict with the *parens patriae* concept and rehabilitation goals of the juvenile justice system. A balanced approach, however, is always used when dealing with serious, violent and repeat juvenile offenders—one that emphasizes enforcement, prosecution, bail, and detention to protect public safety.

There is no agreement among jurisdictions, however, on whether a child has the constitutional right to be released on bail. The U.S. Supreme Court has never decided the issue of whether juveniles have a constitutional right to bail. Some courts have stated that bail provisions do not apply to juveniles. Others rely on the Eighth Amendment against cruel and unusual punishment or on state constitutional provisions or statutes and conclude that juveniles do have a right to bail.

In a bail hearing for a child, the court reviews the charge, the history of the parents' ability to control the child's behavior, the child's school participation, psychological and psychiatric evaluations, the child's desire to go home, and the parents' interest in continuing to take care of the child while awaiting the trial.

Preventive Detention

preventive detention
Keeping the accused in custody prior to trial because the accused is suspected of being a danger to the community.

An issue closely related to bail is **preventive detention,** the practice of keeping a person in custody before trial because of his or her suspected danger to the community. Proponents argue that preventive detention can save potential new victims from harm caused by an offender released on bail. Opponents hold that preventive detention statutes deprive offenders of their freedom because guilt has not been proven. It is also unfair, they claim, to punish people for what judicial authorities believe they may do in the future, as it is impossible to predict with any accuracy who will be a danger to the community. Moreover, because judges are able to use unchecked discretion in their detention decisions, an offender could unfairly be deprived of freedom without legal recourse.

Although the Supreme Court has upheld preventive detention of adults, most state jurisdictions allow judges to deny bail to adult offenders only in cases involving murder (capital crimes), when the offenders have jumped bail in the past, or when they have committed another crime while on bail. However, every state allows for preventive detention of juveniles. The reason for this discrepancy hinges on the legal principle that adults have the right to liberty and juveniles have a right to custody. Therefore, it is not unreasonable to detain youths for their own protection. On June 4, 1984, the Supreme Court dealt with this issue in *Schall v. Martin* when it upheld the state of New York's preventive detention statute. The Court concluded that there was no indication in the statute that preventive detention was used as punishment.[58] (See the Juvenile Law in Review box entitled "*Schall v. Martin.*")

In a study of the effect of *Schall,* the American Bar Association concluded that continued refinement of the detention screening process is needed to achieve the twin goals of public safety and protection of juvenile offenders' constitutional rights.[59] Because preventive detention may attach a stigma of guilt to a child presumed innocent, the practice remains a highly controversial one, and the efficacy of such laws remains unknown.[60]

The Plea and Plea Bargaining

In the adult criminal justice system the defendant normally enters a plea of guilty or not guilty. More than 90 percent of all adult defendants plead guilty before the trial stage. A large proportion of those pleas involve what is known as plea bargaining. **Plea bargaining** is the exchange of prosecutorial and judicial concessions for guilty pleas.[61] It permits a defendant to plead guilty to a less seri-

SCHALL V. MARTIN

FACTS

Gregory Martin was arrested in New York City on December 13, 1977, on charges of robbery, assault, and criminal possession of a weapon. Because he was arrested at 11:30 P.M. and lied about his residence, Martin was kept overnight in detention and brought to juvenile court the next day for an "initial appearance" accompanied by his grandmother. The family court judge, citing possession of a loaded weapon, the false address given to police, and the lateness of the hour the crime occurred (evidence of a lack of supervision), ordered him detained before trial under section 320.5(3)(6) of the New York State code. Section 320.5 authorizes pretrial detention of an accused juvenile delinquent if "there is a substantial probability that he will not appear in court on the return date or there is a serious risk that he may before the return date commit an act which if committed by an adult would constitute a crime." Later, at trial, Martin was found to be a delinquent and sentenced to two years' probation.

While he was in pretrial detention, Martin's attorneys filed a habeas corpus petition (demanding his release from custody). Their petition charged that his detention denied him due process rights under the Fifth and Fourteenth Amendments. Their suit was a class action on behalf of all youths subject to preventive detention in New York. The New York appellate courts upheld Martin's claim on the ground that because, at adjudication, most delinquents are released or placed on probation it was unfair to incarcerate them before trial. The prosecution brought the case to the U.S. Supreme Court for final judgment.

DECISION

The Supreme Court upheld the state's right to place juveniles in preventive detention. It held that preventive detention serves the legitimate objective of protecting both the juvenile and society from pretrial crime. Pretrial detention need not be considered punishment merely because the juvenile is eventually released or put on probation. In addition, there are procedural safeguards, such as notice and a hearing, and a statement of facts that must be given to juveniles before they are placed in detention. The Court also found that detention based on prediction of future behavior was not a violation of due process. Many decisions are made in the justice system, such as the decision to sentence or grant parole, that are based in part on a prediction of future behavior, and these have all been accepted by the courts as legitimate exercises of state power.

SIGNIFICANCE OF THE CASE

Schall v. Martin established the right of juvenile court judges to deny youths pretrial release if they perceive them to be "dangerous." However, the case also established a due process standard for detention hearings that includes notice and a statement of substantial reasons for the detention.

Source: *Schall v. Martin,* 104 S.Ct. 2403 (1984).

JUVENILE LAW IN REVIEW

plea bargaining
The exchange of prosecutorial and judicial concessions for a guilty plea by the accused; plea bargaining usually results in a reduced charge or a more lenient sentence.

ous charge in exchange for an agreement by the prosecutor to recommend a reduced sentence to the court. The plea bargain involves a discussion between the defense attorney for the child and the juvenile prosecutor by which the child agrees to plead guilty to obtain a reduced charge or a lenient sentence.

Few juvenile codes require a guilty or not guilty plea when a petition is filed against a child in juvenile court. In most jurisdictions an initial hearing is held at which the child either submits to a finding of the facts or denies the petition.[62] If the child admits to the facts, the court determines an appropriate disposition and treatment plan for the child. If the child denies the allegations in the petition, the case normally proceeds to the trial or adjudication stage of the juvenile process. When a child enters no plea, the court ordinarily imposes a denial of the charges for the child. This may occur where a juvenile doesn't understand the nature of the complaint or isn't represented by an attorney.

A high percentage of juvenile offenders enter guilty pleas or admissions in juvenile court. How many of these pleas involve plea bargaining between the prosecutor or probation officer and the child's attorney is unknown. In the past it was believed that plea bargaining was unnecessary in the juvenile justice system because there was little incentive for either the prosecution or the defense to bargain in a system that does not have jury trials, criminal labels, or long sentences. In addition, because the court must dispose of cases in the best interests of the child, plea negotiation seemed unnecessary. Consequently, there has long been a debate among experts over the appropriateness of plea bargaining in the juvenile justice system. The arguments in favor of plea bargaining include lower court costs and efficiency. Others believe it is an invisible, unfair, unregulated, and unethical process. When used, experts believe the process requires the highest standards of good faith by the prosecutor in the juvenile and adult system.[63]

In recent years, however, growing public concern about violent juvenile crime has spurred attorneys to increasingly seek to negotiate a plea rather than accept the so-called good interests of the court judgment—a judgment that might result in harsher sanctions for their clients. The extension of the adversary process to children has led to an increase in plea bargaining, creating an informal trial process that parallels the adult system. Other factors in the trend toward juvenile plea bargaining include the use of prosecutors rather than probation personnel and police officers in juvenile courts and the ever-increasing caseloads in such courts.

Plea bargaining negotiations generally involve one or more of the following: (1) reduction of a charge, (2) change in the proceedings from that of delinquency to a status offense, (3) elimination of possible waiver proceedings to the criminal court, and (4) agreements between the government and defense regarding dispositional programs for the child. In states where youths are subject to long mandatory sentences, reduction of the charges may have a significant impact on the outcome of the case. In states where youths may be waived to the adult court for committing certain serious crimes, a plea reduction may result in the juvenile court maintaining jurisdiction.

Little clear evidence exists of how much plea bargaining there is in the juvenile justice system, but it is apparent that such negotiations do take place and seem to be increasing. In one of the most comprehensive studies of juvenile plea negotiation in juvenile court, Joseph Sanborn found that about 20 percent of the cases processed in Philadelphia resulted in a negotiated plea. Most were for reduced sentences, most typically probation in lieu of incarceration, or if an institutional sentence could not be avoided, assignment to a less restrictive environment. Sanborn found that plea bargaining was a very complex process in juvenile court, depending in large measure on the philosophy of the judge and the court staff. In general, he found it to be a device that has greater benefit for the defendants than for the court itself.[64] (The Focus on Delinquency box entitled "Pleading Guilty in Juvenile Court" takes a closer look at juvenile plea bargaining.)

In summary, the majority of juvenile court cases that are not adjudicated seem to be the result of open admissions to the facts rather than actual plea bargaining.

PLEADING GUILTY IN JUVENILE COURT

Although the nature and extent of plea bargaining in the adult court system is well documented, plea bargaining in juvenile court has remained a "low visibility" practice. Recent research by Joseph Sanborn sheds some light on the role of plea negotiation in the juvenile justice system.

Sanborn conducted a survey of all fifty states and the District of Columbia to identify legislative and judicial recognition of juvenile plea bargaining. He also observed practices in three juvenile courts and interviewed court personnel to illustrate the bargaining process.

Sanborn found that forty states recognize plea negotiations in juvenile court and apply some type of control over the guilty plea process. Twenty-five states have formulated rules that control juvenile plea negotiations. Thirteen states have passed legislation that details a judge's obligations when a juvenile pleads guilty; another three states regulate the practice through appellate court ruling. Only ten states have not addressed the issue of juvenile plea negotiations.

Although most states now address juvenile court pleas, the amount of regulation still varies widely. Most but not all jurisdictions that recognize plea bargaining in juvenile court require judges to remind defendants that they are giving up constitutional rights, warn them of possible sentencing outcomes, determine if the plea was voluntary, and establish if there was a factual basis for the plea.

Sanborn's observation and interview data indicate that there are ecological differences in the way the plea bargaining process is carried out. Urban courts may be more likely to institute formal procedures, whereas suburban and rural courts are more likely to conduct plea negotiations informally.

Sanborn concludes that as the juvenile court system becomes more formal and punitive, it is essential for juvenile courts to institute more formal and rigorous proceedings to ensure that admissions are not later lost on appeal. Fairness dictates that youths, some of whom face long incarceration sentences, understand precisely what they are doing and the implication of pleading guilty for both current and future considerations.

Source: Joseph Sanborn, "Pleading Guilty in Juvenile Court: Minimal Ado about Something Very Important to Young Defendants," *Justice Quarterly* 9:126–50 (1992).

Unlike the adult system—where almost 90 percent of all charged offenders are involved in some plea bargaining—plea bargaining in the juvenile court is less common because incentives such as dropping multiple charges or substituting a misdemeanor for a felony are unlikely. Nonetheless, plea bargaining is firmly entrenched in the juvenile process. Any plea bargain, however, must be entered into voluntarily and knowingly; otherwise, the conviction may be overturned on appeal.

Transfer to the Adult Court

transfer process
Transferring a juvenile offender from the jurisdiction of juvenile court to adult criminal court.

One of the most significant actions that can occur in the early court processing of a juvenile offender is the **transfer process.** Otherwise known as **waiver, bindover,** or **removal,** this process involves transferring a juvenile from the juvenile court to the criminal court. Virtually all state statutes allow for this kind of transfer.

waiver, bindover, removal
Terms used to indicate the transfer process has been approved and the juvenile is under the jurisdiction of the adult criminal court.

Historically, the U.S. justice system has made a fundamental distinction between children and adults. The juvenile justice system emphasizes rehabilitation, whereas the criminal justice system emphasizes deterrence, punishment, and social control. Proponents of the transfer process claim that children who commit serious, chronic offenses and who may be hardened offenders should be handled by the criminal court system. In fact, so the argument goes, these children cannot be rehabilitated. Even such well-regarded institutions as the National Council of Juvenile and Family Court Judges have made it their stated policy to favor transfer.[65] The theory is that unless a waiver policy exists children may feel immune from "real" punishment.

Opponents suggest that the transfer process is applied to children unfairly and is at odds with the treatment philosophy of the juvenile court. Furthermore, some children tried in the adult criminal court may be incarcerated under conditions so extreme that they will be permanently damaged. Another serious disadvantage of transferring a child is the stigma that may be attached to a conviction in the criminal court. Labeling children as adult offenders early in life may seriously impair their future educational, employment, and other opportunities.

In reality, however, juveniles often take advantage of decisions to transfer them to the adult court. Although the charge against a child may be considered serious in the juvenile court, the adult criminal court will not find it so; consequently, a child may have a better chance for dismissal of the charges or acquittal after a jury trial.

Today, all states allow juveniles to be tried as adults in criminal courts in one of three ways:

concurrent jurisdiction
More than one court has jurisdiction; the prosecutor then has the discretion of filing charges in either juvenile or adult court.

excluded offenses
Offenses, some minor and others very serious, that are automatically excluded from juvenile court.

judicial waiver
When the juvenile court waives its jurisdiction over a juvenile and transfers the case to adult criminal court.

1. **Concurrent jurisdiction.** The prosecutor has the discretion of filing charges for certain offenses in either juvenile or criminal court.
2. **Excluded offenses.** Certain offenses are automatically excluded (by statute) from juvenile court. These offenses can be very minor, such as traffic or fishing violations, or very serious, such as murder or rape (offense-based waiver). Statutory exclusion accounts for the largest number of juveniles tried as adults in criminal court.
3. **Judicial waiver.** The juvenile court waives its jurisdiction and transfers the case to criminal court. (This procedure is also known as "binding over" or "certifying" juvenile cases to criminal court.) Nearly all states offer provisions for juvenile waivers.

Today thirteen states authorize prosecutors to bring cases in the juvenile or adult criminal court at their discretion; thirty-six states exclude certain offenses from juvenile court jurisdiction; and forty-nine states, the District of Columbia, and the federal government have judicial waiver provisions. As indicated, every state has some provision for handling juveniles in adult criminal court.[66]

Due Process in Transfer Proceedings

Statutes set the standards for transfer procedures. Age is of particular importance. Some jurisdictions allow for transfer between the ages of fourteen and seventeen. Others restrict waiver proceedings to mature juveniles and specify particular offenses. In a few jurisdictions any child can be sentenced to the criminal court system, regardless of age.

More than thirty states have recently amended their waiver policies to automatically exclude certain offenses from juvenile court jurisdiction. About half of these jurisdictions automatically exclude serious offenses. For example, Indiana excludes cases involving sixteen- and seventeen-year-olds charged with kidnapping, rape, and robbery (if a weapon was used or bodily injury occurred); in Illinois, youths ages fifteen and sixteen who are charged with murder, aggravated or sexual assault, or armed robbery with a firearm are automatically sent to criminal court; in Pennsylvania, any child accused of murder, regardless of age, is tried before the criminal court.[67] Other jurisdictions use exclusion to remove minor traffic offenses and public ordinance violations, which are then handled by lower criminal courts. Nonetheless, the trend to exclude serious violent offenses from juvenile court jurisdictions is growing in response to the public demand to get tough on crime. In addition, large numbers of youth (estimated at about 175,000 cases) under age 18 are tried as adults where the upper age of juvenile court jurisdiction is age 15 or 16.

In a minority of states, statutes allow prosecutors to file particularly serious cases either in the juvenile court or the adult court at their own discretion.[68] Prosecutor discretion may occasionally be a more effective transfer mechanism than the waiver process because the prosecutor can file a petition in criminal or juvenile court under concurrent jurisdiction provisions without judicial approval.

Thus, the criteria that affect the decision to transfer the child to the criminal court are found in each state's juvenile court act. Many states, however, favor keeping children in juvenile court rather than transferring them to criminal court. The ineffectiveness of the adult criminal justice system is itself an adequate argument for keeping children in juvenile court.

KENT V. UNITED STATES AND BREED V. JONES

KENT V. UNITED STATES: FACTS

Morris Kent was arrested at the age of sixteen in connection with charges of housebreaking, robbery, and rape. As a juvenile, he was subject to the exclusive jurisdiction of the District of Columbia Juvenile Court. The District of Columbia statute declared that the court could transfer the petitioner "after full investigation" and remit him to trial in the U.S. District Court. Kent admitted his involvement in the offenses and was placed in a receiving home for children. Subsequently, his mother obtained counsel, and they discussed with the social service director the possibility that the juvenile court might waive its jurisdiction.

Kent was detained at the receiving home for almost one week. There was no arraignment, no hearing, and no hearing for petitioner's apprehension. Kent's counsel arranged for a psychiatric examination, and a motion requesting a hearing on the waiver was filed. The juvenile court judge did not rule on the motion and entered an order stating, "After full investigation, the court waives its jurisdiction and directs that a trial be held under the regular proceedings of the criminal court." The judge made no finding and gave no reasons for his waiver decision. It appeared that the judge denied motions for a hearing, recommendations for hospitalization for psychiatric observation, requests for access to the social service file, and offers to prove that the petitioner was a fit subject for rehabilitation under the juvenile court.

After the juvenile court waived its jurisdiction, Kent was indicted by the grand jury and was subsequently found guilty of housebreaking and robbery and not guilty by reason of insanity on the charge of rape. Kent was sentenced to serve a period of thirty to ninety years on his conviction.

Decision

The petitioner's lawyer appealed the decision on the basis of the infirmity of the proceedings by which the juvenile court waived its jurisdiction. He fur-

Since 1966, the U.S. Supreme Court and other federal and state courts have attempted to ensure fairness in the waiver process by handing down decisions that spell out the need for due process. Two Supreme Court decisions, *Kent v. United States* (1966) and *Breed v. Jones* (1975), are set out in the Juvenile Law in Review box because of their significance.[69] The *Kent* case declared a District of Columbia transfer statute unconstitutional and attacked the subsequent conviction of the child by granting him specific due process rights. In *Breed v. Jones* the Supreme Court declared that the child was granted the protection of the double jeopardy clause of the Fifth Amendment after he was tried as a delinquent in the juvenile court.

Today, as a result of *Kent* and *Breed,* states that have transfer hearings provide specific requirements for transfer proceedings in their juvenile code. For the most part, when a transfer hearing is conducted today, due process of law requires that there be (1) a legitimate transfer hearing, (2) sufficient notice to the child's family and defense attorney, (3) the right to counsel, and (4) a statement of the reason for the court order regarding transfer. These rights recognize what *Kent v. United States* indicated: namely, that the transfer proceeding is a critically important action in determining the statutory rights of the juvenile offender.

ther attacked the waiver on statutory and constitutional grounds, stating: "(1) no hearing occurred, (2) no findings were made, (3) no reasons were stated before the waiver, and (4) counsel was denied access to the social service file." The U.S. Supreme Court found that the juvenile court order waiving jurisdiction and remitting the child to trial in the district court was invalid. Its arguments were based on the following:

- The theory of the juvenile court act is rooted in social welfare procedures and treatments.

- The philosophy of the juvenile court, namely *parens patriae,* is not supposed to allow procedural unfairness.

- Waiver proceedings are critically important actions in the juvenile court.

- The juvenile court act requiring full investigation in the District of Columbia should be read in the context of constitutional principles relating to due process of law. These principles require at a minimum that the petitioner be entitled to a hearing, access to counsel, access by counsel to social service records, and a statement of the reason for the juvenile court decision.

Significance of the Case

This case examined for the first time the substantial degree of discretion associated with a transfer proceeding in the District of Columbia. Thus, the Supreme Court significantly limited its holding to the statute involved but justified its reference to constitutional principles relating to due process and the assistance of counsel. In addition, it said that the juvenile court waiver hearings need to measure up to the essentials of due process and

(continued on the next page)

JUVENILE LAW IN REVIEW

(continued from the previous page)

fair treatment. Furthermore, in an appendix to its opinion, the Court set up criteria concerning waiver of the jurisdictions. These are:

- The seriousness of the alleged offense to the community
- Whether the alleged offense was committed in an aggressive, violent, or willful manner
- Whether the alleged offense was committed against persons or against property
- The prosecutive merit of the complaint
- The desirability of trial and disposition
- The sophistication and maturity of the juvenile
- The record and previous history of the juvenile
- Prospects for adequate protection of the public and the likelihood of reasonable rehabilitation

BREED V. JONES: FACTS

In 1971 a petition in the juvenile court of California was filed against Jones, who was then seventeen, alleging that he had committed an offense that, if committed by an adult, would constitute robbery. The petitioner was detained pending a hearing. At the hearing the juvenile court took testimony, found that the allegations were true, and sustained the petition. The proceedings were continued for a disposition hearing, at which point Jones was found unfit for treatment in the juvenile court. It was ordered that he be prosecuted as an adult offender. At a subsequent preliminary hearing, the petitioner was held for criminal trial, an information was filed against him for robbery, and

Youths in Adult Court

The issue of waiver is an important one. Waiver is attractive to conservatives because it jibes with the get-tough policy currently popular in the juvenile justice system. Liberals oppose its use because it clashes with the rehabilitative ideal. Some conservative thinkers have argued that the increased use of waiver can help get violent, chronic offenders off the streets. Barry Feld suggests that waiver to adult court should be mandatory for juveniles committing serious, violent crimes.[70] He argues that mandatory waiver would coincide with the popular "just deserts" sentencing policy and eliminate potential bias and disparity in judicial decision making. A recent detailed analysis by Feld of legislative changes in juvenile waiver statutes indicates that the nature of the offense, rather than the real needs of the offender, dominates the waiver decision. According to Feld, basing waiver decisions on type of offense rather than on the rehabilitative needs of the child has added to what has been referred to as the "criminalization" of the juvenile court.[71]

Another trend has been toward giving original jurisdiction for serious juvenile crimes to the adult courts and then allowing the adult court judge the option of waiving deserving cases back to the juvenile court. Despite these trends toward integrating juveniles into the adult criminal court system, it should be noted that youths cannot be placed in adult correctional facilities until they reach age 16.

Because of the popularity of waiver, the number of youths processed in

he was tried and found guilty. He was committed to the California Youth Authority over objections that he was being subjected to double jeopardy.

Petitioner Jones sought an appeal in the federal district court on the basis of the double jeopardy argument that jeopardy attaches at the juvenile delinquency proceedings. The writ of habeas corpus was denied.

Decision

The U.S. Supreme Court held that the prosecution of Jones as an adult in the California Superior Court, after an adjudicatory finding in the juvenile court that he had violated a criminal statute and a subsequent finding that he was unfit for treatment as a juvenile, violated the double jeopardy clause of the Fifth Amendment of the U.S. Constitution as applied to the states through the Fourteenth Amendment. Thus, Jones's trial in the California Superior Court for the same offense as that for which he was tried in the juvenile court violated the policy of the double jeopardy clause, even if he never faced the risk of more than one punishment; double jeopardy refers to the risk or potential risk of trial and conviction, not punishment.

Significance of the Case

The *Breed* case provided answers on several important transfer issues: (1) *Breed* prohibits trying a child in an adult court when there has been a prior adjudicatory juvenile proceeding; (2) probable cause may exist at a transfer hearing, and this does not violate subsequent jeopardy if the child is transferred to the adult court; (3) because the same evidence is often used in both the transfer hearing and subsequent trial in either the juvenile or adult court, a different judge is often required for each hearing.

Sources: *Kent v. United States,* 383 U.S. 541, 86 S.Ct. 1045, 16 L.Ed.2d 84 (1966); *Breed v. Jones,* 421 U.S. 519, 95 S.Ct. 1779 (1975).

JUVENILE LAW IN REVIEW

adult courts by judicial waiver is significant. In 1995, 9,700, or 1 percent, of all formally processed delinquency cases were transferred to criminal court. Drug law violation cases were the most likely to be transferred to criminal court (4.1 percent), compared with 2.4 percent of person offense cases, less than 1 percent of property offense cases, and 0.4 percent of petitioned public order offense cases.[72] (See Table 14.5.)

Between 1986 and 1994, the number of delinquency cases waived to criminal court increased 60 percent, and then dropped 17 percent from 1994 to 1995. The number of actual cases transferred to criminal court increased from 7,300 in 1986 to 10,800 in 1991, and decreased to 9,700 in 1995 (see Tables 14.5 and 14.6).[73]

The pattern of change in the number of waived cases between 1986 and 1995 varied across offense categories (see Figure 14.1 and Table 14.7). The most dramatic increase in number of waived cases was for person-centered crimes, which rose 125 percent between 1986 and 1994. (In 1995, however, this number dropped, as did rates for most other offense categories.) In 1995 the largest group of cases waived to criminal courts—nearly half of all waived cases—involved person offenses.[74]

Today the principal choice across the nation of a strategy for attacking serious youth crime is to place more juveniles in adult court. This is done by lowering the age of juvenile court jurisdiction, dropping the age for transfer to criminal court, increasing the number of offenses requiring placement in adult court, and giving the prosecutor more discretion to file juvenile cases in the criminal court.[75]

Table 14.5

PERCENTAGE OF PETITIONED DELINQUENCY CASES WAIVED TO CRIMINAL COURT, 1986–1995

Most Serious Offense	1986	1991	1995
Delinquency	1.3	1.5	1.0
Person	2.2	2.4	2.1
Property	1.2	1.2	0.7
Drugs	1.2	4.1	1.3
Public Order	0.7	0.7	0.4

Source: Melissa Sickmund, *Juvenile Court Statistics 1995* (Pittsburgh, Pa.: National Center for Juvenile Justice, 1998).

Table 14.6

PERCENTAGE CHANGE IN PETITIONED DELINQUENCY CASES WAIVED TO CRIMINAL COURT, 1986–1995

Most Serious Offense	Number of Cases			Percentage Change	
	1986	1991	1995	1986–95	1991–95
Total Delinquency	7,300	10,800	9,700	33	–10
Person	2,300	3,600	4,600	100	–27
Property	4,000	4,600	3,300	–18	–29
Drugs	400	1,800	1,200	180	–32
Public Order	600	800	700	8	–13

Source: Melissa Sickmund, *Juvenile Court Statistics 1995* (Pittsburgh, Pa.: National Center for Juvenile Justice, 1998).

Note: Detail may not add to totals due to rounding; percentage change calculations are based on unrounded numbers.

Debating the Waiver Concept

Despite the increased use of waiver, the value of transferring youths to the adult court has been questioned by critics on various grounds.

■ Waivers don't always support the goal of increased public protection.

One alleged shortcoming is that the actual treatment of delinquents in adult court is quite similar to what they might have received had they remained in the custody of juvenile authorities. For example, New York's system has been criticized on the ground that 70 percent of juvenile offenders arraigned in adult court are waived to juvenile court. The processing of these children is a waste of both time and money. Of the remaining children who are tried in adult court, 40 percent get probation; only 3 percent of juvenile offenders tried in adult court received longer sentences than they could have been given in juvenile court.[76]

FIGURE 14.1

Delinquency Cases Waived to Criminal Court, 1986–1995

Source: Melissa Sickmund, *Juvenile Court Statistics 1995* (Pittsburgh, Pa.: National Center for Juvenile Justice, 1998).

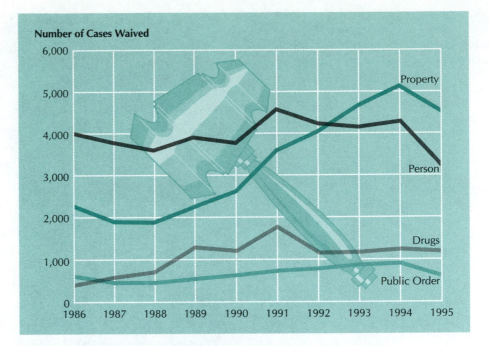

Table 14.7

OFFENSE PROFILE OF DELINQUENCY CASES WAIVED TO CRIMINAL COURT, 1986–1995

Most Serious Offense	1986 (percent)	1991 (percent)	1995 (percent)
Person	31	33	47
Property	54	43	34
Drugs	6	17	13
Public Order	8	7	7
Number of Waived Cases	7,300	10,800	9,700

Sources: Melissa Sickmund, *Juvenile Court Statistics 1995* (Pittsburgh, Pa.: National Center for Juvenile Justice, 1998).

More recent studies support these findings. In the majority of cases involving transferred juveniles sentenced to incarceration, the length of sentence did not exceed three years. This is within the range of options typically available to juvenile courts. In fact, incarcerated, transferred juveniles do not always receive longer sentences than those tried and sentenced in juvenile courts.[77] This has prompted some critics to ask the question, why even bother transferring these children?

■ Waivers add undue burdens to youthful offenders.

Researchers Rudman, Hartstone, Fagan, and Moore are also critical of waivers, albeit on very different grounds. Their research is based on a comparison of a group of waived violent juvenile offenders with a control group of offenders whose cases were retained in juvenile court. The adult court and juvenile court groups were

Opponents of waiver suggest that the transfer process is often applied unfairly and is at odds with the treatment philosophy of the juvenile court. Furthermore, some children tried in the adult criminal court may be incarcerated under conditions so extreme that they will be permanently damaged. Another serious disadvantage of transferring a child is the stigma that may be attached to a conviction in the criminal court. Labeling children as adult offenders early in life may seriously impair their future educational and employment opportunities.

comparable in terms of case characteristics such as offense type, age, and prior offense record. Using data from four jurisdictions, the research team found that processing a waiver case took significantly longer than a comparable juvenile court case (246 days versus 98 days). During most of this added time, the waived youth was held in a detention center. Also, in striking contrast to previous studies, this study found that the waived youths were treated unusually harshly by the adult justice system: 90 percent were convicted; 91 percent of those convicted were incarcerated; and sentences were five times longer than their juvenile court equivalents. For example, the average adult court sentence for murder was 247 months, compared to 55 months for juvenile court sentenced offenders.[78]

■ Transfer decisions may be motivated by administrative and political considerations.

This conclusion was supported by Bortner, who studied the records of 214 youths who were waived to adult court in a western county.[79] These records showed that the waived youths were no more dangerous or unruly than the youths who remained in juvenile courts. Moreover, there was no evidence that these transfers enhanced public safety. Apparently, the juvenile court authorities chose to turn over a small percentage of their clientele—those depicted as the most dangerous element—to the adult courts to convey the appearance of concern for public safety and to satisfy the public appetite for tough treatment of dangerous offenders. In reality, they were able to retain control over the vast majority of youths who were processed by the juvenile system.

■ Transfer decisions are not always carried out fairly or equitably.

prosecutorial discretion
Allowing the prosecutor to determine the jurisdiction by selecting the charge to be filed or by choosing to file the complaint in either juvenile or adult court.

Those who voice this criticism point out that minorities are waived at a rate that is greater than their representation in the population. Jeffrey Fagan and his associates have identified the existence of such racial disparity in decision making from apprehension through the commitment stage.[80] Elizabeth McNulty points out that there is little evidence to support the idea that adult sentencing of juveniles is consistent, equitable, or effective.[81]

Using **prosecutorial discretion** to determine whether to proceed in the juvenile or the criminal justice system is also a much maligned practice (see Table 14.8 for a list of the many factors influencing the waiver decision). Although most states require that a waiver decision be made at a judicial hearing, a few jurisdictions allow the prosecutor to determine jurisdiction by filing a complaint in the juvenile or adult court. In still other jurisdictions, where the juvenile court may have no jurisdiction over certain crimes, the prosecutor can in effect control which court hears the case on the basis of the charge filed against the child. Such an approach eliminates the requirement of a waiver hearing but leaves a great deal of discretion in the hands of the prosecutor.

A recent analysis of juvenile waivers by Frank Zimring argues that, despite its faults, waiver is superior to alternative methods for handling the most serious juvenile offenders.[82] The major argument for waiver rests on the premise that, even though the modern juvenile court is preferable for most juveniles because they are given greater chances for rehabilitation, certain exceptional cases will occur involving serious violent offenses in which the minimum criminal penalty is greater than that available to the juvenile court. Nonetheless, it is equally important to keep in mind the possible consequences of transfers: (1) greater risk to juveniles who could be transferred to an adult jail during trial; (2) punishment that is less swift than juvenile processing; (3) lower conviction rates and shorter incarcerations in the adult system; and (4) higher recidivism rates for youths tried in adult courts.

In summary, the trend has been to increase the flow of juvenile cases to adult courts. This policy change can be attributed to the current get-tough attitude toward the serious, chronic juvenile offender. A number of important questions have been raised about the fairness and propriety of this method of handling serious juvenile cases. The big question is, what is accomplished by treating juveniles like adults? The Case in Point considers the question of waiver.

The issue of waiver has become critical in recent years because transfer to the adult court is viewed as an efficient means of dealing with violent, chronic juvenile offenders. The seriousness of the offense plays a significant role in determining juvenile waiver, as do the number and the nature of prior offenses and prior treatment.[83]

Table 14.8

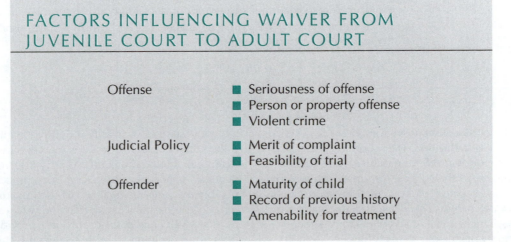

FACTORS INFLUENCING WAIVER FROM JUVENILE COURT TO ADULT COURT

Offense	■ Seriousness of offense
	■ Person or property offense
	■ Violent crime
Judicial Policy	■ Merit of complaint
	■ Feasibility of trial
Offender	■ Maturity of child
	■ Record of previous history
	■ Amenability for treatment

You are a newly appointed judge whose jurisdiction embraces criminal cases heard in the lower criminal court.

One week after his twelfth birthday, Dexter G., an honor student with a strict religious education, had his first contact with the justice system. Dexter was arrested and charged with criminal homicide after he allegedly took his father's rifle, aimed from a third-floor bedroom window, and shot eight-year-old James once in the head as he rode along on his bicycle. James died instantly. Dexter was subsequently released to the custody of his parents.

The law of this jurisdiction requires that all persons charged with murder, regardless of age, stand trial as adults in criminal court. If convicted of murder, Dexter could be sentenced to life imprisonment without parole. The state's Juvenile Court Act has a waiver provision that permits the criminal court judge to transfer the case to juvenile court if the child is under seventeen years of age and if the accused demonstrates that he is amenable to treatment and rehabilitation.

Dexter is a healthy youth with above-average intelligence and no apparent psychological problems. He has shown no emotion or remorse regarding the killing. Psychiatrists who examined Dexter indicate that the boy said he was "playing hunter" when the rifle accidentally discharged.

- If you were the judge, would you transfer the case to the juvenile court for jurisdiction?
- What criteria would you use in making this decision?

Yet studies of the impact of recent changes in waiver statutes have yielded inconclusive results. Meanwhile, more than half of the legislators responding to a national survey on juvenile crime expect to consider waiver legislation that makes it easier to transfer juveniles to adult courts. Clearly the issue of waiver will continue to be debated for some time to come. The Focus on Delinquency box entitled "Transferring Serious Juvenile Offenders to Adult Court" highlights this controversy.

SUMMARY

Many important decisions about what happens to a child may occur prior to adjudication. Detention in secure facilities for those charged with juvenile delinquency and involuntary placement in shelter care for those involved in noncriminal behavior place severe limitations on the rights of the child and the parents. There has been a major effort in the past few years to remove juveniles from detention in adult jails and to make sure status offenders are not placed in secure pretrial detention facilities.

Most statutes ordinarily require a hearing on detention if the initial decision is to keep the child in custody. At a detention hearing the child has a right to counsel and is generally given other procedural due process safeguards, notably the privilege against self-incrimination and the right to confront and cross-examine witnesses. In addition, most state juvenile court procedures provide criteria to be used in deciding whether to detain a child. These include (1) the need to protect the child, (2) the likelihood

TRANSFERRING SERIOUS JUVENILE OFFENDERS TO ADULT COURT

Prior to development of the first modern juvenile court in Illinois in 1899, juveniles were tried for violations of the law in adult criminal courts. The consequences were devastating; many children were treated as criminal offenders and often sentenced to adult prisons. Although the subsequent passage of state legislation creating juvenile courts eliminated this problem, the juvenile justice system did recognize that certain forms of conduct were extreme enough to merit trying children as adults. Today most jurisdictions provide for waiver, or the transfer of juvenile offenders to the criminal courts, by statute. Between 1992 and 1997, forty-eight of fifty-one state legislatures (over 90 percent) made substantive changes to their laws targeting juveniles who commit serious crimes. All but ten states have modified their laws, making it easier to prosecute juveniles in criminal court, and more than half the states have added crimes to the list of excluded offenses.

Three developments led to the increase in the use of waiver procedures: (1) a philosophical shift from an emphasis on rehabilitation to an emphasis on punishment, (2) the increase in violent juvenile crime, and (3) the belief that juvenile courts are not effective.

What is accomplished by treating juveniles like adults? As we've seen, studies of the impact of the recent waiver statutes have yielded inconclusive results. Some juveniles whose cases are waived to criminal court are sentenced more leniently than they would have been in juvenile court. In many states, even when juveniles are tried in criminal court and convicted on the charges, they may still be sentenced to a juvenile or youthful offender institution rather than to an adult prison. The laws may allow them to be transferred to an adult prison when they have reached a certain age. Some studies show that only a small percentage of juveniles tried as adults are incarcerated for periods longer than the terms served by offenders convicted of the same crime in the juvenile court. Moreover, judges tend to sentence sixteen-year-olds appearing in adult court to probation rather than prison. In the end, what began as a get-tough measure has had the opposite effect, while costing taxpayers more money.

Critics view these new methods of dealing with juvenile offenders as inefficient, ineffective, and philosophically out of step with the original concept of the juvenile court. Supporters view the waiver process as a sound method of getting the most serious juvenile offenders off the streets while ensuring that rehabilitation plays a less critical role in the juvenile justice system. No area of juvenile justice has received more attention recently than efforts to redefine the jurisdiction of the juvenile court.

When the twentieth century began, states were following Illinois's lead in rejecting the use of criminal courts and imprisonment to punish children. By transferring more children to adult courts, have juvenile justice policies come full circle in this country?

Sources: James Howell, "Juvenile Transfers to Criminal Courts," *Juvenile & Family Justice Journal* 6:10–13 (1997). Dale Parent et al., *Key Issues in Criminal Justice: Transferring Serious Juvenile Offenders to Adult Courts* (Washington, D.C.: National Institute of Justice, 1997); *Juvenile Justice Reform Initiatives in the States, 1994–1996* (Washington, D.C.: OJJDP, 1997); P. Griffin et al. *Trying Juveniles as Adults in Criminal Court: An Analysis of State Transfer Proceedings* (Washington, D.C.: UJSDP, 1998).

that the child presents a serious danger to the public, and (3) the likelihood that the child will return to court for adjudication.

The intake stage is essentially a screening process to decide what action should be taken regarding matters referred to the court. The law enforcement officer is required to make decisions about court action or referral to social agencies. In addition, it is important for law enforcement agencies and the juvenile courts to have sound working relationships. Their objective is the same: to protect the child and the community.

Throughout the early court stage of the juvenile process, the issue of discretion plays a major role. In the last decade juvenile justice practitioners have made efforts to divert as many children as possible from the juvenile courts and place them in nonsecure treatment programs.

Critics charge that diversion programs actually involve more youths in the justice system than would be the case had the programs not been in operation, a concept referred to as widening the net. Moreover, the effectiveness of diversion as a crime-reducing policy has been questioned.

Those who are held for trial are generally released to their parents, on bail, or through other means, such as on recognizance. Because the juvenile justice system, like the adult system, is not able to try every child accused of a crime or a status offense due to personnel limitations, diversion programs seem to hold greater hope for the prevention and control of delinquency. As a result, such subsystems as diversion, statutory intake proceedings, plea bargaining, and other informal adjustments are essential ingredients in the administration of the juvenile justice system.

An issue related to bail is preventive detention, which refers to the right of a judge to deny persons release before trial on the grounds that they may be dangerous to themselves or others. Advocates of preventive detention argue that dangerous juvenile offenders should not be granted bail and pretrial release because they would then have an opportunity to intimidate witnesses and commit further crimes. Opponents retaliate that defendants are "innocent until proven guilty" and therefore should be allowed freedom before trial.

Prior to the creation of the first modern juvenile court in Illinois in 1899, juveniles were tried in adult criminal courts. However, even with the development of the juvenile court system, it is recognized that certain crimes require that children be tried as adults.

In addition to normal juvenile justice processing, each year thousands of youths are transferred to adult courts because of the serious nature of their crimes. This process, known as waiver, is an effort to remove serious offenders from the juvenile process and into the more punitive adult system. Despite controversy surrounding this practice, most states have modified their laws, making it easier to prosecute juveniles in criminal court. Today, virtually all jurisdictions provide by statute for waiver or transfer of juvenile offenders to the criminal courts. The number of juveniles transferred to criminal court has grown substantially in recent years, although a slight decline occurred in 1995. More research is needed on the impact of transferring juveniles to the adult justice system.

KEY TERMS

transfer hearing	widening the net	waiver
detention	complaint	bindover
shelter care	petition	removal
detention hearing	bail	concurrent jurisdiction
deinstitutionalization	preventive detention	excluded offenses
intake	plea bargaining	judicial waiver
diversion	transfer process	prosecutorial discretion

INFOTRAC COLLEGE EDITION EXERCISES

Read the following article from InfoTrac College edition:

Eight factors to assess in juvenile waivers. Richard J. Gelles. *Behavioral Health* Treatment, Nov 1997

A great deal of controversy surrounds the practice of transferring juveniles to adult court. Many see it as a last resort when dealing with violent juvenile offenders. Others see it as giving up on the child, who is still innocent and therefore not as culpable as an adult. Although each transfer case is looked at individually, the decision to waive is fraught with difficulty. Judges must consider issues such as potential for rehabilitation, past criminal history, and possibility for future harm.

Using the factors that Gelles discusses in his article above, decide whether or not the following hypothetical juvenile offender should be waived to adult court:

James has been charged with the assault of his brother after a heated family argument. James has recently returned from a lengthy stay at the Youth Authority for a previous conviction for numerous violent offences. During his incarceration, he was involved in a number of fights with other inmates and correctional personnel. James has had a history of violent behavior and, according to a court-appointed psychiatrist, has serious anger-management problems. He has also been diagnosed with Attention Deficit Disorder but has not been prescribed any medication. His parents are at their wits end and feel they are unable to care for him anymore. In three years James will turn 18, and the family feels that he will likely end up in prison anyway.

QUESTIONS FOR DISCUSSION

1. Why has the use of jails and detention facilities for children been considered one of the greatest tragedies in the juvenile justice system?

2. Processing juvenile cases in an informal manner—that is, without filing a formal petition—is common in the juvenile court system. Describe some methods of informally handling cases in the juvenile court.

3. The use of diversion programs in the juvenile justice system has become common in an effort to channel cases to noncourt institutions. Discuss the advantages and disadvantages of diversion. Describe diversion programs and their common characteristics.

4. What is the purpose of bail? Do children as well as adults have a constitutional or statutory right to bail? What factors are considered in the release of a child prior to formal adjudication?

5. Under extraordinary circumstances, once juvenile proceedings have begun, the juvenile court may seek to transfer a juvenile to the adult court. This is often referred to as a transfer proceeding. Is such a proceeding justified? Under what conditions? Does the juvenile court afford the public sufficient protection against serious juvenile offenders?

6. Explain the meaning of preventive detention. Is such a concept in conflict with the fundamental principle of presumption of innocence?

7. Do you think plea bargaining for juvenile offenders is desirable? Why or why not?

8. How would you redefine the jurisdiction of the juvenile court?

NOTES

1. American Correctional Association, *Standards for Juvenile Detention Facilities* (Laurel, Md.: ACA, 1991).

2. American Bar Association, *Standards Relating to Interim Status of Juveniles* (Cambridge, Mass.: Ballinger, 1977), p. 4; see also, Robert Shepard, *Juvenile Justice Standards Annotated—A Balanced Approach* (Chicago, Ill.: ABA, 1997).

3. See Community Research Associations, *Michigan Holdover Network—Short-Term Detention Strategies* (Washington, D.C.: U.S. Department of Justice, 1986).

4. Howard Snyder and Melissa Sickmund, *Juvenile Offenders and Victims—A National Report* (Washington, D.C.: OJJDP, 1995), p. 157; Melissa Sickmund et al., *Juvenile Court Statistics—1995* (Pittsburgh, Pa.: National Center for Juvenile Justice, 1998).

5. Sickmund et al., *Juvenile Court Statistics—1995,* p. 38.

6. Ibid., p. 34.

7. Snyder and Sickmund, *Juvenile Offenders and Victims—A National Report,* pp. 143–50.

8. Edward J. Loughran, "How to Stop Our Kids from Going Bad," *Boston Globe* 11 February 1990, p. 42.

9. Ira M. Schwartz and William H. Barton, eds., *Reforming Juvenile Detention—No More Hidden Closets* (Columbus: Ohio State University Press, 1994), p. 176.

10. Belinda McCarthy, "An Analysis of Detention," *Juvenile and Family Court Journal* 36:49–50 (1985).

11. Hubert H. Humphrey Institute of Public Affairs, *The Incarceration of Minority Youth* (Minneapolis: Humphrey Institute, 1986); Katherine Hunt Federle and Meda Chesney-Lind, "Special Issues in Juvenile Justice: Gender, Race and Ethnicity," in Ira Schwartz, ed., *Juvenile Justice and Public Policy* (New York: Lexington Books, 1992), chap. 9.

12. Russell Schutt and Dale Dannefer, "Detention Decisions in Juvenile Cases: JINS, JDs and Genders," *Law and Society Review* 22:509–20 (1988).

13. Charles Frazier and Donna Bishop, "The Pretrial Detention of Juveniles and Its Impact on Case Dispositions," *Journal of Criminal Law and Criminology* 76:1132–52 (1986).

14. L. Rosner, "Juvenile Secure Detention," *Journal of Offender Counseling Services and Rehabilitation* 12:57–76 (1988).

15. David Steinhart, "Objective Juvenile Detention Criteria: The California Experience," in Ira Schwartz and William Barton, eds., *Reforming Juvenile Justice Detention—No More Hidden Closets* (Columbus: Ohio State University Press, 1994), p. 47; see also, David Steinhart, *Status Offenses, The Future of Children—The Juvenile Court* (Los Altos, Calif., David and Lucille Packard Foundation, 1996).

16. American Bar Association, *Standards Relating to Interim Status of Juveniles,* p. 86; Claudia Worrell, "Pretrial Detention of Juveniles: Denial of Equal Protection Marked by the *Parens Patriae* Doctrine," *Yale Law Review* 95:174–93 (1985).

17. Edward Wakin, *Children without Justice—A Report by the National Council of Jewish Women* (New York: National Council of Jewish Women, 1975), p. 43; Ira M. Schwartz, *Justice for Juveniles—Rethinking the Best Interests of the Child* (Lexington, Mass.: D. C. Heath, 1989), chap. 3.

18. S. Smith and D. Roush, "Defining Juvenile Detention Goals: ACA Committee Takes the Lead," *Corrections Today* 51:220–21 (1989); see also Earl Dunlap and David Roush, "Juvenile Detention as Process and Place," *Juvenile and Family Court Journal* 46:1–16 (1995).

19. I. Schwartz, G. Fishman, R. Hatfield, B. A. Krisberg, and Z. Eisikovitz, "Juvenile Detention: The Hidden Closets Revisited," *Justice Quarterly* 4:219–35 (1987); John Criswell, "Juvenile Detention Resource Centers: Florida's Experience Provides a Model for Nation in Juvenile Detention," *Corrections Today* 49:22–26 (1987).

20. *Learning Behind Bars: Selected Educational Programs from Juvenile Jail and Prison Facilities* (Laurel, Ind.: Correctional Education Association, 1989), p. 5; see also, David Roush and Trudy Wyss, *A Resource Manual for Juvenile Detention and Corrections: Effective and Innovative Programs* (Washington D.C.: OJJDP, 1995).

21. Ibid., p. 10.

22. Ibid., p. 13.

23. Schwartz and Barton, eds., *Reforming the Juvenile Justice System—No More Hidden Closets,* p. 176.

24. Juvenile Justice and Delinquency Prevention Act, Sec. 223 (a)(12), 1974, amended 1980.

25. "OJJDP Helps States Remove Juveniles from Jails," *Juvenile Justice Bulletin* (Washington, D.C.: U.S. Department of Justice, 1990).

26. Community Research Associates, *The Jail Removal Initiative: A Summary Report* (Champaign, Ill.: Community Research Associates, 1987).

27. Ibid.

28. Charles Frazier, *Preadjudicatory Detention—From Juvenile Justice: Policies, Programs and Services* (Chicago: Dorsey Press, 1989), pp. 143–68.

29. Ira Schwartz, Linda Harris, and Lauri Levi, "The Jailing of Juveniles in Minnesota," *Crime and Delinquency* 34:131 (1988).

30. See, generally, Ira Schwartz, ed., "Children in Jails," *Crime and Delinquency* 34:131–228 (1988).

31. Schwartz, Harris, and Levi, "The Jailing of Juveniles in Minnesota," p. 134.

32. David Steinhart, "California Legislation Ends Jailing of Children—The Story of a Policy Reversal," *Crime and Delinquency* 34:150 (1988).

33. Henry Swanger, "*Hendrickson v. Griggs*—a Review of Legal and Policy Implications for Juvenile Justice Policymakers," *Crime and Delinquency* 34:209 (1988); *Hendrickson v. Griggs,* 672 F.Supp. 1126 (N.D. Iowa 1987).

34. Melissa Sickmund, Howard Snyder, and Eileen Poe Yamagata, *Juvenile Offenders and Victims: 1997 Update on Violence* (Washington D.C.: OJJDP, 1997).

35. "Assessing the Effects of the Deinstitutionalization of Status Offenders," *Juvenile Justice Bulletin* (Washington, D.C.: U.S. Department of Justice, 1990), p. 1; Snyder and Sickmund, *Juvenile Offenders and Victims—A National Report*, p. 147.

36. Solomon Kobrin and Malcolm Klein, *National Evaluation of the Deinstitutionalization of Status Offender Programs, Executive Summary* (Washington, D.C.: U.S. Department of Justice, 1982); I. Spergel, F. Reamer, and J. Lynch, "Deinstitutionalization of Status Offenders: Individual Outcome and System Effects," *Journal of Research in Crime and Delinquency* 4:32 (1981).

37. M. A. Bortner, Mary Sutherland, and Russ Winn, "Race and the Impact of Juvenile Institutionalization," *Crime and Delinquency* 31:35–46 (1985).

38. Anne L. Schneider, *The Impact of Deinstitutionalization on Recidivism and Secure Confinement of Status Offenders* (Washington, D.C.: U.S. Department of Justice, 1985); for a similar view, see Susan Datesman and Mikel Aickin, "Offense Specialization and Escalation among Status Offenders," *Journal of Criminal Law and Criminology* 75:1246–75 (1984).

39. Duran Bell and Kevin Lang, "The Intake Dispositions of Juvenile Offenders," *Journal of Research in Crime and Delinquency* 22:309–28 (1985); Federle and Chesney-Lind, "Special Issues in Juvenile Justice: Gender, Race and Ethnicity," p. 189; Kimberly Budnick and Ellen Shields-Fletcher, "What About Girls," Fact Sheet 84 (Washington, D.C.: OJJDP, 1998).

40. David Steinhart, "Status Offenders," *The Future of Children—The Juvenile Court,* 1996, p. 96.

41. National Council on Crime and Delinquency, *Standard Family Court Act* (San Francisco, Calif.: NCCD, 1979), p. 12; William Sheridan, *Model Acts for Juvenile and Family Courts,* p. 13; National Conference of Commissioners on Uniform State Laws, *Uniform Juvenile Court Act,* p. 9.

42. Leona Lee, "Factors Influencing Intake Disposition in a Juvenile Court," *Juvenile and Family Court Journal* 46:43–62 (1995).

43. H. Ted Rubin, "The Emerging Prosecutor Dominance of the Juvenile Court Intake Process," *Crime and Delinquency* 26:299–318 (1980).

44. Ibid., p. 318; see also, James C. Backstrom and Gary Walker, "A Balanced Approach to Juvenile Justice," *The Prosecutor* 32:36–38 (1998).

45. Paul Nejelski, "Diversion: The Promise and the Danger," *Crime and Delinquency Journal* 22:393–410 (1976); Kenneth Polk, "Juvenile Diversion: A Look at the Record," *Crime and Delinquency* 30:648–59 (1984).

46. President's Commission on Law Enforcement and Administration of Justice, *Task Force Report: Juvenile Delinquency and Youth Crime* (Washington, D.C.: U.S. Government Printing Office, 1967).

47. Ibid.

48. See Raymond T. Nimmer, *Diversion—The Search for Alternative Forms of Prosecution* (Chicago: American Bar Foundation, 1974); Mark Ezell, "Juvenile Arbitration: Net-Widening and Other Unintended Consequences," *Journal of Research in Crime and Delinquency* 26:358–77 (1989).

49. Edwin E. Lemert, "Diversion in Juvenile Justice: What Hath Been Wrought," *Journal of Research in Crime and Delinquency* 18:34–46 (1981).

50. Don C. Gibbons and Gerald F. Blake, "Evaluating the Impact of Juvenile Diversion Programs," *Crime and Delinquency Journal* 22:411–19 (1976); Richard J. Lundman, "Will Diversion Reduce Recidivism?" *Crime and Delinquency Journal* 22:428–37 (1976); B. Bullington, J. Sprowls, D. Katkin, and M. Phillips, "A Critique of Diversionary Juvenile Justice," *Crime and Delinquency* 24:59–71 (1978); Thomas Blomberg, "Diversion and Accelerated Social Control," *Journal of Criminal Law and Criminology* 68:274–82 (1977); Sharla Rausch and Charles Logan, "Diversion from Juvenile Court: Panacea or Pandora's Box," in J. Klugel, ed., *Evaluating Juvenile Justice* (Beverly Hills, Calif.: Sage, 1983), pp. 19–30.

51. Charles Frazier and John Cochran, "Official Intervention, Diversion from the Juvenile Justice System, and Dynamics of Human Services Work: Effects of a Reform Goal Based on Labeling Theory," *Crime and Delinquency* 32:157–76 (1986); Charles Frazier and Sara Lee, "Reducing Juvenile Detention Rates or Expanding the Official Control Nets: An Evaluation of a Legislative Reform Effort," *Crime and Delinquency* 38:204–14 (1992).

52. Dennis Anderson and Donald Schoen, "Diversion Programs: Effect of Stigmatization on Juvenile/Status Offenders," *Juvenile and Family Court Journal* 36:13–25 (1985).

53. Rausch and Logan, "Diversion from Juvenile Court," p. 20.

54. Frazier and Cochran, "Official Intervention, Diversion from the Juvenile Justice System, and Dynamics of Human Services Work," p. 171.

55. Arnold Binder and Gilbert Geis, "Ad Populum Argumentation in Criminology: Juvenile Diversion as Rhetoric," *Criminology* 30:309–33 (1984).

56. Mark Ezell, "Juvenile Diversion: The Ongoing Search for Alternatives," in Ira M. Schwartz, ed., *Juvenile Justice and Public Policy* (New York: Lexington Books, 1992), pp. 45–59.

57. Mark Soler, James Bell, Elizabeth Jameson, Carole Shauffer, Alice Shotton, and Loren Warboys, *Representing the Child Client* (New York: Matthew Bender, 1989), Sec. 5.03b.

58. *Schall v. Martin,* 467 U.S. 253, (1984).

59. James Brown, Robert Shepard, and Andrew Shookhoff, *Preventive Detention after Schall v. Martin* (Washington, D.C.: American Bar Association, 1985); Michael O'Rourke, "Juvenile Justice—Preventive Detention of Juveniles: Have They Held Your Child Today: *Schall v. Martin,*" *Southern Illinois University Law Journal* 4:315–33 (1985).

60. Jeffrey Fagan and Martin Guggenheim, "Preventive Detention for Juveniles: A Natural Experiment," *Journal of Criminal Law and Criminology,* 86:415–28 (1996).

61. Albert W. Alschuler, "The Prosecutor's Role in Plea Bargaining," *University of Chicago Law Review* 36:50–112 (1968); Joyce Dougherty, "A Comparison of Adult Plea Bargaining and Juvenile Intake," *Federal Probation* (June):72–79 (1988).

62. Sanford Fox, *Juvenile Courts in a Nutshell* (St. Paul, Minn.: West, 1985), pp. 154–56.

63. See Darlene Ewing, "Juvenile Plea Bargaining: A Case Study," *American Journal of Criminal Law* 6:167 (1978); Adrienne Volenik, *Checklists for Use in Juvenile Delinquency Proceedings* (Chicago: American Bar Association, 1985); Bruce Green, "Package Plea Bargaining and the Prosecutor's Duty of Good Faith," *Criminal Law Bulletin* 25:507–50 (1989).

64. Joseph Sanborn, Plea Negotiations in Juvenile Court (Ph.D. thesis, State University of New York at Albany, 1984); Joseph

Sanborn, "Philosophical, Legal and Systematic Aspects of Juvenile Court Plea Bargaining," *Crime and Delinquency* 39:509–27 (1993).

65. National Council of Juvenile and Family Court Judges, "The Juvenile Court and Serious Offenders," *Juvenile and Family Court Journal* 35:13 (1984).

66. Melissa Sickmund, *How to Get Juveniles to Criminal Court, OJJDP Update on Statistics* (Washington, D.C.: Bureau of Justice Statistics, 1994); Eric Fritsch and Craig Hemmens, "Juvenile Waiver in the United States 1979–1995—A Comparison and Analysis of State Waiver Statutes," *Juvenile and Family Court Journal* 46:17–36 (1995).

67. Ind. Code Ann. 31-6-2(d) 1987; Ill.Ann.Stat. Ch. 37 Sec. 805 (1988); Penn. Stat. Ann. Title 42 6355(a) (1982); Patrick Griffin et al., *Trying Juveniles as Adults in Criminal Court: An Analysis of State Transfer Provisions* (Washington, D.C.: OJJDP, 1998).

68. Joseph White, "The Waiver Decision: A Judicial, Prosecutorial or Legislative Responsibility," *Justice for Children* 2:28–30 (1987).

69. *Kent v. United States,* 383 U.S. 541, 86 S.Ct. 1045, 16 L.Ed.2d 84 (1966); *Breed v. Jones,* 421 U.S. 519, 95 S.Ct. 1179, 44 L.Ed.2d 346 (1975).

70. Barry Feld, "Delinquent Careers and Criminal Policy," *Criminology* 21:195–212 (1983).

71. Barry Feld, "The Juvenile Court Meets the Principle of the Offense: Legislative Changes in Juvenile Waiver Statutes," *Journal of Criminal Law and Criminology* 78:471–534 (1987); Paul Marcotte, "Criminal Kids," *American Bar Association Journal* 76:60–66 (1990); Dale Parent et al., *Transferring Serious Juvenile Offenders to Adult Courts* (Washington D.C.: U.S. Department of Justice, National Institute of Justice, 1997).

72. Sickmund et al., *Juvenile Court Statistics 1995,* p. 13.

73. Ibid.

74. Ibid.

75. Robert Shepard, "The Rush to Waive Children to Adult Courts," *American Bar Association Journal of Criminal Justice* 10:39–42 (1995); see also, Kevin Strom and Steven Smith, *Juvenile Felony Defendants in Criminal Courts* (Washington, D.C.: Bureau of Justice Statistics, 1998).

76. Richard Allinson and Joan Potter, "Is New York's Tough Juvenile Law a Charade?" *Corrections* 9:40–45 (1983).

77. Snyder and Sickmund, *Juvenile Offenders and Victims—A National Report,* p. 157; Eric Fritsch, Tory Caeti, and Craig Hemmens, "Spare the Needle But Not the Punishment—The Incarceration of Waived Youth in Texas Prisons," *Crime and Delinquency,* 42:593-610 (1996).

78. Cary Rudman, Eliot Hartstone, Jeffrey Fagan, and Melinda Moore, "Violent Youth in Adult Court: Process and Punishment," *Crime and Delinquency* 32:75–96 (1986).

79. M. A. Bortner, "Traditional Rhetoric, Organizational Realities: Remand of Juveniles to Adult Court," *Crime and Delinquency* 32:53–73 (1986).

80. Jeffrey Fagan, Martin Forst, and T. Scott Vivona, "Racial Determinants of the Judicial Transfer Decision: Prosecuting Violent Youth in Criminal Court," *Crime and Delinquency* 33:359–86 (1987); J. Fagan, E. Slaughter, and E. Hartstone, "Blind Justice: The Impact of Race on the Juvenile Justice Process," *Crime and Delinquency* 53:224–58 (1987); J. Fagan and E. P. Deschenes, "Determinants of Judicial Waiver Decisions for Violent Juvenile Offenders," *Journal of Criminal Law and Criminology* 81:314–47 (1990); see also, James Howell, "Juvenile Transfers to Criminal Court," *Juvenile and Family Justice Journal* 6: 12–14 (1997).

81. Elizabeth McNulty, The Transfer of Juvenile Offenders to Adult Court: Panacea or Problem?, unpublished paper presented at the American Society of Criminology Annual Meeting, Boston, Mass., November 1995.

82. Frank Zimring, "Treatment of Hard Cases in American Juvenile Justice: In Defense of the Discretionary Waiver," *Notre Dame Journal of Law, Ethics and Policy* 5:267–80 (1991); Lawrence Winner, Lonn Kaduce, Donna Bishop and Charles Frazier, "The Transfer of Juveniles to Criminal Courts: Reexamining Recidivism over the Long Term," *Crime and Delinquency,* 43:548–64 (1997).

83. F. W. Barnes and R. S. Franz, "Questionably Adult: Determinants and Effects of the Juvenile Waiver Decision," *Justice Quarterly* 6:117–35 (1989).

Chapter Fifteen

The Juvenile Trial and Disposition

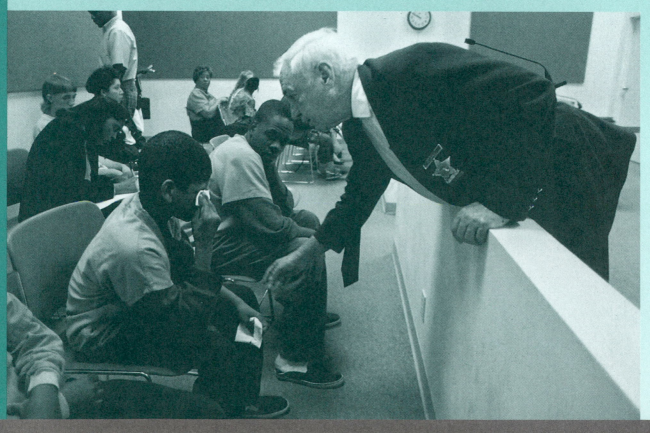

David appeared before a Massachusetts Juvenile Court Judge in December 1998 charged with auto theft. Only twelve years old, he was notorious for having stolen more cars than most people own in their lifetime, and everyone in the juvenile court knew it. Wanting David to spend Christmas at home instead of in a detention center, the judge made him promise that he would not get into further difficulty. Sealing the promise with a handshake, the judge released David. But before the Christmas holidays were over, David was brought into the juvenile court on more serious charges. After being convicted of robbing a fast-food store with two friends, the judge sentenced David to the Department of Juvenile Justice, where he was committed to a secure institution.

Like many other children, David had been involved with government agencies all his life. He was born to an alcoholic mother who beat him regularly. At age 6 an uncle promised him a safe haven but instead repeatedly raped him. David had been in and out of more institutions than he could remember.

Why didn't he keep his promise to stay out of trouble? He had never known anyone to keep a promise to him. If the juvenile court system had more understanding of David's problems and if the proper intervention and prevention programs had been in place, perhaps David would not have been before the court that day.

Unfortunately such careful consideration is a luxury in light of the magnitude of cases handled by the nation's juvenile courts each year. The latest study found that the nation's juvenile courts petitioned and formally processed an estimated 938,400 delinquency offense cases and 73,000 status offense cases (see Figures 15.1 and 15.2). This estimate does not take into account the hundreds of thousands of informally handled or nonpetitioned cases adjusted or diverted by the courts. Thus, the nation's juvenile court system continues to deal with an enormous number of youths who need care, protection, treatment, and control.

Throughout its history, the juvenile court has played a major role in helping to care for troubled youths who come before it. In fact, its influence is

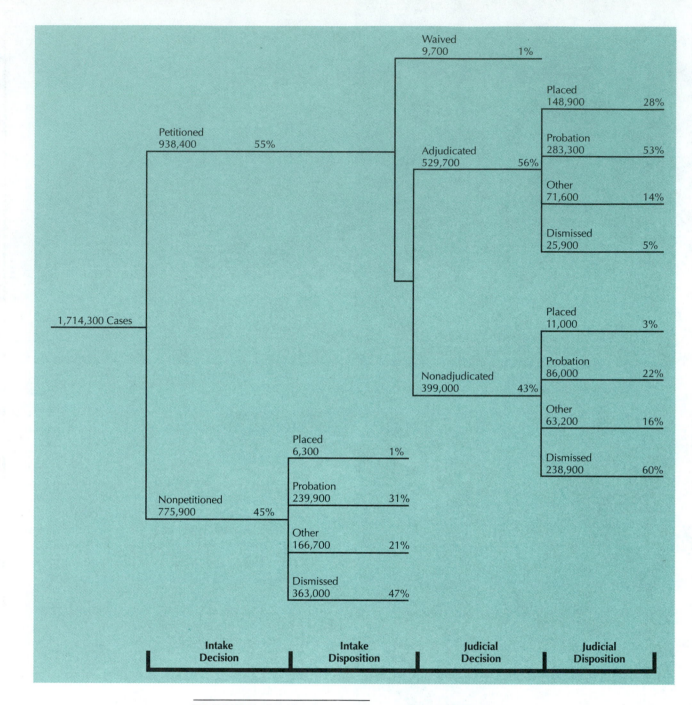

Intake
Decision

Intake
Disposition

Judicial
Decision

Judicial
Disposition

FIGURE 15.1

Juvenile Court Processing of Delinquency Cases, 1995

Source: Melissa Sickmund, *Juvenile Court Statistics 1995* (Pittsburgh, Pa.: National Center for Juvenile Justice, 1998).

Note: Detail may not add to totals due to rounding.

probably greater than that of the adult court because it is also charged with the care and treatment of offenders, not merely with their punishment and control.[1] The court and its representatives must consider their actions carefully, because any decision can have long-term consequences for young offenders who require both treatment and punishment.

In this chapter we describe the adjudication stage of the juvenile justice process. As Figures 15.1 and 15.2 show, about 56 percent of all formally processed cases, or

A car-jacking in progress on a city street corner. Many young juveniles become repeat offenders, and the court's actions can have long-term consequences for young offenders who require both treatment and punishment.

FIGURE 15.2

Juvenile Court Processing of Petitioned Status Offense Cases, 1995

Source: Melissa Sickmund, *Juvenile Court Statistics 1995* (Pittsburgh, Pa.: National Center for Juvenile Justice, 1998).

Note: Detail may not add to totals due to rounding.

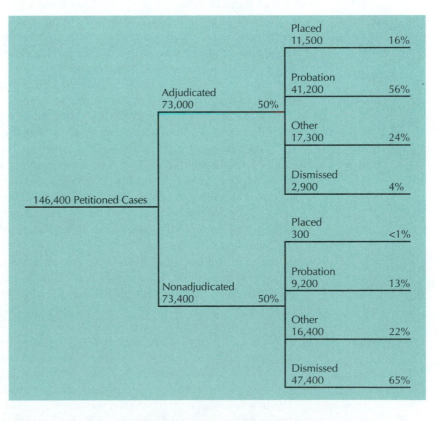

529,700 youths, are adjudicated as delinquent, and 50 percent of all petitioned status offense cases, or 73,000 youths, were adjudicated in 1995.[2] The term *adjudication* refers to the trial stage of the juvenile court proceedings. In this chapter we initially explore the operation of the juvenile court and the role of the important legal actors in the trial and disposition—the juvenile court prosecutor, the judge, the defense attorney, and the probation officer. In addition, we look at the constitutional and due process rights of the child at trial—particularly those rights dealing with counsel and trial by jury—through a detailed analysis of landmark U.S. Supreme Court decisions. Various procedural rules that govern the adjudicatory and dispositional hearings are also reviewed. We conclude the chapter with a discussion of dispositional alternatives and trends in sentencing that affect juvenile dispositions.

The Juvenile Court and Its Jurisdiction

juvenile court
Court that has original jurisdiction over persons defined by statute as juveniles and alleged to be delinquents, status offenders, or dependents.

jurisdiction
Every kind of judicial action; the authority of courts and judicial officers to decide cases.

The **juvenile court** is the centerpiece of the juvenile justice system (Figure 15.3). It plays a major role in controlling juvenile behavior and delivering social services to children in need. Efforts to control juvenile crime depend largely on how the juvenile court is organized and on what laws apply to those who appear before it. Roscoe Pound, one of the most important teachers and writers about jurisprudence in our history, was of the opinion that the juvenile court was one of the great social inventions of the twentieth century.[3]

Today's juvenile court is a specialized court for children. Its organizational structure varies in each state. A juvenile court can be (1) a special session of a lower court of trial **jurisdiction,** (2) part of a high court of general trial jurisdiction, (3) an independent statewide court, or even (4) part of a broader family court. The juvenile court includes a judge, probation staff, government prosecutors and defense attorneys, and a variety of social service programs. The court seeks to promote rehabilitation within a framework of procedural due process. It is concerned with acting both in the best interest of the child and in the best interest of public protection—often incompatible goals. At the same time, the juvenile courts are faced with an increasing and changing workload. They handle almost 5,000 delinquency cases each day, which amounts to more than 1,750,000 cases each year.

Juvenile court jurisdiction is defined by state statutes, constitutional amendments, or state legislation. The New York Family Court, for example, claims its roots from the New York Constitution; legislation serves merely to implement the constitutional mandate and specify the details of the court's makeup and operation. More often, juvenile courts are created by the authority of the legislature. Thus, the jurisdiction itself is generally controlled by legislative enactment.

Most juvenile courts in the United States are established as lower courts of limited jurisdiction as part of a district court, city court, or recorder's court and are limited solely to juvenile delinquency matters. Salaries, physical facilities, and even the prestige of the court can all be directly affected by its jurisdictional location. These factors tend to influence the ability of the court to attract competent personnel, including judges, and to obtain necessary resources from the state legislature.

It is unclear why juvenile courts have been structured as part of lower trial courts in many states. Quite possibly it was to provide local attention to juvenile matters, as some experts believe a lower court relates more efficiently and effectively to the concerns of parents and young people in the local community. In addition, legislators may have seen the juvenile court as an inferior court, relegated to the lowest level simply because of its jurisdiction over children.

However, an increasing number of states are now placing juvenile matters at the highest court of general trial jurisdiction. Here, juvenile cases are tried in the more prestigious courts of general jurisdiction. States that deal with juvenile matters at the highest trial court level have an integrated organizational structure that re-

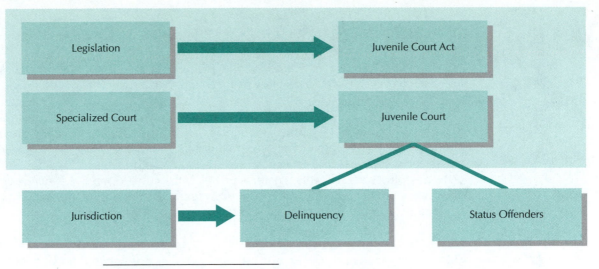

FIGURE 15.3

Juvenile Justice System

sults in more efficient and effective court administration. Such courts are also better able to secure the funding they need to improve physical facilities and hire competent judicial and probation personnel.

Some states have independent juvenile court systems. Such systems may be referred to as statewide juvenile or family courts. These courts often have broad jurisdiction over family matters such as delinquency, neglect, paternity, adoption, child support, and even marriage and divorce. The major advantages to the statewide independent system are that it can serve sparsely populated areas within a given jurisdiction, it permits judicial personnel and others to deal exclusively with children's matters, and it can obtain legislative funding better than other court systems. However, what may be a benefit—obtaining legislative funding—can also act as a detriment. Separately organized juvenile courts encounter resistance from legislators concerned with duplication of effort who may be unwilling to provide resources for the control and prevention of juvenile delinquency.

Family courts have broad jurisdiction over family matters such as neglect, paternity, child support, and delinquency. The key disadvantage of implementing a family court structure is that it requires major reorganization of the existing court system by the legislature. The costs are substantial, especially in the first few years of the court's existence. Where family court structures do exist, little statistical data has been collected that indicate that these courts have reduced delinquency or improved family programs.

It has become apparent to some experts, however, that to treat the related problems of intrafamily crime, divorce, and child neglect in separate courts is to encourage inconsistency in court administration and decision making and to foster ineffective case-flow management. Thus, they believe it would be preferable to deal with juvenile matters in a family court system. Where drug-related juvenile delinquency is on the rise, some jurisdictions have even experimented with juvenile drug courts (see the Policy and Practice box entitled "The Juvenile Drug Court Movement").

Age

The states differ over the age that brings children under the original jurisdiction of the juvenile court.[4] Most states include all children under age 18. Others set the upper limit at under age 17. Still other states have established the juvenile age as under 16.

THE JUVENILE DRUG COURT MOVEMENT

Many nonviolent, substance-abusing adult and juvenile offenders repeatedly cycle through the judicial system because of a lack of intervention measures that would provide the sanctions and services necessary to change their deviant behavior. To address this problem, some communities have established adult and juvenile drug courts. Beginning as a grassroots initiative, drug courts have spread across the nation. Currently, more than two hundred drug court programs are under way, with twenty-five dedicated to juveniles. Local teams of judges, prosecutors, attorneys, treatment providers, law enforcement officials, and others are using the coercive power of the court to force abstinence and to alter behavior with a combination of intensive judicial supervision, escalating sanctions, mandatory drug testing, treatment, and strong aftercare programs.

INCEPTION

Title V of the Violent Crime Control and Law Enforcement Act of 1994 (P. L. 103–322) authorizes the attorney general to make grants to state courts, local courts, and units of local government to establish drug courts. In 1997 the U.S. Department of Justice Drug Court Grant Program appropriated over $30 million to states for the development of drug courts.

The population and caseloads of most juvenile courts have changed dramatically during the past decade. Drug cases have increased 82 percent since 1991, with juvenile courts handling an estimated 125,000 delinquency cases involving drug law violators in 1996. In addition, juvenile arrests involving drug offenses doubled between 1991 and 1995. There has also been a sharp increase in the number of drug cases involving white juveniles. As a result, jurisdictions are trying to determine if juvenile drug courts can effectively deal with the increasing number of substance-abusing juvenile offenders.

THE PROGRAM

Juvenile drug courts face unique challenges not encountered in other juvenile justice programs, such as the need to

- counteract the negative influences of peers, gangs and family members.
- comply with confidentiality requirements in juvenile proceedings while obtaining information to address the juvenile's problems and progress.
- motivate juvenile offenders to change their behavior, especially given their lack of maturity.

At one time, some jurisdictions established age ranges that varied according to the sex or geographic location of the juvenile, but statutes employing these distinctions have been held to be in violation of the equal protection clause or due process clause of the U.S. Constitution. For example, in the case of *Lamb v. Brown*—an Oklahoma statute that allowed females under age 18 the benefits of juvenile court proceedings but limited the same benefits to males under age 16—this variation according to sex was held to be unconstitutional.[5]

A few state statutes describe juvenile court jurisdiction in terms of minimum age. For example, a child may be defined as a person who is under seventeen but over seven years of age. In most states, court jurisdiction is defined by the common law understanding of the responsibility of children. Under the age of seven, children are deemed incapable of committing crimes. There is a rebuttable presumption that children between the ages of seven and fourteen do not have the capacity for criminal behavior. This type of presentation may be overcome or rebutted through

As a result, the juvenile drug court movement has developed special strategies that differ from those of traditional juvenile courts:

- Earlier and more comprehensive intake assessment

- Greater focus on functioning of juveniles and family throughout the court process

- Greater coordination among the court, treatment groups, the school system, and other agencies in responding to the needs of the juvenile and court

- More active supervision of the juvenile's case

- Increased use of immediate sanctions for noncompliance with the drug court program

JUVENILE DRUG COURT IN ACTION

Here is a description of a typical juvenile drug court operation.

The Escambia County Juvenile Drug Court in Pensacola, Florida, is a twelve-month, three-phase approach to treating substance abuse/use/addiction. Phase I lasts approximately two months, Phase II lasts four months, and Phase III lasts six months. The drug court judge supervises and reinforces treatment of up to forty offenders by reviewing reports from the treatment provider to determine the need for either positive or negative incentives to encourage compliance and by holding regular status hearings for program participants. More frequent and intensive treatment services are offered during the early stages of the program. Treatment focuses on motivation and commitment to treatment, the recovery process, development of a drug-free support system, relapse prevention, and preparation for aftercare. Two residential treatment beds are available for the program. Overall, this program provides early intervention and serves as a meaningful alternative to incarceration for the offender who can function adequately in the community with support. The goal of the program is to reduce the recidivism rate for those offenders who successfully complete the program.

Many juvenile justice programs work, others don't. Scientific evidence is needed to establish if juvenile drug courts can be effective in reducing drug use in juvenile offenders.

Source: Marilyn Roberts, Jennifer Brophy, and Carolyn Cooper, *The Juvenile Drug Court Movement* (Washington, D.C.: OJJDP, 1997); Jeffrey Butts, *Drug Offenses in Juvenile Court 1985–1995* (Washington, D.C.: OJJDP, 1997).

introduction of the contrary evidence that shows the child has the capacity to commit a crime. Over the age of fourteen, children are believed to be responsible for their actions. Some states believe below a minimum age the child is powerless to act and therefore not accountable for criminal conduct.

Delinquency

Juvenile court jurisdiction is also based on the nature of the child's actions. If a child commits a crime, the offense normally falls under the category of juvenile delinquency. Definitions of delinquency vary from state to state but most are based on the common element of a maximum age as well as on the fact that delinquency

JUVENILE DELINQUENCY IN THE FEDERAL JUDICIAL SYSTEM

DEFINING DELINQUENCY IN THE FEDERAL COURT SYSTEM

An act of juvenile delinquency is a violation of federal law committed by a person prior to age 18 that would have been a crime if committed by an adult. Under federal law, a person accused of an act of juvenile delinquency may be processed as a juvenile provided the person has not attained age 21.

Adjudication of juveniles in the federal system is limited. Federal law requires that prosecutors restrict proceedings against juveniles to those cases in which they certify to the court that there is a substantial federal interest in the case and

■ the state does not have jurisdiction or refuses to assume jurisdiction;

■ the state with jurisdiction does not have adequate programs or services for juvenile offenders; or

■ the offense charged is a violent felony, a drug trafficking or importation offense, or a firearms offense.

Unlike state-level criminal justice systems, the federal system does not have a separate juvenile justice component. Juveniles are adjudicated by a U.S. district court judge or magistrate in a closed hearing without a jury. After a juvenile has been adjudicated delinquent, a hearing concerning the disposition of the juvenile is held. During the disposition hearing, a juvenile may be ordered to pay restitution, be placed on probation, or be committed to a correctional facility.

TRANSFER TO ADULT STATUS

A person who committed an offense prior to age 18 may be adjudicated as an adult if

■ the offense charged was a violent felony or drug trafficking or importation offense and if the offense was committed after the person's fifteenth birthday.

is an intentional violation of the criminal law (see the Focus on Delinquency box entitled "Juvenile Delinquency in the Federal System.")

As discussed in the previous chapter, there has been an increased use of waivers to adult courts. In recent years state legislatures, concerned about serious juvenile crime, have passed laws automatically excluding serious offenses from the jurisdiction of the juvenile court. For example, a state may exclude crimes punishable by death or life in prison allegedly committed by juveniles over fourteen years of age and robbery committed with a dangerous weapon if the accused is over sixteen years of age. However, such cases can be transferred back to juvenile court from the adult court at the discretion of the adult court judge. Other recent measures call for states to lower the allowable age for transfer of juveniles to age 14, or younger, and even use age 15 or 16 as the upper age for juvenile delinquency jurisdiction.[6]

Such trends reflect a "toughening up" of juvenile justice policy—removing young offenders from the jurisdiction of the juvenile court so that they can be tried and punished as adults and eventually sentenced to adult prisons. However, this does not mean that the juvenile court has totally abandoned its rehabilitative ideals. Some states still require that juveniles manifest a "need for treatment" or supervision before they can be declared delinquents or status offenders; committing an illegal

- the person possessed a firearm during a violent offense and the offense was committed after the person's thirteenth birthday.
- the person had been previously adjudicated delinquent of a violent felony or drug offense.

NUMBER OF DELINQUENTS IN THE FEDERAL SYSTEM

During 1995, U.S. attorneys filed cases against 240 persons for alleged acts of juvenile delinquency. Of these, 122 cases were adjudicated in federal court, representing 0.2 percent of the 56,243 cases (both adult and juvenile) adjudicated during 1995. Almost half of juvenile delinquency cases involved a violent offense (32 percent) or a drug offense (15 percent). Federal prosecutors declined further action against 228 other juveniles referred to them.

Many of the juveniles adjudicated in the federal system are Native Americans. When Native American tribal jurisdictions lack resources or jurisdiction or when there is a substantial federal interest, a U.S. attorney may initiate juvenile delinquency proceedings. Further, the federal government has jurisdiction over certain offenses committed on reservation land.

Of those juveniles adjudicated delinquent during 1995, 37 percent were committed to a correctional facility, 59 percent were placed on probation, and 4 percent received a sentence that did not include supervision or confinement.

JUVENILES IN STATE COURT

In contrast to the federal system, the state systems frequently charge juveniles with delinquency. During 1995 there were more than 1.7 million delinquency cases in courts with juvenile jurisdiction. Juvenile state courts handle virtually all of the juvenile delinquency cases in the United States. Consequently, juvenile prosecution is truly a state responsibility. No federal juvenile court exists in the U.S. federal court system.

Sources: John Scalia, *Juvenile Delinquents in the Federal Criminal Justice System* (Washington, D.C.: U.S. Department of Justice, 1997); 18 United States Code Sec. 5031.

act is not enough for the state to take control of a child. So there is still recognition that the juvenile court's mandate is something other than control and punishment.

Status Offenders

Juvenile courts also have jurisdiction over status offenders, children who commit offenses for which adults are not normally prosecuted. Some juvenile delinquency statutes still include status offenses within their definition, but most states now have separate PINS and CHINS (persons or children in need of supervision) statutes so that separate proceedings can be held for children who are runaways, unmanageable, truant, or incorrigible.

The position of status offenders within the juvenile justice system remains controversial. One of the most difficult problems with such jurisdiction is the statutes themselves. The descriptions of behavior commonly included in these statutes—for example, "unmanageable," "unruly," and "in danger of leading an idle, dissolute, lewd, or immoral life"—have been challenged in court for being unconstitutionally

Status offender statutes typically include behavior that is "unmanageable," "unruly," and "in danger of leading to an idle, dissolute, lewd, or immoral life." Sometimes these definitions are so broad that they have been challenged in court for being unconstitutionally vague and indefinite. However, most statutes have been upheld because of their overall concern for the welfare of the child.

vague and indefinite. However, the courts that have addressed this issue of vagueness have nonetheless upheld the breadth of the statutes in view of their overall concern for the welfare of the child.[7]

The removal of status offenders from secure lockups with delinquent youths has been one of the more successful justice-related policy initiatives (see Chapter 14). Almost all states have legally prohibited incarcerating status offenders with delinquents. For example, a West Virginia court prohibited housing status offenders in "secure, prison-like facilities which also house children guilty of criminal conduct or needlessly subject status offenders to the degradation and physical abuse of incarceration."[8] However, it is not uncommon for judges to get around these prohibitions by holding status offenders in contempt of court if they refuse to honor judicial decrees; a number of states have permitted these youths to then be held in secure detention facilities.[9]

The status offense category often becomes a catchall for offenders who do not fit anywhere else. If there is not enough evidence to support a finding of delinquency, prosecutors sometimes charge youths with being status offenders on the grounds that their behavior endangered their morals, their health, or their general welfare. Defense attorneys should welcome the substitution of categories as it means their clients will not be subject to the same degree of confinement and control as they would be if they had been found delinquent.

Today the juvenile court still retains jurisdiction over status offenses in every state, although processing of these cases varies from virtually no intervention in some locales to highly developed intervention programs in others. Most status offense cases are not formally processed by the court. Many cases are diverted to community service programs or handled in other forums without filing case petitions. Truancy cases, for example, are often processed through local school systems without involving the court.[10]

Juvenile Courtroom Players

The key players in the adjudicatory process are prosecutors, judges, and defense attorneys.

The Prosecutor in the Juvenile Court

juvenile prosecutor
Government attorney responsible for representing the interests of the state and bringing the case against the accused juvenile.

The **juvenile prosecutor** is the government attorney responsible for representing the interests of the state and bringing the state's case against the accused juvenile. Depending on the level of government and the jurisdiction, the prosecutor can be called a district attorney, a county attorney, a state attorney, or a United States attorney. Prosecutors are members of the bar selected for their positions and by political appointment or popular election.

Ordinarily, the juvenile prosecutor is a staff member of the local prosecuting attorney's office. If the office of the district attorney is in an urban area and of sufficient size, the juvenile prosecutor may work exclusively on juvenile and other family law matters. If the caseload of juvenile offenders is small, the juvenile prosecutor may also have criminal prosecution responsibilities.

For the first sixty years of its existence the juvenile court did not include a prosecutor as a representative of the state in court proceedings.[11] The concept of advocacy and the adversary process were seen as inconsistent with the philosophy of diagnosis and treatment in the juvenile court system. The court followed a social service helping model, and informal, noncriminal proceedings were believed to be in the best interests of the child.

As we've seen, these views changed dramatically with the Supreme Court decisions of *Kent v. United States, In re Gault,* and *In re Winship,* which ushered in an era of greater formality and due process rights for children in the juvenile court system.[12] Today, almost all jurisdictions require by law that a prosecutor be present in the juvenile court.

The prosecutor's role in juvenile court is expanding. A number of states have passed legislation giving prosecutors control over intake and waiver decisions. Some have passed concurrent jurisdiction laws that allow prosecutors to decide in which court to bring serious juvenile cases. In some jurisdictions, it is the prosecutor and not the juvenile court judge who is entrusted with making the critical decision of whether to transfer a case to adult court. Consequently, the role of juvenile court prosecutor is now critical in the juvenile justice process.

In the words of the American Bar Association, "An attorney for the state, hereinafter referred to as the juvenile prosecutor, should participate in every proceeding of every stage of every case subject to the jurisdiction of the family court in which the state has an interest."[13] Including a prosecutor in juvenile court balances the respective interests of the state, the defense attorney, the child, and the judge, preserving the independence of each party's functions and responsibilities.

A prosecutor enforces the law, represents the government, maintains proper standards of ethical conduct as an attorney and court officer, participates in programs and legislation involving legal changes in the juvenile justice system, acts as a spokesperson for the field of law, and takes an active role in the community in preventing delinquency and protecting the rights of juveniles. Of these functions, representing the government while presenting the state's case to the court occurs most frequently. In this regard, prosecutors may perform these tasks:

- Investigate possible violations of the law
- Cooperate with the police, intake officer, and probation officer in ascertaining the facts alleged in the petition
- Authorize, review, and prepare petitions for court
- Play a role in the initial detention decision
- Represent the case in all pretrial motions, probable cause hearings, and consent decrees
- Represent the state at transfer hearings
- Recommend, if necessary, physical or mental examinations for children brought before the court

- Seek amendments or dismissals of filed petitions if appropriate
- Represent the state at the adjudication of the case
- Represent the state at the disposition sentencing phase of the case
- Enter into plea bargaining discussions with the defense attorney
- Represent the government on appeal and in habeas corpus proceedings
- Be involved in hearings dealing with violations of probation

The prosecutor has the power either to initiate or to discontinue delinquency or status offense allegations brought against a juvenile. Like police officers, they have broad discretion in the exercise of their duties. Because due process rights have been extended to juveniles, the prosecutor's role in the juvenile court has in some ways become similar to the prosecutor's role in the adult court. Court decisions such as *In re Gault* demonstrate the judicial movement toward developing court procedures for juveniles that are similar to those for adults. However, it is important for the juvenile prosecutor not only to represent the government but also to remain cognizant of the philosophy and purpose of the juvenile court.

Although it may seem evident that prosecutors are beginning to play an expanded role in juvenile courts, the actual impact of their presence is open to debate. To define the role of the prosecutor in juvenile court, some states have attempted to draw up general policy guidelines or principles for juvenile prosecution based on the recent *Prosecution Standards* issued by the National District Attorneys Association.[14] In Prosecution Standard 19.2, Juvenile Delinquency, the prosecutor is defined as an advocate of the state's interest in juvenile court. The state's interest includes (1) the protection of the community from the danger of harmful conduct by the restraint and rehabilitation of juvenile offenders and (2) the concern shared by all juvenile justice system personnel, as *parens patriae,* with promoting the best interests of the child. The prosecutor also has a duty to seek justice in juvenile court by insisting on fair and lawful procedures. This includes ensuring, for example, that baseless prosecutions are not brought, that all juveniles receive fair and equal treatment, and that excessively harsh dispositions are not sought. It also entails overseeing police investigative behavior to ensure its compliance with the law.

Because children are committing more serious crimes today and because the courts have granted juveniles constitutional safeguards, the prosecutor is likely to play an increasingly significant role in the juvenile court system. According to Shine and Price, the prosecutor's involvement will promote a due process model that should result in a fairer, more just system for all parties. But they also point out that to meet current and future challenges prosecutors need more information on such issues as (1) how to identify repeat offenders, (2) how to determine which programs are most effective, (3) how early childhood experiences relate to delinquency, and (4) what measures can be used in place of secure placements without reducing public safety.[15]

Today, prosecutors are addressing the significant problems associated with juvenile crime. A balanced approach has been recommended—one that emphasizes enforcement, prosecution, and detention of serious and repeat juvenile offenders and the use of proven prevention and intervention programs.[16]

The Juvenile Court Judge

juvenile court judge
A judge elected or appointed to preside over juvenile cases and whose decisions can only be reviewed by a judge of a higher court.

Even with the elevation of the prosecutor's role, the **juvenile court judge** is still the central character in a court of juvenile or family law. His or her responsibilities are quite varied and have become far more extensive and complex in recent years. Following *Kent* and *Gault,* new legal rulings have probed the basic legal aspects of the juvenile justice system. In addition, juvenile cases are far more complex today and encompass issues involving social change such as truancy, alcoholism, the use of drugs by children, juvenile prostitution, and violent juvenile crime. Such cases involve problems of both public safety and individualized treatment for children.

Juvenile or family court judges perform the following functions:

- Rule on pretrial motions involving such legal issues as arrest, search and seizure, interrogation, and lineup identification
- Make decisions about the continued detention of children prior to trial
- Make decisions about plea bargaining agreements and the informal adjustment of juvenile cases
- Handle bench and jury trials, rule on the appropriateness of conduct, settle questions of evidence and procedure, and guide the questioning of witnesses
- Assume responsibility for holding dispositional hearings and deciding on the treatment accorded the child
- Handle waiver proceedings
- Handle appeals where allowed by statute and where no prior contact has been made with the case

In addition, judges often have extensive control and influence over other service agencies of the court: probation, the court clerk, the law enforcement officer, and the office of the juvenile prosecutor. Of course, courts differ organizationally and procedurally. Larger courts have more resources to handle the volume of juvenile cases. They may also have unique approaches to addressing juvenile problems, including specialized offender caseloads for drug users, diversion programs, and a whole host of special social services. Smaller courts, in contrast, most likely have little more than a judge, a clerk, and a probation staff.

Juvenile court judges exercise considerable leadership in developing services and solutions to juvenile justice problems. In this role juvenile court judges must respond to the external pressures the community places on juvenile court resources. In fact, research indicates that juvenile court decision making may be influenced more by the needs of the outside community than by the particular philosophy or views of the presiding judge.[17]

According to Judge Leonard Edwards of the Santa Clara, California, Superior Court, who has extensive experience in juvenile and family law, "The juvenile judge must take action to ensure that the necessary community resources are available so that the children and families that come before the court can be well-served."[18] This may be the most untraditional role for the juvenile court judge, but it may also be the most important.

A variety of methods are used to select juvenile court judges.[19] Sometimes, the governor simply appoints candidates chosen by a screening board. In some states judges are chosen in popular partisan elections; in others judges run for office without party affiliation. In a few states the legislature appoints judges. About a dozen states have adopted the **Missouri Plan,** which involves (1) a commission to nominate candidates for the bench; (2) an elected official, usually the governor, to make appointments from the list submitted by the commission; and (3) subsequent nonpartisan and uncontested elections in which incumbent judges run on their records (usually every three years).

In some jurisdictions juvenile court judges handle family-related cases exclusively. In others they preside over criminal and civil cases as well. Traditionally, juvenile court judges have been relegated to a lower status than other judges, with less prestige, responsibility, and salary. Judges assigned to juvenile courts have not ordinarily been chosen from the highest levels of the legal profession. Such groups as the American Judicature Society have noted that the field of juvenile justice has often been shortchanged by the appointment of unqualified judges and staff. In some jurisdictions, particularly major urban areas, juvenile court judges may be of

Missouri Plan
Sets out how juvenile court judges are chosen and specifies that a commission should nominate candidates, an elected official should make the appointment, and the incumbent judge should run uncontested on his or her record in a nonpartisan election, usually every three years.

the highest caliber, but many courts throughout the nation continue to function with mediocre judges. This is especially distressing since the Advisory Council of Judges of the National Council on Crime and Delinquency states:

> Juvenile court has been brilliantly conceived; its legal and social facets are not antithetical, but the preservation of equilibrium between them, which is the key to their successful fusion, depends upon the legal knowledge, social perspective, and eternal vigilance of *one person, the judge*.[20]

Judge Maurice Cohill, former judge of the Juvenile Court of Allegheny County, Pennsylvania, put it most succinctly when he said, "In terms of sheer human impact, the juvenile court is the most important court in the land."[21]

Inducing the best-trained individuals to accept juvenile court judgeships is a very important goal. Where the juvenile court is part of the highest general court of trial jurisdiction, the problem of securing qualified personnel is not as great. However, if the juvenile court is of limited or specialized jurisdiction and has the authority to try only minor cases, it may attract only poorly trained and poorly qualified personnel. Lawyers and judges who practice in juvenile court receive little respect from their colleagues. The juvenile court has a negative image to overcome, because even though what it does is of great importance to parents, children, and society in general, it has been placed at the lowest level of the judicial hierarchy.

One group that has struggled to upgrade the juvenile court judiciary is the **National Council of Juvenile and Family Court Judges.** Located in Reno, Nevada, this organization sponsors research and continuing legal education efforts designed to help judges master their field of expertise. Its research arm, the National Center for Juvenile Justice, in Pittsburgh, offers assistance to courts in developing information processing and statute analysis methods; it also provides legal consultation to judicial groups. Some juvenile practitioners have even created their own bar association to support child advocacy programs.

National Council of Juvenile and Family Court Judges
An organization that sponsors research and continuing legal education to help juvenile court judges master their field of expertise.

The Defense Attorney

As the result of a series of Supreme Court decisions, the right of a criminal defendant to have counsel at state trials has become a fundamental part of the criminal justice system.[22] Today, federal and state courts must provide counsel to indigent defendants who face the possibility of incarceration.

The American Bar Association (ABA) has described the responsibility of the legal profession to the juvenile court in Standard 2.3 of its *Standards Relating to Counsel for Private Parties*. The ABA states that legal representation should be provided in all proceedings arising from or related to a delinquency or in-need-of-supervision action—including mental competency, transfer, postdisposition, probation revocation and classification, institutional transfer, and disciplinary or other administrative proceedings related to the treatment process—that may substantially affect the juvenile's custody, status, or course of treatment.[23]

Over the past three decades, the rules and procedures of criminal and juvenile justice administration have become extremely complex. Specialized knowledge is essential for the adversary process to operate effectively. Preparation of a case for juvenile court often involves detailed investigation of a crime, knowledge of court procedures, use of rules of evidence, and skills in trial advocacy. Prosecuting and defense attorneys both must have this expertise, particularly when a child's freedom is at stake. The right to counsel in the juvenile justice system is essential if children are to have a fair chance of presenting their cases in court.

In many respects, the role of **juvenile defense attorney** is similar to that in the criminal and civil areas. Defense attorneys representing children in the juve-

juvenile defense attorneys
Represent children in juvenile court and play an active role at all stages of the proceedings.

A teen on trial for murder meets with his attorney in Santa Ana, California. To satisfy the requirement that indigent children and their families be provided with counsel at the various stages of the juvenile justice process, the federal government and the states have expanded public defender services.

nile court play an active and important part in virtually all stages of the proceedings. For example, the defense attorney helps to clarify jurisdictional problems and to decide whether there is sufficient evidence to warrant filing a formal petition at intake. He or she also helps outline the child's position regarding detention hearings and bail and explores the opportunities for informal adjustment of the case. If no adjustment or diversion occurs, the defense attorney represents the child at adjudication, presenting evidence and cross-examining witnesses to see that the child's position is made clear to the court. Defense attorneys also play a critically important role in the dispositional hearing. They present evidence bearing on the treatment decision and help the court formulate alternative plans for the child's care. Finally, defense attorneys pursue any appeals from the trial, represent the child in probation revocation proceedings, and generally protect the child's right to treatment.

In some cases, a **guardian *ad litem*** may be appointed by the court.[24] The guardian *ad litem,* nominally used in abuse, neglect, and dependency cases, may be appointed in delinquency cases where there is a question of a need for a particular treatment (for example, placement in a mental health center) and the offender and his or her attorney resist placement. The guardian *ad litem* may advocate for the commitment on the ground that it is in the child's "best interests."[25]

Court Appointed Special Advocates (CASA) programs also advise the juvenile court about child placement. The CASA programs ("casa" is Spanish for "home") have demonstrated that volunteers can investigate the needs of children and provide a vital link between the judge, the attorneys, and the child in protecting the juvenile's right to a safe placement.[26]

Public Defender Services for Children   To satisfy the requirement that indigent children and their families be provided with counsel at the various stages of the juvenile justice process, the federal government and the states have expanded **public defender** services. Three primary alternatives exist for providing children with legal counsel in the juvenile court today: (1) an all-public defender program, (2) an appointed private counsel system, and (3) a combination system of public defenders and appointed private attorneys.

guardian *ad litem*
A court appointed attorney who protects the interests of the child in cases involving the child's welfare.

Court Appointed Special Advocates (CASA)
Volunteers appointed by the court to investigate the needs of the child and help officers of the court ensure a safe placement for the child.

public defender
An attorney who works in a public agency or under private contractual agreement as defense counsel to indigent defendants.

The public defender program is a statewide program organized by legislation and funded by the state government to provide counsel to children at public expense. This program allows access to the expertise of lawyers who spend a considerable amount of time representing juvenile offenders every day. Defender programs generally provide separate office space for juvenile court personnel as well as support staff, and training programs for new lawyers.

In many rural areas where individual public defender programs are not available, defense services are offered through appointed private counsel. Private lawyers are assigned to individual juvenile court cases and receive compensation for the time and services they provide to the child and the family. When private attorneys are used in large urban areas, they are generally selected from a list established by the court, and they often operate in conjunction with a public defender program. The weaknesses of a system of assigned private counsel include assignment to cases for which the lawyers are unqualified, inadequate compensation, and lack of supportive or supervisory services.

Even though public defense services for children have grown in recent years, a major concern is continued provision of quality representation to the child and the family at all stages of the juvenile process. In some jurisdictions today, counsel is available to children only during part of the juvenile proceedings. In other jurisdictions children are not represented in persons-in-need-of-supervision or neglect cases. Often, public defender agencies and the assigned counsel system are understaffed and lack adequate support services. Representation needs to be upgraded in all areas of the juvenile court system.

In Whose Best Interest?   Although juvenile court practice has not traditionally been viewed by the bar with the same esteem as a lucrative corporate practice or adult trial work, defense attorneys must meet the same high standards for competency and professional responsibility when representing a child in the juvenile justice system. Unfortunately, these high standards are not always met.

A number of studies found that having an attorney either makes no difference in juvenile cases or actually results in more damaging dispositions for clients.[27] Juveniles represented by an attorney are more likely to receive institutional sentences than those who waive their right to counsel. Although not all research efforts arrive at this conclusion, sufficient evidence exists that at least in some jurisdictions legal representation may not be in a juvenile's best interest.

One possible reason for this surprising finding is that only the most serious juvenile offenders request counsel, and it is these youths who are most likely to receive an institutional sentence. Another view is that counsel in juvenile court functions in a nonadversarial capacity, furthering the interests of the juvenile court rather than those of the client. Joseph Sanborn found quite a bit of role confusion in the three juvenile courts he studied. Some juvenile court personnel believed the lawyer's role should be one of advocating for the client, whereas others viewed lawyers as guardians who guide juveniles through the treatment process.[28] Some of those Sanborn interviewed thought that attorneys should fight to prove their clients innocent during the trial stage but that once delinquency was established they should revert to the guardian role to obtain the best treatment possible for their clients. Thus, in a case in which the judge believes a child needs placement in a secure facility, the attorney may help convince the client that placement is in his or her best interest rather than use all means to block the incarceration.[29]

The inferior quality of legal counsel in juvenile court has been confirmed by a New York study of juvenile defense work. The study, sponsored by the New York State Bar Association, found significant deficiencies in the quality of legal care given youths by their court-appointed lawyers. In 45 percent of the almost two hundred cases studied, the representation was considered inadequate, and in another 47 percent it appeared that the lawyer had done little or no preparation on the case.

The study also found that lawyers representing juveniles had little knowledge of the statutes governing juvenile law and were unfamiliar with social services available to children. There were frequent instances of insensitivity to the client's feelings, particularly in cases involving sexual issues or abuse.[30] Based on such information, improving legal services for indigent juveniles may be a tough goal to achieve.

Sanford Fox claims, "Few of the rights granted children in the juvenile justice system would have much real meaning without an attorney to assert them or to advise the child when it is in his best interests to waive them."[31] What he didn't say is that the counsel must be knowledgeable enough on the law to be able to use it to protect the client's best interests.

In one of the most comprehensive empirical examinations on right to counsel, Barry Feld analyzed variations in the rates of representation and the impact of counsel on juvenile delinquency and status proceedings in Minnesota in 1986.[32] Feld reported that, overall, only 45.3 percent of juveniles in Minnesota received the assistance of counsel. In counties with high rates of representation, 94.5 percent of juveniles had counsel; in counties with medium rates, 46.8 percent had counsel; and in counties with low rates, only 19.3 percent had counsel.[33] The seriousness of the offense increases the likelihood of representation; many juveniles who commit petty offenses go unrepresented because they waive their right to counsel.

Feld's findings confirm previous research in this area: Youths with lawyers received more serious sentencing dispositions. Almost twice as many youths were removed from their homes and institutionalized in the high-representation counties as in areas where there is low representation. Feld's study provides support for the existence of "varieties of juvenile justice" and suggests that administrative criteria and sentencing guidelines be used to structure dispositional practices in the juvenile court.[34] Sentencing guidelines are created by statute or an independent commission, which bases sentences on the seriousness of the crime and the background of the offenders. The more serious the crime and the more extreme the criminal background, the longer the sentence required by the guidelines. Used in the adult justice system, guidelines often eliminate discretion, prevent judges from considering mitigating circumstances, and reduce the use of probation. Critics argue that guidelines are too rigid, harsh, and overly complex to be adapted in the juvenile court. Feld acknowledges the punitive nature of today's juvenile court and argues that the state must provide appropriate due process protection in this more formal legalistic system.

It appears that a great deal of variation still exists in the extent to which juveniles are represented by counsel at adjudication or dispositional hearings in the juvenile court system.[35] The major reasons for this seem to be:

- Some juveniles are not advised of their right to counsel
- Some defense attorneys do not appear at the hearing
- Pleas of guilty are entered without full explanation
- Juveniles waive their right to counsel, often at the encouragement of parents or some public officer
- Parents are unwilling to retain an attorney
- Public defender services are inadequate

According to some child advocates, juvenile offenders should have an unwaivable right to counsel. But many judicial personnel agree that providing every juvenile with legal counsel would seriously impede the work of the juvenile court. According to Feld, it appears that *Gault*'s promise of counsel remains unkept for most juveniles in most states.[36]

The latest research, a 1995 American Bar Association study, confirmed the fact that many juveniles go to court unrepresented or with an overworked lawyer who provides inadequate representation.[37] According to the report, which was based on a survey of hundreds of juvenile court defense lawyers and defendants, the juvenile court is not being empowered to do the job properly. Today, as juvenile offenders face the prospect of much longer sentences, mandatory minimum sentences, and time in adult prisons, the need for quality defense attorneys for juveniles has never been greater. The report also found that many juvenile court defense lawyers work on more than five hundred cases in one year, and more than half leave their jobs in under two years. The report's recommendations are these:

1. State legislatures need to provide additional funding for the public defenders of juveniles.
2. State and local bar associations need to encourage more lawyers to provide services free of charge to juvenile court defendants.
3. Public defender offices should ensure that lawyers have manageable caseloads.
4. Congress should mandate additional research by holding hearings to identify the quality and accessibility of lawyers in juvenile courts and to evaluate the protection of children's rights in the juvenile justice system.[38]

Despite the constitutional requirements set forth in *Gault* more than thirty years ago, all juveniles are still not represented by counsel. Moreover, studies have shown that the right to counsel may be less of a privilege than the Warren Court had intended because:

■ Court-appointed attorneys may provide inadequate services

■ Public defenders don't always serve their clients' best interests

■ Juveniles who waive their right to counsel may receive more lenient sentences than those who are represented[39]

How do defense attorneys, judges, and prosecutors interact? What actually happens in a juvenile trial? We turn to these questions in the next section.

Adjudication

adjudication hearing
A fact-finding process wherein the juvenile court determines whether there is sufficient evidence to sustain the allegations in a petition.

An **adjudication hearing** is held to determine the merits of the petition claiming that a child is either a delinquent youth or in need of court supervision. The judge is required to make a finding based on the evidence in the case and arrive at a judgment. Adjudication is comparable to an adult trial. Rules of evidence in adult criminal proceedings are generally applicable in juvenile court, and the standard of proof used—"beyond a reasonable doubt"—is similar to that used in adult trials. The majority of juvenile cases do not reach the adjudicatory state, but serious delinquency cases based on violations of the criminal law, situations where juveniles deny any guilt, cases of repeat offenders, and cases where juveniles are a threat to themselves or the community often do reach this stage.

Are adjudication proceedings handled fairly? State juvenile codes vary with regard to the basic requirements of due process and fairness. Most juvenile courts have bifurcated hearings—that is, separate hearings for adjudication and disposition (sentencing). At disposition hearings, evidence can be submitted that reflects nonlegal factors such as the child's home life, relationships, and background.

Although there has not been sufficient research on hearing fairness, there are some indications that minorities may be handled with disproportionate harshness at disposition.[40] For instance, adjudicated cases involving white youth were less likely to result in out-of-home placement in 1995 (26 percent) than cases involving black youths (32 percent) (see Table 15.1).[41] This finding is in line with an earlier study of juvenile court data for 1985 and 1989, which indicated that minority youths are

Table 15.1

PERCENTAGE OF ADJUDICATED DELINQUENCY CASES THAT RESULTED IN OUT-OF-HOME PLACEMENT, BY RACE, 1986–1995

Most Serious Offense	Percentage of Cases that Resulted in Out-of-Home Placement		
	1986	**1991**	**1995**
White (total)	29	27	26
Person	30	31	29
Property	27	24	24
Drugs	26	30	20
Public Order	37	35	32
Black (total)	34	35	32
Person	36	37	32
Property	31	32	30
Drugs	38	40	32
Public Order	36	36	34
Other Races (total)	31	34	31
Person	35	41	35
Property	29	31	29
Drugs	32	40	25
Public Order	37	38	36

Source: Melissa Sickmund, *Juvenile Court Statistics 1995* (Pittsburgh, Pa.: National Center for Juvenile Justice, 1998).

more likely to be referred to and petitioned in court, detained, and placed away from the home after adjudication.[42]

This trend may be partially attributed to the increase in minority drug offenders. However, what sometimes seems to be racial or ethnic bias may actually be a result of legal or socially relevant factors such as the willingness to plea bargain, the seriousness of the crime, school performance, and so on.

Most state juvenile codes provide for specific rules of procedure and a finding at adjudication. These rules require that a written petition be submitted to the court, ensure the right of a child to have an attorney, provide that the adjudication proceedings be recorded, allow the petition to be amended, and provide that a child's plea be accepted. Where the child admits to the facts of the petition, the court generally seeks assurance that the plea is voluntary. If plea bargaining is used, prosecutors, defense counsel, and trial judges take steps to ensure the fairness of such negotiations.

At the end of the adjudication hearing, most juvenile court statutes require the judge to make a factual finding on the legal issues and evidence presented in the child's hearing. In the criminal court, this finding is normally a prelude to reaching a verdict. In the juvenile court, however, the finding itself is the verdict; the case is resolved in one of these three ways:

1. The juvenile court judge makes a finding of fact that the child or juvenile is not delinquent or in need of supervision.
2. The juvenile court judge makes a finding of fact that the juvenile is delinquent or in need of supervision.
3. The juvenile court judge dismisses the case because of insufficient or faulty evidence.

In some jurisdictions, informal alternatives are used, such as filing the case with no further consequences or continuing the case without a finding for a period of time, such as six months. If the juvenile does not get into further difficulty during that time, the case is dismissed. These alternatives involve no determination of delinquency or noncriminal behavior. Because of the philosophy of the juvenile court to emphasize treatment and rehabilitation over punishment, a delinquency finding is not the same thing as a criminal conviction. The disabilities associated with conviction, such as disqualifications for employment or being barred from military service or involvement in politics, do not apply in an adjudication of delinquency.

There are other significant differences between adult and juvenile proceedings. For instance, only a small number of states provide juveniles with jury trials, and in almost all jurisdictions juvenile trials are closed to the public.[43] Because juvenile courts are treating some defendants similarly to adult criminals, an argument can be made that the courts should extend the Sixth Amendment right to a public jury trial to these youths.[44] For the most part, however, state juvenile courts operate without recognizing a juvenile's constitutional right to a public jury trial.

Constitutional Rights at Trial

due process
Basic constitutional principle based on the concept of the primacy of the individual and the complementary concept of limitation on governmental power; safeguards the individual from unfair state procedures in judicial or administrative proceedings; due process rights have been extended to juvenile trials.

In addition to mandating state juvenile code requirements, the U.S. Supreme Court has mandated the application of constitutional due process standards to the juvenile trial. Due process is addressed in the Fifth and Fourteenth Amendments to the U.S. Constitution. It refers to the need in our legal system for rules and procedures that protect individual rights. Having the right to due process means that no person can be deprived of life, liberty, or property without such protections as legal counsel, an open and fair hearing, and an opportunity to confront those making accusations against him or her. Due process is intended to guarantee that fundamental fairness is available to every citizen.

For many years children were deprived of their due process rights because the *parens patriae* philosophy governed their relationship to the juvenile justice system. Such rights as having counsel and confronting one's accusers were deemed unnecessary. After all, why should children need protection from the state when the state was seen as acting in their best interest by providing treatment, care, and protection? As we've seen, this view changed in the 1960s when, under the leadership of Chief Justice Earl Warren, the U.S. Supreme Court recognized the need to reform the juvenile justice system and began to grant due process rights and procedures to minors. As a result of the "due process revolution," a child is now entitled to many of the same due process rights as an adult. As Justice Hugo Black stated in the landmark 1967 case *In re Gault:*

> When a person, infant or adult, can be seized by the state, charged and convicted, for violating a state criminal law, and then ordered by the state to be confined for six years, I think the Constitution requires that he be tried in accordance with the guarantees of all the provisions of the Bill of Rights, made applicable to the states by the Fourteenth Amendment. Appellants are entitled to these rights not because fairness, impartiality and orderliness, in short, the essentials of due process, require them, and not because they are the procedural rules which have been fashioned from the generality of due process, but because they are specifically and unequivocably granted by provisions of the Fifth and Sixth Amendments which the Fourteenth Amendment makes applicable to the states.[45]

The Warren Court set forth the role of due process in juvenile justice through major decisions made during the 1960s, beginning with *Kent v. United States,* dis-

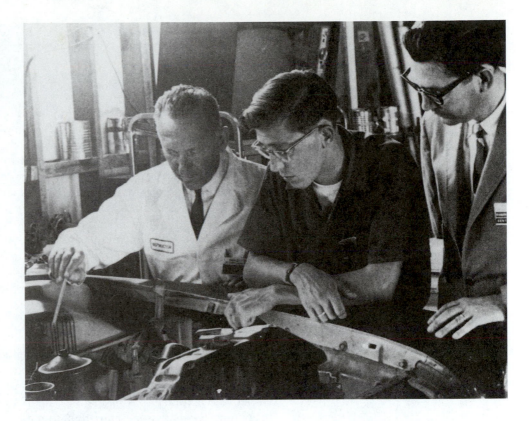

The appeal of Gerald Gault, shown here, heralded in the due process revolution in juvenile justice.

cussed in Chapter 14.[46] In the landmark case of *In re Gault* (1967), the Supreme Court further articulated the basic requirements of due process that must be satisfied in juvenile court proceedings. It held that in an adjudicatory hearing:

■ The child must be given adequate notice of the charges

■ The child and the parent must be advised of the right to be represented by counsel

■ The child has a constitutional privilege against self-incrimination

■ The child has the right of confrontation and sworn testimony of witnesses available for cross-examination[47]

Because of the importance of the *Gault* case in juvenile court proceedings, it is set out in the Juvenile Law in Review box entitled "*In re Gault.*"

The *Gault* decision reshaped the constitutional and philosophical nature of the juvenile court system. As a result, those working in the system—judges, social workers, attorneys—were faced with the problem of reaffirming the rehabilitative ideal of the juvenile court while ensuring that juveniles received proper procedural due process rights. Prior to the *Gault* decision, only a few states required that juveniles be offered the assistance of counsel.[48]

Following the *Gault* case, the Supreme Court decided *In re Winship* in 1970. This case considered the issue of the amount of proof required in juvenile delinquency adjudications.[49] Prior to *Winship*, most juvenile courts judged the sufficiency of evidence in juvenile matters by applying a preponderance of the evidence, or clear and convincing evidence, test. In *Winship*, the Court adapted a stricter standard of proof requiring that delinquency charges in juvenile court be proved beyond a reasonable doubt.

Although the ways in which the traditional juvenile court operates were severely altered by *Kent, Gault,* and *Winship,* the trend toward increased rights for juveniles was somewhat curtailed by the Supreme Court's decision in *McKeiver v. Pennsylvania* (1971). In *McKeiver,* the Court held that trial by jury in a juvenile

IN RE GAULT

FACTS

Gerald Gault, fifteen years of age, was taken into custody by the sheriff of Gila County, Arizona, because a woman complained that he and another boy had made an obscene telephone call to her. At the time, Gerald was under a six-month probation as a result of being found delinquent for stealing a wallet. As a result of the woman's complaint, Gerald was taken to a children's home. His parents were not informed that he was being taken into custody. His mother appeared in the evening and was told by the superintendent of detention that a hearing would be held in the juvenile court the following day. On the day in question, the police officer who had taken Gerald into custody filed a petition alleging his delinquency. Gerald, his mother, and the police officer appeared before the judge in his chambers. Mrs. Cook, the complainant, was not at the hearing. Gerald was questioned about the telephone calls and was sent back to the detention home and then subsequently released a few days later.

On the day of Gerald's release, Mrs. Gault received a letter indicating that a hearing would be held on Gerald's delinquency a few days later. A hearing was held, and the complainant again was not present. There was no transcript or recording of the proceedings, and the juvenile officer stated that Gerald had admitted making the lewd telephone calls. Neither the boy nor his parents were advised of any right to remain silent, the right to be represented by counsel, or any other constitutional rights. At the conclusion of the hearing, the juvenile court committed Gerald as a juvenile delinquent to the state industrial school in Arizona for the period of his minority.

This meant that, at the age of fifteen, Gerald was sent to the state school until he reached the age of twenty-one unless discharged sooner. An adult charged with the same crime would have received a maximum punishment of no more than a $50 fine or two months in prison.

DECISION

Gerald's attorneys filed a writ of habeas corpus, which was denied by the Superior Court of the State of Arizona. That decision was subsequently affirmed by the Arizona Supreme Court. On appeal to the U.S. Supreme Court, Gerald's counsel argued that the juvenile code of Arizona under

court's adjudicative stage is not a constitutional requirement.[50] This decision, however, does not prevent states from giving the juvenile a trial by jury as a state constitutional right or by state statute. In the majority of states, a child has no such right. These major decisions signaling the Supreme Court's determination to evaluate the adjudicatory rights of juvenile offenders are highlighted in the Juvenile Law in Review box entitled "*In re Winship* and *McKeiver v. Pennsylvania.*"

Once an adjudicatory hearing has been completed, the court is normally required to enter a judgment or finding against the child. This may take the form of declaring the child delinquent, adjudging the child to be a ward of the court, or possibly even suspending judgment so as to avoid the stigma of a juvenile record. After a judgment has been entered in accordance with the appropriate state statute, the court can begin its determination of possible dispositions for the child. Table 15.2 on page 572 illustrates the evolution of the juvenile court system in determining judgments.

which Gerald was found delinquent was invalid because it was contrary to the due process clause of the Fourteenth Amendment. In addition, Gerald was denied the following basic due process rights: (1) notice of the charges with regard to their timeliness and specificity, (2) right to counsel, (3) right to confrontation and cross-examination, (4) privilege against self-incrimination, (5) right to a transcript of the trial record, and (6) right to appellate review. In deciding the case, the Supreme Court had to determine whether procedural due process of law within the context of fundamental fairness under the Fourteenth Amendment applied to juvenile delinquency proceedings in which a child is committed to a state industrial school.

The Court, in a far-reaching opinion written by Justice Abe Fortas, agreed that Gerald's constitutional rights had been violated. Notice of charges was an essential ingredient of due process of law, as was the right to counsel, the right to cross-examine and to confront witnesses, and the privilege against self-incrimination. The questions of appellate review and a right to a transcript were not answered by the Court in this case.

SIGNIFICANCE OF THE CASE

The *Gault* case established that a child had the procedural due process constitutional rights listed here in delinquency adjudication proceedings where the consequences were that the child could be committed to a state institution. It was confined to rulings at the adjudication stage of the juvenile process.

However, this decision was significant not only because of the procedural reforms it initiated but also because of its far-reaching impact throughout the entire juvenile justice system. *Gault* instilled in juvenile proceedings the development of due process standards at the pretrial, trial, and posttrial stages of the juvenile process. While recognizing the history and development of the juvenile court, it sought to accommodate the motives of rehabilitation and treatment with children's rights. It recognized the principle of fundamental fairness of the law for children as well as for adults. Judged in the context of today's juvenile justice system, *Gault* redefined the relationships between juveniles, their parents, and the state. It remains the single most significant constitutional case in the area of juvenile justice.

Source: *In re Gault*, 387 U.S. 1; 87 S.Ct. 1248 (1967).

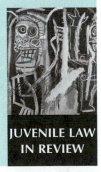

JUVENILE LAW IN REVIEW

IN RE WINSHIP AND *MCKEIVER V. PENNSYLVANIA*

IN RE WINSHIP: STANDARD OF PROOF

Following the *Gault* case came *In re Winship*. This case expressly held that a juvenile in a delinquency adjudication must be proven guilty beyond a reasonable doubt.

(continued on next page)

JUVENILE LAW IN REVIEW

(continued from previous page)

Facts

Winship, a twelve-year-old boy in New York, stole $112 from a woman's pocketbook. The petition that charged Winship with delinquency alleged that this act, if done by an adult, would constitute larceny. Winship was adjudicated a delinquent on the basis of a preponderance of the evidence submitted at the court hearing. During a subsequent dispositional hearing, Winship was ordered placed in a training school in New York state for an initial period of eighteen months, subject to extensions of his commitment until his eighteenth birthday—six years in total. The New York State Supreme Court and the New York Court of Appeals affirmed the lower court decision, sustaining the conviction.

Decision

The problem in the case was whether Section 744(b) of the New York State Family Court Act was constitutional. This section provided that any determination at the conclusion of an adjudicatory hearing must be based on a preponderance of the evidence. The judge decided Winship's guilt on the basis of this standard and not on the basis of proof beyond a reasonable doubt, which is the standard in the adult criminal justice system. The issue in the case was whether proof beyond a reasonable doubt was essential to due process and fair treatment for juveniles charged with an act that would constitute a crime if committed by an adult.

Significance of the Case

Although the standard of proof beyond a reasonable doubt is not stated in the Constitution, the U.S. Supreme Court said that *Gault* had established that due process required the essentials of fair treatment, although it did not require that the adjudication conform to all the requirements of the criminal trial. The Court further said that the due process clause recognized proof beyond a reasonable doubt as being among the essentials of fairness required when a child is charged with a delinquent act. The state of New York argued that juvenile delinquency proceedings were civil in nature, not criminal, and that the preponderance of evidence standard was therefore valid. The U.S. Supreme Court indicated that the standard of proof beyond a reasonable doubt plays a vital role in the U.S. criminal justice system and ensures a greater degree of safety for the presumption of innocence of those accused of a crime.

Thus, the *Winship* case required proof beyond a reasonable doubt as a standard for juvenile adjudication proceedings and eliminated the use of lesser standards such as a preponderance of the evidence, clear and convincing proof, and reasonable proof.

MCKEIVER V. PENNSYLVANIA: RIGHT TO A JURY TRIAL

One of the most controversial issues in the areas of children's rights at adjudication involves the jury trial. Although the Sixth Amendment guarantees the adult criminal defendant the right to a jury trial, the Supreme Court had not seen fit to grant this right to juvenile offenders. In fact, the U.S. Constitution is silent on whether all defendants, including those charged with misdemeanors, have a right to a trial by jury. In the case of *Duncan v. Louisiana*, the Supreme Court held that the Sixth Amendment right to a jury trial applied to all adult defendants accused of serious crimes. However, no mention was made of the juvenile offender. The case of *McKeiver v. Pennsylvania* deals with the right of the juvenile defendant to a jury trial.

Facts

Joseph McKeiver, age 16, was charged with robbery, larceny, and receiving stolen goods, all of which were felonies under Pennsylvania law. McKeiver was subsequently declared delinquent at an adjudication hearing and placed on probation after his request for a jury trial was denied.

In another case, Edward Terry, age 15, was charged with assault and battery on a police officer, misdemeanors under Pennsylvania law. He was declared a juvenile delinquent after an adjudication following a denial of his request for trial by jury.

In an unrelated case in North Carolina a group of juveniles were charged with willful, riotous, and disorderly conduct, declared delinquent, and placed on probation. Their request for a jury trial was denied.

The Supreme Court heard all three cases together on the single issue of whether a juvenile has a constitutional right to a jury trial in the juvenile court system.

Decision

The court was required to decide whether the due process clause of the Fourteenth Amendment guarantees the right to a jury trial in the adjudication of a juvenile court delinquency case. It answered in the negative, stating that the right to a jury trial guaranteed by the Sixth Amendment and incorporated into the Fourteenth Amendment is not among the constitutional safeguards that the due process clause requires at delinquency adjudication hearings. The Court's reasons were as follows:

A jury trial is not a necessary component of accurate fact-finding, as are the procedural requirements stated in the *Gault* case.

Not all the rights constitutionally assured an adult are to be given to a juvenile.

Insisting on a jury trial for juvenile offenders could fully turn the adjudication into an adversary process.

Insisting on a jury trial would not remedy the problems associated with the lack of rehabilitation in the juvenile court.

The preferable approach would be to allow states to experiment and adopt for themselves a jury trial concept in their individual jurisdictions.

The jury trial, if imposed in the juvenile court, would certainly result in a delay, formality, and the possibility of a public trial, which at this point is not provided in most jurisdictions.

Significance of the Case

The *McKeiver* case temporarily stopped the march toward procedural constitutional due process for juvenile offenders in the juvenile justice system. The majority of the Court believed that juvenile proceedings were different from adult criminal prosecutions. The case also emphasized the fact that, as Justice Blackmun said, jurisdictions are free to adopt their own jury trial position in juvenile proceedings. The Court further noted that the majority of states denied a juvenile the right to a jury trial by statute. Thus, the Court believed granting the juvenile offender the right to a jury trial would hinder, rather than advance, the system of juvenile justice in the United States.

Source: *In re Winship*, 397 U.S. 358, 90 S.Ct. 1068 (1970); *McKeiver v. Pennsylvania*, 403 U.S. 528, 91 S.Ct. 1976 (1971).

JUVENILE LAW IN REVIEW

Table 15.2

THE EVOLUTION OF THE JUVENILE COURT

Time Period	Prevailing Public Opinion
Early U.S. history	Children treated the same as adults
Beginning of twentieth century	Juvenile Court Act established in Illinois
First half of twentieth century	Expansion of juvenile courts and rehabilitation model
1950s and 1960s	Public confidence in treatment eroded
In re Gault (1967)	Due process protections introduced
1980s to present	Pendulum moves significantly toward law and order
1990s to 2000	Accountability, punishment, and new dispositions

Disposition

disposition
For juvenile offenders, the equivalent of sentencing for adult offenders; however, juvenile dispositions should be more rehabilitative than retributive.

The stage of the juvenile justice process after adjudication is called **disposition,** the sentencing step of the juvenile proceedings. At this point the juvenile court orders treatment for the juvenile to prevent further delinquency. Adrienne Volenik claims that it is here where the original child-saving philosophy of the juvenile court can come into play.[51]

Disposition is the most important phase of juvenile proceedings.[52] In fact, Paul Piersma and his associates describe the disposition as the heart of the juvenile process.[53] Lindsay G. Arthur, who has spent many years working on behalf of the National Council of Juvenile and Family Court Judges, speaks about the importance and the philosophy of disposition:

> A disposition is not simply a sentencing. It is far broader in concept and in application. It should be in the best interest of the child, which in this context means effectively to provide the help necessary to resolve or meet the individual's definable needs, while, at the same time, meeting society's needs for protection.[54]

The dispositional process has not received much attention from the courts. None of the Supreme Court decisions dealing with juvenile justice refers to its significance. Consequently, one of the most important issues in the disposition is the lack of proper procedure and due process for the child. In most jurisdictions today, adjudication and disposition hearings are separated, or bifurcated. In addition to a separate dispositional hearing, a child is generally accorded the right to counsel.

The Supreme Court has not ruled on the right to counsel at disposition, but counsel's participation is generally allowed either by state statute or unspoken practice. Defense counsel often represents the child, helps the parents understand the court's decision, and influences the direction of the disposition. Others involved at the dispositional stage include representatives of social service agencies, psychologists, social workers, and probation personnel. The information they have supplied about the child's background is often disputed at the disposition, and many states now allow cross-examination at this stage of the juvenile process.

In determining the type of disposition to be imposed on the child, juvenile court statutes often require completion of a **predispositional investigation.** Fox describes the needs and purposes of this report:

predispositional investigation
An investigation usually carried out by a member of the probation staff to acquire information about the child that will allow the judge to make a decision in the best interest of the child.

Individualized justice is often taken to be the most salient characteristic of juvenile court dispositions. In order to have the disposition conform to this ideal, the juvenile court judge requires information about each particular child. This is usually provided by an investigation, usually performed by a member of the probation staff, and report, known as the social study or disposition report.[55]

The Predisposition Report

After the child has admitted to the allegations in the petition or after the allegations have been proved in a juvenile trial, the judge normally orders the probation department to complete a predisposition report. Investigating and evaluating the child prior to juvenile disposition are two of the most important tasks of juvenile probation officers. The predisposition report, which is similar to the presentence report of the adult justice system, has a number of purposes:

- It helps the judge decide which disposition is best for the child.
- It aids the juvenile probation officer in developing treatment programs where the child is in need of counseling or community supervision.
- It helps the court develop a body of knowledge about the child that can aid others in treating the child.
- It serves as a source of information for systematic research in juvenile justice. Many studies are based on analysis of predisposition reports.

The style and content of predisposition reports vary among jurisdictions and also among juvenile probation officers within the same jurisdiction. The requirements for the use of the report, the sources of dispositional information, the techniques for obtaining it, and the conditions of its distribution vary among jurisdictions and are based on rules of law and procedure.

Some juvenile court probation departments require voluminous reports covering every aspect of the child's life. Other jurisdictions require information about the basic facts of the case and only limited details about the child's background. Individual officers bring their personal styles and educational backgrounds to bear on the development of the report. The probation officer who is a trained social worker, for example, might stress the use of psychological data, whereas the probation officer who is a lawyer might concentrate on the child's prior record and how dangerous the child is to him- or herself and to the community.

Sources of dispositional data include family members, school officials, and statements from the juvenile. The results of psychological testing, psychiatric evaluations, and intelligence testing may be relevant to the predispositional report. Furthermore, the probation officer might include information about the juvenile's feelings and attitudes concerning his or her case.

Some state statutes make the predisposition report mandatory. Other jurisdictions require the report only when there is a probability that the child will be institutionalized. Some appellate courts have reversed orders institutionalizing children where the juvenile court did not use a predisposition report in reaching its decision. Access to predisposition reports is an important legal issue. The Supreme Court ruled in the case of *Kent v. United States* that the child and counsel must be given access to the social service report at transfer proceedings.[56] The National Advisory Commission on Criminal Justice Standards and Goals recommends that no dispositional decision be made on the basis of factors or information in a report not previously disclosed to the defense and prosecuting attorney.[57]

In the final section of the predisposition report, the probation department recommends a disposition to the presiding judge. This is a critical aspect of the report as it has been estimated that the court follows more than 90 percent of all probation department recommendations. Again, the purpose of the report is to determine the care or treatment plan the child needs, not the child's innocence or guilt. Consequently, the American Bar Association in its *Standards on Juvenile Justice* recommends seeking the least restrictive alternative in dispositional decision making. Until the more recent trend toward tougher sentencing, this principle of the least detrimental alternative dominated juvenile sentencing practice.

Table 15.3
COMMON JUVENILE DISPOSITIONS

Disposition	Action Taken
Informal consent decree	In minor or first offenses, an informal hearing is held, and the judge will ask the youth and his or her guardian to agree to a treatment program, such as counseling. No formal trial or disposition hearing is held.
Probation	A youth is placed under the control of the county probation department and required to obey a set of probation rules and participate in a treatment program.
Home detention	A child is restricted to his or her home in lieu of a secure placement. Rules include regular school attendance, curfew observance, avoidance of alcohol and drugs, and notification of parents and the youth worker of the child's whereabouts.
Court-ordered school attendance	If truancy was the problem that brought the youth to court, a judge may order mandatory school attendance. Some courts have established court-operated day schools and court-based tutorial programs staffed by community volunteers.
Financial restitution	A judge can order the juvenile offender to make financial restitution to the victim. In most jurisdictions, restitution is part of probation (see Chapter 16), but in a few states, such as Maryland, restitution can be a sole order.
Fines	Some states allow fines to be levied against juveniles age 16 and over.
Community service	Courts in many jurisdictions require juveniles to spend time in the community working off their debt to society. Community service orders are usually reserved for victimless crimes, such as possession of drugs, or crimes against public order, such as vandalism of school property. Community service orders are usually carried out in schools, hospitals, or nursing homes.
Outpatient psychotherapy	Youths who are diagnosed with psychological disorders may be required to undergo therapy at a local mental health clinic.
Drug and alcohol treatment	Youths with drug- or alcohol-related problems may be allowed to remain in the community if they agree to undergo drug or alcohol therapy.
Commitment to secure treatment	In the most serious cases a judge may order an offender admitted to a long-term treatment center, such as a training school, camp, ranch, or group home. These may be either state- or privately run institutions, usually located in remote regions. Training schools provide educational, vocational, and rehabilitation programs in a secure environment (see Chapter 17).
Commitment to a residential community program	Youths who commit crimes of a less serious nature but who still need to be removed from their homes can be placed in community-based group homes or halfway houses. They attend school or work during the day and live in a controlled, therapeutic environment at night.
Foster home placement	Foster homes are usually used for dependent or neglected children and status offenders. Today judges are placing delinquents with insurmountable problems at home in state-licensed foster care homes.

Juvenile Court Dispositions

Historically, the juvenile court has had broad discretionary power to make dispositional decisions after adjudication. The major categories of dispositional choices are (1) community release, (2) out-of-home placements, (3) fines or restitution, (4) community service, and (5) institutionalization. A more detailed list of the numerous possible dispositions open to the juvenile court judge appears in Table 15.3.[58]

The authority to order dispositional alternatives generally stems from the juvenile code. Most state statutes allow the juvenile court judge to select whatever disposition seems best suited to the child's needs, including institutionalization. In some states the juvenile court determines commitment to a specific institution; in other states the youth corrections agency determines where the child will be placed. In addition to the dispositions in Table 15.3, some states go so far as to grant the juvenile court the power to order parents into treatment or to suspend a youth's driver's license.

But state juvenile codes can also put limits on a judge's discretionary power. For instance, many states prohibit confining children in adult institutions.[59] Some states use a minimum age as a criterion for institutional placement, and others limit placement in such facilities to felony offenders only. In other words, there is an almost infinite number of statutory variations on the dispositional process.

Imposition of a particular disposition should be accompanied by a statement of the facts supporting the disposition and the reasons for selecting the disposition and rejecting less restrictive alternatives.[60]

Graduated sanction programs for juveniles are another form of dispositional solution being explored by states across the country. Types of graduated sanctions include (1) immediate sanctions for nonviolent offenders, which consist of community-based diversion and day treatment imposed on first-time nonviolent offenders; (2) intermediate sanctions, which target repeat minor offenders and first-time serious offenders; and (3) secure care, which is reserved for repeat serious offenders and violent offenders. According to Barry Krisberg and his associates, studies of the best graduated sanction programs reveal that they are often more effective than incarceration.[61] The Case in Point explores the disposition process.

The Child's Right to Appeal

final order
Order that ends litigation between two parties by determining all their rights and disposing of all the issues.

appellate process
Allows the juvenile an opportunity to have the case brought before a reviewing court after it has been heard in juvenile or family court.

Juvenile court statutes normally restrict appeals to cases where the juvenile seeks review of a **final order** or a final judgment. Paul Piersma and his associates define a final order as one that ends the litigation between two parties by determining all their rights and disposing of all the issues.[62] A final order is basically an appealable order. The **appellate process** gives the juvenile the opportunity to have the case brought before a reviewing court after it has been heard in the juvenile or family court. Today, the law does not recognize a federal constitutional right of appeal in juvenile or adult criminal cases. In other words, the U.S. Constitution does not require any state to furnish an appeal to a juvenile charged and found to be delinquent in a juvenile or family court. Consequently, appellate review of a juvenile case is a matter of statutory right in each jurisdiction. However, the majority of states do provide juveniles with some method of statutory appeal.

The appeal process was not always part of the juvenile law system. For example, J. Addison Bowman found that in 1965 few states extended the right of appeal to juveniles.[63] Even in the *Gault* case in 1967, the Supreme Court refused to review the Arizona juvenile code, which provided no appellate review in juvenile matters. It further rejected the right of a juvenile to a transcript of the original trial record.[64]

You are a family court judge at a dispositional hearing and are faced with a difficult sentencing decision. John M. was arrested at age 16 for robbery and rape. As a juvenile offender, he was subject to the jurisdiction of the juvenile division of the state family court. After a thorough investigation by the police department, the prosecutor formally filed a petition against John for the alleged offenses. Subsequently, John's mother obtained counsel for him. When the prosecutor suggested that the family court might consider transferring the case to the adult court, John admitted his involvement in the offenses and was sent home pending disposition.

At the disposition hearing the probation officer reported that John was the oldest of three siblings living in a single-parent home. He has had no contact with his father for more than ten years. His psychological evaluation showed hostility, anger toward females, and great feelings of frustration. His intelligence was below average, and his behavioral and academic records were poor. In addition, John seemed to be involved with a local youth gang, although he denied any formal association with the group. This is John's first formal petition in the family court. Previous contact was limited to an informal complaint for disorderly conduct at age 13, which was dismissed by the court's intake department. John verbalizes superficial remorse for his offenses.

To the prosecutor John seems to be a youth with poor controls who is likely to commit future crimes. The defense attorney and court staff see the need for program planning to meet John's needs. As the judge, you recognize the seriousness of the crimes committed by John and have at your disposal a wide range of court services that might help in John's rehabilitation. No one can predict or assess John's future behavior and potential dangerousness.

■ What disposition would you order?

(You may use Table 15.3 as a reference, but feel free to design your own alternative programs.)

Today, however, most jurisdictions that provide a child with some form of appeal also provide for counsel and for securing a record and transcript, which are crucial to the success of any appeal. Because adult criminal defendants have both a right to counsel at their initial appeal and a right to a stenographic transcript of trial proceedings, it would violate equal protection if juveniles were denied the same rights.

Because juvenile appellate review is defined by individual statutes, each jurisdiction determines for itself what method or scope of review will be used. There are two basic methods of appeal: the direct appeal and the collateral attack. The direct appeal normally involves an appellate court review to determine whether, based on the evidence presented at the trial, the rulings of law and the judgment of the court were correct. The appeal of the finding should be heard on the files, records, and transcripts of the juvenile court evidence.

A broader form of direct review is the *de novo* review. A **trial *de novo*** is a complete retrial of the original case based on the original petition. All evidence produced at the first trial can be resubmitted, as can additional evidence. The trial *de novo* appeal is limited to only a few jurisdictions in the nation. It is usually en-

trial *de novo*
A review procedure in which there is a complete retrial of the original case.

countered when a juvenile is originally tried in a court of very limited jurisdiction or in some administrative proceedings before masters or referees.

The second major area of review involves the collateral attack of a case. The term *collateral* implies a secondary or indirect method of attacking a final judgment or order of the court. Instead of appealing the original juvenile trial because of errors, prejudice, or lack of evidence, collateral review uses extraordinary legal writs to challenge the lower court position. Two such procedural devices include the writ of habeas corpus and the writ of certiorari. The **writ of habeas corpus,** known as the "Great Writ," refers to a procedure for determining the validity of a person's custody. In the context of the juvenile court, it is used to challenge the custody of a child in detention or in an institution. The **writ of certiorari** is an order from a higher to a lower court commanding that the case be brought forward for review. This writ is often the method by which the Supreme Court exercises its discretionary authority to hear cases regarding constitutional issues. Even though there is no constitutional right to appeal a juvenile case and each jurisdiction provides for appeals differently, juveniles have a far greater opportunity for appellate review today than in years past.

writ of habeus corpus
Judicial order requesting that a person detaining another produce the body of the prisoner and give reasons for his or her capture and detention.

writ of certiorari
Order of a superior court requesting that the record of an inferior court (or administrative body) be brought forward for review or inspection.

Juvenile Sentencing Structures

least detrimental alternative
Choosing a program for the child that will best foster a child's growth and development.

For most of the juvenile court's history disposition was based on the presumed needs of the child. Although such critics as David Rothman and Anthony Platt have challenged the motivations of early reformers in championing rehabilitation, there is little question that the rhetoric of the juvenile court has promoted that ideal.[65] For example, in their classic work, *Beyond the Best Interest of the Child,* Joseph Goldstein, Anna Freud, and Albert Solnit say that placement of children should be based on the **least detrimental alternative** available in order

On Feburary 1, 1999, Sean Sellers was executed in Oklahoma for a murder committed when he was 16 years old. Should underage minors be put to death for crimes when the law says that they are not old enough to drive, vote, have a checking account, or sign a contract?

to foster the child's growth and development.[66] This should be the goal whether the children are delinquents or status offenders or are neglected, abandoned, or abused.

Views of juvenile sentencing began changing in the late 1980s and early 1990s. In Chapter 14 we discussed the changes in transfer policy that make it easier to waive children to adult court. These changes are evidence of concern about how to handle the chronic juvenile offender. In contrast, there has been a strong push to deinstitutionalize status offenders and to prohibit their incarceration with delinquent youths. Yet, as we shall see in the next section, many states have imposed requirements for greater determinacy and proportionality so that dispositions are more standardized and more punishment-oriented. Some jurisdictions are even suggesting that mandatory sentences of incarceration be used for juveniles convicted of being in possession of a handgun. Other states have adopted reforms under which the adult criminal court may impose both a juvenile and an adult sentence; these blended sentences are discussed later in this chapter.

Determinate versus Indeterminate Sentencing

indeterminate sentence
Does not specify the length of time the juvenile must be held; rather, correctional authorities decide when the juvenile is ready to return to society.

Traditionally, states have used the **indeterminate sentence** in juvenile court. In about half of the states this means having the judge simply place the offender with the state department of juvenile corrections until correctional authorities consider him or her ready to return to society or until the youth reaches his or her legal majority. A preponderance of states consider eighteen to be the age of release; others peg the termination age at nineteen; a few can retain minority status until their twenty-first birthday.[67] In practice few youths remain in custody for the entire statutory period; juveniles are usually released if their rehabilitation has been judged by the youth corrections department, judge, or parole board to have progressed satisfactorily. This practice is referred to as the **individualized treatment model**—each sentence must be tailored to the individual needs of the child.

individualized treatment model
Each sentence must be tailored to the individual needs of the child.

Another form of the indeterminate sentence allows judges to specify a maximum term that can be served. Under this form of sentencing, youths also may be released from incarceration in these jurisdictions if the corrections department considers them to be rehabilitated or they reach the automatic age of termination (usually eighteen or twenty-one). In states that stipulate a maximum sentence, the court may extend the sentence depending on the youth's progress in the institutional facility.[68]

determinate sentence
Sentence that specifies a fixed term of detention that must be served.

A number of states have changed their sentencing policies in an effort to toughen up on juvenile offenders. Some have changed from an indeterminate to a **determinate sentence** in juvenile court. This means sentencing juvenile offenders to a fixed term of incarceration that must be served in its entirety. Other states have passed laws creating **mandatory sentences** for serious juvenile offenders. Juveniles receiving mandatory sentences are usually institutionalized for the full sentence and are not eligible for early parole. The difference between mandatory and determinate sentences is that the mandatory sentence carries a statutory requirement that a certain penalty be set in all cases on conviction for a specified offense.

mandatory sentence
Sentence is defined by a statutory requirement that states the penalty to be set for all cases of a specific offense.

New York's juvenile code gives the adult court original jurisdiction over cases involving fourteen- and fifteen-year-olds who commit serious violent felonies and over cases of thirteen-year-olds who commit murder.[69] If there are mitigating circumstances—for example, if the offender had only a small role in the crime—the adult court judge can waive the case back to the juvenile court. Known as New York's Juvenile Offender Law, this controversial statute reduced the age of criminal responsibility for direct prosecution of youths committing certain offenses in the adult courts and authorized lengthy periods of incarceration.

Probably the best-known effort to reform sentencing in the juvenile court is the state of Washington's **Juvenile Justice Reform Act of 1977.** This act created a mandatory sentencing policy requiring juveniles ages 8 to 17 who are adjudicated delinquent to be confined in an institution for a minimum time.[70] The legislative intent of the act was to make juveniles accountable for criminal behavior and to provide for punishment commensurate with the (1) age, (2) crime, and (3) prior history of the offender. Washington's tough approach to juvenile sentencing is based on the principle of "proportionality." How much time a youth must spend in confinement is established by the Juvenile Dispositions Standards Commission based on the above three criteria. The introduction of such mandatory sentencing procedures standardizes juvenile dispositions and reduces disparity in the length of sentences, according to advocates of a "get-tough" juvenile justice system. The most popular crime legislation being debated among state legislatures across the country is tougher sentences for juvenile offenders of serious and violent crime. The Washington reform statute has been a model for other states.

Evaluating Tough Sentencing Laws

Can such changes in juvenile sentencing statutes have positive outcomes for the operation of the juvenile justice system? One reason for optimism has been the rather dramatic change brought about in the state of Washington by passage of the Juvenile Justice Reform Act of 1977. Research by Tom Castellano found that there was a high degree of compliance with its provisions.[71] The law has moved Washington's juvenile justice system away from informality and disparity and toward the procedural regularity found in the adult system. More than 90 percent of the serious juvenile offenders who came before the court were removed from the community.

However, not all statutory changes have had the desired effect. For instance, although New York's Juvenile Offender Law requires that juveniles accused of violent offenses be tried in criminal court and provides serious penalties comparable to those for adults, Simon Singer and David McDowall conclude that the law's aim of deterring juvenile crime has not been achieved.[72] Since the law lowered the age of criminal responsibility and included family court jurisdiction, many youths ended up receiving lighter sentences than they would have in the family court.

At the time it was enacted, the New York law was considered to be among the toughest in the nation pertaining to crimes committed by juveniles ages 13, 14, and 15. Yet current data indicate that more arrests under the law result in outright dismissal than in any other single disposition.[73]

The growing realization that the juvenile crime rate has stabilized may slow the tide of legislative change in juvenile justice. What is more likely is that states will continue to pass legislation making it easier to transfer youths to the adult court or giving the adult court original jurisdiction over serious cases. Thus, rather than toughening juvenile law for everyone, the system may reserve the harshest measures for the few more serious cases, such as the recent spate of school murders.

The Future of Juvenile Sentencing and Serious Crime

During the past decade, the treatment-oriented philosophy has taken a backseat to the development of more formal and punitive approaches toward juveniles charged with serious crimes. Although more than half of the states still use indefinite sentencing, the trend for the future continues to point toward more determinate and fixed sentences. Does this mean that we have given up on the *parens patriae* philosophy and the century-old vision of the juvenile court movement? Has the system failed us? The Policy and Practice box entitled "Myth or Reality: The Juvenile Court System Is a Failure" examines these questions.

Many experts call for swift and sure sanctions, particularly for violent and repeat offenders.[74] A number of prominent national organizations have also recommended the use of tougher mandatory sentences. For example, the American Bar Association has developed standards that affect the disposition process. Stanley Fisher notes that these standards point to a shift in juvenile court philosophy from the traditional approach of rehabilitation to the concept of just deserts and enhanced penalties.[75] The standards recommend that juveniles receive determinate, or flat, sentences without the possibility of parole rather than the indeterminate sentences that most of them receive now.

The standards further recommend that punishment be classified into three major categories: nominal sanctions, conditional sanctions, and custodial sanctions. *Nominal sanctions* consist of reprimands, warnings, or other minor actions that do not affect the child's personal liberty. *Conditional sanctions* include probation, restitution, and counseling programs. *Custodial sanctions,* which are the most extreme, remove the juvenile from the community into a nonsecure or secure institution.[76] According to the National Conference of State Legislatures, several states have already adapted the minimum/maximum sentencing pattern used in the adult criminal justice system to juveniles. Under this system the offender must serve at least a minimum and up to a maximum amount of his or her sentence.[77]

At a time when much attention is focused on the small group of serious and violent juvenile offenders, a comprehensive, risk-focused balanced model has been recommended by the National Conference of State Legislatures, NDAA, and OJJDP.[78] First-time, nonviolent juvenile offenders receive community sanctions that hold them accountable while providing services aimed at risk reduction and development of resiliency skills. Progressively more punitive and restrictive sanctions are provided for more serious and chronic offenders, ending with secure confinement for the most serious and violent offenders. For example, a recent Connecticut law balances prevention with prosecution of serious repeat juvenile offenders. Legislation in Texas has also toughened sentencing for some juvenile offenders while establishing first offender programs for others (see Chapter 12).

In conclusion, the trend today is to severely increase sanctions for juvenile offenders. Juveniles face the prospect of longer sentences, mandatory minimum terms, and time in adult jails or prisons along with a host of other new tough juvenile crime statutes. State legislatures have focused on the following priorities in juvenile sentencing:

- *Parental responsibility statutes.* Legislative bodies in numerous states have enacted laws holding parents responsible for underaged drinking, graffiti damage, and drunken driving violations. Fines, community service, jail time, and mandatory parenting classes are among the list of punishments being used.[79]

- *Curfew laws.* Curfew laws are becoming commonplace in efforts to reduce delinquency. Seventy-seven percent of major U.S. cities now have curfew ordinances; during the period 1990 to 1997, half of these cities enacted curfew legislation for the first time or updated existing laws.[80] Many cities that have set curfew limits have also gone the extra mile to provide alternative activities for youth.

- *Retributive reforms.* Retributive reforms have led to increased rates of incarceration and longer incarceration terms. The "just deserts" philosophy is resulting in an expansion of punishment for juvenile offenders. Policymakers are legitimizing the concept of punishment for its own sake, and prosecutors are

MYTH OR REALITY: THE JUVENILE COURT SYSTEM IS A FAILURE

Studies show that about 40 percent of all delinquents brought to the juvenile court return. However, a recent review of four hundred programs handling serious juvenile offenders revealed that juvenile justice programs appear to be more effective today than in the past. The current system seems to work even with hard core cases, and supporters point to the fact that the violent arrest rate has gone down 9 percent in the last two years as evidence of success.

Despite this trend, the states are in favor of the prosecutor and the adult criminal court handling serious juvenile offenders. Skeptics believe the unprecedented amount of youth violence in the United States will only become worse in the future.

If the core premises of the juvenile court that impelled its creation one hundred years ago are sound, then labeling it a failure is nothing more than a myth. But the basic premises of the court are under assault. As we approach the centennial of the juvenile court, should we reexamine the assumptions upon which the court was founded? The Center for the Future of Children issued a report entitled "The Juvenile Court in 1996," which listed many important recommendations. Examine these recommendations and determine whether you think they will strengthen the court's ability to handle juvenile crime.

RECOMMENDATIONS

1. Juvenile courts should be at the level of the highest trial court of general jurisdiction in each state.
2. All judges and other judicial officers serving in a juvenile division or juvenile court should be required to have intensive and ongoing training in case law and child development.
3. Juvenile court judges should serve in the juvenile court division for at least two to three years.
4. All courts should work to better coordinate case processing by different branches of the general court that handle family-related matters including the juvenile court.
5. Juvenile courts should encourage the development and use of more alternative dispute resolution techniques.
6. Every youth who is referred to juvenile court for formal processing in delinquency matters should be represented by trained counsel from the time of the detention hearing throughout the court process.
7. The determination as to whether a minor charged with a serious crime should be transferred to the criminal court for trial as an adult is best made by judicial hearing.
8. Communities should ensure that a range of dispositional alternatives, providing a continuum of sanctions from community service and supervised probation to incarceration of juvenile offenders, is available to respond to juvenile crime; particular attention should be given to those models that have shown, through evaluation, success in reducing recidivism.
9. The first line of response to status offenders should be community and public services designed to help children and their families, with court intervention only after services have been offered but have not been successful, or if the child's behavior continues to pose a threat to his or her own safety or well-being.
10. In each state, every effort should be made to assess the data system needs of juvenile courts and to address these needs in a coordinated and complementary manner.

Sources: James Howell, "Five Myths About Juvenile Justice," *Juvenile and Family Justice Journal* 7:21 (1998); Carol S. Stevenson, "The Juvenile Court: Analysis and Recommendations," in *The Future of Children* (Los Altos, Calif.: David Packard Foundation, 1996); Shay Bilchik, *A Juvenile Justice System for the 21st Century* (Washington, D.C.: OJJDP, 1998).

UNITED STATES V. LOPEZ (1995)

FACTS

Alfonso Lopez was a twelfth-grade student at a public high school in San Antonio, Texas, when he was charged with violating the Gun-Free School Zones Act of 1990, having been caught carrying a concealed .38 caliber handgun on school grounds. Confronted by school officials, Lopez explained that he was to be paid $40 to deliver the gun to "Jason" for use in a gang war.

The Gun-Free School Zones Act made it a federal crime for any individual knowingly to possess a firearm at a place that the individual knows, or has reasonable cause to believe, is a school zone (18 USC Sec. 922 (q)). The act defined school zone as "in or on the grounds of a public, parochial or private school, or within a distance of 1,000 feet from the grounds of a public, parochial or private school." In passing the act, Congress relied on its constitutional authority to regulate interstate commerce conferred by the Commerce Clause (U.S. Constitution, Article I, Sec. 8, Cl. 3).

DECISION

Lopez was found guilty in the federal district court and sentenced to six months in prison, two years' supervised release, and a $50 special fine under the Gun-Free School Zones Act. Lopez defended his case by arguing that Congress exceeded its authority under the Commerce Clause. He appealed to the Fifth Circuit Court of Appeals, which reversed his conviction. The U.S. Supreme Court later affirmed the appellate court decision. The Court said that Congress had exceeded its authority in attempting to regulate a local activity—education—without showing a connection between bringing a firearm onto school grounds and interstate commerce.

Chief Justice William Rehnquist wrote that Congress can regulate only activity that "substantially affects" interstate commerce. He pointed out that possession of a handgun on school grounds was not a commercial activity, and therefore, the criminal statute had nothing to do with commerce or any sort of economic enterprise. The *Lopez* case marked the first time in more

taking it as a green light to demand more severe punishments with less treatment emphasis, especially for repeat offenders.[81]

- *Waiver laws.* Perhaps no area of juvenile justice has received more attention of late than that of reforms designed to treat juvenile offenders more like adults. For that reason alone, it is important to note that Alaska, Delaware, Indiana, Louisiana, Minnesota, North Dakota, Oregon, Utah, and West Virginia have added crimes for which juveniles may—or must, in some cases—be prosecuted as adults. More than a dozen states have passed laws to treat juvenile court proceedings more like those of adult courts. This includes fingerprinting and photographing juvenile defendants.[82]

- *Firearm bans.* By 1995 forty states had enacted laws outlawing gun possession by juveniles within a certain distance of a school. Enhanced penalties for crimes involving firearms in school zones, such as mandatory sentences, are being considered by many jurisdictions. Even though the federal Gun-Free School Zones Act of 1990 was declared unconstitutional in 1995 on the ground that Congress lacked constitutional power to regulate gun possession because it is a local

than sixty years that the Supreme Court invalidated federal legislation regulating private parties on the basis of the Commerce Clause.

SIGNIFICANCE OF THE CASE

The Court's decision allowed Lopez to go free. Looking at the broader picture, the Court rejected the government's argument that firearm possession on school grounds would lead to violent crime that would be costly to the economy and provide a substantial relationship to interstate commerce. Second, the Court rejected the notion that firearm possession on school grounds, by substantially disrupting the educational process, would reduce the productivity of the workforce and jeopardize the economy. The Court said that to agree to these ideas would convert Congress's power to regulate interstate commerce into a general police power, disrupting the unique relationship between the federal, state, and local governments.

By enforcing limits on the Commerce Clause, the Court moved to slow down the process of federalizing the criminal law. Nevertheless, it is important to keep in mind that this was a close decision (a 5-4 majority). Justice Stephen Breyer, in his dissent, insisted that educational achievement is intimately connected to economic success and that education is itself an enormous economic enterprise. He, therefore, reasoned that Congress had not violated its powers under the Commerce Clause in adopting the Gun-Free School Zones statute. In light of the Breyer dissent and the continuing arguments over whether state criminal offenses should be made violations of federal law, the true significance of the *Lopez* case and the proper interpretation of the Commerce Clause remain uncertain.

Because gun possession is common for serious juvenile offenders, many states have adopted statutes both to prohibit the possession of handguns by juveniles and gun-free school zone laws. These laws are state laws, thus they are not in conflict with the *Lopez* decision, which had invalidated an act of Congress under the federal Constitution.

Source: *United States v. Lopez*, 115 S.Ct. 1624 (1995).

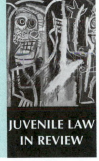

JUVENILE LAW IN REVIEW

matter, laws designed specifically to protect children are being passed at the state level.[83] This trend is illustrated in the Juvenile Law in Review box entitled *"United States v. Lopez."*

■ *Blended sentences*. State sentencing trends indicate that punishment and accountability, in addition to rehabilitation, have become equally important, if not primary priorities, in juvenile justice policy. As a result, many states have created "blended" sentencing structures for cases involving serious and repeat juvenile offenders. Blended sentencing allows the imposition of juvenile and adult correctional sanctions for serious juvenile offenders adjudicated in juvenile court or convicted in criminal court. In other words, this expanded sentencing authority allows criminal and juvenile courts to impose either a juvenile or adult sentence, or both, in cases involving juvenile offenders. When both sentences are imposed simultaneously, the court suspends the adult sanction. If the youth follows the conditions of the juvenile sentence and commits no further violation, the adult sentence is revoked. This type of statute has become popular in recent years, with Connecticut, Kentucky, and Minnesota among the states adopting it since 1994.[84]

The Death Penalty for Juveniles

The most controversial of all sentences, adult or juvenile, continues to be the death penalty. The execution of minor children has not been uncommon in our nation's history. Victor Streib, a law professor and leading expert on the death penalty for children, claims that about 350 juvenile offenders have been executed since 1642. This represents about 2 percent of the total of more than 18,000 executions carried out since colonial times. As of 1998, 67 persons were on death row for capital crimes committed as juveniles. All 67 juvenile offenders on death row had been convicted and sentenced to death for murder.[85]

There has been ample debate on whether children as young as sixteen should be sentenced to death. The U.S. Supreme Court had a chance to resolve this issue in the 1982 case of *Eddings v. Oklahoma* but refused to do so.[86] The case involved a sixteen-year-old boy who killed a highway patrol officer. Although the Court overturned his sentence, it did so on the ground that the trial court had failed to consider his emotional state and troubled childhood when dispensing the death penalty. The Court did not deal with the issue of whether age alone could prohibit a person from being executed. In 1988, however, the Court did prohibit the execution of persons under age sixteen in the narrowly interpreted case of *Thompson v. Oklahoma*. Some justices endorsed the idea that a child should be presumed to be less responsible than an adult when he or she commits a criminal homicide. This decision left unanswered the issue of whether the Constitution prohibits the use of the death penalty for juveniles who were sixteen or seventeen years old when they committed their crimes.[87]

The Supreme Court finally confronted the highly emotional question in 1989 in the cases of *Wilkins v. Missouri* and *Stanford v. Kentucky*.[88] Wilkins was sixteen when he committed murder; Stanford was seventeen. The constitutional question raised by these two cases is basically the same as in the *Thompson* case: At what age does the Eighth Amendment ban the death penalty as punishment, no matter what the crime? Critics of the death penalty believed there was a consensus against executing young people in the United States. Supporters of **capital punishment** argued that juveniles older than age 16 should be held fully responsible for murder. The Supreme Court concluded that states were free to impose the death penalty for murderers who committed their crimes at age 16 or 17. According to the majority opinion, written by Justice Antonin Scalia, society has not formed a consensus that the execution of such minors constitutes a cruel and unusual punishment in violation of the Eighth Amendment.

Those who oppose the death penalty for children, led by Streib, find that it has little deterrent effect on youngsters who are impulsive and do not have a realistic view of the destructiveness of their misdeeds or their consequences. Streib and his associates maintain that the execution of a person who is a child at the time of the crime is cruel and unusual punishment because (1) the condemnation of children makes no measurable contribution to the legitimate goals of punishment, (2) condemning any minor to death violates contemporary standards of decency, (3) the capacity of the young for change, growth, and rehabilitation makes the death penalty particularly harsh and inappropriate, and (4) both legislative attitudes and public opinion reject juvenile executions.[89] Supporters of the death penalty hold that people, regardless of their age, can form criminal intent and therefore should be responsible for their actions. If the death penalty is legal for adults, they argue, then it can also be used for children who commit serious crimes.

What is the situation involving the use of the death penalty abroad? International human rights treaties prohibit anyone who was under eighteen at the time of the crime from being sentenced to death. The International Covenant on Civil and Political Rights, the American Convention on Human Rights, and the UN Convention on the Rights of the Child all have provisions to this effect. More than one hundred countries have laws specifically excluding the execution of juvenile offenders or

capital punishment
Use of the death penalty to punish offenders.

may be presumed to exclude such executions by being parties to one or another of the above treaties. A small number of countries, however, continue to execute juvenile offenders. Five countries since 1990 are known to have executed prisoners who were under eighteen at the time of the crime: Iran, Pakistan, Saudi Arabia, the United States, and Yemen. The majority of known executions of juvenile offenders was in the United Sates (six since 1990).[90]

The fact that the United States is not alone in executing criminals appears to support the retention of the death penalty. However, the fact that so many countries have abolished capital punishment and the trend toward international abolition encourages those who want capital punishment to be abandoned (see the Focus on Delinquency box entitled "Juvenile Death Penalty").

Confidentiality in Juvenile Proceedings

confidentiality
Restricting information in juvenile court proceedings in the interest of protecting the privacy of the juvenile.

Along with the rights of juveniles at adjudication and disposition, the issue of **confidentiality** in juvenile proceedings has also received attention in recent years. The debate centers around whether the practice of restricting information in juvenile court proceedings in the interest of protecting the privacy of juveniles is preferable to the current cry for open proceedings that might increase public exposure for juveniles.[91] The debate on confidentiality in the juvenile court deals with two areas: (1) open versus closed hearings and (2) privacy of juvenile records. Confidentiality, considered by many to be a basic tenet of juvenile justice philosophy, has become moot in some respects as many legislatures have broadened access to juvenile records.

Open versus Closed Hearings

Generally, juvenile trials are closed to the public and the press, and the names of the offenders are kept secret. The Supreme Court has ruled on the issue of privacy in three important decisions. In *Davis v. Alaska* the Court concluded that any injury resulting from the disclosure of a juvenile's record is outweighed by the right to completely cross-examine an adverse witness.[92] The *Davis* case involved an effort to obtain testimony from a juvenile probationer who was a witness in a criminal trial. After the prosecutor was granted a court order preventing the defense from making any reference to the juvenile's record, the Supreme Court reversed the state court, claiming that a juvenile's interest in confidentiality was secondary to the constitutional right to confront adverse witnesses.

The decisions in two subsequent cases, *Oklahoma Publishing Co. v. District Court* and *Smith v. Daily Mail Publishing Co.*, sought to balance juvenile privacy with freedom of the press. In the *Oklahoma* case, the Supreme Court ruled that a state court was not allowed to prohibit the publication of information obtained in an open juvenile proceeding.[93] The case involved an eleven-year-old boy suspected of homicide who appeared at a detention hearing and of whom photographs were taken and published in local newspapers. When the local district court prohibited further disclosure, the publishing company claimed that the court order was a restraint in violation of the First Amendment, and the Supreme Court agreed.

JUVENILE DEATH PENALTY

Victor Streib has released a new report on the death penalty for juvenile offenders covering the last quarter century, 1973 through 1997. In *The Juvenile Death Penalty Today,* Streib says death sentences for juvenile offenders have remained fairly consistent over the past two decades. Executions have been sporadic. No juvenile offenders have been executed since 1993, when there were four executions in six months.

The report includes these statistics:

- A total of 167 juvenile death sentences have been imposed since 1973, or 2.7 percent of the total of 6,180 death sentences imposed for offenders of all ages.

- Over two-thirds of these sentences have been imposed on seventeen-year-old offenders; one-third on offenders ages 16 and 15; none on offenders age 14 or younger at the time of their crimes.

- Of these 167 juvenile death sentences, 67 remain currently in force, or 2 percent of the total death row population of about 3,400.

- Nine death row sentences have resulted in execution; 91 have been reversed.

- Texas leads all other states in death sentences for juvenile offenders with 26 juvenile offenders on death row.

Arrests of juveniles for intentional homicide increased by 90 percent during the ten-year period from 1986 through 1995.

Streib says the number of arrests of juveniles for potentially capital crimes has resulted neither in a comparable rise in juvenile death sentencing nor a significant rise in the number of juvenile offenders on death row. Currently, thirty-eight states and the federal government have statutes authorizing the death penalty for certain forms of murder:

- Of those thirty-nine jurisdictions, fifteen designate age 18 at the time of the crime as the minimum age for the death penalty.

- Four states, Georgia, New Hampshire, North Carolina, and Texas, designate age 17 as the minimum age.

- The remaining twenty states use age 16 as the minimum age, either through an express age in the statutes or by court ruling.

- Fourteen states remain without the death penalty.

Source: Victor Streib, *The Juvenile Death Penalty Today: Death Sentences and Executions for Juvenile Crimes over the Last Quarter Century 1973–1997* (Ada, Ohio: Ohio Northern University, 1997).

The *Smith* case involved the discovery and subsequent publication by news reporters of the identity of a juvenile suspect in violation of a state statute prohibiting publication. The Supreme Court, however, declared the statute unconstitutional because it believed the state's interest in protecting the child's identity was not of such a magnitude as to justify the use of such a statute.[94] Therefore, if newspapers lawfully obtain pictures or names of juveniles, they may publish them. Based on these decisions, it appears that the Supreme Court favors the constitutional rights of the press over the right to privacy of the juvenile offender.

None of the decisions, however, gave the press complete access to juvenile trials. Today, some jurisdictions still bar the press from juvenile proceedings unless they show at a hearing that their presence will not harm the youth. In other words, when states follow a *parens patriae* philosophy, ordinarily the public and press are excluded. However, the court has discretion to permit interested parties to observe the hearings.

Privacy of Juvenile Records

For most of the twentieth century juvenile records were kept confidential by case law, or statute. The general rule was that juvenile court records—both legal and social—were considered confidential and thus inaccessible.[95] Today, however, the record itself, or information contained in it, can be opened by court order in many jurisdictions on the basis of statutory exception. The following groups can ordinarily gain access to juvenile records: (1) law enforcement personnel, (2) the child's attorney, (3) the parents or guardians, (4) military personnel, (5) and public agencies such as schools, court-related organizations, and correctional institutions.

Many states have enacted laws authorizing a central repository for juvenile arrest records. Some states allow a juvenile adjudication for a criminal act, such as rape, to be used as evidence in a subsequent adult criminal proceeding for the same act to show predisposition or criminal nature. In addition, a juvenile's records may be used during the disposition or sentencing stage of an adult criminal trial in some states. Knowledge of a defendant's juvenile record may help prosecutors and judges determine appropriate sentencing for offenders ages 18 to 24, the age group most likely to be involved in violent crime.

Today, most states recognize the importance of juvenile records in sentencing. Many first-time adult offenders committed numerous crimes as juveniles, and evidence of these crimes may not be available or relevant to sentencing for the adult offenses unless states pass statutes allowing access. According to experts such as Ira Schwartz, the need for confidentiality to protect juveniles is far less than the need to open up the courts to public scrutiny and accountability.[96] The problem of maintaining confidentiality of juvenile records will become more acute in the future as electronic information storage makes these records both more durable and more accessible.

In conclusion, virtually every state provides prosecutors and judges access to the juvenile arrest and disposition records of adult offenders. There is a great diversity, however, among the states regarding the provisions for the collection and retention of juvenile records and such information as fingerprinting.[97]

SUMMARY

In this chapter we described two major aspects of the juvenile justice system: adjudication and disposition. Most jurisdictions have a bifurcated juvenile code system that separates the adjudication hearing from the dispositional hearing. Juveniles alleged to be delinquent, as well as children in need of supervision, have virtually all the rights given a criminal defendant at trial—except possibly the right to a trial by jury. In addition, juvenile proceedings are generally closed to the public.

The types of dispositional orders that the juvenile court gives include dismissal, fine, probation, and institutionalization. The use of such dispositions has not curtailed the rising rate of juvenile crime, however. As a result, legislatures and national commissions have begun to take a tougher position with regard to the sentencing of some juvenile offenders. The traditional notion of rehabilitation and treatment as the proper goals for disposition is now being questioned, and some jurisdictions have replaced it with proportionality and determinacy in sentencing procedures. However, many juvenile codes do require that the court consider the "least restrictive" alternative before removing a juvenile from the home.

The predisposition report is the primary informational source for assisting the court in making a judgment about a child's care and treatment. Once a juvenile is found delinquent or in need of supervision, the juvenile court is empowered through the dispositional process to make fundamental changes in the child's life. In recent years a number of states have made drastic changes in juvenile sentencing law, moving away from the pure indeterminate sentence and embracing more structured, determinate forms of disposition. If there is any chance for juvenile crime to be reduced in the future, it may well depend on fair, just, and effective disposition. States are taking unusual approaches to juvenile crime. They have passed laws allowing judges to hand down blended sentences to children found guilty of serious crimes: a juvenile sentence that remains in effect until the defendant turns twenty-one and a suspended adult sentence that can be reinstated if the juvenile has any further brushes with the law.

The most extreme form of punishment is, of course, the death penalty, which in some states can be administered to children as young as sixteen. The use of capital punishment has been the subject of much heated debate, but at present 67 persons remain on death row for crimes committed as juveniles.

Finally, many state statutes require that juvenile hearings be closed and that the privacy of juvenile records be maintained to protect the child from public scrutiny and to provide a greater opportunity for rehabilitation. But this approach may be inconsistent with the public's recent interest in taking a closer look at the juvenile justice system.

KEY TERMS

juvenile court
jurisdiction
juvenile prosecutor
juvenile court judge
Missouri Plan
National Council of
    Juvenile and Family
    Court Judges
juvenile defense attorneys
guardian *ad litem*
Court Appointed Special
    Advocates (CASA)

public defender
adjudication hearing
due process
disposition
predispositional
    investigation
final order
appellate process
trial *de novo*
writ of habeus corpus
writ of certiorari

least detrimental
    alternative
indeterminate sentence
individualized treatment
    model
determinate sentence
mandatory sentence
Juvenile Justice Reform
    Act of 1977
capital punishment
confidentiality

INFOTRAC COLLEGE EDITION EXERCISES

Read the following article from InfoTrac College Edition:

Abolish the juvenile court: youthfulness, criminal responsibility, and sentencing policy. (Symposium on the Future of the Juvenile Court) Barry C. Feld. *Journal of Criminal Law and Criminology* Fall 1997

The origins of the juvenile court were founded on a model of treatment. Recently, many juvenile crimes have had decidedly violent outcomes, leading people to question the necessity of the juvenile court, especially when dealing with these violent offenders. However, some would say that abolishing the juvenile court is akin to giving up on our youth.

What are some problems associated with Feld's proposal to abolish the juvenile court? Focus on such issues as youths tried as adults, the court as social welfare agency, and necessary modifications to the existing criminal courts.

QUESTIONS FOR DISCUSSION

1. Discuss and identify the major participants in the juvenile adjudication process. What are each person's role and responsibilities in the course of a juvenile trial?

2. The criminal justice system in the United States is based on the adversarial process. Does the same adversary principle apply in the juvenile justice system?

3. Children have certain constitutional rights at adjudication, such as the right to an attorney and the right to confront and cross-examine witnesses. But they do not have the right to a trial by jury. Should juvenile offenders have a constitutional right to a jury trial? Should each state make that determination? Discuss the legal decision that addresses this issue.

4. What is the point of obtaining a predisposition report in the juvenile court? Is it of any value in cases where the child is released to the community? Does it have a significant value in serious juvenile crime cases?

5. The standard of proof in juvenile adjudication is to show that the child is guilty beyond a reasonable doubt. Explain the meaning of this standard of proof in the U.S. judicial system.

6. Should states adopt "get-tough" sentences in juvenile justice or adhere to the individualized treatment model?

7. Do you agree with the principle of imposing the death penalty on juveniles found to have committed certain capital crimes?

8. What are blended sentences?

9. Should individuals who committed murder while under age 16 be legally executed?

NOTES

1. Barry Krisberg, *The Juvenile Court: Reclaiming the Vision* (San Francisco: National Council on Crime and Delinquency, 1988); Edward Humes, *No Matter How Loud I Shout: A Year in the Life of Juvenile Court* (New York: Simon and Schuster, 1995).

2. Melissa H. Sickmund, *Juvenile Court Statistics 1995* (Pittsburgh, Pa.: National Center for Juvenile Justice, 1998).

3. Robert Shepard Jr., "Doing Justice to Juvenile Justice," *Juvenile and Family Justice Journal* 6:5–7(1997).

4. See Samuel Davis, *The Rights of Juveniles,* 3rd ed. (New York: Clark Boardman, 1984, 1992); see also, Mark Soler, James Bell, Elizabeth Jameson, Carole Shauffer, Alice Shotton, and Loren Warboys, *Representing the Child Client* (New York: Matthew Bender, 1992).

5. *Lamb v. Brown,* 456 F.2d 18 (1972).

6. National Conference of State Legislatures, *A Legislator's Guide to Comprehensive Juvenile Justice, Treating Juveniles Like Adults* (Denver, Colo.: National Conference of State Legislatures, 1996).

7. 359 Mass. 550(1971); 322 A.2d 58 (1975).

8. State ex rel. *Harris v. Calendine,* 33 S.E. 2d 318 (1977).

9. *O.W. v. Bird,* 461 So.2d 967 (Fla.Dist.Ct.App. 1984); *In re Michael G.,* 214 Cal.Rptr. 755 App. Ct. 1 (1985).

10. Eileen Garry, "Truancy: First Steps to a Lifetime of Problems," *Juvenile Justice Bulletin* (Washington, D.C.: OJJDP, 1996).

11. U.S. Department of Justice, *Prosecution in the Juvenile Courts* (Washington, D.C.: U.S. Government Printing Office, 1973), p. 9.

12. *Kent v. United States,* 383 U.S. 541, 86 S.Ct. 1045, 16 L.Ed.2d 84 (1966); *In re Gault* 387 U.S. 1, 87 S.Ct. 1428, 18 L.Ed.2d 527 (1967); *In re Winship,* 397 U.S. 358, 90 S.Ct. 1068, 25 L.Ed.2d 368 (1970).

13. American Bar Association, *Standards Relating to Juvenile Prosecution* (Cambridge, Mass.: Ballinger, 1977), p. 13; Robert Shepard Jr. "The Prosecutor in the Juvenile Court," *ABA Journal on Criminal Justice* 32:36–40 (1968).

14. National District Attorneys Association, *Prosecution Standard 19.2, Juvenile Delinquency* (Alexandria, Va.: NDAA, 1992).

15. James Shine and Dwight Price, "Prosecutor & Juvenile Justice: New Roles and Perspectives," in Ira Schwartz, ed., *Juvenile Justice and Public Policy* (New York: Lexington Books, 1992), pp. 101–33.

16. James Backstrom and Gary Walker, "A Balanced Approach to Juvenile Justice: The Work of the Juvenile Justice Advisory Committee," *The Prosecutor* 32:37–39 (1988); see also, *Prosecutors' Policy Recommendations on Serious, Violent and Habitual Youthful Offenders* (Alexandria, Va.: American Prosecutors' Institute, 1997).

17. Yeheskel Hasenfeld and Paul Cheung, "The Juvenile Court and a People-Processing Organization: A Political Economy Perspective," *American Journal of Sociology* 90:801–24 (1985).

18. Leonard P. Edwards, "The Juvenile Court and the Role of the Juvenile Court Judge," *Juvenile and Family Court Journal* 43:3–45 (1992); Lois Haight, "Why I Choose to be a Juvenile Court Judge," *Juvenile and Family Justice Today* 7:7 (1998).

19. Sari Escovitz with Fred Kurland and Nan Gold, *Judicial Selection and Tenure* (Chicago: American Judicature Society, 1974), pp. 3–16.

20. National Council of Juvenile and Family Court Judges, "Juvenile and Family Justice," *Juvenile and Family Court Journal* 3:15 (1992).

21. National Council of Juvenile and Family Court Judges, *Annual Report,* 1991 (Pittsburgh, Pa.: National Center for Juvenile Justice, 1991).

22. *Powell v. Alabama* 287 U.S. 45, 53 S.Ct. 55, 77, L.Ed.2d 158 (1932); *Gideon v. Wainwright* 372 U.S. 335, 83 S.Ct. 792, 9 L.Ed.2d 799 (1963); *Argersinger v. Hamlin* 407 U.S. 25, 92 S.Ct. 2006, 32 L.Ed.2d 530 (1972).

23. American Bar Association, *Standard Relating to Counsel for Private Parties* (Cambridge, Mass.: Ballinger, 1977).

24. Howard Davidson, "The Guardian *ad Litem:* An Important Approach to the Protection of Children," *Children Today* 10:23 (1981); Daniel Golden, "Who Guards the Children?" *Boston Globe Magazine* 27 December 1992, p. 12.

25. F. Eastman, "Procedures and Due Process," *Juvenile and Family Court Journal* 22:35–36 (1983), p. 35.

26. Office of Juvenile Justice and Delinquency Prevention, "CASA: Court Appointed Special Advocate for Children," *Juvenile Justice Bulletin* (Washington, D.C.: Department of Justice, 1992); Steve Riddell, "CASA—A Child's Voice in Court," *Juvenile and Family Justice Today,* 7:13–14 (1998).

27. S. H. Clark and G. G. Koch, "Juvenile Court: Therapy or Crime Control and Do Lawyers Make a Difference?", *Law and Society Review* 14:263–308 (1980); David Duffee and Larry Siegel, "The Organization Man: Legal Counsel in Juvenile Court," *Criminal Law Bulletin* 7:544–53 (1971).

28. Joseph Sanborn, "The Defense Attorney's Role in Juvenile Court: Must Justice or Treatment (or Both) Be Compromised?", paper presented at the Academy of Criminal Justice Sciences, St. Louis, Mo., March 15–19, 1987, p. 32; Randy Hertz, Martin Guggenheim, and Anthony Amsterdam, *Trial Manual for Defense Attorneys in Juvenile Court* (Chicago: American Law Institute, American Bar Association, 1991).

29. Sanborn, "The Defense Attorney's Role in Juvenile Court," p. 8.

30. Jane Knitzer, *Law Guardians in New York State* (New York: New York State Bar Association, 1985); David Hechler, "Lawyers for Children: No Experience Necessary," *Justice for Children* 1:14–15 (1985).

31. Sanford Fox, *Juvenile Courts* (St. Paul, Minn.: West, 1984), p. 162.

32. Barry C. Feld, "The Right to Counsel in Juvenile Court: An Empirical Study of When Lawyers Appeal and the Difference They Make," *Journal of Criminal Law and Criminology* 79:1187–1346 (1989).

33. Ibid., p. 1318.

34. Ibid., p. 1346.

35. Clark and Koch, "Juvenile Court: Therapy or Crime Control and Do Lawyers Make a Difference?"; David Aday, "Court Structure, Defense Attorney Use, and Juvenile Court Decisions," *Sociological Quarterly* 27:107–19 (1986); James Walter and Susan Ostrander, "An Observational Study of a Juvenile Court," *Juvenile and Family Court Journal* 33:53–69 (1982); Barry Feld, "*In re Gault* Revisited: A Cross-State Comparison of the Right to Counsel in Juvenile Court," *Crime and Delinquency* 34:392–424 (1988).

36. Barry C. Feld, "The Punitive Juvenile Court and the Quality of Procedural Justice: Dysfunctions between Rhetoric and Reality," *Crime and Delinquency* 36:443–65 (1990).

37. American Bar Association, *A Call for Justice—An Assessment of Access to Counsel and Quality of Representation in Delinquency Proceedings* (Washington, D.C.: ABA Juvenile Justice Center, 1995).

38. "Juveniles Go to Court Unrepresented," *The Boston Globe* 1 January 1996, p. 20.

39. Douglas Dodge, "Due Process Advocacy" Fact Sheet 67 (Washington, D.C.: OJJDP, 1997).

40. Jeffrey Fagan, Ellen Slaughter, and Eliot Hartstone, "Blind Justice? The Impact of Race on the Juvenile Justice Process," *Criminal Delinquency* 33:224–58 (1987).

41. Sickmund, *Juvenile Court Statistics 1995*, p. 32.

42. Edmund McGarrell, "Trends in Racial Disproportionality in Juvenile Court Processing: 1985–1989," *Crime and Delinquency* 39:29–48 (1993).

43. Institute of Judicial Administration, American Bar Association Joint Commission on Juvenile Justice Standards, *Standards Relating to Adjudication* (Cambridge, Mass.: Ballinger, 1980).

44. Joseph B. Sanborn Jr., "The Right to a Public Jury Trial—A Need for Today's Juvenile Court," *Judicature* 76:230–38 (1993).

45. *In re Gault*, 387 U.S. 1, 87 S.Ct. 1428 (1967), at 19.

46. *Kent v. United States*, 383 U.S. 541, 86 S.Ct. 1045 (1966).

47. *In re Gault*, 387 U.S. 1, 87 S.Ct. 1428 (1967).

48. Linda Szymanski, *Juvenile Delinquents' Right to Counsel* (Pittsburgh, Pa.: National Center for Juvenile Justice, 1988).

49. *In re Winship*, 397 U.S. 358, 90 S.Ct. 1068 (1970).

50. *McKeiver v. Pennsylvania*, 403 U.S. 528, 91 S.Ct. 1976 (1971).

51. Adrienne E. Volenik, *Checklist for Use in Juvenile Delinquency Proceedings* (Washington, D.C.: American Bar Association, 1985), p. 42.

52. See, generally, R. T. Powell, "Disposition Concepts," *Juvenile and Family Court Journal* 34:7–18 (1983).

53. Paul Piersma, Jeanette Ganousis, and Prudence Kramer, "The Juvenile Court: Current Problems, Legislative Proposals, and a Model Act," *St. Louis University Law Review* 20:43 (1976); Robert Shepard Jr., "Preparing for the Juvenile Disposition," *American Bar Association Criminal Justice Journal* 7:35–36 (1993).

54. Lindsay Arthur, "Status Offenders Need a Court of Last Resort," *Boston University Law Review* 57:63–64 (1977).

55. Sanford Fox, *Juvenile Courts in a Nutshell* (St. Paul, Minn.: West, 1984), p. 221.

56. *Kent v. United States*, 383 U.S. 541, 86 S.Ct. 1045 (1966).

57. National Advisory Commission on Criminal Justice Standards and Goals, *Report of the Task Force on Juvenile Justice and Delinquency Prevention* (Washington, D.C.: U.S. Government Printing Office, 1976), p. 445.

58. This section is adapted from Jack Haynes and Eugene Moore, "Particular Dispositions," *Juvenile and Family Court Journal* 34:41–48 (1983); see also, Grant Grissom, "Dispositional Authority and the Future of the Juvenile Justice System," *Juvenile and Family Court Journal* 42:25–34 (1991).

59. Criminal Justice Program of National Conference of State Legislatures, *Legal Dispositions* and *Confinement Policies for Delinquent Youth* (Denver: National Conference of State Legislatures, July 1988), p. 3; American Bar Association Institute of Judicial Administration, *Standards on Juvenile Justice, Standards Relating to Dispositions* (Cambridge, Mass.: Ballinger Press, 1977), p. 2.1.

60. Ibid., p. 129.

61. Barry Krisberg, Elliot Currie, and David Onek, "What Works with Juvenile Offenders," *American Bar Association Journal on Criminal Justice* 10:20–24 (1995).

62. Paul Piersma, Jeanette Ganousis, Adrienne E. Volenik, Harry F. Swanger, and Patricia Connell, *Law and Tactics in Juvenile Cases* (Philadelphia: American Law Institute, American Bar Association, Committee on Continuing Education, 1977), p. 397.

63. J. Addison Bowman, "Appeals from Juvenile Courts," *Crime and Delinquency Journal* 11:63–77 (1965).

64. *In re Gault*, 387 U.S. 1 87 S.Ct. 1428 (1967).

65. Anthony Platt, *The Child Savers: The Invention of Delinquency* (Chicago: University of Chicago Press, 1969); David Rothman, *Conscience and Convenience: The Asylum and the Alternative in Progressive America* (Boston: Little Brown, 1980).

66. Joseph Goldstein, Anna Freud, and Albert Solnit, *Beyond the Best Interests of the Child* (New York: Free Press, 1973).

67. Martin Forst, Bruce Fisher, and Robert Coates, "Indeterminate and Determinate Sentencing of Juvenile Delinquents: A National Survey of Approaches to Commitment and Release Decision Making," *Juvenile and Family Court Journal* 36:1–12 (1985).

68. Ibid., p. 9.

69. N.Y.Fam.Ct.Act 753 (1978); also see, New York State Laws of 1976, Chap. 878.

70. Washington Juvenile Justice Reform Act of 1977, Chap. 291; Wash. Rev. Code Ann. Title 9A, Sec. 1–91 (1977).

71. Thomas Castellano, "The Justice Model in the Juvenile Justice System: Washington State's Experience," paper presented at the Academy of Criminal Justice Sciences, St. Louis, Mo., March 15–18, 1987.

72. Simon Singer and David McDowall, "Criminalizing Delinquency: The Deterrent Effects of NYJO Law," *Law and Society Review* 22:Sections 21–37 (1988).

73. New York State Division for Youth, *Research Focus on Youth—Juvenile Offenders*, Vol. 2, No. 1 (1992).

74. Rita Kramer, *At a Tender Age: Violent Youth and Juvenile Justice* (New York: Holt, 1988).

75. Stanley Fisher, "The Dispositional Process under the Juvenile Justice Standards Project," *Boston University Law Review* 57:732 (1977).

76. Robert Shepard Jr., ed., *Juvenile Justice Standards* (Chicago: ABA, 1996).

77. Criminal Justice Program of the National Conference of State Legislatures, *Legal Dispositions and Confinement Policies for Delinquent Youth*, p. 5.

78. National Conference of State Legislatures, *A Comprehensive Guide to Juvenile Justice* (Denver, Colo.: NCSI, 1997); National District Attorneys' Association, *Prosecutors' Policy Statement on Violent Youthful Offenders* (Alexandria, Va.: NDAA, 1997).

79. "Making Parents Pay—Parental Responsibility," *U.S. News & World Report* 12 June 1995, p. 42.

80. William Ruefle and Kenneth Reynolds, "Curfews and Delinquency in Major American Cities," *Crime and Delinquency* 41:347–61 (1995); Alexander Marketos, "The Constitutionality of Juvenile Curfews," *Crime and Delinquency* 40:17–30 (1995); see also, Office of Justice Programs, *Curfew: An Answer to Delinquency* (Washington, D.C.: OJJDP, 1997).

81. Gordon Bazemore and Mark Umbreit, "Rethinking the Sanctioning Function in Juvenile Court, Retributive or Restorative Responses to Juvenile Crime," *Crime and Delinquency* 41:296–316 (1995).

82. "Crime and Sentencing State Enactments, 1995, and Juvenile Crime and Justice State Enactments, 1995," *National Conference of State Legislatures* (Denver: NCLS, 1995); see also, Carol DeFrances, "Juveniles Prosecuted in State Criminal Courts" (Washington, D.C.: Bureau of Justice Statistics, 1997).

83. David Stewart, "Back to the Commerce Clause," *American Bar Association Journal* 81:46–48 (1995).

84. National Criminal Justice Association, *Juvenile Justice Reform Initiatives in the States—1994–1996* (Washington, D.C.: U.S. Department of Justice, 1997).

85. Victor Streib, *Death Penalty for Juveniles* (Bloomington: Indiana University Press, 1987); Paul Reidinger, "The Death Row Kids," *American Bar Association Journal* April: 78 (1989); Victor Streib, *The Juvenile Death Penalty Today: Present Death Row Inmates under Juvenile Death Sentences* (Cleveland: Cleveland State University, 25 August 1992); see also, Sam Verhovek, "Legislator Proposes Death Penalty for Murderers as Young as Eleven," *New York Times* 18 April 1998, p. B10.

86. *Eddings v. Oklahoma*, 455 U.S. 104 (1982); 102 S.Ct. 869.

87. Steven Gerstein, "The Constitutionality of Executing Juvenile Offenders, *Thompson v. Oklahoma*," *Criminal Law Bulletin* 24:91–98 (1988); *Thompson v. Oklahoma*, 108 S.Ct. 2687 (1988).

88. 109 S.Ct. 2969 (1989); for a recent analysis of the *Wilkins* and *Stanford* cases, see the note in "*Stanford v. Kentucky* and *Wilkins v. Missouri*—Juveniles, Capital Crime, and Death Penalty," *Criminal Justice Journal* 11:240–66 (1989).

89. Victor Streib, "Excluding Juveniles from New York's Impendent Death Penalty," *Albany Law Review* 54:625–79 (1990).

90. Associated Press, "Chechen Pair Executed in Public," *The Boston Globe* 19 September 1997, p. 9; National Coalition to Abolish Death Penalty, "Human Rights and Human Wrongs: The Sentencing of Children to Death" (Washington D.C.: National Coalition, 1998).

91. Paul R. Kfoury, *Children Before the Court: Reflection on Legal Issues Affecting Minors* (Boston: Butterworth, 1987), p. 55.

92. *Davis v. Alaska,* 415 U.S. 308 (1974); 94 S.Ct. 1105.

93. *Oklahoma Publishing Co. v. District Court,* 430 U.S. 97 (1977); 97 S.Ct. 1045.

94. *Smith v. Daily Mail Publishing Co.,* 443 U.S. 97, 99 S.Ct. 2667, 61 L.Ed.2d 399 (1979).

95. Linda Szymanski, *Confidentiality of Juvenile Court Records* (Pittsburgh, Pa.: National Center for Juvenile Justice, 1989).

96. Ira M. Schwartz, *Justice for Juveniles: Rethinking the Best Interests of the Child* (Lexington, Mass.: D. C. Heath, 1989), p. 172.

97. National Institute of Justice Update, "State Laws on Prosecutors' and Judges' Use of Juvenile Records" (Washington, D.C.: Office of Justice Programs, 1995).

Part Six

Juvenile Corrections

Over the years there has been a massive effort to remove nonserious offenders from secure institutions and place them in small, community-based facilities. Yet thousands of youngsters are still sent to secure, prison-like facilities each year.

Children in custody have become an American dilemma. Many incarcerated adult felons report that they were institutionalized as youths. Severe punishment seems to have little deterrent effect on teenagers—if anything, it may prepare them for a life of adult criminality. The juvenile justice system is caught between the futility of punishing juveniles and the public's demand that something be done about serious juvenile crime. Even though the nation seems to be in the midst of a punishment cycle, juvenile justice experts continue to press for judicial fairness, rehabilitation, and innovative programs for juvenile offenders.

The two chapters in Part Six describe the correctional treatment of juveniles in the community and in custody. Both approaches seek "the best interest of the child" and "the protection of the community." Although sometimes contradictory, these two major positions dominate the dispositional process.

Chapter 16 discusses efforts to treat juveniles while they remain in society. The most common community disposition employed by the juvenile court is probation. Theoretically, its goal is to rehabilitate the juvenile offender by treatment, guidance, and supplementary programs while the child remains in the community.

Chapter 17 reviews the history and practices of the juvenile institution and discusses efforts to rehabilitate youths in custody. Most secure institutions are not equipped to provide successful treatment for serious juvenile offenders. They often have limited treatment and educational services, as well as antiquated physical plants. One can understand why the training school is under constant judicial scrutiny. Today, a system of graduated sanctions is the recommended mechanism for obtaining treatment and accountability for delinquent offenders in need of court supervision and placement out of the home.

Chapter Sixteen

Juvenile Probation and Community Treatment

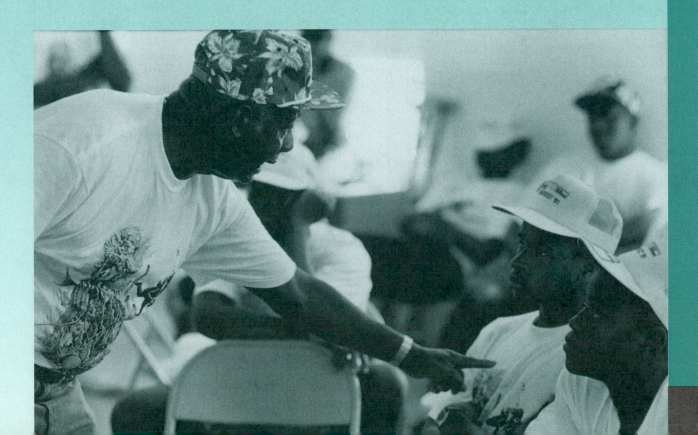

In 1997 a thirteen-year-old juvenile so short he could barely see the judge was on trial for armed robbery. Wearing a Chicago Bulls jacket, John looked more like an elementary school basketball player than a violent juvenile offender. John had been accused of threatening a woman with a knife and stealing her money. This was not John's first offense. At an even younger age he had been arrested for drug possession and placed on probation. While awaiting trial, John stole a car.

Neither his mother nor father accompanied John to the courtroom. John's father had deserted the family, and his mother was under treatment for addiction in a drug clinic. John's caretaker was his maternal grandmother.

The judge presiding in the Cook County Juvenile Court wore a black robe, and attorneys, court personnel, and probation officers were also present. One could sense how the court has shifted from its original informality to a mini-criminal court. After talking with his attorney, John confessed to the armed robbery. The judge ordered a disposition of probation for three years. Some might say that the boy had "beaten the system" again—he was free to go home, under the supervision of the probation department.

These kinds of cases infuriate conservatives and law enforcement officials. Stories like John's suggest that the court is no more than a revolving door and that community treatment programs, like probation, are a failure. According to some juvenile court judges, probation is part of a terrible dilemma that involves only two choices—sending the youth home on probation or incarcerating the youth. As a result, this kind of case has sparked a growing movement to drastically improve and restructure dispositional alternatives for juvenile offenders.

Community treatment refers to a wide variety of efforts to provide care, protection, and treatment for juveniles in need. These efforts include probation, a range of treatment services such as individual and group counseling, as well as restitution and other appropriate programs. The term "community treatment" also refers to the use of nonsecure and noninstitutional residences, such as foster homes, small group homes, boarding schools or semi-institutional cottage living programs, forestry camps, and other outdoor camps. Nonresidential programs where youths remain in their own homes but are required to receive counseling, education, vocational training, and other services also fall under the rubric of community treatment. Parole or aftercare, which is discussed in Chapter 17, is often considered an extension of community treatment. A broader definition of commu-

The term *community treatment* refers to a variety of nonsecure and noninstitutional treatment programs, including residences, small group homes, boarding schools or semi-institutional cottage living programs, and programs where youths remain in their own homes but are required to receive counseling, education, and vocational training. A broader definition of community treatment also includes preventive programs, such as street work with antisocial gangs or early identification and treatment of pre-delinquents. Here a community leader works with a group of neighborhood youth, helping them maintain a conventional lifestyle and encouraging their development.

community treatment
Using nonsecure and noninstitutional residences, counseling services, victim restitution programs, and other community services to treat juveniles in their own communities.

nity treatment also includes preventive programs such as street work with antisocial gangs or early identification and treatment of predelinquents. These programs have been discussed in Chapters 9, 10, and 11.

In this chapter we discuss the concept of community treatment as a dispositional alternative for juveniles who have violated the law and who have been found delinquent or status offenders by the juvenile court. Some feel that any hope for rehabilitation of juvenile offenders and the hope of society for resolving the problems of juvenile crime lie in the use of community treatment programs. Such programs are generally preferable to secure facilities for juveniles because they are smaller, operate in a community setting, and offer creative approaches to treating the juvenile offender. Traditional institutions, in contrast, are costly to operate and offer limited services.

An effective disposition has three objectives: (1) it holds the juvenile offender accountable; (2) it enables the juvenile to become a capable, productive, and responsible citizen; and (3) it ensures the safety of the community.

We begin this chapter with a detailed discussion of probation, examining new and important approaches for providing effective probation services to juvenile offenders. Next, we review restitution, which is being used in many jurisdictions to supplement probation supervision. Next we trace the development of alternatives to incarceration, including community-based, nonsecure treatment programs and graduated sanctions (programs that provide a range of community-based options while reserving secure care for the small percentage of violent offenders). Juvenile court judges generally have considerable latitude regarding the use of various community-based dispositional alternatives, and we focus our discussion on these programs. We conclude the chapter with a review of studies of the best-structured community-based programs, which have proven to be more effective than incarceration.

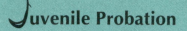

Juvenile Probation

probation
Nonpunitive, legal disposition for juveniles emphasizing community treatment in which the juvenile is closely supervised by an officer of the court and must adhere to a strict set of rules to avoid incarceration.

Although it has many meanings, **probation** usually refers to a nonpunitive, legal disposition for delinquent youths and those in need of supervision, emphasizing maintenance in the community and treatment without incarceration. Probation is the primary form of community treatment used by the juvenile justice system. A juvenile who is on probation is placed and maintained in the community under the supervision of a duly authorized officer of the court. Probation also encompasses a set of rules that must be followed and conditions that must be met for the offender to remain in the community. Probation often refers to an organizational structure—a probation department (either an independent agency or one attached to a court) that manages, supervises, and treats juveniles and carries out investigations for the court.

Juvenile probation is based on the idea that the juvenile offender is not generally dangerous to the community and has a better chance of being rehabilitated within the community. Advocates of probation and community treatment suggest that the alternative—incarceration—can actually encourage juveniles to become further involved in antisocial behavior. Probation provides youthful offenders with the opportunity to be closely supervised by trained personnel who can help them reestablish forms of acceptable behavior in a community setting.

Some see probation as a desirable disposition because, when applied to the right situations, (1) it maximizes the liberty of the individual while at the same time vindicating the authority of the law and effectively protecting the public from further violations of law; (2) it promotes the rehabilitation of the offender by maintaining normal community contacts; (3) it avoids the negative and frequently stultifying effects of confinement, which often severely and unnecessarily complicate the reintegration of the offender into the community; and (4) it greatly reduces the financial cost to the public of an effective correctional system.[1]

Only a judge can order probation. In the majority of jurisdictions, probation is a direct order that is exercised under wide statutory discretion. In particular, the conditions to be followed during the probationary period are subject to the court's discretion. A second form of probation involves ordering that the juvenile be committed to an institution or department of youth services initially, followed by a period of probation.

The Nature of Probation

A probation sentence implies a contract between the court and the juvenile. The court promises to hold a period of institutionalization in abeyance; the juvenile promises to adhere to a set of rules or conditions mandated by the court. If the rules are violated, and especially if the juvenile commits another offense, the probation may be revoked. In that case the contract between the court and the child is terminated, and the original commitment order may be enforced. The rules of probation vary, but they most typically involve conditions such as attending school or work, keeping regular hours, remaining in the geographical jurisdiction, and staying out of trouble.

In the juvenile court, probation is often ordered for an indefinite period of time. Depending on the statutes of the jurisdiction, the seriousness of the offense, and the juvenile's adjustment on probation, youths can remain under the court's supervision until the court no longer has jurisdiction over them, that is, when they reach the age of majority. State statutes determine if a judge can specify how long a juvenile can be placed under an order of probation.

In most jurisdictions the status of probation is reviewed regularly to ensure that a juvenile is not kept on probation needlessly. Generally, discretion lies with the probation officer to discharge the youth if he or she is adjusting to the supervision and treatment plan.

The supervision of a juvenile probationer can be transferred from one state to another if it is necessary for the youth to move from the original jurisdiction. The Uniform Interstate Compact on Juveniles provides jurisdiction over all nonresident juveniles by allowing for the return of runaways to their home state and for supervision of out-of-state children.

Historical Development

Although the major developments in juvenile probation have occurred in the twentieth century, its roots go back much further. In England specialized procedures for dealing with youthful offenders were recorded as early as 1820, when the magistrates of the Warwickshire quarter sessions (periodic court hearings held in a section of England) adopted the practice of sentencing youthful criminals to prison terms of one day, then releasing them conditionally under the supervision of their parents or masters.[2]

In the United States juvenile probation developed as part of the wave of social reform characterizing the latter half of the nineteenth century. Massachusetts took the first step toward development of a juvenile probation service. Under an act passed in 1869, an agent of the state board of charities was authorized to appear in criminal trials involving juveniles, to find them suitable homes, and to visit them periodically. These services were soon broadened and strengthened, so that by 1890 probation had become a mandatory part of the court structure throughout the state.[3]

Probation was a cornerstone in the development of the juvenile court system. In fact, in some states the early supporters of the juvenile court movement viewed probation legislation as the first step toward achieving the benefits that the new court was intended to provide. The rapid spread of juvenile courts during the first decades of the twentieth century encouraged the further development of probation. The two were closely related, and to a large degree, both of these interdependent institutions sprang from the same dedicated conviction that the young could be rehabilitated and that the public was responsible for protecting them.

By the mid-1960s, juvenile probation had become a large, complex social institution that touched the lives of an enormous number of children in the United States. Today, about 550,000 youths are being supervised on informal and formal (court order) probation; approximately half of those cases are formal probation orders where the juvenile was adjudicated a delinquent or status offender.[4] Informal probation is supervised probation prior to any adjudication and formal court order.

More than 50 percent of adjudicated delinquency cases typically result in formal probation. This percentage has remained fairly stable for some time (see Table 16.1) despite increases in the total population of delinquents. In contrast, there has been a discernible decrease in the percentage of status offenders given probation (an 8 percent decrease between 1991 and 1995). In 1995, 56 percent of status offense cases resulted in probation (see Table 16.2). Many of these cases (73 percent) involved truancy as the most serious charge.[5]

These figures show that regardless of public sentiment, probation continues to be a popular dispositional alternative for juvenile court judges. Here are the arguments in favor of probation:

1. For those youths who can be supervised in the community, probation represents an appropriate disposition.

Table 16.1

PERCENTAGE OF ADJUDICATED DELINQUENCY CASES THAT RESULTED IN FORMAL PROBATION, 1986–1995

Most Serious Offense	1986	1991	1995
Delinquency	55	56	53
Person	55	53	53
Property	57	59	56
Drugs	58	51	53
Public Order	49	52	48

Source: Melissa Sickmund, *Juvenile Court Statistics 1995* (Pittsburgh, Pa.: National Center for Juvenile Justice, 1998).

Table 16.2

PERCENTAGE OF ADJUDICATED STATUS OFFENSE CASES THAT RESULTED IN FORMAL PROBATION, 1986–1995

Most Serious Offense	1986	1991	1995
Status Offense	60	64	56
Runaway	53	57	54
Truancy	81	85	73
Ungovernable	61	63	61
Liquor	48	55	57
Miscellaneous	40	38	30

Source: Melissa Sickmund, *Juvenile Court Statistics 1995* (Pittsburgh, Pa.: National Center for Juvenile Justice, 1998).

2. The use of probation allows the juvenile court to tailor a program to the needs and circumstances of each juvenile offender, including those involved in person-oriented offenses.
3. The juvenile justice system continues to have confidence in the balanced rehabilitation model while accommodating demands for legal controls and public protection, even when caseloads may include many more serious offenders than in the past.
4. Probation is often the disposition of choice, particularly for status offenders.[6]

Organization and Administration of Probation

Juvenile probation systems are organized in one of two ways. In the most common form, the juvenile court or a group of courts administers probation services. In the other, an administrative agency such as a state correctional agency, public welfare department, or a combination of agencies provides probation services to the court. The relationship between the court (especially the judge) and the probation staff, whether it is under the court or in a separate administrative agency, is an extremely close one.

In the typical juvenile probation department the leadership role of the chief probation officer is central to its effective operation. In addition, large probation departments include one or more assistant chiefs. Each of these middle managers is responsible for one aspect of probation service. One assistant chief might oversee training, another might supervise and treat special offender groups, and still another might act as liaison with juvenile, police, or community service agencies. The probation officers who investigate and supervise juvenile cases are in direct, personal contact with the supervisory staff.

Each state has its own approach to juvenile probation organization. In some states a statewide probation service exists, but actual control over departments is localized within each district court. Other states have family courts with exclusive original jurisdiction over children aged 18 or under. A state department of juvenile services provides probation services to the juvenile courts in other jurisdictions. Thus, the administration of probation varies from one jurisdiction to another, and there is a considerable lack of uniformity in the roles, organization, and procedures of probation across the states.[7]

Although it appears that juvenile probation services continue to be predominantly organized under the judiciary, recent legislative activity has been in the direction of transferring those services from the local juvenile court judge to a state court administrative office. Whether local juvenile courts or state agencies should administer juvenile probation services is debatable. In years past, the organization of probation services depended primarily on the size of the program and the number of juveniles under its supervision. Today, the judicial–executive controversy is often guided by the amount of money available for these services. Because of this momentum to develop unified court systems, many juvenile court services, including probation, are now being consolidated into state court systems. According to Hurst and Torbet, the transfer of juvenile probation services to state judicial control is consistent with the emerging trend of state funding of courts. Occasionally, local judicial administration of probation has been replaced by state executive control.[8]

In terms of personnel, there are an estimated eighteen thousand juvenile probation professionals working with juvenile offenders in the United States, with a typical average caseload of forty youths. The optimum supervision caseload is about thirty probationers per probation officer.[9]

Duties of Juvenile Probation Officers

juvenile probation officer
Officer of the court involved in all four stages of the court process—intake, predisposition, postadjudication, and postdisposition—who assists the court and supervises juveniles placed on probation.

The **juvenile probation officer** plays an important role in the justice process, beginning with intake and continuing throughout the period in which a juvenile is under court supervision. According to the American Bar Association's standards for juvenile justice, juvenile probation officers are involved at four stages of the court process. At intake, they screen complaints by deciding to adjust the matter, refer the child to an agency for service, or refer the case to the court for judicial action. During the predisposition stage, probation workers participate in release or detention decisions. Intake screening is a critical stage of juvenile processing when a decision is made by an intake officer about the allegations against the juvenile and whether further formal processing is warranted. At the postadjudication stage, they assist the court in reaching its dispositional decision. During postdisposition, they supervise juveniles placed on probation.

Juvenile probation officers provide supervision and treatment in the community. The treatment plan is a product of the intake, diagnostic, and investigative aspects of probation. Treatment plans vary in terms of approach and structure. Some juveniles simply report to the probation officer and follow the conditions of probation. In other cases, juvenile probation officers will supervise children more intensely, monitor their daily activities, and work with them in directed treatment programs.

social investigation report, predisposition report
Developed by the juvenile probation officer, this report consists of a clinical diagnosis of the juvenile and his or her need for court assistance, relevant environmental and personality factors, and any other information that would assist the court in developing a treatment plan for the juvenile.

At intake, the probation staff has preliminary discussions with the child and the family to determine whether court intervention is necessary or whether the matter can be better resolved by some form of social service. If the child is placed in a detention facility, the probation officer helps the court decide whether the child should continue to be held or released pending the adjudication and disposition of the case.

The juvenile probation officer exercises tremendous influence over the child and the family by developing a **social investigation** or **predisposition report** and submitting it to the court. This report is a clinical diagnosis of the child's problems and of his or her need for court assistance based on the child's social functioning. The report evaluates the child's personality and environment and recommends a future treatment plan. Such a report includes analysis of the child's perceptions of and feelings about his or her violations and the child's intellectual and emotional capacity for change. The report should shed light on the value systems that influence the child's behavior and also consider the degree of motivation the child has to solve the problems that cause deviant behavior. The report must examine the influence of family members, peers, and other environmental influences in producing and possibly solving these problems. All of this information is brought together in a complex but meaningful picture of the offender's personality, problems, and environment. These variables must be considered in relation to the possible alternative dispositions available to the court.

Juvenile probation officers also provide the child with supervision and treatment in the community. The treatment plan is a product of the intake, diagnostic, and investigative aspects of probation. Treatment plans vary in terms of approach and structure. Some juveniles simply report to the probation officer and follow the conditions of probation. In other cases, the probation officer may need to provide extensive counseling to the child and family or, more typically, refer them to other social service agencies, such as a local mental health clinic or drug treatment center. Figure 16.1 provides an overview of the juvenile probation officer's sphere of influence.

In summary, the juvenile probation officer's role requires a diversity of skills, including:

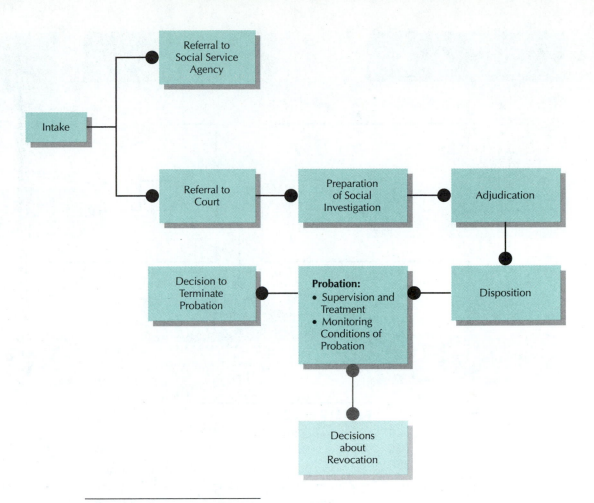

FIGURE 16.1
The Juvenile Probation Officer's Influence

- Providing direct counseling and casework services
- Interviewing and collecting social service data
- Making diagnostic recommendations
- Maintaining working relationships with law enforcement agencies
- Using community resources and services
- Directing volunteer case aides
- Writing predisposition or social investigation reports
- Working with families of children under supervision
- Providing specialized services, such as group therapy and behavior modification counseling
- Supervising specialized caseloads involving children on drugs or children with special psychological or emotional problems
- Making decisions about the revocation of probation and its termination

Performance of such a broad range of functions requires good training. Today, juvenile probation officers have legal or social work backgrounds or special counseling skills. Most jurisdictions require juvenile probation officers to have a background in the social sciences and a bachelor's degree. The probation officer's job is not an easy one. Large caseloads may make the therapeutic goal difficult to achieve. For this reason, overseeing the probationer's compliance with the legal requirements of

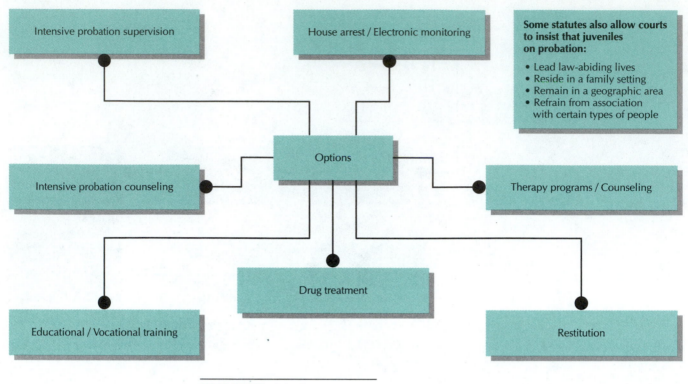

FIGURE 16.2
Conditions of Probation

probation often becomes the probation officer's short-term goal. The conditions of probation serve as the basic foundation of the supervision plan.

conditions of probation
The rules and regulations mandating that a juvenile on probation behave in a particular way.

Conditions of probation are rules and regulations mandating that a juvenile on probation behave in a particular way. They are important ingredients in the treatment plan devised for the child. Conditions can include restitution or reparation, intensive supervision, intensive probation counseling, participation in a therapeutic program, or participation in an educational or vocational training program. In addition to these specific conditions, state statutes generally allow courts to insist that probationers lead law-abiding lives during the period of probation, that they maintain a residence in a family setting, that they refrain from associating with certain types of people, and that they remain in a particular geographic area unless they have permission to leave.

Probation conditions vary, but they are never supposed to be capricious, cruel, or beyond the capacity of the juvenile to satisfy. Furthermore, conditions of probation should relate to the crime that was committed and to the conduct of the child. Typical probation conditions and the options designed to emphasize individual treatment are illustrated in Figure 16.2.

In recent years appellate courts have invalidated probation conditions that were harmful or that violated the juvenile's basic due process rights. Restricting a child's movement, insisting on a mandatory program of treatment, ordering indefinite terms of probation, and demanding financial reparation where this is impossible are all grounds for an appellate court review.

If a youth violates the conditions of probation or breaks the law again, the court can revoke probation. The juvenile court ordinarily handles a decision to revoke probation upon recommendation of the probation officer. Today, as a result of Supreme Court decisions dealing with the rights of adult probationers, a juvenile is normally entitled to legal representation and a hearing when a violation of probation occurs.[10] This means that juvenile probationers are virtually entitled to the same due process protections as adult probationers.

Probation Innovations

Although probation programs have varying rates of recidivism, experts claim they are generally more successful than placement in an institution. As a result, there has been a great deal of experimentation over the years with different probation techniques. However, rule enforcement, guidance, and the use of community services remain the common ingredients for delinquency-reducing programs in probation.

The juvenile justice system, and particularly probation, was founded on the concept of individual rehabilitation. John Augustus, a successful shoemaker and philanthropist, planted the seed of juvenile probation in 1847. He bailed out nineteen children, from ages 7 to 15, and reported back to the court after six months with an evaluation of their performance. From this early reform effort have evolved the intensive probation supervision programs described in the next section.

Juvenile Intensive Probation Supervision

juvenile intensive probation supervision (JIPS)
A true alternative to incarceration that involves almost daily supervision of the juvenile by the probation officer assigned to the case.

Juvenile intensive probation supervision (JIPS) involves treating offenders who would normally have been sent to a secure treatment facility as part of a very small probation caseload that receives almost daily scrutiny.[11] The JIPS model has been met with a great deal of enthusiasm in recent years.

Numerous jurisdictions have adopted programs of intensive probation supervision that have proven more successful than limited probation supervision.[12] The use of intensive probation as a mechanism for removing both children and adults from confinement no doubt will continue to expand. The demonstrated cost benefits of JIPS (about one-third that of confinement) make it an attractive alternative to traditional forms of treatment, such as confinement.[13]

A study by Richard Wiebush that examined the eighteen-month recidivism rate of juvenile felony offenders placed in an intensive probation supervision program found that JIPS was an effective alternative to incarceration.[14] The same study showed that other forms of treatment for juvenile probationers—such as social skills training, counseling, and outdoor adventure programs—may be no more effective than "regular" probation services.[15] Continued research is needed to determine what programs work for what types of juvenile offenders.

In summary, there is some research support for the effectiveness of JIPS as a deterrent to recidivism.[16] Other research, however, shows only marginal benefits. Today, JIPS components can be found in most metropolitan juvenile probation departments in all major regions of the country. They are used as a true alternative to incarceration or other forms of out-of-home placement.[17]

Two successful programs—the Wayne County Intensive Probation Program in Detroit, Michigan, and the Lucas County, Ohio, Intensive Supervision Unit—were independently evaluated and found to be as effective as incarceration at less than one-third the cost.[18] The Wayne County program is highlighted in the Policy and Practice box.

In recent years probation departments have been influenced by juvenile justice policies that shift between crime control and rehabilitation philosophies. The "balanced approach" and restorative justice philosophies evoke new ways of looking at the delivery of probation services.[19] The balanced approach, as previously mentioned, applies a set of complementary principles—community protection, accountability, and competency building—whereas restorative justice promotes the maximum involvement of the victim, offender, and the community in the juvenile process. These two concepts have been combined into the balanced and restorative justice model (which is discussed later in this chapter), and suggests that justice is best served when the community, the victim and the youth receive balanced attention.

WAYNE COUNTY INTENSIVE PROBATION PROGRAM

The Wayne County Intensive Probation Program (IPP) in Detroit, Michigan, is administered by the juvenile court and operated by the court probation department in conjunction with two private, nonprofit agencies under contract with the court: Spectrum Human Services, Inc. and Comprehensive Youth Training and Community Involvement Program, Inc. (CYTCIP). The IPP target population is adjudicated delinquents between ages 12 and 17 who have been committed to the state's Department of Social Services (DSS). The state-funded program was begun in 1983 to reduce the level of delinquency commitments.

Youths referred to the IPP are placed in one of three programs for casework services and supervision: the Probation Department's Intensive Probation Unit (IPU); the In-Home Care Program, operated by Spectrum Human Services, Inc.; or the State Ward Diversion Program, operated by CYTCIP.

The IPU program has the most traditional intensive supervision model of the three programs. It is characterized by low caseloads (a maximum of ten youths per probation officer) and frequent probation officer contacts and surveillance activities. The IPU operates through a system of four steps, with diminishing levels of supervision as the juvenile demonstrates more responsibility and lawful behavior. Probation officers must have two to three weekly face-to-face contacts with youths during the first phase, and at least one face-to-face contact per week during subsequent phases. In addition, telephone contacts to check school attendance, curfew adherence, and home behavior are made on a regular basis. Youths remain in the program from seven to eleven months.

The two private programs have different approaches. The In-Home Care Program employs a family-focused services and treatment approach based on the philosophy that comprehensive family treatment using community resources is needed to alleviate the causes of delinquent behavior. The State Ward Diversion Program is a day treatment program actively involved in several key areas of youths' lives—home, family, school, employment, and community.

The Wayne County Intensive Probation Program was evaluated in 1988. The experimental group consisted of youths assigned to one of the three intensive supervision probation programs; the control group was formed by youth placed in a state institution. Youths were randomly assigned to one of the two groups. The length of the follow-up period was two years.

The overall performances of the experimental and control groups were comparable. Institutionalized youths were slightly less likely to reappear in court than were intensive probation youths; however, this difference disappeared when time at risk in the community was taken into account. The IPP youths committed less serious crimes than the institutional youths, performed better on self-report tests, and were less likely to commit violent crimes measured both by court records and self-report data. It was found that the IPP program was as effective as incarceration at less than one-third the cost. The program saved an estimated $8.8 million over three years. The IPP study shows that a variety of program models can be successful in serving high-risk juvenile offenders in the community.

Source: James C. Howell, ed., *Guide for Implementing the Comprehensive Strategy for Serious, Violent and Chronic Juvenile Offenders* (Washington, D.C.: U.S. Department of Justice, OJJDP, 1995).

Electronic Monitoring

Another program that has been used with adult offenders and is finding its way into the juvenile justice system is **house arrest,** which is often coupled with **electronic monitoring.** This program allows offenders sentenced to probation to remain in the community on the condition that they stay home during specific periods

house arrest
An offender is required to stay at home during specific periods of time; monitoring is done by random phone calls and visits or by electronic devices.

electronic monitoring
Active monitoring systems consist of a radio transmitter worn by the offender that sends a continuous signal to the probation department computer, alerting officials if the offender leaves his or her place of confinement; passive systems employ computer-generated random phone calls that must be responded to in a certain period of time from a particular phone or other device.

of time—for example, after school or work, on weekends, and in the evenings. Offenders may be monitored through random phone calls, visits, or, in some jurisdictions, electronic devices.

Two basic types of electronic systems are used: active and passive. Active systems constantly monitor the offender by continuously sending a signal back to the central office. If an offender leaves home at an unauthorized time, the signal is broken and the "failure" recorded. In some cases, the control officer is automatically notified electronically through a beeper.

In contrast, passive systems usually involve random phone calls generated by computers to which the juvenile offender must respond within a particular time (for example, thirty seconds). Some passive systems require the offender to place his or her monitoring device in a verifier box that then sends a signal back to the control computer; another approach is to have the arrestee repeat words that are analyzed by a voice verifier and compared with tapes of the juvenile's voice. Most systems employ radio transmitters that receive a signal from a device worn by the offender and relay it back to the computer monitoring system via telephone lines. Probationers in an electronic monitoring house arrest program are fitted with an unremovable monitoring device that alerts the probation department's computers if they leave their place of confinement.[20]

Although house arrest has not been evaluated extensively in terms of reducing recidivism, its cost, even with active electronic monitoring, is often less than half that of a stay in a detention facility. Two well-known programs, one in Indiana and the other in North Carolina, appear to operate safely and effectively as alternatives to institutionalization and have become a formal part of probation programming in these jurisdictions.

Joseph B. Vaughn conducted one of the first surveys of juvenile electronic monitoring in 1989, examining eight programs in five different probation departments.[21] Vaughn found that all the programs adopted electronic monitoring to reduce institutional overcrowding and that most agencies reported success in reducing the number of days juveniles spent in detention. In addition, the programs allowed the youths, who would otherwise be detained, to remain in the home and participate in counseling, educational, or vocational activities. Of particular benefit to pretrial detainees was the opportunity to remain in a home environment with supervision. This experience provided the court with a much clearer picture of how the juvenile would eventually reintegrate into society. However, Vaughn found that none of the benefits of the treatment objective in the programs had been empirically validated. The potential for behavior modification and the lasting effects of any personal changes remain unknown.

Since Vaughn's study, there have been some recent indications that electric monitoring can be an effective addition to the range of alternative sanctions. Program evaluations indicate that recidivism rates are no higher than in traditional programs, costs are lower, and system overcrowding is reduced. Also electronic monitoring seems to work better with some individuals than others. Sudipto Roy found that serious felony offenders, substance abusers, and repeat offenders were the ones most likely to fail. Sentence length also predicted failure: the longer the sentence, the more likely the failure. Judges should be aware of these factors when making home confinement decisions.[22]

Electronic monitoring combined with house arrest is being hailed as one of the most important developments in adult and juvenile correction policy. Its supporters claim that electronic monitoring has the benefits of relatively low cost and high security, while at the same time it helps offenders avoid the pain of imprisonment in overcrowded, dangerous state facilities. Furthermore, because offenders are monitored by computers, fewer supervisory officers are needed to handle large numbers of offenders.

Despite these strengths, electronic monitoring also has its drawbacks:

■ Current technology is limited, and existing systems can be affected by faulty telephone equipment.

- Most electronic monitoring/house arrest programs do not provide for rehabilitation services.
- Electronic monitoring may not save money unless it eliminates the need for new institutions.
- Some believe electronic monitoring is contrary to a citizen's right to privacy.[23]

Wilderness Probation

wilderness probation
Programs involving outdoor expeditions that provide opportunities for juveniles to confront the difficulties of their lives while achieving positive personal satisfaction.

Another type of program that seems to be growing in popularity with probation departments is **wilderness probation.** These programs, staffed by probation officers and lay volunteers, are designed to give youngsters a sense of confidence and purpose by involving them in outdoor expeditions.[24] Wilderness programs are used as alternatives to standard dispositions for youths being supervised in the juvenile court. They provide an opportunity for juveniles to confront the difficulties in their lives while achieving positive personal satisfaction. Probation counseling and group therapy are part of this structured program, which is significantly different from a purely recreational field trip. These programs seem to be proving effective with both probationers and institutionalized youths (see Chapter 17 for a discussion of the Outward Bound programs).[25]

Wilderness probation programs, staffed by probation officers and lay volunteers, help give youngsters a sense of confidence and purpose by involving them in outdoor expeditions. They provide an opportunity for juveniles to confront the difficulties in their lives while achieving positive personal satisfaction.

Balanced Probation

In recent years some jurisdictions have turned to a **balanced probation** approach in an effort to enhance the success of probation.[26] Balanced probation systems integrate community protection, the accountability of the juvenile offender, competency, and individualized attention to the offender (see Figure 16.3). Some of these juvenile probation programs offer renewed promise for community treatment. These programs are based on the view that juveniles are responsible for their actions and have an obligation to society whenever they commit an offense. The probation officer establishes a program tailored to the special needs of the offender while helping the offender accept responsibility for his or her own actions. According to Gordon Bazemore, the balanced approach is promising because it specifies a distinctive role and unique objectives for the juvenile probation system.[27]

The balanced probation approach has been implemented with some success, as these examples demonstrate:

1. In inner-city Pittsburgh young probationers in an intensive day treatment program solicit suggestions from community organizations about service projects they would like to see completed in the neighborhood. They work with community residents on projects such as home repair and gardening for the elderly, voter registration drives, painting homes and public buildings, and planting and cultivating community gardens.
2. In Florida young offenders sponsored by the Florida Department of Juvenile Justice and supervised by The 100 Black Men of Palm Beach County, Inc. plan and create shelters for abused, abandoned, and HIV-positive and AIDS-infected infants. Victims' rights advocates also train juvenile justice staff on sensitivity in their interaction with victims and help prepare victim awareness curriculums for youths in residential programs.
3. In cities and towns in Pennsylvania, Montana, and Minnesota, family members and other citizens acquainted with a juvenile offender or victim of a juvenile crime gather to determine the best response to the offense. Held in schools, churches, or other community facilities, these family group conferences are facilitated by a community justice coordinator or police officer and ensure that offenders hear community disapproval of their behavior. Participants develop an agreement for repairing the damage to the victim and the community and define a plan for reintegrating the offender.[28]

Although balanced probation programs are still in their infancy and their effectiveness remains to be tested, they have generated great interest because of their

FIGURE 16.3

Balanced Approach Mission

Source: Gordon Bazemore and Mark Umbreit, *Balanced and Restorative Justice for Juveniles—A Framework for Juvenile Justice in the 21st Century* (Washington, D.C.: OJJDP, 1997), p. 14.

potential for relieving overcrowded correctional facilities and reducing the pain and stigma of incarceration. There seems to be little question that the use of these innovations, and juvenile probation in general, will increase in the years ahead, particularly as the juvenile court with its emphasis on individualized treatment is uniquely organized to provide these programs. Given the $40,000 cost of a year's commitment to a typical residential facility, it should not be a great burden to develop additional innovative probation services.

Restitution

monetary restitution
A requirement that juvenile offenders compensate crime victims for out-of-pocket losses caused by the crime, including property damage, lost wages, and medical expenses.

victim service restitution
The juvenile offender is required to provide some service directly to the crime victim.

community service restitution
The juvenile offender is required to assist some worthwhile community organization for a period of time.

Victim restitution is another widely used method of community treatment. In most jurisdictions restitution is part of a probationary sentence and is administered by the county probation staff. In many jurisdictions independent restitution programs have been set up by local governments; in others restitution is administered by a private nonprofit organization.[29]

Restitution can take several forms. A juvenile can reimburse the victim of the crime or donate money to a worthy charity or public cause; this is referred to as **monetary restitution.** In other instances a juvenile may be required to provide some service directly to the victim **(victim service restitution)** or to assist a worthwhile community organization **(community service restitution).**

Requiring youths to reimburse the victims of their crimes is the most widely used method of restitution in the United States. Less widely used but more common in Europe is restitution to a community charity. In the past few years numerous programs have been set up to enable the juvenile offender to provide service to the victim or to participate in community programs—for example, working in schools for retarded children or fixing up neighborhoods. In some cases juveniles are required to contribute both money and community service. Other programs emphasize employment and work experience.[30]

Restitution programs can be employed at various stages of the juvenile justice process. They can be part of a diversion program prior to conviction, a method of informal adjustment at intake, or a condition of probation. Restitution has a number of advantages.[31] It provides the court with alternative sentencing options. It offers direct monetary compensation or service to crime victims. It is rehabilitative because it gives the juvenile the opportunity to compensate the victim and take a step toward becoming a productive member of society. It also relieves overcrowded juvenile courts, probation caseloads, and detention facilities. Finally, like other alternatives to incarceration, restitution has the potential for allowing vast savings in the operation of the juvenile justice system. Monetary restitution programs in particular may improve the public's attitude toward juvenile justice by offering equity to the victims of crime and ensuring that offenders take responsibility for their actions.

Despite its many advantages, however, some believe restitution supports retribution rather than rehabilitation because it emphasizes justice for the victim and criminal responsibility for illegal acts. There is some concern that restitution creates penalties for juvenile offenders where none existed before.

The use of restitution is increasing around the nation, and many states have developed novel approaches to restitution. In 1977 there were fewer than fifteen formal restitution programs around the United States. By 1985 formal programs existed in four hundred jurisdictions, and thirty-five states had statutory provisions that gave courts the authority to order juvenile restitution.[32] Today, all fifty states, as well as the District of Columbia, have statutory restitution programs in one form or another.[33]

A sample statute from the State Juvenile Code of North Carolina shows the type of statutory language used for restitution programs and the latitude given the juvenile court judge regarding this disposition.

North Carolina Restitution Statute
In the case of any juvenile who is delinquent, the judge may:
(2) Require restitution, full or partial, payable within a twelve-month period to any person who has suffered loss or damage as a result of the offense committed by the juvenile. The judge may determine the amount, terms, and conditions of the restitution. If the juvenile participated with another person or persons, all participants should be jointly and severally responsible for the payment of restitution; however, the judge shall not require the juvenile to make restitution if the juvenile satisfies the court that he does not have, and could not reasonably acquire, the means to make restitution.
(4) Order the juvenile to perform supervised community service consistent with the juvenile's age, skill, and ability, specifying the nature of the work and the number of hours required. The work shall be related to the seriousness of the juvenile's offense and in no event may the obligation to work exceed twelve months.[34]

Alternative Work Sentencing Program (Earn-It)
A Massachusetts program that brings together the juvenile and the crime victim to develop an equitable work program to provide restitution to the crime victim.

An example of a successful restitution program is that developed in the Quincy, Massachusetts, district court. The **Alternative Work Sentencing Program (Earn-It)** handles juveniles referred by the court, the county probation department, and the district attorney's office.[35] The program brings together the youth and the victim of the crime to develop an equitable work program. Program staff members determine the dollar amount of the victim's loss and place the juvenile in a paying job to earn the money needed to make restitution. Some youths are placed in nonpaying community service jobs to work off requirements specified in court orders.

Does Restitution Work?

How successful is restitution as a treatment alternative for juvenile offenders? Most attempts at evaluation have shown that it is reasonably effective, and the OJJDP has expanded the principles underlying restitution and community service into a system improvement model called balanced and restorative justice, which has been discussed in previous sections.[36]

In an analysis of federally sponsored restitution programs, Peter Schneider and his associates found that about 95 percent of youths who received restitution as a condition of probation successfully completed their orders.[37] Factors that related to success were family income, good school attendance, few prior offenses, minor current offense, and size of restitution order. Schneider found that the youths who received restitution as a sole sanction (without probation) were those originally viewed by juvenile court judges as the better risks, and consequently, they had lower failure and recidivism rates than youths ordered to make restitution after being placed on probation.

In another attempt to evaluate restitution, Anne Schneider conducted an in-depth analysis of four programs in different states.[38] She found that the program participants had lower recidivism rates than youths placed in control groups, such as those included in regular probation caseloads. Although Schneider's data indicate that restitution may reduce recidivism, the number of youths who had subsequent involvement in the justice system still seems high.

In short, there is ample evidence that most restitution orders are successfully completed and that youths who make restitution are less likely to become recidivists. (For more on this topic, see the Policy and Practice box entitled "Restitution in Utah.") Existing programs meet the important twin goals of retribution and rehabilitation.[39] However, the number of repeat offenses committed by juveniles who made restitution suggests that, by itself, restitution is not the answer to the delinquency problem.

POLICY AND PRACTICE

RESTITUTION IN UTAH

The statewide Utah Juvenile Court operates a structured juvenile restitution program. In the majority of restitution cases youths make restitution directly in the form of financial payments. Others may be ordered to participate in community service programs to earn money to make restitution. In 1988 financial or community service restitution was used in approximately 30 percent of petitioned cases and 10 percent of nonpetitioned cases. Almost a decade later, restitution was being used in almost 40 percent of all cases in the Utah Juvenile Court System.

Under state law, the Utah Juvenile Court may order youths to repair, replace, or make restitution for victims' property and other losses. Probation officers are authorized to develop restitution or community service plans even in cases where youths are not formally brought before the court by petition. In such cases consent agreements are signed by youths and their parents, and restitution is often paid directly to the victims.

An innovative feature of Utah's approach to juvenile restitution was established by state law in 1979. It permits the court to withhold a substantial portion of fines paid by juveniles to underwrite a work restitution fund. The fund allows juveniles otherwise unable to pay restitution to work in community service projects in the private or public sector to earn money to compensate their victims. The juveniles' earnings are paid directly from the fund to the victims.

During the past decade, the use of restitution has increased in Utah. In 1980 court-ordered restitution paid by juveniles and returned to victims was just under $250,000. By 1990 that amount had increased to more than $550,000, and by 1996 to almost three-quarters of a million dollars.

RESULTS

More than thirteen thousand cases from Utah were studied to assess the association between the use of restitution and subsequent recidivism. Of the probationers ordered to pay restitution, 32 percent became recidivists within a year. In cases involving charges of burglary and theft, which represented the majority of all the cases, significantly fewer youths who were ordered to pay restitution became recidivists than those placed on probation alone. Formal probation cases involving juveniles charged with burglary had a recidivism rate of 31 percent when the disposition included restitution, but 38 percent when probation alone was ordered. In the theft cases the rates were 34 percent recidivism with restitution and 38 percent without it. Restitution combined with probation was consistently associated with lower recidivism rates than probation alone.

In the most recent study of Utah's juvenile court, which was conducted by the National Center for Juvenile Justice for OJJDP, recidivism was lower for informally handled and adjudicated cases involving robbery, assault, burglary, theft, auto theft, and vandalism when juveniles were placed on formal probation and ordered to make restitution than when they were placed on probation without a restitution order. These programs also respond to some key needs of victims by holding juvenile offenders accountable and restoring their loss.

Overall, the results of the study suggest that the use of restitution is a significant factor in reducing recidivism among certain juvenile offenders.

Sources: Administrative Office of the Courts, *Utah Juvenile Court: Restitution and Community Service Program* (Salt Lake City: Administrative Office of the Courts, 1991); Jeffrey Butts and Howard Snyder, *OJJDP Update on Research, Restitution and Juvenile Recidivism* (Washington, D.C.: U.S. Department of Justice, 1992), p. 4; Director of Restitution Programs (Washington D.C.: OJJDP Juvenile Justice Clearinghouse, 1996).

Although appealing in theory, restitution programs may be difficult to implement in some circumstances. Offenders may find it difficult to make monetary restitution without securing new or additional employment. This economic reality makes restitution seem absurd at a time when unemployment rates for youth are high.[40] Because most members of such programs have been convicted of a crime, many employers are reluctant to hire them. Problems also arise when offenders who need jobs suffer from alcohol or drug abuse or from emotional problems. Public and private agencies are likely sites for community service restitution, but their directors are sometimes reluctant to allow delinquent youths access to their organizations.

Another criticism directed at restitution programs is that they widen the net of social control. Some critics claim that those given restitution orders would not have received more coercive treatment under any circumstances. Therefore, instead of being an alternative to incarceration, restitution has become an extra burden on some offenders.[41]

Beyond these problems, some juvenile probation officers view restitution programs as a threat to their authority and to the autonomy of their organizations. It is interesting to note that courts believe police officers view restitution more positively than social workers because the police are quick to grasp the retributive nature of restitution.

Another criticism of restitution programs is that they foster involuntary servitude. For the most part, the courts have upheld the legality of restitution even though it has a coercive element. It has been argued that restitution is inherently biased against indigent clients because a person who is unable to make restitution payments can have probation revoked and face incarceration. To avoid such bias, probation officers should first determine why payment has stopped and then suggest appropriate action for the court to take rather than simply treat nonpayment as a matter of law enforcement.

Finally, restitution orders are subject to the same abuses of discretion as traditional sentencing methods. The restitution orders one delinquent offender receives may be quite different from those given another in a comparable case. To remedy this situation, a number of jurisdictions have been using restitution guidelines to encourage standardization of orders.

Restitution programs may be an important alternative to incarceration, benefiting the child, the victim, and the juvenile justice system. H. Ted Rubin, a leading juvenile justice expert, even advocates that courts placing juveniles in day treatment and community-based residential programs also include restitution requirements in their orders and expect that these requirements be fulfilled during placement.[42] However, all restitution programs should be evaluated carefully to answer these questions:

- What type of offenders would be most likely to benefit from restitution?
- When is monetary restitution more desirable than community service?
- What is the best point in the juvenile justice process to impose restitution?
- What is the effect of restitution on the juvenile justice system?
- How successful are restitution programs?

Community-Based Programs

To many juvenile justice experts, the institutionalization of even the most serious delinquent youths in a training school, reform school, or industrial institution is a great mistake. A period of confinement in a high security juvenile institution usually cannot solve the problems that brought a youth into a

delinquent way of life, and the experience may actually help to amplify delinquency once the youth returns to the community. Surveys indicate that about 30 to 40 percent of adult prison inmates had been juvenile delinquents, and many had been institutionalized as youths. There is little reason to believe a secure institutional experience can be beneficial or reduce recidivism.[43]

A key to comprehensive juvenile justice is providing programs that meet identified problems or needs that have contributed to a juvenile's criminal behavior. Although the merits of rehabilitation versus punishment form an ongoing debate, many agree that warehousing juveniles without attention to their treatment needs does little to forestall their return to criminal behavior. Research has shown that the most effective secure corrections programs provided individualized services for a small number of participants. Large training schools have not proved to be effective.[44]

Because of the problems associated with institutional care, influential policy-making bodies as the National Council of Juvenile and Family Court Judges, the National Council on Crime and Delinquency, and the American Bar Association have recommended that, whenever possible, treatment of serious offenders be community-based. While recognizing the problems presented by the chronic offender, these groups maintain that adequate security can be maintained in community-based programs.[45] Similar initiatives have been promoted by state governments.[46]

Since the early 1970s, Massachusetts has led the movement to keep juvenile offenders in the community. In the mid-1960s its Department of Youth Services housed more than one thousand youngsters in secure training schools. After decades of documenting the failures of the youth correctional system, Massachusetts closed most of its secure juvenile facilities and began a massive deinstitutionalization of juvenile offenders.[47] Today, thirty years after the institutions were closed, the Massachusetts Department of Youth Services operates a community-based correctional system. The vast majority of youths are serviced in nonsecure settings, and the relatively few committed youths are placed in some type of residential setting ranging from group and foster homes to secure facilities and forestry camps.

Initially, many of the early programs suffered from residential isolation and limited services. Over time, however, many of the group homes and unlocked structured residential settings were relocated in residential community environments and became highly successful in addressing the needs of juveniles while presenting little or no security risk to themselves or others.

Roxbury Youthworks, an inner-city program in Boston, is such a private community-based agency controlling juvenile delinquency through a comprehensive range of resources that include (1) evaluation and counseling at a local court clinic, (2) employment and training, (3) detention diversion, and (4) outreach and tracking to help youths reenter the community. Roxbury Youthworks is one of twenty-four independent programs—both residential and nonresidential—under contract with the state youth services department to provide intensive community supervision for almost 90 percent of all youths under its jurisdiction.[48]

There are other historic and pioneering examples of jurisdictions that have reduced the need for high security institutions to treat delinquent offenders. Like Massachusetts, Vermont was one of the early states to move to a noninstitutional system. It closed the Weeks School, the only training school in the state, in 1979. In 1975 Pennsylvania removed youths from the Camp Hill Penitentiary, which had been used to house the most hard core juvenile offenders. Three-quarters of the juvenile inmates were returned to programs in their home communities. The remainder were transferred for short periods of time to small, secure institutions, then released. In 1978 Utah established a system of seven community-based programs as an alternative to traditional institutionalization in the state's Youth Development Center. An evaluation comparing the recidivism rates of comparable groups showed higher rates of success for the alternative program.

Today, the deinstitutionalization movement is still alive. Most recently, Maryland closed its Montrose Juvenile Training School, a facility that had been in operation for nearly three-quarters of a century. More than two hundred youths were released from the school in less than a year. Many of them should not have been there in the first place as they had not committed serious or violent crimes. Nearly half of the youths were released with services and supervision in their own homes. Most of the others were safely placed in smaller, nonsecure residential programs.[49]

In conclusion, we have seen many states reduce the use of institutionalization in favor of nonsecure facilities and community-based programs.[50] The Case in Point highlights the need for such programs and the difficulty in obtaining services for youths in the juvenile justice system.

Encouraging Community Corrections

A number of factors have affected the placement of juvenile offenders in nonsecure community-based facilities. At first reformers emphasized the futility of exposing youths to the hardships of high security institutions. Then, in 1974, the Juvenile Justice and Delinquency Prevention Act tied the receipt of federal funds for juvenile justice programs to the removal of status offenders from institutions. The "deinstitutionalization of status offenders" mandate in the Act specifies that juveniles not charged with acts that would be crimes for adults shall not be placed in secure correctional facilities. Consequently, many states reformed their juvenile codes to support new community-based treatment programs and to remove status offenders from institutions. Most states now have provisions banning the institutionalization of status offenders with delinquents, although in some states repeat status offenders may be placed in secure facilities, either public or private, depending on the state. A few states allow status offenders to be institutionalized with delinquents if their behavior is so unruly that the court finds them unamenable to any other kind of treatment.

The second factor fueling the deinstitutionalization movement was an effort to grant children the general right to services and, in particular, the legal **right to treatment.** When the juvenile justice system places a child in custody, basic concepts of fairness and humanity suggest that the system should supply the child with

right to treatment
Philosophy espoused by many courts that juvenile offenders have a statutory right to treatment while under the jurisdiction of the courts.

You are a juvenile corrections consultant doing a study to determine if dispositional decisions are meeting the needs of youths in juvenile courts.

Jamie B., age 15, was adjudicated a juvenile delinquent. Placed on probation for one charge of shoplifting, he failed to report to the probation officer. Brought into the juvenile court on a second petition, namely being intoxicated and disruptive in public, Jamie admitted to having a substance abuse problem.

At the dispositional stage of the court process Jamie's attorney asked the court to place him in a drug rehabilitation program. The judge suggested that such services could be obtained in a state training school as other less restrictive dispositional alternatives were not available. Concluding that Jamie's behavior constituted a threat to the community and to his own welfare, the court committed the youth to a state training school for an indeterminate period of time not to exceed two years.

A wide variety of dispositional alternatives are listed in the juvenile code of this jurisdiction. Among these are supervised probation, participation in a supervised day program, placement in a residential or nonresidential treatment program, and commitment to a state training school. The legislative preference for a community-based solution to Jamie's problem is reflected throughout the code. Jamie's lawyer challenges the dispositional decision, claiming that the commitment to a training school without first examining the appropriateness and availability of community-based services was judicial error.

■ Do you think the commitment order should be vacated and Jamie's case remanded for a new dispositional hearing? Why or why not?

rehabilitation. The right to treatment (see Chapter 17) often meant providing counseling, education, adequate nutrition, and medical care. Consequently, the cost of maintaining youths in secure treatment facilities has skyrocketed. Considering these costs and the assumed ineffectiveness of institutional treatment, the least restrictive alternative available to treat juvenile offenders in many cases means placement in community-based programs, and this trend has continued over the past three decades.

A word of caution: Although the movement to place juveniles in nonrestrictive, community-based programs continues, the actual number of incarcerated youths has increased in recent years. Almost seventy thousand children are now held in secure and nonsecure public facilities.[51] Secure institutional programs make up more than one-third of public and private facilities and house more than 50 percent of the total juvenile population. Community corrections has supplemented, but not replaced, institutionalization (see Chapter 17).

Today, most states rely on a sophisticated network of small, secure programs for violent youths coupled with a broad range of highly structured community-based programs for the majority of committed juveniles. Many of the community-based programs are operated by private, nonprofit agencies; secure facilities are reserved for only the most serious violent offenders. Many states aim to privatize more of the system and to develop a set of smaller, less intensive, and far cheaper alternatives for those children who do not present a significant risk to the community.

Graduated sanctions, those that deal with a range of immediate, intermediate, and secure care, is another approach to effective treatment for juvenile offenders. Such programs attempt to "grade" sanctions to match the severity of the offense.

Residential Community Treatment

residential programs
Placement of a juvenile offender in a residential, nonsecure facility such as a group home, foster home, family group home, or rural home where the juvenile can be closely monitored and develop close relationships with staff members.

group homes
Nonsecured, structured residences that provide counseling, education, job training, and family living.

How are community corrections implemented with delinquent youths? In some cases adjudicated youths are placed under probation supervision, and the probation department maintains a residential treatment facility. Placement can also be made to the department of social services or juvenile corrections with the direction that the youth be placed in a residential, nonsecure facility.

Residential programs can be divided into four major categories: (1) group homes, including boarding schools and apartment-type settings; (2) foster homes; (3) family group homes; and (4) rural programs.

Group homes are nonsecure, structured residences that provide counseling, education, job training, and family living. They are staffed by a small number of qualified persons, and generally house twelve to fifteen youngsters. The institutional quality of the environment is minimized, and children are given the opportunity to build a close but controlled relationship with the staff. Children reside in the home, attend public schools, and participate in community activities in the area.

Over the past two decades, extensive research has been done on group home settings. Two pioneering community-based residential treatment programs in the field of juvenile corrections have served as models for many other programs. These two programs are the Highfields project and the Silverlake experiment.

Highfields was a short-term residential, nonsecure program for boys that began in 1950. The youths lived in groups of no more than twenty boys in a large home on an estate in Highfields, New Jersey, for periods of three or four months. They were permitted to leave the grounds under responsible adult supervision. They were also granted furloughs over weekends to visit their families and to retain ties with the community. They worked twenty to forty hours a week at a neuropsychiatric clinic. The most important treatment technique was peer pressure exerted through active participation in guided group interaction sessions.

The Highfields project was evaluated by comparing it to a controlled group of boys sent to Annandale, a juvenile reform school in the same state. One year after release, Highfields boys had a lower recidivism rate than Annandale boys. The Highfields project was considered as successful as any training school and was much less expensive to operate. However, the validity of the recidivism rates were questioned because of the difficulties associated with matching the control and treatment groups.[52]

The Silverlake experiment occurred in Los Angeles County in the mid-1960s. Like Highfields, this program provided a group home experience seeking to create a nondelinquent culture for male youths between the ages of fifteen and eighteen. The participants, seriously delinquent youths, were placed in a large family residence in a middle-class neighborhood. Some of them attended local high schools, and many returned to their homes on weekends. Only twenty boys at a time lived in the residence. They were responsible for maintaining the residence and for participating in daily group interaction meetings, whose purpose was to implement program goals. The Silverlake program sought to structure a social system with positive norms by discussing the youths' problems and offering alternatives to delinquent behavior.

To evaluate the Silverlake experiment, researchers selected experimental and control groups at random from youths participating in the program. Those in the control group didn't participate in the daily guided group interactions. There was no significant difference in the recidivism rates of the two groups tested, and it was unclear whether one program reduced recidivism more than the other. As both control group youths and treatment youths lived in the facility, the researchers concluded that the experimental group receiving guided group interaction and the control group were positively affected by the program. Recidivism rates twelve months after release indicated a general reduction in delinquent behavior on the part of participants.[53]

The research on these programs supports the position that they do prevent recidivism—and far more cheaply than imprisonment.

Foster care programs typically involve one or two juveniles who live with a family—usually a husband and wife who serve as surrogate parents. The juveniles enter into a close relationship with the foster parents and receive the attention, guidance, and care they did not receive at home. The quality of the foster home experience depends on the foster parents and their emotional relationship with the child. Foster care for adjudicated juvenile offenders has not been extensive in the United States. It is most often used for orphans or for children whose parents cannot care for them. Welfare departments generally handle foster placements, and funding of this treatment option has been a problem for the juvenile justice system. However, foster home services for delinquent children and status offenders have expanded as a community treatment approach.

Family group homes combine elements of both foster care and group home placements. Children are placed in a private group home that is run by a single family rather than by a professional staff. Troubled youths have an opportunity to learn to get along in a family-like situation and at the same time the state avoids the startup costs and neighborhood opposition often associated with establishing a separate public institution. Family group homes can be found in many jurisdictions throughout the United States.

Rural programs include forestry camps, ranches, and farms that provide specific recreational activities or work for juveniles in a rural setting. Individual programs typically handle from thirty to fifty children. Such programs have the disadvantage of isolating children from the community, but reintegration can be achieved if the child's stay is short and if family and friends can visit.

Most residential programs use group counseling techniques as the major treatment tool. Although group facilities have been used less often than institutional placements in years past, there is definitely a trend toward developing community-based residential facilities.

foster care programs
Juveniles who are orphans or whose parents cannot care for them are placed with families who provide the attention, guidance, and care they did not receive at home.

family group homes
A combination of foster care and a group home in which a juvenile is placed in a private group home run by a single family rather than by professional staff.

rural programs
Specific recreational and work opportunities provided for juveniles in a rural setting such as a forestry camp, a farm, or a ranch.

Although rural programs have the disadvantage of isolating children from the community, they help reintegrate clients into society if the child's stay is short and if family and friends can visit.

Nonresidential Community Treatment

nonresidential programs
Juveniles remain in their own homes but receive counseling, education, employment, diagnostic, and casework services through an intensive support system.

In **nonresidential programs** youths remain in their homes or in foster homes and receive counseling, education, employment, diagnostic, and casework services. A counselor or probation officer gives innovative and intensive support to help the child remain at home. Family therapy, educational tutoring, and job placement may all be part of the program.

Nonresidential programs are often modeled on the Provo program, begun in 1959 in Utah, and on the Essexfields Rehabilitation Project, started in the early 1960s in Essex County, New Jersey.[54] Today, one of the best known approaches is Project New Pride, which has been replicated in a number of sites around the United States. Project New Pride and two other innovative programs are the subject of the Policy and Practice box entitled "Three Model Nonresidential Programs."

Pros and Cons of Community Treatment

The community treatment approach has limitations. The public may have a negative impression of community treatment, especially when it is offered to juvenile offenders who pose a real threat to society. Institutionalization may be the only answer for violent, chronic offenders. Even if the juvenile crime problem abates, society may be unwilling to accept the outcomes of reform-minded policies and practices. For example, it is common for neighborhood groups to actively oppose the location of corrections programs in their community. The thought of a drug rehabilitation center being located across the street sends shivers up the spine of many property owners.

Although some studies of community treatment programs are encouraging, evaluations of recidivism rates do not show conclusively that community treatment is more successful than institutionalization. Some experimental programs indicate that young people can be treated in the community as safely and as effectively as youths placed in an institution. However, commitment to an institution guarantees that the community will be protected against further crime, at least during the time of the juvenile's placement. More research is needed to evaluate the success of community treatment programs.

Much of the early criticism of community treatment was based on poor delivery of services, shabby operation, and haphazard management, follow-up, and planning. In the early 1970s, when Massachusetts deinstitutionalized its juvenile correction system, there were a torrent of reports about the inadequate operation of community treatment programs, based in part on the absence of uniform policies and procedures and the lack of accountability. The development of needed programs was hampered, and available resources were misplaced. Today's community treatment programs have generally overcome their early deficiencies and operate more efficiently than in the past.

Another criticism is that deinstitutionalization results in increased use of pretrial detention for juveniles if judges fear that dangerous children will be treated leniently at adjudication. Also, more children are being transferred to adult courts and subsequently committed to adult prisons.[55]

Despite such criticisms, community-based programs continue to present the most promising alternative to the poor results of reform schools for these reasons:

1. Some states have found that residential and nonresidential settings produce comparable or lower recidivism rates. Some researchers have found that youths in nonsecure settings are less likely to become recidivists than those placed in more secure settings (although this hasn't been proven conclusively).
2. Community-based programs have lower costs and are especially appropriate for large numbers of nonviolent juveniles and those guilty of lesser offenses.

THREE MODEL NONRESIDENTIAL PROGRAMS

PROJECT NEW PRIDE

One of the best known community-based treatment programs is Project New Pride. Begun in 1973 in Denver, Colorado, it has been a model for similar programs around the country.

The target group for Project New Pride is serious or violent youthful offenders from fourteen to seventeen years of age who have at least two prior convictions for serious misdemeanors or felonies and are formally charged or convicted of another offense when they are referred to New Pride. The only youths not eligible for participation are those who have committed forcible rape or are diagnosed as severely psychotic. New Pride believes this restriction is necessary in the interest of the safety of the community and of the youths themselves.

The project's specific goals are to steer these hard core offenders back into the mainstream of their communities and to reduce the number of rearrests. Generally, reintegration into the community means enrolling in school, getting a job, or both. The success of this program revolves around four ideas:

1. *Schooling.* New Pride youths receive alternative schooling and are then reintegrated into the public school system or directed toward vocational training. Some youths get jobs and pursue a general equivalency diploma (GED). Some of them complete high school in the alternative school (certified by the public school system).
2. *Jobs.* New Pride emphasizes vocational training. The staff recognizes that money is the key to independence for these youths, and the most socially acceptable way to get money is to work for it.
3. *Family.* Not only do the youths benefit from intensive counseling but their families also have access to counselors. New Pride encourages family members to visit the project facility to observe the daily operations, involve themselves in their child's treatment, and get to know staff.
4. *Cost-effectiveness.* New Pride community-based programs are extremely cost effective when compared with the cost of placing a child in an institution. In Colorado and New Jersey, for example, it costs approximately $28,000 per year to incarcerate a youth; the cost for placing a youth in Denver New Pride is approximately $4,500.

3. Public opinion of community corrections remains positive. In choosing between two approaches (training schools and community-based programs) for all but the most violent or serious juvenile offenders, more than 71 percent of the respondents in a recent public opinion survey indicated they favored a system that relied primarily on community-based services.[56]

As jurisdictions continue to face high rates of violent juvenile crime and ever-increasing costs for juvenile justice services, community-based programs will play an important role in providing rehabilitation of juvenile offenders and ensuring public safety.

Experts have confirmed the decline of rehabilitation in juvenile justice throughout much of the United States over the past twenty-five years.[57] But several recent **meta-analysis** studies have refuted the claim that "nothing works" with juvenile offenders and have given support to community rehabilitation. Independent studies have concluded that adjudicated delinquents do respond positively to community treatment, and they suggest that rehabilitation is more successful in community rather than in institutional settings. According to Krisberg, the most successful community-based programs seem to share at least some of these characteristics: (1) comprehensiveness, dealing with many aspects of youths' lives; (2) intensive, involving multiple contacts; (3) operate outside the formal juvenile justice system; (4) build on youths' strengths rather than deficiencies; and (5) adopt a socially grounded approach to

meta-analysis
An analysis technique that synthesizes results across many programs over time.

Each participant in New Pride has six months of intensive involvement and a six-month follow-up period during which the youth slowly reintegrates into the community. During the follow-up period, the youth continues to receive as many services as necessary, such as schooling and job placement, and works closely with counselors.

THE BETHESDA DAY TREATMENT CENTER PROGRAM

The Bethesda Day Treatment Center Program in West Milton, Pennsylvania, is another model day treatment program. The center's services include intensive supervision, counseling, and coordination of a range of services necessary for youths to develop skills to function effectively in the community. The program provides delinquent and dependent youths, ages 10 to 17, with up to fifty-five hours of services a week without removing them from their homes. A unique program feature requires work experience for all working age clients, with 75 percent of their paychecks directed toward payment of fines, court costs, and restitution. A preliminary study revealed recidivism rates far lower than state and national norms.

MULTISYSTEMIC THERAPY

Multisystemic Therapy (MST), a nonresidential delinquency treatment program developed by Dr. Scott Henggeler of the Medical University of South Carolina, views individuals as being "nested" within a complex of interconnected systems, including the family, community, school, and peers. The MST treatment team may target problems in any of these systems for change and use the individual's strengths in these systems to effect that change. Treatment teams, which usually include three counselors, provide services over a four-month period for about fifty families per year. In one evaluation the rearrest rate for the MST group was found to be about half that of the group receiving traditional services. In another, the recidivism rate four years after treatment was 22 percent for MST youths, 72 percent for youths receiving individual counseling, and 87 percent for youths who refused either treatment. These evaluation results are a strong indicator of program effectiveness.

Sources: *Project New Pride* (Washington, D.C.: U.S. Government Printing Office, 1985); Shay Bilchik, *A Juvenile Justice System for the 21st Century* (Washington, D.C.: OJJDP, 1998).

understanding a child's situation rather than an individual-level (medical or therapeutic) approach.[58]

Even though the pendulum has swung away from rehabilitation and toward community protection, states continue to develop community-based services.[59] The Policy and Practice box entitled "A Case Study in Juvenile Justice Reform" describes one recently formed program.

SUMMARY

Community treatment encompasses efforts by the juvenile justice system to keep offenders in the community and spare them the pain and stigma of incarceration in a secure facility. The primary purpose of community treatment is to address the individual needs of juveniles in a nonrestrictive or home setting, employing any combination of educational, vocational, counseling, and employment services.

The most widely used method of community treatment is probation. Approximately four hundred thousand youths are currently on probation. They must obey rules given to them by the court and partake in some form of treatment program. Their behavior in the community is monitored by probation officers. If rules are violated, youths can have their probation revoked and suffer more punitive means of control, such as secure incarceration.

Probation may be used at the "front end" of the juvenile justice system for first-time lower risk offenders or at the "back end" as an alternative to institutional confinement for more serious offenders.

A CASE STUDY IN JUVENILE JUSTICE REFORM

In recent decades juvenile justice policy has become more conservative. The implementation of various get-tough strategies has contributed to an increasing juvenile corrections population. Programs of prevention, treatment, and control are necessary to reduce juvenile crime.

The administration of juvenile justice has been reformed significantly in the state of Ohio over the past three years. The primary reform initiative, the RECLAIM Ohio program (Reasoned and Equitable Community and Local Alternatives to the Incarceration of Minors), provides for a community-based response to the problem of youth delinquency through establishment of a local graduated sanctions programs. RECLAIM meets both liberal and conservative ideals by encouraging counties to treat delinquents adjudicated for less serious felonies in their communities and reserving space for more serious offenders in institutions. The program's ability to address both liberal and conservative ideology may be the reason for its success.

The program places a policy and funding emphasis on prevention and early intervention activities that will minimize the need for more costly efforts later. RECLAIM Ohio is a unique program that enables local juvenile courts to respond immediately and effectively to youth misbehavior by developing their own community-based disposition programs or contracting with private and nonprofit organizations to establish them. Several factors led to the enactment of the RECLAIM Ohio legislation. County judges, often faced with pressure from their limited local budgets, thought committing a youth to a DYS secure facility was free, since sending youth to the state juvenile prison system came at no cost to the county. Thus, there was a fiscal incentive in place to commit youths to secure juvenile facilities, no matter how nonviolent the crime for which they had been adjudicated. According to a RECLAIM Ohio program overview, "It was becoming readily apparent that many of the youth committed to DYS (secure facilities)—particularly first-time, nonviolent offenders—would be better served in their local communities."

This sentencing trend helped contribute to significant crowding in juvenile institutions around the state. The overcrowded conditions created a dangerous situation for both residents and staff. The end result was RECLAIM Ohio.

Probation departments have developed restitution programs as a type of community treatment. These involve having juvenile offenders either reimburse their victims or do community service. Although these programs appear successful, critics argue that they are widening the net of social control over young offenders.

Other forms of community treatment are day programs and residential community programs. The former allow youths to live at home while receiving treatment in a non-punitive, community-based center; the latter require that youths reside in group homes while receiving care and treatment.

Despite criticisms, the cost savings of community treatment, coupled with its benign intentions, are likely to keep these programs growing. They are certainly no less effective than secure institutions. Massachusetts, Maryland, Pennsylvania, Florida, and Utah are examples of states that have moved toward deinstitutionalization. Community-based graduated sanctions are as effective and sometimes more effective than traditional incarceration for juvenile offenders. An examination of more than two hundred programs found that the most successful ones are operated in nontraditional community settings.[60]

KEY TERMS

community treatment
probation
juvenile probation officer

social investigation report
predisposition report
conditions of probation

juvenile intensive
   probation supervision
   (JIPS)

ELEMENTS OF REFORM

Designed to provide more local autonomy in the administration of juvenile justice, RECLAIM Ohio is a funding initiative that encourages local juvenile courts to develop or contract for a range of community-based sanction options. The program goals are twofold: to empower local judges with more sentencing options and disposition alternatives for the juvenile offender and to improve the ability of the secure facilities to treat and rehabilitate youthful offenders. RECLAIM Ohio allows local juvenile courts to create a series of different services and sanctions appropriate to the juvenile offenders who come before them.

REFORM STRATEGY

Under the RECLAIM Ohio program, the responsibility for crowding in juvenile facilities and the delivery of services to delinquent youths is not a state or local problem but a systems challenge. The developers of RECLAIM Ohio soon realized that communities lacked resources to treat some juvenile offenders locally with appropriate and cost-effective services.

Since the introduction of RECLAIM Ohio, DYS officials have seen decreased institutional populations and a greater opportunity to address treatment issues for youths in need. However, the best result, according to officials, is the shared effort in reclaiming delinquent children among the juvenile courts, DYS, and other state agencies. This newly created vision would have been unimaginable five years ago, officials report.

Today, RECLAIM Ohio is well received by local courts and appears to be working. A fiscal year 1996 program overview indicates that admissions to DYS decreased 4 percent compared with fiscal year 1995, and more than 10,400 youths were served by community-based programs administered by local juvenile courts and funded with RECLAIM Ohio appropriations.

Sources: *Juvenile Justice Reform Initiatives in the States 1994–1996* (Washington, D.C.: OJJDP, 1997); Melissa Moon, Brandon Applegate, and Edward Latessa, "Reclaim Ohio—A Community-Based Initiative," *Crime and Delinquency* 43:438–57 (1997).

---

house arrest
electronic monitoring
wilderness probation
balanced probation
monetary restitution
victim service restitution

community service
  restitution
Alternative Work
  Sentencing Program
  (Earn-It)
right to treatment
residential programs

group homes
foster care programs
family group homes
rural programs
nonresidential programs
meta-analysis

INFOTRAC COLLEGE EDITION EXERCISES

Read the following articles from InfoTrac College Edition:

Expert policy in juvenile justice: patterns of claimsmaking and issues of power in a program construction. Rebecca D. Petersen. *Policy Studies Journal* Winter 1995

Group work with high-risk urban youths on probation. Harriet Goodman, George S. Getzel, William Ford. *Social Work* July 1996

Read the above two articles from InfoTrac College Edition. Based on Petersen's comments regarding the common approach of policymakers to attempt to correct the behavior of youth rather than the problems of society, how would she react to the youth probation program detailed by Goodman and Getzel?

QUESTIONS FOR DISCUSSION

1. Would you want a community treatment program in your neighborhood? Why or why not?
2. Is widening the net a real danger, or are treatment-oriented programs simply a method of helping troubled youths?
3. If a youngster violates the rules of probation, should he or she be placed in a secure institution?
4. Is juvenile restitution fair? Should a poor child have to pay back a wealthy victim, such as a store owner?
5. What are the most important advantages to community treatment for juvenile offenders?
6. What is the purpose of juvenile probation? Identify some conditions of probation and discuss the responsibilities of the juvenile probation officer.
7. What are graduated sanctions?
8. Has community treatment generally proven successful?

NOTES

1. Robert Shepard Jr., ed., *Juvenile Justice Standards, A Balanced Approach* (Chicago: ABA, 1996).
2. George Killinger, Hazel Kerper, and Paul F. Cromwell Jr., *Probation and Parole in the Criminal Justice System* (St. Paul, Minn.: West, 1976), p. 45; National Advisory Commission on Criminal Justice Standards and Goals, *Corrections* (Washington, D.C.: U.S. Government Printing Office, 1983), p. 75.
3. Ibid.
4. Melissa Sickmund, *Juvenile Court Statistics 1995* (Pittsburgh, Pa.: National Center for Juvenile Justice, 1998).
5. Ibid.
6. Ibid.
7. Hunter Hurst IV and Patricia McHall Torbet, "Organization and Administration of Juvenile Services: Probation, Aftercare and State Institutions for Delinquent Youth" (Pittsburgh, Pa.: National Center for Juvenile Justice, 1993); Patricia Torbet, "Juvenile Probation: The Workhorse of the Juvenile Justice System" (Washington, D.C.: OJJDP, 1996).
8. Hurst and Torbet, "Organization and Administration of Juvenile Services," p. 2.
9. Torbet, "Juvenile Probation."
10. *Morrissey v. Brewer,* 408 U.S. 471, 92 S.Ct. 2593, 33 L.Ed.2d 484 (1972); *Gagnon v. Scarpelli,* 411 U.S. 778, 93 S.Ct. 1756, 36 L.Ed.2d 655 (1973).
11. See, generally, James Byrne, "The Control Controversy: A Preliminary Examination of Intensive Probation Supervision Programs in the United States," *Federal Probation* 50:4–16 (1986).
12. For a review of these programs, see James Byrne, ed., "Introduction," *Federal Probation* 50:2 (1986); see also Emily Walker, "The Community Intensive Treatment for Youth Program: A Specialized Community-Based Program for High-Risk Youth in Alabama," *Law and Psychology Review* 13:175–99 (1989).
13. Edward Latessa, "The Cost Effectiveness of Intensive Supervision," *Federal Probation* 50:70–74 (1986); John Ott, "Bibliotherapy as a Challenging Condition to the Sentence of Juvenile Probation," *Juvenile and Family Court Journal* 40:63–67 (1989).
14. Richard G. Wiebush, "Juvenile Intensive Supervision: The Impact on Felony Offenders Diverted from Institutional Placement," *Crime and Delinquency* 39:68–89 (1993).
15. H. Preston Elrod and Kevin I. Minor, "Second Wave Evaluation of a Multi-Faceted Intervention for Juvenile Court Probationers," *International Journal of Offender Therapy and Comparative Criminology* 36:249–61 (1992).
16. S. H. Clarke and A. D. Craddock, *Evaluation of North Carolina's Intensive Juvenile Probation Program* (Chapel Hill, N.C.: University of North Carolina Institute of Government, 1987).
17. T. L. Armstrong, *National Survey of Juvenile Intensive Probation Supervision* (Washington, D.C.: Department of Justice, Criminal Justice Abstracts, 1988); National Council on Crime and Delinquency, *Juvenile Intensive Probation Programs—The State of the Art* (San Francisco: NCCD, 1991).
18. Barry Krisberg, Elliot Currie, and David Onek, "What Works with Juvenile Offenders," *Journal of Criminal Justice of American Bar Association* 10:20–52 (1995); William Barton and Jeffrey Butts, *The Metro County Intensive Supervision Experiment* (Ann Arbor, Mich.: Institute for Social Research, 1988).
19. Gordon Bazemore and Mark Umbreit, *Balanced and Restorative Justice for Juveniles—A Framework for Juvenile Justice in the 21st Century* (Washington, D.C.: OJJDP, 1997).
20. Richard Ball and J. Robert Lilly, "A Theoretical Examination of Home Incarceration," *Federal Probation* 50:17–25 (1986); Joan Petersilia, "Exploring the Option of House Arrest," *Federal Probation* 50:50–56 (1986); Annesley Schmidt, "Electronic Monitors," *Federal Probation* 50:56–60 (1986); Michael Charles, "The Development of a Juvenile Electronic Monitoring Program," *Federal Probation* 53:3–12 (1989).
21. Joseph B. Vaughn, "A Survey of Juvenile Electronic Monitoring and Home Confinement Programs," *Juvenile and Family Court Journal* 40:1–36 (1989).
22. Sudipto Roy, "Five Years of Electronic Monitoring of Adults and Juveniles in Lake County, Indiana: A Comparative Study on Factors Related to Failure," *Journal of Crime and Justice* 20:141–60 (1997).
23. Joseph Papy and Richard Nimer, "Electronic Monitoring in Florida," *Federal Probation* 55:31–33 (1991); Annesley Schmidt, "Electronic Monitors—Realistically, What Can Be Expected?," *Federal Probation* 55:47–53 (1991).
24. Robert Callahan, "Wilderness Probation: A Decade Later," *Juvenile and Family Court Journal* 36:31–35 (1985); "Wilderness Programs in Probation," *Juvenile and Family Court Newsletter,* vol. 19 (1989), p. 5.
25. Steven Flagg Scott, "Outward Bound: An Adjunct to the Treatment of Juvenile Delinquents: Florida's STEP Program," *New England Journal on Criminal and Civil Confinement* 11:420–37 (1985).
26. Dennis Mahoney, Dennis Romig, and Troy Armstrong, "Juvenile Probation: The Balanced Approach," *Juvenile and Family Court Journal* 39:1–59 (1988).
27. Gordon Bazemore, "On Mission Statements and Reform in Juvenile Justice: The Case of the Balanced Approach," *Federal Probation* 61:64–70 (1992); Gordon Bazemore and Mark Umbreit, *Balanced and Restorative Justice* (Washington, D.C.: Office of Juvenile Justice and Delinquency Prevention, 1994).
28. Gordon Bazemore, *Guide for Implementing the Balanced and Restorative Justice Model* (Washington, D.C.: OJJDP, 1998).
29. Anne L. Schneider, ed., *Guide to Juvenile Restitution* (Washington, D.C.: Department of Justice, 1985); Anne Schneider and Jean Warner, *National Trends in Juvenile Restitution Programming* (Washington, D.C.: U.S. Government Printing Office, 1989).

30. Gordon Bazemore, "New Concepts and Alternative Practice in Community Supervision of Juvenile Offenders: Rediscovering Work Experience and Competency Development," *Journal of Crime and Justice* 14:27–45 (1991); Jeffrey Butts and Howard Snyder, *Restitution and Juvenile Recidivism* (Washington, D.C.: Department of Justice, 1992).

31. Anne Newton, "Sentencing to Community Service and Restitution," *Criminal Justice Abstracts* (Hackensack, N.J.: National Council on Crime and Delinquency, September 1979), pp. 435–68.

32. Anne Schneider, "Restitution and Recidivism Rates of Juvenile Offenders: Results from Four Experimental Studies," *Criminology* 24:533–52 (1986).

33. Linda Szymanski, *Juvenile Restitution Statutes* (Pittsburgh, Pa.: National Center for Juvenile Justice, 1988).

34. N.C. Gen.Laws 7A, 649 (1995).

35. Descriptive materials can be obtained from the Earn-It Program, District Court of East Norfolk, Quincy, Mass. 02169. The Quincy District Court Probation Department was extremely helpful in providing information about this program.

36. Shay Bilchik, *A Juvenile Justice System for the 21st Century* (Washington, D.C.: OJJDP, 1998).

37. Peter Schneider, William Griffith, and Anne Schneider, *Juvenile Restitution as a Sole Sanction or Condition of Probation: An Empirical Analysis* (Eugene, Ore.: Institute for Policy Analysis, 1980); S. Roy, "Juvenile Restitution and Recidivism in a Midwestern County," *Federal Probation* 57:55–62 (1995).

38. Anne Schneider, "Restitution and Recidivism Rates of Juvenile Offenders," *Directory of Restitution Programs* (Washington, D.C.: OJJDP Juvenile Justice Clearinghouse, 1996). This directory contains information on more than five hundred restitution programs across the country.

39. Burt Galaway, "Restitution as Innovation or Unfilled Promise," *Federal Probation* 52:3–15 (1989).

40. William Staples, "Restitution as a Sanction in Juvenile Court," *Crime and Delinquency* 32:177–85 (1986).

41. Barry Krisberg and James Austin, "The Unmet Promise of Alternatives to Incarceration," *Crime and Delinquency* 28: 374–409 (1982).

42. H. Ted Rubin, "Fulfilling Juvenile Restitution Requirements in Community Correctional Programs," *Federal Probation* 52: 32–43 (1988).

43. Bureau of Justice Statistics, *Report to the Nation on Crime and Justice* (Washington, D.C.: U.S. Government Printing Office, 1988), pp. 44–45; Peter Greenwood, "What Works with Juvenile Offenders: A Synthesis of the Literature and Experience," *Federal Probation* 58:63–67 (1994).

44. Greenwood, "What Works With Juvenile Offenders."

45. National Council of Juvenile and Family Court Judges, "The Juvenile Court and Serious Offenders," *Juvenile and Family Court Journal* 35:16 (Cambridge, Mass.: 1984); American Bar Association, Institute of Judicial Administration, Standards on Probation, 1980.

46. Robert Pierce, *Juvenile Justice Reform: State Experiences* (Denver: National Conference of State Legislatures, 1989); National Conference of State Legislatures, *A Legislator's Guide to Comprehensive Juvenile Justice* (Denver: author, 1996).

47. Robert Coates, Alden Miller, and Lloyd Ohlin, *Diversity in a Youth Correctional System* (Cambridge, Mass.: Ballinger Press,

1978); Barry Krisberg, James Austin, and Patricia Steele, *Unlocking Juvenile Corrections* (San Francisco: National Council on Crime and Delinquency, 1989).

48. "Roxbury Agency Offers a Map for Youths at the Crossroads," *Boston Globe* 18 February 1990, p. 32.

49. Jeffrey Butts, *Youth Corrections in Maryland: The Dawning of a New Era* (Ann Arbor, Mich.: Center for Study of Youth Policy, University of Michigan, 1988).

50. J. Blackmore, M. Brown, and B. Krisberg, *Juvenile Justice Reform—The Bellwether States* (Ann Arbor, Mich.: Center for Study of Youth Policy, University of Michigan, 1988).

51. Joseph Moone, *Juveniles in Public Facilities, 1995* (Washington, D.C.: OJJDP, 1997); Melissa Sickmund, Howard Snyder, and Eileen Peo-Yamagata, *Juvenile Offenders and Victims—1997 Update on Violence* (Washington, D.C.: OJJDP, 1997).

52. H. Ashley Weeks, *Highfields* (Ann Arbor: University of Michigan Press, 1956).

53. LaMar T. Empey and Stephen Lubeck, *The Silverlake Experiment: Testing Delinquency Theory and Community Intervention* (Chicago: Aldine, 1971).

54. Lamar Empey and Maynard Erickson, *The Provo Experiment* (Lexington, Mass.: D. C. Heath, 1972); Paul Pilnick, Albert Elias, and Neale Clapp, "The Essexfields Concept: A New Approach to the Social Treatment of Juvenile Delinquents," *Journal of Applied Behavioral Sciences* 2:109–21 (1966); Yitzhak Bakal, "Reflections: A Quarter Century of Reform in Massachusetts Youth Corrections," *Crime and Delinquency* 40:110–17 (1998).

55. Barry Krisberg and Ira Schwartz, "Rethinking Juvenile Justice," *Crime and Delinquency* 29:333–64 (1983); Ira Schwartz, Shenyang Guo, and John Kerbs, "The Impact of Demographic Variables on Public Opinion Regarding Juvenile Justice: Implications for Public Policy," *Crime and Delinquency* 39:5–28 (1993).

56. Ira Schwartz, Juvenile *Justice and Public Policy* (New York: Lexington Books, 1992), p. 217.

57. Dan Macallair, "Reaffirming Rehabilitation in Juvenile Justice," *Youth and Society* 25:104–23 (1993).

58. Mark W. Lipsey, "Juvenile Delinquency Treatment: A Meta-Analytic Inquiry into the Variability of Effects," in Thomas D. Cook et al., eds., *Meta-Analysis for Explanation: A Casebook* (San Francisco, Calif.: Russell Sage Foundation, 1991); Carol Garrett, "Effects of Residential Treatment on Adjudicated Delinquents: A Meta-Analysis," *Crime and Delinquency* 22:287–308 (1985); Ted Palmer, *The Re-Emergence of Correctional Interventions* (Newbury Park, Calif.: Russell Sage Foundation, 1992), p. 69; Barry Krisberg, Elliot Currie, and David Onek, "New Approaches in Corrections," *American Bar Association Journal of Criminal Justice,* 10:51 (1995).

59. Lawrence Sherman, Denise Gattfredson et al., *Preventing Crime: What Works, What Doesn't, What's Promising* (Washington, D.C.: National Institute of Justice, Research in Brief, 1988).

60. James Howell, ed., *Guide for Implementing the Comprehensive Strategy for Serious Violent and Chronic Juvenile Offenders* (Washington, D.C.,: U.S. Department of Justice, 1995); Patricia Torbet and Linda Szymanski, *State Legislative Responses to Violent Juvenile Crime: 1996–97 Update* (Washington, D.C.: OJJDP, 1998), p. 4.

Chapter Seventeen

Institutions for Juveniles

George Yamas, convicted at age 16 of grand theft auto and firebombing, was sent to the Preston Youth Correctional Institution in California, one of the state's most secure detention facilities, where inmates walk single file between two white lines on the pavement and guards routinely pat them down for weapons. With the current emphasis on institutional rehabilitation and accountability, the Preston facility organized "Newborn in Need," a unique program that provides warm clothing and blankets for premature babies. Despite institutional safety concerns—that crochet hooks, knitting needles, and scissors make lethal weapons in an institution—none of the materials has gone missing in the first six months of the program.

Three days a week George Yamas, eighteen years old now, can be found deftly sewing gowns with his tattooed hands. He admits that for two weeks before joining the program he taunted the participants. When he found he could earn community service credits toward early release, he joined the program and now prefers sewing and knitting to working out at the gym. When asked what he gets out of the program, George replies, "I was always negative, now I want to give something back."[1]

When the court determines that community treatment can't meet the special needs of a delinquent youth, a judge may refer the juvenile to a privately run treatment program that specializes in dealing with a particular social problem (such as drug abuse, violent juvenile crime, or juvenile sex offenses). These programs are often administered in secure long-term facilities that limit access to the community. In other cases, an offender may be referred to the state department of youth services for a period of confinement.

Today, correctional institutions operated by federal, state, and county governments are generally classified as secure or nonsecure facilities. Secure facilities restrict the movement of residents through staff monitoring, locked entrances and exits, and interior fence controls. Nonsecure institutions generally do not restrict the movement of the residents and allow much greater freedom of access in and out of the facility.[2]

In the past twenty-five years smaller secure facilities have, for the most part, replaced large bureaucratic institutions in the belief that these programs offer more freedom and a greater chance of rehabilitating young offenders. Many states have closed their large training schools and now rely on smaller institutions handling fewer than forty youths.[3] Violent youths and chronic serious offenders are placed in small, high security treatment units with specialized programs.

Two residents at the Preston Youth Correctional Facility create garments and blankets for the "Newborn in Need" program. Although correctional officers were worried at first that the juvenile offenders might take scissors and needles, none of the materials disappeared during the first six months of the program.

Beyond the secure and nonsecure classifications, there are at least six different categories of juvenile correctional institutions in the United States: (1) detention centers that provide restrictive custody prior to adjudication or disposition, (2) shelters that offer nonrestrictive temporary care, (3) reception centers that screen juveniles placed by the courts and assign them to an appropriate facility, (4) training schools or reformatories for adjudicated youths needing a long-term secure setting, (5) ranch or forestry camps that provide long-term residential care in a less restric-

FIGURE 17.1

Institutional Options for Juveniles

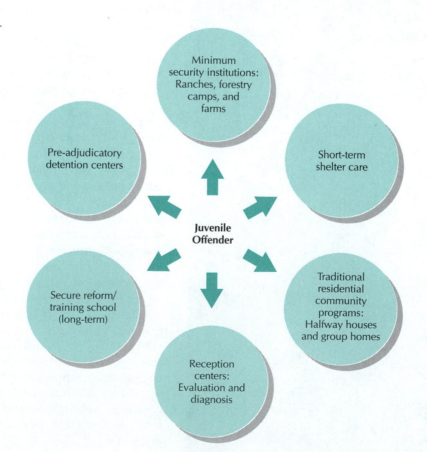

tive setting, and (6) halfway houses or group homes where juveniles are allowed daily contact with the community.[4] Youth correctional systems often incorporate virtually all of these programs (see Figure 17.1).

In addition to these types of institutions, many states develop a juvenile corrections placement matrix—a blueprint for a broad, comprehensive, risk-based continuum of care. This matrix serves to classify, by level and type of placement, the best treatment for each youth, taking into account the severity of the current offense and the risk of future recidivism. High-risk youths who are serious or violent offenders, for example, would be recommended for secure incarceration. The greatest advantage of the matrix format is that it helps state correctional agencies create a large number of classifications, allowing juvenile offenders to be assigned to different security levels and programs[5] (see Table 17.1).

Many experts believe institutionalizing young offenders generally does more harm than good. It exposes them to prison-like conditions and to more experienced delinquents without giving them the benefit of constructive treatment programs. In contrast, offenders in less costly community-based programs often have recidivism rates at least as low as (if not lower than) those in institutions. Nonetheless, secure treatment in juvenile corrections is still being used extensively around the country, and the populations of these facilities continue to grow.

In this chapter we analyze the state of secure juvenile corrections, beginning with some historical background. This is followed by a discussion of life in institutions, the juvenile client, treatment issues, legal rights, and aftercare programs.

Table 17.1

MODEL JUVENILE CORRECTIONS PLACEMENT MATRIX

Seriousness of Offense	High Risk	Risk Level Medium Risk	Low Risk
Violent Offense	violent offender program; assertive sex offender program; secure placement	secure residential program	boot camp; wilderness program
Serious Offense	secure placement; boot camp	intermediate community program	day treatment; specialized group homes
Less Serious Offense	short-term (thirty-day) stay in residential placement; day treatment program of six months: specialized group homes	day treatment; community service	community supervision; mentor program
Minor Offense	proctor program combining tracking with residential services; community supervision	community supervision	limited supervision; use of volunteers

The History of Juvenile Institutions

reform schools
Institutions in which educational and psychological services are used in an effort to improve the conduct of juveniles who are forcibly detained.

Until the early 1800s, juvenile offenders as well as neglected and dependent children were confined in adult prisons. The inhumane conditions in these institutions were among the factors that led social reformers to create a separate children's court system in 1899.[6] Early juvenile institutions were industrial schools modeled after adult prisons but designed to protect children from the evil influences in adult facilities. The first was the New York House of Refuge, established in 1825. Not long after this, states began to establish **reform schools** for juveniles. Massachusetts was the first, opening the Lyman School for Boys in Westborough in 1846. New York opened the State Agricultural and Industrial School in 1849, and Maine opened the Maine Boys' Training School in 1853. By 1900, thirty-six states had reform schools.[7] Although it is difficult to determine exact population of these institutions, by 1880 there were approximately eleven thousand youths in correctional facilities, a number that more than quadrupled by 1980 (see Table 17.2).[8] Early reform schools were generally punitive in nature and were based on the concept of rehabilitation (or reform) through hard work and discipline.

In the second half of the nineteenth century, emphasis shifted from massive industrial schools to the **cottage system.** Juvenile offenders were housed in a compound consisting of small cottages, each of which could accommodate twenty to forty children. A set of cottage parents ran each cottage, creating a home-like atmosphere. This setup was believed to be more conducive to rehabilitation than the rigid bureaucratic organization of massive institutions.

cottage system
Housing juveniles in a compound containing a series of small cottages, each of which accommodates twenty to forty children and is run by a set of cottage parents who create a home-like atmosphere.

The first cottage system was established in Massachusetts in 1855, the second in Ohio in 1858.[9] The system was held to be a great improvement over the earlier industrial training schools. The general feeling was that by moving away from punishment and toward rehabilitation, diagnosis, and treatment, not only could known offenders be rehabilitated but crime among dependent and unruly children could be prevented.[10]

Twentieth-Century Developments

The early twentieth century witnessed important changes in the structure of juvenile corrections. Because of the influence of World War I, reform schools began to adopt a militaristic style. Living units became barracks; cottage groups became companies; housefathers became captains; and superintendents became majors or colonels. Military-style uniforms were standard wear.

In addition, the establishment of the first juvenile court in 1899 reflected the expanded use of institutional confinement for delinquent children. As the number of juvenile offenders increased, the forms of juvenile institutions varied to include forestry camps, ranches, and educational and vocational schools. Beginning in the 1930s, camps modeled after the camps run by the Civilian Conservation Corps became a part of the juvenile correctional system. These juvenile camps centered on conservation activities, outdoor living, and work as a means of rehabilitation.

Los Angeles County was the first to use camps during this period.[11] Southern California was experiencing problems with transient youths who came to California with no money and then got into trouble with the law. Rather than filling up the jails, the county placed these offenders in conservation camps, paid them low wages, and then released them when they had earned enough money to return home. The camps proved more rehabilitative than training schools, and by 1935 California had

Table 17.2

YOUTHS IN CORRECTIONAL FACILITIES, 1880–1980

	1880	1890	1904	1910	1923	1980
Number	11,468	14,846	23,034	25,038	27,238	59,414
Per 100,000 population aged 10–20	97	100	126	125	125	136

Source: Margaret Werner Cahalan, *Historical Corrections Statistics in the United States, 1850–1984* (Washington, D.C.: U.S. Department of Justice, 1986), pp. 104–5.

established a network of forestry camps especially for delinquent boys. The idea soon spread to other states.[12]

Also during the 1930s, the U.S. Children's Bureau, the first federal agency to address juvenile delinquency issues, sought to reform juvenile corrections. The bureau conducted studies and projects to determine the effectiveness of the training school concept. Little was learned from these early programs because of limited funding and bureaucratic ineptitude, and the Children's Bureau failed to achieve any significant change in the juvenile correctional field. But such efforts recognized the important role of positive institutional care in delinquency prevention and control.[13]

Another innovation came in the 1940s with passage of the American Law Institute's Model Youth Correction Authority Act. This act emphasized the use of reception-classification centers. California was the first to try out this new idea, opening the Northern Reception Center and Clinic in Sacramento in 1947. Today, there are many such centers scattered around the United States.

Since the 1970s, a major change in institutionalization has been the effort by the federal government to remove status offenders from institutions housing juvenile delinquents. This initiative also includes removing status offenders from secure pretrial detention centers and removing all juveniles from contact with adults in jails.

This "decarceration" policy mandates that courts use the **least restrictive alternative** in providing services for status offenders. This means that a noncriminal child should not be put in a secure facility if a community-based program is available. In addition, the federal government prohibits states from placing status offenders in separate custodial care facilities that are similar in form and function to those used for delinquent offenders. This is to prevent states from merely shifting their institutionalized population around so that one training school houses all delinquents and another houses all status offenders, but actual conditions remain the same.

Throughout the 1980s and into the 1990s, admissions to public and private juvenile correctional facilities grew substantially.[14] Capacity of juvenile facilities also has increased but not enough to avoid overcrowding. State training schools, in particular, are seriously overcrowded in some states. Private juvenile facilities are playing an increased role in juvenile corrections, in part because of overpopulation in public facilities. Reliance on incarceration has been costly to states: inflation-controlled juvenile corrections expenditures for public facilities grew to more than $2 billion in 1995—an increase of 20 percent since 1982.[15]

Overcrowding often results in problematic conditions. A 1994 report issued by the OJJDP said that crowding, inadequate health care, lack of security, and poor control of suicidal behavior are substantial and widespread in juvenile corrections facilities. Despite new construction, at an average cost of over $100,000 per bed, crowding persists in more than half the states.[16]

least restrictive alternative
Choosing a program with the least restrictive or secure setting that will best benefit the child.

As we enter the twenty-first century, the number of confined juveniles is increasing. Most confined juveniles have committed property or drug offenses, but more than 25 percent have committed violent offenses. Progressively, more punitive and restrictive sanctions are provided for the serious and violent offenders. The remainder of this chapter explores the nature of today's juvenile institutions, the children who inhabit them, and the programs to help them reintegrate into society.

Juvenile Institutions Today: Public and Private

There are approximately 1,100 public and 2,200 private juvenile facilities in operation around the United States, holding an average one-day count of approximately 108,000 youths.[17] In 1995 (latest data) public juvenile facilities held 69,075 juveniles in residential custody, and private facilities held 39,671 juveniles.[18]

Public juvenile facilities include secure and nonsecure facilities used to hold pre- and postadjudicated individuals under the jurisdiction of the juvenile court. Just under 96 percent (66,236) of juveniles in public residential facilities were held for delinquent offenses—that is, offenses that would also be illegal if committed by an adult. A small number were held for status offenses—truancy, running away, possession of alcohol, and ungovernability—offenses that are not illegal for individuals who have reached the age of majority or another age established by law (see Table 17.3).

Private facilities have also played a significant role in juvenile corrections during the past twenty years. Private facilities have traditionally specialized in one particular method of treatment or one type of offender. For example, a private facility might hold one-time status offenders or females who require more intensive psychiatric treatment. Following a decrease in 1993, the population in private facilities increased to its highest level in 1995 (see Table 17.4).[19]

The majority of today's private institutions are small nonsecure facilities holding fewer than thirty youths. Although about 80 percent of the public institutions can be characterized as "closed" and secured, only 20 percent of private institutions are high security facilities.

Table 17.3

JUVENILES HELD IN PUBLIC INSTITUTIONS, 1995

Offensive Type	Total Juveniles	Percent
Total	69,075	100.0
Delinquent	66,236	95.9
Status	1,785	2.6
Other	889	1.3
Unknown	165	0.2

Source: Joseph Moone, "Status at a Glance—Juveniles in Public Institutions, 1995," OJJDP Fact Sheet 69 (Washington, D.C.: U.S. Department of Justice, 1997).

Table 17.4

JUVENILES IN PRIVATE INSTITUTIONS 1991–1995

	1991	1993	1995	Percentage Change 1991–95	1993–95
Total Population	36,190	35,626	39,671	9.62	11.35
Custody Type					
Detained	2,647	2,522	3,229	21.99	28.03
Committed	26,975	26,623	29,457	9.20	10.64
Voluntary	6,568	6,498	6,975	6.20	7.34
Offense Type					
Delinquent offense	14,433	14,292	17,781	23.20	24.41
Status offense	5,274	5,087	5,700	8.08	12.05
Nonoffender/other	16,483	16,264	16,777	−1.86	-0.53
Sex					
Male	25,801	25,874	29,176	13.08	12.76
Female	10,389	9,752	10,495	1.02	7.62
Race					
White, non-Hispanic	20,524	19,373	20,968	2.16	8.23
Black, non-Hispanic	11,555	11,813	13,333	15.39	12.87
Hispanic	3,136	3,431	4,116	31.25	19.97
Other	975	1,012	1,263	29.54	24.80
Age					
Under 10	632	580	626	−0.01	7.93
10 to 15	20,830	19,637	21,655	3.96	10.28
16 to 17	13,089	13,676	15,454	18.07	13.00
18 and older	1,639	1,742	1,967	20.01	12.92

Source: Joseph Moone, "Juveniles in Private Facilities 1991–95," OJJDP Fact Sheet 69 (Washington, D.C.: U.S. Department of Justice, 1997).

Public institutions for juveniles may be administered by any number of state agencies: child and youth services; mental health, youth conservation, health, and social services; corrections; or child welfare.[20] In some states these institutions fall under a centralized corrections system that covers adults as well as juveniles. Recently, a number of states have created separate youth services organizations and removed juvenile corrections from an existing adult corrections department or mental health agency. However, the majority of states still place responsibility for the administration of juvenile corrections within social service departments.

A diversity of administrative arrangements characterizes the organization of institutional juvenile corrections in the United States today. According to experts, there is a preference for a single statewide department of juvenile corrections. This form of organization seems best able to carry out the courts' dispositions, appropriate moneys, and implement effective institutional programs for juveniles. Institutional administration, including financial management and program planning, is not an easy task. Unfortunately, it is the quality of the administration that often determines the effectiveness of a particular facility.

The physical plants of juvenile institutions across the nation vary tremendously in size and quality. Many of the older training schools are tremendously outdated and still tend to place all juvenile offenders in a single building, regardless of the offense. More acceptable structures today include a reception unit with an infirmary, a security unit, and dormitory units or cottages. Planners have concluded that the most effective design for training schools is to have facilities located around a community square. The facilities generally include a dining hall and kitchen area, a storage warehouse, academic and vocational training rooms, a library, an auditorium, a gymnasium, a laundry, maintenance facilities, an administration building, and other basic facilities such as a commissary, a barber shop, and a beauty shop.

The conditions of individual living areas also vary, depending on the type of facility and the progressiveness of its administration. Most traditional training school conditions were appalling, with juveniles living in unbelievable squalor. Today, however, most institutions provide toilet and bath facilities, beds, desks, lamps, and tables. New facilities usually provide a single room for each individual.

Most experts recommend that juvenile facilities have indoor and outdoor leisure areas, libraries, academic and vocational education spaces, chapels, facilities where youths can meet with their visitors, a reception and processing room, security fixtures, windows in all sleeping accommodations, and fire safety equipment and procedures. Because institutions for delinquent youths vary in type and purpose, it is not necessary that they meet identical physical standards. Security measures used in some closed juvenile institutions, for instance, may not be required in a residential community program.

The physical conditions and architecture of secure facilities for juveniles have come a long way from the training schools of the turn of the century. However, many administrators and state legislators realize that more modernization is necessary to meet even minimum compliance with national standards for juvenile institutions. Correctional administrators have described conditions as horrendous, and health officials have cited institutions for violations such as pollution by vermin, rodents, and asbestos.[21] Although some improvements have been made, there are still enormous problems to overcome.

Legal efforts—at the heart of more than twenty-five years of child advocacy—continue to focus on (1) establishing procedures to protect the rights of children in institutions; (2) reducing the number of institutionalized juveniles nationwide; and (3) improving the treatment of incarcerated youth, including providing for adequate medical and educational programs.[22] Later in this chapter we will explore some of the issues surrounding the legal right to treatment.

Trends in Juvenile Corrections

There is little question that tremendous variation exists among the states in the use of juvenile correctional facilities. California is by far the leading state in both its use and the variety of such facilities, housing almost 20 percent of all residents of public and private institutions.[23] The California incarceration rate for juveniles is more than 559 per 100,000 juveniles in the population. In contrast, Texas has an incarceration rate of about 170 per 100,000. New York, another populous state, has almost 3,000 youths in custody and averages an incarceration rate of 200 per 100,000 youths.[24] In 1995 the national average was 245 juveniles per 100,000 in public custody. The highest rate of incarceration in public facilities for delinquent acts is in the District of Columbia, an entirely urban population, where the juvenile custody rate is 594 per 100,000 or more than twice the national average of 245 per 100,000 youths. These numbers indicate that states address the problems of institutional care in different ways.

Currently, six states hold half of all juveniles in custody in public facilities: California, Ohio, Texas, New York, Florida and Illinois. In other words, the aggregate juvenile custody population of a handful of states surpassed that of the remaining states. California has the highest number of juveniles in custody in public facilities with 19,567 (28 percent). The number of juveniles in custody is affected by differences in state laws, policies, and practices, and the upper age of original or extended jurisdiction for juvenile court differs among the states. Under California law, the juvenile corrections system can hold offenders adjudicated in juvenile court much longer than those in other state systems.[25]

Overcrowding and its attendant problems have made states reluctant to increase the number of juvenile residents in their publicly run facilities. Another reason for this reluctance is the enormous expense involved in constructing and running facilities. The average cost of housing one resident for one year is between $40,000 and $50,000, and construction of a new facility is in the millions.

The Institutionalized Juvenile

The best source of information on institutionalized youths is the federal government's Children in Custody (CIC) census. This survey provides timely information on the number and characteristics of children being held in public and private facilities around the nation. Other excellent resources are the Office of Juvenile Justice and Delinquency's "Juveniles Taken into Custody Report" and the "Juvenile Court Statistics Report."

The latest information available (1995) indicates that of the 108,000 youths who were being held daily (see Figure 17.2 and Table 17.5) twice as many were long-term institutional commitments as preadjudication detainees.[26] The census also found that more than 66,000 juveniles were confined for delinquent acts, over 3,500

FIGURE 17.2

Rate for Incarcerated Children, 1985 to 1995

Source: Bureau of Justice Statistics, *Children in Custody 1975–1985* and *Fact Sheet 1987* (Washington, D.C.: U.S. Department of Justice, 1989); Office of Juvenile Justice and Delinquency Prevention, *National Juvenile Custody Trends 1978–1989* (Washington, D.C.: U.S. Department of Justice, 1992); James Austin et al., *Juveniles Taken into Custody—1993* (Washington, D.C.: U.S. Department of Justice, 1995); Joseph Moone, *States at a Glance—Juveniles in Public Facilities, 1995* (Washington, D.C.: U.S. Department of Justice, 1997).

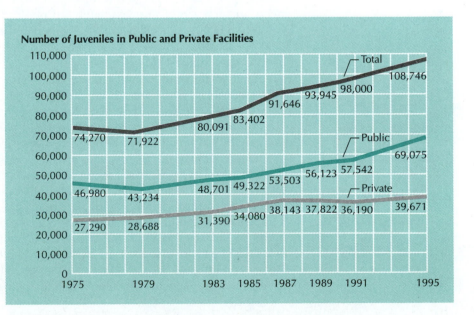

Number of Juveniles in Public and Private Facilities

Table 17.5

NATIONAL TRENDS IN JUVENILE CORRECTIONS, PUBLIC AND PRIVATE, 1979–1995

	1979	1989	1991	1995
Juveniles in custody	71,922	93,945	98,000	108,746
Overall custody rate per 100,000	251	367	357	245
Admission rate per 100,000	2,220	2,974	3,213	3,300
Total expenditures	1,307,684	2,860,818	3,000,000	3,500,000
Total number of juvenile institutions	2,200	3,267	3,200	3,200

Sources: Office of Juvenile Justice and Delinquency Prevention, *National Juvenile Custody Trends 1978–1989* (Washington, D.C.: U.S. Department of Justice, 1992); Barbara Allen Hagen, *Public Juvenile Facilities—Children in Custody, 1989* (Washington, D.C.: U.S. Department of Justice, 1991); James Austin et al., *Juveniles Taken into Custody—1993* (Washington, D.C.: U.S. Department of Justice, 1995); Melissa Sickmund et al., *Juvenile Offenders and Victims, 1997 Update* (Washington, D.C.: OJJDP, 1998).

were confined as a result of status offenses, and more than 1,500 were confined as nonoffenders such as abandoned or neglected children.[27] The one-day count of juveniles held in public facilities rose 47 percent between 1983 and 1995. In addition, minority youths outnumbered white youths in public custody facilities by more than two to one. Minorities represent more than two-thirds of all residents in long-term public facilities. States have undertaken a variety of programs aimed at eliminating any racial disparities in the juvenile justice system in light of the disproportionate number of minorities in institutional care.

The number of youths in public facilities remained virtually unchanged between 1980 and 1985 (about 50,000) but then increased to 56,723 in 1989 and to more than 57,000 in 1991 and to 69,075 in 1995. Private sector institutions experienced an increase of approximately 10 percent between 1983 and 1985 (from 31,000 to 34,000), as well as another 10 percent increase from 1985 to 1989 (from 34,000 to 38,000).[28] By 1995 this figure was 39,671.

The data suggest that despite twenty-five years of decarceration efforts the number of incarcerated youths has increased, a trend that reflects the dominance of a conservative, crime control-oriented policy in some states. Nationally, about 96 percent of the juveniles in public facilities were in custody for a delinquent act.

Although the number of institutionalized youths is on the increase, the CIC data may reveal only the tip of the correctional iceberg. For example, the data do not include many of the minors who are incarcerated after they are waived to adult courts or who have their cases tried there because of exclusion statutes. Most states place underage juveniles convicted of adult charges in youth centers until they reach the age of majority, whereupon they are transferred to an adult facility. In addition, as Ira Schwartz and his colleagues point out, there is a "hidden system" of juvenile control that places wayward youths in private mental hospitals and substance abuse clinics for behaviors that could easily have brought them a stay in a correctional facility or community-based program.[29] This hidden system is an important community resource for mentally ill children and juvenile substance abuse offenders.

These data suggest that the number of institutionalized children may be far greater than that reported in the CIC surveys.[30]

Personal Characteristics

The "typical resident" described in the CIC report is a fifteen- to sixteen-year-old white male incarcerated for an average stay of approximately five months in a public facility or six months in a private facility. Almost 80 percent of all the residents in public and private facilities are male; the remaining 20 percent are female. Most juveniles committed to institutions are between fourteen and seventeen years of age. Private facilities tend to house younger youths, and public institutions provide custodial care for older youths, including a small percentage of youths between eighteen and twenty-one years of age.

Girls in a Marlin, Texas, juvenile facility. According to the most recent surveys, minority youth outnumbered nonminority white youth in public custody facilities by more than 2 to 1. Minorities represent more than two-thirds of all residents in public long-term facilities. Because these data may represent a trend of racial discrimination in juvenile sentencing, some states have undertaken a variety of programs aimed at eliminating any racial disparities in the juvenile justice system.

Racial makeup of the youths differ widely between private and public facilities. More than 53 percent of those in private institutions are white, whereas more than 68 percent of the juveniles held in public facilities are African American or Hispanic. Although the number of white juveniles held in public facilities decreased between 1983 and 1991, the number of African American and Hispanic juveniles in custody remains disproportionately high.

Because of changing social patterns, a juvenile in a public facility today is most likely to be an African American male between fourteen and seventeen years of age who is held for a delinquent offense, such as a property crime. A juvenile in a private facility is more likely to be a white male between fourteen and seventeen years of age who is held for a nondelinquent act, such as running away or truancy.

Although the data show that a majority of juvenile correctional inmates are white, recent research by Barry Krisberg and his associates found that minority youths are incarcerated at a rate three to four times that of white youths and that this overrepresentation is not a result of differentials in their arrest or crime rates. Of equal importance, minorities are more likely to be confined in secure public facilities rather than in open private facilities that might provide more costly and effective treatment.

Minority youths accused of delinquent acts are less likely than white youths to be diverted from the court system into more lenient, informal sanctions and are more likely to receive sentences involving incarceration. Racial disparity in juvenile disposition is a growing problem that demands immediate public scrutiny.[31] In response, some jurisdictions have initiated studies of the extensiveness and causes of racial disproportionality in their own juvenile justice systems.[32] Today, over 65 percent of the juveniles in custody belong to racial or ethnic minorities. (See the Policy and Practice box entitled "Disproportionate Minority Confinement" for more on this topic.)

How do juvenile offenders wind up in correctional facilities? Contrary to popular belief, the majority of residents are not committed for violent crimes such as murder, kidnapping, or violent sexual assault. Most incarcerated youths are person, property, or drug offenders. Thus, the image of the incarcerated delinquent as a violent menace to society is somewhat misleading.

Institutional Adjustment

More than two decades ago shocking exposés of the treatment of institutionalized youths focused public attention on the problems of juvenile corrections. Today, some critics believe the light of public scrutiny has improved conditions within training schools. There is now greater professionalism among the staff, and staff brutality seems to have diminished. Status offenders and delinquents are, for the most part, held in separate facilities. Finally, confinement length is shorter, and rehabilitative programming has increased.

Despite such improvements, the everyday life of male inmates still reflects institutional values. Bartollas, Miller, and Dinitz identified an inmate value system that in many ways resembles the "inmate social code" found in adult institutions. The general code revolves around these principles:

- Exploit whomever you can.
- Don't play up to staff.
- Don't rat on your peers.
- Don't give in to others.[33]

In addition to these general rules, the researchers found that there were separate norms for African American inmates (exploit whites; no forcing sex on blacks; defend your brother) and for whites (don't trust anyone; everybody for himself).

The male inmate code still seems to be in operation. More recent research conducted in five juvenile institutions confirmed the notion that residents formed cohesive groups and adhered to an informal inmate culture.[34] The more serious the youth's delinquent record and the more secure the institution, the greater the adherence to the inmate social code.

Today, male delinquents are more likely to form allegiances with members of their own racial group and attempt to exploit those outside the group. They also scheme to manipulate staff and to take advantage of weaker peers. However, in institutions that are treatment-oriented and where staff–inmate relationships are more intimate, residents are less likely to adhere to a negativistic inmate code.

Culture of the Female Offender

Females have traditionally been less involved in criminal activities than males. As a consequence, the number of females in institutions has been lower than the number of males. However, the growing involvement of girls in criminal behavior and the influence of the feminist movement have drawn more attention to the female juvenile offender. This attention has revealed a double standard of justice. For example, girls are more likely than boys to be incarcerated for status offenses such as truancy, running away, and sexual misconduct. Institutions for girls are generally more restrictive than those for boys, and they have fewer educational and vocational programs and fewer services. Institutions for girls also do a less than adequate job of rehabilitation. It has been suggested that this double standard operates because of a chivalrous male-dominated justice system that seeks to "protect" young girls from their own sexuality.[35]

Over the years the number of females held in public institutions has generally declined. This represents the continuation of a long-term trend to remove girls—many of whom are nonserious status offenders—from closed institutions and place them in less restrictive private or community-based facilities. So, although a majority of males are housed in public facilities today, most female delinquents reside in private facilities.

Institutionalized girls are often runaways seeking to escape intolerable home situations, which can involve abusive or incestuous relationships. Some are pregnant and have no means of support. Many are the "throwaways" of society—those whom nobody wants. Only a few are true delinquents.

The same double standard that operates to bring a girl into an institution continues to exist once she is in custody. Females tend to be incarcerated for longer terms than most males. In addition, institutional programs for girls tend to be strongly oriented toward reinforcing traditional roles for women. How well these programs rehabilitate girls and ready them for life in a quickly changing society is questionable.

Many of the characteristics of juvenile female offenders are similar to those of their male counterparts. These include poor social skills, low self-esteem, and poor home environment. Other problems are more specific to the female juvenile offender, such as sexual abuse issues, victimization histories, educational and vocational inequity, and the lack of placement options.

Although there are more coed institutions for juveniles than in the past, most girls remain incarcerated in antiquated, single-sex institutions that are usually isolated in rural areas and rarely offer adequate rehabilitative services. Results of a federally sponsored survey of institutions across the nation revealed a definite pattern of inequality in services for boys and girls.[36]

Several factors account for the different treatment of girls. One is sexual stereotyping by administrators, who believe that "girls should be girls" and that teaching them "appropriate" sex roles in prison will help them function effectively in society.

DISPROPORTIONATE MINORITY CONFINEMENT

Why is the incarceration rate for African American youths disproportionately high? The disparate treatment of minorities in the U.S. juvenile justice system was brought to national attention by the Coalition for Juvenile Justice (formally the National Coalition of State Juvenile Justice Advisory Groups) in its 1988 annual report to Congress entitled *A Delicate Balance.* In the 1988 amendments to the Juvenile Justice and Delinquency Prevention (JJDP) Act of 1974, Congress required that states address disproportionate minority confinement (DMC) in their state plans. In the 1992 amendments to the JJDP Act, DMC was elevated to a core requirement, with future funding eligibility tied to state compliance. Thereafter, studies were conducted in sixteen states to examine the likelihood of juveniles being incarcerated in a juvenile correction facility before the age of eighteen. These studies showed that African American youths had the highest prevalence rates of all segments of the population in fifteen of the sixteen states. In two states it was estimated that 1 in 7 African American males (compared with approximately 1 in 125 white males) would be incarcerated before the age of eighteen.

Additional research has consistently confirmed that minority overrepresentation has not been limited to confinement in secure facilities. As we've seen, overrepresentation exists at each of the major decision points in the juvenile justice process— arrest, detention, prosecution, adjudication, transfer to adult court, and commitment to secure facilities. Thus, the term "minority overrepresentation" has been used to describe the phenomenon of disproportionately large numbers of minority youths who come into contact with the juvenile justice system at various stages, including, but not limited to, the secure confinement program.

ONE APPROACH TO ASSESSING DMC

During the past decade, the Office of Juvenile Justice and Delinquency Prevention has funded various state approaches to assessing DMC. One such effort is that of Dauphin County, Pennsylvania. The focus of their strategy was to target at-risk minority youths in an effort to prevent delinquency and the potential for arrests.

Dauphin County, including the state capital, Harrisburg, was selected as the first target site because it showed the greatest difference between the proportion of minorities arrested (50 percent) and the proportion of minorities (22 percent) in the at-risk population. Five prevention and intervention programs were put in place for a period of thirty months:

- *The Business Entrepreneur Club.* This program helps young minority females learn work and life skills.

- *Targeted Outreach.* This program helps identify and recruit minority youths within its service area to take advantage of the educational, physical, social, and vocational programs available through the Boys and Girls Club of Harrisburg.

These beliefs are often held by the staff as well, many of whom have only a high school education and hold highly sexist ideas of what is appropriate behavior for adolescent girls. Girls' institutions tend to be smaller than boys' institutions. As a result, they simply do not have the money to offer as many varied programs and services as do the larger male institutions.[37]

In general, it appears that although society is more concerned about protecting girls who act out, it is less concerned about rehabilitating them because the crimes

- *Positive Choice.* This program, previously known as Teens Together, provides minority juveniles with tutoring, homework assistance, and special classes with speakers who address topics of interest and also help youths make positive choices for their future.

- *Project Connect.* This program, now part of the Boys and Girls Club, prevents youths from dropping out of school by improving school attendance and academic achievement and addressing other social and familial needs.

- *Hispanic Center After-School Program.* This program helps at-risk Hispanic students improve their school performance, reducing the rate of school failure and dropping out among Hispanic youths.

The strengths of the approach used in Dauphin County as well as other Pennsylvania counties were (1) active support of state government, (2) effectiveness of the minority confinement subcommittee, (3) utilization of all community resources, (4) use of a data collection approach involving analysis of minority crime rates, and (5) an emphasis on prevention and early intervention.

CONCLUSIONS

The 1995 DMC data show encouraging signs of progress when compared with 1988 data. Although the minority juvenile population who are at risk increased from 12 percent in 1988 to 13 percent in 1995, minority juveniles confined in secure detention and correctional facilities decreased from 73 percent to 66 percent, and minority juvenile arrests decreased from 30 percent to 29 percent. Minority juveniles transferred to adult court, however, increased from 71 percent in 1988 to 72 percent in 1995.

In Pennsylvania overrepresentation of minorities in the juvenile justice system begins at arrest—minorities are arrested at a rate two times their proportion in the general population. Overrepresentation more than doubles again at the preadjudicatory detention stage and increases slightly at the point of commitment to juvenile corrections. More than five times as many minority juveniles are transferred to criminal court compared with their numbers in the general population. Reducing overrepresentation in the early stages by preventing arrests is expected to reduce minority representation at later stages in the system.

Sources: Heidi Hsia and Donna Hamparian, "Disproportionate Minority Confinement: 1997 Update," Juvenile Justice Bulletin (Washington, D.C.: OJJDP, 1997); Melissa Sickmund, Howard Snyder, and Eileen Poe Yamagata, *Juvenile Offenders and Victims—1997 Update on Violence* (Washington, D.C.: OJJDP, 1997); R. E. Decumo, *Juveniles Taken into Custody Research Program: Estimating the Prevalence of Juvenile Custody by Race and Gender* (San Francisco, Calif.: National Council on Crime and Delinquency, 1993).

they commit are not serious. These attitudes translate into fewer staff, less modern buildings, and poorer vocational, educational, and recreational programs than those found in boys' institutions. Ilene Bergsmann points out that little time and effort have been devoted to the female juvenile offender in the last century. She concludes that differential treatment of females and males in the juvenile justice system begins with the schools, continues with law enforcement, and is perpetuated by the correctional system.[38]

Correctional Treatment for Juveniles

Nearly all juvenile institutions implement some form of treatment program for youths in custody: counseling on an individual or group basis, vocational and educational training, recreational programs, and religious counseling. In addition, most institutions provide medical and dental health programs of some kind, as well as occasional legal service programs. Generally, the larger the institution, the greater the number of programs and services offered.

The purpose of these various programs is to rehabilitate the youths within the institutions—to reform them into well-adjusted individuals and send them back into the community to be productive citizens. Despite generally good intentions, however, the goal of rehabilitation is rarely attained. National statistics show that a significant number of juvenile offenders commit more crimes after release from incarceration. Whitehead and Lab's 1989 evaluation of fifty studies of institutional and community-based programs concluded that correctional treatment has little effect on recidivism.[39] An examination of more than four hundred programs, including both community-based and institutional treatment services, was conducted by Mark Lipsey in 1992. His study also used meta-analysis, which synthesizes results of multiple program evaluations. Overall, he reported that juveniles who receive treatment have recidivism rates about 10 percent lower than untreated juveniles in comparison groups.[40] The best intervention programs reduced recidivism between 20 percent and 30 percent, which translates into significant reductions in crime and its costs.

Which programs worked? According to Lipsey, the most successful programs provide behavior training or modification designed to improve interpersonal relations skills, self-control, and school achievement. These programs also tended to be the most intensive in terms of the amount and duration of concentrated attention to youths. Programs of a more psychological nature, such as individual, family, and group counseling, showed only moderate positive effects on delinquents in Lipsey's analysis. And deterrence and "shock" approaches (like "scared straight programs") actually had negative effects; that is, youths who received these treatments had higher recidivism rates than those who did not receive them.

A recent national survey conducted by the National Center for Juvenile Justice collected information on three thousand programs from juvenile justice professionals, including judges, probation officers, and other court personnel. Reviewing these programs, researchers designated 425 of them as "promising interventions." Selected programs include a wide variety of academic, skill development, mentoring, substance abuse treatment, and outdoor programs, with target populations ranging from at-risk children and runaways to gang members and other serious offenders. This compilation demonstrates that there are many models to examine in designing community and institutional programs.[41] The Focus on Delinquency box entitled "Here's a Program that Really Works" describes a very successful residential facility that combines a number of treatment options.

One of the most common problems in efforts to rehabilitate juveniles is a lack of well-trained staff members to run programs. Budgetary limitations are a primary concern when it comes to planning for institutional programs. It costs a substantial amount of money per year to keep a child in an institution, which explains why institutions generally do not employ large professional staffs.

The most glaring problem with treatment programs is that they are not being administered in the way in which they were intended. Although the official goals of many institutions may be treatment and rehabilitation, the actual programs may center around security, control, and punishment. The next sections describe some

HERE'S A PROGRAM THAT REALLY WORKS

The Thomas O'Farrell Youth Center (TOYC), located in rural Maryland, is a thirty-eight-bed, unlocked, staff-secure residential program for male youths committed to the Maryland Department of Juvenile Services. The typical TOYC youth has many prior court referrals, generally for property crimes and drug offenses. On average, juveniles stay at the center for nine months and then receive six months of community aftercare. The TOYC philosophy is to create a community of dignity and respect for all its members. This positive social environment is at the core of all TOYC activities. Each youth who completes the TOYC residential program has a specialized aftercare plan and receives postrelease services from two aftercare workers. Aftercare services include assistance in reentering school, vocational counseling, crisis intervention, family counseling, transportation, and mentoring. Aftercare workers have contact with the youth on at least twelve days each month during the aftercare period.

An evaluation found that the majority (55 percent) of the first fifty-six TOYC graduates had no further court referrals in the postrelease period (an average of 11.6 months). The study also showed a dramatic decline in the number of offenses committed by youths after their stay at TOYC. In the twelve months prior to placement in TOYC, the fifty-six youths were charged with 219 offenses, an average of almost four court referrals each. However, in the year after leaving TOYC, these youths were charged with just 51 offenses, a decline of 77 percent. It was also observed that youths who committed new crimes after leaving TOYC were likely to commit less serious offenses than before. This is an example of an effective privatized staff-secure residential program where there has been a dramatic decline in the number of offenses committed by youths after their institutional experience.

Source: Shay Bilchick, "A Juvenile Justice System for the 21st Century," *Crime and Delinquency* 44(1):89–101 (1998).

---

of the more common treatment approaches that, when used in institutional settings, aim to rehabilitate offenders.

Individual Treatment Techniques: Past and Present

individual counseling
Counselors help juveniles understand and solve their current adjustment problems.

Individual counseling is one of the most common treatment approaches, and virtually all juvenile institutions use this approach to some extent. This is not surprising, as psychological problems such as depression are a real and present problem in juvenile institutions.[42] Individual counseling does not attempt to change a youth's personality. Rather, it attempts to help individuals understand and solve their current adjustment problems. Some institutions employ counselors who may not be professionally qualified, which subjects offenders to a superficial form of counseling.

Highly structured professional counseling, in contrast, can be based on psychotherapy or psychoanalysis. **Psychotherapy,** an outgrowth of Freudian psychoanalytic techniques, requires extensive analysis of the individual's past childhood experiences. An effective, skilled therapist attempts to help the individual solve conflicts and make a more positive adjustment to society by altering negative behavior patterns learned in childhood.

psychotherapy
Highly structured counseling in which a skilled therapist helps a juvenile solve conflicts and make a more positive adjustment to society.

Although individual counseling and psychotherapy are used extensively in institutions and may work well for certain individuals, these treatments are only marginally effective when used alone. Another highly used treatment approach for delinquents is **reality therapy.**[43] In contrast to psychoanalysis, this approach, developed by William Glasser during the 1970s, emphasizes current, over past, behavior by stressing that offenders are completely responsible for their own actions. The object of reality therapy is to make individuals more responsible people. This end is accomplished by giving youths confidence and strength through developing their ability to follow a set of expectations as closely as possible.

The success of reality therapy depends greatly on the warmth and concern of the individual counselor. Unfortunately, many institutions rely heavily on this type of therapy because they believe highly trained professionals aren't needed to administer it. Actually, a skilled therapist is essential to the success of this form of treatment. The therapist must be knowledgeable about the complexity of personalities and be able to deal with any situation that may come up in counseling sessions.

Behavior modification is used in many institutions.[44] It is based on the theory that all behavior is learned and that current behavior can be shaped through a system of rewards and punishments. This type of program is easily used in an institutional setting that offers points and privileges as rewards for behaviors such as work, study, or the development of skills. It is a reasonably effective technique, especially when a contract is formed with the youth to modify certain behaviors. When youths are aware of what is expected of them, they plan their actions to meet these expectations and then experience the anticipated consequences. In this way, youths can be motivated to change. Behavior modification is effective in controlled settings, where a counselor can manipulate the situation, but once the youth is back in the real world, it becomes difficult to use.

In general, effective individual treatment programs are built around combinations of psychotherapy, reality therapy, and behavior modification. Other less formal approaches include personal growth counseling, substance abuse treatment, assertiveness training, and self-image and ego development counseling.

Group Treatment Techniques

Group therapy is more economical than individual therapy because one therapist can counsel more than one individual at a time. Also, the support of the group is often highly valuable to the individuals in the group, and individuals derive hope from other members of the group who have survived similar experiences. Another advantage of group therapy is that a group can often solve a problem more effectively than an individual.

One disadvantage of group therapy is that it provides less individualized attention. Everyone is different, and some group members may need more highly individualized treatment. Others may be shy and afraid to speak up in the group and thus fail to receive the benefits of the group experience. Conversely, some individuals may dominate group interaction, making it difficult for the leader to conduct an effective session. Finally, group condemnation may seriously hurt rather than help a participant.

More than any other group treatment technique, group psychotherapy probes into an individual's personality and attempts to restructure it. Relationships in these groups tend to be quite intense. The group is used to facilitate expression of feelings, to solve problems, and to teach members to empathize with one another.

Unfortunately, the ingredients for an effective group psychotherapy session—personal interaction, cooperation, and tolerance—are in direct conflict with the antisocial, antagonistic, and exploitive orientation of delinquents. This type of technique can be effective when the members of the group are in attendance voluntarily, but such is not the case with institutionalized delinquents, who are often forced to attend. Consequently, the effectiveness of these programs is questionable.

guided group interaction (GGI)
Through group interactions a delinquent can acknowledge and solve personal problems with support from other group members.

Positive Peer Culture (PPC)
Counseling program in which peer leaders encourage other group members to modify their behavior and peers help reinforce acceptable behaviors.

milieu therapy
All aspects of the environment are part of the treatment, and meaningful change, increased growth, and satisfactory adjustment are encouraged; this is often accomplished through peer pressure to conform to the group norms.

Guided group interaction (GGI) is a fairly common method of group treatment. It is based on the theory that through group interactions a delinquent can acknowledge and solve personal problems. A group leader facilitates interaction among group members, and a group culture develops. Individual members can be mutually supportive and can help reinforce more acceptable behavior. Guided group interaction was an instrumental factor in the success of programs at Highfields, New Jersey, and Provo, Utah.[45]

In the 1980s a version of GGI called **Positive Peer Culture (PPC)** became popular in juvenile corrections. PPC programs use groups in which peer leaders encourage other youths to conform to conventional behaviors. The rationale for PPC is that if negative peer influence can encourage youths to engage in delinquent behavior then positive peer influence can help them conform.[46]

Another approach is **milieu therapy,** which seeks to make all aspects of an inmate's environment a part of his or her treatment and to minimize differences between custodial staff and treatment personnel. Like GGI, it also emphasizes peer influence in the formation of constructive values. Milieu therapy attempts to create an environment that encourages meaningful change, increased growth, and satisfactory adjustment. This is often accomplished through peer pressure to conform to group norms.

One early type of milieu therapy, based on psychoanalytic theory, was developed in Chicago during the late 1940s and early 1950s by Bruno Bettelheim.[47] This therapy attempted to create a conscience, or superego, in delinquent youths by getting them to depend on their therapists to a great extent and then threatening them with the loss of the loving and caring relationship if they failed to control their behavior.

Today, institutional group counseling often focuses on drug and alcohol group counseling, self-esteem development groups, and role model support sessions. In addition, because considerably more violent juveniles are entering the system than in years past, group sessions often deal with appropriate expressions of anger and rage and methods for understanding and controlling such behavior.

Educational, Vocational, and Recreational Programs

In addition to individual and group treatment programs, most institutions use educational, vocational, and recreational programs designed to teach juveniles skills that will help them adjust more easily when they are released into the community. Educational programs for juveniles are required in long-term facilities because children must go to school until they reach a certain age. Because educational programs are an important part of social development and have therapeutic, as well as instructional, value, they are an essential part of most treatment programs. What takes place through education is related to all other aspects of the institutional program—work activities, cottage life, recreation, and clinical services.

Educational programs are probably some of the best-staffed programs in training schools, but even at their best, most are inadequate. Training programs must contend with a myriad of problems. Many of the youths coming into these institutions are mentally retarded or have low IQs or learning disabilities. As such, they are educationally disabled and far behind their grade levels in basic academic areas. Most of these youths dislike school and become bored with any type of educational program. Their boredom often leads to acting out and subsequent disciplinary problems.

Ideally, institutions should allow the inmates to attend a school in the community or offer programs that lead to a high school diploma or GED certificate. Unfortunately, not all institutions offer these types of programs. Ironically, more secure

Most juvenile facilities have ongoing vocational and educational programs. Some, such as this California Youth Authority program in Ventura County, offer computer training that will help juveniles gain employment upon their release.

institutions, because of their large size, are more likely than group homes or day treatment centers to offer supplemental educational programs such as remedial reading, physical education, and tutoring. Some more modern educational programs offer computer-based learning and programmed learning modules.

Vocational training has long been used as a treatment technique for juveniles. Early institutions were even referred to as industrial schools. Today, vocational programs in institutions are varied. Programs offered include auto repair, printing, woodworking, mechanical drawing, food service, cosmetology, secretarial training, and data processing. A common drawback of vocational training programs is sex-typing. The recent trend has been to allow equal access to all programs offered in institutions that house girls and boys. Sex-typing is more difficult to avoid in single-sex institutions, because funds aren't usually available for all types of training.

But these programs alone—even those that include job placement—are not panaceas. Youths need to acquire the kinds of skills that will give them hope for advancement.

The Ventura School for Female Juvenile Offenders, established under the California Youth Authority, has been a successful pioneer in the work placement concept. Private industry contracts with the youth authority to establish businesses on the institution's grounds. The businesses hire, train, and pay scale wages for work. Wages are divided into a victim's restitution fund, room and board fees, and forced savings, with a portion given to the juvenile to purchase canteen items. Trans World Airlines (TWA), for example, has established a ticket reservation center on the school grounds. The center handles the overflow phone calls from Los Angeles. Many juveniles have been trained, and a significant number have been employed by TWA or travel agencies upon their release. Ventura also has a program that involves private industry in the manufacture of uniforms at the school. Such skills are often marketable to employers in need of trained workers.[48]

Recreational activity is also an important way to help relieve adolescent aggressions, as evidenced by the many diversionary and delinquency prevention programs that focus on recreation as the primary treatment technique.

In summary, the treatment programs that seem to be most effective for rehabilitating juvenile offenders are those that use a combination of techniques. Programs that are comprehensive, intensive, built on a juvenile's strengths, and that adopt a socially grounded position have a much greater chance for success. Individual treatment alone often fails to address institutional and community issues. Successful programs typically address issues relating to school, peers, work, and community.

The juvenile justice correctional system must confront the challenges of an increasingly violent juvenile population. The next section discusses some of the treatment programs that have been developed for chronic and violent offenders.

Treating Chronic and Violent Delinquents

chronic juvenile offenders
Youths who have been arrested four or more times during their minority; this small group of offenders is believed to engage in a significant portion of all delinquent behavior.

Treating the **chronic juvenile offender** has become a major concern in recent years. Although significant efforts are being made to deinstitutionalize nonserious and status offenders, the question remains what to do with the more serious juvenile delinquents who commit crimes such as rape or robbery. As we've seen, one answer has been to ease waiver rules and standards so that younger children can be transferred to adult courts. A number of states have created concurrent jurisdiction laws, which enable prosecutors to choose whether to bring a case to the adult court or to juvenile court.

An early approach was to incarcerate serious offenders in intensive juvenile treatment programs where their problems could be dealt with while they were isolated both from society and from other juvenile offenders. This policy received impetus from a controversial book, *Beyond Probation,* by Charles Murray and Louis B. Cox.[49] Murray and Cox compared chronic delinquents sent to traditional Illinois training school programs with those in an innovative community-based program, the Unified Delinquency Intervention Services. They discovered a **suppression effect**—a reduction in the number of arrests per year—for those youths who had been incarcerated. Moreover, the suppression effect for youths sent to training school was higher than for those in less punitive treatment programs. Murray and Cox concluded that the juvenile justice system must choose which policy outcome its programs are aimed at achieving: prevention of delinquency or the care and protection of needy youths. If the former is a proper goal for the juvenile justice system, then institutionalization or the threat of institutionalization is desirable.

suppression effect
A reduction of the number of arrests per year for youths who have been incarcerated or otherwise punished.

lifestyle violent juveniles
Juveniles who become more violent when exposed to more serious offenders in institutions.

Twenty years ago Andrew Vachss and Yitzhak Bakal argued that a secure treatment center was necessary to deal with what they called **lifestyle violent juveniles**.[50] If secure placements were not available, there would be (1) increased use of waiver; (2) a dangerous mixing of offender types within an institutional setting (nonviolent youths would be exposed to more serious offenders); (3) collapse and failure of alternative programs, because they would become contaminated by chronic offenders; and (4) the continuing problems of a system that returns dangerous juveniles to communities in far more dangerous condition and at the same time continues to incarcerate nondangerous juveniles within its programs.

Today we realize that secure corrections programs should be reserved only for the most serious and violent offenders; large training schools, in particular, have proven to be ineffective in rehabilitating juvenile offenders.[51] Ira Schwartz, a noted expert in juvenile justice, has recommended that all large training schools be closed. Although incarceration of chronic violent offenders may help keep our streets safer, must we assume that these individuals are "beyond" rehabilitation? Let's review some of the more successful corrections-based institutional programs.

Specialized Programs for Chronic Offenders

Many states have set up specialized programs for chronic violent offenders.[52] These efforts have been aided and funded by the federal government's **Violent Juvenile**

Violent Juvenile Offender (VJO) program

Specialized programs in small, secure settings where youths are gradually reintegrated into the community with intensive supervision.

Offender (VJO) program, which tests innovative strategies for reintegrating chronic violent offenders back into the community.[53]

Some offenders pose such a threat to the public that they must be placed in locked, secure, and specialized types of facilities. Youths in these programs also need a wide range of rehabilitation services. Correctional research has shown that the most effective secure programs limit the number of participants and provide individual services.

VJO youths are placed in small, secure settings and are gradually reintegrated into the community through community-based programs and intensive supervision. The VJO model is based on strengthening the juvenile's ties to positive institutions, providing opportunities for success, and employing a system of rewards and sanctions. Most youths in VJO programs have been adjudicated for major felonies. Jeffrey Fagan conducted in-depth studies of the VJO program and found there were fewer and less serious rearrests with VJO youths than with those in control groups. Fagan concluded that the basic principles of these programs can reduce recidivism among violent juvenile offenders.[54]

Two other programs also merit attention. The Florida Environmental Institute (FEI), also known as "The Last Chance Ranch," targets Florida's most serious juvenile offenders. Located in a remote area of the Florida Everglades, it receives many of its referrals from the adult justice system. (In Florida, a juvenile found guilty as an adult may be returned to the juvenile justice system for treatment.) FEI also offers both residential and nonresidential aftercare programs. The FEI philosophy is based on (1) education, (2) therapeutic hard work, (3) a system of rewards, and (4) a strong aftercare component. Although the recidivism rate is unclear for the FEI, studies of traditional training schools indicate much higher rates—often more than 50 percent.[55] Because of FEI's strong emphasis on education, hard work, social bonding, and aftercare, recidivism rates of juveniles who have gone through the program are substantially less than those of youths who have completed traditional training school programs.

The Capital Offender Program (COP) in Texas is an unusual group treatment program for juveniles committed for homicide.[56] The COP treatment approach focuses on group psychotherapy and seeks to create a sense of personal responsibility and reduce levels of hostility and aggression among youths in the residential center. Research data suggest that the participants showed a lower rearrest rate and a lower reincarceration rate after participating in the program.

Another approach that seems to show promise is the outdoor education and training programs known collectively as Outward Bound. Two of these programs are described in the Policy and Practice box entitled "Juvenile Rehabilitation Strategies: Wilderness Programs."

According to Castellano and Soderstrom, very little is known about the effects of wilderness stress-challenge programs on juvenile recidivism. A study of the Spectrum Wilderness Program in Illinois found that successful completion of the program often resulted in arrest reductions that began immediately and lasted for about one year. Although results of such studies are mixed, these programs are promising alternatives to traditional juvenile justice placements.[57]

Juvenile Boot Camps

boot camps

Juvenile programs that combine get-tough elements from adult programs with education, substance abuse treatment, and social skills training.

Correctional **boot camps** are also being developed for juvenile offenders. Boot camps combine the get-tough elements of adult programs with education, substance abuse treatment, and social skills training. The American Correctional Association's Juvenile Project has studied the concept and sees merit in well-run boot camp programs provided they incorporate these elements: (1) a focus on concrete feelings and increasing self-esteem, (2) discipline through physical conditioning, and (3) programming in literacy as well as academic and vocational education.[58]

In theory, a successful boot camp program should rehabilitate juvenile offenders, reduce the number of beds needed in secure institutional programs, and thus reduce the overall cost of care. The Alabama boot camp program for youthful offenders estimated savings of $1 million annually when compared with traditional institutional sentences.[59] However, no one seems convinced that participants in these programs have lower recidivism rates than those who serve normal sentences. Corbett and Petersilia do note, however, that boot camp participants seem to be less antisocial upon returning to society.[60]

Some juvenile corrections agencies feature shock incarceration programs, with high-intensity military discipline and physical training for short periods of time. The expectation is that the offender in such a boot camp will be "shocked" into going straight. These programs are now being used with young adult offenders and juveniles who have been waived to the adult system in many jurisdictions.

Some experts believe juvenile boot camps fail on several levels. They point out that (1) juvenile boot camps cannot save money unless they have hundreds of beds and the stay is limited to three months—conditions that would make the programs pointless; (2) juvenile boot camps are widening the net by including youths who previously would not have been locked up; (3) juvenile boot camps are often limited to shock incarceration and keep costs down by leaving aftercare to overloaded parole officers; and (4) no documentation exists that boot camps decrease delinquency.[61] Margaret Beyer, a psychologist working with delinquents, also points out that boot camps cannot be effective because they violate the basic principles of adolescent behavior: teenagers want to be treated fairly, reject imposed structure, and respond to encouragement. Beyer believes juveniles will rebel against the imposed structure, punishment, and unfairness of juvenile boot camps.

In 1992 OJJDP funded three juvenile boot camps designed to overcome these objections and the special needs and circumstances of adolescent offenders. The programs were conducted in Cleveland, Ohio; Denver, Colorado; and Mobile, Alabama.[62] Focusing on a target population of adjudicated, nonviolent offenders under the age of eighteen, the boot camp programs were designed as highly structured, three-month residential programs followed by six to nine months of community-based aftercare. During the aftercare period, youths were to pursue academic and vocational training or employment while under intensive, but progressively diminishing, supervision.

Juvenile boot camps apply rigorous, military-style training and discipline in an attempt to reshape the attitudes and behavior of heretofore unruly youth.

JUVENILE REHABILITATION STRATEGIES: WILDERNESS PROGRAMS

In the past, camping or wilderness adventure usually played a tangential role in juvenile rehabilitation programs. In the 1930s the Chicago Area Project developed a summer camping component as part of its delinquency prevention efforts. Many states rotated selected wards from the state training schools through forestry camps, where they worked in fire crews or at maintaining trails. Unlike these early endeavors, the newer programs assign a central role to the outdoor education component. Two well-established and respected programs using these concepts are VisionQuest and the Associated Marine Institutes. Many more use similar techniques.

VISIONQUEST

VisionQuest, a for-profit contractor with headquarters in Tucson, Arizona, is probably the largest program of its type, with annual commitments in excess of five hundred delinquent youths. VisionQuest typically takes youths committed directly by juvenile courts in Pennsylvania, California, and several other states. The length of stay is usually between one year and eighteen months.

To enter the program, each candidate youth must agree to (1) abstain from drugs and sex during his or her commitment, (2) not run away, and (3) complete at least two impact programs, which can include residence in a wilderness camp, cross-country travel on a wagon train, or voyaging on a sailing vessel. In addition to its impact programs, VisionQuest conducts counseling sessions with other family members while the youth is in the program and operates several group homes that facilitate reentry into the community. While they are on the wagon train or in wilderness camp, each youth is assigned to a small group (teepee) of about eight other youths and two junior staff. Each wagon train or wilderness camp consists of thirty to forty-five youths and a similar number of staff. Junior staff members sleep in the teepees with the juveniles and are off duty two days in every seven.

In addition to the wagon trains and sailing programs, VisionQuest is also known for its confrontational style. Committed youths are not allowed to slide by and just "do time." Rather, an individual program is worked out to ensure that each youth is challenged intellectually, physically, and emotionally. When juveniles do not perform up to expectations or begin to "act out," they are "confronted" by one or more senior staff members in an attempt to get them to deal with whatever issues underlie the poor behavior.

ASSOCIATED MARINE INSTITUTES

Associated Marine Institutes (AMI) is the parent agency for a group of nonprofit programs (institutes) located in Florida that use various marine projects as a means of motivating and challenging delinquent youths. Most of AMI's programs are nonresidential, picking up participating youths in the morning and returning them home in the evening, five days a week. During a typical stay of six months in the program, a participating youth will attend remedial classes, learn scuba diving and related safety procedures, study marine biology,

OJJDP undertook impact evaluations for all three sites, comparing recidivism rates for juveniles who participated in the pilot programs with those of control groups. The evaluations also compared the cost-effectiveness of juvenile boot camps with other dispositional alternatives. The findings indicated these successes:

■ Most juvenile boot camp participants completed the residential program and graduated to aftercare. Program completion rates were 96 percent in Cleveland, 87 percent in Mobile, and 76 percent in Denver.

■ At the two sites where educational gains were measured, substantial improvements in academic skills were noted. In Mobile approximately three-quarters of

An environmental camp in Florida, E-Nini-Hasse (Seminole for "Her Sunny Road") helps runaways, drug addicts, and young criminals ages 10–18 turn their lives around.

and participate in some constructive work project, such as refurbishing an old boat or growing ground cover for some commercial site.

AMI also operates a long-term residential program at Fisheating Creek in south-central Florida. In this program, boys committed by the Dade County Juvenile Court spend six months to a year in an isolated work camp. During the first phase, their living conditions are extremely primitive, and their working conditions are rather hard (digging out stumps to clear an airstrip). Graduation to phase two earns participants the right to sleep in air-conditioned quarters and to have better work assignments. The last two phases of the program are spent in one of the nonresidential institutes near their home.

One of the distinctive characteristics of the nonprofit AMI is its heavy reliance on the capitalist spirit. Employee performance is periodically assessed by computerized measures that track GEDs obtained, program completion rate, or subsequent recidivism rate for all of the youths in the program. End-of-year staff bonuses are based on these performance measures and can exceed 10 percent of regular salary. Committed youths can also earn money by participating in various work projects, such as clearing brush, that AMI has contracted to undertake.

Source: Adapted from Peter Greenwood and Franklin Zimring, *One More Chance* (Santa Monica, Calif.: Rand Corp., 1985), pp. 41–42.

the participants improved their performance in reading, spelling, language, and math by one grade level or more. In Cleveland the average juvenile boot camp participant improved reading, spelling, and math skills by approximately one grade level.

■ Where employment records were available, a significant number of participants found jobs while in aftercare.

The pilot programs, however, did not demonstrate a reduction in recidivism. In Denver and Mobile no statistically significant difference could be found between the recidivism rates of juvenile boot camp participants and those of the control

ABOUT FACE: A JUVENILE BOOT CAMP PROGRAM

About Face is a boot camp for nonviolent males ages 14 to 17 who were adjudicated of cocaine trafficking. Participants are sentenced to the program by the Memphis juvenile court. About Face participants spend three months in a nonsecure residential facility (the Memphis Naval Air Station, an active military base), followed by six months of aftercare. During two years, a total of 344 youths participated in the program.

The About Face residential program has four main components:

■ Military training conducted by current and former Navy and Marine personnel. The training includes discipline, drill, physical conditioning, and leadership; however, it intentionally avoids the abusive punitive aspects usually associated with military boot camps.

■ Group and individual counseling. Youths participate in two hours of group counseling each day and a minimum of one hour of individual counseling per week.

■ Education using Navy-designed reading and math immersion techniques, computer-assisted learning, and individualized instruction. Youths receive six hours of educational services per day, not including study time.

■ Spiritual support that includes voluntary attendance at religious services conducted twice a week by members of local African American churches.

During the About Face aftercare component, youths attend weekly two-hour group counseling sessions and receive continued educational assistance.

An evaluation of the program indicated that the juveniles significantly increased their achievement scores, showed some improvement in psychological testing, and improved their understanding of societal obligations. Recidivism data indicated that almost half of the youths were rearrested during a twenty-month period beginning with program entry and concluding with formal discharge. However, later charges were less serious than those incurred in the twelve months preceding entry into the program.

Sources: James Howell, ed., *Guide for Implementing the Comprehensive Strategy for Serious, Violent, and Chronic Juvenile Offenders* (Washington, D.C.: U.S. Department of Justice, 1995); About Face, Youth Service USA, 314 South Goodlett Avenue, Memphis, Tennessee.

groups (youths confined in state or county institutions or released on probation). In Cleveland, pilot program participants evidenced a higher recidivism rate than juvenile offenders confined in a traditional juvenile correctional facilities.

In spite of these mixed results, forty to fifty juvenile boot camps exist in more than thirty states, processing more than 7,500 offenders. They appear to have a place among the array of sentencing options, if for no other reason than to appease lawmakers and the public with the promise of tougher sentences and lower costs.[63] About Face, a boot camp for juvenile drug offenders, is highlighted in the accompanying Policy and Practice box.

In summary, many in correctional programs have been used to treat chronic and violent youths, but little definitive knowledge has resulted from evaluating these programs. It is clear, however, that traditional, large training schools are expensive and counterproductive and that more attention should be focused on evaluating different treatment approaches, intensive services, and community-based sanctions (as described in Chapter 16). New evidence in the 1990s suggests that some well-developed treatment programs can deter and control delinquent behavior. Education, vocational training, and specific counseling strategies can be effective if they are intensive, relate to program goals, and meet the youth's individual needs.[64]

The Legal Right to Treatment

right to treatment
Philosophy espoused by many courts that juvenile offenders have a statutory right to treatment while under the jurisdiction of the courts.

The primary goal of placing juveniles in institutions is to help them adjust positively to reentry in the community. Therefore, lawyers in the field of juvenile justice claim that children in state-run institutions have a legal **right to treatment.**

The concept of a right to treatment was first introduced to the mental health field in 1960 by Morton Birnbaum.[65] He theorized that individuals who are deprived of their liberty because of a mental illness serious enough to require involuntary commitment are entitled to treatment to correct that condition.

Not until 1966 did any court acknowledge such a right to treatment. That year, in *Rouse v. Cameron,* the District of Columbia Circuit Court of Appeals held that mentally ill individuals were entitled to treatment, an opinion based on interpretation of a District of Columbia statute.[66] Although the court did not expressly acknowledge a constitutional right to treatment, it implied that it could have reached the same decision on constitutional grounds:

> Indefinite confinement without treatment of one who has been found not criminally responsible may be so inhumane as to be "cruel and unusual punishment under the Eighth Ammendment."[67]

The constitutional right to treatment suggested by the *Rouse* decision was further recognized in 1971 in *Wyatt v. Stickney.*[68] This case was particularly important because it held that involuntary commitment without rehabilitation was a denial of due process of law.[69]

Of greater significance, however, is the U.S. Supreme Court's decision in *O'Connor v. Donaldson* in 1975.[70] This case concerned the right to treatment of persons involuntarily committed to mental institutions. The Court concluded that, except where treatment is provided, a state cannot confine persons against their will if they are not dangerous to themselves or to the community.

The right to treatment argument has expanded to include the juvenile justice system. One of the first cases to highlight this issue was *Inmates of the Boys' Training School v. Affleck* in 1972.[71] This case analyzed conditions that allegedly violated juvenile constitutional rights to due process and equal protection and that constituted cruel and unusual punishment. *Affleck* was one of the first cases to describe some of the horrible conditions existing in many of the nation's training schools. The court argued that rehabilitation is the true purpose of the juvenile court and that without that goal due process guarantees are violated. It condemned such devices as solitary confinement, strip cells, and the lack of educational opportunities and held that juveniles have a statutory right to treatment. The court also established the following minimum standards for all juveniles confined in training schools:

■ A room equipped with lighting sufficient for an inmate to read by until 10 P.M.

■ Sufficient clothing to meet seasonal needs

- Bedding, including blankets, sheets, pillows, pillow cases, and mattresses, to be changed once a week
- Personal hygiene supplies, including soap, toothpaste, towels, toilet paper, and toothbrush
- A change of undergarments and socks every day
- Minimum writing materials: pen, pencil, paper, and envelopes
- Prescription eyeglasses, if needed
- Equal access to all books, periodicals, and other reading materials located in the training school
- Daily showers
- Daily access to medical facilities, including provision of a twenty-four-hour nursing service
- General correspondence privileges[72]

These minimum requirements were expanded in *Martarella v. Kelly,* which analyzed juvenile treatment facilities and the confinement of persons in need of supervision in New York. The court held that failure to provide these juveniles with adequate treatment violated their right to due process and to be free from cruel and unusual punishment.[73]

In 1974 the case of *Nelson v. Heyne* was heard on appeal in the Seventh Circuit Court of Appeals in Indiana.[74] This was the first federal appellate court decision affirming that juveniles have a constitutional and statutory right to treatment. The court ordered the state to require standards of care and treatment for institutionalized children of the Indiana Boys School.

In *Morales v. Turman* the court held that all juveniles confined in training schools in Texas have a constitutional right to treatment. The court established numerous criteria for assessing placement, education skills, delivery of vocational education, medical and psychiatric treatment programs, and daily living conditions.[75]

The *Morales* case marked a historic step in the effort to extend the civil rights of children in institutions. This landmark case challenged conditions and practices in all five juvenile training schools in Texas. *Morales* has had a national impact, establishing benchmark standards for the treatment of detained juveniles, including access to medical and psychiatric care and meaningful education and appropriate disciplinary treatment.

In a more recent case in New York, *Pena v. New York State Division for Youth,* the court held that the use of isolation, hand restraints, and tranquilizing drugs at Goshen Annex Center was punitive and antitherapeutic and therefore violated the Fourteenth Amendment right to due process and the Eighth Amendment right to protection against cruel and unusual punishment.[76]

Although the U.S. Supreme Court has not ruled that juveniles have a constitutional right to treatment, the cases described here have served as a basis for many substantive changes in the juvenile justice system, most notably in the improvement of physical conditions in juvenile institutions and in the judiciary's recognition that it must take a more active role in the juvenile justice system.

However, the right to treatment has not been advanced in all instances, and the case law does not totally accept a legal right to treatment for juvenile offenders. For example, in *Ralston v. Robinson,* the Supreme Court rejected a youth's claim that he should continue to be given treatment after he was sentenced to a consecutive term in an adult prison for crimes committed while in a juvenile institution.[77] In reaching its decision, the Court rejected the concept that every juvenile offender, regardless of the circumstances, can benefit from treatment. In the *Ralston* case, the offender's proven dangerousness outweighed the possible effects of rehabilitation.

Similarly, in *Santana v. Callazo,* the influential U.S. First Circuit Court of Appeals rejected a suit brought by residents at the Maricao Juvenile Camp in Puerto

Rico on the ground that the administration had failed to provide them with an individualized, comprehensive rehabilitation plan or adequate treatment. The circuit court concluded that it was a legitimate exercise of state authority to incarcerate juveniles solely to protect society from them and that therefore the offender does not have a right to treatment per se. However, courts can evaluate each case individually to determine whether the youth is receiving adequate care.[78]

The future of the right to treatment for juveniles is uncertain. The courts have not gone so far as to order the creation of new programs, nor have they decided what constitutes minimal standards of specific individual treatment. However, federal courts continue to hear on a case-by-case basis complaints that treatment is not up to minimal standards or that inappropriate disciplinary methods are being used. In one such case, *Gary H. v. Hegstrom,* a federal judge ruled that isolation punishments at the McClaren School for Boys in Oregon were excessive and that residents were being denied their right to treatment.[79]

Some experts believe a case like *Gary H.* will eventually reach the Supreme Court and provide an avenue for a definitive decision on the right to treatment. Thus far, minimum standards of care and treatment have been mandated on a case-by-case basis, with some courts limiting the constitutional protections regarding the right to treatment. In light of the new hard-line approach to juvenile crime, it does not appear that the courts will be persuaded to expand this constitutional theory further.

Struggle for Basic Civil Rights

Several court cases and a large amount of publicity have led a number of federal and state groups to develop standards for the juvenile justice system, including its institutions. The most comprehensive standards are those of the Institute of Judicial Administration—American Bar Association; the American Correctional Association; and the National Council on Crime and Delinquency. These standards provide appropriate guidelines for conditions and practices in juvenile institutions and call on juvenile corrections administrators to maintain a physically safe and healthy environment for incarcerated youths.

For the most part, state-sponsored brutality has been outlawed, although the use of restraints, solitary confinement, and even medication for unruly residents has not been completely eliminated. The courts have consistently ruled that corporal punishment in any form, other than for one's own protection, is constitutionally unacceptable and violates standards of decency and human dignity.

Disciplinary systems are an important part of any institutional program. Most institutions maintain disciplinary boards that regulate and hear appeals by juvenile inmates. The case of *Wolff v. McDonnell* focused on due process requirements for disciplinary proceedings in adult institutions.[80] Many state court decisions involving children have affirmed the principles in *Wolff v. McDonnell.* To provide the same rights for juveniles, several sets of standards have recommended similar rules and regulations governing juvenile institutional boards, including notice, representation by counsel, and the right to a written record of proceedings and decision.

Isolation or "administrative segregation" is also an issue that has been subject to court review. The leading case, *Lollis v. New York State Department of Social Services,* concluded that confining a female status offender to a small room for a two-week period was unconstitutional.[81] Virtually all courts have reached similar conclusions. Juveniles may be confined under such conditions only if they are a serious threat to themselves or others; even then, they should be released as soon as possible.

In the past twenty-five years there has been considerable litigation over conditions of confinement. Most of it results from violations of the constitutional rights of the residents. The outcomes of such litigation have become the basis for institutional reform.[82] A recent case on juvenile institutions and the right to treatment is described in the Juvenile Law in Review box entitled "*Alexander v. Boyd, and South Carolina Dept. of Juvenile Justice* (1995)."

Alexander v. Boyd is significant in that it affirmed that juveniles have constitutional rights when they are placed in institutions. The case represents another example in a long line of cases involving the role of the judicial system in remedying constitutional violations in correctional institutions. It also clearly reestablished that the purpose of the South Carolina juvenile law in confining juveniles was not to punish them but to provide training and services to correct their delinquent behavior. Court action continues to be a viable solution to achieving change and reform in the juvenile corrections system.

What provisions does the juvenile justice system make to help institutionalized offenders return to society? The remainder of this chapter is devoted to this important topic.

Juvenile Aftercare

aftercare
Transitional assistance to juveniles equivalent to adult parole to help youths adjust to community life.

Aftercare in the juvenile justice system is the equivalent of parole in the adult criminal justice system. When juveniles are released from an institution through an early-release program or after completing their sentences, they may be placed in an aftercare program of some kind. The belief is that youths who have been institutionalized should not be returned to the community without some form of transitional assistance. Whether individuals who are in aftercare as part of an indeterminate sentence remain in the community or return to the institution for further rehabilitation depends on their actions during the aftercare period.

In a number of jurisdictions the early release of juveniles resembles the adult parole process. A paroling authority, which may be an independent body or part of the corrections department or some other branch of state services, makes the release decision. Juvenile aftercare authorities, like adult parole officers, review the youth's adjustment within the institution, whether he or she is chemically dependent, what the crime was, and other specifics of the case.

parole guidelines
Recommended length of confinement and kinds of aftercare assistance most effective for a juvenile who committed a specific offense.

Some juvenile authorities are even making use of **parole guidelines** first developed with adult parolees. Each youth who enters a secure facility is given a recommended length of confinement that is explained at his or her initial interview with parole authorities. The stay is computed on the basis of the offense record, influenced by aggravating and mitigating factors. The parole authority is not required to follow the recommended sentence but instead uses it as a tool in making parole decisions.[83] Whatever approach is used, several primary factors are considered by virtually all jurisdictions when recommending a juvenile for release: (1) institutional adjustment, (2) length of stay and general attitude, and (3) likelihood of success in the community.

Risk classifications have also been designed to help parole officers make decisions about which juveniles should receive aftercare services.[84] The risk-based aftercare system uses an empirically derived risk scale to classify youths. Juveniles are identified as most likely or least likely to commit a new offense within a period of release to aftercare supervision based on factors such as prior record, type of offense, and degree of institutional adjustment.

Armstrong and Altschuler describe the critical components of a model aftercare program as follows: (1) preparing youths for progressively increased responsibility in the community, (2) facilitating positive youth interaction with peers, (3) working with the offender and community support groups, (4) developing new community resources, and (5) monitoring the juvenile and the community concerning their

ALEXANDER V. BOYD, AND SOUTH CAROLINA DEPARTMENT OF JUVENILE JUSTICE (1995)

This case involved juveniles who were temporarily housed at the South Carolina Reception and Evaluation Center, as well as those confined at three long-term institutions. The juveniles filed a class action suit, claiming that the basic conditions of confinement were so inadequate that they amounted to a deprivation of their Fourteenth Amendment rights.

The Reception and Evaluation Center was the institution designed to receive and evaluate juveniles considered for long-term confinement by the family court. The three long-term institutions, or training schools, were Willow Lane (for female juveniles and younger or less aggressive males), John G. Richards (for older male juveniles), and Birchwood (for the oldest, most aggressive male residents).

After a very thorough analysis of the institutions, the district court found that a number of deficiencies represented constitutional and statutory violations of the juvenile's rights. Among the problems cited were:

1. *Disciplinary practices.* The Department of Juvenile Justice (DJJ) facilities relied primarily on the use of lockup units and CS gas to punish inmates for disciplinary infractions. The suit challenged the procedures by which juveniles were placed in lockup units and the spartan conditions of the lockup cells. CS gas is a potent form of tear gas used primarily for riot control. It irritates the mucous membranes, causes instant pain and spasms in the eyelids, coughing fits, and breathing problems; it also can cause damage to the cornea and potential blindness. CS gas was used on a fairly regular basis in the South Carolina institutions; the defendants' own records show that gas was used on juveniles more than 180 times in 1993.

2. *Fire safety.* The greatest risk of harm was from mattress fires. Mattress fires emit insufficient heat to set off the sprinkler system but cause substantial amounts of smoke, which can be fatal to the occupants of the units if those juveniles are not removed quickly. In each of the two lockup units at the DJJ facilities, the thirty individual cells were secured with individual padlocks. In the event of a fire, each cell must be opened by hand, a time-consuming process that posed a significant risk to the confined inmates.

3. *Food/sanitation.* At trial several juveniles, and even the food services director, testified that cockroaches and other foreign matter were present frequently in the food served to the juveniles.

4. *Classification.* An inadequate system of inmate classification at DJJ facilities meant that potentially dangerous individuals could be housed with less aggressive inmates, causing an unreasonable threat to their physical safety.

5. *Medical services.* Medical facilities at DJJ were stretched to the limit. The institutions relied on three full-time nurses and a handful of part-time nurses to serve a population of almost nine hundred juveniles. (One medical doctor was under contract to visit the facilities once a week for a total of three hours.)

6. *Programs.* Without minimally adequate programming, the agency was simply warehousing the juveniles and abandoning the interest of rehabilitation.

7. *Overcrowding.* The Reception and Evaluation Center frequently experience severe overcrowding. Approximately two thousand juveniles passed through the institution each year.

The district court decision concluded that a constitutional right to treatment exists for juveniles and required that the conditions at the institution must relate to that purpose. The state was given the opportunity to correct all the deficiencies but was not required to release any juveniles placed in the long-term facilities because of existing conditions.

As a result of these programs, risk assessment and classification systems have become major case management tools for community supervision.

Supervision

One purpose of aftercare is to provide an individual with some support during the readjustment period following release into the community. The institutionalized minor is likely to have some difficulty making the adjustment. Individuals whose activities have been tightly regimented for some time may not find it easy to make independent decisions. Second, incarcerated offenders may perceive themselves as scapegoats, cast out by an unforgiving society. Furthermore, the community itself may view the returning minor with a good deal of prejudice; adjustment problems may reinforce a preexisting need to engage in bad habits or deviant behavior.

Juveniles in aftercare programs are supervised by parole caseworkers or counselors whose job is to provide surveillance by maintaining contact with the juvenile, to make sure that a corrections plan is followed, and to show interest and caring to help prevent further mistakes by the juvenile. The counselor also keeps the youth informed of available services that may assist in reintegration and counsels the youth and his or her family on the possible root of the original problems related to the delinquency. Unfortunately, aftercare caseworkers, like probation officers, often carry such large caseloads that their jobs are next to impossible to do adequately.

Research has generally questioned the effectiveness of traditional juvenile parole programs (those involving casework and individual or group counseling).[85] In one of the most impressive research efforts on the effectiveness of juvenile parole, Patrick Jackson randomly assigned subjects from the California Youth Authority to either parole or outright discharge.[86] He found that youths under formal parole supervision were actually more likely to become reinvolved in serious offenses than those simply discharged and left on their own. However, there was relatively little difference between the two groups with respect to the chance of being arrested or serving time in another institution. Jackson found that the longer a person was retained on parole, the greater the chance of his or her being rearrested. Jackson concluded that there are few beneficial elements of parole supervision and many potentially harmful side effects.

Despite the less than encouraging results of the Jackson research, there are indications that juvenile aftercare can be very effective if it is combined with innovative treatment efforts. For example, the Violent Juvenile Offender program discussed earlier combines short-term incarceration with intensive follow-up in what appears to be a successful rehabilitative effort. Jeffery Fagan and his colleagues found that highly structured efforts to reintegrate youths into society can have better results than previously thought possible.[87] The Albuquerque (New Mexico) Girls Reintegration Center is an excellent example of a successful community-based program that prepares female juvenile offenders for their eventual release into the community. The program provides participants with positive role models, involvement in community activities, and relevant school and work experience.

Intensive Aftercare Program (IAP)

A balanced, highly structured, comprehensive continuum of intervention for serious and violent juvenile offenders returning to the community.

The Armstrong and Altschuler **Intensive Aftercare Program (IAP)** model is important because it offers a balanced, highly structured, comprehensive continuum of intervention for serious and violent juvenile offenders returning to the community following placement (see Figure 17.3). The Virginia Department of Youth and Family Services applies this model to its intensive parole program. The program consists of a screening process and treatment plan; a complete physical, psychological, and educational assessment; intensive counseling and treatment team meetings with parents; a reintegration plan that identifies services and service

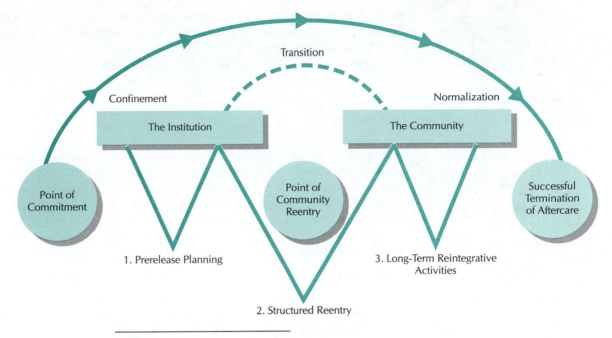

FIGURE 17.3

The Continuum of Intervention for Youth Corrections

Source: David Altschuler and Troy Armstrong, "Aftercare Not Afterthought: Testing the IAP Model," *Juvenile Justice* 3:15–23 (1996).

providers; increased surveillance by aftercare workers; and judicial reviews by the county and adolescent and parent groups in the community. Similar programs have been formed in Denver, Colorado, and Las Vegas, Nevada. The IAP initiative was designed to help public and private correctional agencies implement effective aftercare programs for chronic and serious juvenile offenders.[88]

Aftercare is a very important stage in the juvenile justice process because few juveniles age out of state custody. In 1992, for example, more than 70 percent of juvenile offenders were released to parole or aftercare. Another 10 percent received some other type of conditional release. In some jurisdictions today, the proportion of children released to parole or aftercare is 100 percent.[89] There is almost a total lack of research on juvenile aftercare, particularly with regard to high-risk juvenile offenders, yet intensive aftercare services are crucial to the success of residential treatment programs.

Recent state legislation underscores the importance of aftercare for juvenile offenders. Reform legislation in Connecticut last year created a program of aftercare for youths who have been in state institutions. The program continues to provide services based on need and supervises the offender in the community to protect the public. Other recent programs include:

■ The Texas Youth Commission, which operates an "independent living program" that provides prerelease and transition assistance to male and female offenders ages 16 to 18 who are returning to the community from secure corrections.

■ An aftercare program in Cuyahoga County, Ohio, begins with education and employment training while a youth is incarcerated and continues after the youth is released.

■ The Student Transition Education and Employment program, part of the Cuyahoga County aftercare program, has shown lower reoffense rates for participants than for those involved in more traditional postrelease supervision at only a slightly greater cost per participant.

- A reintegration program for youths released from the New Mexico Boys' School saved the state money by providing aftercare because the boys spent less time in juvenile corrections.[90]

Aftercare Revocation Procedures

A final issue in aftercare for juveniles concerns revocation procedures. Although adult parolees have been entitled to certain procedural rights in revocation proceedings since 1972, the Supreme Court has not yet extended the same rights to juveniles.[91] However, most states have extended these rights to juveniles on their own initiative, as have appellate courts that have considered juvenile aftercare revocation procedures. To avoid revocation, a juvenile parolee must meet the following general conditions, among others:

- Adhere to a reasonable curfew set by youth worker or parent
- Refrain from associating with persons whose influence would be detrimental, including but not limited to persons convicted of crimes or persons of a known criminal background
- Attend school in accordance with the law
- Abstain from drugs and alcohol
- Report to the youth worker when required
- Refrain from acts that would be crimes if committed by an adult
- Refrain from operating an automobile without permission of the youth worker or parent
- Refrain from being habitually disobedient and beyond the lawful control of parent or other legal authority
- Refrain from running away from the lawful custody of parent or other lawful authority

Certain procedural safeguards have been set up to ensure that revocation of juvenile aftercare is handled fairly:

- The youth must be informed of the specific conditions of parole and receive notice of any obligations.
- The youth has the right to legal counsel at state expense if necessary; the right to confront and cross-examine; the right to introduce documentary evidence and witnesses; and the right to a hearing before an independent hearing officer who shall be an attorney but not an employee of the revoking agency.

The use of these procedures has led to improved administrative decision making and adequate constitutional safeguards for juveniles in revocation hearings.

The trend of increased due process rights for parolees may be on the wane. In 1998 the U.S. Supreme Court ordered that legally seized evidence is admissible in adult state parole revocation proceedings. In *Pennsylvania Board of Parole v. Scott,* parole officers conducted a warrantless search of the parolee's home, uncovering weapons the parolee was forbidden to possess.[92] On that basis the defendant's parole was revoked. The state court of Pennsylvania ruled that the search was illegal because the officers lacked reasonable suspicion of a parole violation and held that the Fourth Amendment exclusionary rule (a rule of evidence that excludes illegal evidence at a criminal trial) was applicable in parole proceedings. But the U.S. Supreme Court reversed the lower court and took the position that the exclusionary rule should not be applied outside the context of the criminal trial. This decision will most likely be applied to juvenile aftercare proceedings, and the use of such evidence might result in an increase in aftercare revocations. Further decisions are needed to determine if the Fourth Amendment exclusionary rule is a constitutional requirement in both juvenile and adult revocation proceedings.

SUMMARY

The juvenile institution was developed in the mid-nineteenth century as an alternative to placing youths in adult prisons. Youth institutions evolved over the years from large, closed institutions to today's open, cottage-based education- and rehabilitation-oriented institutions. Most institutions for youths feature libraries and recreational programs and are low-security facilities.

The juvenile institutional population has increased in recent years to more than 108,000 residents, despite efforts to decarcerate status offenders and petty delinquent offenders. Although there has been a shrinking youth population and a stabilization in juvenile arrest rates, there appears to be evidence of higher rates of incarceration in the future. In addition, increasing numbers of youths are being "hidden" in private medical centers and drug treatment clinics. A disproportionate number of minorities are being incarcerated in youth facilities today.

Most institutions maintain intensive treatment programs featuring individual or group therapy. Although a wide variety of techniques are used around the nation, little evidence has been found that any single method is effective in reducing recidivism. Yet the philosophy of treatment and rehabilitation remains an important goal of juvenile practitioners. Recent studies indicate that some programs do work.

The violent offender has come to be recognized as a major social problem. A number of states have set up intensive programs to deal with these hard core offenders.

The right to treatment is an important issue in juvenile justice. Legal decisions have mandated that a juvenile cannot simply be warehoused in a correctional center but must receive proper care and treatment to aid rehabilitation. What constitutes proper care is still being debated, however, and recent federal court decisions have backed off from holding that every youth can be rehabilitated. Gender is also a factor in equal access to treatment resources. Institutions for females generally have fewer vocational and educational programs than those exclusively for male delinquents.

Most institutions have a standard set of rules and discipline. There have been many exposés of physical brutality in youth institutions, and courts have sought to restrain the use of physical punishment on inmates.

Juveniles released from institutions are often placed on juvenile parole or aftercare. However, there is little evidence that this type of community supervision is actually more beneficial than simply releasing youths on their own. Many jurisdictions are experiencing success with community halfway houses and reintegration centers. Some researchers are reaffirming the importance of delinquency prevention, promising new treatment programs and graduated sanctions in juvenile corrections today.[93]

Deciding when to use secure incarceration and providing appropriate programs for serious and violent offenders that include aftercare, are key components to a comprehensive system of juvenile justice. At a time when the amount and seriousness of juvenile crime is significant, strengthening and defining the use of juvenile corrections is vital if the juvenile justice system is to be effective in treating serious offenders.

KEY TERMS

reform schools
cottage system
least restrictive alternative
individual counseling
psychotherapy
reality therapy
behavior modification
group therapy

guided group interaction (GGI)
Positive Peer Culture (PPC)
milieu therapy
chronic juvenile offender
suppression effect
lifestyle violent juveniles

Violent Juvenile Offender (VJO) program
boot camps
right to treatment
aftercare
parole guidelines
Intensive Aftercare Program (IAP)

INFOTRAC COLLEGE EDITION EXERCISES

Read the following article from InfoTrac College Edition:

The legacy of juvenile corrections. Barry Krisberg, *Corrections Today* August 1995

Prior to the 1800s, corporal punishment was the preferred method of dealing with wayward youth. Often this amounted to severe beatings, sometimes resulting in death. With the development of juvenile institutions came what was thought to be less punitive measures. However, these institutions were often extremely harsh and inhumane. Changes in the twentieth century saw the reorganization of the structure of juvenile correctional facilities. Since the 1970s there has been a push for the deinstitutionalization of youthful offenders.

Summarize the history of juvenile corrections according to Krisberg's article. Highlight his concerns regarding the need for change in the housing of youthful offenders in the coming decade.

QUESTIONS FOR DISCUSSION

1. Should status offenders ever be institutionalized with delinquents? Are they really different?
2. What kinds of programs would you implement in a juvenile correctional center?
3. Do you believe juveniles have a right to treatment? Should all offenders receive psychological counseling? What court decisions give credence to your position?
4. Is the use of physical punishment ever warranted in a juvenile institution? If not, how do you reconcile the fact that the Supreme Court has upheld the use of corporal punishment in public schools?
5. Identify and explain the current problems and issues in juvenile corrections. What possible solutions might you suggest?

6. In light of the extensive use of incarceration for juvenile offenders, do you think the trend toward determinate sentences for serious juvenile crime is desirable? Isn't such an approach in direct conflict with decarceration policy?
7. How should society deal with the chronic juvenile offender? Is incarceration the only practical solution?
8. What is meant by the "legal right" to treatment? Do juveniles have such a right? Discuss the meaning of the cases dealing with this issue.
9. Are boot camps for juveniles a dangerous trend and as ineffective as wholesale incarceration of youths in secure institutions?
10. What is the IAP model?

NOTES

1. Dorsey Griffith, "California Criminals Stitch Options in Sewing Program," *Dallas Morning News* 13 December 1998, p. A44.
2. U.S. Department of Justice, *Children in Custody 1975–85—Census of Public and Private Juvenile Detention, Correctional and Shelter Facilities* (Washington, D.C.: U.S. Department of Justice, 1989), p. 4.
3. Edward Loughran, "Juvenile Corrections: The Massachusetts Experience," in L. Eddison, ed., *Reinvesting Youth Corrections Resources: A Tale of Three States* (Minneapolis: University of Minnesota, Hubert Humphrey Institute of Public Affairs, 1987), pp. 11–18.
4. U.S. Department of Justice, *Children in Custody 1975-85*, p. 4.
5. James Howell, ed., *Guide for Implementing the Comprehensive Strategy for Serious, Violent and Chronic Juvenile Offenders* (Washington, D.C.: OJJDP, 1995).
6. For a detailed description of juvenile delinquency in the 1800s, see J. Hawes, *Children in Urban Society: Juvenile Delinquency in Nineteenth Century America* (New York: Oxford University Press, 1971).
7. D. Jarvis, *Institutional Treatment of the Offender* (New York: McGraw-Hill, 1978), p. 101.
8. Margaret Werner Cahalan, *Historical Corrections Statistics in the United States, 1850–1984* (Washington, D.C.: U.S. Department of Justice, 1986), pp. 104–5.
9. Clemons Bartollas, Stuart J. Miller, and Simon Dinitiz, *Juvenile Victimization: The Institutional Paradox* (New York: Wiley, 1976), p. 6.
10. LaMar T. Empey, *American Delinquency—Its Meaning and Construction* (Homewood, Ill.: Dorsey, 1978), p. 515.
11. Edward Eldefonso and Walter Hartinger, *Control, Treatment, and Rehabilitation of Juvenile Offenders* (Beverly Hills, Calif.: Glencoe, 1976), p. 151.
12. Ibid., p. 152.
13. M. Rosenthal, "Reforming the Justice Correctional Institution: Efforts of U.S. Children's Bureau in the 1930s," *Journal of Sociology and Social Welfare* 14:47–73 (1987).
14. Bureau of Justice Statistics, *Fact Sheet on Children in Custody* (Washington, D.C.: U.S. Department of Justice, 1989); Barbara Allen-Hagen, *Public Juvenile Facilities—Children in Custody, 1989* (Washington, D.C.: Office of Juvenile Justice and Delinquency Prevention, 1991); James Austin et al., *Juveniles Taken into Custody, 1993* (Washington, D.C.: OJJDP, 1995).
15. National Conference of State Legislatures, *A Legislator's Guide to Comprehensive Juvenile Justice, Juvenile Detention and Corrections* (Denver, Col.: National Conference of State Legislators, 1996).
16. Ibid.
17. Data in this and the following section come from the federal government's *Children in Custody* series, published biennially by the U.S. Department of Justice, Bureau of Justice Statistics (*Fact Sheet on Children in Custody, 1989*); Austin et al., *Juveniles Taken into Custody, 1993;* also, Melissa Sickmund, *Juvenile Court Statistics 1997* (Washington, D.C.: OJJDP, 1998).
18. Joseph Moone, *States at a Glance—Juveniles in Public Facilities, 1995,* OJJDP Fact Sheet (Washington, D.C.: U.S. Department of Justice, 1997).
19. Joseph Moone, *Juveniles in Private Facilities 1991–95,* OJJDP Fact Sheet (Washington, D.C.: U.S. Department of Justice, 1997).
20. Hunter Hurst and Patricia Torbet, *Organization and Administration of Juvenile Services: Probation, Aftercare, and State Delinquent Institutions* (Pittsburgh, Pa.: National Center for Juvenile Justice, 1993), p. 4.
21. Alan Breed and Barry Krisberg, "Is There a Future?", *Corrections Today* 48:14–26 (1986).
22. "My Twenty Years of Child Advocacy," *Youth Law News* 6:3 (1990); Patricia Puritz and Mary Ann Scali, *Beyond the Walls:*

Improving Conditions of Confinement for Youth in Custody (Chicago, Ill.: American Bar Association Juvenile Justice Center, 1988).

23. Department of Justice, *Children in Custody, 1989* (Washington, D.C.: U.S. Department of Justice, 1991), p. 10; Austin et al., *Juveniles Taken into Custody, 1993,* chapters 1 and 3; Howard Snyder and Melissa Sickmund, *Juvenile Offenders and Victims: A National Report* (Washington, D.C.: OJJDP, 1995), chapter 7; Moone, *States at a Glance,* p. 1.

24. Ibid, p. 13; Office of Juvenile Justice and Delinquency Prevention, U.S. Department of Justice, "Children in Custody, Public Juvenile Facilities, 1987," *Juvenile Justice Bulletin* (Washington, D.C.: U.S. Department of Justice, October 1988), p. 2; Austin et al., *Juveniles Taken into Custody, 1993,* chapters 1 and 3; Snyder and Sickmund, *Juvenile Offenders and Victims: A National Report,* chapter 7; Melissa Sickmund, Howard Snyder, and Eileen Poe Yamagata, *Juvenile Offenders and Victims: 1997 Update on Violence* (Washington, D.C.: OJJDP, 1998).

25. Data from Bureau of Justice Statistics, *Fact Sheet on Children in Custody: Public and Private Juvenile Facilities, 1989* (Washington, D.C.: U.S. Government Printing Office, 1989); Allen-Hagen, *Public Juvenile Facilities—Children in Custody, 1989;* Austin et al., *Juveniles Taken into Custody, 1993,* chapters 1 and 3; Snyder and Sickmund, *Juvenile Offenders and Victims: A National Report, 1997;* Moone, *States at a Glance—Juveniles in Public Facilities, 1995,* p. 2.

26. Joseph Moone, *States at a Glance—Juveniles in Public Facilities, 1995* (Washington, D.C.: U.S. Department of Justice, 1997); Melissa Sickmund et al., *Juvenile Offenders and Victims, 1997 Update* (Washington, D.C.: OJJDP, 1998).

27. Office of Juvenile Justice and Delinquency Prevention, U.S. Department of Justice, "More Juveniles Held in Public Facilities," *Children in Custody, 1989* (Washington, D.C.: U.S. Department of Justice, Bureau of Justice Statistics, September 1989), p. 2; Austin et al., *Juveniles Taken into Custody, 1993,* chapters 1 and 3; Snyder and Sickmund, *Juvenile Offenders and Victims: A National Report, 1997.*

28. "Comparison of Private and Public Placements," unpublished paper, California State University, San Bernadino, 1990, calls for a nationwide effort to evaluate private placements for juvenile offenders.

29. Ira Schwartz, Marilyn Jackson-Beck, and Roger Anderson, "The 'Hidden' System of Juvenile Control," *Crime and Delinquency* 30:371–85 (1984).

30. Rebecca Craig and Andrea Paterson, "State Involuntary Commitment Laws: Beyond Deinstitutionalization," *National Conference of State Legislative Reports* 13:1–10 (1988).

31. Barry Krisberg, Ira Schwartz, G. Fishman, Z. Eisikovits, and E. Gitman, "The Incarceration of Minority Youth," *Crime and Delinquency* 33:173–205 (1987).

32. Craig Fischer, ed., "Washington State Moves to End Juvenile Justice Race Disparity," *Criminal Justice Newsletter* 27:1–8 (1996).

33. Bartollas, Miller, and Dinitz, *Juvenile Victimization,* sec. C.

34. Christopher Sieverdes and Clemens Bartollas, "Security Level and Adjustment Patterns in Juvenile Institutions," *Journal of Criminal Justice* 14:135–45 (1986).

35. Several authors have written of this sexual double standard, see E. A. Anderson, "The Chivalrous Treatment of the Female Offender in the Arms of the Criminal Justice System: A Review of the Literature," *Social Problems* 23:350–57 (1976); G. Armstrong, "Females under the Law: Protected but Unequal," *Crime and Delinquency* 23:109–20 (1977); M. Chesney-Lind, "Judicial Enforcement of the Female Sex Role: The Family Court and the Female Delinquent," *Issues in Criminology* 8:51–59 (1973); idem, "Juvenile Delinquency: The Sexualization of Female Crime," *Psychology Today* 19:43–46 (1974); Allan Conway and Carol Bogdan, "Sexual Delinquency: The Persistence of a Double Standard," *Crime and Delinquency* 23:13–135 (1977); M. Chesney-Lind, *Girls, Delinquency and the Juvenile Justice System* (Pacific Grove, Calif.: Brooks/Cole, 1991).

36. "A Look at Juvenile Female Offenders," *Juvenile Corrections and Detention Newsletter* 2:6 (1988).

37. For a historical analysis of a girls' reformatory, see Barbara Brenzel, *Daughters of the State* (Cambridge: MIT Press, 1983).

38. Ilene R. Bergsmann, "The Forgotten Few Juvenile Female Offenders," *Federal Probation* 53:73–79 (1989).

39. For an interesting article highlighting the debate over the effectiveness of correctional treatment, see John Whitehead and Steven Lab, "Meta-Analysis of Juvenile Correctional Treatment," *Journal of Research in Crime and Delinquency* 26:276–95 (1989).

40. National Conference of State Legislatures, *A Legislators' Guide to Comprehensive Juvenile Justice, 1996.*

41. Ibid.

42. Louise Sas and Peter Jaffe, "Understanding Depression in Juvenile Delinquency: Implications for Institutional Admission Policies and Treatment Programs," *Juvenile and Family Court Journal* 37:49–58 (1985–86).

43. See, generally, William Glasser, "Reality Therapy: A Realistic Approach to the Young Offender," in Robert Schaste and Jo Wallach, eds., *Readings in Delinquency and Treatment* (Los Angeles: Delinquency Prevention Training Project, Youth Studies Center, University of Southern California, 1965); see also, Richard Rachin, "Reality Therapy: Helping People Help Themselves," *Crime and Delinquency* 16:143 (1974).

44. Helen A. Klein, "Towards More Effective Behavior Programs for Juvenile Offenders," *Federal Probation* 41:45–50 (1977); Albert Bandura, *Principles of Behavior Modification* (New York: Holt, Rinehart & Winston, 1969); H. A. Klein, "Behavior Modification as Therapeutic Paradox," *American Journal of Orthopsychiatry* 44:353 (1974).

45. LaMar T. Empey and Steven Lubeck, *The Silverlake Experiment* (Chicago: Aldine, 1971); H. Ashley Weeks, *Youthful Offenders at Highfields* (Ann Arbor: University of Michigan Press, 1958); LaMar T. Empey and J. Rabow, "The Provo Experiment in Delinquency Rehabilitation," *American Sociological Review* 26:679 (1961).

46. Larry Brendtero and Arlin Ness, "Perspectives on Peer Group Treatment: The Use and Abuses of Guided Group Interaction/Positive Peer Culture," *Child and Youth Services Review* 4:307–24 (1982).

47. Bruno Bettelheim, *The Empty Fortress* (New York: Free Press, 1967).

48. California Youth Authority Newsletter, "Ventura School for Juvenile Female Offenders" (Ventura, Calif.: California Youth Authority, 1988).

49. Charles Murray and Louis B. Cox, *Beyond Probation* (Beverly Hills, Calif.: Sage, 1979).

50. Andrew Vachss and Yitzhak Bakal, *The Life-Style Violent Juvenile* (Lexington, Mass.: Lexington Books, 1979).

51. Dan Macallair, "Reaffirming Rehabilitation in Juvenile Justice," *Youth and Society,* 25:104–25 (1993).

52. Barry Krisberg, Elliot Currie, and David Onek, "What Works with Juvenile Offenders," *American Bar Association Journal of Criminal Justice* 10:20–26 (1995).

53. Robert Mathias, Paul DeMuro, and Richard Allinson, eds., *Violent Juvenile Offender* (San Francisco: National Council on Crime and Delinquency, 1984).

54. J. A. Fagan, "Treatment and Reintegration of Violent Juvenile Offenders: Experimental Results," *Justice Quarterly* 7:233–63 (1990).

55. For a description of the Florida Environmental Institute Program, see Howell, *Guide for Implementing the Comprehensive Strategy for Serious, Violent and Chronic Juvenile Offenders.*

56. For a description of the Capital Offender Program, see Howell, *Guide for Implementing the Comprehensive Strategy for Serious, Violent and Chronic Offenders.*

57. Thomas Castellano and Irina Soderstrom, "Therapeutic Wilderness Programs and Juvenile Recidivism: A Program Evaluation," *Journal of Offender Rehabilitation* 17:19–46 (1992); Troy Armstrong, ed., *Intensive Interventions in High Risk Youth:*

Approaches in Juvenile Probation and Parole (New York: Willow Tree Press, 1991).

58. William J. Taylor, "Tailoring Boot Camps to Juveniles," *Corrections Today* (July) 1992, p. 124.

59. Jerald Burns and Gennaro Vito, "An Impact Analysis of the Alabama Boot Camp Program," *Federal Probation* 59:63–67 (1995).

60. Ronald Corbett and Joan Petersilia, eds., "The Results of a Multisite Study of Boot Camps," *Federal Probation* 58:60–66 (1995).

61. Margaret Beyer, "Juvenile Boot Camps Don't Make Sense," *American Bar Association Journal of Criminal Justice* 10:20–21 (1996).

62. Eric Peterson, *Juvenile Boot Camps: Lessons Learned* (Washington, D.C.: OJJDP, 1996); Michael Peters et al., *Boot Camps for Juvenile Offenders* (Washington, D.C.: OJJDP, 1997).

63. Anthony Salerno, "Boot Camps—A Critique and Proposed Alternative," *Journal of Offender Rehabilitation* 20:147–58 (1994).

64. Robert Shepard Jr., "State Pen or Playpen? Is Prevention 'Pork' or Simply Good Sense," *American Bar Association Journal of Criminal Justice* 10:34–37 (1995). Howell, *Guide for Implementing the Comprehensive Strategy for Serious, Violent and Chronic Juvenile Offenders*.

65. Morton Birnbaum, "The Right to Treatment," *American Bar Association Journal* 46:499 (1960).

66. *Rouse v. Cameron*, 373 F.2d 451 (D.C. Cir. 1966).

67. Ibid., p. 453.

68. *Wyatt v. Stickney*, 325 F. Supp. 781 (1971); see also, note, "*Wyatt v. Stickney*—A Constitutional Right to Treatment for the Mentally Ill," *University of Pittsburgh Law Review* 34;79-84 (1972).

69. *Wyatt v. Stickney*, 325 F. Supp. 781 (1971).

70. *O'Connor v. Donaldson*, 422 U.S. 563 (1975).

71. *Inmates of the Boys' Training School v. Affleck*, 346 F. Supp. 1354 (D.R.I. 1972).

72. Ibid., p. 1343.

73. *Martarella v. Kelly*, 349 F. Supp. 575 (S.D.N.Y. 1972).

74. *Nelson v. Heyne*, 491. F. 2d 353 (1974).

75. *Morales v. Turman*, 383 F. Supp. 53 (E.D. Texas 1974).

76. *Pena v. New York State Division for Youth*, 419 F. Supp. 203 (S.D.N.Y. 1976).

77. *Ralston v. Robinson*, 102 S.Ct. 233 (1981).

78. *Santana v. Collazo*, 714 F.2d 1172 (1st Cir. 1983).

79. *Gary H. v. Hegstrom*, 831 F.2d 1430 (1987); see also, David Lambert, "Children in Institutions," *Youth Law News* 8:10–14 (1987).

80. *Wolff v. McDonnell*, 418 U.S. 539 (1974).

81. *Lollis v. New York State Department of Social Services*, 322 F. Supp. 473 (1970).

82. For extensive analysis of juvenile law, see Samuel Davis, *Rights of Juveniles, the Juvenile Justice System* (New York: Clark Boardman, 1993); Joseph Senna and Larry Siegel, *Juvenile Law—Cases and Comments* (St. Paul, Minn.: West, 1992).

83. Michael Norman, "Discretionary Justice: Decision Making in a State Juvenile Parole Board," *Juvenile and Family Court Journal* 37:19–26 (1985–86).

84. James Maupin, "Risk Classification Systems and the Provisions of Juvenile Aftercare," *Crime and Delinquency* 39:90–105 (1993).

85. T. Armstrong and D. Altschuler, "Recent Developments in Programming of High-Risk Juvenile Parolees," in Albert Roberts, ed., *Critical Issues in Crime and Justice* (San Francisco, Calif.: Sage, 1994).

86. Patrick Jackson, *The Paradox of Control: Parole Supervision of Youthful Offenders* (New York: Praeger, 1983).

87. Jeffrey Fagan, Cary Rudman, and Eliot Hartstone, "Intervening with Violent Juvenile Offenders: A Community Reintegration Model," in Robert Mathias, Paul DeMuro, and Richard Allinson, eds., *Violent Juvenile Offenders* (San Francisco, Calif.: National Council on Crime and Delinquency, 1984), pp. 207–31.

88. "Girls Reintegration Center—Albuquerque, New Mexico," *Juvenile and Corrections Newsletter* 2:6 (1988).

89. Snyder and Sickmund, *Juvenile Offenders and Victims: A National Report*, p. 177.

90. A Legislator's Guide to Comprehensive Juvenile Justice, Detention and Corrections, 1996.

91. See *Morrissey v. Brewer*, 408 U.S. 471, 92 S.Ct. 2593, 33 L.Ed.2d 484 (1972). Upon revocation of adult parole, a defendant is entitled to the due process rights of (1) a hearing, (2) written notice of charges, (3) knowledge of evidence against him or her, (4) opportunity to present and cross-examine witnesses, and (5) a written statement of reasons for parole revocation. Most jurisdictions require that these procedures be applied to juveniles.

92. *Pennsylanvia Board of Parole v. Scott*, 118 S.Ct. 2014 (1988).

93. John Wilson and James Howell, "Serious and Violent Juvenile Crime—A Comprehensive Strategy," *Juvenile and Family Court Journal* 45:3–15 (1994); U.S. Department of Justice, *Delinquency Prevention Works—A Program Summary* (Washington, D.C.: OJJDP, 1995).

Concluding Notes
American Delinquency

We have reviewed in this text the current knowledge of the nature, cause, and correlates of juvenile delinquency and society's efforts to bring about its elimination and control. We have analyzed research programs, theoretical models, governmental policies, and legal cases. Taken in sum, this information presents a rather broad and complex picture of the youth crime problem and the most critical issues confronting the juvenile justice system. Delinquents come from a broad spectrum of society; kids of every race, gender, class, region, family type, and culture are involved in delinquent behaviors. To combat youthful law violations, society has tried a garden variety of intervention and control strategies: tough law enforcement; counseling, treatment and rehabilitation; provision of legal rights; community action; educational programs; family change strategies. Yet, despite decades of intense effort and study, it is still unclear why delinquency occurs and what, if anything, can be done to control its occurrence. One thing is for certain, juvenile crime is one of the most serious domestic problems faced by Americans.

Though uncertainty prevails, it is possible to draw some inferences about youth crime and its control. After reviewing the material contained in this volume, certain conclusions seem self-evident. Some involve social facts; that is, particular empirical relationships and associations have been established that have withstood multiple testing and verification efforts. Other conclusions involve social questions; there are issues that need clarification, and the uncertainty surrounding them has hampered progress in combating delinquency and treating known delinquents.

In sum, we have reviewed some of the most important social facts concerning delinquent behavior and posed some of the critical questions that still remain to be answered.

THE STATUTORY CONCEPT OF JUVENILE DELINQUENCY IS IN NEED OF REVIEW AND MODIFICATION.

Today, the legal definition of a juvenile delinquent is a minor child, usually under the age of 17, who has been found to have violated the criminal law (juvenile code). The concept of juvenile delinquency still occupies a legal position falling somewhere between criminal and civil law; juveniles still enjoy more rights, protections and privileges than adults. Nonetheless, concerns about teen violence may eventually put an end to the separate juvenile justice system. If kids are equally or even more violent as adults, why should they be given a special legal status consideration? If the teen violence rate begins to rise again, so too may calls for the abolition of a separate juvenile justice system.

THE CONCEPT OF THE STATUS OFFENDER (PINS, CHINS, AND MINS) MAY BE IN FOR REVISION.

Special treatment for the status offender conforms with the *parens patriae* roots of the juvenile justice system. Granting the state authority to institutionalize non-criminal youth in order "to protect the best interest of the child" cannot be con-

sidered an abuse of state authority. While it is likely that the current system of control will remain in place for the near future, it is not beyond the realm of possibility to see the eventual restructuring of the definition of status offenders, with jurisdiction of "pure" non-criminal first offenders turned over to a department of social services, and chronic status offenders and those with prior records of delinquency petitioned to juvenile court as delinquency cases.

JUVENILE OFFENDERS ARE BECOMING MORE VIOLENT.

Official delinquency data suggests that there has been a decade long rise in the juvenile violence rate. At a time when adult violence is in decline, juvenile offenders are committing murder and other serious felony offenses at an increasing pace. While there has been a recent stabilization in the violence rate, forecasters suggest that an increasing juvenile population portends a long term increase in the overall violence rate.

EASY AVAILABILITY OF GUNS IS A SIGNIFICANT CONTRIBUTOR TO TEEN VIOLENCE.

Research indicates a close tie between gun use, control of drug markets and teen violence. Unless efforts are made to control the spread of handguns or devise programs to deter handgun use, teen-age murder rates should continue to rise.

THE CHRONIC VIOLENT JUVENILE OFFENDER IS A SERIOUS SOCIAL PROBLEM FOR SOCIETY AND THE JUVENILE JUSTICE SYSTEM.

Official crime data indicates that the juvenile violence rate is at an all-time high. Chronic male delinquent offenders commit a disproportionate amount of violent behavior including a significant amount of the most serious juvenile crimes, such as homicides, rapes, robberies, and aggravated assaults. Many chronic offenders become adult criminals and eventually end up in the criminal court system. How to effectively deal with chronic juvenile offenders and drug users remains a high priority for the juvenile justice system.

Chronic juvenile delinquency has unquestionably become a major concept within the field. The best approach to dealing with chronic offenders remains uncertain, but concern about such offenders has shifted juvenile justice policy toward a punishment-oriented philosophy.

THERE IS STILL DEBATE ABOUT WHETHER THE PROPENSITY TO COMMIT CRIME CHANGES AS PEOPLE MATURE.

Delinquency experts are now researching such issues as the onset, escalation, termination and continuation of a delinquent career. There is an on-going debate concerning change in delinquent behavior patterns. One position is that people do not change, conditions and opportunities do. A second view is that real human change is conditioned by life events. If the former position holds true there is little hope of using treatment strategies to change known offenders; a more productive approach would be to limit their criminal opportunities through the use of long-term incarceration. If the latter position is accurate, effective treatment and provision of legitimate opportunities might produce real behavioral changes.

FEMALE DELINQUENCY HAS BEEN INCREASING AT A FASTER PACE THAN MALE DELINQUENCY.

The nature and extent of female delinquent activities changed in the late 1980s, and it now appears that girls are engaging in more frequent and serious illegal activity in the 1990s. While gender differences in the rate of the most serious crimes such as murder still persist, it is possible that further convergence will occur in the near future.

THERE IS LITTLE QUESTION THAT FAMILY ENVIRONMENT AFFECTS PATTERNS OF JUVENILE BEHAVIOR.

Family relationships have been linked to the problem of juvenile delinquency by many experts. Broken homes, for instance, are not in and of themselves a cause of delinquency, but some evidence indicates that single-parent households are more inclined to contain children who manifest behavioral problems. Limited resource allocations limit the single-parent's ability to control and supervise children. In addition, there seems to be a strong association in family relationships between child abuse and delinquency. Cases of abuse and neglect have been found in every level of the economic strata, and a number of studies have linked child abuse and neglect to juvenile delinquency. While the evidence is not conclusive, it does suggest that a strong relationship exists between child abuse and subsequent delinquent behavior. This relationship does not bode well for delinquency rates because the extent of reported child abuse is on the increase. Some experts believe a major effort is needed to reestablish parental accountability and responsibility.

JUVENILE GANGS HAVE BECOME A SERIOUS AND GROWING PROBLEM IN MANY MAJOR METROPOLITAN AREAS THROUGHOUT THE UNITED STATES.

Ethnic youth gangs, mostly males aged 14 to 21, appear to be increasing in such areas as Los Angeles, Chicago, Boston, and New York. National surveys of gang activity now estimate that there are about 700,000 members in the United States, up sharply over the previous twenty years. One view of gang development is that such groups serve as a bridge between adolescence and adulthood in communities where adult social control is not available. Another view suggests that gangs are a product of lower-class social disorganization and that they serve as an alternative means of economic advancement for poorly motivated and uneducated youth. Today's gangs are more often commercially than culturally oriented, and the profit motive may be behind increasing memberships. It is unlikely that gang control strategies can be successful as long as legitimate economic alternatives are lacking. Look for rapid growth in ganging when the current adolescent population matures and limited job opportunities encourage gang members to prolong their involvement in illegal activities.

MANY OF THE UNDERLYING PROBLEMS OF YOUTH CRIME AND DELINQUENCY ARE DIRECTLY RELATED TO EDUCATION.

Numerous empirical studies have confirmed that lack of educational success is an important contributing factor in delinquency; experts generally agree chronic offenders have had a long history of school failure. Dropping out of school is now being associated with long-term antisocial behavior. About ten percent of all victimizations occur on school grounds. School-based crime control projects have not been very successful, and a great deal more effort is needed in this critical area of school-delinquency prevention control.

SUBSTANCE ABUSE IS CLOSELY ASSOCIATED WITH JUVENILE CRIME AND DELINQUENCY.

Self-reported teen substance abuse has increased during the 1990s. Surveys of arrested juveniles indicate sizable numbers of young people are substance abusers. Most efforts in the juvenile justice system to treat young offenders involved with substance abuse seem to be unsuccessful. Traditional prevention efforts and education programs have not had encouraging results.

AN ANALYSIS OF THE HISTORY OF JUVENILE JUSTICE OVER THE PAST 100 YEARS SHOWS HOW OUR POLICY REGARDING DELINQUENCY HAS GONE THROUGH CYCLES OF REFORM.

Many years ago, society primarily focused on the treatment of youth who committed criminal behavior often through no fault of their own. Early in the nineteenth century, juveniles were tried in criminal courts, like everyone else. Reformers developed the idea of establishing separate institutions for juvenile offenders in which the rehabilitation idea could proceed without involvement with criminal adults. As a result, the House of Refuge Movement was born. By the late 1890s the system proved unworkable, because delinquent juveniles, minor offenders and neglected children weren't benefiting from institutional placement. The 1899 Illinois Juvenile Court Act was an effort to regulate the treatment of children and secure institutional reform. *Parens patriae* was the justification to ignore legal formalities in the juvenile courts up until the early twentieth century. In the 1960s, the *Gault* decision heralded the promise of legal rights for children and interrupted the goal of individualized rehabilitation. The 1970s yielded progress in the form of the Juvenile Justice and Delinquency Prevention Act. Throughout the 1980s and 1990s, the juvenile justice system seemed suspended between the assurance of due process and efforts to provide services for delinquent children and their families. Today, society is concerned with the control of serious juvenile offenders and the development of firm sentencing provisions in the juvenile courts. These cycles represent the shifting philosophies of the juvenile justice system.

TODAY, NO SINGLE IDEOLOGY OR VIEW DOMINATES THE DIRECTION, PROGRAMS, AND POLICIES OF THE JUVENILE JUSTICE SYSTEM.

Throughout the past decade, numerous competing positions regarding juvenile justice have emerged. As the liberal program of the 1970s has faltered, more restrictive sanctions have been imposed. The "crime control" position seems most formidable as we enter the new millennium. However, there remains a great deal of confusion over what the juvenile justice system does, what it should do, and how it should deal with youthful antisocial behavior. The juvenile justice system operates on distinctly different yet parallel tracks. On the one hand, significant funding is available for prevention and treatment strategies. At the same time, states are responding to anxiety about youth crime by devising more punitive measures.

TODAY'S PROBLEMS IN THE JUVENILE JUSTICE SYSTEM CAN OFTEN BE TRACED TO THE UNCERTAINTY OF ITS FOUNDERS, THE "CHILD SAVERS."

Such early twentieth-century groups formed the juvenile justice system on the misguided principle of reforming wayward youth and remodeling their behavior. The "best interest of the child" standard has long been the guiding light in juvenile proceedings, calling for the strongest available rehabilitative services. Today's juvenile justice system is often torn between playing the role of social versus crime control agent.

IN RECENT YEARS, THE JUVENILE JUSTICE SYSTEM HAS BECOME MORE LEGALISTIC BY VIRTUE OF U.S. SUPREME COURT DECISIONS THAT HAVE GRANTED CHILDREN PROCEDURAL SAFEGUARDS IN VARIOUS COURT PROCEEDINGS.

The case of *In re Gault* of the 1960s motivated state legislators to revamp their juvenile court legal procedures. Today, the Supreme Court is continuing to struggle with making distinctions between the legal rights of adults and those of minors. Recent Court decisions that allowed children to be searched by teachers and denied their right to a jury trial showed that the Court continues to recognize a legal separation between adult and juvenile offenders.

DESPITE SOME DRAMATIC DISTINCTIONS, JUVENILES HAVE GAINED MANY OF THE LEGAL DUE PROCESS RIGHTS ADULTS ENJOY.

Among the more significant elements of due process are the right to counsel, evidence efficiency, protection from double jeopardy and self-incrimination, and the right to appeal. The public continues to favor providing juveniles with the same due process and procedural guarantees accorded to adults.

A recent report of the American Bar Association on juvenile access to counsel and the quality of legal representation in juvenile court found that the many constitutional protections that adults receive are not actually provided to juvenile offenders. High caseloads, poor pretrial preparation and trial performance, and the lack of dispositional representation are issues where juveniles are being denied due process of law. More resources are needed to implement constitutional procedures so that legal protections are not discarded.

The key area in which due process is required by *Gault* is the right to counsel. While progress has been made in improving the availability and quality of legal counsel afforded youth in delinquency proceedings in the three decades since *Gault,* much remains to be done.

STATES ARE INCREASINGLY TAKING LEGISLATIVE ACTION TO ENSURE THAT JUVENILE ARREST AND DISPOSITION RECORDS ARE AVAILABLE TO PROSECUTORS AND JUDGES.

Knowledge of defendants' juvenile records may help determine appropriate sentencing for offenders age 18–24, the age group most likely to be involved in violent crime. Laws that are being passed include (1) police fingerprinting of juveniles charged with crimes that are felonies if committed by an adult; (2) centralized juvenile arrest and disposition recordholding and dissemination statutes; (3) prosecutor and court access to juvenile disposition records; and (4) limitations on expungement of juvenile records when there are subsequent adult convictions.

THE JUVENILE COURT IS THE FOCAL POINT OF THE CONTEMPORARY JUVENILE JUSTICE SYSTEM.

Created at the turn of the century, it was adopted as an innovative solution to the problem of wayward youth. In the first half of the century, these courts (organized by the states) and based on the historic notion of *parens patriae,* were committed to the treatment of the child. They functioned without procedures employed in the adult criminal courts. When the system was reviewed by the U.S. Supreme Court in 1966, due process was imposed on the juvenile court system. Thirty years have since passed and numerous reform efforts have been undertaken. But the statement of Judge Abe Fortas "that the child receives the worst of both worlds—neither the protection afforded adults nor the treatment needed for children" still rings true. Reform efforts have been disappointing.

WHAT ARE THE REMEDIES FOR THE CURRENT JUVENILE COURT SYSTEM?

Some suggest abolishing the delinquency-status jurisdiction of the courts. This is difficult to do because the organization of the courts is governed by state law. Others want to strengthen the legal rights of juveniles by improving the quality of services of legal counsel. The vast majority of experts believe there is an urgent need to develop meaningful dispositional programs and expand treatment services. Over the last half-century, the juvenile court system has been transformed from a rehabilitative to a quasi-criminal court. With limited resources and procedural deficiencies, there is little likelihood of much change in the near future. On the one-hundredth anniversary of the juvenile court, one important change is the rise of juvenile drug courts for youth struggling with substance abuse.

THE DEATH PENALTY FOR CHILDREN HAS BEEN UPHELD BY THE SUPREME COURT.

According to the *Wilkens v. Missouri* and *Standford v. Kentucky* cases in 1989, the Supreme Court concluded that states are free to impose the death penalty for murderers who commit their crimes while age 16 or 17. According to the majority decision written by Justice Antonin Scalia, society has not formed a consensus that such executions are a violation of the cruel and unusual punishment clause of the Eighth Amendment.

ONE OF THE MOST SIGNIFICANT CHANGES IN AMERICAN LAW ENFORCEMENT HAS BEEN THE EMERGENCE OF COMMUNITY POLICING IN THE FIELD OF DELINQUENCY PREVENTION.

Community participation and cooperation, citizen crime prevention programs, and education programs such as Project DARE (drug education) have become a mainstay of law enforcement in the 1980s and 1990s and have had a particularly significant impact on improving perceptions of community safety and the quality of community life in many areas.

The Violent Crime Control and Law Enforcement Act of 1994, described as the largest piece of criminal legislation in the history of the country and four years in the making, provides major new opportunities for the field of juvenile crime prevention and community policing. Fighting to retain this law's major focus on prevention will be a future goal.

THE USE OF DETENTION IN THE JUVENILE JUSTICE SYSTEM CONTINUES TO BE A WIDESPREAD PROBLEM.

After almost three decades of work, virtually all jurisdictions have passed laws requiring that status offenders be placed in shelter care programs rather than detention facilities. Another serious problem related to the use of juvenile detention is the need to remove young people from lockups in adult jails. The Office of Juvenile Justice and Delinquency Prevention continues to give millions of dollars in aid to encourage the removal of juveniles from such adult lockups. But eliminating the confinement of children in adult institutions remains an enormously difficult task in the juvenile justice system. Although most delinquency cases do not involve detention, its use is more common for cases involving males, minorities, and older juveniles. Juvenile detention is one of the most important elements of the justice system and one of the most difficult to administer. It is experiencing a renewed emphasis on programs linked to short-term confinement.

THE USE OF WAIVER, BIND-OVER, AND TRANSFER PROVISIONS IN JUVENILE COURT STATUTES HAS BEEN GROWING.

This trend has led toward a criminalization of the juvenile system. Because there are major differences between the adult and juvenile court systems, transfer to an adult court exposes youths to more serious consequences of their antisocial behavior and is a strong recommendation of those favoring a crime-control model. Waiver of serious offenders is one of the most significant developments in the trend to criminalize the juvenile court. According to the National Conference of State Legislatures, every state has transfer proceedings. Many states are considering legislation that makes it easier to transfer juveniles into adult courts. States continue to modify age/offense criteria, allowing more serious offenders to be tried as criminals; some are considering new transfer laws, such as mandatory and presumptive waiver provisions.

THE ROLE OF THE ATTORNEY IN THE JUVENILE JUSTICE PROCESS REQUIRES FURTHER RESEARCH AND ANALYSIS.

Most attorneys appear to be uncertain whether they should act as adversaries or advocates in the juvenile process. In addition, the role of the juvenile prosecutor has become more significant as a result of new and more serious statutory sentencing provisions, as well as legal standards promulgated by such organizations as the American Bar Association and the National District Attorneys association. Juvenile defendants also need and are entitled to effective legal representation. Through creative and resourceful strategies, many more states are providing comprehensive representation for delinquent youth. These programs include law internships, attorney mentoring, and neighborhood defender services.

JUVENILE SENTENCING PROCEDURES NOW REFLECT THE DESIRE TO CREATE UNIFORMITY AND LIMITED DISCRETION IN THE JUVENILE COURT, AND THIS TREND IS LIKELY TO CONTINUE.

Many states have now developed programs such as mandatory sentences, sentencing guidelines, and limited-discretion sentencing to bring uniformity into the juvenile justice system. As a result of the public's fear about serious juvenile crime, legislators have amended juvenile codes to tighten up juvenile sentencing provisions. Graduated sanctions are the latest type of sentencing solution being explored by states. The most popular piece of juvenile crime legislation in the near future will be tougher sentences for violent and repeat offenders. Perhaps the most dramatic impact on sentencing will be felt by the imposition of "blended sentences" that combine juvenile and adult sentences. Blended sentencing statutes, that allow courts to impose juvenile and/or adult correctional sanctions on certain young offenders, were in place in twenty states at the end of 1997.

IN THE AREA OF COMMUNITY SENTENCING, NEW FORMS OF PROBATION SUPERVISION HAVE BECOME COMMONPLACE IN RECENT YEARS.

Intensive probation supervision, balanced probation, wilderness probation, and electronic monitoring have become important community-based alternatives over the last few years. Probation continues to be the single most significant intermediate sanction available to the juvenile court system.

RESTORATIVE COMMUNITY JUVENILE JUSTICE IS A NEW DESIGNATION THAT REFERS TO A PREFERENCE FOR NEIGHBORHOOD-BASED, MORE ACCESSIBLE, AND LESS FORMAL JUVENILE SERVICES.

The restorative justice idea pioneered by Gorden Bazemore is understood by examining the relationship between the victim, the community, and the offender. For the *victim,* restorative justice offers the hope of restitution or other forms of reparation, information about the case, support for healing, the opportunity to be heard, and input into the case, as well as expanded opportunities for involvement and influence. For the *community,* there is the promise of reduced fear and safer neighborhoods, a more accessible justice process, and accountability, as well as the obligation for involvement and participation in sanctioning crime, supporting victim restoration, reintegrating offenders, and crime prevention and control. For the *offender,* restorative justice requires accountability in the form of obligations to repair the harm to individual victims and victimized communities, and the opportunity to develop new competencies, social skills, and the capacity to avoid future crime.

VICTIM RESTITUTION IS ANOTHER WIDELY USED AND PROGRAMMATIC METHOD OF COMMUNITY TREATMENT IN TODAY'S JUVENILE JUSTICE SYSTEM.

In what is often referred to as monetary restitution, children are required to pay the victims of their crimes or in some instances provide some community service directly to the victim. Restitution provides the court with an important alternative sentencing option and has been instituted by statute in virtually every jurisdiction in the county.

DEINSTITUTIONALIZATION HAS BECOME AN IMPORTANT GOAL OF THE JUVENILE JUSTICE SYSTEM.

The Office of Juvenile Justice and Delinquency Prevention has provided funds to encourage this process. In the early 1980s, the deinstitutionalization movement seemed to be partially successful. Admissions to public juvenile correctional facilities declined in the late 1970s and early 1980s. In addition, the number of status offenders being held within the juvenile justice system was reduced. However, the number of institutionalized children in the 1990s has increased, and the deinstitutionalization movement has failed to meet all of its optimistic goals. Nonetheless, the majority of states have achieved compliance with the DSO mandate. Because juvenile crime is a high priority, the challenge to the states will be to retain a focus on prevention despite societal pressures for more punitive approaches. If that can be achieved, then deinstitutionalization will remain a central theme in the juvenile justice system.

THE NUMBER OF INCARCERATED YOUTHS CONTINUES TO RISE.

Today, there are over 100,000 youths in some type of correctional institutions. The juvenile courts seem to be using the most severe of the statutory dispositions, that is, commitment to the juvenile institution, rather than the "least restrictive statutory alternative." In addition, there seems to be a disproportionate number of minority youths incarcerated in youth facilities. The minority incarceration rate is almost four times greater than that for whites, and minorities seem to be placed more often in public than in private treatment facilities. The OJJDP is committed to ensuring that the country address situations where there is disproportionate confinement of minority offenders in the nation's juvenile justice system. The overall organization of the juvenile justice system in the United States is changing. Early on, institutional services for children were provided by the public sector. Today, private facilities and programs service a significant proportion of juvenile admissions. In the next decade, many more juvenile justice systems will most likely adopt privatization of juvenile correctional services.

DESPITE THE GROWTH OF ALTERNATIVE TREATMENT PROGRAMS SUCH AS DIVERSION, RESTITUTION, AND PROBATION, THE NUMBER OF CHILDREN UNDER SECURE INSTITUTIONAL CARE HAS INCREASED, AND THE SUCCESS OF SUCH PROGRAMS REMAINS VERY UNCERTAIN.

Nearly all juvenile institutions utilize some form of treatment program for the children in their care. Despite generally positive intentions, the goal of rehabilitation in an institutional setting is very difficult to achieve. Recent studies indicate some programs do work. Those secure programs that emphasize individual attention, reintegrate youths into their homes and communities, and provide intensive aftercare can be successful.

THE FUTURE OF THE LEGAL RIGHT TO TREATMENT FOR JUVENILES REMAINS UNCERTAIN.

The appellate courts have established minimum standards of care and treatment on a case-by-case basis, but it does not appear that the courts can be persuaded today to expand this constitutional theory to mandate that incarcerated children receive adequate treatment. Eventually, this issue must be clarified by the Supreme Court. Reforms in state juvenile institutions often result from class-action lawsuits filed on behalf of incarcerated youth.

A SERIOUS CRISIS EXISTS IN THE U.S. JUVENILE JUSTICE SYSTEM.

How to cope with the needs of large numbers of children in trouble remains one of the most controversial and frustrating issues in our society. The magnitude of the problem is such

that over 2 million youths are arrested each year; over 1.5 million delinquency dispositions and 150,000 status offense cases are heard in court; and drug abuse is a significant factor in more than 60 percent of all the cases referred to the juvenile courts. Today, the system and the process seem more concerned with crime control and more willing to ignore the rehabilitative ideal. Perhaps the answer lies outside the courtroom in the form of greater job opportunities, improved family relationships, and more effective education. Much needs to be done in delinquency prevention. One fact is also certain: According to many experts, the problem of violent juvenile crime is a national crisis. While the good news is that the juvenile crime rate declined in recent years, violence by juveniles is still too prevalent and remains an issue of great concern. Developing programs to fight juvenile violence seems to overshadow all other juvenile justice objectives.

FEDERAL FUNDING FOR JUVENILE DELINQUENCY IS ESSENTIAL TO IMPROVING STATE PRACTICES AND PROGRAMS.

The Juvenile Justice and Delinquency Prevention Act of 1974 has had a tremendous impact on America's juvenile justice system. Its mandates to deinstitutionalize status offenders and remove juveniles from adult jails have spurred change for over two decades. The survival of many state programs will likely depend on this federal legislation. Because the Act has contributed to a wide range of improvements, Congress will most likely approve future financial incentives. Reauthorization of JJDPA is expected in the 106th Congress (1999).

IN 1996, THE COORDINATING COUNCIL ON JUVENILE JUSTICE AND DELINQUENCY PREVENTION, AN INDEPENDENT ORGANIZATION IN THE EXECUTIVE BRANCH OF THE FEDERAL GOVERNMENT, PRESENTED ITS NATIONAL JUVENILE JUSTICE ACTION PLAN.

The Plan is a blueprint for action designed to reduce the impact of juvenile violence and delinquency. It calls upon states and communities to implement the following objectives: (1) provide immediate intervention sanctions and treatment for delinquent juveniles; (2) prosecute serious, violent, and chronic juvenile offenders in criminal court; (3) reduce youth involvement with guns, drugs, and gangs; (4) provide educational and employment opportunities for children and youth: (5) break the cycle of violence by dealing with youth victimization, abuse and neglect; (6) strengthen and mobilize communities; (7) support the development of innovative approaches to research and evaluation; and (8) implement an aggressive outreach campaign to combat juvenile violence. This text provides numerous examples of the innovative and effective strategies that are described in the National Juvenile Justice Action Plan.

TODAY, THE JUVENILE JUSTICE SYSTEM AND COURT OF ONE-HUNDRED YEARS IS UNDER ATTACK MORE THAN EVER BEFORE.

Yet it has weathered criticism for failing to control and rehabilitate juveniles. It is a unique American institution duplicated in many other countries as being the best model for handling juveniles who commit crime. The major recommendations of such important organizations as the National Council of Juvenile Court Judges, the American Bar Association, and the Office of Juvenile Justice and Delinquency Prevention for the new century are (1) the court should be a leader for juvenile justice in the community; (2) people (judges, attorneys, and probation officers) are the key to the health of the juvenile justice system; (3) public safety and rehabilitation are the goals of the juvenile justice system; (4) juvenile court workloads are shaped today and in the future by the increase of substance abuse cases which must be resolved; and (5) the greatest future needs of the juvenile court in particular are resources and funding for more services, more staff, and more facilities.

Glossary

abandonment Parents physically leave their children with the intention of completely severing the parent–child relationship.

academic achievement Being successful in a school environment.

active speech Expressing an opinion by speaking or writing; freedom of speech is a protected right under the First Amendment to the U.S. Constitution.

addict A person with an overpowering physical or psychological need to continue taking a particular substance or drug.

addiction prone personality The view that the cause of substance abuse can be traced to a personality that has a compulsion for mood-altering drugs.

adjudication hearing A fact-finding process wherein the juvenile court determines whether there is sufficient evidence to sustain the allegations in a petition.

advisement hearing A preliminary protective or temporary custody hearing in which the court will review the facts and determine whether removal of the child is justified and notify parents of the charges against them.

aftercare Transitional assistance to juveniles equivalent to adult parole to help youths adjust to community life.

age-graded theory Identifies turning points (such as marriage and career) that can cause delinquents to reverse course and desist from further criminal behavior.

age of consent Age at which youths are legally adults and may be independent of parental control. When an adolescent reaches the age of consent, he or she may engage in sexual behaviors prohibited to youths.

age of onset Age at which youths begin their delinquent careers; early onset is believed to be linked with chronic offending patterns.

aging out (also known as **desistance** or **spontaneous remission**) Frequency of offending or delinquent behavior diminishes as youths mature; occurs among all groups of offenders.

aging-out process The tendency for youths to reduce the frequency of their offending behavior as they age (also called spontaneous remission); aging out is thought to occur among all groups of offenders.

alcohol Fermented or distilled liquids containing ethanol, an intoxicating substance.

Alternative Work Sentencing Program (Earn-It) A Massachusetts program that brings together the juvenile and the crime victim to develop an equitable work program to provide restitution to the crime victim.

anabolic steroids Drugs used by athletes and body builders to gain muscle bulk and strength.

anesthetic drugs Nervous system depressants.

anomie Normlessness produced by rapidly shifting moral values; according to Merton, anomie occurs when personal goals cannot be achieved using available means.

appellate process Allows the juvenile an opportunity to have the case brought before a reviewing court after it has been heard in juvenile or family court.

arrest Taking a person into the custody of the law to restrain the accused until he or she can be held accountable for the offense in court proceedings.

at-risk youths Young people who are extremely vulnerable to the negative consequences of school failure, substance abuse, and early sexuality.

bail Amount of money that must be paid as a condition of pretrial release to ensure that the accused will return for subsequent proceedings; bail is normally set by the judge at the initial appearance, and if unable to make bail the accused is detained in jail.

balanced probation Programs that integrate community protection, accountability of the juvenile offender, competency, and individualized attention to the juvenile offender; based on the principle that juvenile offenders must accept responsibility for their behavior.

balancing-of-the-interest approach Efforts of the courts to balance the parents' natural right to raise a child with the child's right to grow into adulthood free from physical abuse or emotional harm.

barrio A Latino term meaning neighborhood.

battered child syndrome Nonaccidental physical injury of children by their parents or guardians.

behaviorism Branch of psychology concerned with the study of observable behavior rather than unconscious processes; focuses on particular stimuli and responses to them.

behavior modification A technique for shaping desired behaviors through a system of rewards and punishments.

best interests of the child A philosophical viewpoint that encouraged the state to take control of wayward children and provide care, custody, and treatment to remedy delinquent behavior.

bifurcated process The procedure of separating adjudicatory and dispositionary hearings so different levels of evidence can be heard at each.

bindover See **waiver.**

biosocial theory The view that both thought and behavior have biological and social bases.

blended families Nuclear families that are the product of divorce and remarriage; blending one parent from each of two families and their combined children into one family unit.

boot camps Juvenile programs that combine get-tough elements from adult programs with education, substance abuse treatment, and social skills training.

broken home Home in which one or both parents is absent due to divorce or separation; children in such an environment may be prone to antisocial behavior.

capital punishment Use of the death penalty to punish offenders.

chancery courts Court proceedings created in fifteenth-century England to oversee the lives of high-born minors who were orphaned or otherwise could not care for themselves.

child abuse Any physical, emotional, or sexual trauma to a child, including neglecting to give proper care and attention, for which no reasonable explanation can be found.

Children's Aid Society Child-saving organization that took children from the streets of large cities and placed them with farm families on the prairie.

child savers Nineteenth-century reformers who developed programs for troubled youth and influenced legislation creating the juvenile justice system; today some critics view them as being more concerned with control of the poor than with their welfare.

chivalry hypothesis (also known as **paternalism hypothesis**) View that low female crime and delinquency rates are a reflection of the leniency with which police treat female offenders.

choice theory Holds that youths will engage in delinquent and criminal behavior after weighing the consequences and benefits of their actions; delinquent behavior is a rational choice made by a motivated offender who perceives that the chances of gain outweigh any possible punishment or loss.

chronic delinquent offenders See **chronic juvenile offender.**

chronic delinquents See **chronic juvenile offender.**

chronic juvenile offender (also known as **chronic delinquent offenders, chronic delinquents,** or **chronic recidivists**) Youths who have been arrested four or more times during their minority and perpetuate a striking majority of serious criminal acts; this small group, known as the "chronic 6 percent," is believed to engage in a significant portion of all delinquent behavior; these youths do not age out of crime but continue their criminal behavior into adulthood.

chronic recidivists See **chronic juvenile offender.**

classical criminology Holds that decisions to violate the law are weighed against possible punishments and to deter crime the pain of punishment must outweigh the benefit of illegal gain; led to graduated punishments based on seriousness of the crime (let the punishment fit the crime).

cliques Small groups of friends who share intimate knowledge and confidences.

cocaine A powerful natural stimulant derived from the coca plant.

cognitive theory The branch of psychology that studies the perception of reality and the mental processes required to understand the world we live in.

college boy Strives to conform to middle-class values and to move up the social ladder but is ill-equipped to succeed and fated to become frustrated and disappointed.

commitment to conformity The strength of the ties of youths to conventional social institutions predicts their likely behavior; those with poor or negative ties are more likely to indulge in delinquent acts.

community policing Police strategy that emphasizes fear reduction, community organization, and order maintenance rather than crime fighting.

community service restitution The juvenile offender is required to assist some worthwhile community organization for a period of time.

community services Local delinquency prevention services such as recreational programs and drug and alcohol information programs in schools that help meet the community's needs for youths.

community treatment Using nonsecure and noninstitutional residences, counseling services, victim restitution programs, and other community services to treat juveniles in their own communities.

complaint Report made by the police or some other agency to the court that initiates the intake process.

concurrent jurisdiction More than one court has jurisdiction; the prosecutor then has the discretion of filing charges in either juvenile or adult court.

conditions of probation The rules and regulations mandating that a juvenile on probation behave in a particular way.

confidentiality Restricting information in juvenile court proceedings in the interest of protecting the privacy of the juvenile.

containment theory Asserts that a strong self-image insulates youths from the pressure to engage in illegal acts; youths with poor self-concepts and low self-esteem are more likely to engage in crime.

continuity of crime The idea that chronic juvenile offenders are likely to continue violating the law as adults.

control theories Suggest that many forms of delinquent behavior are attractive to all teenagers, but only those who have few social supports (through family, friends, and teachers) feel free to violate the law.

control theory Posits that delinquency results from a weakened commitment to the major social institutions (family, peers, and school); lack of such commitment allows youths to exercise antisocial behavioral choices.

co-offending Committing criminal acts in groups.

corner boy Not a delinquent but may engage in marginal behavior; eventually will marry a local girl and obtain a menial job with few prospects for advancement or success.

cottage system Housing juveniles in a compound containing a series of small cottages, each of which accommodates twenty to forty children and is run by a set of cottage parents who create a home-like atmosphere.

Court Appointed Special Advocates (CASA) Volunteers appointed by the court to investigate the needs of the child and help officers of the court ensure a safe placement for the child.

crack A highly addictive crystalline form of cocaine containing remnants of hydrochloride and sodium bicarbonate, which emits a crackling sound when smoked.

criminal atavism The idea that delinquents manifest physical anomalies that make them biologically and physiologically similar to our primitive ancestors, savage throwbacks to an earlier stage of human evolution.

critical criminologists Analysts who review historical and current developments in law and order to expose the interests of the power elite and ruling classes.

crowds Loosely organized groups who share interests and activities.

cultural deviance theory Links delinquent acts to the formation of independent subcultures with a unique set of values that clash with the mainstream culture.

cultural transmission Cultural norms and values that are passed down from one generation to the next.

culture conflict When the values of a subculture clash with those of the dominant culture.

culture of poverty View that lower-class people form a separate culture with their own values and norms, which are sometimes in conflict with conventional society.

custodial interrogation Questions posed by the police to a suspect held in custody in the prejudicial stage of the juvenile justice process; juveniles have the same rights against self-incrimination as adults do when being questioned.

dark figures of crime Incidents of crime and delinquency that go undetected by police.

degradation ceremony Going to court, being scolded by a judge, or being found delinquent after a trial are examples of public ceremonies that can transform youthful offenders by degrading their self-image.

deinstitutionalization Removing juveniles from adult jails and placing them in community-based programs to avoid the stigma attached to these facilities.

delinquency prevention programs Programs developed by the police in cooperation with social services agencies to provide needed services to juveniles.

delinquent Juvenile who has been adjudicated by a judicial officer of a juvenile court as having committed a delinquent act.

delinquent boy Adopts a set of norms and values in direct opposition to middle-class society and resists control efforts by authority figures.

desistance See **aging out.**

detached street workers Social workers who go out into the community and establish close relationships with juvenile gangs with the goal of modifying gang behavior to conform to conventional behaviors and to help gang members get jobs and educational opportunities.

detention Temporary care of a child alleged to be delinquent who requires secure custody in physically restricting facilities pending court disposition or execution of a court order.

detention hearing A hearing by a judicial officer of a juvenile court to determine whether a juvenile is to be detained or released while juvenile proceedings are pending in the case.

determinate sentence Sentence that specifies a fixed term of detention that must be served.

developmental process At different stages of the life course a variety of factors can influence behavior; factors influential at one stage of life may not be significant at a later stage.

developmental theories Assert that personal characteristics guide human development and influence behavioral choices but that these choices may change over the life course.

developmental view The view that factors present at birth and events that unfold over a person's lifetime influence behavior; developmental theory focuses on the onset, escalation, desistance, and amplification of delinquent behaviors.

differential association theory Asserts that criminal behavior is learned primarily within interpersonal groups and that youths will become delinquent if definitions they have learned favorable to violating the law exceed definitions favorable to obeying the law within that group.

differential reinforcement theory A refinement of differential association theory that asserts that behavior is shaped by the reactions of others to that behavior; youths who receive more rewards than punishments for conforming behavior will be the most likely to remain nondelinquent.

disaggregated Analyzing the relationship between two or more independent variables (such as murder convictions and death sentence) while controlling for the influence of a dependent variable (such as race).

discretion Use of personal decision making and choice in carrying out operations in the criminal justice system, such as deciding whether to make an arrest or when to accept a plea bargain.

disposition For juvenile offenders, the equivalent of sentencing for adult offenders; however, juvenile dispositions should be more rehabilitative than retributive.

disposition hearing The social service agency presents its case plan and recommendations for care of the child and treatment of the parents, including incarceration and counseling or other treatments.

diversion Officially halting or suspending a formal criminal or juvenile justice proceeding at any legally prescribed processing point after a recorded justice system entry, and referral of that person to a treatment or care program or a recommendation that the person be released.

dower system Middle Ages custom of the bride's family giving the groom monetary compensation before a marriage could take place.

drift Idea that youths move in and out of delinquency and that their lifestyles can embrace both conventional and deviant values.

dropouts Youths who leave school before completing their required program of education.

due process Basic constitutional principle based on the concept of the primacy of the individual and the complementary concept of limitation on governmental power; safeguards the individual from unfair state procedures in judicial or administrative proceedings; due process rights have been extended to juvenile trials.

egalitarian families Husband and wife share power at home; daughters gain a kind of freedom similar to that of sons and their law-violating behaviors mirror those of their brothers.

ego identity According to Erik Erikson, ego identity is formed when persons develop a firm sense of who they are and what they stand for.

electronic monitoring Active monitoring systems consist of a radio transmitter worn by the offender that sends a continuous signal to the probation department computer, alerting officials if the offender leaves his or her place of confinement; passive systems employ computer-generated random phone calls that must be responded to in a certain period of time from a particular phone or other device.

equipotentiality View that all people are equal at birth and are thereafter influenced by their environment.

evolutionary theory Explaining the existence of aggression and violent behavior as positive adaptive behaviors in human evolution; these traits allowed their bearers to reproduce disproportionately, which has had an effect on the human gene pool.

excluded offenses Offenses, some minor and others very serious, that are automatically excluded from juvenile court.

extravert A person who behaves impulsively and doesn't have the ability to examine motives and behavior.

familicide Mass murders in which a spouse and one or more children are slain.

family group homes A combination of foster care and a group home in which a juvenile is placed in a private group home run by a single family rather than by professional staff.

Federal Bureau of Investigation (FBI) Arm of the U.S. Department of Justice that investigates violations of federal law, gathers crime statistics, runs a comprehensive crime laboratory, and helps train local law enforcement officers.

feminist theory Asserts that the patriarchal social system oppresses women, creating gender bias and encouraging violence against women.

final order Order that ends litigation between two parties by determining all their rights and disposing of all the issues.

focal concerns The value orientation of lower-class culture that is characterized by a need for excitement, trouble, smartness, fate, and personal autonomy.

foot patrol Police patrolling an area by walking around the community rather than driving about in patrol cars.

foster care programs Juveniles who are orphans or whose parents cannot care for them are placed with families who provide the attention, guidance, and care they did not receive at home.

freebase Purified cocaine crystals that are crushed and smoked to provide a more powerful high than cocaine.

free will View that youths are in charge of their own destinies and are free to make personal behavior choices unencumbered by environmental factors.

gangs Groups of youths who collectively engage in delinquent behaviors.

gateway drug A substance that leads to use of more serious drugs; alcohol use has long been thought to lead to more serious drug abuse.

gender identity The gender characteristics individuals identify in their own behaviors; members of both sexes who identify with "masculine" traits are more likely to engage in delinquent acts.

gender-schema theory Asserts that our culture polarizes males and females, forcing them into exclusive gender roles of "feminine" or "masculine"; these gender scripts provide the basis for deviant behaviors.

general deterrence Crime control policies that depend on the fear of criminal penalties, such as long prison sentences for violent crimes; aim is to convince law violator that the pain outweighs the benefit of criminal activity.

gentrified The process of transforming a lower-class area into a middle-class enclave through property rehabilitation.

graffiti Inscriptions or drawings made on a wall or structure and used by delinquents for gang messages and turf definition.

group autonomy Maintaining subcultural values and attitudes that reinforce the independence of the group and separate it from other cultural groups.

group homes Nonsecured, structured residences that provide counseling, education, job training, and family living.

group therapy Counseling several individuals together in a group session; individuals can obtain support from other group members as they work through similar problems.

guardian *ad litem* A court appointed attorney who protects the interests of the child in cases involving the child's welfare.

guided group interaction (GGI) Through group interactions a delinquent can acknowledge and solve personal problems with support from other group members.

hallucinogens Natural or synthetic substances that produce vivid distortions of the senses without greatly disturbing consciousness.

hashish A concentrated form of cannabis made from unadulterated resin from the female cannabis plant.

hearsay Out-of-court statements made by one person and recounted in court by another; such statements are generally not allowed as evidence except in child abuse cases wherein a child's statements to social workers, teachers, or police may be admissible.

heroin A narcotic made from opium and then cut with sugar or some other neutral substance until it is only 1 to 4 percent pure.

house arrest An offender is required to stay at home during specific periods of time; monitoring is done by random phone calls and visits or by electronic devices.

House of Refuge A care facility developed by the child savers to protect potential criminal youths by taking them off the street and providing a family-like environment.

identity crisis Psychological state, identified by Erikson, in which youth face inner turmoil and uncertainty about life roles.

Illinois Juvenile Court Act of 1899 A major event in the history of juvenile justice, this act served as a model for other states, establishing the special status of juveniles and the emphasis on helping to treat rather than punish young offenders.

indeterminate sentence Does not specify the length of time the juvenile must be held; rather, correctional authorities decide when the juvenile is ready to return to society.

index crime See **Part I offenses.**

individual counseling Counselors help juveniles understand and solve their current adjustment problems.

individualized treatment model Each sentence must be tailored to the individual needs of the child.

inhalants Volatile liquids that give off a vapor, which is inhaled, producing short-term excitement and euphoria followed by a period of disorientation.

in loco parentis In the place of the parent; rights given to schools that allow them to assume parental duties in disciplining students.

intake Process during which a juvenile referral is received and a decision is made to file a petition in juvenile court to release the juvenile, to place the juvenile under supervision, or to refer the juvenile elsewhere.

Intensive Aftercare Program (IAP) A balanced, highly structured, comprehensive continuum of intervention for serious and violent juvenile offenders returning to the community.

interaction theory Asserts that youths' interactions with institutions and events over the life course determine criminal behavior patterns and that these patterns of behavior evolve over time.

interstitial group Delinquent group that fills a crack in the social fabric and maintains standard group practices.

intrafamily conflict An environment of discord and conflict within the family; children who grow up in dysfunctional homes often exhibit delinquent behaviors, having learned at a young age that aggression pays off.

judicial waiver When the juvenile court waives its jurisdiction over a juvenile and transfers the case to adult criminal court.

jurisdiction Every kind of judicial action; the authority of courts and judicial officers to decide cases.

juvenile court Court that has original jurisdiction over persons defined by statute as juveniles and alleged to be delinquents, status offenders, or dependents.

juvenile court judge A judge elected or appointed to preside over juvenile cases and whose decisions can only be reviewed by a judge of a higher court.

juvenile defense attorneys Represent children in juvenile court and play an active role at all stages of the proceedings.

juvenile delinquency Participation in illegal behavior by a minor who falls under a statutory age limit.

juvenile intensive probation supervision (JIPS) A true alternative to incarceration that involves almost daily supervision of the juvenile by the probation officer assigned to the case.

Juvenile Justice and Delinquency Prevention Act of 1974 This act established the OJJDP as an independent agency charged with developing and implementing programs to prevent and reduce juvenile crime.

juvenile justice process Under the paternal *(parens patriae)* philosophy, juvenile justice procedures are informal and nonadversarial, invoked *for* the juvenile offender rather than *against* him or her; a petition instead of a complaint is filed; courts make findings of involvement or adjudication of delinquency instead of convictions; and juvenile offenders receive dispositions instead of sentences.

Juvenile Justice Reform Act of 1977 A Washington state statute that created mandatory sentencing for juvenile offenders based on their age, the crime, and their prior history as an offender.

juvenile justice system The segment of the justice system including law enforcement officers, the courts, and correctional agencies, designed to treat youthful offenders.

juvenile officers Police officers who specialize in dealing with juvenile offenders; they may operate alone or as part of a juvenile police unit within the department.

juvenile probation officer Officer of the court involved in all four stages of the court process—intake, predisposition, postadjudication, and postdisposition—who assists the court and supervises juveniles placed on probation.

juvenile prosecutor Government attorney responsible for representing the interests of the state and bringing the case against the accused juvenile.

klikas Subgroups of same-aged youths in Hispanic gangs that remain together and have separate names and a unique identity within the gang.

labeling theory Posits that society creates deviance through a system of social control agencies that designate (or label) certain individuals as delinquent, thereby stigmatizing youths and encouraging them to accept this negative personal identity.

latchkey children Children left unsupervised after school by working parents.

latent delinquents Youths whose troubled family life leads them to seek immediate gratification without consideration of right and wrong or the feelings of others.

law enforcement The primary duty of all police officers to fight crime and keep the peace.

Law Enforcement Assistance Administration (LEAA) Unit in the U.S. Department of Justice established by the Omnibus Crime Control and Safe Streets Act of 1968 to administer grants and provide guidance for crime prevention policy and programs.

learning disability (LD) Neurological dysfunction that prevents an individual from learning to his or her potential.

learning theory Posits that delinquency is learned through close relationships with others; asserts that children are born "good" and learn to be "bad" from others.

least detrimental alternative Choosing a program for the child that will best foster a child's growth and development.

least restrictive alternative Choosing a program with the least restrictive or secure setting that will benefit the child.

left realism Asserts that crime is a function of relative deprivation and that criminals prey on the poor.

legalization of drugs Decriminalizing drug use to reduce the association between drug use and crime.

liberal feminism Asserts that females are less delinquent than males because their social roles provide them with fewer opportunities to commit crimes; as the roles of girls and women become more similar to those of boys and men, so too will their crime patterns.

lifestyle violent juveniles Juveniles who become more violent when exposed to more serious offenders in institutions.

longitudinal studies A research design that entails repeated measures over time; for example, a cohort may be measured at several points over their life course to determine risk factors for chronic offending.

low-visibility decision making Decisions made by public officials in the criminal or juvenile justice system that the public is not in a position to understand, regulate, or criticize.

mandatory sentence Sentence is defined by a statutory requirement that states the penalty to be set for all cases of a specific offense.

marijuana The dried leaves of the cannabis plant.

Marxist feminists See **radical feminists.**

masculinity hypothesis View that women who commit crimes have biological and psychological traits similar to those of men.

meta-analysis An analysis technique that synthesizes results across many programs over time.

middle-class measuring rods Standards by which teachers and other representatives of state authority evaluate students' behavior; when lower-class youths cannot meet these standards they are subject to failure, which brings on frustration and anger at conventional society.

milieu therapy All aspects of the environment are part of the treatment, and meaningful change, increased growth, and satisfactory adjustment are encouraged; this is often accomplished through peer pressure to conform to the group norms.

minimal brain dysfunction (MBD) Damage to the brain itself that causes antisocial behavior injurious to the individual's lifestyle and social adjustment.

***Miranda* warning** Supreme Court decisions require police officers to inform individuals under arrest of their constitutional rights; warnings must also be given when suspicion begins to focus on an individual in the accusatory stage.

Missouri Plan Sets out how juvenile court judges are chosen and specifies that a commission should nominate candidates, an elected official should make the appointment, and the incumbent judge should run uncontested on his or her record in a nonpartisan election, usually every three years.

monetary restitution A requirement that juvenile offenders compensate crime victims for out-of-pocket losses caused by the crime, including property damage, lost wages, and medical expenses.

moral entrepreneurs Interest groups that attempt to control social life by promoting their own personal set of moral values and establishing them as law.

multisystemic treatment (MST) Addresses a variety of family, peer, and psychological problems by focusing on problem solving and communication skills training.

National Advisory Commission on Criminal Justice Standards and Goals Established in 1973, the commission's report identified major strategies for juvenile justice and delinquency prevention.

National Council of Juvenile and Family Court Judges An organization that sponsors research and continuing legal education to help juvenile court judges master their field of expertise.

natural areas for crime Inner-city areas of extreme poverty where the critical social control mechanisms have broken down.

nature theory Holds that low intelligence is genetically determined and inherited.

near groups Relatively unstructured short-term groups with fluid membership.

negative affective states Anger, depression, disappointment, fear, and other adverse emotions that derive from strain.

neglect Passive neglect by a parent or guardian, depriving children of food, shelter, health care, and love.

neuroticism A personality trait marked by unfounded anxiety, tension, and emotional instability.

neutralization theory Holds that youths adhere to conventional values while "drifting" into periods of illegal behavior; for drift to occur, youths must first neutralize conventional legal and moral values.

nonresidential programs Juveniles remain in their own homes but receive counseling, education, employment, diagnostic, and casework services through an intensive support system.

nuclear family A family unit composed of parents and their children; this smaller family structure is subject to great stress due to the intense, close contact between parents and children.

nurture theory Holds that intelligence is partly biological but mostly sociological; negative environmental factors encourage delinquent behavior and depress intelligence scores for many youths.

Office of Juvenile Justice and Delinquency Prevention (OJJDP) Branch of the U.S. Justice Department charged with shaping national juvenile justice policy through disbursement of federal aid and research funds.

parens patriae Power of the state to act in behalf of the child and provide care and protection equivalent to that of a parent.

parole guidelines Recommended length of confinement and kinds of aftercare assistance most effective for a juvenile who committed a specific offense.

Part I offenses (also known as **index crimes**) Offenses including homicide and nonnegligent manslaughter, forcible rape, robbery, aggravated assault, burglary, larceny, arson, and motor vehicle theft; recorded by local law enforcement officers, these crimes are tallied quarterly and sent to the FBI for inclusion in the UCR.

Part II offenses All crimes other than Part I offenses; recorded by local law enforcement officers, arrests for these crimes are tallied quarterly and sent to the FBI for inclusion in the UCR.

passive speech A form of expression protected by the First Amendment but not associated with actually speaking words; examples include wearing symbols or protest messages on buttons or signs.

paternalism hypothesis See **chivalry hypothesis.**

paternalistic family A family style wherein the father is the final authority on all family matters and exercises complete control over his wife and children.

peacemakers Assert that peace and humanism can reduce crime and offers a new approach to crime control through mediation.

petition Document filed in juvenile court alleging that a juvenile is a delinquent, a status offender, or a dependent and asking that the court assume jurisdiction over the juvenile.

plea bargaining The exchange of prosecutorial and judicial concessions for a guilty plea by the accused; plea bargaining usually results in a reduced charge or a more lenient sentence.

pledge system Early English system in which neighbors protected each other from thieves and warring groups.

Poor Laws English statutes that allowed the courts to appoint overseers over destitute and neglected children, allowing placement of these children as servants in the homes of the affluent.

Positive Peer Culture (PPC) Counseling program in which peer leaders encourage other group members to modify their behavior and peers help reinforce acceptable behaviors.

power-control theory Holds that gender differences in the delinquency rate are a function of class differences and economic conditions that influence the structure of family life.

precocious sexuality Sexual experimentation in early adolescence.

predatory crimes Violent crimes against persons and crimes in which an offender attempts to steal an object directly from its holder.

predispositional investigation An investigation usually carried out by a member of the probationary staff to acquire information about the child that will allow the judge to make a decision in the best interest of the child.

predisposition report See **social investigation report.**

President's Commission on Law Enforcement and the Administration of Justice This 1967 commission suggested that we must provide juveniles with opportunities for success, including jobs and education, and that we must develop effective law enforcement procedures to control hard core youthful offenders.

prestige crimes Stealing or assaulting someone to gain prestige in the neighborhood; often part of gang initiation rites.

pretrial conference The attorney for the social services agency presents an overview of the case and a plea bargain or negotiated settlement can be agreed to in a consent decree.

preventive detention Keeping the accused in custody prior to trial because the accused is suspected of being a danger to the community.

primary deviance Deviant acts that do not redefine the self- and public image of the offender.

primary sociopaths Individuals with an inherited trait that predisposes them to antisocial behavior.

primogeniture Middle Ages practice of allowing only the family's eldest son to inherit lands and titles.

probable cause Reasonable ground to believe the existence of facts that an offense was committed and that the accused committed that offense.

probation Nonpunitive, legal disposition of juveniles emphasizing community treatment in which the juvenile is closely supervised by an officer of the court and must adhere to a strict set of rules to avoid incarceration.

problem behavior syndrome (PBS) Convergence of a variety of psychological problems and family dysfunctions including substance abuse and criminality.

Project DARE An elementary school drug abuse resistance education program designed to prevent teenage drug abuse by giving youths the skills they need to resist peer pressure to experiment with drugs.

prosecutorial discretion Allowing the prosecutor to determine the jurisdiction by selecting the charge to be filed or by choosing to file the complaint in either juvenile or adult court.

psychodynamic theory Branch of psychology that holds that the human personality is controlled by unconscious mental processes developed early in childhood.

psychopathic personality (also known as **sociopathic personality**) A person lacking in warmth and affection, exhibiting inappropriate behavior responses, and unable to learn from experience.

psychotherapy Highly structured counseling in which a skilled therapist helps a juvenile solve conflicts and make a more positive adjustment to society.

public defender An attorney who works in a public agency or under private contractual agreement as defense counsel to indigent defendants.

radical feminists (also known as **Marxist feminists**) Hold that gender inequality stems from the unequal power of men and women and the subsequent exploitation of women by men; the cause of female delinquency originates with the onset of male supremacy and the efforts of males to control females' sexuality.

reaction formation Rejecting conventional goals and standards that seem impossible to attain.

reality therapy A form of counseling that emphasizes current behavior and that requires the individual to accept responsibility for all of his or her actions.

reflective role-taking A process whereby youths take on antisocial roles assigned to them by others.

reform schools Institutions in which educational and psychological services are used in an effort to improve the conduct of juveniles who are forcibly detained.

relative deprivation Condition that exists when people of wealth and poverty live in close proximity to one another; the relatively deprived are apt to have feelings of anger and hostility, which may produce criminal behavior.

removal See **waiver.**

representing Tossing or flashing gang signs in the presence of rivals, often escalating into a verbal or physical confrontation.

residential programs Placement of a juvenile offender in a residential, nonsecure facility such as a group home, foster home, family group home, or rural home where the juvenile can be closely monitored and develop close relationships with staff members.

restorative justice Nonpunitive strategies for dealing with juvenile offenders that make the justice system a healing process rather than a punishment process.

retreatists Gangs whose members actively engage in substance abuse.

review hearing Periodic meetings to determine whether the conditions of the case plan for an abused child are being met by the parents or guardians of the child.

right to treatment Philosophy espoused by many courts that juvenile offenders have a statutory right to treatment while under the jurisdiction of the courts.

role conflicts Conflicts police officers face that revolve around the requirement to perform their primary duty of law enforcement and a desire to aid in rehabilitating youthful offenders.

role diffusion According to Erik Erikson, role diffusion occurs when youths spread themselves too thin, experience personal uncertainty, and place themselves at the mercy of leaders who promise to give them a sense of identity they cannot develop for themselves.

routine activities theory View that crime is a "normal" function of the routine activities of modern living; offenses can be expected if there is a motivated offender and a suitable target that is not protected by capable guardians.

rural programs Specific recreational and work opportunities provided for juveniles in a rural setting such as a forestry camp, a farm, or a ranch.

school failure Failing to achieve success in school can result in frustration, anger, and reduced self-esteem, which may contribute to delinquent behavior.

search and seizure The U.S. Constitution protects citizens from any search and seizure by police without a lawfully obtained search warrant; such warrants are issued when there is probable cause to believe that an offense has been committed.

secondary deviance Deviant acts that redefine the offender's self- and public image, forming the basis for the youth's self-concept.

secondary prevention (also known as **special prevention**) Psychological counseling, psychotropic medications, and other rehabilitation treatment programs designed to prevent repeat offenses.

secondary sociopaths Individuals who are biologically normal but exhibit antisocial behavior due to negative life experiences.

sedatives Drugs of the barbiturate family that depress the central nervous system into a sleep-like condition.

self-control Ability to control impulsive and often imprudent behaviors that offer immediate short-term gratification.

self-fulfilling prophecy Deviant behavior patterns that are a response to an earlier labeling experience; youths act out these social roles even if they were falsely bestowed.

self-reports Questionnaire or survey technique that asks subjects to reveal their own participation in delinquent or criminal acts.

shelter care A place for temporary care of children in physically unrestricting facilities.

skinhead Member of white supremacist gang, identified by a shaved skull and Nazi or Ku Klux Klan markings.

social bond Ties a person to the institutions and processes of society; elements of the bond include attachment, commitment, involvement, and belief.

social conflict theory Asserts that society is in a state of constant internal conflict, and focuses on the role of social and governmental institutions as mechanisms for social control.

social control Ability of social institutions to influence human behavior; the justice system is the primary agency of formal social control.

social development model (SDM) An array of personal, psychological, and community-level risk factors that make some children susceptible to development of antisocial behaviors.

social disorganization Neighborhood or area marked by culture conflict, lack of cohesiveness, a transient population, and insufficient social organizations; these problems are reflected in the problems at schools in these areas.

social disorganization theory Posits that delinquency is a product of the social forces existing in inner-city, low-income areas.

social ecology Theory focuses attention on the influence social institutions have on individual behavior and suggests that law-violating behavior is a response to social rather than individual forces operating in an urban environment.

social investigation report (also known as **predisposition report**) Developed by the juvenile probation officer, this report consists of a clinical diagnosis of the juvenile and his or her need for court assistance, relevant environmental and personality factors, and any other information that would assist the court in developing a treatment plan for the juvenile.

socialization The process of learning the values and norms of the society or the subculture to which the individual belongs.

social learning theory The view that behavior is modeled through observation either directly through intimate contact with others or indirectly through media; interactions that are rewarded are copied, whereas those that are punished are avoided.

social process theories Posit that the interactions a person has with key elements of the socialization process determine his or her future behavior.

social structure theories Explain delinquency using socioeconomic conditions and cultural values.

Society for the Prevention of Cruelty to Children (SPCC) First established in 1874, these organizations protected children subjected to cruelty and neglect at home or at school.

sociopathic personality See **psychopathic personality.**

somatotype school Argued that delinquents manifest distinct physiques that make then susceptible to particular types of delinquent behavior.

special prevention See **secondary prevention.**

specific deterrence Sending convicted offenders to secure incarceration facilities so that punishment is severe enough to convince offenders not to repeat their criminal activity.

spontaneous remission See **aging out.**

status offense Conduct that is illegal only because the child is under age.

stimulants Synthetic substances that produce an intense physical reaction by stimulating the central nervous system.

strain theory Links delinquency to the strain of being locked out of the economic mainstream, which creates the anger and frustration that lead to delinquent acts.

stratification Grouping society into classes based on the unequal distribution of scarce resources.

subculture of violence An identified urban-based subculture in which young males are expected to respond with violence to the slightest provocation.

subcultures Groups that are loosely part of the dominant culture but that maintain a unique set of values, beliefs, and traditions.

substance abuse Using drugs or alcohol in such a way as to cause physical harm to yourself.

subterranean values The ability of youthful law violators to repress social norms.

suppression effect A reduction of the number of arrests per year for youths who have been incarcerated or otherwise punished.

TOP program Police and community prevention effort in which teens are hired to patrol the city's parks and recreation areas.

totality of the circumstances doctrine Legal doctrine that mandates that a decision maker consider all the issues and circumstances of a case before judging the outcome; the suspect's age, intelligence, and competency may be issues that influence his or her understanding and judgment.

tracking Dividing students into groups according to their ability and achievement levels.

trait theory Holds that youths engage in delinquent or criminal behavior due to aberrant physical or psychological traits that govern behavioral choices; delinquent actions are impulsive or instinctual rather than rational choices.

tranquilizers Drugs that reduce anxiety and promote relaxation.

transfer hearing Preadjudicatory hearing in juvenile court for the purpose of determining whether juvenile court should be retained over a juvenile or waived and the juvenile transferred to adult court for prosecution.

transfer process Transferring a juvenile offender from the jurisdiction of juvenile court to adult criminal court.

transitional neighborhood Area undergoing a shift in population and structure, usually from middle-class residential to lower-class mixed use.

trial *de novo* A review procedure in which there is a complete retrial of the original case.

truancy Staying out of school without permission.

underachievers Those who do not achieve success in school at the level of their expectations.

underclass Group of urban poor whose members have little chance of upward mobility or improvement.

Uniform Crime Report (UCR) Compiled by the FBI, the UCR is the most widely used source of national crime and delinquency statistics.

utilitarians Those who believe that people weigh the benefits and consequences of their future actions before deciding on a course of behavior.

victimizations The number of people who are victims of criminal acts; young teens are fifteen times more likely than older adults (age 65 and over) to be victims of crimes.

victim service restitution The juvenile offender is required to provide some service directly to the crime victim.

Violent Crime Control and Law Enforcement Act of 1994 This act made available increased funding for juvenile justice and delinquency prevention.

Violent Juvenile Offender (VJO) program Specialized programs in small, secure settings where youths are gradually reintegrated into the community with intensive supervision.

waiver (also known as **bindover** or **removal**) Term used to indicate the transfer process has been approved and the juvenile is under the jurisdiction of the adult criminal court.

waiver process Transferring legal jurisdiction over the most serious and experienced juvenile offenders to the adult court for criminal prosecution.

watch system Replaced the pledge system in England; watchmen patrolled urban areas at night to provide protection from harm.

wayward minors Early legal designation of youths who violate the law because of their minority status; now referred to as status offenders.

widening the net Phenomenon that occurs when programs created to divert youths from the justice system actually involve them more deeply in the official process.

wilderness probation Programs involving outdoor expeditions that provide opportunities for juveniles to confront the difficulties of their lives while achieving positive personal satisfaction.

writ of certiorari Order of a superior court requesting that the record of an inferior court (or administrative body) be brought forward for review or inspection.

writ of habeus corpus Judicial order requesting that a person detaining another produce the body of the prisoner and give reasons for his or her capture and detention.

zero tolerance policy Mandating specific consequences or punishments for delinquent acts and not allowing anyone to avoid these consequences.

Appendix
Excerpts from the U.S. Constitution

AMENDMENT I (1791)

Congress shall make no law respecting an establishment of religion, or prohibiting the free exercise thereof; or abridging the freedom of speech, or of the press; or the right of the people peaceably to assemble, and to petition the government for a redress of grievances.

AMENDMENT II (1791)

A well regulated militia, being necessary to their security of a free state, the right of the people to keep and bear arms, shall not be infringed.

AMENDMENT III (1791)

No soldier shall, in time of peace, be quartered in any house, without the consent of the owner, nor in time of war, but in a manner to be prescribed by law.

AMENDMENT IV (1791)

The right of the people to be secure in their persons, houses, papers, and effects, against unreasonable searches and seizures, shall not be violated, and no warrants shall issue, but upon probable cause, supported by oath or affirmation, and particularly describing the place to be searched, and the persons or things to be seized.

AMENDMENT V (1791)

No person shall be held to answer for a capital, or otherwise infamous, crime unless on a presentment or indictment of a grand jury, except in cases arising in the land or naval forces, or in the militia, when in actual service in time of war or public danger; nor shall any person be subject for the same offense to be twice put in jeopardy of life or limb; nor shall be compelled in any criminal case to be a witness against himself, nor be deprived of life, liberty, or property; without due process of law; nor shall private property be taken for public use without just compensation.

AMENDMENT VI (1791)

In all criminal prosecutions, the accused shall enjoy the right to a speedy and public trial, by an impartial jury of the state and district wherein the crime shall have been committed, which district shall have been previously ascertained by law, and to be informed of the nature and cause of the accusation; to be confronted with the witnesses against him; to have compulsory process for obtaining witnesses in his favor, and to have the assistance of counsel for his defense.

AMENDMENT VII (1791)

In suits at common law, where the value in controversy shall exceed twenty dollars, the right of trial by jury shall be preserved, and no fact tried by a jury shall be otherwise reexamined in any court of the United States, than according to the rules of common law.

AMENDMENT VIII (1791)

Excessive bail shall not be required, nor excessive fines imposed, nor cruel and unusual punishment inflicted.

AMENDMENT IX (1791)

The enumeration in the Constitution of certain rights shall not be construed to deny or disparage others retained by the people.

AMENDMENT X (1791)

The powers not delegated to the United States by the Constitution, nor prohibited by it to the states, are reserved to the states respectively, or to the people.

AMENDMENT XIV (1868)

Section I. All persons born or naturalized in the United States, and subject to the jurisdiction thereof, are citizens of the United States and of the state wherein they reside. No state shall make or enforce any law which abridge the privilege or immunities of citizens of the United States; nor shall any state deprive any person of life, liberty, or property, without due process of law; nor deny to any person within its jurisdiction the equal protection of the laws.

Table of Cases

Name Index

Subject Index

Amsterdam, 30
Anabolic steroids, 402
Androgens, 94, 253–254
Anesthetics, 400
Anglo Americans. *See* Whites
Anomie theory, 145–148, 159, 347
Antisocial behavior
  attention deficit hyperactivity disorder
    and, 97
  biochemical factors and, 93
  bullying and, 377
  in communities, 378
  developmental theories and, 186
  differential association theory and, 172
  dropouts and, 369
  drug abuse and, 418
  evolutionary theory and, 101
  families and, 279–280, 283
  gangs and, 347
  gender and, 252–255
  general strain theory and, 149, 150
  general theory of crime and, 184
  genetic influences and, 99, 100
  Hirschi's control theory and, 178, 179
  hormonal levels and, 94, 253–254
  individual theory and, 80, 115
  information processing and, 109
  labeling theory and, 215, 218, 219
  learning disabilities and, 96
  mentoring programs and, 501
  multiple pathways and, 189
  offense specialization and, 191
  parenting skills and, 310
  peer relations and, 320–321
  problem behavior syndrome and, 189–190
  psychodynamic theory and, 104–105
  psychological theories and, 101
  school failure and, 364
  self-enhancement theory and, 178
  social development model and, 191, 192,
    193
  social disorganization theory and, 143
  social process theories and, 166
  television and, 107
  trait theory and, 79
Antisocial personality disorder (ASPD),
  111–112, 410
Anti-Violent Crime Initiative (AVCI), 351
Appellate process, 575–577, 604
Apprenticeship movement, 16–17, 18, 478
Area studies, 135–138
Arkansas, 216–217, 300
Arousal theory, 97–98, 111–112
Arrest, 480, 509
Arrest procedure, 480–481, 490, 491, 492
ASET (After School Education Training), 233
Asia, 293, 415
Asian Americans, 132–133, 341, 344–345
ASPD (antisocial personality disorder),
  111–112, 410
Associated Marine Institutes (AMI), 650–651
At-risk youths
  adolescent risk-taking behavior and,
    10–11, 21, 185
  dropouts and, 8–9, 387
  families and, 8, 309
  juvenile delinquency and, 78
  mentoring program and, 500–501

problems of, 8–9
  single-parent households and, 8, 55
  treatment for, 31
Atlanta, Georgia, 43
ATP (Adolescent Transitions Program), 310
Attachment, 178, 180, 181, 281–282
Attention deficit hyperactivity disorder
  (ADHD), 96–97, 111, 286
Australia, 322, 396
Authority conflict pathway, 189, 190
AVCI (Anti-Violent Crime Initiative), 351
Awaiting Disposition of the Court (ADC) unit,
  515

B

Bail, 525–527
Balanced probation, 605, 609–610
Balancing-of-the-interest approach, 302
Baltic states, 293
Bangladesh, 293
Barbiturates, 401
Barrios, 324, 330, 342–343
Battered child syndrome, 287–288
Beacon Community Center Program, 199–200
Behavior modification, 644
Behavioral theory
  differential reinforcement theory and, 173
  general strain theory and, 150
  psychological theories and, 102, 105–108,
    110
Behaviorism, 105
Belief, 179, 180, 181
Berkeley, California, 478
Berlin, 30
Best interests of the child, 20, 550, 557
Bethel, Alaska, 371
Bethesda Day Treatment Center Program,
  621
Bias, 493–497, 499, 613
Bifurcated hearings, 453, 564, 572
Big Brother/Big Sister, 460, 500
Bindover, 530–531, 668
Biochemical factors, 93–94, 101
Biological theory, 250–251
Biosocial theory
  biochemical factors and, 93–94, 101
  child abuse and, 92, 299
  delinquency prevention and, 116, 117
  education and, 361
  equipotentiality and, 92
  evolutionary theory and, 100–101
  gender and, 251–253
  genetic influences and, 98–100, 101
  neurological dysfunction and, 94–98, 101
  punishment and, 90
Birth cohort studies, 60–63
Blackboard Jungle, 325
Blacks. *See* African Americans
Blackville, South Carolina, 371
Blended families, 280
Blended sentencing, 583
Boca Raton, Florida, 43
Bolivia, 419
Boot camps, 648–653
Border control, 419
Boston, Massachusetts
  Boston's Mid-City Project, 157
  child savers movement in, 436

community-based treatment programs
    and, 615
  gangs and, 330, 338, 341, 344, 351
  nature theory and, 113
  police and, 478
  Society for the Prevention of Cruelty to
    Children and, 441
Boyz N the Hood, 322
Broken homes, 258–259, 279–282, 283
Broward County, Florida, 517
Buffalo, New York, 341
Bulgaria, 362
Bullying, 286, 375, 376–377
Bureau of Justice Statistics, 65, 69
Burnouts, 415
Business Entrepreneur Club, 640

C

California
  African Americans and, 494
  child abuse and, 302
  detention and, 512
  drug abuse and, 403, 420
  education and, 362
  forestry camps and, 630–631
  gangs and, 330, 344
  juvenile aftercare and, 658
  juvenile institutions and, 634, 635
  residential community treatment and, 617
California Youth Authority, 63
Cambodian youths, 341
Cambridge Study in Delinquent Development,
  187
Cambridge Youth Survey, 286
Cambridge-Somerville Youth Study, 116
Canada, 377, 396
Capable guardians, 83–84
Capital Offender Program (COP), 648
Capital punishment, 584–585. *See also* Death
  penalty
CAPTA (Child Abuse Prevention and Treat-
  ment Act), 299
Carnegie Corporation, 382
CASA (Center for Addiction and Substance
  Abuse), 375–378
CASA (Court Appointed Special Advocates),
  454, 561
CCTV (closed-circuit television), 303–304, 305
Center for Addiction and Substance Abuse
  (CASA), 375–378
Center for the Future of Children, 581
Center for Research on Women, 264
Centers for Disease Control (CDC), 7, 10–11
Chancery court, 16, 17–18, 438
Chicago, Illinois
  area studies and, 135–137
  curfews and, 501
  gangs and, 324, 326, 327, 329, 330, 331,
    342, 348, 350, 352
  immigrants and, 134
  juvenile courts and, 434
  nature theory and, 113
  violence and, 142
Chicago Area Project, 138, 157, 650
Chicago Bar Association, 22
Chicago Housing Authority, 126
Chicago Intervention Network, 352
Chicago Reform School, 441

Russia, 30, 293
Russian Revolution, 347
RYDS (Rochester Youth Development Study), 338–339, 348

S

St. Louis, Missouri, 339
Samoans, 341, 344
San Diego, California, 280, 329, 417
San Francisco, California, 341, 344, 514, 517
Saudi Arabia, 585
Scandinavia, 376–377
Scavenger gangs, 329
Schizophrenia, 95, 104, 105, 297
School crime. *See also* Juvenile crime
    drug abuse and, 375–378
    juvenile delinquency and, 12
    reduction of, 378–382
    search and seizure and, 485
    social disorganization theory and, 378
    statistics on, 370, 371, 372–378
    victimization and, 67, 378, 380
    weapons and, 370, 372, 377, 378, 487, 582
School Crime Victimization Survey, 370, 372–374
School failure. *See also* Dropouts
    at-risk youths and, 8
    biosocial theory and, 92
    causes of, 364–368
    drug abuse and, 397, 418
    juvenile delinquency and, 360, 362, 363, 364
    labeling theory and, 218
    school failure rationale, 95
Scream, 107
Scream II, 107
SDM (social development model), 191–195
Search and seizure, 481–487
Seattle, Washington, 50, 309, 344
Seattle Social Development Project, 192, 384
Secondary deviance, 214–215, 220
Secondary prevention, 116
Secondary sociopaths, 112
Sedatives, 401
Segmentalization, 135
Self-concept, 177, 214, 245
Self-control
    gender and, 244, 245
    general theory of crime and, 182–185
    juvenile institutions and, 642
    school failure and, 364
Self-enhancement theory, 177–178
Self-fulfilling prophecy, 213, 366
Self-incrimination, 21
Self-labeling, 211, 214
Self-rejection, 213
Self-report data
    age and, 57
    alcohol use and, 48, 396
    bullying and, 377
    chronic offenders and, 63
    drug abuse and, 38, 47, 48, 50, 396, 397
    education and, 46, 47, 363
    families and, 47, 280, 282, 284–285
    gender and, 38, 47, 52, 248, 262
    Hirschi's control theory and, 179
    juvenile delinquency and, 38, 46–50

learning disabilities and, 96
race and, 38, 47, 53–54, 55
social class and, 47, 56, 131, 138
validation of, 49–50
violence and, 142
Sensorimotor stage, 108
Sentencing
    classical criminology and, 80
    defense attorneys and, 562, 563
    detention and, 510
    disposition and, 453, 572
    future of, 579–580, 582–583, 668
    history of, 434
    juvenile justice process and, 577–585
    juvenile records and, 587
    rehabilitation and, 583
    restitution and, 610
    of status offenders, 445
    types of, 433
Serious delinquent gangs, 329
Settlement houses, 319, 435
Seven, 30
Sex Pistols, 345
Sexual abuse
    child abuse and, 289, 290–291, 294, 304, 305, 308
    detention and, 515
    gender and, 245, 259, 264, 639
    prostitution and, 291, 293
Sexual harassment, 264
Sexuality
    adolescent risk-taking and, 10
    at-risk youths and, 8
    dower system and, 14
    gangs and, 333
    gender and, 250, 252, 258, 259, 264, 265–268
    juvenile delinquency and, 29–30
    juvenile justice system and, 445
    personality characteristics and, 111
    psychodynamic theory and, 103
    social class and, 257
    statutory rape laws and, 26–27
    teenage birthrates and, 10
Sexually transmitted diseases, 30, 252, 292
Shelter care, 510, 518, 519, 628
Shock programs, 649
Siblings, 286, 411
Silence of the Lambs, 30
Silverlake experiment, 617–618
Single-parent households. *See also* Families; Parents
    at-risk youths and, 8, 55
    child abuse and, 296, 298
    child care and, 11
    detention and, 513
    family makeup and, 276, 282
    juvenile crime rate and, 44, 45
    labeling theory and, 218
    persistent juvenile delinquency and, 59
    poverty and, 129
    school crime and, 381
    social ecology and, 139
Situational crime prevention, 87–88, 89
Situational factors, 493, 499
Sixth Amendment, 566, 570, 571
Skinheads, 345, 347
Slovak Republic, 362

Social adaptations, 146–148
Social bond
    general theory of crime and, 182–183
    Hirschi's control theory and, 177, 178–179, 180, 181
    interactional theory and, 194–196
    social development model and, 192
Social capital, 198
Social class
    adolescent risk-taking and, 11
    anomie theory and, 148
    arrest procedures and, 492
    child abuse and, 297–299
    child savers movement and, 435–436, 437
    crime data and, 43
    delinquent subculture theory and, 155
    detention and, 513
    differential association theory and, 170, 172–173
    disciplining parents and, 26
    dropouts and, 369
    drug abuse and, 408, 410
    education and, 360, 361, 362, 367–368
    focal concerns and, 153, 154
    gangs and, 324, 329, 345, 346
    gender and, 257, 264–265, 266
    Head Start and, 200
    Hirschi's control theory and, 180
    interactional theory and, 194
    juvenile delinquency and, 55–56, 60, 113
    labeling theory and, 218, 219
    middle-class measuring rods, 155
    peer relations and, 320
    police department policies and, 496–497
    school failure and, 364–365
    self-report data and, 47, 56, 131, 138
    sexuality and, 257
    social conflict theory and, 223, 224, 225
    social reaction theories and, 210
    strain theory and, 134, 144
    stratification and, 129
    tracking and, 367
    underclass, 54, 56, 128, 140, 154, 329, 348, 418, 436
Social conditions
    biosocial theory and, 92
    child abuse and, 294
    choice theory and, 81
    gender and, 252, 263
    individual theory and, 117
    juvenile crime rates and, 44–45
    juvenile delinquency and, 55, 78
    personality characteristics and, 278–279
    poverty and, 127–128
    race and, 54
    social conflict theory and, 220, 222
    social reaction theories and, 208–209
    urban decay and, 126–127
Social conflict theory
    approach of, 234
    branches of, 222–223
    and critical criminology, 220–222
    delinquency prevention and, 228
    education and, 361
    elements of, 223–225
    feminist theory and, 226
    left realism and, 226–227
    peacemaking and, 227–228

Victimization (*continued*)
  school crime and, 67, 378, 380
  social class and, 130
  social disorganization theory and, 141
  in United States, 66
  victim data, 38, 57, 64–70
  victim surveys and, 64–65
  victims' rights and, 32
  young victims and, 66–67
Victims of Child Abuse Act of 1990, 304
Vietnamese gangs, 344
Violence
  adolescent death and, 10
  adolescent risk-taking and, 11
  African Americans and, 55
  arousal theory and, 98
  biochemical factors and, 93
  biosocial theory and, 93
  birth cohort studies and, 62, 63
  child abuse and, 274, 277, 294, 296, 297
  discretionary justice and, 494
  dropouts and, 369
  drug abuse and, 44
  economic conditions and, 44
  education and, 367, 368, 487, 579
  evolutionary theory and, 100
  families and, 282, 285
  gangs and, 319, 322, 325, 327, 328, 329,
    332, 339–340, 344, 347, 416
  gender and, 51, 52, 142, 248–249,
    254–255, 264
  general deterrence and, 85
  general strain theory and, 149, 150
  hopelessness and, 142
  hormonal levels and, 94
  individual theory and, 80
  information processing and, 109
  juvenile courts and, 581
  juvenile crime and, 433, 459, 465,
    476–477, 529, 665
  juvenile delinquency and, 12, 29
  juvenile institutions and, 616, 619, 620,
    627, 638, 647
  juvenile offenders and, 665
  juvenile/police encounters and, 475
  left realism and, 226
  media and, 107–108
  Middle Ages and, 15
  neighborhood violence programs, 500
  neurological dysfunction and, 94, 95
  official delinquency and, 41, 42
  parents and, 164
  personality characteristics and, 111
  prevention of, 454
  prostitution and, 292
  psychodynamic theory and, 102, 105

  radical feminism and, 224
  school crime and, 370, 374
  self-report data and, 142
  sexual abuse and, 308
  social conditions and, 45
  social disorganization theory and, 141
  social ecology and, 140
  social learning theory and, 106
  subculture of, 153, 154
  subcultures and, 152
  television and, 6, 30, 106–108
  transfer process and, 532
  victimization and, 67
  weapons and, 665
Violent Crime Control and Law Enforcement
  Act of 1994 (PL. 103-322), 454, 463, 465,
  552
Violent Juvenile Offender (VJO) program,
  647–648, 658
Virginia, 18, 26, 306, 658
VisionQuest, 650
VJO (Violent Juvenile Offender) program,
  647–648, 658
Vocational training
  community-based treatment programs
    and, 596
  conditions of probation and, 604
  juvenile institutions and, 630, 645, 646,
    653

W

Waiver process. *See also* Transfer process
  adult legal jurisdictions and, 21, 32, 86
  chronic offenders and, 647
  definition of, 21
  general deterrence and, 86
  juvenile justice strategies and, 462
  juvenile justice system and, 454
  plea bargaining and, 529
  sentencing and, 582
  totality of the circumstances doctrine and,
    488
  use of, 668
Washington, 25, 362, 579
Washington, D.C.
  disciplining parents and, 26
  drug abuse and, 396, 407, 417, 425
  judicial waiver and, 531, 532–534
  juvenile institutions and, 634
  plea bargaining and, 530
Watch system, 478
Wayne County Intensive Probation Program,
  605, 606
Wayward minors, 22
Weapons
  adolescent risk-taking and, 10

  ban of, 582–583
  gangs and, 326–327, 342–343, 344
  gender and, 248–249
  gun control programs, 462
  juvenile crime rates and, 45, 46, 459
  race and, 53
  school crime and, 370, 372, 377, 378, 487,
    582
  violence and, 665
Weeks School, 615
West Paducah, Kentucky, 370, 371
West Side Story, 322, 325
West Virginia, 556, 582
Westboro, Massachusetts, 438
Western House of Refuge, 438
Westinghouse Learning Corporation, 200
Wet nurses, 14
White Conference on Juvenile Justice, 465
Whites
  adjudication and, 565
  birth cohort studies and, 62
  correctional agencies and, 455
  detention and, 511, 513, 516
  discretionary justice and, 493–494
  disposition and, 564
  drug abuse and, 552
  families and, 282
  gangs and, 341, 345
  juvenile delinquency and, 53–54
  juvenile institutions and, 638
  poverty and, 132–133
  social class and, 56
  status offenders and, 519
  tracking and, 367
Wickersham commission of 1931, 478
Widening the net, 32, 229, 425, 519, 523–524,
  613, 649
The Wild Ones, 325
Wilderness probation, 608
Wisconsin, 23, 300
Workhouses, 435
Writ of certiorari, 577
Writ of habeas corpus, 577

Y

Yale University Child Center, 500
Yemen, 585
YMCA, 352
Youth Development and Delinquency Preven-
  tion Administration, 462, 463
Youth leadership challenge programs, 233
Youth service bureaus, 349, 454, 498, 522
Youth Violence Strike Force (YVSF), 351

Z

Zero tolerance policy, 378, 379

Photograph Credits

This page constitutes an extension of the copyright page. We have made every effort to trace the ownership of all copyrighted material and to secure permission from copyright holders. In the event of any question arising as to the use of any material, we will be pleased to make the necessary corrections in future printings. Thanks are due to the following authors, publishers, and agents for permission to use the material indicated.

3 © Michael A. Dwyer/Stock, Boston; 5 Jim Alcorn/New York Post Pool/Corbis; 9 © Catherine Leroy/Sipa Press; 15 The Pierpont Morgan Library/Art Resource, NY; 17 Stock Montage, Inc. 24 © Sherman Zent/Palm Beach Post; 29 © Bruce Davidson/Magnum Photos; 36 © James Nubile/The Image Works; 38 © Joel Gordon; 46 © Eugene Richards/Magnum Photos; 51 © Catherine Leroy/Sipa Press; 58 © A. Ramey/Stock, Boston; 68 © Sygma; 77 © Catherine Leroy/Sipa Press; 79 Rogelis Solis/AP/Wide World Photos; 83 © Nick Lacy/Stock, Boston; 91 © Collection Viollet/Gamma Liaison Network; 98 © Frank Siteman/Stock, Boston; 103 © Karen Garber-The Corning Leader/Sipa; 107 Dimension Films/Shooting Star; 125 © Joel Gordon; 127 © Joel Gordon; 136 © Patrick Zachman/Magnum Photos; 141 © Gregg Mancuso/Stock, Boston; 144 © Dorothy Littell/Stock, Boston; 150 © Mark Richards/Sipa Press; 163 © Katherin McGlynn/Impact Visuals; 165 © David Woo/Stock, Boston; 171 © Richard Hutchings/Photo Edit; 179 © Gale Zucker/Stock, Boston; 184 © Joel Gordon; 192 Photo Edit; 207 © Michael Newman/Photo Edit; 209 Montana Standard-AP/Wide World Photos; 213 © McLaughlin/The Image Works; 222 © Bibliotheque Municiple, Besancon, France, © by Erich Lessing/Art Resource; 227 © McLaughlin/The Image Works; 230 Jeff T. Green-AP/Wide World Photos; 241 © Bruce Davidson/Magnum Photos; 246 © Jeffry W. Myers/Stock, Boston; 256 © Myrleen Ferguson/Photo Edit; 261 © Lisa Quinones/Black Star;

267 © Joel Gordon; 273 © Sadin/Liaison/Rapho; 275 © Dan Lo-AP/Wide World Photos; 284 © Joel Gordon; 288 American Humane Society; 294 © Joel Gordon; 298 © Denis LaCuyer/Gamma Liaison Network; 304 © Joel Gordon; 317 © Bob Daemmrich/The Image Works; 326 © Michael Abramson/Black Star; 331 © Robert Yager/Sipa Press; 334 © Nancy Siesel/Saba; 340 © Joel Gordon; 350 © Joe Rodriguez/Black Star; 358 © Joel Gordon; 360 © Elizabeth Crews/Stock, Boston; 371 © Steve Starr/Saba Press Photos; 375 © Joel Gordon; 388 AP-Wide World Photos/Reed Hoffmann/Democrat & Chronicle; 395 © Joel Gordon; 397 © Paul Milette/Palm Beach Post; 400 © Joel Gordon; 409 © Joel Gordon; 411 © Joel Gordon; 422 © Joel Gordon; 431 American Correctional Association; 436 Stock Montage, Inc.; 439 Stock Montage, Inc.; 449 Copyright © 1998 Time, Inc. Reprinted by permission. 459 © Glen Korengold/Stock, Boston; 471 © Joel Gordon; 473 Charles Bennett-AP/Wide World Photos; 483 © Kelly Wilkinson/Indianpolis Star/ Sipa; 489 © Joe Rodrigquez/Black Star; 492 © Bob Strong/Sipa; 502 © Joel Gordon; 507 © Gary Wagner/Stock, Boston; 509 © Ted Fitzgerald; 513 © Jim Whitmer/Stock, Boston; 520 © Joel Gordon; 526 © Jacques Brund/Design Concepts; 538 © Joel Gordon; 546 © Rich Graulieh/Palm Beach Post; 549 Photo Edit; 556 © Mike Mazzachi/Stock, Boston; 561 © Spencer Grant/Photo Edit; 567 AP/Wide World Photos; 577 J. Pat Carter-AP/Wide World Photos; 595 © Tony Arruza/The Image Works; 597 © Jonathan Elderfield/Gamma Liaison Network; 602 © Lee Celano/Gamma Liaison Network; 608 © Joel Gordon; 614 © Bob Daemmrich/Stock, Boston; 618 © Jonathan Elderfield/Gamma Liaison Network; 626 © Gale Zucker/Stock, Boston; 628 Dick Schmidt/Sacramento Bee; 637 © David Woo/Stock, Boston; 646 © A. Ramey/Stock, Boston; 649 © Jacques Brund/Design Concepts; 651 © Charlie Varley/Sipa Press.

1967

President's Commission on Law Enforcement recognizes the problems of the juvenile justice system.

In re Gault, a U.S. Supreme Court decision establishes juveniles have the right to counsel, notice, confrontation of witnesses, and the avoidance of self-incrimination. In general, the court holds that Fourteenth Amendment due process applies to the juvenile justice system, specifically in adjudicatory hearings.

1968

Ginsberg v. New York establishes that it is unlawful to sell pornography to a minor.

1971

Mckeiver v. Pennsylvania establishes that a jury trial is not constitutionally required in a juvenile hearing but states can permit one if they wish.

The Twenty-Sixth Amendment to the Constitution is passed, granting the right to vote to 18-year-olds.

1969

Tinker v. Des Moines School District establishes that the First Amendment applies to juveniles and protects their constitutional right to free speech.

Hirschi publishes *Causes of Delinquency.*

1966

Kent v. United States—initial decision to establish due process protections for juveniles at transfer proceedings.

1970

In re Winship establishes that proof beyond a reasonable doubt is necessary in the adjudicatory phase of a juvenile hearing. A juvenile can appeal on the ground of insufficiency of the evidence if the offense alleged is an act that would be a crime in an adult court.

White House Conference on Children

1972

Wisconsin v. Yoder gives parents the right to impose their religion on their children.

Wolfgang publishes *Delinquency in a Birth Cohort.*

1960   1970

1973

In re Snyder gives minors the right to bring proceedings against their parents.

San Antonio Independent School District v. Rodriguez establishes that differences in education based on wealth were not necessarily discriminatory.

1974

Federal Child Abuse Prevention Act

Buckley Amendment to the Education Act of 1974, the Family Education Rights and Privacy Act. Students have the right to see their own files with parental consent.

Juvenile Justice and Delinquency Prevention Act

1975

Goss v. Lopez establishes that a student facing suspension has the right to due process, prior notice, and an open hearing.

1977

Report of the Committee of the Judiciary, especially concerning the rights of the unborn and the right of 18-year-olds to vote

Juvenile Justice Amendment of 1977

Ingraham v. Wright establishes that corporal punishment is permissible in public schools and is not a violation of the Eighth Amendment.

American Bar Association, Standards on Juvenile Justice

Washington State amends its sentencing policy.

1979

International Year of the Child

1980

National concern over child abuse and neglect

1981

Fare v. Michael C. defines *Miranda* rights of minors.

1982

Efforts to decarcerate status offenders escalate.

1983

The Federal Government focuses its attention on chronic offenders.

1984

Schall v. Martin allows states to use preventive detention with juvenile offenders.

1985

New Jersey v. T.L.O. allows teachers to search students without a warrant or probable cause.

Wilson and Herrnstein publish *Crime and Human Nature,* focusing attention on biological causes of delinquency.

1975   1980   1985